HISTORY

of

Perry County, Pennsylvania

Including Descriptions of Indian and
Pioneer Life from the Time of
Earliest Settlement

Sketches of Its Noted Men and Women
and Many Professional Men

By

H. H. HAIN

————————————

HARRISBURG, PA.
1922

————————————

HAIN-MOORE COMPANY, PUBLISHERS
HARRISBURG, PA.

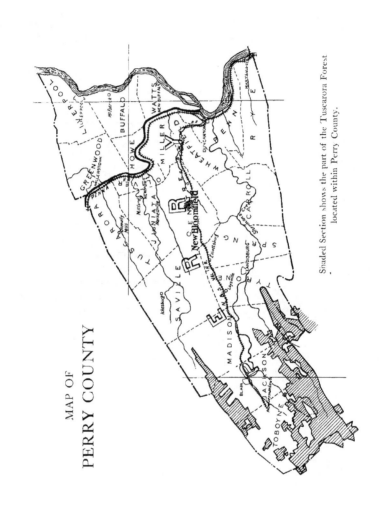

MAP OF
PERRY COUNTY

Shaded Section shows the part of the Tuscarora Forest located within Perry County.

FOREWORD

THE lands lying north of the Kittatinny or Blue Mountain, which were a part of Cumberland County until 1820, when Perry County was organized, form historically one of Pennsylvania's most interesting sections for various reasons. Here, when the world was in formation, geologists tell us, occurred upheavals and an admixture of the elements so unusual that Perry County, as to-day constituted, has more varieties of soil than any other county in the State.

For many years these lands stood at the very verge of the unbroken forests, a veritable out-post of civilization, where the warwhoop of the red men yet echoed through the hills while the pioneer plied axe and saw, as he hewed from the wooded lands a home for himself and his people. Amid such surroundings there was no place for the weakling or timid and thus there came to these lands a race of men and women, fearless and unafraid, who builded their homes, carved from the wilderness their farms, peopled the towns, surged over the borders and became useful citizens of other counties and states. They or their descendants have filled positions of honor and trust, which included the Presidency, the Vice-Presidency of two governments, governorships, chief justices' places on the supreme courts of three different states, and United States senatorships. From no other county have come more illustrious men or those whose ancestry have abided there, considering the small extent of territory and the necessarily attendant small population of a rural county.

This is more than a history of Perry County, as it records much of Indian habitation and devastation and pioneer life long before its lands became a county, which has come down to us through the mists of another day, being principally based on official records and historical accounts of the period, with here and there a tinge of tradition, when well founded, which has descended down the years through generations of responsible people.

Among the first settlers were men and women of mental vigor and talent, and these characteristics became inherent in unborn generations, with the attendant result that Perry County has not only been the birthplace of many men illustrious in the affairs of state, but also of an array of men and women educated in the learned professions, who have held, or hold, responsible positions in their respective communities, all over Pennsylvania and in a large majority of the states of the Union. While the book is in no sense a biographical work, yet it is deemed fit and proper to record the more noted. Unfortunately the list is not complete, as

the whereabouts of some at this time is unknown to the author,
as many letters seeking information remaining unanswered, and
also for the reason that it is difficult to obtain the records of
those of the first half-century or more of the county's existence.
It will serve as a basis for future records.

Of all these things: of the county's beautiful scenery, with its
physical distinction and magnificent mountains, verdant valleys,
rambling and sometimes raging rivers; of its traditions and its
treasures—its homes and its people, the book will go into detail.

It is unfortunate that the work was not undertaken a score of
years ago; but the author, who was just young enough to be included in the last conscription of men for the United States army,
in 1918, during the great World War, at an earlier day never
even dreamed of personally assuming a work of this importance.
Had it been undertaken then, the help of many who have since
passed away could have been enlisted, thus securing data which
has now been lost for all time.

In undertaking the task of writing and compiling a history of
the county of his nativity, the author has not done so under the
impression that he is more able to do so than others, as there are
many more competent. It was principally undertaken by him as
no other had even presumed to do so. A period of almost fifty
years had elapsed since the publication of Wright's History of
Perry County, the only separate history of the county published
since its organization, and which was written in answer to a
call from the Governor for the compilation of a history of every
county of the Commonwealth prior to the Centennial of 1876.

The book's contents are largely the result of development.
While some of the material used dates back to a boyhood scrapbook, and more to the advantages afforded by connection as a
correspondent from boyhood and later as editor of one of the
county newspapers, and a continual collection of historical data
since, yet by far the major portion was gathered, written and
compiled during the past three years. As the prospectus announcing its coming publication was being written, June 28, 1919,
the bells and whistles at the State Capital were pealing forth the
glad tidings that the terms of peace had been signed at Versailles,
and two days later war-time prohibition became effective throughout the Nation.

From the very beginning of writing and compiling this volume
the author has taken the public into his confidence, through
notices in the public press, and at every phase of its compilation,
and with some success. Conjointly with letters seeking information the business end was conducted and its publication assured.
As the book goes to press the proposed edition has been almost
wholly subscribed for. Inexperienced in the writing of a book

the triple method of traveling the territory, with the greater part of which he was already familiar, searching legal records and doing research work in libraries was adopted in the very beginning and continued throughout, and found to be advantageous. His place of residence and occupation made available the wonderful library of the State of Pennsylvania, the library of the City of New York, occupying a block; the Carnegie Library at Pittsburgh, a veritable acreage of books, and others of less importance, an advantage not available a half century ago, when the former history was written. The work has been a pleasant one, done in connection with filling a regular position, and if the reader enjoys the perusal of the volume half as much as the author enjoyed its writing and compilation he is well repaid for his efforts, undertaken largely as a labor of love. His one aim has been to give to posterity all of the many good things pertaining to his native county and its people, in so far as possible, in the form of a single volume. Had its completion been hurried much valuable data would have been lacking.

The history of a county differs from that of a state or nation, its government being largely a part of a greater territory, and necessarily includes matters of state and national importance, as they have a bearing upon local conditions. That tendency is a marked one in so far as Perry County is concerned, for in both the pioneer period and the sectional war time these lands were at the very borderland. In this book there will be found many things which naturally are of the state and nation, but they are here embodied, as their bearing on local matters is of import. To William C. Sproul, Governor of Pennsylvania; Thomas L. Montgomery, then State Librarian, and H. H. Shenk, Custodian of Public Records, the author is indebted for public sanction of the undertaking and for putting at his disposal every facility and advantage for securing information. Should he name the published works of others which he has searched for information it would require pages, as he has gone over many hundreds of them.

In his many trips within and without the county, the latter mostly spent in interviewing former Perry countians, everywhere he met with the kindest consideration and regard and to name a list of all who gave information is also impossible, but they have his most profound thanks for help in the preservation of these historical records. Here and there throughout the book he gives mention to a few who have been of marked assistance. Especial credit is due to Miss Margaret H. Barnett, of New Bloomfield, who carefully read practically all of the manuscript and made necessary corrections and valuable suggestions; to Prof. H. H. Shenk, custodian of Public Records of the State of Pennsylvania, and former Professor of History in Lebanon Valley College, for performing a similar duty; to Dr. George P. Donehoo, secretary of the Pennsylvania Historical Commission and a noted authority on Indian lore, and now State Librarian, for reviewing the Indian chapters, and to the many who read and criticised chapters with which they were especially familiar.

To those who loaned volumes from their libraries we are indebted, and especially so for the valuable scrap books of Miss Minnie Deardorff, Rev. John D. Calhoun, the late Senator Charles H. Smiley and others. Ex-Senator James W. McKee and Attorney George R. Barnett deserve special mention for aiding in research work on many occasions.

The county editors have been uniformly kind and helpful in every way, including the gratuitous use of their columns for furthering the work and for seeking information, and the privilege of searching their files. To Messrs. H. E. Sheibley and W. W. Branyan we are also indebted for the use of a number of the interesting electrotypes which help illustrate the book.

Upon the practical completion of the book notice was given through the public press, inviting any interested persons to read, criticise and correct any misstatements which they might find. The privilege of so doing was open for a period of sixty days.

During the many days spent in the capitol building and state library at Harrisburg the writer was treated with the utmost courtesy and consideration, both by the employees and their chiefs. They are skilled in their respective duties and considerate of the general public, whose business calls them to Capitol Hill.

While the work was in progress death took from us a number of men and women who had offered help in securing material and facts, some of which appears here and there throughout the book. Among these were Prof. L. E. McGinnes, Prof. Daniel Fleisher, Frank Pennell, Mrs. Annie Swartz Hench, wife of Harry F. Hench, and Mrs. Clara Lahr Moore, wife of Dr. E. E. Moore, two cultured and learned women.

As the work took form the impression was made that no matter what proportion it assumed upon completion there would still be a lack of finality, as ever and anon there appeared new (or rather old) data, legend, tradition, and sketches of men— and still more men—who had gone forth from Perry County and its territory and lived lives of honor and distinction. There will be errors, of course, but the statements herein made have all been secured or transferred from historical or other books, public records, newspaper files, scrap-books, etc., except where noted. Where statements have differed the one supported by facts has been used.

H. H. HAIN.

Harrisburg, Pa., January 10, 1922.

CONTENTS

ILLUSTRATIONS

CHAPTER I.

LOCATION, PHYSICAL FEATURES, GEOLOGY, ETC.

PERRY COUNTY, Pennsylvania, is located in the southern central portion of the state, just north of the Kittatinny (Blue) Mountain, its southern boundary being within forty miles of the Mason-Dixon Line, that historic line which not only separated the states of Pennsylvania and Maryland, but which became, politically, the boundary line between the North and the South, on the slavery question. In fact, in much of the legislation appertaining to slavery, this line was the barrier against which two contending forces battled, practically from the time of the formation of the United States until the best blood of the nation was spilled in the four years of war between the States, 1861-65.

Perry County is bounded on the north by Juniata County; on the east by the Susquehanna River, across which lies Dauphin County; on the south by Cumberland County; and on the west by Franklin and Juniata Counties. It contains 564 square miles, according to Smull's Handbook, the official publication of the commonwealth. Groff, in the History of the Juniata and Susquehanna Valleys, gives the square miles as 480; Claypole, the geologist, gives the number at 539, and Wright, in his History of Perry County, makes the number 550, which show considerable variance.

While the size of Perry County is relatively small, yet it is not the smallest county in Pennsylvania, by any means. Twenty-seven others are smaller in area, but many of them have a vastly greater population. It is larger than either Cumberland or Dauphin. Perry County is credited with 564 square miles. The other counties whose area is not so great are as follows: Montour, 130 square miles; Philadelphia, 133; Delaware, 185; Union, 305; Snyder, 311; Lehigh, 344; Lawrence, 360; Lebanon, 360; Northampton, 372; Juniata, 392; Cameron, 392; Wyoming, 397; Mifflin, 398; Fulton, 402; Carbon, 406; Forest, 423; Beaver, 429; Lackawanna, 451; Sullivan, 458; Columbia, 479; Luzerne, 484; Montgomery, 484; Dauphin, 521; Cumberland, 528; Adams, 528; Blair, 534, and Pike, 544.

In population, eleven other counties of the state have less. According to the census of 1920, Perry County's population was 22,875. The counties having less are Cameron, Pike, Forest, Sullivan, Fulton, Montour, Wyoming, Juniata, Union, Snyder, and Potter.

15

seventy-eighth degrees, and almost all of it between the seventy-seventh and seventy-eighth. It lies between the fortieth and forty-first degrees of latitude. A line drawn from Pittsburgh to Reading, Pennsylvania, would pass through New Bloomfield, and one from Johnstown to Reading, through Marysville.

Considered in size, Perry County is one of the smaller counties of the state, and yet it is almost half of the size of the state of Rhode Island, and almost one-fourth as large as the state of Delaware. Its average length is thirty-eight miles, and its average breadth, fourteen miles. Its elevation varies very much. At the mouth of the Juniata it is 357.4 feet above sea level, and at the Gibson mill in Spring Township, it is 471 feet. The old road over Bower Mountain, in Jackson Township, according to Claypole, the geologist, is 950 feet above the valley, 1,350 feet above Landisburg, and 2,000 feet above the level of the sea.

Its location is in the Atlantic slope of the great Appalachian Mountain system, of which Groff* says: "The construction of the underground world is so beautifully simple as a whole, and so curiously complicated in details, that it will ever stand the typical district of the Appalachian Mountain belt of the Atlantic seaboard." The shape of the county resembles roughly a triangle, or rather, a pennant. Its acreage is 360,960, according to the Department of Agriculture of the State.

Along the eastern boundary, where winds the broad Susquehanna, from a point about five miles above Liverpool to below Marysville, where the river breaks through the Blue or Kittatinny Mountain, the distance is twenty-nine miles, or twenty-one by air

---

*George G. Groff, M.D., former Professor of Natural History, Bucknell University.

Gibson's Rock. Gibson's Rock is located along the north side of Sherman's Creek, three miles west of Shermansdale. It is a striking geological formation, of which the county has many, and yet this is a surpassing one in size and interest. Located at the dividing line of Spring and Carroll Townships this mighty crag towers from the bed of Sherman's Creek almost perpendicularly. West of it the old Indian trail, known as the Allegheny Path, crossed the creek to the northern side. Here the mountain evidently once breasted the creek and held back waters which covered several townships, according to geologists. Picturesquely situated, this point has long been a mecca for campers, outings, and picnics. Above it, within sound of the human voice, stood the famous Gibson mansion, and still stands the "Westover" or Gibson mill. In that house was born Chief Justice John Bannister Gibson, Governor William Bigler, and John Bernheisel, representative in Congress from the then Territory of Utah. Governor William Bigler had a brother, John Bigler, who was governor of California at the same time that his brother was governor of Pennsylvania, but John Bigler was born at Landisburg, where his parents resided, prior to coming to the Westover mill in 1809. During the early years of the county's existence a bill passed the Pennsylvania Legislature making Sherman's Creek navigable, and many huge boulders were blown from the creek's bottom, some within the shadow of the great cliff, the drill marks being yet distinguishable.

line. The trend of the river is from north to south, with considerable bend to the west at Duncannon. The southern boundary, starting at the Susquehanna River from a point seven miles north of Harrisburg, the capital of Pennsylvania, follows the crest of the Blue Mountain, adjoining Cumberland County, for fifty-three miles, at an average elevation of one thousand feet above the Cumberland Valley, to the south. The course of the mountain for the first twenty-two miles is almost a straight line, due westward. Then it curves back, northward, to Welsh Hill, and makes a loop, in which lies Green Valley. Going out again to practically the same line from which it receded, to Pilot Knob, it makes a second loop—deeper than the first—which is the location of Kennedy's Valley. Thereafter its course is practically southwest to the Franklin County line for over a dozen miles. The air line distance along the southern border is thirty-eight miles.

The extreme western boundary, which borders Franklin County, is only a little over eight miles, crossing a series of mountains, described further on, at very irregular intervals. From the northwest corner it follows the crest of the Tuscarora Mountain to the Juniata River, the first ten miles being almost straight in a northeastern direction. It then makes two small offsets at the west of Madison Township and assuming the same general direction runs "straight as a crow flies" to the western bank of the Juniata River. At this point the line runs due north for a mile and a half, and thence almost due east about thirteen miles to the western bank of the Susquehanna River.

The mountains in and surrounding Perry County are from six hundred to twelve hundred feet high, measured from the valley levels adjoining, but are eight hundred to sixteen hundred feet above sea level. A brief description of these mountains follows, much of the information being drawn from the works of Professor Claypole, the geologist:

MOUNTAINS.

Kittatinny or Blue Mountain. This mountain is known by various names. Geographers term it the Blue Mountain; the pioneers called it the Kittatinny Mountain, derived from the Indian "Kau-ta-tin-chunk," meaning the main or principal mountain; Conrad Weiser, the Indian interpreter, interpreted it as "the endless mountain"; Richard Peters, the provincial secretary, in a letter to Governor Hamilton, dated July 2, 1750, first officially called it "the Blue Hills"; the residents east of the Susquehanna called it the First Mountain, and the residents of the Cumberland Valley called and many yet call it the North Mountain, as it lies north of that valley. In a provincial record dated May 6, 1752, this mountain is called "Kekachtany" or "Endless Hills," the title which the Delaware Indians applied to it. In the Albany grant of July 6, 1754, for the lands which now comprise Perry County and others, recorded in the provincial records of February 3, 1755, it is called the Kittochtinny or Blue Hills, by which it was known throughout provincial and colonial times in all records. The description at the beginning of this chapter only applies to this mountain in so far as it is the southern boundary of the county. This Indian name, "Kautatinchunk," as quoted in some volumes, is said to have been "Tyannuntasacta" by the Six Nations, and "Kekachtannin" by the Delawares. The name is defined at one place as meaning "steadfast in storm and ever true blue." It is to be regretted that the old Indian name, Kittatinny, has fallen somewhat into disuse. Luther Reily Kelker, in his History of Dauphin County, speaking of the Kittatinny Mountain also being called the Blue or North Mountain, said, "The Indian name alone should be used; any mountain may be blue at a distance, and any one is north of some place."

These mountains (of the Appalachian system) really stretch from a point not far from Newburgh, New York, on the Hudson River, across New York State, New Jersey, Pennsylvania, Maryland, Virginia, and enter North Carolina and Tennessee, being broken by water gaps to let through the waters of the Delaware, the Lehigh, the Schuylkill, the Swatara, the Susquehanna, and the Potomac (at Harper's Ferry). At the southern part of the county its crest-length of fifty-three miles is unbroken by a single water gap. For seventeen miles it runs, with one small zigzag, parallel to Bower Mountain, separated from it by the steep and narrow vale of the north branch of Laurel Run, which starts at the Franklin County line. Both mountains run on thus southwestward through Franklin County, unite and end before reaching Fort Loudon. Bower Mountain is therefore only a return zigzag of Blue Mountain.

It received its name First Mountain from the early settlers of southeastern Pennsylvania, especially those who built their cabins along the Susquehanna River at Columbia, Marietta, and Harrisburg, and had occasion to go up the river in canoes through the water gaps. The *first* mountain they passed by was this mountain, hence the name, First Mountain. The *second* was Cove Mountain, and from the Susquehanna to the Lehigh it has retained the name of Second Mountain ever since; the *third* was the Sharp Mountain of Schuylkill County, which traverses Dauphin County, but does not quite reach the Susquehanna River; the *fourth* was Peters' Mountain, opposite Duncannon. Here, at the mouth of the Juniata the numerals stopped, as the mountains farther up, Berry's and Buffalo, did not run in the same general direction.

In September, 1742, David Zeisberger, the missionary, and a party of friends, among whom was Conrad Weiser, on their way from the settled part of the province "came to a ridge of forest-crowned mountains, across which led a blind trail, full of loose, sharp stones, and close to high rocks the rugged sides of which rendered horseback riding exceedingly dangerous. The mountains being without a name, Conrad Weiser called them 'The Thürnstein,' in honor of Zinzendorf. They were the parallel chains of the Blue Ridge, now known as the Second, Third, and Peters' Mountains."

The western end of the Tuscarora Mountain, Conococheague Mountain, Round Top, Little Round Top, Rising Mountain, Amberson Ridge, Bower Mountain, and Middle or Sherman Mountain, named in order from northwest to southeast, across the western end of the county, are all in a way zigzags of different lengths of one range. The following description from Claypole is given verbatim:

"A woodsman can enter Perry County from Franklin County on the rocks at the top of the West Tuscarora Mountain, and walk along the rocky crest of this range, alternately towards the northeast and towards the southwest, for a total distance of thirty-five miles, reëntering Franklin County from the crest of Bower Mountain, only three miles across from the place where he left it. In all this distance he will keep at nearly the same elevation, say 1,600 feet above ocean level, except at three points, where the wall on the top of which he is traveling is broken down to its base by small streams. One of these water gaps is cut through the West Tuscarora Mountain; a second is made by the head of Sherman's Creek, which cuts through Rising Mountain; the third is made by Houston's Run through the north leg of Bower Mountain. Everywhere else along the line he will find the sharp crested mountain unbroken by gaps, with steep rock-covered slopes or even cliffs always on his right hand, and a gentler, smoother, but still quite steep slope on his left hand. When he turns the east end of a zigzag he will see the mountain crest make a long slope downward into the valleys of Perry County; and when he turns the west ends of the zigzag, he will be on boldly scarped knobs overlooking the shale and limestone valleys of Franklin County. On these knobs he will always reach a somewhat higher elevation above tide. Round Top and Little Round Top are simply the southwestward looking ends of two of the zigzags rather more strongly pronounced than the others."

The district enclosed by these mountains is peculiarly isolated from travel, except along the river. While the extreme western part of the county is bound by this series of mountain ranges, yet the traveler can go through to Amberson Valley, Franklin County, by utilizing the second narrows and the break through Bower's Mountain.

Tuscarora Mountain. The eastern end of the Tuscarora Mountain forms a range alone, along its crest for a distance of twenty-one miles runs the boundary line which separates Perry from Juniata County. Almost straight and continuous, it is broken by a ravine opposite Ickesburg. A small stream flows through this ravine, draining a small glen in the heart of the mountain, three miles in length and a half-mile in width. At this point the mountain has two crests, the county line following the southern. This mountain slopes gently at both ends. In Gordon's History of Pennsylvania and Belknap's Gazetteer of Pennsylvania, both of which were published in 1832, the Tuscarora is referred to as Tussey's Mountain, in these words, "The Juniata River enters Perry County through Tussey's Mountain." There is a mountain by that name farther up the state, but as these two historians called the Tuscarora "Tussey's Mountain" it may have been known to many others by that name and hence the resultant confusion of pioneer and Indian history and legend.

THE HILL RANGES WITHIN.

Surrounded by mountains and the Susquehanna River and penetrated from the east to a small extent by other mountains the interior of Perry County is an extensive wedge-shaped area of open country, traversed by many ranges of hills, which vary from two hundred to five hundred feet above the levels of the streams which drain them. Some of these hills are cultivated in common with the lower soil, a prominent and extensive example being the Middle Ridge, which extends ten miles west from Newport.

Raccoon Ridge. A ridge in Tuscarora Township, starting some distance from the river. At Donally's Mills it is broken by a gap through which flows the south branch of Raccoon Creek.

Ore Ridge. A ridge paralleling the Tuscarora Mountain at its base, comparatively low and located within Tuscarora Township.

Hominy Ridge. The southern boundary of the western half of Tuscarora Township. It is of Chemung shale, which Claypole says is among the poorest, adding "of all the Chemung districts that on Hominy Ridge is the most uninviting. High, steep and rough, it presents little to attract the farmer and the wonder arises why so much of it is cleared."

Limestone Ridge. A wooded ridge starting at the Juniata River below Bailey's Station, on the Pennsylvania Railroad, in Miller Township, and extending westward through the county to the Madison Township line, forming the boundary between Miller and Oliver Townships and separating Spring and Tyrone from Saville. Even west of that its formation exists, to the western end of the county, but it is more broad and is cultivated. North of Andersonburg and Centre it is two and a half miles broad. From New Bloomfield to the Juniata it has double and at some places triple crests. Limestone generally follows its southern surface. The U. S. Geological Survey names this ridge, Hickory Ridge, and the northern crest, Buffalo Ridge.

Mahanoy Ridge. Mahanoy Ridge starts near the Juniata River, in Miller Township, at a point between Iroquois and Losh's Run stations, on the Pennsylvania Railroad, and traverses Miller, Centre, and Spring Townships. At four points in Miller and Centre Townships it is broken by water gaps. Between Green Park and Landisburg it zigzags, coming to an abrupt incline at the latter place in a promontory known as Bell's Hill.

Dick's Hill. This ridge starts in Miller Township, almost five miles west of the Juniata River, and becomes from that point the boundary line between Miller and Wheatfield Townships. It separates Wheatfield and Carroll Townships from Centre and continues into Spring Township, terminating at a point east of a line between Landisburg and Bridgeport, being known as Pisgah Ridge after leaving the Wheatfield Township line. Its central portion is shown in old maps as Iron Ridge, and is sometimes locally known as Rattlesnake Hill. This ridge was probably known as Dick's Hill for its entire length originally, as it is mentioned as being crossed by the old Indian trail to the West as early as 1803, by a woman then 100 years old, as will be noted in our chapter devoted to "Trails, Roads, and Highways." From its eastern gap, through which flows Little Juniata Creek, one of the three earliest churches took its name—the Dick's Gap Church, long since gone to decay. This church was not located along Dick's Hill however, but along Mahanoy Ridge, a short distance north. Dick's Hill was also the site of two pioneer industries, Perry Furnace and Montebello Furnace. Claypole says, "Curving round sharply it sweeps for almost twenty miles under the name of 'Little Mountain' to the Susquehanna River at Marysville."

Pisgah Ridge. See Dick's Hill, immediately preceding.

Pine Hill. This ridge starts in Carroll Township and runs east, forming the dividing line between Rye and Wheatfield. It is, in fact, an extension of the Cove Mountain.

Buck Hills. South of New Germantown, in Toboyne Township, a low range called Buck Hills rises gradually, but irregularly, until it merges into Rising Mountain.

Chestnut Hills. The Chestnut Hills rise in Madison Township, west of Centre, run through Jackson and Toboyne, merge into Amberson Ridge, their ascension being gradual.

Round Top. Right after leaving the county the Conococheague Mountain turns sharply and reënters the county, forming Round Top, which commands the head of Sherman's Valley and is a conspicuous object for many miles. Its course is short, however, and zigzaging again, it passes over the county line to the southwest, with a southeast dip, and continues for about twelve miles as a range known as Dividing Mountain, as it divides Path Valley and Amberson Valley, in Franklin County.

Dividing Mountain. See Round Top.

Little Rount Top. Located in Toboyne Township, south of Round Top.

Rising Mountain. Returning from its long lap into Franklin County the mountain again reënters Perry County and forms the high, broad, stony ridge known as Rising Mountain, lying southwest of New Germantown. To the east lie Buck Hills, which rise gradually into a mountain, hence the name, Rising Mountain.

Amberson Ridge. After Rising Mountain crosses into Franklin it laps and again crosses the line into Perry, being then known as Amberson Ridge. It meets the great fold of Bower Mountain and forms a high knob overlooking Amberson Valley, Franklin County.

Bower Mountain. Bower Mountain is a great level-crested ridge rising near Loysville, passing through Madison Township, gently sloping upward through Jackson Township, and on entering Toboyne it forms a small zigzag and separates into two parts which are unnamed. Named after Nathaniel Bower, whose 200-acre farm saddled its crest.

Mount Pisgah. The highest elevation of the little range of Pisgah Mountains is in Carroll Township. Opposite these mountains, near where Sherman's Creek breaks through at Gibson's Rock, was born John Bannister Gibson, once Chief Justice of the Supreme Court of Pennsylvania. It is also known locally as Pisgah Hill.

Little Mountain. A small ridge lying north of the Blue Mountain, in Rye and Carroll Townships and a short distance into Spring Township.

Slaughterbeck Hill. Sometimes called Michael's Ridge. A conspicuous promontory in Pfoutz Valley, Greenwood Township. It blocks entrance from the west, rising above every other range in the township. Claypole says of it: "It is really a fragment of the great Tuscarora anticlinal which has been cut off by the Juniata River from the main body and constitutes an outlier. In truth the whole of the valley is a continuation eastward of the anticlinal ridge of the Tuscarora, eroded by long ages of frost, rain and sunshine."

Michael's Ridge. See Slaughterbeck's Hill, immediately preceding.

Wildcat Ridge. A high and rugged ridge separating Perry and Pfoutz Valleys, in Greenwood township. It enters Liverpool Township for a short distance, but dies down, the two valleys here being less distinct than farther west. Rough and rocky at places, where wildcats once had a rendezvous, hence the name.

Turkey Ridge. This high ridge, at places farmed to its very top, but mostly wooded, is the dividing line between Perry and Juniata Counties at Liverpool Township. Like Wildcat Ridge it loses much of its steepness as it approaches the Susquehanna River. In pioneer days noted as a great wild turkey territory, from which comes the name, Turkey Ridge.

Half Fall Mountain. In provincial and colonial records, frequently referred to as Half Fall Hills. It lies between Buffalo and Watts Townships, its crest being the township line. It is an extension, across the Juniata, of the converging Mahanoy and Limestone Ridges, the limestone rocks forming almost a complete dam across the river, producing a "half-falls" from which the mountain takes its name. It spans the territory completely between the Juniata and Susquehanna Rivers, being crossed by a public highway. Below Montgomery's Ferry it ends in a conspicuous bluff, near the top of which is a cave supposed to have once been the hiding place of Simon Girty, the renegade, but which records practically confute. (See chapter on Simon Girty.) On a promontory of the mountain here is a protruding rock, which viewed coming from the north over the Susquehanna Trail, presents the profile of an Indian as perfect as can be found, and one which only the Creator, that greatest of artists, could produce.

Mount Patrick. A name sometimes applied to the end of Berry's Mountain at the village of that name.

North Mountain. See Kittatinny Mountain.

First Mountain. See Kittatinny Mountain.

Second Mountain. See Kittatinny Mountain.

Third Mountain. See Kittatinny Mountain.

Fourth Mountain. See Kittatinny Mountain. This is also known as Peters' Mountain and is located opposite to Duncannon, the Cove Mountain being in reality an extension thereof, the Susquehanna water gap cutting through.

Peters' Mountain. See preceding paragraph.

Mount Dempsey. A high promontory of the Blue or Kittatinny Mountain, where it laps, located opposite Landisburg, in Tyrone Township. One of the most picturesque spots in the county. An Indian trail, later used as a bridle path, passes its base.

Buck Ridge. A "breaking down" of Rising Mountain, in Toboyne Township.

Big Knob. A mountain ridge north of Blain.

Little Knob. Twin sister to Big Knob, north of Blain.

"The Crossbar." A wooded ridge running from Big Knob, north of Blain, to the Tuscarora Mountain.

Berry's Mountain and Buffalo Mountain. These two mountains are located in the northeast section of the county, are broken by water gaps by the Susquehanna at Mt. Patrick and Liverpool, are seven and eight miles long, respectively, and unite in a single elevated knob on the east bank of the Juniata River a mile above Newport, known as Round Top, which can be plainly seen from east of the Susquehanna. Both of them have perfectly straight sharp crests, long gentle slopes towards the cove which they form, and outer terraces, that of Berry's facing south and that of Buffalo facing northwest. Unlike the sharp ellipse of Cove Mountain, that of Berry's Mountain is broken by a gap nearly to its base at its western end on the southern side, by a small stream extending into the Juniata. But a high divide behind the gap virtually closes the upper end of the cove. Berry's Mountain runs on through Dauphin County and returns as Peters' Mountain, then Cove Mountain. Buffalo Mountain also reappears on the east side of the Susquehanna under the name Mahantango Mountain, and along its crest runs the north county line of Dauphin to the northwest corner of Schuylkill County. Buffalo Mountain separates Buffalo Township from Greenwood and Liverpool Townships.

As the Dauphin County anthracite coal basin is enclosed at its west end by the Cove Mountain in Perry County, so is the Wiconisco anthracite coal basin enclosed by Berry's and Buffalo Mountains in Perry County. The two coves resemble each other closely in shape, size and position. Within the cove formed by Buffalo and Berry Mountains is located Hunter's Valley, the northern half of Buffalo Township. Berry Mountain, it is said, was named after a family by the name of Berry which resided at its base, below Mt. Patrick, but as it bears the same name east of the Susquehanna it probably derived its name from the fact that immense quantities of berries have always grown along its sides.

Cove Mountain. The Cove Mountain, lying between Duncannon and Marysville, is a sharply recurved ridge, one thousand feet higher than the water level of the water gap below, like the cut-off prow of a canoe-shaped basin—the Dauphin County anthracite coal basin, being the west end of a long-pointed ellipse, the east end of which is Carbon County, beyond the Lehigh River. The Susquehanna River crosses it diagonally at the east, the northern crest being only five miles in length and the southern ten miles. The crest at the extreme west is known as "the horseshoe" to sportsmen and overlooks the fertile Sherman's Valley to the west.

Conococheague Mountain. A beautiful mountain is the Conococheague. It forms a long, straight, even-crested ridge from Madison Township, where it starts, to its termination at Round Top, in Toboyne Township, without break or gap of any character. Over it pass two roads, one leading north from New Germantown to Horse Valley and Juniata County, and the other west over the bend in the range to Concord, Franklin County. At its east end it is a perfect arch, but to the west it becomes a south-dipping range. The Indian word, Conococheague, is recorded as meaning "it is indeed a long way."

Buffalo Ridge. The name applied to the ridge south of the Little Buffalo Creek. Also known as Furnace Hills.

Furnace Hills. See preceding paragraph.

Bell's Hill. The promontory ending of Mahanoy Ridge in Spring Township.

Quaker Hill. An outlying hill of the Pisgah Ridge in Spring Township.

Gallows Hill. In "Little Germany," John Faus (Foose), known as the "King of Germany" on account of his large land holdings, took up 300 acres on June 12, 1794, with which he was assessed in 1820, the date of the county's birth, and on which he had erected a sawmill and a distillery. A tavern was kept on the old mansion farm until 1827. The sign of this tavern was an iron ring suspended from an arm attached to a high post, so suggestive of a gallows that the place came to be known as "Gallows Hill."

Welsh Hill. The point of the Blue Mountain separating Kennedy's Valley from Green Valley, in Tyrone Township.

Pilot Knob. Pilot Knob is the highest spur of the Kittatinny or Blue Mountain, and is located not far from Landisburg.

Middle Ridge. The ridge running west from Newport, through Oliver and Juniata Townships, once wooded, but now a fertile section of farm lands.

Crawley Hill. A high hill in Spring Township, an outlying knoll of the Dick's Hill range, which derived its name from a man named Crawley, who, it is said, was murdered upon it long years ago for his money. His remains were buried near the road which crosses the hill. But a few rods from this road, on the south side of the hill, stood a very small stone schoolhouse in the shadow of a thicket, and tradition tells of the teacher raising a window sash to get a rod without leaving the building, for it appears that at one time the rod was a necessary accessory to every schoolhouse. Tradition may be right, but the writer cannot conceive of any Perry County boy allowing them to remain so handy longer than twenty-four hours. A frame structure later took its place, but it was abandoned. Between Crawley Hill and Mahanoy Hill nestles the famous settlement known as "Little Germany."

Iron Ridge. The name once applied to the ridge just south of Crawley Hill, in Spring Township.

THE KITTATINNY MOUNTAIN GAPS.

Across the crest of the Kittatinny Mountain, where it drops, often slightly, are a number of famous gaps or passes, some of which were the locations of old Indian trails and are mentioned in provincial and colonial records. Starting from the Susquehanna River these gaps in the order named are Lamb's, Miller's, Myer's, Croghan's (now called Sterrett's), Crane's, Sharon's, Long's,

Waggoner's, and McClure's. A concise description of each follows:

Holt's Gap. A small gap in the mountain at a point just west of Marysville, little more than a great depression.

Lamb's Gap. Crosses the mountain almost opposite what was known as Hartman's mill, in Rye Township, now Glenvale. On the Cumberland side it is the boundary line between Hampden and Silver Spring Townships. Elevation, 1,018 feet.

Miller's Gap. Crosses the mountain at a point a short distance southwest of Keystone, the road coming out at Wertzville, Cumberland County. Elevation, 1,080 feet.

Myer's Gap. Almost directly south of Grier's Point. Crossed by a poor road, little better than a trail.

Dean's Gap. The road from Perry County leading up to this gap, which lies almost two miles east of Sterrett's Gap, leaves a point known as "the narrows" and runs in a southeastern direction: another road from the same point runs towards Sterrett's Gap, in a southwestern direction. There is a considerable farm on the mountaintop at this gap, where Dr. Dean long resided, having a considerable medical practice in both Perry and Cumberland Counties. The road on the Cumberland side trended in the direction of Mechanicsburg.

Croghan's or Sterrett's Gap. Of all the gaps across the Kittatinny this one is the easiest for travel and the most noted historically. Through it leads the state highway from New Bloomfield to Carlisle. Across it ran the earliest Indian trail and in pioneer times the old Allegheny Path. Over it passed the great Indian chiefs, the early interpreters, the early traders and the pioneers with their meagre belongings and their first domestic animals. Through its then precipitous passes came those first early missionaries of Scotch-Irish Calvinism carrying to these inland forests the message of the Man of Galilee, and across its picturesque ravines today roll hundreds of motor cars on pleasure and business bent. From a point of greater elevation several hundred feet west can be seen, looking northward, the historic and picturesque Sherman's Valley, nestling between the mountains, one of the famous coves of Pennsylvania, and looking southward, the more extensive and productive Cumberland Valley in all its beauty. The elevation of Sterrett's Gap is 925 feet. As late as 1877, according to Beach Nichols' Atlas of Perry, Juniata, and Mifflin Counties, there was a post office located there known as Sterrett's Gap. At that time there was also a store and tavern there. Authorities give the name of the first tavern keeper as a man named Buller. When the county was created, in 1820, Daniel Gallatin was the tavern keeper. After the middle of the last century there was a new hostelry built, where came the well-to-do from Carlisle, Baltimore and other places, on leisure bent. There came happy throngs, and there were scenes of gayety by day and sounds of revelry by night, but with the growing popularity of the great resorts and the easy methods of travel its fame as a resort passed and a struggling lone tavern remained. In fact, there was a road house there until very recent years, at times being a hostelry of good reputation and again being a rendezvous for those of questionable reputation, its clientele often changing with the change of proprietors. This gap was originally known as Croghan's Gap, by reason of George Croghan's residing near. Croghan was prominent in provincial affairs. An early order of survey was taken out for the lands at this point by John Armstrong, who sold it to Nathan Andrews. It was returned to the land office June 21, 1788, in the name of Ralph Sterrett, who with his brothers John and James Sterrett, warranted

408 acres along the crest of the mountain, extending over three miles east from the gap. Accordingly it came to be known as Sterrett's Gap and so it remains, though the Sterretts are gone long since. Descendants of the Sterretts sold the lands to William Ramsey, of Carlisle. In a mortgage dated June 26, 1830, the Ramsey lands in Rye Township included "850 acres of land, two fulling mills, a woolen factory, three dwelling houses, a wagonmaker shop, stable, shed and part of tavern house and part of orchard at same place." (Part of the tavern and orchard were in Cumberland County, the former being built upon the line.) By right of mortgage James Buchanan, later President of the United States, became owner of a part of these lands in 1835 and was assessed with 250 acres and a fulling mill.

The mountain near the gap slopes so gradually that the approach from Shermansdale and Fishing Creek is very gentle, and abundant springs of water from high levels are available at the very top. There, upon a small plateau, met four early highways from divergent points, which made it an early centre of trade. And thus, at the dawn of the past century, we find an early trading post. There were stores for exchange and sale and shops for repairs, a tavern where man and beast were fed and cared for, and there dwelt an early physician, Dr. Kaechline, until after a severe and intensely cold midwinter night his frozen body was found near the foot of the eastern slope, while a riderless horse at the gap stables gave the alarm, too late. Additional facts may be found in the chapters devoted to Trails, Roads and Highways, and Carroll Township. Something of George Croghan's life also appears in the early chapters of this book.

Crane's Gap. This gap crosses the mountain about three miles west of Sterrett's at an elevation of 1,300 feet. The road enters Cumberland County in North Middleton Township. At an early day it was but a footpath, but in 1848 was made a public road, now long abandoned.

Sharon's Gap. A small gap about a mile west of Crane's gap, called after the original warrantee of the lands. There was once a road there, but it too has been long since abandoned.

Long's Gap. This gap is directly south from Falling Springs, where William Long, on February 3, 1794, warranted 400 acres of land. Its elevation is 1,390 feet. To the older generation it is known as the "Forty Shillings' Gap," tradition having it that a murder was once committed there for the purpose of robbery and that the culprit got but forty shillings. As our monetary system has had no shillings in circulation since our divorce from George III the murder was likely a provincial tragedy.

Waggoner's Gap. Crosses the mountain south of Oak Grove Furnace or Bridgeport. It is mentioned in early provincial annals. The road from New Germantown, via Landisburg, leads through this gap, and was known as the Baltimore Pike in the days when teaming to Baltimore with farm produce was an industry.

McClure's Gap. McClure's Gap crosses the mountain at Welsh Hill, southwest of Landisburg. There is really very little gap to the Perry County side from the hollow on the Cumberland side, formed by the folds in the mountain. It is crossed by a road built in 1821 to connect Landisburg, then the temporary county seat, with Newville, Cumberland County. This gap is mentioned in provincial records as early as 1756. See chapter on "Trails and Highways."

Doubling Gap. Probably named by reason of the doubling of the mountain here. In a number of early publications, one as late as June 11, 1829, however, it was called Dublin Gap, and the springs on the Cumberland side were advertised as "Dublin Gap Springs" as late as 1800. It was first known as McFarlan's Gap, as James McFarlan had located about a thousand acres just below the gap. Court records bear out the fact that it was once known as McFarlan's, as in April, 1891, a petition to the Cumberland County court asked for the laying out of a road from Thomas Barnes' sulphur spring in the gap, formerly known as McFarlan's Gap, to Carlisle. Doubling Gap figures in traditions of the first settlers and was a commanding pass from the Shosshone Indians on the south, to the fierce Tuscaroras in the north, long before white settlers dared invade the section. During the Provincial-Indian wars, an Indian trail from the Susquehanna, starting at the mouth of the Juniata, followed an almost direct course westward across the county territory, through Doubling Gap, thence to the mouth of Brandy Run on the Conodoguinet. Facing Doubling Gap from Cumberland Valley, the eye meets Round Knob, 1,400 feet above tidewater. On top of it is Flat Rock, one of the most noted lookouts in the whole range of mountains. From its vantage point the whole Cumberland Valley lies before you, the South Mountain far below and the tortuous Conodoguinet wending its way eastward. During the period from 1820 to 1846 the hostelry known as the Doubling Gap Springs Hotel was in its heyday, and to it came men of note and prominence from far-off points. With the coming of the railroads and the growth of seaside resorts its fame gradually dwindled until it is little known.

Tuscarora Mountain Gaps.

Unlike the Kittatinny Mountain, to the county's south, the Tuscarora Mountain, along the northern boundary, has few gaps, and only one of importance. The gaps are mentioned in the report of the survey of 1860, which was for the purpose of locating the line between Perry and Juniata Counties.

Waterford Gap. This is the largest gap crossing the Tuscarora Mountain and the one through which crossed that old-time trail, the Allegheny Path. Through it passed the red men on their incursions in and out of Perry County territory and the daring and intrepid fellows who followed them. Along this trail passed the trader, the early postrider, the circuit rider, the pioneer emigrant on his way to the valley of the Ohio, and through it to-day is a highway on which pass great touring cars of the modern world. In early annals it was known as Bigham's Gap, but is described here as Waterford Gap, as that is the official name placed upon it by the County Line Commission. It is also sometimes called the Waterford Narrows. The residents of the east end of Horse Valley travel via this gap in order to trade at East Waterford, Juniata County, their nearest town. The public road traversing this gap extends from East Waterford through into Horse Valley and to New Germantown.

Bigham's Gap. See Waterford Gap, immediately preceding.

Bealetown Narrows. Another gap or break in the Tuscarora Mountain is located southeast of Honey Grove, Juniata County, and is known as the Bealetown Narrows. These narrows permit easy access to and from the eastern portion of Liberty Valley, the road passing near the former site of the Mohler tannery, and thence eastward by Walsingham schoolhouse to Saville and Ickesburg.

Winns' Gap. Winns' Gap is located approximately two and one-half miles east of the Waterford Gap. This gap is only a slight depression in the mountain, and according to local gossip was frequently used by the inhabitants living in the east end of Horse Valley for travel into Tuscarora Valley in Juniata County. This end of Horse Valley is sometimes called Kansas Valley. Only a trail or path crosses this gap.

VALLEYS.

The county of Perry, in itself a part of two of the most beautiful valleys of Pennsylvania, the Susquehanna and Juniata, has within its borders a number of beautiful and picturesque valleys, many of them fertile and whose history dates back to almost the middle of the second century past, when the pioneers braved the untold dangers of the frontier to make their homes here. A brief description of each:

The Susquehanna Valley. The long, broad and fertile drainage area of the Susquehanna River, extending from within New York State, through Pennsylvania to Maryland, the greater part of Perry County being drained into the Susquehanna via Sherman's Creek, which empties into it at Duncannon, and various other streams. Duncannon is located at the most western point of the Susquehanna, the river making a sharp turn to the southeast at that point.

The Juniata Valley. The picturesque valley drained by the Juniata River, extending from the Allegheny Mountains to Duncannon, where the Juniata flows into the Susquehanna. Almost half of the county is drained by the Juniata.

Sherman's Valley. Sherman's Valley comprises the larger part of western Perry County, being drained by Sherman's Creek. It extends from west of New Germantown to Duncannon. For several decades it was at the very frontier of civilization. Across it first moved traffic to the west of the Alleghenies, when roads were yet unknown.

Just how Sherman's Valley got its name will always remain a mystery. There is a tradition that a trader by that name was drowned while crossing Sherman's Creek, but nowhere is there record to substantiate it. However, as early as 1750 both the creek and the valley are referred to by that name. The first person of that name to patent land was John Shearman, and the tract was the first one east of the Haas mill tract in what is now Penn Township. Here Andrew Berryhill took up 331 acres November 26, 1766, and it is named on the warrant as "Sherman's Valley." It was sold to Isaac Jones in 1773 and he transferred it to John Shearman, whose patent is dated November 24, 1781. While John Shearman, as stated, was the first person of that name to patent land, the valley had been named long before that and the first settler may have been only a squatter and not have patented land. In fact, when it is referred to as Sherman's or Shearman's Valley and creek as early as 1750 it was impossible to patent land, as the land office for these lands was not opened until February 3, 1755. Egle's "Notes and Queries," page 454, says it was so named for the original settler, but gives no evidence to substantiate the fact, yet the writer is inclined to give credence to that statement, as it looks plausible. Of actual substantiation, however, there is none. It is even likely that the original name was Sherman and that Shearman is a German corruption, as Shearman has the broad German sound.

Page 454, Egle's Notes and Queries, says: "In going over the files of the *Carlisle Gazette* from 1787 to 1817 we find the original spelling in all references and in official advertisements—so named for one of the early settlers, Jacob Shearman."

Horse Valley. Horse Valley lies between the Tuscarora and Conococheague Mountains, in western Perry County, within the confines of Toboyne and Jackson Townships. It was so named because the farmers of Path Valley, Franklin County, of which it is an extension, used it as a pasture for their horses, before it had been settled. It was once known as McSwine's Valley.

Little Illinois Valley. This is a small valley located in Toboyne Township. The eastern part is cultivated and the western part is wooded. On the north it is bounded by Rising Mountain and Buck Ridge, which is a continuation of this mountain. On the south is Amberson Ridge and Schultz Ridge, a continuation of Amberson Ridge. It is about seven miles long and a mile wide. Brown's Run drains it. The western end of this valley is locally known as Fowler Hollow.

Henry's Valley. Henry's Valley is located in Toboyne and Jackson Townships, between Bower's Mountain and the Kittatinny or Blue Mountain. It is over ten miles long and merges into Sheaffer's Valley. It was named after John Henry, an early settler, who moved to Ohio. It is watered by Laurel Run.

Sheaffer's Valley. Sheaffer's Valley is located in Madison and Tyrone Townships, between Bower's Mountain and the Kittatinny or Blue Mountain, and is in reality a continuation of Henry's Valley. It is about six miles long and is watered by Laurel Run, in this section sometimes called Patterson's Run. In earlier years there was a preaching appointment in this valley, and as so many families named Sheaffer resided in the valley the itinerant missionary, in announcing his services referred to it as Sheaffer's Valley, and the name stuck.

Kennedy's Valley. Kennedy's Valley is located in Tyrone Township, in the cove formed by the folds of the Kittatinny or Blue Mountain, the broad part lying close to Landisburg. Called after the Kennedys, early settlers.

Green's Valley. Green's Valley is also located in Tyrone Township, in the small cove formed by a fold of the Blue Mountain.

Liberty Valley. Liberty Valley lies east of the watershed which runs from the Conococheague to the Tuscarora Mountain, and between these mountains in Madison Township.

Raccoon Valley. The valley lying between the Tuscarora Mountain and Raccoon Ridge in Tuscarora Township. Sometimes termed the Tuscarora Valley. It is watered by Raccoon Creek, eleven miles in length.

Tuscarora Valley. See Raccoon Valley, immediately preceding.

Mahanoy Valley. The valley in Miller Township located between Mahanoy Ridge and Dick's Hill.

Fishing Creek Valley. This valley comprises the most of Rye Township and lies between the Blue Mountain and the Cove Mountain.

Buffalo Valley. The name given in early provincial papers to the territory drained by Buffalo Creek, which rises in Liberty Valley, Madison Township, and flows into the Juniata above Newport.

Pfoutz Valley. The limestone valley which extends from the Juniata River to the Susquehanna River and lies between Wildcat Ridge and Turkey Hills, or the Juniata County line. One of the earliest points settled after the opening of the land office.

Buckwheat Valley. The valley located between Raccoon Ridge and Hominy Ridge, extending west from the Juniata as far as Eshcol.

Big Buffalo Valley. The local name applied to the territory between Hominy Ridge and Middle Ridge.

Little Buffalo Valley. Located between Middle Ridge and Buffalo Ridge, sometimes called Furnace Hills.

Pleasant Valley. A small valley lying south of Mannsville, its location being between Furnace Hills and Limestone Ridge.

Perry Valley. Formerly known as Wildcat Valley. It is located in

Greenwood and Liverpool Townships, between Wildcat Ridge and Buffalo Mountain.

Wildcat Valley. See Perry Valley, immediately preceding.

Hunter's Valley. Hunter's Valley is a cove formed by the Buffalo and Berry Mountain joining at the west, it lying between the two and wholly within Buffalo Township. Named after the many persons of that name who resided there, James Hunter being the original one. Isaiah Hunter, long afterwards an undertaker at Millerstown, was a grandson.

Buck's Valley. Early known as Brush Valley. It lies between Berry Mountain and Half Fall Mountain, in Buffalo Township, extending through Howe to Newport on the Juniata River. Its eastern end joins the Susquehanna River.

Brush Valley. See Buck's Valley, immediately preceding.

"Back Hollow." Located in Toboyne Township, and spoken of by Claypole, the geologist, as "the valley without a name."

Fishing Rod Valley. According to an old map, located in Liverpool Township, south of the wooded ridge, separating it from Susquehanna Township, Juniata County.

The Cove. The Cove is a geological peculiarity. Professor Claypole says its physical features are entirely due to the presence and direction of the Pocono Sandstone Mountain, which crosses the Susquehanna River at Duncannon under the name of Peters,' or Fourth Mountain, runs to the southwest, then curves around, and, turning eastward at the horseshoe returns to the Susquehanna River, which it crosses above Marysville. The Cove is considered the western extremity of the southern angle of the great Pottsville coal basin. It is located in Penn Township.

Limestone Valley. Located between Limestone Ridge and Mahanoy Ridge, starting east of New Bloomfield and running west until it merges into Sherman's Valley near Green Park.

Sandy Hollow. Sandy Hollow is located in Carroll Township. It extends from the township's western boundary in a northeasterly direction, for three miles. It is really a continuation of Sherman's Valley, as Sherman's Creek, after running close to the base of Pisgah Mountain for several miles, turns sharply to the right, while the valley continues ahead.

FEATURES OF DISTINCTION.

The Perry County territory belongs to one of the more important drainage systems of the world. The Susquehanna River, north of the Maryland line, including its tributaries, the West Branch and the Juniata River, drains a territory comprising 21,006 square miles, according to a statement of the Forestry Department of the State of Pennsylvania. Of this immense territory the West Branch drains 6,820 square miles; the North Branch, 5,328; the Susquehanna, from Sunbury to its junction with the Juniata at Duncannon, 1,552; from Duncannon to the Maryland line, 3,895, and the Juniata, 3,411.

As the Christmas season comes around with its pleasing memories and happy greetings, with its gay decorations and beautiful holly wreaths everywhere in evidence, being shipped from southern climes, few probably know that holly grows as far north and actually within the limits of Perry County; yet Prof. H. Justin Roddy, of the Millersville State Normal School, in his geological investigations has found it growing in Greenwood township, near the old home of former superintendent of schools, the late Silas Wright.

On the old Wesley Soule farm in Centre Township, not far from New Bloomfield, there grows one of the most rare plants to be found in America, known as the "box huckleberry." A man named Michaux and his son from France, came to this country over a century ago to make botanical discoveries. They were experts in their line and probably discovered and named more plants in America than any others. They described minutely various plants that were later found to be extinct in the districts named and botanists then thought they had been mistaken. Among these plants was named the box huckleberry, which had been discovered in the mountains of Virginia, which form a part of the same system as do the Perry County mountains. None have been found there since, and their discovery was supposed to have been a mistake or they had become extinct. About 1875 Spencer F. Baird, who later became president of the Smithsonian Institute at Washington, D. C., while making investigations in Pennsylvania, discovered the same plant covering a considerable area (about eight acres) on the Soule farm.

While the species has been found extinct in Virginia, there is one other small plot of it in the state of Delaware, on the banks of the Indian River, near Millsboro. Prof. E. W. Claypole, the geologist, speaks thus of it: "It appears to be a lingering relic of the ancient flora of the county; maintaining itself on the sterile hillside of Chemung shale, but liable to be destroyed by cultivation at any time. It is exceeding plentiful, forming a perfect mat over much of the ground, but its limits are sharply defined without apparent cause." This farm, as well as the Andrew Comp farm and others, was warranted by Robert McClay on March 22, 1793, its extent being 436 acres.

During 1920, another colony of this famous plant, said to be the oldest living thing on earth, was discovered within the borders of Perry County. It is located on the lands of John Doyle, in Watts Township, not far from the Juniata River, opposite Losh's Run Station, on the Pennsylvania Railroad. The discovery was made by Mr. H. A. Ward, of Harrisburg, Pennsylvania, under peculiar circumstances. Near the colony there is a famous fossil rock, which has been visited by geologists of note from many states. Mr. Ward had accompanied a party of geologists there, they being under the leadership of Dr. Benjamin L. Miller, of Princeton University. Being more interested in plants than fossils, Mr. Miller strayed through the ravines of the Half Falls Hills, and in a short time discovered the mass of low shrubbery with bright, shining leaves, being uniformly about ten inches high. He recognized it as the rare box huckleberry (Gaylussacia brachycera), and upon sending specimens to such authorities as Dr. Edgar T. Wherry, of the U. S. Bureau of Chemistry; Dr. N. L. Britten, director-in-chief of the New York Botanical Gardens, and Dr. J. P. Bill, a Harvard instructor, found that he was correct, and that he had discovered that which botanists had been seeking for over fifty years. The main colony occupies the northern slope of a ridge for at least a mile, and covers about two hundred feet in width. It is located on the same chain of ridges of Chemung soil as is the colony at the old Soule property, the two being less than a dozen miles apart. Mr. Ward has since discovered three additional colonies close by. It does not grow from seed, but spreads from the roots, and does not cross streams.

Located in Spring Township are the Warm Springs, the tract of land on which they are located being warranted by Solomon Dentler on March 21, 1793. James Kennedy, who was the owner in 1830, erected bath houses there. John Hipple, who had been sheriff of the county from 1826 to 1829, leased the property in 1830 from Kennedy for a ten-year period and erected a building 40x45 feet in size and other additional bath houses, and in 1831 opened the place as a regular health resort, entertaining those who during previous years had lodged in the surrounding farmhouses. In 1838 Peter Updegraffe, by marriage connected with the owner- ship, was in charge, employing his unoccupied time at farming and conducting a pottery which he had erected. On August 8, 1849, H. H. Etter purchased the property, and in 1850 again opened the house to the public. He built a seventy-five-foot extension to the hotel. The property passed to R. M. Henderson and John Hays, of Carlisle, who leased it to various parties until April 4, 1865, when it was destroyed by fire. Then, on April 11, 1866, the Perry Warm Springs Hotel Company was incorporated by A. L. Spon- sler, Robert M. Henderson, John Greason, Jacob Rheem, John Hays, William T. Dewalt, and John D. Crea (probably Creigh), with a capital stock of $10,000. The resort was again opened, but never attained its former popularity, as the seashore and other resorts which were reached by railroads were then being developed. As late as 1877 lists of guests appeared in the county press. For many years it has not been open as a resort. The property later came into the possession of Abram Bower, and in 1919 it was pur- chased by H. B. Rhinesmith, of New Bloomfield, from the Bower estate.

Sulphur springs abound at various places in Perry County, notably in Wheatfield, Juniata, and Toboyne Townships.

According to Prof. E. W. Claypole, an authority on geology, of the Second State Geological Survey, the earliest fish fossils and the earliest vertebrates found in any part of the world were discovered in Perry County, about 1883, in the Catskill rock formation. He describes these little prehistoric fish as not more than six inches in length, with thin shields protecting their vital organs. He says: "In every link the chain of argument is complete, and Perry County now has the honor of contributing to geology the oldest indisputable vertebrate animals which the world has yet seen." Further on in his report, he says:

"It is a long, long vista through which we look back, by the help of geology's telescope, to see these tiny ancestors of our fishes sporting in the Silurian seas. The Tertiary and Secondary rocks abound with fish. Even in our coal measures we find numerous species. The Devonian seas, as I have already mentioned, swarmed with great armor-clad monsters, some of which I have found in Perry County. These lived millions of years ago, and few can realize what a million means. But earlier than all these swam the little hard-shelled Pennsylvania Palæaspis, as I have called it, in the seas of long ago, before Tuscarora and the Blue Mountains had raised their heads above the waters. To these queer, antiquated forms we must look as the ancestors of some at least of our existing fish, developed by the slow process of nature, by change of environment, by competition in the struggle for existence, and by the inexorable law of the survival of the fittest. The condition of life must then have varied rapidly, for these and every nearly allied form became extinct in Mid-Devonian days; and when our coal measures were laid down they were already as much out of date and as nearly forgotten as are the armor-clad knights of the Middle Ages at the present time. But the mud of the sea bottom received their carcasses, buried them carefully, and has ever since faithfully preserved them, if not perfect, yet in a condition capable of being recognized. And to the geologist that same sea bottom, long since dried and turned to stone, now returns these precious remains. The day of their resurrection has come, and the hammer has brought to light from the rocks of Perry County the identical bones entombed, perhaps, twenty million years ago, when its wearer turned on its back, gave up the ghost and sank to the bottom."

Prof. Gilbert Van Ingen, of the Geological Department of Princeton University, assisted by H. Justin Roddy, has been making geological investigations throughout Perry County in recent years, and the following extract from a personal letter from him in 1921 is self-explanatory:

Referring to your inquiry regarding the salina beds of Perry County. There is only one item that is worthy of mention in a county history, namely, that the salina beds of Perry County contain remains of the most primitive types of fish known in North America. These were discovered by E. W. Claypole, who described them about 1880, in the vicinity of New Bloomfield, and have since been found by me at a certain horizon in the salina group at several different localities scattered throughout the county.

Perry County has practically no minerals. Coal has been found in small quantities on Cove Mountain and on Berry's Mountain in what is known as Pocono sandstone formation, but not in sufficient quantities to pay for mining and marketing.

3

There have been mines in years past of Clinton fossil ore at
Tuscarora Mountain, Millerstown; of Marcellus iron ore in small
basins of Oriskany sandstone in Limestone Ridge at a place
locally known as "Ore Bank Hill," south of Newport, in Miller
Township; on Iron Ridge, south and west of the old Perry Furnace; on Mahanoy Ridge, north and west of New Bloomfield;
at Bell's Hill, north and west of "Little Germany"; on Pisgah
Mountain, near Oak Grove Furnace; at old Juniata Furnace, west
of Newport; at Girty's Notch, on the Susquehanna, and at various
points along the south side of Mahanoy, Crawley's and Dick's
Hills, and back from the Susquehanna River at Marysville.

The only mineral of value ever mined to any considerable extent was iron ore, and that was principally in the vicinity of Millerstown. Ore was first discovered on lands of Abram Addams,
by Peter Wertz, in small quantities. Later the farm descended to
Mr. Adams' daughter, Mrs. McDonald, and George Maus began
actual operations. They were not worked extensively until 1867,
when Beaver, Marsh & Co. operated them and shipped the ore by
boat to their furnace at Winfield, Union County. In 1877 James
Rounsley, an experienced miner, bought the mines and shipped
much ore to that firm as long as their furnace was in operation, or
until 1892. They had built the furnace in 1853. The last ore
shipped from these mines was in 1903, by Mr. Rounsley. There
was another mine located near Millerstown, on the west side of
the river. James Lannigan began operations there in 1868 and
continued until 1875. James Rounsley purchased these mines also
in 1879 and continued their operation until 1901, his continuous
mining lasting for twenty-six years. About 1868 the Reading
Iron Company operated mines on the Thomas P. Cochran farm,
near Millerstown, but did not operate regularly. The Duncannon
Iron Company opened the mines on the Perry Kremer farm, on
the west side of the river, near Millerstown, in 1868, and operated
for about three years. The Reading Company also opened mines
on the Jonathan Black farm about 1868 and mined until 1877.
Other marts to which this ore was shipped was Lochiel, Reading,
and Harrisburg. When the Perry Furnace was in operation the
mines on the Dum farm in "Little Germany," Spring Township,
employed twelve men. With the blowing out of the charcoal furnaces throughout Perry County, about the middle of the last century, these smaller operations ceased. The substitution of coal
and coke for charcoal in the iron industry spelled their end, as coal
was too far away and the product insufficient to pay.

An effort to mine coal in Berry Mountain, near Mt. Patrick,
was made by Baltimore capitalists, the McDonald-Downing Co.,
around the period of the Sectional War. A drift of three hundred
feet was made and at that point it was claimed a three-foot vein

of coal was discovered, said to be too small to operate upon a paying basis. The mouth of the drift is plainly to be seen. Another statement is that the firm offered a Mr. Matchett, a prospector, $10,000 for a three-foot vein.

An old legend is that the Indians once came to a blacksmith shop on what is now the James R. Showaker place, on Shaffer Run, in Toboyne Township, and wanted a horse shod, but were informed by the smith that he had no coal, whereupon they left and in a short time returned with the necessary coal. As coal was not then yet in use the story must be only a legend. Coal was discovered on the Cove Mountain twenty-five years ago, but not in sufficient quantities. The *Perry Forester* of May 24, 1827, said "a very extensive bed of stone coal has been discovered near the mouth of Sherman's Creek, on land belonging to Stephen Duncan." In 1857 the county press reported "a large vein of coal" discovered on the land of D. Lupfer, one and a half miles west of New Bloomfield. A small vein was once discovered in "Little Germany," Spring Township, but it was only three inches thick, soft and easily crumbled.

The great length of the zigzag beds of Lower Heidelberg limestone, aggregating 150 miles, which underlie the surface, makes the burning and marketing of lime an industry worth while, at the same time supplying a fertilizer for the soil. Many of these lime kilns date back to the time of the pioneer.

While Perry County is practically destitute of minerals, yet there have been several cases of great excitement over their reported discovery. Immediately after the close of the Sectional War, in 1865, it was reported that oil had been discovered in Saville Township and two companies were formed for development of the industry. The Snyder Spring Oil Company, with a capital of $50,000, the shares being one dollar each, was formed and leased the farms then owned by Godfrey Burket and William Snyder. The Colier Oil Company leased the lands at the headwaters of Buffalo Creek. It had a capital of $100,000, the shares being of a par value of five dollars. Of course, oil was never found. During 1920 another company was organized, principally by persons from outside the county, to prospect for oil in Perry and Cumberland Counties. They are now sinking their first well near Landisburg.

Crossing Perry County to the south is a remarkable geological trap-dyke formation known as Ironstone Ridge. Nine miles west of Marysville it makes a watershed across Rye Township and its outcroppings continue clear across Cumberland County and are visible in York County. It is probably two hundred feet wide. Three others cross Rye and Penn Townships. Of these a much smaller one than the one described runs about five hundred yards east. Two others cross the Cove slightly northeast, one of which, passing Duncannon, runs across Wheatfield and Watts Townships. They cut mountains and valleys at right angles. Local tradition would have this most prominent trap-dyke, crossing Rye Township, as extending clear south to Tennessee, but Claypole, the geologist, whose position as an authority has never been questioned, has it end in York County. Samuel J. Tritt, for twenty years county surveyor of Cumberland County, who did much surveying in Perry County, also recognized it as first becoming conspicuous in Rye Township, and as extending across Cumberland to the Susquehanna River in York County. Claypole tells us:

"Trap-dykes are ancient cracks in the earth, filled from below by lava, which has hardened into rock. They must be of great depth, for they can be traced along the present surface of the earth for a great distance. The trap-dyke described by Dr. Frazer, in his report on Lancaster County, runs in a straight line (N. E.) forty miles. Many others exist in Adams, York, Lancaster, Dauphin, Lebanon, Berks, Chester, Delaware, Montgomery and Bucks Counties, and in middle and northern New Jersey, southern New York, and New England.

"The most remarkable of them all starts in the South Mountains, and runs in a nearly straight line across Cumberland County (between Mechanicsburg and Carlisle), crossing the Blue Mountain two miles east of Sterrett's Gap." This is the "Ironstone Ridge" spoken of above.

Claypole further says: "At the earliest date to which geology can point back with tolerable certainty in the history of what is now Perry County, the interior of the North American continent was an ocean of unknown extent into which was borne the sand and mud of neighboring lands, swept down by the rivers of that distant age to make the beds of rock which to-day compose the solid land of the United States. The history of this process is written in the rocks."

At another place the noted geologist, speaking of an unusual feature, says: "The volcanic rocks of Perry County may seem strange, but it has long been known that in the southeast of the county occur some rocks of very peculiar nature, totally different from any others. They cut across the line of the bedded rocks quite regardless of their direction. They are very heavy, intensely tough, and highly charged with iron. They are in effect what the geologist calls 'trap-rocks,' what the miner calls 'elvans.' They are composed of material that has been fused, and forced in a fused condition into and between the other rocks, filling up cracks and cavities and baking and hardening by its heat and strata through which it flowed. When cooled the fluid matter became hard, and is now known as intrusive or trap-rock."

CHAPTER II.

EARLIEST RECORDS OF INDIAN INHABITANTS.

WHEN Christopher Columbus, in October, 1492, discovered the Western Continent, which was the preliminary act in the development of this great nation, the lands which now comprise the county of Perry—in Pennsylvania—were, according to all traditions, inhabited by the swarthy, copper-colored race, from that day to be generally spoken of as Indians, on account of the discoverer's mistaken idea that he had crossed the world to the eastern shores of India.

When the first settlements were made in Pennsylvania by the Dutch (not to be misconstrued as referring to the Germans) in 1623, when it was later occupied by the Swedes, the Dutch again, the English, and eventually in 1682 by William Penn and the Quakers, the outlying sections of which Perry was naturally a part, were evidently overrun by these wild tribes, although almost two hundred years had elapsed since the discovery of America.

Then for another period of a half century little is known, except that which comes to us through the misty veil of years and which for want of a better name is known as tradition. About that time, however, the outlying settlements had pushed west to the Susquehanna, and an occasional manuscript, a diary, a letter or a record of one kind or another has been found and preserved. so that one can get a glimpse into the lives of the Indians and the hardy pioneers on the lands which were later to become the county of Perry.

If any other nationality than the English under Penn had settled in Pennsylvania, Perry County would probably not have advanced nearly as rapidly as it did, as the English-speaking people were then as now, the advance agents of civilization. It is significant that those old English charters gave title to the land straight

---

*The chapters of this book relating to the Indians have been passed upon by Dr. George P. Donehoo, of Coudersport, Pennsylvania, noted authority upon Indian History and secretary of the Pennsylvania Historical Commission, and later, November, 1921, appointed State Librarian of Pennsylvania, by Governor Sproul.

Common or popular usage adds the "s" to Indian names, thus Delawares, Tuscaroras, although the names Delaware, Tuscarora, etc., as applied to Indian tribes, is already plural, being applied to a tribe, according to scientific writers. Not belonging to the latter class of writers it has been thought best to add the "s" in this book, as do even many noted writers.

across the continent from ocean to ocean. The following paragraph from George Sydney Fisher's "The Making of Pennsylvania," well illustrates this:

"In nothing is the difference in nationality so distinctly shown. The Dutchman builds trading posts and lies in his ship off shore to collect the furs. The gentle Swede settles on the soft, rich meadow lands, and his cattle wax fat and his barns are full of hay. The Frenchman enters the forest, sympathizes with its inhabitants, and turns half savage to please them. All alike bow before the wilderness and accept it as a fact. But the Englishman destroys it. He grasped at the continent from the beginning, and but for him the oak and the pine would have triumphed and the prairies still be in possession of the Indian and the buffalo." No lands in the world advance and prosper as do those of the English-speaking nations, and be it remembered that among the English-speaking people the American is always in the van.

One of the earliest records of Indian affairs in Pennsylvania is the "Jesuit Relations of 1659," which tells of a tradition of a ten years' war between the Mohawks and the Pennsylvania Indians, in which the latter almost exterminated the Mohawks. This was before either could obtain firearms. To Captain John Smith, of Virginia, posterity is indebted for the very first description, by a white man, of the Indians of the interior of Pennsylvania. Powhatan had told him of a mighty nation which dwelt here which "did eat men." Smith says: "Many kingdoms he described to me to the head of the bay, which seemed to be a mighty river, issuing from mighty mountains betwixt two seas." On the east of the bay Smith found an Indian who understood the language of Powhatan, and he was dispatched up the river to bring down some of them. In a few days sixty of these "gyant-like people" appeared. Smith called all the country Virginia, and from a description by the Indians he drew a map, which is the oldest map of any inland parts of Pennsylvania. He locates five Indian towns, the second lowest down being designated "Attaock," a branch which corresponds to the Juniata. This was probably the Indian village later known as Juniata, on Duncan's Island, further described in the chapter devoted to that island. He described the river as "cometh three or four days from the head of the bay." These Indians were supposed to be of the Andaste tribes, using dialects of the throat-speaking Iroquois. Smith's description tells of their "hellish voice, sounding from them as a voice in a vault." The Iroquois used no lip sounds, but spoke from the throat with an open mouth. Along the shores of the bay Smith found the natives all fearful of the "great-water men," who principally dwelt along the Potomac and the Susquehanna and "had so many boats and so many men that they made war with all the world." Smith

sterdam, of New Netherlands, in which he almost accurately places
the Susquehanna, but without any West Branch or Juniata. During the next fifty years about fifteen maps appeared, all having
practically the same river outline. On all of them just where the
Juniata belongs, there is the name of a tribe called "Onojutta
Haga," the first part of the name meaning a projecting stone, and
the "Haga" being the Mohawk word for people or tribe. They
were a superior race and lived largely by the cultivation of the soil.

When the Dutch began selling firearms to the Iroquois, or Five
Nations, about 1640, they started a military conquest which extended as far west as the Mississippi. Among those destroyed or
subdued and incorporated into their own tribes were the Andaste
tribes in Pennsylvania, which among others included the "Standing
Stone" Indians on the Juniata. By 1676 all were exterminated.
The Iroquois then claimed all the lands of the Susquehanna and
its branches, selling to William Penn and his heirs at different
times what they had gained by conquest. While negotiating for
the sale of lands as early as 1684 the Iroquois spoke of the entire
region as "the Susquehanna River, which we won with the sword."
In 1736 Thomas Penn, then governor, acknowledged their right
by these words: "The lands on Susquehanna, we believe, belong
to the Six Nations by the conquest of the Indian tribes on that
river."

The entire region, which of course included what is now Perry
County, was then a vast deserted space until such time as the Tuscaroras were allowed to settle there. The Delawares and Shawnees later were allowed to settle, the Delawares coming in between
1720 and 1730. During this period not even a trader or pioneer
had ventured there and through this veil of obscurity comes no
record whatsoever of this time. However, the tribal records of
the Hurons and the Iroquois tell of vast numbers of prisoners
being brought to their New York towns from the South, as many
as six hundred at a time, and the inference is that the tribes inhabiting this section were among the captives.

The Tuscaroras had been defeated and driven from their former
abode, and they claimed that the colonists were selling their children into slavery. About 1713 or 1714, they came from the South,
and settled, with the consent of the Five Nations, "on the Juniata,
in a secluded interior, not far from the Susquehanna River." At
a conference with Governor Hunter, of New York, September 20,
1714, a Chief of the Iroquois, said, "We acquaint you that the
Tuscarora Indians are come to shelter themselves among the Five
Nations."

The great path or trail to the southwest was known as the "Tuscarora Path," when the first traders came, and this tribe's principal
settlements were likely responsible for that name, as they were

located in Tuscarora Valley, now in Juniata County; in Path Valley, now in Franklin County, and in what is now Perry County, principally in Raccoon Valley. These lands had not been occupied for from a half to three quarters of a century, or since the conquest by the Five Nations. According to Samuel G. Drake, an Indian antiquarian, "the Tuscaroras from Carolina joined them (the Five Nations) about 1712, but were not formally admitted into the confederacy until about ten years after that; this gained them the name of the Six Nations." They were sometimes known as Mingoes. In all the Albany conferences dated from 1714 to 1722 in which the members of the Five Nations participated the Tuscaroras are not mentioned. After this probationary period of probably ten years on the Juniata, where most of them lived, they were formally assigned a portion of the Oneida territory and had their council-house east of Syracuse, New York. However, all the Tuscaroras did not migrate to New York, some choosing to remain on the Juniata. In 1730 there is record of "three Tuskarorows missing at Pechston" (Paxtang), now Harrisburg. Even to the time of the Albany purchase of the lands north of the Kittatinny or Blue Mountain, in 1754, some of the tribe still inhabited the district. In a letter from John O'Neal to the governor dated at Carlisle, May 27, 1753, is the statement: "A large number of Delawares, Shawnees and Tuscaroras continue in this vicinity —the greater number having gone to the West." As early as 1725 the Conestogas and the Shawnees had begun working their way westward along the Juniata and the West Branch of the Susquehanna.

Among the reports and records of Fort Duquesne was found the following, dated September 15, 1756:

"Two hundred Indians and French left Fort Duquesne to set fire to four hundred houses in a part of Pennsylvania. That province has suffered but little in consequence of the intrigues of the Five Nations with Taskarosins, a tribe on the lands of that province, and in alliance with the Five Nations. But now they have declared that they will assist their brethren, the Delawares, and Chouanons (Shawnees), and consequently several have sided with them, so that the above province will be laid waste the same as Virginia and Carolina." According to that, some were still there in 1756.

About 1730 some Scoth-Irish, who had crossed the Susquehanna, settled in what was then termed the "Kittochtinny or North Valley, near Falling Springs." This was the Cumberland Valley of the present, and the place called Falling Springs was not the settlement by that name in Perry County, but was where the present town of Chambersburg stands. This is the first settlement west of the Susquehanna of which there is record. The woods were then full of Indians.

As George Croghan, the interpreter, who knew the languages of the Shawnees and the Delawares, located in Cumberland County in 1742, the presence of those tribes here is indicated. The Delawares were known among themselves as the Leni Lenape tribe. According to their tradition they were one of two great peoples who inhabited the entire country, the other being the Mingoes.

As the names Juniata and Oneida are derived from the same source the contention is advanced that the Oneidas may have inhabited the Juniata Valley, but according to authorities there is nowhere any evidence to bear out that fact.

An Indian trail led westward along the Susquehanna and Juniata Rivers, crossing the former near what is now Clark's Ferry, at Duncannon; another led over the Kittatinny or Blue Mountain at what was then Croghan's (now Sterrett's) Gap, and a third led over the same mountain at McClure's Gap, the two latter crossing the Tuscarora Mountain. That via Sterrett's Gap was known as "the Allegheny Path," the first great highway to the West. The first white men to enter Perry County territory came over these routes, and the men were known as traders, whose vocation necessitated their going westward as far as the Ohio. There are evidences that these men were traders even before there is record of it. There are some recorded statements pertaining to their operations, but traders then, as now, do not belong to the class which reduce events to writing.

One of them was George Croghan, whose name was given to Sterrett's Gap. Croghan first lived in what was later to become Cumberland County, about five miles from Harris' Ferry (now Harrisburg), and afterwards on the mountain at the Gap, near where the old tavern or road-house stood later. Still later he took up his residence at Aughwick, near Mount Union, in Huntingdon County. As early as 1747 he is mentioned as a "considerable trader." He was well acquainted with the Indian country and with the paths and trails. He continually used the one via the Kittatinny and Tuscarora Mountains, from which one would infer that it was at least preferable to the others. He served the provincial government by convoying expeditions westward for them. He was associated much with Conrad Weiser, the Indian interpreter, and of them there is more further on in this book.

The scope of this book is not wide enough to go into all the details of the often fraudulent, crafty and deceptive actions of some of the pioneers, traders and officials in dealing with the Indians, which in a general way might be said to have been largely responsible for much of the heart-rending suffering of the white settlers and many of the sickening massacres perpetrated upon them. With every setting of the sun the aborigines saw their domain dwindling before the oncoming tide of white pioneers, their favorite hunting grounds encroached upon and the very streams from which came much of their subsistence marred by the building of mill dams. Constantly impressed with such conditions, but a spark was often needed to light the flame of resentment which left death and destruction in its wake.

OF OUR INDIAN INHABITANTS.

The reader is familiar with the life and habits of the American Indian; and from what can be learned in reference to the tribes which dwelt on what is now Perry County soil, they were the exact counterpart of the average member of that race in industry, cruelty and all the other characteristic traits to which they were heir. They hunted and fished for a living, and the territory now embraced in Perry County was noted as a famous hunting ground, evidences of that fact being recorded in provincial records and mentioned in various places in this volume. The only evidences of their industry were the locations of several patches of Indian corn and beans which the women raised.

Their skin was red or copper-colored, their hair coarse and black, and they had high cheek bones. The males were seldom corpulent, were swift of foot, quick with bow and arrow and later with firearms, and very skillful in the handling of canoes. Their home was the tepee or wigwam, a few in after years having log huts. These tepees were a number of poles or saplings covered with skins of animals, the only heat afforded being from fires built upon the ground.

Their only clothing was of skins, which they had a method of curing so that they were soft and pliable and which they often ornamented with paint and beads made from shells. Their moccasins were of deer skin and were without heels. The females often bedecked themselves with mantles made of feathers, overlapping each other similar to their appearance on fowls. Their dress was of two pieces, a shirt of leather, ornamented with fringe, and a skirt of the same material fastened about the waist by a belt. Their hair they made into a thick, heavy plait, which they let hang down the back. Their heads they usually ornamented with bands of wampum or with a small skull cap. The men went bareheaded, with their hair fantastically trimmed, each to his own fancy. The white man, with all his knowledge, has never been able to excel the Indian method of tanning, the result of which was softness and pliability.

The aborigines had a peculiar idea of government. They were absolutely free, acknowledged no master, and yielded obedience to law only in so far as they chose, and yet there existed a primitive system of government which was a faint type of that of our present great republic. They worshiped no graven image, but spoke of "the great spirit" and the "happy hunting grounds." While their ideas of a future were indistinct, yet they possessed a belief in a hereafter. They had much reverence for the forces of nature and measured time by the sun and the moon.

They had rude villages, one of which lay opposite the west end of Duncannon, on Duncan's Island, known as "Choiniata," or "Juneauta," which is known to have existed as late as 1745, the story of which appears in the chapter devoted to Duncan's and Haldeman's Islands. In searching Indian historical data and tradition the knowledge that there was an Indian village in western Perry territory, probably near Cisna's Run, appeared somewhat vaguely. While it is impossbile at this late day to locate it exactly, it is practically certain that it was located on lands owned by the late George Bryner and W. H. Loy, at Cisna's Run, as it was on the north side of Sherman's Creek, on a branch of that creek, surrounding or near a deep spring. On Mr. Loy's lands, almost against the Bryner line, Cedar Spring, five feet deep, is located. Mrs. Jacob Loy, of Blain, well up in years, had as an actual fact from her people, the location of this village. When the writer visited the location, in midsummer of 1919, Mr. Bryner was yet living and pointed out a mound, near the Sherman's Valley Railroad, which resembled a small knoll. From William Adair, an aged man who died many years ago, Mr. Bryner learned that it was once the site of an Indian log hut which he had seen in his youth, probably a lone reminder of the old Indian village.

A neighborhood story connected with an Indian woman that lived in this hut, the last of her clan in the district, follows:

She called on a neighbor, a Mrs. Cisna, grandmother of the late Dr. William R. Cisna, who resided near by. Mrs. Cisna, after washing her hands, mixed the ingredients, and kneading the meal proceeded to bake corn bread, inviting her copper-colored caller to remain for tea, which she did. Shortly afterwards Mrs. Cisna returned the call and was invited to dine. She accepted, and the Indian lady also washed her hands and proceeded to mix the ingredients for corn bread, but mixed them in the water in which she had washed her hands. Not wishing to offend one of the race, Mrs. Cisna ate of this "sanitary" production and, notwithstanding, lived to a ripe old age.

Between the Bryner and Loy homes and Sherman's Creek, opposite the point where the Moose mill is located, was an Indian cornfield. It is a bottom field, lying by the creek, and is as level as a floor. The evidence that this location was thickly populated at one time by the Indians is not only passed down by spoken word and

records, but even in the year this is written—1919—Ex-County
Commissioner A. K. Bryner (since deceased), while plowing a
truck patch for his brother, containing less than two acres, found
a half dozen of fine specimens of Indain arrowheads, which are
in the possession of the writer. In the past few years he has also
found an Indian tomahawk, Indian tanning stones, skinning stones,
many arrowheads, etc. Some years ago, in the same vicinity,
William Adair, the father of Ex-County Commissioner James K.
Adair, plowed up an Indian soapstone pot, a very rare specimen.
The latter curiosity was unearthed on the farm now owned by
A. N. Lyons.

The Lyons or old Adair farm, the Bryner and Loy farms, and
the deep spring are all on the location of the old Indian trail,
known to later generations as the "bridle path," still descernible
on Bowers' Mountain, opposite Cisna's Run, from whence it
crossed westward to Kistler and around the foot of Conococheague
Mountain to Juniata County and the West.

They were, generally speaking, a lazy, listless people, addicted
to the use of rum, which they knew as "walking stick," and lived
on game, fish and mussels, the Susquehanna River at that time
being prolific of the two last named products. Indian cornmeal
was their only grain product, their method of grinding it being
with a bowl and stones. With the coming of the early trader a
market was created at their door for the skins from their game,
for furs for the fair sex. The pay was often in trinkets and
gaudy fabrics for which the red man had a fancy, sometimes in
rum, and even in money, but often the latter went for rum in the
end. In the chapter on Duncan's and Haldeman's Islands there is
a lengthy description of their mode of life by Rev. Brainerd, a
missionary who spent much time among them. In the chapter
dealing with Simon Girty much more of Indian life is to be
learned.

When the pioneers settled the county a few Indians refused to
follow their tribes in leaving their homes—just as many older
people of the present day object to locating in new sections in the
latter years of their lives—and remained. The Indian woman
mentioned above as being located at Cisna's Run, was one of these,
and an old Indian, known as "Indian John," who lived near the
Warm Springs, in Carroll Township, was another. He used to
trade at the store of Thomas Lebo, at the point which later became
Lebo post office, and is said to have been a very old man.

At various places in this book are recorded the taking of cap-
trade at the store of Thomas Lebo, at the point which later became
now owned by Mrs. Charles McKeehan, located between Blain and
New Germantown, which was warranted and settled by John Rhea,
who sold it to a family named Hunter, from whom the early

Briners purchased it in 1809. During an Indian invasion of the valley two of the Hunter children, a boy and a girl, were captured by red men. The girl escaped during the following night and returned, but the boy never came back. Long years afterwards he wrote to George Black, a neighbor, from the far West, making inquiry as to the disposition of his father's estate. George Conner, a black-haired child who was favored by the Indians during his captivity, was captured near Landisburg, but later escaped. He was the ancestor of Mrs. Garland, of Landisburg.

The Indian was the earliest road builder, but his building consisted of making a mere path through the brush either in the most direct line or by the line of least resistance. Evidences of the old Indian trails yet remain, as described under the chapter devoted to trails and roads. Located along one of these old trails over Tuscarora Mountain is a large boulder, weighing many tons and of a size that would fill a large room of an ordinary house, known as "Warrior Rock," famous in legend and story. They also had a line of trails following the mountain tops, so that their perspective was greater. These they used in troublesome periods.

At various places in the county there are old Indian burial places which would substantiate the fact that Indian villages were once located in those vicinities. There is one at Saville post office, in Saville Township. This place was formerly known as Lane's Mill and was a great hunting and fishing ground for the aborigines. Those located here are supposed to have been the ones which came back to the county and did the attacking on the McMillen place, near Kistler. An old legend tells of their getting lead near by for the points of their arrows when they needed it, but if so, their followers—the pale face—has failed to locate it. Several men well up in years by the name of Elliott, who were Indian traders, resided in the locality, from whom descended David Elliott, D.D., LL.D., the noted divine.

There is also legendary evidence of an Indian burial ground at Blain, at the old Presbyterian cemetery. Many arrowheads are found in the vicinity and a few years ago, in excavating for a grave, two skulls were found placed against each other, the skeletons extending in opposite directions. Tradition has it that that was the Indian custom of interment, thus affording some evidence of the location of the Indian burial place at this point. Arrowheads are found even to this day along Sherman's Creek, at New Germantown, Blain, Landisburg, Shermansdale and at many other points. Also at Millerstown and Duncan's Island, in the Juniata River territory.

On Quaker Ridge, near the Warm Springs, in Spring Township, there is an Indian grave surrounded by pine trees. The aged residents of the vicinity also recall the legend of the three Indian graves on the old Burrell farm, in Carroll Township, now owned by Willis Duncan. Near the celebrated Gibson Rock, along Sherman's Creek, is a spring, known to this day as Indian Spring. According to a legend six soldiers sent from the garrison at Carlisle during the Indian uprisings, were waylaid there and murdered.

John Clendenin, a settler in what is now Toboyne Township, was killed and scalped by the Indians near the site of the old Monterey tannery. One of the saddest of all the abductions from Perry County territory was the case of two children from the George Kern farm, bordering New Germantown, in Toboyne Township. Simon Kern, the ancestor, had come from his home in Holland and had located on the farm mentioned. Two small Kern girls were helping work in the fields when lurking Indians carried them away. They traveled a considerable distance when they were overtaken by night. During the night one of the little girls managed to escape while her captors slept and returned to her people. The other remained an Indian captive. Tradition tells of a woman from the stockade at Fort Robinson returning to the farm opposite—the McClure farm—and of her being killed and scalped by lurking redskins.

According to James B. Hackett, long a resident of New Bloomfield, whose father was once a resident of Madison Township, there was an interesting tradition connected with his father's tract of land there which was later owned by Noble Meredith. A man named James Dixon had first located it, but had been driven out by the Indians, and then took up a tract in Centre Township. John Mitchell then warranted it January 28, 1763. Three Indians are supposed to be buried there, and men of the present generation had the graves, then already overgrown mounds, pointed out to them in their early years. On this tract, according to this tradition, was buried a pot or kettle of gold by a squaw, received in return for English scalps turned over to the French. It is supposed to have been left by the Indians when they were hastily driven out. Evidently this story is a mere legend, as the red men were too crafty to tell their white brethren their personal and tribal affairs.

Wright's History names Millerstown as the scene of "either a long residence or probably a fierce battle between the Delawares and the immigrating Shawnees," adding "the location of the conflict was no doubt near the canal bridge, for they were interred in a wide and deep mound, west of the house now the residence of Mrs. Oliver, and found by the workmen who dug the canal." Mentioning an Indian village at or near Newport and one at Millerstown, it says: "These were the only Indian villages in Perry County." As the soil which is now comprised in Perry County was inhabited at different times by different tribes, and as Indian villages were formed by wigwams, which were easily movable, the statement above is hardly borne out by facts.

On Clemson's Island, opposite the town of New Buffalo, located on the Susquehanna River (not Perry County soil, however), was an Indian mound which is remembered by those in very mature years as being quite prominent, but now indiscernible. There are vague accounts of the torturing of whites in Pfoutz Valley, while the relentless savages danced about the fires which tortured and consumed the unfortunates.

THE FIVE NATIONS.

The great western confederacy of Indian nations was styled by the French, the "Iroquois," generally at first being known as "The Five Nations," and later as "The Six Nations." The Mohawks are said to be the oldest of the confederacy, the Oneidas joining them next, the Onondagas third, the Senecas fourth, and the Cayugas fifth. About 1713 the Tuscaroras from the Carolinas placed themselves under the protection of this "League of Nations, but was not formally admitted to membership until about 1722. The Six Nations called themselves "Aquanuschioni," which the interpreter tells us means "United People." The Shawnees, who lived on the west branch of the Susquehanna and in Cumberland County (which then included Perry), were not in this confederacy.

Just when the Five Nations was formed is uncertain. There is a tradition, according to the Jesuit Relations, that before the English settlements were made in America the Susquehannas had almost exterminated the Mohawks in a ten-years' war. Some historians incline to the belief that at that time the Mohawks appealed to kindred tribes along the shores of Lake Ontario for aid and that that was the beginning of the Five Nations. It is probable that the Indian battles fought at Duncan's Island and likely at Millerstown were during this war between the Susquehannas and the Mohawks. Captain John Smith, who explored Chesapeake Bay in 1608, says the inhabitants of the Susquehanna country "made war with all the world," which implies that they were then already at war with the Mohawks.

Kelker's History of Dauphin County says: "In 1633 they were at war with the Alonquin tribes on the Delaware, maintaining their supremacy by butchery." Later they warred with tribes from Maryland and Virginia, and Governor Calvert, in 1642, issued a proclamation declaring them public enemies. The end of the Susquehannas came in 1675, according to the Jesuit Relations, when they were completely defeated and became the prisoners and subjects of their captors, evidently the Mohawks, as Thomas Penn, the provincial governor, later credited the Mohawks with ownership of the lands "by the conquest of the Indian tribes on that river."

The Shawnees were a tribe of Southern Indians, having resided near the Spanish possessions in that territory and being almost constantly at war with their neighbors. As extermination threatened them they appealed to the Five Nations and the English for protection, which was granted them by the treaty of 1701. They settled on the Susquehanna and its tributaries and were later assigned to the lands along the Ohio. However, many of them refused to go, and the others kept traveling back and forth from the Ohio. The Six Nations resided principally in New York State and it was only by permission that the Shawnees were allowed to occupy these lands. As an illustration of the contempt in which they were held listen to this extract from a speech by Cannassetego, diplomat of the Iroquois:

"We conquered you; we made women of you; you know you are women, and can no more sell lands than women; nor is it fit you should have the power of selling lands, since you would abuse it. The land that you claim is gone through your guts; you have been furnished with clothes, meat and drink, by the goods paid you for it, and now you want it again, children as you are. But we find you none of our blood; you act a dishonest part, not only in this, but in other matters; your ears are ever open to slanderous reports about your brethren. For all these reasons we charge you to remove instantly; we don't give you liberty to think about it. Don't deliberate, but move away, and take this belt of wampum."

The Delawares, who jointly with the Shawnees occupied these lands, were very much chagrined at being called women and usually offered other explanations than the real one.

Murder of an Early Trader.*

Many of the early traders, because of their cupidity, took advantage of the Indians by trickery and thus were at times the cause of much trouble to the provincial authorities. Others became the victims of their own greed. An instance of this kind is reproduced here in its original form for various reasons. At that time Duncan's Island, then known as Juniata Island, was a centre for traders and "McKee's Place," which was just around the lower end of Peters' Mountain, was also already inhabited by a number of these people.

In this vicinity resided John Armstrong, or at least that is the impression formed from the fact that among the names on the affidavit are those of Thomas McKee, Francis Ellis, and William Baskins, who were among the searching party, who are known

---

*From Conrad Weiser's journal.
Note.—Shikellamy was sometimes spelled Shickcalamy.

4

to have been inhabitants here, and it is also probable ·that actions of those days were largely as they exist to this day, in which a man's neighbors are those whose aid is first sought whose names are usually used in evidence. There is record of the three pioneers above named being located here in 1752, or eight years thereafter, and they probably were already here in 1744.

Musemeelin was of the Indian tribe that inhabited the Susquehanna Valley. In order to let the rising generation get a glimpse of the methods used to adjust difficulties between the province and the Indians the documentary evidence and communications are printed in full. It follows:

Before Cumberland County was created, when the soil of Perry was yet an Indian domain, in 1744, one John Armstrong, a trader with the Indians west of the Susquehanna, and two of his employes, James Smith and Woodward Arnold, were murdered by an Indian of the Delawares on the Juniata River. Seven settlers, accompanied by five Indians, made a search and found the bodies. The murderer was apprehended and turned over to the authorities, being first imprisoned at the county seat at Lancaster, and later removed to Philadelphia, as his countrymen were about to assemble in conference with the whites at Lancaster, and it was deemed that his presence there might cause friction. The Colonial governor ordered Armstrong's property returned to his people and asked that a delegation attend the trial of the culprit and his execution, if found guilty. A brother of the murdered man, named Alexander Armstrong, of Lancaster County, wrote a letter to the king of the Delawares—Allumoppies—at Shamokin, bearing on his brother's death and also threats made against himself:

April 25, 1744.

To Allumoppies, King of the Delawares: Great Sir, as a parcel of your men have murdered my brother, and two of his men, I wrote you, knowing you to be a king of justice, that you will send us in all the murderers and the men that were with them. As I looked for the corpse of my murdered brother; for that reason your men threaten my life, and I cannot live in my house. Now as we have no inclination or mind to go to war with you, our friends, as a friend I desire that you will keep your men from doing me harm, and also to send the murderers and their companions. I expect an answer; and am your much hurt friend and brother.

ALEXANDER ARMSTRONG.

According to the following deposition the bodies of the murdered men were found after a search was made:

PAXTON, April 19, 1744.

The deposition of the subscribers testifieth and saith, that the subscribers having a suspicion that John Armstrong, trader, together with his men, James Smith and Woodward Arnold, were murdered by the Indians. They met at the house of Joseph Chambers, in Paxton,* and there consulted to go to Shamokin, to consult with the Delaware King and Shikel-

---

*Now Fort Hunter.

lamy, and there council what they should do concerning the affair, whereupon the king and council ordered eight of their men to go with the
deponents to the house of James Berry in order to go in quest of the
murdered persons, but that night they came to the said Berry's house,
three of the eight Indians ran away, and the next morning these deponents,
with the five Indians that remained, set out on their journey peaceably
to the last supposed sleeping place of the deceased, and upon their arrival
these deponents dispersed themselves in order to find out the corpse of
the deceased, and one of the deponents, named James Berry, a small distance from the aforesaid sleeping place, came to a white oak tree which
had three notches on it, and close by said tree he found a shoulder bone,
which the deponent does suppose to be John Armstrong's, and that he
himself showed it to his companions, one of whom handed it to the said
five Indians to know what bone it was, and they after passing different
sentiments upon it, handed it to a Delaware Indian, who was suspected
by the deponents, and they testify and say, that as soon as the Indian
took the bone in his hand, his nose gushed out with blood, and directly
handed it to another. From whence these deponents steered along a
path about three or four miles to the Narrows of Juniata, where they suspected the murder to have been committed, and where the Allegheny road
crosses the creek, these deponents sat down in order to consult on what
measures to take in order to proceed on a discovery. Whereupon most of
the white men, these deponents, crossed the creek again, and went down
the creek, and crossed into an island, where these deponents had intelligence the corpse had been thrown; and there they met the rest of the
white men and Indians, who were in company, and there consulted to go
further down the creek in quest of the corpse, and these deponents further
say, they ordered the Indians to go down the creek on the other side; but
they all followed these deponents, at a small distance, except one Indian,
who crossed the creek again; and soon after, these deponents seeing
some Bald eagles and other fowls, suspected the corpse to be thereabouts;
and then lost sight of the Indians, and immediately found one of the
corpse, which these deponents say, was the corpse of James Smith, one
of said Armstrong's men; and directly upon finding the corpse these deponents heard three shots of guns, which they had great reason to think
were the Indians, their companions, who had deserted from them; and in
order to let them know that they had found the corpse, these deponents
fired three guns, but to no purpose, for they never saw the Indians any
more. And about a quarter of a mile further down the creek, they saw
more Bald eagles, whereupon they made down towards the place, where
they found another corpse (being the corpse of Woodward Arnold, the
other servant of said Armstrong) lying on a rock, and then went to the
former sleeping place, where they had appointed to meet the Indians; but
saw no Indians, only that the Indians had been there and cooked some
victuals for themselves, and had gone off.

All that night, the deponents further say, they had great reason to sus-
pect that the Indians were then thereabouts, and intended to do them
some damage; for a dog these deponents had with them, barked that
night, which was remarkable, for the said dog had not barked all the time
they were out, till that night, nor ever since, which occasioned these deponents to stand upon their guard behind trees, with their guns cocked
that night. Next morning these deponents went back to the corpses which
they found to be barbarously and inhumanly murdered, by very gashed,
deep cuts on their heads with a tomahawk or such like weapon, which had
sunk into their skulls and brains; and in one of the corpses there appeared a hole in his skull near the cut, which was supposed to be made

with a tomahawk, which hole these deponents do believe to be a bullet hole. And these deponents, after taking a particular view of the corpses, as their melancholy condition would admit, they buried them as decently as their circumstances would allow, and returned home to Paxton, the Allegheny road to John Harris'; thinking it dangerous to return the same way they went out. And further these deponents say not.

These same deponents being legally qualified, before me, James Armstrong, one of his majesty's justices of the peace for the county of Lancaster, have hereunto set their hands in testimony thereof.

JAMES ARMSTRONG.

Alexander Armstrong. Thomas McKee, Francis Ellis, John Florster, William Baskins, James Berry, John Watt, James Armstrong, David Denny.

The reader will note that the circumstances stated and those following relate to what was probably the first Indian massacre in the vicinity, that our country was yet in "His Majesty's" domain, and that the nearest county seat was then Lancaster. The massacre was so shocking to the pioneers that a Provincial Council was assembled, the result of which was that the provincial interpreter and Indian agent, Conrad Weiser, was dispatched in the name of the governor to Shamokin, to make demands for several others concerned in the murder.

As this document, the proceedings of the council, has been preserved for posterity, it is reproduced here, spelling, language, etc., just as recorded, probably being the first case for that territory where an Indian Council became necessary to the settlement of a matter which was vital between the Indians and the provincial government.

At a council, April 25, 1744.—"The governor, George Thomas, laid before the Board a letter dated April 22, 1744, from Mr. Cookson, at Lancaster, purporting that John Armstrong, an Indian trader, with his two servants, Woodward Arnold and James Smith, had been murdered at Juniata by three Delaware Indians, and that John Musemeelin and Johnson of Neshalleeny, two of the Indians concerned in the murder had been seized by the order of Shikellamy, and the other Indian chiefs at Shamokin, and sent under a guard of Indians to be delivered up to justice; that one was actually delivered up in jail at Lancaster; but the other had made his escape from the persons to whose care he was committed.

"His honor then sent to the chief justice to consult him about the steps proper to be taken to bring the Indian to his trial, but as he was absent at a Court of Oyer and Terminer in Bucks County, it was the opinion of the Board that the Indian, Musemeelin, should be immediately removed to Philadelphia jail, and that Conrad Weiser should be immediately dispatched to the chiefs of the Delaware Indians at Shamokin to make a peremptory demand in his honor's name of the other murderers concerned, and that Shikellamy and the other Indians there do order immediate search to be made for the goods of which the deceased was robbed, in order to their being put into the hands of his brother for the satisfaction of his creditors, or the support of his family. And at the same time to inform them that the chiefs of the Indians which shall meet at Lancaster on the treaty with our neighboring governments, will be desired to depute some of their number to be present at the trial and at the execution of such as shall be found guilty.

"Conrad Weiser was accordingly sent to Shamokin. He writes in his journal, Shamokin, May 2d, 1744: This day I delivered the governor's message to Allumoppies, the Delaware chief, and the rest of the Delaware Indians in the presence of Shikellamy and a few more of the Six Nations. The purport of which was that I was sent express by the governor and council to demand those that had been concerned with Musemeelin in murdering John Armstrong, Woodward Arnold and James Smith; that their bodies might be searched for, and decently buried; that the goods be likewise found and restored without fraud. It was delivered them by me in the Mohawk language, and interpreted into Delaware by Andrew, Madame Montour's son.

"In the afternoon Allumoppies, in the presence of the aforesaid Indians, made the following answers:

"Brother, the Governor: It is true that we, the Delaware Indians, by the investigation of the evil spirit, have murdered James Armstrong and his men; we have transgressed and we are ashamed to look up. We have taken the murderer and delivered him to the relations of the deceased, to be dealt with according to his works.

"Brother, the Governor: Your demand for the guard is very just; we have gathered some of them; we will do the utmost of what we can to find them all. We do not doubt but that we can find out the most part, and whatever is wanting, we will make up with skins, which is what the guard are sent for to the woods.

"Brother, the Governor: The dead bodis are buried. It is certain that John Armstrong was buried by the murderer, and the other two by those that searched for them. Our hearts are in mourning, and we are in a dismal condition, and cannot say anything at present.

"Then Shikellamy with the rest of the Indians of the Six Nations there present said:

"Brother, the Governor: We have been all misinformed on both sides about the unhappy accident. Musemeelin has certainly murdered the three white men himself, and upon his bare accusation of Neshaleeny's son, which was nothing but spite, the said Neshaleeny's son was seized, and made a prisoner. Our cousins, the Delaware Indians, being then drunk, in particular Allumoppies, never examined things, but made an innocent person prisoner, which gave a great deal of disturbance amongst us. However the two prisoners were sent, and by the way in going down the river they stopped at the house of James Berry; James told the young man, 'I am sorry to see you in such a condition, I have known you from a boy, and always loved you.' Then the young man seemed to be very much struck to the heart, and said, 'I have said nothing yet, but I will tell all, let all the Indians come up, and the white people also, they shall hear it.' And then told Musemeelin in the presence of all the people: 'Now I am going to die for your wickedness; you have killed all the three white men. I never did intend to kill any of them.' Then Musemeelin in anger said: 'It is true, I have killed them; I am a man, you are a coward; it is a great satisfaction to me to have killed them; I will die with joy for having killed a great rogue and his companions.' Upon which the young man was set at liberty by the Indians.

"We desire therefore our brother, the governor, will not insist to have either of the two young men in prison or condemned to die; it is not with Indians as with white people, to put people in prison on suspicion or trifles. Indians must first be found guilty of a crime, then judgment is given and immediately executed. We will give you faithfully all the particulars; and at the ensuing treaty entirely satisfy you; in the meantime we desire that good friendship and harmony continue; and that we may live long together, is the hearty desire of your brethren, the Indians of the United Six Nations present at Shamokin.

"The following is what Shikellamy declared to be the truth of the story concerning the murder of John Armstrong, Woodward Arnold and James Smith from the beginning to the end, to wit:

"That Musemeelin owing some skins to John Armstrong, the said Armstrong seized a horse of the said Musemeelin and a rifle gun; the gun was taken by James Smith, deceased. Some time last winter Musemeelin met Armstrong on the river Juniata, and paid all but twenty shillings, for which he offered a neck-belt in pawn to Armstrong and demanded his horse, and James Armstrong refused it, and would not deliver up the horse, but enlarged the debt, as his usual custom was, and after some quarrel the Indian went away in great anger without his horse to his hunting cabin. Some time after this, Armstrong, with his two companions on their way to Ohio, passed by the said Musemeelin's hunting cabin, his wife, only being at home, demanded the horse of Armstrong, because he was her proper goods, but didn't get him. Armstrong had by this time sold or lent the horse to James Berry; after Musemeelin came from hunting, his wife told him that Armstrong was gone by, and that she demanded the horse of him, but did not get him—and as is thought pressed him to pursue and take revenge of Armstrong. The third day in the morning after James Armstrong was gone by, Musemeelin said to the two young men that hunted with him, come let us go toward the Great Hills to hunt bears; accordingly they went all three in company; after they had gone a good way Musemeelin, who was foremost, was told by the two young men that they were out of their course. Come you along, said Musemeelin, and they accordingly followed him till they came to the path that leads to the Ohio. Then Musemeelin told them he had a good mind to go and fetch his horse back from Armstrong, and desired the two young men to come along; accordingly they went. It was then almost night and they traveled till next morning. Musemeelin said, now they are not far off. We will make ourselves black, then they will be frightened and will deliver up the horse immediately, and I will tell Jack that if he does not give me the horse I will kill him, and when he said so he laughed. The young men thought he joked, as he used to do. They did not blacken themselves, but he did. When the sun was above the trees, or about an hour high, they all came to the fire, where they found James Smith sitting, and they also sat down. Musemeelin asked where Jack was; Smith told him that he was gone to clear the road a little. Musemeelin said he wanted to speak to him, and went that way, and after he had gone a little distance from the fire, he said something, and looked back laughing, but he having a thick throat, and his speech being very bad, and their talking with Smith, hindered them from understanding what he said; they did not mind it. They being hungry, Smith told them to kill some turtles, of which they were plenty, and we would make some bread, and by and by, they would all eat together. While they were talking, they heard a gun go off not far off, at which time Woodward Arnold was killed, as they learned afterwards. Soon after Musemeelin came back and said, why did you not kill that white man according as I bid you? At this they were surprised, and one of the young men commonly called Jimmy, run away to the riverside. Musemeelin said to the other, how will you do to kill Catabaws, if you cannot kill white men? You cowards, I'll show you how you must do; and then taking up the English axe that lay there, he struck it three times into Smith's head, before he died. Smith never stirred. Then he told the young Indian to call the other; but he was so terrified he could not call. Musemeelin then went and fetched him and said to him that two of the white men were killed, he must now go and kill the third; then each of them would have killed one. But neither of them dare venture to talk anything about it. Then he pressed them to go along with him—he went foremost; then one of the young men told the other as they went along, my friend, don't you kill any of the white people, let him do what he will; I have not killed Smith, he has done it himself, we have no need to do such a barbarous thing. Musemeelin being then a good way before them in a hurry, they soon saw John Armstrong sitting upon an old log. Musemeelin spoke to him and said, where is my horse? Armstrong made answer and said, he will come by and by, you shall have him. I want him now, said Musemeelin. Armstrong answered, you shall have him. Come let us go to that fire—which was at some distance from the place where Armstrong sat—and let us talk and smoke together. Go along then, said Musemeelin. I am coming, said Armstrong, do you go before; Musemeelin, do you go foremost. Armstrong looked then like a dead man, and went toward the fire and was immediately shot in his back by Musemeelin and fell. Musemeelin then took his hatchet and struck it into Armstrong's head, and said, give me my horse, I tell you. By this time one of the young men had fled again that had gone away before, but he returned in a short time. Musemeelin then told the young men, they must not offer to discover or tell a word about what had been done for their lives, but they must help to bury Jack, and the other two were to be thrown into the river. After that was done Musemeelin ordered them to load the horses and follow towards the hill, where they intended to hide the goods; accordingly they did and as they were going, Musemeelin told them that as there were a great many Indians hunting about that place, if they should happen to meet with any, they must be killed to prevent betraying them. As they went along, Musemeelin going before, the two young men agreed to run away as soon as they could meet with any Indians, and not to hurt anybody. They came to the desired place, the horses were unloaded, and Musemeelin opened the bundles and offered the two young men each a parcel of goods. They told him that they had already sold their skins, and everybody knew they had nothing, they would certainly be charged with a black action, were they to bring any goods to the town, and therefore they would not accept of any; but promised nevertheless not to betray him. Now, says Musemeelin, I know what you were talking about when you stayed so far behind.

"The two young men being in great danger of losing their lives—of which they had been much afraid all that day—accepted of what he offered to them, and the rest of the goods they put in a heap and covered them from the rain, and then went to their hunting cabin. Musemeelin unexpectedly finding two or three more Indians there, laid down his goods, and said he had killed Jack Armstrong and taken pay for his horse, and should any of them discover it, that person he would likewise kill; but otherwise they might all take a part of the goods. The young man, called Jimmy, went away to Shamokin, after Musemeelin was gone to bury the goods with three more Indians, with whom he had prevailed; one of them was Neshaleeny's son, whom he had ordered to kill James Smith, but these Indians would not have any of the goods. Some time after the young Indian had been in Shamokin, it was whispered about that some of the Delaware Indians had killed Armstrong and his men. A drunken Indian came to one of the Tudolous houses at night and told the man of the house that he could tell him a piece of bad news. What is that? said the other. The drunken man said, some of our Deleware Indians have killed Armstrong and his men, which, if our chiefs should not resent, and take them up, I will kill them myself to prevent a disturbance between us and the white people, our brother. Next morning Shikellamy and some other Indians of the Delawares were called to assist Allomoppies in council.

"When Shikellamy and Allumoppies got one of the Tudolous Indians to write a letter to me to desire me to come to Shamokin in all haste; that the Indians were much dissatisfied in mind. This letter was brought to my house by four Delaware Indians sent express; but I was then in Philadelphia, and when I came home and found all particulars mentioned in this letter, and that none of the Indians of the Six Nations had been down, I did not care to meddle with Delaware Indian affairs, and staid at home till I received the governor's orders to go, which was about two weeks after. Allumoppies was advised by his council to employ a conjurer, as they call it to find out the murderer; accordingly he did and the Indians met; the seer being busy all night, told them in the morning to examine such and such one, they were present when Armstrong was killed, naming the two young men: Musemeelin was present. Accordingly Allumoppies, Quietheyyquent and Thomas Green, an Indian, went to him that had fled first and examined him; he told the whole story very freely; then they went to the other, but he would not say a word, but went away and left them. The three Indians returned to Shikellamy and informed of what discovery they had made. When it was agreed to secure the murderers, and deliver them up to the white people, a great noise arose among the Delaware Indians, and some were afraid of their lives and went into the woods; not one cared to meddle with Musemeelin, and the other that could not be prevailed on to discover anything, because of the resentment of their families; but they being pressed by Shikellamy's son to secure the murderers, otherwise they would be cut off from the chain of friendship; four or five of the Delawares made Musemeelin and the other young man prisoners and tied them both. They lay twenty-four hours and none would venture to conduct them down; because of the great division among the Delaware Indians, and Allumoppies in danger of being killed, fled to Shikellamy and begged for protection. At last Shikellamy's son Jack went to the Delawares. most of them being drunk, as they had been for several days, and told them to deliver the prisoners to Alexander Armstrong, and they were afraid to do it; they might separate their heads from their bodies, and lay them in the canoe, and carry them to Alexander to roast and eat them, that would satisfy his revenge, as he wants to eat Indians. They prevailed with the said Jack to assist them, and accordingly he and his brother and some of the Delawares went with two canoes and carried them off."

No available records remain to show the final disposition of Musemeelin.

According to a record left by John Harris, of Harris' Ferry (now Harrisburg), Jack's Narrows, near Mapleton on the Juniata, came to be named this way. Harris referred to them thus: "Jack Armstrong's narrows, so called from his being there murdered." Other writers claim they were called after Captain Jack, a resolute Indian hater, described elsewhere in this book. While either may be the truth, yet the fact that the murder happened at this point inclines one to believe that the mountain was named after the trader, Armstrong, who was murdered there.

CHAPTER III.

INTRUDING SETTLERS EVICTED.

THE lands now comprising Perry County probably caused the provincial government a greater amount of anxiety during a number of years than any other in Pennsylvania. In a treaty made with the Indians for certain lands west of the Susquehanna River no lands north of the Kittatinny or Blue Mountains were included, yet notwithstanding this fact pioneers, impatient over the delays of the land office, began entering the valleys between the Kittatinny and Tuscarora ranges, as well as north of the latter, erected cabins and started to clear the lands, without the sanction of the provincial authorities, as the following pages show.

A large delegation of Iroquois journeyed to Philadelphia in July, 1742, to receive the second and last payment for the lands which were sold to the proprietary in 1736. Canassatego, a chief, made a speech in which he refers to the Juniata lands, which include the soil of Perry County and which was a matter of contention for years, finally leading to the burning of the cabins of "squatters," as portrayed further on in this chapter. He said:

"We know our lands are now become more valuable; the white people think we do not know their value, but we are sensible that the land is everlasting, and the few goods we receive for it are soon worn out and gone. For the future we will sell no lands, but when our brother Onas (William Penn) is in the country, and we will know before hand the quantity of goods we are to receive. Besides, we are not well used with respect to the lands still unsold by us. Your people daily settle on these lands and spoil our hunting. We must insist on your removing them, as you know they have no right to the northward of Kittochtinny Hills. In particular, we renew our complaints against some people who are settled at Juniata, a branch of the Susquehanna, and all along the banks of that river, as far as Mahaniay, and desire that they may be made forthwith to go off the land, for they do great damage to our cousins, the Delawares."

This was not their first protest, as the governor's reply would indicate. He replied that "on your former complaints against people settling the land on Juniata, and from thence all along the river Susquehanna as far as Mahaniay, some magistrates were sent expressly to remove them, and we thought no person would stay after that." To which the Indians rejoined, "These persons who were sent did not do their duty; so far from removing the people, they made surveys for themselves and they are in league with the trespassers. We desire more effectual methods to be used, and honester persons employed."

The governor promised them this would be done and after letting the period between July 7 and October 5 elapse he issued a proclamation from the contents of which one would infer that the sections most in contention were at the mouth of the Juniata and probably as far as the Juniata County line and in Fulton County and up the Susquehanna as far as Wyoming.

These lands were among the choicest of the Indians, who made their living by hunting and fishing, being especially noted as a great hunting ground for deer, probably excelling all others, as the following extract from a letter by Conrad Weiser, the interpreter, dated April 22, 1749, will show: He was on his way to Shamokin with a messenger from the provincial government to the Indians and met the sons of Shikellamy, at the trading house of Thomas McKee, and delivered to them the message, as he had been informed that all the Indians were absent from Shamokin. In the letter referred to, addressd to Richard Peters, secretary of the province, having just returned from this trip, he writes:

"The Indians are very uneasy about the white people settling beyond the Endless Mountains, on Joniady (Juniata), on Sherman's Creek and elsewhere. They tell me that about thirty families are settled upon the Indian lands this spring, and daily more go to settle thereon. Some have settled almost to the head of Joniady River along the path that leads to Ohio. The Indians say (and that with truth) that that country is their only hunting ground for deer, because farther to the north, there was nothing but spruce woods and the ground covered with calmia (laurel) bushes, not a single deer could be found or killed there. They asked very seriously whether their brother Onas (William Penn) had given the people leave to settle there. I informed them of the contrary, and told them that I believed some of the Indians from Ohio, that were down last summer, had given liberty (with what right I could not tell) to settle. I told them of what passed on the Tuscarora Path last summer, when the sheriff and three magistrates were sent to turn off the people there settled; and that I then perceived that the people were favored by some of the Indians above mentioned; by which means the orders of the governor came to no effect. So far they were content and said the thing must be as it is, till the Six Nation chiefs would be down and converse with the Governor of Pennsylvania about the affair."

The Six Nations having consulted in council on the subject sent a delegation to Philadelphia with remonstrances, but the Senecas had already been there and had been dismissed with £100 and little satisfaction. The Six Nations were given £50. Returning disgusted they killed the cattle and ruined the orchards along the way.

In May, 1750, a conference was held at George Croghan's, in Pennsboro Township, Cumberland County, between the whites and the Indians, to give the Indians the assurance that those who had intruded on their lands on the Juniata should be removed without further delay. Present at the meeting were Richard Peters, secretary of the province; Conrad Weiser, James Galbreath,

George Croghan, George Stevenson, William Wilson, Hermanus Alricks, Andrew Montour, Jac-nec-doaris, Sai-nch-to-wano, Cata-ra-dir-ha, Tohonady Huntho, a Mohawk from Ohio.

Some of these men went away peaceably, upon the promise that when the lands were purchased from the Indians they might return to their claims, but others were morose and went to other sections. Among those to return were Richard Kirkpatrick and John McClure.

Secretary Peters, in an official communication, dated July 2, 1750, recounting the previous troubles along this line, takes credit for having caused the intruders to be driven out in June, 1743. He further says that to the best of his remembrance there were no further encroachments until about 1747, when, among others, "some persons had the presumption to go into a place called Shearman's Creek, lying along the waters of Juniata, and is situate east of the Path Valley, through which the present road runs from Harris' Ferry (now Harrisburg) to Allegheny; and lastly they extending their settlements to big Juniata; the Indians all this while repeatedly complaining that their hunting ground was every day more and more taken from them; and that there must infallably arise quarrels between their Warriors and these settlers, which would in the end break the chain of friendship."

The Indians then threatened to do themselves what the government failed to do, with the result that Richard Peters, secretary of the province, with Conrad Weiser, the interpreter, were despatched to the territory in which the new settlements were located to expel the intruders. They were joined by the magistrates of the county, the delegates of the Six Nations, a chief of the Mohawks, and Andrew Montour, an interpreter. The party met with some resistance, but Mr. Peters, the secretary, was somewhat of a diplomat and gave money to the needy and offered a place of refuge on farms of his own elsewhere. He also gave all of them permission to locate on parts of the two million acres east of the Susquehanna, purchased of the Indians the previous year. Some accepted, and Andrew Lycon was one of them, the town of Lykens, in upper Dauphin County, where he later settled, being named after him.

In the letter from Richard Peters, the provincial secretary, to James Hamilton, the Colonial governor, dated July 2, 1750, among other matters is the following report of this expedition:

"Mr. Weiser and I have received your honor's orders to give information to the proper magistrates against all such as had presumed to settle and remain on the lands beyond the Kittochtinny Mountains, not purchased of the Indians, in contempt of the laws repeatedly signified by proclamations, and particularly by your honor's last one, and to bring them to a legal conviction, lest for want of their removal a breach should ensue between the Six Nations of Indians and this province. We set out on

we are pleased to see on this occasion, and as the council of Onondago has this affair exceedingly at heart, and it was particularly recommended to us by the deputies of the Six Nations, when they parted from us last summer, we desire to accompany you, but we are afraid, notwithstanding the care of the governor, that this may prove like many former attempts; the people will be put off now, and next year come again; and if so the Six Nations will no longer bear it, but do themselves justice. To prevent this, therefore, when you have turned the people off, we recommend it to the governor, to place two or three faithful persons over the mountains, who may be agreeable to him and us, with commissions, empowering them immediately to remove every one who may presume after this to settle themselves, until the Six Nations shall agree to make sale of their land.'

"To enforce this they gave a string of wampum, and received one in return from the magistrates, with the strongest assurances that they would do their duty.

"On Tuesday, the 22d of May, Matthew Dill, George Croghan, Benjamin Chambers, Thomas Wilson, John Finley and James Galbreth, Esqs., justices of the said county of Cumberland, attended by the undersheriff, came to Big Juniata, situate at the distance of twenty miles from the mouth thereof, and about ten miles north from the Blue Hills, a place much esteemed by the Indians for some of their best hunting ground, and there they found five cabins, or log houses, one possessed by William White,* another by George Croghan, another not quite yet finished in possession of David Hiddleston, another by George and William Galloway, and another by Andrew Lycon; of these persons William White, George and William Galloway, David Hiddleston and George Cahoon appeared before the magistrates, and being asked by what right or authority they had possessed themselves of those lands and erected cabins thereon, replied: 'By no right or authority but that the land belonged to the proprietaries of Pennsylvania.' They were then asked whether they did not know they were acting against the law and in contempt of frequent notices given them and in contempt of the governor's proclamation. They said they had seen one such proclamation and had nothing to say for themselves, but craved mercy. Hereupon the said five men being convicted by said justices on their view, the undersheriff was charged with them and he took William White, David Hiddleston and George Cahoon

---

*This is the place where Frederick Starr, a German, with several of his countrymen, are spoken of in provincial annals as having "made settlements on Big Juniata, about twenty-five miles from the mouth thereof (recorded at other places as twenty miles), and about ten miles north from the Blue Hills." That location is impossible, as twenty-five miles (or twenty miles) from the mouth of the Juniata would be in Juniata County, while ten miles north from the Blue Hills would be in the vicinity of Wheatfield or Miller Township, in Perry County. Wright's History places Starr's settlement "probably near the Pennsylvania Railroad bridge over Buffalo Creek," above Newport, and those of Lycon and others "probably in Pfoutz's Valley," while the records of the land office show them to have been in Walker Township, Juniata County. In the letter to James Hamilton, dated July 2, 1750, is this clause, which locates the place in the vicinity of Thompsontown: "About the year 1740 or 1741, one Frederick Starr, a German, with two or three more of his countrymen, made some settlements at the above place, where we found William White, the Galloways, and Andrew Lycon, on Big Juniata, situate at the distance of twenty-five miles from the mouth thereof," etc. As William White and John Lycon returned to their places, after the opening of the land office, February 3, 1754, and took up the lands legally, the location is determined.

into custody, but George and William Galloway resisted, and having got at some distance from the undersheriff, they called to us: 'You may take our lands and houses and do what you please with them; we deliver them to you with all our hearts, but we will not be carried to jail.'

"The next morning being Wednesday, the 23d of May, the said justices went to the log house or cabin of Andrew Lycon, and finding none there but children, and hearing that the father and mother were expected soon, and William White and others offering to become security, jointly and severally, and to enter into recognizance as well for Andrew's appearance at court, and immediate removal as for their own, this proposal was accepted and William White, David Hiddleston and George Cahoon entered into a recognizance of 100 pounds, and executed bonds to the proprietaries in the sum of 500 pounds, reciting that they were trespassers and had no manner of right and had delivered possession to me for the proprietaries. When the magistrate went to the cabin of George and William Galloway (which they had delivered up the day before, as aforesaid, after being convicted and were flying from the sheriff) all the goods belonging to the said George and William were taken out, and the cabin being quite empty, I took possession thereof for the proprietaries; then a conference was held what should be done with the empty cabin; after great deliberation, all agreed that if some cabins were not destroyed they would tempt the trespassers to return again, or encourage others to come there should these go away. So what was doing would signify nothing, since the possession of them was at such a distance from the inhabitants and could not be kept for the proprietaries, and Mr. Weiser also giving it as his opinion that if all the cabins were left standing the Indians would conceive such a contemptible opinion of the government that they would come themselves in the winter, murder the people and set their houses on fire. On these considerations the cabin by my order, was burnt by the undersheriff and company.

"Then the company went to the house possessed by David Hiddleston, who had entered into bond as aforesaid, and he having voluntarily taken out all the things which were in the cabin, and left me in possession, that empty and unfurnished cabin was likewise set on fire, by the undersheriff, by my order.

"The next day, being the 24th of May, Mr. Weiser and Mr. Galbreth, with the undersheriff and myself, on our way to the mouth of the Juniata, called at Andrew Lycon's, with intent only to inform him that his neighbors were bound for his appearance and immediate removal, and to caution him not to bring himself or them into trouble by a refusal. But he presented a loaded gun to the magistrates and sheriff and said he would shoot the first man that dared to come nigher. On this he was disarmed, convicted and committed to the custody of the sheriff. This whole transaction happened in the sight of the tribe of Indians, who by accident had in the nighttime fixed their tent on that plantation; and Lyken's behavior giving them great offence the Shikellamies insisted on our burning the cabin or they would burn it themselves. Whereupon, when everything was taken out of it, Andrew Lycon all the while assisting, and possession being delivered to me, the empty cabin was set on fire by the undersheriff and Lycon was carried to jail.

"Mr. Benjamin Chambers and Mr. George Croghan had about an hour before separated from us; and on my meeting them again in Cumberland County, they reported to me they had been at Sheerman's Creek, or Little Juniata, situate about six miles over the Blue Mountain, and found there James Parker, Thomas Parker, Owen M'Keib, John M'Clure, Richard Kirkpatrick, James Murray, John Scott, Henry Gass, John Cowan, Simon

Girtee and John Kilough, who had settled lands and erected cabins thereon; and having convicted them of the trespass on their view, they had bound them in recognizances of one hundred pounds to appear and answer for their trespasses on the first day of the next Cumberland County Court, to be held at Shippensburg, and that the said trespassers had likewise entered into bonds to the proprietaries in 500 pounds penalty, to remove off immediately with all their servants, cattle and effects and had delivered possession of their houses to Mr. George Stevenson for the proprietaries' use; and that Mr. Stevenson had ordered some of the meanest of those cabins to be set on fire, where the families were not large or the improvements considerable."

But even this did not deter aggression and at a council held at Carlisle in 1753 the Indians again protested the occupation of their hunting grounds and notified the authorities that "they wished the people called back from the Juniata lands until matters were settled between them and the French, lest damage should be done, and then the English would think ill of them." That they had a right to protest is substantiated by the fact that Alexander Roddy, Thomas Wilson, William Patterson, James Kennedy, John and Joseph Scott, and probably others, had located in 1753, in what later became Tyrone Township, then generally known as Sherman's Valley.

As early as 1751 the number of taxables in Cumberland County north of the Kittatinny Mountain was 1,134. Rupp's History says: "These were chiefly Irish and some few Germans, who seated themselves on Juniata River, Sherman's Creek, Tuscarora Path, etc." The first settlements of these intruders on the unpurchased lands began about the year 1740, and increased despite the complaints of the Indians, the laws of the province and the proclamations of the governor.

While the treaty of 1736 gave to the Penns all the lands lying east and south of the Kittatinny or Blue Mountains, yet settlements had been made west of the Susquehanna River prior to that time, special grants having been issued for settlements. When the Penns came the first purchase by them from the Indians included a small domain around Philadelphia. This was at the famous council meeting of 1682. On September 17, 1718, another treaty confirmed that sale and extended the lands as far west as the Susquehanna River. The treaty of 1836 again confirmed the previous ones, when on October 11, twenty-three Six Nation chiefs sold to John, Thomas and Richard Penn all the lands on both sides of the Susquehanna, "eastward, to the heads of the branches or springs flowing into the river; northward to the Kittochtinny Hills, and westward to the setting sun." "Westward to the setting sun" merely meant that south and east of the Kittatinny Mountains all the lands, including those that drained into the Potomac, were conveyed—nothing more—and yet many of the white settlers construed that "westward to the setting sun" to mean anything.

THE ALBANY TREATY.

Perry County is a part of the lands transferred by the Treaty of Albany, on July 6, 1754. The deed bears the names or marks of all the Chiefs and Sachems of the Six Nations and John and Richard Penn and their agents. It conveys to the latter "all the lands lying within the said province of Pennsylvania, bounded and limited as follows: Beginning at the Kittochtinny, or Blue Hills, on the Susquehanna River, thence along the said river a mile above the mouth of a certain creek called Kayarondinhagh; thence northwest by west as far as the said province extends, to its western lines and boundaries; thence along the said western line or boundary to the south line or boundary; thence along said south line or boundary to the south side of said Kittochtinny Hills; thence by south side of said hills to the place of beginning." The price was "400 pounds, lawful money of New York."

Should these boundaries have stood practically the greater part of western Pennsylvania to the Ohio line would have been included, but disaffection appearing among the Indians a conference was held at Aughwick (near Mount Union) in September, 1754, at which the representatives of the various tribes declared that it was not their intention to sell the lands drained by the west branch of the Susquehanna and that they would never agree to any boundary that extended to Lake Erie. The "certain creek" named Kayarondinhagh, is Penn's Creek, which flows into the Susquehanna at Selinsgrove and a line northwest by west would strike Lake Erie about where the city of Erie is now located. The result of this conference was that another treaty was concluded at Easton, Pennsylvania, October 22, 1754, when the boundary lines to the north and west were changed. The line starting above Penn's Creek was made to run "northwest and by west to a creek called Buffalo Creek; thence west to the east side of the Allegheny or Appalachian Hills; thence along the east side of the said hills, binding therewith to the south line or boundary of the said province; thence by the said south line or boundary to the south side of the Kittochtinny Hills; thence by the south side of said hills to the place of beginning." ·

The territory, as thus defined by the revised boundaries, included all of the present counties of Perry, Juniata, Mifflin, Huntingdon, Bedford, Blair and Fulton, almost all of Snyder, about one-half of Centre and portions of Union, Franklin, and Somerset. The Perry County territory is the extreme southern part of this purchase.

During the preceding years pioneers had become familiar with the lands of the new grant and when the land office opened on February 3, 1755, on the very first day, a number of warrants were granted to those who had located their claims. While it has been impossible to give a full list of the warrantees during the early settlement of the county, yet a large number are covered in the early history of the various townships in another part of this volume.

As will be seen in the following chapters many of these pioneers abandoned their homes and fled to more thickly populated sections during the French and Indian War, many more were killed and scalped and still others were taken prisoner by the wily redskins.

The Six Nations were not the occupants of the territory, although in authority. Many of the Delawares and the Shawnees, who were inhabiting it did not take the treaty literally, claiming a sort of ownership by right of occupation. This, in connection with the settlers having come in before the purchase and the troubles between the English and the French and Indians, soon made the land a veritable "dark and bloody ground."

That Andrew Montour, the first authorized citizen of the lands which now comprise Perry County, was sent for by Col. George Washington in 1754, the very year of the purchase of these lands, is attested by Montour's autograph letter, on file in the office of the Secretary of the Commonwealth, at Harrisburg, addressed to Governor R. H. Morris. It follows:

SHERMAN'S CREEK, 16th May, 1754.

Sir: I once more take upon me the liberty of informing you that our Indians at Ohio are expecting every day the armed forces of this province against the French, who, by their late encroachments, is likely to prevent their planting, and thereby render them impossible of supporting their families. And you may depend upon it, as a certainty, that our Indians will not strike the French unless this province (or New York) engage with them; and that, by sending some number of men to their immediate assistance. The reasons are plain, to wit: that they don't look upon their late friendship with Virginia, sufficient to engage them in a war with the French; I therefore think, with submission, that to preserve our Indian allies, this province ought instantly to send out some men, either less or more, which I have good reason to hope, would have the desired effect; otherwise I doubt there will, in a little time, be an entire separation; the consequences of which, you are best able to judge, &c. I am informed, by my brother, who has lately come from the Lakes, that there is at that place a great number of French Indians, preparing to come down to the assistance of the French, at Ohio. I am likewise informed, by a young Indian man (who, by my brother's directions, spent some days with the French at Monongahela), that they expect a great number of French down the river, very soon. I have delayed my journey to Ohio, and waited with great impatience for advice from Philadelphia, but have not yet received any. I am now obliged to go to Col. Washington, who has sent for me many days ago, to go with him to meet the half-king, Mona-

5

catootha, and others, that are coming to meet the Virginia companies;
and, as they think, some from Pennsylvania—and would have been glad
to have known the design of this province, in these matters, before I
had gone.   I am sir, your humble servant,

ANDREW MONTOUR.

THE FRENCH AND INDIAN WAR.

Prior to 1753-54 for a period of probably seventy years the
white settlers of the province and the Indians had gotten along
peacefully in a general way, but about this time things changed.
The Indians joined with the French against the English and
bloody massacres followed. Already Virginia was being desolated and consternation seized the pioneers on every hand. The
inhabitants of the new county of Cumberland, including what is
now Perry County, petitioned Colonial Governor Hamilton for
aid. The petition:

The address of the subscribers of the county of Cumberland, sheweth
that we are now in most imminent danger by a powerful army of cruel,
merciless and inhumane enemies, by which our lives, liberties, estates, and
all that tends to promote our welfare, are in utmost danger of dreadful
destruction, and this lamentable truth is most evident from the late defeat
of the Virginia forces, and now as we are under your honor's protection,
we would beg your immediate notice, we living upon the frontiers of the
province and our enemies so close upon us, nothing doubting but these
considerations will affect your honor, and as you have our welfare at
heart, that you will defer nothing that may tend to hasten our relief.
And we have hereby appointed our most trusty friends, James Burd and
Philip Davies, our commissioners, to deliver this our petition to your
honor, and in hopes of your due attention and regard thereto, we are
your honor's devoted servants, and as in duty bound shall ever pray:

CUMBERLAND, 15th July   1754.

To which was attached the following signatures: Benjamin Chambers,
Robert Chambers, James Carnahan, James McTeer, Charles Morrow, John
Mitchell, Joseph Armstrong, John Miller, Alexander Culbertson, James
Holiday, Nathaniel Wilson, Wm. McCord, James Jack, John Smith, Fran-
cis West, James Sharp, John Ervin, Matthew Arthur, James McCormick,
Charles Magill, George Finly, John Dotter, John Cesna, Joseph Culbert-
son, Samuel Culbertson, John Thompson, John Reynolds, George Hamil-
ton, David Magaw, James Chambers, Hermanus Alricks, Robert Meek,
Archibald Machan, Benjamin Blyth, Joseph McKinney, John Thompson,
Francis Campbell, John Finly, Isaac Miller, John Machan, John Miller,
John Blair, James Blair, James Moore, John Finly, William White, Wil-
liam Buchanan, John Montgomery, Andrew McFarlane, James Brandon,
John Pattison, John Craighead, Wm. McClure, Samuel Stevens, William
Brown, Pat McFarlan, Stephen Foulk, John Armstrong, Stephen Foulk,
Jr., William McCoskry, Charles Pattison, William Miller, John Prentice,
Arthur Forster, William Blyth, Gideon Griffith, Thomas Henderson, An-
drew McIntyre, John McCuer, Reuben Guthrie, George Davidson, Robert
Miller, Thomas Willson, Thomas Lockert, Tobias Hendricks. It was
read in Council, August 6, 1754.

The governor, after giving proper consideration to the urgent
demands of these settlers, in the same month—August, 1754—sent
a message to the Assembly, then in session, urging that immediate

attention be given to the matter and assistance be sent to them. From "Votes of Assembly," 4-319, August, 1754, the document is here reproduced:

"The people of Cumberland and the upper parts of Lancaster County, are so apprehensive of danger, at this critical juncture, from the nearness of French and savages under their influence, that the principal inhabitants have, in the most earnest manner, petitioned me to provide for their protection; representing withal, that a great number would be warm and active in defence of themselves and their country, were they enabled so to be, by being supplied with arms and ammunition, which many of them are unable to purchase at their own private expense. The substance of these several petitions, which I shall likewise order to be laid before you, appears to me, gentlemen, to be of the greatest importance, and well worthy of your most serious attention. You may be assured that nothing which depends on me shall be wanting towards affording them the protection they desire; but you cannot at the same time but be sensible how little it is in my power to answer the expectations without the aid of your house. It becomes then my indispensable duty, and I cannot on any account whatever, excuse myself from pressing you to turn your thoughts on the defenceless state of the province in general, as well as of our back inhabitants in particular; and to provide such means for the security of the whole, as shall be thought at once both reasonable and effectual to the ends proposed; in which, as in every other matter, consistent with my honor, and the trust reposed in me, I promise you my hearty concurrence."

Legislative bodies in those days seem to have been the progenitors of the present-day product; and while the citizens appealed continually, and the Indians wielded the tomahawk assiduously, the members of the Provincial Assembly talked continuously. According to old records all they did was "talk, and talk, and talk."

In 1755, actual hostilities had begun, between the English and the French, in the struggle for the control of America and the settlement of the question as to whether it would be for all time an English-speaking or a French-speaking nation. The frontier settlers were panic-stricken, which is not to be wondered at, for were they not at the the verge of civilization?

The reader will remember that February 3, 1755—that very year—is the date upon which the land office opened at Lancaster for the settlement of the lands which now form the county of Perry.

The Indian nations were divided. Sir William Johnston had induced the Mohawks, the Tuscaroras and the Oneidas to take sides with the British, and the Onondagas, Cayugas and Senecas, to remain neutral—a difficult job. Many of the Canadian Iroquois, however, went over to the French. Of the Susquehannas, Delawares and Shawnees, a part, influenced by Logan, John Thachnechtoris, Scarrooyady, Paxnous, The Belt, Zigarea and Andrew Montour, remained true to the Colonies, offering to estab-

lish a post at Shamokin against the French; but part of them
took up the hatchet.

In the latter part of 1754 the disposition of the French toward
the frontiers was very threatening, and it was proposed to remove
the Indians from Aughwick, in what is now Huntingdon County,
to the mouth of the Juniata. The opinion of George Croghan, the
Indian agent then located at Aughwick, was sought, and his reply
is reproduced here as showing that the settlers at the mouth of
the Juniata River were principally traders. It follows:

"As to moving the Indians to the mouth of the Juniata, I think
it a very improper place, for this reason: it is settled with a set
of white men that make their living by trading with the Indians
that is settled on the river Susquehanna and sells them little else but
spirits, so that it would be impossible to keep these Indians from
spending all their clothing and then they would be forever teasing
your honor for goods. Indeed it is my opinion that were they
to live in any part of the inhabitance, it would be attended with
bad consequences, as there is no keeping them from being inflamed with liquor if they can get at it, cost what it will; besides
it is dangerous for fear of their getting sickness; then they would
say the white people killed them, and while they stay here they are
a defense to the back inhabitants, which I think lays very open
to the enemy, and I think if the government intends to build any
fortifications for the security of the back inhabitants that this
place or some place hereabouts is the properest place."

As this was the year of the Albany purchase of these lands, and
as the land office was not yet opened for settlement, the location
of these traders was evidently on Duncan's Island, then known as
Juniata Island, which was included in an earlier purchase by Penn.

Late in October, 1755, the Indians appeared in the neighborhood
of Shamokin, and early in November committed several murders
of whites under peculiarly cruel and barbarous circumstances.
Not only those on the immediate frontier, but also those farther
to the heart of the settled part of the province were in constant
dread of the savages. A proclamation signed by nine prominent
citizens advised all to repair to the frontiers and be prepared for
the "worst event." The George Gabriel's mentioned in their proclamation was located "below the forks of the Susquehanna, about
thirty miles of Harris' Ferry, on the west side of the river," according to Rupp. The proclamation:

PAXTON, Oct. 31, 1755. From John Harris' at 12 p. m.

To all his majesty's subjects in the Province of Pennsylvania, or elsewhere: Whereas, Andrew Montour, Belt of Wampum, two Mohawks,
and other Indians came down this day from Shamokin (where Sunbury
is now located), who say the whole body of Indians or the greatest part
of them in the French interest, is actually encamped on this side George
Gabriel's, near Susquehanna; and that we may expect an attack in three

days at farthest; and a French fort to be begun at Shamokin in ten days hence. Tho' this be the Indian report; we the subscribers, do give it as our advice to repair immediately to the frontiers with all our forces to intercept their passage into our country, and be prepared in the best manner possible for the worst event.

Witness our hands.

James Galbreath, John Allison. Barney Hughes, Robert Wallace. John Harris, James Pollock, James Anderson, William Work, Patrick Henry.

P. S. They positively affirm that the above named Indians discovered a party of the enemy at Thomas McKee's upper place on the 30th of October last.

Mona-ca-too-tha, the Belt, and other Indians here, insist upon Mr. Weiser's coming immediately to John Harris' with his men, and to council with the Indians.

Before me,   JAMES GALBREATH.

That the matter of calling forth the above proclamation was urgent is attested by the fact that the latter part of the date line shows it to have been despatched at an unusual hour, "From John Harris' at 12 p. m.," is the inscription, and it was likely sent by courier, or as the provincial authorities termed it, "by express."

The above is from the provincial records and also establishes the fact that Thomas McKee had two places, a fact which has confused many writers. McKee was an Indian trader and is mentioned in many records, one being in an earlier chapter of this book, where he was one of a party to help hunt for the murderers of John Armstrong. That he was one of these men would imply that he probably made his headquarters at the lower place, which was at Peters' Mountain, opposite Duncannon; in fact his name frequently appears in matters pertaining to the lower location. The upper location was where McKee's Half Falls is, that place taking its name from him. The "places" were likely trading posts for the exchange of goods and possibly also stopping places for travelers, but the latter is hardly likely, as the country was too little settled to require such accommodation. People yet living remember when Harry McKee, a descendant, owned the farm at the end of Peters' Mountain. He later kept a hotel at the east end of Clark's Ferry bridge.

McKee's store, mentioned in many provincial documents, was near Peters' Mountain, and further proof of the fact is contained in Rupp's History, page 314, where it is stated that William Clapham, commandant at Fort Halifax, wrote Governor Morris, July 1, 1756, saying he would leave a sergeant and twelve men at Harris', twenty-four at Hunter's Fort, twenty-four at McKee's store, each in command of an ensign, and Captain Miles and thirty-seven men at Fort Halifax, naming the points in order coming up the river.

Camerhoff, the Moravian bishop, on January 13, 1748, after being at one of McKee's places, described him thus: "McKee

holds a captain's commission under the government; is an extensive Indian trader; bears a good name among them, and drives a
brisk trade with the Allegheny country." McKee's wife was
either a white woman who had been reared among the Indians or
was herself an Indian, probably the former. There is record that
she could speak little English. Various stories appear in historical
works as to her origin. Certain it is that, if she were even reared
among the Indians to her must be credited the half-savage nature
of Alexander McKee—son of Captain Thomas—who was the fellow renegade of Simon Girty. His rearing among the Indians,
where his father traded, probably also contributed to it. He was
George Croghan's assitant at Pittsburgh as Deupty Indian Agent
to the British. When a lad at the store below Peters' Mountain
he probably became acquainted with young Simon Girty, who lived
a few miles below. The reader is referred to the chapter on Simon
Girty for further description of the younger McKee.

In a letter* addressed to "Mr. Peters, Secretary of the Province, dated Conococheague, Nov. 2, 1755, John Potter, sheriff of
Cumberland County, after telling of the great Indian massacres in
Great Cove (now Bedford County), says: 'I am much afraid
that Juniata, Tuscarora and Sheerman's Valley hath suffered;
there are two-thirds of the inhabitants of this valley who have
already fled, leaving their plantations; and without speedy succour be granted I am of the opinion this county will be laid desolate and be without inhabitants. Last night I had a family of upwards of an hundred women and children, who fled for succour.
You can form no just idea of the distress and distracted condition
of our inhabitants, unless you saw and heard their cries.'"

In a letter also dated November 2, 1755, to Governor Morris,
signed by John Armstrong,† is this: "We have sent our expresses everywhere and intend to collect the forces of this lower
part; expecting the enemy at Sheerman's Valley, if not nearer at
hand. I am of the opinion that no other means than a chain of
block houses along or near the south side of the Kittatinny Mountain, from Susquehanna to the temporary line, can secure the lives
and properties even of the old inhabitants of this county, the new
settlements being all fled, except those of Sheerman's Valley whom,
if God do not preserve, we fear, will suffer very soon. I am your
honor's disconsolate, humble servant," etc.

The only man, as far as official records show, who inhabited the
territory which is now Perry County, to fight in the French and
Indain War with the army was Andrew Montour, the Indian
agent and trader, who resided on Sherman's Creek, near where

*Rupp's History.
†Provincial Records.

Montour's run empties into it. In one of his official communications to Governor Morris, Braddock says he has forty or fifty Indians with him and has taken into the service Andrew Montour and George Croghan. Coming from such a source it is evidently not only official but authentic. Another man, Alexander Stephens, who later resided in Perry County territory, and became a captain in the Revolution, was a soldier in this war and was present at Braddock's defeat. He was a private in Capt. Joseph Shippen's company of Col. William Clapham's regiment.

Most of the Indians deserted the Braddock expedition, and with some reason. Braddock advanced with great pomp and his method of fighting was bad, in so far as Indian warfare was concerned. Scarroyady, a chief, in an address to the Provincial Council, said:

"It is now well known to you how unhappily we have been defeated by the French near Minongelo (Monongahela). We must let you know that it was the pride and ignorance of that great general that came from England. He is now dead; but he was a bad man when he was alive; he looked upon us as dogs, and would never hear anything that was said to him. We often endeavored to advise him and to tell him the danger he was in with his soldiers; but he never appeared pleased with us, and that was the reason that a great many of our warriors would not be under his command."

The following letter shows that Montour was mistrusted, and also illustrates the distressed condition of the territory at that period:

"CARLISLE, Sunday Night, November 2, 1755.

"*Dear Sir:* Inclosed to Mr. Allen, by the last post, I sent you a letter from Harris', but I believe forgot, through that day's confusion, to direct it.

"You will see our melancholy circumstances by the governor's letter and my opinion of the method of keeping the inhabitants in this county, which will require all possible despatch. If we had immediate assurance of relief a great number would stay; and the inhabitants should be advertised not to drive off, nor waste their beef cattle, &c. I have not so much as sent off my wife, fearing an ill precedent, but must do it now, I believe, together with the public papers and your own.

"There are no inhabitants on Juniata, nor on Tuscarora by this time, my brother William being just come in. Montour and Monaghatootha are going to the governor. The former is greatly suspected of being an enemy in his heart—'tis hard to tell—you can compare what they say to the governor to what I have wrote. I have no notion of a large army, but of great danger from scouting parties.   JOHN ARMSTRONG."

INDIAN MASSACRES ON COUNTY SOIL.

With the defeat of General Braddock in western Pennsylvania by the French and Indians on July 9, 1755, the Indians took the warpath and laid waste all outlying settlements. The land office for the settlement of these lands had only opened the third day of the preceding February and the new settlers were unable to locate in the territory until the coming of spring. They had cleared a few acres of land on which was growing their first crop when the Braddock defeat occurred.

Evidently learning of the outrages of Indians elsewhere a brave family named Robinson,* the father's name being George Robinson, and their neighbors erected a log fort and stockade on a tableland of the Robinson farm for the protection of the citizens in case of attack by the Indians. That it was built during this first year of the settlement of Perry County soil is attested by Robert Robinson in his narrative telling of the Woolcomber tragedy along Sherman's Creek. According to Rupp, the historian, that and other murders occurred in Sherman's Valley towards the close of December, 1755—the first year of the settlement of these lands.

The story of Robert Robinson is recorded in †Loudon's Narratives, the first part of it relating to the first battle fought with the Indians after Braddock's defeat, in which his brother lost his life. It follows:

"Sideling Hill was the first fought battle after Braddock's defeat. In the year 1756 a party of Indians came out of Conococheague to a garrison named McCord's Fort, and killed some and took a number of prisoners. They then took their course near to Fort Littleton. Captain Hamilton, being stationed there with a company, hearing of their route at McCord's Fort, marched with his company of men, having an Indian with them who was under pay. This Indian led the company, and came on the tracks of the Indians and soon tracked them to Sideling Hill, where they found them with their prisoners, and having the first fire, but without doing much damage, the Indians returned the fire, defeated our men and killed a number of them. My brother, James Robinson, was among the slain. The Indians had McCord's wife with them; they cut off Mr. James Blair's head and threw it in Mrs. McCord's lap, saying that was her husband's head, but she knew it to be Blair's."

---

*The name is variously spelled Robison, Robeson, and Robinson. It is believed that the first method was the original, but as official publications of the state use the latter and as the descendants also do, that method is used in our pages.

†For much of the information contained in this chapter posterity is indebted to Archibald Loudon, author of Loudon's Narratives. His father, James Loudon, was a pioneer in what is now Tuscarora Township, Perry County, and in Bull's Hill graveyard there the oldest stone marks his grave. Archibald Loudon thus got his information at first hand, there being no tradition about it.

Robinson further says: "In 1756, I remember of Woolcomber's family on Shearman's Creek; the whole of the inhabitants of the valley was gathered at Robinson's, but Woolcomber would not leave home; he said it was the Irish who were killing one another; these peaceable people, the Indians, would not hurt any person. Being at home and at dinner, the Indians came in, and the Quaker asked them to come and eat dinner; an Indian announced that he did not come to eat, but for scalps; the son, a boy of fourteen or fifteen years of age, when he heard the Indian say so, repaired to a back door, and as he went out he looked back, and saw the Indian strike the tomahawk into his father's head. The boy then ran over the creek, which was near to the house, and heard the screams of his mother, sisters and brother. The boy came to our fort and gave us the alarm; about forty went to where the murder was done and buried the dead." The scene of this tragedy was the Burchfield farm, near Cisna's Run.

Loudon's Narratives also states that in the year 1755 Peter Shaver, John Savage and two other men were killed at the mouth of Shaver's Creek, or Juniata, by the Indians.

In February, 1756, Captain Patterson, with a party of scouts, went up the Susquehanna and reported the woods, from the Juniata to Shamokin, to be filled with Indians. Encountering a party of Indians they scalped one, which later proved to be the son of Shikellamy's sister.

In Loudon's Narratives are the following details of another scalping: "February, 1756, a party of Indians from Shamokin came to Juniata. They first came to Hugh Micheltrees, being on the river, who had gone to Carlisle, and had got a young man, named Edward Nicholas, to stay with his wife until he would return—the Indians killed them both. The same party of Indians went up the river where the Lukens now live—William Wilcox lived on the opposite side of the river, whose wife and eldest son had come over the river on some business—the Indians came while they were there and killed old Edward Nicholas (in some books the name is given as Nicholson) and his wife, and took Joseph, Thomas and Catharine Nicholas, John Wilcox, James Armstrong's wife and two children prisoners. An Indian named Cotties (Cotter), who wished to be captain of this party, when they did not choose him, did not go with them. He and a boy went to Shearman's Creek and killed *William Sheridan and family, thirteen in number. They then went down the creek to where three old persons lived, two men and a woman, called French, whom they killed; of which he often boasted afterwards, that he

---

*Those killed at this time were William Sheridan, a Quaker, his wife, three children and a servant; William Hamilton, his wife and daughter and a man and two women whose last name was French.

and the boy took more scalps than the whole party." Some historians locate the scene of this tragedy as "being within ten miles of Carlisle, a little beyond Stephens' Gap," evidently meaning Sterrett's Gap. The location of the French home is uncertain at this distant day, but was probably in the vicinity of Dellville, as the description says they *went down* the creek from the Sheridan home. There is little doubt that the Sheridan family lived along the creek on the farm long known as the Levi Adams farm, above Dellville. According to the statement of Rev. L. C. Smiley, Mrs. Ludwig Cornman, when near ninety years of age, pointed out to his mother the location of the graves, which her father, Philip Foulk, had shown her, telling her the story, exactly as printed above and in Provincial Annals. It is in the meadow, adjoining the W. A. Smiley farm, and the Sheridan house stood between the sites of the present Adams house and barn. For years a long stone, deeply set in the ground and projecting, marked the graves, but Mr. Adams found it inconvenient to farm around it and broke it off with a sledge hammer on a level with the bottom of the furrow. Mr. Smiley, at a later period while working in the same meadow with Mr. Adams, was informed by him that at the time he was unaware of the stone being a marker of so historic an incident or he would not have removed it.

Of the murder on Sherman's Creek of ten persons there remains an affidavit made almost a decade later, being dated February 28, 1764, and signed by Alexander Stephens, then of the county of Lancaster. He says Cotties, or Cotter, came back for a canoe which the murderers had left and admitted that he was of the party that killed these settlers.

On October 1, 1757, near Fort Hunter—opposite Marysville— this Indian named Cotties saw a young fellow named William Martin,* gathering chestnuts, and killed him. In later years he got his just deserts. After the Indian war was over he appeared at Fort Hunter and boasted of the friendship he had had for the settlers. An Indian named Hambus, who had been friendly all the while, called him a liar and told of him causing all the trouble possible and of seeing him kill Martin. An altercation ensued, but the white settlers stopped it. Later in the day Cotties became drunk and while asleep the other Indian sunk his tomahawk into his skull.

Robert Robinson, mentioned a number of times in these pages, was a hero and well known to Archibald Loudon, both being from Perry County territory. In introducing his narratives Mr. Lou-

---

*This William Martin was the second son of Samuel Martin, of Paxtang, whose uncle James had warranted the Fort Hunter property. He was a brother of Captain Joseph Martin, who became owner of the Martin mills, in what is now Howe Township, upon the death of his father.

don thus refers to him: "Robert Robinson, who was an eye witness of many of the transactions related by him, was wounded at Kittanning, when it was taken by Colonel, later General John Armstrong, and a second time at Buffalo Creek, when two of his brothers fell victims to savage fury. From our long acquaintance with this man, who is now no more, we can have no hesitation in believing the narratives correct, to the best of his remembrance."

The French left unturned no stone in their efforts to enlist the Delawares and often they were successful by preying upon the savage disposition through intrigue and deception. The following letter from Captain McKee to Edward Shippen, headed "Foart at Hunter's Mill, Ap'l 5th, 1756," is an example of their schemes:

"*Sir:* I desire to let you No that John Secalemy, Indian, is Come here ye Day before yesterday, about 4 o'clock in ye afternoon, & Gives me an account that there is a Great Confusion amongst ye Indians up ye North branch of Susquehanna; the Delawares are a moving all from thence to Ohio, and wants to Persuade ye Shanowes along with them, but they Decline Goeing with them that course, and as they still incline to join with us, the Shanowes are Goeing up to a Town Called Teoga, where there is a body of ye Six Nations, and there they Intend to Remain. He has brought two more men, som women & som children along with him, and Sayeth that he Intends to live & Die with us, and Insists upon my Conducting him down to where his Sister and children is, at Canistogo, and I'm Loath to leave my Post, as his Honor was offended at ye last time I did, but can't help it, he Desires to acquaint you that his sister's son was killed at Penn's Creek, in ye scrimege w'th Cap't. Patterson. This with Due Respect from Sir, your Hum'l Ser't,

"THOMAS McKEE."

There were many encounters between the English and the Indians. Loudon, in his narratives, says that few of the achievements equal that of Samuel Bell, a wealthy farmer of Cumberland It follows:

"Samuel Bell and his brother, George Bell, after Braddock's defeat, agreed to go into Shearman's Valley to hunt for deer, and were to meet at Croghan's (now Sterrett's) Gap, on the Blue Mountain; by some means or other they did not meet, and Samuel slept all night in a cabin belonging to Mr. Patton, on Shearman's Creek. In the morning he had not traveled far before he spied three Indians, who at the same time saw him; they all fired at each other; he wounded one of the Indians but received no damage, except through his clothes by the shots; several shots were fired on both sides, as each took a tree; he took out his tomahawk and stuck it into the tree behind which he stood, so that should they approach he might be prepared. The tree was grazed by bullets and he had thoughts of making his escape by flight, but on reflection had doubts of his being able to outrun them. After some time the two Indians took the wounded one and put him over a fence and one took one course and the other another, taking a compass so that Bell could no longer secure himself by the tree, but by trying to ensnare him they had to expose themselves, by which means he had the good fortune to shoot one of them dead. The other ran, took the dead Indian on his back, one leg over each shoulder; by this time Bell's gun was again loaded and he ran after the Indian until he came within about four yards, fired and shot through the dead Indian and lodged his ball in the other, who dropped the dead man and ran off. On his return, coming past the fence where the wounded Indian was, he despatched him but did not know he had killed the third Indian until his bones were found afterwards."

The prominent Bell families of the past and the present generations located in Rye Township are, however, not descendants of this same family.

In a letter by James Young dated July 18, 1756, at Carlisle, to "the Hon. Gov. Morris," among other things is another reference to Sherman's Valley, as follows:

I left Shamokin early on Friday morning in a battoe; we rowed her down to Harris' Ferry before night, with four oars. There is but one fall above those you saw, not so bad as those at Hunter's; it is about four miles from Fort Halifax. I came here yesterday noon hoping to find money sent by the commissioners to pay the forces on this side of the river as they promised, but as yet none is come. Neither is Colonel Armstrong come, and I find but sixteen of his men here, the rest having gone to Shearman's Valley to protect the farmers at the harvest, so when the money comes I shall be at a loss for an escort. I am informed that a number of men at the forts whose three months is expired agreable to their enlistments have left their posts and expect their pay when I go there. This may be of bad consequence and I heartily wish there were none enlisted for less than twelve months. I am persuaded the officers would find men enough for that time.

The distress of the frontier settlements at this time had became a tragedy and any attempt to portray their sufferings and fears would prove a failure. In the fall of 1755 the country west of the Susquehanna and north of the Blue or Kittatinny Mountain had three thousand men fit to bear arms, and in August, 1756, exclusive of the provincial forces, there were not one hundred, fear having driven the greater part from their homes into the more settled part of the province. Governor Morris, in his message to the Assembly, August 16, 1756, said: "The people to the west of the Susquehanna, distressed by the frequent incursions of the enemy and weakened by their great losses, are moving into the interior parts of the province, and I am fearful that the whole county will be evacuated, if timely and vigorous measures are not taken to prevent it."

The Assembly were inclined to disregard the appeals, but the frequent reports of additional outrages impelled them to pass a measure providing for the appropriation of forty thousand pounds which was to be raised by taxing the proprietary estates. The governor, being indebted to the proprietaries for his position, vetoed the bill. The proprietary, however, made a contribution of five thousand pounds, which was applied to the defence of the frontier. Governor Morris and the Assembly not being able to agree on the matter of protecting the frontier from the ravages of the Indians the entire matter, including the petitions from citizens, was laid before the King of Great Britain, who ordered a hearing before a committee of the Privy Council. At this hearing Cumberland County (which included Perry) and the Assembly were represented by counsel and the Assembly was criticized for its conduct in relation to the public defense dating as far back as 1742.

Upon consideration of the report of the committee the Privy Council went upon record that the Legislature of Pennsylvania, as of every other county, was bound to support its government and its subjects; that the measures heretofore adopted by the Assembly for that purpose were improper, inadequate and ineffectual; and that there was no cause to hope for other measures while the majority of the Assembly consisted of persons whose avowed principles were against military service; who, though not a sixth part of the inhabitants of the province, were admitted to hold offices of trust and profit, and to sit in the Assembly without their allegiance being secured by the sanction of an oath.

The massacres which followed Braddock's defeat were principally laid to King Shingas (Shingask), the greatest Delaware warrior of his period. Among the settlements that fell prey to him was Sherman's Valley, says Rupp, the historian. He was a small personage but his savagery is said to have been unrelenting.

Those who had not fled or whose interests lay in the desolated territory petitioned the governor, council, and assembly for protection against the relentless foe, the same being read in Council, August 21, 1756. Among the signatures are the ancestors of many Perry Countians. The petition:

To the Honorable Robert Hunter Morris, Esq., Lieut. Governor of the Province of Pennsylvania:

The address of part of the remaining inhabitants of Cumberland County, most humbly showeth, that the French and their savage allies, have from time to time made several incursions into this county, have in the most inhuman and barbarous manner murdered great numbers of our people and carried others into captivity, and being greatly emboldened by a series of success, not only attempted but also took Fort Granville on the 30th of July last, then commanded by the late Lieutenant Edward Armstrong, and carried off the greater part of the garrison, prisoners, from whom doubtless the enemy will be informed of the weakness of this frontier, and how incapable we are of defending ourselves against their incursions, which will be a great inducement for them to redouble their attacks, and in all probability force the remaining inhabitants of this county to evacuate it. Great numbers of the inhabitants are already fled, and others preparing to go off; finding that it is not in the power of the troops in the pay of the government (were we certain of their being continued) to prevent the ravages of our restless, barbarous and merciless enemy. It is therefore greatly to be doubted that (without a further protection) the inhabitants of this county will shortly endeavor to save themselves and their effects by flight, which must consequently be productive of considerable inconveniences to his majesty's interest in general, and to the welfare of the people of this province in particular.

Your petitioners being fully convinced of your honor's concern for a strict attention to his mâjesty's interest, have presumed to request that your honor would be pleased to take our case into consideration, and, if agreeable to your honor's judgment, to make application to his excellency, General Loudon, that part of the troops now raising for his excellency's regiment may be sent to, and for some time, continued in some of the most important and advantageous posts in this county, by whose assistance we may be able to continue a frontier if possible, and thereby induce the remaining inhabitants to secure, at least, a part of the immense quantity of grain which now lies exposed to the enemy and subject to be destroyed or taken away by them; and also enable the provincial troops to make incursions into the enemy's country, which would contribute greatly to the safety and satisfaction of your honor's petitioners— and your petitioners, as in duty bound shall ever pray, &c.

The signatures: Francis West, John Welch, James Dickson, Robert Erwin, Samuel Smith, Wm. Buchanan, Daniel Williams, John Montgomery, Thomas Barker, John Lindsay, Thomas Urie, James Buchanan, Wm. Spear, James Pollock, Andrew McIntyre, Robert Gibson, Garret McDaniel, Arthur Foster, James Brandon, John Houston, Patrick McCollom, James Reed, Thomas Lockertt, Andrew Dalton, John Irwin, Wm. Blyth, Robert Miller, Wm. Miller, James Young, John Davis, John Mitchell, John Pattison, Samuel Stevens, John Fox, Charles Pattison, John Foster, Wm. McCaskey, Andrew Calhoun, Jas. Stackpole, Wm. Sebbe, Jas. Robb, Samuel Anderson, Robert Robb, Samuel Hunter, A. Forster, Nath. Smyth.

ATTACK OF FORT ROBINSON.

Of the attack on Fort Robinson during harvest time in 1756 there is record, as the narrative of Robert Robinson, of that hardy pioneer family of Robinsons, was preserved for posterity by Loudon, the historian, in his work known as Loudon's Narratives. The Indians had murdered some persons in Sherman's Valley in . July and waylaid the fort in harvest time. They kept quiet until the reapers had gone into the clearings to harvest, when a chance shot at a mark by Robert Robinson caused them to imagine they were discovered. But let us listen to his story, just as related:

"The Indians murdered some persons in the Shearman's Valley in July and waylaid the fort in harvest time, and kept quiet until the reapers were gone; James Wilson remaining some time behind the rest and I not being gone to my business, which was hunting deer, for the use of the company. Wilson standing at the Fort gate I desired liberty to shoot his gun at a mark, upon which he gave me the gun and I shot. The Indians on the upper side of the fort, thinking they were discovered, rushed on a daughter of Robert Miller and instantly killed her and shot at John Simmeson. They then made the best of it that they could and killed the wife of James Wilson, and the widow Gibson and took Hugh Gibson and Betsy Henry prisoners. The reapers being forty in number, returned to the fort and the Indians dispersed."

While the Indian was scalping Mrs. Wilson, Robert Robinson took a shot at him, wounding him, but he escaped.

The story of Hugh Gibson, who was carried away by the Indians at that time, reads like romance. It is recorded by Archibald Loudon, that first historian from Perry County territory, in his book, Loudon's Narratives, as follows:

"I was," says Gibson, "taken captive by the .Indians, from Robinson's fort, in Shearman's Valley, in July, 1756, at which time my mother was killed; I was taken back to their towns, where I suffered much from hunger and abuse; many times they beat me most severely, and once they sent me to gather wood to burn myself, but I cannot tell whether they intended to do it or to frighten me; however, I did not remain long before I was adopted into an Indian family, and then I lived as they did, though the living was very poor. I was then about fourteen years of age; my Indian father's name was Busqueetam; he was lame in consequence of a wound received by his knife in skinning a deer, and being unable to walk, he ordered me to drive forks in the ground and cover it with bark to make a lodge for him to lie in, but the forks not being secure they gave way and the bark fell down upon him and hurt him very much, which put him into a great rage and calling his wife, ordered us to carry him on a blanket into the hut and I must be one that helps to carry him in; while we were carrying him I saw him hunting for the knife, but my Indian mother had taken care to convey it away, and when we had got him again fixed in his bed, my mother ordered me to conceal myself, which I did; I afterward heard him reproving her for putting away the knife, for by this time I had learned to understand a little of their language. However, his passion wore off and we did very well for the future.

"Some time after this all the prisoners in the neighborhood were collected to be spectators of the cruel death of a poor, unhappy woman, a prisoner, amongst which number 1 was. When Colonel Armstrong destroyed the Kittanning fort this woman fled to the white men, but by some means lost them and fell into the hands of the Indians, who stripped her naked, bound her to a post, and applying hot irons to her whilst the skin stuck to the iron at every touch, she screaming in the most pitiful manner, and crying for mercy, but these ruthless barbarians were deaf to her agonizing shrieks and prayers, and continued·their cruelty till death released her from the torture of those hellish fiends. Of this shocking scene at which human nature shudders, the prisoners were all brought to be spectators.

"I shall omit giving any account of our encamping or decamping, or our moving from place to place, as every one knows this is the most constant employment of Indians. I had now become pretty well acquainted with their manners and customs, had learned their language and was become a tolerable good hunter—was admitted to their dances, to their sacrifices and religious ceremonies. Some of them have a tolerable good idea of the Supreme Being; and I have heard some of them very devoutly thanking their Maker, that they had seen another spring and had seen the flowers upon the earth. I observed that their prayers and praises were for temporal things. They had one bad custom amongst them; that if one man kill another, the friends of the deceased, if they cannot get the murderer, they will kill the nearest akin. I once saw an instance of this: two of them quarreled and the one killed the other, upon which the friends of the deceased rose in pursuit of the murderer, but he having made his escape, his friends were all hiding themselves; but the pursuers happened to find a brother of the murderer, a boy concealed under a log; they immediately pulled him out from his concealment; he plead strongly that it was not him that killed the man; this had no weight with the avengers of blood; they instantly sunk their tomahawks into his body and despatched him. But they have some rules and regulations among them that are good; their ordinary way of living is miserable and poor, often without food. They were amazingly dirty in their cookery; sometimes they catch a number of frogs, and hang them up to dry; when a deer is killed they will split up the guts and give them a plunge or two in the water and then dry them and when they run out of provisions they will take some of the dried frogs and some of the deer guts and boil them till the flesh of the frogs is dissolved, then they sup the broth.

"Having now been with them a considerable time, a favorable opportunity offered for me to regain my liberty; my old father, Busqueetam, lost a horse, and he sent me to look for him; after searching some time I came home and told him that I had discovered his tracks at some considerable distance and that I thought I could find him; that I would take my gun and provisions and would hunt for three or four days and if I could kill a bear or deer I would pack home the meat on my horse; accordingly I packed up some provisions and started towards the white settlements, not fearing pursuit for some days, and by that time I would be out of the reach of the pursuers. But before I was aware I was almost at a large camp of Indians, by a creek side; this was in the evening and I had to conceal myself in a thicket till it was dark and then passed the camp, and crossed the creek in one of their canoes. I was much afraid that their dogs would give the alarm, but happily got safe past. I traveled on for several days, and on my way I spied a bear, shot at and wounded him, so that he could not run, but being too hasty ran up to him with my tomahawk; but before I could give a blow he gave me a severe stroke on the leg, which pained me very much, and retarded my journey much longer than it otherwise would have been. However I traveled on as well as I could till I got to the Allegheny River, where I collected some poles, with which I made a raft and bound it together with elm bark and grape vines, by which means I got over the river, but in crossing which I lost my gun. I arrived at Fort Pitt in fourteen days from the time of my start, after a captivity of five years and four months."

Hugh Gibson, mentioned as being taken captive, was the son of David Gibson, who came from County Tyrone, Ireland, about 1740 and settled in Lancaster County, where Hugh was born in 1741. His mother's maiden name was Mary McClelland. The father died while Hugh was quite young and the widowed mother, with her three children, Hugh, Israel, and Mary, removed to the vicinity of Fort Robinson, then Tyrone Township, to be near her brother, William McClelland, who resided near Centre church. During that summer season of 1756, when Indian uprisings were common and the war whoop resounded through the forests, the widow and her children had taken refuge in the stockade at Fort Robinson. With her eldest son Hugh, Mrs. Gibson was out in the woods looking for their cattle, when she was shot down and scalped and her son chased and captured. He was carried away to the Indian town of Kittanning and adopted into an Indian family to take the place of a son killed in battle with the Cherokees. His initiation into the tribe is said to have been by washing him thoroughly in the river which he was told washed away his white blood. From then on he was called brother by the Indians.

He had been compelled to witness the cruel death of a captive and when the Indians thought that he entertained thoughts of escape he was told that he would be served the same death and was treated with extreme cruelty. In one instance he was set to carrying wood to be used in his own death by burning at the stake. Happily this threat was never carried out. When Armstrong took the Indian town of Kittanning with his company from Carlisle, Gibson was kept in the rear in the woods with the old men, squaws and children but he was near enough to hear the sound of the guns as they battled. After the fall of their stronghold they retreated to the region of the Muskingum River in Ohio, where, at the point where its two branches joined, was located a large Delaware town. In fact, that was the extreme western point to which traveled those early missionaries, Rev. Duffield and Rev. Beatty, who were the first advance agents of Christianity in Perry County territory.

After his return to the settled portion of the province he resided with his maternal uncle, William McClelland, near the scene of his capture, later marrying a Miss Mary White, of Lancaster, and rearing a large family. After the Revolutionary War he removed to Crawford County, Pennsylvania, where he died at an advanced age, July 30, 1826. Rev. Dr. George Norcross, the prominent divine so long pastor of the Second Presbyterian church of Carlisle, was a descendant, being his great-grandson.

BASKINS FAMILY ABDUCTED.

Some time after Braddock's defeat Fort Granville was erected at a place called Old Town, on the bank of the Juniata, some distance from the present site of Lewistown, then Cumberland, now Mifflin County, where a company of enlisted soldiers were kept, under the command of Lieutenant Armstrong. The position of the fort was not favorable. The Indians had been lurking about there for some time and knew that Armstrong's men were few in number, sixty of them appeared July 22, 1756, before the fort, and challenged the garrison to combat; but this was declined by the commander, in consequence of the weakness of his force. The Indians fired at and wounded one man belonging to the fort, who had been a short way from it, yet he got in safe; after which they divided themselves in small parties, one of which attacked the plantation of one Baskins, near Juniata, whom they murdered, burnt his house and carried off his wife and children; and another made Hugh Carroll and family prisoners.

The Indians on one occasion murdered a family of seven persons on Sherman's Creek; from there they passed over the mountain at Croghan's (Sterrett's) Gap, wounded a man, killed a horse and captured a Mrs. Boyde, her two sons and a daughter upon the Conodoguinet Creek.

The Shawnees and Delaware Indians, aided and abetted by the French, continued their hellishness until 1757, when negotiations

6

Indians were used as guides and interpreters by the provincial troops and the troops were constantly aided by the pioneers. From a report from Col. John Armstrong dated Carlisle, July 11, 1757, the following extract relating to Sherman's Valley is made: "On Wednesday last Lieutenant Armstrong marched with forty soldiers, accompanied by Mr. Smith, the Indian interpreter, and ten Indians, into Sherman's Valley, where some of the enemy had been discovered. They were joined by thirty of the country people who wanted to bring over their cattle from that place. On Thursday they found the tracks of the enemy and followed them with spirit enough until evening, when the tracks made toward this valley; next morning the Cherokees discovered some tracks bearing off to the westward, upon which they said they were discovered and that those bearing towards the westward were going to inform a body of the enemy, which they said was not far off; upon which the lieutenant told the interpreter that his orders particularly led him to make discovery of the enemy's encampment (if any such there was) and to know whether any were drove off for their support. But two or three of the bravest of the Indians freely told the interpreter that their young men were afraid that the enemy discovered them and therefore no advantage could at that time be got; nor could the interpreter prevail on them to stay any longer out. The lieutenant reconnoitered the country towards Juniata, and returned last night without any discovery of a lurking party of the enemy behind us."

Even if a few had remained north of the Kittatinny or Blue Mountain to attend to the stock, or if trips were made across the mountain for that purpose, yet Sherman's Valley was practically abandoned in 1756, in so far as actual residence was concerned. The settlers had gradually gone back, however, until in 1763, as the next chapter will show, they were again driven from their homes by a devastating and relentless Indian warfare.

CHAPTER IV.

TREATY OF PEACE, BUT A DEVASTATING INDIAN WARFARE.

I N 1758 the provincial authorities and the Indians made a
treaty of peace and friendship at Easton, and, generally speaking, the Indian massacres were over; yet unattached bands
of marauding savages appeared at times and committed murders.
In fact the war between the English and the French still continued
until 1762. A secret confederacy had also been formed by the
Shawnees and the various tribes along the Ohio and about Detroit for the purpose of attacking simultaneously the English posts
and settlements on the frontiers, and the territory which is now
Perry County was certainly not only the frontier, but the "front
line."

This was termed by the frontier inhabitants, the Pontiac War,
by reason of Pontiac, a chief of the Ottawas, being the evil genius
who was one of the principals in the inception. The province had
dealt leniently—too leniently—with the Indians and a treaty of
peace was usually accompanied by expensive and numerous presents, which in reality put a premium on war, as there could be
no treaties of peace without the necessary preceding war. A certain day was set apart and the frontiers everywhere were to be
attacked at the same time. A bundle of small rods had been given
to every tribe and one was to be withdrawn on the morning of each
day, and on the date of the withdrawal of the final rod the general
attack was to have been made. From the bundle going to those
who were to attack Fort Pitt, at the present site of Pittsburgh,
a squaw, not in sympathy with the movement, drew a few rods.
This accounts for the actions of the Indians in attacking that place
ahead of the designated day, which news was hurried abroad and
which put some settlements on their guard.

Their plan was deliberate and skillful. The border settlements
were to be invaded during harvest, the people, corn and cattle destroyed and the land thus laid waste. Traders had been invited
among them and these were first put out of the way, their goods
being plundered. The country was then put at the mercy of scalping parties and desolation followed in their wake. It is said the
roads were literally covered with women and children seeking
refuge at Lancaster and Philadelphia. The forts at Presque Isle,
Lebeuf and Venango had been captured and the garrisons massacred. For Ligonier was barely saved. The soil of Perry was

overrun by these western Indians and fortunately records exist
which show some of the horrors, but many of them were in such
exposed places that no one was left to tell the tale.

In correspondence to the *Pennsylvania Gazette,* dated Carlisle,
July 12, 1763, is the following, which covers the horrible situation, not only of what is now Perry, but of Juniata and of Cumberland:

"I embrace this first leisure since yesterday morning to transmit you a
brief account of our present state of affairs here, which indeed is very
distressing; every day almost affording some fresh object to awaken the
compassion, alarm the fears or kindle into resentment and vengeance every
sensible breast, while flying families obliged to abandon house and possession, to save their lives by a hasty escape; mourning widows, bewail-
ing their husbands surprised and massacred by savage rage; tender parents lamenting the fruit of their own bodies, cropt in the very bloom of
life by a barbarous hand; with relations and acquaintances pouring out
sorrow for murdered neighbors and friends, present a varied scene of
mingled distress.

"When, for some time, after striking at Bedford, the Indians appeared
quiet, nor struck any other part of our frontiers, it became the prevailing
opinion, that our forts and communication, were so peculiarly the object
of their attention, that, till at least after harvest, there was little prospect.
of danger over the hills, and to dissent from the generally received sentiment was political heresy, and attributed to timidity rather than judgment, till too early conviction has decided the point in the following
manner.

"On Sunday morning, the 10th inst., about nine or ten o'clock, at the
house of one William White, on Juniata, between thirty and forty miles
hence, there being in said house four men and a lad, the Indians came
rushing upon them, and shot White at the door, just stepping out to see
what the noise meant. Our people then pulled in White and shut the
door; but observing through a window the Indians setting fire to the
house, they attempted to force their way out at the door; but the first
that stept out being shot down, they drew him in and again shut the door;
after which one attempting an escape out of the window on the loft,
was shot through the head and the lad wounded in the arm. The only
one now remaining, William Riddle, broke a hole through the roof of the
house, and an Indian who saw him looking out, alleged he was about to
fire on him, withdrew, which afforded Riddle an opportunity to make his
escape. The house, with the other four in it, was burned down, as one
McMachen informs, who was coming to it, not suspecting Indians, and
was then fired at and shot through the shoulder, but made his escape.

"The same day, about dinner time, at about a mile and a half from said
White's, at the house of Robert Campbell, six men being in the house,
as they were dining, three Indians rushed in at the door, and after firing
among them and wounding some, they tomahawked in an instant one of
the men; whereupon one George Dodds, one of the company, sprang back
into the room, took down a rifle, shot an Indian through the body, who
was just presenting his piece to shoot him. The Indian being mortally
wounded, staggered, and letting his gun fall, was carried off by three
more. Dodds, with one or two more, getting upon the loft, broke the
roof in order to escape, and looking out saw one of the company, Stephen
Jeffries, running, but very slowly, by reason of a wound in the breast,
and an Indian pursuing; and it is thought he could not escape, nor have

we heard of him since, so that it is past dispute, he also is murdered. The first that attempted getting out of the loft was fired at and drew back; another attempting was shot dead; and of the six, Dodds, the only one, made his escape. The same day about dusk, about six or seven miles up Tuscarora, and about twenty-eight or thirty miles hence, they murdered one William Anderson,* together with a boy and girl all in one house. At White's were seen at least five, some say eight or ten, Indians, and at Campbell's about the same number. On Monday, the 11th, a party of about twenty-four went over from the upper part of Shearman's Valley, to see how matters were. Another party of twelve or thirteen went over from the upper part of said valley; and Col. John Armstrong, with Thomas Wilson, Esq., and a party of between thirty and forty from this town, to reconnoitre and assist in bringing in the dead.

"Of the first and third parties we have heard nothing yet; but of the party of twelve, six are come in, and inform that they passed through the several places in Tuscarora, and saw the houses in flames, or burnt entirely down. That the grain that had been reaped the Indians burnt in shocks and had set the fences on fire where the grain was unreaped; that the hogs had fallen upon and mangled several of the dead bodies; that the said company of twelve, suspecting danger, durst not stay to bury the dead; that after they had returned over the Tuscarora Mountain, about one or two miles on this side of it, and about eighteen or twenty from hence, they were fired on by a large party of Indians, supposed about thirty, and were obliged to fly; that two, viz: William Robinson and John Graham, are certainly killed, and four more are missing, who it is thought, have fallen into the hands of the enemy, as they appeared slow in flight, most probably wounded, and the savages pursued with violence. What farther mischief has been done we have not heard, but expect every day and hour, some more messages of melancholy news.

"In hearing of the above defeat, we sent out another party of thirty or upwards, commanded by our high sheriff, Mr. Dunning, and Mr. William Lyon, to go in quest of the enemy, or fall in with and reinforce our other parties. There are also a number gone out from about three miles below this, so that we now have over the hills upwards of eighty or ninety volunteers scouring the woods. The inhabitants of Shearman's Valley, Tuscarora, &c., are all come over, and the people of this valley, near the mountain, are beginning to move in, so that in a few days there will be scarcely a house inhabited north of Carlisle. Many of our people are greatly distressed, through want of arms and ammunition; and numbers of those beat off their places have hardly money enough to purchase a pound of powder.

"Our women and children, I suppose must move downwards, if the enemy proceed. To-day a British vengeance begins to rise in the breasts of our men. One of them that fell from among the twelve, as he was just expiring, said to one of his fellows: 'Here, take my gun and kill the first Indian you see, and all shall be well.' "

The following is an extract from a letter dated the next day, July 13, 1763, to the same paper, and continuing the report of the relief forces sent north of the Kittatinnies:

"Last night Colonel Armstrong returned. He left the party, who pursued further and found several dead, whom they buried in the best manner they could, and are now all returned in. From what appears the Indians are traveling from one place to another, along the valley, burning

---

*William Anderson was killed without warning, while reading the Bible.

the farms, and destroying all the people they meet with. This day gives
an account of six more being killed in the valley, so that since last Sunday
morning, to this day, twelve o'clock, we have a pretty authentic account
of the number slain, being twenty-five, and four or five wounded. The
Colonel, Mr. Wilson and Mr. Alricks are now on the parade, endeavoring
to raise another party, to go out and succor the sheriff and his party consisting of fifty men, which marched yesterday, and I hope they will be
able to send off immediately twenty good men. The people here, I assure
you, want nothing but a good leader and a little encouragement, to make
a very good defense."

The result of these marauding expeditions is best summed up
by the *Pennsylvania Gazette* of July 28, 1763, in which is the following statement:

"Our advices from Carlisle are that the party under the sheriff, Mr.
Dunning, mentioned in our last, fell in with the enemy, at the house of
one Alexander Logan, in Shearman's Valley, supposed to be about fifteen,
or upwards, who had murdered the said Logan, his son, and another man
about two miles from said house, and mortally wounded a fourth, who is
since dead; and that at the time of their being discovered they were
rifling the house and shooting down the cattle, and it is thought, about to
return home with the spoil they had got. That our men, on seeing them,
immediately spread themselves from right to left, with a design to surround them, and engaged the savages with great courage, but from their
eagerness rather too soon, as some of the party had not got up when the
skirmish began; that the enemy returned our first fire very briskly; but
our people, regardless of that, rushed upon them, when they fled, and were
pursued a considerable way, till thickets secured their escape, four or five
of them it was thought being mortally wounded; that our parties had
brought in with them what cattle they could collect, but that great numbers
were killed by the Indians, and many of the horses that were in the valleys carried off; that since the 10th inst. there was an account of fifty-
four persons being killed by the enemy.

"That the Indians had set fire to houses, barns, corn, wheat and rye,
hay; in short, to everything combustible; so that the whole country
seemed to be in one general blaze; that the miseries and distresses of
the poor people were really shocking to humanity, and beyond the power
of language to describe; that Carlisle was become the barrier, not a single
inhabitant being beyond it; that every stable and hovel in the town was
crowded with miserable refugees, who were reduced to a state of beggary
and despair; their houses, cattle and harvest destroyed; and from a
plentiful, independent people, they were become real objects of charity
and comiseration; that it was most dismal to see the streets filled with
people, in whose countenances must be discovered a mixture of grief,
madness and despair; and to hear, now and then, the sighs and groans
of men; the disconsolate lamentations of women, and the screams of
children, who had lost their nearest and dearest relatives; and that on
both sides of the Susquehanna, for some miles, the woods were filled
with poor families, and their cattle, who made fires, and lived like savages, exposed to the inclemencies of the weather."

From a letter dated July 30, 1763, at Carlisle, the following
account is taken. It relates of the efforts made to save a part of
the harvests:

"On the 25th, a considerable number of the inhabitants of Shearman's
Valley went over, with a party of soldiers to guard them, to attempt

saving as much of their grain as might be standing, and it is hoped a considerable quantity will yet be preserved. A party of volunteers, between twenty and thirty, went to the farther side of the valley, next to the Tuscarora Mountain, to see what appearance there might be of the Indians, as it was thought they would most probably be there, if anywhere in the settlement; to search for, and bury the dead at Buffalo Creek, and to assist the inhabitants that lived along, or near the foot of the mountain, in bringing off what they could, which services they accordingly performed, burying the remains of three persons; but saw no marks of Indians having lately been there, excepting one track, supposed about two or three days old, near the narrows of Buffalo Creek hill; and heard some hallooing and firing of a gun at another place."

The murders at the home of William White, previously mentioned in this chapter, were in harvest time and the reapers, as the harvest hands were then termed, were all in the house, it being the Sabbath day, when the redskins surprised them. Robert Robinson's account of many of these murders is almost parallel with that of the accounts printed on the foregoing pages, but he goes farther. He tells of receiving the news at Edward Elliott's, where he and others were harvesting; how John Graham, John Christy and James Christy heard the firing of guns at the William Anderson home early in the evening, and of their investigation and carrying the news to Elliott's. His account further says:

"Graham and the Christys came about midnight. We, hearing the Indians had got so far up the Tuscarora Valley, and knowing Collins' famliy and James Scott's were there about harvest, twelve of us concluded to go over Bigham's Gap (the entrance to Liberty Valley) and give those word that were there; when we came to Collins' we saw that the Indians had been there, had broke a wheel, emptied a bed and taken flour, of which they made some water gruel; we counted thirteen spoons made of bark; we followed the tracks made down to James Scott's, where we found the Indians had killed some fowls; we pursued on to Graham's; there the house was on fire and burned down to the joists. We divided our men into two parties, six in each; my brother with his party came in behind the barn, and myself with the other party came down through an oats field; I was to shoot first; the Indians had hung a coat upon a post on the other side of the fire from us; I looked at it and saw it immovable, and therefore walked down to it and found that the Indians had just left it; they had killed four hogs and had eaten at pleasure. Our company took their track, and found that two companies had met at Graham's and had gone over the Tuscarora Mountain. We took the run gap, the two roads meeting at Nicholsons; they were there first, heard us coming and lay in ambush for us; they had first fire; being twenty-five in number and only twelve of us—they killed five and wounded myself. They then went to Alexander Logan's, where they emptied some beds and passed on to George McCord's.

"The names of the twelve were William Robison, who acted as captain; Robert Robison, the relator of this narrative; Thomas Robison, being three brothers; John Graham, Charles Elliott, William Christy, James Christy, David Miller, John Elliott, Edward McConnel, William McAlister, and John Nicholas. The persons killed were William Robison, who was shot in the belly with buckshot and got about half a mile from the ground; John Elliott, then a boy about seventeen years of age, having emptied his gun, was pursued by an Indian with his tomahawk, who was within a few perches of him when Elliott had poured some powder into his gun by random, out of his powder horn, and having a bullet in his mouth, put it in the muzzle, but had no time to ram it down; he turned and fired at his pursuer, who clapped his hand on his stomach and cried 'och,' then turned and fled. Elliott had run a few perches further, when he overtook William Robison, weltering in his blood, in his last agonies; he requested Elliott to carry him off, who excused himself by telling of his inability to do so, and also of the danger they were in; he said he knew it, but desired him to take his gun with him, and, peace or war, if ever he had an opportunity of killing an Indian, to shoot him for his sake. Elliott brought away the gun and Robison was not found by the Indians.

"Thomas Robison stood on the ground until the whole of his people were fled, nor did the Indians offer to pursue, until the last man left the field; Thomas having fired and charged a second time, the Indians were prepared for him, and when he took aim past the tree, a number fired at him at the same time; one of his arms was broken; he took his gun in the other and fled; going up a hill he came to a high log, and clapped his hand, in which was his gun, on the log to assist in leaping over it; while in the attitude of stooping a bullet entered his side, going in a triangular course through his body; he sunk down across the log; the Indians sunk the cock of his gun into his brains and mangled him very much. John Graham was seen by David Miller sitting on a log, not far from the place of attack, with his hands on his face, and blood running through his fingers. Charles Elliott and Edward McConnel took a circle round where the Indians were laying, and made the best of their way to Buffalo Creek; but they were pursued by the Indians; and where they crossed the creek there was a high bank, and as they were endeavoring to ascend the bank, they were both shot and fell back into the water.

"Thus ended the unfortunate affair; but at the same time it appears as if the hand of Providence had been in the whole transaction, for there is every reason to believe that spies had been viewing the place the night before, and the Indians were within three quarters of a mile from the place from which the men had started, when there would have been from twenty to thirty men perhaps in the field reaping, and all the guns that could be depended upon were in this small company, except one, so that they might have become an easy prey, and instead of those five brave men who lost their lives three times that number might have done so.

"A party of forty men came from Carlisle to bury the dead at Juniata; when they saw the dead at Buffalo Creek they returned home. Then a party of men came with Captain Dunning; but before they came to Alexander Logan's his son John, Charles Coyle, William Hamilton, with Bartholomew Davis, followed the Indians to George McCord's, where they were in the barn; Logan and those with him were all killed, except Davis, who made his escape and joined Captain Dunning. The Indians then returned to Logan's house again, when Captain Dunning and his party came on them, and they fired some time at each other; Dunning had one man wounded.

"The relief parties took back with them what cattle they could secure, but the Indians had killed a large number and had taken all the horses upon which they could lay hands."

By the latter part of July, 1763, there were 1,384 refugees from north of the Kittatinny Mountain domiciled in barns, sheds or other temporary place of refuge at Shippensburg, having fled from their homes.

The victory of Colonel Henry Bouquet over the Indians in western Pennsylavnia, in 1764, gave the settlers new courage and they gradually returned to Sherman's Valley and the territory east of the Juniata River, and by 1767 many of the best locations in the county had been warranted.

*There is record of the heirs of Robert Campbell, mentioned in this chapter as being cruelly murdered by the Indians, warranting lands in Tuscarora Township in 1767, four years after his death.

†The Alexander Logan, whose death at the hands of the Indians is here described, was the owner of lands near Kistler, later long owned by the McMillens.

COUNTY CITIZENS RECIPIENTS OF CHARITY.

When Perry Countains have been contributing to charity—to flood and famine sufferers everywhere, to India, France, Belgium, Armenia, the Harrisburg and other hospitals—little did many think that in its provincial days, before it arose to the dignity of a "little commonwealth," its people were the objects of charity, owing to their being driven out by the Indians from their homes. Such, however, was the case. The refugees, who were in Carlisle, were relieved to some extent in their great distress by the generosity of the Episcopal churches of Philadelphia. On July 26, 1763, Richard Peters, the rector of Christ church and St. Peters, in Philadelphia (the same man who was secretary of the province), represented to the vestry "that the back inhabitants of this province are reduced to great distress and necessity, by the present invasion" and proposed that some method be formed for collecting charity for their relief. A preamble was drawn up and a subscription paper started. At the next meeting the wardens reported that they had collected £662, 3s. Of course that amount of money needed systematic distribution and the Philadelphia congregations corresponded with persons in Cumberland to ascertain the extent of the distress. William Thomson, an itinerant missionary for the counties of York and Cumberland, and Francis West and Thomas Donellon, wardens of the Episcopal church at Carlisle, sent a reply in which, among other statements, is this: "We have taken pains to get the number of the distressed, and upon strict inquiry, we find seven hundred and fifty families have abandoned their plantations, the greatest number of which have lost their crops, some their stock and furniture, and besides, we are informed that there are about two hundred women and children coming down from Fort Pitt. We also find that sums of money lately sent up are almost expended, and that each family has not received twenty

---

*See chapter on Tuscarora Township.
†See chapter on Madison Township and on "Frontier Forts."

shillings upon an average." The letter also tells of the great distress and says that smallpox and flux are raging among the homeless. Upwards of two hundred of these families were in Carlisle and the remainder in Shippensburg, Littlestown, York and other places. However, it must be remembered that they were not all from Perry County territory, but from what is now Fulton, Franklin, Bedford and farther west, as well as from the outlying districts of Cumberland County itself.

In recounting the result of this report and appeal Rev. Dorr, in his Historical Account of Christ and St. Peters' Church, says:

"In consequence of this information, a large supply of flour, rice, medicine, and other necessaries, were immediately forwarded for the relief of the sufferers. And to enable those, who chose to return to their plantations, to defend themselves against future attacks of the Indians, the vestry of Christ church and St. Peters were of opinion that the refugees should be furnished with two chests of arms, and half a barrel of powder, four hundred pounds of lead, two hundred of swan shot, and one thousand flints. These were accordingly sent with instructions to sell them to prudent and good people as are in want of them, and will use them for their defense, for the prices charged in the invoice."

PIONEER RUNNERS.

During these trying periods the pioneers employed men who were dispatched as runners to give settlers notice of impending danger. They were accustomed to hunting, immune to hardships and with a thorough knowledge of the country. There were thirty in the territory west of the Susquehanna and south of the Juniata to the Allegheny Mountains. They were a lot of intrepid, resolute fellows, on the order of our present admirable troops of State Constabulary, and were in the command of a man who had been a captive of the Indians for several years and knew their traits, but whose name unfortunately fails to be recorded. According to Votes of the Assembly, Sept. 17, 1763, the Colonial legislators were appealed to for assistance in retaining this body of scouts in existence.

The terror of the citizens subsided but little until Colonel Bouquet conquered the Indians in 1764 and compelled them to solicit peace. A condition of the peace terms was that the Indians were to give up all the women and children which they held in captivity. Among them were many who had been seized as mere children and had grown up among the savages, learning their language and forgetting their own. Their affections were even with the savages. Some mothers found lost children but others were unable to identify theirs. The separation between the Indians and the captives was heart-rending, the red men shedding many tears and the captives leaving reluctantly. Many of these captives later voluntarily rejoined the Indians. Some had married Indians, but from choice,

records tell us. A girl who had been captured at the age of fourteen and had married an Indian and was the mother of several
children, said: "Can I enter my parents' dwelling? Will they be
kind to my children? Will my old companions associate with the
wife of an Indian chief? Will I desert my husband, who has been
kind?" During the night she fled to her husband and children.

A great many of these prisoners were brought to Carlisle, among
them the captives from Perry County. Colonel Bouquet advertised
for those who had lost children to come and look for them.
Among those who came was an old lady who had lost a child many
years before, but she was unable to identify her. With a breaking heart the old lady told Colonel Bouquet her sad story, relating
how she used to sing to the little one a hymn of which the child
was so fond. The colonel requested her to sing it then, in the
presence of the captives, and she did, the words being:

> "Alone, yet not alone am I,
>   Though in this solitude so drear;
> I feel my Saviour always nigh,
>   He comes my every hour to cheer."

As the sweet voice of the mother so beautifully sang the words,
from among the captives sprang a young girl and rushed into her
mother's arms.

During the time of the French and Indian War, 1756-61, the
world was largely at war. The ships of France and England even
carried it to the great high seas.

Capture and Release of Frederick Stump.

In January, 1768, a party of Indians visited a pioneer, Frederick
Stump, later known as the "Indian killer," at his cabin on Middle
Creek (now in Snyder County), and differences arising, he
and his employe, named Ironcutter, killed the Indians and also
those at a cabin four miles distant, so that the news would not
reach the Indian settlements. The bodies were thrown into the
creek and floated down it to the Susquehanna; one was found
along the shore near what is now New Cumberland, Pa., then
below Harris' Ferry. It was interred by James Galbraith and
Jonathon Hoge, who reported it to John Penn, then provincial
governor. One William Blythe traveled to Philadelphia and under
oath stated that he had seen Stump at the home of George Gabriel
and heard his story, in which he admitted the murders.

Penn issued a proclamation offering a reward for Stump and
Ironcutter, promising to punish them with death and notifying the
Indians of what he had done. Sir William Johnson sent an urgent message to the Indians, saying, "If they know any of the
relatives of these persons murdered at Middle Creek, to send them

to him, that he might wipe the tears from their eyes, comfort their afflicted hearts and satisfy them on account of their grievances."

As soon as Capt. William Patterson, formerly of Lancaster County, but then residing on the Juniata, heard of the murders he went, without waiting orders of the authorities, with a party of nineteen men, and arrested Stump and Ironcutter, and delivered them to John Holmes, the sheriff, at Carlisle. Aware that the Indians would be exasperated at hearing of the murders he sent a messenger to the west branch country to them, telling of the arrest. As the messages and replies are of much historical interest they are reproduced in full. First, his official report:

CARLISLE, January 23, 1768.

Sir: The 21st instant, I marched a party of nineteen men to George Gabriel's house, at Penn's Creek mouth, and made prisoners of Frederick Stump and John Ironcutter, who were suspected to having murdered ten of our friend Indians near Augusta; and I have this day delivered them to Mr. Holmes at Carlisle jail.

Yesterday I sent a person to the Great Island, that understood the Indian language, with a talk; a copy of which is enclosed.

Myself and party were exposed to great danger, by the desperate resistance made by Stump and his friends, who sided with him. The steps I have taken, I flatter myself, will not be disapproved of by the gentlemen in the government; my sole view being directed to the service of the frontiers, before I heard his honor the governor's orders. The message I sent to the Indians I hope will not be deemed assuming an authority of my own, as you are very sensible I am no stranger to the Indians, or their customs. I am, with respect,

Your most obedient humble servant,

W. PATTERSON.

The message to the Six Nations, in the west branch country:

JUNIATA, January 22, 1768.

Brothers of the Six Nations, Delawares, and other inhabitants of the West Branch of Susquehanna, hear what I have to say to you:

With a heart swelled with grief, I have to inform you that Frederick Stump and John Ironcutter hath, unadvisedly, murdered ten of our friend Indians near Fort Augusta. The inhabitants of the province of Pennsylvania do disapprove of the said Stump and Ironcutter's conduct; and as proof thereof, I have taken them prisoners, and will deliver them into the custody of officers, that will keep them ironed in prison for trial; and I make no doubt, as many of them as are guilty, will be condemned, and die for the offence.

Brothers, I being truly sensible of the injury done you, I only add these few words, with my heart's wish, that you may not rashly let go the fast hold of our chain of friendship, for the ill-conduct of one of our bad men. Believe me, brothers, we Englishmen continue the same love for you that hath usually subsisted between our grandfathers, and I desire you to call at Fort Augusta, to trade with our people, for the necessaries you stand in need of. I pledge you my word, that no white man there shall molest any of you, while you behave as friends. I shall not rest by night nor day until I receive your answer.

Your friend and brother,

W. PATTERSON.

The following answer to the above was received from the Indians:

February 11th, 1768.

Loving Brother: I received your speech by Gertham Hicks, and have sent one of my relatives with a string of wampum, and the following answer:

Loving Brother: I am glad to hear from you. I understand that you are very much grieved, and that the tears run from your eyes. With both my hands I now wipe away those tears; and as I don't doubt but your heart is disturbed, I remove all the sorrow from it, and make it easy, as it was before. I will now sit down and smoke my pipe. I have taken fast hold of the chain of friendship; and when I give it a pull, if I find my brothers, the English, have let it go, it will then be time for me to let go too, and take care of my family. There are four of my relatives murdered by Stump; and all I desire is, that he may suffer for his wicked action; I shall then think that people have the same goodness in their hearts as formerly, and intend to keep it there. As it was the evil spirit that caused Stump to commit this bad action, I blame none of my brothers, the English, but him.

I desire that the people of Juniata may sit still in their places, and not put themselves to any hardships, by leaving their habitations; whenever danger is coming, they shall know it before it comes to them.

I am, your loving brother,

SHAWANA BEN.

To Capt. William Patterson.*

The governor's proclamation offered £200 for Stump's apprehension, but not knowing of his arrest, delayed the publication for a short period, lest news of it should reach him, and in order to accomplish his arrest in a more secretive manner.

The council of the province advised Governor Penn to write to General Gage and Sir William Johnson, informing them of the murder and of the steps he was taking, and to ask Sir William to communicate the same to the Six Nations, as soon as possible, "in the best and most favorable manner in his power, so as to prevent their taking immediate resentment for this unavoidable injury, committed on their people, and to assure them of the firm and sincere purposes of this government to give them full satisfaction at all times for all wrongs done to the Indians, and to preserve the friendship subsisting between us and them inviolable."

But before these letters and the proclamation of Chief Justice Allen reached the magistrates and sheriffs, Stump and Ironcutter as previously stated, had been lodged in jail; however, before they were brought to trial they were rescued from prison.

As white settlers had from time to time been scalped in Perry County territory there was a certain sympathy went out to Stump and Ironcutter with the result that on January 29, 1768, a party of seventy or eighty armed men, supposed to be mostly from Sherman's Valley, appeared at the Carlisle jail and overpowered

*Provincial Records.

the sheriff, John Holmes, and the jailer and released the two prisoners, who until that time had been kept in the dungeon. A half dozen prominent citizens who hastily appeared to aid the sheriff included Ephraim Blaine, who was formerly a Toboyne Township citizen and of whose later prominence this book elsewhere goes into detail.

While this murder and the subsequent rescue did not happen on Perry County soil, yet they are dwelt on at some length here owing to the fact that the greater part of the rescuers were supposed to be from Sherman's Valley. Owing to possible complications with the Indians the murders by Stump and Ironcutter and their subsequent delivery from jail produced a great wave of excitement in the entire colony. Governor John Penn cited the officers and magistrates to appear before him, reprimanding the latter for their conduct in advising the retention of the prisoners at Carlisle instead of delivering them to Philadelphia, as required by the warrant. Tradition implies that the sheriff and jailer were passive actors in this jail delivery.

Exploits of Captain Jack.

There are traditionary tales connected with "Captain Jack" and his operations in Perry County, but as county lines in those days were not in existence, his exploits may properly belong to the whole Juniata and Cumberland Valleys. He was a white man, but was variously termed the "black hunter," the "black rifle," the "wild hunter of the Juniata," the "black hunter of the forest," but principally "Captain Jack." His real name was Patrick Jack, in all probability. He entered the forest section of Pennsylvania, somewhere in the Juniata Valley, with a few companions, built a cabin, cleared a little land and made his living by hunting and fishing, not having a care. He was a free and easy, happy-go-lucky type of man until one evening in 1752, when he returned from a day in the woods to find his cabin burned, his wife and children murdered. From that moment for over a year he forsook civilization, lived in caves, protected the frontier settlers from the Indians and seized every opportunity for revenge that presented itself. He was the terror of the Indians and the guardian angel of the pioneers. On an occasion, near Juniata—the name of the Indian town on Duncan's Island, opposite the west end of Duncannon— about midnight on a dark night, a family was suddenly awakened by the report of a gun. Jumping from their cots they saw an Indian fall to rise no more. The open door exposed to view the "wild hunter," who called, "I saved your lives," and vanished into darkness. He never shot foolishly and his keenness of vision was as unerring as his aim. He formed an association to defend the settlers against savage aggressions. On a given signal they would unite. During 1756 his exploits were often heard of from the Conococheague in Franklin County, to the Juniata River. To some he was known as the "Half-Indian," and Colonel Armstrong, in a letter to the governor, said: "The company under the command of the Half-Indian, having left the Great Cove, the Indians took advantage and murdered many." Through Colonel·Croghan —for George Croghan had been made a colonel—he also proffered his aid to Braddock. "He will march with his hunters," says the colonel, adding, as a further description, "they are dressed in hunting shirts, moccasins, &c., are well armed and are equally regardless of heat and cold. They require no shelter for the night—they ask no pay." As Captain Jack wanted to go free of the restraint of camp life and army regulations General Braddock refused his services. Braddock was a strict disciplinarian and despised the Indian method of fighting. He wanted to attain a signal victory over the French without using those methods or the help of others who used them. However, he had already accepted a company of Indians under Captain George Croghan. He never lived to discover his error in refusing Captain Jack's services or the fact that the Indian method of fighting excelled that of marching in the open, clad in gaudy uniforms, with drums beating and banners flying. There is no doubt that among Captain Jack's daring men were some whose homes were within the confines of what is now Perry County.

While some historians give his name to Jack's Mountain, in the Juniata Valley, John Harris says the mountain was named after Jack Armstrong, who was murdered at its base by the Indians. The latter is probably the truth, as Captain Jack's activities were principally' in the territory now known as Perry and Franklin Counties.

There is evidence of Captain Jack once owning property, the location being described as "on back Crike, Joning Matthew Arthor's pleas, operward of ye sad Creek," in Antrim Township, later Franklin County. In 1748 this property passed from John Ward to Matthew Arther, who owned the adjoining place. In November, 1767, Arther sold it to Patrick Jack, same being recorded in Book C, Volume 1, at the Cumberland County courthouse.

An early writer, in referring to Doubling Gap, located on the Blue or Kittatinny Mountain, further clinches the fact that the Sherman's Valley was one of the principal scenes of the activities of Captain Jack. It follows: "The place for many miles around is invested with many historical facts and legends connected with the early settlements of the country. It was in the adjoining valley (Sherman's) and on these mountains that Big Beaver, a chief of the Shoshones, with his tribe, in 1752 and for years before had their hunting grounds, having been driven in 1677 from Carolina and Georgia. This valley (Sherman's) was the grave of many of his children and the scene of many a massacre. It was where the far-famed and many-named Captain Jack—the Black Rifle, the Wild Hunter, etc.—entered the woods, built his cabin and cleared a little patch of land within sight of a spring and amused himself with hunting and fishing."

Some authorities credit Captain Jack's real name as being Joseph Ager, or Aiger, who settled in Cumberland County in 1851, but the writer is inclined, after careful research, to believe that he was no other than Patrick Jack. However, the actual establishment of his real name and his early history must forever remain an unfathomed mystery. Of Herculean proportions and of swarthy complexion he was supposed by some to have been a half-breed. Colonel Armstrong, in a letter to the governor, terms him "the Half-Indian." Others term him a white man with a past. The following, from Hanna's "The Wilderness Trail," is self explanatory: "Captain William Patterson, who lived on Tuscarora Creek, was a bold, resourceful, frontiersman and Indian fighter, whose exploits, with those of his father, furnished much of the material for the legendary history of the fictitious 'Captain Jack,' the Wild Hunter of the Juniata." That much of the history of Captain Jack is lengendary is true, but that he was a fictitious character only is disproved by the previous pages, the extracts being from provincial history and records.

In the possession of Miss Margaret D. McClure, of Bradford, a daughter of William McClure, one of Perry County's noted sons, are two old documents left by her father, which also show that Captain Jack was very real. They follow:

The 2nd Battalion, Penna. Regiment, commanded by
Lt. Colonel Clayton, Camp Fort Loudon, August 16, 1764.

John Morrison, Soldier in Colonel Clayton's Company, discharged by Dr. Plunkett's orders from any further service in the above Regiment.

Given under my hand this   PATRICK JACK,
day, 16th August, 1764.   Capt. Lieut.

These are to certify:

That the three Marching Companies from the Second Battalion met at Studler's Mill upon the 15th of this m. and proceeded to elect a Major, when it appeared upon summing of the Poll that Capt. Patrick Jack and Elias Davison, 1st Lieut., had each of them eighty-two votes.

August 22, 1776,   BY THEO. McPHERRIN,
Fort Conococheague.   One of the judges of the election.

They throw further light on the length of his services, as the first shows service as early as 1764 and the last as late as 1776.

7

FORTS IN AND NEAR THE COUNTY.

The horrible atrocities which occurred during the summer and fall of 1755 almost depopulated the lands which now comprise Perry County, as well as others, and the provincial authorities took steps to allay fear and safeguard the pioneers by a line of forts extending from the Delaware River across the province to the Maryland line and at other outlying places. George Croghan was commissioned to select the site of three, in Cumberland County, which were located as follows: Fort Granville, in present Mifflin County; Patterson's, in present Juniata County, and at Sideling Hill, now in Bedford County.

Among the forts mentioned in provincial history is Fort Augusta, built by Colonel Clapham's regiment, which was located where the present town of Sunbury stands. Joseph Greenwood—after whom Greenwood Township was named later—and George Gabriel acted as guides for the regiment of soldiers which Colonel Clapham was conducting to Fort Augusta, as their signatures to an affidavit dated June 2, 1756, verifies. On account of the better trail the movement of troops was conducted up the Perry County side. A member of this regiment was Ensign Samuel Miles, who twenty years later was a colonel commanding a Continental regiment in the army under Washington. In a journal kept by him he tells of this early trip up the west side of the Susquehanna to the site of Sunbury.

Fort Robinson was built by the members of that brave and intrepid family by the name of Robinson, resolute woodsmen inured to hardship, toil and danger, and their neighbors who inhabited Sherman's Valley, as a place of refuge from Indian attack. It was a log fort, surrounded by a stockade. It occupied a site on the present Edward R. Loy farm, near Centre Church, being located on a tableland with a good view of the surrounding country. At its edge was a bluff, the shelter of which was sought in escaping to the fort. The lowlands below were heavily wooded with large oak and maple, which also afforded protection in going to the fort. A spring was located at the foot of the bluff where water was secured with the least exposure, the distance from the stockade being only the steep bank—probably twenty feet. It was not under provincial control, at least there are no records to prove such fact. The Robinsons figured prominently in pioneer life. A brother of George Robinson, who located the fort and stockade was a member of Colonel Armstrong's expedition to Kittanning. George Robinson warranted the tract on which the fort was located, the fort being built in 1755. The fort was evidently in the nature of a block house, surrounded by a stockade built of heavy planks or poles. It was located along the famous Allegheny or

Traders' Path and was the only source of protection for the traveler along the Allegheny Path between the Kittatinny or Blue Mountain and the Tuscarora. There are no traces of the pioneer battlements, nothing to indicate the part played by these hardy pioneers in the struggle for settlement and civilization.

While called a fort it would probably have come under the term of stockade. The stockades of that period were practically all of one style. They consisted of oak logs, about seventeen feet long, set in a ditch four feet deep, the logs being usually about a foot in diameter. Around the inside was erected a platform of logs about four or five feet from the ground, upon which the pioneers stood and aimed their guns trough port holes made in the logs. This additional elevation gave them a considerable advantage in reconnoitering the surrounding country.

Speaking of the Fort Robinson site "Frontier Forts of Pennsylvania" queries, "Could there be a place in our commonwealth more worthy of the fostering care of her people?" Working along that line during 1920, the centenary of Perry County's organization, the author of this volume took up with the State Historical Commission the advisability of marking the site with a proper stone and inscription, with the result that that Commission will agree to have the bronze inscriptions placed upon a native boulder (as being appropriate to pioneer life) if some local organization will agree to arrange for its future care. Plans are now under way for its consummation and within another year this historic site will probably be marked for all time.

In a list of provincial forts prepared by Jay Gilfillen Weiser, of Middleburg, in 1894, and published in "Frontier Forts of Pennsylvania," the only fort credited to Perry County is Hendrick's, built in 1770. This is an error, as Hendrick's fort was located in what is now Snyder County.

On a map which appears in "Frontier Forts of Pennsylvania," showing the disposition of the provincial troops in the Western District for the winter season of 1764, in the territory which now comprises Perry County, are located two detachments, one marked "A. Grove's, an officer and 20 men," and the other, "Fisher's an officer and 20 men." The location marked Grove's is near the centre of western Perry, vicinity of Fort Robinson, and Fisher's, approximately where the county seat is located.

While Fort Halifax is in Dauphin County, it is to be noted here that it was, with the exception of Fort Hunter, the only fort really built by the province along any border of the present county · of Perry, Fort Robinson being built by the pioneers themselves, according to the only records available. Fort Halifax stood a half mile above where the present town of Halifax now stands, and was garrisoned with provincial troops. Commissary General Young, in a report to the governor and council, said that "Fort Halifax was in a very bad location, being built beyond two ranges of hills and nobody living near it, none could be protected by it; that it is no station for batteaux parties, having no command of the channel, which runs close to the western shore, and is besides, covered with a large island (Clemson's) between the channel and the fort, so that numbers of the enemy may, even in daytime, run the river, without being seen by that garrison, and that though the fort, or blockhouse at Hunter's was not tenable, being hastily erected and not finished, yet the situation was the best upon the river for every service, as well as for the protection of the frontiers."

The purpose of the construction of Fort Halifax at that location is uncertain, as records show that but two families resided anywhere in the vicinity, and the river channel was on the opposite side, with the Clemson Island between. In all probability it was erected as a convenient and safe place to lodge during the two-day trip from Fort Hunter to Fort Augusta, which was located where Sunbury now stands. It was dismantled and abandoned in 1763. Clemson's Island, lying in the river opposite the fort, was the home of a considerable number of Indians, who could easily have annihilated a large party.

Fort Hunter was a provincial fort located opposite the site of the present town of Marysville, on a small promontory, where Fishing Creek enters the Susquehanna River, on the eastern side. It is in Dauphin County and one of the two provincial forts erected along the county's border. The property is now, or was lately, in the possession of John Reilly. Its location, described in provincial records as being "where the Blue Hills cross the Susquehanna," gave it command of the passage through this water gap and of the river itself, affording a place of rendezvous for the batteaux which carried supplies to Fort Halifax and Fort Augusta at Shamokin (now Sunbury). It was a blockhouse, surrounded by a stockade, and occupied the site of the present Reilly mansion. It was erected about 1755, as it is spoken of in official records as early as January 10, 1756, as "the fort at Hunter's mill." Its location was at a very romantic spot, noted for its picturesque outlook. In 1814 Archibald McAllister erected a large storage house upon its ancient foundations. Not far above the site are the famous "Hunter's Falls," where the river narrows to pass through a gap and where its waters are deep and swift, as they rush over immense ledges of rock which the waters of the centuries have failed to yet wear away.

Fort Bigham, a strong blockhouse, surrounded by a small stockade, commanded Bigham's Gap on the Juniata County side, through which lay the famous Allegheny Path to the West. It was on the "plantation" of Samuel Bigham, a Scotch-Irish settler who had

located in the Tuscarora Valley in 1754. With Bigham came John
and James Gray and Robert Hoag, who joined in the erection of
the fort as a place of refuge. Other settlers used it also until
June, 1756, when it was attacked and burned by the Indians, who
killed or took prisoner all who had sought refuge therein, the total
being twenty-three persons. It was rebuilt in 1760 by Ralph Sterrett, described by Jones, in his History of the Juniata Valley, as
"an old Indian trader." In this fort his first child, William Sterrett, was born. It is related of Sterrett that upon an occasion an
Indian tired and hungry, passing his way, was invited in and
given a meal and tobacco. He had even forgotten the occurrence
when, in 1763, the Indians again being on the warpath, he heard
a noise and looking out saw an Indian in the moonlight. He
coolly demanded his business, when the Indian recalled the hospitality and stated that the Indians were as plenty as the pigeons
in the woods and before another night they would be at Fort
Bigham to scalp and kill. Nearly all the settlers of the valley
were in the fort and were awe-stricken. They immediately began
preparations and long before daybreak a train of pack horses,
carrying them and their belongings was crossing Perry County
soil, via the Allegheny Path, to Carlisle.

Until recent years there stood on the Preston A. McMillen
farm, about a mile northeast of Kistler, in northeast Madison
Township, a log building which had been used both as a residence
and as a fort. Families by the name of Logan had taken up these
lands, which included the farms now owned by Lucian McMillen,
Linn J. McMillen, and Preston A. McMillen. On this latter
property this building was erected for both a residence and the
protection of the surrounding families. Some logs from the building were used for the construction of the McMillen barn and are
pointed out to the inquirer. It was on the nature of a blockhouse.
The property on which the fort was erected is now in the hands
of the fifth generation of McMillens, one of Perry County's substantial families. As fast as possible the Indians replaced their
bows and arrows with firearms and the residents of these farms
frequently had to seek shelter from the redskins. On one occasion a hog had been killed and was being prepared for use in the
cellar when an attack was made and a bullet struck above the cellar
door, imbedding itself five and one-half inches in a walnut log.
Many people yet living saw this log when a part of the old building. The marks of other bullets could be plainly seen. When
things got too serious the settlers would flee to the mountains, all
wooded, and escape to Carlisle. The logs were hewed on both
sides, some of them being almost two feet in width. In an Indian account of Robert Robinson, elsewhere, he tells of a Captain
Dunning seeking Indians and coming to a certain house (Alex-

ander Logan's) after the fight on Buffalo Creek. This old block-house was Logan's home. A favorite pastime of the McMillens of a century ago was "digging" bullets from these old logs.

Where the Tressler Memorial Lutheran church at Loysville now stands once stood a log cabin equipped like a blockhouse, the rear room being without windows and having portholes. This prop-erty was later owned by John Kistler, father of Rev. Kistler, who was a missionary to India about 1860.

While there is no official record of there having been a fort at New Buffalo, during the early settlements, yet, according to old records Henry Meiser, of what is now Snyder County, put his children in chaff bags and escaped to New Buffalo, where there was a temporary fort for refuge. Evidently Fort Halifax—oppo-site New Buffalo—was referred to.

Some of the earlier homes were equipped with portholes, for use in case of an Indian attack. One of these was the house on the Thomas Adams farm, near New Germantown, in Toboyne Township, now owned by Milo N. Willhide, its location being just south of Sherman's Creek.

That those daring provincials located at these forts were kept busy is attested by their many reports which are a part of the Pennsylvania Archives. A letter from Capt. James Patterson, commandant at Fort Hunter, dated January 10, 1758, and ad-dressed to "the Honorable William Deney, Esq'r, Governour and Commander in Chief of the Province of Pennsylvania," follows:

"Fort Hunter, Jan'ry ye 10th, 1758.

"I took with me 19 men & ranged from this Fort as far as Robinson's Fort, where I lodged, keeping a guard of six men & one Corporal on Centry that night. The sixth day I marched towards Hunter's Fort, ranging along the mountain foot very diligently till I came to the Fort that evening, my men being so afflicted with sickness; I could not send out till the eighth day, Lieu't Allen, with 14 men, went to Range for three days. On the 12th day Lieu't Allen, with Eighteen men & one Serjeant ranged along the mountain about 14 miles from this Fort, where he met Cap't Lieu't Weiser with his party & returned back towards this Fort the next day & came to it that night. The fifteenth, Lieu't Allen, with 18 men, kept along the Frontier till the 25th & came to this Fort that night.

"Hearing of Indians harbouring about Juniatta, on the 28th of De-cember, I took 15 men with me up the Creek, and about 14 miles from the mouth of it I found fresh tracks of Indians on both sides of the Creek & followed the tracks about four miles up the said Creek, where I lost the tracks, but I still kept up the Creek 'till I gott up about 25 miles from the mouth of said Creek, where I encamped that night. The In-dians I found were round me all night, for my Dogg made several attacks towards the Woods as if he saw the Enemy and still run back to the Centry. On the 3d of January I returned down the Creek in some Canoes that I found on said Creek, and when I came about nine miles down I espied about 20 Indians on the opposite side of the Creek to where I was. They seemed to gett themselves in order to fire upon the men that were in Canoes. I immediately ordered them all out but two men that let the Canoes float close under the shore, and kept the Land in readiness to fire upon the Enemy, as soon as they moved out of the place where they lay in Ambush, but I could see no more of them. On the 5th day of January I came to this Fort."

It will be noted that Captain Patterson terms the Juniata, "the Creek." Fourteen miles from the mouth of it, where he found the Indian tracks, would have been at the vicinity where Buffalo Creek empties into the Juniata, above Newport. Having gone up twenty-five miles from its mouth and returned nine he saw twenty Indians. That point was probably in the vicinity of Old Ferry, midway between Newport and Millerstown, but of course there is no way of telling the exact locations, they probably varying a mile or two either way.

These provincials were kept very busy by the duties of their position; but, with the success of the British arms, the scene of action shifted, during 1758, and until Pontiac's war in 1763, this pioneer garrison had little to do.

CHAPTER V.

SIMON GIRTY, THE RENEGADE.

I N that section of Perry County lying between the Juniata and Susquehanna Rivers and along the banks of the latter there is a mountain promontory below Montgomery's Ferry, almost jutting to the river's edge, which bears to this day the name of "Girty's Notch," said to have been named after Simon Girty, the renegade, who betrayed his own race to join the redskins and later the British. It is in Watts Township, almost on the Buffalo Township line and along the Susquehanna Trail—the state highway to the north. On approaching this promontory from the northeast there can be seen, half-way up the craggy rocks, the face of a man—albeit an Indian—the outline of which no sculptor could improve, put there by the Great Creator of the universe and which tradition would have us believe is the counterpart of the Girty profile.

There is record of the elder Simon Girty's once being a property owner, but not here. In 1743 he cleared a tract of thirty acres in Dauphin County, near the Susquehanna River, and made some improvements. He resided on this place several years. Becoming indebted to Thomas McKee, the storekeeper, in a sum upwards of £300 the land subsequently came into the possession of McKee.

The Alexander McKee, referred to in connection with Girty, the renegade, in the following pages, was a son of this Thomas McKee, the trader, who kept a store immediately below Peters' Mountain, in Dauphin County, opposite Allen's Cove. He was an Indian agent for the British government and became a pronounced tory.

The activities of Simon Girty, the renegade, in the provincial affairs were of such magnitude that a brief account is not out of place here, especially as his father—also named Simon Girty—was one of the men ejected from Perry County soil prior to the lands being opened for settlement, mentioned at several places in this book.

Almost opposite Marysville, Perry County, there empties into the Susquehanna River a small stream known as Fishing Creek. A few hundred yards from its mouth, prior to 1730, several brothers by the name of Chambers erected a grist mill and the place came to be known as Chambers' Mill. It was the same family of Chambers which settled at Chambersburg, Pennsylvania, in 1736,

scale as a trader with the Indians, he married Mary Newton, an
English girl. They became the parents of four boys, Thomas,
born in 1739; Simon, with whom this story deals, born in 1741;
James, born in 1743, and George, born in 1745. The name is variously spelled, "Girty," "Girte," "Gerty," and sometimes "Girtee."
In a list of traders licensed in 1747 Simon Girty, the elder, does
not appear; in a list of traders unlicensed of the same date, it
does appear. However, the list of 1748 contains his name among
those licensed.

The lands lying west of the Susquehanna River and north of the
Kittatinny or Blue Mountain, which includes the present county of
Perry, had not been opened to settlement yet, but nevertheless,
by the spring of 1749 there were more than thirty families already
located there. The sheriff of Lancaster County having authority
over all the lands west of the Susquehanna except York County,
three magistrates and a provincial agent were sent to what is now
Perry County soil to warn the people to leave immediately. Little
heed was given to their words and others also went in and located.
Among these was Simon Girty, in 1749, with his wife and little
brood, settling on Sherman's Creek, but their career there was
suddenly terminated, as eight provincials appointed by the constituted authorities, accompanied by a deputy sheriff of the new
county of Cumberland, proceeded to carry out by force the desires
of the Indians and the commands of the authorities. After burning five cabins of settlers near the Juniata they proceeded to Sherman's Creek, where Girty and nine other trespassers were found.
Each had settled on a separate tract and had erected a cabin.
These were also burned and the owners bound over to appear at
Shippensburg, then the seat of justice of the new county, in the
sum of one hundred pounds each. In view of the others having
remained when notified to leave during the previous year this occurrence can hardly be viewed with great discredit to Girty. From
here he went back to Chambers' Mill.

Girty, the elder, was a drinking man of the "spree" type, and
met his death at Chambers' Mill on one of these occasions. One
story tells of a neighbor knocking him in the head and bearing off
Mrs. Girty as a trophy of his prowess; another tells of a neighborhood difficulty in which Girty was the challenger to a duel and in
which his antagonist put the sword through him, but both are only
traditionary tales. Even Theodore Roosevelt, in his "Winning of
the West," erroneously has him "tortured at the stake, tomahawked finally by a papoose held up by its father for that purpose," doubtless confounding that circumstance with the one happening at the death of Turner, the man who married Girty's
widow and who was tortured at the stake at Kittanning, as described further on in this chapter.

The facts, according to the Magazine of American History, are these: He was killed in a drunken revelry by an Indian known as "the fish," at his home in the latter part of 1751. His death must needs be avenged and the avenger in this case was John Turner, who made his home with Girty, who killed "the fish" and thereby fulfilled the theory of "an eye for an eye," etc. Turner's reward came later, when, early in 1753, at Paxtang he was united in marriage to Mrs. Girty, described as a woman of unblemished character.

In 1756, Turner, his wife and the four Girty boys, for their better protection, were in the fort known as Fort Granville, located near the present town of Lewistown, Pennsylvania, where Turner was a second lieutenant. On July 22 a band of over a hundred Indians and twenty-three Frenchmen from Fort Duquesne arrived at the fort and challenged its occupants to combat, which was declined by the commander, Captain Edward Ward. All of Ward's men were provincials in the pay of Pennsylvania. Not far away Sherman's Valley, comprising practically all of western Perry County, was depopulated by reason of the Indian massacres and expeditions, yet much grain had been sown and was now ripe with no reapers to venture forth without protection. Captain Ward determined to guard the harvesters and took all his men save twenty-three to Sherman's Valley, thinking the French and the Indians had gone.

In this he was mistaken, as they were only abiding their time. On the very day in which he marched, they began a furious attack and by a feint, entrance was gained through a ravine to within thirty or forty feet of the fort. The lieutenant in charge, Edward Armstrong, and a private were killed, three wounded and the fort set on fire. The enemy then offered quarter if they would surrender and Turner, then in charge, opened the gates. The fort was consumed in the flames and all were taken prisoners, including Turner, his wife and the four Girty boys. Simon Girty was then fifteen years old. The fort was sacked before its fall and the prisoners were compelled to lug the loot to the limit of their endurance. Tradition says Turner's share was a hundred pounds of salt. The trip was over the Allegheny Mountains to Kittanning, where there was an Indian village from which this band of Indians were largely recruited.

Turner, tradition says,—and it is only tradition,—was recognized as the man who had slain "the fish" (who was the murderer of the elder Girty) at Chambers' Mill and his doom was sealed. Be that as it may, the evidence and records of his execution are more than tradition. "They tied him to a black post, danced around him, made a great fire and, having heated them red-hot, ran gun barrels through his body. Having tormented him for three hours, they scalped him alive, and at last held up a boy with a hatchet in his hand to give the finishing stroke," says Gordon in his History of Pennsylvania. His wife sat on a log near by with their young son and with the four Girty boys, compulsory beholders of the horrible affair.

The family was shortly broken up, never to be reunited. Simon was turned over to the Senecas, one of the Six Nations, and speedily learned their language. James was given to the Shawnees and George to the Delawares, all being adopted. The other brother, Thomas, had been recaptured by the whites in an attack upon Kittanning, within forty days of his first captivity. The Dalawares and the Shawnees, notwithstanding the fact that the Indians had made a treaty of peace with the English at Easton in 1757, remained hostile along the Ohio. During the autumn of 1858, however, they sent their representatives to Easton, Pennsylvania, and too formed a treaty of peace. As a result all white prisoners were delivered up at Pittsburgh, and among them were the three Girty boys, their mother (Mrs. Turner) and her young son, John Turner.

Having lived the wild life of the red men for some time the boys were rough and crude and now almost grown into young manhood. Their location at Pittsburgh placed them among a rough and uncouth element, as it was a mere trading post and frontier fort with the attending influences. The principal business was trading with the Indians and the linguistic ability of these boys, Simon being but eighteen and his brothers younger, made their services invaluable, for collectively they could speak the languages of three different Indian nations. Simon, who had been with the Senecas, now became popular with the Delawares, took up their language, and in a short time could speak it fluently. One of the principal Delaware warriors—Katepakomen—liked him so well that he assumed his name. The capture of this Indian pretender, "Simon Girty," by Colonel Henry Bouquet in 1764, when he marched with his men west of the Ohio, is responsible for conflicting historical accounts, many of which assume that it was the real Simon Girty.

Simon, and perchance his brothers also, became popular among a certain class of the white population surrounding the post and an incident of historical preservation is that he voted at the first election (1771) when Bedford was made a county, including practically all the territory of western Pennsylvania. Two years later (1773) Westmoreland County was created, with the capital at Hannastown, about thirty-five miles east of Pittsburgh, and it then comprised all of these western Pennsylvania lands. The student of history will recollect how Pennsylvania and Virginia clashed for that territory, Pennsylvania contending that much of the land even along the Ohio belonged to the province, while Virginia's contention was that that state owned even the location where Pittsburgh now stands and where the post was then located. In the same year Lord Dunmore, governor of Virginia, visited the section and took measures for its being made a part of his state. Simon Girty took sides with Virginia. At the October sessions of court of that year a warrant was issued for his arrest for a misdemeanor, the grand jury having found a true bill, but he escaped. Dr. John Conolly, of Pittsburgh, was the leader of the Virginians, who, with an armed force, assailed the court at Hannastown and sent three of the justices to jail in Virginia. Pennsylvania's champion was Arthur St. Clair, also of Pittsburgh, who caused Conolly's arrest and had him imprisoned at Hannastown.

Not only the boundary troubles, but others threatened the new country. As the tide of emigration broke through the Alleghenies and rolled westward in a continuous stream towards the Ohio Valley the continuous conflict of the red and white races was again uppermost. Southwest of Pittsburgh the Shawnees and the Mingoes were on one side and the Virginians on the other. In this war Simon Girty was an active participant. Taking sides with Virginia in the boundary dispute when his own state was concerned, naturally he could easily do so then. When Lord Dunmore reached Pittsburgh with the northern branch of the Virginia army Girty became his interpreter as well as a scout. Dunmore had also with him several scouts whose frontier deeds made them famous, but of a type the opposite of Girty. The criticism of Roosevelt covering this phase in his "Winning of the West" is "At the moment he was serving Lord Dunmore and the whites; but he was by taste, habits and education a red man, who felt ill at ease among those of his own color."

Lord Dunmore's war did not lessen the severity of the boundary dispute around Pittsburgh and Girty was made a second lieutenant on his return from the expeditions against the Indians. The immediate effect of this was to give Virginia immunity from Indian troubles at the west and to give Pennsylvania resumption of its trade with the Indians. But the Revolutionary War was at hand and after the battle of Lexington patriotism west of the mountains put all else to rout and at conventions held at Pittsburgh and Hannastown practically everybody gave expressions to their sentiments, among them being the supporters of Lord Dunmore, who rallied to the Whigs, with a single exception or two, which did not include Girty.

On May 1, 1776, he was appointed an interpreter by the Colonial government to interpret for the Six Nations at Pittsburgh, which practically meant for the Senecas. His wage was to be four-eights of a dollar per day. On August 1 it was found necessary to discharge him for ill behavior.

He then exerted himself in getting recruits for the patriot army for which he expected a captain's commission. In this he failed, but was made a second lieutenant in Captain John Stephanson's company of one-year men. The company was sent to Charleston, but for some reason he was not with them, but on detached duty. Early in August (1776) he resigned his commission. He was then already plotting with the Indians. General Hand, on assuming charge of the military affairs at Pittsburgh, discovered that there was doubtful loyalty among some of the inhabitants. Alexander McKee, an influential trader who had come from that part of the province lying east of the mountains, being especially suspicioned. He and Girty were friends. He was paroled to the immediate vicinity. There was a movement on foot to murder all the Whigs and turn the government over to Hamilton, the lieutenant governor, located at Detroit, and Girty was suspected of being in the plot and was arrested and confined in the guardhouse. He soon broke out, just to show that he could, but returned of his own accord and was imprisoned. Later he was examined by a magistrate and acquitted. Being restored to confidence, during the fall he was sent to meet the Senecas, living on the upper waters of the Allegheny, who were supposed to be hostile to the United States. He would have been held by them as a spy but managed to escape.

Finally from authentic reports it became known to General Hand that Alexander McKee was making preparations to leave Pittsburgh to join the enemy. On December 29, 1777, he was ordered to York, Pennsylvania, there to answer orders of the Continental Board of War, but the tory made excuses and was allowed to remain. On February 7, 1778, he was again officially ordered to York, but feigned illness and was permitted to remain. Meanwhile he was secretly preparing to take as much of his property as was portable with him and at the earliest possible moment start for the Indian country on his way to Detroit. He had influenced Girty to join in the flight and on the night of March 28, 1778, McKee and his cousin, Robert Surphlit, together with Matthew Elliott, Simon Girty, a man named Higgins and two negroes belonging to McKee departed for the Indian country and Detroit, traitors to the land of their birth.

Many reasons are advanced for Girty's disaffection, but the persuasion of McKee and Elliott certainly had much to do with it. Farther than that all must be conjecture. Perchance its inception may have dated back to the burning of that cabin of his father by the provincial authorities along Sherman's Creek—now a part of Perry County—which, as a child he sat by and saw, but of which he did not comprehend the meaning.

However, desertions to the enemy did not stop with the seven. Others were disaffected, including part of the garrison at Fort Pitt. On the night of April 20 a boat was stolen by some, who fled down the Ohio. They were overtaken at the Muskingum River by a party sent in pursuit and the ringleaders killed or captured. Six soldiers and two civilians escaped. Of those taken two were shot, one hanged and two whipped, being given one hundred lashes each. Their leaving caused great consternation among the settlers, some even wanting to desert their claims in fear of the Indians. John Proctor, of Westmoreland County, wrote to Thomas Wharton, president of the Supreme Executive Council of Pennsylvania, on April 26, as follows: "Captain Alexander McKee, with seven (six) other villains, is gone to the Indians; and since then there are a sergeant and twenty-odd men gone from Pittsburgh, of the soldiers. What may be the fate of this country, God only knows, but at present it wears a dismal aspect."

Girty never possessed real estate, as sometimes stated, hence he left nothing behind. He could neither read nor write, so left no paper which could shed any light upon his actions. Up to the time of his desertion he was not quite so black as painted by many historians, as his connections with the provincial government will attest. True, he drank, gambled, associated with questionable people, yet he was not at that time "an inveterate drunkard," "an outlaw," "a redskin of the worst type," etc. Now, however, he became a renegade, a deserter and a traitor to his country—what a threefold record of infamy those words imply!

In all the American settlements west of the Allegheny Mountains watered by the Ohio and its tributaries, there were not to be found three other persons so well fitted as were McKee, Elliott and Girty to work upon the superstitions of the western Indians for evil to the patriot cause; and General Hand feared the worst, thinking they had gone over to the Indians. He and Colonel Morgan at once prepared "addresses" and had them sent to the Delawares. Others fearing to carry the messages, John Heckewelder and Joseph Bull, Moravian missionaries, offered to carry them to Coshocton. They were searching for the whereabouts of missionaries of their church who had gone into the Ohio valleys. They found the Delawares about to take up arms against the Americans. According to Heckewelder, the renegades had stopped at their town and told them that the patriot armies were cut to pieces, that General Washington was killed, that there was no more congress, that the English had hung some of the members and taken the remainder to England to hang them there, and that the few thousand Americans who had escaped the British soldiers were now busying themselves west of the mountains for the purpose of killing all the Indians beyond the Ohio—even the women and children.

The renegades had left Coshocton, but "White Eyes," the Delaware chief, sent the following figurative message out to the Shawnees and the Mingoes: "Grandchildren, ye Shawnees! Some days ago a flock of birds that came on from the east lit at Goschoching (Coshocton) imposing a song of theirs upon us, which song has nigh proved our ruin! Should these birds, which, on leaving us, took their flight toward the Scioto, endeavor to impose a song on you likewise, do not listen to them for they lie."

However, the words of "White Eyes" were of no avail to his grandchildren on the Scioto. The renegades had there met James Girty, who was easily persuaded to join them. The Shawnees were wavering and he was largely responsible for turning them from all thoughts of peace with the United States. It was about the middle of June when the original party (James Girty not being along) reached the open arms of Lieutenant Governor Hamilton at Detroit. He immediately appointed Girty as interpreter of the Six Nations, the renegade thus becoming an employee of the British, for his services receiving two dollars per day. McKee was made a captain of the British Indian Department. On June 15, 1778, the Supreme Executive Council issued a proclamation adjudging them traitors. Hamilton sent Simon Girty to the Mingoes and James Girty to the Shawnees, each instructed to give the best possible service both in interpreting and fighting. Until this time neither had the blood of a fellow countryman upon his hands. From now on this can not be said of them. For their future attitude Hamilton was largely responsible.

Upon their reaching the Indian tribes a war party was started for Kentucky, both being along. The party brought back seven scalps, a woman named Mary Kennedy and seven children as prisoners.

Simon Kenton, the scout, had left Boone's station in Kentucky to cross the Ohio, being accompanied by Alexander Montgomery and George Clark. They ran across some horses in the rich prairies and by the use of salt and halters succeeded in stampeding seven towards the Ohio. The river being wild the party was delayed in crossing and were overtaken by the Indians. Clark escaped, Montgomery was killed and scalped, and Kenton was tied upon the back of one of the wildest horses. After plunging, kicking and rearing the animal finally followed the others. At four different villages he was beaten and made to "run the gauntlet," almost losing his life each time. Later, while seated on the floor of the council house with his face blackened, a sure sign of being doomed, in walked Simon Girty, his brother James, John Ward and an Indian with the eight captives spoken of above and the seven scalps. Kenton was temporarily removed but was shortly brought back. He recognized the hated traitor. Girty threw down a blanket and with a scowl ordered him upon it. He hesitated and Girty impatiently jerked him upon it. Girty did not recognize him and proceeded to quiz him for information. To the inquiry as to where he lived he replied "In Kentucky." To other questions Kenton gave answers which were intended to lead his interrogator astray. Finally he was asked his name and replied, "Simon Butler," the name he was known by along the frontier. Girty embraced him on the spot and told him he was condemned to death, but that he would use every means to save his life. His pleas were effective, as the Indians relented.

A short time afterwards a party of Indians returned from the vicinity of Wheeling defeated by the whites, some having been killed and others wounded. Determined to be avenged they sent to Girty to appear with Kenton, which he did. He again interested himself, but by an overwhelming vote it was decided to burn him at the stake. However at Girty's request he was taken by the Indians to Upper Sandusky to suffer the torture. Through the intercession of a trader there he escaped death, being sent to Detroit. Subsequently he fled and finally arrived safely in Kentucky.

Captain John Clark had commanded a relief party with provisions for Colonel Gibson at Fort Laurens, and on his return Girty and seventeen redskins attacked them and killed two, wounding four and taking one prisoner. The remainder, including the captain, fought a defensive fight back to the fort. Lieutenant Governor Hamilton, getting restless, had previously captured Vincennes, and Clarke knew that if he didn't get Hamilton and Vincennes that Hamilton would get him. Accordingly on February 7, with a force of 126 men he started, and on February 25 captured Hamilton and the fort. Girty, in attacking Clark, had gained possession of correspondence of Colonel Gibson, which he took to Detroit, but Hamilton had already been captured. In the correspondence Gibson revealed the fact that Girty, if captured, could expect little mercy from him. At first this caused a feeling of despondency which developed into resentment and vindictiveness against his countrymen far greater than before.

Girty met an American named Richard Conner at Coshocton and told him to "tell the Americans that I desire to be shown no favor, neither will I show any." George Girty, who had been a second lieutenant of the Colonial troops, also deserted and on August 8, 1779, arrived at Detroit, the third of the family to become a renegade. He was made an interpreter and assigned to the Shawnees. Deer skins (known as "bucks" and "does") were worth about a dollar each and were in some cases used as currency. Hence, a charge to George Girty reads: "To salt at

8

Shawnees towns, 4 bucks; to 116 pounds flour, 14 bucks; to bag flour, 2 bucks; to tobacco, 3 bucks."

A party of "Virginians" from near where Brownsville, Pennsylvania, now stands, went to New Orleans for supplies. They had returned to about three miles below where the little Miami joins the Ohio when Simon and George Girty, Matthew Elliott and a hundred Indians attacked them, killing David Rogers, the captain, and forty-one others of the party and taking five prisoners. The Indians lost but two, with three more slightly wounded. They captured a quantity of rum, forty bales of dry goods, and a "chest of hard specie."

On one occasion Simon Girty saved the life of an eighteen-year-old boy, Henry Baker, who had been captured by a small war party near Wheeling. He was taken to Upper Sandusky, where he was placed with nine other prisoners, captured Kentuckians. All were compelled to "run the gauntlet." The boy, being fleet of foot, easily ran it, which so enraged a young Indian that he knocked him down with a club after reaching the council house. The nine Kentuckians were burned at the stake, one a day until all had perished. Baker was compelled to witness all this. Then it was his turn. An old chief ordered him taken out and tied to a stake. Seeing a white man approaching on horseback, he resisted somewhat and then ran up and implored the rider to save him. It was Simon Girty, who at once interceded in his behalf. The savages relented and let him go, sending him to Detroit as a prisoner. He escaped and reached his home in safety.

On one occasion (1781) Simon Girty had a narrow escape from death. Captain Brant, while drinking intoxicants, boasted of his prowess and told how he single-handed had captured a number of the enemy. Girty's envy was awakened and he promptly told Brant that he lied. The latter immediately struck him in the head with his sword, making an ugly scar which he carried to his death and which he later boasted of as "having received it in battle." It was many weeks before he could even sit up.

Heckewelder, the Moravian missionary, in 1782, saw Simon Girty frequently, he being at that time the constant companion of Dunquat, the half-king of the Wyandottes. He had then become more inhuman and savage than ever. The winter was cold, food was scarce, the cattle were dying for want of food, there was little wood to burn and the tents were small, many were living on the carcasses of the starved cattle; yet when the missionary's wife had prepared for themselves a little food, from their scanty lot, in walked Simon Girty and a Wyandotte Indian and helped themselves. The half-king had lost two sons in battle the previous fall and was very resentful against the whites. Girty now called himself "Captain Girty" and would instigate among the Wyandottes all the trouble possible for the Moravians.

On one occasion Christian Fast, of Westmoreland County, Pennsylvania, and of the part which later became Fayette County, a boy of seventeen was captured. He was wounded before being made prisoner but his life was spared. He was adopted by a Delaware family which had lost a son in a skirmish. Naturally young Fast became melancholy at times. Thoughts of home would steal upon him, and on one of these occasions he had proceeded into the woods and was sitting on a log musing. He was suddenly accosted by a white stranger and asked what he was thinking about. He replied that he had no company and felt lonesome. "That is not it," said the stranger. "You are thinking of home; be a good boy and you shall see your home again." The speaker was Simon Girty, who had taken a liking to the boy, who later did escape and reached his own home in safety.

While three of the Girty boys were renegades, the fourth, Thomas Girty, lived in Pittsburgh, rather a respected citizen.

Captain Crawford, who was a fellow officer with Girty in the Virginia militia of a period before, was captured and was burned at the stake, and among the witnesses of the spectacle was the renegade. Crawford was undressed, and tied to a stake about fifteen feet high by a rope which was attached to the ligaments of his wrists. The rope was of a length to permit his walking around the post two or three times, returning the same way. The fires were six or seven yards from the post. About seventy loads of powder were shot into his body and then his ears were cut off. On every side were tormentors with burning faggots and if he turned about to escape torture he again met with it. In the midst of these tortures Crawford called to Girty and begged to be shot. In derision Girty replied that he had no gun, and laughed heartily, all his gestures showing that he was delighted with the spectacle. After almost two hours of torture Crawford fell upon his stomach and was then scalped. Hot coals were applied to him, but he again raised himself to his feet and walked around the stake, seeming more insensible to pain than before. Dr. Knight, who was also captured at the same time, was a witness up until this point when he was led away.

Girty then told Knight to prepare for death but not there, as he was to be burned in one of the Shawnee towns. With fearful oaths he told him that he need not expect to escape death, but should suffer it in all its agonies. Colonel John Gibson had threatened to trepan him, if captured, and he told Knight that some prisoners had informed him that if the Americans got him they would torture him, but that he didn't believe it. He asked Knight's opinion, but he, having just witnessed the awful proceedings with

Crawford, was so unnerved that he could not reply. Knight was sent to the Shawnee town under the guard of a single Indian, whom he killed and then escaped, finally arriving at Pittsburgh half starved.

George Girty was about as blood-thirsty as his brother Simon. John Stover had been of the same war party as Crawford and Knight, and was later condemned to the stake. He was tied to the stake and George Girty cursed him and told him he was about to get what he deserved, but suddenly a storm broke and the Indians sought cover, Stover in the meantime breaking his bonds and escaping.

The news of peace between the United States and Great Britain did not reach Fort Pitt until May, 1783, and incursions into the settlements by small war parties of savages were still carried on. Simon Girty led one to Nine Mile Run, within five miles of Pittsburgh, and took a few scalps. This was the renegade's last trip into the state of his birth. In July, 1783, after five years of almost constant life among the red men he returned to Detroit, where he made his home for a short time. In 1784 he journeyed to the Indian country for Catharine Malott, who, as a girl in her teens, was taken prisoner on the Ohio River in 1780. She was now grown to womanhood and wanted to escape savage life, which was, no doubt, her only reason for marrying the renegade, which she did late that year, settling on the Canadian side. He was still a British government agent and was often on the American side urging the Indians to harass the new government.

It appears nowhere that Girty possessed courage, yet his cowardice is attested by hundreds of acts of a disreputable nature. About 1798 he and his wife separated, as she could not stand his cruel treatment. Later they lived together again. When the Americans came to take possession of Detroit he got so frightened that he hurriedly swam the river on horseback. He was almost six feet tall, with black hair, a full face, a massive head, and black eyes. He was bronzed by exposure, and dressed in Indian fashion, being adorned with paint and feathers, and he looked every inch an Indian.

He died on his farm, in Canada, granted him by the British government for his perfidy, in 1818, although many historians, including Roosevelt, in his "Winning of the West," mistakenly have him killed in battle at Proctor's defeat on the Thames. Of the four brothers, Thomas alone led a civilized life.

Girty became an Indian of his own free will, acquired their habits, participated in their councils, inflamed their passions, and goaded them on to the most cruel tortures of captives; and he deserves to go down in history as one of the most desperate and degenerate characters in its annals. There ever rankled in his bosom a dreadful hatred against his country, and while he had all the vices of both civilized and uncivilized peoples, he had the virtues of neither.

Tradition would have Simon Girty, the renegade, use the cave or "notch" near the top of Half Falls Mountain, known as Girty's Notch, as a hiding place and observatory during the Indian troubles from 1754 to 1764, but there are official records, as stated, during these years, which connect him indisputably with the territory lying west of Pittsburgh. It is no pleasure to the writer, whose birthplace was within a half dozen miles of the location and whose childhood was enlivened by tales of Girty's prowess and deviltry, to mar this tradition, but history not only fails to bear it out, but furnishes evidence of his activities having been in an entirely different region.

Consul Willshire Butterfield, in his History of the Girtys, severely criticizes the accounts of Simon Girty as contained in *Wright's History of Perry County, which was published many years ago and which were probably taken from newspaper articles of the period, as the facilities for research at that time were limited. Many of the errors in reference to Girty are caused by confusing father and son, both being named Simon.

In the vicinity of Landisburg there is a tradition that Girty's perfidy was the result of his not having been given the command of the whites during a skirmish at Wagner's woods, near that town. Like the other tales which connect the renegade with Perry County territory, there is nothing to it, as he never was in the territory save as a boy of eight years, when his father was a squatter, and later in crossing the territory when twelve to fifteen years of age, with his stepfather and family on their way to Fort Granville, near Lewistown. As stated, their capture at that place was in 1756 and Girty's perfidy dates from 1776 to 1778, and its actual occurrence was at Pittsburgh.

That the renegade was a thorough Indian at heart is proven by the fact that in 1792, when a Great Council of all the northwestern tribes was convened on the Maumee, he was the only white man admitted, among the others being forty chiefs of the Six Nations, who counseled peace.

---

*In an article in the Newport (Pa.) *Ledger* in later years Mr. Wright wrote: "From reliable information in the writer's possession the renegade never visited these places (Girty's Notch) and could not have given them his name."

CHAPTER VI.

DUNCAN'S AND HALDEMAN'S ISLANDS.

IN announcing the intention to publish this book the statement was made that the history of Duncan's and Haldeman's Islands, while located in Dauphin County, would be included for the reason that the business and social activities of every nature—except legal—are with the Perry County side of the river, and for the additional reason that the history of one merges into the other. The only reason why these two islands are not a part of Perry County is that in the old Indian grant to Penn the line was made the western bank of the river. Logically they should be a part of Perry County, and in 1819 a strong effort was made to have them attached to Cumberland County (of which Perry was then a part), but it was defeated. Then, a year later, when Perry County was formed, they probably could have been attached to Perry, but no effort was made. As this chapter contains much of Indian life it is inserted here, rather than later.

Originally the Juniata's waters joined with those of the Susquehanna at two points, one being a channel at the north end of Duncan's Island, thus forming between the rivers an island, originally known as Juniata Island to the natives. This channel was known to early rivermen as "the gut." Marcus Hulings connected it with the mainland by a causeway, so that pack horses could pass over. Although it retains the name "island," it is in reality no longer an island, as the channel at the upper end has long since been filled in, the same having been done when the Pennsylvania canal was building. During the great floods of 1846 and 1889 the embankment was swept away and each time was rebuilt at great expense, the first time by the state, then in possession of the canals, and the last time by the Pennsylvania Railroad, at an expense of $60,000. Across it passed that great artery of traffic, the Pennsylvania canal, and over it now passes the William Penn highway and the Susquehanna Trail. Much of this fill-in was dug out when the highway was put through recently, and whether this was discreet only another great flood will tell, but rivermen contend that it will again break through.

Duncan's Island is almost two miles long, and almost all of it is now the property of William H. Richter. It contains approximately 300 acres of land. During the first decade of the Nineteenth Century a village sprang up at its southern point and was named Benvenue. It still exists, but is now largely summer cottages. Here once stood the Indian village of "Choniata" or "Juneauta," of which there is record as early as 1654 and as late as 1745. From this lower point of the island a long, covered wooden bridge spans the Susquehanna to Clark's Ferry, a station on the Northern Central Railway, and an iron bridge spans the Juniata to a point near Juniata Bridge, a station on the main line of the Pennsylvania Railroad.

When the Pennsylvania canal was in operation the mule teams which drew the boats crossed the Susquehanna bridge on a tow-path built on the outside, towing the canal boats across the river at this point, through Green's dam—now commonly referred to as the Clark's Ferry dam. The original ferry over the Juniata was conducted by the Baskins family, some of whose descendants to this day live near by.

In Watson's Annals the following statement is to be found: "This island was the favorite home of the Indians and there are still many Indian remains. At the angle of the canal, near the great bridge, I saw the mound covered with trees, from which were taken hundreds of cartloads of human bones, and which were used with the intermixed earth as filling materials for one of the shoulders or bastions of the dam. What sacrilege! There were also among them beads, trinkets, etc."

During the latter part of the last century and the beginning of the twentieth the writer was a resident of the near by vicinity and knows of many arrowheads, Indian hatchets, skinning stones, etc., being found on the islands, and present day residents say they are still being found, especially when turning up the ground. As late as 1916 the Susquehanna Archæological Expedition, of which Mr. George P. Donehoo, the noted authority upon Indian and Colonial history, was a member, found many evidences of Indian occupation upon Duncan's Island. They gathered many hundred specimens of Indian origin, including banner stones, hatchets, arrow points, etc. The upper end of the island is even now covered with cracked stones used at fireplaces. On one of the paths at the lower end of the island, Dr. Moorehead, of the Expedition, found an unsual specimen—a half-finished banner stone. The so-called Indian mound was dug into, but no traces of Indian work found there.

Duncan's Island, even to the eye, but more so to memory, seems a spot of fascination and romance, and its uncounted historical data, like its silt levels, is more or less submerged. It was here that tradition would have two powerful tribes, the Delawares and Cayugas, fight for days until the eddying river inlets along shore were crimsoned. To tell the tale we have only vast quantities of broken spearheads and arrows, and they are but mute evidence, but to the winner (the Cayugas, already familiar with firearms)

the strategic point between the rivers and the oncoming civilization was probably worth all it cost. Luckily a few records exist
which makes it possible to get a glimpse into those early days.

Marcus Huling, who came from Marcus Hook, Pennsylvania,
is credited by various historians as probably being the first settler
of Duncan's Island, but there is no record to bear this out, but
there are records relating to Hulings which disprove it. The first
settler was William Baskins, referred to farther on. Hulings
owned the point between the two rivers, long owned by Dr. Reutter's heirs. Rupp, the historian, gives the date as 1735. That he
was there in 1744 is practically certain, as he was one of the
searching party which hunted for the murdered man Armstrong
in that year. (See "Murder of an Early Trader," chapter 2.)
The locality is still the home of some of Hulings' descendants.

In a rough draft submitted to the province to protect his own
claim Hulings has left to posterity the names of a few of the
first settlers of these lands and the vicinity, as the following pages
will show, and at no place does he claim either ownership or occupancy. The Hulings family was of Swedish descent and on settling between the rivers he built the causeway over the strip of
water connecting the two rivers and started a ferry over the
Juniata. Trade at that time, it will be remembered, was all done
with pack horses. Later he owned a toll bridge there, which at
his death passed to Rebecca Hulings Duncan.

With Braddock's defeat in 1755 came all the horrors of Indian
warfare, and the scattered settlers in and around Perry County
were obliged to flee. However, home, then as now, was dear to
these pioneers, and some of them lingered long. Being apprised
of the near approach of the redskins Marcus Hulings, grasping a
few valuables, placed his wife and youngest child upon a large
black horse and fled to the point of the island. His other children
had previously gone to seek safety. Having forgotten something
and thinking the Indians might not have arrived he ventured to
return to the house. After carefully reconnoitering he entered
and found an Indian upstairs "coolly picking his flint." He par-
leyed with the Indian to escape death and got away. The delay
caused his wife to believe him murdered and she swam the Susquehanna on horseback, although the water was high. When he
arrived at the point he crossed in a light canoe and they finally
reached Fort Hunter, having been preceded by the Baskins family
and other fugitives. Here the inhabitants of Pextang (Harrisburg) had rallied for defense.

In 1756 Mr. Hulings went to the western part of Pennsylvania
and became the owner, whether by purchase or patent we do not
know, of the point of land located between the Monongahela and
Allegheny Rivers, where they meet and form the Ohio, and where

Pittsburgh now stands. Becoming discontented he sold this west-ern property for £200 and returned to the one on the Juniata.

While in western Pennsylvania encroachments were made on his lands in what is now Watts Township, Perry County, and he protested, as the following letter still in existence, shows:

"FORT PITT, May the 7th, 1762.
"To William Peters, Esq., Secretary to the Propriatories in land office in Philadelphia, &c.:

"The petitioner hereof humbly sheweth his grievance in a piece of un-cultivated land, laying in Cumberland County (now Perry), on the North-west side of Juneadey, laying in the very Forks and Point between the two rivers, Susquehanna and Juneadey, a place that I Improved and lived on one Year and a half on the said place till the enemeyes in the beginning of the last Warrs drove me away from it, and I have had no opertunity yet to take out a Warrant for it; my next neighbor wass one Joseph Greenwood, who sold his improvement to Mr. Neaves, a merchant in Philadelphia, who took out a warrant for the S'd place, and gave it into the hands of Collonel John Armstrong, who is Surveyor for Cumberland county; and while I was absent from them parts last summer, Mr. Arm-strong runed out that place Joyning me, for Mr. Neaves; and as my place layes in the verry point, have encroached too much on me and Take away part of Improvements; the line Disided between me and Joseph Greenwood was up to the first short small brook that emptyed into Sus-quehanna above the point, and if I should have a strait line run'd from the one river to the other with equal front on each River from that brook, I shall not have 300 acres in that survey; the land above my house upon Juneadey is much broken and stoney. I have made a rough draft of the place and lines, and if Your Honor will be pleased to see me righted, the Petitioner hereof is in Duty bound ever for you to pray; from verry humble serv't. MARCUS HULINGS."

Accompanying the above was a note to Mr. Peters, which shows that Hulings also had a claim on the south (west) side of the Juniata. The note:

"May ye 17th, 1762.
"Sir: I have left orders for Mr. Mathias Holston, living in Upper Merrion of Philadelphia county, to take out two warrants for me, one for the Point between the two Rivers, and one for the Improvements I have in the place called the Onion bottom on the south side of Juneadey right opposite to the other, where I lived six months before I moved to the other place; from your humble servant, MARCUS. HULINGS."

"Accompanying these letters was the rough draft spoken of in the first letter, an attempted description of which follows: Three islands are marked. The one now known as Duncan's is marked "Island" and the house upon it as "Widow Baskins." The large island in the Susquehanna known as Haldeman's is marked "Is-land" and three houses located, the lower one being marked "Fran-cis Baskins," the next a third up on the east side, "George Clark," and a little above the centre, "Francis Ellis." On the east bank of the Susquehanna, almost opposite, is a house marked "James Reed," while between the centre of the island and the western shore is a small triangular island.

On the point between the Susquehanna and Juniata Rivers is Hulings' residence. Some distance from the point is a straight line running from river to river, marked "this is the way I want my line," while above, on the west bank of the Susquehanna, nearly opposite the James Reed house, is "Mr. Neave's house." Farther up the river, opposite a small island, is another house also marked "Francis Ellis." A circuitous line shows where Neave's line crossed that of Hulings. On the south side of the Juniata, below the mouth thereof, is a house marked "William Kerl," and opposite the points of Duncan's Island is "James Baskins'." Farther up, in the plot called the "Onion bottom," is another house marked "Marcus Hulings." Beyond this, on the south side of the Juniata, is a house marked "Cornelius Acheson," who is also credited with encroaching on Hulings' "Onion bottom" property. On the east side of the Susquehanna River Peters' Mountain and "the narroughs" are marked. As Hulings likely came to these fertile lands with provincial sanction and probably insistence to induce settlement it is believed that his claims, which also appear to be founded on prior right, were adjusted to his satisfaction.

In 1788 Marcus Hulings died. During the earliest years of their life in that vicinity Mrs. Hulings on more than one occasion forded the Susquehanna on horseback with a bag of grain which she took to the mill at Fort Hunter. Marcus, the eldest Hulings' son, did not return with the family to this vicinity, but remained in Pittsburgh, where he established a ferry at what is now the foot of Liberty Street, over the Monongahela River. It was afterwards known as Jones' Ferry. He was later employed in moving military stores on the rivers in that vicinity and in other work in behalf of the government and pioneers. Another son located in the western part of the province and was the owner of Hulings' Island, in the Allegheny River.

Thomas Hulings, the youngest son, became the owner of the estate in the East. He died in Buffalo Township in 1808. His first wife was a daughter of General Frederick Watts, of Revolutionary fame. Their oldest daughter, Rebecca, married Robert Callendar Duncan, a son of Judge Duncan, of Carlisle and it is through him that Duncan's Island gets its name, he eing the grandfather of Mr. P. F. Duncan, cashier of the Duncannon National Bank; Mrs. William Wills and Mrs. Frank McMorris, of Duncannon, the line of descent coming through Benjamin Stiles Duncan.

As previously stated, Duncan's Island was the seat of an Indian village, known as "Juneauta," in fact the island was known by that name among the Indian tribes. There is a tradition which is strongly substantiated that at one time the Cayugas and the Delawares fought a battle here. To David Brainerd, a graduate of

Yale College and a distinguished missionary, posterity is indebted for a glimpse into the utter debauchery and dissoluteness of the tribe of Indians located here, and in all probability a counterpart of the lives of Indians generally in those days. It is the first record of the Shawnees in these islands.

He became so devoted to the gospel that he consecrated his whole life to the evangelizing of the savages. He came down the Susquehanna afoot and on May 19, 1745, he landed at the Indian town of Juneauta. In his diary he says, evidently discouraged:

"Was much discouraged with the temper and behavior of the Indians here; although they appeared friendly when I was with them last spring. and then gave me encouragement to come and see them again. But they now seem resolved to retain their pagan notions, and persist in their idolatrous practices."

On September 20 he again visited the island and while his descriptions as recorded in his diary are rather long they are reproduced here in full. He says:

"Found them almost universally very busy in making preparations for a great sacrifice and dance. Had no opportunity to get them together, in order to discourse with them about Christianity, by reason of their being so much engaged about their sacrifice. My spirits were much sunk with a prospect so very discouraging; and especially seeing I had this day no interpreter but a pagan, who was as much attached to idolatry as any of them, and who could neither speak nor understand the language of these Indians; so that I was under the greatest disadvantages imaginable. However I attempted to discourse privately with some of them, but without any appearance of success; notwithstanding, I still tarried with them,

"In the evening they met together, nearly 100 of them, and danced around a large fire, having prepared ten fat deer for the sacrifice. The fat of the inwards they burnt in the fire while they were dancing, which sometimes raised the fire to a prodigious height; at the same time yelling and shouting in such a manner that they might easily have been heard two miles or more. They continued their sacred dance nearly all night, after which they ate the flesh of the sacrifice, and so retired, each one to his own lodging.

"I enjoyed little satisfaction, being entirely alone on the island, as to Christian company, and in the midst of this idolatrous revel; and having walked to and fro till body and mind were pained and much oppressed. I at length crept into a little crib made for corn and there slept on the poles."

The next entry is dated Lord's day, Sept. 21, and continues:

"Spent the day with the Indians on the island. As soon as they were well up in the morning I attempted to instruct them, and labored for that purpose to get them together, but soon found they had something else to do, for near noon they gathered together all of their conjurors and set about half a dozen of them playing their juggling tricks and acting their frantic, distracted postures, in order to find out why they were then so sickly upon the island, numbers of them at that time being disordered with a fever and bloody flux. In this exercise they were engaged for several hours, making all the wild, ridiculous and distracted motions imaginable, sometimes singing, sometimes howling, sometimes extending their hands to the utmost stretch, spreading their fingers; they seemed to push with them as if they designed to push something away, or at least keep it off at arm's end; sometimes stroking their faces with their hands, then spurting water as fine mist; sometimes sitting flat on the earth, then bowing their faces to the ground; then wringing their sides as if in pain or anguish, twisting their faces, turning up their eyes, grunting, puffing, &c.

"Their monstrous actions tended to excite ideas of horror, and seemed to have something in them, as I thought, peculiarly suited to raise the devil, if he could be raised by anything odd, ridiculous and frightful. Some of them, I could observe, were much more fervent and devout in the business than others, and seemed to chant and mutter with a great degree of warmth and vigor, as if determined to awaken and engage the powers below. I sat at a small distance, not more than thirty feet from them, though undiscovered, with my Bible in my hand, resolving, if possible, to spoil their sport, and prevent their receiving any answers from the infernal world, and there viewed the whole scene. They continued their horrid charms and incantations for more than three hours, until they had all wearied themselves out, although they had in that space of time taken several intervals of rest, and at length broke up, I apprehended, without receiving any answer at all.

"After they had done powwowing I attempted to discourse with them about Christianity, but they soon scattered and gave me no opportunity for anything of that nature. A view of these things, while I was entirely alone in the wilderness, destitute of the society of any one who so much as 'named the name of Christ' greatly sunk my spirits and gave me the most gloomy turn of mind imaginable, almost stripped me of all resolution and hope respecting further attempts for propagating the gospel and converting the pagans, and rendered this the most burdensome and disagreeable Sabbath which I ever saw. But nothing, I can truly say, sunk and distressed me like the loss of my hope respecting their conversion. This concern seemed to be so great and seemed to be so much my own, that I seemed to have nothing to do on earth if this failed. A prospect of the greatest success in the saving conversion of souls under gospel light would have done little or nothing towards compensating for the loss of my hope in this respect; and my spirits were so damp and depressed that I had no heart nor power to make any further attempts among them for that purpose, and could not possible recover my hope, resolution and courage by the utmost of my endeavors.

"The Indians of this island can, many of them, understand the English language considerably well, having formerly lived in some part of Maryland, among or near the white people, but are very drunken, vicious and profane, although not so savage as those who have less acquaintance with the English. Their customs, in various respects, differ from those of the other Indians upon this river. They do not bury their dead in a common form, but let their flesh consume above the ground, in closed cribs made for that purpose. At the end of a year, or sometimes a longer space of time, they take the bones when the flesh is all consumed and wash and scrape them and afterwards bury them with some ceremony. Their method of charming or conjuring over the sick, seems somewhat different from that of the other Indians, though in substance the same. The whole of it among these and others, perhaps, is an imitation of what seems, by Naaman's expression (Kings 2-11) to have been the custom of the ancient heathen. It seems chiefly to consist in their 'striking their hands over the diseased, repeatedly stroking them, and calling upon their god;' except the spurting of water like a mist and some of the other frantic ceremonies common to the other conjurations which I have already mentioned.

"When I was in this region in May last I had an opportunity of learning of the notions and customs of the Indians, as well as of observing many of their practices. I then traveled more than 130 miles upon the river, above the English settlements, and in that journey met with individuals of seven or eight distinct tribes, speaking as many different languages. But of all the sights I ever saw among them, or indeed anywhere else, none appeared so frightful, or so near akin to what is usually imagined of infernal powers, none ever excited such images of terror in my mind as the appearance of one who was a devout or zealous reformer, or rather restorer of what he supposed was the ancient religion of the Indians. He made his appearance in his 'pontifical' garb, which was a coat of bear skins, dressed with the hair on and hanging down to his toes; a pair of bear-skin stockings and a great wooden face painted, the one-half black, the other half tawney, about the color of the Indians' skin, with an extravagant mouth cut very much awry; the face fastened to a bear-skin cap, which was drawn over his head.

"He advanced toward me with the instrument in his hand which he used for music in his idolatrous worship, which was a dry tortoise shell with some corn in it, the neck of it drawn on to a piece of wood, which made a very convenient handle. As he came forward he beat his tune with the rattle and danced with all his might, but did not suffer any part of his body, even his fingers, to be seen. No one would have imagined from his appearance or actions that he could have been a human creature, if they had not had some intimation of it otherwise. When he came near me I could not but shrink away from him, although it was then noonday, and I knew who it was; his appearance and gestures were so prodigiously frightful. He had a house consecrated to religious uses, with divers images cut upon the several parts of it. I went in and found the ground beat almost as hard as a rock, with their frequent dancing upon it. I discoursed with him about Christianity. Some of my discourse he seemed to like, but some of it he disliked extremely. He told me that God had taught him his religion and that he would never turn from it, but wanted to find some who would join heartily with him in it; for the Indians, he said, were grown very degenerate and corrupt. He had thoughts, he said, of leaving all his friends and traveling abroad in order to find some who would join with him; for he believed that God had some good people somewhere who felt as he did. He had not always, he said, felt as he now did, but had formerly been like the rest of the Indians until about four or five years before that time. Then, he said, his heart was very much distressed, so that he could not live among the Indians, but got away into the woods and lived alone for months. At length, he said, God comforted his heart and showed him what he should do, and since that time he had known God and tried to serve Him; and loved all men, be they who they would, so as he never did before.

"He treated me with uncommon courtesy and seemed to be heart in it. I was told by the Indians that he was opposed to their drinking strong liquor with all his power; and that, if at any time he could not dissuade them from it by all he could say, he would leave them and go crying into the woods. It was manifest that he had a set of religious notions which he had examined for himself and not taken for granted upon bare tradition; and he relished or disrelished whatever was spoken of a religious nature, as it either agreed or disagreed with his standard. While I was discoursing he would sometimes say: 'Now, that I like; so God has taught me,' &c., and some of his sentiments seemed very just. Yet he utterly denied the existence of a devil and declared there was no such creature known among the Indians of old times, whose religion he supposed he was attempting to revive. He likewise told me that departed souls went southward and that the difference between the good and bad was this: that the former were admitted into a beautiful town with spiritual walls and that the latter would forever hover around these walls in vain attempts to get in. He seemed to be sincere, honest and conscientious in his own way and according to his own religious notions, which was more than I ever saw in any other pagan. I perceived that he was looked upon and derided among most of the Indians as a precise zealot, who made a needless noise about religious matters, but I must say that there was something in his temper and disposition which looked more like true religion than anything I ever observed among other heathen. But alas! how deplorable is the state of the Indians upon this river! The brief representation which I have here given of their notions and manners is sufficient to show that they are led captive by Satan at his will in the most eminent manner; and methinks might likewise be sufficient to excite the compassion and engage the prayers of God's children for these, their fellow men, who 'sit in the region of the shadow of death.'"

September 22 the entry is as follows:

"Made some further attempts to instruct and Christianize the Indians on this island, but all to no purpose. They live so near the white people that they are always in the way of strong liquor, as well as the ill example of nominal Christians; which renders it so unspeakably difficult to treat with them about Christianity."

The following summer (1746) Brainerd again passed up the Susquehanna valley and made the following notations in his diary:

August 19. Lodged by the side of the Susquehanna. Was weak and disordered both this and the preceding day, and found my spirits considerably damped, meeting with none that I thought godly people.

August 21. Rode up the river about 15 miles and lodged there, in a family which appeared quite destitute of God. Labored to discourse with the man about the life of religion, but found him very artful in evading such conversation. Oh, what a death it is to some, to hear of the things of God! Was out of my element, but was not so dejected as at some times.

August 22. Continued my course up the river, my people now being with me who before were parted from me. Traveled above all the English settlements; at night lodged in the open woods, and slept with more comfort than while among an ungodly company of white people. Enjoyed some liberty in secret prayer this evening; and was helped to remember dear friends, as well as my dear flock, and the church of God in general.

Brainerd returned down the river in October, weak and feeble from exposure in the outdoors, never again to return to his beloved work. He died in New England in the following October.

Jones' History of the Juniata Valley, in speaking of Indian hostilities, says:

"That they had many fierce and sanguinary struggles among themselves is well authenticated. A battle almost of extermination was once fought between two tribes at Juniata—now known as Duncan's Island—within the memory of many Indians who were living when the whites settled among them. This island must have been a famous battleground—a very Waterloo—in its day. When the canal was in progress of construction, hundreds of skeletons were exhumed; and to this day stone arrowheads can be found upon almost any part of the island."

Rupp, in his history, recites an early Indian story of the Baskins family having been furnished the information by Mitchell Steever, Esq., of Newport, Pa. The William Baskins referred to was a granduncle to the late Cornelius and James Baskins, who will be remembered by many readers of this volume and whose descendants yet reside in various parts of the county.

It appears that at one time Baskins had a crop of grain maturing on Duncan's Island while the Indians were on a rampage. He had previously removed his family to Fort Hunter for security, what was known as Fort Hunter in those days, being an outpost opposite to the present town of Marysville. With part of his family Baskins had returned to cut his grain. While engaged in reaping they were startled by a war whoop close by, but seeing neighboring Indians they were not alarmed. But they were deceived, as the savages soon gave them to understand that they were after scalps. They all fled, hotly pursued, toward the house, but Mr. Baskins, caught in the act of getting his gun, was shot dead and scalped. His wife, a son of three, and a daughter of seven years were abducted. A man named McClean was also in the field, but plunged into the Juniata and swam to "Sheep Island" (above the iron bridge on the Juniata) and concealed himself in the cleft of some rocks on the far side and thus eluded capture.

As a captive nearing Carlisle Mrs. Baskins escaped from the Indians. The daughter was taken to the Miami country, west of the Ohio, then an unbroken wilderness, where she was held in captivity for more than six years, when, in conformity with a treaty made with the Indians, as mentioned in a previous chapter of this book, she was returned. She later married a man named John Smith, whose descendants lived in Newport, Pa., during the middle of the last century. The lad, who was captured at the same time, was taken to Canada, where he was raised by Sir William Johnston, who didn't know his name and who had him baptized "Timothy Murphy."

This Baskins lad ("Timothy Murphy") had a venturesome life. He was one of the chief riflemen of Morgan's celebrated sharpshooters. At the battle of Bemis Heights Morgan selected a few of his best marksmen and directed them to make General Fraser, of the British troops, their especial target. A number fired with no effect, but at the crack of Murphy's gun Fraser fell.

Shortly after the battle of Monmouth, three companies of Morgan's troops were sent into Schoharie, New York. Among these was Murphy, and the tories set an extra price upon his scalp, which it was never necessary to pay, although many Indians tried for it. He had grown into a stout, well-built man, with jet-black hair and eyes and was handsome. While the tories failed to get him here he had many hairbreadth escapes, but usually in the nick of time something turned up to save him. At one time he possessed a double-barreled rifle, an unknown weapon to the Indians. He was being chased by a party, and, although he could usually get away, now they were gaining on him. He turned and shot one and succeeded in getting behind a tree where he quickly reloaded the empty chamber. As they again gained on him he stopped and shot another, but they resumed the chase, desiring to capture him alive and torture him before a slow fire. They were again gaining and in despair he jumped behind a tree, and as they advanced shot a third one. They immediately fled and in after years "Murphy" learned that they had seen him fire three times without reloading and that they thought he had "a great medicine of a gun that would shoot forever."

When the war was over, "Murphy," true to the characteristics of his forbears, became a farmer. Records tell of his death occurring from a disease contracted while saving the children of a neighbor during a winter flood.

When peace was declared and the independence of the colonies became a fact many of the Schoharie Indians returned to settle among the people whose buildings they had burned and whose relatives they had killed and scalped. Of the worst of his tribe was an Indian named Seths Henry, who had killed more than any other and who would sometimes leave upon a dead body a war club containing many notches cut therefrom. He too came back and one day started to call on the different settlers. Not unstrangely "Murphy" followed him and there is no record to show that the Indian arrived anywhere in this world.

Then, there began strange disappearances of tories and Indians and coincident there was always a fire of brush in the same vicinity in which might have been found their ashes. The remaining renegades and savages took the hint and left the community.

Timothy Murphy became a wonderful stump speaker and a political power in Schoharie County. He brought William C. Bouck into public life and later to the gubernatorial chair of New York. His mother, the widow of William Baskins, the first settler of Duncan's Island, remarried, her second husband being Francis Ellis. He established a ferry across the Susquehanna during the Revolution and carried on the business for many years.

After the Baskins boy's capture by the Indians he was first heard of through Alexander Stephens, grandfather of Alexander H. Stephens, Vice-President of the Confederacy, and father of the late James Stephens, of Juniata Township, by a peculiar mark on the head. He later visited Perry County and the island and James Smith, his nephew, when in Canada during the War of 1812, visited him near a place called Malden, and found him to be the owner of a large estate.

The original Clark's Ferry crossed the Susquehanna at a point about the centre of Duncannon, its western landing being at the point where Clark's run empties into the river. The Indians had a place in the vicinity where they forded the river, which they knew as "Queenashawakee." The Juniata they knew as "Choiniata," or "Juneauta." In 1733 John Harris, who had a lust for land, had erected a cabin and cleared some fields on the island near "the white rock on the riverside." This caused a complaint by the Indians. This was on Haldeman's Island.

At a Council held at Philadelphia Shikellamy, the Indian chief, through Conrad Weiser, the interpreter, asked whether the proprietary government had heard of a letter which he and Sassoonan had sent to Harris, asking him to desist from making a plantation at the mouth of the "Choinata," where he had built a house and was clearing fields. They were informed that Harris had only built that house for carrying on trade; that his plantation on which were houses and barns was Pextang (now Harrisburg), where he dwelt and from which he was not supposed to remove, and that he had no order or permit to make a settlement on the "Choinata." Even if he had built his house for trading purposes Shikellamy said "he ought not to have cleared fields." He was informed that Harris had probably only cleared as much land as was needed for raising corn for his horses, to which Shikellamy rejoined that he "had no ill will to John Harris, in fact it was not his custom to bear ill will, but he is afraid that the warriors of the Six Nations, when they pass that way, may take it ill to see a settlement made on lands which they had always desired to be kept free from settlement." He was further informed that care would be taken to issue the necessary orders.

In 1806 Robert C. Duncan, a son of the celebrated jurist, Thomas Duncan, of the Supreme Court of Pennsylvania (having married Rebecca Hulings), moved to Duncan's Island, where he spent the remainder of his days. It is from him that the island takes its name. His brother Stephen resided in what is now Perry County, near the mouth of Sherman's Creek, and was the founder of the Duncannon Forges, the forerunner of the Duncannon Iron Company. He subsequently removed to Washington, D. C., where he died. Robert C. Duncan had two sons, one of whom was Dr. Thomas Duncan, born in 1814, a celebrated physician and a prominent member of the Pennsylvania Legislature. The other was Benjamin Stiles, born in 1816, who went to Arkansas in his boyhood, where he resided until 1858. He was a real estate operator and laid out a section of Arkadelphia, which is known to this day as "the Duncan Addition." He returned to Duncan's Island and

9

engaged in farming, residing in the house in which he was born until his death, which occurred in 1870.

Sherman Day, in his Historical Collections of Pennsylvania (1843) pays to Mrs. Duncan, widow of the late proprietor of Duncan's Island, the following tribute:

"About half a mile above the village (Benvenue), Mrs. Duncan, the accomplished widow of Robert C. Duncan, still resides in the family mansion, where the traveler who chooses to tarry in this delightful region may find accommodations—not a hotel, with its bar and bottles, and blustering loafers; but in a comfortable, well-furnished gentleman's *home,* with its quiet fireside, and books, and intelligent society and amiable tea table."

The old register of this hotel, beginning with February 6, 1841, is in the possession of Mr. P. F. Duncan, her grandson, and is a matter of much curiosity to the present day generation. Travel was then either overland or by packet. One entry reads thus: "Rev. Thomas C. Thornton and lady;" also four children, "all the family on the way to Clinton College, Mississippi." On another line is "Dr. D. L. N. Reutter, residence, Breach at Duncan's Island." Susan Ickes Harding, a daughter of Dr. Jonas Ickes, was one of the travelers. Mrs. Harding later became a noted philanthropist in Central Illinois. Another name of interest is that of Lucretia Mott, a pioneer in woman's suffrage, "on her way to Clearfield."

Among the earlier residents of the island during the past century were the Garmans, who settled there in 1828, Samuel Garman, long ticket agent and telegrapher for the Northern Central Railway at Clark's Ferry and now living retired at Millersburg, being a descendant. A man by the name of Updegraff built the "point house" in 1834. This was the house where the late J. L. Clugston lived, he who long kept a general store at the inlet lock. The Carpenter family came from Newport in "the forties," and of some of that family more appears in the chapter devoted to "River and Canal Transportation." Their sons who grew to manhood were James, John, Thomas and George, and their daughter, Elizabeth, became the first wife of Stiles Duncan, owner at that time of Duncan's Island. She died September 25, 1857, aged twenty-four years.

The channel between the two islands once was deep and swift, but years of constant deposit of silt has left it far less deep and its waters seem not nearly so swift as in the days of yore. Duncan's Island has gone through some famous flood experiences, of which there is an account in the chapter devoted to Rivers and Streams, elsewhere in this book.

Both Duncan's and Haldeman's Islands are a part of Reed Township, Dauphin County, which was created by an act of the

John Kelton. Charles Williams and John Lee (trader) are designated as "Freemen." John Kelton was the collector.

The dam across the Susquehanna, at the mouth of the Juniata, generally known as the Clark's Ferry Dam, was originally known as Green's Dam, by reason of the contractor's name having been Abbott Green. Mr. Green was born at Penn's Creek, Snyder County, and there grew to manhood. During the spring seasons he floated rafts down the river and thus became familiar with river traffic. He moved to Lewisburg and engaged in contracting upon the public works then under construction by the state. The construction of this dam—in that period a noted undertaking—was the crowning work of his life.

Duncan's Island Methodist Church. Rebecca Duncan, a resident of Duncan's Island, at a very early day of Methodism, opened her home for the preaching of that faith. Through her efforts and at her expense the school board later added a second story to the public school building, which she donated to the cause for the use of the Methodists. In it regular services were conducted until the great flood of 1865, when, on March 16th, it was destroyed by the onrushing waters. The word was preached by the pastors of the Duncannon charge. At various times, and sometimes for long continuous periods, there have been Sunday school sessions of an undenominational character held in the public school building on Duncan's Island.

The Clark's Ferry Bridge. The building of the Clark's Ferry bridge was, in that day, a considerable undertaking. It was to span the Susquehanna at a point above the location of the ferry conducted by the Clarks, and, as it was to be a part of a great highway across the state, men from five counties composed the commission which was organized for its erection. The commissioners appointed for that purpose were as follows: Christian Gleim, Archibald M'Allister, Innis Green and Abraham Gross, of Dauphin County; Robert Clark, John Boden, and Dr. Samuel Mealy, of Cumberland County (then including Perry, from which section these three men came); William Bell, Lewis Evans, David Hulings, Robert Robinson, and John Irwin, of Mifflin County (then including Juniata); William Steel, Patrick Gwinn, and Maxwell Kinkead, of Huntingdon County, and James Potter, John Rankin, and John Irwin (Penn's Valley), of Centre County. The commission organized on Wednesday, May 22, 1818, by electing John Boden, chairman, and Christian Gliem, secretary. They began their duties by holding their first view of a site on June 3, 1818. On April 17, 1837, a span of the bridge gave way and one end lodged upon a pier and could not easily be removed. It was then set on fire and floated down the river as it fell, a mass of flaming timber. Destruction of parts of the bridge by fire and flood at various times is told in the chapter devoted to "Rivers and Streams."

While to the present generation it is a very, very ordinary structure, yet it is described in a noted State History of 1844 as "a wooden bridge on the Barr plan, resting upon many piers, the whole constructed with an elegance and strength equal to if not surpassing any public work in the country." Harry McKee long kept a hotel at the east end of the bridge and also owned the first farm below the point of Peters' Mountain, which had descended from his ancestor, Thomas McKee, the trader, spoken of in our Indian chapters.

When the Clark's Ferry bridge burned on May 14, 1846, the destruction being credited to incendiarism, an arrest was made and the verdict of guilty in the Dauphin County courts—for both landings of the bridge are in Dauphin County—doomed the defendant to a term of years in the Eastern penitentiary, although he then and in after years protested his innocence. According to two men who have long resided in Perry County, one (Jesse M. Pines) recently passing away, his contention may have been right. The incident is printed here for that reason and also as showing methods of travel, etc.

Many years afterwards, over forty years ago, in the later seventies, George Boyer, now an associate judge of Perry County, and Jesse Pines took an extensive horseback ride over parts of central and northen Pennsylvania. In the upper part of the state in a mountainous section known as Seven Mountains, above Towanda, they came upon a mountain tavern near a place known as Unityville, where they stopped for lodging. In a forlorn, forsaken section of the forest they took turns at sleeping, as the proprietor and the Negro porter's appearance seemed to forbode anything but good. They were the only occupants of the hotel. During the evening one of the travelers chanced to refer in some way to Clark's Ferry. The colored fellow became agitated and, when asked if he had ever been there, replied that he had, but that he left the night that the bridge burned. Further questioning was of no avail, as all efforts to get him to say another word about Clark's Ferry were futile. Why did he leave the night the bridge burned?

THE MINING OF RIVER COAL.

Farther up the Susquehanna lay the rich anthracite coal beds. From them for generations down the river with the tide drifted deposits of the very smaller sizes of coal, which settled in various places where the current was not swift, forming coal beds upon the river's bottom. When coal from the mines was selling very cheaply and when the canals were hauling it at a very low rate the mining or digging of this coal by pumping from the river bed would have been unprofitable and was·not even considered, but with coal prices going up annually about 1890 there sprang up a business of pumping this coal by suction, and several outfits followed it for years. The coal is from the Wilkes-Barre and Wyoming districts, principally. In the early days of coal mining, sizes smaller than pea were thrown to the huge dumps until they became virtual mountains, containing millions of tons. Many of them were located along the Susquehanna and contributary streams, and from these immense culm banks spring freshets and rainy seasons carried the deposits of coal, which rivermen say exist clear to the Chesapeake Bay and at some places have been found to be five feet in depth.

The coal operations at Green's Dam, commonly known as the Clark's Ferry Dam, commenced in the vicinity of Benvenue in 1890. Like many other industries it began in a small way, the coal being taken out by hand scoops and canoes, followed by small flats of three-ton capacity, for stove use. Shortly after Santo & Pease, of Harrisburg, arrived with a steam outfit, with which they loaded canal boats for transportation to Harrisburg. This was followed by others and, in 1894, a Mr. Squires, a Wilkes-Barre machinist, built and put in operation the largest plant on the river, with the late George B. Lukens as foreman. This plant was bought in June, 1897, by B. F. Demaree, a Newport business man, who retained Mr. Lukens, and added four fifty-ton flats to the plant. With these and two canal boats the coal was conveyed to Harrisburg, where it was largely sold to the public utility plants. Rail shipments followed in 1902, and the orders were at times for amounts from 500 to 5,000 tons. This coal found its way to such buyers as Dickinson College, the Philadelphia Rapid Transit Company, the Arbuckle Coffee Company, etc. The beginning of the erection of the stone arch railroad bridge across the Susquehanna near Marysville necessitated the closing of the canal and the end of that method of shipping. The Pennsylvania Railroad Company then put in a siding near Clark's Ferry, where the coal was loaded by derricks, operated by both horse-power and steam. With increased automobile traffic the State Highway Department stopped the swinging of derricks over the highway, and it became necessary to introduce the hydraulic system of loading, which has materially increased the output. The ice flood of 1919 made a breach in the dam and injured the coal business materially, which for thirty years flourished there, and may, eventually mean its ending. There has been an annual increase in the production; in 1897 it was as little as 8,000 tons, while in 1920 it totaled 150,000 tons. An average of thirty men have been employed by the various firms operating. The Demaree plant is now owned by Harry V. Lukens, who purchased it in 1908. Another operator is H. E. Lukens, his father, who, about 1899, purchased the outfit started by a Mr. Seiler, of Dalmatia, in 1893. The third plant still in the business is that of Hicks Brothers, of Auburn, Pennsylvania, who purchased out the plant of John Zeigler, about 1912, which he had operated as early as 1901. In fact, Mr. Zeigler and John Briner had converted an old river steamer, known as the "Shad Fly," into a coal dredge, the previous year, but had dissolved partnership, Mr. Briner retaining the outfit, but retiring from the business about 1904.

BALD EAGLE ISLAND.

While Bald Eagle Island is a part of Dauphin County, yet its location in the Susquehanna River at Montgomery's Ferry is but a few hundred feet from the Perry County shore line. That it is a part of Dauphin County comes from the fact that the county line is stated in the act creating the county as "to the westward of the Susquehanna." The order of survey dated October 23, 1809, to George Eckert, "of Strasburgh Township, and county of Lancaster," and John Shura, "of the township of Upper Paxton, and county of Dauphin," describes it as "Bare Island, opposite the lands of John Huggins, on the Cumberland County shore and about a quarter mile below Berry's Falls or riffles." It is signed by Governor Snyder, the third governor of Pennsylvania. Through this earliest of records one learns the fact that it was once known as Bare Island. It is now owned by Mr. James D. Bowman, of Millersburg, who has a fishing lodge there, which was erected by Mr. Christian S. Albright, about 1902, and which he remodeled and enlarged in 1909. Mr. Bowman is an adept fisherman and seldom fails to furnish to the many large and joyous gatherings assembled there at his command, a luncheon of black bass.

Bald Eagle Island has long been a source for finding many Indian relics, which would imply that it was probably an Indian camping ground. From an Indian standpoint it possessed two distinct advantages; one being the lookout both up and down the river, and the other that it was an ideal fishing ground, which it still is. There was also an early fording here, the width of the river at this point during low water being not over five-eighths of a mile. The island contains approximately five acres, not including the sand bar at the north end. A third of a century ago the Harrisburg Young Men's Christian Association used it as their annual camping ground. The name Bald Eagle was given to the island by reason of the fact that there once stood on it a large and high pine tree, on which for many years the eagles had their nests

CHAPTER VII.

COMING OF THE TRADER.

WHO the first white man was that set foot upon the soils of present Perry County must forever remain a mystery, for there were no records kept of matters of that nature. However, it must have been some trader or adventurer. In the days of the early settlement of the province the Indians even from afar journeyed to the seaboard to trade with the newcomers. The skins and furs they brought became so valuable abroad that, many years before settlements in the interior were even dreamed of, the trader traveled the fastnesses of the mountains and ascended the rivers in quest of gain. Often the worst class of men went into the business of trading and penetrating the forests, built up a business with the Indians.

There is record of James LeTort, a trader who "went out" from Carlisle as early as 1727. As the "Allegheny Path" was the route of travel to "Allegheny on the branch of the Ohio," where he traded, he was evidently among the first white men to travel this territory. LeTort's date of settlement at Carlisle is said to have been in 1720. By 1735 there were over twenty regular traders journeying back and forth across the county to the Ohio

In fact, even earlier—as early as 1704, Joseph Jessup, James LeTort, Peter Bazalion, Martin Chartier and Nocholas Goden, all Frenchmen, were traders with the Indians on the Susquehanna and with those west of the Alleghenies, via the old Indian trail, supposed even then to have been the "Allegheny Path."

That traders even carried on a traffic in rum at that early day is substantiated by a protest made July 23, 1727, at a council held at Philadelphia by the Chiefs of the Five Nations, with Madame Montour as interpreter. It follows:

"They desire that there may be no settlements made up Susquehannah higher than Pextan (now Harrisburg), and that none of the settlers thereabouts be suffered to sell or keep any rum there, for that being the road by which their people go out to war, they are apprehensive of mischief if they meet with liquor in these parts. They desire also, for the same reasons, that none of the traders be allowed to carry any rum to the remoter parts where James Letort trades, that is Allegheny, on the branch of the Ohio. And this they desire may be taken notice of, as the minds of the chiefs of all the Five Nations, for it is all those nations that now speak by them to all our people."

After considering the matter over night the governor, on the following day, replied, through the same interpreter:

"We have not hitherto allowed any settlement to be made above Pextan, but, as the young people grow up, they will spread, of course, yet it will not be very speedily. The governor, however, will give orders to them all to be civil to those of the Five Nations, as they pass that way, though it would be better if they would pass Susquehannah above the mountains. The sale of rum shall be prohibited both there and at Allegheny; but the woods are so thick and dark we cannot see what is done in them. The Indians may stave any rum they find in the woods, but, as has been said, they must not drink or carry any away."

These old documents are the basis for the inference that pioneers were even then presuming to settle above the Kittatinny or Blue Mountain; at least, the Indians were apprehensive and were early going on record as opposed to any such aggression.

More than one of these traders had ulterior motives. The French and the English were contending for the lands of the great West, and to the Quaker—who largely ruled the province—it became almost a necessity, owing to religious convictions and personal interests, that traders' licenses be given only to English settlers and traders and to those of the Protestant faith, barring the French Papists and with them communication to the French on the Ohio.

The traders carried their goods on packhorses and the Indians were an easy prey to their cupidity and avarice. In fact, many of the early troubles of the province were reaped by reason of seed sown by unprincipled and inconsiderate traders. Among prominent early traders were George Croghan, Thomas McKee, Jack Armstrong, Francis Ellis, and William Baskins.

OF THREE PROVINCIALS.

So closely were three early interpreters associated—one the first authorized settler of the territory which now embraces Perry County—with the provincial life of the district that it is deemed expedient to briefly give a few facts about them and their actions during that important epoch of Pennsylvania life, when "the border" was the term used in referring to the lands along the Kittatinny or Blue Mountains. The names of Conrad Weiser, George Croghan, and Andrew Montour are inseparably associated with the pioneer life of the section, as well as of the province in general.

CONRAD WEISER, THE DIPLOMATIC INTERPRETER.

Conrad Weiser, of all the Indian interpreters who were interested in this territory, was the most prominent. In fact, he was the most prominent in the provincial annals of Pennsylvania. That he crossed and recrossed the county's territory via the old Indian trail past Gibson's Rock there is evidence. He kept a diary, and in August, 1754, he stopped at Andrew Montour's, the following entry being dated September 1 of that year:

"Crossed the Kittatinny Mountains at George Croghan's (now Sterrett's) Gap and Sherman's Creek, and arrived that day at Andrew Montour's, accompanied (from Harris' Ferry) by himself, the half-king, another Indian and my son. I found at Andrew Montour's about fifteen Indians, men, women and children, and more had been there, but had gone.

"Andrew's wife had killed a sheep for these some days ago. She complained that the Indians had done great damage to the Indian corn, which was now ready to roast."

Weiser had much to do with the Indian affairs which attended the early settlement of Perry County soil. Three different provincial governors had entrusted him with manifold Indian affairs where diplomacy was required and Weiser, the peacemaker, had succeeded. What William Penn preached about treating the Indians squarely Conrad Weiser practiced. Had he not induced the Five Nations to remain neutral, and had they cast their lot with the French the chances are that to-day we would be a French dependency, as the occasion for the Revolution might not have arisen, and we would have likely remained a more or less weak French dependency instead of a virile English-speaking nation which soon became independent. When George Washington came to Berks County in 1760 to attend the funeral of Conrad Weiser, the future father of his country stood at the open grave and made the remark, "Here lies a man whom posterity will never forget." Weiser was a farmer, an interpreter, a trader and a merchant, having a store in Reading. As he was so great a factor in the Indian negotiations relating to the Perry County territory it is deemed expedient to give this concise account in this book.

He was born in Germany in 1696, and came to America with his parents during the reign of Queen Anne, when fourteen years of age. His father was a blacksmith and lived on the Mohawk River, near a settlement of the Mohawk Indians. Conrad was sent by his father to reside with an Indian named Tajuajanont, that he might learn the Indian tongue. He became popular with the Indians and obtained great influence over them even as a boy. When twenty-six he was adopted by the family of the Turtles, a distinctive caste. In 1729 he came to Pennsylvania, and for the remaining thirty years of his life he was connected with the provincial government of Pennsylvania as an interpreter. He made his home—but he was seldom there—at Heidelberg, in Lancaster (now Berks) County. His duties kept him continually going to the most distant localities, and sometimes farther than the boundaries of the province, to attend conferences with the Indians, principally the Six Nations. As a man of honor and trust he had the implicit confidence of both the settlers and the Indians. He was withal, adroit, skillful and diplomatic.

In March, 1748, instructions were given to Weiser for a projected trip to the Ohio, the object being to cement further the good-

commissioners for that purpose, and built a house and store there which stood until recent years. One of the men who accompanied Weiser on one of these trips through Perry County territory is named as William Franklin, a son of Benjamin Franklin, and who later became governor of New Jersey.

GEORGE CROGHAN, TRADER AND INTERPRETER.

Of the men who had much to do with Indian affairs in what is now Perry County, next in importance to Conrad Weiser stood George Croghan, the trader and interpreter. He was an Irishman by birth and came to this country in 1742, stopping at the Harris Ferry (now Harrisburg) for a while. Soon after becoming an Indian trader he located in Cumberland County, near what is now Hogestown, and about eight miles from Harris' Ferry. He first traded in a rather restricted district, the limits of which were to Aughwick (near Mt. Union) and Path Valley, later going as far as the Ohio River. As early as June, 1747, he is mentioned "as a considerable trader." His long residence among Indians enabled him to become thoroughly familiar with both the life and the habits of the Delaware and Shawanese tribes. For that reason he became invaluable to the province. Later on he is supposed to have lived at Sterrett's Gap for a time, as the gap was long known as Croghan's. Afterwards he removed to Aughwick.

His first letter while in the employ of the province is dated "May 26th, 1747," and is addressed to Richard Peters, secretary of the province. With it he enclosed a letter from the Six Nations, some wampum and a French scalp taken along Lake Erie.

Governor Hamilton, in a letter to Governor Hardy, dated July 5, 1756, in speaking of Croghan, who was at one time suspected of being a spy in the pay of the French, says:

"There are many Indian traders with Braddock—Croghan among others, who acted as a captain of the Indians under a warrant from General Braddock, and I never heard of any objections to his conduct in that capacity. For many years he had been very largely concerned in the Ohio trade, was upon that river frequently, and had a considerable influence among the Indians, speaking the language of several nations, and being very liberal, or rather, profuse, in his gifts to them, which, with the losses he sustained by the French, who seized great quantities of his goods, and by not getting the debts due him from the Indians, he became bankrupt, and since has lived at a place called Aughwick, in the back parts of the province, where he generally had a number of the Indians with him, for the maintenance of whom the province allowed him sums of money from time to time, but not to his satisfaction. After this he went, by my order, with these Indians, and joined General Braddock, who gave the warrant I have mentioned.

"Since Braddock's defeat, he returned to Aughwick, where he remained till an act of assembly was passed here granting him a freedom of arrest for ten years. This was done that the province might have the benefit of his knowledge of the woods and his influence among the Indians; and immediately thereupon, while I was last at York, a captain's commission was given to him, and he was ordered to raise men for the defense of the western frontier, which he did in a very expeditious manner, but not so frugally as the commissioners for disposing of the public money thought he might have done. He continued in the command of one of the companies he had raised, and of Fort Shirley, on the western frontier, about three months; during which time he sent by my direction Indian messengers to the Ohio for intelligence, but never produced me any that was very material; and having a dispute with the commissioners about some accounts between them, in which he thought himself ill-used, he resigned his commission, and about a month ago informed me that he had not received pay upon General Braddock's warrant, and desired my recommendation to General Shirley, which I gave him, and he set off directly for Albany; and I hear he is now at Onondago with Sir William Johnston."

On his return from the Johnston conference he bore a commission as a deputy agent of Indian affairs.

Croghan had settled permanently at Aughwick in 1754 and had built the fort and stockade there. He was appointed by the province, in 1755, to locate three forts in what was then Cumberland County—one at Patterson's, on the Juniata; one at or near Lewistown, to be known as Fort Granville, and one at Sideling Hill, now Bedford County. He recruited men and garrisoned them very quickly. In December of 1754 he had written Secretary Peters, asking that no one sell liquor to the Indians on account of the bad consequences, but admitting that he gave them a keg once a month for a frolic. As an official he was noted for promptness. After the evacuation of Fort Pitt we find Croghan there for a while. On a trip down the Ohio the French captured him and took him to Detroit. When liberated he returned to New York. He died in 1782. In March, 1749, he was appointed a justice of the peace of Lancaster County, to which the soil of Cumberland yet belonged. In 1748 there is record of him having a trading house on the Ohio. Croghan and Andrew Montour were largely associated in business.

France claimed the vast country west of the Alleghenies, watered by the Ohio and Mississippi Rivers, and was attempting to establish her claim by locating military posts from the great lakes to the Mississippi and along the Ohio and Allegheny Rivers. The Indian tribes were numerous and war-like. Croghan saw the importance of detaching them from the French by means of presents and the most favorable trading terms. His suggestions were wisely heeded by the Provincial Council. He had a thorough knowledge of all the Indian trails and the territory of the tribes between the Susquehanna and the Ohio. At Carlisle, on April 4, 1756, he filed an account of his "losses occasioned by the French and Indians driving the English traders off the Ohio." While two of the items of probable great value have no actual valuation named, those which do total 881 pounds.

On June 27, 1767, Croghan and two kinsmen petitioned the New York Council, on behalf of themselves and others, to purchase 40,000 acres of land between Otsego Lake and "Caniadcuagy" Lake, and between the head branches of the Susquehanna. On November 25, 1767, a return was made of a survey for him and his associates for 100,000 acres.

In fact, the journals of George Croghan are an epitome of the Indian history of the period. In 1750, according to it, he was on the Ohio, enroute to the Shawnee towns; the next season he outwitted Joincaire on the Allegheny. In 1754 he was on the Ohio, after Washington had passed, and in 1760-61 he was on a trip to Detroit, via Lake Erie, in the company of Roger's Rangers. In 1765 he toured down the Ohio towards Illinois and was captured by Ouiatanon, later making peace with Pontiac and returning.

Next to Sir William Johnson, George Croghan was the most prominent figure among the British Indian agents during the period of the later French wars and Pontiac's conspiracy. A pioneer trader, traveler and government agent, no other man of his time knew as much of the coming great West and the counter currents, intrigues, etc., connected therewith. It was as deputy of Sir William Johnson that he conducted the difficult negotiations at Fort Pitt and Detroit in 1758-61 and those in Illinois in 1765, by which Pontiac was brought to terms. His winning adherents for the English among the wavering allies of the French, beyond the bounds of the province, at Sandusky and Lake Erie, was but one of his diplomatic feats. He first won the attention of Conrad Weiser, who recommended him to the provincial authorities, where his first service began in 1747, continuing through the active years of his life. At the beginning of the Revolution he appeared as a patriot, but later became the object of suspicion, and in 1778 he was proclaimed officially by the colony as a public enemy.

Andrew Montour, First Authorized Settler.

Andrew Montour was the first authorized settler of the lands which now comprise Perry County. He was a half-breed, the oldest son of Madame Montour, and the brother of the celebrated Catharine Montour. There was a conference held at George Croghan's (Sterrett's Gap) in May, 1750, and among those present were Richard Peters, secretary of the province; Conrad Weiser, James Galbreath, George Stevenson, William Wilson, Hermanus Alricks, George Croghan, Andrew Montour, three Indian delegates from the Five Nations, and one from the Mohawks, when the effort was made to drive from the lands north of the Kittatinny Mountain those who had settled there, the territory not having as yet been purchased from the Indians.

They were driven from the lands on which they had settled, and on April 18, 1752, Andrew Montour was commissioned by the governor to settle and reside upon these Indian lands, the Indians on July 2, 1750, having petitioned for such occupation, and arrangements having been made with them for such occupation, at a place considered most central, to see that the lands were not settled upon and to warn off any who had presumed to settle there. He was also to report the names of any who did settle there that they might be prosecuted. He chose to settle on a stream which to this day bears his name, Montour's run, flowing through Tyrone Township. Just how honest Montour was in fulfilling this responsible position is a matter of conjecture, but there is evidence that the Indians were still protesting a year later at a Carlisle council about encroachments. In fact, Montour was not only suspected by the provincial authorities of neglecting his duty here, but he was on more than one occasion suspected of double dealing with the Indians of the West and the province.

He was present at the conference at George Croghan's probably in the capacity of an interpreter for Tohonady Huntho, the representatives of the Mohawks from Ohio, for he was an expert interpreter, speaking the language of the various Ohio tribes as well as the Iroquois. His name will be found in our Indian chapters. He was an interpreter and later a trader. Hanna, in The Wilderness Trail, says: "Madame Montour and her son, Andrew Montour, were the most picturesque characters in the colonial history of Pennsylvania."

There is evidence that William Patterson, John and Joseph Scott, James Kennedy, Alexander Roddy, Thomas Wilson and others had located in Sherman's Valley during 1753, not a great distance from the Montour place, but whether he notified the authorities is not known, but it is a fact that he brought in his brother-in-law, William Dason, and allowed him to locate a claim, according to an affidavit of William Patterson some years thereafter.

His mother, the famous Madame Montour, was not a daughter of a governor of Canada, as sometimes stated. Her father, Pierre Couc, a Frenchman, emigrated to Canada. By an Indian wife he had a number of children, some of whom took the name of Montour. In 1694 his son, Lewis Couc, or Montour, was severely wounded by the Mohawks, near Fort Lamotte, on Lake Champlain. Madame Montour (a daughter of Lewis), then a ten-year-old girl, is supposed to have been captured at this time by the Five Nations and adopted. Her first appearance in history is at an Albany conference, August 24, 1711, where she acted as interpreter. She seems to have been educated. She married Carondowana, or the "Big Tree," who had adopted the name of

Robert Hunter, governor of New York. He was of the Oneida tribe, a great captain of the Five Nations, and fell at the hands of the Catawbas in 1729. When a treaty was made in Philadelphia in 1734 the proprietess of the province publicly condoled with the widow—a rather belated function, as viewed in our day. She was handsome and spoke French, being the object of some social activity while in Philadelphia. Her duplicity later became apparent to the provincial authorities.

The settlement of Andrew Montour on Montour's run was never surveyed to him, although he took out a warrant for 143 acres adjoining the site of Landisburg. By a warrant dated July 11, 1761, he was granted 1,500 acres of land on the Juniata River in what is now Mifflin County. He took it in two separate tracts, the aggregate of which was over 2,500 acres. His Indian name was Sattelihu. In 1753 the French had set a price of £100 on his head. In the French and Indian War he was a captain of a company of Indians on the English side. He accompanied Conrad Weiser on his mission to the settlements of the Six Nations. He was for almost forty years in the service of Pennsylvania, Virginia, and under Sir William Johnson. He often accompanied the Moravian missionaries, Count Zinzendorf and Bishop Spangenburg, to the Indian towns. To Count Zinzendorf posterity is indebted for a pen picture of Andrew Montour. His description: "His face is like that of a European, but marked with a broad Indian ring of bear's grease and paint drawn completely around it. He wears a coat of fine cloth of cinnamon color, a black necktie with silver spangles, a red satin vest, pantaloons, over which hangs his shirt; shoes and stockings, a hat and brass ornaments, something like the handle of a basket, suspended from his ears." He died prior to 1775.

Andrew Montour's first wife was a daughter of Allumoppies, King of the Delawares. The Province of Pennsylvania educated his children in Philadelphia as proteges of Governor Robert Hunter Morris. These were the first children to be sent away to school from the soil which now comprises Perry County. Even in that day the call for an education was in the atmosphere of these lands.

He is first mentioned by Conrad Weiser in 1744 when he interpreted his Iroquois into Delaware. He assisted in nearly all the important Indian negotiations from that time until the treaty of Fort Stanwix in 1768, being employed in turn by the Pennsylvania, Virginia, and New York governments and the Ohio Company. In 1754 he was with George Washington at the surrender of Fort Necessity. Several times he warned the settlers of impending raids, among other services bringing word of the Pontiac outbreak. He accompanied Major Rogers as captain of Indian

10

forces, when the latter went to take possession of Detroit, and in 1764 commanded a party against the recalcitrant Delawares. He received for his services several grants of land in western Pennsylvania, as well as money.

In the autumn of 1750 Conrad Weiser reported to the governor of the province that the French agent Joincaire was on his way to the Ohio with a present of goods and orders from the governor of Canada to drive out all English traders. Governor Hamilton detailed George Croghan and Andrew Montour to hasten thither and by use of a small present and promise of more to try and counteract the intrigues of the French and retain the Indians in the English interest.

At a meeting of the commissioners of the province at Carlisle, October 1, 1753, Montour was associated with such illustrious lights as Richard Peters, Isaac Norris, and Benjamin Franklin. Conrad Weiser said of Montour "that he was faithful, knowing and prudent." He operated among the more western Indians and was rewarded financially for keeping track of their movements.

While Andrew Montour was sometimes under suspicion of double dealing he always maintained his position with the provincial government in one capacity or another. In proof of his connection at the time of the French and Indian troubles, also of his actual residence in what is now Perry County before the Albany treaty of July 6, 1754, as the authorized representative of the provincial authorities, the following letter is here reproduced:

SHERMAN'S CREEK, 16th May, 1754.

Sir: I once more take upon me the liberty of informing you that our Indians at Ohio are expecting every day the armed forces of this province against the French, who, by their late encroachments, is likely to prevent their planting, and thereby render them impossible of supporting their families. And you may depend upon it as a certainty, that our Indians will not strike the French, unless this province (or New York) engage with them; and that by sending some number of men to their immediate assistance. The reasons are plain; to wit: that they don't look upon their late friendship with Virginia, sufficient to engage them with a war with the French; I therefor think, with submission, that to preserve our Indian allies this province ought instantly to send out some men, either less or more, which I have good reason to hope, would have the desired effect; otherwise, I doubt there will, in a little time, be an entire separation; the consequences of which you are best able to judge, &c. I am informed by my brother, who has lately come from the Lakes, that there is at that place a great number of French Indians, preparing to come down to the assistance of the French, at Ohio. I am likewise informed, by a young Indian man (who, by my brother's directions, spent some days with the French at Monongahela), that they expect a great number of French down the river very soon. I have delayed my journey to Ohio and waited with great impatience for advice from Philadelphia, but have not yet received any. I am now obliged to go to Colonel Washington, who has sent for me many days ago, to go with him to meet the half-king, Monacatootha, and others, that are coming to meet the Virginia companies; and, as they think, some from Pennsylvania—and would have been glad to have known the design of this province, in these matters, before I had gone.

I am, sir, your very humble servant,

ANDREW MONTOUR.

To Gov. H. R. Morris.

He had correspondence with the governor and council, and this letter to the governor was copied from Montour's autograph letter on file in the office of the Secretary of the Commonwealth at the State Capitol in Harrisburg.

As early as 1744 we find that "Andrew Montour, Madame Montour's son, interpreted an Indian message from the Mohawk language to that of the Delawares." During the same year he was also the interpreter in the Jack Armstrong murder case, which appears earlier in this book. In that year we also find him as captain of a party of Iroquois warriors, marching against the Catawbas, of Carolina. He fell sick and was obliged to return to Shamokin. In May, 1745, he accompanied Weiser and Shikellamy to Onondaga with a message and instructions from the governor of the province. In June, 1748, he was introduced by Weiser to the president of the council of the province, at Philadelphia, and recommended as "faithful and prudent." During 1754 George Washington sent for Montour to meet him at Ohio, and he (Montour) wrote to Secretary Peters, of the province, from his residence on Sherman's Creek, the above letter, urging the immediate necessity of sending men and arms to resist the impending French invasion. Montour and George Croghan proceeded to Monongahela and there, on June 9, found Washington. He commanded a mixed company of whites and Indians under Washington.

At a conference, October 24, 1759, at Pittsburgh, Montour and George Croghan met General Stanwix, and Montour lit the "pipe of peace." In 1761, May 22, at a conference at the State House in Philadelphia, Montour was the official interpreter. In 1768, at a conference at Fort Pitt, between George Croghan, deputy agent Indian affairs, and the Six Nations, Delawares and Shawnees, Montour was the interpreter. He filled the same position October 24, 1768, at a great congress with the Indians at Fort Stanwix.

During 1769, on November 3, at the junction of Loyalsock Creek and the West Branch, a tract of land was surveyed to Andrew Montour. It contained 880 acres and was called Montour's Reserve.

CHAPTER VIII.

COMING OF THE PIONEERS.

THE frontier of the early Eighteenth Century was still east of the Susquehanna. Beyond lay the forests, the hills, the rivers and bands of Indians sometimes hostile when they emerged. By the middle of the century adventurers—mostly Scotch-Irish—had carried settlement across that river and were clamoring for the right to cross the Kittatinny or Blue Mountain to settle. When that section was thrown open they not only quickly settled it, but passed on, and crossed the Alleghenies to the Ohio. While that was happening in Pennsylvania the New Englanders made their way to the Mohawk Valley of New York, then on to the Seneca territory and along the shores of the Great Lakes, and to the south through the Cumberland pass and over the hills of the Carolinas was trickling civilization from the southern seaboard to Kentucky and Tennessee.

*The date of the opening of the land office for the settlement of the lands which comprise Perry County was February 3, 1755, early in the very year of Braddock's defeat, and almost coincident with the time when that noted general was moving towards Braddock's Field—as it later came to be known—where the British, because of their pride and contempt for the advice of experienced officers, paid for the Indian dissatisfaction of the previous year at Albany, in connection with the purchase of these very lands. Has it ever occurred to the reader how closely the Perry County lands are related to the historic Braddock defeat?

Settlers had come in in large numbers during 1755; but owing to the defeat of Braddock and the attending defection of the savages, which created a reign of terror and bloodshed throughout the province, few claims were located and settled upon between that year and 1761. While there was still much land open to settlement south of the Blue or Kittatinny Mountain there was a scarcity of water as compared to the north side. These earliest set-

---

*Legendary and traditional information, unless backed up by supporting facts, is not to be relied upon. Various persons have furnished statements that their ancestors were settlers of the Sherman's Valley and other parts of Perry County as early as 1741, 1743, and various other dates. Careful investigation has been made in provincial records, and nowhere can there be found any permanent settlements prior to the late summer of 1753, save those who came in as squatters and intruders and were dispossessed, mention of which appears in the chapters relating to the Indians, elsewhere in this book.

tlers were mostly Scotch-Irish, and it is a remarkable fact that they invariably sought lands near the headwaters of streams, a characteristic likely instilled deep in the race. If they could but get their habitations near springs or running water they regarded it of more advantage than having them on more fertile soil where the matter of water was a question. And it must be remembered that in Perry County these springs and streams come welling to the surface of the earth, pure, and clear, and cold, from vast subterranean caverns in the heart of the hills.

Prof. Wright. in his history, states that there is not a single farm in Perry County of one hundred acres or more which does not have running water upon it.

With these early Scotch-Irish came a few English, many Germans coming in later. The provincial government at first made an effort to place the different nationalities in different sections, but soon found it difficult of accomplishment and a failure when done. The Scotch-Irish, as spoken of in America, are not Irish at all, but Scotch and English, who fled religious persecution at home at the hands of Charles I (1714-1720) and found refuge in Ireland, and their descendants. The term is of American origin and use and is identical with the English term, Ulstermen. It denotes no mixture of blood of the two races, as they did not intermarry. They entered Ireland and took up the estates of Irish rebels, confiscated under Queen Elizabeth and James I. James I, by the way, was king of Scotland, and as James VI encouraged his Presbyterian subjects to do this. Many of them had migrated early in the Seventeenth Century, about seventy-five years before the founding of Pennsylvania. Towards the middle of the same century Cromwell confiscated Irish lands and emigration increased further, many English being among them. The Scotch were principally Saxon in blood and Presbyterian in religion, devout Christians, while the native Irish are Celtic in blood and Roman Catholic in religion. The races are distinct in Ireland to this day, which accounts largely for the eternal Irish question, which at this very time (1920) has the British Kingdom at wit's end.

The settlement of Irish and Germans north of the Kittatinny was often the cause of neighborhood and family feuds, which existed even after the organization of the county, as there is record of such a fight in the spring of 1823, when one of the participants, fearing that he "had killed the dutchman," fled to Indiana, where he became an honored citizen.

In his Making of Pennsylvania, Sydney George Fisher says: "The thought and enterprise of New England has been built up entirely by Congregationalists; well on to one-half of the social fabric of Pennsylvania has been built up by Presbyterians, and there is scarcely a state in the Union where the influence of Calvinism had not been powerfully felt." In the original settlement of Perry County territory this Scotch-Irish element was a large factor and their descendants are among the foremost in its affairs and among those sent out to wider fields, one of whom, when this is written, occupies the Vice-Presidential chair of the United States. See biography of Thomas R. Marshall further on in this volume.

The struggle for the possession of the new world was at first confined to six nationalities: the Spanish, French, English, Dutch, Swedes, and Portuguese. The Germans, distracted by their own political divisions, seemed to have no desire to colonize. They finally appeared in Pennsylvania half a century after most of the English colonies had been established, but *they came as immigrants under the protection of the English nation,* at first encouraged by the Quakers, and later by the British Government, says Fisher. They came principally from the Palatinate; from Alsace, Swabia, Saxony, and Switzerland. They had been held in more or less subjection at home, and many of the earlier immigrants were a very crude people. Pastorius tells of the Indians even considering them so. He relates: "An Indian promised to sell one a turkey hen. Instead he brought an eagle and insisted it was a turkey. It was refused, and the Indian to a Swede, a bystander, remarked that he thought a German, just arrived, would not know the difference." Later they came in larger numbers and of a more intelligent class. The German element, often referred to in our state, as the Pennsylvania Dutch, has been variously estimated as composing from one-third to one-half of the population of Pennsylvania, and has had a great influence in the development of the state and of Perry County, where their descendants are a thrifty and enterprising element. In the blood of thousands of Perry Countians and their descendants who have gone abroad is a strain of German steadfastness and perseverance which has sent men to the gubernatorial chair of not only our own state, but of others, and to the highest legislative body in the world. See biographies of noted men. In some counties the German element has lived unto itself, using the German language, with little or no intermarriage with other elements, thus causing practically no advancement. This was not so in Perry County. The children attended the public schools and soon learned to use English, the parents learning it in turn, and to-day of this original German stock not one family uses the German language in the home. However, about 1890 a German colony located in Watts Township, built a small church, and a few of the parents of these families may still use it, while the children speak English. The Germans were mostly of the Lutheran and Reformed faith. These older settlers and their descendants have had considerable contempt for a few of the newer who continually talked of "The Fatherland."

Thomas Kilby Smith, in his "Commonwealth of Pennsylvania," says of the type of Germans which settled Perry County:

"The members of the Lutheran and Reformed Churches, who represent the second phase of German emigration to Pennsylvania, were of a higher type than their predecessors, most of them belonging to the middle classes and not to the peasantry, as were the great majority of the sects who preceded them. Like the Scotch-Irish and the Welsh, they have mingled with the community in general and have been absorbed into the population of the state, abandoning any peculiarities of language or custom that they may have had at the time of their arrival. They have engaged in various occupations, with a tendency, however, to remain in the towns rather than in the country districts. Being less numerous than the Pennsylvania Dutch and more rapidly assimilated, they have made less impression, as a separate people, on the civilization of the state than the Germans who preceded them. Generally speaking, they have been prosperous, have adhered closely to their respective churches, relinquished their native tongue, and pursued industriously their various occupations. With a few exceptions, they have not taken a prominent part in politics or public affairs, except in lines of philanthropy, education and music."

In the matter of noted men from the county the two races, now much intermarried, vie with each other as to the number which the county has sent forth.

Speaking of the German element, Prof. Wright, in his history (1873), says: "Pfoutz's Valley is still characteristically a German settlement, though there are many persons unable to converse in any but the English language. For our fertile soil the German is slowly exchanging his language; his children receive an English education in the free schools, without dissent. In fact, many of our best scholars were the children of German parents." He adds, "Although the soil of Perry County was first settled by English-speaking people, the farming population is now largely composed of German origin."

Prof. W. C. Shuman, formerly of Perry County, in his "Genealogy of the Shuman Family," says of the Germans: "The Germans have profoundly influenced the history of Pennsylvania for about 200 years. They have been slow, self-centered and nonprogressive; but they have also been honest, industrious and thrifty; and in the main, they have been on the right side of all great issues."

The Indian troubles of 1763 again retarded settlement, but the victory of the noted Colonel Henry Bouquet in Ohio, in 1764, caused the Indians to pretty generally desert the central Pennsylvania territory, and a tide of immigration from the eastern section of the province began, and, owing to imperfect titles to their lands in Chester County, later brought to the territory such men as John Hench, Jacob Hipple, Jacob Hartman, Frederick Shull and

Zachariah Rice, whose descendants are legion, and hundreds of others. By 1767 many of the best plots were taken, and by 1778 the greater part of the lands.

The selling of emigrants into servitude for the payment of their passage across the ocean was practiced. George Leonard, an early settler of the lands which comprise Perry County, was sold in that manner when but six years old, his father having died while aboard and his body cast into the sea, according to the custom.

The western part of Perry County, generally speaking, impresses one with the fact that it was settled before the eastern section, or the part lying between the rivers, and records verify it. All through western Sherman's Valley are to be found stone houses more than a century old, built by artisans whose work has stood the test, whose wage was likely a very meagre one and whose hours possibly were numbered only by the number of hours of daylight. Their work will ever stand a monument to early craftsmanship. At only one other part of the county are there many of these old landmarks, and that is Millerstown. (See chapter on Millerstown.) The one on the Solomon Bower farm, in Jackson Township, now owned by Assemblyman Clark Bower, was built in 1794, when George Washington was President. An end was built to it in 1834 and a second story added in 1870. The large stone house on the C. A. Anderson farm, at Andersonburg, is another fine example. It was built in 1820. The adjoining barn was erected in 1821.

It is difficult for the present generation, with its modern homes, many lighted by electricity and gas; with water piped throughout and a multitude of accessories to make life easy and comfortable; with its modern method of travel in parlor cars at fifty miles an hour; with automobiles equipped and finished finer than the grandest carriage, and traveling thirty miles an hour (according to law); with stores and shops existing at which anything may be purchased; with telephones in one's home whereby he may talk to another state in a few minutes, and hundreds of other conveniences unnamed and unenumerated, to realize the extreme needs and crude methods and equipment of these pioneers of civilization, who braved the rigors of the early winters and the dangers of the redskins to build in the wilderness a home and to wrest from the savage a state.

When the pioneer wended his way over the Kittatinny or Blue Mountain the country was a vast forest, whose creeks and rivers were destitute of bridges and could only be crossed with safety at given points, and not at all when the waters were high. There were no roads, but only the trails and paths used by the red men and the traders. There were no houses, no cleared lands, no schools, nothing but the eternal stillness which one yet experiences when traveling afoot in the fastnesses of the mountain. Upon entering the forest their very first act was to cut the timber and hew boards with an axe for the erection of their homes, for at first there were even no sawmills. Instead of their floors being sawed and planed, as are ours, they were split and hewed. Indeed, there were some that had no floors save the earth upon which they were built, even the old church at Dick's Gap being floorless.

While the little log house was yet in course of erection the trees were being felled on "the clearing," which was to be the first field of the new home, and by the time of its finishing a "patch" was ready for planting or sowing. Then, while it was growing, there were other lands to clear, a barn and other buildings to be built; and eternal vigilance was necessary to prevent the coming of the savage with his tomahawk, in search of scalps. There was no machinery and the crudest methods of slow and tedious operation were necessary to the raising and threshing of crops. In fact, the threshing of a crop, which is now done in a day or two on the great majority of farms, then required months, as the tramping out of grain on the barn floors, with horses, and the use of the "flail" were the only available methods of extracting the grain.

The furnishings of the pioneers were as crude as the cabins themselves, the tables and benches being of wood, split and hewed, until the advent of the "up-and-down" sawmill. Dishes, plates and spoons were of pewter, bowls were fashioned from wood, and squashes and gourds supplied receptacles for water. The clothing was of homespun and homemade, the women and girls being busy with spinning wheel and needle during the long winters. The men dressed in hunting shirts and moccasins, later in knee pants with buckles. When the first schools were established the clearing of lands and threshing during the long winters, and the spinning and sewing to make the family clothing, kept many from school, even the few months when schools were in session. Tallow candles were used as lights, and there are many men and women yet living who can well remember when their people used tallow candles as their only lights, save perchance a rare oil lamp "when company came."

Gradually roads were built and travel was either afoot, on horseback or by wagon, all of which was slow and required much time. Settlements were widely separated and the nearest town was in the Cumberland Valley, then known as the "Kittochtinny Valley." Large families were the rule and it was no uncommon thing for a family to have over a dozen children, five or six children being considered a small family. Many of the most prominent families of the district were large. To-day the reverse is the case and hundreds of families in the same territory number from one to three children, the family of a half-dozen being considered large. Mr. William Morrison, of New Germantown, a man of mature years,

those who took them in. In fact, hospitality in the early days was not confined to any one section, and it is said of our first President, General Washington, that his family "did not sit alone to dinner for twenty years." In the provincial days the public stopping place was an "ordinary," later it became a "tavern," and still later a "hotel," which name it retains, with variations, such as "hostelry," "road house," "tea room," etc.

Some folks attached considerable importance to certain days and certain signs, "planting in signs" being largely practiced. The modern way of planting in fertile ground, well prepared and duly cultivated, seems to be an improvement. These signs were regarded as foretelling the state of the weather, of health, and whether seed should be planted. One certain day broke ice if it found it, and formed it if there was none (rather a contrary sort of day and emblematic of a certain type of people); other days were "bad days" or "good days" for planting or sowing seeds, others for building fences and roofing buildings, and still others for slaughtering stock and weaning stock and even babies. It is not strange that many of these old notions prevailed, for they were bequeathed from sire to son and from mother to daughter for centuries; they came with the Pilgrim and the Cavalier from across the sea and formed a sort of tradition among all classes. The belief in witchcraft and sorcery is practically gone, yet once in too was a part of the belief of many in widely scattered sections of the Union. Even in our own day certain customs known to our earlier years have since been replaced and proven fallacious, and things now generally acceptable will, in the coming years, seem as strange to the populace as does witchcraft to us now.

For many decades Bear's Almanac, a Lancaster publication, was a part of the literature of every farm home, and largely continues so.

In the early days the currency was "eleven penny bits," "fi' penny bits," "levies" and shillings, eight shillings making one dollar. The big cents of copper appeared in 1792 and bore on their face the head of Washington, and on the reverse side a chain of thirteen links, emblematic of the thirteen original states.

Wild animals roamed at will and some were beasts of prey, among them being bears, panthers, wolves, wild cats, etc. Bears were seen in Horse Valley as late as 1885. Wolves were bad and even the graves had to be covered with stones in early times to insure their safety from these animals. "The Narrows," below Mt. Patrick, was once a dangerous place owing to its being the habitation of wolves. Near Crawley Hill, in Spring Township, there is a small area of rocks, probably fifteen feet high, known to this day as "the wolf rocks," and which tradition says was so named by reason of it having been a rendezvous for wolves when they still inhabited the forests. It is yet a den for foxes. The Fishing Creek Valley (Rye Township) was a place noted for wolves even to the present generation, and there are men of fifty years who can remember them. On January 21, 1829, George Hollenbaugh, of Toboyne Township, was hunting, and entered a cavern in the mountains, but quickly retraced his steps, a bear following him out. He shot it, and another appeared. It too was despatched. He then went for help to carry away the animals, when a third appeared and was shot, according to the *Perry Forester,* Perry County' first paper.

There is record of a Mr. Magee, who was grandfather of Alexander Magee, sheriff of Perry County in 1841-43, going to the door of his home, in Toboyne Township, one night when he heard a scream. He stepped out, axe in hand, and killed a panther, which was just ready to pounce upon him. Deer, rabbits and squirrel were common, and venison graced the table of the pioneer on many occasions. The meats of these animals were salted down for use during the long winters. Wild turkeys, pheasants and partridges roamed the forests, and during certain seasons wild pigeons collected in vast numbers. The streams, unpolluted and at first free of dams, were alive with fish, principally bass, pike and trout. After the severe winters shad, rockfish, salmon and perch ascended the streams, thus probably augmenting a supply of provisions which had become largely depleted.

During the summer of 1919 the late George Bryner (born in 1832) recalled how his Grandmother Hench, who resided near the McMillen farms, in the vicinity of Kistler, Madison Township, used to describe the howling of the wolves and tell of using powder, which they would ignite at night, to scare the animals from their cattle. It appears that wolves scent trouble with the smell of powder, as do many other wild animals.

The Susquehanna and Juniata country was once the home of that great and picturesque bird, the American eagle, and to this day Bald eagles inhabit the shores, including Perry County territory, but in very small numbers. Their passing is attributed to the propensity for killing by a certain class of hunters, who never should have been permitted to shoulder a gun. The Bald eagle was here when the pioneer came, and unmolested, continued until the last century was well passed, when they began to be viewed as thieves, with the result that only a few stragglers remain. In an interesting booklet, by that wonderful lover of outdoor life, Col. Henry W. Shoemaker, appears this paragraph relating to the method of their passing, which is of interest to this section:

"Charles Lukens, of Duncan's Island, near the mouth of the Juniata River, states that a hunter, now residing at Halifax, killed a Bald eagle on Peters' Mountains in 1910. He made ready to take the carcass to Harrisburg to claim a bounty, but on learning that it was a protected bird abandoned the trip, and it is not known what became of the eagle. Charles Smith, an intelligent farmer residing on Haldeman's Island, states that it was formerly not an extraordinary occurrence to see Bald eagles soaring over the island and the river, but for several years he has not seen any. The Rev. B. H. Hart, of Williamsport, who owns an island not far from Liverpool, says Bald eagles were formerly seen in fair numbers along the river and at his island, though he cannot recollect having seen any for several years."

Slowly sailing across the heavens their *eagle* eyes would detect a fish in the water hundreds of yards away, and at one fell swoop would fasten it between their beaks, and carry it to their young in the crags of the mountain where they nested. Their nests were built of sticks and twigs and were huge affairs when compared with the nests of other birds. It is related that when a tree upon which a pair nested, in a neighboring county, was cut, a small wagonload of kindling was gathered from the nest. Naturalists tell that these birds would tear down and rebuild their nests entirely, every third or fourth year, and in the intervening years would only rebuild the top or finishing part.

Passing of the Buffalo.

Many, many years ago this land was overrun by great herds of Buffalo, especially that portion of Pennsylvania which comprises the tablelands lying between the Juniata and Susquehanna Rivers. Part of Perry County, of course, is included in this domain, and Buffalo Township, Perry County, was named to perpetuate the memory thereof. There is a chapter in this book relating to Buffalo Township, which was, by the way, the author's birthplace. Its lands belonged to Greenwood Township, which was a part of Fermanagh Township—one of the original townships of Cumberland County, when that county was formed. Buffalo Township became a separate unit in 1799, the very year in which the illustrious Washington, the first President of the Republic, passed away. Even before one of the county's townships was named Buffalo, we find in annals relating to the pioneers and the Indians the name of Buffalo Creek, which rises in present Madison Township, in the section known as Liberty Valley, and flows into the Juniata above Newport, and which was most probably named by the red men themselves. Then, besides Buffalo Creek and Buffalo Township, there is Buffalo Church, Buffalo Mills, New Buffalo, etc., within the limits of Perry County.

In 1655 a man named Vonder Donk published a history, in which he said: "Many of the Netherlanders have been far into the country more than seventy or eighty leagues from the river and seashore. We frequently trade with the Indians who come more than ten and twenty days' journey from the interior." He says that half of the buffaloes have disappeared and left the country, and now "keep mostly to the Southwest, where few people go." The beavers, of which eighty thousand are killed annually, are also mostly taken far inland, there being few of them near the settlements.

Vast herds of buffalo once roamed the Susquehanna Valley, as they later did the plains of the great West, ever receding before the westward sweep of the pioneer. W. T. Hornaday says that the animals used to roam the country west of the Susquehanna, between Harrisburg and Sunbury, and the West Branch country of the Susquehanna. Other writers say that as late as 1773 there were probably as many as twelve thousand bison in the herds that came to this part of the country. Like Perry, Union County perpetuates the name in three of its nine townships and in other ways. According to Col. Henry W. Shoemaker, along Buffalo Path Run, in that county, can be plainly seen the marks made by the herd, although none have traveled it for almost a century and a half.

The country between Buffalo Township, in Perry County, and the three Buffalo Townships in Union County, and westward in northern Snyder and southern Union Counties, will ever be memorable as the scene of the "last stand" in Pennsylvania of the dwindling buffalo herd, in December, 1799. A coincidence, not strange however, is that Buffalo Township was created by the Cumberland County court—for Perry was yet a part of Cumberland—within ninety days prior to this incident. Almost four hundred animals, unable to escape because settlements had grown up which entirely surrounded them, had remained hidden in the fastnesses of the mountains to the west of Snyder and Union Counties. That last winter of the closing Eighteenth Century was severe and, desperate for want of food, they braved the Middle Creek section of that territory, scenting a barnyard haystack of a settler. They broke through the stump fence and trampled to death the cattle and sheep within the enclosure. The owner and a neighbor succeeded in killing four.

The shots and attacking dogs drove them further down the valley to a cabin which stood near where Troxelville, Snyder County, is now located, being in the northwest section of that county. There the wounded leader of the herd, wild with rage, broke down the door and entered the cabin. As many as could enter followed. They were so tightly jammed in the cabin that the only way to get them out was to tear it away and release them. The mangled bodies of the wife and children of the owner, crushed beyond description, were beneath them when released.

Naturally this state of affairs needed immediate attention, and messengers went up and down the valley summoning hunters to help exterminate the herd. Fifty men responded and started to hunt the bison which had fled to the mountain. In the meantime more snow had fallen and their tracks were obliterated. After a two-day search they were found, buried to their necks in snow, at a spot near Weikert, along Penn's Creek, in the southwest section of Union County—the "blind end" of Buffalo Valley. Surrounded by snow of awful depth, almost frozen and at the verge of starvation thus perished the last herd of buffalo in the lands of William Penn. In January, 1801, a straggler was found and despatched at Buffalo Crossroads, near Lewisburg. A strange coincidence in this connection is that the last elk in the state was killed near the same spot, though not until almost a century later—1878.

Early Maps Showing Locations.

Modern map makers for the great trunk lines of railroads show almost straight lines of these arteries of travel, yet the tourist finds his train taking innumerable curves while traveling over these "straight lines." Naturally all maps radiate from the given centre in the eye of the producer, and it is not strange to find, in the many old maps available, some things which are practically correct, and much that is drawn from conjecture and description, surrounding the known locality. The inaccuracies of these old maps, with the facilities at hand for securing information, can be much more readily excused than the modern ones "with intent aforethought to deceive." A man named Visscher published a map of New Netherlands in 1655 which shows with some degree of accuracy the course of the Susquehanna River, but with no west branch of it or no Juniata. During the following half century about fifteen different maps all contain the same river outline. West of the river, about where the Juniata belongs, he locates an Indian tribe known as the "Onojutta Haga."

Lord Baltimore had a map maker named Augustine Herman make a map of Maryland for him in 1670, and it shows Maryland coming up to the Blue or Kittatinny Mountain, including part of the Cumberland Valley. It shows a group of mountains about where Perry County is located and a note along the edge carries the information that "beyond these mountains the streams run to the west, either into the Bay of Mexico or the South Sea; that the first one discovered, a very great stream, is the 'Black Minquas' River (the Ohio), on which lived the tribe of that name; that there was a branch of this river (the Conemaugh) opposite the Susquehanna (Juniata), which entered at some leagues above the fort." In 1698 Gabriel Thomas published a map, which places at least a part of Cumberland County in Virginia; in fact, Virginia long claimed a large part of western Pennsylvania.

A man named Nicholas Schull, probably the most noted map maker of those early days, made a map of the new county of Cumberland which was authorized by an act of Parliament in January, 1759. Of the present names we find Kittatinny and Tuscarora Mountains, Horse Valley, Juniata and Susquehanna Rivers. Where the Cocolamus Creek is located he has a stream named the "Kakonalamus Creek." "Shareman's Creek" is also on this map. In the Blue Mountain he designates one gap and names it "Stevenson's." At a point near the present Perry-Juniata County line a lone settler is designated as "Barber's."

In 1770 a map appeared by W. Schull, with practically the same outlines but another settlement marked "Logan's," located on the line of the trail from Carlisle to Fort Shirley. The Conococheague Mountain is also marked and Logan's appears close to it. Croghan's Gap (Sterrett's) also appears for the first time. Other streams added are Juniata Creek, Buffalo Creek and Wild Cat Run. Near the site of Millerstown, on the bend of the Juniata below Newport, and near Marysville appears the word "Saut." (Salt, in Scotch.)

When the commonwealth was new and its first governor, Thomas Mifflin, was in office, a map appeared which contained the names of the four townships then existing in what is now the county of Perry, as follows: Toboyne, Tyrone, Rye, and Greenwood. "Buffalo Hills," "Mahanoy Hill," and "Limestone Ridge" appear for the first time. Many mills are already marked, an account of which appears in our chapter relating to "Old Landmarks, Mills and Industries."

On a map in the Book of Deeds, page 128, in the office of the Secretary of the Commonwealth, the territory opposite the Cove and located in Dauphin County, between the Blue and Peters' Mountains, is designated as "Saint Anthony's Wilderness."

CHAPTER IX.

PERRY COUNTY IN THE REVOLUTIONARY WAR.

IT has virtually been handed down to us from father to son, even from Plymouth Rock and Jamestown, that somewhat like another nation, we were in a sense a chosen people—that something greater than human foresight, something greater than finite wisdom had guided a persecuted people to these shores and bestowed vision and faith upon those in whom rested the stupendous and responsible task of erecting a new government upon an unheard of scheme and following a new standard of life.

Strangely enough, the first suggestion of a union of the American colonies came from the Province of Pennsylvania, and from its proprietor, William Penn, who, as early as 1697, suggested it. The pioneers had crossed the ocean to be free, but as the colonies grew in size and in trade they found that the same forces that drew them from the mother country now drew them together. In 1754 Benjamin Franklin, another Pennsylvanian, elaborated upon the Penn idea.

When the first congress of deputies assembled at New York on October 7, 1765, the discerning ones saw in it a gleam of coming independence. When the heel of British oppression had descended with heavy tread upon the rights and privileges of the provinces and they arose in their wrath against the mother country, the pioneers who inhabited that part of Cumberland County which is now Perry, were unable to offer much cash, as the Indians had twice driven them from their homes, scalped and carried off many, stolen what they could conveniently remove and burned or destroyed the remainder. Under such circumstances they were a people who really needed the help of others instead of being called upon for help, yet notwithstanding they gave of their substance, and to the first blast of the bugle calling recruits they responded. The first settlers to return after the second Indian invasion in 1763 went back in 1765, so that but ten years had elapsed until the necessity arose to defend the colonies. An effort, fathered at Philadelphia, to have the different sections of the province send delegates to a meeting there on July 15, 1774, to consider the indignities perpetrated upon the provinces, was no doubt responsible for the following described meeting:

Echoing down the centuries is this first official record relating to independence coming from Cumberland County, of which the Perry County territory was an integral part. England, through

II

its German-speaking king, was oppressing the colonies, especially New England, and a public meeting "of the freeholders and freemen" was held Tuesday, July 12, 1774, at Carlisle, with John Montgomery, Esq., in the chair. These resolutions show the patriotic spirit of those days, just as boys from Perry showed it in 1918 at Chauteau Thierry and the Argonne Forest in the World War, and as it was shown by Perry Countians in all the intervening wars. The resolutions:

1. Resolved, That the late act of the Parliament of Great Britain, by which the port of Boston is shut up, is oppressive to that town, and subversive of the rights and liberties of the colony of Massachusetts Bay; that the principle upon which the act is founded, is not more subversive of the rights and liberties of that colony, than it is of all other British colonies in North America; and therefore the inhabitants of Boston are suffering in the common cause of all the colonies.

2. That every vigorous and prudent measure ought speedily and unanimously to be adopted by these colonies for obtaining redress of the grievances under which the inhabitants of Boston are now laboring; and security from grievance of the same or of a still more severe nature, under which they and the other inhabitants of the colonies may, by a further operation of the same principle, hereafter labor.

3. That a congress of the deputies from all colonies will be one proper method for obtaining these purposes.

4. That the same purposes will, in the opinion of this meeting, be promoted by an agreement of all the colonies not to import any merchandise from nor export any merchandise to Great Britain, Ireland or the British West Indies, nor to use any merchandise so imported, nor tea imported from any place whatever till these purposes shall be obtained; but that the inhabitants of this county will join any restriction of that agreement which the General Congress may think it necessary for the colonies to confine themselves to.

5. That the inhabitants of this county will contribute to the relief of their suffering brethren in Boston, at any time when they shall receive intimation that such relief will be most seasonable.

6. That a committee be immediately appointed from this county to correspond with the committee of this province, or of the other provinces, upon the great objects of the public attention; and to coöperate in every measure conducting to the general welfare of British America.

7. That the committee consist of the following persons, viz: James Wilson, John Armstrong, John Montgomery, William Irvine, Robert Callendar, William Thompson, John Calhoon, Jonathon Hoge, Robert Magaw, Ephraim Blaine, John Allison, John Harris, and Robert Miller, or any five of them.

8. That James Wilson, Robert Magaw, and William Irvine be the deputies appointed to meet the deputies from other counties of this province at Philadelphia on Friday next, in order to concert measures preparatory to the General Congress.   JOHN MONTGOMERY, *Chairman.*

The new nation, the United States of America, had come into being because the people could not help it, and as a protest against indignities, taxes and officers forced upon them by the mother country, rather than because of a great desire for it. In the resolutions adopted at this Cumberland County meeting, including what is now Perry, the colonies, it will be noted, are named "British America." Most Americans then held allegiance to their states more so than to a union of all, and many believed it possible to continue thus, independent of each other except pledged to work together on foreign affairs. For a period of eleven years—from 1776 to 1787—such a government, in fact, existed. George Washington, soon to be the first President of the United States, in the meantime was conducting a movement for a united nation, by taking the matter up with the various state governors and otherwise. But there was no unanimity. When the Constitutional Convention met in Philadelphia in 1787 two great men—Adams and Jefferson —were absent in Europe as envoys; Patrick Henry, wedded to "state's rights," refused to attend, and John Hancock, Richard Henry Lee, and Samuel Adams, all fearing a too central government, remained away. Perry Countians will do well to remember that among the representatives was James Wilson, then only twenty-three years of age, of Cumberland (then their county), whom all historians agree was the most learned lawyer in the convention and who afterwards became a justice of the United States Supreme Court. In 1778 he removed to Philadelphia. He was elected to Congress in 1775 and 1782. He died in the South, in 1798, and his remains rested there until within the last two decades, when they were disinterred and removed to Philadelphia.

James McLene was a member from the county to the Provincial Conference of June, 1776, and of the Constitutional Convention of the same year, as well as a member of the Supreme Executive Council from Cumberland County in 1778-79, serving in the last named body from Franklin County from 1784 to 1787.

Continental Congress adopted resolutions on May 15, 1775, recommending the adoption of a state government by each colony. This resulted in a provincial conference held at Philadelphia on Tuesday, June 18, which met at Carpenters' Hall, and chose Thomas McKean president. It was unanimously resolved that a convention should be called to form a new government. The qualification for voters or electors were made as follows: must have attained the age of twenty-one years, have lived in the province one year or more, must have paid either a provincial or county tax, and swear that he would no longer bear allegiance to King George. Representatives to the convention needed the same qualifications, and in addition an affidavit that he "would oppose any measures that would interfere with or obstruct the religious principles or practices of any of the good people of the province," and still further, sign a declaration of faith in the Trinity and in the Divine inspiration of the Old and New Testaments. It was determined that each county should have eight representatives or members, the election of whom should be held on Monday, July 8, and that four thousand, five hundred militia be raised to join a flying camp to consist of ten thousand men in the middle colonies.

The convention met on Monday, July 15, in Philadelphia, and Benjamin Franklin was chosen president. It continued, including adjournments, until September 28, when the Constitution of Pennsylvania was adopted and signed. The lawmaking power of the state was vested in a House of Representatives, the members of which were to be chosen annually by ballot on the second Tuesday of October, to meet the fourth Monday of the same month, no member of which could serve over four years. This body was to choose annually the state treasurer and delegates to the United States Congress, of which no one could be a member for more than two years successively and not be eligible for membership again until three years had elapsed. Until a proper apportionment could be made each county was to have six members of this Assembly.

When the threatened storm approached, our people were equally firm in their determination to resist all oppression. They made preparations, adopted measures and organized for defense. From the American Archives, Vol. II, page 516, the following is reproduced, being the contents of a letter from a gentleman writing May 6, 1775, from Carlisle, the county seat:

"Yesterday the county committee met from nineteen townships, on the short notice they had. About three thousand men have already associated. The arms returned amount to about fifteen hundred. The committee have voted five hundred effective men, besides commissioned officers, to be immediately drafted, taken into pay, armed and disciplined, to march on the first emergency; to be paid and supported as long as necessary, by a tax on all estates, real and personal, in the county; the returns to be taken by the township committees; and the tax laid by the commissioners and assessors; the pay of the officers and men as usual in times past."

"This morning we met again at eight o'clock; among other subjects of inquiry this day, the mode of drafting or taking into pay, arming and victualling immediately the men, and the choice of field and other officers, will among other matters be the subject of deliberation. The strength or spirit of this county, perhaps may appear small, if judged by the number of men proposed; but when it is considered that we are ready to raise fifteen hundred or two thousand, should we have support from the province; and that independent, and in uncertain expectation of support, we have voluntarily drawn upon this county, a debt of about £27,000 per annum, I hope we shall not appear contemptible. We make great improvements in military discipline. It is yet uncertain who may go."

On June 22, 1775, the "Colony of Pennsylvania," the name province having become obsolete, was authorized to raise eight companies of expert riflemen, instead of six companies, as authorized by the Continental Congress on the preceding June 14, to proceed to join the army near Boston. The result was that nine companies responded. Cumberland (always remembering that it still included Perry) sent one under command of Captain William Hendricks, its first offering upon the altar of liberty. It was one of two companies to be assigned to accompany General Benedict Arnold (he who later became a traitor) in his difficult and historical march through Maine to the stronghold of Quebec. Captain Hendricks is recorded as a brave and good officer, but doomed to be killed in the attack January 1, 1776. These men were all enlisted in June, 1775.

Cumberland County then embraced all of Perry, and this company was composed also of men from the present counties of Juniata and Mifflin (also a part of Cumberland), and at this late date there is no way of distinguishing the sections to which each inhabited, hence the entire list is reprinted.

Roster of Captain Hendricks' Company.

Captain, William Hendricks. Killed at Quebec.
First Lieutenant, John McClellan. Died on march, November 3, 1775.
Second Lieutenant, *Francis Nichols.
Third Lieutenant, George Francis.
Sergeants, Dr. Thomas Gibson, of Carlisle (died at Valley Forge, winter of 1778) ; *Henry Crone, *Joseph Greer, *William McCoy.

Privates:

*Edward Agnew.
George Albright.
*Thomas Anderson.
*Philip Boker, w. at Quebec.
*John Blair.
*Alexander Burns.
*Peter Burns.
*William Burns.
John Campbell, k. at Quebec.
*Daniel Carlisle.
*John Corswill.
*Roger Casey.
*Joseph Caskey.
*John Chambers.
*Thomas Cooke, later a lieutenant.
*John Cove.
John Craig, later a lieutenant.
*Matthew Cumming.
Arthur Eckles.
*Peter Frainer.
*Francis Furlow.
*William Gommel.
*John Gardner.
*Daniel Graham.
*James Greer.
*Thomas Greer.
*John Hardy.
Elijah Herdy.
*John Henderson, w. at Quebec.
*James Hogge.
*James Inload.
*Dennis Kelley, k. at Quebec.
*Wm. Kirkpatrick.
*Robert Lynch.
*David Lamb.
*Thomas Lesley.

John Lorain.
*John McChesney.
*Daniel McClellan.
*Richard McClure.
Henry McCormick.
Henry McEwen.
*Archibald McFarlane, escaped.
*Barnabas McGuire.
*John McLinn.
John McMurdy.
*Jacob Mason.
*Philip Maxwell.
*George Morrison.
*George Morrow.
Edward Morton.
*Thomas Mordoch.
*Daniel North.
*Daniel O'Hara.
*William O'Hara.
*John Ray.
*James Reed.
George Rinehart.
*Edward Rodden.
*William Shannon.
*William Smith.
*William Snell.
*Robert Steel.
Hugh Sweeney.
Edward Sweeney.
*Abraham Swaggerty, w. at Quebec.
Matthew Taylor.
*Henry Turpentine.
*Michael Young.
*Thomas Witherof.
*Joseph Wright.

Those marked with an asterisk (*) were captured.

Colonel William Irvine was commissioned in January, 1776, as commander of the Sixth Battalion, Pennsylvania Troops. One of the companies, under Capt. William Bratton, of what is now Mifflin County, contained soldiers whose homes were within the confines of present Mifflin, Juniata, and Perry Counties. The roster of that company follows:

William Bratton, Capt.
Thomas McCoy, Lieut.
Amos Chapman, Sergt.
Thomas Giles, Sergt.
Timothy O'Neil, Sergt.
Edward Steen, Drummer.
John Waun, Fifer.

Privates:

Beatty, John.
Carman, William.
Carter, Patrick.
Daley, John.
Donovan, Daniel.
Edgarton, Edward
Elliott, James.
German, Henry.
Giles, Thomas.
Gilmore, Michael.
Hall, David.

Henry, Francis.
Higgins, James.
Lee, Fergus.
Lloyd, Peter.
Lowden, Richard.
McCay, Gilbert.
McCay, Neil.
McDonald, Patrick.
McGhegan, John.
McKean, John.
Martin, Peter.
Moore, Fergus.
Prent, John.
Redstone, William.
Rooney, Peter.
Ryan, John.
Shockey, Patrick.
Simonton, James.
Simonton, Thomas.
Taylor, John.

On March 15, 1777, the battalion was reorganized at Carlisle, and became the Seventh Pennsylvania Regiment of the Continental Army. The men composing it were paid and mustered out, at Carlisle, during April, 1781. Captain Bratton was wounded at the Battle of Germantown, and a township in Mifflin County was named in his honor.

In several other companies there were a few men from what is now Perry County territory, but how to distinguish them is a question. In the above roster, however, any one familiar with the names of Perry County families will easily distinguish many of them.

After January 1, 1776, this company became a part of the First Regiment of the Army of the United Colonies, commanded by General George Washington, later to become first President of the United States.

Thacher's Military Journal described the men of this battalion as follows:

"Several companies of riflemen have arrived here from Pennsylvania and Maryland, a distance of from five hundred to seven hundred miles. They are remarkably stout and hardy men, many of them exceeding six feet in height. They are dressed in rifle shirts and round hats. These men are remarkable for the accuracy of their aim, striking a mark with great certainty at two hundred yards' distance. At a review a company of them, while on a quick advance, fired their balls into objects of seven-inch diameter, at a distance of two hundred and fifty yards. They are now stationed on our lines and their shot have frequently proved fatal to British officers and soldiers."

French were found upon them, but no one was able to read them. Arnold and Despard had been in the habit of going hunting within the limits of their parole, but were now barred from leaving town. Accordingly they broke their fowling pieces, declaring that no d—— rebel should ever burn powder in them. During their confinement there a man named Thompson, from what is now Perry County, enlisted a company of militia in that district and marched them to Carlisle. Whether eager to display his recruits or not we know not, but at night he drew his company up in front of this stone house and "swore lustily," records tell us, "that he would have their lives, as Americans who were prisoners in hands of the British were dying of starvation."

Through the entreaties of this same Mrs. Ramsey, Captain Thompson, who had formerly been an apprentice to her husband, was induced to leave. He departed, with a menacing nod of his head, and the exclamation, "You may thank my old mistress for your lives." The next morning she received a very polite note from the British officers thanking her for saving them from the valiant Captain Thompson. They were later removed to York, and before leaving sent to Mrs. Ramsey a box of spermacetti candles, a rare article in those days, with a note thanking her for her many kind favors. She returned them with a polite note to the effect that she was too staunch a Whig to accept a gratuity from a British officer. Despard was executed in London in 1803 for high treason, and with Arnold's fate the reader is familiar.

Committees of Observation were appointed throughout the colonies, the committees representing the home county being composed of James Wilson, John Montgomery, Robert Callendar, William Thompson, John Calhoun, Jonathan Hoge, Robert Magaw, Ephraim Blaine, John Allison, John Harris, Robert Miller, John Armstrong, and William Irvine.

Throughout the colonies there appeared here and there sympathizers with the mother country, known in their day as "tories," and the prototype of their ilk known as "copperheads" during the war between the States and as "German-Americans" and "pacifists" during the recent great World War. The English language does not contain words loathsome enough to describe men of that class, who gladly enjoy the pleasures, advantages and protection which their land affords, and yet are traitors of the foulest stripe. That such an one had settled north of the Kittatinny Mountain, in the territory which later became Perry County, is recorded with deep regret, but from the public records his infamy passes to posterity. The affidavit is self-explanatory:

"Cumberland County, ss.:

"Before me, George Robinson, one of His Majesty's Justices, for said county, personally appeared Clefton Bowen, who, being duly examined and sworn, doth depose and say: that some time in the month of January last, he, this deponent, was in the house of John Montgomery, in Tryone Township, in company with a certain Edward Erwin, of Rye Township, and this deponent says he then and there heard said Erwin drink damnation and confusion to the Continental Congress, and damn their proceedings, saying they were all a parcel of damned rebels, and against spring would be cut off like a parcel of snowbirds, and more such stuff.

"Sworn and subscribed before George Robinson, 19th February, 1776.
"CLEFTON BOWEN."

In addition to Erwin there were a number of others of the same ilk who left the territory soon after the British gained possession of Philadelphia and joined them there. The list includes, according to the Pennsylvania Archives, Alexander McDonald, Kennet McKenzie, and Edward Erwin, all of Rye Township, farmers on small farms, and William McPherson, William Smith, and Hugh Gwin, of Tyrone Township. The latter was a laborer and McPherson and Smith, blacksmiths. Their property was confiscated.

A citizen by the name of Job Stretch, who had taken up lands in what is now Juniata Township, was an intense loyalist during the Revolution, but began finding things getting "too warm" for him and left for Canada, where he settled.

LEADS CORNWALLIS' ARMY INTO CAPTIVITY.

To one from within the limits of what now comprises Perry County was accorded one of the greatest honors of the entire Revolution. When the army of the mighty Cornwallis, the British general, laid down their arms, at Yorktown, the entire army, save the officers, was placed in charge of the command of Colonel George Gibson (father of the late Chief Justice Gibson), under whose command they were marched to York, Pennsylvania, where they were prisoners of war. Imagine, if you can, the army of that great empire, prisoners, in the hands of a native of the soil which comprises our little county of Perry.

*Almost seventy years after the ending of the Revolution, on March 2, 1856, the last funeral in Perry County of a soldier of the Revolution occurred. It was that of William Heim, of Jackson Township, father of Rev. John W. Heim, who was the last survivor. He was aged about ninety-five years and could relate from memory many of the incidents which resulted in the declaration of war. The funeral of Andrew Losh, of Wheatfield Township,

---

*William Heim was not recruited from this territory, however, but moved here from Northumberland County in 1815 and became a citizen. He was ninety-five years of age, and 150 horsemen escorted his funeral cortege, this being the only instance of this kind on record here. He is said to have asked the national government for a pension in his later years, but being unable to furnish other evidence than the existence of his name on the company roll, he never received it. The state rewarded his services with a small annuity.

occurring after his death on April 12, 1849, at the age of ninety-eight, was the next last of Revolutionary veterans.

Another prominent name connected with the Revolution from the local territory was that of Capt. Alexander Stephens, who had located near the Baskins' Ferry (now northern Duncannon). He wed a daughter of James Baskins and became the grandfather of Alexander H. Stephens, Vice-President of the Confederacy, to whom a chapter in this book is devoted. The head of this particular Stephens clan in America was an intelligent man, as evidenced by various documents from his pen which we have been privileged to read. He entered the war as a private in the Fourth Company of the Fifth Battalion of the Cumberland County contingent. He was also in the French and Indian War, being present at Braddock's defeat as a member of Capt. Joseph Shippen's company of Col. William Clapham's regiment.

Some of the Patriots.

George Albright, one of the first settlers of Buck's Valley, went to serve his country, his wife, a servant girl and several small boys doing the farming. Mrs. Albright and the servant girl carried bags of grain to the river on horseback. Leaving their horses there they placed the grain bags in canoes and went down the river to the nearest mill, then at Dauphin. While they waited until the grain was ground and they rowed the precious load of flour up the river, the distance being about fifteen miles. Albright returned home at the close of the war and was a respected citizen of the little valley the balance of his days.

Benjamin Bonsall, Sr., of Greenwood Township, served at Valley Forge with Washington during the dark days when they had little to wear and little to eat. Aged eighty-nine years, he died in 1845.

Thomas Brown, of Tyrone Township, patriot to the core, provided in his will for the reading of the Declaration of Independence over his open grave, after which the minister was to pray for him and his beloved country.

Andrew Burd, a fourteen-year-old boy from Greenwood Township, entered the army as a fifer and served seven years, being mustered out in time to get his first vote.

Edward Donelly, of Buckwheat Valley, was a member of the Colonial militia.

The Smiley family, of Carroll Township, had five members in the Revolution, as follows: Thomas Smiley, an ensign in Colonel Watts' battalion; John, George, William, and Samuel Smiley.

William Wallis, who was a resident of what is now Juniata Township, Perry County, served through the Revolution and received for pay a certificate of service, which he exchanged for a set of blacksmith tools later on.

David Focht, one of Perry County's first settlers, a resident of Jackson Township, was in the army.

Note.—According to information given to Mrs. Lelia Dromgold Emig, author of the Hench-Dromgold genealogy, a number of Revolutionary soldiers are interred in the following cemeteries: Loysville cemetery, John Hench, Michael Loy, John Hench II, and John Yohn; Donnally's Mills, Edward Donally and George Hench; cemetery on ridge near Elliottsburg, Frederick Shull; George Hench, Duncannon.

Benjamin Essick, of Liverpool Township, served in the militia and lived to be ninety-three.

Alexander Gaily, a resident of the Cove, Penn Township, served in the Revolution and lived until 1842, being then 102 years old.

Andrew Lynch, of Tuscarora Township, was in the service of his country during the Revolution.

*William Patterson, of Petersburg, Rye Township (Duncannon), was in the service a year, and in later years used to tell of "the tories" mustering on Young's Hill.

Frederick Watt, later general in the patriot army, whose biography appears elsewhere in this book, was wounded in the mouth at the Wyoming massacre, where he served with Colonel Zebulon Butler, who fought British, tory, and Indian forces of thrice his strength.

Englehart Wormley, one of the first settlers, was in the battle of Long Island. He died in 1827.

Greenwood Township also furnished John Buchanan, whose descendants long lived in the same vicinity; Robert Moody, William Rodgers, William Philips, and others.

The state pensioned disabled Revolutionary soldiers, and among the documents in the Bureau of Public Records at Harrisburg, is a deposition, No. 317, relating to Robert Pendergrass, a sergeant, pensioned April 12, 1821, at $48 per annum. The oath of Hugh Sweeny is executed before Jacob Fritz, a Perry County justice, which makes it practically certain that Sweeny was from Perry. Pendergrass was likely from Cumberland. Part of the deposition verifieth "that he (Sweeny) was well acquainted with Pendergrass, that he enlisted in Capt. John Hays' company, that they both marched from Carlisle on the sixth of April, 1776, on their way to Kenedy (Canada), that Pendergrass remained in the service four years, all of which time they were acquainted and part of the time messmates."

Capt. Jonathon Robison, of Sherman's Valley, was a son of George Robinson, and suffered much in the Indian wars. Although above fifty years of age he entered the Colonial Army. With his company he was in the battle of Princeton, being stationed there for some time to guard against the British and to act as scouts and intercept foraging parties.

Joseph Martin, a resident of what is now Howe Township, who became a captain in the Revolution, sold a house on the south bank of the Juniata, March 26, 1776, for fifty pounds, with which to purchase his horse and equipment for the army. After spending that bitter winter with Washington's army at Valley Forge, he was taken with camp fever, and started for home, but never arrived. Whether he perished in the wilderness or was captured and tortured to death by the British, as tradition says, will never be known.

*Silas Wright, in his History of Perry County, says: "The Tories mustered their troops during the Revolutionary War on Young's Hill," adjoining Duncannon. He probably based the statement upon that of one William Patterson. That fact, often quoted, seems legendary, as Duncannon (then known as Clark's Ferry) was not laid out in lots until 1792, and according to a reliable tradition, there were only eight houses from the cabins surrounding the old forge to Clark's Run as late as 1830. When the Revolution was taking place there evidently were very few houses there, and just where these Tories came from would be hard to determine. Furthermore, there are provincial records of all Tory movements and Tories and nothing like that appears in the annals of the province, while even the few British sympathizers within the territory are recorded as will be seen in the foregoing pages.

In the Loysville cemetery also rests Abraham Smith, a Revolutionary soldier, but from what territory is not known. John Ramsey, who resided in the county, was another. Valentine Ritter was in the Revolution from Berks County, and after the war located near Loysville.

Adam Smith, great-grandfather of the late John M. and Alvin Smith, of Newport, served in the Continental Army, but not from what is now Perry County.

Peter Kipp served with the Sixth Company of Second New York Artillery in the patriot army, his name appearing on the rolls until July 10, 1783. At the close of the war he settled in Buck's Valley, Buffalo Township, where he married Margaret Finton. He was a tailor and followed his trade, going from house to house, as was the custom. His brother Jacob, who enlisted in the same unit on the same day, was killed in the battle of the Brandywine.

George Hench, who had settled in Perry County before the Revolution, was a fifer in the army.

John Stewart, a Revolutionary soldier of Carlisle, settled in Perry County prior to 1800, and his descendants live in the county.

In the Millerstown cemetery, besides Benjamin Bonsall, who died in 1845, aged 89 years, are buried two other Revolutionary patriots. Ephraim Williams, a cabinetmaker, died August 15, 1843, aged 86 years, and Robert Porter (grandfather of the late T. P. Cochran), who was 86 at his death and said to have been an officer.

Francis DeLancey, located on a farm near Kistler, after serving in the Revolution under General Lafayette, with whom he came from France. He was first married to a French woman in New York, from whom are descended William and Oliver DeLancey, attorneys, whose father was Bishop DeLancey. Dr. C. E. DeLancey and brothers are his grandsons from the second marriage. He lived to be eighty-three.

David Mitchell, who first resided upon the farm from which the lands for the county seat of Perry County were taken, was in the Provincial Army under Forbes and Bouquet, as a subaltern officer, and served in the Revolution as a major in Colonel Frederick Watts' battalion. He was appointed by Governor McKean, in May, 1800, as brigadier general of the militia of Perry and Franklin Counties. He represented his county (then Cumberland) continuously in the legislature for twenty years, from 1786 to 1805, and was a presidential elector in 1813 and 1817. He was a son of John and Agnes Mitchell, and was born July 17, 1742, in what later became Cumberland County. He died May 25, 1818, on the Juniata, above Newport.

That the territory which later became Perry County did well in the way of furnishing men who then resided there or had previously been residents, as officers, is not a matter of question. By referring to the chapter in this book devoted to the Blaine family it will be noted that Ephraim Blaine,* once a resident of the vicinity of Blain, Perry County, was Commissary General of the Colonial Army and the associate of General George Washington. There appears the story of his wonderful saving of the Revolutionary army, which places him second only to Washington himself. Near the close of 1776 or the beginning of 1777, when battalions began

---

*In the Manuscript Division of the Congressional Library, Washington, there is a valuable collection of Letters of Col. Ephraim Blaine. (See page 629.)

to be designated by numerals, we find Col. Ephraim Blaine in charge of the First Battalion. His service must have been brief there as he is soon found to be filling the responsible post of Commissary General. The Second Battalion was commanded by Col. John Allison, described as "a justice of the peace of Tyrone Township, over the mountain, and a judge of the county, but after his retirement, for he was now past middle life." In 1778 we find the Fourth Battalion commanded by Colonel Jonathon Robison, "of Sherman's Valley." The battalion composed entirely of men "from north of the mountain," was commanded by Col. Frederick Watts, and another by Major David Mitchell.

While the Revolution was waged by the British government, yet it was largely a personal war of the German-speaking George III, who could not get enough of his own people interested to fight their own kinsmen, but had to fall back on hirelings—the Hessians —who fought for pay. Strangely enough, the histories in our public schools are not specific upon that fact, which is largely responsible for the feeling against Great Britain in America, although we dwell alongside of one of their great dependencies and not a single fort worthy of the name guards the four thousand-mile border on either side—unlike that of the old German monarchy, along whose borders frowned huge fortresses on every hand. The writer, however, holds no brief for the British Empire, neither has he any patience with those who would give that nation equal rights in the Panama Canal.

The Continental Congress, July 18, 1875, recommended that "all able-bodied, effective men between sixteen and fifty years of age should immediately form themselves into companies of militia, to consist of one captain, two lieutenants, one ensign, four sergeants, four corporals, one clerk, one drummer, one fifer, and about sixty-eight privates; the companies to be formed into regiments or battalions, officered with a colonel, lieutenant colonel, two majors, and an adjutant or quartermaster; all officers above the rank of captain to be appointed by the provincial authorities."

COLONEL FREDERICK WATTS' BATTALION.

Although occupation of the county territory was in its primary stage practically the whole of the Seventh Battalion of Cumberland County Militia, with Colonel Frederick Watts in command, was recruited here, and the battalion became a unit July 31, 1777, in the patriot army, although many of the men had been in the service at an earlier date. There is record of some of them as early as the beginning of 1776, and Colonel Watts was present at the surrender of Fort Washington, November 16, 1776. Early in 1776 there is record of the forwarding of an order for funds to cover the expense of forwarding his men to camp.

The Staff.—Colonel, Frederick Watts; Lieutenant Colonel, Samuel Ross; Major, David Mitchell; Adjutant, Thomas Bolan; Quartermaster, Albert Adam.

First Company.—Captain, James Fisher; First Lieutenant, Thomas Fisher; Second Lieutenant, Robert Scott; Ensign, Joseph Sharpe.

John Montgomery.	Patrick Cree.
James Baxter.	Hugh Evans.
Francis McGarvey.	Alexander Akins.
William Robertson.	George Brown.
Ross Mitchell.	Robert Boggs.
James Shields.	Thomas Williams.
Samuel Hutchinson.	John Campbell.
James Gaudy.	James Rhea.
Benjamin Chambers.	Robert Purdy.
James Edmondstone.	Isaac Somers.
James Roddy.	Robert Walker.
James Menoch.	Robert Chew.
Edward Nicholson.	Robert Heatly.
Thomas McIntire.	James Ardery.
William Ferguson.	John Piper.
John Black.	George Biddle.
Mathias Sweezy.	

The rank and file of this company is named as fifty-eight, yet the above-named is a copy of the roll of July, 1777, as printed in the State Archives.

Second Company.—Captain, James Power; First Lieutenant, David Marshall; Second Lieutenant, Samuel Shaw; Ensign, John Kirkpatrick.

David Carson.	John Hunter.
Andrew Shaw.	Thomas McKee.
James Smith.	William McCoy.
William Elliott.	John McCoy.
William McConnell.	George McLeve.
John Crawford.	David Baird.
Samuel Byars.	David McClintock.
Archibald Kinkead.	Samuel Glass.
Andrew Everhart.	James White.
Robert Creigh.	Robert Johnstone.
James Horn.	John Phillips.
John McNaughton.	Benjamin Hillhouse.
Alexander Fullerton.	Patrick Killian.
Daniel Mulhollin.	Richard Taylor.
James Barker.	William Smiley.

The number of this company is named as sixty-seven, yet the above names are all that appear in the State Archives, as of September, 1777.

Third Company.—Captain, William Sanderson; First Lieutenant, George Black; Second Lieutenant, John Simonton; Ensign, Archibald Loudon.

William Murray.	David McClure.
George Dixson.	George Brown.
George Wallace.	Thomas Adams.
Michael Kirkpatrick.	David Hartnis.
Thomas McTee.	Samuel Galbreath.
Robert McKebe.	William Carns.
William Miller.	James Gaily.
William Chain.	John Sedgwick.
John Sanderson.	Robert McCabe.
John McLean.	William Gardner, Jr.
John McCown.	John Neeper.
David Miller.	Alexander McCaskey.
Thomas Noble.	Thomas Hamilton.

Thomas Smiley.
John Devlin.
Hance Ferguson.

John Ewing.
James Maxwell.

The total enrollment of this company is named as forty-six, but the above are the only names on the State Archives list of October, 1777.

Fourth Company.—Captain, William Blain; First Lieutenant, James Blain; Second Lieutenant, William Murray; Ensign, Allen Nesbit.

James Cameron.
Michael Marshal.
John McCallaster.
John Ardery.
John Baker.
Joseph Childers.
Charles McCarty.
William Galbreath.
Robert Boyd.
Robert McClurg.
James Findley.
John Douglass.

Hugh Gormly.
John Marshall.
William McClintock.
James McClure.
John Smith.
William Brown.
Robert Galbreath.
Abram Johnston.
John McBride.
David Martin.
William Cunningham.
John Taylor.

The above is the list as recorded in the Pennsylvania Archives for October, 1777, although the number is quoted in some records as fifty-one.

Fifth Company.—Captain, Frederick Taylor; First Lieutenant, Daniel Hart; Second Lieutenant, Matthew McCoy; Ensign, Thomas Watson.

Hans Kilgees.
Edward O'Donald.
Pattrick Grant.
Robert McClintog.
James Wymer.
Matthew Merrot.
Richard Morrow.
William Watson.
Hugh Miller.
Clifton Bowen.
Richard Stewart.
Robert Huev.
William Williams.
Daniel Graham.
Hugh Gibson.
Joseph Nelson.
Andrew Kinkead.

William Spottwood.
Thomas Shedswick.
Andrew Linch.
Robert Irwin.
Hugh McCraghan.
James Miller.
Thomas Purdy, Jr.
William Taylor.
James Maxwell.
William Martin.
Andrew Irwin.
John Faddon.
Samuel Glass.
Robert Adams.
William Neeper.
William Adams.
John Gardener.

Evidently the clerk of this company erred in spelling proper names; O'Donald is likely O'Donnel; McClintog, McClintock; Wymer, Weimer; Shedswick, Sedgwick; Linch, Lynch; McCraghan, McCracken; Faddon, McFadden, and Gardener, Gardner.

Sixth Company.—Captain, Edward Graham; First Lieutenant. Samuel Adair; Second Lieutenant, Samuel Whittaker; Ensign, George Smiley.

William Cree.
William Lewis.
Francis McQuoan.
John Coulter.
Thomas Boyd.
Matthew White.
Hugh Law.
William McKee.
James Kerr.
Thomas Barnet.
Robert Dawson.
Samuel Ewing.

John Jamison.
Henry Heatly.
Alexander Brown.
John Kellem.
James Nelson.
Thomas Shaw.
Samuel Raynev.
Joseph Gormely.
John Marshall.
Michael Marshal.
William Carson.
William Blaine.

Hugh McClintock.
John Rea, Jr.
John Elliott.
John Smylie.
Alexander Gaely.
Moses Hays.

Edward West.
Henry Glass.
Alexander McCoy.
James Thompson.
John Nelson.
John Nelson, Jr.

In January, 1778, according to the Pennsylvania Archives, the enrollment was as above, yet it is quoted at some places as seventy-eight.

Seventh Company.—Captain, John Buchanan; First Lieutenant, William Nelson; Second Lieutenant, James Ewing; Ensign, Benjamin Junkin.

Samuel McClelland.
Daniel Stuard.
James Hodkins.
John Riddle.
Matthew Kerr.
John Miller.
James Hamilton.
Samuel Ncesbit.
John Cowburn.
William Shehan.
Joseph Kirkpatrick.
John Smith.
David McKee.
Henry Kelly.
Alexander Kelly.
John Ross.
George Logan.
John Cord.
James Byard.

Samuel Fisher.
Robert Graham.
John Camble.
Daniel Marrit.
Thomas Elliott.
Patrick Kain.
Alexander Murray, Esq.
William Erwin.
Henry Savage.
Moses Kirkpatrick.
Peter Patterson.
William McKee.
Archibald Marrin.
Robert Cumins.
Thomas Willson.
John Kinkead.
Adrew Kinkead.
Robert Neelson.

The State Archives contained the above list only, yet the roster is quoted at some places as containing fifty-five names.

Eighth Company.—Captain, Thomas Clark; First Lieutenant, Joseph Neeper; Second Lieutenant, William Hunter; Ensign, James Fergus.

James Officer.
George Morrah.
Robert Wiley.
Samuel Barnhill.
James Carson.
John McKebe.
William Kerr.
Henry Skivington.
Robert Murray.
John McCurry.
Joseph Kilpatrick.
William Murphy.
Matthew McBride.
Michael Walters.
John Wright.
William McKebe.
William Logan.
Thomas Townsley.

George Douglas.
John Cree.
Robert Holliday.
John Mitchell.
Joseph Patten.
Joseph Shields.
Matthew Morrison.
Michael Baskings.
Alexander Maxwell.
George Miller.
Richard Stuard.
John White.
Andrew McKee.
James McKebe.
Thomas McIntire.
Joseph Sharp.
John McClintoch.

CHAPTER X.

PERRY COUNTY TERRITORY IN THE WAR OF 1812.

JUST what part the lands which now comprise Perry County played in the War of 1812, or more properly, the Second War with Great Britain, is of interest. Not only did it furnish many men, but across it ran the nearest route to Niagara, whence sped United States government couriers from the National Capital to the frontier. Coming from Washington, the route lay through Sterrett's Gap, via the site of New Bloomfield and over Middle Ridge, to Rider's Ferry, thence across the Juniata. There was then no valley road from Bloomfield to Newport as at present, for there was no Bloomfield and no Newport at that time. One of the relay places, where horses were exchanged, was at Sterrett's Gap. Whether there was another before Middle Ridge it is not possible to say. On the top of Middle Ridge (now in Juniata Township), three-fourths of a mile south of Milford, on the Carlisle-Sunbury road, stood the White Ball Tavern, then kept by Philip Clouser. There horses were again exchanged. Just at the foot of Middle Ridge, on the same road, located on the north bank of the Little Buffalo Creek, John Koch (Kough) kept the Blue Ball Tavern, and as the courier would pass his place a horn signaled the White Ball Tavern (Clouser's) at the top of the ridge, so that on the arrival of the courier there the steed would be in waiting, and scarcely a minute consumed in resuming the journey. There were no telegraph or telephone lines in those days, and that was the only available method of sending dispatches. It is remarkable how quickly the journey was made by the frequent change of horses and the occasional relief of messengers.

This war was occasioned largely by the British policy of searching American vessels and impressing seamen, on the subterfuge that they were British subjects. Anticipating the war, President Madison had called the American Congress a month earlier, in 1811, and it authorized a call for 100,000 volunteers, the quota of Pennsylvania being 14,000. Governor Simon Snyder issued a call for that number of troops on May 12, 1812. Three times the number responded. The Perry County companies which responded were not assigned until 1814. The United States declared war June 18, 1812. Early that year Governor Simon Snyder called for a force of one thousand militia to help repel the British invasion of the northern frontier. Cumberland County (to which Perry then belonged) raised over half that number, a large part of whom came from the lands which now constitute Perry, and all of whom were volunteers. The others came from Franklin, York, and Adams, being drafted men, principally. These soldiers constituted the Eleventh Regiment, or Division, under the command of General Porter. They were in immediate command of Colonel James Fenton, Lieut. Colonel Robert Bull, and Majors Galloway and Marlin. Lieutenant Colonel Bull was from what is now Tuscarora Township, Perry County, his father having been Henry Bull, who built the first grist mill in Raccoon Valley, now known as the Donnally Mill, being owned by L. E. Donnally, a former member of the General Assembly. They were mustered in at Carlisle, marched to Pittsburgh, and from there to Black Rock Fort—now the site of the city of Buffalo, New York—which they reached about April 1.

This expedition consisted of two brigades. They embarked July 2. The first landed about a mile below Fort Erie and the second about a mile above. A battery of "long sixteens" was soon placed in position and under a flag of truce the fort was given two hours to capitulate. When the time expired 137 men, including the officers, marched out and surrendered. At three o'clock, on the 5th, delay having been occasioned by getting supplies of food, the army of 3,500 men marched against the enemy's army. Indians had annoyed the pickets by firing upon them from concealed points. Volunteers were called for and three hundred from the Eleventh Regiment responded, among them officers who exchanged their swords for guns. This was the beginning of the Battle of Chippewa, in which Colonel Bull, the brave Perry Countian, figured. Every man who went with General Porter was ordered to leave his hat behind and go with head uncovered. The Indians tied up their heads in muslin and blackened their faces with burned wood. In less than an hour General Bull, Major Galloway and Captain White, with a number of private soldiers, were surrounded by the redskins, who had concealed themselves in high grass and permitted the main body to pass, so that they might secure the officers. They were made to disrobe and their clothing divided. Major Galloway and Private Wendt were stripped of their boots and compelled to march through thorn and stubble "until their feet were pierced through and through," as Wendt afterwards said. Silas Wright, in his History of Perry County (1873), further describes the event:

"The party had advanced their prisoners but a short distance until they were halted, and there was evidently an Indian dissatisfied about something. They started again and had scarcely gone more than half a mile when the dissatisfied Indian, then in the rear, whooped loudly, raised his rifle and shot Colonel Bull through the body. The ball entered the left shoulder and come out through the right breast. After he was pierced by the bullet, Colonel Bull raised himself on his elbow, reached out his hand to Major Galloway, and said, "Help me, Wendt, I am shot." The help implored by the dying man was prevented by the Indian who had shot him, coming up, sinking his tomahawk into his head and scalping him. This act, so contrary to all laws of human warfare, was no doubt in compliance with the order of General Riall, which was in substance, not to spare any who wore the uniform of militia officers, while those who wore the regular officers' uniform were to be brought into camp in safety. To this fact we ascribe the fate of a brave soldier and a good officer." Colonel Bull was a religious man and during his service was often among the sick, encouraging and helping them. His age at the time was thirty-five years.

Those from within the confines of what is now Perry County who served there, are as follows:

CAPTAIN JAMES PIPER'S COMPANY.

Privates:

Michael Donally, Tuscarora.
Jacob Hammaker, Watts.
Daniel Fry, Greenwood.
Abraham Fry, Greenwood.
Joseph Fry, Greenwood.
George Wendt, Liverpool T.
Frederick Burd, Greenwood.
John Staily, Liverpool.
Jacob Potter, Buffalo.
Jacob Liddick, Buffalo.
Peter Werner, Buffalo.
Andrew Hench, Buffalo.
Joseph Fry was killed by the Indians at Chippewa, July 5th.

CAPTAIN DAVID MORELAND'S COMPANY.

David Moreland, Capt., Jackson.
Robert Thompson.
John Neiper.
Amos Cadwallader.
John Kibler, Landisburg.
John Steigleman.
Richard Rodger.
George Strock.
James Adams.
John Abercrombie.
Sebastian Waggoner.
James Rodgers.
David Beems.
John Myers.

Privates:

Barkley, William, Saville.
Bower, Jacob, Saville.
Comp, ——, Centre.
Dissinger, George, Tyrone.
Dissinger, ——, Tyrone.
Evinger, Peter, Jackson.
Gutshall, George, Jackson.
Gutshall, Jacob, Toboyne.
Garland, John, Madison.
Goodlander, John, Madison.
Hockenberry, Jos., Toboyne.
Jacobs, John, Saville.
Johnston, William, Toboyne.

Kiner, Jacob, Tyrone.
Kessler, Peter, Toboyne.
Kessler, David, Toboyne.
Kessler, Adam, Tohoyne.
Mealy, Dr. Samuel, Millerstown.
Otto, Peter, Toboyne.
Ruggles, Moses, Madison.
Robinson, George, Saville.
Ross, Samuel, Tyrone.
Strock, George, Saville.
Strock, Joseph, Saville.
Stump, William, Toboyne.
Schreffler, John, Toboyne.
Schreffler, George, Toboyne.
Stambaugh, Philip, Tyrone.
Sheafer, Jacob, Tyrone.
Sheafer, Wm., Tyrone.
Swanger, Peter, Tyrone.
Stroup, ——, Madison.
Scott, ——, Liverpool.
Sponenberger, ——, Liverpool.
Stewart, Richard, Tyrone.
Topley, John, Landisburg.
Weaver, Michael, Toboyne.
Wolfe, Adam, Tyrone.
Wolfe, George, Tyrone.
Wilson, Joseph, Tyrone.
Welch, Robert, Tyrone.

The following additional names are found on a muster roll, made out September 22, 1814:

Askins, William.
Bergstresser, George.
Bower, Jacob.
Bergstresser, Solomon.
Bice, Samuel.
Bower, Peter.
Buck, George.
Dougherty, Robert.
Deckard, Philip.
Dunbar, Robert.
Dansville, Thomas.
Ewens, Moses.
Fry, Daniel.
Fry, Joseph (killed July 5th).
Fry, Abraham.
Gillam, Jacob.
Gurhard, Isaac.
Gallagher, John.
Hollenbaugh, Henry.
Hoobler, John.
Hollenbaugh, Mathias.
Hays, Robert.
Hammaker, Joseph.
Hamilton, John.
Hockenberry, Joseph.
Irwin, George.
Jordan, David.
Kennedy, Archibald.
Kelsey, George.
Kenny, Jacob.
Ledech, Jacob (Liddick).
Mores, John.

Buck, Robert.
Burd, Frederick.
Byers, Joshua.
Baughman, John.
Comp, Daniel.
Kiner, Jacob.
Clark, Thomas.
McMurray, Ezekiel.
McCoy, Thomas.
Morton, James.
Miller, William.
Neeper, James.
Potter, Jacob.
Presser, Henry.
Gray, George.
Rogers, Robert.
Ross, Henry.
Shaw, George.
Sleighter, John.
Shumbaugh, George.
Sheets, Samuel.
Stambaugh, Jacob.
Tate, William.
Taylor, Joseph.
Wilson, Joseph.
Wendt, George (taken prisoner July 5th).
Wilson, Samuel.
Wallace, William.
Young, Abraham.
Rouse, Godfrey.
Shreffler, John.

That these men were in action and at the front is proven by the notations as to Joseph Fry being killed and George Wendt captured. The company was also in the field at the date of the roster.

When Washington had been burned by the British and the news reached Landisburg, Dr. John D. Creigh enrolled an entire company in the short space of two days. It was known as the Landisburg Infantry and completed its organization on September 6, 1814. It was at once accepted by Governor Snyder and assigned to the second post of honor in the Pennsylvania line. Upon October 2 it was encamped on Bush Hill, near Washington. The roster:

CAPTAIN JOHN CREIGH'S COMPANY.

John Creigh, Capt., Tyrone.
Henry Lightner, Landisburg.
Thompson, ——, Jackson.
Carl, Isaiah, Tyrone.
Neeper, ——, Tyrone.
Lackey, Henry.
Cadwallader, Amos, Tyrone.

Privates:

Bollinger, Daniel, Millerstown.
Curry, John.

Carl, David, Tyrone.
Dunbar, George.
Dunbar, John.
Dunkelberger, Benj., Tyrone.
Ernest, Jacob, Landisburg.
Foose, Michael,
Frederick, Jacob.
Fullerton, Joseph.
Gibson, Francis, Landisburg.
Henderson, Wm., Tyrone.
Hipple, John.

Holman, Conrad.
Ickes, Samuel.
Jones, Nathan, Landisburg.
Jones, Samuel, Landisburg.
Johnson, John, Saville.
Jennings, Israel, Millerstown.
Keck, Stephen.
Lightner, Jacob, Landisburg.
Landis, John, Landisburg.
Landis, Samuel, Landisburg.
Lynch, ———.
Mahoney, John, Landisburg.
M'Cracken, Benj., Tyrone.
Marsh, Joseph, Tyrone.

Power, John, Tyrone.
Roddy, Alex., Tyrone.
Stambaugh, Daniel, Tyrone.
Smith, Philip, Tyrone.
Sheibley, Barnett, Tyrone.
Sheibley, Solomon.
Sheer, ———.
Swarner, George.
Simons, George, S., Tyrone.
West, George, Tyrone.
Wilson, William, Tyrone.
Whitmer, Barney, Tyrone.
Zeigler, ———.

John Gabel, of Howe Township, also served in this war, but with what unit is unknown.

Michael Donnally, of what is now Tuscarora Township, was one of the men who volunteered to go aboard Commodore Perry's fleet, then operating on Lake Erie, expecting to stay a few days at the utmost, but just four weeks elapsed before he got back to his company.

Perry Countians and residents of the Juniata Valley have reason to be proud of their record in this war. Although the British never set foot on Pennsylvania soil, the state at one time had more men in the field than any other, as well as having paid a larger share of the expense. On the pretext that they were not obliged to leave their own state, General Van Rensselaer, of New York, refused to cross the line into Canada. General Tannehill, with a brigade of two thousand Pennsylvanians, including local men, welcomed the chance and promptly crossed into the enemy's country.

CHAPTER XI.

THE PROVINCE AND "MOTHER CUMBERLAND."

A HISTORY of Perry County would be incomplete without reference to the founder of the province, the province itself, and to Cumberland County—Mother Cumberland—during the sixty-six years when Perry County soil was an integral part of its domain, before attaining countyhood in its own right. William Penn, the proprietor, has left his impress upon the land and its people, never to be effaced. He was born in London, England, October 16, 1644, being a son of Sir William Penn, an admiral in the English Navy, and Margaret Jasper Penn, daughter of a Rotterdam merchant. He was educated at Christ Church, Oxford, where, on hearing Thomas Loe, an eminent Quaker, he thought well of his principles, and a few years later publicly professed them. In consequence of this action he was twice turned out by his father. In 1668 he began preaching and writing on the principles of the Quakers. For this he was twice imprisoned and once brought to trial.

In 1680 Penn petitioned Charles II for a grant of land in America, the Crown being in the debt of his father to the extent of some sixteen thousand pounds. On March 4, 1681, the great seal was affixed to the document which gave to him a grant in America—practically the Pennsylvania of to-day, which the king named in honor of his father. It gave to Penn almost unlimited powers, the exceptions being the levying of taxes and the vetoing of legislation. Here he founded a province where men might worship God according to the dictates of their individual conscience. Until 1776 Penn and his heirs were the feudal lords of the land, with an exception of two years under William III. Penn died in England in 1718. The provincial history is largely of the pioneers and the Indians, the part of which relates to Perry County territory appearing in the early chapters in this book devoted to the Indians.

Prior to the establishment of the Constitution of 1790 Pennsylvania had various methods of government. The Dutch began to rule in 1609 and continued until 1638; the Dutch and Swedish rule covered the period from 1638 to 1655, when the Dutch authority again became absolute and lasted until 1664. The chief executive was then known as Vice Director. The conflict between the English and the Dutch led to the establishment of English rule from 1664 to 1673, when the Dutch Deputy Governor reëstablished the rule of his race. The English, in turn, regained their

sioned one or more of them for seven years. They held the courts.
Two persons were to be voted for for sheriff and the Council was
to commission one. The county commissioners and assessors of
taxes were to be elected by the people, thus embodying in the State
Constitution the principles which brought on the revolution, the
right of the people to tax themselves.

This early province is now the great Commonwealth of Pennsylvania, with its sixty-seven subdivisions known as counties. It is
one hundred and seventy-six miles in width from the New York
State line to Maryland, and three hundred and three miles in
length from Ohio to New Jersey. It contains 45,215 square miles
of territory and is almost as large as England and Wales combined; it is one-third larger than Ireland and larger than Holland,
Denmark, and Belgium combined. It is the only one of the thirteen original states having no coast line along the Atlantic Ocean.
Of the thirteen it has exerted greater influence upon the nation
than any other, and its history has been more interesting. The
Maryland and Virginia claims to a part of the Pennsylvania domain
in the south and west and the claims of Connecticut in the Wyoming Valley, and the various Indian troubles and wars, were some
of the early difficulties of the province. The pioneers and later
settlers, unlike many of the other colonies and provinces, were not
a single people but those of many nationalities. Here were to be
found the types and sects of more religious beliefs than anywhere
else, and that is largely true to this day. Here were the beginnings
of popular government by the people. Here transportation first
developed and manufacturing started. On Pennsylvania soil were
fought battles which helped in *making* the Union and the greatest
battle in helping *preserve* the Union. Within its borders liberty
was proclaimed and that great compact between the states—the
Constitution, was adopted. No other state in the Union has been
so typical of world progress. It is second in population, while in
land area it stands thirty-second.

Pennsylvania originally had but three counties. When William
Penn first visited the province in 1682—his visit covering almost
two years—he laid out three counties, Philadelphia, Bucks, and
Chester, whose boundaries were not clearly defined, but Chester
had charge of the legality of everything as far west as settlements
were then made. While there were no settlements at that time in
what is now Perry County, had such been the case it would have
been necessary to journey to West Chester to have legal action.
These original counties had seals, adopted by the provincial legislature. That of Philadelphia was an anchor, of Bucks a tree, and
of Chester a plough.

The settlements of the colonists were pushing farther and farther into the wilderness, as immigrants came in from across the

seas, and the necessity of having official and legal advantages closer
at hand in order to avoid far journeys to the courts caused the
citizens to petition for the erection of a new county out of the
"upper part of Chester." The petition was granted and by an act
of the Provincial Assembly, May 10, 1729, Lancaster County became the fourth county of the present great commonwealth, then
in embryo. It extended westward as far as the province. From
that date any legal matters from what is now the territory comprising Perry County would necessarily have been adjusted at Lancaster, the county seat of Lancaster County. But the territory
was uninhabited.

The continual westward trend, which has practically continued
to this day, with the attending desire for local courts, caused the
residents west of the Susquehanna to petition for the formation
of separate counties, and in 1749 York County, including the present county of Adams—it being the fifth county and formerly a
part of Lancaster—was laid out. Cumberland, a year later—1750
—was the sixth county created. Thus the nearest county seat to
the territory comprising Perry County, was that of Chester, then
that of Lancaster, and later that of Cumberland. It became a part
of Cumberland in 1754, where it was destined to remain for sixty-
six years, or until 1820, when it "came into its own."

In presenting a petition to the Provincial Assembly representations were made by the inhabitants of the "North Valley," as the
territory was then known, who resided west of the Susquehanna
River, that "owing to the great hardships they laid under, of being
very remote from Lancaster, where the courts were held—some
of them one hundred miles distant—and the public offices kept,"
etc., a new county was to be desired. The act of January 27,
1750, creating Cumberland County, gave the boundaries as follows:

"That, all and singular lands lying within the Province of Pennsylvania,
to the westward of Susquehanna, and northward and westward of the
county of York, be erected into a county, to be called Cumberland;
bounded northward and westward with the line of the province, eastward
partly with the river Susquehanna, and partly with said county of York;
and southward in part by the line dividing said province from that of
Maryland."

Literally that would have included all of Perry and of Pennsylvania to its northern border, but the lands north of the Kittatinny
or Blue Mountain had not then yet been purchased from the Indians. Consequently no townships were designated in the old records as lying north of the mountains, until after the Albany purchase of 1754. Neither were any justices appointed in or for
that territory. Notwithstanding that fact the author of the bill
creating Cumberland County used poor judgment, in including
within its borders, lands which were not yet purchased from the

Indians, and there is little wonder that squatters went into the territory and located claims. Mention of a number of these squatters occur throughout this book, and among the names are the forefathers of many present day inhabitants. Information was not disseminated nearly so easily in provincial days and it is unfair to charge these squatters with disobeying the laws, when they probably inferred from the language creating Cumberland County that it meant just what it said, which was not the case.

This wonderful domain, when taken literally, included all of Pennsylvania lying west of the Susquehanna River, except York County. From it all the counties west of the Susquehanna have been carved, either directly or indirectly, Perry being the last to attain separation.

Cumberland County was named after a maratime county of England, on the borders of Scotland. When the Scotch-Irish began settling the Cumberland Valley at first the Six Nations still inhabited it. This was about 1730 or 1731. When Cumberland County was organized it had but 807 taxable citizens.

The first Cumberland County courts, after the county's establishment in 1750, were held at Shippensburg, but were transferred to Carlisle in 1751, when the town was laid out. In those days the session of Orphans' Court were sometimes held in the various districts, and there is at least one reference to it being held on the north side of the Kittatinny or Blue Mountain while the lands yet belonged to Cumberland. The records state that it was held "at William Anderson's," which location was at what is now Andersonburg.

Carlisle, the new county seat, early became an educational centre, which it is to this day. Dickinson College opened in 1783, and in 1833 came under the influence of the Methodist Church.

While Perry was yet a part of Cumberland "the Father of His Country," President George Washington, visited Carlisle. Incidentally, that title—the Father of His Country—was first applied to him in Baer's Almanac, published at Lancaster, Pennsylvania. It was quickly adopted by the public press and will be used as long as time lasts. It was but fit and proper that that appropriate title should be first applied to him by a Pennsylvanian, for while he was born in Virginia and died in Virginia, yet he spent the greater number of his mature years in Pennsylvania. No less a historian than Ex-Governor Pennypacker is responsible for the latter statement.

In 1787, in a list of field officers selected to command the militia of Cumberland County, is the following: Toboyne, Tyrone, and Rie (Rye)—Lieutenant Colonel, John Davidson; Major, Michael Marshall.

In 1795 the Senate of Pennsylvania voted to make Carlisle the State Capital, but the House refused to concur.

During the period immediately prior to the Revolution, during that war and afterwards, while Perry County was yet a part of Cumberland, its residents had great reason to admire a fellow citizen who was a noted lawyer, a statesman and a patriot who was one of the signers of the Declaration of Independence, that great document which has given civilization everywhere a new impetus. James Wilson was born in 1742 and was foremost in all matters pertaining to the province, later to the colony, and still later to the state. His influence upon the Constitution of the United States—second only to that of the Declaration of Independence—was probably greater than that of any other member of the convention. Largely to his addresses, efforts and public articles was due the ratification of the Constitution by Pennsylvania. In 1791 he established the first law school in America in connection with the University of Pennsylvania. In 1789 President Washington appointed him a justice of the United States Supreme Court.

It was from Cumberland County, remembering that Perry County was an integral part at that time, that "Molly Pitcher" went forth to the army and the battle of Monmouth, from whence has come her fame. Her maiden name was Ludwig, and she was wed to a man named Hays. At that time a number of wives of soldiers were allowed to accompany the army on errands of mercy —to care for the wounded. They were the forerunners of the Red Cross nurses of our time. Mrs. Hays was one of these women and was carrying water to the soldiers when she saw her husband fall at the battle of Monmouth. She immediately took his place and fought courageously until the close of the battle, and her name, "Molly Pitcher," came by reason of her carrying water for the soldiers. She later married again, but it is as "Molly Pitcher" that her name will descend for all time as one of the heroines of that great conflict.

During the first thirty-two years that Perry County territory was a part of Cumberland County there stood in Carlisle a pillory, a whipping post and stocks, where offenders paid the penalty for crime. The Act of 1786 did away with that form of punishment. A considerable crime of that day was larceny, and the law provided that for the first offense of that nature the person so convicted should be publicly whipped on his bare back, with stripes well laid on to the number of twenty-one. Later offenses carried a larger number. Murder, arson, burglary, robbery and witchcraft were punishable by death. After 1785 the public whippings ceased, but records show that 150 persons were so punished. Of these seventeen were in addition sentenced to stand in the pillory for one hour, and six of them had both ears cut off and nailed to the pillory. These latter were convicted of horse stealing and passing counterfeit money.

From 1779 to 1787, in Cumberland County, eleven men and women were sentenced to be hanged, three for murder, three for robbery, two for burglary, two for counterfeiting, one for rape, one for arson, and one for an unmentionable crime. The early judges were laymen and were known as justices of the peace. According to a statute three were required to preside at trials. The Act of April 3, 1791, provided for a president judge, learned in the law. The old guardhouse, near one of the entrance gates of the Carlisle Indian School, now again a military post, was built by Hessian soldiers, captured by General Washington's army at the battle of Trenton, and sent to Carlisle as prisoners of war.

A signer of the famous document known as the Declaration for the Colony of Pennsylvania was John Creigh, one of the nine representatives. Creigh was the father of Dr. Creigh, long a physician at Landisburg, and the grandfather of Rev. Dr. Thomas Creigh, born in Landisburg, a noted divine. Of German origin, transplanted to Ireland, he came to this country in 1761. He was a lieutenant colonel of the Continental Army and a member of the Provincial Conference which met in Carpenter's Hall in June, 1776. In February, 1778, directed by Congress, he administered the oath to six hundred and forty-two citizens of Carlisle and vicinity. He died February 17, 1813.

At the last election for Governor of Pennsylvania while Perry was yet attached to Cumberland, in 1817, William Findlay was nominated by the (then) Republicans, and General Joseph Heister, by the disaffected branch of the party known as "The Old School" and the Federalists. Findlay was elected and was the governor who signed the act creating the new county of Perry, but at the following election for governor, in 1820, General Heister was elected as his successor.

Even during the term of George Washington as first President of the United States insurrection broke out—and in our own favored Pennsylvania. Historians term it "the Whiskey Insurrection" of 1794. The farmers, and especially of western Pennsylvania, distilled whiskey in large quantities, that being their principal source of revenue. When the United States passed an act laying an excise on liquor the measure was very unpopular in that section, and although a people of a generally peaceful disposition, they resisted the law. Perry County's territory, as stated, was still a part of Cumberland, and Carlisle was its county seat. Troops were raised at once to stand by the government and force submission of the insurrectionists. This was the occasion of President Washington's visit to Carlisle, where he reviewed four thousand men under arms, many of them from north of the Kittatinny or Blue Mountain.

Among these troops was the young attorney, David Watts, son of General Frederick Watts, born in Wheatfield Township, and the first lad from Perry County territory to secure a college education, who joined the troops as a private. Alive to the danger of any refusal to support the government and resolute in his opposition to the "whiskey boys," who planted a "liberty pole" near Carlisle, he shouldered an axe and alone, unaided and unarmed, rode to the spot where it stood and felled it to the ground, although there was a public threat to shoot any one who offered to disturb it. Whether the planting of this "liberty pole" of 1794 was the forerunner of the "personal liberty" party of the beginning of the Twentieth Century the reader must be left to conjecture. Another member of the Cumberland militia company, the Carlisle Infantry, who helped quell the insurrection was Francis Gibson, eldest son of George Gibson, who died at Gibson's Mill in 1856.

As the territory now comprising Perry County was yet a part of Cumberland during the agitation attending the adpotion of the Constitution of the United States the following episode from Rupp's History will be of interest to the reader:

"In December, 1787, a fracas occurred between the Constitutionalists and Anti-Constitutionalists. A number of citizens from the county assembled on the 26th (at Carlisle), to express, in their way, aided by the firing of cannons, their feelings on the actions of the convention that had assembled to frame the Constitution of the United States, when they were assaulted by an adverse party; after dealing out blows they dispersed. On Thursday, the 27th, those who had assembled the day before met again at the courthouse, well armed with guns and muskets. They, however, proceeded without molestation, except that those who had opposed them also assembled, kindled a bonfire and burned several effigies. For that temerity several, styled as rioters, were arrested and snugly lodged in jail. They were subsequently, on a compromise between the Federalists and Democrats, liberated. The Federalists were the Constitutionalists."

While Perry was a part of Cumberland, Jacob Alter was elected to the Pennsylvania Legislature twenty-one consecutive times upon the Whig ticket. His only sister became the wife of Governor Joseph Ritner, of Pennsylvania. Cashier James T. Alter and D. Boyd Alter, of the First National Bank of New Bloomfield, are of the third generation of this noted family. William Anderson, who resided at Andersonburg, also represented Cumberland in the legislature.

Among others located north of the Kittatinny or Blue Mountains who represented Cumberland County in the legislature before Perry County was formed was David Mitchell, who served for more than twenty years. (See chapter on Revolutionary War.) He resided first on the Barnett farm at New Bloomfield, but sold it to Thomas Barnett and removed, first to Raccoon Valley, but soon to the well-known Mitchell place, in the Juniata, north of Newport, in Oliver Township. His father was Colonel John Mitchell, commander of the Cumberland County Militia, whose remains lie in the Poplar Hill graveyard, on the McKee farm, west of New Bloomfield. An interesting document, the text of which is here reproduced, refers to soldiers from north of the mountain, as well as south, all of which was then Cumberland County. It is in connection with the military career of the elder Mitchell, who came to America from Ireland, because while enraged at a member of parliament who voted against an issue to which he was pledged, struck him, which either meant banishment or death. It follows:

"In Council, September 2, 1780.

"*Sir:* His excellency, the President of the State, having received orders from General Washington to dismiss the militia for the present, but to hold themselves in readiness to march at an hour's warning; we hereby direct you to discharge the Cumberland Militia now under your command at Lancaster on the conditions above expressed. At the same time expressing our warmest acknowledgments of the readiness with which your militia have turned out on this occasion and make no doubt, but on every future call, they will manifest the like zeal in the cause of the country.

"Your Most Honorable Servant,

"WILLIAM MOORE, *Vice-President.*

"To Colonel John Mitchell, Commanding the Cumberland Militia at Lancaster."

Robert Mitchell, of the third generation, being a son of David, was one of the first board of county commissioners of Perry County, and was interviewed by Prof. Silas Wright, the historian, in 1872, from which interview we quote:

"I am now in my ninetieth year; was one of the first board of county commissioners of Perry County; have lived on this place since I was three years old. I remember when the deer were so plenty that, from September to January, thirty-seven were driven into the Juniata River below the rope ferry."

Cumberland County, its people and its traditions, more than any other in the state, resembles the original counties of Bucks, Philadelphia, and Chester, formed by William Penn, along the Delaware. Just as that section was the nucleus of the millions east of the Susquehanna, so was Cumberland the nucleus of that vast population west of the Susquehanna, occupying a far greater territory. Just as that section takes pride in its traditions, its institutions and its ancestry, so does Cumberland. And why not? With its institutions, dating back almost to the time of Penn; its traditions and its location, as the very outpost of civilization for decades, and again at the very borderland of sectional strife, its importance historically is self-evident.

Inextricably intertwined with the history and development of the province and of old Mother Cumberland is the series of warrants, patents, sales and land grants of this then frontier of civilization. In a volume the size of this it has been impossible to give any great number of them, yet, in the history of each township, some of the more important are recorded. While squatters or intruders had presumed to settle within the borders of the county, as now constituted, and had been dispossessed and in some cases their cabins burned, yet there is evidence that a considerable number again went in before the opening of the land office on February 3, 1755. The purchase of 1754, consummated on July 6, had likely no sooner been proposed than the lure of the land, like a magnet, drew the hardy pioneer across the Kittatinny Mountain for a choice parcel which his eyes had previously feasted upon. The fact that claims of that very first day mention the names of others as "adjoining them" is in itself evidence that entry had already been made. As an example, take the very property on which the county seat is located. According to an affidavit of James Mitchell, taken before David Redich, prothonotary of Washington County, Pennsylvania, October 19, 1801, and read before the Board of Property, which met at Lancaster:

"In September, 1753, William Stewart, father of John (party to the suit), made an improvement, which was the first made in that part of the county, on a tract of land now lying in Cumberland County, bounded as follows: Beginning at the mouth of Stewart's branch of Little Juniata (Creek); then northerly, to a gap in the Mahanoi Mountain, and not to cross said mountain, which line was agreed between John Mitchell, father of the deponent, who assisted Stewart in building a house on said tract some time in the fall of 1753, and Stewart moved in with his family the next spring, cleared ground and raised a crop that season."

The land here in dispute consisted of 348 acres and was known as the Bark Tavern tract, being located in Centre Township, the lower boundary being near the stone house formerly owned by Andrew Comp.

This affidavit, however, specifically states that the line "was agreed between John Mitchell and William Stewart" and names the date as September, 1753, which proves that Mitchell had then already located the county seat tract. While he had located it and agreed with "an adjoiner" upon the line, yet he had not then erected an improvement upon it as the affidavit by James Mitchell (the son of John) says that William Stewart "made an improvement, which was the first made in that part of the county." If the affidavit is accepted at all from a historical standpoint, and there appears no reason why it should not be, then it must be accepted in its entirety, which establishes 1753 as being the exact date of the entry of the Mitchells and many others into Perry County territory, the advance guard of the pioneers.

There is quite a distinction attached to the original territory—Perry and Cumberland Counties. In the capital at Washington—

in the Hall of Fame—provision has been made for the various states to place statues of their two most illustrious sons. The State of Georgia has chosen Alexander H. Stephens—congressman, statesman, governor—and Dr. Crawford Long—discoverer of anæsthesia—as Georgia's most representative citizens. Both are the sons of natives of this original county. As stated at a number of places in this book and in a separate chapter devoted to Mr. Stephens, his father, Andrew Stephens, was born at Duncannon. Mr. Long's ancestry were from Cumberland County. Three brothers named Long—Samuel, Andrew, and another—with their father, emigrated from Ulster, Ireland, to Cumberland County before the Revolution. They came of staunch stock—Scotch-Irish Presbyterians—and their name in Britain is associated with shipping and banking through generations. Of these brothers, Samuel went to Georgia, another went West, and the third remained in Carlisle. Samuel was born in 1753 and fought in the Revolution as an ensign, from which one would infer that he was barely grown to manhood when he came to America. He married Ann Williamson about 1776. About 1790 a colony of Scotch-Irish Presbyterians left the Cumberland Valley and went to Georgia, settling in Madison County. Of that colony Samuel Long was one of the leaders. With him went his small son, James, who became the father of Dr. Crawford Long. A few years earlier another colony had preceded these people to Georgia, where they suffered many hardships, yet, in spite of settling in a wilderness, they built at Paoli, the second Presbyterian church to be erected in the state of Georgia—the New Hope Church, of which Samuel and later James Long were elders. With the Longs there went to Georgia the Groves, McCurdys and Cartlidges, all reliable families who in after years left their impress on the state. Anæsthesia, as the reader is aware, causes insensibility to pain and other external impressions. Before the discovery of surgical anæsthesia surgery was very painful and many patients died from shock due to pain. There has long been a contention as to who was the discoverer of anæthesia, but Dr. Long's experiments and regular use of it date to March 30, 1842, predating the actual use by the others of from two to four years. Four Americans—Jackson, Wells, Morton, and Long—claimed the discovery. The Medical Association of Georgia, in 1910, unveiled a marble monument to the honor of Dr. Crawford Long at Jefferson, Georgia, and in the infirmary connected with the University at Athens, Georgia, is a Long Memorial. In 1912 the University of Pennsylvania unveiled in its medical building a bronze medallion with the inscription.

"To the memory of Crawford W. Long,
who first used ether as an anæthetic in surgery,
March 30, 1842."

A life-sized marble statue of Dr. Long stands in Paris and the state of Georgia has well chosen him one of its two immortals for the Hall of Fame in the National Capitol.

James Long, the lad who left Cumberland County, married Elizabeth Ware and became a state senator of Georgia. His noted son, Dr. Crawford Long, was born at Danielsville, Georgia, November 1, 1815. At the University of Georgia, where he graduated at nineteen, his roommate and best friend was Alexander H. Stephens, later vice-president of the Confederacy. At the age of twenty-three he was graduated at the University of Pennsylvania in the medical course. He specialized in surgery in the New York hospitals for two years. In 1841, then twenty-six, he located at Jefferson, Georgia, and in 1851 he located at Athens, Georgia, where he practiced until his death on June 6, 1878. When Georgia decided to go out of the Union Dr. Long said, "This is the saddest day of my life," He was a Whig in politics.

OLD ELECTION DISTRICTS.

The Continental Congress in session in Philadelphia passed a resolution on May 15, 1776, in reference to the election of representatives from each county. Prior to that time the proprietary government ruled and practically everything was done by appointment instead of by election. A new régime had now begun and at the provincial conference held in Carpenter's Hall, Philadelphia, June 18 to 25, the counties were divided into districts. Cumberland County was divided into three districts, the third being composed of the townships of Tyrone, Toboyne, Rye, Milford, Greenwood, Armagh, Lack, Derry, and Fermanagh. This district comprised all of what is now Perry, Juniata and Mifflin Counties. The voting place was to be "at the house of Robert Campbell, in Tuscarora Valley," being in what is now Juniata County.

The Act of June, 1777, changed the county from three to four districts. the third being composed of Tyrone, Toboyne, and Rye, the voting place to be at William McClure's—the farm now occupied by the county home at Loysville. All the territory east of the river which then comprised Greenwood Township was in the fourth district, the voting place being at James Purley's, in Fermanagh Township, now in Juniata County.

[1]"By the Act of September 13, 1785, entitled 'An act to regulate the general elections of this commonwealth and to prevent frauds therein,' the state redistricted, and voting places fixed in each district. Cumberland County was thrown into four districts. The first was within her present limits. The second was composed of the townships of Rye, Tyrone, and Toboyne. with the voting place 'at the house of William McClure, Esq., in the township of Tyrone.' The third district embraced Greenwood, with the townships of Fermanagh, Milford, and Leck (Lack) (now Juniata County), with the voting place fixed at the house of Thomas Wilson (Port Royal), in the township of Milford.'

"The citizens of Rye and Greenwood were much inconvenienced by the long distance to the voting places, especially Greenwood, and petition was

1. For much of the information as to old election districts we are indebted to William H. Sponsler's historical article on the subject, prepared and read before the Philomathean Literary Society at New Bloomfield Academy, many years ago.

13

made to the legislature asking relief, which was granted by Act of September 10, 1787, of which Section IV is in these words: 'And whereas, a number of the freemen of the townships of Greenwood and Rye, in the county of Cumberland, have, by their petition set forth that their distant situation from the place of holding their general elections is found inconvenient, and have, therefore, prayed this General Assembly to enact a law by which the said townships shall be made a separate district for the holding of their general elections. Therefore,' etc.

"The fifth section accordingly erects Rye and Greenwood into the sixth district of Cumberland, with its voting place 'at the mill late the property of David English, and known by the name of English's Mill' (at the mouth of Buffalo Creek, near Newport).

"By the Act of the 19th of September, 1789, this sixth district was bereft of a portion of the territory, that part of Greenwood lying north of Turkey Hills, which, by an act passed 29th of same month, was made into a separate election district of Mifflin County.

"After Rye was taken from Tyrone and Toboyne, it was found that McClure's, which had, no doubt, been selected with a view to accommodate the Rye Township people, as well as the other two townships, was inconvenient and the inhabitants asked that a more convenient place be established. The Act of September 30, 1791, was enacted to remedy this among others, and the place of election was fixed 'at the house now occupied by George Robinson, in Tyrone Township (now Edward R. Loy's, Madison Township).

"In 1787 the township of Rye and that part of Greenwood lying south of the Half Falls Mountain were erected into a separate election district, with its voting place 'at the Union schoolhouse, in the town of Petersburg, in Rye Township.'

"The next change was made by the Act of March 8, 1802, Juniata Greenwood and that part of Buffalo Township lying north of the Half Falls Mountain had their place of holding elections fixed 'at the house now or lately occupied by William Woods, at Millerstown, in the township of Greenwood.'

"By the Act of March 21, 1803, the townships of Tyrone and Toboyne heretofore together, are separated, each to constitute an election district of itself. Tyrone was to vote 'at the schoolhouse in the town of Landisburg,' and Toboyne 'at the house now occupied by Henry Zimmerman, in said township.'

"By the Act of February 11, 1805, Buffalo Township was made a separate election district, with a voting place 'at the house now occupied by William Thompson, in Buffalo Township.'

"By the Act of March 19, 1816, it was provided that 'the electors residing within the eastern part of Greenwood Township be divided as follows: beginning in the narrows of Berris (Berry's) Mountain; thence westerly above the summit of the said mountain, six miles; thence northerly by a line parallel with the river Susquehanna to the line of Cumberland County; thence easterly along the said line to said river; thence down said river to the place of beginning, shall hold their general elections at the house of Henry Raymon,' now in Liverpool Township.

"By the thirty-second section of the Act of March 24, 1818, the voting place of Buffalo Township was changed to the house of Frederick Deal, in said township, and by the twelfth section of the Act of March 29, 1819, the township of Saville was erected into a separate election district, with voting place 'at a schoolhouse near Ickesburg, in said township.'

"In 1820, when the county was separated from Cumberland as a new county the election districts and voting places were as follows: Toboyne, house of Henry Zimmerman; Tyrone, schoolhouse, Landisburg; Saville, schoolhouse, North Ickesburg; Buffalo, house of Frederick Deal; East Greenwood, house of Henry Raymon; Rye, Union schoolhouse, Petersburg; Juniata and West Greenwood, W. Woods' house, Millerstown.

"A change was made in 1860, and the following were made the voting places: At the schoolhouse in Germantown district; at Zimmerman's tavern for the lower district of Toboyne; at the schoolhouse in Landisburg for Tyrone Township; at the schoolhouse near Ickesburg for Saville; at John Koch's (Kough's) tavern for the northern district of Juniata Township; at the Union schoolhouse near the Methodist Church in Wheatfield Township; at Colonel Bovard's tavern for Rye Township; at the house of Straw, for Buffalo Township; at the house of John Gardner, Millerstown, for Greenwood Township; at the house of John.Eberling, in Liverpool Township.

"At this time a new district was made composed of parts of Juniata, Wheatfield, Tyrone, and Saville Townships, bounded as follows: Beginning at the mouth of Little Buffalo Creek in Juniata Township; thence up said creek to the house of John Smith, in Saville Township, including said house; thence by a straight line to the house of Abraham Kistler, in Tyrone Township, including said house; thence by a straight line to Jacob Shatto's sawmill in said township; thence down the summit of Iron Ridge, to the house of John Greer, in Wheatfield Township, including said house; thence along the summit of Dick's Hill to Johnston's sawmill in said township; thence by a straight line to Dick's Gap, in Juniata Township; thence along the summit of Mahanoy Hill to the house of Alexander Watson, on the bank of Juniata River, including said house; thence up said river to place of beginning.

"A few years later, as townships were erected, separate election districts were made embracing the townships, and, with the exception of Madison Township, each township is an election district to-day. The north end of Madison was cut off into a separate district called Sandy Hill or Northeast Madison, which practically is a separate township, with the single exception of in the election of justices of the peace, both districts voting for the same candidates for this one office."

Newport borough is the only town in the county which has two separate election districts, the first and second wards.

Several special acts relating to polling places in Perry County were passed by the Pennsylvania Legislature. That of March 4, 1842, added Henry's Valley to Tyrone Township for voting purposes, and that of March 12, 1849, added part of Juniata Township to Saville Township, and made Ickesburg the polling place. An Act of March 6, 1849, annexed to Greenwood Township for election purposes "all that part of Juniata Township, commencing on the Juniata River, on division line of Perry and Juniata Counties, thence along said line on Tuscarora Mountain until it comes opposite the upper line of Samuel Black's farm, thence along said upper line to top of Raccoon Ridge one mile, thence south to Patton's schoolhouse, thence along the Oliver Township line to the Juniata River."

In a general election district bill vetoed by Governor Bigler and passed over his head by the House on January 19, 1844, and by the Senate, January 22, 1844, parts of Tyrone, Saville, and Madison Townships were made an election district, with the voting place at Andesville (now Loysville). It was repealed by an Act of March 9, 1844, less than sixty days later.

LEWIS, THE ROBBER.

The history of Lewis, the robber, is of no consequence in this book, except in so far as his depredations and abode concerns the territory, as he was a native of Carlisle, but even left there when he was but three years old. The year of the organization of Perry County was, strangely enough, coincident with the passing of Lewis, who died July 13, 1820, in the Bellefonte jail, when only thirty years of age, a victim of his own bad life. The very first issues of the *Perry Forester* tell of his capture and later of his death. There are those who uphold him as a gentleman robber, who stole from the rich to give to the poor, but his own confession, dated the day before his death, belies that assertion, as he pleads guilty to almost the whole category of crime, save murder. However, in some instances he did steal from the rich to give to the poor, if tradition be true; and tradition is persistent, in newspaper and locality. This story appears with slight variations at various places.

On one occasion Lewis dropped in to rob a home and the lady occupant told him she was a widow, had no money and that the constable was coming to take her cow for her overdue taxes, accompanying the statement with tears. Lewis asked her the amount of the taxes and gave her an amount of money sufficient to pay them, telling her to say nothing of the fact that he had been there or where she had gotten the money. As he was hungry she gave him a meal. Shortly after he left, the expected officer of the law came, the taxes were paid and he departed, but on his way home Lewis held him up and not only got the tax money, but all that he had. Lewis is said to have remarked that that was the best investment he ever made.

He roamed the country from the Susquehanna west as far as Fayette County, and was a notorious counterfeiter, according to his own confession. He was always in search of victims to rob. One of his favorite resorts was in the Kittatinny or Blue Mountains, north from Doubling Gap Springs, where there was a cave, which was the size of an ordinary living room, being formed by a projecting rock. The spot is known to hunters to this day, its location having been handed down from one generation to another. Time has wrought much in its destruction by the disintegration of the rock by the elements, partly filling the cave. From a point not far from the cave he had a fine view of the valleys below and the trails up the mountain. From that point he watched for officers of the law, and confederates in the valleys below used to display danger signals to him when strangers were in the vicinity. One of these confederates was reputed to be a man named Moffitt, and on entering the cave at one time officers found among other

things an almanac bearing his name. Near the big spring at Mt.
Patrick is one of the places where tradition would have a rendezvous of Lewis. This may have been possible, as there is a well
founded tradition that a stranger once called on Peter Musselman,
at Liverpool, to have a tooth drawn, and that he "later found it to
have been Lewis, upon whose head was a price." Mr. Musselman,
by the way, was in France as a student during the trying period
of the French Revolution.

But Lewis didn't learn his deviltry in this vicinity, as the follow-
lowing brief account of his life will show:

David Lewis was born in Carlisle, Cumberland County, Pennsylvania, March 4, 1790, and was one of a numerous family of
children; and according to his deathbed confession he grew up
"without regard for men and little fear of God." Three years
later his father was made a deputy district surveyor and removed
to Northumberland County, where he died several years later,
while David was yet a small boy. He remained with his mother,
doing occasional farm labor for farmers until 1807, when he left
home. After trying several avocations he enlisted in the army at
Bellefonte. A petty offense caused the sergeant to endeavor to
arrest him, but he ran away. Some time later, using the assumed
name of Armstrong Lewis, he enlisted in Capt. Wm. N. Irvin's
company of artillery in the United States service, at Carlisle. He
did this in order to get the bounty money and then decamp, but
failed. He then decided that he would study law and tried to get
out of the army for that purpose by having a writ issued. After
a tedious hearing before John D. Creigh, then associate judge of
Cumberland County, he was remanded into the army. This hearing caused an inquiry to be made into his past life and it was discovered that he had once before enlisted in the army under his
right name and deserted.

The rumbling of the second war with Great Britain was already
heard, and according to the strict military discipline of the time
Lewis was sentenced to be executed. His mother, then living in
Centre County, rode overland on a horse loaned by Judge Walker,
to aid him. Eventually he was reprieved in so far as the death sentence was concerned, but was sentenced to life imprisonment. He
was first imprisoned, attached to a ball and chain, but gradually
ingratiated himself into the good graces of the guards and effected
his escape. Once free Lewis escaped to a small cave north of
Carlisle, where he remained until long after nightfall, when hunger
drove him forth. Arousing a woman who lived by the wayside
he was served a cooked meal and given a bed, but before morning
he decamped and departed for Centre County, where his mother
lived, crossing the Kittatinny or Blue Mountain, and traveling
across what later became Perry County.

Later, meeting an itinerant tin peddler of a nomadic clan which frequented the countryside in those days, he learned of a concern at Burlington, Vermont, which issued counterfeit bills, and forthwith made a trip there and in due time headed for Pennsylvania, a counterfeiter with his wares ready for the market. While passing through New York State he bought a horse of a General Root, then a candidate for office and paid for it with counterfeit bills. He was soon detected and jailed in Troy, where, through a girl friend of the sheriff's daughter, he effected his escape on a Sunday night while the sheriff was at church. In company with the girl, whom he promised to marry, he arrived in Albany the next evening and kept his word and had the marriage ceremony immediately performed.

The next day Lewis imparted to his unsuspecting girl-wife the less criminal of his actions. Up to this time he had kept her in ignorance of any previous improprieties and insisted that his prosecution in the horse purchase was really persecution on account of politics. During the several days following, Lewis and his wife traveled to New York, the latter having secured passage on the wagon of a Yankee, bound to New York with his wares. In New York Lewis soon associated with his kind and became an ordinary sneak thief and burglar, according to his own confession. There he belonged to a gang which signed a parchment with their own blood.

After a time in New York, where he had personally robbed Mrs. John Jacob Astor of much finery which she had purchased, he was accused by his accomplices of not turning in all of the same to the general "fund." He became disgusted and with his wife traveled to New Brunswick, New Jersey, and set up housekeeping. Leaving his wife there he journeyed to Princeton, posed as a Southern planter and by gambling fleeced the students out of hundreds of dollars. As soon as the holiday recess was over at Princeton Lewis moved on to Philadelphia, where he resumed sneak thieving. He had conceived a plan there to lure to the country Stephen Girard, the wealthy banker, and hold him for a ransom, but his small daughter's illness recalled him to New Brunswick.

After spending some time at home he started for the Canadian lines, but became penniless and hired to a farmer. Hardly had he done so until the farmer's team was impressed into the service of the United States Army. Lewis drove it away, and when it was no longer needed he "drove it away" again, but towards his old haunts in Pennsylvania, selling it as soon as he could. He was then traveling under the fictitious name of Peter Vanbeuren. He landed at Stoyestown, Pennsylvania, where he learned from another crook that his wife was dead and buried.

In the mountains near there he joined a band of counterfeiters and, when they made some accusation against him, he waited until they slept and robbed them. This wealth he claims to have put in a bottle and buried, forgetting the place, but as his whole life was crooked his statements, too, must not be taken too seriously. In his confession he tells of stealing a horse in Maryland, coming to Cumberland County and getting arrested for passing counterfeit money, escaping to see his family, returning to Cumberland County with other counterfeiters and embarking in the business there.

This establishment was in the South Mountain. Lewis then tells of proceeding to Landisburg, where he passed a $100 counterfeit note to a Mr. Anderson, a merchant, whose place was in the building owned by the heirs of George Patterson. Passing through Roxbury, Strasburg, and Fannettsburg, he gathered in $1,500 in real money, which he deposited in the Bedford bank. He was arrested and found guilty of counterfeiting, his sentence being ten years in the penitentiary, but Governor Findlay pardoned him after serving a year. He returned to Bedford to get his money, but it was refused. Here he fell in with a man named Rumbaugh, but traveling under the name of Conelly, and another who called himself Hanson. The three overtook a drover, who was returning westward on horseback, and robbed him, tying both man and horse to a tree, with a threat of death if he tried to get away. Lewis here prevented the other two from killing the drover, saying they would have to kill him first. The drover got away and aroused the community. The robbers made for the Juniata River country but were captured and returned to Bedford. They escaped from there and after some more robberies, recaptures and escapes, they turned to the Juniata River country again, with which they were familiar, and made an effort to reach New York State. According to the "Life and Adventures of David Lewis," being exhausted they stopped at a tavern below Lewistown. Sheriff Samuel Edmiston learned of it and with a posse of about thirty men went to the hotel. One man was sent in to carelessly discover whether or not they were there. He returned and reported them in bed. The posse closed in and a half-dozen brave men quietly ascended the stairs and found them sleeping. On awakening Lewis he immediately reached for a weapon, but the sheriff overpowered him. When taken to the Bedford jail, he said it wouldn't hold him long, and it didn't. The sheriff, as an extra precaution, had handcuffed him, but he slipped the cuffs and escaped. They later got to Clearfield County, and one day recklessly began shooting at a mark, which aroused the neighborhood and they were surrounded, but defied the posse. The result was that Lewis was shot through the arm, which shortly thereafter, July 13, 1820, caused his death, and that Conelly was shot in the groin and died in a few hours.

When Lewis escaped from the Bedford jail he was in irons, according to the public press of the period. He succeeded in getting to a near by woods, where, by use of a file, he cut the irons from his person. The advertisements describing him make him "six feet tall, square shoulders, reddish hair, speaks quick and has a fierce look."

While Lewis is supposed to have had no education, his confession belies that supposition, both from the standpoint of language and logic. He flays the Carlisle lawyers and the public officials, naturally, for had it not been for them he might have had easier sailing. Endeavoring to find a cause for what he terms his "misfortunes and crimes," he says:

"When I look back upon my ill-spent life, and endeavor to discover the cause or source from which all my misfortunes and crimes have sprung and proceeded, I am inclined to trace their origin to the want of early instruction. Had my widowed mother been possessed of the means of sending me to school, and afforded me the opportunity of profiting by an education during the early part of my youth, instead of being engaged in idle sports and vicious pursuits, I might have been employed in the studies of useful knowledge, and my mind by this means have received an early tendency to virtue and honesty from which it would have not afterwards been diverted. But, alas! She was poor, and the Legislature of Pennsylvania—I blush with indignation when I say it—had made no provision, nor has she yet made any adequate one, for the gratuitous education of the children of the poor. Until this is done and schools are established at the public expense for teaching those who are without the means of paying for instruction, ignorance will cover the land with darkness, and vice and crime run down our streets as a mighty torrent."

The writer feels like apologizing for publishing this account, but if it will show at least one boy the value of his free schooling, where his mind is kept on useful things, instead of those of a vicious nature, it is not done in vain. The fact that Lewis' life, through dissipation, vice, exposure and crime, was only thirty short years, will also impress the youth of the land as they see about them men and women of sixty, seventy, and even eighty, enjoying all the comforts of life, a tribute to lives of honesty, discretion and labor.

This chapter would not be complete without adding that Lewis came of good people, that he was the only member of his family who trod the crooked pathway and that his children lived honest and straightforward lives. About 1845 a handsome young woman —a daughter of the robber by a second marriage—resided with her mother at Harrisburg, Pennsylvania's capital, where she attracted much attention by her frank, open, womanly bearing.

CHAPTER XII.

PERRY COUNTY ESTABLISHED.

B Y an act of the State Legislature of the Commonwealth of
Pennsylvania Perry County was created, the act being signed
by the governor, William Findlay, on March 22, 1820. It
was the fifty-first county of the state. The territory was a part
of the lands covered by the Indian treaty at Albany, New York,
July 6, 1754, of which mention is made elsewhere. The lands
covered by this treaty were all embraced in Cumberland County
at that time, and the northern part was formed into counties, the
last one being Mifflin, in 1789.

When Perry County was formed it comprised the seven townships of Cumberland County lying north of the Blue Hills, or
Kittatinny Mountains. Tyrone, early being known as "the everlasting State of Tyrone," was the oldest of these townships, being
erected in 1754. The other six were Toboyne, 1762; Rye, 1766;
Greenwood, 1767; Juniata, 1793; Buffalo, 1798; and Saville,
1817.

The population of these townships was considerable, and with
the incoming of new settlers, frequent trips to the county seat at
Carlisle were necessary in connection with the new claims, over
roads which were at some seasons of the year almost impassable.
The fact that most of the changes in property in those days occurred
around the first of April, when the roads were at their worst, and
that the shortest routes lay over the Kittatinny Mountain, no doubt,
actuated the movement for the new county, with a county seat
within easy distance. In conformity with this desire petitions
were presented to the State Legislature then in session and the act
creating Perry County was passed.

With the passing years the residents of what is now Perry—of
the Sherman's Valley and the land between the rivers—became
discontented as a part of a county whose seat of justice was south
of that great natural barrier, the Kittatinny or Blue Mountain,
and not at all central. In fact, the physical features of the entire
territory of Cumberland at that time were such that there could
be no logical central point to locate a seat of justice: nature had
decreed it otherwise. Those located north of the Kittatinny had
to travel distances which were as far as forty miles to the county
seat; unlike those of the south side they could not return to their
homes the same day, and were thus necessitated securing hotel
accommodations, which cost thousands of dollars annually. The

home on account of a vow that "no child of mine shall first open his eyes on the Cumberland side of the mountain."

Eventually, after years of consideration and when the small body of original enthusiasts had grown to a vast majority of the residents of the northern section, petitions were prepared and circulated, with the end in view of presenting them to the Pennsylvania General Assembly in session at Harrisburg, praying that a new county be formed. The petitions were printed and a timeworn one is in the possession of W. H. Sponsler, a New Bloomfield attorney-at-law. At several places words are obliterated by the ravages of time, but are supplied for the purpose of making clear the meaning of the instrument, the contents of which follow:

The Petition,

Of the subscribers residing in that part of Cumberland County called Shearman's Valley, situate on the north side of the Blue Mountain, to the Honorable the Senate, and House of Representatives, of the Commonwealth of Pennsylvania, in General Assembly met, at their session of 1819-20,

Humbly Showeth,

That your Petitioners again renew their prayers for a division of Cumberland County, because its local situation, and the convenience and prosperity of the people of Shearman's Valley, imperiously require a division. The local situation of Cumberland County, is as follows, viz: It is bound on the north by the Tuscarora Mountain, on the south by the South Mountain. The Blue Mountain runs through the County, nearly east and west, making a natural division of said County into two valleys, nearly of equal territory and population. Carlisle, our present seat of Justice, is situate in the Valley on the Southern side, not more than six miles from the south boundary, and in the most eligible and central part of it, on the very spot where it ought to be, had Shearman's Valley never been attached thereto. On the north side of the Blue Mountain, lies Shearman's Valley, our proposed new county, which is in length east and west, from forty-eight to fifty miles; and the general breadth, from sixteen to eighteen miles; containing twenty-two hundred taxable inhabitants. We have forty-eight Grist and Merchant Mills, sixty Sawmills, ten Fulling Mills, eight Carding Machines, four Oil Mills, one Forge, one Furnace, two Tilt-hammers and one Powder Mill; we have beautiful settlements, fertile and well cultivated lands, and wealthy inhabitants, yet notwithstanding all our local advantages for want of a division the people from the upper end of Shearman's Valley have to travel thirty-six, and the people from the lower extreme, have to travel about forty miles, to Carlisle, our present seat of Justice; and that is not all, we have to cross and recross, that almost insuperable barrier, the Blue Mountain, besides the Connodoguinet Creek, which is often times not fordable and in going by Bridge, those from the upper end of Shearman's Valley, have to travel seven additional miles in going to or coming from Carlisle.

There are a number of counties in the State, which have neither the population, extent of territory nor fertility of soil that either the old or new counties would have if divided, and a great many more, that the whole amount of lands, are not valued so high, as is the land in Cumberland County.

Therefore, in point of numbers and wealth, we consider ourselves altogether competent to support a County and the administration of Justice;

for if a division was granted, our saving in travelling expenses, and lying at Court in Carlisle, at so great distance from home, would amount in short time to a sum sufficient, to make our Public Buildings; and Justice could be administered, for much less than one-half the expense, that the whole County now costs. For the intercourse between the people on this side, and the people on the other side the Blue Mountain, is so trifling, that it rarely happens, that any suit of importance comes before the Court, where persons from both sides are concerned. But the Court being occupied by parties both from one side or the other; so that while causes from the south side of the Blue Mountain are before the Court, the people from the north side, who have causes depending, are obliged to lie with their witnesses, at great expense, very often for several courts successively, which in most cases increases the expenses above the matter in controversy: and moreover, it gives the wicked, unjust and troublesome, a complete triumph over Justice, because many would rather give up their just rights, than seek Justice at such a vast expense, and further, the people on this side of the Blue Mountain, have been at their full share of expenses, in building a Court House, a house for the public offices, a Jail and Penitentiary at Carlisle; all which they are willing to give up their part of, to the people on the other side, if the Legislature will pass a law to divide the County.

It would be a moderate computation, to say that each taxable inhabitant of our proposed new County, would have to go to Carlisle, at least once a year, on business, either to Court, or some of the public offices; the expenses upon the average, with loss of time, cannot be computed at less than three dollars per man. If we were divided, there would be a saving of at least one-half, say 3300 dollars, to the people of this side, in the bare item of travelling expenses and loss of time. Besides there would be a saving of at least double that sum in Mileage of Sheriffs, Jurors, and Witnesses, to say nothing of the saving to the estates of widows and orphans. Upon the whole, the people on this side of the Blue Mountain, at a moderate calculation sustain a loss of at least 10,000 dollars per annum for want of division.

We ask part of no other County, we ask barely what nature intended, by rearing a stupendous Mountain, dividing the present large boundary of Cumberland County into two Valleys nearly equal; each of which being sufficiently large for a County, and the people on our side, labour under the most intolerable inconvenience, by reason of their having to cross the Mountain, whenever business of a public nature is to be transacted.

Therefore, your petitioners most sincerely pray that your Honorable body, will pass a law, to divide Cumberland County, making the summit of the Blue Mountain the division line.

And we further pray, that the Governor be authorized to appoint three or five disinterested, respectable, Judicious and honest men, living out of the County, to explore our new County, and fix a scite for the seat of Justice, and your petitioners as in duty bound will ever pray.

We, the undersigned living on the south side of the Blue Mountain pray the representatives of Pennsylvania, in general assembly met now in session of 1819-20 to grant the people of Shearman's Valley a County north of the Blue Mountain separate from Cumberland County and your petitioners as in duty bound will pray, etc.

The words "that your petitioners again renew their prayers," in the beginning of the petition, imply that previous effort or efforts had been made towards separation from Cumberland County, but attempts to find facts relating thereto have been unavailing. While the language of the petition is more or less crude, the reasons presented were plausible, as any person having even a small knowledge of legal procedure must readily see. Who were the leading spirits that urged it and later saw it an accomplished fact? No records remain to tell, but a perusal of the early citizens whose names stand forth in the county's first years must necessarily include many of them. Having pressed to success their design it would be but natural to see them play a leading part in the affairs of their new county.

To the south lay Carlisle—staid, pedantic, historic, aristocratic and the seat of a government military post. It seemed strange to that town "that a country of sparse population, with no towns of importance and only a river or two and a few mountain streams for transportation and selling mostly 'hoop poles' and furs" should have a desire to become a separate county. Its formation would be a great blow to the commerce and trade of Carlisle, as to it went largely the trade of the entire Sherman's Valley, taken thence by those who went on legal errands; and from Carlisle came the opposition to the birth of the new county. Until then the Sherman's Valley people were largely tied economically to Carlisle; but the building of the canals and later the railroad changed the course of trade. The automobile has again somewhat reversed trade conditions for residents of the vicinity of Shermansdale. At the time of the passage of this act William Anderson, of the Perry County territory, was one of the three members of the legislature from Cumberland County.

The text of the act creating the new county follows:

THE LEGISLATIVE ACT CREATING PERRY COUNTY.

An act erecting part of Cumberland County, into a separate county to be called Perry.

Sec. 1. *Be it enacted by the Senate and House of Representatives of the Commonwealth of Pennsylvania, in General Assembly met, and it is hereby enacted by the authority of the same,* That from and after the first day of September next all that part of Cumberland County lying north of the Blue Mountain, beginning on the summit of the Blue Mountain, where the Franklin County line crosses the same, and running thence along the summit thereof an eastwardly course to the river Susquehanna, thence up the west side of the same to the line of Mifflin County, thence along the Mifflin County line to the summit of the Tuscarora Mountain, thence along the summit of the same to the Franklin County line, thence along the same to the place of beginning, be and the same is hereby declared to be erected into a separate county to be called Perry.

Sec. 2. *And be it further enacted by the authority aforesaid,* That the inhabitants of the said county of Perry from and after the first day of September next, shall be entitled to and at all times thereafter have, all and singular the courts, jurisdictions, offices, rights and privileges, to which the inhabitants of other counties of this state are entitled by the Constitution and laws of this commonwealth.

Sec. 3. *And be it further enacted by the authority aforesaid,* That the several courts in and for the said county of Perry, shall be opened and held at such house in the town of Landisburg, as may be designated by the commissioners of said county, to be elected at the next general election, until a courthouse shall be erected in and for said county, as is hereinafter directed, and shall be then held at said courthouse, at which place the returns of the general election in and for the county of Perry shall be made.

Sec. 4. *And be it further enacted by the authority aforesaid,* That the suits which shall be pending and undetermined in the Court of Common Pleas of Cumberland County, on the first day of September next, where both parties in suit or suits shall at that time be resident in the county of Perry, shall be transferred to the Court of Common Pleas of Perry County, and shall be considered as pending in said court, and shall be proceeded on in like manner as if the same had been originally commenced in said court, except that the fees on the same due to the officers of Cumberland County, shall be paid to them when recovered by the prothonotary or sheriff of Perry County; and the prothonotary of Cumberland County shall on or before the first day of September next purchase a docket, and copy therein all the docket entries respecting the said suits to be transferred as aforesaid, and shall on or before the first day of November next, have the said docket, together with the records, declarations and other papers respecting said suits, ready to be delivered to the prothonotary of Perry County; the expense of said docket and copying to be paid by the prothonotary of Perry County, and reimbursed by the said county of Perry, on warrants to be drawn by the commissioners of Perry County on the treasurer thereof.

Sec. 5. *And be it further enacted by the authority aforesaid,* That all taxes or arrears of taxes laid or which have become due within the said county of Perry before the passing of this act, and all sums of money due to this commonwealth for militia fines in the said county of Perry, shall be collected and recovered, as if this act had not been passed: *Provided always,* That the money arising from county taxes assessed or to be assessed within the limits of the county of Perry, subsequently to the first day of November last, shall from time to time, as the same may be collected, be paid into the treasury of the county of Cumberland for the use and benefit of the county of Perry; until a treasurer shall be appointed in the county of Perry, and the treasurer of the county of Cumberland shall keep separate accounts thereof, and pay the same to the treasurer of the county of Perry as soon as he shall have been appointed; and whatever part of said taxes may remain uncollected in the county of Perry at the time of the appointment of the treasurer thereof, the same shall be collected in the usual manner, and paid into the treasury of the county of Perry.

Sec. 6. *And be it further enacted by the authority aforesaid,* That the sheriff, treasurer, prothonotary and all such officers as are by law required to give surety for the faithful discharge of the duties of their respective offices, who shall hereafter be appointed or elected in the said county of Perry, before they or any of them shall enter on the execution thereof, shall give sufficient security in the same manner and form and for the same uses, trusts and purposes, as such officers for the time being are obliged by law to give in the county of Cumberland.

Sec. 7. *And be it further enacted by the authority aforesaid,* That the sheriff, coroner and other officers of the county of Cumberland, shall continue to exercise the duties of their respective offices within the county of Perry, until similar officers shall be elected or appointed, as the case may be, agreeably to law within the said county; and the persons who shall be appointed associate judges for the county of Perry, shall take and subscribe the requisite oaths or affirmation of office before the prothonotary of the Court of Common Pleas of the county of Cumberland, who shall file a record of the same in the office of the prothonotary of the Court of Common Pleas of Perry County.

Sec. 8. *And be it further enacted by the authority aforesaid,* That the inhabitants of the county of Perry shall elect one representative and the county of Cumberland two, until otherwise altered, and in conjunction with Cumberland County one senator to serve in the legislature of this commonwealth in the same mode, under the same regulations, and make return thereof in the same manner, as is directed by the fifteenth section of this act.

Sec. 9. *And be it further enacted by the authority aforesaid,* That the governor be and he is hereby authorized and required, on or before the first day of September next ensuing, to appoint three discreet and disinterested persons, not resident in the counties of Cumberland or Perry, whose duty it shall be, to fix on a proper and convenient scite for a courthouse, prison and county offices within the aforesaid county of Perry, as near the centre thereof, as circumstances will admit, having regard to the convenience of roads, territory, population and the accommodation of the people of the said county generally; and said persons, or a majority of them, having viewed the relative advantages of the several situations contemplated by the people, shall on or before the first day of September next, by a written report under their hands or under the hands of a majority of them, certify, describe and limit the scite or lot of land which they shall have chosen for the purpose aforesaid, and shall transmit the said report to the governor of this commonwealth; and the persons so as aforesaid appointed, shall each receive three dollars per diem for their services out of the monies to be raised in pursuance of this act: *Provided always,* That before the commissioners shall proceed to perform the duties enjoined on them by this act, they shall take an oath or affirmation before some judge or justice of the peace, well and truly and with fidelity to perform said duties without favor to any person, according to the true intent and meaning of this act.

Sec. 10. *And be it further enacted by the authority aforesaid,* That it shall and may be lawful for the commissioners of the county of Perry who shall be elected at the next annual election, to take assurance to them and their successors in office of such lot, or lots or piece of ground as shall have been approved of by the persons appointed as aforesaid, or a majority of them, for the purpose of erecting thereon a courthouse, jail and offices for the safe keeping of the records; and the county commissioners are hereby authorized to assess, levy and collect in the manner directed by the acts for raising county rates and levies, a sufficient sum to defray the expenses thereof, and also are hereby authorized to assess, levy and collect for the purpose of building a courthouse and prison, which they are hereby authorized to erect, a sufficient sum to defray the expenses thereof.

Sec. 11. *And be it further enacted by the authority aforesaid,* That the said county of Perry shall form a part of the district composed of the counties of Cumberland, Franklin and Adams for the election of members of congress.

Sec. 12. *And be it further enacted by the authority aforesaid,* That the judges of the Supreme Court shall have like powers, jurisdictions and

authorities within the said county of Perry, as by law they are vested
with and entitled to have and exercise in other counties of this state;
and the said county is hereby annexed to the southern district of the Supreme Court.

Sec. 13. *And be it further enacted by the authority aforesaid,* That the
county of Perry shall be annexed to and compose part of the ninth judicial district of this commonwealth and the courts in said county of Perry
shall be held on the Monday after the courts in Franklin County.

Sec. 14. *And be it further enacted by the authority aforesaid,* That all
certioraries directed to and appeals from the judgment of any justice of
the peace of the said county of Perry, and all criminal prosecutions which
may originate in the said county before the test day hereinafter mentioned,
shall be proceeded in as heretofore in the Courts of Common Pleas and
Quarter Sessions of the county of Cumberland, and all process to issue
from the courts of the said county of Perry, returnable to the first term
in said county, shall bear test on the third Monday of November next.

Sec. 15. *And be it further enacted by the authority aforesaid,* That the
judges of the district elections within each of the said counties of Cumberland and Perry after having formed the returns of the whole election
for senator within each county in such manner as is or may be directed
by law, shall on the third Tuesday in October in each year send the same
by one or more of their number to the courthouse in the borough of Carlisle in the county of Cumberland, when and where the judges so met
shall cast up the several county returns, and execute under their respective hands as many returns for the whole district as may be requisite, and
also transmit the same as is by law required of the return judges in other
districts.

Sec. 16. *And be it further enacted by the authority aforesaid,* That in
all cases when it would be lawful for the sheriff, jailor, or prison keeper
of the county of Perry, to hold in close custody the body of any person
in the common jail of the said county, if such jail were at this time erected
in and for the said county, such persons shall be delivered to and kept in
close custody by the sheriff, jailor or prison keeper of the county of Cumberland, who upon delivery of such prisoner to him or to them at the
common jail in said county of Cumberland shall safely keep him, her or
them until they be discharged by due course of law, and shall also be an-
swerable in like manner and liable to the same pains and penalties as if
the persons so delivered were liable to confinement in the common jail of
Cumberland County; and the parties aggrieved shall be entitled to the
same remedies against them or any of them, as if such prisoner had been
committed to his or their custody by virtue of legal process issued by
proper authority of the said county of Cumberland: *Provided always,*
That the sheriff of Perry County be allowed out of the county stock of
said county, ten cents per mile as a full compensation for every person
charged with a criminal offense which he may deliver to the jail of Cumberland County by virtue of this act, on orders drawn by the commissioners of Perry County on the treasury thereof.

Sec. 17. *And be it further enacted by the authority aforesaid,* That the
sheriff, jailor and prison keeper of the county of Cumberland shall receive
all prisoners as aforesaid, and shall provide for them, according to law,
and shall be entitled to the fees for keeping them, and also to such allowance as is by law directed for the maintenance of prisoners in similar
cases, which allowance shall be defrayed and paid by the commissioners
of the county of Perry out of the county stock.

Sec. 18. *And be it further enacted by the authority aforesaid,* That the
sixteenth and seventeenth sections of this act shall be and continue in

force for the term of three years, or until the commissioners of Perry County shall have certified to the court, that a jail is erected and ready for the reception of prisoners and approved of by the court and grand jury, who shall enter their approbation, signed by them, on the record of said court; and from thenceforth it shall be lawful for the sheriff of Perry County, to receive all and every person or persons who may then be confined in the jail of Cumberland County, in pursuance of this act, and convey them to the jail of Perry County, and to keep them in custody until they be discharged by due course of law.

Sec. 19. *And be it further enacted by the authority aforesaid,* That the poorhouse establishment, which will be included in the county of Perry, shall be and continue to be conducted as heretofore for the term of four years, from and after the passage of this act, and at the expiration of the said four years, the commissioners of Cumberland County shall remove their paupers into their own county.

(Passed March 22, 1820. Recorded in Penna. Laws, No. XVIII, p. 11.)

The northern boundary of the new county, described as "thence along the Mifflin County line," refers to the present Juniata County line, as Juniata had not then yet been taken from Mifflin and made a separate county.

When Cumberland County was erected in 1750, the eastern boundary line was made specific, as Cumberland's lands were to lie "to the westward of the Susquehanna." Whether that was the intention of those who drew the act or not will never be known, but when Perry County's territory was taken from Cumberland, it inherited that boundary line. This line has never been changed by man, save that by two special acts of the Pennsylvania Legislature, islands in the Susquehanna River have become a part of Perry. The Act of March 7, 1856, detached from Upper Paxton Township, Dauphin County, an island "by the name of Crow's Island, to be attached to and hereafter become a part of Perry County." The Act of March 21, 1868, detached from Middle Paxton Township, Dauphin County, and annexed to Penn Township, Perry County, the island below Duncannon, known as Wister's Island. Just where the county line would be drawn at these two points has never been determined.

The northern line, as stated in the act erecting Perry County, starts at the Susquehanna at the line of Mifflin County (now the southern line of Juniata County), "thence along the Mifflin County line to the summit of the Tuscarora Mountain." The act creating Mifflin County designated the southern boundary thus: "Beginning at the Susquehanna River where the Turkey Hill extends to said river; thence along said hill to Juniata, where it cuts Tuscarora Mountain, thence along the summit of said mountain to the line of Franklin County." Consequently, on Turkey Hill, the ridge which lies between Liverpool and Greenwood Townships of Perry County and Susquehanna and Greenwood Townships of

14

Juniata County, is the county line of that part of the county lying east of the Juniata. To residents of that section of the county "Turkey Hill" is known as Turkey Ridge, and the first valley north of it (in Juniata County) is known as Turkey Valley.

An act of the Pennsylvania Legislature, December 23, 1824, authorized the appointment of John Harper, of Cumberland County; John Cox, of Franklin County, and Robert Clark, of Perry County, to run the line dividing Cumberland and Perry.

Perry County had been erected for fourteen years before the northern boundary line was run by surveyors. An act of the Pennsylvania Legislature of April 14, 1834, authorized its survey, and David Hough, of Mifflin County; Samuel Wallick, of Juniata County, and Jason W. Eby, of Cumberland County, were appointed commissioners to conduct it. They were required to run the line before June 15, 1834. They were to make duplicate drafts of the survey, inserting the courses and distances "in words, at length," and to furnish a copy to the prothonotary of each county, to be "thereafter considered a public record." Evidently their task was not entirely completed until the time limit, yet the fifth section of an act of April 4, 1835, ratified it and declared it to be of the same effect as if finished at the appointed time. According to records Jason W. Eby did not act, the other commissioners running the line. In all probability the line then designated did not meet with the approval of all, for on April 2, 1860, an act was passed by the legislature to rerun that part of the line located west of the Juniata river. James Woods and Mitchell Patton, of Perry County, and George W. Jacobs, of Juniata County, were appointed commissioners for that purpose. The line was to be located by September 1, 1860, and was to be marked "upon the ground, by distinct and permanent marks, wherever and as often as the said division line crosses any public road or highway and at other convenient distances, on the aforesaid line." Like the previous commissioners, they were instructed to make duplicate drafts, but with the specific provision that they were to be "with courses and distances plainly laid down, with reference to the improvements through which said line may pass, one of which they shall deposit in each of the prothonotary's offices of the aforesaid counties, as soon thereafter as practical, which shall be considered as a public record." The courses and distances are merely statistical and are not considered of enough importance to reproduce here. They may be referred to at the courthouse in either Perry or Juniata Counties. The survey of 1860 differed little from that of 1834.

The western county line was the original line between the ancient township of Fannett and Toboyne, Cumberland County. Fannett became a part of Franklin County and Toboyne, a part of

Perry County. This old line sufficed until 1841, when, on April 28, the Pennsylvania Legislature passed an act "for the purpose of running and marking the lines between Franklin and Perry Counties." Abraham S. McKinney, of Cumberland County; John Johnston, of Perry County, and Andrew Wilson, of Franklin County, were appointed commissioners to run the line. To them was left little but the actual surveying, as the language of the act commanded them to leave the entire Amberson Valley in Franklin County, and the entire Sherman's Valley in Perry County. The line was to start "at the corner of Cumberland and Franklin Counties, on the top of the Blue Mountain; thence by a line in the direction of Concord, to the summit of the next mountain; thence along the summit of said mountain as far as practicable, so as to leave the entire valley of Amberson, in the county of Franklin, and to divide the mountain territory as equally as possible between the two counties; thence along the summit of the Round Top, to the most practicable point on the Conococheague Mountain, leaving .the entire valley called Sherman's Valley, in the county of Perry; and thence to the corner between Franklin, Perry and Juniata Counties; and said commissioners are required in all cases (in running said division line), to keep as near possible to the summit of said mountains." A year's time was allotted in which to complete the task and triplicate copies of the survey made, one each for the offices of the prothonotary of Perry and Franklin Counties and a third for the office of the surveyor general. This survey was a complicated affair to tackle, as anyone familiar with the various laps of the mountains there can readily realize.

There is a legend that at the northeastern corner of Perry County, in the river, there is a rock which is supposed to be the corner stone of five counties: Northumberland, Dauphin, Perry, Juniata, and Snyder. This is another of those local legends which is not borne out by facts. The fact is that but three, Dauphin, Perry, and Juniata Counties, meet at the river shore at that point. Juniata has a short stretch of river frontage, which bars Snyder from touching, and the Dauphin-Northumberland line would touch the shore considerably below the Perry-Juniata line. A similar legend, relating to the northwestern boundary, would have four counties, Perry, Juniata, Huntingdon, and Franklin, centre at a common corner. Save that of Huntingdon, the other three do meet there.

When Perry County was formed Landisburg was designated as the temporary county seat, pending the selection of a permanent site, and its residents immediately, as noted elsewhere, began a campaign to secure that advantage permanently. During the time the town was the county seat, the courts were held in a log building, located at the northwest corner of Carlisle and Water Streets.

It was unfinished, "chunked and daubed." The entire first floor was occupied by the court room, while the second floor was divided by board partitions into an office for the county commissioners, a room for the grand jury and a room for the traverse jury. The entrance to the second story was by a rude open stairway from the court room. The judge's "bench" was made of unplaned boards and was located on a raised platform at the northern end of the room. At its front was a shelf, the top of which was used to write upon or for placing documents, etc. The counsel table was an ordinary pine dinner table. The clerks' desks were very ordinary wooden affairs and the seats in the court room ordinary board benches. A small one-story dwelling adjoined it on the west, on Water Street, in which lived a tanner by the name of Allen Nesbit, whose small tanyard was located on the same lot. He rented the building to the new county for fifty dollars a year. With the exception of the commissioners' office the other county offices were located in the homes of the officials. The first sheriff, Daniel Stambaugh, and also his successor, Jesse Miller, had the office in the house located on the northeast corner of Centre Square, the first sheriff dying there during his term. The house is now owned by the S. P. Lightner estate, Mrs. Lightner occupying the property.

The register and recorder's office was located on Water Street, in a stone house belonging to Mrs. Robert Shuman at this time. This building had once been a hotel operated by W. P. West. Its erection was started in 1794 and it was completed in 1809. The rear part, or addition, was built of logs and in it at one time was a factory in which nails were made by hand, machine-made nails being then unknown.

The prothonotary's office was located in the parlor of the Patterson brick building, on Carlisle Street, until 1826, when removed to the new courthouse at New Bloomfield. William B. Mitchell was the prothonotary. This lot was bought December 11, 1811, by Jacob Fritz and sold to Samuel Anderson, who built the brick building. After 1826 it passed to Henry Fetter, who was a merchant there for years.

John Topley, Sr., was the court crier. Court was called by small boys ringing a bell along the street. Until each obtained a church building of its own the court room was the place of worship of the Presbyterian and Methodist congregations. When the courthouse at New Bloomfield was completed and the county seat removed the old courthouse became the property of Robert Gibson, who used it for a cabinet maker's shop until 1840, when he razed it and built the present building, which is now owned by D. B. Dromgold.

The first court of common pleas ever held in Perry County was convened in Landisburg on December 4, 1820. John Reed, originally of Westmoreland County, was the president judge, and William Anderson and Jeremiah Madden were the associate judges. David Stambaugh was sheriff. The first grand jurors were William English, Henry Bellin, William Brown, Jacob Weibley, and Joshua Jones, of Juniata Township; Andrew Linn, Peter Moses, Philip Fosselman, Christian Simons, Henry Hipple, Thomas Kennedy, and John Eaton, of Tyrone Township; Conrad Rice, John Milligan, Thomas Milligan, Moses Oatley, Jacob Burd, and Jacob Keiser, of Saville Township; William Arbigast, of Greenwood Township; William Potter, of Buffalo Township; Samuel Willis, of Rye Township; Nicholas Burd, John Kogan, and Daniel Motzer, of Toboyne Township.

The first traverse jurors were George Beard, John Linn, John Staily, Josiah Roddy, Jacob Reiber, George Arnold, Charles Elliott, John Moses, Peter Baker, John Elliott, John Holland, Robinson Black, Samuel Linn, Andrew Mateer, Thomas Black, Nicholas Ickes, Frederick Peale, Samuel Grubb, John Purcell, Jushua North, Jr., Charles Wright, John Keiser, William McClure, Jr., Michael Horting, Benjamin Leas, Sr., Daniel Bloom, Owen Owen, Philip Deckard, John Hallopeter, John Snyder, John Rumbaugh, Jacob Dubbs, and Samuel Thompson. They were paid for five days, except Nicholas Ickes, who was present only four days, at the rate of $1.00 per day and twelve and one-half cents per mile, one way, and the total cost of this jury was $223.25.

The constables at this time were: George Fetterman, Buffalo Township; John O'Brian, Greenwood Township; Thomas Martin, Juniata Township; Daniel McAllister, Rye Township; Mathias Moyer, Saville Township; John Cree, Tyrone Township; Abraham Kistler, Tyrone Township, and James McKim, Toboyne Township. The grand jury were paid $1.00 per day and six cents per mile circular, and for two days, the total cost of the first grand jury having been $73.48. The auditors were paid $2.00 per day, and the constables were paid $1.00 per day, but no mileage, for attending court.

The first record of a conveyance was a recorded deed from Jacob Sole, of Juniata Township, to Elizabeth Sole, of Millerstown, dated March 11, 1820, for three acres of land in Juniata Township, the consideration being $1.00. The first mortgage recorded was given by Samuel Stroop, of Tyrone Township to John Shuman, of Greenwood. The first proceedings in Orphans' Court was on December 4, 1820, when Caleb North, of Greenwood, was appointed guardian of Julia Power, minor daughter of James Power, late of Juniata Township. The first letters testamentary issued by the register of wills were those of Christian Seiders, of

The first justices of the peace of the new county were as follows, the transcript being taken from the Executive Minutes:

Friday, November 17, 1820.

The governor this day appointed and commissioned the following named persons to the office of justice of the peace in and for the districts hereafter mentioned in the county of Perry, that is to say: David Bloom, Robert Adams, and Jacob Bargstresser for the district composed of the township of Toboyne, in the said county, lately district number ten, in the county of Cumberland; Jacob Fritz, John Taylor, Jacob Stroop, William Power, and Henry Titzel for the district composed of the township of Tyrone, including the township of Saville, in the said county of Perry, lately district numbered eleven, in the county of Cumberland; John Ogle, John Owen, and John White, in and for the district composed of the township of Rye, in the county of Perry, lately the district numbered twelve, in the county of Cumberland; George Monroe, Benjamin Bonsall, Frederick Orwan, and James Black in and for the township of Juniata, in the said county of Perry, lately the district numbered thirteen in the said county of Cumberland; Caleb North, John Huggins, John Purcell, Samuel Utter, John Turner, Abraham Adams, Willian Linton, and Richard Bard, in and for the district composed of the township of Greenwood and Buffaloe, in the said county of Perry, lately the district numbered fourteen, in the county of Cumberland.—*Executive Minutes, Volume Eleven, page 251.*

Other justices of the peace commissioned during the county's very first years were as follows:

1822.   John Kooken, Toboyne; Robert Thompson, Buffalo; Francis Gibson, Tyrone; Thomas Gallagher, Liverpool.

1823.   Andrew Linn and George Baker, Saville; Frederick Speck, Wheatfield.

1824.   Joseph Martin, Juniata; Alexander Rogers, Wheatfield; George Mitchell, Liverpool.

1825.   Jacob Bloom and James R. Scott, Toboyne; Alexander Branyan, Rye.

Just why Perry County was so named has often been asked. Why was this name selected rather than some other? It will be remembered that the battle of Lake Erie was one of the greatest events of the War of 1812, or our Second War with England, that Commodore Perry was the hero, and that the war was over but six years before the erection of the county. But the great outstanding reason was that Commodore Perry died on August 23, 1819, at the Port of Spain, Island of Trinidad, and the news of his death had just reached our shores in the year of the county's creation; and that his death, like that of Ex-President Theodore Roosevelt in 1919, was the occasion of much grief, the erection of memorials, etc. Not only was he honored by the naming of Perry County, Pennsylvania, in memory of him, but counties elsewhere are so named. There are Perry Counties in nine other states, as follows: Alabama, Arkansas, Illinois, Indiana, Kentucky, Mississippi, Missouri, Ohio, and Tennessee.

And so it was named Perry—after Commodore Oliver Hazard Perry, who in 1812, as a young lieutenant, was sent to take charge of the fleet of boats on Lake Erie, who unfurled a blue flag bearing in white letters the dying words of the gallant Lawrence, "Don't give up the ship;" who succeeded in overcoming the powerful British boats and sent to General Harrison the famous dispatch, "We have met the enemy and they are ours—two ships, two brigs, one schooner and one sloop;" and who saved the young nation from an enemy's entrance over the lakes. He was in charge of the whole West Indian fleet as commodore at the time of his death.

A newspaper notice of the period, relating to the death of the hero for whom the new county of Perry was named, may not be inappropriate here:

NORFOLK, September 25.

Died. On the 23 of August, on board the United States schooner, Nonsuch, at the moment of her arrival at Port of Spain, in the Island of Trinidad, Commodore Oliver Hazard Perry. He was taken with yellow fever on his passage from the town of Angostura, and although he was attended by two able physicians, he was reduced to the greatest extremity on the fourth day of his illness. Sensible to his approaching dissolution, he called his officers together, and communicated his last wishes. His remains were interred at Port of Spain, on the 24th of August with naval and military honors.

Pennsylvania counties have been named under probably eight distinct classes, as follows: First, after English shires or counties; second, from Indian derivation; third, of sentimental suggestion; fourth, geological, geographical or faunal titles; fifth, topographically; sixth, of local historical connection; seventh, of political significance; eighth, in honor of patriots, etc. It is the last named and largest class which includes Perry.

A story, in connection with the locating of the temporary county seat at Landisburg, which is persistent, coming from a dozen widely separated sources, and always the same, is, it is believed, worthy a place here. The reader may pass judgment upon it. On all occasions the scorner turns up, but when this one turned up Perry Countians were in no humor to be ridiculed, having just came into their own after the opposition of Carlisle citizens, especially. The new county had just been created and the first court was to be held in an improvised courthouse in Landisburg. A number of young men from Carlisle came over and one of them kept up a continual interrogation, "Where's the town clock?" This angered a man named Power, and strangely enough Power was the next man to whom he put the question. A brawny arm shot out and the inquirer went down, but true to the species, he retorted, "There it is; it struck one."

Strange as it may seem, within two years after the separation of Perry County from "Mother Cumberland," there were petitions out for their merging, and strangest of all, the plan advocated was to annex Cumberland to Perry. A copy of the petitions was printed in the *Perry Forester*, Perry County's first paper, on February 7, 1822. It follows:

PETITION.

"To the Senate and House of Representatives of the Commonwealth of Pennsylvania, in General Assembly met. Sheweth:

"That on account of the great dissatisfaction which prevails in the borough of Carlisle, and the surrounding country, by reason that they have been separated from the county of Perry, and which has much increased our taxes, and not only this, but our once thrifty and flourishing old borough of Carlisle, has become delirious and inconsolable on account of the separation—and further, as we would prefer the name of *Perry* to that of *Cumberland,* because the latter savors something of royalty, being taken from the Duke of Cumberland in England, which your petitioners deem to be repugnant to the principles of our republican government; we therefor pray your honorable bodies to pass a law annexing Cumberland to Perry County, and that the seat of Justice may be located at Landisburg.

"And your petitioners in duty bound will pray, &c."

When the new county of Perry was formed the keepers of taverns, as they were then known, were holding licenses granted by the Cumberland County court. Accordingly the first licenses granted in Perry County were in 1821. From the Divisions of Records at the State Capitol a copy of the return to the state is made. It follows:

A list of the tavern keepers of Perry County to whom licenses have been granted by the Court of General Quarter Sessions of the Peace for said county, at January and April terms, 1821, and for which licenses have been delivered to William Power, Esqr., Treasurer of Perry County, viz:

At January Sessions, 1821.

David Pfautz, John Woodburn, George Eckerd, John Flurie, Henry Zimmerman, Anthony Brandt.

At April Sessions, 1821.

Andrew Tressler, John Foose, Thomas Craighead, Jr., Michael Sypher, John Hipple.

Henry Lightner, John Strawbridge, Gilbert Moon, Henry Long, John Dunkelberger, Thomas Paul.

Christian Hipple, Peter Wolf, John Miller, Peter Musselman, Frederick Rinehart, Henry Landis, George Wilt.

Benjamin Leas, James Baird, Peter Shively, John Snell, Daniel Gallatin, Jonathan Harmon.

Frederick Smiley, George Billow, John Neiper, John Rice.

County of Perry, S.S.

I, Henry Miller, Esquire, Clerk of the Court of General Quarter Sessions of the Peace, held at Landisburg for the County of Perry, do hereby certify that the within is a true statement of the tavern keepers of Perry County licensed by the Court at the January and April sessions, 1821, and that thirty-four licenses have accordingly been delivered to William Power, Esqr., Treasurer of Perry County.

                    In testimony whereof I have hereunto set my hand and affixed the Seal of said Court this fifteenth day of May, (Seal)   in the year of our Lord, one thousand, eight hundred and twenty-one.   HENRY MILLER,
Clerk of the Quarter Sessions.

To James Duncan Esq., Auditor
General of the Commonwealth of
Pennsylvania.

The following is the first return from the new county of Perry to the State Treasurer, being copied from the original document in the Bureau of Records at the State Capitol:

Wm. Powers, Esq., Treasurer of Perry County in account with the State of Pennsylvania.

Dr. With amount of eight licenses to retail foreign merchandise and liquors to the following persons, viz: to Robert H. McClelland, Henry Fetter, Abraham Fulweiler, George Tharp, Henry Walters, Philip Bosserman, Edward Purcell, Isaiah Clark, at fifteen dollars each, ...cash $120.00
With amount of ten licenses to retailers of foreign merchandise only to the following persons, viz: to Thomas Cochran, David Moreland, William Irwin, Nathan Van Fossen, Daniel Okeson, Thomas Gaulagher, John Rice, Anthony Black, Robert Welch, Peter Beaver, at ten dollars each, ... cash 100.00

                                                $220.00

Cr. With treasurer's commission, $217.75, at five per cent, $10.88
With amount paid constables for making returns of eighteen retailers of foreign merchandise and liquors at 12½c each, ... 2.25
                                                13.13

    Balance due state, ... $206.87
Settled and entered at the Auditor General's office,
              December 14, 1821.

FIRST RECORDS OF THE COMMISSIONERS' OFFICE.

*The first minute book of the commissioners of Perry County, which, according to the inside of the cover, cost $3.75, has the following inscribed on page 1:
                "Landisburg, Oct. 26th, 1820.

    "Agreeably to previous arrangements Thomas Adams, Jacob Huggins & Robert Mitchell, Esquires, duly elected Commissioners for the County of Perry met at the house of Michael Sypher and after having taken and subscribed the oaths of office required by the Constitution and laws of the Commonwealth of Pennsylvania,

---

    *For the interesting data from this first minute book of the first Board of County Commissioners we are indebted to Walter W. Rice, attorney-at-law, New Bloomfield, Pa.

"Appointed Jesse Miller Clerk to their Board for the term of one year and agreed to allow him Forty eight dollars pr. annum.

"Oct. 27th.

"Commissioners met. A full Board.

"Agreed with Jacob Albert for him to make the necessary seals for the different county offices at seven dollars per seal to be delivered on or before the 1st of Dec. next.

"Oct. 28th.

"Commissioners met. A full Board.

"Appointed William Power, Esqr., Treasurer for one year (commission 2 per cent for all monies by him rec'd and paid out according to law)."

This old minute book further shows that, on Nov. 6 and 7, 1820, Messrs. Huggins and Mitchell, Commissioners, "attended at Carlisle for the purpose of obtaining the original assessments of 1820 to get them transcribed, and that, on Nov. 8, 1820, Mr. Mitchell, having obtained the said assessments together with a transcript of the Treasurer's book of Cumberland County for the monies paid by the collectors of Perry County, returned to Landisburg and met Mr. Adams. These two met on the 9th, 10th, 11th and 12th of Nov., 1820, and on the 21st "a full Board" met and agreed with George Dunbar "for the making of a bench for the Judges of the Court & a counsel table." On Nov. 24th, 1820, the Board met for the purpose of "selecting jurors and comparing assessments." On that day the first order on the county treasury was granted to Robert Mitchell for $28.00 for pay as Commissioner from Oct. 26th, 1820, to Nov. 24th, 1820. On Nov. 25th, 1820, the Commissioners bought of William Power "6 candlesticks & 3 pair snufflers for $4.00," which were paid for by order No. 41 given on Feb. 2d, 1821. On Dec. 4th, 1820, order No. 2 was given to James Beatty "for $26.90 pay of the election officers of Juniata District for holding 2 elections in 1820." In the first part of the minute book the words "order given" were used, but later on "O. G." indicates that payment was ordered. On Dec. 5th, 1820, order No. 4 was given to David Grove, return judge for Toboyne Township, for $25.20 "pay of election officers of said District for holding 2 elections in 1820." On the same date an order was given to Alexander Magee, for $12.00 "for a transcribing docket to transfer suits from Cumberland County to Perry County." On Dec. 6th, 1820, orders for $20.00 and $26.00 were given to Thomas Adams and Jacob Huggins respectively for their pay as Commissioners from Oct. 26th, 1820, to Dec. 6th, 1820, "both days inclusive." These bills of the Commissioners evidently included their expenses, as no bills were presented for expenses. On Dec. 8th, 1820, orders were granted to Jacob Albert for $49.00 for seven seals for the county offices, George Dunbar for $9.00 for carpenter work and Andrew Martin $9.75 for making chairs. Robert McCoy was paid $50.00 for transcribing into a docket for the Court of Common Pleas of Perry County the record of the suits in the Cumberland County Court between persons residing in Perry County. On Jan. 30th, 1821, John Diven was paid $12.00 for making a jury wheel, and Alexander C. Martin was paid $2.58 "for the tuition of paupers as per acct." The witnesses were paid 50 cents per day and 3 cents per mile circular. An ink stand was bought from Samuel A. Anderson for 31 cents.

On Feb. 2d, 1821, Abraham Fulweiler was paid $106.87 for stoves, pipes, etc., and William Power $6.45 for candlesticks, wood, etc.

On Feb. 17th, 1821, the Commissioners met to lay the tax for 1821, and apportioning the rates on the different townships. Messrs. Huggins and

Mitchell held appeals on April 16th, 1821, at Clark's Ferry, on the 17th at Montgomery's Ferry, on the 18th at Capt. Frederick Rinehart's for Greenwood Township, on the 19th at the Blue Ball for Juniata Township, and all three Commissioners held appeals on the 20th at Ickesburg for Saville Township, on the 21st at Zimmerman's tavern for Toboyne Township, and on the 23d at their office for Tyrone Township. On the latter day they paid Robert Kelly, Teacher, $5.91 for tuition of paupers in Saville Township. On the 24th they paid William Charters 20 cents for candles. On April 30th, 1821, they paid John Jones $12.00 for a wolf scalp, and on May 1st, they paid William B. Mitchell $0.75 for two old fox scalps.

The records show that the office of tax collector was not a very desirable one in those days. Henry Kline, the Collector selected for Tyrone Township, refused to serve and paid a fine of $20.00. Robert Cree was then selected; he refused, and a suit was commenced against him for the fine.

The County Commissioners in the first few years of the existence of the County received $1.50 per day, and their yearly compensation averaged about $107.00. The Commissioners now receive $1,000.00 and their expenses per year.

The amounts of the tax duplicates and collectors for the year 1821 were as follows:

Daniel Motzer, Toboyne Township,	$1,200.26
Henry Kline, Tyrone Township,	1,575.89
Nicholas Ickes, Saville Township,	692.54
Philip Bosserman, Juniata Township,	915.22
Anthony Kimmel, Rye Township,	754.71
Isaac Pfoutz, Greenwood Township,	863.99
Henry Steaphen, Buffalo Township,	421.25
Total,	$6,423.86

A total of the duplicates for the county in 1920 was $62,950.64.

On Sept. 7, 1821, an order was given to Jacob Bishop, Keeper of the prison of Cumberland County, for $102.15 for maintaining 5 prisoners sent from Perry County. The daily charge was 20 cents. Among the items 104 lbs. beef at 5 cents per lb. and 8 quarts of soap at 6¼ cents per quart. One of the prisoners made 45 pairs of shoes in 15 weeks, and a credit at the rate of 40 cents per pair was allowed for his labor.

The election boards in those times consisted of 3 judges, 1 inspector and 2 clerks.

On Oct. 24, 1821, Jesse Miller was reappointed Clerk to the Commissioners and his salary was increased to $100.00 per annum.

On Nov. 3d, 1821, $10.00 was paid for one year's rent for the office of the Commissioners. On Dec. 6, 1821, $51.50 was paid to Allen Nesbet for one year's rent for the Court House and 6 mos. interest on the first semi-annual payment.

On Dec. 7, 1821, $27.00 was paid to William McClure, Deputy Attorney General, as his fees in 9 criminal cases.

On Dec. 7, 1821, $5.00 was paid to John Albert for "a bell to call the court."

On March 12th, 1827, the Commissioners held their last meeting in Landisburg and removed their offices to Bloomfield.

CHAPTER XIII.

THE FIGHT FOR THE COUNTY SEAT

IN the locating of its county seat Perry County had almost as much trouble as the United States had had just three decades before, when for a long period Trenton, New Jersey, and the present site were rivals; when, in 1789, the Commonwealth of Pennsylvania, in the United States Senate, offered to deed ten miles square around any one of seven towns, which included Harrisburg and Carlisle, and when it was proposed to select a site on the Susquehanna instead of the Potomac.

COURTHOUSE AT NEW BLOOMFIELD.

In accordance with the provisions of the act creating the county Governor William Findlay was empowered to appoint a commission of three men from without the county to select a location for the county seat. This commission was appointed eight days later and was composed of William Beale, of Mifflin County; David Maclay, of Franklin County, and Jacob Bucher, of Dauphin County. The following extract from the Executive Minutes, Volume 11, page 168, records the appointment:

Thursday, March 30th, 1820.

The Governor this day appointed and commissioned the following named persons to the offices annexed to their names, respectively, that is to say.

William Beale, of Mifflin County, David Maclay of Franklin County, and Jacob Bucher of Dauphin County, to be commissioners to fix upon a proper and convenient site for a Court house, prison, and County offices, within the County of Perry, as near the Centre thereof as circumstances will admit, having regard to the convenience of roads, territory, population and the accommodation of the people of the said County generally; and the said Commissioners, or a majority of them having viewed the relative advantages of the several situations contemplated by the people, were required on or before the first day of September next by a written report under their hands or under the hands of a majority of them, to certify, describe and limit the site, or lot of land which they shall choose for the purpose aforesaid, and to transmit the said report to the Governor; and to do all other matters and things required of them in and by an act of the General Assembly, passed on the 22d day of March last, entitled, "An Act erecting part of Cumberland County into a separate County to be called Perry."

There have been many political fights in Perry County during the past century, but from what can be gleaned from old newspapers and records that county seat fight eclipsed them all. The many different locations proposed complicated the situation. Landisburg, with a taste of the dignity attached to the temporary seat of justice, put up a stiff fight. An old subscription list shows that the citizens obligated themselves for $1,610.00 to help secure it. Cedar Run (vicinity of Cisna's Run, Madison Township), then in Toboyne Township, raised the sum of $2,907.00. There was a provision that the plot to be used was to be that of Helfenstine and Ury (now Wm. H. Loy's), who agreed to raise the amount to $5,000.00, on such condition.

Casper Lupfer offered a free site on his "plantation" which was adjoining the present site of New Bloomfield, later owned by W. A. Sponsler, then John R. Adams, and now in the possession of Robert E. McPherson. Inhabitants of Millerstown and vicinity offered a site in Raccoon Valley, Tuscarora Township, opposite Millerstown, owned by Henry Lease. Other proposed locations were Clark's Ferry (now Duncannon), Reider's Ferry (now Newport), George Barnett's (the present site), Captain William Powers', west of New Bloomfield, Elliottsburg, and Douglas' place, near Green Park.

Before the matter was finally decided and the present location selected there were four different commissions appointed to select a site. Public meetings were held at various places over the new county and petitions gotten out protesting against different sites and favoring others. The first commission, after examining the various sites offered, which required twelve days of their time, which shows that they covered it pretty thoroughly, decided on the site on the farm of William Powers, about two miles west of New Bloomfield. On the back of the report are the signatures: David Maclay, W. Maclay, W. Beale and J. Bucher. How "W. Maclay" came to have an interest in it records do not tell, but he was not on the original appointment. Their first meeting was in June, 1820, and they made their report August 26, 1820. Millerstown held a meeting, December 2, and resolved "that the commission did its duty by locating it at the centre of the county."

Hardly had the report been made public when Landisburg, on December 2, held a public meeting to protest. A resolution was passed opposing the site as a place "having no intersection of roads, no direct intercourse with adjacent counties—a strong point with Landisburg—destitute of good water, good mills or even mill sites." Protests came from all over the new county. At the meeting of the next legislature many citizens of the county petitioned for another commission, which was granted by an act dated April 2, 1821, which required that the new commission should examine sites and report before June 1. This commission was composed of William Irwin, of Centre County; Isaac Kirk, of York County, and Christian Ley, of Lebanon County.

At times a story has been told of William Powers and the commission digging a well and getting no water, of Powers and his negro servant hauling water into the well and of the commission, "discouraged, resolving to stop work on the well." Nothing in any record, in any newspaper, or used by the opposition at the time would help to substantiate that story, and it is one of those mythical stories which sometimes gain considerable circulation, but which are unfounded and will not stand when scrutinized. Had such been the case the other points seeking the location would have grasped the information quickly and utilized it. Furthermore, the commission had neither the authority nor the time to go into the well-digging business.

The following entry appears on Executive Minutes of the State, Volume 11, page 359:

Saturday, April 28th, 1821.

Under the authority contained in an Act of the General Assembly passed the second day of the present month, entitled, "A supplement to an Act entitled 'An Act erecting part of Cumberland County into a separate County to be called Perry,'" the Governor this day appointed William Irwin, of the County of Centre; Isaac Kirk, of the County of York, and Christian Ley, of the County of Lebanon, Esquires. Commissioners to review the scite lately determined upon by the Commissioners appointed in pursuance of the original act aforesaid, for the seat of justice of the County of Perry, and if they, or a majority of them shall be of opinion that the said scite does not combine the interests and advantages of the inhabitants of the said County generally, then, and in that case, they or a majority of them, are authorized and required to select and fix upon some other scite for a Court house, prison, and County offices, within the said County of Perry, as near the Centre thereof as circumstances will admit,— they, the said Commissioners to execute the said Commission according to the true intent and meaning of the above recited Act of Assembly, and of the ninth section of the Act to which the same is a supplement; and to make a report to the Governor in writing, under their respective hands and seals, on or before the first day of June, next, certifying, describing and limiting the scite or lot of ground which shall have been chosen by them as aforesaid.

Sites were proposed by a committee of one from each township, but in the voting the result was as follows: Clark's Ferry (now Duncannon), 5; Barnett's, 2; Landisburg, 9; county poor farm, 0.

This second commission located the site at Reider's (now Newport), which resulted in indignation meetings being held in the other sections of the county. The fact that it was seven miles from the centre of the county resulted in another lot of petitions

to the State Legislature, which, at the next session, on March 11, 1822, passed an act which created the third commission, the members of which were named in the act.

On Friday, September 14, 1821, a meeting was held at the home of Captain William Powers to protest against the site at Reider's Ferry. The delegates to this meeting were:

Buffalo.—Col. Robert Thompson, Frazer Montgomery.
Juniata.—Wm. English, Finlaw McCown, John Kyser.
Rye.—John Chisholm, Abraham Brunner.
Saville.—Robert Hackett, Andrew Linn, Conrad Rice.
Toboyne.—Wm. Anderson, Robert Adams, Col. John Urie.
Tyrone.—Francis Gibson, Allen Nesbit, Wm. Wilson.

This third commission was composed of Moses Rankin, of York; James Hindman, of Chester; Peter Frailey, of Schuylkill; David Fullerton, of Franklin, and James Agnew, of Bedford. They were to report before June 1, 1822. From Executive Minutes, Volume 11, page 527, is reproduced their official notification from the chief executive:

Wednesday, March 27th, 1822.

A certified copy of the Act of the General Assembly passed the eleventh instant entitled "A supplement to an Act entitled 'An Act erecting part of Cumberland County into a separate County to be called Perry,'" was this day transmitted by mail to each of the Commissioners named therein, to wit: Moses Rankin, of York County; James Hindman, of Chester County; Peter Frailey, of Schuylkill County; David Fullerton, of Franklin County, and James Agnew, of Bedford County; who were at the same time respectively notified that the Governor by virtue of the power in the said Act of Assembly given to him, has fixed upon the seventh day of May, and the Town of Landisburg, in the said County of Perry, as the time, and place of meeting of the said Commissioners.

This commission—the third—decided upon Landisburg as the proper location. A few days later, on June 5, citizens from the five eastern townships held a meeting at the home of John Koch, which history tells us was at Blue Ball, Juniata Township, and appointed a committee to draw up an address to the citizens of the county on the subject. Frazer Montgomery, John Harper, and William Waugh composed the committee, whose report recited at length reasons why the county seat should not be located at Landisburg, which was within three miles of the Cumberland County line, and protested the unjustness of the location to the county at large. On October 16, 1822, a meeting of the citizens of Juniata and Buffalo Townships was held at the home of Meredith Darlington to discuss the merits and demerits of the various proposed sites. Of this meeting there is some record; Francis McCowen was the chairman and William Power, Jr., secretary. Resolutions were passed proposing the site first selected on the Power farm, west of New Bloomfield. This site, we are told, is at the exact centre of the county.

15

That weapon of every cause, the petition, was again brought into being and stated that three different commissions had been appointed under acts of the Pennsylvania Legislature, the last commission having moved the location to Landisburg, a place which is within three miles of the Cumberland County line and a distance of thirty-four miles from the eastern settlement. The proposed place for its location on the Power farm is named as the admitted centre of territory and population as near as circumstances will admit.

On November 16, 1822, a public meeting of protest was held at the home of John Fritz, at the Bark tavern, in Rye Township (now Centre, near New Bloomfield), for the purpose of electing delegates and recommending or requesting the citizens of the other townships to do likewise, such delegates—two from each township—to meet at the home of John Fritz on December 10, 1822, to designate a place for the location of the county seat, and draft a petition accordingly. No record of the meeting is handed down to posterity, yet it evidently was held, for on December 23, 1822, Mr. Mitchell, a member of the legislature, presented to the House twenty-one petitions, signed by eight hundred of the inhabitants of the county, praying that the seat of justice for the new county be fixed at the point suggested by the first commission. The member of the General Assembly from Perry County at that time was not Mr. Mitchell, but F. M. Wadsworth, and again history fails to tell us why the petitions was not presented by him. The commission having fixed the site at Landisburg, as far as they were concerned, reported, and an act for the confirmation thereof came before the House on Monday, February 24, 1823, and after considerable discussion passed first reading. It came up on Tuesday for second reading, and a Mr. Todd proposed a substitute for the act, naming Barnett's farm instead of Landisburg. On a vote this proposition for the Barnett farm was defeated fifty-six to thirty. The bill was killed in the Senate by a proposition to create another commission.

The fourth commission was appointed by Governor Joseph Heister, in accordance with an act passed March 31, 1823, being composed of the following men: Joseph Huston, of Fayette; Abner Leacock, of Beaver; Cromwell Pearce, of Chester; Henry Sheete, of Montgomery, and Dr. Phineas Jenks, of Bucks. The first stated meeting of this commission was to be at the home of Meredith Darlington, on Wednesday, May 28, 1823, but the weather being stormy, they postponed business until Friday. On that day they met at Landisburg and decided to ignore all three of the sites previously chosen. Then, on Monday, June 2, 1823, they decided to locate the county seat on the farm of George Barnett, in Juniata (now Centre) Township, within about two miles of the Powers location, the one named by the first commission.

They reported, and in January, 1824, the act was introduced in the legislature, when Jacob Huggins, then the member of the General Assembly from Perry County, presented nine petitions for confirmation of this site and nine petitions for the site at Landisburg. On February 5, 1824, he again presented petitions, which shows that those early Perry Countians had contracted the petition habit. On this occasion there were nine for the New Bloomfield (or Barnett) site and seven for Landisburg. On February 27 he presented seven for Landisburg and one for New Bloomfield. The matter had now narrowed down to the two sites and Mr. Huggins stated that he was privileged to withdraw the petitions of Abraham Reider and William Power.

The report of this fourth commission is on record in the office of the custodian of public records at the State Capitol and is reproduced below:

To Joseph Hiester esquire Governor of the Commonwealth of Penna.

Sir: In compliance with an Act of the Legislature of this State passed the 31st day of March, 1823, entitled An Act Supplementary to an Act entitled A Supplement to an Act erecting a part of Cumberland County into a separate County to be calld. Perry and in accordance with our appointment we the undersigned Commissioners wiz: Abner Laycock, Cromwell Pearce, Henry Sheets and Phineas Jenks, having met (for the purpose of carrying the requisitions of the said act into effect) at the house of Meredith Darlington in Juniata Township on the 28th day of May and after taking the requisite oaths proceeded to view the several sites contemplated by the people as well as those fixed upon by former Commissioners.

And from the view we have taken of the territorial bounds of said County, the relative situation of its inhabitants, convenience of roads, waters etc. we are of opinion that neither of the sites fixed upon by former Commissioners are calculated to combine the interests or render that satisfaction and accommodation to the Citizens of said County contemplated by the law under which we act.

Therefore we have after due deliberation unanimously agreed, and have located a site for the seat of Justice of Perry County on the farm of George Barnett in Juniata Township described and bounded as follows, viz: Beginning at a Post in the field west of the barn South 68 degrees West 9 perches & two tenths from a wild Cherry tree then from said post South 64 degrees West 34.2 perches to a post thence North 26 degrees West 41 perches to a post thence North 64 degrees East 34.2 perches to a post thence South 26 degrees East 41 perches to the place of beginning, which lot or parcell of ground as above described we do hereby adjudge and confirm as far as our power extends as laid down by said act to be the proper site to erect the Court house, prison and County offices of said County of Perry upon, and as such make report and return the same to the Governor as we are by law directed.

Given under our Hands this second day of June An dom 1823.

A. LACOCK.   HENRY SCHEETZ.
CROMWELL PEARCE.   PHS. JENKS.

Apropo of the location having been finally determined the following documents, in the possession of the Barnett sisters, of New Bloomfield, may be of interest:

"30th of May, 1823.

"Know all men by these presents, that I, George Barnett, of Juniata township, in the county of Perry, do bind myself, my heirs, executors, or administrators to give as a donation for the use of Perry County, five acres of Land in Case the Seat of Justice be Located on my farm, but none of the principal springs to be included in said five acres, but is hereby Reserved for the use of the Town & I will also Give five acres of woodland for the use of the County of Perry."   Geo. Barnett.

Present, Jeremiah Madden.

A copy of the original petition used in order to have the present location chosen is also reproduced, the signatures being omitted. It follows:

"May, 1823.

"To Joseph Huston & others, Esquires, Commissioners appointed by an act of the General Assembly passed the 31st day of March, one thousand, Eight Hundred and twenty three to fix and locate the Seat of Justice in Perry County.

"The Petition of the Citizens of said County Humbly Sheweth,

"Whereas the Seat of Justice has been located by three different set of Viewers in said County but not to the Satisfaction of a Majority of the Inhabitants of our County we therefore Humbly set fourth and Represent the Plantation of Mr. George Barnett in our County it being the most Centerable scite for the Seat of Justice accommodated with Roads from the four quarters of the County and a Variety of never failing springs in a wholesome Pleasant situation. We are of opinion had the seat of Justice in our County been located on the above said Plantation by any of the former Viewers the Contest now would be at an end—and if fixed there now it would have the same Effect.

"We therefore Pray to take the above into Consideration & your Petitioners will Ever Pray, &c."

On April 12, 1824, George Barnett conveyed to the commissioners of Perry County eight acres and one hundred and thirty-six perches of land which was selected as the county seat site by the commission appointed under the Act of March 31, 1823. The deed bears the date of April 12, 1824.

A century has rolled around; the gig, the phaëton and all of their kind have been superseded by the automobile for trips of any length and, after all the phases of the contest have been settled, the experience of a century shows that in the final conclusion 'twas well done, and to-day an automobile from one end of the county can reach the seat of justice as quickly as from the other.

In 1849 and again about 1886 movements were begun in efforts towards having the county seat removed to Newport, but with no success. The movement inaugurated in 1849 went so far as to have a bill introduced into the legislature changing the county seat, but it was reported negatively and died, and with it the attendant agitation. The later movement, while resulting in nothing in so far as the changing of the county seat was concerned, was the beginning of the movements which resulted in two railroads, the Perry County and the Newport & Sherman's Valley, being built into western Perry County.

Three other near-by Pennsylvania counties, Mifflin, Adams, and Franklin, each had three commissions before the sites of their seats of justice were finally determined, but Perry County required the fourth.

With the final conclusion of the location of the seat of justice "on George Barnett's farm" the officials of the new county got busy to comply with the sections of the act creating it, one of which—Section 10—authorized the county commissioners to accept title to the site selected and to "assess, levy and collect money to build a courthouse and prison." As these matters could not be done in a short time the act—Section 16—provided that "all prisoners of Perry County shall be kept in the Cumberland County jail for the term of three years, or until the commissioners of Perry County shall have certified to the court that a jail is erected and approved by the court and grand jury." Then, on May 17, 1824, the commissioners of the new county of Perry advertised that twenty-five lots on the public ground recently conveyed to the county by George Barnett would be sold at "public vendue" on Wednesday, June 23, 1824. By referring to the chapter in this book relating to "Bloomfield Borough, the County Seat," the reader may learn something of the sales of these first lots, also of the taking up of this plot of land by the pioneers.

Three sales of lots were held to dispose of the lands donated by George Barnett to the county of Perry. The first was on June 23, 1824, and Robert Elliott, Samuel Linn, and John Maxwell, the commissioners, sold lots to the value of $1,913, one-third of which was payable in cash on August 3d, and one-third annually for the two succeeding years. On September 14, 1826, a second sale was held by Robert Mitchell, Abraham Bower, and Abraham Adams, then commissioners, and lots disposed of to the amount of $594. The third sale was on June 28, 1828, when Abraham Bower, John Owen, and George Mitchell, the board of commissioners, sold a single lot for the original price, $200, on which the former bidder had paid $32 and then defaulted. Thus it will be seen that the county not only received the ground for its public buildings, but also $2,539.00 from the sales of lots. In addition $267.50 was subscribed and paid in cash into the treasury of the new county.

The contract for the jail was first let. On July 7, 1824, the county commissioners, Robert Elliott, Samuel Linn, and John Maxwell, advertised for proposals for erecting a stone jail, the dimensions of which were to be 32x50 feet, two stories high, with walls two and one-half feet in thickness. The lower floor was to

have four rooms and the upper one six. John Rice was the contractor, the cost to be $2,400, but its final cost proved to be $2,600.
The few prisoners from the new county were transferred back
from Cumberland on its completion. John Hipple was awarded
the contract on October 1, 1827, to build a stone wall enclosing the
jail yard at a cost of $950, which he completed the following year.
This original jail, with slight alterations and improvements served
the use of the county for the remainder of the century. On April
4, 1902, bids were received for the erection of a new brick jail,
not to be enclosed by the ancient high wall, in which was also to
be the residence of the sheriff. Dean & Havens, contractors, received the contract at $26,000, but changes in the plans increased
its cost to over $30,000. It was occupied January 1, 1903. It is
modern in every respect, it is said, but not greatly needed in Perry
County. On many occasions there have not been any prisoners
within its walls, and the average population is less than two persons.

At the election of 1824 Robert Mitchell and Abraham Bower
succeeded John Maxwell and Robert Elliott on the board of commissioners, the other member being Samuel Linn. On April 11,
1825, they advertised that they would receive proposals until August 30th for the erection of a new brick courthouse, forty-five
feet square. In September the contract was awarded to John
Rice for $2,975, but later the height of the walls was increased
and a cupola added to the contract. The building was completed
in 1826 at a cost of $4,240. The courthouse then erected was in
use until 1868, when the grand jury authorized the county commissioners to make any alterations and additions that might be
necessary for the increasing business of the county, then about to
enter its second half-century of existence. It was considerably
enlarged and modernized and including the cost of the clock tower
cost a trifle over $25,000, the citizens of the town donating ap-
proximately $300 towards purchasing the clock. While these
alterations were being done the county offices were installed in the
basement of the Presbyterian Church, and the sessions of court
were held in the old Methodist Church on High Street. A new
addition was erected in 1892 to the north end of the building at a
cost of about $20,000. In it are the offices of the register and
recorded and prothonotary, on the first floor, and the jury rooms
and the law library on the second floor.

The removal of the public documents from Landisburg to
Bloomfield took place on March 12 and 13th, 1827.

CHAPTER XIV.

TRAILS AND HIGHWAYS.*

THE story of the settlement of Perry County territory is also the story of the first road westward over the Allegheny Mountains to the Ohio, which was then the "Far West." The travel on streams was by canoe, and on land, following the trails made by the Indians through the forests, first on foot, the original manner of travel; later on horseback, and with the advent of roads, in carriages and wagons. These Indian trails were generally direct, reaching the gaps in the mountains and following streams, when the route was not too circuitous. The continual use of given routes, even afoot, soon created paths, which the Indians termed trails, and which often later became pack horse paths, then roads or highways, some even becoming main highways or turnpikes. Some were narrow and never became utilized for vehicles, but were used by the pioneer circuit rider, who came after the Indians had departed, and by the pioneers before roads became general. These were then known as bridle paths and some of them are yet distinguishable. One such is over the end of Bowers' Mountain, near Cisna's Run, and another around the foot of Mt. Dempsey, opposite Landisburg, in Sheaffer's Valley, and not far from Sherman's Creek. Both are known to the oldest residents of these localities from their earliest recollections.

One of these old Indian trails led from New York State, southwest across Pennsylvania, to the Potomac, contiguous to Perry County soil, through present Juniata County. It was known as the Tuscarora Path, hence the names of two of the valleys through which it passed, *Tuscarora* and *Path*. Its proximity to the county territory is largely responsible for the seeming ease with which the Indian warriors reached here even from remote points to wield the tomahawk and scalping knife.

The through trail to the West, as far as the Ohio, first known as the "Allegheny Path," led through Croghan's (now Sterrett's)

---

*In discussing the inception of this volume with Prof. H. H. Shenk, custodian of public records of the Commonwealth of Pennsylvania, to whom we are indebted for many suggestions and much encouragement, he remarked that the history of roads and highways was very much neglected, a fact which has proven true, in so far as Perry County is concerned at least. An effort has been made to record the earlier roads with partial success. Following the first Indian trails in the province, roads or highways were laid out, the main ones being at first known as "The King's Highways," for the pioneers had not yet arrived at the point where freedom was even considered.

Gap, across what is now Perry County, over Tuscarora Mountain, through Shade Gap, Black Log, Aughwick, Frankstown, and Hollidaysburg, crossing the Allegheny Mountains at or near Kittanning Point. It was the great highway to the West and was used by George Croghan, Andrew Montour, Conrad Weiser and other traders, interpreters and government representatives as far back as records are available. It was in general use by traders in 1740 and succeeding years. It was then an old Indian trail and it was but natural for these men to use it. It became known as the "Traders' Path" and as "The Horseway." It descended in turn to the pioneers, but they were men of vision and soon regular roads were laid out and built.

Watson's Annals tells of a Mrs. Murphy, who died at the age of 100, in 1803, and who remembered "that the first 'Indian track' to go westward was across Simpson's Ferry, four miles below Harris', then across the Conodoguinet at Middlesex, then up the Kittatinny Mountain across Croghan's (Sterrett's) Gap, thence down the mountain and across Sherman's Creek at Gibson's, thence by Dick's Gap, thence by Sherman's Valley, by Concord, to the burnt cabins, thence to the west of the Allegheny."

The route westward varied at points, or rather, at some places there were several routes, but this oldest of routes over Perry County's domain, was likely the main trail to which these other routes led.

John Harris, who had been westward in 1748, left a diary which mentions the following points with intermediate distances:

"From my ferry to George Croghan's, 5 miles; to Kittatinny Mountain, 9; to Andrew Montour's, 5; to Tuscarora Hill, 9 (Conococheague Mountain is intended) ; to *Thomas Mitchell's sleeping place, 3; to Tuscarora, 14; to Cove Spring, 10; Shadow of Death, 8; Black Log, 3; 66 miles to this point."

"Starting at Black Log, to Aughwick, 6; Jack Armstrong's Narrows (so called from his being murdered there), 8; to Standing Stone (about 14 feet high and 6 inches square), 10; total, 24 miles."

The "standing stone" referred to is where Huntingdon is now located. There was a route from Croghan's via Robert Dunning's and McAllister's Gap, west of Perry County, to Path Valley, but six miles of it through the gap were at the bottom of a chasm, over a bed of stones and rocks, which the waters of ages had washed bare, and the descent into Path Valley was very steep and stony for an additional mile, so that the route over the Perry

---

*Thomas Mitchell's sleeping place was in that part of Madison Township known as Liberty Valley. It is mentioned by John Harris, in his table of distances from Harrisburg to Logstown, in 1754, and by Conrad Weiser. Mitchell was an Indian trader as early as 1848 and is supposed to have made a shelter at this point.

County territory became the popular one. This old path, known as the Allegheny Path, the Traders' Path, etc., came through Croghan's (now Sterrett's) Gap, followed the south side of Sherman's Creek to a point west of Gibson's Rock, where it crossed to the north, continuing westward to where Montour's Run joined the creek; from there it passed onward by Fort Robinson, crossing the Conococheague Mountain's end near the present Sandy Hill road, past Thomas Mitchell's sleeping place (the old Meminger place), in Liberty Valley, via Bigham's Gap to the Tuscarora Valley. A tradition has the path crossing the Conococheague at a point between Andersonburg and Blain, but the late Prof. J. R. Flickinger, himself a resident of the immediate vicinity, wrote "it seems improbable that a crossing so difficult would be selected, when nature had provided an easier passage at a point almost as direct." The sleeping places mentioned at various places were usually either hollow logs, bark or sapling huts or abandoned Indian shacks, and no record remains as to the nature of the "Thomas Mitchell sleeping place." It likely took its name from the fact that he either improvised it or that he was the first one known to use it. A deed on record in the Perry County courhouse, executed in 1811, mentions the Meminger place as the location of "Mitchell's Sleeping Place." Thomas Mitchell was an unlicensed trader in 1747, and in the minutes of the Provincial Counsel for November 15, 1753, is mentioned as a man of no character. Authorities differ as to the route, as the following paragraph shows.

In describing this old Indian trail across the county Prof. A. L. Guss, the historian, says: "The path by way of Bigham's Gap is largely misunderstood. Liberty Valley was an impregnable thicket of laurel and spruce. No early trader or adventurer passed through it. It took much and hard labor to make a path through it. The west Tuscarora and the Conococheague Mountains form an anticlinal axis, with Horse Valley scooped out of the crest. Just where they begin to separate the broadened mountain has ravines on each side, and it was along these ravines that the early path led over the mountains. The old 'traders' road' passed up a ravine north of Andersonburg and came down a ravine at Mohler's tannery, in Liberty Valley, and crossed directly over the depressed end of the Tuscarora Mountain by Bigham's Gap."

It was contended by the province at the treaty of Albany in 1754 and admitted by the Indians (the Six Nations) that "the road to Ohio is no new road; it is an old, frequented road; the Shawnees and Delawares removed thither about thirty years ago from Pennsylvania, ever since which that road has been traveled by our traders at their invitation, and always with safety until within these few years." The reader will note that it was then already called an "old, frequented road."

That the first official journey of a representative from the colonies bordering the Atlantic seaboard to the lands west of the Alleghenies—that mighty empire of the West—was made over this old Allegheny Path, through the territory now comprising Perry County, is an historical fact. That notable journey of Conrad Weiser at the instance of the English colonies in 1748 was the occasion. Of course there were other trails to the West, but this was at that time the principal one. "There were later three great Indian paths from the East to the West through western Pennsylvania," says Thwaite's "Early Western Travels." "The southern led from Fort Cumberland, on the Potomac, westward through the valleys of Youghiogheny and Monongahela, to the forks of the Ohio, and was the route taken by Washington in 1753, later by Braddock's expedition, and was substantially the line of the great Cumberland National Road of the early Nineteenth Century. The central trail, passing through Carlisle, Shippensburg, and Bedford, over Laurel Mountain, through Fort Ligonier, over Chestnut Ridge to *Shannopin's town, at the forks of the Ohio, was the most direct and became the basis of General Forbes' road and later the Pennsylvania wagon road to the Ohio. But the older, or Kittatinny Trail, was the oldest and most used by the Indian traders. It was this route that Conrad Weiser followed. From Croghan's (in East Pennsboro Township, Cumberland County) he passed over into the valley of Sherman's Creek (now in Perry County), crossing Sterrett's Gap and the Tuscarora Mountains via Standing Stone (now Huntingdon). There was also a fourth trail, still farther north, by way of Sunbury and the West Branch to Venango."

Of the place where the Kittatinny Trail, more generally known as the Allegheny Path, crossed the Allegheny Mountains, Jones, in his History of the Juniata Valley (1889) says: "It is still visible in some places where the ground was marshy, close to the run; the path is at least twelve inches deep and the very stones along the road bear the marks of the iron-shod horses of the Indian traders." As late as 1796 Carlisle was an important point for the starting of pack horse trains for Pittsburgh and the Ohio region.

There are records to show that this old Allegheny Trail was taken by the northern section of Liuet. Col. John Armstrong in his expedition against the Indians at Kittanning in 1756. They show that the expedition left Carlisle in August, Colonel Armstrong being personally in charge, "going via Sherman's Valley." At Fort Shirley additional recruits were received.

---

*Shannopin's town was named after a chief of that name, who died in 1749. It was situated on the Allegheny River where the present city of Pittsburgh stands.

When the English and French rivalry for the possession of America came to its inevitable end—war—Conrad Weiser, an agent for the provincial government, was sent to the Ohio for the purpose of conciliating the Indians, as was the custom, with valuable presents. At the same time his duties were not unlike those of a spy. He was to ascertain their strength, location, mood and prestige, and at the same time learn the objects of the French. With the party on this trip was a son of Benjamin Franklin, George Croghan, and Andrew Montour, and there is record of their using this route over Perry County soil.

When there was pressing need of military operations against the French on the Ohio, in 1754, and ways and means were under consideration, there was no other highway; and Governor Morris described it as "only a horseway through the woods and over the mountains, not passable with any carriage." Travel was not diverted from this road or trail until a year later, 1755, when the southern route was made. over the Alleghenies via the route which is to-day known as the Lincoln Highway, in order to enable Braddock and his army to march against Fort Duquesne. In May of that year the province agreed to send three hundred men, in order to cut a wagon road from Fort Loudon, Franklin County, to join Braddock's Road near the "turkey foot," three miles from the forks of the Youghiogheny.

In the introductory remarks in the chapter relating to churches, there is an account of a Presbyterian missionary, Rev. Charles Beatty, passing over this route in 1766. It was then only an Indian trail over which the pioneers had entered the county's territory. However, it became the first road to be laid out in the new purchase covered by the Albany treaty. In 1761 the Cumberland County court ordered it laid out as a public highway between Carlisle and Sherman's Valley. Viewers appointed by the court recommended that the road be opened "through the lands of Francis West (vicinity of the Gibson mill) and others, from Carlisle, across the mountain, and through Sherman's Valley, to Alexander Logan's, and from thence to the gap in the Tuscarora Mountain, leading to Aughwick and Juniata, as the nearest and best way from the head of Sherman's Valley to Carlisle." The removal of the timber was about all that was required in making a roadway in those days.

This old Allegheny Path should be taken over in its entirely by the State Highway Department, if for no other reason than that it was the first roadway to the West, but another great reason is that a good road is needed. not only by the public but by the state. whose reserve—the Tuscarora Forest—it passes through. There are only certain small links which need to be improved. From Carlisle to a locality known as Dromgold there is already a state road. The stretches from Dromgold to Landisburg, from a mile west of Landisburg to Loysville, and from the Waggoner Mill bridge, via Fort Robinson, Kistler and Walsingham, to Honey Grove, in Juniata County, is all that requires to be taken over. A fair road already exists over these stretches, but there is no reason why the entire old Allegheny Path should not be kept up at state expense. Representative Clark Bower introduced a bill to that effect in the legislature of 1920-21, but it failed. That bill should be introduced at each and every session until the great commonwealth, in a way, perpetuates the first great highway to the West.

There were trails along the Juniata and Susquehanna Rivers, entering the county above Duncan's and Haldeman's Islands, the latter going into the Susquehanna country and New York State and known as the Susquehanna Trail, and the former being of a local nature, as the traffic from Harris' Ferry westward preferred the more direct line across present Perry County, via Black Log and Aughwick. Hardy, in "The Wilderness Trail," says another traders' path north of the Juniata was joined by the Shamokin Path near what is now Mifflintown, and was crossed by the Tuscarora Path near present Port Royal, Pennsylvania. He also says: "One branch may have led directly up the river from the Shawnee towns on Big Island (now Haldeman Island), and on the mainland, opposite, at the mouth of the Juniata; if so the first stage may have been by canoes, as the river, from the island to what is now Newport, is hemmed in in some places by mountains." Tradition differs from that statement and we are inclined to be with tradition in this case. The Indians had a fording, known as "Queenashawakee," where Clark's Run enters the Susquehanna in Duncannon Borough, and there was a trail from there through the hills via the old Dick's Gap Church, to below the present location of Newport, which was four miles shorter than the river route, and it was but natural for the Indian to take the shorter route. That there was a trail over this route is proven by the fact that the church was located along the old trail and that the first stage line likewise followed the trail. Furthermore, the average Indians hardly found canoes available for "through traffic."

Further on in "The Wilderness Trail" is this reference to a branch of the Allegheny Path which connected with the Susquehanna Trail: "Bishop Cameroff, who traveled along the east bank of the Susquehanna from Paxtang to Shamokin in the winter of 1748, notes in his journal that after crossing to the north side of Wiconisco Creek, near its mouth, on January 12th, he came to a house a short distance beyond, where he halted. Here his host informed him that on the west bank of the Susquehanna, opposite to his home, 'began the great path to the Allegheny country, estimated to be three or four hundred miles distant.' This must have been in what is now Buffalo Township, Perry County."

· The inception of the first road to what is now Juniata and Mifflin Counties dates to 1767, when a petition was presented to the Cumberland County court to open a road from Sherman's Valley to the Kishacoquillas Valley. In May, 1768, viewers reported in favor of "a carriage road from the Sherman's Valley road, beginning two and three-quarter miles from Croghan's (now Sterrett's) Gap, running through Rye Township and across the Juniata River at the mouth of Sugar Run, into Fermanagh (now Greenwood) Township, and thence through the same and Derry Township, up the north side of the Juniata into the Kishacoquillas Valley." This road was the first to be built into these two counties. There was also a petition during the same year for a road from Baskins' Ferry on the Susquehanna to Andrew Stephens' Ferry on the Juniata.

At the January term of court in 1771 a petition was presented asking that a road be opened from James Gallagher's, on the Juniata River, to William Patterson's, thence to James Baskins' Ferry, on the Juniata River. At the April term of court of the same year the request of the petitioners was granted and it was ordered opened as a "bridle path." At the same term of court a petition was presented asking for a road from William Patterson's mill, on Cocolamus Creek, to Middle Creek. This was probably intended to extend to Middleburg, Snyder County.

James Gallagher's was near where Thompsontown is now located, and William Patterson's at Cocolamus Creek, below Millerstown. Baskins' Ferry was at the north end of Duncannon.

Then came the American Revolution and road building was farthest from the thoughts of men. Their whole thought was of liberty and the preservation of that freedom which had caused them to brave the dangers of crossing the sea. During the provincial days when the proprietary government was in power slow progress was made with the building of roads, but when the change was made from province to colony improvements began. In 1787 a commission was appointed to survey a road to connect the Frankstown branch of the Juniata with the Conemaugh at Johnstown. A year later it was contracted for, and in 1790 completed. Another Frankstown road was authorized in 1792, south of the previous one. In 1788, at the January term of the Cumberland County courts a road was recommended to be laid out from the Reed Ferry on the Susquehanna, to Boston Shade's mill, on Cocolamus Creek. There was an act passed April 13, 1791, which is known as the Improvement Act. It granted £300 for the improvement of a road from the mouth of the Juniata to David Miller's (now Millerstown) on the Juniata, through Dick's Gap.

There was a road from Carlisle to Sunbury at a very early date. On February 3, 1794, William Long warranted 400 acres of land located in what is now Spring Township, which is described as "adjoining lands on the west this day granted to John Long, and on the north by lands now in the possession of John Caven, and to join the great road leading from Carlisle to Sunbury." This "great road" passed through Long's Gap over the Blue Mountain. It was originally a pack horse route or bridle path from the South to the Susquehanna River, thence along to Sunbury.

In 1803, at the August term of court held at Carlisle, a petition was presented, requesting the erection of a bridge across Cocolamus Creek, on the post road from Harrisburg to Lewistown, near the junction of the creek with the Juniata River. This road was washed out by a flood, but its location was between the present road and the old canal bed, where the Patterson mill was located. Until recently there were traces of it. This old petition set forth that during winter this road was almost impassable, by reason of backwater from the river and ice blocking the fording. While it is here named as "the post-road" yet the fact remains that the Juniata Mail Stage Company did not begin operations until 1808, but the mails were carried over the route on horseback as early as 1798.

When the first through route was made through the Juniata Valley to Pittsburgh, now known as the "Old State Road," it did not take the river route from Clark's Ferry to Newport, but followed the old Indian trail via Pine Grove, in what is now Miller Township, where Woodburn's tavern, an old and well-known road house, was located. Later this part of the route was abandoned and it followed the river bank.

In the fall of 1806 petitions favoring a turnpike along the Juniata were in circulation. On March 4, 1807, the State Legislature enacted a law to incorporate a company for building a turnpike from Harrisburg via Lewistown and Huntingdon, to Pittsburgh. This turnpike, which has been known by various names, frequently as the Allegheny pike, entered Perry County at the head of Duncan's Island and ran west along the Juniata through Millerstown. For many years this was a turnpike, then it relapsed into the township road class, and in 1889, the Johnstown flood year, the high water washed out a section of five miles in Watts Township, which remains vacated to this day, by an order of the Perry County court, the township claiming it as a too expensive piece of road to keep in order. As this route is now a part of the William Penn Highway an effort is under way to have the state rebuild it, which should be done.

The first section, from Harrisburg west, was not built until 1822, however. By an act of the Pennsylvania Legislature, dated in March, 1821, two turnpike companies were chartered, the Harrisburg & Millerstown Turnpike Company and the Millerstown & Lewistown Turnpike Company. The location of two of the tollgates were at the Miller pottery, in Howe Township, and at a point above Millerstown, known as "the burnt house." The lower company in 1825 had as commissioners: George Mann, of Cumberland County, and the following Perry Countians: John Fry, Robert Clark, Cadwallader Jones, Peter Stingle, Robert Mitchell, John Rider, Francis Beelen, Joseph Power, Thomas Power, and Caleb North. Among the fourteen commissioners of the Millerstown & Lewistown Company were James Freeland and Abram Addams. Mr. Addams, whose eldest daughter became the mother of Governor James A. Beaver, was an influential man in the community and the new county and took a great interest in turnpike affairs. The turnpike was completed in 1825 and the subscription books opened at Millerstown. It was in use until 1857, when the county authorities took charge, the turnpike companies having abandoned it owing to the building of the canal and railroad, which took away the principal part of the traffic.

The Harrisburg & Millerstown Turnpike Company, with a pike of twenty-six miles, had $25,000 individual subscriptions and a state grant of $40,000, and the Millerstown & Lewistown Turnpike Company had $70,000 individual subscriptions and a grant of $39,500 from the state. Shares were $50, and the average cost per mile about $2,000.

Before the advent of the canal and railroad the overland traffic was largely done with large covered wagons, known as Conestoga wagons, by reason of their being built at Lancaster, on the banks of the Conestoga. These wagons, usually with a tar can hanging beneath, had four-inch tires and were often drawn by six or eight horses or mules, with jingling bells attached to the hames. Queerly enough the drivers of these wagons fastened the name upon a present-day tobacco product. They liked to smoke to while away the time, and at Pittsburgh there was a great demand for a cigar which would smoke for a long period. As the demand came from these drivers of Conestoga wagons a cigarmaker rolled a long cigar, which he could sell at a low price—four for a cent— and named it the "Conestoga." The product immediately became popular, but the word was too long and became Americanized as "stogies," and sometimes mistakenly called "tobies." To accommodate these drivers and their teams, road houses sprang up along the turnpike at approximately every ten or twelve miles. There are records which tell of a dozen or more large Conestoga wagons, with six or eight horses each, waiting to be ferried at Clark's Ferry, the western end of which was then at Clark's Run, near the centre of present-day Duncannon. The ferry house, or road house, still stands and is occupied by Joseph Smith as a dwelling.

As an example of what was done over the old mud roads, before the building of the turnpikes, in 1817, twelve thousand wagons passed over the Allegheny Mountains to Baltimore and Philadelphia, each with four or six horses, and carrying a load of from 3,500 to 4,000 pounds. The cost from Pittsburgh to Philadelphia was $7 to $10 per hundredweight. About 1885 the rate over the Pennsylvania Railroad was three-fourths of a cent per mile for each ton, or about $2.60.

When the turnpike was built through the county in the territory which now comprises Howe Township, one of the smallest townships in the county, inns or taverns were opened, known as Fahter's Falls tavern, Fetterman's tavern, and Red Hill tavern. The latter became a famous stopping place for the picturesque old Conestoga wagons on which the traffic of the new nation was largely transported. It was later long in the possession of Alfred Wright. Fetterman's was in the building now owned by Heister Moretz, along the William Penn Highway (now under construction) where the roads join, and Fahter's Falls (later Juniata Falls) was later kept by John Patterson, and is now known as the Lewis Steckley homestead.

The late Thomas H. Benton, in his "Thirty Years in the United States Senate," in discussing the establishment of the first national turnpikes, from the Atlantic seaboard to the Ohio, says:

"The absolute necessity for a public highway from the Atlantic seaboard to the inland cities of the republic, which were fast springing into existence, in the great West, were so great that the Whigs had no difficulty in procuring the necessary appropriations for the survey, location and construction of a national road from tidewater at Philadelphia and Baltimore to the Ohio."

An act of the Pennsylvania Legislature dated March 29, 1813, authorized the appointment of commissioners "to make an artificial road from Millerstown to the Franklin County line, to go through McKessonburg, and thence via Daniel Sprenkle's."

The road from Perry County, over the mountains to Concord, Franklin County, was built in 1820. By reference to the chapter in this book entitled Postrider and Stagecoach, it will be seen that during the second year following, 1822, the United States Government established a mail route over this new highway, from Clark's Ferry (now Duncannon) to Concord.

The McClure's Gap road was built in 1821. It connects Landisburg (which was then the temporary county seat) with Newville, Cumberland County. The following bond, etc., is published here as of historical value and will show the names of the commissioners and bondsmen, etc., without further description. It follows:

Know all men by these presents that we James W. Allen of Frandford township, Cumberland County and State of Pennsylvania and Benjamin Rice of Tyrone, Perry County and same State (Commissioners appointed by an Act of Assembly for improving the State for to lay out open and improve the road over the North mountain between Landisburg and Newville at McClures Gap, and Jacob Alter Esquire of West Pennsboro township and James Laird Esquire of Frankford township in the County of Cumberland aforesaid, are held and firmly bound unto his Excellency Joseph Hiester Governor of Pennsylvania in the just and full Sum of Eight hundred Dollars money of the United States: To the which payment well and truly to be made to the Said Joseph Hiester or to his legal Attorney or Successor in office, we do hereby bind ourselves our heirs executors, or administrators jointly Severally, firmly by these presents: Sealed with out Seals and dated the fifteenth day of May, one thousand Eight hundred and twenty one.

The CONDITION of the above obligation is Such that if the above bounden James W. Allen and Benjamin Rice as commissioners above Stated, Shall well and truly apply Such monies as may be put into their hands for the purpose of opening and improving Said Road agreeable to the intent and meaning of Said Law and Settle and adjust their accounts in manner therein directed, then the above obligation to be void, otherwise to remain in full force and virtue in Law.

Signed and Sealed in
presence of

Paul L. Peirce	James William Allen (Seal)
John Dickson	Benjamin Rice (Seal)
William McCrea	Jacob Alter (Seal)
John Lefever	James Laird (Seal)

(Indorsed) 28th May 1821. The within bond. and Security are approved in open Court, by the judge thereof.   John Reed
                                                                            James Armstrong
                                                                            Isa. Graham.

Cumberland County Vs.

I do Certify the above and foregoing to be a true Copy of the original as the Same remains filed of Record in the office of the Court of General Quarter Session of the Peace in and for Said County.

In witness whereof I have hereunto Set my hand and the Seal of the Same Court at Carlisle the 28th May A. D. 1821.

J McGinnis Jr.
Clk C. Q. S.

James Allen and Benjamin Rice Commissioners under the 71st Section of the twenty-sixth day of March 1821 have received credit in this Office for four hundred dollars the amount expended for the improvement for which money was appropriated in and by that Section.

Auditor Generals   James Duncan
Office 27th Match. 1823.   Auditor Genl.

The road from the George Barnett farm, on which New Bloomfield is located, to Sterrett's Gap, was laid out in 1824. There was once a military road to the Canadian frontier projected which was to have crossed Perry County. From the *Perry Forester* of September 14, 1826, we note the fact, as follows: "Major Long, of the engineer department, passed through Bloomfield, in this county,

16

on Thursday last, engaged in the duty assigned to him by the United States Government, of viewing a national military road from Washington to a point on our northern frontier."

The Act of April 14, 1827, appointed Solomon Bower, Jacob Stambaugh, Jr., and Robert Elliot, of Perry County, and Abraham Waggoner and John Hays, of Cumberland County, commissioners to lay out a state road from Landisburg to Carlisle, by way of Waggoner's Gap. The *Perry Forester* of May 24, 1827, tells of viewers having inspected the Waggoner Gap road and found it to have a grade of only four and one-half degrees, or one-half a degree less than the specifications, which fixes the time of the building of that road. In 1829 Nicholas Ickes, J. Kibler, and Robert Elliott, of Perry County, and William Wharton and Henry Hackett, of Mifflin County, were appointed commissioners to locate a state road from Landisburg, by way of Ickesburg and Run Gap, to Mifflintown. The State Legislature of 1826-27 provided for the opening of an additional state road via Long's Gap, which was built in 1828.

During 1827 and 1829 the Pennsylvania Legislature authorized the opening of roads from Union County to Liverpool; from Innis, Huntingdon County, to Landisburg; from Lewistown to Shippensburg, via New Germantown and Three Square Hollow.

The state road leading from a point opposite Harrisburg to Petersburg, now Duncannon, was opened in 1829. The commission who viewed the route and located it was composed of John Clendenin, A. Wills, Alexander Branyan, R. T. Jacobs and Robert Clark. Even before its construction there was a very rough and stony way along the river, the last vestige of the old Indian trail. Prior to the opening of this state road the main travel was over the mountain, about two miles from the river, via Miller's Gap.

By an act of the Pennsylvania Legislature, of April 19, 1844, John Wily, Robert Mitchell, Jesse Beaver, Thomas Cochran, and Michael Steever were appointed commissioners to lay out a state road from Reider's Ferry (now Newport) to the west end of Millerstown bridge, by the nearest and best route between those points. When Carroll Township was laid out in 1843 part of the boundary was described as being "along the great road leading to Clark's Ferry," which shows it as a then important highway. Its route lay through Grier's Point and Wheatfield Township.

An Act of February 14, 1845, authorized the Perry County commissioners to pay Jackson Township $250 to help build a road from McFarland's tannery to the Cumberland County line, its outlet in Cumberland County being at McCormick's Mill.

The road across the Blue Mountains at Crane's Gap was formerly a footpath. In 1848 the road was built, but it is now little used. About a mile farther west from Crane's Gap is a small gap known as Sharron's, after James Sharron, who warranted lands about 1769. There was once a road there also, but it was vacated many years ago.

The Act of April 12, 1855, appointed Samuel O. Evans and William Cox, of Juniata County, and Jesse Beaver, of Perry, to lay out a road "from the turnpike gate east of Thompsontown, in Juniata County, down Pfoutz Valley to the bridge over the Cocolamus Creek, in Perry County." An act fifteen days later, April 27th, appointed John P. Thompson and John M. Jones, of Juniata County, and Lewis Gilfillen, of Perry County, to lay out a road "from a point on the public road leading from Dunn's Mill to Mifflintown, at or near Hibbsfield, in the county of Juniata; thence from a point on road leading from Thompsontown to Liverpool, on lands of Christian Coffman, near the bridge over the Cocolamus Creek, in Perry County."

At the April term of court in 1859 viewers were either appointed or reported in the laying out of thirty-four different roads. At the January term of 1861 there were thirty-three, with many at other courts during the intervening period and shortly before and thereafter, which would fix that as the period when the greatest road development occurred.

An Act of March 6, 1873, required the county commissioners to appropriate $300 towards the erection of a bridge over the Big Buffalo Creek, on the road leading from the tanyard owned by Rev. J. J. Hamilton, to Elliottsburg, at Spriggle's fording.

That part of the William Penn Highway directly opposite Newport occupies the old roadway which was often the cause of trouble. The original road led from Greenwood Township, over the turnpike across the hill, and by Red Hill Church, to Newport. An act of the legislature was passed March 21, 1865, authorizing the county commissioners to pay $500 to aid Howe Township in making a road recently laid out, from the east end of the Newport bridge to a point on the Harrisburg and Millerstown turnpike, at the foot of Buffalo Mountain. Another act, dated March 20, 1869, authorized the county to pay $2,000 more towards the same road and to issue bonds for the amount. It named Lewis Gilfillen, Dr. J. E. Singer, and Isaac Wright as commissioners to build it. There was a provision that as soon as $3,500 was contributed the contract was to be let. Michael Hartzell evidently had the contract, as an act of April 24, 1873, required that the county commissioners pay him $1,865 of moneys so appropriated. After the 1889 flood it was again impassable, but was finally rebuilt largely by the progressive business men of Newport.

But one new state highway was granted by the Legislature of 1921-22, and that was the one provided for in a bill introduced by Representative Clark M. Bower, of Perry County, providing for a new outlet from western Perry County. The present road, descending into Path Valley, has a very steep grade and is a dangerous route, with the result that it was little traveled. The new route is really a very old one, long since abandoned. It was in use by the pioneers. It leaves Perry County by circling Big Round Top and drops into Franklin County by an easy grade to Burns' Valley and the iron bridge near Doylesburg, where it joins route 45 of the highway system. It opens up a route from Dry Run and Concord which saves forty miles on the trip to Harrisburg. It connects with the Lincoln Highway at Fort Loudon, and to the traveler from the Susquehanna and lower Juniata Valleys it means a saving of forty miles on a westward trip. It passes through the Tuscarora State Forest and through a mountainous section unequaled in Pennsylvania for beauty.

The reader can readily realize the discomforts of travel in those early days, yet they had no terrors for even a woman when she had the blood of the brave coursing her veins, as the following will show: Peter Hartman, an early settler, had married Elizabeth Oelwein, of Chester County, a relative of Gen. Anthony Wayne, and who had inherited the vigor and indomitable bravery of the Wayne family. In the summer of 1794, when her first child was but six months old, she started from Buffalo Mills (located in what is now Saville Township, Perry County) on horseback with the baby, and traveled 120 miles to see her relatives in Chester County, using bridle paths where there were no roads. Being a tactful woman she met with kindness all along the route. This was a most remarkable journey in that day and under those circumstances. There are many Perry Countians of to-day who can be proud that they have coursing in their veins the same blood as that of that Revolutionary hero, General Anthony Wayne.

In those pioneer days, Perry County territory, with the methods of travel then available, was as far from Philadelphia as the Mississippi Valley is to-day, with our really wonderful and speedy railroad trains. In fact, a letter will now go from Philadelphia to Denver, Colorado, in the same length of time that was then required to carry it from Philadelphia to Carlisle.

There being only trails at first the horseback method was the only one available, even for the transportation of weighty products. Pack horses, each of which carried a burden of about two hundred pounds over the mountains, were usually in groups of fifteen, with two men in charge. In passing along hills and mountainsides the loads frequently came in contact with the ground. About 1800, at Harris' Ferry, five hundred horses were fed and rested during a single night, which shows the extensiveness of the traffic.

With roads came that first vehicle, known as the "gig," and in use when the new county of Perry came into being. Then came the carriage, known as the "Dearborn," for milady, and to be succeeded by all varieties of carriages and buggies down to the fashionable "Jenny Lind," even to this day in use. Our century, however, has brought the motor vehicle into popular use, and the automobile is more common to-day than was the good carriage of forty years ago. As early as 1906 there were but 48,000 in the entire United States, but to-day (1920) the total approximates almost 6,000,000. In the interim the bicycle was a popular vehicle for personal trips, enjoyment and business from about 1890 until the advent of the automobile, but its use is now chiefly confined to business trips of a few blocks.

"Pack Saddle Path," known to all hunters as far back as they can remember, starts at the lower end of Lew Run, in Tyrone Township, and crosses the Kittatinny Mountain to the Wagner farms in North Middleton Township, Cumberland County. Evidently this run should be called Lewis Run, as tradition says that a colored slave named Lewis is buried near the run.

On March 24, 1851, an act of the Pennsylvania Legislature authorized the formation of the Millerstown, Andersonburg and New Germantown Plank Road Company. The capital was to have been $25 per share, and the number of shares 800. The road was to pass through Ickesburg. The commissioners named in the act were Samuel Black, Robert Elliott, Isaac Kinter, Wm. B. Anderson, Thomas Boal, Andrew Shuman, W. Blair, James Milligan, Samuel Liggett, Simon Kell, James Irvin, Jacob Shuman, Kirk Haines, T. P. Cochran, Jacob Bixler, W. I. Jones, G. W. Parsons, Wm. Rice, Solomon Bower, and George Black.

A plank road was once projected from a point upon the Pennsylvania Railroad, via New Bloomfield, to New Germantown. By an act of the Pennsylvania Legislature, dated April 12, 1851, the Sherman's Valley Plank Road Company was incorporated, with forty-three stockholders. Section 1 of the act reads:

"Be it enacted, etc., That Henry Rice, George Stroop, James Macfarland, Benjamin McIntire, Jonas Ickes, David Lupfer, H. F. Topley, George Barnett, Sr., John Campbell, Conrad Roth, Jr., John R. McClintic, George B. Arnold, Finlaw McCown, Alex. B. Anderson, A. C. Kling, Wm. A. Sponsler, John A. Baker, John B. Topley, Samuel McKnight, C. W. Fisher, Lindley Fisher, John Charters, Joseph Bailey, James Black, Jacob Smith, Samuel Leiby, Joshua E. Singer, John W. Bosserman, John Demaree, John Beaver, Wm. T. Shively, Jesse L. Gannt, George S. Hackett, Daniel Gannt, James F. McNeal, John Rice, David Adams, Joseph McClure, James Kay, John Ritter, John Tressler, Wm. B. Anderson, and Solomon Bower be and are hereby appointed commissioners to open books, receive subscriptions, and organize a company by the name and style of 'The Sherman's Valley Plank Road Company,' with power to construct a plank road from such point on the Pennsylvania Railroad as a majority in value of the stockholders shall determine, through New Bloomfield, to New Germantown, Perry County, with all the authorities and subject to all the provisions and restrictions of the act regulating turnpike and plank road companies, passed the 26th day of January, 1849, and its supplements, excepting so much thereof relating to tolls as discriminates in favor of wheels of the width of four inches and upwards; and the said company shall have power to regulate their tolls within the limits prescribed by said act, without reference to the width of wheels in any case, and excepting also such other portions of said act as may be inconsistent therewith."

The capital stock was made 550 shares, the par value of which was $20. Privilege was given to use any road then in existence, save that twenty feet was to be left for the public use, free of toll as before, and the proportionate cost of the part used to be paid for. The road was never built. Many of the older people of the present generation well remember these men, some of whom lived until very recent years.

Pennsylvania has long been noted for bad roads, but on May 31, 1911, a bill passed the Pennsylvania Legislature creating a State Highway Department, and since that time various bills have been passed for the rebuilding of the state highways, which have been taken over since the passage of the original act. The voters of Pennsylvania at an election in 1919 voted to bond the state for fifty millions to help construct roads. Through Perry County runs two great highways of the state system, the William Penn Highway and the Susquehanna Trail. As a part of this great expenditure, during 1920 a contract was let by Lewis S. Sadler, chief of the State Highway Department, for the construction of 41,753 feet of eighteen-foot road from the west end of Clark's Ferry bridge (in Dauphin County) to the line between Watts and Buffalo Townships (in Perry County). The contract went to Mac-Arthur Bros. Company, of New York, at $481,784.55. It is built of one-course, reinforced concrete, and is almost eight miles in length, over six miles of which are in Perry County. The present governor, Wm. C. Sproul, was always interested in better highways, and while a member of the State Senate many years ago, fathered the "Sproul Good Roads Bill." He may be said to be the pioneer good roads enthusiast of Pennsylvania.

CHAPTER XV.

OLD LANDMARKS, MILLS AND INDUSTRIES.

WHEN the pioneers first delved into the forests of what is now the county of Perry and hewed from them their primitive, homesteads which soon blossomed forth with vegetables and grain, they, of necessity, had to cross the Blue Mountain to the Cumberland Valley to have their grain ground into flour and meal. But that condition was short-lived, for at their very doors was the force of streams flowing away, which, if dammed, would drive the machinery of innumerable mills. Thus came the building of the first mill. The lands were not open to settlement until 1755, it will be remembered; and after Braddock's defeat in June of that year, the Indian uprising drove practically all the settlers out of the territory until it was thought safe to return. The Roddy (Waggoner) mill was built either during the first year of settlement, 1755, or in 1762, the year of the return of the pioneers, as it was taxed in 1763, while Perry was under the jurisdiction of Cumberland County. Its history is as interesting as the story of Paul Revere or other tale of province or colony with which all are familiar. When the war whoop of the wily red men resounded through the forest, the valuable millstones imported from France were taken from their places and sunk in the mill race until all danger had passed and it was safe for the family to return.

The flouring mill was one of Pennsylvania's original manufacturing industries and remains one of importance to this day. During the growth of the Perry County territory there have been many mills erected, and until the advent of the steam mill this section had more mills than any other in Pennsylvania. There was a reason for this in the many water-power locations available, for be it remembered that Perry County has more springs and streams than any other, when its comparatively small extent is considered. Of some of these mills the history follows, or is contained in the chapters of the various townships, but as earlier records are few and far between, there will be omissions, of course.

On a map published in 1791, when the first governor, Thomas Mifflin, was in office, no less than ten gristmills are located by name, and there are a number merely marked "mill." At the mouth of the Cocolamus Creek, in Greenwood Township, was Shade's mill, now the J. Keely Everhart mill. Above Duncan's Island, on the Susquehanna, is one designated as Vaux's mill, and at Berry's Falls (Mt. Patrick) a third. Along the entire length of Sherman's Creek there are four mills, three being merely marked "mill," and the fourth designated as West's, now known as the Gibson mill, and owned by S. V. Dunkelberger. On Fishing Creek Shortis' mill appears at the source, and Kincris' mill at its mouth, where Marysville is now located. On the Little Juniata two are marked, near its mouth, probably being the Duncannon mill and the old Haas mill. In the Cove one is also marked. At Buffalo Creek's headwaters Linn's mill is designated, and near "Buffaloe Hills" is Robinson's. At the mouth of the Little Buffalo is English's mill, later known as M. B. Eshelman's, and now as the T. H. Butturf mill.

As early as 1814 two townships in western Perry, not to mention the other large extent of the county, had twenty-eight gristmills, Toboyne having ten and Tyrone eighteen. In 1792 the county territory had thirteen flour mills. When the county was erected, in 1820, there were forty-eight.

There is record of Marcus Hulings, an early resident of Perry County, being authorized to erect a dam and mill at the mouth of Sherman's Creek, on September 15, 1784. While there is no record of its building, yet it was probably then already built, as the great ice flood in the winter of 1784 is recorded as having "swept away gristmill of Marcus Hulings, situated on Sherman's Creek, three-fourths of a mile from its mouth," according to the diary of Jacob Young, Sr. It either had been built prior to its authorization, as the year 1784 appears in both cases, or was under construction at the time, if Mr. Young's date is correct. The authorization date is from the public records.

In those early days when roads were few and trails and bridle paths were the avenues of traffic, it was no uncommon thing to go to mill by horseback, the women frequently performing that duty while the husband and sons were carving farms from the forests. Many of these trips at first were ten to fifteen miles to the mill and back, and some much farther, tiresome journeys, indeed, especially by bridle paths and with the probability of even meeting redskins on the way.

At that period the mills were more or less of a rude and simple construction. A clumsy water wheel, with intermediate cogs put the machinery in motion. From a hopper the wheat was fed to the stones, where a rough bolting cloth separated the wheat from the bran. The present milling machinery is one of the most remarkable inventions and is in general use.

The Waggoner Mill. Alexander Roddy was the builder of the first mill in the territory, upon the site of the present Waggoner mill, it having been long known as the Roddy mill. He first came to Tyrone Township from Chester County and located on what later became the Stambaugh farm and erected a cabin of poles near the spring at the picnic grounds of a generation ago. This was before 1754, the year of the treaty with the Indians for these lands, and he was accordingly driven out with other "squatters," in fact, tradition has him driven out several times. He evidently did not return to the Stambaugh tract, for as early as March, 1755, he is mentioned as an adjoiner of a warrant just east of this mill tract. He did not warrant the mill tract though until May 13, 1763. The previous year, 1762, was the time of the return of the great number of settlers to the territory, and it is likely that he built the mill that year, as it was already on the tax list of 1763.

The Waggoner mill is located on Roddy's Run, between Centre and Loysville, in Madison Township, one and a half miles west of Loysville. The warrant calls for "one hundred and forty-three acres, including his improvements, and adjoining John Byards (Byers), George Robinson, Roger Clark, James Thorn and William Officier, in Sherman's Valley." In research work it has been found that frequently settlers lived for years on a place before applying for a warrant. In the case of the adjoining James Thorn tract Provincial Secretary Peters attached a note, dated April 22, 1763, which helps bear this out. It says: "The land for which this warrant is granted, having been settled upwards of nine years ago, the interest and quit rents *is* to commence from the 1st of March, 1754."

In March, 1763, the stream is mentioned as the dividing line between Tyrone and Toboyne Townships, upon the erection of the latter: "Alexander Roddy's mill run to be the line." As the mill race had to be constructed and as the dam originally covered twenty-three acres of ground, he evidently had been there long enough before this to dig the race and build the dam—a task of no mere days. The first mill, on the site of the present mill, was built of logs, but was torn down and replaced by the present one in 1812. There is a reliable family tradition that there was no mill yet in the Tuscarora Valley, now in Juniata County, and that women came alone to the mill on horseback by way of Bigham's Gap (Bealetown). After the erection of the first mill Indian uprisings were still occurring, and when conditions became alarming the millstones, even in those days imported from France, were removed from the mill and sunk in the mill race until the danger was over. Fort Robinson was less than a half mile to the west, and to this the owners fled for protection.

The dam was washed out by the great flood of 1889. At times when the dam has been cleaned as many as thirty bushels of fish have been captured, but those were the days when the game and fish laws were less drastic. There was also an old "up-and-down" sawmill and a clover mill here at one time, the clover mill still standing.

Alexander Roddy later located in Virginia, where he died before 1786, as at that date a property transaction refers to his tract as "the late Alexander Roddy's." His son, James Roddy, became the owner, and for some years it changed hands frequently. In 1784 James More purchased it at sheriff's sale. In January, 1793, James Irvin bought it, but two months later sold it to Henry Rickard. In 1804 David Showers purchased it, and the next deed is from the sheriff to Frederick Bryner, who erected the present mill in 1812. In 1816 he sold it to his son, Henry Bryner. At executor's sale in 1831, it passed to William Miller, who sold it to Jacob Weibley and John Weidman in 1837.

On March 29, 1839, it was purchased by Benjamin Waggoner, and it is still in the ownership of the Waggoners. The new owner was an experienced mill man and came from a generation of millers. His father, John Waggoner, as early as 1785 had purchased the Garwood stone mill, located in Kennedy's Valley, and in 1805 had built the Snyder mill at Bridgeport (near Landisburg). Benjamin Waggoner's brother, John Waggoner, was the owner of the Patterson mill. Benjamin Waggoner operated the Waggoner mill until his death in 1850. In August, 1854, Moses Waggoner, a son, purchased it from the heirs and erected the commodious brick dwelling house adjoining. He died in possession in 1876.

The mill is now owned by W. H. Waggoner* (who has since died) and his sister, Harriet B. Waggoner, who purchased it from the heirs. Mr. Waggoner can remember when the flour was packed in barrels and hauled to Baltimore to market. They are descendants of the original owner, Alexander Roddy, who was their great-grandfather and who was three times driven from the mill to seek protection at the fort at Robinson's. A brother John E. Waggoner, is a merchant and postmaster at Centre, to whom, as well as the owners, we are indebted for much information. As late as 1917 W. H. Waggoner picked up an Indian skinning knife near the mill, and Indian arrow darts are frequently found. In 1900 the mill was equipped as a roller mill and draws a large trade, even from points afar. The first mill dam was almost one-fourth mile farther up the stream.

The Martin Mill. That a gristmill was located in what is now Howe Township, then a part of Greenwood, before the Revolution, is fully established by public records. That its location was

---

*W. H. Waggoner died in 1921. He resided in the Great West for many years, being in the cattle business from Texas as far north as British Columbia. When the Indians still inhabited the West, train guards were employed, and for a time Mr. Waggoner filled that position on the Union Pacific. The death of his wife, leaving two motherless girls, one but a few months old, necessitated his return to Pennsylvania.

at the creek west of the farm now or lately owned by Lewis Steckley, near the Henry Moretz place, between the William Penn Highway and the river, is likewise established. While the work on this
book was in progress, J. M. Martin, a prominent attorney of Minneapolis, came East, and with Rev. Frank T. Bell, then the pastor
of the Newport Methodist Episcopal Church, went to the traditional location of this old gristmill, the property of their common
ancestor, Samuel Martin, and still found a part of one side of the
overgrown foundation, near the mouth of the run—then "Brightwell's Run"—and the spring near which stood the first stone house
of his son Joseph, afterwards Captain. That the sawmill and
gristmill were actually built is proven by the fact that they were
devised by the will of Samuel Martin, dated August 23, 1769, to
his son Joseph, being designated as "all the plantation which I
bought from Robert Brightwell, with mills thereon, and all and
every of the locations in Greenwood Township, etc." Samuel
Martin also owned the property on the south side of the Juniata,
on which many years later was located the old Caroline furnace,
near Bailey Station. Historical records relate to all the properties,
and for that reason are included in one description, under this
head. The time of passing of this old mill is veiled in obscurity.
That it was one of the first few mills within the limits of what is
now Perry County is a fact.

Samuel Martin, who located and built the mill, was a son of
Joseph Martin, one of the first settlers of present Dauphin County
(then a part of Lancaster), who located 300 acres of land at Paxtang, now a suburb of Harrisburg, in 1738, part of which is now
known as "Willowdale Farm" and owned by Mrs. Alice Motter
Lescure, of Harrisburg. The brick house built there by Samuel
Martin, the son, in 1760, is still standing. From there came
Samuel Martin, who located, on November 18, 1768, by application No. 5263, 300 acres of land, "on the north side of the Juniata,
adjoining Brightwell's Run and Buffalo Hill, including the improvements bought of James Mahanna." Samuel Martin, however, never resided here. The mills here were in charge of his
son Joseph, later a captain in the Revolution. On the same day,
this son, Joseph, made a like location of 300 acres, "on the north
side of the Juniata, and including a run called Brightwell's Run,
joining Samuel Martin, Cumberland County." Samuel also located
200 acres at about the same time, on the south bank of the Juniata.
This is the land on which the Caroline furnace was long afterwards built. Samuel Martin, by his will, dated August 23, 1769,
proved in Lancaster County, June 6, 1770, devises to his son Joseph "the plantation I purchased of Robert Brightwell, in Greenwood Township, Cumberland County, and mills thereon, with all
and every of the locations in Greenwood Township," and with one

location on the south side of the Juniata, described as being "at the
Upper Falls, below the Great Bend in the Juniata." By the terms
of Samuel Martin's will, the devise to Joseph of the two plantations or locations, together with "the Dam Stalion Colt, and his
Saddle and Bridle, with a pair of oxen commonly called Duk and
Brown, also a low Plantation Wagon," was coupled with the provision that "my son Joseph shall pay the remaining part of the
payment due unto John Bowman for the plantation willed and bequeathed unto my son John." The devise of the Bowman plantation is made to the son John on the condition that he "make no
charge for any part or parcel of his work done by him to or making the mills on the plantation I purchased from Robert Brightwell, in Greenwood Township, Cumberland County," which shows
that he was one of the actual builders of this primitive mill.

Joseph Martin, evidently, to secure this charge upon his land,
gave a mortgage to the executors of Samuel Martin, dated January 24, 1771 (recorded in Book C-1, p. 141, at Carlisle), for 250
pounds, 19 shillings and 4 pence, mortgaging 300 acres in Greenwood Township, "bounded by Juniata on the south, with gristmill
thereon; also 200 acres in Dublin* Township (now Miller) on
the south side of the Juniata, above the falls adjoining Dick's
Hill."

On March 26, 1776, Joseph Martin and wife, by deed, recorded
in Book 1, page 101, in Carlisle, conveyed to Hugh Miller, eight
acres with house, being a "divided fifth of forty acres, bounded
west by land of Hugh Miller, north by Juniata River, east by
Samuel Hutchinson, south by William Oliphant." This deed was
not acknowledged, but proven September 4, 1789, by affidavit of
Ann Martin (then Ann McCoy), formerly widow and relict of
Joseph Martin, deceased. This hasty unacknowledged deed evidently furnished Joseph with the money to purchase his equipment
for the Revolutionary War. While in the army, the mortgage was
foreclosed (Carlisle records, D-1, p. 557), but 400 acres on the

---

*The name Dublin Township, as recorded at Carlisle, is evidently an
error of the transcriber, as the location became a part of Tyrone Township in 1754, the very year of the purchase of the lands from the Indians.
Then in 1766, when Rye Township was formed, it was within its borders,
and when Miller Township was erected in 1852 it was within its confines.
Dublin Township is located in Huntingdon County. The Evarts-Peck
History of the Susquehanna and Juniata Valleys, page 731, says of it:
"The formation of Dublin Township, in 1767, is so imperfectly defined as
to the eastern limits that nothing can be determined by it. It was to
bound 'Ayr and Fannett Townships on the one side,' but Lack Township
is not mentioned, and there are no dividing lines as to Ayr or Lack. The
first Dublin assessment, in 1768, shows no transfer of names from Lack.
The only thing that places any part of Dublin east of Shade Mountain is
that it was to join on Fannett, which lay on the other side of the Tuscarora Mountain." That the Martin property is the one located in Miller
Township, however, is certain, as the description "above the falls joining
Dick's Hill," implies. It is now in possession of Mrs. L. C. Zimmerman.

north side with gristmill and improvements, was in 1787 deeded back to the widow, then Ann McCoy, with remainder to the three children of Captain Joseph Martin, Samuel, Mary, and Joseph.

The heirs, in attempting to sell this land in November, 1805 (deed recorded Carlisle, Q-1, p. 486), found it necessary in order to supply evidence of a lost deed, to take testimony in "Perpetuam Rei Memoriam." The record of this is in the docket of Cumberland County, Pennsylvania, at Carlisle, for 1800 and 1803, and pertains to 100 acres of the tract on the north shore of the Juniata, purchased from Robert Brightwell, who had purchased from Frederick Stoner, and recites that the deed from Stoner bore date between the year 1763 and 1767; "that the title to the same tract of land and possession of the same did come by diverse deeds of sale and devises to Joseph Martin, father of the petitioner (Samuel), *that in the year 1777, the said Joseph Martin marched as a captain* to serve a tour of militia, *and that he died before his return;* that the petitioner and all the children of said Joseph were then infants; that the said deed, during the infancy of the children of the said Joseph Martin, has been lost or mislaid, so that it can not now be found," etc.

Capt. Joseph Martin,* after spending the winter at Valley Forge, was taken with camp fever, and started home, but "died before his return." His fate was never known. Whether he died in the wilderness, or according to a tradition, was captured by the British and died in a British "black hole," has never been known. His three children afterwards moved to Lewistown, Pennsylvania, where Samuel and Joseph became rivermen, engaged in transportation by arks between Lewistown and Columbia, from 1800 to 1823.

This old Martin location is historic in more ways than one. While Samuel Martin located this land on an application from the province, yet, in his will and in other legal papers it is spoken of by him as "having been purchased of Robert Brightwell." The fact is that a warrant and original order of survey were first obtained on April 30, 1765, by a certain Frederick Stoner, who sold

---

*Captain Joseph Martin was the great-grandfather of Mr. J. M. Martin, of Minneapolis, and of the father of Rev. Bell, the pastor of the Newport Methodist Church, spoken of in the beginning of this sketch. The three generations named are noted historically in three different fields. Samuel Martin erected pioneer mills, almost at the beginning of settlement; Captain Joseph Martin, of the next generation, became a martyr to the patriot cause, and Samuel and Joseph Martin, of the following generation, were pioneer rivermen in traffic when it was done with the ancient water craft known as arks. Captain Joseph Martin was married to Ann (Nancy) Baskins, of Duncan's Island, and his two sons, Samuel and Joseph, were born at the home of their grandparents there, while their father was a captain in the Continental Army. Their mother, by the way, was a cousin of the grandmother of Alexander H. Stephens, notable as the Vice-President of the Confederacy.

and conveyed his interest to Robert Brightwell on March 17, 1768. After eight months it passed to Samuel Martin, it would appear, both by purchase of the previous right and by warrant from the province, thus assuring title. The improvements of James Mahanna are taken to refer to an improvement probably made by a squatter, who had no title to the lands. On January 2, 1880, it was conveyed by Samuel and Joseph Martin, two of the heirs of Captain Joseph, to James McGinnes, Sr. (the husband of their only sister Mary). He, in turn, sold to William and James Power, by agreement dated November 7, 1801, thirty-seven acres, at the western boundary, including the mills. On November 16, 1805, his executors gave the deed accordingly. The patent from the state for a part of this original tract was issued to John Patterson, August 19, 1803, of another portion to his son John, July 25, 1863, and remained in his possession for many years. At its eastern boundary the latter kept a famous road house in turnpike days, and there was located the post office known as Fahter Falls, and later as Juniata Falls.

The Patterson Mill, near Millerstown. The first mill erected on the Cocolamus Creek, near its mouth, in Greenwood Township, was built by William Patterson. Jones' History of the Juniata Valley describes it as a "tub mill" and states that it was carried away by a flood. It was built prior to 1771, for in that year it is named as a point on the road leading from John Gallagher's to Baskins' Ferry. Shuman's mill, at the same point, was built before 1805, for in that year John Shuman is assessed with a grist- and sawmill. John Shuman had come from Lancaster before 1800 and, after building the mill, operated it until his death, in 1818. In that year Col. John Shuman, his son, bought it and 190 acres of land, for $9,000. In 1827 he sold the mill to George Shuman for $5,000. It then passed through the hands of George Maus, Sylvester Bergstresser, and others. Its location is a half mile east of Millerstown, and it is now owned and operated by J. Keely Everhart.

The Rice Mill. While the Rice mill lays no claim to being the first mill to be erected in what is now Perry County, its history is over a century and a third in years and it is the oldest original mill building to remain standing in the county. It is located near Landisburg. in Tyrone Township, on Montour Creek, near the Kennedy's Valley bridge. It was on this creek that the first authorized settler, Andrew Montour, from whom it takes its name, was located, the provincial authorities giving him permission so that he would see that no others would settle in the territory until such time as the lands were purchased from the Indians. In fact, he later warranted 143 acres, located between Landisburg, Montour's Creek and Sherman's Creek, which in 1788 was surveyed

visit in 1919, the life of a wheel being about twenty-four years, according to information furnished by John A. Saucerman, the present proprietor.

These old mills used burrs in the grinding of the grain and were not as speedy as modern roller equipment, yet a little incident handed down in the Rice family shows that even in that early period things were sometimes done with speed, although the facilities were crude. It was related to us by Mrs. A. K. Rice, whose husband was the proprietor until his death a few years ago, she in turn having received the information from the preceding generation. Jeremiah Rice, of the second generation to own the mill, cut wheat in the morning with an old-fashioned cradle, the implement in use in those days for that purpose; threshed it with the flail, that crude and noisy implement which extracted the grain from the hulls; ground the wheat into flour in the Rice mill and turned it over to Katharine, his good wife, who baked bread of it and served fresh and warm to the hungry harvest hands for supper —the entire operation occurring between sunrise and sunset.

Adjoining the old mill stands the old Rice distillery, now used as a storage room, in the basement of which appears the inscription, painted on a beam, "Last stilling, 1822." The brick house, located above the mill, along the stream, was erected in 1822. It is the equal of any summer residence to be found anywhere, and it is little wonder that the fifth generation of the Rice family is still in possession, the owner being John A. Saucerman, who is married to a daughter of A. K. Rice.

There was a sawmill there built in 1842. The gristmill is used now only as a chopping mill.

The Stokes Mill, Once the Blaine Mill. The mill known to the present or recent generation as the Stokes mill was the one built by James Blaine as early as 1778, as it was assessed in that year, and later around it sprang up the settlement now called Blain, the final "e" being dropped. This James Blaine is the one and same man from whom sprang the famous Blaine family, which produced the noted Commissary General of the Revolution, Ephraim Blaine, and at a later day a noted statesman and the candidate of the Republican party for President of the United States, James G. Blaine. The mill later must have come into the possession of James S. Blaine, for on April 20, 1820, the very year of the organization of Perry County, it passed to David Moreland. By inheritance it passed to his daughter, Diana Gitt, who was united in marriage to Anthony Black, to whom she transferred it on December 20, 1830. On December 21, 1846, Anthony Black's administrator deeded it to Thomas, Wayne, and James Woods. They, in turn, sold it to Isaac Stokes on October 1, 1857. He owned it until

April 1, 1905, at which time it was purchased from him by William H. Book, the present owner and operator. It is equipped with rolls.

This title is traced for the reason that there has existed a difference of opinion as to who built the mill, Silas Wright, in his History of Perry County (1873) crediting William Douglas with its building, and Professor Flickinger, as a contributory editor of the Evarts-Peck History of the Susquehanna and Juniata Valleys (1886), asking, "If Douglas built the mill, then where was the gristmill situated for which James Blaine was assessed in 1778?" Mr. Flickinger was a native of western Perry and long principal of the Central State Normal School at Lock Haven. He adds that Douglas was the first postmaster, the office being called Douglas' Mill. The fact is that the first post office was called Moreland's, being established in 1820, the very year of the county's erection, but in 1822, when the mail contract was let it was already known as Douglas' Mills.

There is no record of Douglas locating or purchasing lands in that vicinity, and the mill is on the original James Blaine location. There is a probability that he was the lessee of the mill, probably for a long period, and that it came to be known as Douglas' Mill. Should there have been an office there before 1820 and Douglas the postmaster, then, evidently with Mr. Moreland's purchase in 1820, the name was changed to Moreland's, and in a very short time restored to Douglas' Mills. One fact is clear, and that is that Douglas never owned the mill, else the records of the recorder of deeds are wrong.

Up to the time of the ownership of Andrew Black the mill and the farm were always owned by one and the same party, but he sold the farm to James McNeal, who conducted a large tannery at the northern end of Blain, and the mill passed as previously stated.

The Endslow Mill. Before 1778, in which year it was already assessed in the name of James Miller, the Endslow mill was built in what was then Toboyne Township, but in that part of the township which later became Jackson Township. Its location is one mile east of Blain. John Moreland, an uncle of the late David Moreland, of Blain, married Jane, the daughter of James Miller, and her patrimony was this mill and forty acres of land. In 1822 it passed to James McNeal, whose son-in-law, Samuel Endslow, became the next owner, obtaining possession about 1840. In 1869 his son, William S. Endslow, became the owner and operated the mill until about 1908, when he retired from both milling and farming. About 1883 the mill, which was already the second one to occupy the site, was burned by incendiaries, and was rebuilt by Mr. Endslow. Upon his retirement he sold both mill and farm to his son, George S. Endslow, now of Lancaster County, who still owns it

17

in use. On a corner of the foundation of this old historic landmark is this inscription plate: "U. S. Geological Survey; Elevation above sea level, 471 feet. A. D. 1903." The original mill is
described as being a "log structure, with only one run of stone."
It will be noted that the top story is not of stone. The original
mill tract is spoken of as containing seventy-eight acres.

The Eshelman Mill, now Butturf's. Just when the Eshelman,
or Butturff mill, in Oliver Township, at Newport's very border,
was built, cannot be stated exactly. It is built on a tract of land
which once comprised 185 acres and which was warranted June 5,
1772, to William West, Jr., from whom it passed on September 3
of the same year to David English. That the mill was built before
April 22, 1790, is sure, as on that day the sheriff sold it to Christopher Myers. In December, 1790, it was purchased from him by
Dr. Daniel Fahnestock, of Warrington, York County. In 1814 it
was assessed in the name of Joseph Zinn. At that time the original
stone building, 50x60 feet in size, included all of the mill, but
Amos Overholtzer, who purchased it in 1873, built the brick story
to it and added improved machinery. A sawmill, plaster mill and
dwelling house with nine acres of land, were a part of the establishment. M. B. Eshelman, who purchased it in 1876, from Mr.
Oberholtzer's administrator for $17,500, added the latter. Mr.
Eshelman's heirs sold it to T. H. Butturf, in 1902, for $5,200.

The Mt. Patrick Gristmill. Shall I ever forget it? Not while
memory lasts. Geo. Blattenberger, Jr., friend of my father's, was
the miller, and to him came the grists from the countryside to be
ground into flour for the family bread. Although many years
have passed since I made my last trip there and heard the jolly
greeting and the ringing laugh of the miller, who now sleeps the
sleep that knows no waking, in the cemetery on the heights above
Liverpool, it seems as but yesterday. The way from home led
along the Pennsylvania Canal, and in its palmy days many boats
were passed on the way, and occasionally the nifty little steamer of
Col. T. T. Weirman, the superintendent, would be passed. It was
an innovation in those days. Opposite the mill was an overflow,
where the waters of the canal fell over the side of an aqueduct
to the bed of the valley stream crossing beneath, with a swish and
a roar that drowned ordinary speaking. The trip to the mill was
never labor, as the welcome of Mr. Blattenberger, whose heart
was in the right place, far repaid any seemingly hardships.

Just when this mill was built, or when the first mill was built
at that site, is unknown, but a map of 1791 shows a mill located
at "Berry's Falls." As the locations are identical the inference is
that it was built prior to 1791. While the property was not patented until November 10, 1829, it had been warranted long before
and made into a farm. It was early owned by a man named Bru-

baker, and in August, 1834, was sold as the estate of Peter Ritner (a brother of Governor Ritner) to Simon Gratz, who transferred it to Simon Cameron in trust for the Lykens Valley Coal Company, who desired it for a landing for their coal flats which brought coal across the river to the new Susquehanna Canal. In 1841 it was purchased by George Blattenberger, Sr., familiarly known as "Judge," having been an associate judge of the county. He owned it until 1889, when it was purchased by Adam Barner, who died in 1890. It is now owned by his son, George A. Barner. The transfer of 1834 names the place as having a sawmill, a merchant mill, a plaster mill, a flour mill, a trip-hammer, and a distillery. The mill has been dismantled and the building removed and, when completed, "the Susquehanna Trail" will pass over the site.

The farm originally included all of Mt. Patrick, the mill property, the Jacob McConnell place, and the S. E. Bucke farm. The distillery was located across the creek from the mill, on the millhouse plot. The fulling mill was at the forebay of the gristmill and the sumac mill at the Jacob McConnell place.

The Old Snyder or Hackett Mill. John Sanderson, who owned eleven hundred acres of land in one body, near Elliottsburg, in Spring Township, was assessed with two stills and a gristmill in 1792. Upon his death he devised the land covering this mill site to his nephew, George Elliott. In 1831 George Elliott conveyed to George S. Hackett 400 acres upon which was erected the mill and a distillery. In 1850 he sold it to Alexander Topley, of Bloomfield, and upon his death, in 1854, his administrator conveyed it to Robert and Isaac Jones. A year later they sold it to John Snyder, who operated it until about 1873, when it was found to be unprofitable to continue operations. Mr. Snyder died on the premises in 1882, and in 1907 the old mill property passed to Silas W. Moyer, the present owner.

The Snyder Mill, now Hooke's. In 1805 John Waggoner, the father of Benjamin Waggoner, the first of the clan of that name to own the Roddy mill, erected a mill near Bridgeport, which is now known as Snyder's mill. There is an article of agreement on record dated 1805 in which Thomas Ross grants to Mr. Waggoner the privilege of "joining" his mill dam to lands of his. At the same time he was the owner of the mill in Kennedy's Valley, assessed to Robert Garwood in 1782, and which he purchased a few years later. There is record of his residence in Kennedy's Valley until his death, and the presumption is that he built the Snyder mill as an investment.

Mr. Waggoner died in 1834, and among other things in his appraisement was ninety-two barrels of whiskey, and one barrel of peach brandy appraised at $8.00 per barrel, for which $1.75 per barrel was paid to convey it to Baltimore in wagons. His estate was unsettled for years, and in 1854, the sheriff, by proceedings in partition, deeded these lands, "having thereon erected a large brick house, log barn, and a large stone merchant mill and other outbuildings to Joseph McClure and William W. Snyder. Mr. McClure died and his heirs conveyed his half to James McClure, from whom, in 1861, Mr. Snyder secured entire ownership. Mr. Snyder operated the mill until his death in 1893. In 1902 the property was conveyed to Dr. B. P. Hooke (a son-in-law of Mr. Snyder), who died in 1903, and by will devised it to his son, B. P. Hooke, the present owner.

The Bear Mill. The Bear mill is located on Sherman's Creek, in Madison Township, south of Centre, and about one and one-half miles from Loysville. It is on a tract warranted by John Scouller in 1787. It was erected prior to 1814, at which time Englehart Wormley was assessed with it. In 1835 it was in possession of John Wormley. The brick mill which replaced the first structure was erected in 1841. Henry Bear came into possession and he and his son, Wm. F. Bear, operated it for many years. In 1889 it was purchased by Jos. B. Lightner, who in 1910 sold to Ida Wolfe, and from her in 1915 it was purchased by the Tressler Orphans' Home and an electric light plant installed.

The Patterson Mill. In 1753, as indicated in a case before the provincial governor, William Patterson had located on Laurel Run, Tyrone Township. He did not, however, warrant lands until 1766, when he took up four hundred acres, some of which is still in possession of the Patterson family. In 1814 Francis Patterson had a sawmill there, and soon after erected an oil mill. These two, and a chopping mill were operated by Thomas Patterson in 1825. Then, in the period between 1830 and 1840, Fahnestock and Ferguson built a scythe and edge-tool factory there. John Waggoner, a son of the sire of the Waggoner family of millers, then purchased it and turned the oil mill and the chopping mill into a gristmill. After 1840 Solomon Hengst also conducted a foundry there for a few years. William A. and James F. Lightner later came into possession of the mill, and in 1887 sold to Martin L. Rice, who after operating it for some years, in 1903 sold it to the Oak Extract Company, and from that time it has been dismantled as a mill.

Bixler's Mill. The old Bixler flour mill is located on Tousey's Run, in Madison Township, and is still in operation, the present miller being George E. Beck, and the place being often known as Beck's Mills. It was built in 1812-1814 by Zalmon and Azariah Tousey, brothers, who had purchased the property containing 345 acres, March 7, 1812, from Hugh Hamilton, whose holdings comprised over six hundred acres and was known as "Hamiltonia."

This mill is located on the tract warranted by Hugh Alexander, February 3, 1755, the day the land office was first opened to settlement for Perry County. It contained 344 acres. In 1801 this property was transferred to Hugh Hamilton, a son of John Hamilton and Margaret Alexander, the warrantee's daughter. The new owner was also possessor of the 400 acres which adjoined and which was warranted by John Hamilton, which made the tract a large one as noted above. Jacob Bixler and John Flickinger, in 1836 bought it from the administrators of the Touseys and in a few years divided it, the mill going to Bixler with ninety acres of land, and the rest of the lands to Flickinger.

A mute reminder of the early settlement of this young couple and the erection of their home lies in the office of the old mill. It is the corner stone of the old house, which Bixler tore away in 1840, it being a two-story log house. It is of marble, with an inscription arranged as in the accompanying diagram.

```
        ┌ ─── ─── ─── ─── ─── ┐
        |           A          |
        |     H           M     |
        |  S        1766      N  |
        └ ─── ─── ─── ─── ─── ┘
```

The A is evidently the initial of the family name, Alexander, and the H and M on a lower line probably refer to the first initials of the builders, Hugh and Martha. The date probably is connected with the early occupation of the lands. The S. and N. evidently refer to the directions of the compass, and the stone was evidently used to mark their claim.

In 1846 Jacob Bixler rebuilt the east end of the mill from the foundation, and in 1870 remodeled the interior and put in two turbine water wheels, the first in the county. He also built the adjoining woollen mill in 1853, of which more elsewhere. The firm was later known as Jacob Bixler & Sons.

The present owner, George E. Beck, purchased the property and mills from the Bixler heirs in 1888 and does a good business. The mill is of the old-fashioned burr variety and the stones used in grinding the grain are secured in France, none as satisfactory being obtainable elsewhere.

Before the county was dotted with its many merchandising places the Bixler mill made blankets and yarns, and besides wholesaling them also ran a wagon over the county doing a retailing business. Upon this wagon appeared in neat lettering: "Centre Woollen Mills, Bixler & Bro., Blankets, Yarns, etc." Many Perry Countians, even of middle age, can remember its regular trips. It still stands in a shed at the mills, a mute reminder of a passing age. Even the advertisements on its sides link the past with the present, for among the names are those of persons yet living, who were then in business. The names:

"Bentzell & Bro., Tailors, New Bloomfield.

"Ensminger Livery, New Bloomfield.

"A. P. Nickel, Undertaking, New Bloomfield.

"Chas. B. Stewart, Watches, New Bloomfield.

"Wm. H. Smith, Coach Maker, New Bloomfield.

"John A. Martin, Harness, New Bloomfield."

The old woollen mill was operated until 1910. It still contains the old looms, but the only work done there is the carding of wool on a small scale and principally as an accommodation, for the raising of sheep in the county has decreased as the years have passed. The mill contained an old "hand-mule" spinner, with 160 spindles. Bixler's Mills was once a thriving settlement, and in 1884 a post office was established there named Bixler, since replaced by rural delivery. Jacob Bixler was the son of a miller, Jacob Bixler, Sr., who came from Dauphin County in 1818 and built the mill near Eshcol, in Saville Township.

Other Mills. The history of the various other mills, many of them dating back a century, appears in the various chapters devoted to the townships and boroughs of the county, to be found elsewhere in this book.

SAWMILLS.

The lands of Perry County were not long settled by any of the white race before there began springing up here and there along the various streams, numbers of the old-fashioned water-power sawmills, known largely as "up-and-down" sawmills. On them were sawed the huge trees, which were fashioned into boards and shingles for the building of the early homes. There were so many of these at various times and places that it is impossible to give with any degree of thoroughness their locations and owners. Through them the primeval forests were turned into dwelling houses, barns, outbuildings, churches, bridges, schoolhouses, and the forerunner of the brick and cement pavement—the old-time boardwalk. The drainage basins of practically all important streams were locations of one or more of these early manufacturing plants. In a single community of which Shermansdale was the centre, there were the McCord mill near Pisgah, the Smiley mill on Smiley Run, the McCaskey mill in northern Carroll, the Stauffer mill in a gorge of the mountain along Sherman's Creek, the Rebert (now Smith's) mill west of that village, and that of John H. Louck, two miles east of Shermansdale, where he also had a gristmill and post office known as Louck's Mills, to which the mails were carried from Carlisle by postrider. The proprietors of four of these mills—the McCord, Smiley, McCaskey, and Louck's—

now rest within fifty feet of each other, in the Presbyterian cemetery near Shermansdale, while their mills, later developed into the "thundergust" type, have long since been swept away by the floods from the very hills which their industry denuded, and of which it was the contributing cause. Some of these old milldams were strongly constructed and even the immense force of successive floods has failed to remove the large boulders which were used in their construction, among those being that at the Louck mill. In 1814 Tyrone Township alone had eighteen such mills. Later the steam mill with its circular saw largely did the work of these more primitive mills.

The date of the probable entry into Perry County forests of the steam sawmill, quoted elsewhere as about 1870, is no doubt correct, as that is the year in which a Mr. Coulter, of Mechanicsburg, put a mill in "Allen's Swamp," at the western end of the Cove Mountain, between that mountain and Pine Hill. It took almost four years to saw the lumber, and the sale of the outfit took place in 1874. When that operation was started deer were still plentiful and were often seen by the woodsmen. A heavy growth of timber long covered the lands which comprise Perry County.

In the vicinity of "The Narrows," near the Rye-Carroll Township line, there were four of these up-and-down sawmills. They were owned by Conrad Brubaker, Adam Nace, Henry Sykes, and Adam Luckenbaugh. James Sykes also had a fulling mill there, carding wool and weaving blankets. In connection with the settlement known as "The Narrows," the change in population might be noted here. Between forty and fifty persons then resided there, while to-day there is one lone house.

That part of Perry County which included present Juniata Township and which in 1795 included all of Tuscarora and Oliver, and parts of Centre and Miller Townships, was once heavily wooded. In the assessment lists of that year twelve sawmills were enumerated. There were also two gristmills, two tanyards and two distilleries, the latter both operated by George Hildebrand. With the cutting of the timber came the development of the land.

Sixty years ago there were at least three sawmills on Sugar Run, the small stream which empties into the Juniata opposite Cocolamus Creek. All did considerable business, yet to-day there seems to be hardly enough water there to turn a wheel.

FULLING MILLS.

On a previous page of this chapter, in connection with the Bixler gristmill, is a description of the Bixler fulling mill, which was but one of a number of fulling mills located throughout the county, where wool was carded and clothing manufactured. Mention of these mills is made in the various chapters relating to the townships in which they were located. One of these mills was operated by George Gutshall, at New Germantown, he also having a chopping mill. He was the grandfather of Mrs. Wilson Morrison, yet living in that town, who remembers how they "carded wool into round rolls almost a yard in length, from which the women spun the yarn." Homespun clothing was then in general use. Mrs. Morrison also tells of how they sowed flax, pulled, dried and threshed it, using a "flax-break" to divest it of the outside shell. Although but a young girl she helped in this work.

"Stills" and Distilleries.

At an early day, before the coming of the canal and the railroads, the surplus products of the farms in the line of grains and fruits were distilled into liquors. Fruits when ripe, had either to be dried or distilled into liquors for preservation. Surrounded by these conditions the pioneers would either erect stills or take their apples and peaches, usually loaded in large English wagonbeds which held from forty to eighty bushels, and have them distilled into brandy and applejack, for which the distiller received one-half the product. It was not unusual to see a long line of wagons awaiting their turn at these distilleries. Grains were also distilled into liquors, as the product in that condensed form required far fewer trips to the far-away Baltimore market. There was also a demand for these products and the state even made concessions to encourage the industry, which has long since passed out of Perry County life, and which the Eighteenth Amendment to the Constitution of the United States this year—1920—eliminated for all time.

Owing to these conditions the Perry County territory teemed with "stills" and distilleries. As early as 1814 Tyrone Township alone had seventeen stills on the assessment roll. Liquor seems to have been in very general use during that early period and the price was extremely low. Rye whiskey sold from thirty-three to thirty-seven cents a gallon. Peach brandy was quoted at the same prices, and applejack at twenty-five cents per gallon.

The locations of many of these old stills are to be seen or are pointed out by the residents. They were principally in western Perry and in a few instances the stillhouses are still standing. The one on the Lucian R. McMillen farm at Kistler, Madison Township, is in good repair, and those at the Rice mill, in Tyrone Township, and Manassas Gap, three miles south of Blain, in Jackson Township, still stand. A partial list of locations follow:

On the old Shearer farm, now owned by David Beaston, above McLaughlin's, in Toboyne Township.

On the James Johnston farm, in Toboyne Township, one mile above New Germantown.

On the farm of Clark Bower, in Jackson Township.

At Manassas Gap, three miles south of Blain. Operated by Philip Stambaugh about 1830. The building still stands on the property of David Rowe, Jr.

The Hackett distillery on Reisinger Brothers' farm, in Madison Township, at a place locally known as Pine Grove, near Kistler.

A half-mile west of Blain.

On the J. E. Lyons farm, at Andersonburg.

The stone distillery on the Lucian R. McMillen farm at Kistler, Madison Township. In good condition.

On George Palm farm, one and one-half miles east of Kistler.

Near the Lutheran Church at Saville, Saville Township.

The Conrad Ernest still at Stony Point, three miles east of Blain.

At Kistler, just west of the Lutheran Church.

On the J. S. Lightner farm, one and one-half miles southeast of Cisna's Run.

The Baughman distillery, near Rock schoolhouse, in Saville Township.

Near the M. E. Chapel in Madison Township.

One on the W. Scott Irvine farm, in Saville Township.

On the John and Solomon Briner farm on Sherman's Creek, one and one-half miles south of Loysville, now owned by Edward Briner.

On Montour's Run at Rice's mill, near where it joins Sherman's Creek. It still stands.

The Wagner still, later Egolf's, in lower Kennedy's Valley, Tyrone Township. In business as late as 1868.

Keck's distillery, on the Adam Wentzel farm at Bridgeport, in Spring Township. It burned in 1874, but had ceased operations a few years previous.

On the Joseph Lightner place, "Still House Hollow," Tyrone Township.

In Landisburg, near Water Street.

On the Junkin place in Spring Township, now owned by George Dum.

On the farm of Samuel Ebert, north of the Tressler Orphans' Home.

At Elliottsburg, in Spring Township.

Near Jackson schoolhouse in Saville Township, about a mile north of Elliottsburg.

In "Little Germany," Spring Township, built by John Fuas (Foose).

On property of S. W. Moyer, a short distance east of Elliottsburg.

On the Abraham Bower farm, at Falling Springs.

On Swartz farm, west of New Bloomfield, south of former steam mill.

On the J. L. Kline farm, in Liverpool Township's eastern extremity.

On the steam mill property, below Liverpool, a distillery was in operation as late as 1869. The property is now owned by Mrs. John Williamson.

At Mt. Patrick, on the western bank of the creek from the gristmill, long known as the Blattenberger mill, now Barner's.

On the J. R. Wright farm in Greenwood Township. This is the property which was once owned by Rev. Britton E. Collins, but, of course, he was not the operator of a distillery, but had only purchased a farm on which one had been located.

At Falling Springs, in Spring Township, where Abraham Bower resided and operated it.

Between Pine Hill and Sherman's Creek, at Billow's old fording.

Sponsler's distillery, New Bloomfield, site of foundry, Carlisle Street.

Along Little Buffalo Creek, in Juniata Township, owned and operated by Abram Flurie.

THE TANNING INDUSTRY.

The tanning of leather dates back to the time of the red men, whose product was so finely tanned that one of Perry County's greatest tanners tells us it has never been equaled by the whites. Accidentally discovered by letting a hide lie among some oak bark over winter the Indians experimented until they had perfected a system. Their most delicate work was produced by using the brains of the deer. A history of this little mountain-bound county without something of its tanning industry and mention of the tanner's apprentice who became Pennsylvania's most noted journalist and a national figure (Col. A. K. McClure), would not be a history at all. At first the tanneries followed the bark to be used in tanning, locating in the very midst of the forests, but later the bark followed the tanneries, as they were located along the transportation lines, many of the inland tanneries going out of existence.

The tanning industry in America is, in fact, one of the original industries, and was from the early days one of the vocations of the pioneers. Perry County at one time was among the leading counties of the state in the tanning business, and had tanneries in many localities, but to-day only three remain, the Beaver tannery, near Blain, the Bechtel tannery at Newport, and the Rippman tannery at Millerstown. Although some of these tanneries are out of existence for a half-century an attempt has been made to record their locations, in so far as possible:

Ahl's tannery, in Henry's Valley, Toboyne Township. Samuel Lupfer ran it for years.

Tannery one mile above Fairview Church, in Toboyne Township, now run as a chopping mill. Once owned by E. A. McLaughlin, now by Samuel Slemmons.

Tannery in New Germantown, in Toboyne Township, near where M. E. Church stands. Once owned by William D. Humes.

Beaver tannery at Monterey, Toboyne Township. Israel Lupfer ran it for years. One of the three tanneries still in operation. Now owned by Silas W. Gutshall.

Cook's tannery, in Horse Valley, Toboyne Township, near church.

Tannery in Henry's Valley.

Mohler's tannery in Liberty Valley, Madison Township. Built by Milligan & Beale.

The McNeil tannery at Blain, on the Harry N. Hall farm. Burned in 1878.

The George Hench tannery at Centre, on present Robert Hench farm. Once the largest tannery in the county.

The Titzell tannery, between Green Park and Elliottsburg, operated until about 1870.

The Shearer tannery, owned by the father of Ex-Sheriff H. C. Shearer between Green Park and Landisburg, in Tyrone Township.

The Hench & Black tannery in Landisburg.

The Diven tannery in Landisburg.

Tannery in Kennedy's Valley, Tyrone Township, last operated by "Colonel" Wm. Graham, now the Newton Reisinger farm.

Tannery in Sheaffer Valley, Tyrone Township, where Harry Kiner resides.

Tannery at Oak Grove, Tyrone Township, recently owned by Henchs, now in the possession of Thomas Bernheisel.

The Abraham Wertz tannery in Tyrone Township, on Carlisle road, three miles from Landisburg, now the Al. Dunkelberger farm.

Tannery one mile above Elliottsburg, in Spring Township, last owned by a Mr. Wentzell.

Loysville tannery, on property now owned by Mrs. William Kell.

The tannery of Daniel A. Bear's heirs, in Spring Township.

The tannery at Dromgold's corner, in Carroll Township, operated by T. M. Dromgold.

The Ickesburg tannery, erected in 1821.

The tannery above Ickesburg, long known as the Swartz tannery.

The Eshcol tannery, erected by William Rosensteel.

The tannery at Roseburg, Saville Township.

The Millerstown tannery, one of the very first. One of the three still in operation. Now owned by J. G. H. and C. A. Rippman, Jr.

The North tannery, in Greenwood Township.

The Newport tannery, now owned by the Elk Tanning Company. One of the three still in operation.

The Jordan tannery, at Walnut and Front Streets, Newport.

The Peale tannery, opposite the old jail, in New Bloomfield.

Tannery one mile west of New Bloomfield, operated as early as 1843, by Israel Lupfer.

The tannery near Nekoda store, in Greenwood Township, known as Shellenberger's.

The tannery at Allen's Cove (later Cove Forge, and now Covallen), where A. G. White (father of James A. White, of Shermansdale) built the Good Hope tannery and carried on the tanning business.

The tannery which John Bowers built at Mannsville and which he operated as late as 1871, when he died.

The tannery on Hominy Ridge, Juniata Township, operated by Robert Stephens. Residents who can remember to 1856 say it had then already ceased to operate. One stone building still stands.

The William Fosselman tannery, in Tuscarora Township, later the property of James Davis, and now owned by McClellan Lineaweaver. Out of business prior to 1870.

Before the building of the narrow gauge road—the Newport & Sherman's Valley—through western Perry County, and after the tanneries in western Perry had largely become extinct, the transportation of bark from that section to the Newport tannery was extensive, and those old bark wagons drawn by four- and six-horse teams are well remembered by many yet living. During the bark season long lines of them passed down the main valley highway daily.

The first tannery in the county was built by Joshua North, on the James Patterson farm, in Greenwood Township, before 1800. The bark was chopped into bits with axes in those days, instead of being ground. This tannery was later known as Jordan's. Just when North built the tannery is unknown, but in 1776 Joshua

North, tanner, and Caleb North, storekeeper, came from Chester County and bought a number of tracts of land, including the old tannery farm. It probably was built soon after that. The Norths also bought the island in the Juniata, long known as North's Island, and being located at the old Rope Ferry Dam. In 1800 Joshua North built the Millerstown tannery, selling to Isaac Mc-Cord in 1816. During the ownership of Mr. McCord he also bought the Jordan tannery and closed it down. He also erected the stone house, which is the present home of J. H. G. Rippman, in 1822, and began the erection of a new tannery in 1824. In 1849 Henry Hopple purchased the plant from the McCord heirs for $2,500, and modernized it by the introduction of steam in 1867. Two years later he sold it to Joseph Howell, of Philadelphia, for $6,000.00. He erected a new steam tannery in 1870. In the meantime it had become Howell & Company, who were overcome with financial difficulties, and the property was purchased in 1882 by Charles A. Rippman, a skilled tanner and business man, at assignee's sale. He put in modern leeches and modernized it throughout with improved machinery. In 1901 Mr. Rippman sold it to two of his sons, J. G. H. and C. A. Rippman, Jr., who are the owners at this time. This tannery has two claims to distinction. One is that it was awarded the highest award for its product —oak tanned sole leather, at the World's Fair at Chicago in 1893, and the other is that it is an independent concern, altogether within the control of its owners. Few tanneries to-day lay claim to that distinction. Charles H. Rippman has been identified with the tanning trade in Perry County longer than any other man, and his product had a state-wide reputation.

The Beaver tannery is located in Jackson Township, two miles south of Blain. It was established prior to 1835 by a man named Ebright, and has been in continuous operation ever since, being the only inland tannery in the county from among the large number to remain in operation. The present tannery building was erected in 1849 by Samuel Mateer. The output is rough leather, harness leather and lace leather. This tannery has been operated by three generations of Gutshalls. Capt. Samuel Gutshall owned and operated it for some time prior to 1860. His son, David Gutshall, then became owner and operated it until 1896, when the present owner, Silas W. Gutshall, assumed charge, since which time he has operated it.

The Newport tannery dates back to 1872, when John A. Bechtel & Son purchased a plot of three acres of land in Oliver Township, adjoining Newport Borough on the west, and extending from Third to Front Street. This part of the township has since been taken into the Newport Borough. The Bechtels erected on this site a two-story stone tannery, which is still in use and now owned by the Elk Tanning Company, Ridgway, Pa. John A. Bechtel died in 1875, and the business was then conducted by the remaining member of the firm, his son, H. H. Bechtel. After the sale of this tannery (and another which he owned at Reed's Gap) to the Elk Tanning Company in 1893, he became associated with the American Oak Leather Company of Cincinnati, Ohio, and at the time of his death, July 13, 1914, was vice-president of that company. Horace Beard, who was a grandson of John A. Bechtel, was the first superintendent appointed by the Elk Tanning Company, serving from 1893 to 1900, when he became division superintendent of a group of tanneries, including the Newport tannery, which he held until his death, April 7, 1911. Edward G. Sheafer succeeded Mr. Beard as superintendent from 1900 to 1914, when he was transferred to a Southern tannery, and John G. Culver appointed superintendent, serving from 1914 to 1916. Mr. Culver was succeeded by George P. Bistline, a native of Perry County, who is the present superintendent. This tannery increased its capacity and has been kept in first-class condition, employing a large number of men steadily from the time of its erection. It has been idle only sixty days since its erection in 1872. Oak tanned sole leather has always been manufactured at this plant, and from 4,000 to 5,000 tons of rock oak bark are consumed annually, most of which is purchased in Perry and surrounding counties.

Quite a number of the employees have worked in the tannery for a long period of years, four men having an average of over forty years' service. While labor troubles throughout the country prevail this is a matter of interest. Two of these employees have been with it over forty-five years and two others over thirty-five, at this time (1920). These men and their length of service are George W. Taylor, 48 years; James Gardner, 46 years; George Shull, 37 years, and William Gardner, 37 years.

EARLY IRON INDUSTRY.

There is a Jewish legend that when the temple at Jerusalem was completed the king gave a feast to the workmen and artificers employed in its construction. The story went abroad that the particular craftsman who had done the most to complete the great structure should have the seat of honor next to the king. A blacksmith claimed the place and the populace clamored. The great Solomon commanded that the man be allowed to speak, whereupon he asked how these builders could have erected the temple without the tools which he had wrought out of iron. Solomon decreed that "the seat is his of right; all honor to the iron worker." During a residence, while a newspaper proprietor, of more than a dozen years in Duncannon, the one iron town in Perry County, I saw men toil amidst red-hot furnaces, while others slept, to produce iron from the raw material. The scene is so vivid in my memory to this day that I join in saying "all honor to the iron worker," and especially those early pioneers, who wrought better than they knew, who established primitive plants within the confines of our forests and who were the heralds of the present great iron and steel industry of the nation.

The very first one of these primitive plants within the county's boundaries, of which we can find record, is the Boyd forge, in Carroll Township. In 1793 William Boyd warranted 105 acres in eastern Carroll, at Boyd's Fording, and settled there. He erected several blacksmith forges and began the manufacture of nails. The iron was brought from Carlisle and slit by him into rods, and by himself and his three sons manufactured into handmade nails. This plant was still in operation when the county was formed.

As early as 1804 there is record of the Lewis forge, located on Cocolamus Creek, in Greenwood Township, near Millerstown, being in operation. Its employees were mostly negroes who lived in a colony of huts surrounding the plant. In describing it in his history (1873) Wright says: "The old forge hammer, broken through the eye, still remains in the dried-up race, while the stone abutment breastwork of the dam, on the east side of the creek, may still be seen." It was known as Mt. Vernon forge and was built by General James Lewis in 1804.

General Lewis was one of the proprietors of Hope furnace, west of Lewistown, and operated the Mt. Vernon forge in connection with it. He was a Berks County ironmaster, and James Blaine, of the vicinity of Blain, Perry County, was married to his daughter. In fact, Mr. Blaine helped him build Hope furnace in 1797 and Mt. Vernon furnace in 1804. On the retirement of Mr. Lewis, Mr. Blaine operated the forge. He later sold to a man named M'Gara, who failed, the property coming into the possession of Purcell & Woods. William P. Elliott and William Power purchased from them and rebuilt the forge, but failed in 1817, and the property reverted to Purcell & Woods. From then it was never operated. The forge had two fires and two large hammers, which were supplied with charcoal from Forge Hill and pig metal from Hope furnace and Juniata furnace in Centre Township.

Landisburg was the site of an early nail factory. It was located on Water Street, in the rear part of a building started in 1794 and not completed until 1809. The front part is of stone, and the rear was built of logs. It is now owned by Mrs. Robert Shuman, and in it was located the office of the register and recorder when Landisburg was the temporary county seat. Just when the factory moved therefrom is not known, but in the *Perry Forester* of June 21, 1821, appears the advertisement of the manufacturer, Joseph

H. Kennedy, who offers "10-penny and 8-penny nails at 10 cents per pound." He add that "wheat will be received at 40 cents, and rye at 27 cents, in exchange."

The various chapters of this book covering the townships tell of many early industries, among them the construction of a scythe and edge-tool factory by Peter Fahnestock and a Mr. Ferguson, during the period between 1830-1840. It was located in Tyrone Township and had also a tilt-hammer attached. Between Landisburg and Oak Grove, in Spring Township, Peter Moses built a large stone blacksmith shop and manufactured screw augers. At his death, in 1824, his son, also named Peter Moses, succeeded him.

During the first half of the Nineteenth Century various furnaces and forges were erected throughout the county, but near its end but two remained in business, the furnaces at Duncannon and Newport. At this time but one, the Newport furnace, remains, and it is in operation but a small part of the time. The first of these furnaces to be built was the Juniata furnace. The inland furnaces ceased operations owing to the expensive hauls of the finished product to railroad sidings, and the Duncannon furnace was dismantled owing to the necessity of obtaining the raw materials from far distant points at heavy cost. The first geological survey of Perry County, made in 1839-40, was largely responsible for the extension of the early furnace industry in Perry and adjoining counties, as the existence of deposits of iron ore was fully established at that time.

Juniata Furnace. The lands upon which Juniata furnace in Centre Township, was later erected, were warranted by James McConaughy in 1766, and later became the property of William Power, then a large landowner in what is now Perry County. About 1808 Power and David Watts, of Carlisle, erected, on a small stream which flows through the property, a small furnace, which later came to be known as Juniata furnace. They operated it for several years, and in 1824 the Watts heirs and Power leased the furnace to John Everhart, of Chester County, for a ten-year period. He erected a forge, and in 1825 put the furnace in blast, continuing operations for several years.

During May, 1833, Charles Postley & Son, of Philadelphia, purchased the furnace property and 3,500 acres of land, which included a gristmill at the mouth of the run, paying therefor $19,500. During January, 1834, Postley & Company advertised for "sixteen stone and four potter hollowware moulders to work at the Juniata Iron Works." From Postley title had passed entirely to his sons, who sold it to John McKeehan and Matthew S. Henry in 1837. In a year or two James McGowan acquired the interest of Henry. Another furnace had been added further up the stream, and under McGowan's supervision both furnaces were operated. This firm built the gristmill, which later came to be known as Shoaff's mill.

There was a large ore bank on the tract. A settlement had grown up around it, comprising eleven tenement houses, coal house, storehouse, warehouse, carpenter shop, blacksmith shop and the gristmill. About 1849 the furnace was abandoned and the mill passed to the ownership of William R. Shoaff. In 1855 the casting house and the office were destroyed by a cyclone which hit the section. The property is now in possession of Ellis Shoaff, the mill having long since ceased operations.

Fio Forge. Fio forge, in Wheatfield Township, was built on a plot of ground which was warranted in 1766 by Benjamin Abram and which contained 207 acres. In 1827 Israel Downing and James B. Davis purchased twenty-three acres and began the erection of the forge, which they had almost completed in July, 1828, when they sold to Jacob Lindley and Frederick Speck. They owned and operated it until 1841, when it passed to Elias Jackson, Samuel Yocum, and Daniel Kough, who at the same time operated Mary Ann furnace in Cumberland County. It later passed to a man named Walker, who retained Kough as manager. On March 14, 1846, a great flood on Sherman's Creek carried away the dam and the plant was abandoned.

Oak Grove Furnace. Oak Grove furnace was located in Spring Township on a tract of land purchased from Christian Heckendorn, in February, 1827, by Adam and John Hays. In a paper dated October, 1825, Heckendorn advertised three hundred acres of land for sale, describing it as an excellent location for a furnace, having ore within a half-mile. The new owners contracted with John Miller February 20, 1827, for "the right for twenty-one years to dig and haul iron ore from any part of land on which Miller lives and has his tanyard, at twenty dollars per year for every year they dig ore." On March 16th of the same year they contracted with Thomas March and John Souder to pay each fifteen dollars per year for a like privilege. During the same year they built Charlotte furnace, it being put in blast on December 4, 1827, under the management of Colonel George Patterson. It was operated until 1828, its capacity being twenty-five tons of metal per week.

It was refitted during 1828-29 and was again put in blast in 1829, its name being changed to Oak Grove furnace. It passed from the ownership of Adam and John Hays to that of Hays & McClure, John Hays remaining in the firm. In 1831 a post office was established there with John Hays as postmaster. In the meantime McClure retired from the management and John Hays continued until January 6, 1834, when he sold the furnace, his ore rights and 2,500 acres of land to Jacob F. Plies, for $22,000. It

18

was later under the ownership of Plies, Hess & Company and of Jacob F. Plies & Company, the latter company being composed of Christian Thudium and Frederick Boger. It was abandoned about 1843 and the property passed to Christian Thudium. With its passing also passed the post office, but many years later another was established near by and was known as "Lebo." The James McCormick heirs obtained possession of the property and owned it for many years. During the ownership of both Hays and Plies plates were manufactured or cast here for the old-fashioned "ten-plate stoves."

Montebello Furnace. The old Montebello furnace, in Wheatfield Township, was located on a tract of land warranted by William Baskins in 1766, which contained 238 acres. Its location was on Little Juniata Creek, several miles above King's mill, and near where Montebello Park, a popular amusement resort flourished during the early days of the Perry County Railroad. In 1834 Jacob Lindley, Elizabeth and Hannah Downing and William Logan Fisher purchased this and an adjoining tract, "for the purpose of building a furnace thereon." It was built in a year or two, and after a few years passed to Fisher, Morgan & Company, who operated it until 1846 or 1848, when it was abandoned. It had a capacity of from twenty-five to thirty tons of iron per week. When the latter firm secured possession it was run in connection with the Duncannon iron plant, then owned by the same firm. They built a stave mill near the forge, which was in use until 1875, when it was destroyed by fire. The company owned and leased large timber tracts, from which the wood was cut and used for the burning of charcoal. The limestone and ore was hauled in wagons from the canal wharf at Losh's Run Station, on the Pennsylvania Railroad, and the finished product transported in the same way to the firm's Duncannon plant. In April, 1837, when the entire Mahanoy Ridge burned over the industry lost three thousand cords of wood by fire. The *Forester* pronounced this conflagration "a grand and imposing spectacle," instead of speaking of the great loss.

Perry Furnace. Perry furnace was located on a tract of land warranted by Anthony Shatto, which later came into the possession of William Power. In 1837 Jacob Loy, John Everhart, and John Kough, trading under the name of Loy, Everhart & Company, purchased several hundred acres of land and erected Perry furnace, where they began the manufacture of hollowware and ten-plate stoves. After running the plant for ten years they had financial difficulties and the property was sold to Peter Cameron. The barn of Edward Comp is located on the site of the old furnace.

Perry furnace was abandoned about 1848. During its operation the timber was cut from a piece of woodland about three miles

long and over a mile wide, and burned into charcoal. The iron
ore mostly was procured at the Dum farm, in that section of
Spring Township known as "Little Germany." After being reduced to "pig iron" it was hauled overland by wagon to the Duncannon rolling mills, a distance of twelve miles. The limestone
used in melting the ore was secured on the furnace farm. At one
time a village of a dozen houses was located there, being occupied
by the employees. On a single acre of ground there are nine
springs, any one of which would be ample to supply a single farm
with water. Half of them are phosphorous.

Caroline Furnace. Travelers over the lines of the Pennsylvania
Railroad will note that there stands not many rods east of Bailey
Station a stone stack almost overgrown with vines. It is a mute
reminder of the early furnace industry of Pennsylvania. There
stood Caroline furnace. Even the very lands on which it stood
have a historical setting. Samuel Martin, who located this claim
of two hundred acres, on a part of which later stood Caroline furnace, also warranted an extensive acreage on the northern side of
the Juniata, on which he built a gristmill and a sawmill. The property is described as being "at the Upper Falls, below the great bend
south of Newport." John Bowman had evidently some prior claim
on the property at Bailey Station, in Miller Township, as it is referred to in Samuel Martin's will as the property purchased of him.
In a mortgage it is mentioned as "above the Falls, adjoining Dick's
Hill." Caroline furnace was erected by John D. Creigh in 1836,
and began operations the same year. It later came into the possession of Joseph Bailey, later a congressman of the United States.
His residence, with numerous additions, still stands. Very little
seems to have been recorded of this old industry.

Cove Forge. About 1863 several hundred acres of land were
purchased in the Cove, Penn Township, about one and one-half
miles east of Duncannon, by Wm. McIlvaine & Sons, of Reading,
who in April, 1864, began the erection of a forge, long known as
Cove forge. It was put in blast in September, 1865, with six fires,
being run by water-power. A sexton hammer was operated by
steam. On their lands they made charcoal for use in their own
furnaces. It was operated for about twenty years. The large
dam erected above the plant was put in by this firm, the lands now
being owned by Robert C. Neal, whose father, Robert C. Neal,
a Harrisburg capitalist, erected a fine mansion on the property,
turning it into a gentleman's country estate. It was located upon
the original Thomas Barnett tract, described in the chapter relating to Penn Township. The local passenger station was long
known as Cove Forge, but within the past decade it has been
changed to Covallen, significant of Allen's Cove, long the name
by which the Cove was known.

The Duncannon Iron Works. The location of this plant is at
the point of land lying just north of where Sherman's Creek enters
the Susquehanna. It is on part of a tract of 220 acres, warranted
June 2, 1762, to George Allen and surveyed to Robert Jones. In
1827 it passed to Stephen Duncan and John D. Mahon, who immediately began the erection of a forge, which began operations in
the summer of 1828. In February of the same year the firm
bought ninety-four acres and the lower gristmill, a sawmill, and a
distillery from Robert Clark, and on April 17 they purchased 1,231
acres of land, comprised in three different tracts, from Andrew
Mateer. The firm's advertisement called for men to go to work
on July 31, 1828. The little plant run until July 9, 1829, when it
was destroyed by fire, the loss being stated as from $1,500 to
$2,000. It was at once rebuilt and in operation by December
of the same year. The firm of Duncan & Mahon then operated
the forge until 1832 or 1833, when they leased it to John Johnston
& Company, who also operated and were the owners of Chestnut
Grove forge, in Adams County. This firm then operated it until
the dissolution of the firm in September, 1834. The stock on hand
was disposed of by public sale early in 1835 and in the spring of
1836 the property of Duncan & Mahon passed to William Logan
Fisher and Charles W. Morgan. It included the forge, which they
operated for a short time, and about six thousand acres of land,
mostly timber land.

This firm was the forerunner of the Duncannon Iron Company.
They erected the old rolling mill in 1837-38, on the site of the old
forge, which they tore down. This first rolling mill was rather
primitive, being but 60x100 feet. Its capacity was five thousand
tons of bar iron per year. The first nail factory was erected by
them in 1839 and began operations in 1840. Prior to its erection
Fisher & Morgan had been sending their bar iron in flats to New
Cumberland, where it was manufactured into nails by Roswell
Woodward. When the Duncannon nail factory was completed
that plant was dismantled and the twenty-five nail machines taken
to Duncannon and installed. The new plant then had a capacity
of twenty thousand kegs per annum. On March 14, 1846, a flood
coming down Sherman's Creek, washed away the dam and part
of the rolling mill. The mill and dam were rebuilt. This flood
also took the Juniata River bridge and the eastern span of the
Susquehanna River bridge. The furnace was erected in 1853.
Its capacity was twenty tons per day. It was remodeled in 1880,
its capacity then being fifteen thousand tons per year. The year
1860 was a bad one for the plant. The nail factory burned on
January 10th and the rolling mill dam was again washed out on
May 11th. The nail factory was rebuilt at once and the number
of machines increased to forty-six, many being added later. The

output then reached 100,000 kegs of nails annually. The dam was never rebuilt, as steam had already been used in part in the operation of the rolling mill.

In the meantime the firm had become Fisher, Morgan & Company, and on February 1, 1861, their interests were purchased by the newly organized Duncannon Iron Company, the old firm retaining an interest in the stock of the new concern. The transfer of lands included about eight hundred acres. The new firm was under the management of John Wister, later for many years its president, and without doubt the greatest ironmaster ever interested in any Perry County plant. When Fisher, Morgan & Company sold to the Duncannon Iron Company they retained Montebello furnace (which had ceased operations), and 3,469 acres of land, which they sold in June, 1885, to John Wister, as trustee of the Duncannon Iron Company. The iron storage house was burned November 1, 1871. The old stave mill, built when the first nail factory was erected, was burned in the spring of 1875, and a new one immediately erected on the south bank of Sherman's Creek. On March 12, 1882, the rolling mill was burned down and again rebuilt at once. On the evening of November 28, 1888, the main building of the nail factory was entirely destroyed by fire and the machinery badly damaged. It too was immediately rebuilt, on the opposite side of Sherman's Creek. The large stone office building of the Duncannon Iron Company was built in 1866, being occupied January 14, 1867. It is 35x54 in size, with the main office room sixteen feet in height. The company store dates back to the time of the first forge, erected in 1828. Who the early managers of the company store were it is impossible to state. W. J. Stewart was the manager as early as 1871. His successor was Abram Hess, who was succeeded in 1882 by S. A. E. Rife. The store closed in 1908.

John Wister was for over half a century connected with the Duncannon Iron Works, rising from errand boy to president and general manager. He was born in Germantown, Philadelphia, July 15, 1829, the son of William and Sarah Logan (Fisher) Wister, the former of German and the latter of English descent. He was educated in the Germantown Academy. He arrived at Duncannon, via packet boat and on foot, November 2, 1845, to enter the employ of an uncle, skilled in the iron business, and his first position was that of office boy. He was then a tall, athletic young lad of but sixteen summers. From that position of office boy he became the noted president and general manager of the Duncannon Iron Company, skilled along every operation of the iron business, for he had made it a study. When he first came the operation of the plant was still furnished by the waters of Sherman's Creek, and without any tariff on iron the workers at the

Sherman's Creek. The road was to begin at the eastern end of the bridge, at a point not exceeding one-fourth of a mile therefrom, and to cross to the west bank of the Juniata, passing through or near Petersburg (now Duncannon), and to terminate at or near the mouth of Sherman's Creek, the distance being two miles. The directors were Cornelius Baskins, president; Amos A. Jones, Jacob Keiser, Thomas Duncan, Thomas K. Lindley, John B. Topley, John Charters, and Jacob Clay. They were likewise the directors of the bridge. This old railroad was used and operated by the Duncannon Iron Company in transporting to and from their plant raw material and the finished product, shipments being made and received at Benvenue by canal boat. The cars were drawn by horses and mules. The bridge over which the railroad crossed the Juniata River was washed away in 1845 and was rebuilt. On March 17, 1865, it was again washed away. The iron company then erected a warehouse at Aqueduct, reshipping by rail from there to Duncannon. After that the road was no longer used, although its rails lay for a number of years.

Marshall Furnace. The lands upon which Marshall furnace, in East Newport, was built, was purchased of Elias Fisher, and in 1872, Egle, Philips & Company erected the furnace, which later passed into the possession of the Marshall family, of Philadelphia. Major Peter Hiestand was long superintendent of this furnace, which ran rather regularly until about 1900, but which has run intermittently since, owing to its distance from raw material.

CHAPTER XVI.

THE EARLIEST CHURCHES.

IT seems strange that these shores should have been hidden so long and that they should be reserved for settlement until after the Reformation. Could it have been mere chance, or was it the work of an all-wise Creator? Did He reserve these lands for the most enlightened Christian people of that age—for those western Europeans, the Pilgrim, the Puritan, the Holland Dutch, the Friend, the German, the Scotch-Irish, and all that noble band who braved the dangers of the deep and the terror of the red men that they might worship God according to their own free will?

The men who founded Pennsylvania were intensely religious; many of them came here to have freedom of religious worship; they lived in a period when religious doctrines were the great absorbing questions of life, so much so that the present generation cannot realize the zeal of their ancestry. They had family worship in their homes. The Father's business was their first consideration, and they builded well, for notwithstanding any seeming laxity of religion, even the sneering cynic does not enter the state of wedlock nor have the last sad rites for a member of his family occur without calling upon the ministry and the church, thus recognizing its sanctity and Divine inspiration.

Those churchmen of generations ago and even of the passing generations were men of stability and worth who stood foursquare in their communities and were as solid and trustworthy as the very hills which surrounded them. Even to-day, is it not largely so with the active churchmen—those who attend and participate and whose names are upon the church books for more than business reasons? Of course there were prejudices in those days, but they have largely turned to dust, buried bigotries of a departing age. In all the writer's many travels over the territory during the past few years in only two cases did he note any evidence of prejudice in regard to sect upon the part of those interviewed and one of the interviewed is now numbered with the departed. Joint services are held in many towns and communities by the various denominations, and this passing of prejudice is a heritage largely due to the "union Sunday school picnics" of yesteryear, when the men and women of to-day were boys and girls and knew their neighbor of another creed was just as good a fellow and that there was really little difference—and no vital one— in their beliefs. And this community spirit is growing!

Some of the old-time preachers were often loud in their discourses, and sometimes long. Many of them preached much of the relentlessness of God towards evildoers, instead of dwelling upon His love and forgiving spirit, ofttimes shouting or thundering their remarks. It is, however, even said of Jonathan Edwards, the prominent New England theologian, whose life was passed in benevolence, that he delighted in describing the fierceness and relentless cruelty of God.

Bancroft, the historian, says: "He who will not honor the memory and respect the influence of John Calvin knows but little of the origin of American liberty," and it was the creed of John Calvin that first carried the Gospel into the territory now comprising Perry County. The Scotch-Irish were the first to settle Perry County territory, and with them came Calvinism and Presbyterianism. Here, in the heart of the forests, they planted the first churches, one of which is to-day a bulwark of strength in western Perry, in the famous Sherman's Valley. In those early days the church had more or less dominion as to where buildings should be erected and where dividing lines should be drawn in the intervening territory. That that question came up early in the settlement is evidenced by the fact that the Presbytery of Donegal—practically the predecessor of the Carlisle Presbytery—at a meeting held April 24, 1766, appointed a committee "to attempt to settle matters respecting the seat of a meetinghouse or meetinghouses to be erected in Sherman's Valley." It was to meet the Wednesday after the third Sabbath of June. It was composed of Rev. Robert Cooper, Rev. George Duffield, and the following elders: Colonel Armstrong (with William Lyon, alternate), Thomas Wilson and John McKnight, the elders to devote the previous Tuesday "to reconnoitre."

This committee met at George Robinson's—close to the present location of Centre church—on July 2. After two days devoted to hearing testimony and deliberating the committee came to the conclusion "that there ought to be a church at Alexander Morrow's or James Blain's (where there was already a graveyard) for the upper end of the valley, and one at George Robinson's for the centre." Settling the place of the location for the lower meetinghouse was deferred until further light could be obtained. (Records of Presbytery for 1766, pp. 186-189.) These incidents predate the forming of the General Assembly of the Presbyterian Church in America, which convened first in 1788.

To a little book printed in London, in 1768, entitled "The Journal of a Two-Months' Tour, with a view of Promoting Religion Among the Frontier Inhabitants of Pennsylvania, and of Introducing Christianity Among the Indians to the Westward of the Allegheny Mountains," we are indebted for a glimpse of the early

The statement that they came to the Ross home *in the night* is an example of the perils and discomforts which attended these early purveyors of the Word, for it must be remembered that they were unattended by any who knew the way and that roads were then unknown, the vast forests being broken only by trails and paths.

In the entry following Rev. Beatty tells of his visit to that temple in the woods, not built by hands, but where for over a century historic Centre Presbyterian Church has stood and where it has ministered to a people who braved dangers untold to erect their homes in a land still a forest primeval, and to their descendants. He says:

"Tuesday, 19th.—Rode four or five miles to a place in the woods, designed for building a house for worship, and preached, but to a small auditory; notice of our preaching not having been sufficiently spread. After sermon, I opened to the people present the principal design of the synod in sending us to them at this time; that it was not only to preach the Gospel, but also to enquire into their circumstances, situation, numbers, and ability to support it."

"The people not being prepared to give us a full answer, promised to send it to Carlisle before our return. After sermon we proceeded on our way about five miles and lodged at Mr. Fergus's. The house where he lives was attacked by the Indians in the late war, the owner of it killed, and, if I am not mistaken, some others. While the Indians were pillaging the house and plantation, in order to carry off what suited them, a number of the countrymen armed came upon them; a smart skirmish ensued, in which the countrymen had the better. The Indians were obliged to fly, and carried off their wounded, but left all their booty behind them."

The place here referred to was the home of Alexander Logan, which was later occupied by Mr. Fergus. It is located near where Sandy Hill post office was later established, in Madison Township, and was long owned by George McMillen. From the Logan place the party traveled along the south foot of Conococheague Mountain, crossing it by the ravine north of Andersonburg, and mistakenly calling it the Tuscarora Mountain. In passing down the north side they came to where Mohler's tannery was located in a succeeding generation, and crossed Liberty Valley via Bigham's Gap to the Tuscarora Valley, now in Juniata County.

Just how the Gospel came to be first carried west of the Kittatinny Mountains is of interest to all. The origin of the missionary tour of Rev. Charles Beatty and Rev. George Duffield to the distressed frontier, harassed by the Indians, and to the Indians themselves, seems to have been an action of The Corporation for the Relief of Poor and Distressed Presbyterian Ministers of New York, as an extract from their minutes reads:

"November 16, 1762.—At a meeting of the Corporation in the city, it was agreed that the board appoint some of their members to wait on the synod at their next meeting, and in their name request that some mis-

sionaries be sent to preach to the distressed frontier inhabitants, and to
report their distresses, and to let us know when new congregaticns are
a forming, and what is necessary to be done to promote the spread of the
Gospel among them, and that they inform us what opportunities there
may be of preaching the Gospel to the Indian nations in their neighborhoods."

It was then agreed that the necessary expenses of these missionaries be paid by this board. To many Perry Countians it may be
a surprise that the Gospel was first carried to their county by
missionaries.

After mentioning the beginning of Centre Church in 1766 and
that of Dick's Gap about the same time, Rev. D. H. Focht, in his
valuable and painstaking volume, "The Churches Between the
Mountains," says: "Besides these two instances we have not found
a single reference to churches in Perry County (territory) until
1790." He fails to mention the organization of the Upper Church
at Blain at the same time, that Limestone Ridge (or Sam Fisher's
Church") existed coincidentally, and that Dick's Gap joined with
the Sherman's Creek Church as early as 1778 in calling Rev.
Thom, all of which were long prior to 1790. Farther back in his
own book (page 286) he tells of the St. Michael's Lutheran
Church in Pfoutz Valley being organized as early as 1770 to 1773,
and of the purchase of their grounds February 15, 1776, on which
they erected a building which they used for both school and church
purposes, also long prior to 1790. This is not mentioned here in
the way of criticism, but to correct a general misunderstanding
that prevails by reason of the paragraph cited above, which is
sometimes quoted.

Early last century many of the Scotch-Irish had begun to move
westward and the new population, coming in their wake and often
purchasing their lands, was mostly of German extraction, whose
religion was principally Lutheran and German Reformed. At
first their services were almost exclusively in German, but gradually were replaced with English. Then came the Methodist
Church, with youth, zeal and earnestness, holding its meetings in
homes and schoolhouses and conducting great camp meetings in
the woods. Other denominations followed until to-day there are
ten, eight of which have numerous churches, and of the remaining
two one has two churches, and the other a single church.

The Presbyterians had been holding services and building
churches within the limits of what is now western Perry County
for several decades before the advent of the Lutherans to any extent, although the Lutherans of that section east of the Juniata,
about 1770, were holding meetings and were about organizing St.
Michael's Church, in Pfoutz Valley. Rev. Focht, in his "Churches
Between the Mountains," says the Lutheran people were occasionally visited by ministers of their own churches before 1774,

according to tradition, and that afterwards they enjoyed frequent visits from Rev. John G. Butler, who was pastor of the Lutheran Church of Carlisle from 1780 to 1788. Shortly after that Rev. John Timothy Kuhl, of Franklin County, began visiting the members in Sherman's Valley, and in 1790 he moved among them and became the first regular pastor, having a large field and preaching once every six weeks at each place. In an old document belonging to the congregation at Loysville, it is written: "In the year of our Lord 1790, the Germans in Sherman's Valley secured the Evangelical Lutheran minister, the Rev. John Timotheus Kuhl, as their pastor." Rev. Focht, in his volume, further says: "The late Mr. George Fleisher, of Saville Township, who died in 1855, aged eighty-four years, when nineteen years old, with a team moved Rev. Kuhl's family and effects from Franklin County to this valley. Rev. Kuhl resided near where Loysville is now located. From the above documentary evidence, we infer that he visited and preached to the members scattered at various points in the whole valley. Before the erection of Lebanon Church at Loysville, he preached in barns and private dwellings at different places in that neighborhood. Encouraged by a minister living in their midst, and united in their desires and efforts, the membership proceeded, in 1794, to build a house of worship at Loysville, which they denominated Lebanon Church." The history of the building of that church appears further on. The George Fleisher referred to was the grandfather of the various heads of the Fleisher families located about Newport some years ago and yet, viz: George, John, Amos, Prof. Daniel, etc.

There has never been a Catholic church in Perry County. While the canal was building, during 1827-28, services were held occasionally in homes, as the employees were largely Irish Catholics. Their number was occasionally reduced by a death, and they purchased from John Huggins a plot of ground on the lands lying close to Liverpool and opened a cemetery. There was but one tombstone in it and it marked the grave of John Doyle, a hotel keeper. The Liverpool folks have known it as "the Irish cemetery."

With the settlement of both English-speaking and German-speaking people in this territory the two languages were in general use, but the public business was conducted in English. The German element was loath to give up their language and, although their children were learning and speaking English, they contended against the preaching of the word in English in their churches. The most prominent example of this was that of Rev. John William Heim, pastor of the Loysville Lutheran Charge. When the West Pennsylvania Synod met at New Bloomfield in September, 1842, some of the ministers preached in the English language. Members of the congregation at Bloomfield—also a part of his charge—knew the necessity of introducing the English language and urged him to have an associate pastor who could preach in English. This he refused to do, with the result that an English Lutheran church was organized in June, 1844, and held its meetings in the school-house, and later in the Presbyterian Church. This condition existed until 1850, after the death of Rev. Heim, which occurred the previous year, when the two Lutheran churches were again put under one pastorate. But, as late as 1853 there was a requirement that one-third of the preaching should be in German.

In the early years of settlement it was a common thing to travel long distances to church, over bridle paths and roads hardly worthy of the name. George and Alexander Johnston, of Toboyne Township, the latter the father of Dr. A. R. Johnston, of New Bloomfield, were members of the United Presbyterian Church at Concord, Franklin County. They were born in 1802 and 1805, and died in 1872 and 1864, respectively, so that even to almost the middle of last century, it appears, it was not uncommon to travel a long way to divine worship. George W. Gehr, long a newspaper correspondent, tells of Elliottsburg citizens walking to New Bloomfield, before the building of the schoolhouse at Elliottsburg, in which the first services were held; telling how the young ladies tripped along barefooted until they came to the gristmill site west of the county seat, where they put on shoes and hose and proceeded to church. This was a custom in various parts of the county. H. E. Sheibley, editor of the *Advocate,* at New Bloomfield, recalls the time when his people attended the United Presbyterian Church at Duncannon, making the ten-mile trip by carriage. Ann West Gibson, the mother of the celebrated Chief Justice Gibson, went from the Gibson mill, at the Spring-Carroll line, to Carlisle to attend the services of the Church of England (Episcopalian). In fact, many of the first pioneers crossed the Kittatinny to Carlisle to church before they had churches in their communities.

There seems to be a diminishing of the number of the little country churches which once dotted the wayside, as population seeks the great centres and since labor-saving machinery has made less labor requirements upon the farms; and in many cases when one enters those that remain the attendance seems to be considerably less than in the years gone by. Of course families are also smaller, and the introduction of motor cars has also had its effect, but the passing of these churches is indeed to be regretted. They were a leading factor in the breaking down of sectarianism, they fostered the best in life and were to newcomers in the community a refuge from homesickness and loneliness. They were, along with being houses of worship, also, to the country just what

thirteen now holding worship. Groves, homes, schoolhouses, and even barns were used for early meetings. Few churches have burned. Some have passed away through the loss of population in their respective settlements. Several have been removed and built elsewhere. Some have been flooded by high waters during river floods.

The clergymen of Perry County are, as a rule, a zealous and industrious body, and Sunday school work and the opposition to the liquor traffic has had their almost united enthusiastic support. Many of them have gone to larger and broader fields. For decades ministerial associations have been in existence in Newport and Duncannon, and in 1920 the Ministerial Association of Western Perry County was organized at Loysville with Rev. G. R. Heim, of Blain, as president, and Rev. F. H. Daubenspeck, of Ickesburg, as secretary. Rev. A. R. Longanecker, of Loysville, and Rev. E. V. Strasbaugh, of Blain, were much interested in its organization.

The old-time prayer meeting will be remembered by many of the readers of this book, and through the years they will see a vision of one and recall the kindly voice of a devout worshiper whose presence is no longer felt, but whose example in the community is remembered to this day. Many years ago, Jacob Crist, one of the good and substantial citizens of New Bloomfield, wrote for the *Perry Freeman* a poem which is here reproduced in part, not for any especial literary value, but as a pen picture of an old-time prayer meeting:

PRAYER MEETING OF THE PAST.

BY JACOB CRIST.

Only the aged ones can know
Of prayer meetings, long ago,
How Christian men, and women too,
Did worship God, sincere and true.

Most happy and sincere they felt,
When side by side in prayer they knelt;
Then rise and sing while one would lead,
"Alas! and did my Saviour Bleed."

Then one would lead in prayer again,
Would read a chapter and explain,
Then sing about that Crimson Flood,
"There is a Fountain filled with Blood."

And "Come Thou Fount" they all would sing
And, "Children of the Heavenly King"
And ofttimes sing that hymn of praise,
"Awake my soul in joyful lays."

Then kneeling down without delay
In happy mood they all would pray,
Then sing some brother's favorite choice
With cheering sound, and strengthened voice.

And Cennick's hymn, in highest tone,
"Jesus, my all to heaven is gone";
Then too, well nigh beyond control,
Sing "Jesus, lover of my soul."

Then for the mourners all would pray,
That Christ would wash their sins away;
Then rise and make their voices ring,
"O for a thousand tongues to sing."

The "mourners' bench" was always there,
Where penitents would kneel for prayer,
And Christians would with talk sincere,
Encourage them to persevere.

And Jones' invitation hymn,
Which is pathetic and sublime;
"Come, humble sinner, in whose breast"
Was sung and anxious souls were blest.

One custom then, seems no more so,
Then men and women both would go;
Now women mostly do attend,
While men their evening elsewhere spend.

Schoolhouses then were Bethels true,
And men did not object thereto;
The fuel too was not refused,
But during winter, freely used.

Lit candles hung around the wall,
Would dimly shine within the hall,
And ofttimes when they shone too dim,
Some brother would with snuffers trim.

Oft when the meeting knelt to pray,
Bad boys would laugh, and talk and play,
And then the leader would complain
About their want of sense and brain.

Sometimes his strictures were severe,
And sometimes earnest and sincere;
But boys are boys, as they are yet,
And good advice would soon forget.

Near ten, the leader would propose
To bring the meeting to a close;
Then rise and sing—ere they would go—
"Praise God, from whom all blessings flow."

Outside the girls would find their beaux
Where they would stand each side in rows,
And when some one would get the "fling."
Then cheers and laughs and whoops would ring.

Soon would the people homeward go,
Some better, others so and so,
And thus repeat it o'er and o'er
Or find excuse to go no more.

19

sexton. In the graveyard, with an extant of several acres, are tombstones bearing dates as early as 1766. It is the last resting place of heroic and prominent people. The church is in the midst of the most historic section of Perry County, in itself being the most historic of the religious organizations. About the old church building there stood on guard two members of the flock with guns while the rest worshiped, as protection against the stealthy encroachment of Indians. Worshipers came carrying their guns, ready for any attack.

The trustees of Centre Church in 1819, when it was chartered, were John Linn, John Creigh, Thomas Purdy, William McClure, Charles Elliott, Samuel McCord, David Coyle, Robert Elliott, and Samuel A. Anderson.

In 1767 the first church was erected of logs, with dovetailed corners. There were no arrangements for fire, even in severe weather. Two services were held on Sunday and lunches were brought along by the attendants who remained for the second service. As early as 1760 there had been requests for a preacher to the Donegal Presbytery, but the churches were not organized. However, preachers were sent. In 1766 the Presbyterian churches of Sherman's Valley asked for organization, and the Missionary Board of the Presbyterian Church sent Rev. Charles Beatty to visit the frontier settlements. (See previous pages.)

In 1793 a stone church was erected in place of the log structure. It is said that some of the logs of this first church still are a part of the barn on the old Wormley farm, below Waggoner's. The third church was built in 1850, to which has since been added the Sunday school section. The entire church has also been remodeled several times.

After some investigation three churches were organized, as follows: the old Dick's Gap Church, Centre Church, and Blain, then called the Upper Church. April 14, 1767. Presbytery approved it. The "Limestone Church"(Samuel Fisher's), near Green Park, had already been partly erected, but Presbytery refused to organize it on account of it being too near Centre Church. In 1772, however, the request was granted and it, with Centre and Upper (also sometimes called Toboyne) united in a call to Rev. William Thom, but he declined. No pastor was secured until 1778, when Rev. John Linn was installed and remained until his death in 1820. In the meantime the "Limestone" Church was abandoned and in 1823 the congregation at Landisburg was organized. A Rev. Gray filled in as a supply for several years. From 1826 to 1831 Rev. James M. Olmstead was pastor of the Upper churches. From 1831 to 1836 Rev. Lindley C. Rutter served, followed by Rev. Nelson until 1842. Rev. George D. Porter followed in 1844 and remained until 1851, also preaching for the Millerstown church.

Rev. George S. Ray, a supply, filled in until 1854, when Landisburg joined in with Centre and Blain. Then came Lewis Williams, who was pastor until he died in 1857. Rev. John H. Clark served 1857-62, and Rev. J. H. Ramsey 1863-67.

Blain then united with Ickesburg. Centre and Landisburg called Rev. Robert McPherson, who remained until 1881. It was supplied until 1883, when Rev. John H. Cooper. filled the place until 1885, first as stated supply, then as pastor.

From 1867 until the present time—a period covering more than a half-century—Centre Church has had but six ministers, the sixth being the present pastor, as follows:

        1868-81   —Rev. R. M. McPherson.
        1883-85   —Rev. John H. Cooper.
        1887-1910—Rev. Wm. M. Burchfield.
        1910-14   —Rev. George H. Miksch.
        1915-17   —Rev. Hugh R. Magill, M.D.
        1919   —Rev. Carl G. H. Ettlich.

During the pastorate of Rev. Burchfield, in 1895, Landisburg, Blain (or Upper Church), and Buffalo (near Ickesburg) were detached from Centre Church.

Of the "old stone church," built in 1793, Rev. William A. West, who wrote the History of the Presbytery of Carlisle, said: "The writer remembers well its appearance in his boyhood days, when he enjoyed the annual treat of a visit at his maternal grandfather's, close by. In style, in appearance, and in arrangement it was like nearly all the stone churches of that day." Rev. D. H. Focht, in his "Churches Between the Mountains," says that "the old church building was not erected until 1793," but fails to state that that was the second church to be erected there.

Blain Presbyterian Church. The question of locating the first Presbyterian churches in the territory which now comprises Perry County came up at Donegal Presbytery's meeting April 24, 1766, and the committee sent to "reconnoitre" reported that there ought to be a church at Alexander Morrow's or James Blaine's (where there was already a graveyard) for the upper end of the valley, and one at George Robinson's for the centre." The people of the upper end erected their church near James Blaine's, near where the "Upper Church" still stands, and adjoining the graveyard spoken of. This James Blaine was the father of Ephraim Blaine, the Perry Countian who was Commissary General during the Revolutionary War, and from him descended that great statesman, James G. Blaine, younger generations adding an "e" to the name. See chapter in this book entitled The Blaine Family.

The early records of this church are missing, but according to the annals of Presbytery and early historical records there was an organized congregation where Blain now stands as early as 1767, in which year it united in a call with the churches at Centre and Dick's Gap to Presbytery for recognition and the services of a pastor. There is no evidence of the erection of a church then and the meetings, as they were known, were likely held in the homes. September 8, 1772, it united with Centre and "Sam Fisher's Church" ("Limestone" Church, near Green Park) in extending a call to Rev. William Thom to become pastor, but he did not accept. They probably had a building by this time. In 1777 they called Rev. John Linn, and from then to 1868 its pastors were the same as those of Centre Church. (See preceding pages.) In that year the Blain and Ickesburg churches united to form a charge. Rev. J. J. Hamilton, residing in Saville Township, was pastor from 1869-75; Rev. Robt. McPherson, stated supply, 1877-81, and Rev. J. H. Cooper, residing in Blain, in 1884-85. Following Rev. Cooper, Rev. Wm. Burchfield was pastor of this church, Buffalo (near Ickesburg), Centre, and Landisburg, from 1887 to 1895, when Centre became a separate charge, Rev. Burchfield continuing until 1910. It then became known as the Landisburg charge. The minister resided in that town. The pastors were:

> 1896-97 —Rev. Hugh G. Moody, stated supply.
> 1898-1902—Rev. A. F. Lott.
> 1904- —Rev. Will H. Dyer.

Following that period the regular pastors of Centre Church were again in charge, as follows:

> 1910-14—Rev. George H. Miksch.
> 1915-17—Rev. Hugh R. Magill.

During 1920-21 Rev. Carl G. H. Ettlich, pastor of Centre Church, was the stated supply pastor. In 1921 the Church Hill Cemetery Association was chartered and took over all the property of the church, which, as an organization, will cease to exist. Through removals and deaths the membership of the Upper (Blain) Church had become very weak and the Presbytery had proposed selling the same, which resulted in the incorporation of this cemetery association, the incorporators being James A. Noel, H. M. Hall, Dr. A. R. Johnston, and others. The church will be kept in repair for occasional meetings. This is a step in the right direction. These old landmarks should be preserved, as nearly as possible, in their original state.

The first church was a long, low, log building near the schoolhouse on "Church Hill." The present church, built long ago, stands adjoining a small grove. While there is no evidence obtainable yet, one is inclined to believe that this lot was given for church purposes by James Blain, who warranted the tract in 1765 on which it is located, as the application for recognition by the Presbytery is dated early the next year, April 14, 1766.

"Limestone Church." There was an early Presbyterian church located at Green Park, being located on the site of the old burying ground on the John Garlin farm. It was known as the "Lime-stone" or "Lower Church," and sometimes as "Sam Fisher's Church," and its people formed the first organization in 1766, but the Presbytery declined to give it regular standing on account of its nearness to Centre Church. The meetinghouse lot contained thirty-six acres, and it was surveyed in 1768. A log church was erected and after continuous appeals Presbytery consented June 24, 1772, and this church, Centre Church, and the Upper churches called Rev. William Thom, but he declined. Supply ministers then filled in until 1777, when a call was tendered Rev. John Linn, who was installed in June, 1778. He was in charge until his death in 1820. This church had been abandoned, however, before his death, and its place was filled by the organization of the Landis-burg church a few years later. It is known in some records as "Same Fisher's Church," as it was located upon a thirty-six-acre plot which he took up for church purposes. It is about six miles below Centre Church. In this old cemetery sleep the Fulwilers, Fosters, Neilsons, McClures, and other noted families.

Dick's Gap. According to all records and to tradition the old Dick's Gap Church, in Miller Township, Perry County, was one of the first churches to be erected within the borders of what is now Perry County, if it could be called a church. It was built of logs, but for over thirty years was not filled between the logs with mortar. It is said to have had an old-fashioned clapboard roof and no floor, the attendants sitting on stumps and logs.

Rev. John Edgar, who wrote a history of the Presbyterian churches of Perry County, made a careful search of all records, and considerable information is drawn from his research.

The pioneer settlers of Sherman's Valley, which includes prac-tically all of the county lying west of the Juniata River, asked Donegal Presbytery for ministerial instruction in 1760. Six years later they again appealed to the same source for church organiza-tion. Both appeals were answered. After visits by several pio-neer preachers three churches were organized, as follows: Dick's Gap, which was located four miles east of New Bloomfield and three miles west of Bailey's Station, on the present line of the Pennsylvania Railroad; Centre Church, the present site of the same organization, and the Upper Church, at Blain. Presbytery approved this arrangement on April 14, 1767, and these churches remained under the supervision of Donegal Presbytery until the organization of the Carlisle Presbytery, October 17, 1786.

Dick's Gap was contemporary with the two upper churches named above and joined the Sherman's Creek Church in call-ing a pastor at the same time as the upper churches called the

Rev. John Linn. The Dick's Gap Church called Rev. Hugh Magill in 1777, and the Sherman's Creek Church called him in 1778. He refused to preach during 1777-78-79, and Presbytery all the while sent supplies to these two churches. Among these supplies were Rev. John Hoge, Rev. Waugh, Rev. William Linn, Rev. John Linn, Rev. Cooper, Rev. Henderson, Rev. Johnson, Rev. Mc-Mordie, Rev. Caldwell, Rev. Wilson, Rev. Speer, and Rev. McLane. Near the beginning of the last century Dick's Gap Church was abandoned and Middle Ridge Church took its place.

The church was 18x20 in size, and its exact site is to-day a matter of question. It is described shortly after the half of the last century had fled as being in "an unenclosed graveyard, in which trees of great age are growing near to and even upon graves, and many graves are covered with boulders, seemingly to prevent ravages of wolves."

Mrs. Jane Black, mother of the late Isaac G. Black, of Duncannon, remembered this old church in 1797, when still in an unfinished state; built of pine logs, the spaces between the logs were not filled, but she also recollected that in 1798 a coat of mud plaster remedied that. It was, she says, roofless—wherein she differs from other accounts—and she remembers that her grandfather, John Graham, and Robert Johnson, were two of the elders, having heard that they dated back to about 1773, and they were still living in her time. Mrs. Black was born June 3, 1790, and was a daughter of John Stewart, who resided near "the Loop" of Sherman's Creek. She died May 1, 1881, in Philadelphia, at the home of her son, Isaac G. Black. To her memory posterity is indebted for many of the few facts relating to this early church. She became a church member in 1805, but her memory dated back to when she was about seven, when she went with her mother and her grandfather, John Graham, who was an elder, to communion services in the old church. This must have been about 1797. Within the church, which was without floor, the stumps of trees had been allowed to remain, and on these were placed split logs for seats. This church was a regularly organized one, but the only pastor ever called did not accept. The History of Presbytery shows it had very little nucleus and no growth.

According to Mrs. Black she went to church on horseback, riding behind her mother, while her grandfather would lead her horse by the bridle, passing through "Dick's Gap Trail." She recalled being told by her people that in earlier years guards were stationed outside the church to be on the lookout for Indians. Long lines of people came on horseback, often two on a horse.

The consensus of opinion is that the old church stood to the east or left of the present Church of God, and somewhat nearer the ridge which runs in the rear of the church. The mother of George

Barrick, of Newport, who lived to a ripe old age, and who died almost a half century ago, remembered when the church still stood, and gave its location as being near where the present Church of God stands. There is a gap in the ridge known as Dick's Hill, which probably accounts for the name Dick's Gap. It has long since ceased to be known by that name, and is now called Pine Grove, an unfortunate change in the eyes of those historically inclined. On account of a man by the name of Stingle warranting land near by and building a sawmill, it had been known as Stingle's Gap

As early as 1793 the church on Sherman's Creek was one of three churches—the other two being Dick's Gap and the one at the mouth of the Juniata—which were supplied pastors by Presbytery. The Sherman's Creek Church was so close that it drew support from the one at Dick's Gap. In the meantime almost all of the communicants lived long distances to the north, and they built Middle Ridge Church in 1804, having organized the previous year. Thus abandoned Dick's Gap day of usefulness passed with the ending of 1803. It stood for some years, an abandoned pile of logs.

It is said that Marcus Hulings, the pioneer, and his wife, lie buried in the surrounding graveyard. According to tradition an old Indian trail led by this church, which is probably true, as these pioneers seemed to follow the trails of the departing race. Tradition says also that there are graves of both traders and Indians there. There is no way of proving the latter statement and it is left to the reader to conjecture.

The church was built upon lands warranted by Nicholas Robison, in 1766, according to Rev. Focht's "Churches Between the Mountains." According to Mr. T. W. Campbell, a native and resident of the neighborhood, the old Indian trail is supposed to have passed by the site of Charles O. Houck's home, at the foot of Dick's Hill, on the Newport-Duncannon road, the residence once having been an old tavern but converted into a dwelling by Mr. Houck's ancestors. Rev. Focht erred in stating "by whom or for whom it was built it is now impossible to say," as there are many records to show that it was of the Presbyterian faith. The covering of the graves with stones does not prove that they are Indian graves, as there is record that the pioneers used that method in order to keep them from molestation by wolves.

There are some things about this old church that are hard to understand. If it was built in 1767 why was it not "chunked and daubed" between the logs until 1798, and why was it yet roofless in 1797? Both these statements were made by Mrs. Black, a reputable and religious woman, and are evidently true, yet they naturally cause inquisitiveness. That a people would meet in that kind of a building for over thirty years, without giving it even the ordinary advantages which their homes possessed is indeed strange. Might it have been that they early saw their error of location and in the following years used it only as a sort of camp meeting place during the summer months? From the silence of the long departed years there comes no voice to tell us.

Shermansdale Presbyterian Church. The date of organization and early history of Sherman's Creek Presbyterian Church—the forerunner of the Shermansdale Church—are enveloped in obscurity. In all probability the location of the church at Dick's Gap, in 1767, was meant to suffice for the lower end of that part of Perry County lying west of the Juniata. The language of the committee conveys that thought. In October, 1777, a call from Dick's Gap went to Rev. Hugh McGill. When its acceptance was being considered the following spring the name of the Sherman's Creek Church first appears in the minutes of Presbytery (1778), in regard to the proportion of his time each should have. According to these minutes the two churches are referred to as "the united congregations of Dick's Gap and Sherman's Creek." In 1779 Rev. McGill reported to Presbytery "on account of a disagreement in his congregation respecting the places of public worship, and his apprehension of their inability to support him," he desired to relinquish his call. A noteworthy fact is that from then on the Sherman's Creek Church asked for supplies independently.

Just when the first church was built is a mystery, but it was located between Fio Forge and Dellville (on the Charles Zeigler farm), where an old graveyard marks the site. There rests Swisshelm, said to have been a squatter on the Zorger farm. A brown stone, on which the name is still legible, marks his grave. The church was sometimes referred to as Swisshelm's. Various volumes mark the date as 1804, but that date is wrong, as the following facts will show: Owing to the congregation's place of worship being close to that of "the church at the mouth of the Juniata" (the forerunner of the Duncannon Presbyterian Church), in 1801, there is record of its being moved, first to Boyd's, now known as the Matlack farm, and in 1802 "to Swisshelm's," now the Adam Zorger property. Tradition has it that at these first two locations, at the graveyard in the Zeigler field, and at Boyd's fording, at the Matlack farm, were built small places of worship. On October 8, 1802, "verbal application was made to Presbytery for supplies every month to preach at the house of John Fitzhelm (Swisshelm)." In 1804, at Pine Hill, about one hundred yards from Sherman's Creek, and two and a half miles east of their present church, a log church was erected. There this people worshiped until 1843, when the church was taken down and the best of its material used in the erection of the present church. There, in an old graveyard, rest the Wests, Smileys, Hendersons, and others.

This church is located a half mile north of Shermansdale, upon lands donated by William Smiley. The congregation was incorporated by an act of the Pennsylvania Legislature dated April 16, 1829.

The church was served altogether by supplies until 1804, when Rev. Joseph Brady was installed, on October 3, his call including the churches at the mouth of the Juniata and Middle Ridge, which comprised one charge until Middle Ridge was abandoned in 1841. He served until his death, which occurred April 24, 1821, being pastor when the county was organized. Rev. John Noblock served from 1826 to 1830. Rev. Matthew B. Patterson was pastor from 1831 to 1853, and Hezekiah Hanson, from 1854 to 1856. Then, from 1857 to 1867 Rev. William B. Craig served the Shermansdale church and the New Bloomfield church, with which it had been united. Then Duncannon and Shermansdale were separated from New Bloomfield, and Rev. William Thompson was called in 1868 and remained until 1873, when Duncannon was separated from it. Rev. S. A. Davenport was pastor from 1878 to 1880, before and after which it was filled by supplies, two of which were Rev. J. J. Hamilton and Rev. J. A. Murray, D.D. For one year, covering 1883-84, Rev. J. C. Garver, of the Landisburg charge, was pastor, since which time the pastors have been the same as those of the New Bloomfield church, with which it is united. See New Bloomfield chapter.

Middle Ridge Church. Dick's Gap Church, in Miller Township, was, according to all available records, one of the first churches located in what is now Perry County. When services were no longer held there Middle Ridge replaced it. The organization was effected in 1803, and the church built in 1804. In that year (1803) Rev. Joseph Brady was called to the charge, which included this church and the ones at the mouth of the Juniata (Baskins') and Sherman's Creek (Swisshelm's). He was installed in October, 1804, and served until his death in 1821, being buried in the Presbyterian cemetery which occupies the bluff above northern Duncannon.

Supplies were then sent by Presbytery, among them being Rev. Gray, who served Centre and Middle Ridge for six months, covering one winter. In November, 1826, Rev. John Niblock was installed and served until his death, which occurred in August, 1830, at the age of thirty-two years. His remains lie buried in the Middle Ridge graveyard, near the corner of the old church foundation. During January, 1831, Rev. Matthew Patterson began supplying the three churches, and in November was installed as their regular pastor. He filled the position until April 13, 1842, when the membership had dwindled and Presbytery dissolved the congregation and directed the membership to unite with New

Bloomfield or Millerstown, which churches had come into existence in the meantime.

When the church was no longer used by the Presbyterians, the Associate Reformed people—known as the seceders—began worshiping in it and continued to do so until 1860. While the Presbyterians held their services there they were attended by folks from as far as New Bloomfield, Millerstown, and other equally distant points. There is an authentic account of young folks coming from New Bloomfield on horseback to catechize, among them being Eve, a daughter of John and Catharine (Lesh) Smith. On their arrival Samuel Leiby, a youth, helped the fair Miss Smith from her horse, and his gallantry won him a wife, who became the maternal ancestor of the prominent Leiby families of Perry County. By an act of the Pennsylvania Legislature of April 16, 1829, the churches at Middle Ridge, the mouth of the Juniata, and Sherman's Creek were incorporated. The trustees were urged to sell the building, but failed to do so, and no longer in use, it became the object of marauders, who tore out and carried off pews, tore the doors from their hinges, and even removed a part of the roof. The stove had been loaned to the school board and was destroyed when the schoolhouse was burned. Every vestige, save the foundation, has gone to decay.

The mode of journeying to the old church was either on foot or horseback. Behind the husband often rode the wife, and perhaps a small child, and in many cases a mother rode with a small child in her arms. Naturally those residing at the greatest distances started first, and as they passed others joined, crossroads contributing large delegations. Traveling two abreast they frequently arrived in great troops from different directions. The services were held twice each Sunday, the first one in the morning and the other in the early afternoon, lunches being carried along to be eaten during the intervening period. Later "the Tilburry," a two-wheeler, came into vogue, and a few were in use by attendants.

When Rev. Edgar, to whose historic articles we are indebted for no little material used in our descriptions along religious lines, was a resident of the county, a Miss Black, of Millerstown, sent him a relic of that early period. It is described by him as "a little, oblong piece of metal, marked 'M. R.,' and distributed to the members a day or two before communion, to entitle them to a place at the sacramental table."

This church was, originally, well founded and substantial. When the call was sent Rev. Brady in 1803, it offered sixty pounds for one-third of his services. Sherman's Creek Church and the church at the mouth of the Juniata offered fifty pounds each, later raising the amounts to sixty.

There was an early Sabbath school started here in 1823 or 1824, which was well attended. Its first superintendent was Ralph Smiley, an unmarried man, and the owner of Fravel's mill, south of Witherow's, whose remains lie interred in the old graveyard at New Bloomfield.

The Gap Church. There was an early church located in Half Falls Mountain Gap, erected about 1780, near a beautiful spring, on lands which were vacant until near the middle of last century. It is supposed to have been burned down in 1800. Professor Wright, the historian, states that "the foundation stones may still be seen (1880) and the spot recognized." There was no graveyard there. The existence of this church has been questioned, but Mrs. William Kumler, all her life a resident of the immediate vicinity, was told of it by her aunt, Mrs. Mary Baird, who described how they used to ride to and from the church there on horseback, which substantiates its existence.

That this church really existed, although it has been questioned, is further attested by a statement of I. E. Stephens, a life-time resident of Bucks Valley, Buffalo Township, who says: "The people in an early day worshiped in a church situated on the top of Half Falls Mountain. It was used by the inhabitants of Buck's Valley and those of Watts Township. This church was destroyed by fire in 1800." Learning of its existence from an old resident Mr. Stephens soon found himself at the mountain top, on the road leading from Buck's Valley to New Buffalo. At the township line, on the crest of the mountain, stands a large oak tree. Taking thirty steps due west, and then thirty due south, he found the remnant of the old foundation, through which now runs a wood road.

Judging the matter by deduction, it is to be presumed that there was an earlier church than either Buck's Church, in Buck's Valley, or the old Union Church at the Hill, in Watts Township, for there was an early religious spirit pervading the community in the very early years and, not far from this location, at the Richard Baird place (at the forks of the road near the Richard Callin residence), was started one of the first Sunday schools in Perry County. Further deduction is possible, for Rev. Focht, in his "Churches Between the Mountains," says this primitive Gap Church was burned down *"about* the beginning of the century." From his volume it is also to be learned that a graveyard already existed where the Hill Church now stands, and that the first church there was built during the period from 1804 to 1809. If the Gap Church existed and burned about that time, its replacement in the community at another and better location within a very few years would be logical. Rev. Focht names Rev. Mathias Guntzel and Rev. John Herbst, Lutheran ministers, as preaching there, the former from about 1789 to 1796, and the latter from 1796 for a few years.

St. Michael's Lutheran Church. When the land office opened in 1755 there were at least three Germans who warranted lands in Pfoutz Valley. In the succeeding years many others followed, and thus that section of Perry County became the pioneer Lutheran community of the county and had the first regularly organized congregation. Shortly after the expeditions of the Indians, which ceased in 1764, they were visited by ministers who held occasional services. Then, some time between 1770 and 1773 the congregation was regularly organized. Baptismal records date back to October, 1774, Rev. Michael Enderlin then being the pastor, and remaining such until April, 1789. This was the seventh congregation to organize in what is now Perry County, and the first outside of the Presbyterian faith. The deed to the church grounds, dated February 15, 1776, reads in part as follows:

"This Indenture, made the fifteenth day of February, in the year of our Lord, one thousand, seven hundred and seventy-six, by and between John Fouts, of Greenwood Township, in Cumberland County, and Province of Pennsylvania, of the one part, and John Long and Philip Huber and the whole Lutheran congregation of the township, county and province aforesaid, of the other part."

While the person who wrote the deed wrote the name "Fouts," yet inscribed the signature is plainly Pfautz—now spelled Pfoutz. It was recorded at Carlisle, June 13, 1788.

Prior to the deed's execution a large schoolhouse had been erected upon the grounds, and in it the early settlers worshipped from 1770 until 1798, as the building was their property. After the last incursion of the Indians in 1763, when many of the residents of this section were cruelly massacred, and prior to the erection of the school buildings services were held in the homes. It was on these grounds that these victims were buried, before either school building or church was there. Fearing surprise from the Indians when funerals were held the men carried their guns. They also came to church services carrying their guns. At that time the surrounding cemetery was the only one in the valley. Tradition tells of pioneers being tied to the hickory tree (now gone) at the corner of the church land and made targets for the deadly arrows of the red skins. It is said that the graveyard was started by the interment of their bodies. In "The Churches Between the Mountains," Rev. D. H. Focht says: "No graveyard, and no place of worship in Perry County, is as old as this," which he evidently later found to be incorrect, as his introduction gives the credit for the first congregations to Centre and Dick's Gap. From the same authority it is learned that "on the 19th of March, in the year 1798, the church edifice was erected, and on the 25th of May, 1800, the church was consecrated," the services being in German. It was a log building, about 35x45 feet in size, with a gallery on three sides. The pulpit was high and supported by a post, and the seats had high and erect backs. The organ was on the gallery fronting the pulpit, and was not used as late as 1820, having become ruined. This old church stood until 1847, when it was replaced by a new one. In 1802 the congregation purchased an additional acre of ground from John Long for one dollar. With no free school system in sight, it appears the proceeds of the land were to go towards the support of the schoolmaster, who was also to lead the singing in the church and play the organ. For many years a congregational school was maintained there. The ministers were:

1774-89 —Rev. Michael Enderlin.
1789-1800—Rev. Matthias Guntzel.
1800-04 —Rev. John Herbst.
1805-14 —Rev. J. Conrad Walter.
1815-33 —Rev. John William Heim.

During the pastorate of Rev. Walter, Rev. George Heim was his assistant. Other ministers conducted baptismal and other ceremonies during these years, but a careful perusal of Rev. Focht's book will not show them as regular pastors, although a number of historians have so stated. Then followed:

1833-35—Rev. C. G. Erlenmeyer.
1835-42—Vacant.
1842-43—Rev. Andrew Berg.
1843-47—Vacant.
1847-51—Rev. William Weaver.

Rev. Weaver found but three members of the congregation left, but immediately began a movement for building a new church. At a congregational meeting in March, 1847, a building committee was appointed, consisting of David Kepner, Joseph Ulsh, Frederick Reinhard, John Ulsh, and George Beaver. The carpenter work was contracted for at $680, and the masonry done separately. The corner stone was laid in June, and in the fall it was dedicated. Rev. Weaver resigned in 1851, and the pastorate was vacant until October, 1856. Pastors since then have been:

1856-59—Rev. Josiah Zimmerman.
1859-61—Rev. Jacob A. Hackenberger.
1861-62—Rev. William O. Wilson.

In April, 1862, it became attached to the Liverpool charge, since which time the ministers have been the same. See Liverpool chapter.

Lebanon Lutheran Church. In 1790 the Lutherans were organized at Loysville by Rev. John Timothy Kuhl, who that year began visiting the different sections of Sherman's Valley in the interests of that denomination. Rev. Kuhl's family came from Path Valley, and George Fleisher, of Saville Township, who died in 1855, aged eighty-four years, hauled their household goods over the mountains, he being then a boy of nineteen. Private homes and barns were the scenes of many of these early meetings. Martin Bernheisel and Michael Loy donated two acres and forty-two perches of land in 1794 for the erection of a church and school building. The building was about 30x40 in size, and in 1808 was weatherboarded and painted white, from that time on being known as "the white church." John Calhoun superintended the building and a building committee consisted of Michael Loy, George Hammer and Peter Sheibley. While the majority of the congregation were Lutherans yet the Reformed denomination was an equal owner. It was in use until 1850.

March 2, 1851, a new church was dedicated, the pastors then being Rev. F. Ruthrauff, Lutheran, and Rev. C. H. Leinbach, Reformed. Its construction was of brick and its cost about six thousand dollars. In 1883 it was remodeled at a cost of about $2,500.

Rev. Kuhl served as pastor until 1796. The following five years Rev. John Herbst, of Carlisle, acted as supply. Then came Rev. Frederick Sanno, and later Rev. John Frederick Osterloh, who resided on a farm in Saville Township and also occupied the pulpits at New Bloomfield, St. Peter's (Spring Township), and Fishing Creek (Rye Township). In May, 1815, Rev. John William Heim became pastor, and until 1828 his pastorate included not only almost all of Perry County, but all of Juniata and Mifflin. In that year he moved to Loysville and died there on December 27, 1849.

After Rev. Heim's death Sherman's Valley was divided into three charges, the Upper Circuit including Loysville (Lebanon) church, Zion, St. Peter's, and Ludolph's (Little Germany). The middle, or Bloomfield charge, to include also Ickesburg, Shuman's, Bealor's, and Newport, and the lower, or Petersburg charge, to include that church, Pisgah, Fishing Creek, Billow's, and New Buffalo.

The congregation at Loysville had built a parsonage and bought fifteen acres of land as early as 1828. While Rev. Heim was pastor as early as 1815, he did not reside in Loysville until this parsonage was built, and he then gave up his appointments in Mifflin County. While pastor here he found time and money wherewith to purchase a farm and erect a gristmill. In 1833 he gave up the congregations east of the Juniata so that they might be formed into a separate charge, and in 1835 he gave up those in Juniata County for a similar reason. In 1842 he still had eight churches in Perry County.

The church erected in 1851 was used jointly by the Lutherans and Reformed faiths until 1909, when a separation took place, the interest of the Lutherans having been purchased by the Reformed people, who still use the edifice. In that year the Lutherans erected a new church, known as the Tressler Memorial Church, the cost of which was $16,000. Its seating capacity is five hundred, and it is one of the finest churches in the county.

Until 1850 the services were held entirely in German, but in that year Rev. Frederick Ruthrauff began preaching alternately in English. He resigned in 1852. In 1853 Rev. Reuben Weiser followed, but was elected as president of Central College of Iowa in 1856. Rev. Philip Willard then served two years. The succession of ministers from then on is as follows:

Rev. G. M. Settlemover. 1859-61.   Rev. John F. Dietrich, 1877-80.
Rev. Peter Sahm, 1862-69.   Rev. F. Aurand, 1880-83.
Rev. Daniel Sell, 1869-71.   Rev. W. D. E. Scott, 1883-1906.
Rev. John B. Stroup, 1873-74.   Rev. Geo. A. Royer, 1907-14.
Rev. Isaiah B. Crist, 1875-77.   Rev. A. R. Longenecker, 1914-20.
Rev. J. G. C. Knipple. 1921-

Rev. John William Heim was the pastor of this church for thirty-four years. In the spring of 1824, at Eastertide, he received into membership a class of seventy persons.

Loysville Reformed Church. The history of the Reformed congregation's church home is identical with that of the Lutheran Church, described above, as the two bodies were joint owners of the old Lebanon Church. The first minister of the Reformed congregation was Rev. Jacob Scholl, who became pastor in October, 1819, although there were earlier ministers of that faith who held occasional services, one probably being Rev. Ulrich Heininger, who traveled Sherman's Valley. Rev. Scholl served until 1841, when he was succeeded by Rev. Charles H. Leinbach, who served until 1859. A list of the pastors since that time will be found under the Landisburg Reformed Church.

St. Peter's Church. Two miles east of Landisburg, in Spring Township, stood St. Peter's Church, built in 1816-17, and dedicated in the spring of 1817. While its inception is shrouded in obscurity yet it is known to have been a preaching station when Loysville Church was formed in 1790, the ministers from Carlisle stopping to attend to the spiritual needs of the members.

Historians place the probable date of first services as 1788, and 1809 as about when the Lutheran and Reformed congregations were organized there. Prior to 1815 both congregations had worshiped in a school building which stood on the site now occupied by St. Peter's Union Church. This school building was likely the property of the two congregations.

December 23, 1815, is the date of an agreement between the two congregations to build a church, in which it was stated that

20

owing to the increasing number of Germans in that vicinity and the rapid growth of the congregations, the schoolhouse was too small for further worship. The new church was built on lands given for the purpose by John Gamber, and was dedicated in the spring of 1817. It was a log structure, 35x40 feet in size, and had a gallery on three sides, a cup-shaped pulpit mounted on a high post, and high, unpainted seats. The building committee was Henry Kell, Reformed, and John Miller, Lutheran.

This old landmark stood until 1857, when on September 20th the present brick church was dedicated, taking its place, and belonging to the German Reformed people, the Lutherans having at the same time erected their own church. On April 28, 1824, $800 was paid to Samuel Ickes for fourteen acres of land for a parsonage for the pastor of the "German Reformed Presbyterian Church," by Philip Stambaugh, trustee of Zion Church in Toboyne Township; Henry Kell, trustee of Lebanon Church in Tyrone Township; Philip Kell, trustee of St. Peter's Church in Tyrone (now Spring) Township; William Hipple, trustee of Fishing Creek Church (now Rye) Township; Casper Lupfer, trustee of Christ's Church in Juniata Township. Here the pastor resided for many years.

Rev. Alfred Helfenstein, pastor at Carlisle, was the first one to come over the mountain and hold services. On October 3, 1819, Rev. Jacob Scholl assumed the regular pastorate of the Sherman's Valley charge, which extended as far as New Bloomfield. By 1838 the work had become so extended on this charge that it was divided. Rev. Scholl remained at the Landisburg end until 1841, when he accepted a call to the lower end and remained pastor of the New Bloomfield charge until his death on September 4, 1847. His successor, Rev. C. H. Leinbach, served sixteen and a half years. From then on the pastors have been the same as those found under the Landisburg Reformed Church. See Landisburg chapter.

Mt. Zion Lutheran Church. The Mt. Zion Lutheran Church's home was jointly with St. Peter's Reformed in the old Union church building just previously described, and was known as St. Peter's Lutheran congregation. In 1857 this old church was dismantled and each congregation built its own church. The Lutheran then became Mt. Zion, and was dedicated May 30, 1858, Rev. Philip Willard then became the pastor. Stephen Losh was the contractor and the contract price was $2,300.00. George Sheaffer, Jeremiah Dunkelberger, and Joseph Dunkelberger were the building committee. It was extensively repaired in 1882 and again in 1894. Starting with Rev. John F. Osterloh, in 1809, the ministers have been the same as those of the Lutheran Church at Loysville. See chapter relating to Tyrone Township.

Mt. Pisgah Lutheran Church. The Lutherans of Carroll Township were among those who first attended church at Carlisle, crossing the Kittatinny Mountain. Later they worshiped at Mt. Zion, described above, and at St. Peter's, in Spring Township. They had preaching services occasionally at Reiber's schoolhouse by Rev. Keller and Rev. Heyser, of the Carlisle churches. In 1838 they began holding their own services regularly, every four weeks, and a year later became a regularly organized congregation.

Their church is located in Carroll Township, on the southern side of Sherman's Creek, and is near the site of Sutch's schoolhouse, which was built between 1775 and 1780. There is an old graveyard there where many pioneers sleep. In 1842 Abraham Jacobs donated a lot for church purposes, with a proviso that when the Lutherans were not using it for their services it was to be available for any Christian denomination. A frame church was built and dedicated September 24, 1842. Its pastors were:

Rev. John Ulrich, 1838-42.   Rev. Levi T. Williams, 1842-45.
Rev. Jacob Kempfer, 1842.   Rev. Lloyd Knight, 1845-49.
Rev. Jacob Martin, 1850.

In 1851 the church united with the Petersburg (now Duncannon) charge, whose pastors served it until 1870, since which time it has had no regular services. During June, 1920, it was reopened for a service by Rev. Longanecker, pastor of the Loysville church. Pastors of two other denominations joined in a community service, designed to keep this old landmark from passing.

Other Churches. The history of all the churches throughout the county, save these very early ones, appears in the chapters devoted to the various townships and boroughs. Where facts are missing, and there are some, letters sent out for information remained unanswered, with the necessarily attendant result.

Oldest Burial Ground. Just which is the oldest burial ground in the county is at this late date a matter of conjecture. In the Evarts, Peck & Richards History of the Juniata and Susquehanna Valleys, Horace E. Sheibley says:

"The site of the old Sherman's Creek Church, near Shermansdale, is marked by an old graveyard, on what is known as the Zeigler property, between Fio Forge and Dellville, and where tradition claims that the first white man buried in the county was laid. In it are interred ancestors of the Stewarts and Kirkpatricks, of Duncannon." Swisshelms are also among those buried there.

The Sherman's Creek Church, which was the forerunner of the present Shermansdale Presbyterian Church, can be traced back to 1778, when it first appeared in the records of Presbytery, but it may have been organized before that or been a community affair for a time. Likewise, it may have been built where burials had previously been made.

In 1766 three church organizations were formed within the limits of the present county; where Centre Church now stands, at

Dick's Gap, and at or near Blain. In the cemetery at Centre, among other old stones, is one bearing the following legend:

> Here lies the body of
> Martha Robison,
> Who departed this life
> December 22, 1766,
> In the 81st year of her age.

What relation she was to that memorable Robinson family which so often befriended the persecuted pioneers and much of whose history is recorded in these pages, must forever remain unknown, but barring tradition, her interment must have been among the first. So soon after the entry of the settlers in 1755 did the Indians arrive that there may have been no deaths at that time, but the returning settlers came back in large numbers in 1762, and it is hardly likely that there were no deaths in over four years among all the number, so that in the opinion of the writer the death of Martha Robison was not the first, but it is the first of which we could find record. Tradition has pioneers buried in the St. Michael's Lutheran churchyard in 1763, after massacres by the Indians. During the Indian invasion of 1755 there were also deaths, but where burial took place is not known. The tradition as to the old Sherman's Creek yard containing the first grave of a white man may be correct. In the cemetery at Loysville are a number of graves of persons who died prior to 1800, which attests the fact that this was a burying ground already over a century and a quarter ago. The Blain burial ground already existed in 1766.

Wilson College Planned. Eighteen miles north of Mason and Dixon's line, at Chambersburg, in the beautiful Cumberland Valley, Wilson College, a leading women's college is located. Its first board of trustees was appointed at a meeting in the Presbyterian Church at Duncannon, at which time it was decided to open the college. Members of the Presbytery of Carlisle began a movement in 1868 for the formation of a college, and laid their representations before the spring meeting of Presbytery at Greencastle, April 15, 1868. It was favorably received and referred to the Committee on Education, which met at Duncannon, in June, 1868. There the action was favorable and the first plans of that great institution were made in Perry County. The Pennsylvania Legislature chartered it March 24, 1869. Its location was determined by a gift of great value by Miss Sarah Wilson, which enabled the trustees to purchase the residence of that former Perry Countian, Col. A. K. McClure, together with its fifty-two acres of adjoining lands, to-day the college grounds.

CHAPTER XVII.

THE COUNTY SCHOOLS, PAST AND PRESENT.

THE first schools anywhere, ordained of God, were families, where parents taught their children to live in the fear and admonition of the Lord. Undoubtedly, as many facts in this book will verify, the early settlers of this territory brought with them from their homes Christian principles, which caused them to think early of their education along secular as well as religious lines. The early churches were used as schools in some instances, and where there was a schoolhouse and no church the condition was reversed, and the "meetings," as they were then known, were held in the schoolhouses.

When William Penn became the proprietary of the Province of Pennsylvania he was not unmindful of the necessity of an educational system, for he knew that a free government depended on an intelligent people for its success as well as its perpetuity. The second Assembly convened at Philadelphia in 1683, and on March 10th of that year enacted the following law with reference to the education of the children of the province:

"And to the end that the Poor as well as the Rich may be instructed in good and commendable learning, which is to be preferred before wealth,

"Be it enacted by the authority aforesaid, That all persons within this Province and territories thereof, having children, and all the Guardians or Trustees of Orphans, shall cause such to be instructed in reading and writing, so that they may be able to read the Scriptures, and to write by the time they attain to the age of twelve years, and that then they be taught some useful trade or skill, that ye poor may work to live, and the Rich, if they become poor, may not want, of which every county court shall take care; and in case such Parents, Guardians or Overseers shall be found deficient in this respect, every such Parent, Guardian or Overseer shall pay for every such child five pounds, except there should appear an incapacitie of body or understanding to hinder it."

While the law referred to the province generally yet it is considered especially applicable here, as Perry County has ever been considered one of the foremost counties in the state in an educational way. It shows that the early legislators of the province were concerned with education and that the courts by that act received their first authority to require attendance at school.

When the State Constitution of Pennsylvania was adopted in 1790 it contained a provision for the establishment of schools throughout the commonwealth, that the poor might be taught gratis and that the arts and sciences should be promoted through one or more institutions of learning, but left to the legislature the fram-

309

superior quality of brains. In our highest position in the land, the Presidency, this is well illustrated in the cases of George Washington, Abraham Lincoln, and Theodore Roosevelt, Washington and Roosevelt being children of the more wealthy, and Lincoln being born in a log cabin and poor even when he attained that great office. This charity idea had been tried before. About 1750 about £20,000 were raised in Europe for the purpose of opening charity schools among the Germans in America. Some were opened, but the Germans did not welcome the idea of charity. The object then had a double purpose, that of weaning them from their language, and with a political object in view. It ended in failure.

The early settlers of the county territory experienced all the privations incident to frontier life. The first settlers were either driven out or murdered, and not until after the Revolution was it possible to do anything with a view to permanency. The first schools were usually community affairs, and the branches taught were the rudimentary spelling, reading, writing, and arithmetic. The houses were built of logs and were very crude. The desks or tables and the seats were made of boards and slabs, and the windows had greased paper in place of window glass.

A sparse population extending over a wide extent of country, mainly covered with dense forests and destitute of roads and bridges, was not conducive to the establishment of good schools within convenient distances. The occupations of the pioneers also were such that the time to be devoted to education was limited, owing to the necessity of clearing lands and erecting houses and other farm buildings, while, at the same time planting and harvesting the products of the soil to maintain a livelihood. There was no labor-saving machinery then and agricultural operations were of necessity slow and tedious. The threshing of the crops, now done in a day or two, then required months, as the "flail" was the "machinery" then in use to get the grain from the stalk. The daughters of the pioneers were just as much needed in the homes, as then all clothing was made by hand, and the operations of the spinning wheel and the needle (there being no sewing machines), along with the other household duties, required their constant attention.

The schools in those days were ruled to a great extent by cruel methods of punishment and humiliation. The "locking out of the teacher" was a holiday and last-day custom in many parts of the county. At Millerstown, during one of these frolics, Valentine Varnes, the teacher, had an arm injured, the use of which was impaired for the balance of his life. Many pupils had no books at all. Others had perchance a Bible, a speller or an old English reader. A few had slates. Fewer still had foolscap paper. These were invariably boys, as it was considered unnecessary for girls to learn to write or "figure." The few who had copy books were also the possessors of goose quills, as Joseph Gillett did not invent the steel pen until 1820. By introducing machinery in manufacture the price became as low as twenty-five cents each, after which a few found their way into the schools. There was no uniformity in the use of textbooks, each pupil bringing such as the family possessed. History, geography, grammar, physiology, and algebra were unknown in the schools of that day. In 1823 the Columbia Standard spelling book was the one in general use in the new county.

No attention was given to elementary sounds, yet many good spellers came out of our earlier schools; in fact, the scholars of a half century ago were probably better spellers than are their descendants of to-day, but the present-day pupils have far more branches. When geography was first taught the method was to have the pupil learn all the states and their capitals, even singing them in order to memorize. Blackboards were practically unknown until about 1850. The teachers wrote the copy for the copy books of foolscap paper. Shortly after the organization of Perry County the old log schoolhouses were gradually replaced by frame structures, which had better light, but were not nearly so warm. About the middle of the last century the red brick buildings began replacing the frame, being known universally as "the little red schoolhouse."

For those who disparage these early pioneer schools or "the little red schoolhouse," which followed in their wake the writer has little sympathy, as the fine new high school building in many a place is but the fruition of the seed sown over a century ago; and we know that with the hundreds of disadvantages under which they labored, they did well, and builded better than they knew. These new high school buildings with plastered and papered walls, fine desks, books galore, heated throughout at the same temperature, no matter what the condition of the weather, are the logical successors of these little log schoolhouses just as much as is the fine modern passenger train with its vestibuled cars the successor of the Conestoga wagon and the packet boat. Without the one we would never have progressed to the other. Practically all great institutions and machines are the results of progression and the products of many minds and years of experience and experiment.

Throughout the state there was more or less opposition to progress in education. A strange coincidence along this line is worthy of reproduction here. A number of young men decided that they wanted an academy at Bath, Northampton County, so as to secure a more advanced education. They decided to canvass the community for subscriptions, and among others upon whom they called was George Wolf, a German who was located in the neighborhood. He refused, remarking in broken English, "Dis etication and dings make raskels." He later on relented and helped build the academy. In inducing the subscription his young caller mentioned his two sons, George and Philip, as probable future beneficiaries of the school, and suggested that his favorite son, George, might get an education and some day become governor, to which he replied, "Vell, den, when my George is gobernor, he will be queer times." The sequel is that George Wolf got his English education in that academy and did become the governor of his state, and one of the most illustrious of his time, being the first governor to call attention to the appalling condition of ignorance which faced the commonwealth.

The passage of the act of 1834 to a great extent can be credited to Governor Wolf, who in 1833 had become acquainted with the fact that while there were *four hundred thousand* children of school age in the state there were but *twenty thousand* in school, or while one was getting an education there were nineteen others growing up illiterate. In his annual message to the legislature he mentioned these facts and appealed for legislation to remedy this appalling condition.

The first effort at establishing a free school system in the state was in 1820, when a Dr. Cummings, a member of the Pennsylvania Legislature, introduced a bill to establish one. It failed to pass and the author was not reëlected, as that act caused him to be regarded as a dangerous man and his constituency felt disgraced by his actions. Henry Beeson, of Fayette County, introduced another in 1825. It too failed.

All the legislative acts prior to 1834 are generally known as acts of pauper legislation, but the legislature of that year passed the common school act which is to-day the basis of our public school law. This act completely revolutionized school affairs. School directors were elected in every district, arrangements were made for new buildings, taxes were levied and assessed, teachers were employed, and the children of the rich and the poor met on a common level. In some districts of Perry County for a year or two the provisions of the act were not accepted, but generally speaking, it was the other way. In some counties it was opposed for many years; in one where the population was mostly German, two-thirds of the districts did not adopt it until after 1850, and some as late as 1864. These German communities had a sort of a parochial school system of their own which they feared would be destroyed. As an example, of the local aversion to the free school system, John Bair, Sr., father of John Bair, later president of the Peoples' Bank of Newport, refused to let his children attend the free schools of Buffalo Township for the first two terms.

When the free school law became effective in 1834 the court did not appoint directors to serve until the necessary elections took place the following spring. In 1836, the first year after the introduction of the system, Perry County stood third in the state in its support. Of the thirteen districts then reporting Toboyne Township was the only one to stand out against acceptance. In 1837, Millerstown, then in Greenwood Township, had a five-months' term. As early as that year Saville Township had twelve female and five male teachers. In the remainder of the county there were only four other females employed. When it passed the representative from Perry County, then but recently formed, was John Johnston, the second son of George and Margaret (Russell) Johnston, emigrants who had come from Ireland and settled in Toboyne Township. He was of athletic build and weighed more than two hundred pounds, was well read, and was supporting Thaddeus Stevens in the passage of the bill, when he was interrupted by a member of slight stature, with the interrogation, "What do you raise in Perry County?" Quick as a flash he retorted, "We raise men," and his erect and well formed body, coupled with his ability and quick wit, at once substantiated the statement. Within recent years the writer had a similar experience along the same line. Being queried by several companions as to "what Perry County produced," the retort was, "The county school superintendents of both your counties," for the one interrogater was from Lancaster County, Pennsylvania, where Prof. Daniel Fleisher was then county superintendent, and the other was from Mercer County, New Jersey, where Prof. Joseph M. Arnold is superintendent of schools.

These early schools were open for but short periods, from one to three months, but the Act of 1854 made the minimum term four months. It was increased to five months in 1872, to six months in 1887, and to seven months in 1899. In 1893 a law was passed providing for the furnishing of free textbooks to all pupils.

Every step in advancement along educational lines in the state has been fought, and when the Act of 1854 created the office of county superintendent of schools it was considered a mighty unpopular piece of legislation, and in nearly all of the counties of the state the position carried a niggardly wage to the new official, the school directors being the final authority on salary. However, the influence of the county superintendency soon became apparent in the improved condition of the schools, in the higher standards of teachers, and in a greater interest in education generally. The organization of teachers' institutes and the establishment of normal schools were two of the indirect results of the institution of the county superintendency. As an example of the salaries first paid county superintendents, note the following: Lancaster County

paid $1,500, the only county in the state to pay over $1,000. Only
four counties in the state paid $1,000, all the rest being below $800
per annum. For a large county Berks was the most conspicuous,
paying but $250, or $50 less than Perry County. Wyoming paid
$150, and Fulton and Pike $100, or less than $9 per month.

Previous to the creation of the position of county superintendent
the individual efforts of the teachers and directors, owing to isola-
tion, were practically lost on account of the lack of supervision.
Though there were advanced ideas in effect here and there, there
was no way of their getting into general use. Those first county
superintendents must have found as many varieties of teaching
methods and customs as there were schools.

Col. Alexander K. McClure, himself a Perry Countian, in his
book, "Old-Time Notes of Pennsylvania," published in 1905,
speaking of the period when the county was young, among other
things, says:

"Free schools were unknown and the few who dared to advocate them
did not venture to seek political preferment. The crossroad schoolhouse
was found in every community, but it was usually the centre of a neighborhood five or six miles in diameter. Every schoolhouse had its teacher
during the winter season, for which he was usually paid so much by the
parent for each scholar, and "boarded around" with his patrons. Teaching
was confined to reading, writing, and arithmetic, and I well remember the
hostility aroused among a large portion of my school district (located in
Madison Township) when the violent innovation of teaching grammar
was made. It was long resisted, but finally succeeded to the extent of
permitting the teacher to teach it, although there were very few who accepted what was generally regarded as such a needless feature of education for their sons. The one green memory I have of the occasional
school of that time is that of the holiday frolic. It was then that the
school children had not only absolute freedom to bar their teacher out and
keep him out even with hot pokers if he tried to climb through a window,
until he compromised by giving them a liberal supply of apples and nuts.
If the teacher had walked away, as he presumably might have done, without undertaking to force his way into the schoolhouse, he would have been
promptly dismissed by the school authorities, and, while a majority of the
parents of children would have flogged their boys severely at any other
time for the antics they played upon the teacher in the holiday season,
they were expected even by the strictest of parents to take a full hand in
the holiday battle, and the boy who gave the teacher the bravest fight was
the hero of the hour. If the teacher fought his way into the schoolhouse
or entered it by compromise with the boys, the moment he was within the
sanctuary of his authority discipline was instantly resumed, but there could
be no punishment for the scholars who were in the fight.

"I well remember the early battles in the neighborhood in which I
lived made for the acceptance of the free school system. The original
free school law was very crude, but it was the best that could be obtained
at the time, and it cost the brave Dutch (meaning German) Governor
(Wolf) who signed it, and many who had supported it, defeat before the
people. It was not compulsory, and at any spring election a certain number of citizens could call for a vote on the acceptance of the free school
law, and many times did the few Scotch-Irish in the neighborhood make

a brave struggle for the acceptance of free schools, but they were voted down half a dozen times or more by the united vote of the Germans and others who opposed taxation for free education. Our school system was thus of little value, and advancement in it was very slow until Curtin became sceretary of the commonwealth, in 1855, when it was made a distinct department and placed in charge of the assistant secretary of the commonwealth, the late Henry C. Hickok, who had heart and soul in the cause, and under Curtin's direction gave the free school system of our state a standing that commanded general respect.

"Strange as it may seem in this enlightened age, with Pennsylvania enjoying the most liberal educational policy of any state of the Union, the free school system was simply a crude, crippled, and in some localities, very generally decried system of free education of the children of the state. It had been passed by Thaddeus Stevens a quarter of a century before, but the public sentiment of the state was so overwhelmingly against it in many communities that it was impossible to make it a homogeneous and beneficent system. The same year that the law was passed, the people of the state elected a legislature that was openly and positively averse to free schools, and a bill repealing the entire system had reached a position of final passage in the house, when Stevens, the author of the original bill, delivered the most effective speech of his life, and doubtless one of the ablest and most eloquent, as it literally made the house take pause and defeat its own openly proclaimed purpose. For many years thereafter, notably in the German counties of Berks, Lehigh, and others, delegations were chosen to the legislature on the distinct issue of "no free schools," and it was nearly or quite a generation after the passage of the original bill that the acceptance of the free schools of every district was made mandatory.

"The law as first enacted authorized any township to accept the free school system by the vote of the majority at the spring elections and put it into operation, but in some sections of the state there were entire counties in which there was not a single accepting district. I well remember, when a small boy, the special interest taken by my father and other Scotch-Irish residents of the township to have the free school system accepted. They called election after election from year to year, but suffered defeats for a decade or more, as the Germans, as a rule, were bitterly opposed to enforced education. Although Governor Wolf, a distinct representative of the old German element of the state, with his home among the Germans of Northampton, had approved the school bill, a very small percentage of the Germans of the state supported it, and it cost him his reëlection, as when he was nominated for a third term a large element of the Democrats bolted, nominated Muhlenberg, of Berks, as a second Democratic candidate, and thus divided the Democratic vote and elected Ritner governor."

That there never was a school at the old Dick's Gap Church, as sometimes stated, is evident from the fact that schools were conducted only in winter, and that this building was not "chunked and daubed" as late as 1797. Just where the first school may have been opened in the county will probably never be known, but within the limits of what is now Perry County there was opened the first *free* school in Pennsylvania west of the Susquehanna River. It was located a quarter-mile west of Barnett's mill, near New Bloomfield, on the Carlisle road, and was not only built at the expense of George Barnett, owner of the lands upon which it was located, but was proclaimed by him to be free to any and all children of the neighborhood. He even paid the salary of the teacher and furnished the fuel for the heating of the schoolroom. A pioneer and real philanthropist among those of his day who believed in education, George Barnett became the progenitor of a family which has left its mark in legal, educational, literary, medical and business lines. Two of his descendants have been elected president judge of the courts of his county. Just when this building was erected cannot be told, but as the lands passed to George Barnett on May 10, 1804 (previous ownership having been vested in his father, Thomas Barnett), it was subsequent to that time. During 1815 a Mrs. O'Donnell was engaged as teacher, but the school had then been in operation for a number of years, which places the date of its erection somewhere between 1804 and 1815. Whether Mrs. O'Donnell taught as early as Miss Gainor Harris, at Blain, is questioned, but the teaching period of the one was practically coincident with that of the other. The school at Blain, however, was a pay school then, as all were save the Barnett school at New Bloomfield.

That both the first free school west of the Susquehanna prior to the free school act and the first school to be declared a free school under that act should have been located within the boundaries of the county of Perry is an interesting coincidence, and a fact. In the sketch relating to Chief Justice Daniel Gantt, of Nebraska, to be found elsewhere in this book, the statement is made which verifies it. The facts are these, from the diary of the late chief justice, now in possession of his heirs, near Lincoln, Nebraska: To help pay his expenses while reading law at New Bloomfield, he taught a subscription school (as all schools then were save the one previously mentioned) in Buffalo Township, at Colonel Thompson's, in the part which later became Watts Township. Interested parties from that community had ridden horseback to Harrisburg to learn of the legislation pertaining to free schools. Hearing that the bill had passed, they rode home during the night and arrived before morning with the news. When the future chief justice opened his school in the morning he proclaimed it a free school—his diary says the first school in the commonwealth under that act. As the act had then only passed the legislature and was still unsigned by the governor his statement that it was the first to open under the act is no doubt correct. From the same source the statement comes that Buffalo Township at once accepted the free school law, the first township in the commonwealth to do so.

Perry County was one of the very first counties in the state to hold teachers' institutes. The origin of the first one dates back to a letter written by Samuel S. Saul, of Duncannon, dated June 7, 1854, and published in the county press. It suggested the forming of a teachers' association. The call for the first County Teachers' Institute followed, being issued July 15, 1854, and signed by Samuel S. Saul, Joseph Ogle, William Brown, Albert E. Owen, James G. Turbett, and R. I. Heim. It was held at New Bloomfield, in the academy, on Wednesday, August 9, 1854. The first officers were: Rev. R. Weiser, Loysville, president; John A. McCroskey, New Bloomfield, secretary; committee on constitution and by-laws: A. Owen, J. R. Titzel, W. Glover, J. A. McCroskey, and Charles A. Barnett; committee on work: A. D. Owen, J. R. Titzel, and George Tressler. This committee suggested as needing attention: 1. Small pay of teachers; 2. Incompetent teachers; 3. How to procure the best knowledge of the art of teaching; 4. School books; 5. Duties of teachers; 6. Authority of teachers in school government. The institute recommended Page's Theory and Practice of Teaching and the following textbooks: Webster's spellers, McGuffey's readers, Emerson's arithmetics, Smith's elementary grammar and Parker & Fox's advanced grammar, and Mitchell's geographies and maps.

Then the further meetings seem to be confusing. Prof. Silas Wright recorded that on October 26th of the same year an institute was held in Landisburg, and that on January 12, 1855, another was held at New Bloomfield, at which the name the "Perry County Teachers' Institute" was adopted. That would place three meetings very close together. The files of the county press place the second meeting on March 20, 1855, with A. R. Height, president, and Albert Owen, secretary, and continuing over Tuesday, Wednesday, Thursday, and Friday. It also places the next at Landisburg, September 7, 1855, with Daniel Gantt, president; Henry D. Woodruff, vice-president; Noble Meredith, secretary; F. M. McKeehan, treasurer, and an executive committee consisting of Rev. George S. Rea, R. I. Heim, and D. Kistler. In the meantime a Perry County Teachers' Association had been formed in April, 1855, with the following officers: Daniel Gantt, president; D. Kistler, vice-president; Noble Meredith, secretary; F. M. McKeehan, treasurer, and an executive committee consisting of R. I. Heim, Henry Titzel, and C. S. Toomey. As the officers of the Landisburg session, in the main, were the same as the officers of this association, it is presumed that the meeting of April was merely to form the permanent organization.

Until 1869 the institute was held at various places, but since then regularly at the county seat. State Supt. Thomas H. Burrowes was the first instructor from without the county. At the session of 1856 Chas. A. Barnett (later judge) presented the subject of English Grammar. Among the early instructors were Professors Wickersham, Brooks, and Raub. At the session of 1869 H. C. Magee and G. C. Palm tied on a spelling contest for first place.

At the session of 1870 Henry Houck, later to become famous in educational circles, and Silas Wright were among the instructors. Shortly afterwards local institutes were started in the various towns, covering two evenings and the intervening Saturday, and they are continued to this day, community centres for educational thought. Their usefulness and value are attested by the large number of educators who have been connected with them and have gone abroad to serve other communities. The custom of issuing the proceedings of the Teachers' Institute in pamphlet form was begun in 1877.

The curriculum of the grade public schools at this time includes spelling, reading, writing, arithmetic, geography, English grammar, United States history, and physiology. History was not required until 1867, and physiology was added in 1885.

An act of the Pennsylvania Legislature, dated April 12, 1866, extended to Perry and Indiana Counties the provisions which had been granted to the counties of Lancaster and York the previous year. This was the legislation which authorized the county to appropriate $200 annually to get instructors for the annual institute of one week. Another act was passed relating to the Perry County Teachers' Institute. It is dated March 19, 1872, and authorized the payment of the salaries of the teachers while attending institute.

Mr. John S. Campbell, long connected with educational work in Perry County, during 1920, compiled for the *Newport News* a historical sketch of the actions of early Newport school boards, taken from the minutes. At a meeting November 26, 1855, it was resolved "that all the teachers within the district of Newport are hereby required to personally attend the meeting of the Perry County Teachers' Institute, to be held in New Bloomfield, and beginning on December 17, 1855, and that during the sessions of the same they shall all be allowed their pay for the time thus spent as fully as if they were actually engaged in teaching in town district," and "that Messrs. Alfred M. Gantt and W. S. Marshall, our teachers, be requested to meet the board each on an evening on their return from attendance at the institute and in a lecture give an account of the doings and action of said institute with the advantage it may be to the teachers and children under their care, which lectures at the option of Messrs. Gannt and Marshall shall or may be public." That may have been the first or one of the first boards to pay teachers for attending institute. Mr. Gannt's salary then was $26 per month, and Mr. Marshall's, $25. There were then two single room buildings. In 1860 a night school was conducted by G. McKey. During that year the borough had two schools, paying the teachers $25 and $28 per month.

In the chapters of this book relating to the various townships and boroughs the locations of the earliest schools are given, as it was considered to be more appropriate there than in this general chapter. It will be noted that the first schoolhouses, established almost coincident with the settlement of the pioneers, were invariably built of logs, being "chunked and daubed," with few windows, and in some a log being omitted from the regular order so as to let in light. The reader should not consider this fact as disparaging, as the homes of that pioneer period were practically all built in the same manner. These first schoolhouses in many cases were built by the communities by voluntary contributions and labor. They usually occupied as much ground as their dimensions, playgrounds being then unthought of. They had long desks built along the outside walls, the benches upon which the children sat being the same heighth for all ages. A large wood stove occupied the centre of each of these primitive buildings. The teachers were either the early ministers or men who merely taught long enough to amass enough to pay their way to other fields, using the profession as a "stepping-stone"—an unfortunate condition which has to this day followed in its wake. The schools were conducted for pay at a stated price per quarter.

The old Monterey schoolhouse in Toboyne Township, which burned about five years ago, still had the oldest type of furniture which ever graced a schoolroom in the county. The site of this building is now surrounded by state forest lands of the Tuscarora Forest. The East Horse Valley school, in the same township, also has homemade furniture, but of a somewhat later type. The oldest schoolhouse still standing in the county is in Blain Borough, but is no longer in use as such.

According to an announcement in the *Perry Forester* of November 15, 1827, the new county had a night school in its very early years. It follows:

Night School.

The Subscriber will commence a Night School on Monday, the 26th instant. Persons desiring of improving themselves in the common rudiments of learning, and cannot well spare the daylight, will please make immediate application.   JAMES B. COOPER.
Landisburg, November 15, 1827.

During the period from 1851 to 1853 there was a night school at Millerstown, among the students being the late William Kipp, later a justice of the peace in that town for many years.

Dr. J. R. Flickinger, once county superintendent of Perry County Schools and for many years prior to his death principal of the State Normal School at Lock Haven, Pennsylvania, related an early incident in connection with a schoolhouse which stood as late as 1808 in what is now Jackson Township, on the farm later known as the Wentz place. It follows:

"A wedding party was expected to pass the schoolhouse on a certain day, and when they were reported to be coming by a boy stationed on the outside, the teacher took all his pupils to the roadside and stationed them in rows on both sides of the road, and when the wedding party passed through the ranks the teacher had instructed them to make a profound obeisance to the bride and groom. The result happened as the shrewd teacher expected, the happy groom treating him to the contents of his flask."

Pupils from the west end of Liberty Valley traveled to Sandy Hill, where an early schoolhouse stood near a spring at the foot of the hill south of the Sandy Hill store. They traveled across the foot of Conococheague Mountain over a path trod by bears as late as 1870. During the shortest days of the year these pupils had to take their breakfasts before daylight and start for school, and it was long after nightfall that they returned to warm firesides and supper. At Loysville, in Tyrone Township, the teacher and family occupied one end of the schoolhouse. In some counties that was the general custom. By neighborhood or community spirit sometimes a schoolhouse, save the roof, was on the stump at the rising of the sun, and when the sun went down, the building was finished.

On March 28, 1814, a bill passed the Pennsylvania Legislature authorizing the land office to make a clear title to lands for a school in Toboyne Township, Cumberland County—now Perry. In the *Perry Forester* there was a notice published for a school meeting to be held May 7, 1825, the call being signed by William B. Miller, Jesse Miller, and Jacob Fritz. This was doubtless for the purpose of carrying out the provisions of the Act of 1825.

The *Peoples' Advocate* ran an educational department as early as April 11, 1855, being the first paper in the county to run such a department. Others soon followed. The same paper, beginning August 1, 1877, published a series of articles on "History of Education in Perry County."

During the earlier years of the existence of the public schools many experiments naturally were made, a notable one being in Newport Borough in 1854, when the school board decided to have eight months' school, divided into the following terms: First term, May, June, August, and September; second term, November, December, January, and February. That system left a two months' vacation during March and April, and the other vacations, one in July and one in October.

During the period of the War Between the States many teachers who were most efficient and who had the most experience were called to the colors, with the attending result that inexperienced boys and girls were requisitioned to fill their places, thus lowering the educational standard for a time. That condition had its counterpart in the recent World War when salaries became so high in other lines that many left the profession and others were called to the colors.

21

During the period of educational development, from prior to the War Between the States to almost the end of the century the public schools of the county, especially the country districts, were attended by many scholars who had reached young manhood and womanhood, a condition which no longer exists. With the years the average age of the pupils has decreased, and in few country schools can any pupils over fifteen years of age be found, and in the borough schools few over seventeen. During the sessions of 1873-74 there were 185 pupils in private schools, and 6,198 under sixteen years of age, and 1,606 beyond that age in the public schools. Yet it should be remembered that, in so far as the educators of note from the county are concerned, to a very great extent they were products of that period, and largely of the country schools.

Ex-County Supt. Silas Wright, in a report to the state and later in various historical articles in speaking of the visitation of schools by the board of directors, said: "From 1874 to 1878 the directors of Buffalo Township visited the schools as a whole board a number of times during the term and carefully inspected the condition of the schools. This was the period of most marked progress." The fact that Mr. Wright made the statement and singled out Buffalo Township infers that that was the initial proceeding of that kind in the Perry County schools. The records at New Bloomfield show the election of the following men who composed the boards there during the years of that period, who instituted that method: John C. McGinnes and Ezra Patton, 1872; George W. Potter and Robert B. Fritz, 1873; Samuel Bair and Jacob McConnell, 1874; Henry Hain and Michael Seiler, 1875; Jacob Charles and Josiah Bair, 1876.

In 1836 Wheatfield Township paid its teachers $14.25 a month. In 1838 there were eighty schools in the county, with terms ranging from three to seven months. The salaries were from $15.00 to $23.00 per month. In 1840 Buffalo Township dispensed with schools altogether in order to use the funds to build schoolhouses. There were fifty-five schools in the remainder of the county, with male teachers getting from $15.00 to $22.00, and females $12.00 per month.

When the law creating the office of county superintendent of schools came into effect, in 1854, there were in Perry County 108 schools in session with an attendance of 5,984 pupils. The male teachers received an average salary of $18.50, $11.40 being paid females. In 1855, the law being effective for the first time, the number of schools had increased to 138, and the salaries for males averaged $22.75, and that of females, $18.72 per month. The highest salary paid that year was $30.00. In 1876 salaries had advanced to an average of $30.57 for males, and $28.51 for females.

Later on, during the period around 1890, salaries had become very low in many of the country districts, Tuscarora Township one year paying as little as $15.00 a month, and Carroll Township paying $17.00 to some of its teachers.

By 1877 there were 181 schools in the county, conducted in 160 schoolhouses, of which 119 were frame buildings, thirty-six brick and stone, and five of logs: The grounds of 118 were reported as of sufficient size, and of five as suitably improved. Of the buildings five had been built that year, twenty-four were unfit for use, 119 had suitable furniture, and twenty-eight injurious furniture. Of the teachers five held permanent certificates, five professional, and the remainder were chosen from among 222 who held provisional certificates. Their average age was twenty-seven years, thirty-eight had no experience, seventy-seven had over five years, three intended to make teaching a permanent business, five had attended a state normal school, two had graduated there, three were reported as failures, and the average grade of provisional certificates was 1.9, with ten applicants rejected. The estimated number of children of school age not in school was 634. There were thirty-four graded schools, 169 well classified, twenty-three examinations held by the superintendent, and 115 directors present. The higher branches were taught in eight schools and the Bible read in all of them. There were five academies in the county, with 270 pupils attending, and ten teachers employed. There were 4,056 males and 3,472 females in attendance in the public schools. The teaching staff was composed of 142 males and thirty-nine females. The average salaries of males was $28.08 and of females, $28.05. The mill rate averaged 4.14 mills and the state appropriation to the county was $6,870.66. Carroll Township paid the smallest salaries, $18 per month. The Duncannon Borough principal got the highest salary, $60 per month.

The Perry County schools were represented at the Philadelphia Centennial in 1776 by an exhibit containing:

A.—A History of Perry County, by Prof. Silas Wright, once county superintendent of schools.

B.—A map of Perry County, showing the division of townships, location of towns and villages, mountains, streams, and iron ore deposits. It was a pen and ink sketch by L. E. McGinnes, later superintendent of the Steelton schools.

C.—Specimens of the work of pupils in the common branches, examination questions, and a table of school statistics of the county.

The laws governing the public schools of Pennsylvania had become so extensive and complicated that, upon the report of a special commission to investigate the subject, a school code was adopted at the special session of the Pennsylvania Legislature in 1911. Among other provisions was that of a state board of education, a state superintendent and assistants, thirteen state normal schools, teachers' institutes, a teachers' retirement fund, school libraries and medical supervision and inspection of the schools.

A strange contrast is that of the past and the present in the teaching profession. During the last quarter of the past century there were many applicants for almost every school, even at the very low salaries then paid, while now there are very often not enough applicants to supply the schools, although the salaries are more than double what they then were. A. J. Magee, now proprietor of Alfalfa Stock Farm at Sanford, Colorado, recalls that in "the seventies," when he was the successful applicant for the Shenandoah school, near Ickesburg, in Saville Township, there were seventeen applicants. That township then paid $31 per month for No. 1 certificates; $27 for No. 2; $23 for No. 3, and a further reduction, regardless of grade, for beginners. During recent years the high salaries paid in other lines induced many of the best teachers to adopt other vocations, with the result that teachers' salaries had to be advanced or a backward step taken with the schools.

With a decrease of population, owing to smaller families and fewer families, the wayside school buildings are dwindling in number. Taking but one district in the county as an example (Spring Township), two have dropped out in the Perry Furnace section, there being none between Jericho and Springdale, a distance of not less than six and one-half miles. Between Union and Germany there are none, the distance being more than three miles.

During the past century, especially in the country districts, the spelling school and the literary society, conducted during evening hours, were a source of instruction as well as entertainment, not only for those of school age, but for the public generally. In these spelling schools it was the custom for two "choosers"—a position of favor—to "choose sides," words being pronounced alternately to the "sides," the "side" having the last contestant standing being the winner. Some are still held, but their number is few as compared with the days of yore. The literary societies produced the best talent in their respective neighborhoods, the debates giving many a youngster his or her first chance "to speak in public." There are yet a number of these societies in existence and showing real life, but as a whole, like the spelling school, they passed their zenith with the end of the century.

The modern trend seems to be to pass over the common branches too briefly, as an instance in the neighboring city of Harrisburg well illustrates. During a very recent year the Colonial Dames of that city offered three prizes of $10, $5, and $2.50 for the best essays along patriotic lines from scholars. The first two prizes were carried off by foreign-born children on better grammatical expression, better spelling, and better penmanship, all of which shows that heritage alone cannot win against ambition.

Liverpool Borough was the first school district in Perry County to have a graduating class, the year being 1884, and the principal, E. Walt Snyder, later a physician at Liverpool and Marysville.

The first teacher in Perry County to be retired under the provision of the Teachers' Retirement legislation was T. W. Tressler, of Juniata Township, who was retired in 1920. The previous winter Mr. Tressler had taught his fifty-third term. As it is but eight-six years (in 1920) since the advent of the free school system it will be seen that he was identified with it for more than sixty per cent of the time since its inception. Those fifty-three terms were consecutive, save a single break of one term. During the fifty-three years but one day was missed owing to illness. That record is remarkable.

Among the teachers who taught for long periods is Capt. G. C. Palm, late of near Sandy Hill, who taught over fifty terms and was once a candidate for county superintendent of schools. His first term was taught at the Sandy Hill school and he had eighty pupils. He was then sixteen years old, and fifteen of his pupils were older than he was. Mr. Palm was 82 years of age in February, 1921, which would place the time of his entry into the profession in 1855. The late John W. Soule, of Centre Township, was another veteran teacher, having taught thirty terms. The late Wm. A. Meminger was another veteran, having taught thirty-one consecutive terms. He began teaching in 1862. He was also a surveyor for twenty-three years and long a justice of the peace in Newport. J. J. Asper began teaching in 1875 and still teaches, having been out of the schoolroom but one or two years during that time. G. H. Rumbaugh has also taught about that long.

Abner Knight, father of the late Erastus L. Knight, of Newport, taught in the county schools for forty years.

In the public press the first county superintendent quoted the late J. A. McCroskey, of New Bloomfield, as a good teacher of that period. Henry Thatcher, father of the noted Thatcher boys, taught quite a number of terms, as also did Daniel Gantt, who became chief justice of Nebraska. Two others who taught many terms were John S. Campbell and S. E. Bucke, Mr. Campbell having taught over forty terms.

An early teacher in Perry County, soon after its creation as a county, was Ann Watts, who afterwards became a missionary in the home field. She taught in the vicinity of Nekoda, Greenwood Township. One of the early teachers was Thomas Cochran, at Millerstown. Another who taught eight years in the public schools soon after their establishment was John Raffensperger, born in the very year of the county's erection.

by conducting entertainments and holding small social affairs. The
New Bloomfield school even purchased a most expensive encyclo-
pædia. Numerous literary societies are held, and at Duncannon
the schools had their own entertainment course. At a number of
places, notably the Blain Vocational School and at a number of
Buffalo Township schools, hot lunches were provided by the pupils, under direction of the teacher. The Newport schools have
their own publication, "The Blue and White," and a number of the
lower grades have a school garden on lands owned by the school
district in another section of the town. New Bloomfield has a
school orchestra. A number of schools measure and weigh the
children and look after their general health. Many of the town
schools have track teams, basketball teams and baseball clubs. So
far, Tyrone Township has led the movement for consolidation, by
closing four schools and selling the buildings. A new central
school at Loysville replaces them. Even a village the size of Ickesburg has educational advantages now which a very few years ago
were not enjoyed by many boroughs of much larger population.
The former high school there was transformed into that of a three-
year alternating type in 1920, but in 1921 it was changed to a four-
year course with two teachers, by the Saville Township school
board. To it go the advanced pupils from the entire township.
Being a rural county and the towns considerably separated, field
day exercises were not instituted until 1921, when the Blain Vocational School carried off first honors. The score by points was:
Blain, 66.50; Newport, 52.50; Landisburg, 37; Duncannon, 34;
Bloomfield, 22.

The Blain Vocational School is an outgrowth of the Blain-
Jackson Joint High School, which had as principal Newton Kerstetter from 1914 to 1920. During the winter of 1916-17 Mr.
Kerstetter, looking towards the advancement of the schools, introduced the subject of vocational training to the citizens, who sanc-
tioned it, and the Blain Vocational School came into being with the
opening of the term of 1917-18. In 1920 the State Department
classed it as one of the three best vocational schools in the state.
As an example of the advantage secured by the change it might
be noted that during its last year as a joint high school the state
appropriation was $172, and the payments to teachers was $735,
while during its first year as a vocational training school it received
from the state $2,637.50, which added to $586.38 tuition from non-
resident pupils, totaled $3,223.88. During the latter year the pay-
ments to teachers was $3,045.

The trend of education in the country districts is towards the
consolidation of schools, and spells the passing of the small one-
room building in many places. The Blain Vocational School is an

example; the Landisburg joint high school is another. Penn and
Saville Townships established central high schools. Late in 1921
Centre school, in Wheatfield Township, burned, and that township
is considering the erection of a central school at Roseglen.

It may be of interest to know just who were the first persons
from Perry County territory to graduate from college, to get a State
Normal diploma and to secure a business education. David Watts,
the only son of General Frederick Watts, born in what is now
Wheatfield Township, on October 29, 1764, matriculated at Dickinson College, founded in 1783, and graduated with the very first
class, the first college man born in the territory comprising the
county. He became one of the greatest lawyers of his day and
the father of Judge Frederick Watts, the third judge to sit regularly on the Perry County bench. The first graduate of a State
Normal School was Silas Wright, born in Greenwood Township,
who graduated at Millersville, the first school of that description
in Pennsylvania, in 1865. Prof. Wright was the superintendent
of the Perry County schools for three terms and the author of the
only separate History of Perry County before this volume. The
first woman graduate of a State Normal School was Miss Anna
Froelich, born in Duncannon, who also graduated at Millersville, in the class of 1882. Miss Froelich was also the first Perry
County woman to become a school principal, having been principal
of the Duncannon High School in 1885. She was long a member
of the faculty of the Central State Normal School, at Lock Haven,
and is now a member of the faculty of the Millersville State Normal School. The first native to take a business course that we
could find record of was Hugh Hart Cummins, of Liverpool, who
later became President Judge of Lycoming County.

As something of an indication of where Perry County stands
educationally in the commonwealth, no less than three of her sons
have been honored with the presidency of the State Educational
Association. At the annual meeting held in Pittsburgh, in 1902,
Junius R. Flickinger, a native of Madison Township, was the presiding officer. At the Altoona meeting, in 1906, Lemuel E. Mc-
Ginnes, who was reared to manhood in Buffalo Township, was the
president. In 1917 the meeting was held at Johnstown, and
Charles S. Davis, who was born in New Bloomfield, presided.
That as many as three school men from little Perry should be
selected to preside over the deliberations of this important educational body in but little more than sixty years of its existence, is
an honor that has come to no other locality in the state outside of
the larger cities. At the present time John C. Wagner, born in
Saville Township, is treasurer of the State Association, having
been such since 1917. Mr. Wagner is superintendent of the Carlisle schools. Of the three named above who were presidents of

the State Association, Mr. Flickinger was long principal of the Central State Normal School at Lock Haven, Mr. McGinnes was long superintendent of the Steelton schools, and Mr. Davis was then principal at Steelton and succeeded Mr. McGinnes as superintendent, the latter two having been associated in the work at Steelton for thirty-six years.

Two of Perry's sons, David Loy Tressler, and Charles W. Super, became college presidents, the former of Carthage College in Illinois, and the latter of Ohio University, while a third, Junius R. Flickinger, became principal of the Central State Normal School of Pennsylvania. Others became founders of academies, county superintendents in various states and counties, while still others— many in number—became superintendents, principals and teachers.

The rolls of educational institutions throughout the land contain and have contained for many years the names of hundreds of Perry Countians. Of the academies patronized the New Bloomfield Academy (now the Carson Long Institute) and Mercersburg have been the leading ones. The State Normal Schools at Shippensburg, Millersville, and Lock Haven, in the order named, have had the larger number of those preparing to teach, while among the colleges, those most patronized have been Dickinson, the University of Pennsylvania, State, Gettysburg, Franklin & Marshall, and Bucknell. Among women's colleges Wilson probably leads. There is usually a Perry County Club at the Shippensburg institution, at State College, and ofttimes at other institutions. Invariably the county is represented on leading athletic teams in these institutions, and even more frequently upon the staff of the literary clubs.

While Perry County has always been in the van in so far as education in Pennsylvania is concerned, yet many of its school buildings, especially in country districts, are not the models of neatness as are the homes which contribute the children as pupils. The number which need paint inside and out is large. In dozens no papering has been done since their erection many years ago. Other counties are in the same plight, yet that fact does not mitigate the circumstances in the least. A county which has given to the country at large four governors, three chief justices of as many states, two college presidents, and educators like J. R. Flickinger and L. E. McGinnes, not to mention dozens of others, cannot afford to let any building in the county remain in any but first-class shape.

The only joint high school in the county, except the Blain Vocational School, is at Landisburg, being maintained by that borough, Tyrone and Spring Townships. It was started in 1914, the first principal having been Rev. Thomas Matterness. The first township in Perry County to establish a township high school was Penn, in 1895, in the room formerly occupied by the Lower Duncannon High School. It was later consolidated with the Duncannon Borough High School. During 1919 the county teachers formed an association and held their first annual picnic at Groff's Woods. In 1920 a second picnic was held. The program consisted of educational topics.

Public schools have proven that education is the greatest defense of a free people, that ignorance is a curse to any nation, and that their existence is the best guarantee of the rights granted by the Constitution. They are the virtual cradle of our democracy and, in the classrooms and upon the playgrounds meet upon an equal footing the sons and daughters of the wealthy and the poor. There are instilled the lessons of democracy and there are taught the first principles of fraternity. A writer has well said "the battleground of the world is the heart of the child," and that government fails at its source which ceases to make ample provision for the development and nurture of its future citizens.

County Superintendents of Schools.

Until the creation of the office of county superintendent of schools the public schools made slow progress, but from then on the schools became systematized and made great progress. Perry County has been unusually fortunate in having the highest type of men fill this important office—educators of the type of Kerr, Wright, Flickinger—and, in fact, one might well mention any one of them and still be within the truth in saying that they were men well above the average, even in educational circles.

Shortly after the passage of the act creating the position the first convention to select a county superintendent of schools was held in the courthouse at New Bloomfield, June 5, 1854. Joseph Bailey, then a state senator, residing in Miller Township, was chosen as president, and James L. Diven, of Landisburg, as secretary of the convention. An effort to make the salary $600 per annum was lost and it was placed at half that amount. There was a contest in which three ballots were taken, Rev. Adam R. Height, of Mechanicsburg, winning the election and thus becoming the first county superintendent. He had just located in the county that year—March 1—as pastor of the New Bloomfield Lutheran charge. The candidates nominated and votes received were as follows:

Rev. A. R. Height, Bloomfield, ...	42	47	51
William Brown, Penn, ...	33	42	49
Rudolphus Heim, Landisburg, ...	6	11	
Albert A. Owen, Landisburg, ...	16		
Henry Titzel, Juniata, ...	4		

Henry G. Milans, New Bloomfield; Rev. Solomon Bingham, Penn, and David Brink, Liverpool, were also nominated but were withdrawn before balloting began.

Rev. Height's term is noted for his promptness in familiarizing himself with the work of the county's schools, his efficiency, and his energy. He used the public press to report his visits and make suggestions towards standardizing the schools.

Three years later, at the triennial convention, Rev. Theodore P. Bucher was elected. He was a theological student, but recently graduated, and had attained prominence by opening the Mount

PROF. SILAS WRIGHT.
Ex-County Supt. of Schools and author of "A History of Perry County."

Dempsey Academy at Landisburg. Another advantage possessed by him was that he had been a clerk in Thatcher's store at Newport as a boy, and his manliness and exemplary behavior was known of among a large circle of people. He continued teaching at the academy during the summer months while filling the office.

During the summer of 1859 Superintendent Bucher resigned, and Lewis Barnett Kerr, of Tuscarora Township, was appointed, his commission being dated September 1, 1859. So successfully did Prof. Kerr fill the position that he was elected at the third triennial convention, which met in May, 1860. Prof. Kerr's work stands high in Perry County educational circles, even to this day.

On May 4, 1863, at the fourth triennial convention, Jacob Gantt, of Millerstown, was elected over William R. Cisna, of Madison Township, on the fifth ballot, by a majority of fourteen votes. Other candidates voted for were L. B. Kerr, Tuscarora Township; L. O. Foose, Juniata, and S. H. Galbraith, New Bloomfield. Three years previously the salary had been increased from $300 to $400 annually, but at this convention it was again placed at $300, but Superintendent Gantt, at a special meeting after his election succeeded in having it raised to $500 per year.

In May, 1866, the fifth convention chose Silas Wright, of Greenwood Township, on the third ballot, over Jacob Gantt, of Millerstown, and George W. Lesher, of Duncannon. Prof. Wright was graduated from the Millersville State Normal School in 1865 and was the first State Normal graduate in the county. When elected county superintendent he was under twenty-five years of age.

In May, 1869, at the sixth convention, Lewis B. Kerr was again elected, having a majority of eight votes over Silas Wright, his closest competitor. There were eleven ballots and four candidates.

The seventh convention occurred May 7, 1872, and fixed the salary at $700 per annum. George C. Welker, of Liverpool, was chosen over G. C. Palm, on the third ballot, by a majority of eight votes. Before the ending of the first year of his term Superintendent Welker died, and Silas Wright was appointed, his commission dating April 1, 1873. So acceptably did Prof. Wright fill the position that at the eighth convention in May, 1875, he was elected over six competitors on the first ballot.

At the ninth convention in May, 1878, S. B. Fahnestock, of Duncannon, was elected over Rev. John Edgar. At the tenth convention, May, 1881, Junius R. Flickinger, of Madison Township, defeated S. B. Fahnestock, of Duncannon, for reëlection. At the eleventh convention, in May, 1884, Prof. Fahnestock was again a candidate but was defeated by E. U. Aumiller. At the twelfth convention, in 1887, Prof. Aumiller was reëlected over G. C. Palm and E. Walt Snyder, and at the thirteenth convention he was again reëlected, his opponent then being John S. Arnold.

The fourteenth convention, in 1893, selected Joseph M. Arnold, the other candidates being Silas Wright and J. Albert Lutz. Mr. Arnold was reëlected at the fifteenth convention, in 1896, but later resigned and was succeeded by E. H. Bryner, by appointment of the governor. The salary was made $1,000 per annum in 1896. At the sixteenth convention, in 1899, and the seventeenth, in 1902, Mr. Bryner was reëlected, the latter time over John C. Wagner. The salary was made $1,500 in 1899, and $1,475, according to a provision of the state law, in 1902. In 1905, at the eighteenth convention, Mr. Bryner was elected for the third time, his competitors being D. A. Kline, S. S. Willard, J. L. L. Bucke, and F. A. Hamilton. Superintendent Bryner resigned in October, 1905, and S. S. Willard was appointed by the governor to fill the vacancy.

The nineteenth convention, in 1908, brought the closest vote since the first election, when Rev. Height led William Brown by but two votes. At this convention the vote was D. A. Kline, 83, and S. S. Willard, 81. At the twentieth convention, in 1911, Mr. Kline had no opposition and was reëlected. The salary was made $15 for every school up to 100 and $5 for each additional school, which made it $1,945. At the twenty-first convention, in May, 1914, Professor Kline was again elected without opposition, for a term of four years, at a salary of $1,940. For the first time the convention was held on the first Tuesday of April, 1918, instead of in May. This was the twenty-second election and Prof. Kline was again selected without opposition. According to statute the salary is now $2,490.

Of the men who have filled the position Rev. A. R. Height, Rev. T. P. Bucher, J. R. Flickinger, S. S. Willard, and D. A. Kline were college graduates. Silas Wright, S. B. Fahnestock, E. U. Aumiller, E. H. Bryner, and D. A. Kline were state normal school graduates, and Lewis B. Kerr, Jacob Gantt, and George C. Welker were educated in the common schools and academies. It will be noted that Prof. D. A. Kline, the present incumbent, is the only one graduated from both college and normal school. While there have been twenty-two elections to the superintendency and four appointments to fill vacancies created by death and resignation, yet but twelve men have filled that responsible position. *Prof. Kline has had four elections, or more than any other. Prof. Aumiller and Prof. Bryner were elected three times. Prof. Wright's name was voted on at more conventions than any other, being balloted for in the convention of 1866, 1869, 1872, 1875, and 1893, being successful in 1866 and 1875. Of the appointees, Messrs. Kerr, Wright, and Bryner were successful in succeeding themselves.

In 1921, the State Legislature having created the position of assistant county superintendent, Albert J. Deckard, principal of the Marysville schools, was appointed to that office.

---

*Prof. Kline was selected for the fifth time, April 11, 1922.

CHAPTER XVIII.

ACADEMIES AND PUBLIC INSTITUTIONS.

PERRY COUNTY, owing to its small extent of territory, has never had within its borders one of the higher institutions of learning, neither has it had a State Normal School. It was, however, in earlier years, the home of a number of academies and soldiers' orphans' schools, two of which have grown into other institutions of more than local note. The New Bloomfield Academy has become the Carson Long Institute, with students from all over the world, and the Loysville Academy, later the Loysville Orphans' Home, has become the growing Tressler Orphans' Home of the Lutheran Church in America. In the following pages an endeavor has been made to record the history and growth of these institutions, and the passing of those which no longer exist.

THE ACADEMIES.

Perry County during the past century was the location of quite a number of academies, and their impress has been left not only within its borders, but from among the students at these various institutions went forth educators and professional and business men into many parts of Pennsylvania, and into many of the other states of the Union. The passing of these institutions, in a way, is to be regretted, for they gave to the boys and girls a chance to learn, near their own homes, more than the common schools afforded. Of course the borough high schools have now largely taken their places in so far as the teaching of the higher branches is concerned. Of these academies the ones to remain in existence, the New Bloomfield Academy, now the Carson Long Institute, and the Loysville Academy, now the Tressler Orphans' Home, the history to date is noted. Of the others time has erased much information, but briefly their history follows:

The First Academy. From Presbyterian records it is noted that Rev. James Brady, of Carlisle, was called on March 10, 1803, to become pastor of the church at the mouth of the Juniata (predecessor of the Duncannon Presbyterian Church), of Dick's Gap Church and of Sherman's Creek Church. He was installed October 3, 1804, and "located on a farm,, where he opened an academy" and conducted that work along with his duties along religious lines. He died April 24, 1821, and his remains are interred in the cemetery on the heights, above Juniata Bridge Station, at the junction of the two rivers. While the date of the establishment of this first

came the first president of Carthage College in Illinois—the first native Perry Countian to attain so great an honor in the educational world. In 1862, when disunion was threatened, Mr. Tressler became captain of Company H, 133d Penna. Volunteers, in the United States Army, and with his company went many boys from the institution. In 1865 it became a Soldiers' Orphan School, one of the first in the United States, with Capt. David L. Tressler as principal. That action destined it to become a perpetual home for orphans, for the attention of the Lutheran Church was thereby attracted to it as a home for orphan children, which it is to this day, being fully described in the following pages under the title, The Tressler Orphans' Home.

Charity School. In 1842 citizens of Madison Township erected on lands of Mr. Samuel Hench a building which was known as "Charity School." Little data remains as to it.

Andersonburg Academy. This academy was started by Alexander Blaine Anderson, in the house now owned and occupied by W. Scott Moose, in Madison Township, on the Blain road. It was once known as "Sunnyside Academy." Dr. W. R. Cisna was once principal, assisted by Rev. J. J. Kerr, pastor of the Duncannon Lutheran Church, it then being known as Sherman's Valley Institute. As Rev. Kerr's incumbency at Duncannon was from 1875 to 1878, the period was within those three years. In 1866 Martin Motzer rented the building and turned it into a Soldiers' Orphans' School, under which head it is described in the succeeding pages. While an orphan school an additional building was erected and remained standing until 1919, when it was torn down and the timber which remained in good condition was used in St. Mark's Lutheran Church at Kistler.

Duane Academy (Strain's School). During the summer of 1856 Rev. John B. Strain opened an academy, known as Duane Academy, in the dwelling of Mr. Jacob Super, near St. Samuel's Lutheran Church, in Juniata Township. It was later conducted in the schoolhouse which stood on the ground now occupied by St. Samuel's Church. Rev. Strain had as his assistant his sister, Miss Hannah Strain. Dr. C. W. Super, later president of the Ohio University, now of Athens, Ohio, attended this school for a term. Another student was the late Prof. W. C. Shuman, long principal of the Chicago Evening Schools, and a teacher in the Cook County Normal School.

Markelville Academy. On the hill at Markelville, then known as Bosserman's Mills, there stood a building locally termed "Washington Seminary." In the spring of 1855 a school known as Buffalo Creek High School was opened in this building. The law providing for the election of county superintendents of schools had just gone into effect during the previous year, and Rev. A. R.

22

Height, a Lutheran clergyman, was made the county superintendent. He was also chosen principal of this school and filled the positions simultaneously. A year later, in 1856, the school was called the Buffalo Creek High School and Perry County Normal Institute, and in 1857 the first part of the title had been dropped and it was known as the Normal Institute at Markelville and so advertised, the name of the town in the meantime having been changed to Markelville. He was succeeded by Rev. George S. Rea, a Presbyterian clergyman, who in 1801 gave place to Prof. G. W. Leisher, later a Lutheran clergyman. In 1866 Prof. C. W. Super—now Dr. Super—tried to resuscitate the academy, which the fortunes of war had disturbed. He was succeeded by Alexander Stephens and Adam Zellers, in turn. As an evidence of its large attendance, in 1860 it was attended by 112 boarding students. In 1867 George Markel erected a two-story frame academy building in which the school was continued and the students boarded. This building had fifteen rooms for students and the basement was above street level and was intended for classroom use. It was Mr. Markel's intention to make the school a permanent institution, but his death caused its discontinuance. Prof. John S. Campbell, of Newport, states (1920), "It is a pity that this man was called away," he having had personal knowledge of his ability and energy.

Mount Dempsey Academy. Rev. T. P. Bucher founded the Mount Dempsey Academy, which he then called the Landisburg Classical School, at Landisburg, on April 8, 1856, its location being in the basement of the Reformed Church.* It closed about 1864, largely because the War Between the States called the young men to arms. Rev. Bucher was elected county superintendent in 1857 and filled that position in connection with his work at the academy. Later principals of the academy were F. A. Gast, David Evans (later superintendent of the Lancaster County schools), Rev. R. X. Salem, William H. Sheibley, S. H. Galbreath, Rev. G. C. Hall, S. C. Cooper, J. C. Sheibley, and Lewis B. Kerr (later superintendent of the Perry County schools). Rev. Samuel Wagner, still a resident of the county and long a noted minister, was one of the students. Many lawyers, physicians and ministers secured the rudiments of their education at this pioneer institution. The late George Patterson, of Landisburg, interviewed by the author in 1919, while engaged in the compilation of this book, was a student at this institution in 1861.

Willow Grove Female Seminary. This institution was short-lived. It had its headquarters in the Judge Junkin home, one mile northeast of Landisburg, and was presided over by Miss E. J.

---

*See church on page 202, in left foreground.

Petherfridge, of whom the *Freeman* said: "As a female instructor
she is inferior to none in the state." Board and washing was $1.50
per week. Tuition was $4 and $5 per quarter. Other rates were:
French, $3.00; drawing and painting, $6.00; piano, $8.00. The
attendance was limited to twenty students. This evidently is identical with the school authorized by a special act of the Pennsylvania
Legislature passed June 12, 1840, designated as "a female seminary or public school for the education of female youths in the
English or other languages, the useful arts, sciences and literature,
by the name, style and title of the Landisburg Female Seminary."
The act named John Junkin, Samuel A. Moore, Henry Fetter,
James Diven, Sr., Peter Hench, John Stambaugh, and James Mc-
Clure, as trustees.

Susquehanna Institute. In 1860 Prof. Bartlett opened the Susquehanna Institute in the basement of the United Presbyterian
Church at Duncannon, being the first principal. It was continued
for a short time by Rev. William B. Craig, the Presbyterian pastor.

Duncannon Academy. Largely through the efforts of Dr. T. L.
Johnston and Dr. H. D. Reutter, who were its directors, the Duncannon Academy was established in 1890, the sessions at first being
held in Pennell's Hall, and the following year on the second floor
of Odd Fellows' Hall. Seventy pupils were enrolled in 1890.
Prof. Thomas M. Stalford, of Athens, was the principal, and Prof.
W. F. Kennedy, later superintendent of the Lewistown schools,
assistant. Its life was but two years.

The Blain School. For over fifty years a summer normal was
conducted at Blain, but often under different managements.
Among the instructors were such men as Gard C. Palm, S. E.
Harkins, and Rev. Rentz.

Juniata Valley Normal School. That a State Normal School
was not located somewhere in Perry County is not the fault of
Prof. Silas Wright, but rather of the citizenship of the communities; for Mr. Wright strained every effort to have it done. The
general apathy—sometimes even yet displayed towards incoming
things, industrial plants, etc.—was the barrier against which
Prof. Wright's efforts spent their force, and the project failed.
Looking towards the establishment of the State Normal School of
the Sixth District within the borders of the county, the Juniata
Valley Normal School was opened on April 8, 1867, in the new
brick schoolhouse at Newport, for which $12.50 a month was paid
as rental. The attendance at the first term was 141, a remarkably
good showing. Two terms were conducted, the first being from
April 8 to June 28, and the second from July 29 to September 17.
The second session had an attendance of ninety-seven; of these
twenty-two were not attendants at the first term. During the first

session, on May 3, the Normal Echo Literary Society was organized.

Newport not having displayed as much interest as Millerstown, which offered its school building rent free for the school, the sessions of 1868 began in the Millerstown school building on April 8, with an attendance of 140. At the very first term (in Newport) the theory class numbered forty-one, a number which it always exceeded in later years. The instructors were teachers of prominence, and beside Professor Wright were Nannie J. Alexander (Millersville, '66), a cultured musician; M. M. Rutt, of the same class at Millersville; Mina Kerr, and Prof. Charles W. Super, who taught ancient languages and German, and who later became president of the Ohio University. During 1875 Professor Super got a temporary leave of absence from his position as head of the department of Ancient Languages and German in Wesleyan College in Ohio, in order to teach the languages for Mr. Wright.

A list of textbooks in use in the Juniata Valley Normal School at Millerstown in 1868, follows: Raub's and Sander's Union Spellers, Sander's Union Readers, Kidd's Elocution, Kerl's Grammars, Trench's Study of Words, Brook's Arithmetics and Geometry, Ray's New Algebras, Payson, Dunton & Scribner's Penmanship, Bartholomew's Drawing, Coppee's Elements of Rhetoric and Logic, Mitchell's Political and New Physical Geography, Apgar's Map Drawing, Seavey's and Goodrich's History of the United States, Sheppard's Constitution, Gray's Botany, Hillside's Geology, Quackenbo's Natural Philosophy, Wickersham's School Economy and Method's of Instruction, Haven's Mental Philosophy, Hickok's Moral Science, Harkness' Latin, etc.

A "calendar" of the Juniata Valley Normal School at Millerstown for 1868 follows:

"First term of twelve weeks, opens April 6; closes June 26, 1868.

"Last term of eight weeks, opens August 3; closes September 26, 1868.

"The Faculty: Silas Wright, M.E., principal; Nannie J. Alexander, B.E.; Mina J. Kerr, and O. P. Wright (pupil assistant)."

The location is described as being "easy of access by private conveyance or stage from every section of the county, and from east or west on the Pennsylvania Central Railroad." The price of boarding for the session of five months is named as $60. Prof. Silas Wright organized this school and was always its principal, save for a few weeks of the second summer term of 1871.

A glance over several old programs of the Normal Echo Literary Society recalls names of other days, many of whom attained distinction, with a few still living and active in business. The first anniversary of the society was celebrated Friday evening, May 29, 1868, the officers being:

A. M. Markel, Markelville. President.
Amanda Passmore. Newport, Secretary.
Mina J. Kerr, Donally's Mills, Editress.
Charles H. Heffley, Duncannon, Critic.

On the program were P. S. Lesh, May N. Donally, Mina J. Kerr, and Alfred M. Markel. A debate was a part of the program, the question being, "Resolved, that human language is of Divine origin." The speakers on the affirmative side were S. B. Fahnestock, Wm. N. Ehrhart, O. P. Wright, and H. C. Magee; those on the negative side were H. C. Gantt, W. W. Haines, C. A. Frank, and J. R. Runyon.

The second anniversary was celebrated Friday evening, May 28, 1869, the following being the officers:

S. B. Fahnestock, Millerstown, President.
Josephine Debray, Millerstown, Secretary.
L. C. Zimmerman, Editor.
M. E. Haines, Critic.

On the program were H. C. Magee, Laura E. Goodman, Haly L. Kerr, H. C. Gantt, L. C. Zimmerman, and P. S. Lesh. The question for debate was, "Resolved, that the crusades were beneficial to Europe." Those assigned to the affirmative were O. P. Wright and Perry K. Brandt, and those assigned to the negative were Wm. N. Ehrhart and J. S. Runyon.

Prof. John S. Campbell, long one of Perry County's prominent educators, with the terse comment, "It did a good work," expresses the opinion of all who have any knowledge of the great work of the Juniata Valley Normal School. Dozens of its students became educators, lawyers, physicians, ministers of the Gospel, bankers, business men and intelligent farmers and homemakers.

CARSON LONG INSTITUTE, FORMERLY NEW BLOOMFIELD ACADEMY.

Almost from its beginning as a town and the location of the county seat New Bloomfield became greatly interested in education. Much of the credit for this interest was then due to the families of men like George Barnett and Alexander Magee. There is hardly a state in the Union to-day in which there are no former attendants of New Bloomfield Academy and Carson Long Institute, many of whom have risen to positions of prominence and trust. To name over a list of these students is like calling a roll of honor. The writer's knowledge goes back only to the proprietorship of William Grier, but there was already at that time something about the institution which impressed him with its importance as a substantial educational center.

In March, 1830, there was a call in the *Perry Forester* for a meeting to consider the advisability of establishing an academy, but for some reason which has not come down to the present gen-

ward the erection of suitable buildings, and the purchasing of a necessary library, mathematical, geographical and philosophical apparatus for the use of the academy, on condition that one thousand dollars be contributed by those interested. Robert Finley was employed as principal in May, at four hundred dollars per annum. "The barracks" then became the temporary home of the academy, the trustees agreeing to rent from John Smith, the owner, one-half of the building, for which they were to pay him $21.29 and taxes for the year, for the use of the same from May 21 until April 1 of the next year. Arrangements were at once made for desks, benches and chairs, and on May 21 the term began. The schoolroom was the one in which Mr. Finley had started the seminary and was in use until 1840, when the brick academy building was completed. The hours were fixed at from 8 to 12 a. m., and from 2 to 5 p. m. Instruction was to be given in the following branches:

First class—Geography, English grammar, bookkeeping, arithmetic, and modern history, at three dollars a quarter.

Second class—Natural history, natural philosophy, ancient history and algebra to quadrated equasions, at four dollars a quarter.

Third class—The Greek and Latin languages, chemistry, astronomy, rhetoric, logic, the higher branches of mathematics, mental and moral philosophy, and evidences of Christianity, at five dollars a quarter.

On August 3 the first quarter ended, twenty pupils having been in attendance. An examination was held that day, also an election of trustees at which the following were chosen: Robert Elliot, John D. Creigh, Thomas Patterson, John Gotwalt, J. R. McClintock, and B. McIntire.

On August 18, 1838, at a meeting of the trustees the following resolution was passed:

Resolved, that the trustees will receive proposals from persons who have sites to locate the building for the academy, and request them to state particularly the location, boundary, quantity and terms upon which it can be had; that the proposals be handed to the trustees on or before ten o'clock a. m. of the first of September next.   JOHN D. CREIGH, *Secretary.*

In answer to the resolution propositions were received from George Barnett (two), John D. Creigh, William Power, and Jeremiah Madden. Later others were received from Mrs. Miller and Messrs. Mehaffy, Ickes, Klinepeter, and Clark. At the meeting of the board on September 21 one of those proffered by George Barnett, was selected. The site then selected was on a knoll east of the Barnett homestead. Evidently with the history of the selection of the county seat and its petitions still fresh in their minds a petition was gotten out requesting that the site be changed to one at the west end of the borough, in consideration of which a further contribution of $241 was pledged. The request was not granted, but the supporters of the west end plan continued the agitation with the result that, at a meeting of the trustees on March 1, 1839, the following action was taken:

"WHEREAS, the sum of one thousand dollars has been subscribed by individuals to aid the funds of the academy, a part of which is subscribed on condition that the site of the academy be removed to the north end of Carlisle Street; therefore,

"*Resolved*, That the present location of the site for the academy be and the same is hereby changed to the north end of Carlisle Street, and a committee be appointed to enter into a contract with Mr. George Barnett for four acres of land at said place, on such terms as they may agree upon.

"*Resolved*, That public notice be given by advertisements, that the trustees will receive proposals on the 14th of March for building a house of brick or stone, to be thirty feet by sixty feet from out to out and twenty-three feet high from top of foundation. to have a cupola and also a portico or vestibule in front of steps.

The contract having been let to Dr. Jonas Ickes he immediately began work, and it was completed and occupied in 1840. By private subscription a bell was purchased in Philadelphia, at a cost of $65.60.

In 1842, owing to a demand, a steward was appointed and it was opened as a boarding school for both teachers and pupils. In September, 1850, the trustees appointed two of their number to confer with the Presbytery of the Presbyterian Church in reference to selling the property and academy to that denomination. The movement was unsuccessful. In 1852 the trustees decided to apply to the legislature for the enactment of a law enabling them to transfer the real estate and property to the commissioners of the county and that it be a county institution, the county to assume the indebtedness. On petition to the legislature such an act was passed and signed by Governor William Bigler, a Perry County native, April 1, 1852, providing that the commissioners with others appointed by the court act as trustees. On December 4, 1852, by resolution of the trustees the president of the board was authorized to transfer by deed all the real estate belonging to the academy, which was done January 3, 1853. Under the county's management the school took on new life, and in January, 1854, the county grand jury recommended that an additional building be erected for the better accommodation of the pupils.

Finlaw McCown, a former trustee and a former county commissioner, had in the meantime bequeathed to the trustees of the academy the sum of four hundred dollars for the purpose of helping to erect an additional building. Upon the commissioners being notified of the bequest and of the action of the grand jury they absolutely refused to grant any assistance towards the erection of an additional building and even withheld the right of any company or association of so doing. Upon such refusal the trustees appointed a committee to secure grounds situated in proximity to the academy for the purpose of erecting such building as their needs

this noted institution, through the magnanimity of Theodore K. Long, comes to the new corporation without the payment of a cent or without any indebtedness whatsoever.

For over four score years this school has successfully prepared students for college, teaching and business, literary and professional life. Its graduates are on the honor rolls of Yale, Harvard, Princeton, and Wilson, as well as on those of many less noted institutions. The graduating class of 1921 was the forty-eighth. While the institution was in its infancy and during its earlier years there were no graduating classes, yet young people were being prepared for college and teaching from its very organization.

A list of the principals who have been in charge of the school from the date of its organization follows, the date named being the beginning of the period for which they served:

1838—Robert Finley.
1839—Rev. Matthew B. Patterson.
1842—J. M. Stearns.
1843—Samuel Ramsey.
1845—Rev. Martin Smith.
1850—Rev. Matthew B. Patterson.
1853—William S. Post (elected but did not serve).
1853—Charles A. Barnett.
1858—James A. Stephens.
1862—George S. Rea.
1864—James A. Stephens.
1869—T. A. Snively.
1870—A. R. Keiffer.
1870—W. H. Dill.
1872—Rev. John Edgar.
1877—J. R. Flickinger.
1881—Rev. John Edgar.
1883—J. R. Flickinger.
1884—William H. Schuyler.
1889—Joseph M. Arnold.
1893—Geo. W. Wagonseller (from November to February, 1894).
1894—H. E. Sheibley (Spring term).
1894—George B. Roddy.
1895—Oliver J. Morelock.
1896—H. C. Mohn.
1905—Julian C. Plau (September to end of year).
1906—George B. Roddy (January to June).
1906—L. E. Strohm.
1908—A. J. Shumaker (January to June).
1908—John F. Buckheit.
1912—Donald C. Willard.
1918—Theodore K. Long (February to September).
1918—George F. Schneider.
1920—John W. Weeter.

The Orphan Schools.

From the vortex of the Sectional War, while it was still being waged with all the energy of two equally red-blooded antagonists, save that one was not burdened with the taint of secession, there arose in Pennsylvania the beginning of a system of Soldiers' Orphans' Schools, which has always stood abreast of the most advanced states of the Union. In fact, in the annals of the centuries there is no prior record of any state or nation adopting as their wards all the dependent children of slain and injured defenders. As two of the early institutions devoted to the education of these orphans were located within the limits of Perry County it is a matter of interest to record a word of their start.

On his way to church on Thanksgiving Day, 1862, Governor Andrew G. Curtin was met upon the street by two children asking aid. Being of a sympathetic nature he stopped and inquired their condition and the reason for it. Promptly came the reply, "Father was killed in the war." He gave them a liberal contribution and passed on into church; but the Thanksgiving sermon grated harshly upon his ears, as he thought of the children of soldiers fallen while fighting for the preservation of their country begging upon the streets. That was the beginning of Soldier Orphan Schools. In a few weeks the Pennsylvania Legislature met and in his message Governor Curtin said: "I commend to the prompt attention of the legislature the subject of the relief of the poor orphans of our soldiers who have given, or shall give, their lives to the country during this crisis. In my opinion their maintenance and education should be provided for by the state. Failing other natural efforts of ability to provide for them, they should be honorably received and fostered as the children of the commonwealth."

The legislature refused to adopt a measure that might bind the state for heavy expenditures, but authorized the governor to expend $50,000, which the Pennsylvania Railroad had contributed for use in any way deemed best for the prosecution of the war, the governor to use his discretion in its expenditure. Thus there came from that great corporation the money which provided the beginning of that heroic institution—the Soldiers' Orphan School. To what better project could it have been devoted?

Section 2 of the rejected bill gave any school then in existence the right to apply to be recognized as a suitable school for the instruction and training of destitute children, and Section 6 provided that in no case must the cost per child per annum exceed $100. With this slender appropriation at his command Governor Curtin appointed Thomas H. Burrowes, LL.D., superintendent, on June 16, 1864, and from it grew the wonderful result. The intention at the beginning was to have a school in each of the twelve

State Normal School districts. Provision was also made that the children should be neatly clothed in uniforms, well fed, and trained in employment as well as intellectually. Several institutions in the state had already taken up work in the same line on their own responsibility, but the first schools to come to the aid of the system after its beginning were those at Paradise, McAllisterville, Mount Joy, Quakertown, and Orangeville. The legislature of 1865 appropriated $75,000 to continue the work. By January 1, 1866, that amount was utterly exhausted and the legislature delayed passing any act, quibbling over various differences. It was then that Governor Curtin executed a shrewd move. On March 16th three hundred and forty-five soldiers' orphans from McAllisterville, Mount Joy, and Paradise arrived at Harrisburg on the noon trains and, neatly uniformed, gave an exhibition of their training before the surprised legislators, with the result that $300,000 was appropriated, four times the amount of the previous year, and from that day their existence was assured. Among those who spoke was Master Frank A. Fry, of McAllisterville, he who later edited the *Newport News* for many years. By the end of 1866 twenty-four schools in the state were caring for the younger children, and twelve for the older ones. Of these the Andersonburg School and the Loysville Home were Perry County institutions. Of the smaller children the former had 32 boys and 22 girls, and the latter, 66 boys and 52 girls.

In 1867 a general statute, covering every phase of requirements for these schools, passed the legislature. During that year the cost of the larger pupils was $150 per annum, with $25 additional for clothing, and that of the smaller ones from $105 to $125, including clothing.

THE ANDERSONBURG SCHOOL.

Through the influence of Martin Motzer and Alexander Blaine Anderson, during the fall of 1865, Dr. Thomas H. Burrowes, Superintendent of Soldiers' Orphans' Schools, visited Mr. Anderson's building in Madison Township, above Andersonburg. It was a large brick building, then in use as an academy. Dr. Burrowes' said of it: "This is a beautiful location for a school; one of the best I have yet selected. This must certainly be a healthy locality." Mr. Motzer rented the building and took possession in the spring of 1866. The first pupils arrived on September 20, 1866, and on October 16th the school opened with Prof. William H. Hall as principal. Miss Laura J. Milligan followed in a short time as assistant teacher. By the close of the second year the number of pupils had increased to 117, and another building, 35x50 feet, was erected. On December 1, 1872, Prof. Hall became a joint owner, with Mr. Motzer, but retained the principalship. On

stands in the very front rank. Just as he reached the top in the field of his choice, would he have reached it should he have chosen the law. During the first eighteen months of the existence of this school W. H. Minich was its superintendent, G. V. Tressler succeeding him. It was established in 1865.

In 1867 the General Synod of the Lutheran Church, through Rev. Philip Willard purchased the building and five acres of land, and it became the home of both church and soldiers' orphans. During the first two years of the church ownership it was leased to Philip Bosserman, with Rev. John Kistler as superintendent. An additional plot of twenty-seven and one-half acres was then purchased by the trustees, who had been named by the Church. On June 1, 1869, it was placed under the charge of Rev. Willard as superintendent. When he took charge the institution had eighty soldier orphans and eighteen wards of the Church. By 1876 the proportion was sixty-two soldiers' orphans and forty-six Church wards. The original brick building was 40x60, three stories high. Upon taking charge for the Church, Rev. Willard erected a frame building, 20x48, the first floor being a dining room and the second a dormitory. In 1875 the old cooking house was torn away and a new brick one, 30x50. two stories high, replaced it. It had separate departments for cooking, for baking, for washing, and for shower baths.

This school under the long control of Father Willard, as Rev. Willard came to be known, had a fine reputation with the state authorities, as their many reports testify. Among the early teachers were: George Sanderson, George W. Weaver, Ira Wentzel, Herman F. Willard, S. S. Willard, L. A. Haffley, G. M. Willard, A. M. Paff, and Misses Nettie Willard, Elsie Berg, Hattie Anstadt, and M. L. Willard. Its further history follows:

THE TRESSLER ORPHANS' HOME.

This wonderful institution, where so many hundreds of children have found an early home, is the result of an early academy opened in the basement of Lebanon Church, at Loysville, in 1853, of which Josiah R. Titzell was principal. J. T. Ross succeeded him for a year or two. Education was then a leading topic, and there was a demand for an institution for higher education. In 1855-56 Col. John Tressler erected a three-story brick building, with a large auditorium on the first floor and twenty rooms on the other floors, to which the school was transferred. The first principal was John A. Kunkelman, who was succeeded by a son of the founder, David L. Tressler. In 1862, when the dismemberment of the nation was imminent, Mr. Tressler accepted a captaincy in the United States Army and with him went almost the entire male enrollment of the little institution.

J. H. Menges and J. Carver, of the West Pennsylvania Synod. Almost at its beginning as a joint school for the orphans of the state and of the Church (June 1, 1869) there were eighty soldiers' orphans and eighteen Church orphans.

Improvements began almost immediately upon the transfer to the Church, and have never ceased, but have kept abreast of the times. In 1872 a frame building was erected for a dining room and dormitory, later being used as part of the Industrial School. In 1874 a two-story kitchen and bakery was built, and in 1875 a large and substantial barn was built. These buildings sufficed for about a decade. Then, in 1884, a large building with basement and three stories was erected at a cost of $10,000. Its purpose was for schools, kitchen, and boys' dormitory. In 1887 the adjoining George Shaffer property, a house later used as a hospital, and thirteen acres of land, were purchased for $2,300. Two years later fire escapes were added to all buildings to comply with a new state law. During that year Rev. Philip Willard, after twenty-one years of persistent and splendid labor in the upbuilding of the Home, retired from the superintendency. He was temporarily succeeded by Major J. G. Bobb, of Carlisle, Pennsylvania, from November, 1889, to July, 1891. Charles A. Widle had come to the institution in July, 1890, as disciplinarian, and upon the retirement of Major Bobb in July 1891, he became temporary superintendent until June, 1892, when he was elected to fill the position, and has been continued in office ever since, a period of thirty-one years, counting the temporary service. Mr. Widle had been a teacher in the public schools of Butler and Lawrence Counties, from whence he had been called to the service of Soldiers' Orphans' Schools, first to McAllisterville, then to Chester Springs, and later to Harford, Susquehanna County, from which place he came to the Tressler Home in 1890.

During the period of time when the soldiers' orphans were cared for there remained services for which the Home was not compensated, and in 1890 a check for $21,000 was received from the state in full for all overdue payments and for any services for which compensation had not been made. The present excellent library was started in 1892, under the direction of Miss Emma Eppley, who was the matron, with about 700 volumes. The Home issues a small monthly paper telling of its work and needs which was started in May, 1892, a printing plant having been put in that year. Its principal work is that of the Church. Through its installation many of the boys of the institution have been enabled to learn the printing trade and hold positions in many states.

In 1894 an extension, 39x15, was added to the original academy building for a girls' dormitory and bath rooms. In the same year steam heat and gas light were introduced into the main buildings.

system was installed. In 1903 an adjoining tract of land containing fifty-two acres was purchased from George W. Loy, for $2,500, the funds being supplied by private contributions. A year later the Samuel Burkhart farm, near Bloserville, in Cumberland County, was left to the Home by will. Owing to its separation from the Home by a great mountain and a long distance, it was sold by order of the Cumberland County courts and the funds placed in charge of a trustee for the benefit of the Home.

The reservoir and sewer system was constructed in 1904, and a boys' dormitory and school building in 1905-06. Owing to the increasing size of the Home and the necessarily increasing size of the number of employees, a double frame house was purchased in Loysville for $2,000 in 1909, for their accommodation. The Jacob L. Minich plot of ten acres of fine farm land adjoining the Home, was purchased during the same year, and also a tract of twenty-two acres from John H. Shumaker, for $2,000.

The Annie L. Lowry Memorial Hospital was erected in 1909, being a gift through her executor, Elwood Bonsall, Esq., of Philadelphia, who donated $8,500 from the residuary funds of her estate under a provision of her will, which directed that such funds be applied to "such charities as he deemed most worthy." In 1910 a modern system of sewage was installed to replace the old and then obsolete system, at a cost of $1,556. During 1910 the old hospital was removed to a new location and fitted up for employees of the Home, and upon its former site a home for the use of the superintendent was erected at a cost of $4,500. In 1913 the ice house was built, and in 1914 brick refrigerating rooms of an approved type were installed.

During 1913-14 the Sharetts Memorial, costing $10,000, was erected by Luther T. and Edward H. Sharetts, of Keymar, Maryland. It houses the printing department, now grown to considerable size, the gymnasium and the band room. In 1914 the Emeline Loy Murray Memorial was erected. It is a one-story brick building, 26x45 feet, being a modern and up-to-date kitchen. During 1913-14 a deep well was sunk to augment the water supply.

The year 1914 is important in the life of the Home from another standpoint. As noted the Home had increased its acreage at various times, but in 1914 the large and fertile Arnold farm adjoining the Home, consisting of 182 acres with farm buildings, and a number of valuable springs, was purchased for $18,225. Its purchase was made possible through a gift or annuity of $14,000 from Fred and Margaret Mehring, brother and sister, of Keymar, Maryland.

In 1909 a movement was begun for the installation of electricity for lighting purposes, and in 1910 the Sherman's Valley Electric Light, Heat & Power Company, connected with the institution, was chartered by the commonwealth. Bear's mill, in Madison Township, had been abandoned some years before for milling purposes. The mill, with all its water rights, was purchased from Jos. B. Lightner. The dam was rebuilt of concrete and all the waterways renewed and a new turbine wheel with new electrical outfit placed in the mill, where, since, January, 1910, electric current is made to light the whole institution, also all residences and churches in Loysville. All industrial operations of the Home are driven by this plant. It is now planned that in 1921 the power of the Weaver mill will be added to this plant, which will enable the company to give service to Landisburg, Elliottsburg and intervening points as well as serve the growing institution.

During the spring of 1915 the Bear Mill farm, surrounding the light plant, with a total acreage of 132, of which sixty is in cultivation, was purchased. Its purchase was not made from the point of desirability in so far as the farm land is concerned, but as an essential to the water-power and the electric plant.

On the first day of the year, 1919, the Home got possession of the Weaver mill, an old, well-established and well patronized flour and feed mill, for which $5,000 was paid. With it was a house, barn and sixteen acres of rough land. The management foresaw that the capacity of the light plant would soon be overtaxed with only the power from the Bear mill, which was the reason for this purchase. An additional twenty-eight acres of bottom and adjacent hill lands were purchased for $375, in order to be sure of title to all necessary water rights. April 1, 1920, the Home paid $4,000 for the David H. Kleckner place, just east of and adjoining the Home buildings, consisting of a house and five acres of land. It was purchased on account of water rights, as water from the springs on the Mehring addition flowed through it, and for that reason the Home was not at liberty to decrease the flow of the stream. These springs have since been enlarged and connected with the water main and an electric pump installed, and this valuable additional water supply made available for the institution.

Owing to incapacity it became necessary to replace the sewage plant in 1917 and a new plant of the Imhoff type was installed. It was built after plans approved by the state and is supposed to endure for a long period of years. Cement porches were added to the Fritz dormitory in 1918-19, through a bequest of $2,000 from Mrs. Charles S. Weiser, an original member of the Board of Lady Visitors.

In June, 1919, one of the most modern of all the group of buildings was completed and given over to the Home by the Pittsburgh Synod. It is known as the Pittsburgh Synodical Dormitory, and is the home of forty boys from eight to twelve years of age. Its cost, with furnishings, was $20,000.

The Home grounds was the scene of much building activity during the summer of 1921. Among the projects is a large pavilion, seating 1,300 persons, on the campus for out-door entertainments; a second nursery building, by the West Pennsylvania Synod for the home of twenty children from three to six years of age; a dormitory for girls of eight to twelve years, by the Allegheny Synod; a dormitory for forty older boys and a vocational school building, by the East Pennsylvania Synod. The completion of these projected buildings will see the plans of the present management fairly well through.

The printing plant at this institution is most complete, having grown from a few fonts of type and a small job press to its present size. There is printed the *Orphans' Home Echoes,* for which a charge of fifteen cents per year is made, with a price of ten cents per year in clubs. Its circulation is over 8,000. For thirty years, or since its beginning in May, 1892, Mr. W. L. Gladfelter, a prominent paper manufacturer of Spring Grove, Pennsylvania, has donated all the paper used in its publication, which in the past year alone amounted to five tons. Thirty-three church papers are printed at the plant, most of them being monthlies, and from four to thirty-two pages in size.

This institution closed its year in June, 1919, with an enrollment of 262, and the year of 1920 with an enrollment of 282, which shows its wonderful growth in taking care of orphan children of the Church since its start with but the small number of eighteen under Rev. Philip Willard in 1869. During the last year twenty-five boys and twelve girls were sent from the Home, and thirty-five girls and twenty-two boys admitted. There is always a large waiting list. The health of the children is unusually good; on only a few occasions in the fifty or more years of its existence have epidemics brought death to the inmates. The public schools of the surrounding districts have a seven-months' term, while the Home has a nine-months' term, with grades from the kindergarten to the third year in high school. Of the teachers during the 1919-20 session, one was a college graduate, four State Normal graduates, and two held provisional certificates in the county. Vocal and musical instruction is under the charge of a special teacher. There is a girls' orchestra and a boys' band, each under the instruction of a tutor. These musical organizations go on tours and give exhibitions in Lutheran communities. During 1920 the band was on a lengthy tour to western Pennsylvania. Religious instruction is a part of the daily program, morning and evening services of a brief nature being conducted as the children sit at table in the dining room. A Sunday school is conducted in the chapel. That idleness is detrimental is taught in the Home by assigning to the pupils such tasks as they can perform. The boys assist in the housekeeping in their own quarters, and with the heavier work about the kitchen, dining room and grounds; with such farm work as they are able, and in the printery and elsewhere. The girls are employed at the various phases of housework, in the kitchen, dining room, laundry and sewing room. Plans are being made for vocational training. The Alumni Association devotes its funds to helping pupils to a higher education.

The farming operations on the lands belonging to the Home are in themselves no small matter, and it is from them that comes much of the product which sustains it. The yield of wheat last year was 1,220 bushels; of corn, after filling two 100-ton silos, 4,225 bushels, and of other crops accordingly. Forty fat hogs were butchered and twenty-two large steers fed and marketed. Two tractors are used in the cultivation of the lands. Donations from individuals and the various congregations connected with the synods supporting the Home are of frequent occurrence and consist of a variety of things from valuable and useful articles down to the smallest things of use in the home. A modernly equipped dairy furnishes all the milk and butter products from the Home herd. Not considering the products of the Home it costs about $48,000 annually to sustain the Home.

In a word we are proud to have within the borders of Perry County this wonderful institution, supported entirely by voluntary contributions. As a native Perry Countian the author believes that he expresses an opinion that is unanimous. Children who are deprived of either parent, or of father and mother, are denied or deprived of many of the inherent rights of childhood, and it is into this breach that the Tressler Orphans' Home steps and gives the orphan children of Lutheran parents a home, plenty of food for the development of their bodies, proper clothing for their protection, a liberal education and the ability to work. A nurse is in continual attendance and a physician within a moment's call. It is a creditable work that has been so successfully conducted for a period of over a half-century by practically two men, Rev. Philip Willard and Charles A. Widle, the present superintendent, and one of whom the great Lutheran denomination should be proud.

The County Home.

Before the formation of Perry County, the county home of Cumberland County was located at the site of the present Perry County Home. On April 12, 1810, the directors of the poor and of the House of Employment of Cumberland County purchased from Adam Bernheisel, of Tyrone Township, his farm of 112 acres, the same having been warranted by William McClure in 1763. The sum paid was $5,196.36. In those days contracting was not done in the modern way and the records show that on

October 8, 1810, the contract for masonry on the County Home was let to Robert Cree for $1,900, for carpenter work to George Libey (Leiby) for $1,850, and for plastering to Thomas Redding for $230—making the cost of the entire building $3,980. The building was located east of the present one and sufficed at that time for all the territory which comprised Cumberland County, which, of course, included the territory of present-day Perry.

When Perry County was formed the institution became the property of the new county, with the proviso that the poor of Cumberland County be allowed to remain for several years, which condition was carried out. The previous owner, Adam Bernheisel, had erected a brick dwelling house, which was used by the steward as a residence. In 1839 the almshouse was burned to the ground and was rebuilt at once, Samuel Shuman being the contractor. The building erected at that time stood until 1871, when it was replaced by the present one.

The present County Home is a four-story building of brick, containing about seventy rooms. Its partitions are of brick and the stairways are of iron. Its cost was approximately $60,000, including improvements. The county commissioners who were in office at the time of its building were John Stephens, Zachariah Rice, and J. A. Leinaweaver. J. R. Shuler was their clerk. It is located on the road connecting Loysville with Landisburg, and the fine farm produces much of the edibles of the large family which is housed in the institution. Those who are not aged and whose health is good help in the many duties around the farm and home. The equipment belongs to the county. There is record of the court appointing visitors to the County Home during the period of 1850-1860.

The steward at this time is Robert Eaton, under whose management, with the able assistance of Mrs. Eaton, the Home is conducted in a practical manner. The building is neat, clean and in order, and the farm in good shape. The present board of directors is composed of G. W. Dunkle, of Duncannon; S. A. Shope, of Marysville, and E. M. Wilt, of Andersonburg.

The clerk and secretary to the board of directors from January 1, 1882, to January 1, 1911, was H. D. Stewart. Since then Samuel Ebert is the incumbent.

As showing some of its activities the following facts are copied from the financial statement of 1920: Seven outdoor physicians over the county were paid $189.75 for attending the poor. Six undertakers were paid $300 for burying eleven persons, all save one in other parts of the county. Merchandise amounting to $2,-627.54 was purchased for the institution, being mostly for food and clothing. The salaries and expenses of the three directors, the steward, the matron, the farmer, the clerk, the minister, the attorney, and the physician only total $2,058.82, surely a creditable showing. Products not used at the Home retailed for $1,051.37, which more than covered the cash expenditure of $1,005.53, for the current needs of the Home and farm. Outdoor relief checks totaled $1,295, and outdoor relief through stores amounted to $191.06.

The number of inmates at the Home in the beginning of the year was fifty-six, twenty-six males and thirty females. During the year three males and three females were admitted. Two were dismissed and one died, which closed the year with twenty-six males and thirty-three females. Tramps were relieved to the number of 150, one being a female. During the year the following clothing and bedding were made at the Home: 100 sheets, 100 pillowcases, 25 bedspreads, 10 chaff ticks, 75 towels, 6 tablecloths, 58 aprons, 19 dresses, 15 comforts, 12 pillows, and 10 children's dresses.

The farm produced 600 bushels of wheat, 1,000 bushels of oats, 2,500 baskets of corn in the ear, four bushels of clover-seed, 500 bushels of potatoes, five bushels of sweet potatoes, six bushels of turnips, fifteen bushels of onions, fifty bushels of tomatoes, and 2,000 heads of cabbage, besides all the small garden vegetables used at the Home. The pork dressed, weighed 6,000 pounds, and the beef, 900 pounds.

At the formation of the new county the first steward was George Hackett. Beginning in 1839—the records prior to that having been destroyed by the fire which burned the building—the stewards were:

1840-43—Daniel Minich.	1870-74 —Joseph S. Bistline.
1844-50—Benjamin Rice.	1875-76 —Isaac B. Trostle.
1851 —H. Kleckner.	1876-79 —Henry P. Lightner.
1852-54—Benjamin Balthauser.	1879-82 —T. P. Orner.
1855-57—Jacob Balthauser.	1882-90 —P. G. Kell.
1858-59—Samuel P. Campbell.	1890-1911—John R. Boden.
1860-62—Thomas W. Morrow.	1911-12 —Irwin I. Rice.
1863-66—John Hopple.	1912-14 —Wm. J. Rice.
1867-69—Jeremiah Minich.	1914- —Robert J. Eaton.

The following paragraph, from the *Perry Forester,* of April 14, 1824, tells of the removal of the first of the inmates of Cumberland County, by the officials of that county:

"About forty of the paupers belonging to Cumberland County, passed through Landisburg this morning from the poorhouse in this county, on their way to Cumberland, attended by the commissioners and some of the overseers of that county. About ten of the Cumberland poor have been left by the overseers to be boarded, which makes about twenty in all, in the Perry County poorhouse at present." That word pauper is happily no longer in use in the county press.

CHAPTER XIX.

POSTRIDER AND STAGECOACH.

CARVED in large granite letters along the Eighth Avenue side of the massive New York post office building is this inscription:

> "Neither rain nor snow nor heat nor gloom of night stays these couriers from the swift completion of their appointed rounds."

Herodotus, who lived some twenty-five centuries ago, was the author of those words, but he was referring to the military couriers of the Persian Cyrus—tireless horsemen who sped from place to place throughout the empire. And yet they seem not inappropriate to the army of postmen from the time of the postrider down to their present-day successors in city and country or to those tireless workers who work through the night on speeding trains, distributing the mails for the four corners of the earth. When storms rage and equinoctial torrents fall the city carrier and rural delivery man are on their "appointed rounds." They are the only representatives of the great United States government who come to every man's door.

When Cumberland County was established in 1750 there was no regular post from Philadelphia, neither did such exist at the time of the Albany treaty in 1754, nor when the first settlers warranted lands in what is now Perry County a year later. The troubles with the Indians were largely responsible for the establishment in 1757 of a weekly horseback post, history recording it as "intended to better enable the governor and the assembly to communicate with 'his majesty's' subjects on the frontier." The first regular post from Philadelphia to New York started in 1756, and from Harrisburg to Pittsburgh, in 1786.

Just when the first route was established that carried the mails to Perry County territory is unknown, but in 1798 Postmaster General Joseph Habersham issued proposals for carrying the mails, *once in two weeks,* over the following routes: "From Harrisburg, by Clark's Ferry, Millerstown, Thompsontown, Mifflintown, Lewistown, Huntingdon, Alexandria, Bellefonte, Aaronsburg, Mifflinburg, Lewisburg, Northumberland, and Sunbury to Harrisburg. The mail to leave Harrisburg from October 15 to April 15, every other Monday at 6 o'clock a. m.; returning the next Monday, by 7 p. m. Other seasons of the year in proportion to days' length."

With the turnpike came the stagecoach, considered a great affair in that day. They continued to run until the advent of the packet boat and even then ran during the winter months when the canal could not be operated. John and James Patterson, of Millerstown, drove the stagecoach which operated between that place and Clark's Ferry about the time of the building of the canal. A whip with four-in-hand was then the admiration of the youngsters, as are aëroplanes of to-day. So regularly did they run upon schedule time that residents of the wayside referred to their passing to set their clocks, we are told.

In the days when the mails between Philadelphia and Pittsburgh were carried by stagecoach a Perry Countian had a unique experience. Isaiah Clark, a Millerstown merchant, was on his way to Philadelphia to purchase goods, and when near Philadelphia the stagecoach was held up by three outlaws known as Wilson, Poteet, and Porter. According to the late John A. Baker's version of the affair, Clark counseled the occupants to resist, as the stage was well filled. With pointed pistols facing them, however, all stood while they were searched and robbed. One man hastily secreted his purse in one of the cushions by ripping it and thus saved his belongings. The mail pouch was rifled, which at that time was a capital offence. The robbers being apprehended, Wilson and Poteet are said to have been hanged. Porter, who turned "state's evidence," was pardoned by President Andrew Jackson.

The earliest record of an effort to run a stage line into the county was made in 1808, announcement to the public being made as follows:

JUNIATA MAIL STAGE.

The subscribers beg leave to inform the public. that on the 3d day of May next, their Stage will commence running from Harrisburg by the way of Clark's Ferry, Millerstown, Thompsontown, Mifflintown, Lewistown, Waynesburg, and Huntingdon, to Alexandria, once a week. Leave the House of Mr. Berryhill, Harrisburg, every Tuesday, at 1 o'clock p. m., and arrive at Alexandria on the Friday following; returning, leave Alexandria every Saturday morning and arrive at Harrisburg on Tuesday morning.

As the company have procured elegant and convenient Carriages, good Horses, and careful drivers, they flatter themselves that the passage of those who may please to favor them with their custom, will be rendered safe, easy and agreeable.

Fare for travelers, 6 cents per mile, each entitled to 14 pounds baggage, gratis; 150 pounds baggage equal to a passenger.

JOHN WALKER,	GEORGE MULHOLLAN,
JOHN M'CONNELL,	THOMAS COCHRAN,
GEORGE GALBRAITH,	JOHN M. DAVIDSON,

April 14, 1808. ROBERT CLARK.

N. B. Horses and chairs will be procured at the different towns, for those passengers who wish to go off the road or proceed further than Alexandria.

On the afternoon of May 3 the stage "Experiment" arrived at Clark's Ferry, crossed Duncan's Island and arrived at Millerstown before nightfall. Such was the beginning of an enterprise which was to continue many years and which was in that day an innovation. The route was later extended to Pittsburgh and connected with a similar one at Harrisburg for Philadelphia.

In April, 1828—twenty years later—this line of stages began running daily from Harrisburg to Pittsburgh. In the meantime it had progressed from once a week to three times a week. About 1830 the three sections of stage lines was converged into two, with the terminus of each at Huntingdon, the eastern section being operated by Calder, Wilson & Co. Passengers were then conveyed from Philadelphia to Huntingdon in two days, and from Huntingdon to Pittsburgh in three and a half days. By 1832 it had so far advanced that passengers arrived at Huntingdon by 4 o'clock of the second day, and at Pittsburgh by evening of the third day. To attain this speed the coaches ran both day and night, as the trains do. At this same period an accommodation line was run by day from Harrisburg to Pittsburgh, making the trip three times a week and consuming three and a half days.

Nature then was the same as now, and the elements frequently caused serious delays in the mails, sometimes as much as several days. The line was not without competition, and with the building of turnpikes during the period was enabled to progress as it did.

Before the organization of Perry County, on May 26, 1817, and also in 1819, J. Meigs, then postmaster general, advertised for bids to carry the United States mails over seventy-one routes in Pennsylvania, among which were the following routes through or contiguous to Perry County territory:

Route 49. From Harrisburg by Halifax, Selinsgrove and Sunbury, to Northumberland, twice a week, 55 miles. Leave Harrisburg every Sunday and Wednesday at 4 a. m., and arrive at Northumberland next day by 11 a. m. Leave Northumberland every Monday and Friday at 2 p. m., and arrive at Harrisburg next day by 6 p. m.

Route 68. From Harrisburg by Clark's Ferry, Millerstown, Thompsontown, Mifflintown, Lewistown, McVeytown and Huntingdon to Alexandria, twice a week, 100 miles. Leave Harrisburg every Tuesday and Saturday at noon, and arrive at Alexandria Thursday and Monday by 6 p. m. Leave Alexandria every Saturday and Thursday at 6 a. m., and arrive at Harrisburg Tuesday and Saturday by 9 a. m.

Route 70. From Carlisle by Wagner's Gap, Landisburg and Shower's Mill to Douglas' Mill, once a week, 24 miles. Leave Carlisle every Friday at 5 a. m., and arrive at Douglas' Mill by 2 p. m. Leave Douglas' Mill every Thursday at noon and arrive at Carlisle by 6 p. m.

Two years later, in 1819, the above routes were again advertised and the following one in addition:

Route 73. From Frederickstown, Maryland, by Creagertown, Maryland; Emmittsburg, Maryland; Gettysburg, Stary's, Carlisle, Shearman's Creek, Millerstown, Straubtown, Mt. Pleasant Mills and Selinsgrove to Sunbury, once a week, 129 miles. Leave Fredericktown every Tuesday at 2 p. m., and arrive at Sunbury Friday by 6 p. m. Leave Sunbury every Saturday at 6 a. m., and arrive at Fredericktown by Tuesday at 10 a. m.

At the time of the county's organization, in 1820, there was a weekly mail from Carlisle to Landisburg, according to an announcement in the initial issue of the *Perry Forester,* the new county's first newspaper, printed at Landisburg July 12, 1820. The first mails carried into the county and through it were carried on horseback. An original route ran through Landisburg to Carlisle, and that part of it exists to this day, having passed from horseback to stagecoach, and now to automobile. When first established the mail was carried over this route once a week, then twice a week, later three times a week, and for many years daily. As trails became roads so the old stagecoach, the prototype of the ones seen in present-day moving picture shows, succeeded the horseback method, and the celebrated Rice stage lines became known not only throughout Perry County, but over the state and in many other states. There are many men and women living today, not yet past their "early forties," who rode on these famous stages. The Rice family at Landisburg owned these routes and were the original mail contractors in the territory.

At the present time, early in 1920, the mails leave Landisburg in the morning, exchanging mails at Alinda and Shermansdale, in Perry County, and at Carlisle Springs, in Cumberland County (the latter service discontinued), returning in the afternoon. This and the Ickesburg-Newport route are the only original post roads yet in use in the county.

Another of these early contract routes where the mails were forwarded by horseback was from New Germantown to Landisburg. The first contractor was William Gray, whose nephew, Wilson W. Morrison, carried the mails in saddlebags thrown across the horse's back. This was about 1853, as near as Mr. Morrison can recollect, for with Mrs. Morrison, he still resides at New Germantown. The distance was about seventeen miles, and the courier left New Germantown at seven in the morning and returned about six in the evening, stopping for the exchange of mails at Loysville, Centre, Andersonburg, and Multicaulisville (now Blain). He first carried it once a week, and later twice a week. The late W. H. Waggoner (1919) distinctly remembered the boy postrider on this route. Samuel Ebert, of Loysville, also distinctly remembers when it was carried by Mr. Morrison in saddlebags, in 1848, on its weekly trip, each Saturday. Samuel Lupfer, born 1825, carried the mail when a boy from, New Bloomfield to Milford (now

Wila). In 1851 there was a similar horseback route from Ickesburg to Landisburg, Roseburg being served on the way, with the late Prof. Wm. C. Shuman as postboy. Jacob Shuman was the contractor. Long years afterwards Prof. Shuman recalled swarms of locusts, which often struck him in the face while riding the mail route, that being "locust year." Jacob and Henry Stambaugh were early postmen out of Landisburg.

As recent as "the late sixties" (prior to 1870) a stagecoach made two trips a week over the mountain from New Germantown to Concord, Franklin County, carrying the United States mail and passengers. Later it was changed to three trips a week. Some of the original patrons still reside along the route.

According to a tradition, which is in all probability true, there was once a through mail route to the West via Liberty Valley and through what is now the McClure State Forest. According to a state forest report one of the main forest roads has been developed from this original trail or route.

In the original issue of the *Perry Forester*, dated July 12, 1820, appears the following advertisement, which shows the method of travel of the period:

Harrisburg and Bellefonte

Mail Stage.

This line will commence running on the

First Day of April

next. The Stage will leave Buffington's Inn, at Harrisburg, every Friday at noon, and arrive at Bellefonte every Sunday afternoon; returning, leave Bellefonte every Wednesday morning, and arrive at Harrisburg every Friday morning.

Fare For Passengers.

From Harrisburg to Clark's Ferry,	$1.00
From Clark's Ferry to Millerstown,	1.00
From Millerstown to Lewistown,	2.00
From Lewistown to Bellefonte,	2.00
From Harrisburg to Bellefonte,	6.00

Way passengers, 7 cents a mile; 17 lbs. of baggage allowed to each passenger—all above that weight to be charged as follows: 150 lbs. at the rate of proportion. All baggage at the risk of the owner.

Clark's Ferry, March 17, 1820.   ROBERT CLARK & Co.

The Huntingdon, Juniata Mail Stage leaves Harrisburg as usual every Tuesday at noon.

Two years later a stage line was put on between Clark's Ferry (now Duncannon) and Concord, Franklin County, as the following announcement, also from the *Perry Forester*, will show:

Clark's Ferry, Landisburg and Concord.

United States Mail Coach.

This line has commenced running—

The coach will leave Clark's Ferry every Wednesday morning at 4 o'clock, passengers take breakfast at Landisburg and arrive at Concord the same evening. Returning leaves Concord on Thursday morning and arrive at Clark's Ferry the same evening.

The line is connected with the Northern route to Pittsburg, so that passengers can go on to Harrisburg without delay.

Fare For Passengers.

From Clark's Ferry to Landisburg,	$1.00
From Landisburg to Concord,	1.25
Way passengers, per mile,	.06¼

Fourteen pounds baggage allowed to each passenger—all packages above that weight to be charged as follows: 150 lbs. at the weight of a passenger, greater or less weight in proportion. All baggage at the risk of the owner. Robert Clark.

April 11, 1822.

The *Perry Forester* announced this route May 10, 1821, but it appears not to have started until March 6, 1822. The original announcement called for a route "from Clark's Ferry via Landisburg, Douglas' Mill, and Concord, to Fannettsburg."

Robert Clark, of Clark's Ferry (now Duncannon), on October 23, 1822, announces a stage line from Bellefonte, Philipsburg, Franklin, and Meadville. On March 23, 1825, a line was announced as starting from Clark's Ferry, through New Bloomfield via Ickesburg, to Landisburg, the first day; to Concord via Douglas' Mill (Blain), the second day; back to Ickesburg via Landisburg the third day, and to Clark's Ferry via Bloomfield the fourth day.

There was once a mail route from Liverpool to New Berlin, Union County.

On June 12, 1828, another route was announced through the new county. It was to leave Millerstown at 6 o'clock on Thursday and pass through Milford and Bloomfield to Landisburg, returning the same day. On Friday at 6 o'clock it was to leave Millerstown, going via Liverpool, Montgomery's Ferry, Thompson's Crossroads, and Clark's Ferry, to Bloomfield. The next morning, Saturday, it was to start from Bloomfield and go to Carlisle via Landisburg and Sterrett's Gap. Clark abandoned the lines after a time and the mails were again carried by postriders until the advent of the Rice stage line.

The mails, when first started to be carried with any regularity, were carried once every two weeks, and then by horseback. The route from Harrisburg to Huntingdon required four days' travel each way. One of the offices was at Clark's Ferry, then where Clark's Run enters the Susquehanna at what is now Duncannon. Storms, freshets with impassable streams, icebound streams and the "indisposition" of the carrier caused innumerable delays.

Upon the completion of the Pennsylvania Canal in 1829-30 a line of daily packets was put on from Columbia to Harrisburg by

Calder & Wilson, and the mails came to Columbia by rail, to Harrisburg by packet, and continued further by stagecoach, more remote sections using the horseback method. The packets ran until superseded by the railway service in 1849. It may interest the reader to know that the first overland mail route was only inaugurated April 3, 1860, when a rider and pony left St. Joseph, Missouri, and arrived at Sacramento, California, April 11th. This route later used stagecoaches. When ponies were yet in use and the mail carried in saddlebags William F. Cody (Buffalo Bill) was one of the riders. The postage was $5 per half-ounce and 200 letters were carried on the initial trip. In 1861, according to the provisions of a bill passed by Congress the rate for letters to the Pacific slope was made 10 cents.

In early days there were no envelopes, nor postage stamps, and a return from Perry County to the state in 1826 is cited as an example. It was not enclosed in any envelope or wrapping, but was sealed with red sealing wax, the method then in use, and marked Landisburg, Pa., 1826. It was addressed to David Mann, Auditor General, and on one corner, underscored, are the words "On Public Service." Opposite that, in place of stamps, the figures "12½." Another document is addressed to Jacob Huggins, Esq., Member of Assembly, Harrisburg. It is sealed the same way and is marked "Clark's Ferry, July 21, 1825." It is a petition to have a justice of the peace appointed for New Bloomfield, the county seat, and states that "the jail is completed and the prisoners confined therein; we are in such cases compelled to go miles to the nearest justice." John Harper was appointed.

Postage stamps were first used in 1847. The postage rate had been fixed in 1790 at six cents per half-ounce for thirty miles, and were graduated up until the rate was twenty-five cents for four hundred miles or more. The first great reduction in postage was in 1845, when the rate upon letters was made five cents per half-ounce for less than three hundred miles, and ten cents for greater distances. In 1851 letter postage was decreased to three cents for distances less than 300 miles, and in 1855 prepayment of postage was made compulsory.

The whole post office idea originated with John Hamilton, of New Jersey, whose father was Andrew Hamilton, governor of the Province of Pennsylvania from 1701 to 1703. Philadelphia had no post office until 1700. Jonathan Dickinson announced in 1717 that "a regular post has just been established between Virginia and the northern colonies, once a month in summer, and once in two months in winter."

The inauguration of a number of the old Perry County stage lines dates to the following periods:

Landisburg to New Germantown, 17 miles, in 1855, with Zach. Rice, Jr., as contractor.

Landisburg to Newport, 17 miles, in 1852, with Zach. Rice, Sr., as contractor.

Ickesburg to Newport, 16 miles, in 1864, with Samuel L. Rice as contractor.

Ickesburg to Millerstown, 12 miles, in 1864, with Samuel L. Rice as contractor.

On January 10, 1856, the Post Office Department advertised for bids for carrying the mails over the following routes, for four years, from July 1, 1856, to July 1, 1860:

From Newport, by Juniata (now Wila), Bosserman's Mills (now Markelville) and Roseburg, to Ickesburg, 16 miles and back, three times a week, Mondays, Wednesdays, and Fridays.

From Newport, by New Bloomfield and Elliottsburg, to Landisburg, 19 miles and back, six times a week.

From Elliottsburg, by Andesville (now Loysville), Centre, Andersonburg and Blain, to New Germantown, 18 miles and back, twice a week, Tuesday and Friday. (Just before starting the contract, on June 25, this was changed to tri-weekly.)

From Millerstown, by Donally's Mills, to Ickesburg, 14 miles and back, three times a week.

Zachariah Rice, Sr., was awarded the contracts, and subcontracted the routes, principally to his sons. In fact, Mr. Rice was one of the largest mail contractors in the state, at a little later period. At one time he had over five hundred contracts, the great majority of which he sublet. The Perry and Cumberland County routes, however, were operated by him and his sons, of which he had seven. These Rice brothers are remembered by many people yet in middle life whose first glimpse of the outer world came after an overland trip in one of the Rice stages. They were Samuel L. Rice, Jesse Rice, William Rice, Henry C. Rice, James C. Rice, Zachariah Rice II, and Joseph A. Rice. Several of them, in turn, had become large mail contractors in far-away states. In inland hamlet and town in Perry County these famous Rice stages were awaited just as anxiously in their day as are the overland trains of to-day, with their missives of love and devotion and those other tidings which bring pain and anguish to the human heart. Their rumble is but a memory.

Once, during the period from 1860 to 1870, the Rices were outbid and they then continued the stage line from New Germantown to Newport on their personal account, the passage between the two points dropping to as low as 25 cents. The Newport-New Bloomfield line was discontinued in 1892.

With the advent of the railroads mail began to be carried in pouches to and from central distributing points, Harrisburg being that point in so far as Perry County was concerned, but in 1864, the railway postal service was inaugurated with the distribu-

24

tion of letters and other mail en route, a system which had become so perfected by the end of the past century that it was a marvel. Through the distribution of the mails on moving trains, when arriving at an important junction point like Pittsburgh, the mails are all routed and ready for dispatch over the various connecting railroads to all points of the compass. The system is the work of no one man, but is the result of experiment and many different men's minds for over a half century. Almost a half hundred Perry Countians find employment in this branch of the government service.

Since the termination of the World War of 1914-18 a number of different routes throughout the United States have been established for the carrying of the mails by aëroplane, but without material success. They are more or less of a novelty and are not practical yet, and it is to be doubted if they ever will be. Their cost far exceeds any material advantage to be gained. From the two crests of Berry's Mountain at and opposite Mt. Patrick, where it is broken by the Susquehanna River, there is suspended a mighty strand of telephone wire. On September 7, 1920, one of these through mail flyers, passing low and following the river through the fog, struck this long wire and was instantly killed, his machine being wrecked upon the rocks of the river.

Some Early Post Offices.

A volume known as "The Gazetteer of Pennsylvania," published in 1832, contains a list of all the post offices in Perry County, with the incumbents at that period. The list:

Andersonburg, James R. Morrison.	Liverpool, James Jackman.
Beelen's Ferry, Francis Beelen.	Millerstown, Edward Purcell.
Clark's Ferry, Eleazer Owen.	Montgomery's Ferry, Wm. Montgomery.
Douglas' Mills, Anthony Black.	
Elliottsburg, Henry C. Hackett.	New Bloomfield, Joseph Duncan.
Ickesburg, William Robert.	New Buffalo, John Livingston.
Juniata, John W. Bosserman.	New Germantown, James Ewing.
Juniata Falls, Alexander Watson.	Newport, Ephraim Bosserman.
Junction, John B. Klein.	Oak Grove Furnace, John Hays.
Landisburg, Francis Kelly.	

The locations of some of these offices will puzzle many. Beelen's Ferry was on the Juniata near present Bailey Station, in Miller Township. Clark's Ferry was at the west end of that ferry at its early landing at Clark's Run, near the centre of Duncannon Borough, in the house now owned and occupied by Joseph Smith. Duncannon and even Petersburg did not then exist. Douglas' Mill was where Blain is. Juniata was at Milford, now Wila post office. Juniata Falls was at the Patterson tavern, now Lewis Steckley's, in Howe Township, on the Allegheny turnpike. Junction was at the junction of the Juniata and Susquehanna Rivers, in Watts Township. The other places named are known to the present generation.

Opposite this lower location of Clark's Ferry, right below the point of Peters' Mountain, was the location of another post office, known at that time as Peters' Mountain, the location being in Dauphin County.

The Douglas' Mill office was the successor of Moreland's, established in 1820, mentioned in the *Perry Forester* of November 25, 1820. Ickesburg was also established that year. Montgomery's Ferry is spoken of as early as 1821. There was once an office at Thompson's Crossroads, in Watts Township. In September, 1827, John H. Thompson was appointed postmaster there.

There was also a post office known as "Mumper's Farm," as the *Perry Forester* of June 8, 1826, tells of its being removed to New Germantown and Robert Kerr's appointment as postmaster. The post office at Milford (then Jonestown) was opened in March, 1827, but was called "Blacksford," with Samuel Black as postmaster. In December of the same year its name was changed to Juniata, and Samuel Beaver was appointed postmaster The post office at Juniata Falls, Buffalo Township (now Howe), was opened in June, 1828, with Alexander Watson as postmaster, and Elliottsburg, in July, 1828, with Henry C. Hackett as postmaster. That known as "Junction," was opened in July, 1830, with John B. Klein as postmaster. It is described as being "above the point where the Northumberland and Juniata Canals unite." During the same year, or early in 1831, an office was established at "Oak Grove Furnace," with John Hays as postmaster. Early in 1834 an office was opened at Roseburg, with Thomas J. Stevens as postmaster. There was once a post office at Bailey Station, called Bailysburg, but it was discontinued in 1855.

An official list of the post offices located within Perry County at this time are as follows:

Alinda.	Ickesburg.	Millerstown.
Andersonburg.	Landisburg.	New Bloomfield.
Blain.	Liverpool.	New Buffalo.
Centre.	Logania.	New Germantown.
Cisna's Run.	Loysville.	Newport.
Duncannon.	Markelville.	Shermansdale.
Elliottsburg.	Marysville.	Wila.
Green Park.		

The total number is twenty-two. The last ones discontinued were Saville and Montgomery's Ferry. About the time of the introduction of the rural delivery service there were fifty-two.

With the advent of rural delivery many Perry County post offices were discontinued. In 1890 there were fifty-two offices, as follows:

Acker.	Green Park.	Mount Patrick.
Alinda.	Grier's Point.	Nekoda.
Andersonburg.	Hench.	New Bloomfield.
Berlee.	Ickesburg.	New Buffalo.
Bixler.	*Juniata.	New Germantown.
Blain.	Keystone.	Newport.
Centre.	Kistler.	Pfoutz Valley.
Cisna Run.	Landisburg.	Reward.
Cove.	Lebo.	Roseburg.
Dellville.	Liverpool.	Sandy Hill.
Donally's Mills.	Logania.	Saville.
Dromgold.	Loysville.	Scyoc.
Duncannon.	Mannsville.	Shermansdale.
Elliottsburg.	Markelville.	Sterrett's Gap.
Erly.	Marsh Run.	Walsingham.
Eshcol.	Marysville.	Wardville.
Falling Springs.	Millerstown.	*Wila.
Ferguson.	Montgomery's Ferry.	†Olmsted.

ESTABLISHMENT OF THE RURAL ROUTES.

There are twenty-seven rural mail routes starting from Perry County post offices, serving the population of Perry and some of the residents of Dauphin, Juniata, and Snyder Counties, as follows: Andersonburg, Blain, Elliottsburg, Marysville, and Ickesburg, one route each; Landisburg, Liverpool, Loysville, and Shermansdale, two each; New Bloomfield and Newport, three each; Duncannon and Millerstown, four each. The initiative action towards securing this service within the county is to be credited to Amos Fleisher, then of Oliver Township, and H. G. Swartz, of New Bloomfield. In the former case the route was granted, with George E. Fleisher, a son, as carrier of Newport route No. 1, and in the other, H. G. Swartz was himself appointed carrier of New Bloomfield route No. 1. These were the first two routes to be started in Perry County and began the same day, July 1, 1903. The routes:

Route.	Established.	Original Carrier.	Present Carrier.
New Bloomfield:			
1	July 1, 1903	H. G. Swartz	Ernest M. Stambaugh.
2	Jan. 15, 1904	H. L. Soule	H. L. Soule.
3	Jan. 15, 1904	D. W. Bruner	P. S. Dunbar.
Newport:			
1	July 1, 1903	Geo. E. Fleisher	Geo. E. Fleisher.
2	Feb. 1, 1904	E. E. Taylor	E. E. Taylor.
3	Feb. 1, 1904	H. H. Deckard	H. H. Deckard.
Duncannon:			
1	Feb. 1, 1904.	M. C. Lindemuth	M. C. Lindemuth.
2	Nov. 15, 1904	Jno. W. C. Kugler,	Jno. W. C. Kugler.
3	Nov. 15, 1904	Chas. W. Mader	Max B. Lightner.
4	Aug. 1, 1905	C. Allen Depugh,	Ian M. Lightner.

*Juniata was later called Wila.
†Olmsted established some time later.

Millerstown:

  1......Nov. 1, 1904 .... Wm. A. Blain .... Wm. A. Blain.
  2......Nov. 1, 1904 .... Harry E. Walker .... Harry E. Walker.
  3......Jan. 2, 1908 ..... Sellers C. Nipple .... Sellers C. Nipple.
  4......Feb. 1, 1908 ..... Thos. J. Nankivell ... Thos. J. Nankivell.

Shermansdale:

  1.......1903 .... H. C. Gutshall .... H. C. Gutshall.
  2......1904 .... C. S. Henderson ..... C. S. Henderson.

Andersonburg:

  1......Jan. 15, 1904 .... John E. Lyons .... John E. Lyons.

Blain:

  1......Jan. 15, 1904 .... Miles D. Garber ..... Miles D. Garber.

Landisburg:

  1......Oct. 15, 1904 .... H. M. Rice .... H. M. Rice.
  2......Oct. 15, 1904 .... Wm. H. Eby .... May S. Lightner.

Marysville:

  1......Jan. 16, 1905 .... Newton L. Kapp* .... Edgar S. Smith.

New Germantown:

  1......Feb. 1, 1905 .... R. W. Johnston ...... R. W. Johnston.

Liverpool:

  1......April 15, 1905 ... L. C. Reifsnyder ..... Cleveland Hoffman.
  2......April 15, 1905 ... Jay W. Staley .... Jay W. Staley.

Elliottsburg:

  1......June 1, 1909 .... H. R. Foose .... H. R. Foose.

Ickesburg:

  1......June 1, 1914 .... J. Clair Gray .... J. Clair Gray.

Loysville:

Two routes were originally established at Loysville, with L. C. Bixler and W. C. Bailor as carriers. Mr. Bixler lost his life when his home burned, and Mr. Bailor resigned. Route 2 was then merged into route 1 and connecting routes, with Samuel D. Wilson as carrier.

Route 1, from the Liverpool office, is unique, delivering mail to four townships and three counties. It starts in Liverpool Township, Perry County, passes through Susquehanna Township, Juniata County, and Perry and Chapman Townships, in Snyder County, returning through Liverpool Township, Perry County.

The carriers of Perry County are progressive, and in 1911 succeeded in having the annual convention of the State Association of Rural Carriers meet at New Bloomfield, the only instance within our recollection where a state body convened within the limits of the county.

The annual salary of carriers in 1905 was graded from $504 for a twelve to fourteen mile route, to $720 for a route of twenty-four or more miles, the carrier to furnish and keep up his own conveyance. This service was first begun in Pennsylvania in 1896.

*Mr. Kapp resigned the Marysville route in September, 1905, and from December 20, 1905, to April 16, 1919, W. T. White was the carrier.

We are indebted to H. L. Soule for assistance in compiling the rural route data.

The following bit of verse may not be inappropriate here, written by one reared in that part of Perry so aptly termed "The Land Between the Rivers," and adapted from Colonel Shumaker's *Altoona Tribune:*

TWO PENNSYLVANIA RIVERS.

BY H. H. HAIN.

In the Allegheny foothills
    Where the Juniata starts;
In central Pennsylvania,
    Far from city street and marts,
There's a wooded land of beauty,
    Deep ravine and mountain crest,
Which the river just inherits
    As it rambles from the West.

In the rugged New York highlands
    Coming from a glistening lake,
The charming Susquehanna flows
    Through many a mountain break.
It waters vale and fertile plain
    As in volume it comes forth,
And crosses Pennsylvania,
    As it rambles from the North.

As these rivers gather body
    Since their sources they have fled,
They trend toward each other,
    Until they meet and wed;
And then, through gorgeous mountain gaps
    The waters swish away,
Until they lose identity
    In the bosom of the bay.

As the waters flow toward the sea,
    Through the very heart of the hills,
You can hear the intonations,
    From the rocky falls and rills,
Of the crafty, stealthy red man
    As he crooned an Indian song;
The very echo of the waters
    Has the sound of Indian tongue.

These Pennsylvania waters,
    Whose banks touch mart and mine,
Come from the very Northland,
    Crossing the "Mason-Dixon Line";
They've been flowing through the ages,
    Untold men have loved the streams
As they've wandered toward the ocean,
    Flowing through a land of dreams.

Harrisburg, Pa., July 2, 1921.

The Susquehanna River.

A writer of seventy years ago, in a magazine article, speaking of the Susquehanna, called it "the Alpha and Omega of Nature's gift to the State—the first and noblest in beauty as it is in extent and position." That writer's name has been lost to posterity, but the quotation will go down the ages. It is the longest unnavigable river on the American continent and traverses a veritable empire. On its way it receives the waters of the Unadilla, the Chenango, the West Branch, and the Juniata Rivers, and of many creeks whose names are often writ in Indian and pioneer annals: Penn's Creek, Sherman's Creek, the Conodoguinet, the Swatara, the Conewago, and the Conestoga. Passing farming districts where fine grains and fat cattle evidence the fertility of the soil, it passes mountain crag and peak, breaking through great mountains on its way to the sea. At Sunbury it kisses Shikellamy Heights, named after that old Indian chief who played so important a part in the history of the province, on one side, and Old Fort Augusta on the other. Leaving Perry County it passes through one of the famous water gaps and lazily flows by the State Capital—Harrisburg—named for a famous pioneer, and tumbles over the Conewago Falls, that ancient terror of rivermen. After its long journey over the lands of the immortal Penn, the founder of the greatest of states, it broadens into that majestic body of water, the Chesapeake Bay, later to join the broad Atlantic, where rides the commerce of a world.

The Susquehanna rises in New York State, Lake Otsego being its headwaters. New York State, it will be remembered, has many lakes, but Lake Otsego is noted as being the most beautiful from a scenic point of view, and the Susquehanna, true to form, has lavished beautiful scenery along its entire course—scenery unsurpassed anywhere. This lake is nine miles in length and over a mile wide, and James Fennimore Cooper, the author, says that "Deerslayer" called it "Glimmerglass." The town located on the lake is Cooperstown, named after Cooper, the famous author. Its principal tributary in New York State is the Chenango River, which joins at Binghamton.

The West Branch, the main tributary, rises in Cambria County, Pennsylvania, and joins the main river at Sunbury. The Susquehanna is really the most important river of Pennsylvania, it and its tributaries draining thirty-three of the sixty-seven counties of the state. It flows in a southerly direction and empties into the Chesapeake Bay. It was named by the Indians "Sa-os-que-ha-an-unk," meaning a "long, crooked river," says Heckewelder.

During the last half of the Seventeenth Century there were published a dozen or more different maps of the Atlantic slope section of Pennsylvania, and on almost all of them, on the western side of the Susquehanna, about where it is joined by the Juniata, appears the name "O-no-jut-ta Ha-ga," the headquarters or abode of an Indian tribe. According to experts Haga is the Mohawk word for people or tribe, and the first part of the name means a projecting stone. The similarity in sound between "O-no-jut-ta" and Juniata will be noticed.

The Susquehanna is over a half-mile wide passing Perry County. Geologists tell us that the land above the Blue or Kittatinny Mountains must at one time have been an immense lake, as the water gaps through the mountains would indicate. The Susquehanna is over four hundred miles long.

The first white man to navigate the Susquehanna River, was Captain John Smith, of Virginia. He sailed several miles up the river from the Chesapeake Bay, in 1608, being met by Susquehanna Indians who then inhabited Lancaster County. Smith said of the Indians, they are "of many kingdoms to the head of the bay, which seemed to be a mighty river issuing from mighty mountains, betwixt two seas."

From the north three Dutch settlers from Albany had come part way down the river in 1614, and had gone overland to the Lehigh and the Delaware. A Frenchman, Etienne Brule, in the service of Champlain, Canada's first governor, left the vicinity of Oneida, New York, in 1615, and spent the following winter exploring along the river "that debouches in the direction of Florida," and followed it "as far as the sea, and to the islands and lands near them." This description would indicate that he had crossed Pennsylvania and reached the Chesapeake Bay.

It is a historical fact that in the year 1723 some Germans from the Province of New York, leaving Schoharie, traveled through the forest in a southwesterly direction until they reached the Susquehanna, where they made canoes and with their families floated down the river until they reached the mouth of the Swatara, at Middletown. They then worked their way up the creek until they reached the Tulpehocken, where they settled.

In 1797 Louis Philippe, the Duke de Nemours, and the Duke de Berri visited Newtown Point, now Elmira, New York, having traveled on foot to that place from Canandaigua, a distance of seventy miles. They then went down the Susquehanna River upon an ark to Harrisburg, says French's *Gazette* of New York. This was probably the earliest record of long navigation upon its waters.

In September, 1700, William Penn bought all the Susquehanna country from the Indians, through Governor Dongan, of New York, for approximately five hundred dollars. Following is a copy of the deed:

"September 13, 1700; Widaugh and Andaggy-Junkquagh, Kings or Sachems of the Susquehanna Indians, and of the river under that name, and lands lying on both sides thereof, deed to W. Penn all the said river Susquehannough, and all the islands therein, and all the lands situate, lying and being on both sides of the said river, and next adjoining the same, to the utmost confines of the lands which are, or formerly were, the right of the people or nation called the Susquehannough Indians, or by what name soever they were called, as fully and amply as we or any of our ancestors, have, might or ought to have had, held or enjoyed, and also confirm the bargain or sale of said lands unto Col. Thomas Dongan, now Earl of Limerick, and formerly Governor of New York, whose deed of sale to Governor Penn we have seen."

However, this purchase seems not to have held, as later purchases of the same territory at different periods shows.

Before the building of the McCall's Ferry dam in the Susquehanna River, large numbers of shad came up the river every spring and there were a number of fisheries. In earlier years there were as many as four at Marysville. There was another at Duncannon, operated as late as 1900, and the Wrights operated one above Newport for many years. There were also a number of others.

The Susquehanna River touches the northeastern corner of the county five miles above Liverpool, and is its eastern boundary from that point until it touches the shores of Cumberland County, over thirty miles below. Its width varies very little covering this distance. Its waters are shallow and the only navigation on it are a number of ferries which cross, the ones at Liverpool and Millersburg being chartered and having regular traffic.

On entering the county it flows in an almost southern direction, until it touches Duncannon Borough, which is the most western point it strikes in the state. Here it bends sharply to the southeast, passing through the famous Susquehanna water gap, crossing the Cove section for a distance of five miles, where it breaks through a second water gap, that of the historic Second Mountain, above the Borough of Marysville and below the Borough of Dauphin. The fall of the river through the Cove is estimated at 1.58 feet per mile, and from the Cove to Rockville bridge, 2.69 feet per mile.

From Mahantonga, above Liverpool, to the Rockville bridge, or practically while passing the breadth of Perry County, a distance of thirty and one-half miles, the river has a total fall of eighty-one and one-half feet, or at the average rate of two and two-thirds feet per mile. Its average fall is said to be two feet to the mile on its long course.

There are three principal drainage rivers of Pennsylvania, the Ohio, the Susquehanna, and the Delaware. The Susquehanna drains far the largest acreage of the domain, as the following figures will testify: Delaware and tributaries, 6,710 square miles, 4,214,400 acres; Ohio and tributaries, 16,760 acres, 10,598,400 square miles; Susquehanna and tributaries, 21,390 acres, 13,685,600 square miles.

THE SUSQUEHANNA.

BY BENNETT BELLMAN.

Throw broad thy gleaming waters bright,
　O Susquehanna! in thy flow,
And let me lie and dream to-night
　Of days which once I used to know.
O river rolling from the dawn
　Of a new world and century,
Not yet, not yet, shall be thy song,—
　That in the future, yet must be.

O broad, blue river, in thy beams
　I see around me now the lands,
Already growing dim like dreams,
　In which are warring, savage bands.
They come again as in a dream,
　Their shadows moving to and fro;
And watch-fires on the hills that gleam
　In the red sunset's crimson glow.

Now like some gleaming sword all bright,
　Unsheathed by some great God of old,
Thou severest with thy liquid light
　The darkness which is round thee rolled.
The turbid Tiber still doth flow
　By temples, aqueducts and domes;
It but of dead days past doth know
　When heroes round it made their homes.

But thou, O river rolling on,
　It is the future which is thine;
A future when a brighter sun
　On brighter days shall proudly shine.
And in the distant years to come,
　Like fable, will it still be told
How a strange race, whose lips are dumb,
　Named thee in time, far passed and old?

THE JUNIATA RIVER.

The Juniata will ever live in song and story. There is music in its very name. Both branches, born in the foothills of the Allegheny Mountains, a part of the great Appalachian system, join and wind in and out by mountain crag and fertile valley, breaking through mountain ranges and introducing to the traveler as charming and picturesque scenery as nature has bestowed anywhere. Favorite haunt of Indian hunter; at different times the home of different tribes; its banks traversed by native trails later used by early traders; that primitive water-way—the Pennsylvania Canal —hugging its side; the standard railroad of America—like the canal, named after the great state, Pennsylvania—along its banks! Those are only milestones in the passing of the centuries of Juniata lore. Of its tales of love and devotion, of confidence and ambition, and of energy and success there will be no end so long as civilization exists and its waters flow towards the sea.

The Juniata River enters Perry County above Millerstown, cutting across the county to a point above Duncannon, where it joins the Susquehanna. The Juniata is formed by two branches, the main stream bearing the name Juniata, and the other being known as the Raystown Branch. The Juniata rises near Hollidaysburg, in Blair County, flowing northeast until it reaches Tyrone, where it turns abruptly to the southeast, forming for a little way the boundary between Blair and Huntingdon Counties, continuing in the same general direction through Huntingdon County.

The source of the Raystown Branch is a short distance west of Raystown, in Bedford County. Its general course is to the northeast until it unites with the Juniata, midway between Huntingdon and Mapleton, the two branches forming the Juniata River, proper. Flowing southeast it again forms a county boundary for a short distance, between Huntingdon and Mifflin. From Mount Union until Lewistown its trend is again northeast, but from that point through Juniata and Perry, until it joins the Susquehanna near Duncannon, its trend is generally southeast.

During the latter half of the Seventeenth Century a number of maps of the province and the Atlantic seaboard were published which showed the Susquehanna River practically correct, but giving little description of the country west of the Susquehanna. On practically all of them, on the west side of the Susquehannna, where the Juniata is located appears the words "Onojutta Haga," as described before. The French maps from 1700 to 1725 show a small stream there named "Cheneaide." Isaac Taylor, a Chester County surveyor, in 1701, made a map of the Susquehanna, on which he has marked the mouth of a large stream "Cheniaty."

To Heckelelder, the Moravian missionary, we are indebted for a slight description of the Juniata. He says: "This word (Juniata) is of the Six Nations. The Delawares say Yuchniada or Chuchniada. The Iroquois had a path leading direct to a settlement of Shawnees residing somewhere on this river; I understood where Bedford is. Juniata is an Iroquois word, unknown now. The Indians said that the river had the best hunting ground for deer, elk and beaver."

The word Juniata has been variously spelled by map makers, traders, provincial officials, interpreters, missionaries and historians, as Soghneijadie, Cheniaty, Choniata, Chiniotta, Chiniotte, Juniada, Scokooniady, Chiniotto, Juneauta, Joniady, Scohonihady, Schohonyady, Junietto, Juniatia, Juniatta, Junieta, Junitia, Juneata, Juniatto, Juneadey, Coniata, and Juniata, as it is spelled to-day. It was first used in the present form by the provincial secretary, July 7, 1742, according to provincial records.

Prof. A. L. Guss, of Juniata County, who devoted much time to the study of Indian legends, and traditions, says: "The name Juniata, like Oneida, is derived from onenhia, onenya, or onia, a stone, and kaniote, to be upright or elevated, being a contraction and a corruption of the compound." The name was handed down to the traders and pioneers, who probably never saw these old maps.

In the report of the Second Geological Survey of Pennsylvania, Prof. E. W. Claypole said:

"In ordinary weather the Juniata water carries about eight grains of earthy sediment, or about one pound for every one hundred cubic feet of water.

"In ordinary weather the Juniata water carries about eight grains of deep, with a current flowing about two miles an hour; that is twenty-four million cubic feet of water pass Millerstown every hour, carrying two hundred and forty thousand pounds (120 tons) of rock sediment. In other words, one million cubic yards of the rock waste of Juniata, Mifflin, Huntingdon, and Blair Counties pass through Perry County down the Juniata River to the sea every year. The water basin from which this river sediment comes measures about ten billion square yards. Its average loss per year is, therefore, about the ten-thousandth of a yard. If we take into account the gravel and stones rolled down the river in flood times, and carried down by ice, it will be safe to call it the five-thousandth of a yard.

"The whole surface of the Juniata country has, therefore, been lowered, say one foot in fifteen hundred years, or three thousand yards in thirteen million, five hundred thousand years; that is supposing the climate was always the same, and the Juniata River never did more work than it does now. But there is good reason for believing in earlier ages the erosion was more violent; this time may be reduced to ten, or even five million years."

The lands through which the Juniata flows are more or less hilly, its waters washing the base of many different mountains. Between these mountains are fertile and well watered valleys.

The Juniata of song and story! The very name of the river speaks of love and devotion, of pathos and poetry, and its romantic and enchanting scenery has on more than one occasion been the object of beautiful sketch or charming poem. While taking a trip along the Juniata on a packet boat, during the first half of last century, Marian Dix Sullivan wrote the words of the following poem, which were soon set to music, and a few of the older generation yet remember when The Blue Juniata was on the lips of every one, for in those days a new song was not turned out with each waning day. Marian Dix Sullivan, by the way, was a matron, the wife of John W. Sullivan, of Boston, whose father, General Sullivan, was a Revolutionary hero. She was a daughter of Timothy Dix, a sister of General John A. Dix, and also of Dorothea L. Dix, the great philanthropist who did so much for sick and wounded soldiers during the Sectional War. She was born near the beautiful Merrimac River, in New Hampshire, and died in

1860. While the title of her poem was The Blue Juniata, the song publisher put it out under the title of "Sweet Alfarata."

There is no great poetical merit in the lines, but they caught the popular fancy and were sung everywhere, throughout the States. Girls and pets and boats and other things were named Alfarata, and the name still survives. The frequency with which the name appears in the song is accounted for by the very few words that rhyme with Juniata. The poem follows:

THE BLUE JUNIATA.

BY MARIAN DIX SULLIVAN.

Wild roved an Indian girl,
    Bright Alfarata,
Where sweep the waters
    Of the Blue Juniata.
Swift as an antelope,
    Through the forest going,
Loose were her jetty locks
    In wavy tresses flowing.

Gay was the mountain song
    Of bright Alfarata,
Where sweep the waters
    Of the Blue Juniata;
Strong and true my arrows are
    In my painted quiver;
Swift goes my light canoe
    Adown the rapid river.

Bold is my warrior true—
    The love of Alfarata;
Proud waves his snowy plume
    Along the Juniata.
Soft and low he speaks to me,
    And then, his war cry sounding,
Rings his voice in thunder loud,
    From height to height resounding.

So sang the Indian girl,
    Bright Alfarata,
Where sweep the waters
    Of the Blue Juniata.
Fleeting years have borne away
    The voice of Alfarata,
Still sweeps the river on,
    The Blue Juniata.

Then, in 1865, came the sequel to "The Blue Juniata." Rev. Cyrus Cort was pastor of the First Reformed Church of Altoona— a mission at that time. He had organized it in 1862, and in the course of raising money to erect a church, made a number of trips along the Juniata. He wrote the poem on one of these trips in August, 1865. For long years afterwards he was the pastor of the Greencastle, Pennsylvania, Reformed Church, where the author of

this volume met him and heard him preach in 1891. He was a
man of fine physical proportions and an eminent divine. While he
had written the poem in August, it had remained a personal matter
with him until the following month, when, traveling overland from
Chambersburg to Mercersburg with Rev. Dr. Harbaugh in his carriage, he showed it to his distinguished host, who was the editor
of a magazine known as "The Guardian." Dr. Harbaugh insisted
on having the permission of publishing it, but not until early the
next year was it granted. It appeared in the March number, and
after that Dr. Cort wrote and had published many beautiful hymns,
poems, historical sketches, etc. He was much interested in the
gathering of historical data and of the marking of historical sites,
and, during the compilation of this volume, probably the greatest
compliment given the writer by a noted Pennsylvanian, himself a
pastmaster in the same line, was to have his interest in things historical compared with that of Dr. Cort. The words of his beautiful poem follow:

RESPONSE TO "THE BLUE JUNIATA."

BY REV. CYRUS CORT.

The Indian girl has ceased to rove
  Along the winding river;
The warrior brave that won her love,
  Is gone, with bow and quiver.

The valley rears another race,
  Where flows the Juniata;
There maidens rove, with paler face
  Than that of Alfarata.

Where pine trees moan her requiem wail,
  And blue waves, too, are knelling,
Through mountain gorge and fertile vale,
  A louder note is swelling.

A hundred years have rolled around,
  The red man has departed,
The hills give back a wilder sound
  Than warrior's whoop e'er started.

With piercing neigh, the iron steed
  Now sweeps along the waters,
And bears, with more than wild deer speed,
  The white man's sons and daughters.

The products, too, of every clime
  Are borne along the river,
Where roved the brave, in olden time,
  With naught but bow and quiver.

And swifter than the arrow's flight,
  From trusty bow and quiver,
The messages of love and light
  Now speed along the river.

The engine and the telegraph
  Have wrought some wondrous changes,
Since rang the Indian maiden's laugh
  Among the mountain ranges.

'Tis grand to see what art hath done,
  The world is surely wiser.
What triumphs white man's skill hath won
  With steam, the civilizer.

But still, methinks, I'd rather hear
  The song of Alfarata—
Had rather chase the fallow deer
  Along the Juniata.

For fondly now my heart esteems
  This Indian song and story;
Yea, grander far old nature seems,
  Than art in all its glory.

Roll on, thou classic Keystone stream,
  Thou peerless little river;
Fulfill the poet's brightest dream,
  And be a joy forever.

As generations come and go,
  Each one their part repeating,
Thy waters keep their constant flow,
  Still down to ocean fleeting.

And while thy blue waves seek the sea,
  Thou lovely Juniata,
Surpassing sweet thy name shall be,
  For sake of Alfarata.

SHERMAN'S CREEK.

Just as Sherman's Valley is the most important valley locally to Perry County, so is Sherman's Creek the most important stream. Like the valley of the same name, which it drains, it is supposed to have been named after an early settler, but records veil the fact in obscurity. Clarence W. Baker, a noted local historian who resided at New Bloomfield and assisted his father in editing The *Freeman*, said the stream was named after an old Indian trader named Sherman (or Sheerman), who plied his vocation in that particular territory many years ago. He is said to have been a veritable "Leather Stocking," sleeping outdoors and killing as many as sixty deer in a season. He and his horse were drowned in the creek which bears his name, at Gibson's Rock, through the animal being hampered with packs of furs. The writer is inclined to give credence to this story. The source of Sherman's Creek is variously given, but through Forester Bryner, who is familiar with every foot of the territory, its actual source is authoritatively given.

Its headwaters rise in the mountains of Toboyne Township, in the extreme western part of Perry County. The general opinion is that the real head of the stream is in a swampy area on the northwestern slope of the Rising Mountain, known as "the bear ponds." These ponds are located in a depression in the mountain which forms a small basin, being drained by what is locally known as Patterson Run. In wet seasons "the bear ponds" overflow and contribute to this stream, but during dry seasons the ponds are usually reduced to small swampy patches of ground, and the main run is fed by a large spring near the southern terminus of the gap or cut through which the stream flows from the Rising Mountain, following a narrow ravine between the north slope of the Rising Mountain and the south slope of the Little Round Top. It emerges near the eastern base of the Big Round Top and unites at this point with what is locally known as the Barnhart Run. This run rises in a small valley formed by the union of the Big Round Top and the Conococheague Mountain. The big spring located approximately five miles west of New Germantown, on the south side of the state highway leading from the former place to Concord, is one of the principal feeders of the Barnhart Run, especially during dry seasons. From the junction of these streams Sherman's Creek flows in a northeastward direction through the Sherman's Valley, passing near the south side of New Germantown and continuing in the same direction towards Blain. In this distance it is fed by numerous small streams flowing from the north and south. In addition to the smaller streams, several larger streams which have their source in the mountains of the same township, contribute to the waters of this creek. Brown or Fowler Run, which rises in the head of Fowler Hollow, on the south side of the Rising Mountain at a point just a little west of "the bear ponds," on the Rising Mountain, flows northeastward through the Little Illinois Valley and empties into the creek at Mt. Pleasant. Houston Run and Laurel Run, which are still farther south, have their source practically as far west as the headwaters of Sherman's Creek and flow in the same direction through long narrow valleys parallel to the main Sherman's Valley, the Houston Run emptying into the creek approximately one mile southeast of Blain, and the Laurel Run emptying into the same stream about one mile west of Landisburg.

Sherman's Creek flows in an almost eastern direction, draining the greater part of western Perry County and emptying into the Susquehanna River at Duncannon. Its history dates back to provincial times, when it was crossed by the first main trail to the West, known as the Allegheny Path. Its main tributary is Montour's Run, named after the first authorized settler of Perry County soil. It is spanned by many bridges erected by the county.

25

Various floods have overflown its banks, but mention of them follows later in connection with the high waters on the rivers. Many gristmills line its banks; in fact, it was one of the original streams which drove the machinery of the many pioneer mills for which Perry County territory was noted and from along its banks flour was transported to the starving Continental armies. Many old-fashioned up-and-down sawmills also lined its banks. Along its banks in childhood there played children whose names have since graced the pages of history of many states of the Union and of the mighty nation itself. As noted elsewhere it was once made navigable for smaller craft by an act of the Pennsylvania Legislature. Scenic beyond description at many points its trend led it towards the Susquehanna River through Fishing Creek Valley, but the barrier of the famous Ironstone Ridge diverted it northward and it made a detour around Cove Mountain and enters the Susquehanna at Duncannon.

Other Streams.

Buffalo Creek. This historic stream, mentioned in Indian history, rises in Liberty Valley, Madison Township, and drains the northern section of western Perry, emptying into the Juniata above Newport. It also is spanned by several county bridges. It is noted for its picturesqueness. Its name perpetuates the fact that long years ago large herds of Buffalo once roamed the forests of our county's territory.

Little Buffalo Creek. Separates Juniata Township from Centre, flows through Oliver, and empties into the Juniata at Newport.

Little Juniata Creek. Originates in the extreme western part of Centre Township and flows through Centre, Wheatfield, Penn and Duncannon Borough to the Susquehanna.

Cocolamus Creek. Rises at the foot of Shade Mountain, near Evendale, in Juniata County, flowing through Greenwood Township, emptying into the Juniata River below Millerstown.

Montour's Run. See Sherman's Creek, above.

Raccoon Creek. In Tuscarora Township. Empties into the Juniata, near Millerstown.

Fishing Creek. In Rye Township. Flows into the Susquehanna at Marysville.

Horse Valley Run. This stream rises in Horse Valley, in western Perry, and flows through the Waterford Narrows, where the mountain breaks, passing into Tuscarora Creek, Juniata County. It is joined by Laurel Run from Liberty Valley, just before entering the narrows.

Jobson's Run. This stream rises in Liverpool Township and enters Greenwood Township, Juniata County, at the extreme southwest corner of that township, flows northwest and joins the west branch of the Mahantango Creek, northwest of Oriental, Juniata County.

McCabe's Run. Drains Kennedy's Valley.

Laurel Run. Drains Sheaffer's Valley.

Guntur Run. Guntur Run is the only stream that rises in western Perry and flows westward. Rising at the watershed it flows about one and one-half miles through Perry County soil and then crosses to Franklin County. It continues to near Forge Hill, turns south and flows through a gap in the Kittatinny, entering the Cumberland Valley north of Roxbury.

Other Streams. There are dozens of others in the various communities, mostly smaller ones.

From John L. McCaskey, a consulting engineer connected with the Westinghouse Electric Manufacturing Company of Pittsburgh, himself a native Perry Countian, comes the following expert opinion:

"Nature was niggardly in her treatment of Perry County in coal beds; not enough in any coal pockets, except to burn the fingers of the would-be operators, but lavish, doubly lavish in her sharing the gift of the white coal (electric motive force) in her scores and scores of waterfall in creeks and rivers. More, doubly so now, than could be used in furnishing power for operating mills and all farm machinery, besides lighting and also heating every church, school, dwelling, barn and all other necessary buildings. I safely predict that the residents of a century hence will not have a building unwired for both heat and light and that power will be used for all domestic purposes, including irrigation, to be secured by the mere throwing of a switch. Its citizens are already to be congratulated for utilizing in part, the unlimited supply of white coal. From it will be developed the utilization of air nitrates and other elements into abundant fertilization and the restoration of worn-out soils."

High Rivers and Floods.

Where rivers of the length and importance of the Juniata and Susquehanna exist, with huge basins draining continuous rainfall and accumulated melting snows, there will naturally be times when the raging waters attain the flood stage, for be it remembered that if the Susquehanna drained one more county it would drain the soils of over half of the counties of the commonwealth. The records available of high waters upon these rivers give the dates of the earlier floods as being in 1744, 1758, 1772, 1784-85, and 1787. Of the first three little information, save that the rivers were raging torrents, is left to posterity. During the winter of 1784-85 there was a flood known to this day as "the ice flood." Historical records fail to tell much about it save that "it carried away all fences and buildings on the lowlands." Near the mouth of Sherman's

Creek it carried away Marcus Hulings' gristmill. During the fall of 1787 there was a flood known as "the pumpkin flood," getting its name from the fact that in the Wyoming Valley it was severe and carried away many thousands of pumpkins from the fields of the Yankees, as the Connecticut farmers who had located there, were known. It is said that these innumerable pumpkins dancing on the waves and riding the tide "looked like so many jewels studding it." As the river receded the pumpkins were strewn in profusion over the lowlands.

Then there were the floods of 1800; August, 1814; August, 1817, 1840, 1846, 1847, 1865, 1867, 1868, 1881, 1889, and another great ice flood in 1920. On the Juniata there is mention of a "great overflow" in 1810, also known as a "pumpkin flood." Its worst havoc was in the vicinity of Mifflintown. Of these floods accounts are vague about those of 1800, 1814, and 1817. The flood of 1840, on the Juniata, carried away two spans of the Mifflintown bridge. The high waters of 1846 were at their worst on March 16. (Some authorities say March 18.) This flood reopened the channel above Duncan's Island which originally connected the Juniata and Susquehanna Rivers. Sherman's Creek, as usual, was higher the two previous days and swept away part of the Fio Forge dam, the puddle mill of the iron works at Petersburg (now Duncannon) and the Sherman's Creek covered bridge. All the bridges on Cocolamus Creek were swept away. The Juniata River bridge, above Duncannon, and the eastern span of the Susquehanna River bridge were also carried away. On May 14 of the same year the balance of the Susquehanna River bridge burned. It was rebuilt, and on September 10 and 11, 1850, was again entirely consumed by fire. On March 18, 1859, it was partially blown down. The bridge over the mouth of Sherman's Creek, swept away in 1840, was not rebuilt until 1846, an act of the Legislature of April 10th of that year having authorized the county commissioners to reconstruct it.

In September, 1847, the Juniata's waters were seething and carried away the bridges at McVeytown and Port Royal, two spans of the Mifflintown bridge (the second such occurrence), and the east half of the Millerstown bridge, which fell at 11 p. m. The Millerstown bridge was rebuilt during the winter by Isaac Kirkpatrick, who fell from the trestle work and was drowned under the ice. His son Garrett finished it, he being then less than seventeen years of age. Before he was twenty-one he contracted for and built the Newport bridge. The reader will recall that the bridges of this period were all covered wooden bridges. On May 11, 1860, the rolling mill dam on Sherman's Creek, near Duncannon, was washed away. The late William Wertz, of Newport, had a faint recollection of the flood of 1847, although he was but four years old. The unusual sight of folks going to and from their homes in boats is what impressed him.

The great flood of 1865 came tearing down the Susquehanna Valley on March 17th, 18th, and 19th, carrying destruction in its course. At Duncan's Island it swept away the building which was used jointly as a Methodist church and school building. The first story contained two schoolrooms, for in those days the island was more thickly populated, with boating and river traffic at their height. The second story had been added by the school board for a Methodist church, at the earnest solicitation of Rebecca Duncan, who stood the entire expense of its addition and its furnishing for worship. On the opposite side of the river, at Duncannon, the waters filled the first stories of the homes on Market Street as far north as Ann Street, to a depth of five feet. The Juniata bridge was in danger and the Duncannon Iron Company, which conducted a small railway over which its products were hauled from the island to the plant, ran their train of cars on it for its protection, but both bridge and cars were swept away. The iron company's warehouse on the island was also torn from its foundations and swept down the river. At Duncannon the waters were twenty-two feet above low water mark. *W. J. Roberts, yet living and now residing in South Dakota, was then employed in the vicinity and saw the bridge swept away. It landed on Wister's Island, below Duncannon. Surrounding the old stone tavern there were two barns and some other buildings, but when the waters receded the old stone tavern was found to be the only remaining structure. Buildings of all kinds went down the river in the torrent. Cornelius Baskins then again resumed operating the old ferry of his ancestors. On February 15, 1867, the eastern span of Sherman's Creek bridge at Duncannon was swept away. In 1868 the waters were again eighteen feet above low water.

In 1881 there was an ice flood on the Juniata, and for the third time two spans of the Mifflintown bridge were carried away. On February 11 it was at its height, and at 5 p. m. the two western spans of the Millerstown bridge went, and in their course carried with them the two western spans of the Newport bridge. Aaron Shreffler rebuilt these two spans at Newport, and the bridge was opened for traffic on October 8, 1881.

While Sherman's Creek is ordinarily a stream which peacefully flows along, carrying the waters of the larger part of western Perry, yet there have been times when it was a raging torrent, leaping over its banks and the adjoining meadows, a veritable river, wild with rage. In 1886, on January 4th and 5th, it reached its greatest height. At that time at the old Gibson mill, "West-

---

*Mr. Roberts died just previous to this book's going to press, early in 1922.

over," it rose to such a great height that it entered the lower doors of the mill, which stands across the meadws on a considerable elevation and is run by the waters of another stream. To realize its wildness at the time one must be familiar with the surroundings here described. This flood was the result of a three-day rain, combined with melting snow.

In its course through the county this flood carried away seven covered bridges, and at Duncannon it undermined and washed away a pier of the iron bridge of the Pennsylvania Railroad, dropping two spans and carrying away the engine and twelve cars of a freight train which was passing at the time. Eight of these cars belonged to the Duncannon Iron Company. Anthony Baldwin, the conductor; Henry McCahan, assistant conductor, and R. M. Turbett, brakeman, lost their lives while in the performance of their duties on the train. All three of the men were residents of Huntingdon, Pennsylvania, the train being known as the Huntingdon local. The engineer, Wm. Noel, and John S. Miller, conductor of the Duncannon Iron Company's ore train, which was combined with the other train, were swept away by the flood, but were rescued at Allen's Cove, some miles below.

The indebtedness of Perry County with the beginning of 1889 was comparatively small, but after several days of heavy and continuous rain, on May 30, 31, and June 1, came the great onrushing waters down Sherman's Creek, Buffalo Creek, the Juniata and Susquehanna Rivers and all their tributaries—the same flood which almost annihilated Johnstown, Pennsylvania—and washed away the bridges, including the three large covered wooden bridges at Millerstown, Newport, and Duncannon, with the result that the county debt grew to enormous proportions through their rebuilding. They had been made free many years ago, as had the toll roads. These river bridges connecting main highways should be a part of the state highway system and should be built by the state.

During the autumn of 1894, four years after the flood, the State Forestry Commission of Pennsylvania communicated with the commissioners of the various counties, asking them the cost of the repairs and renewals of highways and bridges damaged and destroyed by high water since and including the Johnstown flood. William B. Anderson, then clerk to the Perry County board of commissioners, itemized and submitted the following report, the cost totaling almost a hundred thousand dollars:

1889	$13,261.29
1890	53,764.10
1891	6,710.07
1892	11,848.92
1893	14,048.97
Total	$99,633.35

boatyard buildings and lumber and the lumberyard of Sweger & Shreffler. According to a reliable estimate the losses amounted to $204,600.

Mr. S. M. Shuler, a prominent Liverpool merchant, kept a diary during the greater part of his life, devoted chiefly to the weather, and from it the entries of June 1, 2 and 3, 1889, form a pen picture of conditions all along that noted river during this devastating flood. It follows:

June 1, 1889.—Boom logs commence running. A number caught here. River very high. Great amount of damage done in the town. The report is that two spans of the Millerstown and Newport bridges are gone. Newport partly under water. Only one train out of Liverpool, and that was the repair train from Sunbury, which removed the big slide below the station. A freight train passed up at 5:15. The logs running thicker than before. Millions and millions of dollars worth of property destroyed. Logs ran balance of day and no doubt all night, along with bridges and almost anything.

June 2, 7 a. m.—The river and canal one at George C. Snyder's and below town and still rising one and one-half inches an hour. Great destruction along the whole river.

9:30 a. m.—The river at a standstill. Water on the towpath in front of W. H. Miller's blacksmith shop.

10:30 a. m.—The river still on a stand and, from what D. Brink and F. Rowe say, wants about eighteen inches of being as high as in March, 1865.

12:00 m.—Logs still running.

2 p. m.—River commenced to fall. Great amount of damage all along the river and canal, but the most damage was on the Juniata River; it was five feet higher than ever known. Up to 4 p. m. the Juniata fell about eight feet, and the Susquehanna about six inches.

June 3.—River fell about two and a half feet last night. First freight down. Mail train down with daily papers. No mail.

During the onrush of the waters Mr. Shuler measured and recorded the rise and fall at periods covering June 1 and 2. The figures are here reproduced:

JUNE 1, 1889—RISE.

6 to 7	3½ inches	11 to 1 (2 hours)	5	inches
7 to 8	3 "	1 to 2	2½ "
8 to 9	3 "	2 to 3	2 "
9 to 10	2½ "	3 to 5 (2 hours)	3½ "
10 to 11	2½ "	5 to 6	1½ "

JUNE 2, 1889—RISE AND FALL.

6 to 7	1¾ inches	10 to 11	½ inch
7 to 8	1¼ "	11 to 12 on a stand.
8 to 9	½ "	12 to 1 on a stand.
9 to 10	½ "	1 to 3 fell 1 inch.

Heavy rains of March 4 and 5, 1920, caused the ice-bound Juniata to break on March 6 and take with it the ice upon the Susquehanna to a point near Covallen Station, on the Pennsylvania Rail-

road, below Duncannon, where the huge cakes of ice jammed into
a massive gorge, damming back the waters and inundating the low-
lying section of the town. The waters attained a depth of just
two feet less than in 1889 at this point. At this point the Pennsylvania Railroad tracks follow a high fill which extends far out
in the river from the original shore, and the waters reached its top
and sent whirling upon the railroad ton upon ton of ice. This is the
third serious ice flood of which there is record. The winter had been
a hard one and the ice was from twenty to thirty inches in thickness. The ice-bound Susquehanna and Juniata on this occasion
broke all records for extensive freeze-ups. The rivers were frozen
over on December 20, 1919, and successive cold waves only tight-
ened the artificial bridge which remained upon the Juniata until
March 6, 1920, or seventy-seven days, and upon the principal
course of the Susquehanna several days longer. Previous long
records of ice-bound waters on these rivers were in 1882-83 and
1917-18, the latter being during the period of the great World
War. Each of these winters the river was ice-bound but fifty-nine
days, and during each there were great misgivings as to what might
happen, but when the ice moved there were no great losses or
alarming incidents. The 1920 ice flood was at its worst at the
vicinity of Duncannon. The lower part of Duncan's Island was
inundated and considerable damage done to the cottage colony.
Below Duncannon there is an island in the Susquehanna, known
as Wister's Island, upon which resided the family of Jacob Auxt,
the island being a part of the Fred Smith dairy farm. Auxt refused to heed a warning and remained upon the island. He was
driven with his family to the second story and the waters finally
compelled him to vacate that and place the family upon the limbs
of a large cherry tree. A rescuing party from the mainland, headed
by J. R. McKibben, manager of the Perry County Telephone and
Telegraph Company, found the family wrapped in blankets,
perched upon the forks of the tree, where they had spent the
greater part of the preceding long and gloomy night.

There were very high waters at many other times upon these
rivers, but hardly to be named in the same class as those narrated
above. In February, 1882, the Susquehanna's waters were high,
and John W. Albright, of New Buffalo, undertook to row across
the river to Halifax. Unable to stem the tide he was being carried down the river to a sure death when he called for help. His
cries for help attracted one William Reed, upon shore, who secured
a rope, mounted a horse and rode to the Clark's Ferry bridge, six
miles down the river, where he dropped the rope to the waters
below and drew Albright to the bridge. He had been in the boat
two and a half hours during a blinding snowstorm. The point
where he was rescued was within three hundred feet of the breast

of the Clark's Ferry dam, where his small craft would have suffered destruction and where sure death awaited him.

Very high waters occurred within the county in September, 1843. Sherman's Creek and Buffalo and Little Buffalo Creeks overflowed their banks, and along Buffalo Creek Bosserman's mill dam and the county bridge at Milford were swept away. B. Waggoner's dam, on a branch of Sherman's Creek, and John Wormley's and Rev. Heim's mill dams. on Sherman's Creek, were also swept away, as was a bridge which crossed it in Madison Township.

EARLY PERRY COUNTY FERRIES.

With the Susquehanna River skirting the entire eastern boundary of the county, and with the Juniata cutting it into two sections it was necessarily the location of many ferries prior to the period of bridges. Of all the ferries for the transportation of vehicles, Crow's Ferry, below Liverpool, alone remains, and it is soon time that the great Commonwealth of Pennsylvania should erect a bridge there, as it is on a much-traveled route and as there is no bridge from Duncannon to Selinsgrove, a distance of thirty-five miles. As these old ferries were a part of the county's early life they are briefly described.

CLARK'S FERRY.

Those words to the present-day generation mean the small settlement at the east end of the Clark's Ferry bridge over Green's dam, now generally spoken of as the Clark's Ferry dam. To a former generation they had a different meaning. They meant the ferry, which crossed the Susquehanna from the end of Peters' Mountain to the point where Clark's Run flowed into the Susquehanna River, about the centre of the territory comprising Duncannon Borough. There the Indians had a fording, which they knew as "Queenashawakee," and there later the traders and the pioneers crossed, for it was on the first through road to Huntingdon and Pittsburgh. O'er it trailed the famed Conestoga wagon trains of that earlier day on their way to the Ohio Valley. With the increase of travel came a ferry. The Clarks operated it so long that the name became inseparably connected with it, and even later followed to the location above, over which crossed the boats of the Pennsylvania Canal. In 1808 it became a part of the route of the stagecoach line to Huntingdon and Alexandria.

John Clark, who lived at the west end of the ferry, has often been credited with having established the ferry. He had built many years before the stone tavern, which still stands and which is owned and occupied by Joseph Smith as a dwelling. The date of the establishment of the ferry has also been a question variously answered. That the ferry was established in 1788 and that Daniel Clark was the pioneer ferryman comes down the years through the starting of an opposition ferry by Francis Ellis, who evidently advertised his ferry and thus caused the following notice to be inserted in the *Oracle,* a paper printed in Harrisburg, in July, 1800:

"Clark's Ferry, fourteen miles above Harrisburg.—The subscriber has conducted the ferry for twelve years past without the assistance of newspaper bombast; but an advertiser in the last *Oracle* makes it necessary. Francis Ellis takes the liberty of inviting travelers to Mathias Flam's landing, where he has no right or privilege whatever, except that of usurpation and force, for which he and Mathias Flam both stand indicted. He also boasts of the sobriety and experience of his ferryman, additional buildings, &c., &c.

"All I wish to inform the public is that I am still in possession of both sides as formerly, with the same hands, same flats, and same buildings, ready to receive passengers on both sides. I hope my long experience and attention to this ferry may satisfy the public that no exertion will be wanting on my part to merit a continuance of their favors—and to defeat the efforts of this modern adventurer, and support the credit and interest of this ferry."   DANIEL CLARK.

Clark's Ferry Dauphin side,
    July 1, 1800.

There was also a tavern on the Dauphin side of this ferry, probably in the possession of this Daniel Clark. The ferry was in operation until 1838, when the Juniata Bridge Company erected a bridge, from which date its business rapidly told of the end. Before the days of the canal and railroads, over this ferry and the old turnpike passed the stream of Conestoga wagons, bearing the traffic of the early settlers and the merchandise of western Pennsylvania. In the old inn-yard could be seen often a dozen or more of these wagons, drawn by six or eight horses, which were being fed while awaiting their turn to be ferried. The Robert Clark, who was one of the proprietors of the pioneer stage line in 1808, was a son of John Clark, who kept the tavern at the western landing of the ferry, now the Smith house.

That the ferry was located at this old location in 1832 is proven by the following from Gordon's Gazetteer of Pennsylvania, published in that year: "Clark's Ferry (and post office), located upon the Susquehanna, below the confluence of the Juniata with the Susquehanna and above the town of Petersburg." Petersburg was the old or original part of Duncannon located adjoining the Juniata Creek and the Susquehanna.

THE BASKINS' FERRY.

The Baskins' Ferry, established at the Juniata's mouth, where the rivers meet, dates back almost to the first settlement. The exact date cannot be determined, but as early as the spring of 1767 the Cumberland County Court was presented with a number of petitions, among them being one to open a road "from Baskins' Ferry, on the Susquehanna, to Andrew Stephens' Ferry, on the Juniata," which shows that it was then already in existence. The Baskins' Ferry is here mentioned as on the Susquehanna. Its west shore could almost be considered that, as it was almost at the very mouth of the Juniata. It was owned and operated by James Baskins. It was at this old ferry that Capt. Alexander Stephens, grandfather of the noted Alexander H. Stephens, Vice-President of the Confederacy, first beheld and fell in love with the ferry-man's fair daughter, who later became his wife. The ferry was operated by various generations of the Baskins family until 1839, when the bridge over the river at that point was built. Cornelius Baskins, Sr., a grandson of James Baskins, then operated it. When the great flood of 1865 swept away the bridge Mr. Baskins at once reëstablished the ferry. It was during the time of the ending of the great Sectional War, and hundreds of government mules and horses were ferried across the Juniata. The rates charged were ten cents for a passenger, fifteen cents for each horse, twenty-five cents for a horse and carriage, and fifty cents for a team and conveyance. Over this early ferry went the trader, the itinerant missionary, the circuit rider, the tradesman, the drover, Indians, travelers, hunters and the varied traffic of that early day. Over the bridge at the same point now goes the traffic of the countryside, the tourist in palatial car and attendant traffic of another generation.

An act of the Pennsylvania Legislature passed April 12, 1866, recognized "Mitchell and Cornelius Baskins as having conducted a ferry at that point for over fifty years, and (as the bridge had been taken away by a flood) empowered them to make good and convenient landings on both sides, and as having the exclusive right. A provision of the act required that the fees be approved by the Perry County Courts. Cornelius Baskins had established a tavern in the stone house on the western bank, near the landing at one time. In connection with the ferry at this period the following may be of interest. When the bridge was swept away in 1865 it was not rebuilt. A special act of the Pennsylvania Legislature made its rebuilding mandatory by January 1, 1874, the cost not to exceed $18,000. A further act of April 10, 1873, allowed Perry County to borrow money for that purpose and be bonded for the amount. When the flood of 1889 again swept away the bridge Jacob Johnson reëstablished the ferry under the old charter of Cornelius Baskins and conducted it until the iron bridge was built. The poet has pictured the place in verse:

ON THE BRIDGE WHERE THE RIVERS MEET.

BY CHARLES JOHNS.

Years ago, when the wind was low
  And the east was dim with grey
And the west was red with the sunset glow,
  And the daylight ebbed away,
And never a sound came through the night
  Save the rush of the waters fleet,
I stood where I stand in the waning light,
  On the bridge where the rivers meet.

The years have come and the years have gone,
  And have left their marks on me;
But the river unchanged speeds gaily on
  To the ever changing sea;
The hills are unaltered far and near,
  And the still scene is complete;
I alone seem changed, and linger here,
  On the bridge where the rivers meet.

OTHER FERRIES.

Miller's Ferry. This ferry was established as early as 1788, for in that year an article in the Columbian Magazine mentions it. Its location was over the Juniata at Millerstown, and David Miller, who had purchased 222 acres of land where Millerstown is located, in 1780, was the owner. It was operated until 1839, when a bridge was erected over the river at that point. An earlier bridge company had been incorporated in 1814 to build a bridge over the Juniata "at Miller's Ferry, in Cumberland County."

Reiders' Ferry. The ferry across the Juniata River at Newport was established at an early day by Paul, John and Daniel Reider, sons of Paul Reider. The exact date of its establishment is unknown, but it was not prior to 1804, as in that year they only came into possession of the property, and statements show that it was started "after coming into possession of the property." During the war of 1812-14 this ferry was crossed by dispatch riders carrying messages from the National Capital to the Canadian frontier. It was in existence until 1851, when a bridge was erected at that point, although the Reiders' Ferry Bridge Company had been first chartered April 4, 1838.

Rope Ferry. The Rope Ferry was located at North's Island, between Millerstown and Newport, on the Juniata. It was so named by reason of the method of ferrying canal boats across the dam from the canal on one side to that on the other, as at that point all canal boats were taken across by a rope attachment, being further described in the chapter devoted to "River and Canal Transportation."

Fetterman's Ferry. Fetterman's Ferry crossed the Juniata, several miles east of the present site of Newport. The Howe Town-

ship end was known as Fetterman's Ferry, and the Miller Township end as Power's Ferry. At the Miller Township side was a
stone tavern, the walls of which still stand, on the Oliver Rice farm.

Power's Ferry. See Fetterman's Ferry, immediately preceding.

Beelen's Ferry. In 1814 Francis Beelen warranted 328 acres of
land, at the present site of Bailey Station, on the Pennsylvania
Railroad. He established a parade grounds there for the state militia and conducted a ferry. This ferry also crossed the Juniata,
from Howe to Miller Townships. Beelen's Ferry and post office
were described in Gordon's Gazetteer of Pennsylvania (1832) as
being "on the right bank of the Juniata River, in Juniata (now
Miller) Township, eight miles northeast of New Bloomfield,
twenty-three miles from Harrisburg, and 129 miles from Washington City." There was once an effort made to capitalize a ferry
company there, as noted in "Special Legislation" in this book.

Sheaffer's Ferry. This ferry was only for foot passengers and
was for long years conducted by Reuben Sheaffer and family,
crossing the Juniata at what was originally known as Poor Man's
Spring, now Iroquois Station, on the Pennsylvania Railroad. Mr.
Sheaffer was one of the most experienced rivermen, and no member of his family was unskilled in the same line.

The Flamm or Watts Ferry. Mathias Flamm, who resided on the
east side of the Susquehanna River, and David Watts, who resided
on the west side, near the junction of the two rivers, operated a
ferry over the Susquehanna before 1799, as an act of the Legislature of March 8, 1799, confirms. The location is stated thus:

"Whereas, Mathias Flamm owns land on the east side of the Susquehanna, opposite the mouth of Juniata, and David Watts on the west
side, where the state road crosses the Susquehanna, and that they have
established and maintained a ferry at the place for a number of years,
they are empowered by law, at this date, to establish and keep same in
repair, and build landings, etc."

The Hulings' Ferry. Marcus Hulings lived on the point of land
between the rivers, long known as the Reutter farm, for a year
prior to 1755, when the Indian invasion drove him away. He came
back in 1762, and there is record that he operated a ferry over the
Juniata at that point, having built a causeway over the channel
which connected the two rivers above Duncan's Island. As he
says nothing of having had a ferry, when petitioning for the restoration of his lines in 1762, it evidently was subsequent to this.

Liverpool Ferry. The Liverpool Ferry is older than the town
of Liverpool, for when John Huggins laid out that town in 1808
he reserved "to himself, his heirs and assigns forever all ferries
and ferry rights, now made or hereafter to be made or erected."
On May 21, 1834, he conveyed all of that one-half or west side
of ferry known by the name of Liverpool Ferry, to Richard and

Robert Rogers. There may have been a reason for this, as evidently the Rogers brothers were operating a ferry of their own as early as 1819, probably from the Dauphin side, as the following advertisement in the Harrisburg *Republican* of December 31, 1819, would indicate:

The subscribers beg leave to inform the public that they have established a ferry on the Susquehanna River at Liverpool, Cumberland County. They have provided good craft and employed careful and attentive ferrymen, who will be ready at all times to accommodate those who may wish to cross the river at that place, with the least possible delay.

RICHARD ROGERS.

December 24, 1819.   ROBERT ROGERS.

The purchase of the Huggins' interests may have been the means of combining rivals. On August 4, 1832, they in turn sold to Daniel Bogar, who on March 24, 1838, conveyed it to Isaac Meck. Twenty years later, after gaining a competence, Mr. Meck sold it to John Shank. A charter was granted for this same ferry in 1867 to William Inch. Subsequently Peleg Sturtevant and H. F. Zaring owned and operated it under the Inch charter for years, or until 1894, when they brought suit against Israel Ritter and Sons for infringing upon their rights by running ferry boats in opposition. The difficulty was finally settled by Ritter & Sons buying the rights of Sturtevant & Zaring and thus gaining sole control. They then sold to Chas E. Deckard and brothers, who later sold to Chas. H. Snyder. With others Mr. Snyder formed a corporation or stock company and a charter was issued to the new corporation, known as the Liverpool Ferry Company, which is now managed and controlled by H. A. S. Shuler.

Crow's Ferry. Crow's Ferry is the main ferry between Duncannon and Sunbury, where the Susquehanna is bridged. It is located at a point on the river a few miles below Liverpool, and its eastern terminus is at the town of Millersburg, Dauphin County. It is a gateway from the famed Lykens Valley and Pottsville to the West, on a much-traveled route, and should be bridged by the state. It is noted for romantic beauty and is a famous picnic resort. From that point a fine view of the river is to be had. According to tradition there was a ferry there before Millersburg existed. Over it passed the immigration westward from the Pottsville section in pioneer times. The ferry was operated by Isaac Crow as far back as 1860. Some time after this George and Joe Kramer started to ferry from the east side of the river, the Crows ferrying from the west side. About 1865 both parties took out charters and both thought them good to ferry only one way. On April 12, 1872, an act of the Pennsylvania Legislature gave to "Isaac Crow, his heirs and assigns the right to make landings as far north as the canal lock below Liverpool and as far south as Mt. Patrick, and on the east side of the river, along the line of the Borough of Millersburg." Two years prior to that time Levi McConnell has been employed by Isaac Crow to run the ferry, and in 1872 he and Richard McConnell bought it. About the same time the Kramers sold their charter to Joseph Johnson. After a few years of ferrying one way by both parties the owners found that if the charters were good for ferrying one way they were good for the other. Then was begun a famous law suit that extended over fifteen years and only terminated when Levi McConnell bought the charter rights from Ramsey Moyer, who then owned the Kramer charter.

The owners since then have been as follows: The half interest owned by Levi McConnell was sold by him to George W. Seiler in 1902, from whom it passed to his father, J. A. Seiler, in 1905. In 1906 Walter Hunter purchased this interest and is the present owner. The half interest owned by Richard McConnell was sold by his administrator in 1896 to H. M. Hain, who sold it to Annie (McConnell) Miller and P. E. McConnell in 1898. Two years later the latter bought the former's share. P. E. McConnell, in 1904, sold to John Travitz, who sold to Thomas Radle in 1907. Mr. Radle still owns this interest.

Montgomery's Ferry. The date of the establishment of Montgomery's Ferry, across the Susquehanna, is unknown, but it was established by William Montgomery and, as he acquired the property on November 17, 1827, it was probably after that time. This ferry has also long ceased operations. At its eastern landing are located the great McClellan coal yards. In Dauphin County this ferry was known as Moorehead's Ferry, by reason of a family of that name residing there, from whom sprang Congressman Moorehead and the noted Pittsburgh Mooreheads.

Moorehead's Ferry. See Montgomery's Ferry, immediately preceding.

Baughman's Ferry. The history of this ferry is veiled in obscurity, but when the New Buffalo lots were advertised in 1820 the advertisement locates them at Baughman's Ferry. In his deeds Jacob Baughman reserved "to himself, his heirs and assigns forever, the exclusive right to the ferry and fisheries on the river opposite the town. In 1823, his executor, in advertising lots, omits "at Baughman's Ferry," and states the location as five miles above Clark's Ferry, from which one would infer that the Baughman Ferry was out of business.

CHAPTER XXI.

RIVER AND CANAL TRANSPORTATION.

Oh! Boatman, blow that horn again,
For never did the listening air,
Upon its joyous bosom bear
So wild, so soft, so sweet a strain!

What though thy notes are sad and few,
By every common boatman blown,
Yet is each pulse to nature true,
And melody in every tone.—*Selected.*

THIS book would not be complete without containing something of that old canal life, of the alluring call of the canal, with its fascinating and enchanting hours upon and along those old and historic waterways and of the scenic beauty of their courses. Located along two as picturesque rivers as drain any territory in the United States, passing through fertile field and valley, by high and towering mountains, their very edges hugging precipitous bluffs, behind which the sun was hidden long before sunset, their shadows cooled the brow of many a boatman during his long and tiresome hours. Those were halcyon days, but they are gone forever. The mighty monster propelled by steam, its very metal creaking with energy, has grasped from that generation the commerce of the continent and hauls many, many times the product in a very small part of the time consumed on the canal. But the canals played a great part in the development of the nation, and it is yet a question whether the State of Pennsylvania did not make a mistake in their sale. If we had canal transportation to-day, would we not be burning cheaper coal? Canals are still in use in other states for the transportation of goods that are not in an immediate hurry.

The history of the first waterways goes back to the time when the forests still resounded with the war whoop of the red men. The earlier recollection of traffic on and along the Juniata and Susquehanna Rivers has been handed down in song and story. Perchance, even before the Indian there may have been a race here and they may have used the waters for transportation, but there are no records or any evidence supporting such fact. In the case of the Indians, however, actual occurrences, even with dates, are available. Elsewhere in this book is an account, among others, of the bringing down the river of two Indians from Shamokin (now Sunbury), charged with murder. Evidently they had no larger craft than

thing larger was needed, and the batteau followed. John Harris, the original settler of what is now our beautiful State Capital, in a letter dated Paxton, April 17, 1756, says:

"The canoes that must be employed for service on our river, are in general too small; therefore, it is absolutely necessary to have a small number of battoes (batteaux) immediately made, as they will carry a much larger burden, keep but the same number of hands employed in working them up the river as our small canoes will, and will certainly answer the purpose better, as the sides will be higher to keep out the waves in our falls, many of which will be always to pass through, and in high winds, which may sometime happen. There will not be the least danger of passing up and down this river in a battoe, when a canoe must be unloaded or damage her cargo; therefore, as I think myself a judge of our river navigation and the most necessary and serviceable vessels to be employed in it, I think it my duty to write you this letter, and also to inform you that William Chestnut will supply you with suitable plank, upon getting directions to make the battoes; the boards, I imagine, are not to be sawed after the common manner." I am, sir,
                         Your most obedient servant,
                                      JOHN HARRIS.

There is record of the waters of the Juniata and Susquehanna being used for transportation of surplus farm products as early as 1794. In that year an "ark," the name given it by the builder, built by an enterprising German miller named Kryder, of near Huntingdon, and laden with flour, floated down the rivers to Baltimore, braving the terrors of the falls at various points, especially below Middletown, where navigation with small craft was then considered impossible. His success caused the building of many arks; and when the stages of the waters permitted it the following years, they came down the rivers laden with flour, grain and whiskey, on their way to possible markets. Until the advent of the canals they were largely in use. Shortly afterwards the Conewago Canal at York Haven was commenced, and when completed, in 1797 or 1798, keel-bottom boats passed through. Columbia then became a mart of importance, a great deal of the trade in wheat being drawn from Middletown. In a few years, however, these boats were plying clear through to the bay.

The use of keel-bottoms on the Juniata and Susquehanna Rivers was very common prior to the coming of the canal, and in the fall of 1919, the late Prof. L. E. McGinnes, superintendent of the Steelton (Pennsylvania) schools, told of his father having done his marketing with them over the Juniata between Patterson's (now the Lewis Steckley place, in Howe Township) and Newport, early in the last century.

Even between the canoe and the batteau the row boat found a place, and it remains to this day. After the ark and used coincidentally were the large flats or boats, which carried much greater tonnage than the arks, and which transported down the river huge loads of produce, such as beef, pork, grain, lumber, etc. Coming up stream these boats were poled, usually by four or six men, who placed their poles on the river bottom at the front end of the boat and walked its length, consecutively taking their places, thus constantly keeping the boat in motion. Rings had been placed in rocks in the river where there were falls and with the use of ropes and a windlass the boats were drawn up over the falls, otherwise an impossibility. Several iron rings yet remain at the Iroquois Falls, in the Juniata. This was done at the falls below Liverpool and at Mt. Patrick, and at the latter place the tourist can see to-day a narrow neck of land overgrown with bushes, jutting down stream from the falls, about a hundred feet from the Perry County shore. This was originally a wall built by these early boatmen to help get their boats over the falls, the channel being wider at the top so as to divert additional water into this waterway. Not far from this old waterway at Mt. Patrick, at the same falls, is a place in the river known as "the salmon hole." It covers approximately three acres of water, the depth of which is uniformly about eighteen feet.

These old "arks," which carried the traffic before the days of the canal, did a considerable business. From figures available from eight up-river counties in 1824 it is found that there was floated down the river 823,000 bushels of wheat, 17,500 bushels of cloverseed, 9,200 barrels of whiskey, and 3,260,000 pounds of pork. When the arks were in use E. Bosserman and James Everhart built one at Newport, and from the old Kough warehouse took down the river a cargo of flour and pig iron, the latter being manufactured by Mr. Everhart at Juniata furnace, and sold at Port Deposit. The Koughs were grain and commission merchants, and this was the first lot of flour for export ever brought to Newport. Among farmers who built arks were the Wagners and Grubbs, of Liverpool, whose boats were windlassed up over the falls at Conewago, Mt. Patrick, and below Liverpool.

Following the arks came the raft, especially for transporting the immense lumber product from the northern part of the state; and until recent years, when the spring freshets were passing towards the sea, they carried with them annually millions of feet of lumber ready for market. Liverpool, Montgomery's Ferry, and New Buffalo were points at which the raftsmen "tied up" for the night and for days during bad weather, and many were the tales told by old rivermen of the times had at the old-time taverns in these towns, when rafting was in its heyday. At these places the rafts frequently extended for a mile in both directions from the town.

Almost a quarter of a century before the building of the first "ark" on the Juniata, the province was busily interested in waterway transportation, even on smaller streams, as the following incident will show. The Provincial Legislature of 1771, on March

9th, passed an act which declared the Susquehanna and Juniata Rivers public highways, but made no appropriation to improve them. By the act of February 6, 1773, Sherman's Creek was also declared a public highway. A man named James Patton had constructed a dam across the creek near its mouth, and persons residing near by made a protest, claiming it conflicted with navigation, hence the passage of the bill. It follows, in part:

Section one provides that "the said James Patton, and all and every person claiming under him, and all and every person or persons whatsoever, having already erected any milldam or other obstruction across the said creek, where the same has been or can be made navigable for rafts, boats or canoes, shall make open and leave the space of twenty feet in breadth near the middle of said dam, at least two feet lower than any other part thereof; and for every foot that the dam is or shall be raised perpendicular from the bottom of said creek, there shall be laid a platform, either of stone or timber, or both, with proper walls on each side, to confine the waters, which shall extend at least six feet down the stream, and of breadth aforesaid, to form a slope for the water's gradual descent, for the easy and safe passage of boats, rafts and canoes through the same."

This section further provides as a penalty for not constructing these dam chutes within eight months six months' imprisonment or £50 forfeiture, one-half to the informer and the other half to the overseers of the poor of the township wherein the offender resides.

Section two provides against the construction of "any wear, rack, basket, fishing dam, pond, or other device or obstruction whatsoever within said creek" for catching fish, with a penalty of one month's imprisonment "without bail or mainprize," or £10 fine.

Section three makes it the duty of the constables of the respective townships adjoining the creek to inspect the dams therein and make information against offenders. This they must do every month throughout the year, under a penalty of twenty shillings.

Section four provides against fishing at the chutes of the dams so constructed, by net or seine, within twenty perches above and below the same, under a penalty of £5.

Section five is a proviso to prevent the construction of the act to preclude fishing with a seine or net at other places in the stream.

Section six declares the stream a public highway as far as the same is navigable for rafts, boats or canoes.

Section seven provides that James Patton's dam shall not be affected in any way other than is specified by the act.

The session of the Pennsylvania Legislature appropriated two thousand dollars, February 17, 1816, to remove obstructions and improve navigation on Sherman's Creek, between Craighead's milldam and the junction of the creek and the Susquehanna River. A commission, consisting of Francis Gibson, George Stroop, John Maxwell, William Power, Samuel Anderson, John Creigh, Moses Watson, Isaiah Carl, and Robert Adams, was appointed to superintend the work. The time was extended until 1822 to complete the task. The creek was at that time made navigable for small craft as far as Gibson's Rock.

A special act of the legislature, passed April 14, 1827, required the commissioners of Perry County to pay the commissioners appointed by an act of the same body for removing obstructions from Sherman's Creek.

Marcus Hulings also figures in the placing of a dam in Sherman's Creek. On August 28, 1768, he took out an order of survey for a tract of thirty acres which was located on Sherman's Creek, above the Duncannon Iron Company's plant, and upon which was a mill site. Evidently familiar with the Patton case he took precaution to obtain the authority of the State Legislature in 1787 to erect a dam in the stream. He died the following year and there is no record of the dam being built.

Odd as it now seems the Pennsylvania Legislature, in January, 1791, actually passed a bill which, among others, made navigable Little Juniata Creek, which empties into the Susquehanna River at Duncannon. Of course the springs and streams are less copious than when the county was wooded, but that stream has either dropped off wonderfully in the volume of water flowing or else there were some mighty queer proceedings in legislative halls even in those early days. An Act of February 5, 1794, made "the Cocolamus Creek of Cumberland and Mifflin Counties, from the mouth thereof to the forks at Daniel Cargill's," a public highway.

The first iron steamboat to ply the Susquehanna was built near York, on the Codorus, for which it was named, and was launched in 1825. It was sixty feet long, had a nine-foot beam and was three feet high. It weighed six tons and when empty drew only five inches of water. Each ton of contents caused it to sink an inch further into the water. It went up the river as far as Oswego and Binghampton. Its receipts were small, and two years later it was sold for junk. During the winter of 1825-26 it was moored at Montgomery's Ferry, in Perry County.

The *Miltonian,* published at Milton, Pennsylvania, May 11, 1826, said:

" 'The Susquehanna and Baltimore' arrived at Northumberland on Monday last. She is able to ascend the river at the rate of about five miles an hour. At Liverpool she took Mr. Grove's eighty-foot keel boat, heavily laden, in tow. Notwithstanding, it did not in the least impede her progress, for she reached Northumberland in six hours, a distance of twenty-six miles. On May 3 one of her boilers burst at Nescopeck Falls and injured thirteen people whose names are known. Two New York State men were blown overboard and not recovered."

During the administration of Governor Bigler an appropriation was made for removing the obstructions from the channel of the Susquehanna River and to George Blattenberger, later associate judge of the county, was entrusted the work. Upon its completion he returned an unexpended balance to the state treasury, and for this he was commended in the governor's message to the legislature.

COMING OF THE CANALS.

Whose suggestions first brought the matter of canals to the attention of the public the writer does not know, and history fails to agree; but to William Penn, founder of the Province of Pennsylvania, this book is inclined to give that credit. During one of Penn's periods of residence in the province, he made a trip up the Susquehanna as far as Middletown, and probably Harrisburg. As early as 1690 he was arranging for a second settlement or city in the province, upon the Susquehanna River. "It is now," says Penn, "my purpose to make another settlement, upon the river Susquehanna, that runs into the Chesapeake, and bears about fifty miles west from the Delaware, as appears by the common maps of the English dominion in America. There I design to lay out a plan for building another city, in the most convenient place for the communication with the former plantations in the East; which by land is as good as done already, a way being laid out between the two rivers, very exactly and conveniently, at least three years ago; and which will not be hard to do by water, by benefit of the river Schuylkill; for a branch of that river lies near the branch that runs into the Susquehanna River, and is the common course of the Indians with their skins and furs into our parts, and to the provinces east and west, Jersey and New York, from west and northwestern parts of the continent, from whence they bring them."

As early as April 6, 1790, Timothy Matlack, John Adlum and Samuel Maclay were appointed commissioners to survey and examine the Swatara, the Susquehanna, Sinnemahoning Creek and the Allegheny River with a view towards promoting an inland waterway. This route via the Swatara Creek is the one mentioned by Penn, in the above statement, it being described as "the branch that runs into the Susquehanna River." This was the actual beginning of the subject of canal construction.

As early as 1791 a "Society for Promoting the Improvements of Roads and Inland Navigation" existed in Pennsylvania and devoted much of its time to the exploration of the various waterways and routes considered most feasible for connecting the Delaware with the waters of the Ohio and the lakes. Under authority granted by the legislature surveys were made and reports submitted. New York, Maryland, Virginia and the Carolinas were working along the same lines. About this time (1791 to 1827), when the Americans were displaying such enthusiasm and energy in opening up their extensive domain, came the intelligence of the success of steam power on the railroads being built in England, and the inauguration of the new system of passenger transportation between Manchester and Liverpool. Notwithstanding the Americans went ahead and completed their waterways.

Prior to this, as early as 1761, commissioners had been appointed by the proprietary "to clear, scour, and make the Schuylkill navigable for boats, flats, rafts, canoes and other small vessels, from the ridge of mountains commonly called the Blue Mountains, to the river Delaware." After this initial step the Schuylkill at many places was dammed into long deep pools, which were connected by canals with a depth of six feet, carrying boats of two hundred-ton capacity. Following the appointment of the commission, previously mentioned, in 1790, Governor Thomas Mifflin, in his message to the legislature in 1791, said:

"The very laudable attention paid to the survey of roads and rivers is a conclusive proof of the importance of the subject, while it furnishes an example highly deserving of your imitation. Every day, indeed, produces an additional incentive to persevere in improvements of this kind. The commercial policy of insuring the transportation of our produce from the interior counties to the capital is dependent upon the ease and facility of the communications that are established throughout the state; and when we consider Pennsylvania, not only as the route that actually connects the extreme members of the Union, but as a natural avenue from the shores of the Atlantic to the vast regions of the western territory, imagination can hardly paint the magnitude of the scene which demands our industry, nor hope exaggerate the richness of the reward which solicits our enjoyment."

The committee reported on February 19, 1791. They reported on the Delaware towards New York State and towards Lake Ontario; on the Lehigh and Schuylkill and connections of the latter leading towards the Susquehanna, and on the Juniata and the north and west branches of the Susquehanna. The report was comprehensive and upon its foundations later were erected the extensive public waterways which carried the trade of the state for decades.

During the very infancy of Perry County, and while Governor Heister was in office, the greatest question before the people of Pennsylvania was the construction of canals to reach the inland counties. An act of the Pennsylvania Legislature dated March 27, 1824, provided for the appointment of commissioners to promote the internal improvement of the commonwealth. A commission of three was to investigate the feasability and explore a route for a canal from Harrisburg to Pittsburgh, by way of the Juniata and Conemaugh Rivers. A report was made, and after enacting several laws and repealing others, five commissioners were authorized to examine routes through Chester and Lancaster Counties, then by the west branch of the Susquehanna and from the mouth of the Juniata to Pittsburgh. The people had little faith in the railroads building in England, then attaining success, but stood by their early belief in inland waterways.

Then, on that eventful day, July 4, 1826, ground was first broken at Harrisburg for the "Pennsylvania Canal," to be in its day a mighty artery of traffic, and yet to be so soon superseded by one of far greater proportions. An office was opened at Millerstown and James Clark was made superintendent of the Juniata division. On July 15, 1827, advertisements appeared asking for bids for the construction of sixteen miles of canal between Lewistown and Mexico, Juniata County, on the east side of the Juniata; for fourteen miles from Mexico to a point opposite North's Island, below Millerstown, also on the east side, and for fifteen miles, extending from North's Island to a point opposite the extreme northern point of Duncan's Island. On May 13, 1828, bids were called for for the construction of the old aqueduct, which crossed the Juniata at Duncan's Island, and thirteen houses of wood, stone or brick for the use of lock tenders. The distance from this old aqueduct to Clark's Ferry dam was 1.58 miles.

While the canal was building, on February 23, 1828, the following appeared in the *Mifflin Eagle:*

"The work on the canal progresses rapidly; many sections are now more than half completed. The sections in the Narrows appear to get along slower than the rest. This is occasioned in a great measure by the high water, which has prevented the work from going on. The Juniata has not been frozen over this season, and ever since the middle of December it has been on what is termed by boatmen good 'arking order.' We saw five arks pass down on Tuesday last. This is the first winter, in the recollection of our oldest citizens, that the river has remained clear of ice."

Some of these citizens must surely have attained the age of seventy, whose recollection would date back at least sixty years, so that here is a traditional weather record dating back to probably 1768, to the very days of the early pioneers.

In the fall of 1828 plans for the building of the canal from Lewistown to Huntingdon, a distance of forty-five miles, were consummated. The canal was built and completed by the summer of 1829, and on August 27th of that year the first boat came up the canal from Harrisburg, being in command of Cornelius Baskins, of "Upper Clark's Ferry," a name then applied to what later was known as Baskinsville, and now a part of Duncannon. The freight consisted of a quantity of merchandise and seven thousand bricks, which were consigned to John Hipple, then sheriff of Perry County, and residing at New Bloomfield. On September 22 the water was let into the first level of the Juniata Canal at Lewistown. On October 30 the entire line from Lewistown to Duncan's Island was filled with water and placed in service. In November the first packet boat to ply the canal, drawn by two white horses, went from Mifflintown to Lewistown, conveying a party of ladies and gentlemen and members of the legislature.

On November 5, 1829, a packet boat, probably the same one, arrived at Newport from Mifflin laden with members of the legislature and other persons of prominence. According to descriptions of the period it "was drawn by two white horses and set off in fine style with the flag flying at her head, amid the shouts of the people and the cheering music of the band on board."

The canal was completed from Lewistown to Huntingdon the following year, and by 1834 the line was open from Philadelphia to Pittsburgh, by using the railroad of eighty-two miles to Columbia and the portage road from Hollidaysburg to Johnstown, a distance of thirty-six miles. Regular packet lines for the transportation of passengers and freight were established and continued until about 1850, when the advent of the railroads caused the business to be unprofitable. For the hauling of freight, however, the canal did a large business almost to the end of its existence. The Juniata Canal was last used in 1898. Its entire cost was $3,525,000.

The following notice in the *Pittsburgh Gazette* of March 24, 1834, heralded the arrival of the first lot of goods via the Portage railroad and canal:

"We have, to-day, the pleasure to announce the arrival of the first lot of goods, by the way of the Portage Railroad. It was the packet boat, General Lacock, Captain Craig, arrived this morning from Johnstown, with goods in thirteen days from Philadelphia."

The only locks on the Juniata Canal in Perry County, below the Millerstown dam, were located in Miller Township, below the point known as Trimmer's Rock, and below Iroquois, near the home of J. Warren Buckwalter, once a member of the General Assembly from Perry County.

The celebration of National Independence Day, July 4, 1830, was a gala day at Millerstown, when the "splendid new canal boat, "Pennsylvania," was launched with a public ceremony. This was the first boat to be built west of Harrisburg.

At the "Rope Ferry," between Newport and Millerstown, the canal was transferred to the eastern bank of the Juniata, which is described by John T. Faris, in his "Seeing Pennsylvania," thus:

"In the days when the canal was in its glory there was a pool below Millerstown, formed by a state dam in the river. On this pool boats passed 'by means of an endless rope stretched across the river and passing around a large pulley on the canal side.' When a signal was given, one of the pulleys was turned by water power; this put in motion the rope, and the boat attached to the rope was moved in its turn. This was one of the interesting sights of travel by canal that led N. P. Willis to write, in 1840:

"Of all the modes of travel in America, the least popular—and the most delightful, to our thinking—is traveling on the canal. The packet boats are long drawing rooms, where one dines, sleeps, reads, lolls, or looks out of the window; and, if in want of exercise, may at any time get a quick walk on the towpath, and all this without perceptible motion, jar, or sound

across by being towed from a "wooden towpath" built along the south side of the bridge spanning the Susquehanna at that point.

Owing to the far greater expense required to build a canal on the Dauphin County side of the river it was located along the west bank on the Perry County side. The following is from the report of the Canal Commissioners in 1827, covering that phase:

"In the latter end of May, the location of a line from the mouth of the Juniata to Northumberland was commenced by Mr. Simon Guilford. He was instructed to examine both sides of the Susquehanna with the utmost care, to present an estimate of each, and further, to ascertain whether the river might be advantageously crossed at any intermediate point, so as to place the canal partly on one side and partly on the other. At the meeting of the board on the 2d of July, a report was received from Mr. Guilford, accompanied by an estimate, from which it appeared that a canal on the east side would cost $1,018,758, and on the west side, $472,298. Strong representations were at the same time made, from Dauphin and Northumberland Counties, in favor of the east side, to all of which the utmost respect was paid. But the vast difference of expense was thought by the board to leave them no choice, and a location was adopted, beginning at Duncan's Island, and extending up the west side to a point opposite Northumberland."

George Blattenberger, once associate judge of Perry County, was a contractor for sections of both the tidewater canal and the Wiconisco Canal, as well as for a section of the Philadelphia & Erie Railroad. Under Governors Shunk and Bigler, by their appointment he was supervisor of the Susquehanna Canal from Clark's Ferry to Milton.

During the last lays of September, 1829, the water was let into the upper levels of the Susquehanna division, aptly described by a narrative from a writer in Hazard's Register, during October, 1829, as follows:

"It is with pleasure that we are enabled to announce to our readers, from undoubted authority, that the water is now flowing down the Susquehanna division of the Pennsylvania Canal. The water was first introduced two weeks since, and is now three feet high at Selinsgrove, and last Saturday had passed down the canal as far as Liverpool, and is gradually passing on; the whole line being in complete order to receive water. No break or defect of ny kind has been found, though the water now occupies twenty-seven miles of canal, a circumstance highly honorable to the talents and attention of Mr. Guilford, the engineer, and to the contractors, who executed the work. Boats are frequently passing with parties of pleasure from Selinsgrove to Sunbury and Northumberland."

(Signed "Aurora.")

During 1830 regular traffice was carried on continuously until the water was taken out of the canal for the winter months. This was the first year of the operation of this division. The cost of the entire Susquehanna Canal was $4,804,000. The matter of compensation for services shows comparatively the difference between that period and this of almost a hundred years later. In

1832 the chief engineer, then known as the "principal engineer," received $2,000; division superintendents, $3 per day; assistant engineers, 2.50 per day; supervisors, $2.50 per day; foreman, $1.25 and $1.50 per day, and lock tenders, $10 per month and free house rent.

By 1834 six hundred and seventy-three miles of the public works had been completed, as the state's credit had been good, but unfortunately the immense system was too expensive for the state's finances at that period and was not managed in an economical manner, with the result that by 1841 the state debt was over $42,000,000, and work ceased.

The building of the canals through the new county of Perry brought to the county a lawless element, and riots and brawls were of frequent occurrence. One of the worst of these was during April, 1828, in Dolton's tavern, at Montgomery's Ferry. At that time F. Montgomery had his shoulder fractured and John O'Regan diet two weeks later from a fractured skull. Justice of the courts of the new county decreed that three of the rioters serve ten years in the penitentiary, and from then there was less trouble with this element.

The first coal from the Lykens Valley coal fields was shipped from Mt. Patrick by the Lykens Valley Coal Company, over the Pennsylvania Canal, beginning in 1846. The coal was brought sixteen miles over a primitive railroad from Bear's Gap to Millersburg, the little cars being run upon flats fitted with tracks. These were ferried across the Susquehanna, where the tracks of another narrow gauge railroad ran from the canal to the river's edge, on which the small cars were transported to the canal's side and their contents dumped into canal boats for transportation to various marts of trade. After the completion of the Wiconisco Canal the trade was diverted that way.

For a number of years packet boats plied the waters of both the Juniata and Susquehanna Canals. Near their junction stood the historic Amity Hall tavern, a road house of the early days, which was an important stopping place and where many persons of importance tarried. The packet boat leaving Williamsport in the evening would arrive at "the Junction" and Amity Hall at noon the following day, having traveled eighty-seven miles. These boats were of light construction and the teams used in hauling them were relayed. The boatmen have an association which meets annually, usually at Rolling Green Park, near Selinsgrove, and at their meeting in 1920 Mrs. H. G. Houseworth, whose maiden name was Bingaman, of Trevorton,—a one-time cook on these packet boats—was in attendance. She is now eighty-seven years of age. She recalls that the through fare was $2, including a bunk and breakfast, and that the fare was $1 either way to Milton, the half-way point. Being eighteen years of age at the time would place the period as 1851.

According to Mr. Lewis Messersmith, of Howe Township, whose age is eighty-four years (1921), the first packet boat was owned by William Calder, of Harrisburg, and the captain was A. C. Clemson, of Newport. Captain Clemson was the father of C. L. Clemson, for years road foreman of engines on the Middle Division of the Pennsylvania Railroad, now retired. Just as in railroading to-day, many of the old boatmen were Perry Countians. There were at one time three merchant lines, says Mr. Messersmith, the Ohio Line, the Union Line, and the Kiess Line. The other boats were owned by individuals. A grocery boat from Philadelphia, owned by Captain Barnes, delivered groceries along the canal. Two section boats from Pittsburgh delivered wines and liquors as far east as Columbia. Capt. John Weaver, of Saltsburg, was the owner of two boats, the "Effort" and the "Lucinda," which were run day and night, Mr. Messersmith having been one of the drivers.

Captain Clemson died in Newport in 1888. He was a noted old-time captain of the packet boat lines and left a record which follows: In 1845 he became captain of the "Northumberland," running from Harrisburg to Williamsport. The line had three boats. The other two were the "Williamsport," captain, D. Blair, and the "Harrisburg," captain, I. D. Murphy. He ran the "Northumberland" two years and then began running the "Kishoquillas," on the Juniata Line, running from Harrisburg to Hollidaysburg. This line had three other boats, as follows: the "Delaware," captain, R. H. Morton; the "Philadelphia," captain, I. L. Elliott, and the "Monongahela," captain, S. D. Carnes. Mr. Morton was soon succeeded by Captain G. W. Hooper. Captain S. H. Walters succeeded Hooper, who died of cholera. The completion of the Pennsylvania Railroad to Lewistown shortened the route, as exchange of passengers was then made there. This withdrew one boat from the service. When the railroad was completed to Mount Union, the exchange of passengers was made there, and another boat was withdrawn. Later the exchange was made at Huntingdon, the railroad having been built to that place. The boats were taken to Virginia, on the completion of the railroad to Hollidaysburg, and sold to a packet line plying from Richmond to Lynchburg. The first fast packet boat was run on the Pennsylvania Canal in 1835. It was exclusively for passengers and was towed by three horses. All the boats before that time were slow packets, with amidship for freight, and the bow and stern cabins for passengers, the boats being towed by two horses. These Juniata boats were the Calder boats and were known as the "Pioneer Line." In 1837 an opposition line known as "The Express," was started. It ran only one season, Mr. Calder buying it, but during that season there was great rivalry, the blocking of locks and the cutting of tow lines being but parts of the deviltry to delay the opposition. The names of other boats were the "South America" and the "Comet."

Other captains were Drum, Collins, Hicks, Hall, and Daniels, from New York State; Vogelsong and Libhart, from Marietta; Green, Donelson and Williams, from Mifflintown; Wilt, William Sayford, Charles Keller and James Murphy, of Harrisburg. On the Susquehanna Line were Captains John Huff, of Milton; John and Samuel Huggins and George Walker, of Liverpool. The Harrisburg office stood on the site of the old Pennsylvania Railroad depot. At that time it took four days to put passengers through to Pittsburgh, according to Captain Clemson. The connecting train left Philadelphia at 8 a. m. and arrived at Harrisburg at 3 p. m.

The first canal boat to cross the Allegheny Mountains was a section boat of three parts. The cars were dropped into the basin at Hollidaysburg and the pieces floated upon them. They were then pulled to the first plane, by an engine; from there they were pulled up the mountain with a stationary engine and a large wire cable. They were then let down the western side in the same manner until they reached Johnstown, where they were dropped into the canal, united and sent on their way to Pittsburgh. This boat was called the "Hit or Miss."

During the boating period Liverpool and New Buffalo lived and thrived, largely through this industry, and the product of their shops and boatyards sailed the internal waterways well in many states. There were two boatyards at Liverpool, the upper owned by Joseph Shuler, and later by John W. Murray, and the lower one by George Walker, John Sheats, and Henry Hoffman at different times.* At one time over fifty boat owners resided in Liverpool and engaged in the occupation of boating. New Buffalo also had two boatyards.

The routes pursued by the boatmen, when the canal traffic was at its height, were from Lock Haven, on the west branch, and Pittston, on the east branch of the Susquehanna, and from Hollidaysburg, on the Juniata, to Philadelphia and New York, via Havre de Grace, Maryland, over Chesapeake Bay to Chesapeake City, Maryland; then over the Chesapeake and Delaware Canal (fourteen miles) to Delaware City, Delaware; then by tug up the

---

*Among boatmen interviewed for information (1919-20) were Ambrose L. Sterick, who boated from 1859 until 1900; S. E. Klinger, who began boating in 1865 and whose pair of boats was among the very last to transport ties, grain, etc., from Liverpool to Sunbury, and John Trimmer, for three decades a boatman.

Delaware Bay and River to Philadelphia and Bordentown, New Jersey; then over the Raritan Canal (forty-five miles) to New Brunswick, New Jersey, and from there to New York by tug over the Newark and New York Bays.

Another route was from Havre de Grace, Maryland, (sixty-four miles) by tug down the Chesapeake Bay to Baltimore.

Another route left the Pennsylvania Canal at Middletown, Dauphin County, over the Union Canal to Lebanon and Reading, then over the Schuylkill Canal to Philadelphia, a distance of seventy-seven miles.

The principal traffic over the Pennsylvania Canal was the coal from the mines to the large cities, farm produce and lumber being next in order; but in its entirety it was as varied as freight traffic is to-day. On the return trips merchandise, fish, plaster, etc., usually filled the boats.

The Legislature of February, 1899, voted to abandon the Pennsylvania Canal, the vote being 176 to 4, in favor of abandonment. The Juniata Canal was abandoned in 1898, the large aqueduct was removed from across the Juniata above Duncannon, in 1899, and the Susquehanna Canal abandoned on May 1, 1901.

The packet boats seem to have still been in existence in 1876, when the Centennial was held at Philadelphia, as the following advertisement of that period will show:

"Persons wishing to visit the Centennial can go in no cheaper and pleasanter manner than by canal packet, run by Captain Koontz, of Port Royal. Fare $7. The boat will anchor close to the Exhibition Grounds and will remain from 8 to 10 days, where you can have lodging free, and meals 20c each, or if you prefer can board yourself. This is a pleasant way for families and parties to visit the city. Persons can get in the boat at Newport. The next trip made by the boat will be about the last of September. For further particulars address John Dunbar, Port Royal, Pa."

Among the canal and rivermen inseparably connected with the old canal days was Thomas B. Carpenter, born in Newport in 1838, and who moved to Duncan's Island as a boy with his father's family. He followed the canal as boy and man, first as driver, then bowsman, then captain, with the missing period of the days when the States warred, when he served three different enlistments in the Union army. He then returned to the canal and became a pilot over the Clark's Ferry dam, being the last man to remain in that employment with the canal's closing days. Another of that Carpenter family, his brother James, and Jacob Johnston were famous pilots at the same point, but with decreasing business over the waterway took positions elsewhere.

Daniel N. L. Reutter was one of the contractors who helped build the canal, being at that time extensively engaged in contracting. Later he kept a drug store in Harrisburg, but in 1843 he settled on the farm in Watts Township, at the junction of the Juniata and Susquehanna, where he lived the balance of his life. He brought with him his little son, George N. Reutter, then eight years of age, who later studied medicine and practiced from that point during the balance of his lifetime, also becoming a member of the General Assembly. He became the father of seven children, two dying in infancy, and one becoming a physician, the late Dr. H. D. Reutter, of Duncannon. Both D. N. L. Reutter and Dr. George N. Reutter lie buried in the Reutter private cemetery, located upon a bluff near the stone farmhouse.

The second boat built north of Harrisburg was built in Perry County, at Liverpool, in 1829, and curiously enough by a man who had located in Perry County during the very year of its formation, Michael Shank. He was the father of the late Mrs. E. D. Owens and had been a German ship carpenter. He named the boat "Lorenzy Dow."

A rather unusual occurrence happened during the great War Between the States. It was in 1861. Fred Sterick's boat was assigned the task of transporting one hundred soldiers—Company B, Sixth Pennsylvania Reserves—from Selinsgrove to Harrisburg. The men were under command of Captain Roush and Lieutenants Epler and Hardin.

In the days before the railroad was built along the Juniata, among the travelers over the canal and the Portage Railroad were many men of note. An unusual occurrence is cited. Towards the close of 1835, on the passenger list of a packet boat, was Joseph Ritner, governor-elect on an Anti-Masonic platform, on his way to Harrisburg, and Henry Clay, on his way to the opening of Congress, as loyal a Mason as existed. They dined at the same table and were agreeable companions.

The payment of a bill rendered April 1, 1837, to the Commonwealth of Pennsylvania, by Alex. Glazer, a canal boat captain, for service recalls the days when local military operations occupied quite a conspicuous place in life, and also shows that such features were a part of the life of Liverpool. The copy:

To cash for storage at Harrisburg, ...	.37½
To freight in 1,025 lbs. arms and accoutrements from Harrisburg to Liverpool, ...	5.00

While excavating for the construction of the canal near Newport a stone, shaped like a Greek cross, was unearthed. It was unmistakably not the work of nature, and upon being thoroughly cleansed it was found to contain hierglyphics, plainly marked by the use of a sharp-pointed instrument. Those who saw it thought it might have been possessed by the Indians, possibly a gift of the French in Canada. The hierglyphics bore no resemblance to any Indian characters or marks known, so it was thought evidently the

27

property of some earlier race who probably once inhabited the territory. It was shipped to the Historical Society at Philadelphia, but never arrived at its destination. Zenas J. Gray, in "Prose and Poetry," says "Careful research has revealed the story. About 1771 two Jesuit priests came from Canada with the design of founding a mission among the Juniata Indians, reaching the valley near the site of Newport. The priests cut the cross out of native sandstone and it formed part of their rude altar. Failing in their object to build a church the cross was buried and the Jesuits, with the Indians, went towards the setting sun."

The historic old aqueduct which carried the canal across the Juniata River at the head of Duncan's Island, is but a memory, yet in its day was considered quite an engineering feat. Several of the piers still stand and the small flag station of the Pennsylvania and a summer cottage colony, both somewhat above, are alone reminders of the name.

Old taverns lined the banks of the canals. In 1846 John Bair, then a young man, later president of the Newport Deposit Bank, built a hotel at Girty's Notch which he conducted for six years. Besides that one, there were others at "the Junction," New Buffalo, Montgomery's Ferry, Mount Patrick, and Liverpool. John Huggins, of Liverpool, was collector of canal tolls there until his death in 1859. Henry Wilt Shuman, once a leading lumber merchant of Liverpool, had as many as six boats in the business, and John D. Snyder, engaged in the tie business at a later day, had a contract to furnish 50,000 ties annually to the Central Railroad of New Jersey.

The naming of boats oft betokened the love of a member of the family, the patronage of a business man, or the political preference of the owner. A few chosen at random, follow: Lewis Beasom's line of boats were the "William Bosserman," the "John W. Geary," the "Fickes & Brother," and the "Kough Bros." William Wertz, of Newport, called one "Abraham Collins," and another "Parish No. 35." Mr. Wertz made two trips as far as Lake Champlain and Fort Henry with his boats, the time consumed being a month and five days. He discontinued boating in 1892. Jacob and Daniel Bowers, of East Newport, owned the "Frank E. Billings," the "T. H. Milligan," the "Mina," the "John Hoffer," and the "Mollie," but quit boating in 1889.

Prominently connected with the canal for twenty-three years was George Boyer, now an associate judge of Perry County, the last fifteen of which he was supervisor. John A. Lineaweaver, who was county commissioner in 1870, was for thirty-three years located at the inlet lock at the Millerstown dam.

Among the boatmen who resided in Liverpool were: S. E. Klinger, Edward Stailey, John N. Ritter, Charles Fritz, G. W.

Wilt, Jacob Murray, William Ritter, James J. Stailey, Sr., David Shumaker, J. D. Shure, Ambrose Sterrick, William Cook, John Thompson, John Wentzel, W. C. Fortney, I. B. Free, Martin Horting, Isaac Sturtevant, S. N. Snyder, Jacob Gilbert, David Ritter, Albert Shuler, Jere Lowe, Daniel Funk, Samuel Derr, Peter Derr, John Trimmer, David Lenhart, Michael Deckard, John Beigh, Allen Klinger, Jerome Beigh, Frank Beigh, Oscar Beigh, Newton Funk, Peter, Jacob and Harry Shumaker, William Murray, William Portzline, George W. Snyder, Silas Snyder, C. Murray, John Kough, and Daniel Roush.

From Montgomery's Ferry came the three Fortney brothers, Charles, William, and Jacob; Valentine Arndt and Farmer Bair. The island (Duncan's) contributed Henry Heikel, David Miller, John Briner, John Lukens, and others. New Buffalo's contingent included Joseph Steele, J. P. Motter, T. J. Free, Brandt Free, George Rider, Nathaniel Noblet, William and Samuel Hammaker, John Shumaker, and Calvin Liddick.

A BOATING SONG.

BY "MYRRHA" (MRS. EMMA F. CARPENTER).

The boatman's horn! The boatman's horn!
We hear it in the early morn,
When blushing day is newly born;
It sounds across the waters fair,
And quivers in the morning air,
In notes that shadow forth no care.

The boatman's call! The boatman's call!
We hear it 'mid the water's fall,
Uprising, clear above it all;
"Prepare the lock! Our barge is here;
Our steady team has borne us near;
Open the gates, the way make clear."

To work, to work! The boatman springs,
The heavy line he forward brings,
And round the post he deftly flings;
His good, strong arm holds hard the rope,
Which creaks and groans, as one 'thout hope,
Then soft—the strain is loosened up.

The barge sinks down along the wall
Of darksome lock, where shadows fall,
Around, about and over all;
Then slow, the ponderous gates swing round,
And "go ahead," the magic sound—
A joyful "open road" is found.

"Take up the line," the boatman cries,
To do his bid the driver flies,
And to his team he shrilly cries,
'Get up, get up; now Kate, go on,
And Doll, and Jane, you're good and strong,
The day ahead is very long.

The turbid waves with gentle splash,
Around our barge doth play and dash;
The sunlight over all doth flash;
But come there wind, or sleet, or snow—
In sunshine bright, when rude winds blow,
We steady work and onward go.

THE BOATMAN'S CALL.

BY ZENAS J. GRAY, A PERRY COUNTIAN.

Awake, awake, lockkeeper! Let the boat drop through,
  We're drivin' hard to reach the lower bay;
Autumn's fadin' mighty rapid, winter's comin', too,
  Then the horn will cease its callin' night and day.
Open wide the drippin' gates, fill up the slimy lock,
  The water is impatient to rush on;
Hear the bugle notes a tootin' far away, then wander back,
  Like the memory of friendships lost and gone?

By fair romantic valleys, where Juniata's tide
  And Susquehanna's waters float along,
Through echoin' mountain passes—Old Kittatinny's pride—
  I've sat on deck and sang the joyous song.
The boatman's life has charms, the recollection's plain,
  I like to go a dreamin' of the past;
Though my forehead is wrinkled, my heart is young again,
  And I know the sentiment will always last.

I've been snubbin' 'long the towpath nearly fifty years,
  I've seen my share, had tears and frolics, too;
The steam cars have outdone us, we're crowded to the rear,
  The boatmen's shadows grow more dim and few;
The packet is no longer seen—it's rate of speed too slow
  To suit this age of rush and enterprise.
Soon the locks will be deserted, the grizzled captains go
On the final trip beyond the nightless skies.

CHAPTER XXII.

BUILDING OF THE PENNSYLVANIA RAILROAD.

THE main line of the four-track system of the Pennsylvania Railroad, the standard railroad of America, passes through Perry County, being located along the western banks of the Susquehanna and Juniata Rivers. It is America's model railroad as well as its historic railroad. When the great effort was made to rend in twain the Union it was to the Pennsylvania Railroad and to its vice-president, Thomas A. Scott—later its president—that Abraham Lincoln, President of the United States, turned, and the large part played by both Scott and the Pennsylvania Railroad in that immortal struggle is a matter of history. While the early history of the railroad in a general sense is not a part of the history of Perry County, yet, in a greater sense, it is, as its tracks cross the county, its lines transport practically all the traffic to and from the county, and hundreds of Perry Countians from the time of its building to now, have been at all times in its employ. For these reasons and others it is deemed proper to record something of its building and history, as well as a word of early railway history in general. So closely were the early days of railroads and canals in Pennsylvania related that it is difficult to write of one without including much of the other. For that reason the reader is referred to the chapter on The Coming of the Canals, elsewhere in this book.

Strangely enough, of the first twenty miles of the original Pennsylvania Railroad to be let and graded, thirteen were within the limits of Perry County, as the part east of Harrisburg was a state improvement yet at that time. Few people, probably have been aware of this.

As early as 1800, in England, a work entitled "Recreations in Agriculture," by Dr. James Anderson, suggested the construction of railroads at the sides of turnpikes. His descriptions were so graphic that they might have almost passed for a description of the early railroads. Up to 1825 the only railroads constructed were used for the transportation of coal and other heavy tonnage. The completion of the Liverpool and Manchester Railroad, in England, in 1829, was virtually the beginning of passenger traffic and general freight shipments over a system of rails.

In the United States, upon the termination of the Revolutionary War, the people began giving their attention to the matter of transportation. Gradually but steadily the tide of emigration had extended westward from the Atlantic seaboard, leaped the Alleghenies and pushed on to the valley of the Ohio. An immense population was foretold and it was essential to have outlets for the products of their toil. That great channel of trade in subsequent years—the Mississippi River—was virtually closed to Americans, as a large part of its territory was held by a different nation, which at that time was not on very amicable terms with the new United States. Under the authority of the State Legislature surveys were made for canals or waterways to connect the Delaware with the Ohio. Over the Alleghenies these waterways were to be connected by roadways. As steam power had not yet been applied to locomotives these connecting roads were to be merely turnpikes. Pennsylvania was the first state to begin these improvements. The Lancaster turnpike, extending from Philadelphia to Lancaster, was the first extensive turnpike to be completed in the United States. The United States government never embarked in public improvements to any great extent, and what was done had to be done by individual and state enterprise. New York State led the way by constructing the Erie Canal, and Pennsylvania followed closely with her more extensive system of general improvements.

The first railroads to be built here were modeled after those of the English, the locomotives being of English manufacture. In that way the guage of four feet, eight and one-half inches was introduced. Different roads built different guages, and the present system of universal shipments was found impossible under such a system, so that standardization followed. One of the first railroad projects inaugurated in America was in Pennsylvania, when the State Legislature, on March 31, 1823, passed an act incorporating a company to construct a railroad from Philadelphia to Columbia, a town on the Susquehanna River in Lancaster County, a distance of eighty miles. The concession was granted to John Stevens, among whose fellow incorporators were Horace Binney and Stephen Girard. They failed to build. The railroads of England were too new and the people had too little faith in them to turn from their favorite canal projects.

Pennsylvania having inaugurated a system of public improvements, it must be said to her everlasting credit that she persevered and consummated their construction—a vast work in that early day. A canal from Columbia to Philadelphia was considered impractical, and the legislatures of 1827 and 1828, believing private enterprise incapable of the undertaking, authorized the canal commissioners to locate a route for a railroad between those points, to be completed within two years. By the same acts they were commanded to locate a road from Huntingdon to Johnstown, and two million dollars were appropriated to carry on the work. This was the actual beginning of the Columbia and the Portage Railroads, works of great magnitude in their day and generation, one of which—the Portage road—by reason of the peculiarity of its construction and the great barrier to be overcome, will ever stand as a monument to those early pioneers who were not only building a railroad but were making a state and creating a nation. The fact that New York State, in 1826, had completed the Erie Canal, and that it was carrying a product of almost seventy millions annually to the seaboard, spurred them on. That canal had taken from Philadelphia her commercial supremacy and considerably stimulated the growth of her rival, New York City. Self-preservation made action necessary, and two million dollars annually were appropriated for years to complete the public works. This great expenditure taxed the resources of the young state to the utmost, and among the means of raising revenue was the extension of the charter of the Bank of Pennsylvania in 1830, for eighteen years, on condition that it loan the state four millions at five and one-half per cent, towards the completion of the canals and the railroads.

While the state was pushing through the main line, individuals and firms were constructing railroads within its borders. Among these were the Harrisburg and Portsmouth, and the Philadelphia and Trenton Railroads, both of which are now a part of the main line of the Pennsylvania system. In 1833 the canal commissioners were directed by the State Legislature to complete the Columbia Railroad with double tracks, and the Portage Railroad with a single track, and to complete the main line of the canal. It was promptly done, and in 1834 the entire line from Philadelphia to Pittsburgh was opened to trade and travel. As finished it consisted of the following sections:

1. Columbia Railroad, from Philadelphia to Columbia, eighty-two miles in length.

2. Eastern division of canal, from Columbia to Hollidaysburg, one hundred and seventy-two miles.

3. Portage Railroad. from Hollidaysburg to Johnstown, thirty-six miles.

4. Western division of canal, from Johnstown to Pittsburgh, one hundred and four miles, making a total of three hundred and ninety-four miles.

Being thus broken and requiring reshipping of freight, which was both tedious and expensive, it never proved remunerative to the state, but to the country through which it passed it was a marvel of development, and our inland counties—including Perry—owe to it much of their early development.

The first railroad from Philadelphia to Columbia was operated by horses, instead of locomotives. The "cars" were something larger than the later stagecoaches, and horses were changed every twelve miles. About 1836 locomotives replaced the horses. The cars were the property of individuals and a freight toll was charged

these planes, and during the twenty years it was in use no serious accident occurred. Boats carrying through freight were later built in sections, which were placed upon trucks and thus transported over the Alleghenies.

A general convention was assembled at Harrisburg, March 6, 1838, to urge the building of a continuous railroad across the state. A southern route, via Bedford and Somerset, was considered and pronounced practicable, with the exception of about fifty miles over the Alleghenies between Bedford and Franklin Counties, where it was suggested that the turnpike be resorted to. A second route was the one up the Susquehanna to Northumberland, thence via the headwaters of Bald Eagle Creek to the headwaters west of the mountains. It was deemed a feasible route, but too circuitous. The third or middle route suggested was the one that is practically the route of the Pennsylvania Railroad of to-day. It was via the Juniata and the Conemaugh Rivers, crossing the Alleghenies by a series of curves, among which is the famous horseshoe curve. Great as was the need it was not until 1846 that the project assumed tangible shape. On April 13th of that year, the act to incorporate the Pennsylvania Railroad Company passed the Pennsylvania Legislature. Its capital was made seven and one-half millions, with the privilege of increasing to ten millions. This act also provided that in case the company should have three millions actually subscribed and one million actually paid into the treasury, and fifteen miles under construction at each end of the line prior to July 30, 1847, the law granting the right of way to the Baltimore & Ohio Railroad from Cumberland, Maryland, to Pittsburgh, should be null and void. These conditions were complied with, and Governor Shunk granted a charter to the company, and on August 2d issued a proclamation declaring the privileges which had been granted to the Baltimore & Ohio Railroad Company abrogated.

That piece of legislation is of peculiar importance to Perry Countians, for it was a native of Perry County who proposed it. William Bigler, then speaker of the Senate, who later became governor, was the man. He represented Armstrong, Indiana, Cambria and Clearfield Counties—a district that was divided upon this question—yet manfully made a plea for the road through the central part of the state. He ardently supported the friends of the Pennsylvania Railroad in procuring the charter, and in passing the act which gave municipal and other corporations the power to subscribe to its capital stock, without which it could not have been built and which was fiercely opposed in the legislature. (See chapter in this book devoted to Governor Bigler.) For a time this action met with much opposition in Allegheny County and the southwestern counties of the state, but when they saw the resourcefulness of its projectors and the energetic manner in which construction was pursued their antagonism was changed to friendship, and to-day Allegheny County and Pittsburgh are zealous of its very reputation, for there is located its greatest junction, and railroad and city interests are interwoven to a remarkable degree.

On June 22, 1846, books were opened throughout the state for the sale of the stock of the company. Public meetings were held, a house-to-house canvass was made in Philadelphia, and the newspapers were untiring in endorsing the project. The grading of the first twenty miles of the road west of Harrisburg was let on May 16, 1847. (According to President Rea the date would be July 10th.) Over half of this stretch was within the limits of Perry County. The railroad was then called the Pennsylvania Central Railroad. During that summer a city daily contained the following: "The great central railroad—that imperishable chain, destined to more closely unite the interests of the East and the West of this continent—is rapidly progressing along the banks of the Juniata. Day by day the engineers and workmen may be seen surveying, arranging, digging and blasting away, by which the highest, most rugged and rocky bluffs bordering the river crumble and are subdued, forming the foundation for this life-artery of Pennsylvania." On November 26th of the same year, forty additional miles were let, carrying the part under contract to the eastern end of Lewistown. About the same time the company let a contract for fifteen thousand tons of rails, with the stipulation that they were to be manufactured in Pennsylvania. The City of Philadelphia subscribed two and a half millions that year, and Allegheny County followed the next year with a subscription of a million.

On September 1, 1849, the first section, from Harrisburg to Lewistown, a distance of sixty-one miles, was opened for travel. During 1849, what was virtually a "fleet" of canal boats, were engaged in hauling to Hollidaysburg the rails with which to lay the tracks west of the mountains. On December 10, 1852, the line had been completed and the first through train run from Philadelphia to Pittsburgh, using the Portage road as part of the route. On February 15, 1854, the new line had been completed entirely, and the first through train was run over it, not using the Portage route. The public works had cost the state a fortune and were unprofitable. A demand for their sale grew, and accordingly on April 27, 1854, the legislature passed a bill providing for the sale of the main line. No buyer could be found under its provisions. An act of 1855 also proved ineffectual, but an act of May 16, 1857, finally consummated the sale. The price was $7,500,000. In 1864 the company turned its attention to the introduction of steel rails and stimulated their manufacture in America.

When the Pennsylvania Railroad was organized, eight directors were elected by the stockholders, of whom J. Edgar Thompson was one, and one by the City of Philadelphia. Allegheny County elected two directors, and one of them was Thomas Scott, so that the new board contained two of the greatest railroad men yet produced in America. The board then elected an additional director. Mr. Thompson was made president. The State of Pennsylvania then owned the line to Dillerville (west of Lancaster), sixty-nine miles in length. There the tracks were joined to the Harrisburg, Portsmouth (Middletown), Mt. Joy and Lancaster Railroad, thirty-six miles in length. At Harrisburg the 248 miles of the Pennsylvania Railroad started.

According to the diary of the late Jacob Young, the first Pennsylvania locomotive steamed into Duncannon on July 16, 1849. No further notation is made. About that time John D. Crilly, who had published the *Perry County Standard* and kept a hotel at New Bloomfield, purchased a hotel at Newport and operated a stage line. His son, D. F. Crilly, now a retired and wealthy real estate operator and builder of Chicago, aged eighty-two, then a boy of eleven years, thus describes the entry of the first train into Newport:

"At this time the Pennsylvania Railroad was being built through Newport, which was the main line to the West. The scholars of the school there were given a recess to see the first train pass through the town, which was quite an event. The crew of the train allowed the townspeople to climb aboard to take their first railroad ride. On the return trip those so honored were obliged to jump from the train, as it did not stop in passing through the village. No one was hurt, however, in detraining."

An early description of the road about Duncannon is interesting:

"Passing the point of the rocks by a sharp curve to the west the traveler soon crosses the beautiful Sherman's Creek and his ears are saluted with the heavy reverberations of the forge, the roar of the waterfall and the busy noises of the rolling mills. The evidences of industry and thrift are conspicuous in this locality, and the enterprise of William Logan Fisher has erected there a monument durable as brass. Pig, bar, rolled and hammered iron, nails and spikes, are products of these works. Anthracite coal is brought by canal from the Shamokin region, and various localities, some of which are very distant, are laid under contribution for the best varieties of ores.

"Dealers in lumber from the principal cities and from the various towns on the river below Harrisburg resort to the island to make their purchases and secure pick of the market.

"Passing along a rocky sidehill for a distance of nearly two miles the train usually stops at Aqueduct. Here passengers for the Susquehanna region are transferred to the packet boat, which, after receiving its cargo of human freight, crosses the Acqueduct and is towed by horses to Williamsport, on the west branch of the Susquehanna.

"Leaving our friends in the packet to the enjoyment of their bilge water and mosquitoes and to all the comforts of narrow berths, crying babies, and the chances of suffocation, enjoyments which a shower of rain is sure to greatly enhance, we will bid adieu to the blue hills of the Susquehanna and its broad, shining waters and wend our way to the sources of the gently flowing Juniata, where they gush forth in copious streams from the broad bosom of the Alleghenies."

When the turnpikes were built, often termed the national roads, they had tortuous grades reaching two hundred feet to the mile, on which the commerce of the nation was to be tediously and laboriously transported at an average of fifty miles in each twenty-four hours. For years those roads served, and then came the canal, a considerable improvement. Charles Dickens, the noted English author who used it, left evidence that it was a "vast improvement in comfort over the dusty, lumbering stagecoach." Then came the railroad and, although slow and somewhat tedious at first, its projectors were real benefactors. Its successful completion in the face of natural barriers and to the astonishment of the world, worked a revolution in commerce, and to its builders the American people should ever be grateful.

Prior to the days of the railroads the stagecoach was the popular mode of travel, and various lines were operated from different points. John D. Crilly, who kept a hotel at New Bloomfield and also published the *Perry County Standard,* operated a line of stagecoaches from New Bloomfield, but later sold his hotel and paper there and opened a hotel in Newport, operating his line of stages from there. The advent of the railroad made the business unprofitable.

As a member of the House of Representatives, the late A. K. McClure, another native Perry Countian, figured in the sale of the public works, by proposing the abolishment of the canal board, a body that had attained an unsavory reputation. In his "Old-Time Notes of Pennsylvania," he says:

"The Pennsylvania Railroad Company took possession of the main line on the 1st of August, 1857, and in his annual message Governor Pollock congratulated the people of the state upon the consummation of the sale. He said: 'The many approve; the few complain, those most who have gained an unenviable reputation by reckless disregard of the public interests as exhibited in the extravagant, useless and fraudulent expenditure of the public money for selfish or partisan purposes.' The sale embraced only the main line, including the canals and railroads owned by the state between Philadelphia and Pittsburgh, but one year later the legislature of 1858 sold all the remaining state canals to the Philadelphia & Erie Railroad, and I felt a great pride in being able, as a member of the house, to propose and help pass unanimously an act of five lines abolishing the canal board that had been a fountain of debauchery and profligacy for many years. Governor Pollock exerted a powerful if not a controlling influence in accomplishing the sale of the main line, that became the first development of the progressive policy that has made the Pennsylvania Railroad Company the greatest railway system in the world."

While the railroad traffic was very slow at first, yet as early as 1854, on July 6th, a new train was put on which was scheduled to make the trip from Philadelphia to Pittsburgh in thirteen hours—fast time, indeed, for the equipment then in use. The mail trains of the summer schedule of 1853 were designated as follows: Fast line at Newport—west at 5:19, east at 11:38; Slow Line at Newport—west at 2:01, east at 1:35. The "slow line" was the local train.

The railroad at first was a single track, with two passenger trains each way daily. The freight trains ran three times a week each way. All trains were drawn by very small engines in comparison with those now in use, but their huge funnel-shaped smokestacks were many times the size of those of to-day. Mixed trains (freight and passenger) were run over the main line as late as 1877, and are remembered by the older people of this generation. Market cars, owned by individuals, were run. E. B. Fleck, of Newport, and B. F. Alexander, of Duncannon, were the owners of two of them.

To-day no railroad is more carefully managed than the Pennsylvania System, and over its tracks daily pass hundreds of trains, instead of two or three each way, as in that early period. Its interlocking electric signal system, its trackwalkers and its corps of men trained in their especial lines so guard traffic that there have been whole years in which the life of a single passenger was not lost—a most remarkable occurrence. Its operations represent approximately one-eighth of all the railroad operations of the United States. Its lines penetrate Delaware, the District of Columbia, Illinois, Indiana, Kentucky, Maryland, Michigan, Missouri, New Jersey, New York, Ohio, Pennsylvania, Virginia, and West Virginia. In this territory live over 50,000,000 people, or over half the population of the United States.

Charles E. Pugh, who later rose to fame in railroad circles, was for a number of years the P. R. R. ticket agent at Newport.

CHAPTER XXIII.

PROJECTED AND OTHER RAILROADS.

SHOULD all the railroads have been built which were projected through the county, it would certainly have had the most ample facilities along that line of any county in the state. The first attempt to build a local road was made when, on May 5, 1854, the Pennsylvania Legislature passed an act incorporating the Duncannon, Landisburg & Broad Top Railroad Company, with a capital of $800,000, and authorizing the construction of a railroad from a point at or near Duncannon, Perry County, to a point on Broad Top Mountain, in Bedford County, passing through Sherman's Valley via Shermansdale, Landisburg and Bixler's Mills, and through East Waterford, Juniata County. The act incorporating this line was signed by Governor William Bigler, himself a native Perry Countian, and the incorporators were Charles W. Fisher, John Souder, Abraham L. Bowman, David Mickey, Jacob Billow, Henry H. Etter, Christian Thudium, Dr. James Galbraith, Gen. Henry Fetter, David Kochenderfer, Jacob Bixler, George Hench, Wm. B. Anderson, Samuel Milligan, Arnold H. Fahs, George Johnston, Wm. Kirk, Col. Geo. Noss, Alexander Blair, of Perry, Juniata and adjoining counties. A year later, May 5, 1855, the name was changed by an act of the legislature, to the Sherman's Valley & Broad Top Railroad, and the eastern terminus changed from Duncannon to "at or near the mouth of Fishing Creek" (now Marysville). Its route was also changed so as to touch Burnt Cabins, in Fulton County. Then, on May 12, 1857, another act authorized the management "to extend the road by the most practical route to connect with the Connellsville & Portage Railroad and the Allegheny-Portage Railroad. Two years later, March 31, 1859, another act authorized the name of the line to be changed from the Sherman's Valley & Broad Top Railroad to the Pennsylvania-Pacific Railroad Company, with the power to extend the line westward to Maryland and Virginia (now West Virginia). On April 1, 1863, another act repealed all acts in so far as the change of name was concerned and named it the South Pacific Railroad Company. It was not begun within the time specified by the act, and on February 18, 1868, the time was extended for five years, dating from March 31, 1869. The road never was built, but grading was begun in 1857 at a point on the south side of Sherman's Creek, near Shermansdale, and extensive fills were made. The part graded was almost two miles in length.

431

In the meantime, on April 17, 1866, the Duncannon, Bloomfield & Broad Top Railroad Company was incorporated, with a capital of $1,000,000, and with power to construct a railroad from a point at or near Duncannon, Perry County, to a point at Broad Top Mountain, in Bedford County, via New Bloomfield, and with the authority to connect with any railroad at either end. On February 27, 1868, the amount of the capital was reduced to $750,000, and the route changed so as to pass through Loysville. The incorporators interested in the building of this line and in the selling of its capital stock were Benjamin F. Junkin, Joseph R. Shuler, William A. Sponsler, Griffith Jones, John Wister, and Henry D. Egolf. The bill empowered them to increase their number to twenty-five. At the end of forty-eight hours $24,000 was subscribed at Duncannon and New Bloomfield, and $2,000 at Loysville. Notwithstanding this auspicious start—for so it would have been considered in those days—the road never was built.

On March 7, 1872, the Sherman's Valley Railroad Company was chartered with Henry Foulk, Henry Brown, B. F. Hall, Abram Bower, James Galbraith, John Stambaugh, D. B. Milliken, W. W. McClure, A. M. Egolf, Samuel Spotts, Samuel Shoemaker, A. Farnham, George Hench, John Bixler, John Martin, George M. Loy, George Johnston, E. A. McLaughlin, and Jacob Espy, any five of them being authorized to start a railroad line at or near Marysville, via Shermansdale and Landisburg, to or near Loysville. There was an authorized capital of two thousand shares at $50 each. Like its predecessors, this road was never built, but its later projection seems strange indeed. A line had been projected in Adams County, March 11, 1872, known as the Bendersville Railroad Company, and on October 9, 1873, the Bendersville Extension Railroad Company was incorporated, "with authority to construct, equip, operate and maintain a railroad from a point on the Bendersville Railroad, near Bendersville, Adams County, to a point on the Sherman's Valley Railroad, near Landisburg, Perry County, a distance of about sixty miles. Just how the line was to cross the Kittatinny Mountain the reader must be left to conjecture. Nevertheless, on November 17, 1873, the three lines merged, in conformity with the act of April 26, 1870, under the name of the People's Freight Railway Company. The stockholders of the Adams County lines were to receive a share of common stock for each share of their holdings, and the Sherman's Valley stockholders were to receive one-tenth of a share of preferred stock for each of their shares. The capital was to have been 2,000,000 shares of the par value of $50. The directors were mostly from around Philadelphia, Joseph Bailey, of Baileysburg, having been the only Perry Countian. The Sherman's Valley stockholders met at Sherman's Hotel, Landisburg, November 17, 1873, and unanimously agreed to the merger, as signed by Abraham Bower, president, and Benj. F. Hall, secretary. After a lapse of almost ten years this road was again resurrected, and at a meeting held January 26, 1882, to elect officers, the name was changed from the People's Freight Railway Company to the Pennsylvania Midland Railway Company, and the capital stock was made $200,000, with 10,000 shares at $50 each. The officers then elected were: President, H. H. Bechtel; directors, O. H. P. Rider and John M. Smith, Newport; George F. Ensminger and J. L. Markel, New Bloomfield; W. F. Sadler and I. H. Graham, Carlisle. February 14th following, Mr. Ensminger was made president, and Mr. Bechtel took his place as director, having resigned the presidency. This is the last public record of this line, which, like some of the others, was built only on paper.

BUILDING OF THE PERRY COUNTY RAILROAD.

The Duncannon, Bloomfield & Loysville Railroad Company was chartered on April 3, 1872, with authority to build a line from Duncannon, via New Bloomfield, to Loysville, but like its predecessors, it resulted in nothing tangible. Its capital stock was $100,000, being two thousand shares of stock, the par value of which was $50. It had been surveyed, however. The original incorporators of this line were George Hench, Jacob Bixler, Samuel Gutshall, W. W. McClure, James McNeal, John A. Magee, John A. Baker, B. F. Junkin, John R. Shuler, John H. Sheibley, John Jones, Wm. R. Swartz, O. B. Ellis, John McAlister, Jr., and James Swartz. Over a decade later, on February 3, 1887, the Perry County Railroad Company secured its charter. In 1889, the road was begun and built as far as New Bloomfield. Maginnis & White were to grade the 11.1 miles for $32,199, but failed. Peter McGovern, of Tyrone, finished the contract. During the next two years it was extended to Loysville and Landisburg, as the newly built Newport & Sherman's Valley Railroad was diverting all traffic that way. The first locomotive ran into New Bloomfield, September 12, 1889, although the official opening was in October. After operating the Perry County Railroad for many years it met financial reverses, and it was sold to David Gring, who changed the name to the Susquehanna River & Western Railroad. It passed to Rodney Gring at his father's death, and in 1921, when the Newport & Sherman's Valley Railroad was sold on foreclosure proceedings, that road was purchased by interests connected with the Susquehanna River & Western, and the part lying to the west of Bloomfield consolidated with that line. As the Newport & Sherman's Valley was a narrow gauge line, the part taken over is to be standardized. When the Perry County Railroad was in existence Charles H. Smiley was long the president,

28

and S. H. Beck was its superintendent until he was killed, April 29, 1899.

The capital of the Perry County Railroad was $100,000, with 2,000 shares at $50. The incorporators were Frank Mortimer, president; B. F. Junkin, Chas. A. Barnett, John A. Magee, John H. Sheibley, Silas W. Conn, John Adams, M. B. Strickler, James W. Shull, R. S. Minick, Wm. Grier, A. R. Johnston and E. R. Sponsler. The extension to Loysville was built by the Perry County Railroad Extension Company, incorporated May 27, 1891, its incorporators being Chas. H. Smiley, president, he having been made president of the Perry County Railroad in the meantime; John H. Sheibley, Reuben S. Minick, B. F. Junkin, D. B. Milliken, Abraham Bower, George Patterson, H. C. Shearer, Samuel Ebert, L. C. Zimmerman, R. H. Moffitt (Harrisburg), and Wm. Miller (York). The extension was merged with the main line June 2, 1892. The sale to David Gring was on September 14, 1903, the name being then changed to Susquehanna River & Western, with Martin Mumma, J. D. Landes, B. M. Eby, James M. Barnett, Edward R. Sponsler and W. H. Sponsler as directors.

BUILDING OF THE NEWPORT & SHERMAN'S VALLEY RAILROAD.

As early as April 10, 1873, the Pennsylvania Legislature granted a charter to build a narrow gauge road from Newport westward through the Sherman's Valley. The capital was only $25,000, in $25 shares, with privilege of increasing to five thousand shares, but the company was authorized to issue and sell bonds so that the road could be constructed. Its projectors were from Newport, New Bloomfield and the entire Sherman's Valley. The original incorporators were James Everhart, Joseph W. Frank, B. F. Miller, Wm. Bosserman, J. B. Leiby, Thos. Milligan, Wm. S. Mitchell, Nicholas Miller, David Mitchell, Josiah Fickes, Amos Clemson, Henry Troup, C. J. T. McIntire, J. A. Magee, C. A. Barnett, W. A. Sponsler, Isaac Wright, A. J. Fickes, J. W. S. Kough, Thos. Milliken, H. H. Bechtel, Frank Eagle, P. Bosserman, C. Roth, Robert Neilson, John Minich, H. P. Lightner, Benj. Ritter, Andrew Loy, Samuel Shoemaker, George Hench, Jacob Bixler, Martin Motzer, Israel Lupfer, J. F. McNeal, Samuel Gutshall, Jacob Kreamer, J. R. Dunbar, Wm. Stambaugh, Wm. S. Mitchell, James B. Leiby, Jesse L. Gantt, Wilson Darlington, Isaac Hollenbaugh, John A. Fisher, George Stroup, Jacob Shively, Wm. H. Minich, John W. Gantt, James G. Ferguson, David Clark, Solomon Gray, Wm. Woods, John Bixler, George L. Ickes, Blain Grosh, George Hench (of Blain), Thomas Campbell, and Henry Cooper. Any route selected was permitted, and a three-year limit placed on the time to begin construction. The matter again dropped until, in 1890, the Newport & Sherman's Valley Company was chartered

and the construction started on its line from Newport, via Loysville, to New Germantown, 29.1 miles westward. David Gring,
interested in its construction, had owned and operated the Dia-
mond Valley narrow gauge road, and much of that road's material
was used in the construction of the Sherman's Valley line. The
first train ran into Loysville, February 16, 1891. An extension,
to be known as the Path Valley Railroad, was begun in 1893, but
after working upon its grading for a year it was abandoned. The
Newport & Sherman's Valley Railroad operated until 1921, when
it was sold at foreclosure, and purchased by George H. Ross and
Rodney Gring, as trustees for the Susquehanna Coal Company,
which is a subsidiary of the Pennsylvania Railroad Company. The
part from Newport to Bloomfield Junction was then abandoned
and the remainder became a part of the Susquehanna River &
Western, and will be standardized. The directors of the company
are Rodney Gring, George H. Ross, Charles H. Bergner, James
W. Shull, James M. Barnett, William H. Sponsler, E. R. Sponsler,
L. M. Wentzell, and P. F. Duncan.

The Newport & Sherman's Valley Railroad Company was chartered July 30, 1890, with David Gring as president, and H. H.
Bechtel, W. H. Gantt, A. V. Caldwell, R. W. Cline (Harrisburg),
W. A. Denehey (Harrisburg), W. A. P. Johnston (Harrisburg),
and B. M. Eby, as directors. The capital was $180,000, with 3,600
shares at $50. Of the whole number David Gring had 1,500
shares. Others named on the charter were J. H. Irwin, C. W.
Smith, Philip Bosserman, John Fleisher, Horace Beard, Geo.
Fleisher, D. H. Spotts, Marx Dukes, A. B. Demaree, T. H. Milli-
gan, J. S. Butz, Sr., J. S. Butz, Jr., T. H. Butturf, Frank A. Fry,
W. H. Minich, and S. H. Gring. The date of the charter of the
Path Valley extension was October 24, 1893.

The building of the two roads, the Perry County Railroad and
the Newport & Sherman's Valley line, was really the result of an
effort made by Newport in the "latter eighties" to have that town
made the county seat. The late J. R. Flickinger was then the member from Perry County in the General Assembly, and gave New
Bloomfield "a tip" that unless they could secure a railroad the
change would be hard to avert. The county seat, spurred on by
what appeared to them as their death blow, begun an effort for a
railroad. In a single day E. R. Sponsler and James W. Shull,
then young attorneys, secured subscriptions for $27,000 of stock
in New Bloomfield alone. With the building of the Perry County
Railroad, Newport, then as now the leading business town in the
county, had visions of its trade being diverted, and then was born
the rival railroad—the Newport & Sherman's Valley.

The Sherman's Valley, much of which is rich and productive
in soil, was without railroad communication for a long time, but

eventually got these two lines, which have now, however, been combined into one. That two railroads should have been built traversing the western part of Perry County was a monstrous mistake. As to which one should have been built there will always be a division of opinion, depending upon the section in which persons reside, on what interests they have, and all the attending and interlocking conditions to which humans are heir. The writer bears no brief for either section, knows the people of both sections, having lived among both, and knows that barring personal interests, all are a broad-minded people.

Following the building of the Pennsylvania Railroad there was an effort made to build a railroad from Millersburg, Dauphin County, to connect with the Pennsylvania Railroad at Bailey's Station, on the Pennsylvania line below Newport. An act of the Pennsylvania Legislature dated April 12, 1851, incorporated a company composed of George Blattenberger, Joshua Hartshorn, Benjamin Parke, Henry Buehler, Jacob M. Haldeman, Robert J. Ross, James McCormick, John Patterson, John Reifsnyder, Sr., Job R. Tyson, J. Edgar Thompson, and Robert Faries, who were authorized to open books, receive subscriptions and organize the Millersburg & Baileysburg Railroad Company. There were to have been six thousand shares, the par value to be $50. The road was never built.

Many years ago a survey was made through the Raccoon Valley, from Millerstown, passing through the townships of Tuscarora, Saville, and Northeast Madison, touching the villages of Ickesburg and Saville, and passing north of the Conococheague Mountain through Liberty Valley, to Honey Grove, Juniata County. Nothing resulted.

At an early date in the Pennsylvania Railroad's history the advisability of a direct line west was apparent. A civil engineer, a Dane named Hagey, in its employ, ran a line in 1847, which was almost identical with the present line of the Susquehanna River & Western from Duncannon to New Bloomfield. Too many ridges of the Shade Mountains were in the path of the proposed route. During October, 1869, another civil engineer, a Mr. Barrett, surveyed a route passing New Bloomfield to the East Broad Top coal fields. In 1879 H. L. Preisler, a civil engineer and a native of Landisburg, ran a line from New Bloomfield to Losh's Run, at the expense of a number of New Bloomfield attorneys, but the resources were not available for its building. In 1880 a line was surveyed from New Bloomfield to Newport, but the grade was found too heavy and the expense too great for the estimated income.

On May 20, 1903, a charter was granted for a railroad from Selinsgrove Junction, Northumberland County, crossing the Susquehanna River to the west bank, thence south through Snyder, Juniata and Perry Counties, via the route of the old Pennsylvania Canal, crossing the Juniata River, to a point on the Pennsylvania Railroad, near Aqueduct Station, thence through to the Enola yards. The capital stock was $350,000, and officials of the Pennsylvania Railroad were the incorporators. It was known as the Southern Central Railway.

An electric line was once projected to operate an electric street railway from Marysville to Duncannon, and through the latter town. The Perry County Electric Railway was chartered July 23, 1902, with E. J. Stackpole, president, and Herman P. Miller, W. Harry Baker, Edward E. Jauss and Wm. P. Miller on the board. The capital was $50,000, with 1,000 shares at $50. All were Harrisburg residents. No effort was made to construct the line.

CHAPTER XXIV.

THE SUNDAY SCHOOL MOVEMENT IN PERRY.

WHILE the Sunday school movement from the broad standpoint dates back to Robert Raikes and 1780, yet the history
of the start of local schools in individual communities is
largely lost, as few permanent records were kept; but that they
came, that they multiplied to almost countless numbers, that they
girdle the earth, and that they are one of the greatest benefactions
to civilization, is no question. Their mission is to study the Bible,
which, even apart from its divine inspiration, should be more universally read and studied, for it is the greatest summary of human
wisdom and a model of classic English. Almost all of us read it
too little.

In Pennsylvania there is record of an early Sunday school in
connection with a church at Pittsburgh, in 1815. In 1819, Rev. John
George Lochmann, D.D., pastor of Zion Lutheran Church, Harrisburg, organized the first one in the State Capitol for the teaching
of Scripture. By referring to the history of the Duncannon Presbyterian Church, elsewhere in this book, it will be seen that the
Sunday school connected with that church (organized in 1816),
then known as "the church at the mouth of the Juniata," was the
first one to be formed within the limits of what is now Perry
County, and the only one to be organized while the territory was
yet a part of Cumberland. The organization of this school is
accredited to Mrs. Campbell and her sister, Miss Harriet Miller,
of Carlisle, and the former's daughters, Sallie and Julianna. The
ladies evidently remained in the community for a time, as Mrs.
Campbell is quoted as being the first superintendent opening the
school with prayer, save on occasions when Isaac Kirkpatrick, the
first elder of that church, was present. The first teachers were
Mrs. Campbell; her sister, Miss Harriet Miller; her daughters,
Misses Sallie and Julianna Campbell, Mrs. Matilda Duncan, Miss
Hannah Duncan, Miss Elizabeth Hackett, and Miss Isabella Wilson. The attendance was about forty. It is well to remember that
to women does Perry County owe its initiatory Sunday school
work, and, to a great extent, the successful carrying on of its
many Sunday schools during the past century.

Unless tradition and records exist which it has been impossible
to uncover, this was the first Sunday school in the county's territory. According to records compiled, there was one organized in
Landisburg in 1821. The *Perry Forester* of September 27, 1821,

contains a half-page of "Regulations for the government of the
Landisburg Sunday school," which shows that it had been but recently organized then, instead of in 1822, as frequently stated. It
collected fines for absences, as follows: From the superintendent,
six cents; from directors, six cents each, and from teachers, three
cents each. Either in 1823 or 1824 one was organized at the Middle Ridge Presbyterian Church, and continued for several years.
Ralph Smiley was its first superintendent. He was a bachelor and
the owner of Fravel's mill, south of Witherow's, near New Bloomfield, and lies buried in the old graveyard on High Street, New
Bloomfield. In the year 1824 one was organized in Buck's Valley,
Buffalo Township, in the log schoolhouse, on the Richard Baird
place (at the forks of the road near the Richard Callin home).
This old school building is yet remembered by Mrs. Mary (Buck)
Kumler, who attended school there in later years. In 1825 there
was one in the Linn schoolhouse, near Ickesburg. In 1828 one
was organized at Loysville. In 1830 there were ten organized
schools within the county. The number grew slowly but surely,
at first, with the result that a County Bible Society was organized
in 1846, at Landisburg, and existed for a number of years (at
least, until 1855), being the forerunner of the Perry County Sabbath School Association, which is conducted practically along the
same lines, but likely with more energy. The Sunday schools contributed to its support and sent delegates. On August 24, 1871,
at Loysville, the Perry County Sabbath School Association was
organized, largely through the efforts of Rev. S. E. Herring, then
pastor of the Reformed Church at Blain. The State Sabbath
School Convention had been held at Harrisburg, June 14 to 16,
1871, and twenty persons from Perry County attended, which
probably presaged the formation of the county organization two
months later. The meeting at Loysville was in response to a public
call and was followed by a second meeting the same year, at New
Bloomfield, on November 14th and 15th. At the first convention
eighteen schools were all that were represented, with an attendance
of forty persons, although there were then many more schools in
existence. A constitution was adopted, however. The most important subject up for discussion was, "Should Sunday schools be
open all the year?" It was unanimously decided that they should,
wherever possible. The officers of the first convention were: S. E.
Herring, of Blain, president; Rev. Sell and J. L. Diven, Landisburg, secretaries; J. B. Habecker, of Newport, treasurer. The
constitution adopted provided for five vice-presidents and entrusted
the direction of the work to an executive committee, consisting of
three ministers and two laymen.

At the second annual convention, in the Union Church, in Newport, May 14, and 15, 1872, fifty schools were represented by

eighty-one delegates. At the third convention, in New Bloomfield, in 1873, the late Judge B. F. Junkin was elected president, the first layman to fill the position. The forty-eight schools then represented at the convention had 3,264 scholars and 578 teachers. Results were increasing and in 1876, when the convention met at Ickesburg, seventy-two schools reported 4,873 scholars and 874 officers and teachers. Thirty-four schools at that time already were open throughout the year, and the rest for periods varying from as low as three to nine months. The 1883 convention at Millerstown had an innovation, when the Centennial Band held a concert in the public square in the evening for the benefit of the delegates. A children's mass meeting was also held after the school hour. The county yet had toll bridges, and passage over the Juniata River bridge at that point was given free to delegates from entire western Perry. There were then 115 schools in the county, seventy-two being represented by delegates and reports. The organization of the first Home Department was not reported until the convention of 1900.

Rev. Homer G. McMillen, a scion of the noted McMillen family of Madison Township, was a field worker for the State Sunday School Association during the summers of 1904, 1905, and 1906, being assigned to cover his home county of Perry. He organized the county into ten districts and was the pioneer in modern Sunday school work, organizing cradle rolls, home departments, teachers' training classes, etc., through district institutes, which were held in every district during three consecutive summers and have been continued since. During the first summer he traveled 1,539 miles, held nine district institutes, and visited thirty-two Sunday schools. During the succeeding two years his work was approximately the same. This gave to the work its greatest impetus.

With his coming to Penn Township, Perry County, to reside, Arthur K. Lefevre, of Harrisburg, "yet in his twenties," became associated with the work of the Sunday schools and in 1910, at the Marysville convention, he was made president of the County Association. Largely up to that time the presidency of the County Association was passed out as a sort of honor, and very few of the many fine and honorable men who occupied it did much work, outside of their own Sunday schools, in an organizing way, between conventions. With Arthur Lefevre it was different. He was what modern parlance terms "a live wire," and during the two years in which he was president of the County Association he was continually on the job, holding conferences, visiting the schools, using publicity in the county press to keep the work before the public, and putting new life into every department of the work. He set the pace, and to him is largely due the aggressive spirit and work now being so ably conducted under the leadership of David S. Fry, of Newport, who has been president of the County Association since 1915, save for one year.

Following is a list of the county presidents, secretaries, and the dates and places where the county conventions have been held:

Yr.	President.	Secretary	Place and Date.
1871	Rev. S. E. Herring	Rev. Sell	Loysville, Aug. 24.
1871	....	I. L. Diven	Bloomfield, Nov. 14, 15.
1872	Rev. H. C. Cheston	I. G. Black	Newport, May 14, 15.
1872	....	....	Duncannon, Oct. 15, 16.
1873	Rev. James Crawford ..	Rev. Mr. Smith	Millerstown, May 13, 14.
1874	Hon. B. F. Junkin	Rev. R. MacPherson ..	Bloomfield, May 12, 13.
1875	Rev. Mr. Winebeggler .	Rev. W. H. Herbert	Landisburg, May 11, 12.
1876	Capt. F. M. McKeehan .	E. P. Titzell	Newport, May 30, 31.
1877	W. W. McClure	Rev. F. L. Nicodemus ..	Loysville, May 30, 31.
1878	Rev. F. S. Lindaman, ..	Rev. Deitrich	Ickesburg, May 22, 23.
1879	Rev. J. Frazier	David Mickey	Blain, May 27, 28.
1880	Rev. R. MacPherson ...	David Mickey	Bloomfield. May 18, 19.
1881	Wm. Willis	David Mickey	Landisburg, May 31, June 1.
1882	Rev. Geo. W. Crist ...	Rev. J. W. Ely	Bloomfield, May 30, 31.
1883	Rev. W. R. H. Deatrich	Rev. W. B. Glanding ...	Millerstown, May 15, 16.
1884	Rev. R. F. McClean ...	Rev. T. M. Griffith	Newport, May 20, 21.
1885	Rev. J. H. Cooper	Rev. W. J. Grissinger ..	Loysville, May 26, 27.
1886	Prof. E. U. Aumiller ..	H. H. Rice	Landisburg, May 20, 21.
1887	Rev. J. T. Wilson	Josiah W. Rice	Duncannon, May 31, June 1.
1888	Capt. F. M. McKeehan .	W. W. McClure	Elliottsburg, May 31, June 1.
1889	Rev. A. B. Stoner	Chas. S. Losh	Ickesburg, May 28, 29.
1890	L. B. Kerr	Chas. S. Losh	Bloomfield, June 4, 5.
1891	Rev. J. Y. Shannon ...	W. W. McClure	Blain, June 3, 4.
1892	Rev. S. C. Alexander ..	Mr. Rice	Loysville, June 2, 3.
1893	J. B. Lahr	W. H. Kell	Newport, June 6, 7.
1894	J. B. Lahr	W. H. Kell	Liverpool, June 5, 6.
1895	J. B. Lahr	W. H. Kell	Duncannon, June 4, 5.
1896	Rev. F. T. Wheeler ...	W. H. Graham	Bloomfield, June 9, 10.
1897	Rev. W. D. E. Scott ..	A. C. Lackey	Blain, May 18-20.
1898	Rev. W. D. E. Scott ..	A. C. Lackey	Marysville, May 18-20.
1899	Wm. R. Swartz	J. W. Morrow	Loysville, May 16, 17.
1900	Rev. T. C. Strock	A. C. Lackey	Duncannon, May 7, 8.
1901	Rev. F. T. Wheeler ...	Lillian Flickinger	Ickesburg, June 18, 19.
1902	Rev. J. B. Lau	Sarada McLaughlin ...	Newport, May 13. 14.
1903	*		
1904	William Rounsley	Sarada McLaughlin	Blain, May 10, 11.
1905	Milton E. Kline	Sarada McLaughlin	Millerstown, June 6, 7.
1906	Rev. C. A. Waltman ...	Edna Souder	Duncannon, June 20, 21.
1907	Rev. W. S. Sturgeon ..	Mary Dum	Elliottsburg, May 21, 22.
1908	Rev. J. B. Baker	Mary Dum	Blain, June 2, 3.
1909	Rev. P. H. Moover	Mary Dum	Newport, June 22, 23.
1910	A. K. Lefevre	Mary Dum	Marysville, June 1, 2.
1911	A. K. Lefevre	Mary Dum	Newport, May 11, 12.
1912	D. S. Fry	Mary Dum	Liverpool, June 25, 26.
1913	Chas. Bothwell	Mrs. W. C. Patterson ...	Duncannon, May 8, 9.
1914	Chas. Bothwell	Catharine Long	Bloomfield, May 7, 8.
1915	D. S. Fry	Catharine Long	Marysville, May 5, 6.
1916	D. S. Fry	Puera Robinson	Blain, May 3, 4.
1917	D. S. Fry	Puera Robinson	Newport, May 2, 3.
1918	D. S. Fry	Puera Robinson	Duncannon, May 8, 9.
1919	C. M. Bower	Mrs. George W. Hain ..	Ickesburg, May 7, 8.
1920	D. S. Fry	Mrs. George W. Hain ..	Millerstown, May 12, 13.
1921	D. S. Fry	Mrs George W. Hain ..	Elliottsburg, May 4, 5.

*The convention of 1903 was to have been held at Blain, but was postponed.
David Mickey was the first statistical secretary. elected in 1882 and serving to 1884. Other statistical secretaries were P. G. Kell, 1885-1905; Sarada McLaughlin, 1906-1907; Clara E. Waggoner, 1908-1909; Gertrude Fickes, 1910; Thersa Zimmerman, 1911; Daisie V. Kuhn. 1912-1915. (In 1916 the office of statistical secretary was abolished, the duties being merged with those of the corresponding secretary.)

The office of corresponding secretary was created in 1904, when Mame Seager was elected, who served in 1905 also; Sarada McLaughlin, statistical secretary, was elected also corresponding secretary in 1906, but the latter title was dropped in 1907, and seemed to be used interchangeably with statistical secretary till 1911, when Daisie V. Kuhn was elected, to be followed in 1912 by Puera B. Robinson. who held the office until July 1, 1918, when she resigned and was succeeded by Mrs. George W. Hain. then Miss Emma Roberts.

The treasurers of the County Association were J. B. Habecker, 1871, 1872, 1874; Ezra P. Titzel, 1873; E. A. Flickinger, 1875; Henry Smith, 1876, 1877; Hon. J. A. Baker, 1878-1885; John Heim, 1886-1887; J. A. McCroskey, 1888-1889; H. E. Bonsall, 1890-1897; J. B. Lahr, 1898-1911; E. D. Bistline, 1912-1915; Chas. S. Brunner, 1916 to 1922.

Perry County has been ably represented at the many conventions of the State Association, and at two World Conventions, that at Switzerland, in 1913, and in Japan, in 1920. The latter two were attended by Mrs. Carrie Eby Jeffers and Mrs. Margaret Frank Sefton.

Rev. William Weaver, who filled the Liverpool Lutheran charge from early in 1847 until early in 1851, preaching at Liverpool, at Christ's Church (known as the White Church) in Perry Valley, at Millerstown, at St. Michael's in Pfoutz Valley, at St. James' in Turkey Valley, at Richfield, and at St. John's (Neiman's Church), organized more Sunday schools than any other minister in the history of thé county. He organized thirteen schools in his territory, but the last three of the churches named above were in Juniata County, and it is only fair to assume that some of the Sunday schools also were located there. However, should such have been the case, the number formed in Perry County still entitles him to the credit of organizing more than any other person, according to all available records.

The adoption of the International Uniform Lessons occurred on Thursday, April 18, 1872, at the Fifth National Sunday School Convention, at Indianapolis, Indiana. It was at 4 o'clock p. m., under a special order of business, and under the leadership of B. F. Jacobs. That date and circumstances are of great import as from then on the Sunday school work became systematized and of great power. Its effect was soon noticeable in Perry County.

The State Sabbath School Association has presented gold medals to three Perry Countians for having had a record of attendance covering fifty years of Sunday school work. They went to Mrs. John T. Glass, of Duncannon, who was a teacher in the Methodist Sunday school there for over fifty years, and to Samuel Reen, long a resident of Newport, now residing at Blain, and David Ritter, of Liverpool. Mrs. Glass and Mr. Ritter died during the past two years.

Earlier in this book appears a cut of "Grandfather" Jacob Buck, one of Perry County's pioneers in Sunday school work in the country districts. He was but one of a devoted body of men and women to whom is largely due the foundation work of the Sunday school movement.

Considerable data in reference to the County Association was originally compiled by Robert W. Diven and David S. Fry, of Newport, S. H. Bernheisel, of New Bloomfield; Mrs. Sarada (McLaughlin) Burkholder, formerly of Roseburg, Perry County.

CHAPTER XXV.

THE LIQUOR QUESTION.

ON January 16, 1920, the centenary of the formation of Perry County, the Constitutional Prohibition Amendment became the law of the land. Prior to that time half of the United States had voted against liquor. Perry County had "gone dry" in March, 1918, after Associate Judge George Boyer took office, the President Judge, Jeremiah N. Keller, being opposed to licenses. They joined and refused every application at the session of license court that year. The licenses for the sale of liquor expired March 31, 1918.

But the trend has long been towards the elimination of intoxicants. Maine had barred liquor as early as 1850. The first step was made about one hundred years ago, when Sunday schools were organized all over the country. While the study of Scripture was the object, that Scripture contains within its pages many references to strong drink, and its admonitions have been sinking into the minds of the sixth generation. Then, almost fifty years ago, the Sunday schools adopted business principles and made the lesson for all schools identical each Sunday, and in each quarter they placed one temperance lesson. In the opinion of the writer that had as much to do with the elimination of the liquor traffic as any one thing which ever happened. The second generation of those boys who attended Sunday school had become voters, and many of the first generation of the girls who attended are the mothers of boys who vote. Then, the business interests found that the drinking workman was inferior to the one who did not drink, and the attendant result of these and other conditions is the adoption of the Eighteenth Amendment to the Constitution. Even as early as 1832 the George Hench tannery, in Perry County, would employ only men of temperate habits.

Perry was a "middle of the road" county. Sometimes one side would win in a political contest, and sometimes the other, but there are many references here and there along the way showing a trend toward temperance. One of the earliest was a call for the organization of a temperance society in Perry County, made by B. McIntire, over his signature, on January 14, 1833, the date of the meeting to be February 26th. Another was a remonstrance from the town of Ickesburg, objecting to the licensing of a hotel, presented to the Perry County courts as early as the April term, 1833.

Its signers were ancestors of many notable Perry Countians. It follows:

The petitioners, inhabitants of Saville Township, beg leave respectfully to represent that the large and beautiful tavern stand in the town of Ickesburg (occupied for the last year by Mr. Edward Miller), is now purchased by Mr. John Elliot, and will by him be occupied for the present year as a temperance house of entertainment; that we place the utmost confidence in said Elliot as a man well qualified for that business; that he will be provided with everything necessary for the entertainment of strangers and travelers, and that we believe he will be able conveniently to furnish lodging at any time and to any number that may be expected to call in that place. Your petitioners therefore believe that there is no necessity for any other tavern in said town, and more especially for one in which spirituous liquors would be sold, which would only tend to injure the morality, peace and comfort of the community. Should any person therefor apply we would respectfully ask your honors to refuse them such license; and we are in duty bound to pray.

Robert Elliot.	William Irvine.	A. Linn.
William Milligan.	George Baker.	Henry Thatcher.
Frederick Hartman.	Alexander Patterson.	Samuel Reed.
John B. Baker.	David Coyle.	George Billman.
Alexander Robison.	George Sanderson.	Robert Irvine.
Moses Hall.		

By 1835 there were temperance societies at Landisburg, Buffalo Township, Millerstown, and New Bloomfield.

John Staily entered the liquor business at Liverpool, and in 1865 erected a large brick building to extend better accommodations to the public. A year later, in 1866, he suddenly saw things from a different standpoint and, without even mentioning the fact to his family, emptied all the liquors from containers and closed the bar. Before that, in 1860, Mrs. Emily Gray had changed her hotel at New Germantown to a no-license place, after having conducted the sale of liquor there for almost thirty years. The place was known as the "Travelers' Rest." That was before the internal revenue laws covered the liquor business and a license then cost $7.50, with larger-sized glasses of whiskey being sold at three cents, according to Wilson W. Morrison, still residing in that town.

The first temperance ticket nominated and voted for in the county was in 1871. In 1872 there was a campaign in Pennsylvania against alcoholic liquors which resulted in a local option law, but through reaction it was soon repealed. Under it Perry County voted "dry." Largely through the evils of intemperance was it possible to pass the high license law of 1887. The temperance element, however, were dissatisfied with that measure and succeeded in getting before the voters, in 1889, a constitutional amendment, but it was defeated by a large majority. From then on the efforts for the abolition of the liquor business were principally made a matter of education through the Sunday schools and other moral agencies, as stated in the beginning of this topic.

the county thirteen Sunday schools, more than any other person. The late Jacob Billow, of Carroll Township, was an ardent pioneer temperance advocate, and delivered many talks and addresses against the liquor traffic, the title of one of his lectures being "The Three-Legged Stool." His efforts were not confined to Perry County.

Other notable facts connected with the long war waged against liquor in Perry County are that Daniel Gantt, a New Bloomfield attorney who later became the first chief justice of Nebraska, was president of the Sons of Temperance, formed in New Bloomfield in 1846; that in the same year the Sons of Temperance was organized at Duncannon; that at the January term of the courts in 1850 there was presented the accounts of a "Committee" of a man declared "a habitual drunkard"; that among the early editors John A. Baker, George W. Sloop, and John A. Magee printed very, very many articles bearing against the traffic, and that in later years Wm. C. Lebo practically made his paper a temperance paper instead of a political one, no doubt sacrificing considerable business to principle.

During the earlier years of the county's existence there were many taverns, and it seems to have been a common thing to have had the drinking habit. Every village and hamlet had at least one tavern. New Bloomfield at one time had five. When the Pennsylvania Canal was dug, according to a historical sketch compiled by the late Rev. Logan, in Millerstown, "nearly every house was a hotel." Liverpool, during the same period, had many, and other towns also had a very considerable number. In the days of our grandfathers it was thought almost impossible to harvest a crop without a goodly supply of whiskey for the harvesters. In the poor farm account of receipts and expenditures, dated March 20, 1823, one of the items of disbursement read as follows: "To sundry persons, for labor on farm, harvesting, liquors, etc., $75.04." The late W. H. Waggoner had told to him on more than one occasion by his mother, who was an attendant, that at the wedding of Rev. John Linn whiskey in jugs was there for the guests.

Among the old letters and documents found in the William Anderson, Sr., home at Andersonburg, now occupied by Arthur Anderson, was one which shows that liquor was used at funerals:

Recd. from John Nelson and William Anderson, executors of the last will and testament of William Anderson, deceased, the sum of two pounds, one shilling and nine pence, being for whiskey used at the funeral and on that occasion of the deceased, February 2, 1802.

Recd. by me, WILLIAM CAMPBELL.

At the election of October 10, 1854, a prohibitory liquor law was voted upon throughout the county, and the result of the vote was 1,297 for the law, and 1,939 against it. The larger towns, Bloomfield, Liverpool, Millerstown and Petersburg (Duncannon), with Penn Township, were the only places carried against liquor. Newport was the only town of considerable size, supporting the liquor end. Two other county-wide ballots of later periods, 1873 and 1889, are matters of record. That of 1873 was on the question of local option, and the majority on the temperance side was 579. Duncannon and Millerstown were the only two towns voting in favor of license at that time. The other election was on June 18, 1889, on the adoption of a prohibitory amendment, when the county swung about and voted for liquor by 306 majority. Marysville was the only town in the county to give a majority for liquor, however. The state at that time voted to retain liquor, giving the majority of 188,027 votes. The vote by districts follows:

	1854		1873		1889	
	For Liquor	Against Liquor	For Liquor	Against Liquor	For Liquor	Against Liquor
Blain Boro.	Not formed		Not formed		23	33
Bloomfield Boro. ...	41	61	30	93	42	94
Buffalo Twp.	94	15	63	65	67	50
Carroll Twp.	98	66	75	107	121	100
Centre Twp.	101	54	49	109	95	76
Duncannon Boro. ..	Not formed		108	89	66	101
Greenwood Twp. ..	85	71	61	68	78	59
Howe Twp.	Not formed		26	34	35	16
Jackson Twp.	107	50	117	54	119	41
Juniata Twp.	148	56	40	69	66	58
Landisburg Boro. ..	41	40	19	57	11	62
Liverpool Boro.	59	74	34	139	89	92
Liverpool Twp.	101	56	55	71	92	33
Madison Twp.	116	89	87	72	87	48
Marysville Boro. ...	Not formed		59	81	98	51
Millerstown Boro. .	14	65	37	16	38	56
Miller Twp.	41	8	32	92	40	5
New Buffalo Boro..	17	15	24	42	19	25
Newport Boro.	67	39	70	148	90	141
Oliver Twp.	70	32	32	67	92	48
Penn Twp.	63	81	128	119	166	84
Petersburg Boro. ...	26	93	Name changed to Duncannon			
Rye Twp.	57	23	65	33	84	36
Sandy Hill Dist. ...	Not formed		28	93	41	83
Saville Twp.	129	106	57	115	70	147
Spring Twp.	138	45	82	122	128	85
Toboyne Twp.	96	50	73	25	52	75
Tuscarora Twp. ...	Not formed		26	71	54	55
Tyrone Twp.	115	75	85	128	103	114
Watts Twp.	49	11	43	15	48	11
Wheatfield Twp. ...	57	22	57	47	100	29
Totals	1939	1297	1662	2241	2214	1908
Majorities ...	642			579	306	

This table to the uninformed may be further explained. At the time the first vote was taken (1854) Blain Borough was a part of Jackson Township; Howe Township, a part of Oliver; Marysville Borough, a part of Rye Township; Sandy Hill District, a part of Madison Township, and Tuscarora Township, a part of Juniata Township. Duncannon was then Petersburg.

CHAPTER XXVI.

THE COUNTY'S PUBLIC OFFICIALS.

DURING the century of Perry County's existence its officials, largely, have been men of character, stability and intelligence—in fact, creditable representatives of their constituency. They have come from every walk of life, and while some of them have been college men, the greater part have been products of the little schoolhouses by the crossroads and the wayside, with perchance a term or two at an academy or a normal school.

The first officers of the county were: John Fry, member of the general assembly; John Reed, president judge; William B. Mitchell, prothonotary; Benjamin Leas, register and recorder; Daniel Stambaugh, sheriff; William Power, treasurer; Thomas Adams, Jacob Huggins, Robert Mitchell, county commissioners; William Smiley and A. Fulweiler, auditors. Of these the only one to attain promotion politically was Jacob Huggins, who became a member of the General Assembly in 1823, serving with distinction. In fact, it was the opinion of Mr. Huggins which was requested by that body and which finally clinched the location of the new county seat at New Bloomfield.

Other county commissioners who later attained the coveted place in the General Assembly were George Beaver, in 1842; Thomas Adams, in 1854; Charles C. Brandt, in 1857, and Clark Bower, in 1918. Mr. Bower is also the third member of the Bower family to have representation on the board of county commissioners. Solomon Bower was made a commissioner in 1828, his son Solomon Bower, in 1875, and his grandson, Clark Bower, in 1908, all being elected from the same district and having resided in the same house.

Among the clerks to the county commissioners, the first, Jesse Miller, became a noted figure in state and nation, and at least two others attained distinction. William N. Seibert, who was clerk in 1871, became president judge of the district composed of Perry and Juniata Counties in 1912, and James W. McKee, who was clerk in 1885, became State Senator of the district composed of Perry, Juniata and Mifflin Counties, in 1901. The first election of Congressmen in Pennsylvania was in 1788, in conformity with the Constitution of the United States, adopted the previous year. It provided that until an enumeration of the inhabitants could be made, which was to be done within three years after the first meet-

ing of Congress, and an apportionment then to be made thereunder, Pennsylvania was to have eight members. At the election
of 1788, there being no districts, they were elected by the state at
large. That method may have continued for some years, no records being available to show that the apportionment was made
until 1802.

MEMBERS OF THE UNITED STATES CONGRESS.

While there have been those of Perry County birth who have
served in the United States Congress, they are spoken of elsewhere, the list here being only those elected from Perry County
who have represented the district of which Perry County is a part.
*The district, as noted below, has varied much in the course of the
century. The present Congressman, Benjamin K. Focht, is editor
of the Lewisburg (Union County) *Saturday News,* but his birthplace was at New Bloomfield, Perry County, where his father was
a pioneer Lutheran minister. The list:

1834—Jesse Miller.	1862—Joseph Bailey.
1845—James Black.	1872—John A. Magee.
1860—Benj. F. Junkin.	

*Following each decennial census a new apportionment of the state into
congressional districts is made, and only once since its formation has the
same district been allowed to stand for the next decade in so far as Perry
County's placement is concerned. That was during the Sectional War,
when far greater duties than reapportionment occupied the minds of men,
and the district was allowed to remain as before. Before Perry became a
county, the act of April 2, 1802, made Dauphin, Cumberland, Huntingdon
and Mifflin the Fourth District, with two members. Juniata County was
then still a part of Mifflin.

Ten years later, in the act of March 20, 1812, Cumberland, Franklin and
Adams composed the Fifth District, to which the Perry County territory—
still a part of Cumberland—then belonged. It had two members. The act
creating Perry County, in 1820, placed it in this district.

The act of April 2, 1822, made Adams, Franklin, Cumberland and Perry
the Eleventh District, with two members. This was the same territory as
before, but Cumberland County had been divided by the erection of Perry
from its northern half.

On June 9, 1832, an act made the Thirteenth District include Cumberland, Perry and Juniata, with one member. Since that time each district
has had but one member.

In 1843, on March 25, an act was passed which made Cumberland, Perry
and Franklin the Sixteenth District.

In 1852, on May 1, York, Cumberland and Perry was made the Sixteenth
District, and in the act of April 10, 1862, it was not changed, save that it
was designated the Fifteenth District, instead of the Sixteenth.

The act of April 28, 1873, created the Eighteenth District, composed of
Franklin, Fulton, Huntingdon, Juniata, Snyder and Perry.

The act of May 19, 1887, threw Perry into a totally new territory with
Dauphin and Lebanon, comprising the Eighteenth District.

On July 11, 1901, the district was again changed and designated as the
Nineteenth, composed of Perry, Juniata, Mifflin, Huntingdon, Fulton,
Franklin, Snyder and Union. It is the largest territorial district in Penn-
sylvania—a commonwealth in itself. There are no cities within its borders.

The act of April 27, 1909, amended the last previous act, but left Perry in
the same district, designated as the Seventeenth. Until a reapportionment
act is passed the state will have four members-at-large.

As a matter of interest it might be stated that there has been an increase of the number of members of Congress every ten years, except that after the census of 1840 there was an actual reduction of ten. The greatest increase was after the census of 1870, when fifty members were added. The membership is now 435, while that of the British House of Commons, representing a population of only one-half of the United States, is 701 members.

MEMBERS OF THE STATE SENATE.

Previous to 1790 the legislative duties of Pennsylvania were performed by one body—the House of Delegates—but the new Constitution provided for two, a Senate and a House of Representatives. It fixed senatorial districts, which were to remain so until the first enumeration of taxable voters and an apportionment thereunder, and made the term of office four years. Districts were first formed by an act of assembly in 1794, and an act was passed requiring a new apportionment every seven years. The Constitution of 1838 changed the length of the term to three years, and in 1874 it was again placed at four years. *By different apportionments the district has been of various sizes and uncertain outline. Immediately preceding the present apportionment the district for years was composed of Perry, Juniata and Mifflin Counties. At the present time it is composed of Cumberland, Perry, Juniata and Mifflin Counties. Perry Countians were elected as follows:

1830—Jesse Miller.
1844—Wm. B. Anderson.
1846—Robert C. Stewart.
1851—Joseph Bailey.
1857—Henry Fetter.
1864—Kirk Haines.
1867—C. J. T. McIntire.
1881—Charles H. Smiley.
1901—James W. McKee.
1917—Scott Leiby.

*For a period including 1837 to 1843 Perry was in a district with Mifflin, Juniata, Union and Huntingdon. For a period covering 1864 to 1870 Perry was included in a district with Huntingdon, Blair, Centre, Mifflin and Juniata, with the right to elect two senators. For a period covering 1872 to 1876 Perry was included with Snyder, Union and Northumberland.

MEMBERS OF THE GENERAL ASSEMBLY.

According to population Perry County is entitled to but one Member of the General Assembly. At times it was part of another district, as the footnotes will show. Its representatives contain the names of many of the best families of the county, as follows:

1820-21—John Fry.
1822-23—F. M. Wadsworth.
1824-25—Jacob Huggins.
1826-27—Jesse Miller.
1828-29—W. M. Power.
1830-31—James Black.
1832-33—John Johnston.
1834-37—F. Rinehart.
1837-38—Wm. Clark.
1838-41—Wm. B. Anderson.
1842   —George Beaver.
1843-45—Thos. O'Bryan.

1846 —Eleazer Owen.	1872-73 —Joseph Shuler.[3]
1847-49—John Souder.	1874 —J. H. Sheibley.[3]
1850-52—David Stewart.	1875-76 —G. N. Reutter.
1852 —David Shaver.	1877-78 —D. H. Sheibley.
1854 —Thomas Adams.	1879-82 —M. B. Holman.
1855-56—Kirk Haines.	1883-86 —Wm. H. Sponsler.
1857 —Charles C. Brandt.	1887-88 —J. R. Flickinger.
1858 —Charles C. Brandt.[1]	1889-92 —W. R. Swartz.
1859-60—John Power.[1]	1893-96 —J. W. Buckwalter.
1861 —Wm. Lowther.[1]	1897-1900—J. Harper Seidel.
1862 —Jesse Kennedy.[1]	1901-03 —John S. Arnold.
1863 —John A. Magee.	1903-06 —Samuel B. Sheller.
1864 —Charles A. Barnett.	1907-08 —John D. Snyder.
1865-66—Geo. A. Shuman.[2]	1909-10 —W. N. Kahler.
1867 —Geo. A. Shuman.[2]	1911-14 —L. E. Donally.
1868-69—John Shively.[2]	1915-18 —John S. Eby.
1870-71—D. B. Milliken.[2]	1919-22 —Clark Bower.

[1] With Cumberland County.
[2] With Franklin County.
[3] With Dauphin County.

PRESIDENT JUDGES.

Until 1851 the president judges, the associate judges, and the judges of the Supreme Court were appointed by the governor, and held their offices during life or good behavior. An amendment to the Constitution in 1850 provided for an elective judiciary, and on April 15, 1851, the enabling legislation was passed to carry out its provisions. The term was placed at ten years.

YEARS OF INCUMBENCY:

1820-39—John Reed.	1892-1900—Jeremiah Lyons.[1]
1839-48—Samuel Hepburn.	1900-01 —L. E. Atkinson.[1]
1849-51—Frederick Watts.	1902-11 —James W. Shull.
1852-71—James H. Graham.	1912-18 —Wm. N. Seibert.[2]
1872-81—Benjamin F. Junkin.	1918-19 —J. N. Keller.[2]
1882-91—Charles A. Barnett.	1920- —James M. Barnett.[3]

[1] Jeremiah Lyons died, and L. E. Atkinson was appointed by the governor to fill the unexpired term.
[2] William N. Seibert died, and J. N. Keller was appointed by the governor to serve until the election of a successor.
[3] James M. Barnett elected on the Non-Partisan ticket, under the new law.

ASSOCIATE JUDGES.

The year of election is given, the term starting with the first of the succeeding year.

1820—W. B. Anderson.	1852—Jesse Beaver.
1820—Jeremiah Madden.	1852—George Stroop.
1832—John Junkin.	1854—J. Martin Motzer.
1836—Robert Elliot.	1856—John Reifsnyder.
1842—James Black.	1859—David Shaver.*
1844—G. Blattenberger.	1861—Philip Ebert.
1849—John A. Baker.	1862—Isaac Lefevre.
1851—John Rice.	1862—Samuel Lupfer.*

*David Shaver died in office. Samuel Lupfer appointed by the governor to fill the vacancy.

1864—Jacob Sheibley.
1867—John A. Baker.
1869—George Stroup.
1872—John A. Baker.
1874—John Bear.
1877—Samuel Noss.
1879—William Grier.
1882—William Gladden.
1884—Joseph B. Garber.
1887—Samuel Woods.
1889—Henry Rhinesmith.
1891—James Everhart.

1894—John L. Kline.
1896—George M. Stroup.
1899—Isaac Beam.
1901—John Fleisher.
1904—Jacob Johnston.
1906—George Patterson.
1909—Lucian C. Wox.
1911—S. W. Bernheisel
1915—Wm. A. Meiser.
1917—George E. Boyer.
1921—Wm. A. Meiser.

COURT REPORTER.

When the act of assembly requiring the appointment of court reporters was passed, the position was filled by the appointment of Joseph F. Cummings, of Sunbury, in 1878, by President Judge Benj. F. Junkin, and he has served continuously ever since, under Judges Junkin, Barnett, Lyons, Atkinson, Shull, Seibert, Keller and James M. Barnett. As early as 1867 Mr. Cummings, then but fourteen years of age, had entered the employ of the Philadelphia & Erie Railroad Company. He studied shorthand during his spare hours and was taken into the office of the general superintendent of the line—the first shorthand writer in any of its offices. After serving there for over a year an act of assembly was passed requiring the appointment of shorthand reporters by the courts. Judge Junkin's appointment also covered Juniata County, and Judge Bucher appointed him in a like capacity in the counties of Union, Snyder and Mifflin. He served with Judge Bucher in that district to the end of his second term, when he was appointed reporter for Northumberland County, although he had done special reporting there as early as 1874. During his early court reporting he found time to take a three years' course at the Millersville State Normal School. He has also served as reporter for various state commissions and boards, and for ten years, from 1899 to 1910, was official reporter of the State Senate, being thus engaged during the completion of the new state capitol and during the contest over the United States Senatorship between Matthew Stanley Quay and others.

REGISTERS AND RECORDERS.

1820—Benjamin Leas.
       A. Fulweiler.
1824—Jacob Fritz.
1830—John McKeehan.
1836—Jere. Madden.
1839—John Souder.
1842—John Souder.
1845—Geo. W. Crane.
1848—Geo. W. Crane.
1851—Robert Kelley.
1854—John Campbell.
1857—George Spahr.
1860—Samuel Roth.
1863—William Grier.
1866—William Grier.
1869—Thos. J. Sheibley.
1872—Joseph S. Smith.

1875—Geo. S. Briner.
1878—Geo. S. Briner.
1881—Josiah W. Rice.
1884—Joseph S. Smith.
1887—Nathaniel Adams.
1890—Nathaniel Adams.
1893—James W. McKee.
1896—James W. McKee.
1899—J. C. Lightner.
1902—J. C. Lightner.
1905—Chas. L. Darlington.
1908—Chas. L. Darlington.
1911—Chas. L. Depugh.
1915—Chas. L. Depugh.*
       Wm. F. Swartz.*
1919—Wm. F. Swartz.

*Chas. L. Depugh died in office, and was succeeded by Wm. F. Swartz.

SHERIFFS.

1820—Daniel Stambaugh.	1871—D. M. Rhinesmith.
1823—Jesse Miller.	1874—J. W. Williamson.
1826—John Hipple.	1877—James A. Gray.
1829—Josiah Roddy.	1880—J. W. Beers.
1832—Wm. Lackey.	1883—H. C. Shearer.
1835—M. Stambaugh.	1886—Jerome B. Lahr.
1838—Joseph Shuler.	1889—George M. Ritter.
1841—Alexander Magee.	1892—Joseph A. Rice.
1844—Henry Cooper.	1895—Charles L. Johnson.
1847—Hugh Campbell.	1898—William H. Kough.
1850—Samuel Huggins.	1901—Charles L. Johnson.
1853—Benj. F. Miller.	1904—Abram L. Long.
1856—James Woods.	1907—E. T. Charles.
1859—Benj. F. Miller.	1911—James M. Baer.
1862—John Sheibly.	1915—D. L. Kistler.
1865—John F. Miller.	1919—Paul Flurie.
1868—Jere Rhinehart.	

*PROTHONOTARIES.

The dates given are the dates of election.

1820—Wm. B. Mitchell.	1876—David Mickey.
1821—Henry Miller.	1879—Alex. B. Grosh.
1824—Wm. B. Mitchell.	1882—Alex. B. Grosh.
1829—George Stroop.	1885—Jacob E. Bonsall.
1835—John Boden.	1888—Jacob E. Bonsall.
1839—Alex. Topley.	1891—S. S. Willard.
1842—Alex. Topley.	1894—S. S. Willard.
1845—Joseph Miller.	1897—J. Wesley Stephens.
1848—Peter Orwan.[1]	1900—J. Wesley Stephens.[2]
1851—James L. Diven.	1902—G. Warren Stephens.[2]
1854—James L. Diven.	1905—G. Warren Stephens.[3]
1857—David Mickey.	Grafton Junkin.[3]
1860—James G. Turbett.	1906—George B. Shull.
1863—John C. Lindsay.	1909—George B. Shull.
1864—David Mickey.	1913—Harry W. Robinson.
1867—Charles H. Smiley.	1917—Harry W. Robinson.
1870—J. J. Spoonenberger.	1921—H. Russell Campbell.
1873—J. J. Spoonenberger.	

*The prothonotary was clerk of the Court of Common Pleas, Court of Quarter Sessions, Court of Oyer and Terminer, and the Orphans' Court. About 1843 the Orphans' Court was placed in charge of the register and recorder.

[1] John A. Baker was appointed to fill the vacancy caused by the death of Peter Orwan.

[2] J. Wesley Stephens died in office, November, 1900, and was succeeded by his son, G. Warren Stephens, his deputy.

[3] G. Warren Stephens died in office, November 15, 1905, and was succeeded by Grafton Junkin.

COUNTY TREASURERS.

Showing date of election.

1820—William Power.	1835—David Lupfer.
1823—R. H. McClelland.	1838—David Deardorff.
1827—Geo. Stroop.	1841—Wm. Lackey.
1830—John Wilson.	1844—Henry Rice.
1832—Robert Kelley.	1847—David Lupfer.

1849—Jonas Ickes.
1851—George Spahr.
1853—Thomas Clark.
1855—John R. Shuler.
1857—H. D. Woodruff.
1859—David J. Rice.
1861—John H. Sheibley.
1863—James McElheny.
1865—Samuel Smith.
1867—James McElhaney.
1869—Wm. Tressler.
1871—Isaac N. Shatto.
1873—Geo. W. Spahr.
1875—John R. Boden.

1878—Wm. Rice.
1881—Ephraim B. Weise.
1884—Wm. A. Lightner.
1887—Thomas J. Clark.
1890—John W. Kell.
1893—L. H. C. Flickinger.
1896—H. C. Gantt.
1899—Wilson D. Messimer.
1902—Lawrence F. Smith.
1905—D. C. Kell.
1908—Lawrence F. Smith.
1911—Robert A. McClure.
1915—Charles S. Brunner.
1919—James A. Noel.

County Commissioners.

The dates preceding the names of the members of the diffe
boards are the dates upon which they assumed office.

1820—Thomas Adams.
1820—Jacob Huggins.
1820—Robert Mitchell.
1821—Robert Elliott.
1822—Samuel Linn.
1823—John Maxwell.*
1824—Robert Mitchell.
1825—Abraham Adams.
1825—Abraham Bower.
1826—John Owen.
1827—George Mitchell.
1828—Solomon Bower.
1829—John Junkin.
1830—Jacob Kumbler.
1831—Alex. Bryan.
1832—Frederick Orwan.
1833—Jacob Kumbler.
1834—George Beaver.
    Andrew Shuman.
1835—Cadwalader Jones.
1836—George Beaver.
1837—C. Wright.
    J. Zimmerman.
1838—Wm. White.
1839—M. Donally.
1840—Geo. Charles, Sr.
1841—Robert Adams.
1842—Robert Kelly.
1843—T. P. Cochran.
    Isaac Kirkpatrick.
1844—Wm. Messinger.
1845—Nicholas Hench.
1846—John Patterson.
1847—Geo. Titzell.
1848—Thomas Adams.
1849—Jacob Sheibley.
1850—Fenlow McCowen.
1851—Chas. C. Brandt.
1852—George Stroup.
1853—John Myers.
1854—William Power.
1855—Jacob Bixler.
1856—Lawrence Gross.

1857—James B. Cooper.
1858—Thomas Campbell.
1859—Henry P. Grubb.
1860—Henry Foulk.
1861—William Kough.
1862—William Wright.
1863—J. Kochenderfer.
1864—Perry Kreamer.
1865—John Wright.
1866—William Hays.
1867—George S. Bruner.
1868—John Stephens.
1869—Zachariah Rice.
1870—J. A. Leinawever.
1871—W. B. Stambaugh.
1872—George W. Bretz.†
1873—William Brooks.
1874—James Whitner.
1875—Joseph Ulsh.
1875—David Smith.
1876—J. Wesley Gantt.
    Solomon Bower.
    George Campbell.
1879—J. Wesley Gantt.
    John W. Charles.
    Henry Shumaker.
1882—James B. Black.
    Samuel Barner.
    Daniel Shaffer.
1885—U. H. Rumbaugh.
    Aaron Shreffler.
    Edward Hull.
1888—Silas W. Snyder.
    John Martin.
    George W. Burd.
1891—William B. Gray.
    William Kumler.
    Wilson D. Adams.
1894—Josiah Clay.
    D. P. Lightner.
    Isaiah Mitchell.
1897—Aaron Shreffler.
    A. K. Bryner.

1879—Wm. B. Gutshall.
1900—Thomas F. Martin.
    James Rhinesmith.
    Jacob Fleisher.
1903—William R. Dum.
    James K. Adair.
    Abraham Bistline.
1906—J. B. Jackson.
    W. H. Leonard.
    John S. Bitner.
1909—Clark M. Bower.

McClellan Woods.
William H. Smith.
1912—Reuben Beers.
    Jonathan Snyder.
    William H. Lyter.
1916—J. C. Hench.
    Jonathan Snyder.
    Allen R. Thompson.
1920—W. C. Smith.
    M. C. Woods.
    G. W. Meck.

*In May, 1825, Col. John Maxwell died, and the court appointed Abraham Bower to fill the vacancy. Mr. Bower was then elected to the full term in October, 1825, and Abraham Adams was elected to fill the unexpired term of one year of the Maxwell term.

†George W. Bretz died during his term, February 16, 1874.

COMMISSIONERS' CLERKS.

While not an elective office, the list of clerks to the board of county commissioners is given here, as much of the work of the board was entrusted to these men between the meetings of the board. The list:

1820-23—Jesse Miller.
1824-29—Josiah Roddy.
1830-36—N. Eby.
1837-53—William Wilson.
1854-57—H. G. Milans.
1858 —A. C. Kling.
1859 —Lewis Orwan.
1860-62—Benjamin Belford.
1863-64—B. P. McIntire.
1865 —Wm. Wright.

1865-70—Jno. R. Shuler.
1871-75—Wm. N. Seibert.
1876-81—Calvin Nelson.
1882-84—C. W. Rhinesmith.
1885-90—James W. McKee.
1891-99—Wm. B. Anderson.
1900-02—James S. Cameron.
1903-13—D. H. Meck.*
1913-21—Charles J. Swartz.*
1921 —D. C. Kell.

*D. H. Meck, appointed Sealer of Weights and Measures, resigned, and Charles J. Swartz was appointed. Mr. Swartz died in 1921, and was succeeded by D. C. Kell.

DISTRICT ATTORNEYS.

Prior to 1850 the office of district attorney was an appointive one. In that year it became an elective one. The incumbents of the office with date of election until the present time, have been:

1850—Benj. F. Junkin.
1853—C. J. T. McIntire.
1856—J. B. McAlister.
1859—F. Rush Roddy.
1862—Ephraim C. Long.
1866—Lewis Potter.
1869—Benj. P. McIntire.
1872—Jacob Bailey.
1875—J. C. McAlister.
1878—J. C. Wallace.
1881—Jas. W. Shull.
1884—Richard W. Stewart.

1887—J. C. McAlister.
1890—Lewis Potter.
1893—Luke Baker.
1896—W. H. Kell.
1899—James M. Sharon.
1902—James M. McKee.
1905—James M. McKee.
1908—Walter W. Rice.
1911—James M. McKee.
1915—James M. McKee.
1919—James M. McKee.

CORONERS.

There is so little business for that official in Perry County that the office has continually gone unsought. Those elected to that office have been:

1841—Michael Steever.
1845—Dr. Jonas Ickes.
1846—Jacob Steele.
1847—John McKenzie.
1848—James R. Gilmore.
1851—Wm. L. Stephens.
1853—James R. Gilmore.
1854—John Bretz.
1855—James H. Case.
1856—James H. Case.
1859—Philip Ebert.
1860—Joseph Eby.
1861—Patrick McMorris.
1862—Jacob M. Miller.
1863—B. P. Hooke.
1864—James Crawford.
1865—Samuel Stiles.
1866—Dr. James B. Eby.

1867—Cyrus Clemson.
1870—Joseph Swartz.
1871—Dr. Geo. N. Reutter.
1872—Dr. Geo. W. Eppley.
1873—Geo. W. Zinn.
1874—Geo. W. Zinn.
1879—Samuel Stites.
1882—Andrew Traver.
1885—George Shrom.
1888—George A. Ickes.
1889—J. H. Bleistein.
1893—C. E. Gregg.
1896—W. S. Groninger.
1899—W. R. Brothers.
1901—H. M. Smiley.
1911—George W. Gault.*
1919—Geo. W. Gault.

*In the interim between 1911 and 1919, no nominations made by either party for this office.

COUNTY SURVEYORS.

This office, once considered of importance, is now unsought. Until 1850 it was appointive, but in that year it became an elective office. The incumbents, with date of election:

1850—James Woods.
1856—James B. Hackett.
1859—Samuel Arnold.
1862—Daniel Rife.
1865—M. B. Holman.
1871—Samuel Galbreath.
1874—James Bell.
1877—David Mitchell.
1880—John Rynard.
1883—Wm. J. Stewart, Jr.

1886—Wm. A. Meminger.
1889—Silas Wright.
1892—James A. Wright.
1895—Silas Wright.
1898—Silas Wright.
1901—Silas Wright.
1904—Silas Wright.
1907—J. L. L. Bucke.
1910—Gard C. Palm.
1919—J. L. L. Bucke.*

*In the interim between 1910 and 1919, no nominations by either party for this office.

COUNTY AUDITORS.

1820—Wm. Smiley.
   A. Fulweiler.
1821—Robert Kelly.
1822—John Purcell.
1823—George Mitchell.
1824—John West.
1825—Henry Fetter.
1826—John Junkin.
   David Stewart.
1827—William Wilson.
1828—William Roberts.

1829—William Cook.
   Alexander Magee.
1830—Jonas Ickes.
1831—Wm. Adams.
1832—Samuel Beaver.
1833—Jacob Bloom.
1834—M. Donelly.
1835—Alex. F. Topley.
1836—Robert Adams.
   —S. Darlington.
1837—D. G. Reed.

1837—H. R. Wilson.
1838—John Charters.
1839—Hugh Campbell.
1840—Jesse Beaver.
1841—Thomas McKee.
1842—Hugh Campbell.
1843—Michael Steever.
1844—J. B. Zimmerman.
1845—James B. Hackett.
    T. M. Graham.
1846—James L. Diven.
    Peter Sheibley.
1847—John Witherow.
    Martin Motzer.
1848—Francis Mickey.
1849—W. J. Graham.
1850—W. S. Mitchell.
1851—D. Kochenderfer.
1852—John Wright.
1853—Robert Dunbar.
1854—W. Bosserman.
1855—Robert C. Boden.
1856—W. A. Morrison.
1857—Francis English.
1858—Joseph W. Frank.
1859—A. McKenzie.
1860—Geo. A. Shuman.
1861—Samuel Beaver.
1863—Philip Huston.
1864—Alex. G. White.
1865—Geo. W. Bretz.
1866—Simon H. Fry.
1868—George H. Hench.
1869—Jonathan Michener.
1870—John English.
1871—S. H. Baker.
1872—Wm. A. Meminger.
1873—David Messinger.
1874—G. Sheibley.

1875—John F. Stouffer.
1879—James C. Hill.
1881—Geo. A. Sheibley.
1884—Chester L. Steele.
    David Boyd.
    Wm. H. Jackson.
1887—Wm. Adams.
    John H. Murray.
    Sam'l E. Arnold.
1890—Jas. C. Bistline.
    Chas. S. Henderson.
    Wm. H. Gelbaugh.
1893—H. L. Stephens.
    C. S. Henderson.
    Jno. A. Rhea.
1896—S. L. McKeehan.
    Cyrus Smith.
    F. S. Gibson.
1899—S. L. McKeehan.
    McClellan Woods.
    Chas. L. Kline.
1902—Harry E. Wilt.
    McClellan Woods.
    Chas. E. Zerfing.
1905—S. L. McKeehan.
    C. A. Smith.
    Jacob Wolf.
1908—D. R. Kane.
    C. A. Smith.
    Jacob Wolf.
1911—D. R. Kane.
    S. M. Shuler.
    Jacob Wolf.
1915—D. R. Kane.
    S. M. Shuler.
    H. R. Campbell.
1919—S. M. Shuler.
    Nelson I. Zeigler.
    Cloyd E. Wolf.

DIRECTORS OF THE POOR.

The following men have been members of the different boards which have had charge of the county home and the supervision of aid to the outside poor.

The record starts with 1839, the county home having been burned that year, and previous records destroyed.

1839—John Tressler.
1840—Samuel Hench.
1841—Jacob Bixler.
1842—Lewis Mickey.
1843—John Ritter.
1844—Jacob Weibley.
1845—None appears elected.
1846—Charles Wright.
1847—Peter Hench.
1848—Robert Hackett.
1849—Thomas Black.
1850—Moses Uttley.
1851—George Titzell.
1852—Henry Lackey.

1853—Samuel Arnold.
1854—Samuel Milligan.
1855—James McClure.
1856—William Kerr.
1857—Henry Rhinesmith.
1858—Jacob Bernheisel.
1859—John Gensler.
1860—William Kell.
1861—John Stephens.
1862—John Ritter.
1863—John Weldon.
1864—John Arnold.
1865—Peter Shaffer.
1866—John Dum.

1867—Geo. Hoobaugh.
1868—John Flickinger.
1869—John Newcomer.
1870—John S. Ritter.
1871—John Patterson.
1872—Samuel Dunkelberger.
1873—Wm. J. Graham.
1874—John Swartz.
1875—Abraham Long.
1876—Samuel Sigler.
1877—Benj. F. Bealor.
1878—John D. Stewart.
1879—Geo. C. Snyder.
1880—Isaac Hollenbaugh.
1881—Benj. Bistline.
1882—O. S. Green.
1883—John Acker.
1884—Jos. Flickinger.
1885—John Garman.
1886—John Wilt.
1887—John Freeland.
1888—Jacob W. Wagner.
1889—John Swartz.
1890—John Freeland.
1891—George I. Rice.
1892—Benjamin H. Inhoff.
1893—George D. Taylor.

1894—John Wilt.
1895—Darius J. Long.
1896—George D. Taylor.
1897—James S. Peck.
1898—Darius J. Long.
1899—J. B. Free.
1900—Zach M. Dock.
1901—D. M. Hench.
1902—I. B. Free.
1903—Zach M. Dock.
1904—D. M. Hench.
1905—James A. Wright.
1906—S. S. Orris.
1907—Samuel M. Rice.
1908—James A. Wright.
1909—W. A. Lightner.
1911—S. S. Orris.
1911—E. R. Loy.
1911—S. S. Orris.
1913—W. Harry Smith.
1915—E. R. Loy.
1915—S. A. Shope.
1917—Geo. W. Dunkle.
1919—S. A. Shope.
1919—E. M. Wilt.
1921—Geo. W. Dunkle.

COUNTY SCHOOL SUPERINTENDENTS.

1854—Rev. Adam R. Height.
1857—Rev. T. P. Bucher.[1]
1859—Lewis B. Kerr.[4]
1860—Lewis B. Kerr.
1863—Jacob Gantt.
1866—Silas Wright.
1869—Lewis B. Kerr.
1872—Geo. C. Welker.[2]
1873—Silas Wright.[4]
1875—Silas Wright.
1878—S. B. Fahnestock.
1881—J. R. Flickinger.
1884—E. U. Aumiller.

1887—E. U. Aumiller.
1890—E. U. Aumiller.
1893—Joseph M. Arnold.
1896—Joseph M. Arnold.[3]
1896—E. H. Bryner.[4]
1899—E. H. Bryner.
1902—E. H. Bryner.
1905—E. H. Bryner.[3]
1906—S. S. Willard.[4]
1908—D. A. Kline.
1911—D. A. Kline.
1914—D. A. Kline.
1918—D. A. Kline.
1922—D. A. Kline.

[1]Resigned September 1, 1859.
[2]Died March 11, 1873.
[3]Resigned.
[4]Appointed by governor to fill vacancy.

CHAPTER XXVII.

THE BENCH AND BAR.

WITH the land grant to William Penn of the territory comprising Pennsylvania, Charles II conferred the power of establishing courts and appointing judges. The Orphans' Court was modeled after the Orphans' Court of London. There is also a Common Pleas Court, a Court of Quarter Sessions, and Oyer and Terminer, all of which are convened and held simultaneously by the same judge or judges. The decisions of the judge or judges are subject to appeal and review by the Superior and Supreme Courts, the highest courts of the commonwealth. The state is divided into judicial districts, some of which are comprised of two or more counties. Where a judicial district is comprised of two or more countes, there are elected in each county of the district, two associates. These are usually termed lay judges and are not required to be learned in the law. Perry County is in this class and, with Juniata County, comprises the Forty-First Judicial District, according to the Act of April 9, 1874. Prior to this, by the Act of April 11, 1835, Cumberland, Juniata and Perry comprised the Ninth Judicial District. The Act of Assembly of 1722 is a codification of the prior acts into one general law. Under the Constitution of 1776 and the conventions of 1790, 1836 and 1873 the system was revised and strengthened.

At the time of the formation of Perry County as a political unit there were no resident attorneys within its confines, consequently it was the bar of the "mother county"—Cumberland—that furnished the legal staff for the institution of the local courts. At that time Judge John Reed, originally a Westmoreland County man, was president judge of Cumberland County, and upon him was conferred the honor of instituting the courts of the new county. Landisburg was selected as the temporary county seat, and in a log building, fully described in the chapter entitled "Perry County Established," the first courts were held. In early days, the county being yet in its pioneering period, the principal business of the attorneys was with trials pertaining to land titles. Sometimes almost the entire period of the courts' sessions were devoted to such litigation. The attorneys who specialized along this line were known as "land lawyers," and a number of members of the Carlisle bar were men who had thus attained fame. Among these were David Watts, Thomas Duncan, Andrew Carothers, and others. As far west as the Allegheny Mountains these men were retained in legal contests of this nature.

After the discovery of coal in Schuylkill County the fact that many of the mountains there, which were underlaid with coal, extended westwardly across the Susquehanna River, where there was also supposed to be coal, caused capitalists from Philadelphia and elsewhere (about 1796) to warrant the mountain lands and have them surveyed, even before the fertile valley lands were claimed.

BENJAMIN JUNKIN,
First Judge Elected from Perry County.

Without any geological knowledge whatever these men went ahead and took up mountain tracts which were even devoid of timber, let alone coal. Overlapping surveys and encroachments were fought out in the courts with as much avidity as if the lands had been underlaid with diamonds. The lawyers were equally ignorant of the fact that the mountains of this section were barren of coal and naturally fought with all the skill and ability which they possessed, with the result that there has been built up in the courts of the state a land system as perfect as any in existence to this day, and one which has established precedents that are now followed by many other states. The fact that Perry County was then in its formative period in many ways, drew the talent of men such as these to the county.

During the first year of the county's existence—in fact, at the very first session of the courts—John D. Creigh and M. Wadsworth were admitted to practice at the Perry County bar. Descendants of Mr. Creigh are prominent to this day in Perry County. In 1821 Alexander Mahon, a man of distinguished oratorical power; William McClure, Geo. A. Lyon, Alexander A. Anderson, John Williamson, Samuel Riddle, and Charles B. Penrose came over from Cumberland County and were admitted to practice in the Perry County courts. In 1822-23 Andrew G. Miller, Robert Wilson, Thomas McDonald, Baldwin Campbell, and Samuel Douglas followed. Of these latter named men no knowledge was handed down to posterity, in so far as the records available show.

In 1824, however, came men who were heard and known, some even intimately, by such men as B. F. Junkin, once a member of the United States Congress, and long a member of the Perry County bar, former judge of the courts, and known personally to many who will read these words. To the recorded descriptions of Judge Junkin we are indebted for much of our material along this line.

Of these lawyers Frederick Watts probably stood at the head of the list, but we shall let Judge Junkin describe him: "We remember with pleasure his admirable method of addressing a jury. When we first came to the bar, and indeed always, it was a treat to listen to his pleading, and we never lost one word he uttered, for no one moved or spoke or withdrew attention until he closed." About the same time came Samuel Alexander, described as a logical reasoner, preëminent for knowledge and skill, genial, witty, a musician and scientist, with a wonderfully developed sense of humor. In 1825 Benjamin McIntire was admitted. He located here and practiced law in Perry County practically all his life, dying in 1882. The same year came Richard P. Creigh, E. B. Leonard, and William D. Ramsey, but they did not practice steadily.

In the years of 1827-28 came William Ayres, Charles B. Power, Charles McClure, Hugh Gallagher, N. Smith, and Moses McClain, all living out of the county and being only engaged in special cases, except Charles B. Power. Andrew Carothers, a crippled man from Carlisle, also came over to practice and sat in a chair while addressing a jury. John R. McClintock was admitted in 1829 and practiced during his lifetime, to 1874. From 1840 to 1845 Joseph Casey lived here and practiced the profession. He was quite successful, but left to locate in Union County. He was afterwards elected to Congress, became state reporter, and finally chief justice of the Court of Claims of the United States, 1863 to 1870. From 1842 to 1851 James McFarlane lived here and practiced successfully. He then removed to Bradford, where he was wed, and while still practicing his profession he wrote the article on "Coal Formations" for Appleton's Encyclopedia, which gave him national fame.

Admitted to the bar in 1848, Wm. A. Sponsler was one of the older school of attorneys, the colleague of McIntire, Junkin, Potter and others of the period before and after the War between the States. He was born January 28, 1827, in Cumberland County, and removed with his parents to Perry County when but six years old. He studied in the offices of Benjamin McIntire and was admitted to practice in 1848. He possessed a thorough knowledge of the law, and as a pleader before the bar was unexcelled. He died January 15, 1897.

Benjamin McIntire, son of Thomas McIntire, was born in Cumberland County in 1798, and studied law at Carlisle with Charles B. Penrose, locating at Landisburg, and moving to New Bloomfield, when the county seat was moved there. He was once deputy attorney general for Perry County and also was a member of the draft board for Perry, Cumberland and York Counties during the Sectional War.

Charles J. T. McIntire was a son of Benjamin McIntire, and was born January 3, 1830, in New Bloomfield. He graduated at Dickinson College in 1847, and studied law in his father's offices. He was admitted to the bar in 1851. He was twice elected district attorney and served in the State Senate in 1868-70, when the district was composed of the counties of Perry, Juniata, Mifflin, Huntingdon, Blair, and Center. He died in 1886.

Charles H. Smiley was born at Shermansdale, Perry County, on May 9, 1844. He served in the War between the States, and after his return was elected prothonotary of the county, serving from 1867 to 1870. Concurrently he was a law student in the office of Charles A. Barnett, and was admitted to the bar in 1872. From 1881-84 he served the district composed of the counties of Perry, Juniata, and Mifflin in the State Senate. During the last quarter of the last century Mr. Smiley was one of the leading attorneys at the county bar. He was a forceful speaker and had a thorough knowledge of the law. He died March 18, 1912.

Lewis Potter, a native of Buffalo Township, was a noted pension attorney after the Sectional War.

Of later attorneys admitted to the bar who left Perry County, W. D. Ard is now located at Washington, D. C.; W. H. Kell resides at Steelton, Pennsylvania; R. B. Gibson located at Erie; Grafton Junkin is at Rome, Georgia; Arthur C. Lackey is in New

York; James R. Magee, in the government service, few being in active practice. J. J. Kintner is located and practicing at Lock Haven, Pennsylvania. In 1914 and in 1919 he was an unsuccessful candidate for the nomination for judge of the Supreme Court. In 1919 he was elected district attorney of Clinton County by "stickers," his name not appearing on the ballot. George R. Barnett and Scott S. Leiby retain their residence in the county, but have their offices at Harrisburg. George Black Roddy, James M. Sharon, D. L. Detra, William S. Seibert, and J. R. Flickinger are dead, the latter having long been principal of the Central State Normal School at Lock Haven. William S. Snyder practices at Harrisburg.

Following is a list of the attorneys who have practiced at the Perry County bar, since the county's organization, in 1820:

ATTORNEYS AT THE PERRY COUNTY BAR.

Name.	Preceptor.	Date Admitted.
John D. Creigh		December, 1820
Fred'k M. Wadsworth		December, 1820
Charles D. Davis		September, 1821
Benjamin McIntire	Charles B. Penrose	January, 1825
Richard M. Creigh	John D. Creigh	January, 1825
Edward B. Leonard	Andrew Caruthers	January, 1825
Charles B. Power		April, 1825
Samuel Creigh		January, 1829
J. R. McClintock	Charles B. Power	January, 1829
Samuel Ramsey		April, 1829
Abner C. Harding		January, 1830
Fred'k E. Bailey		April, 1839
Joseph Casey	C. B. Penrose and Judge Reed	January, 1839
Henry C. Hickok		April, 1841
Samuel G. Morrison		November, 1842
Paul Corrigan	B. McIntire	August, 1843
Daniel Gantt	Joseph Casey	August, 1843
James McFarlane		August, 1843
George W. Power		August, 1843
Mitchell Steever	Daniel Gantt	April, 1844
John L. Gallatin	Samuel G. Morrison	April, 1844
Benjamin F. Junkin	Samuel Hepburn	April, 1845
A. B. Anderson	Benjamin McIntire	April, 1846
Wm. A. Sponsler	Benjamin McIntire	April, 1848
C. J. T. McIntire	Benjamin McIntire	January, 1852
J. Don Carlisle		January, 1852
Wm. R. Shuler		August, 1856
Samuel B. Richey	B. F. Junkin	April, 1856
John B. McAlister	Wm. A. Sponsler	January, 1856
Charles A. Barnett	B. F. Junkin	August, 1857
Roswell M. Russell	Benjamin McIntire	January, 1858
Rush T. Roddy	Benjamin McIntire	April, 1858
Henry G. Milans	B. F. Junkin	January, 1859
Joseph Bailey	Benjamin McIntire	April, 1860
Joseph H. Arnold	Benjamin McIntire	April, 1861
William M. Sutch	B. F. Junkin	April, 1861
E. C. Long	Benjamin McIntire	January, 1862
A. H. Burkholder	Benjamin McIntire	January, 1862
Lewis Potter	Wm. A. Sponsler	January, 1863
David L. Tressler	Benjamin McIntire	January, 1864

Name.	Preceptor.	Date Admitted.
John F. L. Sahm	Benjamin McIntire	April, 1865
John D. Nelson	W. A. Sponsler	October, 1866
W. W. Whitmer	Benjamin McIntire	January, 1867
Jacob Gantt	Wm. A. Sponsler	April, 1867
Charles L. Murphy	B. F. Junkin	April, 1867
James H. Grier	Wm. A. Sponsler	August, 1867
Martin Liggett		April, 1868
Benj. P. McIntire	C. J. T. McIntire	October, 1868
W. S. Milligan	W. H. Miller	January, 1869
James H. Ferguson		August, 1869
Wm. N. Seibert	Wm. A. Sponsler	August, 1869
Jacob Bailey	C. J. T. McIntire	October, 1870
Calvin Neilson	Wm. A. Sponsler	May, 1872
Charles H. Smiley	Chas. A. Barnett	August, 1872
A. M. Markel	Chas. A. Barnett	August, 1873
J. E. Junkin	B. F. Junkin	October, 1873
J. C. McAlister	Wm. A. Sponsler	May, 1874
Wilson Lupfer	C. J. T. McIntire	August, 1874
Wm. H. Sponsler	Wm. A. Sponsler	April, 1876
John C. Wallis		April, 1876
Theo. K. Long	Harvard Law School	April, 1878
Fillmore Maust	Wm. H. Sponsler	December, 1881
R. H. Stewart	Chas. A. Barnett	December, 1881
James W. Shull	Wm. H. Sponsler	April, 1881
Edward R. Sponsler	Wm. A. Sponsler	August, 1881
C. W. Rhinesmith	Wm. N. Seibert	December, 1883
William Orr	Chas. A. Barnett	December, 1883
George R. Barnett	Chas. H. Smiley	August, 1884
J. L. Markel	B. F. Junkin	August, 1884
J. W. McKee	Wm. H. Sponsler	August, 1884
J. R. Flickinger	Chas. H. Smiley	August, 1885
Luke Baker	Chas. H. Smiley	April, 1891
James M. Sharon	Chas. A. Barnett	November, 1891
James M. Barnett	Chas. A. Barnett	April, 1892
Wm. S. Seibert	Wm. N. Seibert	January, 1893
John C. Motter	Wm. A. Sponsler	April, 1893
Wm. H. Kell	James W. Shull	April, 1894
J. J. Kintner	Chas. H. Smiley	April, 1894
Arthur C. Lackey	Dickinson Law School	April, 1895
R. B. Gibson	Dickinson Law School	April, 1894
James M. McKee	Chas. A. Barnett	April, 1898
Geo. Black Roddy	Chas. H. Smiley	November, 1898
Wm. D. Ard	J. L. Markel	April, 1900
Grafton Junkin	B. F. Junkin	August, 1900
Walter W. Rice	Chas. A. Barnett	August, 1901
Wm. S. Snyder	Jas. A. Stranahan	November, 1902
Chas. H. Smiley, Jr.	Chas. H. Smiley	January, 1905
James R. Magee	Columbia Law School	April, 1916

The Bench.

Before Perry County became a separate political unit, from the soil which is now comprised within its borders, there went out one of the greatest jurists, not only of the state but of the nation, a man whose opinions are quoted to this day not only in the land of his birth, but abroad. We refer to John Bannister Gibson, former Chief Justice of the State of Pennsylvania. An entire chapter devoted to the life of Mr. Gibson will be found in this book.

At the time of the institution of the courts of Perry County there was a life tenure of office connected with the judiciary, but in 1838 this was changed to an appointive term of ten years. Judge Reed, who was in charge of the courts in the new county, presided until that time. He is said to have been a learned jurist, a pleasant and amiable gentleman, and strong socially. After leaving the bench he practiced for over ten years in the judicial district over which he formerly presided. He died January 19, 1850, aged about 65 years.

On Judge Reed's retirement Samuel Hepburn became judge, being appointed by Governor Ritner. Although quite a young man when appointed and without extensive experience at the bar, he was apt, accurate, and acquitted himself with credit upon the bench. He lived at Carlisle, at which place he died.

The third judge was Frederick Watts, of Carlisle, who was appointed by Governor Johnson, assuming office in 1849. The Constitution, as amended, however, made the judiciary elective, and his term thus ended in December, 1851, although it would have been seven more years. Of the talents of Mr. Watts we have spoken in the previous pages among the early practitioners. As a judge he maintained his reputation as an accurate, prompt and efficient jurist. A man without fear, expressing his convictions without regards to consequences. Former Judge Junkin thus described him: "What he believed he said, and what he believed was generally right, and he, more than any other judge who ever sat on this bench, was less careful to conceal his own convictions as to what the verdict of a jury ought to be." Judge Watts was a grandson of General Frederick Watts, who was a resident of what is new Perry County, and a son of David Watts. Watts Township, Perry County, was named in honor of Judge Watts. He resided at Carlisle, where he died. See biographical sketches devoted to several members of the Watts family elsewhere in this book.

Judge James H. Graham was the fourth man to fill the position and the first one to be elected by the people. Perry was then in the old Ninth Judicial District, and over it Judge Graham presided for twenty years, a fitting tribute to the new elective system. He was pronounced a man of great legal ability, a sound reasoner, observant, discerning and rapid in decision. His home was at Carlisle, where he resided until his death.

Benjamin F. Junkin was the fifth man to sit upon the bench of Perry County, the second to be elected by the people, and the first citizen of the county to fill the position. He was a son of John Junkin, by his first wife, and was born November 12, 1822, in Cumberland County. His father, in April, 1823, purchased the Stroop farm, between Green Park and Landisburg, and removed to the new county when it was less than three years in existence.

30

He graduated at Marshall College at Mercersburg, in 1853. He taught school in the Mississippi valley, and on his return to New Bloomfield became the principal of the New Bloomfield Academy —now the Carson Long Institute. In the meantime he was reading law in the office of B. F. Junkin and was admitted to practice law in August, 1857. In 1863 he was elected to the state legislature. He was subsequently appointed register in bankruptcy, which appointment he held until the repeal of the bankrupt law. He was elected president judge in 1881. He died January 29, 1917, having returned to active practice. His high moral standards and sense of right, coupled with a thorough legal knowledge, gave him a wide judicial reputation.

The seventh president judge to preside was Jeremiah Lyons, who was elected in 1891, being the fourth to attain the judgeship by election. He was a son—one of thirteen children—of Nicholas and Sarah (Yohn) Lyons, and was born in Saville Township, Perry County, September 16, 1839. He was educated in the common schools and at Markelville Academy. He read law with Ezra Doty, of Mifflintown, and was admitted to the bar there in 1863. He practiced at Mifflintown until his election to the bench, November, 1891. His election came through a four-cornered contest, the conferees of both parties of the two counties failing to agree on a nominee. He was a member of the electoral college in 1876. He was president of the First National Bank of Mifflintown from its organization until his election as judge. He died in November, 1900, while on a visit to Philadelphia. Judge Lyons was a man of the people. He was learned in the law, frank in manner, and of a genial nature.

The eighth president judge, L. E. Atkinson, came to the position in 1900, by appointment, to fill the unexpired term of Judge Lyons. Mr. Atkinson was born in Juniata County, June 16, 1841, and educated in the common schools and at Airy View and Milnwood Academies. He graduated in medicine at the University of New York in 1861, entered the medical department of the Union Army, serving throughout the war. He was disabled during the war so that he had to use crutches and could not follow the practice of medicine. He then read law with Edmund S. Doty, and was admitted to the bar in 1870. He was a member of Congress for two terms. Judge Atkinson was untiring and had a thorough knowledge of the law.

James W. Shull, still in active practice at New Bloomfield, became the ninth judge, having been elected on the Republican ticket in 1901. Mr. Shull was born in Spring Township, November 5, 1856, the son of Samuel and Elvina (Albert) Shull. He was educated in the public schools of Penn and Wheatfield Townships, at Prof. Wright's Normal School at Millerstown, and at the New

Jeremiah N. Keller, through appointment to fill the vacancy caused by the death of Judge Seibert, became the eleventh man to fill the judgeship. The appointment was valid only until the next regular judicial election. He was born in Juniata County, August 1, 1858. He was educated in the public schools, at Airy View Academy, and graduated from the Central State Normal School at Lock Haven in 1883. He taught in his home county for five years, two of which he was principal at Mifflintown. He read law with L. E. Atkinson, and was admitted to the bar in 1888. He represented his county in the legislature in 1896-97. He practices his profession at Mifflintown.

The present president judge, James M. Barnett, the twelfth to fill the position, is a son of Charles A. Barnett, who was the sixth judge of Perry County. He was born in New Bloomfield, May 24, 1870. His mother was Mary (McClure) Barnett. He was educated in the public schools, the New Bloomfield Academy, and at Princeton College, now Princeton University. He was the Republican nominee in 1911, but was defeated by Wm. N. Seibert, largely on the temperance question, then the foremost issue. He was elected in 1919, the first to be elected upon a non-partisan ticket, that being the law then in force. He read law with his father, and was admitted to the bar in April, 1892. Judge Barnett has a wide reputation as a lawyer. His administration so far has met with public approval at home and abroad.

SPECIAL LEGISLATION RELATING TO PERRY COUNTY.

Throughout this book, at various places there will be found the record of special legislation pertaining to Perry County, and, in most instances it is not considered necessary to refer to it again. This legislation naturally dates to the very act creating Perry County, printed elsewhere in full.

Before the county's erection, special legislation relating to the territory was passed, the more important being the act of February, 1773, making Sherman's Creek a public highway and authorizing James Patton to construct a dam in the creek; that of March 13, 1795, authorizing Wm. Beatty to erect a dam in the Juniata River from Sheep Island, near it mouth, to the west bank of the river; that of March 8, 1799, authorizing Matthias Flam and David Watts to establish a ferry on the Susquehanna at or near the mouth of the Juniata; that of March 29, 1813, authorizing the appointment of commissioners to make an artificial road from Millerstown to the Franklin County line, "to go through McKessonsburg, and thence via Daniel Sprenkle's." and that of March 28. 1814, incorporating the Millerstown Bridge Company.

The first special act relating to Perry County after its establishment was one passed March 15, 1821, pertaining to the appeals, etc., from the judgment of justices of the peace (of that part of Cumberland which became Perry) which happened after March 22, 1820, transferring them to the Perry County courts.

Another was passed April 2, 1821, and related to fences in Perry and Cumberland Counties, boroughs excepted. Section 2 provided that a fence four and a half feet high be a legal fence.

The acts relating to the location of the county seat appear in the chapter relating to that subject.

The act of April 23, 1829, authorized Stephen Duncan and John D. Mahon, their heirs and assigns, "to erect, build and support a good and substantial bridge over Sherman's Creek, in Perry County, at the mouth of said creek," and to

"Erect a gate upon or near said bridge and collect the tolls hereinafter granted, from all persons passing over the same with horses, cattle, carts and carriages, or on foot, that is to say: for every coach, landau, phaëton, stage wagon or other pleasure carriage with four wheels, drawn by four horses or mules, the sum of twenty-five cents; and for every such carriage drawn by two horses or mules, the sum of eighteen cents, and for every such carriage drawn by one horse or mule, the sum of twelve and a half cents; for every wagon drawn by four horses or mules, twenty cents; for every chaise, riding chair, sulky, cart, or other two-wheeled carriage, sleigh or sled, with two horses or mules, the sum of twelve and a half cents, and so in proportion, if more horses or mules are added to the number herein mentioned; and for every such carriage drawn by one horse or mule, the sum of ten cents; and for all the above description of carriages drawn in whole or in part by oxen, two oxen to be estimated equal to one horse; for a single horse and mule rider, the sum of six cents; for every led horse or mule, three cents; for every foot passenger, two cents; for every sheep or swine, the sum of half a cent; for every head of horned cattle, the sum of one cent."

A further provision said that "the tolls authorized should not be taken from any person or persons going to or returning from public worship on the Sabbath, going to or returning from funerals, going to or returning from training in the military, or persons going to or returning from general or township elections." Section 3 provided that if the commissioners saw proper the grand jury could appoint a jury of twelve to place a valuation upon the bridge and a sale made to the county on the condition that the bridge be free.

An act of April 8, 1833, authorized John Everhart, of Juniata Township, "to erect a wing dam in the Juniata, on the east side thereof, at or near Juniata Falls," for the purpose of using water power.

The Perry County Mutual Fire Insurance Company was incorporated by the act of April 18, 1843, by Finlaw McCowen, David Darlington, John Gotwalt, John Witherow, David Deardorff, John Rice, John McBride, David Lupfer, Joseph Casey, James Black, Samuel Leiby, John Junkin, Henry Fetter, Wm. B. Anderson, Abram Addams, Thomas Cochran, Robert Elliot, Abram B. Demaree, Jacob Evinger, and Jacob Shearer. Among the provisions of the act was a requirement that $50,000 be subscribed before the act become effective, that the first thirteen names constitute the board of directors, and that a twenty-five-year limit be placed on the act becoming effective. A supplementary act of April 10, 1845, gave the company the privilege of writing insurance in any county of the commonwealth. By a provision of a blanket bill covering various subjects, dated March 25, 1852, members of the company were made competent witnesses in suits brought against the company, unless individually parties to the suit. By an act of February 25, 1858, the number of directors was reduced to twelve, and a number of provisions of the company relative to insurance, defined.

An effort was once made to build a bridge at Liverpool, as the act of April 29, 1844, shows. It provided for the incorporation of a company for the erection of a bridge at or near Liverpool. The shares were to be $25 each and the following commissioners appointed in the act: From Dauphin County, Jacob Seal, James Freeland, G. W. Finney, John Sherer and Israel Carpenter; from Perry County, F. Rinehart, S. Shuler, Isaac Meck, D. Steward, J. H. Case, H. W. Shuman and James Jackman.

The recent general act relating to the establishment of the office of sealers of weights and measures was not a new law, but rather the revival of an old one. Such an act became effective, upon its signature, April 15, 1845, and on April 14, 1859, its provisions were repealed in so far as Perry, Cumberland and Clarion Counties were concerned. John W. Gotwalt was once the incumbent in Perry County.

The act of March 11, 1850, made it illegal to erect a free bridge within one mile of a toll bridge over the Juniata River. The act of March 11, 1851, compelled the supervisors to open a road from Finlaw McCowen's (the Oliver Rice farm, in Centre Township) to Caroline Furnace (Bailey's Station), in Miller Township. That and other minor acts relating to Perry County were passed at that session.

The Odd Fellows' Hall Association of Perry County was incorporated March 22, 1850, for the purpose of building an Odd Fellows' hall at Liverpool.

A temperance hall had been built at Ickesburg, and the act of April 17, 1854, authorized its sale, and the money to be returned to contributors. The lot had been conveyed to Robert Elliott by James Milligan and Eleanor, his wife.

The act of March 8, 1856, authorized the county to borrow annually a sum not to exceed $1,000.

An act of March 27, 1865, related to the office of jury commissioner.

The act of March 27, 1866, provided that "no license be issued to any person, or persons, to sell spirituous, vinous, malt or brewed liquors, for drinking purposes, in the borough of Duncannon, in Penn Township, or within two miles of the same." Six years later, the act of May 12, 1871, repealed the former act.

By an act of February 11, 1868, Centre Township was authorized to use for school purposes any bounty money for volunteers collected by special taxation and yet in their hands.

A special act of March 18, 1868, was passed and provided for the protection of wild turkeys in Perry County and prohibited their being killed "except from October 1 to January 1."

By an act dated March 21, 1868, the island (Wister's) in the Susquehanna River, then a part of Middle Paxton Township, Dauphin County, was annexed to Penn Township, Perry County. It was designated as containing fifty acres, more or less, and belonging to Langhorne Wister, having thereon erected a tenant house and barn, and located about a mile from the mainland of Dauphin County and about 200 yards from the Perry County shore, and cultivated by the owner in connection with his farm in Perry County.

An act dated March 25, 1868, applied to Perry County the provisions of an act passed April 18, 1853, relating to Westmoreland County, which provided that bridges which were erected by the county must be kept in repair by the township or townships in which they are located, in the same manner prescribed by law in relation to public roads.

Perry County was included in the act of April 9, 1868, passed for "the relief of citizens of certain counties whose property was destroyed, damaged or appropriated to the public service and in the common defense, in the war to suppress the rebellion."

The act of April 11, 1868, authorized the county commissioners to pay $600 to the supervisors of Jackson Township for the erection of a public bridge over Houston's Run, at a point near Baltozer's foundry, where the main road from Blain to Newville crosses that stream.

The act of March 12, 1869, gave to justices of the peace of the county the right to empanel a jury of six for the trial of certain cases. Another act signed the same day created the law library.

The act of February 10, 1871, incorporated the Bailey's Station Rope Ferry Company, with a capital of $25,000. The directors named in the act were Isaac Meck, George Blattenberger, David Deckard, John Stephens, John Herr, Lewis Acker, Joseph Bailey and George Hoffman.

The Perry County Mutual Benefit Association was incorporated by the Pennsylvania Legislature, March 9, 1872, with John R. Shuler, William McKee, Robert N. Wallis, Lewis Potter, Charles L. Murray and J. W. Gotwalt as incorporators. Section 2 required the payment of an assessment of $1.10 by the membership on the death of any member.

The act of April 12, 1872, gave to "Isaac Crow, his heirs and assigns" the right to make landings as far north as the canal lock below Liverpool, and as far south as Mount Patrick, and on the east side of the Susquehanna, along the line of the borough of Millersburg.

The act of April 10, 1873, authorized the county commissioners to borrow a sum not exceeding $9,000 to build a bridge over the Juniata River.

Early legislation appears odd to this generation. For instance, the act of March 23, 1818, authorizing the building of the Clark's Ferry bridge provided for 1,000 shares at $25 each, seemingly an insignificant sum in our day for such a project.

CHAPTER XXVIII.

*THE PUBLIC PRESS.

PERRY COUNTY has not only had many able men connected with newspaper publications, but it has given to the nation one of a quartet of the greatest of American editors, the late Col. Alexander K. McClure, who for so many years was the editor of the *Philadelphia Times*, at that time a paper with a political influence that extended over the entire nation. Elsewhere in this book is a chapter which relates to his life. Compared with those of other counties, Perry County has several papers and a number of newspaper men who are the equals of those to be found anywhere upon the country press, and whose product equals and excels very many city publications. During the past century men connected with the press of Perry County have not only represented their constituents in the legislative halls of the state, but of the nation as well.

During practically the whole period of the writer's connection with the newspaper business, during the last decade of the past century, the press of the county was edited by the following: New Bloomfield, *People's Advocate and Press*, John H. Sheibley; *Perry County Democrat*, John A. Magee; *Perry County Times*, Frank Mortimer; *Perry County Freeman*, John A. Baker, and later by A. B. Grosh; *Newport News*, F. A. Fry; *Newport Ledger*, George Shrom; *Liverpool Sun*, J. A. Zellers; *Duncannon Record*, H. H. Hain. There was a paper at Marysville at times, as stated elsewhere. My colleagues of those days, all men of mature years, are now dead. However, H. E. Sheibley, now editor of the *People's Advocate and Press*, and James S. Magee, of the *Perry County Democrat*, were associated with their fathers in those days, and while their names did not appear "at the masthead," they did much of the real editorial work.

Before the county of Perry was created there were no newspapers published within its borders, the papers from Carlisle, the old county seat, being generally read and patronized. The act of the legislature creating the new county of Perry was signed by the

---

*To the author this topic is of especial interest, as his connection with the press as correspondent, as editor of one of the county papers and as an occasional contributor to several papers since then, covers the entire period of his activity since his twelfth year, when he became a regular weekly correspondent from his section for the *Duncannon Record*, then under the management of J. L. McCaskey, signing the crude efforts with the suggestive nom de plume, "Juvenile."

governor, March 22, 1820, and inside of four months, on July 12, 1820, the first copy of a Perry County newspaper, the *Perry Forester,* appeared at the new county seat, Landisburg, its editors and owners being Alexander Magee and H. W. Peterson. In fact, these two men had entered the new county with rival schemes. A notice in the first issue of the new paper substantiates the fact that Alexander Magee, who had been in the printing business in Carlisle, had proposed publishing a paper to be known as the Gazette, and that H. W. Peterson one known as *The Telescope,* but that they had pooled their interests and compromised with the name *Perry Forester.* It follows:

"Those gentlemen, holding subscription papers for the *Perry Gazette* and *The Telescope,* issued by Alexander Magee and H. W. Peterson, will please transmit them to this office, as soon as possible; or the names and places of residence of the subscribers they may respectively contain, as H. W. Peterson and Alexander Magee have entered into partnership."

(Signed) Editors.

This first paper's cost was $2.50 per annum, but "those who pay six months in advance, every six months, will be charged $2.00." The first issue contained much literary matter, a lengthy introduction, and the following paragraph: "An apology is due our readers for the scanty supply of news in this week's *Forester.* We have not yet received any papers of any account from which we could make extracts." Another article touched upon the very poor postal facilities, as follows: "We labor under a great inconvenience in this place, on account of the arrival of but one mail a week. We sincerely hope that some proper arrangement will soon be made by the good citizens of Landisburg to receive, at least, two mails a week; and to run a post once a week from this place to Millerstown." In an early copy an article tells of the seat of justice not yet being fixed, and another article tells of the capture of Lewis and Connelly, the robbers, on July 2, at Bellefonte, with the added paragraph: "The above information we have received from a young gentleman of respectable appearance direct from Bellefonte, who passed through Landisburg on Thursday last," thus showing the pioneer method of transmitting important events. The issue of July 26th tells of Lewis' death. A crop report of an early issue says: "The harvest is reported fine; corn and potatoes are promising well." "Selected Toasts" were a prominent feature of each issue for a time, there probably being a demand for them by the populace else they would not have appeared. Many volumes contained much literary material. That the use of liquor was also being combated is proven by the many articles appearing against drunkenness and the fruits of intemperance. The issue of September 16, 1820, stated that the proprietors would take wheat, rye, corn, hams, butter, tallow and rags, in payment of subscription.

Francis Gibson, a brother of the future Chief Justice Gibson, writing under the nom de plume of "The Bard of the Vale," furnished considerable verse of a rather problematical value, often of a personal nature.

In the issue of April 14, 1824, over nine hundred pieces of unseated lands were advertised. Evidently the facilities of the publishers were somewhat limited, as in certain issues the type used in publishing the text varies from six point to twenty-four point. The use of words at that time were not especially complimentary on occasions, more especially so between gentlemen of the press, and some of them would not be appropriate in a volume such as this. On one occasion a rival was referred to as "something like a polecat in a menagerie—more offensive than formidable." In the issue of January 1, 1823, appears a "Carrier's Address," two columns in length, and asks for "a fip or two." The issue of June 23, 1834, appears with column rules inverted, in mourning over the death of the illustrious General Lafayette, who had died on May 20th, but news of which had just reached America. Andrew Jackson's "Truth is mighty and will prevail," was long carried at the *Forester's* masthead. Mr. Magee was the ancestor of the present Magee family, who edit and publish the *Perry County Democrat,* the successor of the *Perry Forester,* and the papers have been issued by the Magees since, excepting for about two decades. They have been a power in Democratic politics and have held many offices, the crowning one being when the late John A. Magee served his congressional district in the popular branch of the United States Congress. Mr. Peterson later edited a paper in Lebanon County. He then removed to Gault, upper Canada, where he died later, having in the meantime been a probate judge. The name of this first paper seems, looking down the years, singularly appropriate, for was not the county then still almost a vast forest? It was at first a four-column, four-page paper. Mr. Peterson retired January 13, 1821, and Mr. Magee on January 26th increased it to a five-column paper.

When the county seat was finally located at New Bloomfield Mr. Magee made arrangements to follow, and April 9, 1829, the *Forester* appeared from there. He published the *Forester* until March 1, 1832, when he sold it to David A. Reed, who edited it until February 14, 1835, when he sold it to Dr. Jonas Ickes, Peleg Sturtevant becoming the editor. It was published by them until February 13, 1836, when, according to tradition, it was discontinued. That statement, however, seems doubtful, although it has appeared in many volumes and historical articles, for on February 16, 1837, the *Democrat* refers contemptuously to an editorial which appeared in the *Forester* the preceding week, accusing the junior or nominal editor of hiding behind Messrs. Porter & Gangewer.

Later, on May 4, 1837, the *Democrat* says that "We have just been informed that William M. Porter, Esq., has this day sold the printing office of the *Perry Forester* to Mr. Allen M. Gangewer. It appears to be the fate of that office to change hands semi-annually." References are also made in the *Democrat's* columns during August and September, 1837, to the *Forester,* and as late as May 3d, and August 23, 1838, and in July, 1839. Another evidence that the last issue was not that of February 13, 1836, is that not a word of its discontinuance appeared in that issue. Neither did any such notice appear in the following issue of the Democrat, which would have been the case had it absorbed the *Forester.* The actual date of its passing, is however, obscure. That it no longer existed in 1844 is proven by an article in the *Freeman* telling of the death of David A Reed, which states that he "was once editor of the *Forester,* formerly published in this place."

The Liverpool Mercury, called after a paper in Liverpool, England, of the same name, was the second paper to be established in Perry County. It was started by John Huggins, of a then prominent family in eastern Perry County. It was started July 1, 1831, and was a five-column, four-page paper. The subscription price was $2 per year. In June, 1836, it was moved to New Bloomfield, and published by James B. Cooper, who then owned it, as *The Mercury and Perry Intelligencer.* He sold to Stroop & Sample, who merged it with the *Perry County Democrat.*

George Stroop and James E. Sample, on October 7, 1836, started the publication of *The Mercury and Perry County Democrat,* a five-column, four-page paper. In December of the same year it was made a six-column paper. Sample retired November 16, 1837, and from Stroop, who was an associate judge of the county at one time, in January, 1854, it passed to his son, George Stroop, and John A. Magee, a son of the early proprietor of the *Forester.* In 1858 Stroop sold his interest to Magee, whose son, James S. Magee, is the present owner. John A. Magee was connected with it until his death, on November 18, 1903. In 1867 it had become a seven-column paper, and in 1871 added another column. Its title had early changed to *The Perry County Democrat.*

The Perry Freeman, later changed to the *Perry County Freeman,* was a product of the slavery agitation, as its name implies, and was established by the late John A. Baker, June 21, 1839. In politics it was Whig, and later, like the Whigs, it became Republican. It was started as a six-column folio, and later added a column. On June 19, 1854, the *Freeman* appeared in a new dress, typographically, and began publishing local news. In fact, up until about that period all of the papers were devoted mostly to literary articles and to politics. John A. Baker was a remarkable man of wide knowledge, and it was through him that the late noted editor,

seven-column folio. When the American party was a vital factor in 1854 this paper supported it, and did so until 1856. During the interim the Missouri Compromise had been repealed, and a mighty force arose throughout the land, and organized the Republican party. Its principles became the *Advocate's* principles, and so remain until this day, no one guarding them more sacredly than did the Sheibleys, father and sons. Of course the lengthy name soon changed to the present day title, the *People's Advocate and Press.* It was increased to eight columns in 1866. A disastrous fire in 1873 burned the plant, ruining the type and machinery. A. B. Anderson, one of the projectors, in the earlier years was much interested in its editorial output. It was during only a few years that the paper was a stock concern, John H. Sheibley early purchasing the other interests. He owned and controlled it until his death, December 1, 1900, since which time it has remained the property of his sons, William B. and Horace E. Sheibley, the latter being the editor and manager. He was reared amid the surroundings of a printing office, and is a graduate of Franklin and Marshall College. Horace E. Sheibley is now dean of the newspaper publishers of the county. The *Advocate* has the distinction of having had an employee on its rolls longer than almost any paper in the state. With a lapse of a single year the late James P. Laird was connected with that paper for forty-five years, mostly in the capacity of foreman.

Frank Mortimer was a merchant in New Bloomfield as early as 1865, and two years later, in 1867, started a little monthly advertising sheet. Along with his advertising he ran some local news. It was popular and a demand for more frequent publication caused him to make it a weekly in 1869, the price being one dollar per year. It attained a very large circulation at one time. It was neutral in politics. He conducted his paper and his mercantile business jointly until 1889, and then sold the latter and devoted his entire time to the paper. On August 1, 1904, he sold the paper to William C. Lebo, who had learned the trade with him, and who is still the publisher. Mr. Lebo continued the paper neutral in so far as regular political parties were concerned, but made it a strong supporter of temperance and a foe of the liquor traffic. *The Times* was the first Perry County paper to have a power press.

During the Lincoln campaign, in the fall of 1860, a publication appeared at New Bloomfield known as *The Test*. The name of no editor or proprietor appears. It started during the first week of August and, according to the *Advocate* of November 21, 1860, *The Test,* the Breckenridge paper, lately put out in New Bloomfield, has been discontinued."

W. R. S. Cook. This firm was then in possession until January 30, 1880, when Mr. Cook and Frank A. Fry became the owners, under the firm name of Cook & Fry. They made an eight-column paper of it. On May 1, 1880, Mr. Fry leased the interest of Mr. Cook and secured entire control. Later purchasing this interest he remained at the head of the plant until his death, October 18, 1918. The paper then became the property of his sons, David S. and George R. Fry. It was made a semi-weekly, January 2, 1914, the only one in the county. Charles Woods English, who retired as foreman of the *News* in 1921, was connected with that paper for over thirty-eight years, a fine record, having entered the office to learn the printing trade soon after the entry of the late F. A. Fry.

While Millerstown has no weekly publication now, it has been the birthplace of several. January 1, 1857, the first number of the *Millerstown Gazette* appeared under the hands of Levi Klauser, and was issued as a five-column folio, 12x18 in size. It was published at Millerstown until April 22, 1858, when it was removed to Newport and the name changed to the *Newport Gazette.* Here it was continued until September, 1859, by Klauser & Bowman, when it ceased publication.

George Shrom began the publication of the *Millerstown Ledger,* a seven-column folio, May 1, 1875, and continued it until November 25, 1876, when it was removed to Newport, and the name changed to *The Ledger.* In 1882 it was made an eight-column paper, and the name changed to the *Newport Ledger.* It was edited by Mr. Shrom until his death, November 14, 1907. His son, Harry K. Shrom, then edited it until his death, August 24, 1908, aged but 33 years, when his sister, Miss Lorena Singer Shrom, who assumed charge, beautifully wrote: "I can only whisper gently to you, my precious and beloved brother, my comrade, chum and friend, Harry Kenower Shrom, has fallen asleep." Miss Shrom edited it a short time, when, for various short periods it was edited by others, and then discontinued.

The *Duncannon Record* has been more unfortunate than any paper in the county, by reason of the frequent changes in ownership, although several others in their earlier years equaled it. The *Record* was established during the spring of 1873, by Abner J. Hauck, of Mechanicsburg, over the storeroom long kept by Miss Lydia Fenstermacher, on Market Street. It suspended on April 20, 1874, and then it was taken over by a stock company composed of town merchants, and Horace G. Vines and Sylvester S. Sheller became the publishers, Mr. Sheller remaining about two years. Later Rebecca Sheller (Schiller) became the editress, being succeeded by Clarence J. Passmore. In 1878, Henry J. Lupfer bought a half-interest in the plant, and later the other half. He then sold a half-interest to Rev. G. W. Crist, and it was operated by

31

the next three years worked in the Johnson Type Foundry at Philadelphia, as a journeyman printer. In 1853, with others, he formed a stock company and became the first editor of *The Peoples' Advocate and Press,* shortly thereafter securing entire control. In that capacity he served until his death, which occurred December 1, 1900. A staunch Republican, his masterly pen was ever busy in advancing that cause, as well as those things which tend to community betterment.

Another of these prominent older editors was Frank Mortimer, of *The Times.* Born in Franklin, Massachusetts, March 14, 1829, he was educated in the common schools of his native state. He was admitted to the New York bar in 1853, having read law there with his brother, Samuel Mortimer, but he never practiced. He entered the Sectional War as a captain of Company L, Ninth New York Militia. He was later captured and confined in a Confederate prison, but escaped while being removed to another prison, and found his way to the Union lines. In 1864 he came to Perry County and engaged in the mercantile business at Green Park, removing to New Bloomfield the next year, where he was in business until 1889, only selling his store then so as to devote his entire time to *The Times,* which had grown from a small advertising medium. He sold his office August 1, 1904, and removed from the county.

Francis Allen Fry was connected with the *Newport News* as editor and proprietor for almost four decades. He was the eldest son of William Allen and Mary Louise (Price) Fry, and was born at Ickesburg, September 15, 1852. Bereft of a father, who died in Harwood Hospital, Washington, D. C., while in the service of his country, on November 2, 1863, as a member of Company A, Twelfth Pennsylvania Reserves, he entered the McAlisterville Soldiers' Orphans' School, May 12, 1865, remaining four years. He then became a member of the family of Col. George McFarland, State Superintendent of Soldiers' Orphans' Schools, where he learned the rudiments of the newspaper business, as Col. McFarland was then publisher of the *Temperance Vindicator.* His first connection with the *News* was on December 2, 1876, and from then on he never left it, becoming its editor in January, 1800. In that capacity he remained until his death, October 18, 1918. Mr. Fry's personality shone through his columns, which were ever open to the advancement of his town and county.

George Shrom, once connected with the *Newport News* as editor, and for over three decades editor of the *Newport Ledger,* was born at Carlisle, February 4, 1841. In his fifth year, a gun in the hands of a twelve-year-old boy, destroyed the sight of one of his eyes, the other also being blind for seven weeks. He was educated in the Carlisle public schools, and then learned printing in the office of the *Carlisle American*. He worked at his trade until 1869, when he purchased the *Newport News*, which he published until 1874. In May, 1875, he started the *Millerstown Ledger*. Eighteen months later he removed the plant to Newport, changing the name to the *Newport Ledger*, which he published until his death, November 14, 1907. His son, Harry Kenower Shrom, then assumed the editorship, but within a year he too passed away. With the other papers Mr. Shrom's columns were ever open to the betterment of his community.

The amount of space available in this book bars anything biographical in reference to the many others who have been connected with the press, those mentioned standing out either as pioneers or as having had almost a lifetime connection in that field.

The making of a country weekly newspaper requires the assistance of a thoroughly trained force of correspondents or reporters. There have been and still are some correspondents of the press of Perry County who deserve especial mention. Of those who have passed away are Wm. A. Holland, "the Inkstand Man," of Duncannon, who was a philosopher; George W. Gehr, of Elliottsburg, who, along with his news also contributed many historical and descriptive articles; G. Cary Tharp, of Liverpool, noted for his ability as a correspondent as well as a writer of poems; Chas. S. Losh, of Lebo, a versatile writer; W. W. Welker, of Liverpool; J. B. Jackson, of New Buffalo, and E. P. Titzel, of Millerstown. Among those still living, but who have left the county, were C. Deane Eppley, who as a mere lad started to correspond, and who helped build the Panama Canal, and still holds a responsible position there; S. Nevil Gutshall, now of the *Lewistown Daily;* Dr. O. L. Latchford, now practicing in Philadelphia, and George H. Zinn, now residing in Lancaster County. Of those still living within the county, many of them "still on the job," are John A. Bartruff, whose "Chaff From Wheatfield" marks him also as a philosopher; H. H. Sieg, of Duncannon, long an interesting regular; Harry B. Kell, of Blain, who has no superior in the state; John W. Bernheisel, of Loysville, who laid down his pen about a year ago owing to age, after a continuous service of about forty years; Miss Anna McCaskey (now Mrs. R. E. Flickinger), of Shermansdale; W. Scott Fritz, of Saville; Miss Mary E. Sheibley, of Landisburg; Cloyd A. Wolf, of Southwest Saville; Fred Hamilton, of Marysville; Samuel M. Kistler, of near Mannsville, who has seldom missed a week in twenty years; R. C. Foltz, of Landisburg, and former Associate Judge J. B. Garber, of Andersonburg. Doubtless there are others worthy of mention, but these are outstanding figures.

CHAPTER XXIX.

BANKS AND CORPORATIONS.

ALTHOUGH Perry is a comparatively small county and the population of its largest town is but about two thousand, although no large manufacturing establishments are within its borders and its soil—generally speaking—is not so fertile as those of some other counties, yet within its confines are to be found an exact dozen of banks, financed practically altogether by Perry Countians, whose stability is shown by their statements. In a number of instances their stock, when it occasionally reaches the market at all, sells at many times its par value. Of the banks now in existence, the Duncannon National Bank is the oldest national bank, although the First National Bank of Newport was in business longer, but under the name of the People's Bank, and not as a national bank. The Duncannon National Bank building was also the first building to be exclusively devoted to banking to be built in the county, having been erected in 1889. P. K. Brandt, of the First National Bank of Newport, served as cashier, 1876 to 1922, and P. F. Duncan, of the Duncannon National Bank, has been the only cashier of that bank since it began business, January 2, 1890. Prior to the establishment of banks the larger stores and business firms did more or less of a banking business, there being then little checking, as few had accounts in banks at other points. The south side of the county banked at Carlisle, and the river section at Harrisburg. The Duncannon Iron Company acted in the capacity of banker for the Duncannon section, while in other sections merchants, warehouse men, etc., filled the need.

Before banks were so numerous, and before Duncannon had a bank, the safe of the Duncannon Iron Company was used for the storage of large sums of cash, which were despatched to and from the Harrisburg banks as commerce demanded. Naturally this attracted the attention of yeggmen, and during the night of February 12, 1867, the vault and safe were blown open, the noise being covered by a passing train and the attendant noises of the big iron mill, so that it was not discovered until morning. The burglars carried away ten thousand dollars in currency and six thousand dollars in bonds. They had come and gone unseen, except that John Dudley, an Iron Company employe, had noticed a character known as "Jimmie Hope," get off the afternoon train on the side opposite the station. "Hope" had a criminal record, and months afterwards Mr. Dudley met him in Philadelphia and caused his arrest. He was tried, convicted, and served three years in the Eastern penitentiary at Philadelphia, known as "Cherry Hill." Another one was captured later, but failed to be convicted.

The banking business in Perry County dates back only to 1866, in which year two banks were established. The first one to open its doors was the Perry County Bank, started at New Bloomfield by Sponsler, Junkin & Company, September 20, 1866, and continuing until 1894. It opened for business in the office of the Perry County Mutual Fire Insurance Company, where it remained until the spring of 1868, when the building now occupied by the First National Bank of New Bloomfield was completed for its occupancy, and for residential purposes.

The second bank to be formed that year was the Newport Deposit Bank. It began business on December 12, 1866, in the present Butz building (then known as the Wright building), where Miss Sara Adams now (1920) conducts a millinery store. Perry Kreamer was president; Isaac Wright, cashier, and Charles A. Wright, teller. It reorganized March 23, 1867, with John Wright as president, and Isaac Wright as cashier, who remained in office until 1872, when another reorganization took place. Thomas H. Milligan then became president; Isaac Wright, cashier, and J. M. Wright, teller. In 1876, J. H. Irwin became cashier, remaining until it quit business in 1895. In 1877 it was moved from the Butz building to the location now occupied by the Citizens' Bank.

The Juniata Valley Bank, of Mifflintown, opened a branch bank in the Minich building, on Market Street, Newport, in September, 1873, with J. H. Irwin as cashier, and continued business until 1876, when Mr. Irwin was elected as cashier of the Newport Deposit Bank, and it discontinued business. The Farmers' Bank, of Liverpool, was organized in July, 1871, with M. B. Holman as president, and J. C. Weirick, cashier. It continued in business until 1879. The Farmers' Bank, of Millerstown, was organized December 21, 1872, by electing Perry Kreamer president, and William S. Rickabaugh, cashier. Samuel Clever and T. J. Kreamer were later cashiers. Its capital stock was fixed at $50,000. It quit business December 21, 1878. It conducted a branch bank at Newport in 1873 and later. Of these first five banks none are in business.

FIRST NATIONAL BANK OF NEWPORT.

This bank started in business on August 19, 1875, as the People's Bank, of Newport, with a capital of only $15,000. Dr. J. E. Singer was its first president, and W. S. Rickabaugh, its first cashier. Its first board of directors was composed of P. M. Kepner, H. C. Lewis, John Bair, Jerome Hetrick, Charles K. Smith, and James B. Leiby. Dr. Singer died in 1881, and John Bair became president, and so remained until 1893, when it was reorganized and became the First National Bank of Newport, with Dr. James B. Eby, president; William C. Pomeroy, vice-president, and William Wertz, secretary. The directors other than the officers were: George T. Kepner, S. W. Seibert, Joseph W. Stimmel, and C. K. Smith. Presidents since then have been Rev. S. W. Seibert, beginning with January, 1911; Wm. Emenheiser, January, 1913, who served until his death in February, 1916, when A. W. Kough succeeded him. The new bank building was erected in 1893, the year of the First National's organization. *P. K. Brandt, the cashier, has served in that capacity since 1876. The present board of directors (1920) is composed of A. W. Kough, T. H. Butturf, J. Emory Fleisher, Singer Smith, James E. Smith, Amos L. Gelnett, and Frank M. Snyder. In 1921 W. R. Bosserman was selected to fill the vacancy on the board caused by the death of Singer J. Smith. July 1, 1920, its statement showed undivided profits of $12,000, and surplus fund of $125,000. The time deposits amounted to $186,347, and individual deposits subject to check, $182,887. Its capital stock is $50,000.

CITIZENS' NATIONAL BANK OF NEWPORT.

The Citizens' National Bank of Newport dates from April 28, 1905, James E. Wilson, a resident of Duncannon, becoming its cashier, and still occupying that position. Its first officers were John Fleisher, president; W. H. Gantt, vice-president; Chas. A. Rippman, Chas. W. Smith, Horace Beard, and Dr. J. F. Thompson, of Liverpool, directors. Its present officers and directors (1920) are: Dr. J. H. McCullogh, president; C. L. Bair, vice-president; C. W. Smith, J. C. Swartz, C. E. Noll, and Dr. L. A. Carl. During 1916 this bank purchased the Graham Hotel property, at the corner of Market and Second Streets, and turned the building into a business block and apartments. July 1, 1920, its statement showed undivided profits of $14,502, and a surplus fund of $40,000. The time deposits amounted to $216,631, and the deposits subject to check to $154,333. The capital stock is $50,000.

THE DUNCANNON NATIONAL BANK.

The oldest national bank in Perry County is the Duncannon National Bank, opened January 1, 1890, in a new building, the first in the county to be built exclusively for banking purposes. Its first officers were John Wister, president; Jos. M. Hawley, vice-president, and P. F. Duncan, cashier. The first board of directors were John Wister, Wm. Rotch Wister, Jos. M. Hawley, Samuel Sheller, George Pennell, Dr. T. L. Johnston, G. C. Snyder,

---

*P. K. Brandt retired January, 1922, and was succeeded by G. H. Frank

plus and profits, June 30, 1920, were $21,676.26, and the deposits, $248,758.82.

THE FIRST NATIONAL BANK OF MARYSVILLE.

The First National Bank of Marysville was chartered August 6, 1904. The original officers were: J. W. Place, president; J. Harper Seidel, and J. W. Beers, vice-presidents, and James E. Wilson, cashier. The directors were: J. Harper Seidel, J. W. Beers, J. W. Taubert, H. J. Deckard, E. Walt Snyder, C. S. Wise, J. S. Bitner, J. W. Place, and A. B. Patterson. In 1905, F. W. Geib succeeded J. E. Wilson as cashier. The present board of directors and officers are: J. W. Beers, president; E. B. Leiby and H. J. Deckard, vice-presidents; F. W. Geib, cashier; H. E. Hess, Z. T. Collier, and E. Walt Snyder. June 30, 1920, the undivided profits were $14,482.34, and the surplus fund, $15,000. The deposits amounted to $288,736.68. The capital stock is $50,000. This bank occupies its own brick building, erected exclusively for banking purposes.

FIRST NATIONAL BANK OF MILLERSTOWN.

The First National Bank of Millerstown was chartered April 4, 1904, with Charles H. Rippman, president. At the end of three months Mr. Rippman resigned, and A. H. Ulsh has been president since that time. James Rounsley has been the vice-president since its organization. The first cashier was James E. Rounsley, who served from the date of organization, April 4, 1904, to the time of his death, November 5, 1918. T. Clair Karchner, of Juniata County, has since filled the position. The first board of directors was composed of C. A. Rippman, James Rounsley, J. G. H. Rippman, C. A. Rippman, Samuel L. Beaver, George W. Fry, John G. Ludwick, and A. H. Ulsh. The present board consists of A. H. Ulsh, James Rounsley, D. A. Lahr, T. P. Cathcart, L. A. Dimm, and George W. Fry. June 30, 1920, the surplus and profits were $30,894.25, and the deposits, $282,176.82. Its new stone banking building faces the public square. The capital stock is $25,000.

FIRST NATIONAL BANK OF LIVERPOOL.

The First National Bank of Liverpool was chartered for business August 13, 1906, and opened October 15, 1906. The first officers were Chas. H. Snyder, president; John D. Snyder, vice-president, and H. A. S. Shuler, cashier. The directors were Chas. H. Snyder, John D. Snyder, George W. Snyder, G. A. Gale, and John H. Weirick. The present officers are: Wm. L. Lenhart, president; J. D. Snyder, vice-president, and H. A. S. Shuler, cashier. The board of directors consists of W. L. Lenhart, J. D. Snyder, Lafayette Grubb, George W. Snyder, and H. A. S. Shuler.

The bank occupies its own brick building. An effort was made to burglarize it by yeggmen in 1921, but its improved safeguards made their efforts futile. June 30, 1920, its surplus was $12,500, and its undivided profits, $2,017.55. Its deposits amounted to $190,280.43.

People's National Bank of Duncannon.

The People's National Bank of Duncannon was organized July 5, 1907, with Chas. S. Boll, president; Emanuel Jenkyn, vice-president, and Geo. O. Matter, cashier, the officers also being directors. The other directors were: Dr. B. F. Beale, Chas. A. Disbrow, Chas. L. Harling, S. W. Lehman, Dr. H. W. McKenzie, Allen D. Michener, I. L. Phillips, Adelaide Schiller, Sylvester S. Sheller, Enos Smith, Allen R. Thompson, and McClellan Woods. The present officers are: Sylvester S. Sheller, president; Dr. B. F. Beale, vice-president; M. N. Lightner, cashier, the former two also being directors. The other directors are: S. B. Sheller, Miss A. Schiller, E. S. Glass, Geo. M. Zerfing, J. James Dowdrick, Charles Harling, J. W. Mumper, and G. A. Hemperly. The capital is $25,000, and the deposits in a recent statement were $145,000.

The Ickesburg State Bank.

The Ickesburg State Bank was first organized on October 30, 1917, but did not open for business until August 15, 1918. It occupies a new stone banking building erected for that purpose. Its first officers were: C. A. Meiser, president; Elmer Rice, vice-president, and J. F. Rumbaugh, cashier. The first directors were: C. A. Meiser, Elmer Rice, S. G. Beaver, E. L. Ernest, John Diven W. G. Hench and W. B. Shull. The present board of directors and officers are the same, save that A. W. Shelly takes the place of Mr. Meiser as president and on the board of directors. The capital is $25,000. During the night of March 28, 1922, the bank was burglarized, $3,800 being taken from safety deposit boxes of its patrons, which loss the bank assumed.

First National Bank of Loysville.

The First National Bank of Loysville was chartered November 28, 1919, and opened for business January 2, 1920. Its first officers were: Wm. T. Morrow, president; H. O. Ritter, vice-president, and B. Stiles Duncan, cashier. The first board of directors was composed of B. Stiles Duncan, Dr. Wm. T. Morrow, H. O. Ritter, E. G. Briner, J. E. Garber, L. R. McMillen, and Theorus Bernheisel. In 1921 James Rhinesmith and John H. Shumaker were added to the board. The officers then were B. Stiles Duncan, president; Dr. Wm. T. Morrow, vice-president, and W. H. Soule, cashier. June 30, 1920, six months after its opening, its surplus and undivided profits were $5,486.90, and its deposits, $27,798.48. Its capital stock is $25,000.

Note.—At Newport during the period between 1895, after the room was vacated by the People's Bank, and 1905, when it was again occupied by the Citizens' Bank, a bank was established known as the Perry County National Bank, its existence having been but a few years.

THE FARMERS' AND MECHANICS' MUTUAL FIRE INSURANCE CO.

The Farmers' and Mechanics' Mutual Fire Insurance Company was organized in August, 1872, with George Hoobaugh, president; William W. McClure, secretary, and Jacob Sheibley, treasurer. The directors were Henry Cooper, James A. Gray, David Clark, John Kochenderfer, and Bryan Gibney. Mr. Hoobaugh and Mr. McClure filled the positions of president and secretary for twenty-three consecutive years. June 28, 1879, this company absorbed the risks of the Farmers' and Mechanics' Mutual Fire Insurance Company of Madison, Jackson and Toboyne Townships, which had its headquarters at Blain. From its organization until December 31, 1920, the company paid claims of $130,246.21. The salaries that year totaled only $1,150, while the insurance in force totaled $4,607,391. The losses during that year were only $5,650.06.

Since the organization of the company, forty-eight years ago, there have been thirty assessments, totaling fifty-four mills on the sum total of written risks, or an average of one and one-eighth mills, on the dollar at risk, per annum. On account of the diminishing population of the country districts, during the last fifty years, many homes were abandoned and left uncared for, which naturally increased the fire hazard, yet this company has had very few losses, and a loss account considerably lower than the average of the companies insuring in Pennsylvania. This appears as evidence of the honesty of Perry County people.

David H. Sheibley served the company as their treasurer nine years, and John A. Bower served the company as one of the board of directors for nine years, and as their secretary for twenty-four years. In the year 1916 the charter was amended, permitting the company to carry insurance in the boroughs or towns of Perry County. The present officers are: President, Joseph C. Waggoner, elected in 1913; secretary, Milton R. Bower, elected in 1919; treasurer, A. B. Dum, elected in 1920; directors, James M. Stambaugh, Ezra D. Bupp, Amos L. Dum, Jacob Fleisher, William Turnbaugh.

TELEPHONE COMPANIES.

As near as the facts can be learned probably the first telephone line in Perry County was at Bailey's Station, in Miller Township, where it connected the old-time water station with the telegraph tower a quarter of a mile away. This was a private line used for railroad business only. The first line of a semi-public nature was the one built by the old Perry County Railroad Company, from New Bloomfield, to connect with the offices of the Duncannon

Iron Company, the Duncannon National Bank, and the mercantile establishment of Samuel Sheller, at Duncannon.

In so far as the general public is concerned the real telephone construction only began in 1904, when the Perry County Telephone Company was organized to build a line from New Bloomfield to Loysville, Landisburg, and Bridgeport. The first officers were as follows: Dr. D. B. Milliken, president; J. C. Wagner, secretary; J. R. Wilson, treasurer; George B. Dum, manager The officers were also on the board of directors, with the following others: Dr. L. M. Shumaker, Wm. Dum, Thomas Martin, H. M. Keen, Charles Kennedy, John A. Bower, and B. H. Sheibley. This is less than two decades ago, yet a strange fatality seems to have pervaded the board, for only Charles Kennedy, J. C. Wagner and J. R. Wilson are living. This company was the pioneer one, and from it has come the splendid telephone network which covers the county.

In 1907 it was incorporated with the same officers, save that J. J. Wolfe, of Loysville, was made manager. The directors under the reorganization were Dr. D. B. Milliken, James Moose, Wilson Gray, D. H. Sheibley, and R. J. Makibben. The lines were extended to Blain, New Germantown, Ickesburg, and Shermansdale in 1908, and a line running from Marysville to Duncannon and Newport was purchased in 1910. In 1914 a controlling interest was purchased in the lines through Pfoutz Valley and from Millerstown to Ickesburg. The original line had eleven telephones, in 1904. When incorporated, in 1907, there were forty-seven, and early in 1920 there were almost thirteen hundred. On October 1, 1918, the free service area was extended over the whole county. R. J. Makibben, the present manager, was also president of the company for a period of ten years and is a practical telephone man, having served in every capacity from a messenger boy in Harrisburg, in "the eighties," to the head of the company.

The first telephone line to operate between the two rivers was incorporated March 2, 1909, as the Pfoutz's Valley Telephone Company. The organizers and stockholders were A. T. Holman, A. L. Long, George Rebok, and H. E. Ritter, the latter two remaining with the company a short time, when the business was conducted by Messrs. Holman and Long. At the death of A. T. Holman, his stock was purchased by the Perry County Telephone Company, who own one-half the stock. The Pfoutz's Valley Telephone Company has 220 stations, and conducts two exchanges one at Millerstown and one at Liverpool. The present officers are: J. R. Makibben, president; A. L. Long, vice-president; Geo. W. Fry, treasurer; J. C. Wagner, secretary.

There are also a number of smaller companies, two of which operate lines in Buck's Valley, Buffalo Township.

CHAPTER XXX.

COUNTY'S EARLY YEARS—A COMPARISON.
(1820-1860.)

PERRY COUNTY'S organization was almost coincident with the organization of the Union and of Pennsylvania. When it became a county in 1820 the fifth President of the United States, James Monroe, was only serving the third year of his eight-year term. At the first fall election in the new county President Monroe was on the ticket and was reëlected. It was the noted "era of good feeling" and it would seem that if ever a President had an easy chance for a third term that man was Monroe, although Washington, Jefferson, and Jackson could have had a third.

Alexander K. McClure, the prominent editor and historian, who was born in Perry County, says:

"Monroe's reëlection in 1820 presents the singular political spectacle of his success without having been formally nominated by any party, and without a single electoral vote being cast against him. That had occurred in Washington's two elections, but it was not believed possible that, with the bitter partisan disputes which immediately followed Washington's retirement, any man could ever be chosen for the Presidency without more or less of a contest. Monroe's administration had no serious political or diplomatic problem to confront, and the country was rapidly recovering from the war and was proud of the achievement of the American Army and Navy in the second contest with the English."

In fact, one electoral vote was cast by a New Hampshire elector against Monroe, but he had been elected as a Monroe elector and gave as his excuse "that he was unwilling that any other President than Washington should receive a unanimous electoral vote.

Colonel McClure also tells us:

"Monroe had the most unruffled period of rule ever known in the history of the republic. Washington, with all his omnipotence, was fearfully beset by factional strife and the wrangles of ambition on every side, and there was no period of his two administrations in which he was not greatly fretted by the persistent and often desperate disputes among those who should have been his friends; but Monroe had an entirely peaceful reign, with the single exception of the slavery dispute over the Missouri question. At the close of his term Monroe retired to his home in Virginia entirely exhausted in fortune. For several years he acted in the capacity of justice of the peace, but his severely straightened circumstances finally compelled him to make his home with his son-in-law, in New York, where he died in 1831, and like Jefferson and Adams, on the Fourth of July."

These facts are introduced here principally to show what manner of man was President and what the conditions were nationally at the time of Perry County's beginning. President Monroe, like three of his predecessors, was a Virginian, but less aristocratic and far from being in such affluent circumstances. There were but five cabinet positions in those days, and during the Monroe reign the occupants of these offices were: State Department, John Graham, Richard Rush, and John Quincy Adams; War Department, Isaac Shelby and John C. Calhoun; Treasury Department, W. H. Crawford; Navy Department, B. Crowninshield and S. Thompson; Post Office Department, R. J. Meigs; Attorney General, William Wirt.

Just a year previous to the new county's organization Alabama had been admitted into the Union, and in the same year (1820) Maine was admitted, with Missouri following the succeeding year. In fact, 1820, was the date of the Missouri Compromise, that piece of national legislation which lulled to sleep the slavery agitation for about twenty-five years before it broke out afresh and eventually almost disrent the Union. During the previous year the first steamboat had crossed the Atlantic.

Perry County had existed as a new county less than three years when President Monroe enunciated the famous "Monroe Doctrine," sending it to the United States Congress on December 2, 1823. It follows:

"We owe it, therefor, to candor, and to the amicable relations existing between the United States and those powers, to declare, that we should consider any attempt on their part to extend their system to any portion of this hemisphere as dangerous to our peace and safety." In the *Perry Forester* those words show no undue prominence over the rest of the lengthy message. Probably no State paper ever issued was more potent for good than that one. More than seventy years later President Grover Cleveland, in dealing with England on the Venezuela dispute, reiterated the doctrine in these words: "Europe ought not to intervene in American affairs, and any European power doing so will be regarded as antagonizing the interests and inviting the opposition of the United States."

It was during James Monroe's administration, also, that the first White House wedding occurred, the bride being a niece of the President. Later, March 9, 1820, the President's second daughter was married. It was an exclusive home wedding, the public men and their families being uninvited. Of it the *Washington Intelligencer* said:

"On Thursday evening last (March 9), in this city, by the Reverend Mr. Hawley, Samuel Lawrence Governeur, Esq., of New York, to Miss Maria Hester Monroe, daughter of James Monroe, President of the United States."

There is a great contrast between this inconspicuous description of a society event of national importance, then, and the flaming "scare heads" running entirely across a page that characterized reports by some dailies in connection with White House weddings of the last decade or two.

The early period of the county's history, a matter of two-score years, was, in fact, coincident with that of the nation's history in which the ever-growing sectional question of slavery was the vital issue of the day. Missouri having been admitted as a state, at the celebration in Perry County on Independence Day, 1821, the following toast was drunk—toasts at that time being a popular form of entertainment: "The admission of Missouri territory into the Union—We greet her as a sister, but heartily despise slavery." Among the volunteer toasts was this by Thomas Craighead: "Long corns and short shoes to the enemies of the republic."

The Florida War, a rather insignificant war, occurring about the time when Perry County became a county, was waged with few soldiers, yet a Perry Countian, William D. Boyer, of New Bloomfield, who died on March 14, 1854, served through it. There may have been others, but no records could be found.

The year 1820 is memorable for another event of importance. In that year George III, held in contempt in America, died, and the next year Napoleon's career was ended by death. In the year 1824 the first protective tariff measure was introduced in the American Congress, being opposed by the South and strangely by New England. Political leadership, which up to this time was preëminent in the South, began passing to the North. In the fall elections there were four candidates all of one party, the Democratic-Republican, for the Presidency, and the election was thrown into the House of Representatives, which chose John Quincy Adams. From this time the demarkation along political lines became more acute, the question being whether Adams' successor should be from the South or the North. His opponents were slaveholders and their Northern friends. His supporters were National Republicans, Whigs, and Republicans. Clay and Webster were the bright lights of the United States Senate.

In 1826 a man named Morgan, of New York State, threatened to publish the secrets of Free Masonry. His presses were destroyed and he was never heard of again, according to records of the period. This aroused considerable agitation and, in 1826, there sprang up in many states a party known as the Anti-Masonic party. The end of 1838 saw the ending of that party's existence, but during its life there was an Anti-Masonic ticket nominated and voted for in Perry County. During this period the Masons was not the only organization aimed at, but was designated because it was the most prominent. There was a general antipathy to secret societies, but especially towards the Masons. The political party in Pennsylvania erected upon that protest supported Joseph Ritner for governor in 1829, but he was defeated. He was again defeated three years later, but in 1835 was elected.

On the Fourth of July, 1826, the fiftieth anniversary of American National Independence, two noted men, John Adams and Thomas Jefferson, died, both having been Presidents of the United States and signers of the Declaration of Independence. This fiftieth anniversary, or semi-centennial, was celebrated throughout the United States. Two Perry County towns, Landisburg and New Bloomfield, celebrated it. During this year Noah Webster revised the proofs of his famous dictionary. In 1829 Andrew Jackson became President and instituted the policy of "to the victors belong the spoils." During this year South Carolina and Georgia affirmed the doctrine of nullification, which was the forerunner of secession in 1860. During Jackson's term New England organized its first Anti-Slavery Society.

The county was in its eleventh year (1833) before Chicago was laid out and the first lot sold. During this year James Monroe, who was President of the United States when the county was organized, passed away on July 4. As early as 1833 throughout the new nation newspaper plants were destroyed, public halls burned, homes dismantled and citizens of other sections imprisoned and even flogged in the agitation on the slavery question. In 1834 Great Britain liberated the slaves in its colonies and Abraham Lincoln entered politics and was elected to the Illinois Legislature. McCormick patented the reaper during this year.

During 1837 the youthful Queen Victoria became the ruler of England, and many of us in middle life well remember her notable reign, a veritable lifetime. This was the year of an inflated money panic, when even Perry County issued "scrip." Martin Van Buren was chosen to succeed Andrew Jackson as President. During 1839 the Whig party was organized, principally from the National Republicans. Although the election was fifteen months away the new party soon thereafter held a convention in Zion Lutheran Church, Harrisburg, then building, and nominated William Henry Harrison, who was elected in 1840. This building still stands and is in regular use as a place of worship. It is the red brick church in the foreground seen when leaving the Pennsylvania Railroad Station. This campaign was the first one in which the people took a real interest and in which torch-light processions, etc., were introduced, with the slogan, "Tippecanoe, and Tyler, too." It was broadly heralded that Harrison "lived in a log cabin and drank hard cider." The new party's majority was almost a million and a half of votes, and took from the Democratic party the executive power, which it had held for forty years. Van Buren was the first man to occupy the Presidential chair who was born on American soil and the only one who served as Vice-President during the hundred years between 1800 and 1900 to be elected to the Presidency. Tyler was the first Vice-President to inherit the Presidency.

In 1840 the electric telegraph was first patented by Morse. President Harrison, who had been active in politics since 1797 when he was secretary of the Northwest Territory, died a month after inauguration, having contracted pneumonia through exposure on inauguration day to a chilly rain. As stated, Maine became a state in the same year as Perry became a county. It was followed by Missouri in 1821, Arkansas in 1836, Michigan in 1837, Florida and Texas in 1845, Iowa in 1846, Wisconsin in 1848, etc. In the year that gave Perry birth there were only twenty-three states in the Union, as against forty-eight at this time. There were none west of the Mississippi River at that time.

In his "Recollections of Half a Century," Col. A. K. McClure tells of a personal experience in Perry County during the Harrison-Van Buren campaign of 1840. From it we quote:

"In those days the rural community was fortunate that had a weekly mail. Daily newspapers were unknown in the country, and the people had to depend solely upon their local newspapers for their news. * * * On Friday, two weeks and three days after the Presidential election of 1840 in Pennsylvania, a number of neighbors were gathered at my father's, at what was then known as a 'raising.' The custom of those days was for the neighbors to be summoned when any one of them was ready to erect the frame or log work of a building, and spend the day or afternoon in fulfilling the kind neighborly offices which have almost been entirely effaced by the progress of civilization. What a builder would now do in an hour with machinery the neighborly gathering would give a day to the same task, and make it, besides, one of generous hospitality and enjoyment. Friday was the day on which the weekly mail arrived, and the Whigs and Democrats who enjoyed their political spats, as both claimed the state for their respective parties, were anxious to have the weekly paper to decide the attitude of the Keystone State. I was dispatched to the post office, a mile or more distant, in time to be there when the postboy arrived, with instructions to make special haste in returning. My father was one of the few liberal men of that day who received both the Democratic and Whig local newspapers, so that the anxious company was insured of information from the organs of both parties. When the mail arrived at the post office I seized the Whig paper, and was delighted to find a huge coon over the Pennsylvania returns, and the announcement that the state had gone for Harrison by 1,000 majority. In generous pity I opened the Democratic paper to see how it would accept the sweeping disaster, and to my utter consternation, it had a huge rooster over the Pennsylvania returns, and declared that the state had voted for Van Buren by 1,000 majority. I took the shortest cut across the fields to bring the confusing news to the anxious crowd that was awaiting it, and both papers were spread open and both sides went home rejoicing in the victory. Of course, they all felt that there was a strong element of doubt in the conflicting returns, but the matter was quietly dismissed without complaint for another week, and it was fully two weeks later when the official vote was finally received that gave the state to Harrison by 305 majority. * * * The difference between the relations of the people and the public men they wor-

shiped in the present and half a century ago can hardly fully be appreciated in this wonderfully progressive age. Then travel was a luxury
that few could enjoy and was almost wholly confined to those who found
it a necessity. It was not only tedious and tiresome, but expensive far
beyond the means of the great mass of the people. The great men of that
day were idolized by their partisans as we now pay homage to the statue
of some great leader as it poses on the pinnacle of the temple with its
imperfections obliterated by distance."

These were the principal political and national events in the nation during the first two decades of the county's history, 1820-
1840, and are here printed by way of comparison.

In Pennsylvania, at the time of the formation of Perry County,
William Findlay, of Franklin County, was governor, being the
fourth to fill the office, having been inaugurated on December 16,
1817, and serving until December 19, 1820, when Joseph Heister,
of Berks County, became his successor. At that time slavery was
still lawful in Pennsylvania, and Governor Findlay was the owner
of a slave whom he freed in 1817, with the declaration, "The principles of slavery are repugnant to those of justice, and are totally
irreconcilable with that rule which requires us to do unto others
as we would wish to be done by." It was usual in those days to
chain slaves together and thus they passed across Pennsylvania,
especially the southwestern part. Under the Constitution of 1790,
then in effect, the patronage of the governor was immense. With
few exceptions he had the power to appoint all state and county
officers. The erection of the state capitol was begun about this
time. Up until then the state legislature had met in the old courthouse of Dauphin County at Harrisburg. There was no executive
mansion—not even an executive chamber—for the transaction of
the business pertaining to the governorship. The population of
Harrisburg in 1820 was only 2,990.

According to Dr. Lyman Abbott, in *The Outlook,* during the
first fourth of the last century drunkenness was common and there
were no temperance societies. Slavery existed in half the United
States and there were no anti-slavery societies; there were no labor
laws and from ten to sixteen hours of work were required, and
there were public schools in only half of the United States. While
things had improved over the pioneer period, yet the heating of
homes was by open fires and air-tight stoves, with no warm rooms
save the kitchen. Candles and whale-oil lamps furnished light.
Goodyear had not yet discovered the uses of India rubber and the
heavy boots of the period were well greased to turn water. Medicine was hardly a science and surgery practically in its infancy,
as anesthetics were unknown; amputations were made in a rude
way. Tuberculosis ran rampant and people were of the opinion
that night air was unhealthy and slept in closed rooms. Cholera
visited our shores every summer and yellow fever was epidemic

in our Southern cities. both of which have been abolished by science. Even long years afterwards when passenger trains ran fifteen to twenty-five miles an hour it was considered a wonderful feat.

Of life in those early days of the new county let us again recall the words of one born and reared in Perry County. Col. Alexander K. McClure, in his "Old-Time Notes of Pennsylvania," says:

"The memory of the people of those days that comes to me with the sweetest incense is that of the serene content that prevailed among all classes and conditions. No one possessed great wealth, but none were so poor that they could not have food and raiment unless hindered by serious illness. In such cases there were always prompt and generous ministrations. The sick and the sorrowing of every community were known in almost every household, and where there was want there was always a most willing supply. No matter how people differed in politics or in religion, or on any of the other questions which at times divided rural communities, the duty of caring for the children of sorrow was accepted by all. Religion was the common law, and Sunday was made a day of most tedious and laborious worship. The neighborly feeling that was cherished by all was one of the most beautiful attributes of human nature, and it is a misfortune that it has almost wholly perished as the railroad, the telegraph, the newspaper and all the other many agencies of progress have transformed our rural communities of long ago into the unrest of modern and better civilization. There can be no great transformation of the tastes and habits of a people without some loss of that which should have been preserved; but, discounted by all the unrest that modern civilization has brought, it has made men and women stronger and nobler, and has vastly greater sources of restraint than were thought of in the quiet days of the contented rural life. The house in which I was born and reared, although a brick building and comfortably furnished, never had a lock on door or window, and the burglar, or even the petty sneak thief, was entirely unthought of."

FIRST JUSTICES OF THE PEACE.

From documents in the Bureau of Records in the State Capitol at Harrisburg it has been found possible to give the original list of the first justices of the peace for the new county of Perry. Evidently power to appoint them was delegated to the court, as the following would imply:

LANDISBURG, Sept. 6, 1821.

To Andrew Gregg:

Enclosed I hand you a list of all the justices of the peace who have been appointed in Perry County, agreeable to your direction, in your circular of the 17th of July last, but which I did not receive until the 30th of the same month. I could not get all the information on the subject, before our court, which commenced on the 3d instant.

Very respectfully,

ABM. FULWEILER.

The List:

Jacob Barkstraser, Toboyne, residence Toboyne.
Daniel Bloom, Toboyne, residence Toboyne.
Robert Adams, Toboyne, residence Toboyne.

Jacob Fritz, Tyrone and Saville, residence Landisburg.
Wm. Power, Tyrone and Saville, residence Landisburg.
Samuel Linn, Tyrone and Saville, residence Landisburg.
Jacob Stroop, Tyrone and Saville, residence Tyrone.
*Henry Titsel, Tyrone and Saville, residence Tyrone.
Wilson McClure, Tyrone and Saville, residence Tyrone.
John Taylor, Tyrone and Saville, residence Saville.
John Owen, Rye, residence Rye.
John White, Rye, residence Rye.
John Ogle, Rye, residence Rye.
Robert Clark, Rye, residence Rye.
Frank Orwan, Juniata, residence Juniata.
Benjamin Bonsall, Juniata, residence Juniata.
James Black, Juniata, residence Juniata.
George Monroe, Juniata, residence Juniata.
John Purcell, Greenwood and Buffalo, residence Millerstown.
Caleb North, Greenwood and Buffalo, residence Millerstown.
Abraham Adams, Greenwood and Buffalo, residence Millerstown.
John Turner, Greenwood and Buffalo, residence Greenwood.
Samuel Utter, Greenwood and Buffalo, residence Greenwood.
William Linton, Greenwood and Buffalo, residence Buffalo.
Richard Bard, Greenwood and Buffalo, residence Buffalo.
John Huggins, Greenwood and Buffalo, residence Liverpool.

---

*Has not acted; pays no attention to the duties of justice of the peace.

Fees were small in those days, roads were bad and evidently some duties were also offensive, as the record of an old suit will verify. A suit was instituted by the Commonwealth of Pennsylvania vs. George Leiberich to recover the license ($5.00) for selling wines and liquors, the summons being dated December 11, 1826. At the December court Robert Welch, constable of Tyrone Township, returned it marked "not served for want of time." The summons was turned over to David Miller, constable of Wheatfield Township, on February 5, 1827. At the February court he returned it marked "not served for want of time." On April 12, 1827, it was reissued to Miller, and at the April session he returned it marked "not served." On May 7 it was reissued to him and (strangely enough) by the May court it had been properly served and George Leiberich, the defendant, and his clerk, appeared and proved that he had not sold any wines or "foreign" liquors. His business tax of $10.00 he had paid at the proper time. This suit was brought at the office of Samuel Linn, of Tyrone Township, from whose docket the transcript, on file at the Capitol, was made.

The county's early years, not unlike the beginning of time, were marred by a brotherly quarrel, resulting in its first murder. The court, in December, 1823, sentenced the convicted man to the Eastern Penitentiary, the verdict having been "in the second degree." With the affair this book has nothing to do and the matter is merely introduced here to show the method of travel, the time consumed, and the cost at that period. The sheriff's bill for expenses of taking the prisoner to Philadelphia read like this:

To stage fare from Carlisle to Philadelphia, sheriff, guard and prisoner @ $8.75,	$26.75
To ditto, sheriff and guard back,	17.50
To 7 days spent by sheriff in taking prisoner from Landisburg to city @ $2.00,	14.00
To 7 days for guard @ $1.00,	7.00
To sheriff's expense for 7 days @ $1.50,	10.50
To guard's expense for 7 days @ $1.50,	10.50
To expenses of prisoner @ $1.00,	3.00
To amount paid for keeping prisoner at night,	1.00
To ditto,	.50
Total,	$90.25

During 1829, a prisoner, convicted for manslaughter, was taken to Philadelphia to the penitentiary. The county seat was then at New Bloomfield, and the route taken was another, via Clark's Ferry (now Duncannon). The stage fare had decreased considerably over what it had been six years before. It will be noticed that the word *sundries* had already reached the public records of the new county. The bill:

To taking prisoner from Bloomfield to Clark's Ferry with Dearborn (a type of carriage) and horse, including sending Dearborn back and expenses at ferry,	$2.47
To stage fare (prisoner and staff) from Clark's Ferry to Philadelphia,	10.00
To stage fare (sheriff) from Phila. to Harrisburg,	4.00
Tavern bill at Buehler's, going down,	.94
Tavern bill at Womelsdorf, going down,	.75
Tavern bill at Reading, going down,	1.00
Jailer, for keeping prisoner at Reading,	.37½
Tavern bill at H. Styer's,	.68¾
Stage driver, from office to pen. with prisoner,	.50
Tavern bill for sheriff in Philadelphia,	2.00
Tavern bill at Styer's, returning,	.31
Dinner at Womelsdorf, returning,	.37½
Bill at Buehler's, returning,	1.00
Conveyance and expenses from Hbg. to Bloomfield,	4.00
Sundries, for which no vouchers were taken,	2.00
For six days for sheriff @ $2.00,	12.00
	$42.90

When the county was new, almost at its very beginning, at the December session of 1823, an indictment was brought against a justice of the peace, the charge being that he entered (June 11, 1821) a judgment and when it was paid kept the money; that on July 9, 1821, he gave another judgment, and when it was paid him he withheld part of it three months and later paid the balance, and that he refused to pay the prosecutor's attorney. The indictment is marked "A true bill as to the first two charges in the indictment and an ignoramus as to the third." The commission of the justice was revoked by Governor Shulze, May 27, 1824. The first special election was held on February 26, 1828, to fill the office of member of assembly, owing to the resignation of Jesse Miller. At the election William Power defeated Jacob Huggins.

The return of 1822 shows the tavern keepers (then the term used) by townships, but it must be remembered that these early townships were much more extensive than are those of the same names at this time, as will be noted in the history of the various townships in this book. The list for 1822 follows:

February Sessions, 1822.

Toboyne Township.—Henry Zimmerman.
Tyrone Township.—John Hubler.
Greenwood Township.—David Pfoutz, Anthony Brandt.
Rye.—John Woodburn.

April Sessions, 1822.

Tyrone Township.—John Long, John Hipple, Andrew Tressler, John Foose, Gilbert Moon, Jonathan Dunkelberger, Henry Lightner, Thomas Craighead, Samuel Shoemaker, James Kennedy.
Greenwood Township.—John Miller, Frederick Rinehart, Peter Musselman, Benjamin Leas, Peter Wolf, George Wilt, John Knight, Philip Brady.
Rye.—Peter Yoder, Frederick Smiley, David Gallatin, James Kirkpatrick, George Billow.
Saville.—John Strawbridge, William Roberts.
Juniata.—Joseph Jones, George Eckert.
Toboyne.—John Snell, David Koutz, John Baird.

September Sessions, 1822.

Tyrone.—Abraham Shively, David Heckendorn.
Saville.—Gotleib Sheaffer.
Juniata.—Alexander Watson, Abraham Rider, Dr. John Eckert, John Koch, Joseph Power, Francis Beetem.
Greenwood.—William Waugh, Henry Landis, John Stailey.
Rye.—Henry Layman, John Fritz, Peter Harrup.
Buffalo.—Joseph Sheaffer, Magdalena Baughman, William Montgomery, James Freeland.

While the number of licenses granted at the Quarter Sessions for the year 1821 totaled but thirty-four, yet by 1829 the number had almost doubled, sixty-four being granted to the following persons. However, it is hardly possible to believe that they were all for hotels, as in the earlier years merchants ofttimes sold "wet goods" as well as dry goods, but of course had to be licensed. The list:

January Sessions, 1829.

Saville.—William Roberts.
Buffalo.—Rachel Freeland, Thomas Wells, Michael Albright, Joshua Byers.

Juniata.—David Lupfer, James McNamee, Dr. Jonas Ickes, Conrad Roth.
Toboyne.—John Zimmerman.
Wheatfield.—Abraham Bruner.
Rye.—Leyman Jackson.

April Sessions, 1829.

Greenwood.—John Shuman, James McClelland, Philip Brady. David
Rickabaugh, William Hunter, George Keely, William McGowan, Eli Miller, John M. Schoch.

Toboyne.—Daniel Koutz, Thomas B. Jacobs, Daniel Sheaffer.

Tyrone.—David Heckendorn, John Adams, Abraham Sheibley, George
S. Hackett, Robert Welsh, John Kibler, Gilbert Moon.

Saville.—Mathias Myers.

Rye.—Robert Boner, Charles Bovard, George Billow, Daniel Gallatin.

Wheatfield.—John Cougler, Robert McCoy, John Fritz, David Miller,
James Baskins, John Strawbridge.

Liverpool Township.—John Stailey, Frederick Rinehart, Philip Etter,
Samuel Sipe, Richard Knight, Philip Moyer, James Stewart.

Buffalo.—Alexander Watson, John Miller, Joseph Sheaffer, Charles L.
Berghaus, William Montgomery, John Livingston.

Juniata.—John Comp, John Baskins, Margaret VanCamp, John Sipe,
David Deardorf, Jonathan English. John Rice, Henry Ewalt, Robert
Cochran.

The first census enumerator having in charge the taking of the
census of Perry County was John Wilson.

In 1824 the clerk of the courts returned the following list of
retailers to the state as doing business in the new county: Anthony
Black, Samuel Abernathy, Henry Fetter, William McClure, Abra-
ham Fulweiler, Robert H. McClelland, William Roberts, James
Black, Ephraim Bosserman, George Tharp, John Rice, William
Irvine, Nathan VanFossen, Richard Stewart (liquors only), Jacob
Hollenbaugh, Edward Purcell, Isaiah Clark, Robert B. Cochran
& Co., Mealy & Beaver, Henry Walters, John K. Boyer, and
Thomas Gallagher.

In 1825 the following new ones appear: Robert Welch, Robert
Bous & Kepner, George Lebrich, Jonas Ickes, Frederick Baker
& Co., and John Everhart. In 1826 others entered business pursuits, as follows: Valentine Smith, Henry Brinton, John Bosserman, and George D. Lecky. The names of the last three are almost defaced by time and the writer has tried to decipher them.
During that year the county treasurer remitted $125 for twenty-
five state maps.

In 1827 there were twenty-four returns for selling merchandise
only, and sixteen for merchandise and liquors. New names appeared as follows: Daniel Gallatin, Cadwallader Jones, Jonathan
Lesh, Roger Claxton, Israel Downing. Ezra Squire, Dodd & Co.,
John Salmon, and Alexander Rogers.

For the first time, in November, 1828, the dealers' returns were made to the state, showing the townships in which the mrechants were located. Those marked with a * also sold liquors. The list:

Buffalo:
*William Parson.
*Roger Claxton.
*Patrick Downey.
Bouz & Kepner.
Catharine Urban.

Juniata:
*Alexander Rogers.
*Robert H. McClelland.
*Black & Beaver.
Black & Beaver.
John Everhart.
John Hipple.
Jonas Ickes (apothecary).
John Rice.

Rye:
Daniel Gallatin.
John Mateer.

Liverpool:
*George Tharp.
*Henry Walters.
*John Salmon.

Saville:
William Roberts.
Valentine Smith.

Toboyne:
. Anthony Black.
George D. Leckey.
Ewing & Morrison.
James Davidson.

Tyrone:
*Abraham Fulweiler.
*Henry Fetter.
*William McClure.
Cadwallader Jones.

Wheatfield:
*William Clark.
*William Irwin.
*Richard Stewart.

Greenwood:
*Samuel Mealy.
*Robert B. Cochran.
*Isaiah Clark.
*Edward Purcell.

It will be noted that Black & Beaver had two places, one of which sold dry goods and the other wet goods.

In 1829 the following new entries were reported: Toboyne, Benjamin Fosselman & Co., James Ewing;* Tyrone, Carothers & Stroop,* Bernard Sheibley; Greenwood, Samuel and Jacob Beaver; Juniata, Fulweiler & Bosserman,* John W. Bosserman.

The State Legislature of 1833-34 passed an act placing a tax upon retailers of foreign merchandise. In conformity with that law R. H. McClelland, then county treasurer, published a list of the dealers within the county, as required by the sixth section of the act. Under the classification, "Retailers of wines and spirits," appears no names. Under "Retailers of merchandise other than wines and liquors," appears the names of Samuel Abernathy, Nathan VanFossen, and William Roberts. Under "Retailers of merchandise, including wines and liquors," are Anthony Black, Henry Fetter, Abraham Fulweiler, Robert H. McClelland, James Black, Ephraim Bosserman, Edward Purcell, Isaiah Clark, Samuel Mealy & Beaver, Henry Walters, and George Tharp. Under this latter list are the following names, marked "refused to take out license": William McClure, John Rice, William Irwin, Jacob Hollenbaugh, Robert Cochran & Co., and Frederick Baker.

By 1837 the retail merchants of the county had increased considerably and we find the following names on the return made to the state:

Tyrone:
  Henry Fetter.
  A. & S. Black.
  Pleis, Frering & Thudium.
  Michael Kepner.
  C. Jones.
  Wm. Dalton.
  Jos. Welch.

Toboyne:
  Ewing & Morrison.
  David Moreland.
  Adams & Row.
  James Ewing.

Madison:
  John Reed.
  Fetter & Dunbar.
  R. & J. Hackett.

Saville:
  John Rice.
  James Milligan.
  John English.

Juniata :•
  Wm. Bosserman.
  Murphy & Orwan.
  Smith & Everhart.
  Abraham B. Demaree.
  Samuel Leiby.
  Gantt & Etter.
  John T. Robison.
  R. B. Jordon.
  John English.

Carroll:
  Egolf & Mickey.
  John Wallace.

Wheatfield:
  Jacob Keiser.
  Richard Stewart.
  Lindley & Fisher.
  William L. Fisher.

Centre:
  Charles Portley.

Buffalo:
  Mitchell & Steever.
  George W. Urban.
  William Jackson.
  William A. Dickenson.

Greenwood:
  I. & T. Beaver.
  Jacob Emerick.
  Isaiah Clark.
  D. & I. Strawbridge.
  Henry Thatcher.

Bloomfield Boro:
  Alexander Magee.
  John Rice.
  Thomas Black.
  William Lackey.

Liverpool Boro:
  Samuel Mealy.
  Walters & Jackman.
  William Walters.
  John Reifsnyder & Co.

Toboyne then included Blain; Tyrone included Landisburg; Juniata included Newport; Wheatfield included Duncannon; Greenwood included Millerstown, and Buffalo included New Buffalo. Various townships were still unformed and were a part of the older townships.

The early stores did some queer advertising. On July 19, 1820, the following appeared: "Dry, Goods, *including* Straw Bonnets, Hardware, Glass and Queensware, Brandy, Spirits and Wine." The prices for tailoring in 1825 were: Making fashionable coat, $3.50; next quality, $3.00; homemade cloth, $1.50; fashionable pants, $1.00.

The first appointee from Perry County to carry the returns of a presidential election to the office of the Secretary of the Commonwealth was John M. McKeehan, in 1824.

At the quarter session of April, 1828, an indictment was brought against one Joseph Jones for keeping a "tipling house." In November, 1829, and August, 1834, similar indictments were before the courts.

Early tavern keepers were at times inclined to "drift into verse" in their advertising. An advertisement in the fifth number of the *Perry Forester,* dated August 9, 1820, contains the following:

Come, gentlemen, try my good whiskey;
Come drink "a glass," 'twill make you "frisky";
Come, weary traveler, try my brandy;
'Tis very good—'twill make you handy.

Come breakfast, dine and sup with me,
    At my own table;
Put up your nags—for a small fee,
    Just in the stable.
Come lodge with me—I've beds aplenty,
    (And not a flea;)
Come try my fare, 'tis all good ware,
    Just as you'll see.
Need I say more, you to invite?
    No, I think not
"Put up" with me, if but one night;
    And then you'll see
    What I have got.

Under date of April 14, 1832, signed by John Junkin and A. Branyan, county commissioners, a statement of the valuations of personal property is made to the state, as follows:

Township.	Taxable Property.	Personal Property.
Juniata,	200,400	8,008
Liverpool,	125,120	7,780
Wheatfield,	165,900	9,730
Rye,	142,706	7,620
Saville,	167,700	4,700
Centre,	17,175	2,790
Greenwood,	144,813	8,890
Buffalo,	181,820	6,090
Tyrone,	375,360	12,760
Tohoyne,	311,690	29,030

The first traveling show to visit Perry County exhibited in Landisburg, September 7, 1826. The original show of the noted Dan Rice exhibited in New Bloomfield on October 4, 1855.

Those early settlers realized that the fruits of the earth constitute the reward of labor, and the plow, the harrow, the scythe and the grain cradle were plied in season, so that the valleys and pasture lands were soon stocked with cattle and the cribs and bins filled with grain. The surplus produce of the county in those days consisted of wheat, rye, oats, flour, whiskey, peach and apple brandy, livestock and salted provisions. Fishing during the spring and fall seasons with nets and fish baskets where channels were walled up added to the supply of food. Wild pigeons were plentiful. Lands were still being cleared of brush and trees and the burning of clearings was made a gala affair, as were the early husking bees and barn dances. Grain cradlers received 75 cents per day and reapers and mowers (scythe) half of that amount. In other instances the wage was $1.00 per day for cradlers and very rarely, $2.00. Farm hands received $5.00 to $7.00 per month, including their board. Until 1846 there were no sewing machines, and until 1847 postage stamps were not used.

When the panic of 1837 struck the country its effect was felt in Perry County as elsewhere, and the new county, then less than two decades in existence, was forced to issue paper currency for a time, rare specimens still being in existence. The text of the money was as follows: "This will entitle the Bearer to receive from the County of Perry the sum of Twenty-five Cents, payable on demand in current Bank Notes at the Treasurer's Office in Bloomfield. Per Resolution of the Board of County Commissioners, passed July 1, 1837."

Singing schools were conducted in the various communities and many men and women of mature years recollect well this ancient institution where they got their first (and ofttimes only) musical education. A notice of what was probably one of the first of these schools appeared in the *Perry Forester*—Perry County's first paper —on November 15, 1827. It follows:

Singing School.

The lovers of Sacred Harmony, of Landisburg and vicinity, are informed that a meeting will be held at Mr. J. B. Cooper's schoolroom, on Monday evening next, with a view of making up a singing school, where all persons desirous of encouraging the same, are invited to attend.

(Signed) MANY.

In 1821 the Landisburg Harmonic Singing Society already existed, R. H. McClelland being the secretary. On November 23, 1826, the Handelian Society was organized at Union schoolhouse, four miles east of Landisburg. In 1852 the New Bloomfield Singing School held a public concert in the courthouse.

The preparation and burial of the dead a century ago was also done in the most primitive way. Outside of the large cities the undertaker was still unknown. All cabinetmakers made coffins, which were unlined. A handfull of the most delicate shavings. covered with a piece of muslin tacked over them, sufficed for a pillow. Bodies were invariably dressed in shrouds, usually of cambric muslin. The bottom of the coffin was also covered with muslin, upon which the body was placed and covered with a part of the same piece of muslin, which was known as the "winding sheet." The casket was painted with a crude stain. Ice was as yet unknown as a preserver and embalming undreamed of, so that funerals followed deaths inside of twenty-four hours. Without telegraph and telephone lines and with mails far apart it was necessary to convey the news of deaths to relatives by special messengers. As an example an actual occurrence is quoted. When Henry Thatcher lived at New Buffalo and Charlotte Catharines Albert, Mrs. Thatcher's mother, died at her home near Landisburg, on February 4, 1846, her nephew, John Smith, carried the sad news overland on horseback.

The following incident is also illustrated of the customs of the early part of the last century: Upon the death of Abraham Smith, who was buried in the cemetery at Loysville, the body was conveyed to the grave in a large four-horse wagon, the friends riding in the same conveyance, as hearses were not then in use in the country districts, and even spring wagons were unknown. The late D. H. Smith, of "Little Germany," and later of Duncannon, was a descendant of this family.

Before the county's establishment, in 1780, when Francis West died at his home near the Gibson mill, the interment was made at Carlisle, and the body was borne across the Kittatinny or Blue Mountain in a wagon, the friends following in wagons, on horseback and afoot, over rough roads for a distance of fifteen miles. Having been a prominent man the cortege was attended by prominent men from the north side of the mountain. A delegation of prominent Carlisle men met the procession outside of that town and claimed the honor of replacing them, which was resented and a free-for-all fight followed, after whch they jointly accompanied the remains to the place of interment and spent the balance of the day in a custom then too much in vogue, but happily no longer tolerated.

In those days boys were bound out to learn trades, at a very small compensation, and often for only their clothes and boarding. The time to be served was usually three or four years and sometimes, when the years stretched out ahead, the time seemed so far off that the apprentice ran away. In cases like that he usually secured his first publicity, as one of the advertisements from the old *Perry Forester* will show. In this case the advertiser seems disgusted, offering only six cents and "no thanks" for the return of the apprentice:

Six Cents Reward.

RUNAWAY from the subscriber, living in Toboyne Township, Perry County, on Saturday, the 21st of February, inst., Augustus Waggoner, an apprentice to the shoemaking trade—about fifteen years of age—had on when he went away, Linsey pantaloons and roundabout jacket, an old black coat, old shoes and stockings, an old hat and good linen shirt. Whoever takes up said apprentice so that I get him again, shall have the above reward, but no charges will be paid nor thanks given for their trouble.

ANDREW BEISHLEIN.

February 26, 1824.

According to an advertisement in the *Perry Forester* of April 12, 1830, placed there at the instance of Samuel Linn, executor of

Abram Fulwiler, milady of that period wore as dainty lingerie as her sister of the present day, as the materials offered for sale comprised a very extensive assortment and one that would have done credit to many stores of a much later day. The word "consorts" was then much used instead of wives, carriages were called Dearborns just as the most common motor cars are called Fords, and farms were plantations in many cases, until about 1823. The stores, in their advertisements, invariably used "a good assortment of liquors" as part of their stock in trade. An advertisement of Mary Scott, of Carlisle, in the *Forester,* stated that she "will purchase flaxseed, flour and whiskey," all of which were extensively produced north of the Kittatinny Mountain. Patent medicines were already on the market in 1825, one advertiser offering a wonderful "panacea." The newspaper files show many columns of advertisements praising their merits. The picnic of our day was the "celebration" of those days, even being so termed as late as 1855.

The census of 1840 showed that Perry County, then in its twentieth year, had eight furnaces which produced 2,951 tons of cast iron, and two forges and rolling mills which produced 1,300 tons of bar iron. These furnaces and forges consumed 16,152 tons of fuel and, including mining operations, employed 339 men. The capital invested in them totaled $303,150. There were then twenty-three tanneries which tanned 9,720 sides of sole leather and 4,814 sides of upper leather. They employed fifty-eight men and the capital invested amounted to $56,550. There were thirty-one other leather manufacturers, such as saddlers, whose product was valued at $14,715. Thirteen distilleries distilled 31,475 gallons, the capital invested being $8,590. Four potteries turned out $2,100 worth of manufactured product. There were then fifty-seven stores, with a capital of $169,200, five lumber yards with a capital of $1,600 and employing fifty-seven men and sixty men engaged in transportation. Fisheries were operated which produced a product worth $14,335, and twenty-two barrels of tar was manufactured which sold for $1,893, employing five men. Bricks and lime were manufactured to the value of $7,269. There were seven fulling mills and five woollen manufactories which manufactured goods worth $4,370, their capital being $8,700. Two printing offices and two weekly papers supplied the populace with literature. Their capital was $2,000. There was one "rope walk," the value of whose product was $3,000, the capital invested being $2,200. The value of carriage plants was $685, and of their product was $2,000. Twenty-four flour mills manufactured 11,200 barrels of flour, and twenty-six gristmills ground grain. There were 120 sawmills of the "up-and-down" type. The furniture manufactured was valued at $3,679, and the capital invested $1,760. The value of other

33

manufactured goods was $14,910, and the capital invested $5,905. The total capital invested in manufacturing was $264,024. Eight houses of brick and stone and seventy-seven of lumber were erected. The cost of constructing or building was $38,842.

According to a record of 1840 the lands of Perry County were classified at that time as follows:

Limestone land, cleared, ...	13,410	acres
Limestone land, uncleared, ...	6,050	"
Slate land, cleared, ...	46,660	"
Slate land, uncleared, ...	58,120	"
Gravel land, cleared, ...	53,100	"
Gravel land, uncleared, ...	21,610	"
Sand land, uncleared, ...	5,040	"
Mountain or rock, ...	68,240	"
Known to contain iron ore, ...	40	"
Cleared land of all kinds, ...	139,000	"
Uncleared land fit for cultivation, ...	54,000	"
Unfit for cultivation, ...	74,100	"

The average value of cleared land at that time is stated as $25 per acre, and of woodland, $5 per acre. The whole value of the cleared land was estimated as $1,527,000, and of all the uncleared land, $787,000.

The census of 1840 contained the following in reference to the young county:

Number of horses and mules, ...	4,383	
Number of cattle, ...	15,043	
Number of swine, ...	21,485	
Value of poultry, ...	$6,403	
Wheat raised, ...	200,638	bushels
Barley raised, ...	411	"
Oats raised, ...	192,258	"
Rye raised, ...	143,519	"
Buckwheat raised, ...	37,052	"
Indian corn raised, ...	150,095	"

In an old "State Book of Pennsylvania," printed in 1846, devoted to the geography, history, government, resources, etc., of the state, is a map of the state in which Perry County is included in a belt known as the "Iron Mountain Counties," which runs from the Maryland line north to include Lycoming and Northumberland Counties. The Cumberland and Lebanon Valleys—really one valley—is known as the Kittatinny Valley on the same map. The area of Perry County is given as 540 square miles, and the population as 17,096. The property value is quoted as $2,895,758, and the population of the county seat as 412. The minerals are enumerated as iron ore "in great quantities" and limestone. It then had fifteen townships and six boroughs. It says "the boroughs are Bloomfield, Liverpool, Newport, Petersburg (now Duncannon),

Landisburg, and New Germantown, and the villages are Ickesburg, Duncannon, Millerstown, and Buffalo." The public improvements are noted as the Susquehanna Canal, from the mouth of the Juniata at Duncan's Island, up the eastern line of the county, and the Juniata Canal, from the same point, up the Juniata; the northern turnpike from Duncan's Island along the Juniata and several large bridges. Educationally the county was credited with one academy, one hundred common and some private schools and about thirty churches. Politically at that time Perry had one member of assembly and was joined with Cumberland in the election of a senator and with Cumberland and Franklin in the election of a congressman. The townships at that time were Buffalo, Carroll, Centre, Jackson, Greenwood, Juniata, Liverpool, Madison, Oliver, Penn, Rye, Saville, Toboyne, Tyrone, and Wheatfield. Liverpool was then the largest town in the county, with 454 inhabitants. Newport, Millerstown, and Bloomfield all followed closely, with over 400 each.

One of the county's early contractors was Peter Bernheisel, a son of John B. and Catharine (Loy) Bernheisel, born August 18, 1806, in Sherman's Valley. Recognizing a larger field for his industry, he located at Harrisburg, where he was a contractor from 1832 to 1859. Among his contracts in Dauphin County was the erection of the county jail and the Market Square Presbyterian Church, built in 1841, and burned March 31, 1858.

A surveyor who did work over the county during the middle of the last century was James H. Devor, who came to the county from Shippensburg in 1845. He was known as "the blacksmith lawyer" and practiced that profession also for almost twenty years.

Most salaries were not princely in those days, even for office of great import. In 1833 the annual salaries of a number of governors of states was as follows: Rhode Island, $400; Vermont, $750; New Hampshire, Indiana, and Illinois, $1,000.

During the earlier years of the county's existence a popular method of worship was in the groves and woods; and the camp meetings of that period were largely attended by those who went there to worship instead of as a pleasure trip, which is so largely the case in this modern day. Among these old camp meeting grounds, the Bruner grove, in Centre Township, was used as early as 1830, and sometimes in recent years also, but for the first fifty years camp meeting was almost an annual event. Both the Methodist and United Brethren denominations have occupied it. In 1834 Rev. S. T. Harding had the meetings in charge. Rev. S. W. Seibert, an Evangelical minister, and the father of the late President Judge William N. Seibert, held many camp meetings, one of which was at the Ricedorf place in Juniata Township, in 1849. He also had charge of the camp meetings in Buffalo Township.

A typical camp meeting was long held by the United Brethren and other denominations in Wm. Stouffer's woods, near Shermansdale. The tents (mostly rude wooden structures) were erected in an oblong block. In the middle of one end was the speakers' stand, with a sounding board. Board seats, nailed to logs, occupied the enclosed space, save the aisles. Here were held, as at various other places, great harvest home camp meetings, with their renewals of faith and repledging of vows. The impression made by these old camp meetings, canopied by huge forest trees, while the glaring light gave a colorful effect, with their songs of Zion, are vivid in the minds of many living to-day. As a general thing these camp meetings have passed away, but an occasional one is still held, but not like those of old.

Those of the present generation remember the frequent articles of the late John Rice, of Little Germany, a settlement in Spring Township, relating to Andrew J. Smolnicker and the Peace Union. Smolnicker was an eccentric character who came to the county and purchased a tract of land at sheriff's sale for the erection of a new church. The land had belonged to a man by the name of Eldridge, who resided in Baltimore, and was located near the top of Tuscarora Mountain, in Tuscarora Township. Here in 1853-54 Smolnicker erected a church, 20x40 feet in size. It was also used as a residence by him. He published a book about that time, which contained the dogma which he preached. It was proposed to build steps up the mountain, but it never was done. Smolnicker was nominated by the National Peace Union Convention, at Baltimore, for the Presidency of the United States.

John Hartman, an early settler, built a tavern on top of Tuscarora Mountain, at the gap over the mountain and at the county line between Perry and Juniata Counties. As the modern prize fight is to the generations of this period so were the bare fist fights of early days, and it was here that the "bullies" of Perry and Juniata used to show their prowess. Almost a century later two descendants, unknown to each other, met there in the wilds and the following conversation took place: "Good morning, sir!" reply, "Good morning!" "What are you looking for?" "Hunting for the ruins of the old Hartman tavern!" "I am too, but here is all that is left of it!" "Who are you?" "Wesley Fuller!" "Who are you?" "John M. Hartman!"

During the early period of the county's history the law of the state required the enrollment of all able-bodied men between the ages of eighteen and forty-five, who were assigned to companies, battalions, etc., the officers being elected at a special election held for that purpose. There were two training days during May and June. The first was known as muster day and a penalty of one dollar was imposed for failure to report. As all did not have guns, canes helped to augment the supply of "arms." The second day was parade day and the battalions were reviewed, being commanded by mounted regimental officers in uniform. The parade grounds were usually near a road house or tavern. The ladies, accounts tell us, attended the festivities, which were not unlike the modern carnival. This system became unpopular and with the advent of the Mexican War it began to decline. Landisburg was the headquarters of the Landisburg Guards, the Landisburg Artillery, and the Perry Rangers. The location of one of these old mustering grounds was at the "Rope Ferry," below Millerstown, the near-by hotel being kept by the captain, George Kelly. About 1830 it was changed to Millerstown. Liquor was then more or less in general use. Two old orders echo down to posterity from this old "Rope Ferry" mustering ground: "Move up into solemn column!" and "'Rest any one coming back from dinner 'toxicated." Among the officers of the State Militia was Andrew Loy, who resided on the Fort Robinson farm, having been appointed by Governor Wolfe, in 1835; Robert Fulton Thompson, of Watts Township, who was a colonel prior to the Mexican War; George Shuman, of near Millerstown, a captain, of whom Priscilla, his daughter (wife of Dr. Mahlon J. Davis), said, "I thought my father was a second George Washington, when he was captain of the militia, and had stripes on his trousers and a red plume on his hat"; William Kough, father of Amos W., John, and William Kough, now or late of Newport; Lieut. Colonel John Tressler, of Loysville, commissioned by Governor Wolf; Capt. Zephaniah Willhide, of the Montgomery Cadets, commissioned April 26, 1851, by Governor Johnson and renewed by Governor Bigler; Colonel Robert McCoy, of Duncannon, whose daughter, Mrs. Adaline Brown, still lives and tells of the big review when the militia paraded in all their gay trappings in the fields where Baskinsville is now located, and John Kibler, colonel of the Thirty-Ninth Regiment.

During this militia period Perry County citizens sometimes became attached to important titles. In 1843, on the list is Brigadier General Henry Fetter. During that year Camp Perry was the scene of the military festivities, being located on the George Barnett farm at a point three hundred yards east of Bloomfield. Not only did all the local units encamp there, but the United States mounted artillery from Carlisle Barracks were their guests. The units at Camp Perry were:

> Landisburg Artillery, Capt. Fenstermacher.
> Landisburg Guards, Captain Wilson.
> Newport Guards, Captain Cochran.
> Bloomfield Light Infantry, Capt. Casey.
> Juniata Hornets, Capt. Moyer.
> Perry Hornet Riflemen, Capt. Diven.
> Green Mountain Riflemen, Capt. Hall.

Several of these companies had been but recently organized, yet all were well uniformed according to the county press. The Green Mountain Riflemen from Ickesburg was a crack company during the period from 1830 to 1840. Daniel W. Flickinger was once its captain, but was promoted to major. In 1840 he moved to Juniata County. His son, Rev. Robert E. Flickinger, is an able Presbyterian minister located at Rockwell City, Iowa, as well as the author of four or five noted historical volumes. Three brothers of Major Flickinger were also members of the Green Mountain Riflemen. At an earlier period Brigadier General David Mitchell was in charge of the militia of Perry and Franklin Counties.

That rumblings of the coming storm of secession were apparent is shown by the numerous cases in which the matter of disunion was spoken of. In the drinking of toasts at the military meetings, then so common, or at public celebrations, the matter of the Union was ever to the fore. When the Union troops of the county met at the house of John Patterson, at Juniata Falls (now the Steckley place, in Howe Township), on January 8, 1834, Dr. W.B. Mealey, a prominent physician, proposed the toast, "The union of the States —may it be perpetual and enduring to the end of time; it must and shall be preserved." This is merely cited here as an example of those at all other celebrations, as various public meetings were then termed. In fact disunion had shown itself in 1828 and again in 1832, when President Andrew Jackson quickly crushed it.

Public sales were long known as public "vendues," which title often appeared in sale bills as late as 1880. It appears that public "vendues" were sometimes held for the renting or leasing of lands, according to data taken from an advertisement dated October 22, 1819. On Monday, November 29, at the home of Major Leyman, at Clark's Ferry (now Clark's Run, Duncannon), Robert Clark held a public vendue to rent the following:

1. Elegant merchant mill and farm adjoining Petersburg, with a good dwelling house and barn.
2. Complete sawmill at the mouth of Little Juniata Creek, near the other mill, with a lot of ground of about two acres.
3. The Petersburg farm, containing 216 acres, with good dwelling house and barn, and about one-half of the farm clear land under good fence.
4. Farm and ferry at the mouth of Sherman's Creek, with good dwelling house, barn and orchard.
5. Farm adjoining Clark's Ferry, Major Jones and others, containing 120 acres, half clear land, house, barn, etc.
6. Noted tavern stand, opposite mouth of Juniata, Dauphin County, with large dwelling house, still house and fifty acres of land.

In the earlier days, when hunting and fishing helped provide a part of the livelihood of many families, most men were good marksmen, and shooting matches were of frequent occurrence and largely attended. There was a great rivalry between the sections on opposite sides of the Kittatinny Mountain, and with the forming of the new county, the rivalry became more marked, but the Perry County lads were usually the winners, according to newspaper records.

Before the advent of railroads and long afterwards cattle for markets elsewhere were driven overland in large droves and many, even in middle life, well remember of it. Among Perry Countians long engaged in that business was George Johnston, of Toboyne Township, who bought his stock in western Pennsylvania and eastern Ohio and drove the herds eastward over the Allegheny Mountains. Mr. Johnston met Margaret Russell, of Miami County, Ohio, and they were wed in May, 1835, making the journey eastward via Cincinnati. From there they took a boat up the Ohio River to Pittsburgh, and from that point came via the Pennsylvania Canal and inclined planes over the Allegheny Mountains to their home here. Contrast the methods of travel and transportation then and now. Oxen were used as beasts of burden by the earlier residents, and, while the writer is no patriarch by any means, he still remembers seeing at least one ox team on the streets of each of the two principal business town of the county. The many four and six-horse teams from western Perry, as they brought their heavy loads of bark, potatoes, wheat, corn and other produce to the shipping point at Newport are remembered by those of middle life.

Early Trade With Baltimore.

Before the Pennsylvania Canal and the Pennsylvania Railroad were built, and even after the construction of the canal, much of the marketing of Perry County products was done at Baltimore, Maryland, the goods being conveyed in old English wagons which got their motive power from four- and six-horse teams. [1] At least one of these wagons is yet in use in the county, the writer having passed it near Centre Presbyterian Church on the way to Loysville with a load of grain, in July, 1919, while engaged in seeking material for the publication of this book. It is now in the possession of Mr. Walter Moose, who got it from an uncle, John Moose, it originally having been the property of his grandfather, Samuel Moose. The tires were originally of one-inch iron, but now it is

---

1. While passing this historic wagon the writer accompanied Mr. John Waggoner, postmaster at Centre, in his automobile, he being a descendant of the famous family of millers of that name. At the time, we were in sight of the home where Col. A. K. McClure spent his boyhood days, the site of old Fort Robinson and of Centre Presbyterian Church. Within a mile either way were the old Bixler flour and fulling mills and the Waggoner gristmill, whose history goes back over a hundred years, and the birthplace of the late Prof. Junius R. Flickinger, principal of the Lock Haven State Normal School.

tired with one-half inch iron, which reduces the height of the rear wheels from six feet to seventy-one inches. The tires are four inches wide, and at the present price of iron would cost about fifty dollars for the four wheels.

The wagons on the downward trip were laden with the products of the county flour mills, tanneries, distilleries, and farm, including pork, beef, clover-seed, grain, etc. On the homeward trip the load was principally fish, merchandise, etc. It took about two weeks to make the round-trip in these (English-bed) wagons, which were the prototype of the "prairie schooner," which later played so great a part in the colonization of the western frontiers of the United States. They were covered with canvass and the feed boxes and blankets were attached to the rear by chains when not in use. The sleeping was often done in fair weather beneath the wagons, and when inclement often on cots or benches in bar rooms.

These wagons were equipped with chains to keep the wagon bed from spreading, and on one of the last trips to Baltimore before the advent of the railroad Daniel Minich's team lost this chain. He missed it shortly afterwards near the Waggoner mill, in Madison Township, and went back a distance to search for it, being assisted by W. H. Waggoner, then a boy, but late the proprietor of this mill, but the search was unsuccessful. About 1913, when the state took over the highway passing the mill and its improvement was under progress Mr. Waggoner had charge of the men and the chain was dug up in the vicinity of where the original search was made, a mute reminder of that early method of transportation. It was over a foot under ground and had lain there for over a half century.

Of the pioneers engaged in this business were Samuel Moose, mentioned above; Daniel Gutshall, father of Mrs. Wilson Morrison, New Germantown; Henry Hench, of near Ickesburg; Jonathan Swartz, Ickesburg; Thomas Adams, Toboyne; Harry C. Boden, Duncannon, and David Stambaugh, of Elliottsburg. There were many others, but of them the records are vague. Henry Hench made teaming between the two points a regular business, and on account of his proficiency with large teams was known as "Whip-cracker Harry." The commerce in part consisted of distilled liquors in barrels, and the strength of David Stambaugh is a matter of record, he being able to load a barrel of whiskey unaided, a herculean task. In an old ledger which belonged to Harry C. Boden, who also carried on a regular traffic between the two points, the accounts bear date of 1799 and 1800. Many of its pages are pasted together, it having been utilized for a scrapbook. Among the articles brought back by him as entered in the ledger are sugar in barrels, coffee in bags, salt purchased by the bushel, shot in bags, pepper and tea in kegs, etc.

Others engaged in trafficking to Baltimore were James McNeal, who came from Virginia and settled in what is now Jackson Township, in 1795, he being the maternal grandfather of William S. Endslow; Robert Mitchell, who was a member of the first board of county commissioners; Abraham Bower, grandfather of Abraham Bower, of Falling Springs, a farmer who also operated a still; Major John Zimmerman, who was robbed of a bale of goods worth $50 on September 2, 1826, at Reistertown, where he had put up for the night; Henry Rice, born April 1, 1812, and the father of Henry Rice, later county treasurer; William Woods;, Samuel Endslow, and Wayne Woods, of Blain.

When the canal and railroad, with its old single-track system, came through the county, this traffic from western Perry was diverted to Newport, and Thomas Adams then kept two six-horse teams busy, and many of the older residents yet remember them, as there was a bell attached to the hames of each horses' harness, and the tinkling of these bells could be heard long before the teams came into view.

When these early wagoners sold goods of great value at Baltimore they run many chances of being robbed between there and their homes by crooks who kept track of them. When Philip Boyer left Baltimore, having closed a business deal, he was shadowed by one of these crooks, and on December 18, 1823, when he arrived at Peters' Mountain (opposite Duncannon), he was attacked and, after pulling him from his horse, his portmanteau was seized, he was stripped of his great coat, his undercoat, his pantaloons, his cravat, and with a dirk knife his belt was cut and his money taken. It consisted of twelve fifty-dollar bills on the Bank of Baltimore, ten fifty-dollar bills on the Mechanics' Bank of Baltimore, eight fifty-dollar bills on the Union Bank of Baltimore, and $80 in five- and ten-dollar bills.

David Gutshall, born in 1835, residing at Blain, was along with his father, Daniel Gutshall, when a lad. He tells of the wagoners carrying their folding cots along in the wagons and of placing them in bar rooms and hallways to sleep. Daniel Gutshall was a farmer, yet in a single year he managed to make thirteen trips to and from Baltimore for the A. R. Foss tannery, hauling leather on the downward trip and bringing back raw hides. Among the things recollected by the present Mr. Gutshall was that whiskey was in general use and sold for three cents a glass. York Springs tavern or inn was one of the stopping places for farmers on their way to and from Baltimore. It was not far from the present town of York Springs, in Adams County.

From that section of Perry County lying east of the Juniata the traffic was principally to Pottsville, Lancaster, and Philadelphia, which were nearer than Baltimore. The wagons used were of the same type and the traffic of the same nature. Newton Williamson, a resident of Liverpool, now in his eighty-first year (1920), distinctly recollects when this traffic was in existence, he being then a young lad.

THE POLITICAL TREND.

The germ of party differences began almost with the birth of the nation. 'Twas during the term of the immortal Washington that Thomas Jefferson and Alexander Hamilton, representing different ideas relative to government and having antagonistic conceptions of power and its use, began thinking along party lines. During the first half-century of the county's existence political matters occupied a very conspicuous part of the young nation's affairs and in no other section did the political tides ebb and flow with greater violence than in Perry. The surge of the tide bore to the shores the wreckage of the Anti-Masonic party, the Whig party and the American party, all great political factors in this great commonwealth and in the nation, and it is from their wreckage that originated and developed the great Republican party, the party of Lincoln, Grant, Garfield, Blaine, Roosevelt, and Harding, which was to succeed the historic Democratic party in continuous rule of the nation for a quarter of a century.

The *Perry Forester,* Perry County's first newspaper, of November 15, 1827, contains an account of an early political meeting held in the courthouse on November 7th. The officers elected were: President, Judge Madden; vice-presidents, George Barnett, Dr. Joseph Foster. C. B. Power, Esq., John Chisholm, and George Monroe, Esq., were named a committee "to draft an address to the citizens of the county." A committee on correspondence consisted of Peter Ritner, Esq., Samuel Linn, Esq., and George Monroe, Esq. Peter Ritner was a brother of Governor Ritner and owned the farm at Mt. Patrick long known as the Blattenberger farm. He was chosen a delegate to the convention to be held in Harrisburg the succeeding January. The secretaries were G. Monroe and Jacob Gantt. The meeting passed resolutions favorable to John Quincy Adams and Henry Clay. The above from a report of the secretaries.

In the same issue is an account of the Jackson meeting held the night previous, from the pen of the *Forester's* editor. It follows:

"The Jackson meeting at Bloomfield, on Tuesday evening, the 6th instant, notwithstanding the inclemency of the weather, was most numerous and respectable. The court room was filled to overflowing. Nothing can exceed the zeal with which any measures connected with the elevation of the Hero of Orleans is hailed among nine-tenths of the people of the county, of which this meeting gave ample testimony. We are confident the administration men cannot poll 200 votes out of 2,000 in the county."

A petition dated June 1, 1824, to Gabriel Heister, Esq., Surveyor General of Pennsylvania, asked the appointment of George Mitchell, as deputy surveyor, in these glowing words: "We take it for granted that it will be a leading consideration with you in making your appointments to select the most confidential, capable and deserving men." The statement then follows "that he is well versed in geometry, trigonometry, an excellent and practical surveyor and an accurate and neat draughtman; that he would cheerfully submit his competency as a surveyor to a critical examination by those well versed in the business, and that as a politician he has ever been a firm, active and undeviating Democrat-Republican." Among the signatures are J. Miller, H. B. Mitchell, Alex. Magee, John Hipple, Frederick Rinehart, Jr., and Jacob Huggins, then member of assembly from Perry County. Another dated April 16, 1825, asks the appointment of Alexander Branyan to succeed John Ogle, deceased, as justice of the peace for a part of Rye Township, as "he is a fit person, who has always been a firm and undeviating Republican." It is signed by Thomas Barnett, Robert Branyan, William, David and Isaac Ogle, James and Cornelius Baskins, John McKenzie, Frederick Barnett, Jacob Keel, Jacob Weiser, and Richard Stewart.

In those early days with political issues ever to the fore, some strangely worded petitions appear. There is one on file in the Bureau of Records at Harrisburg, at the Capitol, asking an appointment as justice of the peace of Dr. James R. Scott. It is addressed to Governor Shulze. It describes the candidate as a man "who is eminently qualified to discharge the duties of said office; moreover, he is a member of that Great Democratic Family which constitutes the basis of our Republican Government." It is dated April 18, 1825. Another to Governor Shulze, asking the appointment of Alexander Rogers, of Rye Township, "lately district No. 12 in the county of Cumberland," as justice of the peace to succeed Joseph Ogle, who died. It says "he has ever been a firm, undeviating Democrat and an active politician." Of the attainments necessary to conduct the office it is mute. Rogers was commissioned August 11, 1824. A petition of the citizens of Liverpool and Buffalo Township asks the appointment of George Mitchell as a justice of the peace, describing him as "well qualified," but omits reference to politics.

So frequent is the remark made that as a nation we are degenerating, politically, that the following from McClure's Old-Time Notes of Pennsylvania, written by a Perry Countian who for virtually a half-century was in the very vortex of politics, is here reproduced as showing the opposite trend:

"It is a common and very erroneous belief that the political battles of the early days were much more dignified, and much more free from dishonest manipulation than the political contests of the present (1905). The student of our history who carefully studies the early political contests of Pennsylvania will find that a degree of political intolerance prevailed even among the more intelligent citizens that would not now be tolerated in any community. Party leadership, as a rule, was more blindly followed than it is to-day, as few even of the more enlightened people accepted any political literature but that which came from a county party organ, or from other partisan sources. Party revolts were as common then as now, and often precipitated the most desperate and defamatory contests, and the state political struggle of 1838 between Ritner and Porter has never been approached in any modern political struggle in reckless prostitution of the ballot or in malignant, wanton defamation. No political journal with any pretension to decency could print to-day against a candidate any of the many defamatory articles which swept over the state like a tempest in 1838. A larger measure of fraud has doubtless been perpetrated in modern elections, but as far as the limited opportunities of that day offered, the game of fraud was played to the limit. One township in Huntingdon County returned 1,060 majority for Ritner in a district where there were not two hundred citizens. The excuse given for the vote was that there was a breach in the canal and that some 800 laborers had been employed, when it would not have been possible to give employment to half that number. The new railroad in Adams County for which Stevens had obtained state aid, and that was commonly known in political circles as "the tapeworm," swelled the majority in Adams up in the thousands, and dual returns for members of the legislature in the county of Philadelphia led to the creation of two houses at Harrisburg and wrote the history of the Buchshot War to shame the annals of the state."

The adoption of the Constitution of 1838 made a marked change in Pennsylvania. Prior to that time the governor possessed almost unlimited power. He appointed all the judges of the entire commonwealth and they were commissioned for life or during good behavior. He also held the appointive power for deputy attorneys general—those who executed the duties of district attorneys before the creation of that office—the associate judges and the justices of the peace. At that time the term of office of the governor was not limited to a single term and this vast patronage was largely used to secure a reëlection or build up a political dynasty.

Although the Republican party of a later day was to a great extent the successor of the Whig party of the time of Henry Clay, the Whig party of that time embraced many of the most decided pro-slavery men, and the Democratic party of the period contained many men who became active and persistent Republicans.

In 1838 the names of fourteen candidates were voted for for sheriff of Perry County, at the general election on October 9th. Joseph Shuler, a Whig, was the successful candidate, receiving 824 votes. Prior to this only Democrats were elected to the more important offices.

Before the canals were purchased by the Pennsylvania Railroad, the office of canal commissioner was filled at the general elections. It was an office of importance and eagerly sought.

Unfortunately, as the years passed, no historian recorded the ebb and flow of the county's political tides, and only occasionally do we find a slight record of them or their relation to the larger affairs of the state and nation. Of the Clay-Polk campaign for the Presidency, in which the latter won, it was different. While history calls Polk the original "black horse," such is far from the truth. Virginia backed Polk and he was nominated as part of a new but unavowed policy pertaining to slavery. The motive lay in the fact that the South "saw the handwriting on the wall," and if slavery was to be continued as a permanent institution its territory must be extended. Accordingly the plan was to annex Texas, a republic where slavery thrived, with the right of division into four additional states, as well as the acquisition of additional territory from Mexico. Up to that time the Democratic party had a majority rule in their nominations. Van Buren had a majority of delegates to the convention but not two-thirds. The convention adopted the two-thirds rule by a vote of 148 to 118. As no President was ever elected without the support of the Commonwealth of Pennsylvania until the Cleveland campaign of 1884, the contest of 1844 largely hinged upon the election for governor of Pennsylvania, which was held in October, prior to the general election, just as the Maine elections of the present period largely show the drift of political thought. Of that campaign in Perry County, McClure's "Old-Time Notes of Pennsylvania" says:

"The leaders of both sides realized the vital importance of the contest in this state, and I well remember how earnestly and desperately it was contested. I was a boy not more than half-way through the teens but I was living in the political centre of the mountain forests of my native county, and cherished a devotion for Clay that has never been repeated in all the many political struggles I have seen. The supporters of Clay as a rule literally worshiped him. He was their idol, their political deity, and they believed him to be the noblest, the grandest, the ablest and the most chivalrous of men, while his opponents met him with a tempest of defamation, publicly charging him on the hustings and through every newspaper opposed to him as a gambler, a libertine, a horse racer, a Sabbathbreaker and a murderer. The Whigs responded by charging Polk with disgraceful littleness, studied hypocrisy and the offspring of a traitor."

The slow manner of communication, before the days of the telegraph and telephone, is well illustrated in an instance taken from the writing of Colonel McClure. Governor Moorehead, who presided at the convention which nominated Gen. Zachary Taylor for the Presidency, wrote to Mr. Taylor, advising him of the fact. We quote:

"At that time the prepayment of postage was not compulsory, and unpaid letters were charged from five to ten times the present rate of postage. President Morehead promptly mailed a letter to General Taylor at Baton Rouge, Louisiana, notifying him of the nomination, but several weeks elapsed without any response. The telegraph was then in its infancy and unthought of as an agent, except in the most urgent emergency, and Governor Morehead finally sent a trusted friend to visit General Taylor and inquire why his letter of acceptance had not been given. Every political crank, as well as many others in the country, had been writing letters to General Taylor on the subject of the Presidency, very few of whom prepaid their letter postage. Old Rough and Ready vexed beyond endurance, at the tax thus imposed upon him, gave peremptory orders to the postmaster to send to the dead letter office all unpaid letters addressed to him."

In the gubernatorial fight of 1848 between Johnston and Long-street, the latter was reported elected. The Democrats at New Bloomfield immediately held a public celebration, only to learn a few days later that their candidate was defeated. The Whigs then held a celebration in honor of Governor Johnston's election. When Johnston was a candidate the second time, in 1852, he visited New Bloomfield during the campaign. Among those taking part in that meeting was Mr. Ickes, a Revolutionary hero who was ninety years of age.

The gubernatorial campaign of 1851 was conducted along very strenuous lines, and Governor Johnston spoke at Liverpool, Petersburg (Duncannon) and Bloomfield, during September.

The Whig element almost all became Republicans when, in 1854, the Kansas-Nebraska bill made slavery extension the Democratic program. The North was stirred as never before, and Horace Greely declared that Douglas and Pierce had made more abolitionists in three months than Garrison and Phillips could have made in half a century. In earlier days the West had clung to the South politically, but the development of the railroads to the Atlantic seaboard in the preceding dozen years created a stronger physical bond between the West and the East than the Mississippi had done between the West and the South. This, and the fact that the East furnished the principal home market for Western products, and provided most of the supplies for which these were exchanged, was the economic reason for the agricultural West breaking away from the agricultural South and joining the manufacturing East. Pennsylvania, however, still gave its electoral vote to the Democrats in 1856. The vote in Perry County was Millard Fillmore, Whig, 1,407; James Buchanan, Democrat, 2,135; John C. Fremont, Republican, 521. When the campaign was on the county was wild with excitement. A monster Democratic meeting was staged at New Bloomfield, the county seat town then being but thirty-two years in existence. Thomas Adams, of Toboyne Township, a radical Democrat, who was engaged in wagon transportation from western Perry to Newport, turned out with a sixteen-horse team, decorated with bunting, bells and flags. Wilson Morrison, yet living at New Germantown, attended, he being then a young man. According to his statement when "the lower county delegation" arrived, it passed up Main Street, New Bloomfield, to the mill, turned north to High Street, east to Carlisle Street, and as the head of the parade came down Carlisle Street to the court-house, the rear of the parade was just passing. In the parade, among other features, was a team of six oxen, with an attendant opposite each ox bearing a pail. In the Polk-Dallas and Shunk-Henry Clay campaign one of the features of the Democratic parade was a hickory tree which had been dug from the woods and mounted on a wagon, according to a reliable tradition. David Gutshall, of Blain, distinctly remembers this campaign.

With the defeat of General Winfield Scott for the Presidency of the United States in 1852, the great Whig party virtually went to pieces. Shortly thereafter a mysterious political organization, based upon opposition to foreign immigration and known as the "Know Nothing" party, began to be heard of and spread with remarkable rapidity over the entire United States. It seemed especially hostile to Catholics and foreigners. It was, in point of fact, a secret organization and got its name through the fact that its adherents when questioned invariably said that they knew nothing. The local organizations began forming about 1854 and absorbed most of the old Whigs as well as many of the Democrats, especially those who were dissatisfied with the faction then in power. In 1855 this party had a ticket in the field and carried Perry County, the entire ticket being elected by a majority of about two hundred votes. The motto of the Know Nothings, "Put only Americans on guard," was a mighty good one, even though the party passed away, and might well be used by the present-day political parties. And by "Americans," the writer does not mean simply those born on American soil, but good, honorable men, without the taint of any hyphen, or any other ism save Americanism, in their systems.

On August 2, 1856, a public meeting was held at the county seat as a protest against "the wrongs perpetrated in Kansas." It was attended by three notables who delivered addresses. They were Governor Ford, of Ohio; Andrew G. Curtin, then Secretary of the Commonwealth of Pennsylvania, and Hannibal Hamlin, governor-elect of Maine—one a governor, one a governor-elect, and the third soon to be the great war governor of Pennsylvania. The parade features are designated as the Liverpool Sax Horn Band, the Patterson (now Mifflin) Band, a fourteen-horse team, and the Millerstown delegation carrying the flag of the 113th Regiment, Pennsylvania Volunteers, which was at the battles of Chippewa, Lundy's Lane, and other battles along the lakes in the Second War with Great Britain. It was carried by Dr. Mealy, a Millerstown physician, at the battle of Chippewa. The flag was perforated by a cannon ball and by other shots.

Three days later, Agust 5, 1856, a public meeting was held in the courthouse, the call being signed by 340 citizens of the county. It declared for "Free Kansas and no Popery." Jesse Beaver presided. The speakers were Joseph Casey, General Samuel C. Pomeroy, and a Mr. McAfee, of Kansas, and B. F. Junkin. The parade contained 700 determined men, many of them affiliated with the camps of the Junior Sons of America, then flourishing at Duncannon, Newport, and Bloomfield.

In connection with the birth of the Republican party an occurrence which happened at New Bloomfield is worthy of note. Samuel Wiggins, one of the first members of the new party and the first man in the county to declare himself unconditionally an abolitionist, determined to celebrate the birth of the new party on election night. Benjamin F. Junkin, late president judge, was at that time holding the onerous office of burgess of the borough, and appealed to him not to build a bonfire within the borough limits. Mr. Wiggins then placed barrels of shavings, boards, boxes and other inflammable material on his wagon and drove to the eastern borough line, on the Newport road, where he started the fire. The matter caused an excitement and drew a crowd. He kept marching around his bonfire and cheered for the new party, declaring that it was "a small fire, but one that would burn all over the Union." The Wiggins home, on the square at the county seat, was painted a dark steel gray, and was to some "the black Republican headquarters." There every evening during the War between the States the populace would gather to hear Mrs. Wiggins read the war news from the daily papers brought to town over the noted Rice Stage Lines. There they discussed the outcome of each campaign and the qualifications of the changing commanders, always uniting in the belief that the North would win.

The Democratic National Convention first met at Charleston on the 23d of April, 1860, and after wrangling for ten days adjourned to meet at Baltimore on the 18th of June. The bolters from the Charleston convention adjourned to meet in Richmond on the 11th of June, but on meeting they adjourned until the 21st, being three days after the meeting of the regular convention in Baltimore, with the view of harmonizing on a ticket, if possible. The Baltimore convention declared Douglas the Democratic nominee, and the Richmond convention then rejected both Douglas and the platform, and nominated Breckenridge and Lane. John Reifsnyder, of Liverpool, was a delegate to the Charleston and Baltimore conventions. While at Charleston he attended a sale of slaves, and a small negro boy, seeing his kindly face and evidently comparing it with the average customer's, begged that he buy him. Mr. Reifsnyder came home very much dejected and realized that it probably meant disunion and war. When informed that Fort Sumter had been fired upon his only comment was, "So soon?" On August 6, 1860, Andrew G. Curtin was again at New Bloomfield, then the nominee of the new Republican party for the governorship of Pennsylvania, to which he was triumphantly elected. During the Curtin campaign for the gubernatorial chair all seemed serene until the Philadelphia *Evening Journal,* an organ of the American party, withdrew its support from Curtin, stating that he was a Catholic, which, if true, meant a sweeping defeat. Rev. James Linn, a native of Perry County, then living at Bellefonte, Pennsylvania, where he was pastor emeritus of the Presbyterian Church, immediately gave to the press a public notice stating that he had baptized Curtin in his own church, and that Curtin had always been a member of his congregation, thus reaction saved his election.

In the elections of 1862 the Democrats carried the Pennsylvania Legislature on joint ballot, having a majority of one vote. John A. Magee represented Perry Conty, and was renominated in 1863, the elections then being annual. His opponent on the Republican ticket was Charles A. Barnett, and the election was the closest contest of any importance since the formation of the county. Mr. Magee had 2,310 votes, and Mr. Barnett 2,311, a majority of one. Later Mr. Magee became a member of the United States Congress and Mr. Barnett became president judge of the Forty-first Judicial District, being elected, however, by the Democratic party this time. In the election of 1864 Abraham Lincoln lost the county, the vote being 2,018 for Lincoln, and 2,148 for George B. McClellan. Four years later General Grant carried it over Seymour, the Democratic nominee, for the Presidency, by over two hundred votes. In the nation the Republicans came into power with Lincoln's inauguration in 1861, and remained in power until the inauguration of Grover Cleveland in 1885—practically a quarter of a century.

Colonel McClure, in his "Old-Time Notes of Pennsylvania," has the following two paragraphs relating to political matters during the closing years of the sectional war which are of interest to Perry Countians:

"The burning of Chambersburg, on the 30th of July, by General Mc-Clausland's forces, precipitated new conditions in my section of the state. Most of the residents in the town were entirely homeless and business was suspended. An extra session of the legislature was promptly called by Governor Curtin and $100,000 appropriated that was apportioned among the most needy. While nearly all the property destroyed was insured, the insurance was lost, as the destruction was caused by a public enemy. The people of Chambersburg were, therefore, largely without capital or credit to resume their various occupations, and despair very generally prevailed in all business and industrial circles.

"J. McDowell Sharpe, the leading Democratic member of the Chambersburg bar, was then a member of the house, and after various conferences on the subject, it was decided that I should accept the Republican nomi-

34

nation for the house, with the general expectation that both of us would be elected, to have an active Democrat and Republican in the next legislature to secure a liberal appropriation from the state. The district was composed of Franklin and Perry Counties, and a Democrat and Republican were nominated in each county. The district was naturally Democratic and the people of the smaller county of Perry were not greatly enthused by the undeclared but generally well understood purpose that Franklin would elect both members of the house. It was a demand that I could not hesitate to obey, and as the national battle could be well fought between the October and November elections I remained at home and devoted my entire time to the care of the suffering people of the town and to the contest in the district; but I was in constant communication with the leading men of the state, and before the October election I was well convinced that there was danger of the state being close or lost in October. Three weeks before the election I was in Washington and gave the President a statement of the unfavorable condition, and urged him to have Cameron appreciate the peril and make an aggressive campaign. He conferred with Cameron on the subject and Cameron assured him that the state would be Republican by a large majority. The result was practically a Republican disaster. There were no state officers to lose, but a number of Republican congressmen fell in the race who should have been successful. Sharpe and I were elected by the common interest felt by both parties in Chambersburg and generally throughout the county in favor of state aid to those who suffered from the destruction of the town, and the Republican congressmen in several districts were saved only by the army vote."

THE COUNTY IN THE MEXICAN WAR.

When the Mexican War came on traffic in America was still principally overland and by canal and the larger waterways. Congress passed the act on May 13, 1846, declaring war upon Mexico by authorizing the President of the United States to employ the militia, naval and military forces of the United States, and to call for and accept the services of 50,000 volunteers. General Taylor had previously entered Mexican territory with his army of occupation, and the battles of Palo Alto and Resaca de la Palma had already been fought. The President called upon the governor of Pennsylvania for six regiments of volunteers "to be held in readiness to serve for twelve months unless sooner discharged." Within thirty days enough men for nine regiments had volunteered. The order for mustering in the troops did not come from the War Department until November. The troops went by boat, via the Ohio and Mississippi Rivers. The First Regiment was organized at Pittsburgh, but included none from this section. The Second Regiment was organized at Pittsburgh, January 5, 1847. Others followed later.

This war was so distant from Washington, in those days of difficult travel, and was so easily accomplished and so devoid of disaster to the American cause that it was a mere ripple as compared to several of our later wars.

Perry County furnished a lieutenant, Michael Steever, and sixty-six privates, which were mainly recruited from the Landisburg Guards and the Bloomfield Light Infantry, Perry County's two crack militia companies of that day. They participated in the Battles of Beuna Vista, Vera Cruz, Cerro Gordo, Contreras, Cherubusco, Molino Del Rey, and Chapultepec. Their districts are not given. The roster:

Lieutenant:
Michael Steever.

Privates:
Applegate, Hezekiah.
Allison, Joseph.
*Bistline, George.
Blain, William.
Baker, Fred'k.
Brown, Alexander.
Bolmer, Jacob.
Boyer, John.
Barnhart, Martin.
Baskins, Daniel.
*Boden, Hugh.
Black, David M.
Coheck, Daniel.
Charles, Henry.
Cornyn, Barnard.
Dayton, Hezekiah.
*Evinger, Peter.
Etter, Bayard H.
Elliott, James.
Ernest, ———.
Frank, Hiram.
Ceysinger, Saml.
Hipple, William.
Hatter, George.
Huggins, Samuel, Jr.
Horting, ———.
*Holland, John.
Johns, ———.
Miller, Marshall.
Miller, Dr. G. A.

McGowan, James.
*O'Bryan, Thos.
Peary, George.
*Peck, Samuel.
Rosley, Charles.
Roller, Samuel.
Rodgers, Robert.
Stump, David.
Sweger, Henry.
Sweger, Samuel.
Sweger, Levi.
Simmons, Samuel.
Shatto, Isaac H.
Snyder, John.
Shull, William.
Scholl, George K.
*Sipe, Samuel B.
Shoch, John.
Sullenberger, Joseph.
Shuman, J. Stroop.
Simons, John.
*Titzell, William H.
Tagg, Wilson.
Tweed, Jesse.
Trotter, William.
Varnes, ———.
Wiseman, Andrew.
White, David.
Williams, John.
Woodmansel, W.
Wolf, Samuel.
Whitsel, Daniel.
Willis, William.

Samuel Simons, a blacksmith from Perry County, also served in the Mexican War, but enlisted with the Cameron Guards, of Dauphin County.

One of these soldiers, Samuel Roller, captured a Mexican flag at the gates of the City of Mexico. Mr. Roller had this flag in his possession until his death. With it he appeared in several parades at the soldiers' reunions of over a score of years ago. After his death Samuel B. Sheller, of Duncannon, a former member of Assembly, purchased the flag and presented it to the state.

PART OF PROPOSED COUNTY OF DeKALB.

Physically the lands which comprise Perry County make it logically a separate political division, as the western part is in reality

———
*Died or lost.

a great cove, and the eastern end is practically an extension of that cove along the northern side. Notwithstanding that fact, however, there was once an effort made to have the extreme western part form a part of a new county, to be named DeKalb. From the *Perry Freeman* of March 13, 1846, comes the information that on March 13, 1836, Representative Means introduced into the legislature a bill to make a new county, to be called DeKalb, out of parts of Cumberland, Franklin and Perry. The division line was to have been as follows:

"All those parts of Cumberland, Franklin and Perry lying and being within the following boundaries, to wit: Beginning at a point on the Adams County line, near, but southwest of Southampton furnace (including said furnace within the new county), thence east by said line to the line between Newton and Dickinson Townships in Cumberland County, thence north by said line and the West Pennsborough Township line, crossing the turnpike east of Stoughstown, to a point immediately east of the town of Springfield, thence by a straight line to the ford in the big spring below McFarland's mill, thence by a straight line to the bridge over the Conodoguinet Creek northeast of Newville, thence by the state road to McCormick's mill, thence to the eastern line of Toboyne Township in Perry County, thence by said line to the summit of Conococheague Ridge, thence by said ridge to the road leading from Shippensburg to Waterford, thence by said road to the crossing of the Perry and Juniata County lines, thence by said line to the corner of Huntingdon and Franklin Counties, thence by the Huntingdon County line to the corner of Metal and Fannett Townships in Franklin County, thence by the line of said townships to their corner on the North Mountain, thence by a line running immediately west of Orrstown, to a point on the Adams County line, the place of beginning."

Naturally the bill was reported unfavorably. It was illogical and a wild scheme. What its purport was is probably unknown to the present generation, but Shippensburg seems to have been the most logical place for the county seat, and probably therein lies the secret. The size of the new county would have been approximately that of Snyder County, judging by a look at the map.

THE RUSH FOR GOLD.

Perry Countians and native Perry Countians who had located elsewhere, joined in the rush for gold in '49 and the following years, and, from among their number, furnished to the Golden State a governor. John Bigler was the man, and he was the third governor of California, while at the same time his brother, William Bigler, was governor of Pennsylvania, the only instance in America where brothers were governors of different commonwealths at the same time. While John Bigler failed to find gold, he did find a place in the hearts of California's pioneers. The biography of these two prominent Perry Countians is of such importance that it is covered in another chapter.

Henry Ulsh came from Germany and settled in what is now Liverpool Township, where his son Joseph was born in 1804. When the quest for gold lured the adventurous to California, Joseph Ulsh and his three sons, Reuben, Leonard K., and John W. Ulsh, were among the number, going in 1851. To-day the trip is possible in considerable less than a week, but then no railways spanned the continent and they went, via New York, sailing on the United States mail steamship, Ohio. They arrived at Aspinwall and proceeded up the Jaguar River to Archipelago. There Joseph Ulsh was made captain of the mule team which transported the baggage of over six hundred passengers to Panama. The three sons made the journey on foot, traveling from the first dawn of day, until the shades of night were falling. At Havana, a small town on their route, they were ordered to stop by native soldiers, but the order was disregarded, when they were fired upon, but luckily not hit. At Panama they took the ship, "Isthmus of Panama," and reached San Francisco forty-two days after leaving New York. Joseph Ulsh returned the following year, but his sons remained and worked in the mines four years, earning sufficient to purchase several farms. Upon their return from San Francisco, in 1855, the Panama Railroad had been completed, which reduced the time of the trip over the isthmus from four weeks to four days. Their return trip occupied only twenty four days, or little more than half the time consumed in going.

Jacob Shearer, who came from Frederick, Maryland, and located in Tyrone Township, in 1843, was another whom the lure of gold drew to California. He had learned tanning and was in the business here, but left for California, where he located at Park's Bar, Yuba County, remaining there almost eight years. While there he was elected to represent Yuba County in the California Legislature for two years. He returned to Perry County in 1857. He was the father of the late H. C. Shearer, once sheriff of Perry County.

Abraham Vandling, of Liverpool, was another emigrant in '49, and remained in California, where he died in 1877. Others who went, in 1855, were Joseph McClure, James McClure (son of James), Peter Bernheisel and a Mr. Robinson, of Tyrone Township, and Samuel McClure, William McCardle and William Rhinesmith, of Jackson Township.

Another who went via the Isthmus of Panama was Abram Clouser of near Newport, who long remained in that state, but later returned to Perry County, where he spent the last five years of his life, dying in 1907. In later years when the Klondike fever drew thousands to Alaska among the number were Mr. and Mrs. W. Scott Toomey and Harvey Wilson, a brother of Mrs. Toomey's.

SLAVES OWNED IN PERRY COUNTY.

Slavery in America dates to the early period of the English colonies, when negroes were imported into them and sold as slaves. With the sanction of no law, save that of common consent, the traffic became an awful and debasing system. The introducing of slave labor was not confined to any particular section or colony, and both Cavalier and Puritan were owners of slaves. However, it was in the Southland, with its broad plantations, where slave labor could be most profitably employed, that it grew to its greatest magnitude and sunk its fangs the deepest. The original list of offenses in the protest against the Mother Country, in 1776, when freedom and liberty were sought, first brought forward prominently the question of slavery—for how could liberty be asked by a people which themselves held other men in bondage? There, even before the colonies became a nation, already appeared that great question, which, eventually, almost wrecked the Union. The protest against King George in that original list follows:

"He has waged cruel war against human nature itself, violating its most sacred rights of life and liberty, in the persons of a distant people who never offended him, captivating and carrying them into slavery in another hemisphere, or to incur miserable death in their transportation thither. This piratical warfare, the opprobrium of infidel powers, is the warfare of the Christian king of Great Britain. Determined to keep a market where men should be bought and sold, he has at length prostituted his negative for suppressing any legislative attempt to prohibit and restrain this execrable commerce."

The paragraph was objected to by the Georgia delegation in the Congress of the Colonies and was expunged from the document for the sake of unanimity, and almost a century later in many states men weltered in blood to settle for all time that which *for unanimity* was passed over. Just as studiously did the Articles of Confederation of 1781 avoid mentioning the subject, either by endorsement or censure, yet there are evidences that the leading men of both North and South at that time looked with disfavor upon it. In 1789 the Constitution of the United States was adopted, and at that early day a threat of disunion appeared, thereby again compromising the matter. While the word slavery was not mentioned in that great document, yet in deciding the basis of representation in Congress and the proportion of taxation to be borne by each state, the apportionment among the respective states was made by adding to the whole number of free population, "three-fifths of all other persons," a stipulation which gave the slave-holding states a predominant position in the national government; and yet it was probably the only way out, as any direct action against slavery precluded the formation of our great republic.

Strangely enough, one of the very first acts of the new Congress under the Constitution was to prohibit the introduction of slavery in that great and extensive domain then known as the Northwest Territory, comprising the present states of Ohio, Indiana, Illinois, Michigan, Wisconsin, and Iowa. Thomas Jefferson wrote the measure and the entire South supported it. Even at that time the better opinion of the South recognized slavery as a great moral evil. With the addition of the Louisiana purchase of 1803 and the opening of the great Mississippi valley to settlement the breeding of slaves became a profitable business, and from a financial stand-point an asset of many of the Southern states with the result that, instead of having an apology for the traffic, they began to endorse it, and by the time Perry County was organized, in 1820—in that very year—Missouri was admitted as a slave state.

The Province of Pennsylvania early had an experience on the matter of slavery. Benjamin Furly, a Rotterdam merchant born in 1636, to whom William Penn submitted his famous Frame of Government for advice and criticism, wrote the first protest against slavery on this side of the Atlantic, in these words: "Let no blacks be brought in directly, and if any come out of Virginia, Maryland, or elsewhere, in families that have formerly bought them elsewhere, let them be declared (as in ye West Jersey Constitutions) free at eight years' end." Mr. Furly was largely interested in the founding of the Frankford Company, and Francis Daniel Pastorious, the agent of that company and a German Quaker, in 1688, wrote the first protest against slavery ever adopted in America. In 1790 Pennsylvania had 3,737 slaves, and by 1820, when Perry County was organized, the number had dwindled to 211. The census of 1830 still showed four slaves owned in Perry County, but the next census, 1840, showed none. The mother county—Cumberland—had 223 slaves in 1790; 228 in 1800; 307 in 1810, and 17 in 1820.

In speaking of the great slavery question, which eventually led to the War Between the States, and which is forever settled in so far as the United States is concerned, the average reader locates the slave states south of the Mason and Dixon line, and such, in fact, is the case. However, slavery was originally not confined to the South, alone, but existed throughout the North, including Pennsylvania and even our own native Perry County, but not on so extensive a scale. There were several slaves still owned in Perry County after its organization, as the following advertisement taken from an issue of the *Perry Forester* of 1826 and other facts will show:

"For sale, a healthy, stout mulatto man, aged about 22 years. To be sold as the property of Rev. John Linn, deceased."

In the issue of the same paper, dated December 2, 1920, an advertisement of sale of some of the effects of Rev. John B. Linn includes "the unexpired time of a Mulatti Boy, aged 15 years." Whether this boy was not then sold and is the one appearing in the advertisement of 1826 we have no way of determining, yet believe such to be the case.

The slave was not only *owned,* but was to be *sold,* and furthermore was the property of a minister of the Gospel and a very pious one. Had this same minister lived a quarter of a century later he would likely have been thundering from his pulpit against the very system of which he had been a beneficiary. On August 17, 1822, Cassanda Campbell, of Landisburg, registered "a male child named Jeremiah, born March 7, 1822, of negro woman Junian, the property of Cassanda Campbell."

From an early issue of the *Forester* the following advertisement is copied, which shows that Northern slaves sometimes ran away, but also shows that not much excitement was created, as the huge reward of six cents would indicate:

Six Cents' Reward.

Ran away from the subscriber, living in Toboyne Township Perry County, on the second of June inst., an indented

' Mulatto Man,

aged about 22 years; who calls himself James Diven, but is better known by the name of Pad. He had on, when he ran off, a brown underjacket, tow check pantaloons, and half-worn roram hat. Whoever takes up said runaway and returns him to the subscriber, shall have the above reward, but no other charges will be allowed.   ANDREW LINN.
Toboyne Township, June 22d, 1826.

John Shuman died at Millerstown, March 7, 1807, and the following interesting story told by his granddaughter, Caroline, of Iowa, in 1913, when she was in her seventy-seventh year, recorded in the "Genealogy of the George Shuman Family," page 112, relates to another slave owned on soil which is now comprised within the borders of Perry County:

"My grandparents had a slave named Sam. My grandmother gave him his freedom and he went West. At the burial of my grandfather (prior to his emancipation), Sam carried my father to the grave; and while standing at the grave, one of my father's shoes fell off his foot, down into the grave and was covered up."

Her father, Michael Shuman, was then a little child in his fourth year. Another slave and his wife, also a slave, were baptized and admitted into membership in a Perry County church, St. Michael's Lutheran Church, in Pfoutz Valley, according to the "Churches Between the Mountains," by Rev. D. H. Focht. The negro's name was "Bob," and the date of their admission, according to the church record, was July 5, 1776.

But of all the slave owners within the borders of what is now Perry County, Francis West, the grandfather of Chief Justice Gibson, Rev. William West, and the wife of Rev. David Elliott D.D., was the chief, having had six at one time. Mr. West came to this country from "Westover," the ancestral home in England, in 1754, and first settled in Carlisle, where he was an early justice of the peace and for many years the presiding justice. While he is credited with living in Carlisle by some authorities and dying there, his will, dated September 6, 1781, and probated December 31, 1783, refutes that statement, as he speaks of the lands in Tyrone Township "where I live" (Book D. p. 193, Register of Wills, Carlisle). In this will he gives his Northumberland County lands and his "mulatto boy, Chamont," to his son William; to his son Edward, a tract of land in Tyrone Township, called "Clover Hill," excepting sixty acres at the east end, and adjoining the survey of William West, Sr., a tract on Sherman's Creek called "Upper Bottom," and a tract of land adjoining Alexander Diven's, reserving all the walnut and pine trees fit for sawing; to his sons, William and Edward, and his brother-in-law, Alexander Lowry, the tract of land where he lived, with the mills, and the sixty acres from the "Clover Hill" tract, including the afore-mentioned timber reserved and his "negro wench called Poll," to rent or lease and apply the one-half "to the maintenance and support of his daughter Ann, the wife of George Gibson, during her natural life, and the other half to the maintenance and support of Francis Gibson, son of the said Ann and the other lawful issue of the said Ann (she to have preference in leasing), at her death to be sold and divided among the issue, share and share alike." To Ann he gave also his stills, with vessels and utensils. To Edward West he bequeathed his negro man, named "Sligo," his mulatto man named "Jacob," and his mulatto child named "Lewis," also 250 acres of land in Fermanagh Township, and the residue not otherwise devised. To his granddaughter, Mary Mitchell, he gave a tract of land in Tyrone Township, together with a mulatto child named "Nila," but in case she die without heirs then it was to go to the three named executors for the use of Ann West Gibson and her heirs. A codicil dated April 24, 1782, revoked the disposition of the "negro wench Poll" to the executors and gave her to his son Edward, and another codicil, dated July 12, 1783, took from his son, William West, the Northumberland County lands and his mulatto boy "Chamont," and devised them to John Donnelson, of Philadelphia, merchant, "in trust for sole use and benefit of said son, William West," but with the stipulation that "at the request of said William West they be sold to said William West, or any other persons, and the benefits accrue to William West."

It will be noted that the will disposes of six slaves. There is no available record known to the writer of the final disposition of these slaves.

In 1778 James Blain (the father of Ephraim Blain, Commissary General of the United States, and ancestor of James G. Blaine, the statesman), was assessed in Toboyne Township (then Cumberland County, now Perry, with "a gristmill, a still, and a negro."

Another man to be assessed with a slave in 1820, the year of the county's creation, was William Anderson, after whom the village of Andersonburg was named, and who represented Cumberland County in the legislature before the formation of Perry. He had married Isabelle Blaine, of the famous Blaine family, and his own daughter Isabelle became the wife of Alexander McClure and the mother of the noted journalist, Alexander K. McClure, long editor of the *Philadelphia Times*. The last man to own a slave in Perry County was William Anderson, whose son, A. B. Anderson, was an attorney at New Bloomfield; that was about 1827, the negro's name being "Bob," according to the late Alexander Blaine Grosh, a descendant, who gave the information to the writer in 1919.

The escape of slaves was not altogether foreign to Perry County, either, as an advertisement of February 6, 1818, signed by John B. Gibson, advertises for a lost slave. While the advertisement does not state which John B. Gibson it was, yet there is no doubt that it was he who later became the celebrated chief justice, as the will of Francis West, his grandfather, gave several slaves to trustees for his daughter Ann, which at her death was to descend to her issue, one of whom was the future chief justice.

Even that unspeakable crime, which fosters lynching in the South and occasionally in the North, was not unknown to Pennsylvania at the early day of Perry County's formation. An early issue of the *Perry Forester* tells of the attack of a negro, the victim being a ten-year-old girl, near Carlisle—within six miles of the Perry County line.

On November 6, 1858, Mary Barton (colored) died in Buffalo Township, aged about sixteen years, the newspaper account of her death stating that "she was formerly employed in the family of Dr. Grosh as a bound girl."

The Quakers who at first controlled the provincial affairs were not opposed to slavery, and even William Penn, with all his religious scruples, owned slaves. As early as 1688 the Friends or Quakers had agitated the subject, and in 1758 further traffic in slaves was abolished by them. In 1776 they decided that all slaves held by them must be set free. As early as 1778 an effort was made to abolish slavery in the province, but was unsuccessful. On March 1, 1780, by a vote of thirty-four to twenty-one, Pennsylvania, then a colony instead of a province, enacted a law to gradu-

ally free the slaves, being the first in the Union to do so, nothwith-
standing that Massachusetts was the abolition centre. While the
law was enforced yet the census of 1840 still showed sixty-four
slaves in Pennsylvania. When this act of 1780 passed in order to
prevent slave owners evading the law it was made mandatory to
register the births of all children born to slaves after that date,
and a heavy penalty was attached for failure so to do.

ANTI-ABOLITION FEELING IN COUNTY.

That there was, even as late as "the thirties" of last century an
anti-abolition feeling in the North, in Pennsylvania, and even in
Perry County, may be a surprise to many, yet such is the truth and
the facts came down the generations through old newspaper files.
On January 17, 1837, an abolitionist was to speak in New Bloomfield, the county seat, in the basement of the Presbyterian Church.
When he appeared, with a band, a riot was threatened, and upon
the intervention of wiser heads, and more prudent friends, he was
conducted to his lodgings, amid the hoots and jeers of the crowd.
But, even that occurrence pales into insignificance when it is
known that there was actually held in the Perry County courthouse an anti-abolitionist meeting, at which resolutions were passed
protesting against the freeing of the slaves. The resolutions which
appear a little farther on, while adopted in Perry County, might
easily be mistaken for a series adopted in any South Carolina
county, or, in fact, in any of the slave-holding states. The second
resolution classes slavery as "repugnant to no precept of the Christian religion." While the resolutions uphold slavery, yet the seventh one shows that slavery was really repugnant to the very men
who passed them, as the seventh one admits that they would "not
submit for one moment" to slavery in the North. Those very men,
in the following years, themselves became abolitionists, and their
sons marched away under the flag of their country in "the sixties."
Captain Tressler, the son of a member of the resolution committee,
organized a company composed principally of his pupils at the
Loysville Academy, and joined the Union forces at the front.

On April 4, 1837, according to the *Perry County Democrat* of
April 6 of that year, a largely attended anti-abolition meeting was
held in the Perry County courthouse, and that the attendants were
men of prominence is evidenced by the names of those among the
list of officers and upon the resolution committee. Many of their
descendants of to-day are likewise prominent in county affairs.
The verbatim account of the meeting from the old files follows:

"In pursuance of public notice a meeting of the friends of the integrity
of the Union, and opposed to the wily schemes of modern abolitionism,
convened in the courthouse, in the borough of Bloomfield, Perry County,
on Tuesday evening, the 4th of April, instant, and organized by appointing

Mr. Jacob Shearer, president; Martin Stambaugh, Esq., Solomon Bower, Esq., Cornelius Baskins and Samuel McKenzie, vice-presidents, and Dr. James H. Case and Francis English, secretaries.

"On motion Dr. Joseph Speck, James Wilson, Col. S. Loy, Dr. J. Foster, E. Dromgold, Edward Miller, Esq., and C. Jones, Esq., were appointed a committee to draft a preamble and resolutions expressive of the sense of the meeting, who retired some time and reported the following which was agreed to:

"WHEREAS, The spirit of dissension is abroad in our happy land, having for its object a no less mighty aim than the destruction of our Republican Union, under which we enjoy so many political, civil and religious liberties, and

"WHEREAS, The total abolition of slavery among a degraded race of beings who are incapable of appreciating or enjoying the blessings of freedom, is the dangerous watch-cry with which the unsuspecting and uninformed are incited to participate in this prostration of the Constitution and laws, it becomes the imperative duty of every well wisher to his country, as it is one of his guaranteed rights to express his humble but honest opinions on a subject so momentous in itself, and so ruinous in its consequences. Misguided philanthropy may find some extenuation for calamities inflicted, in the purity of its motives; but in questions so fraught with danger as the present, all should be held criminal who aid in raising a *demon* of discord, which some kindred spirit of a master mind first invoked in charitable accents, but with fiendish intent. Therefore, be it

"*Resolved,* That the present exciting question of the Abolition of Slavery in the Southern States of this Union, is one raised by a total ignorance of the moral condition of the people for whom they wish to legislate; or by minds darker than the tawny skins of the objects of their pretended commiseration, seeking in scenes of excitement some degree of elevation, which times of peace and contentment could not call forth with honor to themselves or usefulness to their country.

"*Resolved,* That the question of Slavery is, of these United States, one in all its features purely political, being repugnant to no precept of the Christian religion, or the practice of its apostles; and the advocates of abolition who would proclaim slavery sinful and un-Christian in the midst of their mad zeal, ought to remember that the Founder of Christianity was born among slaves, and disseminated His divine commandments among them; but never by word or deed declared their bondage sinful; nor did he ever meddle with any of the established political institutions of his country.

"*Resolved,* That we approve of slavery, so far only, as an evil which cannot at once be removed; and that the people among whom it exists, are more capable of determining the time when it should cease, than we, who are happily distant from it. The Southern states are not culpable for its introduction, as it was imposed against their counsel, when colonies, by the mother country.

"*Resolved,* That slavery is recognized by the Constitution of the United States and Congress has no right to legislate upon the subject; and any attempt to enforce the question of Negro Emancipation upon that body, evinces in the petitioners an equal ignorance of the rights of the States, and the true interests of the slaves.

"*Resolved,* That inasmuch as the Constitution declares that 'All rights not delegated to the General Government, are reserved to the States, respectively,' it is the duty of every friend to its provisions to see that the

States are protected in the just rights of legislating on subjects exclusively within their province, and that the integrity of the constitutional compact be preserved.

"*Resolved*, That until some practicable mode can be devised to remove the colored population entirely from the country with the consent of the people of the slave-holding states, their emancipation would be the greatest curse to the non-slave-holding states, as it would bring upon them all the evils of a mixed and a degraded population.

"*Resolved*, That the people of Pennsylvania have no more right to abolish slavery in the South, than those of the South have to establish it within our borders—a thing we would not submit to for one moment.

"*Resolved*, That we approve of the proposition to hold a state convention of the Friends of the Union, at Harrisburg, on the first Monday of next month, and that this county should send delegates to the said convention."

Perry County did send delegates to that convention to the number of eighteen, or at least that number were named, upon motion, to attend it, and among those named the reader may discover the name of an ancestor—a loyal Unionist and abolitionist of a later day. The delegates named were as follows: Dr. Joseph Speck, George S. Hackett, Dr. Joseph Foster, R. R. Guthrie, W. B. Anderson, M. Stambaugh, John McGowan, Dr. J. H. Case, C. Baskins, Wm. White, W. Messinger, E. Dromgold, James Loudon, P. Orwan, S. Bower, Joseph Ulsh, Frederick Orwan, and Henry Fetter.

The Underground Railroad.

That "the Underground Railroad" once operated in Perry County may seem incredible to some, yet such is a fact. As far back as 1726 several Quakers had settled along the Susquehanna River in Lancaster County, having brought their slaves with them. In a few years their slaves were liberated, and in 1787, when Samuel Wright laid out the town of Columbia, provision was made for the settlement of free colored people in the northern part of the borough. Quakers in Maryland and Virginia freed their slaves and they settled in Columbia. In that way other Southern colored people (slaves) heard of that town and its provision for them, and it became a refuge for runaway slaves. Naturally when slaves had good masters they had no desire for freedom, but those who were owned by men of the type of the novelist's "Simon Legree," took a chance for liberty. In escaping they only dared travel by night, as their detection often meant their return. Some traveled, only guided by the North star, while others followed mountain chain or river. Large numbers entered Pennsylvania via the Susquehanna River territory, York, Gettysburg, and Hagerstown. Slave hunters often traced them to these Pennsylvania border towns, where all trace seemed to vanish. Throughout the North kind-hearted families who were opposed to slavery as an institution helped these unfortunates to food and shelter, the homes of some

of them coming to be known as "stations" and the system of escape, as "the Underground Railway." It had no charter, no officials, no organization, yet was encouraged by public sentiment.
Carlisle, but little over a half-dozen miles from the southern Perry
County border, was a "station" on the "underground" route, and
Landisburg and Ickesburg, two Perry County towns, "stations"
of somewhat less import, but nevertheless a part of the system.
So secretly was this system operated that even neighbors were not
aware that adjoining farms harbored runaway slaves throughout
the day, and there are descendants of some of those who helped
whose eyes will scan these pages.

The name came about from the fact that when owners or agents
from the South followed slaves and suddenly lost all trace of them,
they were ironically informed that "there must be an underground
railroad somewhere." With the passing of the fugitive slave law
in 1850 the hunting of runaway slaves became a regular business.
Many of these slaves went to Canada and remained there until
freedom became assured. By 1852 "the underground railroad"
was in full swing. On at least one occasion a slave was drowned
in Perry County in attempting to flee from his master. On
July 8, 1841, Coroner David Tressler held an inquest upon the
body of a colored man drowned above Newport, in the Juniata.
He was one of three negroes who were pursued as runaway slaves,
under the technical charge of having robbed their master. They
were traveling along the bank between the canal and river, closely
pursued by their master, and when they arrived at the Millerstown
dam they found that that point of land terminated. Two escaped
to North's Island (now the property of A. W. Kough), where they
were captured, and the third, as stated, was drowned. The captured two again escaped. The record shows that their master
gladly stood the expense of the inquest and burial.

CHAPTER XXXI.

PERRY COUNTY IN THE SECTIONAL WAR.
(THE CIVIL WAR.)

ALMOST a century had sped after the realization of freedom, before the climax came to the perplexing slavery question, which was the cause of secession, and had there been no secession there would have been no War Between the States. From the very beginning of slavery on our shores it was a thorn in the side of the nation, then only in embryo; for, it was unpopular from a moral standpoint to many in "the Land of the Free"—a revolting practice which was contrary to the principles on which the government was founded. Outside of that one mooted question the traditions of the North and the South were of the same proud origin. They were of one blood. They had shown heroism and won distinction on field and forum side by side. It seems strange and almost impossible that they should have misunderstood each other or attributed cowardice to one another.

The Presidential election of 1860, on which much hinged, occurred at a momentous period in the history of the nation. The vexed question of the admission of Kansas into the Union under the Lecompton Constitution, which was claimed by the Republicans as being fraudulently concocted by the pro-slavery party, and which was also opposed by a powerful element in the Democratic party headed by Stephen A. Douglas, was to result in a schism in the latter party, which eventually caused four candidates to be placed in the field. When the votes were counted it was found that the young Republican party had won on a platform opposing slavery, and that Abraham Lincoln, the tall, gaunt, intelligent young giant from the Middle West would be the next President of the United States. Within sixty days after the election the oft threatened secession had become a fact.

A great many Northerners would not have offered their lives to efface slavery, to limit the territory in which slavery was permissible, or to meddle with the question in any other way; but with the matter of the withdrawal of any part of the Union they were deeply concerned. Perry Countians, generally, were of that class.

The author is indebted to Rev. H. F. Long, a veteran of the 162d Regiment, Seventeenth Pennsylvania Cavalry, and a native Perry Countian, for help in revising this chapter. Rev. Long was twice wounded at Cold Harbor, losing an arm in the battle. He was also an eye witness when Levi R. Long, a brother of Senator Long, of Kansas, lost a leg at Falling Waters.

Even President Lincoln, while opposed on general principles to slavery, in a letter written as late as August 22, 1862, to Horace Greely, in reply to a public letter addressed to him through the *New York Tribune,* says, among other things:

"I would save the Union. I would save it the shorest way under the Constitution. The sooner the national authority can be restored the nearer the Union will be "the Union as it was." If there be those who would not save the Union unless they could at the same time save slavery, I would not agree with them. If there be those who would not save the Union unless they could at the same time destroy slavery, I would not agree with them. My paramount object in this struggle is to save the Union, and is not to save or destroy slavery. If I could save the Union without freeing any slave I would do it, and if I could save it by freeing all the slaves I would do it; and if I could save it by freeing some and leaving others alone I would also do that.

"What I do about slavery and the colored race I do because I feel it helps save this Union. I shall do less whenever I shall believe what I am doing hurts the cause, and I shall do more whenever I shall believe that doing more will help the cause. I shall try to correct my errors, when shown to be errors, and I shall adopt new views so fast as they appear to be true views."

South Carolina had seceded on December 17, and all America looked forward to what Governor Curtin, the newly elected executive of Pennsylvania, would say in his inaugural address, which came a month later, and which would likely interpret, in words, the feeling of the entire North. Lincoln's inauguration would come about six weeks thereafter, but Curtin would be likely to strike the keynote of Northern thought, Pennsylvania being the keystone for the preservation of the Union as it had been in its formation almost a century previous. Of Governor Curtin's entire address everything hinged upon his opinion of secession and, strange as it may seem, that paragraph was written by a native Perry Countian, Colonel A. K. McClure. Governor Curtin had sent business friends and educated and shrewd young men into the South and was in possession of their reports. His only hope was that Pennsylvania, while maintaining thorough loyalty to the Union, would exercise a wholesome influence on the border states of Virginia and Kentucky, and restrain them from joining the Confederate movement.

Perry Countian Writes Secession Edict.

Governor Curtin was entirely satisfied with every part of his inauguration address save that of the relation of the state to the nation. There was no precedent in the civilized world covering just such a situation—the secesssion of part of a republic. Mr. Curtin himself was the one to criticise his own paragraph. He finally suggested that his five friends, then in consultation with him, the hour being three o'clock in the morning, go to their rooms and each write the paragraph for the inaugural as he thought it should be written, all to meet again at ten in the morning. At that hour each man had his paragraph ready for submission. Morton McMichael being the senior of the party, his paper was read first, and without comment. Colonel William B. Mann, next in seniority, followed. Curtin then called for Col. A. K. McClure's paper and McClure read it. McMichael requested its rereading, after which he requested the withdrawal of his own and the adoption of the McClure paragraph, in which Colonel Mann joined. Secretary Slifer and Attorney General Purviance joined in the demand and did not present their papers. Curtin cordially accepted the paragraph and seemed greatly relieved that all had finally agreed upon the declaration which Pennsylvania should make. The inaugural address was well received and was heralded throughout the North as the general attitude to be pursued by the entire section. Those words will ever stand as a legacy to the entire nation, but more particularly so to the fellow natives of Perry who lived to see their boyhood friend McClure help write in the annals of the ages the fact that "government of the people, by the people, and for the people" shall not perish from the earth. Here follows the clear ringing statement:

> "Ours is a National Government, and has within the sphere of its actions all the attributes of sovereignty, and among these are the right and duty of self-preservation. It is based upon a compact to which all the people of the United States are parties. It is the result of mutual concessions which were made for the purpose of securing reciprocal benefits. It acts directly on the people and they owe it a personal allegiance. No part of the people, no state, nor combination of states can voluntarily secede from the Union, nor absolve themselves from their obligations to it. To permit a state to withdraw at pleasure from the Union without the consent of the rest is to confess that our government is a failure. Pennsylvania can never acquiesce in such a conspiracy, nor assent to a doctrine which involves the destruction of the government. If the government is to exist, all the requirements of the Constitution must be obeyed, and it must have power adequate to the enforcement of the supreme law of the land in every state. It is the first duty of the national authorities to stay the progress of anarchy and enforce the laws, and Pennsylvania, with a united people, will give them an honest, faithful and active support. The people mean to preserve the integrity of the National Union at every hazard."

When secession was sweeping the South from its moorings, every state which went out gave added strength to the Confederacy and weakened the Union just that much. As one of the border states Kentucky refused to join the movement and thus helped sustain the government, and it must be remembered that that action was largely through the stand of the governor, and that there then sat in the governor's chair James Fisher Robinson, the son of Perry

35

Countians, Jonathan and Jane (Black) Robinson, who had migrated from Sherman's Valley to Kentucky.

It is not within the province of this book to go into the history of the war, save as it affected Perry County or Perry Countians, as in the cases just quoted.

The inauguration of Governor Andrew Gregg Curtin occurred January 15th, but even before that, scenting the trend of events, an offer of volunteers, in fact of an entire company, was made by John A. Wilson, captain of the Washington Artillery, of Blain, Perry County, who dispatched the following letter to James Buchanan, President of the United States and Commander in Chief of the Army, but in whose hands the nation was as a drifting derelict upon the great high seas:

                                        BLAIN, PA., Jan. 12, 1861.

HON. JAMES BUCHANAN:
    Dear Sir: Not knowing how soon your honor will have need of the services of the uniformed volunteers to suppress the Southern fire-eating disunionists, we hereby tender the services of our company, subject to your orders. The following are the names. We number about seventy-five members.   Very respectfully,
                              JOHN A. WILSON,
                                    Captain Washington Artillery.

Nowhere else, from coast to coast or from the lakes to the gulf, did patriotism ring more true than in the little mountain-bound county of Perry, which was at the forefront in every war, whether for freedom or the preservation of the Union. The attack on Fort Sumter was all that was needed to unite opposing partisans and send men to the front in large numbers.

Just as in the recent World War, the Sectional War was a young men's war, largely, as over a million Union soldiers entered the service when they were twenty-one, and over 600,000 before they reached that age. This was also true of the Perry County contingent, many of whom were men of the early twenties and younger.

The growing sectional feeling which precipitated the war found those of one section either visiting the other or there on buisness bent, and it was with difficulty that the homeward trip was made, as no sooner had Lincoln's call for men gone forth than a band of steel spanned the country. David Mitchell, a Perry Countian, and General McCausland had a contract to build a railroad in Virginia at the time, and Mr. Mitchell, being a Northerner, had to make a hasty exit.

When war became inevitable, Governor Curtin's call for volunteers brought to the State Capital hundreds of men over every intersecting railway and highway, and it was necessary to have a place of encampment and for the organization of units. The result was that a field north of Harrisburg was leased and was designated

Camp Curtin. The city has long since spread over the ground and its location at the present time would be designated as lying between the Pennsylvania Railroad and Fifth Street, and extending from Watts' Lane southward to Maclay Street. There, from April, 1861, until the last tent was removed in September, 1865, were equipped the finest contingents of fighting men that ever issued from any home base. It was the military camp that has been located closest to Perry County soil, although Camp Meade, near Middletown, during the Spanish-American War, was but ten miles further. All the fatalities were not of the battlefield. In the rush of troops to the front accidents sometimes occurred, the late Prof. L. E. McGinnes recalling to the writer's memory one such which took place opposite Montgomery's Ferry, which took the lives of four or five young soldiers on their way to the front, which created a deep impression on him as a lad.

The writer has no faith in the "conscientious scruple" plea, save as an excuse for cowardice. Unfortunately there were a few in Perry County who made this plea, the evidence of which is on file in the Bureau of Records at Harrisburg. Persons enjoying all the rights of a free land should also be held responsible for its preservation and maintenance, along with the rest, when its existence is threatened. While the Sectional War has long since passed, it is hardly far enough in the background of history to justify the placing of the four names here; but all must be glad that the number was *but four*. The war had not progressed very long before it became necessary to draft men for service, which was the occasion for these men thus going on record. John R. Shuler, of Liverpool, superintended the draft in Perry County.

The Perry County territory, so long upon the very border of Indian warfare, was again destined to be the actual Northern border of the great sectional war. Through it passed scouts and spies, and when General Lee crossed the Potomac and entered the Cumberland Valley, although the harvest was ripe, almost everybody began retreating over the mountains and across the Susquehanna with their families and stock. Property was hidden and buried, but the various gaps crossing the Kittatinny or Blue Mountain were literally packed with a vast train of men, women and children, horses, cattle, and even other animals. The town of Blain, in Perry County, resembled a huge horse market, according to Rev. J. D. Calhoun, of Washington, Illinois, then a lad of thirteen, residing at Blain. In the vicinity of Green Park, according to S. H. Bernheisel, long a New Bloomfield merchant, the hand boards were torn from their posts to confuse spies, and many refugees arrived seeking safety. Rye Township was a haven for many horses and much other livestock. To the Confederate credit it must be said that no destruction of grain crops or buildings was permitted,

General Lee's orders against the wanton destruction of property being complied with to the letter. Milroy's command was scattered among the mountains in small squads as far west as Altoona. The last echo of the Southern advance into Pennsylvania came from the immense battle-train—almost twenty miles long—that left Lee at Gettysburg on the 4th and lumbered southward, leading the retreat. To escape Union cavalry it crossed the South Mountain and turned southward at Greenwood to the Potomac, along an unfrequented road at the mountain base, where it was witnessed only by the two small villages of New Guilford and New Franklin. The wagons were largely filled with wounded, the less seriously wounded traveling on foot. It took thirty-four hours to pass a given point.

When General Ewell, of the Confederate Army, led his raiders far into the Cumberland Valley and took possession of Carlisle, June 27, 1863, many of the supporting cavalry contingent arrived at Carlisle Springs, within a mile of the Perry County line. Fearing foraging trips to the county, especially that part known as Sherman's Valley, the home folks, even including the women and the clergy, rushed to Sterrett's Gap and fortified the top of the mountain commanding the approach with a wall of rocks, stones and boulders. No attack was made, neither was an attempt to cross discovered on the part of the Perry Countians, who kept at the work even during the night, but it is supposed that spies for the raiders discovered that the place had been fortified. From that point a dozen well-armed men would have held many men at bay. Evidences of these rude fortifications still remain. Among the younger men who went there armed, some of whom later entered the Union Army, were John Dice, Samuel Hall, Henry Kocher, Jesse Nace, and Frank Raum. This entry into the Cumberland Valley occurred late in June, and the entry into Carlisle, on Saturday, June 27, 1863. On Sunday, June 28, half of the congregation at the Presbyterian Church was composed of Confederate officers in uniform. On Monday, June 29, they destroyed the railroad bridge at the east end of Carlisle, and on the 30th the town was shelled by General Fitzhugh Lee, when signals from the South Mountains called away the invader, who passed on to Gettysburg, where that world-famous battle opened the next day. As the gray columns passed away Perry Countians and those who had fled to the county for safety breathed a sigh of relief. The reverberation of the cannonry at Gettysburg—forty miles away—could be distinctly heard as it echoed along the mountains. It was at this time that Rev. D. H. Focht, father of Congressman B. K. Focht, went to the mountains with the emergency men, which experience caused his death a little later. When border raids were anticipated or actually occurring many refugees or fugitives from border counties would arrive at Ickesburg and other towns. Alexander Barnes then kept a hotel at Ickesburg, and at such times his hostelry was packed.

THE FAMOUS RIDE DOWN SHERMAN'S VALLEY.*

Many of the famous rides of men and women of history have been immortalized by poet and painter. Almost every schoolboy and girl can recite the stirring stanzas which tell of the daring rides of Paul Revere and Sheridan, but few people even residing in the territory know of the dashing ride of Benjamin S. Huber, a young Chambersburg lad, down the main highway through Sherman's Valley, bearing to Governor Curtin the minutest facts relating to the invasion of the North by General Lee, during the great conflict between the States for the preservation of the Union. The vast conflict at Gettysburg so occupied the minds of the entire nation that Ben Huber's ride, which helped turn that battle to a victory for the Union forces, seemed a mere passing episode and was forgotten.

When the seemingly innumerable waves of gray were sweeping through the streets of Chambersburg hey had thrown outposts far in every direction and had cut the telegraph wires, so that no facts from back of Lee's lines could get to Harrisburg, to the ear of that great war governor, Andrew G. Curtin, who in turn could acquaint the Northern forces of the facts and the direction taken by Lee. The more active loyal men of Chambersburg knew the great necessity of getting to Governor Curtin the facts and especially the fact that the infantry had taken the Gettysburg road. General Knipe, of Harrisburg, with a weak force, could not contend with Lee's immense army and his forces were practically only harassing the advance outposts. Between him and Chambersburg was a virtual barrier of gray. To Benjamin S. Huber, a country lad, went the task of getting the facts to the governor. He was one of a brave lot of young and daring fellows used in that service from about Chambersburg, others being Shearer Houser, J. Porter Brown, Anthony Hollar, Sellers Montgomery, T. J. Grimeson, Stephen W. Pomeroy, and a Mr. Kinney.

According to the records of the period Huber carried no notes, but was to personally meet the governor and convey to him not only the fact that the infantry took the Gettysburg road, but the approximate number of men and supplies and the multitude of things which might be desired in the way of information. He made his way up a ravine and being familiar wih the mountain he crossed through a gap known as the "Three Square Hollow" road,

---

*Not to be confused with the ride of Stephen W. Pomeroy, down the Tuscarora Valley, a few days later.

above Blain, having succeeded in getting a horse. On swiftly
mounted steed he sped through Blain, Andersonburg, Loysville, and
New Bloomfield, arriving at Newport, where he took a Pennsylvania
Central train—as the Pennsylvania trains were known in that day
—and was carried to Harrisburg, where he laid before the governor the information which was flashed to General Meade and
turned that warrior and attendant victory towards Gettysburg.

Again let us draw from a Perry County author. Col. A. K. Mc-
Clure, in his "Lincoln and Men of War Times," says:

"Lee then commanded the largest and the most defiant army the Confederates ever had during the war. General Ewell's corps, over twenty
thousand strong, encamped on my farm (at Chambersburg), and thence
General Rhodes and Early made their movements against York and Harrisburg. On the 26th of June, General Lee entered Chambersburg with his
staff, and it is needless to say that his movements were watched with intense interest by all intelligent citizens. Early and Rhodes were already
operating on the lines of the Susquehanna, and Lee's army was so disposed
that it could be rapidly concentrated for operations in the Cumberland
Valley and against Philadelphia or thrown south of the South Mountain
to operate against Washington. Lee held a brief council in the Centre
Square of Chambersburg with General A. P. Hill and several other officers, and when he left them intense anxiety was exhibited by every one
who observed them to ascertain whether his movements would indicate
the concentration of his army in the Cumberland Valley or for operations
against Washington. When he came to the street where the Gettysburg
turnpike enters the square, he turned to the right, went out a mile along
that road, and fixed his headquarters in a little grove close by the roadside, then known as Shetter's woods. When Lee turned in that direction,
Benjamin S. Huber, a country lad, happened to be present, and, as he had
already exhibited some fitness for such work, he was started immediately
overland for Harrisburg to communicate to Governor Curtin the fact that
Lee's movement indicated Gettysburg as his objective point. Lee was
fated to lose three days in valuable time at his headquarters in the quiet
grove near Chambersburg, as his cavalry had been cut off from him by
encountering our cavalry forces in eastern Maryland, and he could get no
information whatever of the movements of the Union Army."

Not until the night of the 29th, however, when the Confederate
wagon train was hurried through Chambersburg towards Gettysburg, was it certain that that was the objective point. Stephen
W. Pomeroy, of Strasburg, with a despatch telling that fact sewed
inside the lining of the buckle-strap of his trousers, managed to get
to his father's home, secured a horse and hurried through the gap
of the mountain from Path Valley to Tuscarora Valley, where he
secured a fresh horse and sped down that valley to Port Royal,
arriving between two and three o'clock in the morning. The message was quickly sent to Governor Curtin, but unsigned, as the
lad was so exhausted that he left at once.

The following bit of verse which first appeared in Colonel Shoemaker's *Altoona Tribune*, may not be inappropriate here:

BEN HUBER'S RIDE.
BY H. H. HAIN.

Of the famous rides of yesteryear,
Of Sheridan and Paul Revere;
Of those daring rides on worthy steed,
Have been read by men of every creed.
The Union of States was almost rent
By insurrection and discontent,
On the part of the South in '63—
'Twas the aftermath of slavery;
Lee, with his army in fettle fine,
Crossed the Mason-Dixon line,
And in Chambersburg, where the ways diverge,
A halt occurred in the onward surge;
Lee and his staff, in conference there,
In bold relief in the public square,
Decided the route of those clad in gray
As they marched forth in battle array.

To points far out outposts were flung,
And wires were cut—No word of tongue
Could hope to pass the band of steel;
The town was 'neath a despot heel.
To get facts to Governor Curtin then,
Was a task worthy of any man.
Ben Huber quietly stole away
And slipped through mountain pass that day,
And how those Northern lads did rally
As he sped down the Sherman's Valley,
Telling that Lee, awaiting his fate,
Had entered the loyal Keystone State.
On fiery steed he ne'er drew rein,
At Newport swung aboard a train,
And soon poured into the governor's ear
Details of Lee's army drawing near;
And instantly the Union code
Flashed, "Lee takes Gettysburg road."

Northern troops then turned that way,
Ben Huber's ride had saved the day.
At Gettysburg the tide was turned,
And into the hearts of men were burned,
The Union shall not be rent in twain,
But undivided ever remain,
And guarantee to all and each
The words of Lincoln's famous speech,
That the government of Freedom's birth
Shall never perish from the earth.

Harrisburg, Pa., May 11, 1921.

This record of Ben Huber's daring ride down Sherman's Valley, when every echo of the clattering hoofs spelled the beginning of the end of disunion, comes not only from one source, but is a part of the annals of the great Sectional War, when the swords of brothers met in mortal combat. In a volume by Lieut. Joshua

Smith, entitled "From Gettysburg to Appomatox," he relates the incident and so graphically that it is here reproduced:

"The latter part of June it was discovered at Chambersburg that Lee was moving towards Gettysburg. The Confederates having possession of the Cumberland Valley and all lines being down, it was difficult to communicate with Harrisburg, so that the authorities there might know of the movements of the armies.

"On June 26, 1863, Ben S. Huber, a young lad, volunteered to carry a dispatch to Governor Andrew G. Curtin, apprising him of Lee's movements and the probable concentration of the armies at Gettysburg. Huber rode through the 'Three Square Hollow,' through New Germantown, Blain, Andersonburg, Loysville, New Bloomfield and at Newport intercepted a Pennsylvania Central train, and soon appeared before the governor with the very important intelligence, being identified by some reliable parties from Chambersburg. The authorities acted accordingly and our troops were ordered to move toward Gettysburg. The fact that Perry County harbored so many refugees with their horses and the significant ride of young Huber through Sherman's Valley, indicates that it was the extreme northern border of the great war drama of the sixties."

The acts of the Pennsylvania Legislature covering the payment of border raid claims, dated April 9, 1868, and May 22, 1871, names the counties damaged by raids, and includes York, Cumberland, Adams, Franklin, Fulton, Bedford, and Perry. The latter act authorized the appointment of a commission, consisting of two members from each of these counties, to consider the claims presented.

While the Cumberland Valley was in the hands of the Confederates Surgeon William W. Bowles, of the Confederate Army, wrote a letter from Shippensburg to his former instructor, Charles A. Barnett, late judge of Perry County, he having been a student at the New Bloomfield Academy while Mr. Barnett was principal.

Colonel A. K. McClure graphically sums up a few facts of the Battle of Gettysburg, which follow:

"The Battle of Gettysburg was not only fought on Pennsylvania soil, but in no other important battle of the war was Pennsylvania heroism so generally and so conspicuously displayed. General Meade, a Pennsylvanian, was suddenly thrust into the command of the Army of the Potomac only three days before the Battle of Gettysburg began, and he was the chieftain who won the greatest of all the Union victories in the fratricidal strife. General Reynolds, another Pennsylvania soldier, was charged by Meade with the responsible duty of making the reconnaissance in force that precipitated the battle in the undulating plains between Gettysburg and Cashtown, where the heroic Reynolds fell early in the action when his single corps was driving the enemy. General Hancock, another Pennsylvanian, was hurried to Gettysburg by Meade after the report of the defeat and death of Reynolds, and authorized to decide whether the discomfited corps at Gettysburg should fall back upon Meade's line or whether Meade should advance the entire army. It was Hancock's command that received and repulsed Pickett's charge with the Philadelphia brigade in the Bloody Angle. Hancock lay on the field severely wounded until he was able to send the cheering report to his chief that the final charge of the enemy not only resulted in failure, but in the almost annihilation of the charging columns. Sykes, another Pennsylvania soldier, commanded his corps and performed heroic service in the many conflicts of the memorable field. Birney, another Pennsylvania soldier, commanded Sickels' corps after Sickels had fallen in the bloody conflict in the Peach Orchard, and the last clash of arms at Gettysburg was made by part of the Pennsylvania Reserves, led by the heroic McCandless, who closely followed Pickett's retreat, and who recovered the position the enemy had won from Sickels the day before, with many prisoners and 5,000 stand of arms.

"Armistead, the only officer of Pickett's command who successfully crossed the stonewall into the Union lines with a number of his followers, was struck by the Sixty-ninth Pennsylvania that forced them to accept surrender or death, and it was there that Armistead, the hero of the gray, and Cushing, the hero of the blue, made the high-water mark of American heroism for the entire Civil War. Thus four Pennsylvania soldiers—Reynolds, Hancock, Sykes, and Birney—commanded corps in the great decisive battle of the war, and to these must be added the gallant Gregg, the Pennsylvania trooper, who met the attack of Stuart's whole cavalry force as more than 10,000 cavalrymen made the hills tremble in the shock of battle, and won a victory quite as important tô the Union cause as was the repulse of Pickett's charge. No half-dozen other states of the Union furnished such a galaxy of chieftains as did our grand old commonwealth in the desperate and bloody conflict that decreed the continued life of the greatest republic of the world's history."

While it is impossible to go into any general detail of the various soldiers, yet there are a few facts here recorded, which are but illustrative and almost had their counterparts in many other cases. Many families sent two, three, four, five, and even six sons to defend the flag. From a little home one mile east of Blain, on the Ickesburg road (in Jackson Township), went six stalwart sons of Cornelius Baker and wife, the son Samuel falling in action near the close of the war. The Blain G. A. R. Post was named after him. A younger brother—a mere lad—went to Harrisburg to enlist, but was rejected on account of his youth. From Saville went five sons of Mrs. Ellen Hall, all of whom returned safe, yet one's life was saved by the deflection of a bullet by a little pocket Testament which he carried. I may be pardoned for mentioning another. From the farm of John Hain, Sr. (grandfather of the writer), in Howe Township, went five sons, the younger, Frederick Hain, dying at Washington, D. C., ten days after the battle of Antietam, where he was wounded. His remains lie in the Centre Union churchyard, in Buck's Valley. Sheridan's famous ride was viewed by a number of Perry Countians, several contingents being at Cedar Creek, as will be seen in the brief description of companies, farther on, with their muster rolls. The story is told of a man named Brown, from Toboyne Township, an expert fifer, who crossed the Kittatinny or Blue Mountain, when honorably discharged. The first notice his family had of his coming home was when they heard afar the sweet notes of his fife playing, "Oh, My Poor Nelly Gray."

George A. Shuman, a Perry Countian, was made a major, June 16, 1865. During the war he had a part in thirty-six engagements. A horse was shot beneath him at Lafayette and another at Fair Garden. At Thompson's Station eleven holes were left in his clothing and a bullet cut his beard. At Readyville a ball battered the scabbard of his saber. On his return from the war he brought with him his faithful war horse, and for years she occupied a prominent place in the parades at the county soldiers' reunions. She was captured in South Carolina and Major Shuman had ridden her on Sherman's March to the Sea. She lived to be thirty-seven, although blind. At New Albany, Indiana, Major Shuman, with some of his men, were captured by Confederate General Morgan's men. Upon learning that they belonged to the same fraternity General Morgan ordered returned to him his watch and revolver, which had been appropriated. After the war Major Shuman was engaged in breeding thoroughbred messenger horses.

Sadly enough when the Union of States was almost rent by secession, the second officer of the Confederate government was Vice-President Alexander H. Stephens, the son of a native Perry Countian, his father having been born at Duncannon, as told in a sketch of Mr. Stephens, elsewhere in this volume. Like even the wife of the great President, Abraham Lincoln, whose brothers were in the Confederate service, there were other Perry County descendants, and even natives, who wore the uniform of gray. In the hearts of a very few conflicting emotions labored, for their kin —yes, even their own sons—were fighting in opposing armies. The most noted of these was General James A. Beaver, whose uncle, Thompson McAlister, once a representative in the Pennsylvania Legislature from Franklin County, had located in Covington, Virginia, where he raised a Confederate regiment and marched to Manassas, participating in the battle. However, his heart was not in the cause and he resigned and returned home. He had married a Miss Addams, a sister of the governor's mother. He was also an uncle of Mrs. Beaver, whose maiden name was McAlister. Rev. William Cochran, a noted Presbyterian minister, who had been born in Millerstown, and was long located in Missouri, had a son in blue and one in gray. He came North during that trying period and preached in Perry County. Alexander Moreland, a son of Captain David Moreland, of the War of 1812, left Blain, Perry County, and located in Jackson, Missouri, where he had married a lady of considerable wealth and strong Southern proclivities. He had entered mercantile life and when the storm broke between the North and South he became a supporter of the Confederacy, enlisted as a private, was awarded a commission, and when General Lee led his powerful Southern army into Pennsylvania, he was among the commissioned officers in command. Frederick Watts

Hulings, a grandson of Marcus Hulings, the pioneer, and also of General Frederick Watts, and the son of Thomas and Elizabeth (Watts) Hulings, born in what is now Perry County, removed to the South and was once speaker of the House of Representatives of Tennessee. He was a captain in the Confederate service, but in attempting to get on a passing train during the war period, was injured so badly that he died from the effects.

While no soldier enlisting from Perry County attained such noted designation, yet two native Perry Countians who went to the front, became brigadier generals on the Union side, and later both men became governors of commonwealths of this great land. General James A. Beaver, who became governor of Pennsylvania, entered the service as a lieutenant, and General Stephen Miller, who became governor of Minnesota, entered the service as a lieutenant colonel. The names of both are enshrined in the hearts of their people. Biographies of both appear elsewhere in this volume, and show them not only to have been brave and good men, but men of the highest character in every respect.

Rev. W. R. H. Deatrich, D.D., long a Reformed minister in Perry County, was arrested on July 1, 1863, near Chambersburg, by order of General Imboden, of the Confederate Army, on suspicion of robbing his mail, and was marched on foot along with his cavalry to Gettysburg, a distance of twenty-four miles. Wearing a silk hat and weighing over two hundred pounds, with the thermometer over ninety degrees in the shade, the trip was anything but enjoyable. While a prisoner there he witnessed the famous Pickett charge from the Confederate side. He was given his release pass on July 3.

Just as women served in the recent World War so did they serve their country within certain lines during the great sectional struggle. Miss Sarah M. Kerr, later the wife of Major Peter Heistand (long residents of Newport), was one of the Pennsylvania telegraphers during the war when the men were needed elsewhere, being stationed at the Spruce Creek tower.

At various times during the war different contingents were on President Lincoln's guard. One Perry Countian so placed was the late David H. Smith, of near Elliottsburg, later of Duncannon. When President Lincoln was delivering his famous Gettysburg speech, Mr. Smith was stationed immediately behind him.

Benjamin McIntire was provost marshal during part of the war period, his successor being Hiram Fertig. Dr. Joseph Swartz, of Duncannon, was surgeon of the 166th Regiment, and Dr. J. M. Miller, of Newport, assistant surgeon of the 172d Regiment.

At the end of the Pennsylvania Central Railroad bridge, at Marysville, a block house was built to guard against invaders, according to Wright's History.

THE LIST OF SOLDIERS FROM PERRY COUNTY.

It is impossible to give a complete list of the Perry County soldiers during the Sectional War, as many went to Camp Curtin at Harrisburg, to enlist and did not give their residence, and consequently were credited to Dauphin County. Others enlisted in regiments from other counties, and as the government did not keep a record of their residences in the official rosters, it is impossible at this late day to make a correct list without spending years at the work, and even then its correctness would be doubtful. The lists printed in the following pages are drawn from various volumes, regimental records and other publications, being corrected where they were known to be wrong. While they are almost all from Perry County, there will be found some from other counties, which belonged to Perry County companies. They follow:

THREE MONTHS' SERVICE—SECOND REGIMENT, COMPANY D.

This company was mustered into the service of the United States on April 21, 1861, and, their time having expired, they were mustered out on July 26th, having been on guard duty in Maryland and Virginia, but escaped action at the front. Their eagerness to go at the very beginning of the war showed their mettle, and they were the vanguard of a vast array of Perry Countians, who, in a steady stream flowed into the Union lines. The enrollment for this company began on the very day of President Lincoln's call for troops. Three days later, on April 18th, it was off for the front. The names:

H. D. Woodruff, Capt., Bloomfield.
J. H. Crist, Newport.
C. K. Brenneman, Newport.
Joseph Fry. Bloomfield.
Jacob Stump, Centre.
James Hahn, Newport.
George Stroop, Bloomfield.
George W. Topley, Bloomfield.
Wm. H. Troup, Oliver.
DeWitt C. O'Bryan, Newport.
George Kosier, Bloomfield.
Daniel Howard.
Charles Weber, Newport.

Privates:

Albright, H. A., Newport.
Arnold, John H., Madison.
Allwood, Wm. H.
Bergstresser, Jacob, Carroll.
Best, J. Edwin.
Barnes, William H.
Bent, Charles C.
Becker, Philip.
Baldwin, Isaac, Millerstown.
Clouser, Wm., Centre.
Clouser, Isaiah W., Centre.
Clay, Samuel, Centre.
Campbell, John W., Bloomfield.
Charles, Eli B., Buffalo.
Dial, George.

DeBray, G. Smith, Millerstown.
Duncan, Wm. C.
Eby, James B., Bloomfield.
Egolf, John F., Bloomfield.
Etter, Isaac, Newport.
Elliott, John B., Saville.
Ernest, Wesley H., Millerstown.
Ferguson, John F.
Fertig. Wm. R., Millerstown.
Fertig, John H., Millerstown.
Gardner, Reuben S., Newport.
Hostetter, Wm. S.
Holt, Frank.
Heany, Thomas J.
Hartzell, Adam J.
Howell, John W., Greenwood.
Heany, James M., Juniata.
Holman, Daniel.
Idal, Comly.
Jumper, Conrad.
Lynch, Michael C., Bloomfield.
Lutman, Daniel W., Centre.
Leiby, Benj. F., Newport.
Maxwell, David.
Mastha, Lewis.
Mysel, George.
Moore, George.
McDonald, Thomas, Carroll.
M'Clintock, John.
Orwan, George W., Centre.

Orwan, Samuel B., Centre.
Orwan, Martin V. B., Centre.
Power, Wash. A., Centre.
Rumbaugh, H. S.
Robeson, Amos, Bloomfield.
Rider, Thad. C., Newport.
Rider, Oliver P., Newport.
Roddy, Lewis, Newport.
Swartz, John M., Newport.
Sanno, George, Newport.

Swartz, Daniel, Jr., Newport.
Shively, David P., Newport.
Sullenberger, Jacob, Newport.
Shultz, Van Buren, Newport.
Smith, Joseph F., Newport.
Watts, Andrew, Newport.
Wallace, Wm. M., Newport.
Weilly, Wm. C., Newport.
Wright, Thomas, Newport.
Wright, Charles J., Millerstown.

THREE YEARS' SERVICE—THIRTY-SIXTH REGIMENT, COMPANY B.
(Seventh Reserve.)

The Thirty-Sixth Regiment of the Union Army included Company B of Perry Countians, as well as a considerable number in Companies A and H. The regiment was organized in the early summer of '61, under command of Colonel Elisha B. Harvey, of Wilkes-Barre. It was mustered at Camp Wayne, near West Chester. The state uniformed and equipped it. Company B was mustered in on May 4th. It was assigned to duty in the Second Brigade, commanded by General Meade. This company, as a part of the Seventh Reserve Regiment, participated in a skirmish at Great Falls on the Potomac, and in the engagements at Gaines Mill, Charles City Crossroads, the Seven Days' Fight on the Peninsula, Groveton, South Mountain, Antietam, Fredericksburg, and the Wilderness. In the latter engagement, April 5, 1864, part of the regiment (272 officers and men) were taken prisoners and not released till the close of the war. They had become separated from supporting troops in the tangled wilderness. The private soldiers were sent to Andersonville prison, where sixty-seven died. The remnant of Company B was mustered out on June 16, 1864. The roll:

John Jameson, Capt., Liverpool.
John Q. Snyder, Capt., Liverpool.
H. Clay Snyder, Capt., Liverpool.
George K. Scholl, Liverpool.
John Deitrick, Liverpool.
W. H. Deifenbach, Liverpool.
Amos W. Hetrick, Liverpool.
Henry H. Winters, Liverpool.
John J. Hamilton, Liverpool.
Benjamin Huff, Liverpool.
Wm. H. Portsline, Liverpool.
Justus W. Eshelman, Liverpool.
Samuel Haas, Liverpool.
Harrison McCracken, Howe.
John Grimes.
William Newkirk.
James Hebel, Buffalo.
Philip Klinger.
T. Kirkpatrick, Penn.

Privates:

Adams, Matthew, Howe.
Bowers, Michael W., Greenwood.
Bitting, Lewis, Greenwood.
Boyer, John B., Newport.
Beaumont, Elias, Liverpool.
Billman, Wm.
Blakely, Joseph C.
Bowers, Edward.
Brown, George W., Liverpool.
Chamberlain, John, Liverpool.
Cluck, John, Liverpool.

Dewalt, Wm. H.
Deemer, John.
Derr, John, Liverpool.
Duffy, James C.
Deitrick, Leonard, Liverpool.
Free, Wm.
Foley, George, Liverpool.
Grissinger, Geo., Liverpool T.
Glaze, John M.
Griffin, Andrew H.
Gebhart, Charles.
Glaze, Stephen F.
Hain, John S., Howe.
Hebel, John C., Buffalo.
Hassinger, John F., Buffalo.
Huggins, Jacob, Buffalo.
Hilbert, Jonathan, Howe.
Heckard, James.
Holmes, John W., Buffalo.
Hebel, David, Buffalo.
Hebel, Alfred, Buffalo.
Harmon, Fred'k H.
Harmon, Calvin R.
Harmon, Newton C.
Holman, Jacob, Liverpool.
Keiser, Leonard, Liverpool.
Keagy, William, Liverpool.
Keller, William T.
Laning, John S.
Larzalier, James, Millerstown.
Liddick, Daniel, Howe.
Leitzel, Solomon, Howe.

Lowe, Thomas, Liverpool T.
Lenhart, Isaac R., Liverpool T.
Lindsay, William, Liverpool T.
Light, Jacob, Buffalo.
Liddick, Jeremiah, Buffalo.
Liddick, Benj. F., Buffalo.
Miller, William, Howe.
McConnell, Thomas, Howe.
McLaughlin, C., Liverpool.
Myers, Lewis, Liverpool T.
Monroe, John, Liverpool.
McKnight, John A., Liverpool T.
Matchett, George, Liverpool.
McLaughlin, James, Liverpool.
Potter, Joseph, Buffalo.
Preisler, Rudolph.
Portsline, Silas.
Reen, Christopher C., Liverpool T.
Reen, Frederick, Liverpool T.
Rinehart, Fred'k, Greenwood.
Ritter, Israel, Liverpool.
Rice, Elias.
Shoemaker, Jacob, Liverpool.
Sheibley, D. P., Spring.

Shuler, Henry H., Liverpool.
Sheibley, James P., Landisburg.
Stephens, Joseph, Buffalo.
Snyder, James, Liverpool T.
Shatto, David, Liverpool T.
Staily, Jere. J., Liverpool.
Smith, George.
Tagg, Richard.
Temple, Robert.
Ulsh, William.
Vandling, Wesley, Liverpool.
Wingard, William.
Welsh, Elias.
Weikell, William.
Williamson, G. W., Liverpool.
Winters, Joseph, Liverpool.
Williamson, Cyrus, Liverpool.
Wagner, John, Liverpool T.
Winters, Isaiah D., Liverpool.
Williamson, J. W.
Wolf, Alfred.
Williamson, P. E., Liverpool.
Walker, William.
Zitch, John.

At Fredericksburg Lieut. John Q. Snyder and John Cluck each lost a-leg. Amos W. Hetrick, William Newkirk, and George W. Brown were killed at Gaines Mill. Leonard Deitrick, Jacob Holman, Jeremiah J. Staily, and Elias Rice were taken prisoners. The date of Elias Rice's capture was May 5, 1864. He was confined at Andersonville, where he died September 3d of the same year. His remains rest in grave 7,716. Elias Rice Post, at Landisburg, was named in his honor. Many others were wounded.

Three-Year Service—Forty-Second Regiment, Company B.
("Bucktails.")

The war had but virtually started, when the company previously mentioned (Company B, Thirty-Sixth Regiment) was mustered in, yet just one month later, to the day, the "Bucktails," Company B, Forty-Second Regiment, was sworn into the Union Army. It was the company recruited at Duncannon and mustered in June 4, '61, with Langhorne Wister as captain, but who was soon promoted to colonel and assigned to the 150th Regiment, September 4, 1862. Thomas B. Lewis succeeded him as captain. In organizing this regiment the intention was to include only companies of skilled marksmen, principally from the lumbering districts of the state. It was encamped at Camp Curtin, at Harrisburg, and was placed under command of Colonel Charles J. Biddle, the lieutenant colonel being Thomas L. Kane, largely instrumental in its organization, and later promoted to brigadier general. The regiment participated in the action at Dranesville, and six companies of which Company B was one, in the action at Mechanicsville, where the regiment's loss was terrific through guarding the rear of the division in retreat. According to Bates' History of the Pennsylvania Volunteers but 125 men and six officers returned. At Gaines Mill, the next day, twenty-six more men were lost. At Charles City Crossroads the regiment was almost annihilated. It also took part in the second battle of Bull Run. The four detached companies then rejoined the regiment and participated in the actions at South Mountain and Antietam, Fredericksburg, and Gettysburg, entering the latter fight on the afternoon of the second day's battle. In 1864 it engaged in the Battle of the Wilderness, and in the actions at Spottsylvania, on the Po and at Bethesda Church. It was mustered out on June 11, 1864. Captain Lewis had a brilliant war record, having distinguished himself at the "Devil's Den" in the Gettysburg fight. He was the last of the Bucktail captains, having lived until 1917. The roll of Company B:

Langhorne Wister, Capt., Duncannon.
Thomas B. Lewis, Capt., Duncannon.
John A. Culp, Duncannon.
William Allison, Duncannon.
Philip E. Keiser.
Joel R. Spahr, Bloomfield.
Fred'k A. Perry, Duncannon.
Thomas J. Belton, Duncannon.
Charles W. Tierney.
Robert B. Bothwell, Duncannon.
J. W. Mutzebaugh, Duncannon.
Lemuel K. Morton, Carroll.
John O'Brien, Penn.
Mark Burke.
Joseph H. Meck, Wheatfield.
Hiram G. Wolf.
J. H. Mutzebaugh, Duncannon.
John W. Parsons, Watts.
Henry J. Jones, Duncannon.
Jacob E. Stuckey.
Samuel Galbraith.
John Wilkinson, Duncannon.

Hood, John, Duncannon.
Hayner, Edward.
Irvin, W. H. H.
Jones, Nicholas Y., Penn.
Jamison, John.
Jumper, Conrad.
Johnson, Wm. H.
Kugler, Charles.
Lenig, Joshua.
Lewis, John B., Penn.
Lehman, Peter.
Lawler, Joseph T.
Mayall, Miles A., Penn.
M'Callum, George.
Mell, John H.
Myers, Jacob.
Mitchell, Samuel M., Greenwood.
Meck, Solomon.
Meck, John C.
Metz, Andrew J., Carroll.
Magee, Ambrose B., Carroll.
McCloud, Jacob.
Pressley, William.
Pennell, John, Wheatfield.
Parsons, Theodore A., Watts.
Roberts, Thomas C.

Privates:

Arnold, George L.
Branyan, Robert H., Penn.
Branyan, James A., Penn.
Breckbill, Jeremiah.
Burns, James E.
Bolden, James, Penn.
Black, Isaac G., Duncannon.
Barth, John.
Cook, George L., Penn.
Caswell, Edward.
Duncan, Joseph, Penn.
Dile, George L.
Davis, Enoch R.
Evans, David.
Ebright, George W.
Etter, Jacob, Newport.
Fissell, William A., Penn.
Fissell, John A., Penn.
Farnsworth, Samuel.
Foster, Erastus R., Penn.
Fleck, Ephraim B., Duncannon.
Furlong, Philip.
Foran, Patrick.
Green, Thomas G., Penn.
Gillespie, T. W.
Holland, Wm. A., Penn.
Hartzell, Isaiah, Penn.

Richard, Davis.
Reynolds, John, Penn.
Rennard, Charles.
Raup, George, Penn.
Sweger, Absalom, Penn.
Shively, Thomas J., Duncannon.
Shively, George W., Spring.
Smith, John C.
Staekle, John F., Howe.
Sheaffer, Oliver.
Stevenson, Wm. M., Duncannon.
Stewart, Levi.
Snyder, Truman K., Duncannon.
Shatto, George W., Duncannon.
Shatto, Alexander, Duncannon.
Sayers, John.
Spear, Samuel.
Spahr, George H.
Seiler, Reuben, Liverpool T.
Seiler, John, Buffalo.
Shatto, John E.
Topley, Samuel A., Bloomfield.
Valentine, Robert B.
Vansant, James N.
Walker, James.
Watson, George C.

George Raup and Samuel Galbraith were killed at Dranesville; Theodore A. Parsons and John Sayers, at Charles City Crossroads; Thomas J. Belton and Samuel Spear, at Gettysburg; Conrad Jumper, at South Mountain, and William Allison, at Antietam. The G. A. R. Post at Duncannon was named in honor of Lieutenant Allison. Ambrose Magee was also killed in action.

THREE-YEAR SERVICE—FORTY-SIXTH REGIMENT, COMPANY D.

While Perry County had no company in the Forty-Sixth Regiment, yet Company D contained a number of Perry County men. This regiment was raised during the summer of '61 and organized at Camp Curtin, September 1. Colonel Joseph F. Knipe was at its head. This regiment was in the action at Winchester, at Cedar Mountain charged three times across an open wheat field, each time being driven back by a superior force; at Antietam, Chancellorsville, and Gettysburg. In the advance on Atlanta they also fought in eleven actions, including Kenesaw Mountain and Peach Tree Creek. Atlanta was captured September 1, and ten days later the regiment was moving with the army on Sherman's march to the sea, capturing Fort McAlister. The Perry County men in Company D were:

Albright, John A.
Bachman, Wm. H.
Chisholm, John W.
Foster, Francis A.
Shelly, John, Watts.
Smith, Joseph S.
Tromble, Solomon.

On July 20, 1864, John Shelly lost a leg in the action at Peach Tree Creek.

THREE-YEAR SERVICE—FORTY-SEVENTH REGIMENT, COMPANY D.

Perry County was contributing men in a speedy manner. It had already put two entire companies in the field, besides many other man, yet when the Forty-Seventh Regiment was organized, two Perry County companies were on its roster. Company D was mustered in on August 31, '61, and Company H, on September 19. These companies, with their regiment, were ordered to Key West, Florida, to open St. John's River and to garrison Forts Jefferson and Taylor. February, 1863, it was transferred to the command of General Banks' army in Louisiana and was assigned a part in the Red River Expedition, being in action at Sabine Crossroads, La., Pleasant Hill, and Cane Hill. On July 5, 1863, it was transferred to the Army of the Shenandoah, under Sheridan, arriving from Louisiana on July 12th. It was assigned to the Nineteenth Corps then engaged in expelling the invader from Maryland, and in the defense of the National Capital. These companies participated in the battles of Opequan (Winchester), Fisher's Hill, and Cedar Creek. This regiment was the only one from Pennsylvania serving in the Red River Expedition. Among the regimental officers from Perry County were Elisha W. Baily, surgeon, and Rev. W. D. C. Rothrock, chaplain, the latter mentioned for bravery in every action. The enrollment of Company D follows, and immediately thereafter, Company H. Company D:

Henry D. Woodruff, Capt., Bloomfield.
George Stroop, Capt., Bloomfield.
George Krosier, Capt., Centre.
Samuel A. Auchmuty, Penn.
George W. Clay, Centre.
Jesse Meadith, Landisburg.
James Crownover, Centre.
John G. Miller, Duncannon.
John V. Brady, Penn.
Isaac Baldwin, Millerstown.
Theodore R. Troup, Oliver.
William R. Fertig, Millerstown.
Henry Heikel, Duncannon.
Alexander D. Wilson, Bloomfield.
Frank M. Holt.
Edward Harper, Newport.

Jacob P. Baltozer, Madison.
John E. D. Roth, Bloomfield.
Noble Henkle, Juniata.
Benj. F. Shaffer, Spring.
Wm. D. Hays.
William Powell, Tuscarora.
James Downs.
James T. Williamson.
Cornelius Stewart, Penn.
Saml. A. M. Reed, Bloomfield.
George Rohm.
Wm. P. Weaver.
Francis Brown.

Privates:

Albert, James E., Juniata,
Anthony, John M.

Anthony, Benj F.
Auker, Joseph, Greenwood.
Bender, Amos.
Brady, Wm. F., Madison.
Baltozer, B. F., Madison.
Brady, Atkinson M., Madison.
Brady, Leonard W., Madison.
Baskins, James C., Penn.
Bowing, Ephraim.
Blain, Lewis, Juniata.
Barnes, Wm. H.
Barton, Uriah.
Bullard, Aaron.
Hamilton, Blanchard.
Berrier, George.
Bistline, Joseph, Juniata.
Baltozer, Geo. W., Madison.
Bullard, John.
Bryan, Albert C.
Carpenter, Thos. B., Duncannon.
Clouser, Wm. H., Bloomfield.
Clouser, John D., Bloomfield.
Clay, John B., Centre.
Clouser, Ephraim, Centre.
Charles, Eli B., Buffalo.
Clouse, Wm.
Charles, Jacob, Buffalo.
Collins, William.
Coulter, Wm. H., Buffalo.
Crook, David.
Donahoe, John F.
Diller, Oliver P.
Dill, Washington, Penn.
Deitzinger, John.
Ewing, Wm. H.
Earhart, Wm., Juniata.
Egolf, John F., Tyrone.
Fertig, Franklin M.
Foreman, Henry.
Forman, Levi.
Frank, David R., Howe.
Foltz, William, Carroll.
Foltz, Michael, Carroll.
Foltz, Henry W., Carroll.
Foltz, George W., Carroll.
Foley, George, Liverpool.
Foose, Samuel.
Gohn, Samuel.
Gibson, George H., Spring.
Hershey, Wm. A.
Harper, Martin, Newport.
Humes, Alexander, Sandy Hill.
Harper, Wm. G., Newport.
Haas, John W., Liverpool.
Isett, George S.
Jordan, Anthony.
Jury, George W.
Jones, Harrison.
Kirkpatrick, Wm., Penn.
Kosier, Wm. S.
Kochenderfer, Geo.
Keim, John.
Keim, A. F., Newport.
36

Kosier, Jesse.
Kern, Samuel M.
Leary, Jeremiah.
Lickel, Simon.
McCarty, Timothy.
McCuskey, James.
McKee, William A.
Mysel, George.
Myers, John C.
McClure, Wm. H.
McCully, John.
Messimer, Josiah.
Messimer, Geo. W.
Messimer, Lemuel.
Myers, Joseph.
Myers, Amon.
Mays, William.
Musser, Alexander.
Mehaffie, Andrew.
Newkirk, Reuben H.
O'Neil, Hugh.
Prothero, Fred'k.
Petre, Peter.
Peterson, Aaron.
Powell, Andrew.
Power, Wash'gt'n A.
Porter, Robert.
Powell, Solomon.
Powell, John, Jr.
Powell, David, Jr.
Raffensperger, S.
Rhoads, Wm. H.
Reynolds, John W.
Rigler, Geo. H.
Robinson, Wm. H.
Reynolds, Jesse D.
Rose, David.
Shannon, Ellis.
Sailor, Cyrus J.
Stall, Abraham.
Smith, Albert G., Carroll.
Smith, Wm. D., Carroll.
Smith, James, Carroll.
Shaffer, Jesse M.
Smith, Wm. J.
Sowers, George.
Sellers, Joseph M.
Shaffer, Wm.
Stites, Wm. D.
Shaver, Joseph B.
Snyder, Emanuel.
Small, Jerome Y.
Souder, William.
Shaffer, Michael.
Stroop, Wm. J.
Swartz, Daniel.
Tagg, Richard.
Tagg, James D.
Topley, George W., Bloomfield.
Tagg, Wilson.
White, Wesley M.
Weimer, Samuel.
Weiand, Benj.

Wright, Thomas.
Woodrow, James.
Work, Washington, Duncannon.
Work, Andrew, Duncannon.
Wantz, John.

Williams, Andrew J.
Wetzel, William, Spring.
Wantz, Jonathan.
Wagner, Samuel, Spring.
Zook, Daniel S.

Solomon Powell and Jonathan Wantz were captured at Pleasant Hill, La., where both died in June, '64. Samuel Wagner was lost at sea from the U. S. S. Pocohontas. Alexander Musser was killed at Pocotaligo, S. C. Harrison Jones, John F. Egolf, Joseph Auker, and Jerome Y. Small were killed at Cedar Creek and are buried in the National Cemetery at Winchester, Virginia, the remains of Egolf and Auker in lot 10, and those of Small in lot 25.

THREE-YEAR SERVICE—FORTY-SEVENTH REGIMENT, COMPANY H.

This company's record is the same as that of Company D, immediately preceding. The roster:

James Kacey, Capt., Elliottsburg.
Reuben S. Gardner, Capt., Newport.
Wm. W. Geety.
James Hahn, Greenwood.
C. K. Breneman, Newport.
Alfred Billig.
David H. Smith.
George Reynolds.
John A. Gardner, Newport.
John S. Snyder.
Michael, C. Lynch, Bloomfield.
Robert H. Neilson, Centre.
John P. Rupley.
Isaac C. Foye.
James F. Naylor.
Isaac Billett.
Daniel Urich.
Daniel K. Smith, Newport.
Daniel W. Fegley.
Elkana Sweger, Centre.
Amos T. Brown, Carroll.
Henry C. Weise, Millerstown.
John Clemmons, Greenwood.
John Kitner.
Wm. M. Wallace, Toboyne.
George W. Harper, Newport.
Daniel Reeder, Spring.
P. W. Stockslager.
James J. Kacey, Spring.
George W. Albert, Juniata.
Edw. H. Marchley.
John H. K. Boyer, Newport.
George Kipp, Newport.
Allen McCabe, Newport.

Privates:

Anderson, John, Newport.
Albert, James, Juniata.
Andrews, Valentine.
Bernheisel, Luther, Tyrone.
Bear, George W.
Bupp, Augustus, Newport.
Bucher, Edward M.
Burd, Abraham, Newport.
Brooks, William, Penn.
Bollinger, Henry.

Briner, Jerome, Tyrone.
Baldwin, Charles E.
Bigger, Alexander.
Bistline, Daniel, Tyrone.
Barry, William.
Beers, Henry W.
Campbell, Oliver H.
Cooper, John.
Cunningham, Robert.
Clay, John D., Centre.
Deily, Edward F.
Duncan, James.
Dunlap, Milton H., Penn.
Dessmer, James R.
Durham, John H.
Dorman, William.
Davenport, Valent.
Deitz, Augustus.
Detrick, Peter, Liverpool.
Dumm, Wm. F., Spring.
Eckerd, Harrison, Greenwood.
Evans, John.
Fink, Emanuel.
Fosselman, Daniel.
Flint, Dwight H.
Fry, Robert.
Faling, Michael.
Frank, David R., Newport.
Foose, Samuel, Duncannon.
Fisher, Daniel W.
Fink, Simon C.
Gechenbaugh, Daniel.
Gusler, Wm. H., Centre.
Garris, Henry F.
Guera, Emanuel.
Gardner, Jacob R.
Galbraith, James.
Hammaker, Isaiah, Watts.
Hammaker, Thomas, Watts.
Hostetter, Jacob C.
Huggins, Samuel, Newport.
Hartshorn, John.
Heenan, Michael.
Hoffman, George W.
Henderson, Isaac.
Horting, Michael, Newport.

Haney, Thomas J., Juniata.
Hutcheson, Wm.
Hammaker, Adam, Watts.
Hammaker, Jacob, Watts.
Horting, Ananias, Newport.
Hall, James.
Haywood, Thomas.
Hayes, William.
Harper, Martin, Newport.
Holmes, John W., Newport.
Idall, Comly.
Johnson, Cyrus, Greenwood.
Jassum, Edward.
Kingsborough, R. A.
Kochenderfer, Daniel, Saville.
Knech, Wm. H.
Keim, John M., Wheatfield.
Kingsborough, R. R.
Klotz, Charles.
Liddick, Jacob, Buffalo.
Liddick, Jacob II, Buffalo.
Laub, Aaron.
Leedy, Henry.
Louden, Adam, Watts.
Liddick, Adam, Watts.
Liddick, John H., Buffalo.
Liddick, Wm.
Lowe, James.
Long, John D., Newport.
Liddick, John.
Lupfer, Michael, Jackson.
Lightner, Sterrett, Madison.
Labar, Lorenzo.
Lightman, John.
Morton, Edward J.
McCoy, David, Penn.
McLaughlin, Peter, Toboyne.
Mowery, Henry.
McKibben, Robert.
Miller, Walter C., Juniata.
Morian, John.
Meyers, John H., Juniata.
Messimer, Benjamin, Bloomfield.
McIntire, John.
Mullen, Patrick.
Naylor, Jacob.
Newman, Edw.
Nagle, John, Liverpool.
Orner, John, Newport.
O'Brien, Wm. H., Newport.
O'Connor, Michael.
Orris, Nicholas I.

Purcell, Dennis.
Reichner, Michael.
Rider, James, Newport.
Radabaugh, S. M.
Rider, John W., Newport.
Reed, Samuel A. M., Bloomfield.
Robinson, Wm. H., Bloomfield.
Robinson, Jason T., Bloomfield.
Rickenbaugh, Jacob.
Ridgway, John.
Shelley, William.
Shipley, Parkinson H.
Seiders, Jeremiah.
Smeigh, Michael, Bloomfield.
Schofield, John J.
Sailor, Lewis W.
Simpson, James.
Stamp, William.
Stitler, William.
Schlocter, Isaac.
Simonton, Wm. J.
Saylor, Lewis W.
Shull, William, Newport.
Smedley, Francis J.
Smith, Thomas.
Stoutsaberger, H.
Sweger, George, Centre.
Saylor, Alexander, Greenwood.
Small, Charles H.
Smith, Jeremiah, Millerstown.
Stambaugh, Henry.
Smith, George H.
Shelley, Joseph.
Smith, Joseph.
Shepley, Henry.
Shaffer, Stephen.
Shaffer, Reuben.
Schofield, William.
Thompson, David.
Thornton, Benj.
Thompson, Wm. R.
Turpin, George.
Warner, Charles F.
Watt, Michael.
Wright, Joseph A., Howe.
Watt, Frederick.
Waggoner, Jefferson.
Whealand, John.
Yohn, John, Jr., Tuscarora.
Yohn, Daniel, Tuscarora.
Yohn, John, Sr.
Zinn, George W., Newport.

Wright's History adds the name of Wm. S. Kosier, corporal, to the list, but omits ninety-five of the other names.

Many of this brave little band sleep on Southern soil. Henry Shepley, who died December 10, '64, and Stephen Shaffer, who died January 8, '65, passed away in a Confederate prison at Salisbury, N. C. Nicholas I. Orris and Wm. F. Dumm were killed at Pleasant Hill. William Barry was killed at Sabine Crossroads. John McIntire, Valentine Andrews, Michael Heenan and Joseph Shelly were killed at Cedar Creek and their remains rest in the National Cemetery at Winchester, the first three in lot 10, and the last named in lot 9.

The action at Pocotaligo, South Carolina, was hard on the company. Many were injured, among whom was Daniel Reeder, who lost an arm. Peter Deitrick, Jason T. Robinson, Henry Stambaugh, and Jefferson Waggoner were killed in action.

THREE-YEAR SERVICE—FORTY-NINTH REGIMENT, COMPANY A.

While the Forty-Ninth Regiment contained no company from Perry County, yet it contained a number of Perry County men in Company A, and is important to Perry Countians for further reasons. Company E, of Lewistown, had as its captain, Henry A. Zollinger, of Newport, who had, prior to that time, been interested in recruiting the Logan Guards and Burns' Infantry. Succeeding its first colonel, Thomas M. (Marcus) Hulings—descendant of Marcus Hulings, a Watts Township pioneer—was made colonel of the regiment. He had been first lieutenant of the Logan Guards, of Lewistown, the first company to reach the National Capital in the War Between the States. He had then been major of the Forty-Ninth. He took part in the Peninsular campaign under McClellan, in General Hancock's brigade. At Young's Mill and Williamsburg (where Hancock's fame began), Hulings was a brave officer. At Spottsylvania he fell, pierced by a bullet.

This regiment was organized during September, '61, and was assigned to General Hancock's (First) Brigade. At Williamsburg, North Carolina, many prisoners of the Fifth North Carolina Regiment were captured. The regiment participated in the actions at Young's Mill, Williamsburg, Savage Station, Charles City Crossroads, Malvern Hill, Crampton's Gap, Antietam, Fredericksburg, Gettysburg, Spottsylvania, Cold Harbor, Winchester, and others. The Perry Countians in Company A:

Ernest S. David, Corporal, Millerstown.
William Attig, Millerstown.
Samuel McClenehan, Millerstown.
John P. Patterson, Millerstown.
Jacob R. Runyan, Millerstown.

THREE-YEAR SERVICE--SEVENTY-SEVENTH REGIMENTAL BAND (CO. C).

While no Perry County company was a part of this regiment, yet a large part of the Regimental Band were from Perry County, being members of Company C, of Mifflin County, before being assigned to the band. It was encamped at Camp Wilkins, near Pittsburgh, in October, '61. It was engaged in the actions at Shiloh, Murfreesborough, Liberty Gap, Chickamauga, Kenesaw Mountain, Peach Tree Creek, and a number of others. The Perry Countians in the band:

Geo. W. Monroe, Leader, Liverpool.
Arndt, John J., Liverpool.
Haas, Henry, Liverpool.
Monroe, A. Worley, Liverpool.
Nagle, Daniel, Liverpool.
Orwan, Lewis W., Liverpool.
Shure, Jacob D., Liverpool.
Shuman, Wm. A., Liverpool.
Shuler, Samuel M., Liverpool.
Welzer, George C., Liverpool.
Zinn, William A., Newport.

THREE-YEAR SERVICE—SEVENTY-EIGHTH REGIMENT, COMPANY K.

A number of Perry Countians were enrolled in Company K, of the Seventy-Eighth Regiment, although the county had no company therein. The names:

John Deitrick, 1st Lieut., Liverpool.
J. J. Spoonenberger, Liverpool.
C. R. Buffington, Liverpool.
David O. Ritter, Liverpool.
Henry Derr, Liverpool.
Peter Derr, Liverpool.
John Ditty, Buffalo.

None of these men were privates.

THREE-YEAR SERVICE—NINETY-SECOND REGIMENT, COMPANY A.

The Ninety-Second Regiment, otherwise known as the Ninth Cavalry, had within its organization one entire company of Perry Countians, Company A, with other detachments in Companies B, C, G, H, L, and M. It was organized at Camp Cameron, Harrisburg, in the fall of '61. Assigned the duty of combating Morgan, the raider, they captured 291 of his men at Gallatin, Tennessee, and were in action with his troops at Spring Creek and Tompkinsville, Kentucky. They were in the actions at Perryville, Holstein River, Franklin, Shelbyville (Tenn.), Elk River, Cowan, Lafayette (Ga.), Chickamauga, McMinnville Road, Lovejoy, Macon, Bear Creek, Waynesborough, Louisville, Blacksville (S. C.), Aiken, Lexington, and Averysborough (N. C.). On April 13, '65, the Ninth received a messenger under a flag of truce. It was a message from the Confederate General Johnston to General Sherman, proposing a surrender of the Southern Army. A detachment of the Ninth also escorted General Sherman, when he advanced to meet General Johnston. It will be noted that the Ninth was in the very last action east of the Mississippi in that great struggle. The roster:

COMPANY A.

Griffith Jones, Capt., Duncannon.
Geo. J. K. Farrall, Capt.
John Boal, Capt.
Wm. M. Potter, Capt., Wheatfield.
Charles Webster.
Charles A. Appel.
Eugene S. Hendrick.
Eleazer Michener, Penn.
Thos. D. Griffith.
Sam'l H. Schneck.
Harry S. O'Neil.
Jacob H. Low.
John M. Graybill, Penn.
James B. Hammersly.
James M. Haney, Juniata.
Wm. H. Coleman, Greenwood.
James H. Marshall.
Henry K. Myers, Newport.
Thomas J. Foose, Duncannon.
Henry Kroh, Bloomfield.
B. H. Branyan, Penn.
M. B. P. Stewart, Duncannon.
Robert McEliget.
Henry Haverstick.
Wm. Rodemaker.
Wm. G. Sheets, Duncannon.
Rudolph Wire.
Josiah Sweezy, Greenwood.
James W. Kennedy, Tyrone.
George W. Pennell, Wheatfield.
John A. Haney, Juniata.
Tighlman Miller.
Stephen B. Boyer.
John A. Gilmore, Millerstown.
Charles Dixon.
John H. Noss, Duncannon.

Privates:

Albright, Louis M., Buffalo.
Albright, Fred'k.
Allen, Samuel.

Barrett, John.
Bechtel, David S.
Buchanan, David K., Greenwood.
Banely, Augustus.
Bellman, Samuel S.
Brass, Luke.
Boyer, Samuel.
Bates, Paul Q.
Barrick, Daniel W., Tuscarora.
Burd, John W., Juniata.
Billow, John W., Greenwood.
Beasom, John, Greenwood.
Benner, Ferd I.
Coup, Michael.
Cassidy, Edwin S., Newport.
Carroll, Jeremiah.
Dunn, John B.
Donohue, Hugh.
Donally, John, Tuscarora.
Dailey, Thomas.
Emerson, George S.
Ellenthorp, Sol. B.
Ebert, Augustus, Duncannon.
Ebright, Benj.
Ettine, Philip.
Frank, Cyrus A., Liverpool.
Foster, Martin.
Fritz, John T., Centre.
Foose, Cornelius, Duncannon.
Finton, Jacob, Howe.
Grubb, Isaac, Greenwood.
Gintzer, Lewis F.
Gates, James P.
Greek, John W.
Grier, Cyrus.
Gelbaugh, John T.
Gunderman, D. V., Greenwood.
Grove, John M.
Haines, Wm. M. D., Greenwood.
Hamersly, Ellis T.
Himes, Charles H.

Hoffman, Oscar **T.**
Hozan, George.
Hite, John.
Huggins, Jacob, Buffalo.
Hamilton, Samuel.
Hazzard, John.
Hosan, John.
Irely, Samuel.
Jones, Ezekiel, Howe.
Jones, Henry C., Penn.
Jones, Isaac.
Kelley, David.
Kauffman, Wm. H., Greenwood.
Kenely, David.
Kern, Jacob, Toboyne.
Kemmerer, Jacob.
Lesh, Peter S., Juniata.
Liddick, Wm., Buffalo.
Lamberton, W. H.
Linn, Samuel B.
Long, Abraham W., Greenwood.
Lowe, John H., Newport.
Liddick, John W.
Metz, Henry H.
Matauer, Victor.
Mountz, John.
Masonhimer, John.
Musser, John S., Newport.
Mutzebaugh, Wm., Penn.
Murray, Lewis E., Liverpool.
Mitchell, Charles, Greenwood.
Miller, David H., Penn.
Mott, Michael.
Mitchell, John.
McClintock, John S., Carroll.
McDonald, Robert, Carroll.
McCoy, Isaac, Penn.
McCann, Robert S., Duncannon.
McConnagha, E.
McCoy, Alexander, Penn.
McClintock, Wm., Carroll.
Nixon, Robert.
Omer, Joseph, Millerstown.

Owens, Davis A., Wheatfield.
Phillips, Lazarus.
Potter, Hiram, Wheatfield.
Palmer, Solomon P.
Parks, Noah.
Pines, Reuben M., Liverpool.
Pennell, Robert, Wheatfield.
Parsons, George B., Watts.
Rose, William, Wheatfield.
River, George, Spring.
Rice, Ephraim, Spring.
Reynolds, Thomas C., Spring.
Ricedorff, Daniel W.
Shingler, John.
Sager, Richard N.
Shaw, Albert.
Shuman, Peter S.
Stutzholtz, John.
Shearer, Reuben, Duncannon.
Smith, Michael.
Sheibley, David R., Spring.
Sheaffer, Israel E., Greenwood.
Showers, David.
Stodter, John H.
Smith, George.
Seisholtz, George.
Thompson, Joseph A.
Toland, John M., Penn.
Tallant, Sidney.
Volzer, Christian.
Wertz, George W., Greenwood.
Wiley, James R.
Wellman, Hiram.
Walter, Frederick.
Winters, Josiah.
Wright, Josiah, Greenwood.
Wiley, William T.
Wells, William.
Wilson, Robert.
Winters, Isaac I.
Wilson, John.
Young, Levi, Duncannon.
Yeager, Edward G.

Capt. John Boal was killed at Averysborough; Tighlman Miller, bugler, at Louisville; Philip Ettine and Cornelius Foose, at Stone River, and M. B. P. Stewart and David Showers, at Griswoldsville, Ga. Benjamin Ebright was captured and sleeps in grave 3,823, at Andersonville. Alexander McCoy was captured and died in a prison camp at Goldsborough, N. C.

COMPANY B.

Elias Heiney, Juniata.   William Reed, Liverpool.

COMPANY C.

Geo. A. Shuman, 2d Lieut., Carroll.
Jacob Coller, 1st Lieut., Saville.
Samuel F. Spohn, Tyrone.
Jere. W. Weibley, Saville.
Samuel P. Gutshall, Jackson.
Jacob B. Sheafer, Spring.
Samuel W. Fickes, Juniata.
Wm. R. Fertig, Millerstown.
James P. Cree, Landisburg.

Henry Baker, Saville.
Cornelius Baker, Saville.

Privates:

Anderson, James A., Jackson.
Attig, Henry H., Millerstown.
Baker, Samuel, Saville.
Linn, William S., Tuscarora.
Lahr, Jerome B., Greenwood.

Messimer, W. D., Bloomfield.
Noll, Samuel, Spring.
Raffensberger, Jere., Juniata.
Ricedorff, Daniel.
Scott, Walter A., Bloomfield.
Smeigh, Walter H., Centre.
Sheafer, David L., Tyrone.

Sheafer, Charles H., Tyrone.
Saylor, Allen, Newport.
Stone, Simon, Newport.
Stambaugh, Wm., Tyrone.
Spohn, John P., Spring.
Tressler, Henry L., Juniata.
Zeigler, Reuben, Oliver.

COMPANY G.

Arnold, John H., Bloomfield.
Grosh, Alex. B., Blain.
Gingrich, Aaron H., Saville.
Heinbach, Chas., Greenwood.

Hohenshildt, D. M., Madison.
Jones, John, Juniata.
Lackey, Geo. S., Carroll.
Laird, James P., Bloomfield.

John Jones was killed at Solemn Grove, N. C.

COMPANY H.

Geo. A. Shuman, Capt., Carroll.
Henry Fritz, Centre.

James P. Cromleigh, Duncannon.

COMPANY I.

Henry K. Myers, First Lieut., Newport.

COMPANY M.

Shottsberger, M., Greenwood.
Shottsberger, Jesse, Greenwood.

Webster, Edmund, Greenwood.

REGIMENTAL OFFICERS FROM PERRY, NINETY-SECOND REGIMENT.

Roswell M. Russell, Lieut. Col., Bloomfield.

Griffith Jones, Major, Duncannon.
Thomas Foose, C. S., Duncannon.

THREE-YEAR SERVICE—104TH REGIMENT, COMPANY F.

Perry County had Company F in the 104th Regiment, organized in November, '61. It participated in the actions at Fair Oaks, Allen's Farm, Peninsula, Malvern Hill, and Harrison's Landing. The regiment also participated in the attack in front of Petersburg, Virginia. The roll of Company F:

Joel F. Fredericks, Capt., Bloomfield.
David C. Orris, Saville.
Wm. Flickinger, Madison.
Wm. E. Baker, Saville.
Richard P. Hench, Saville.
William A. Boden, Saville.
William C. Marshall, Howe.
A. J. Kochenderfer, Saville.
Solomon E. Bower, Saville.
Irvin Kerr, Tuscarora.
William Jacobs, Tuscarora.
Henry B. Hoffman, Greenwood.
Martin L. Liggett, Saville.
John E. Miller, Juniata.

Privates:

Briner, John H., Tyrone.
Baker, John T., Saville.
Bender, Benj. F., Saville.
Blain, George W., Juniata.
Chamberlain, L.
Coller, Andrew, Saville.
Crawford, Andrew, Millerstown.
Ernest, David, Millerstown.
Flickinger. J. R., Saville.
Flickinger, Geo. W., Saville.
Flickinger, J. W., Saville.

Fritz, George W., Centre.
Fry, James, Tuscarora.
Flickinger, H. W., Juniata.
Gallatin, Albert, Bloomfield.
Ickes, John, Saville.
Jacobs, Henry S., Tuscarora.
Kepner, James, Tuscarora.
Kepner, Robert M., Tuscarora.
Kerr, Ephraim, Tuscarora.
Kline, Jacob.
Kochenderfer, T. M., Saville.
Kline, George L., Duncannon.
Mickey, Augustus, Carroll.
Miller, Davidson.
Reeder, David, Spring.
Reisinger, Jacob, Saville.
Reisinger, Philip O., Saville.
Reisinger, Wm. H., Saville.
Rice, Absalom.
Rice, Benj.
Rice, Conrad S.
Shuman, Jacob B.
Simonton, Hamilton.
Swartz, Frederick N.
Trostle, Solomon.
Witmer, William W.
Zimmerman, O. P.

THREE-MONTH SERVICE—106TH REGIMENT, COMPANY C.

Monroe, John, Liverpool.   Mitchell, James, Liverpool.

THREE-MONTH SERVICE—107TH REGIMENT, COMPANY B.

This regiment was organized in March, '62, and contained a number of Perry County men. It participated in the actions at Cedar Mountain, Second Battle of Bull Run, South Mountain, Antietam, Fredericksburg, Chancellorsville, Gettysburg, and others. The roster of Company B's Perry County men:

David W. Wagner, Spring.   James R. McIlhenny, Bloomfield.
John Kozier, Saville.   Benjamin Keck, Spring.

All were minor officers. David W. Wagner was captured at the Weldon Railroad and died a prisoner at Salisbury, N. C. James R. McIlhenny was killed in the same action. John G. Frow, of Perry County, was the surgeon of this regiment.

NINE-MONTH SERVICE—133D REGIMENT, COMPANY G.

This regiment was organized during the summer of '62 at Camp Curtin, Harrisburg. It contained three companies from Perry County, Company G, commanded by Capt. F. B. Speakman, later promoted to the colonelcy; Company H, commanded by Capt. David L. Tressler, and Company I, commanded by Capt. Albert I. Demaree. In the attack on Fredericksburg the regiment lost over a hundred and fifty men. It also participated in Chancellorsville. It was mustered out the latter part of May, '63, the term of service having expired. Perry Countians who were field and staff officers were: F. B. Speakman, colonel; Edward C. Bender, adjutant, killed at Chancellorsville, and Robert M. Messimer, sergeant major. Company G's roster:

F. B. Speakman, Capt., Bloomfield.   Beaver, Solomon, Saville.
Wm. H. Sheibley, Capt., Landis-   Bumbaugh, Wm.
burg.   Beichler, Peter, Toboyne.
Joel F. Fredericks, Bloomfield.   Bender, Edward C., Bloomfield.
James B. Eby, Bloomfield.   Baxter, Solomon, Spring.
David C. Orris, Saville.   Collins, Michael.
Wm. L. Spanogle, Saville.   Clouser, Thomas.
George B. Roddy, Landisburg.   Clouser, Wm.
William A. Boden, Saville.   Dernbaugh, Lewis.
John Jones, Juniata.   Flickinger, Jacob R., Madison.
Jere. J. Billow, Bloomfield.   Flickinger, Geo., Madison.
John N. Belford, Bloomfield.   Fry, David, Greenwood.
John S. Wetzell, Spring.   Finley, Chas.
Samuel Baker, Saville.   Gussler, Wm. H., Centre.
Jonas F. Bistline.   Heckman, Albert J.
James L. Moore, Centre.   Hohenshildt, D. B., Madison.
Daniel L. Smith, Centre.   Holman, Abraham, Greenwood.
Isaac B. Trostle, Centre.   Hench, Richard, Saville.
F. A. Campbell, Centre.   Hayner, Henry C.
Wm. Flickinger, Centre.   Hostetter, Jacob C.
F. M. Witherow, Centre.   Heim, George, Tyrone.
Chas. C. Hackett, Bloomfield.   Hartman, Joseph.
                                            Jacobs, Wm., Newport.
           Privates: Kough, Wm., Juniata.
                                            Kell, Philip, Tyrone.
Anderson, Thomas, Jackson.   Kistler, David S., Sandy Hill.
Baughman, Isaac, Tuscarora.   Lupfer, Wm., Bloomfield.
Baker, John, Tuscarora.   Lupfer, George, Centre.
Bucher, Adam, Tuscarora.   Liddick, Jacob L., Buffalo.
Brown, Samuel, Tuscarora.   Miller, Wm., Howe.
Beaver, John, Jr., Centre.   Morrow, Robert, Tyrone.
Beaver, Jacob, Centre.

Messimer, Geo. W., Bloomfield.
Miller, Wm. K.
Miller, Davidson.
Markel, Jacob, Juniata.
Mehaffie, Wm., Saville.
Morrow, James S., Tyrone.
Mathers, James, Saville.
Miller, Jacob, Juniata.
McKee, James S., Bloomfield.
Noll, Moses F., Centre.
Neilson, James G., Centre.
Orris, Eli, Saville.
Powell, Hanford, Tuscarora.
Reiber, Geo. W., Tuscarora.
Robinson, David E., Tuscarora.

Rhinesmith, Jacob, Toboyne.
Rhule, Jacob, Toboyne.
Smith, William, Tuscarora.
Sweger, Nicholas, Centre.
Smeigh, John.
Shatto, Wm.
Shearer, Henry C., Tyrone.
Shreffler, Henry, Tyrone.
Sutch, Wm. M., Bloomfield.
Spanogle, Abram.
Topley, Lemuel, Bloomfield.
Toomey, Henry A., Juniata.
Woods, James E., Jackson.
Witherow, John M., Centre.
Zeigler, Reuben.

James Mathers and Jacob Miller were killed at Fredericksburg. Many others were wounded there.

COMPANY H.

David L. Tressler, Capt., Tyrone.
Henry Keck, Spring.
Hiram A. Slighter, Spring.
Augustus McKenzie.
John Rynard.
George Tressler, Tyrone.
Robert A. Murray, Landisburg.
Peter Lightner, Tyrone.
Samuel H. Rice, Tyrone.
William Power, Tyrone.
Lewis Sweger, Centre.
J. A. Raudenbaugh, Centre.
Jacob Rowe, Madison.
John A. Boyer, Newport.
Gardner C. Palm, Tyrone.
Josiah E. Tressler, Tyrone.
Levi Steinberger, Tyrone.
Robert M. Messimer, Bloomfield.
Lemuel T. Sutch, Bloomfield.
John S. Kistler, Sandy Hill.

Privates:

Albright, John, Newport.
Bear, Henry, Spring.
Bergstresser, Jacob, Carroll.
Bergstresser, J. W., Carroll.
Baltozer, Benj., Jackson.
Bryner, John H., Tyrone.
Bryner, Geo. W., Tyrone.
Briggs, Samuel, Carroll.
Baker, A. J., Jackson.
Calhoun, Wm. F., Saville.
Craig, Joseph, Centre.
Clouser, Joseph W., Centre.
Campbell, John W., Juniata.
Chestnut, Anderson.
Clellan, Allen, Spring.
Clouser, Simon W., Centre.
Dumm, Wm. R., Spring.
Dromgold, Michael, Saville.
Elder, David P., Newport.

Harris, James C., Saville.
Hutchison, Wm., Tuscarora.
Jumper, George, Centre.
Keck, Solomon.
Kepner, Erasmus D., Saville.
Lightner, David P.
Mehaffie, Amos, Saville.
Mehaffie, John S., Saville.
Mehaffie, David, Saville.
Minich, Wm. H., Tyrone.
Messimer, W. D., Bloomfield.
March, Jesse, Bloomfield.
Milligan, Thos. H., Newport.
Morrison, Emanuel, Toboyne.
Minich, Henry, Tyrone.
McKee, William A., Bloomfield.
McIlhenny, James, Bloomfield.
McCaskey, Fred, Saville.
Neely, David.
Owen, Isaiah P.
Pennell, Geo., Wheatfield.
Rice, Samuel, Jr.
Riggleman, George W.
Rhodes, Samuel, Carroll.
Rhea, Wm. M., Toboyne.
Robinson, Samuel, Toboyne.
Reed, John A., Jackson.
Scheaffer, John B., Jackson.
Smith, Samuel B., Juniata.
Smith, Josiah R., Juniata.
Sowers, Emanuel, Tyrone.
Stuckey, John J., Newport.
Stump, John K.
Swartz, Francis W.
Stutsman, Jacob B., Juniata.
Van Camp, J. E., Miller.
Van Dyke, James.
Weller, John C., Tyrone.
Witmer, Joel W., Saville.
Wagner, David T., Spring.
Yohn, James, Tuscarora.
Zeigler, John A., Sandy Hill.

Quite a number from this company were wounded at Fredericksburg.

COMPANY I.

Albert B. Demaree, Capt., Newport.
Hiram Fertig, Millerstown.
Samuel R. Deach, Millerstown.
William A. Zinn, Newport.
George S. DeBray, Millerstown.
Levi Attig, Millerstown.
Joseph R. Tate, Newport.
Jacob B. Wilson, Greenwood.
Frank Thomas, Centre.
J. Fetter Kerr, Tuscarora.
S. P. McClenegan, Millerstown.
Joseph S. Bucher, Tuscarora.
Wm. Howanstine, Tuscarora.
David Snyder, Millerstown.
William S. Linn, Tuscarora.
Jefferson Franklin, Newport.
John Beasom, Greenwood.
Benj. M. Eby, Toboyne.
William Stahl, Millerstown.
Mahlon T. Bretz, Newport.
David H. Scott, Millerstown.
Geo. S. Goodman, Millerstown.

Privates:

Attig, Henry H., Millerstown.
Attig, Peter, Millerstown.
Bender, Cloyd C., Greenwood.
Beasom, Lewis, Greenwood.
Beaumont, J. L. S., Liverpool.
Boyer, Samuel K., Watts.
Butz, John C., Newport.
Boyer, Jacob K., Millerstown.
Beatty, Robert T., Newport.
Brown, Alex. M., Tuscarora.
Bistline, David, Toboyne.
Bretz, John C., Howe.
Clouser, Wm. H., Juniata.
Cox, William H., Howe.
Cox, Joseph, Howe.
Carwell, Jere. M., Greenwood.
Clouser, Isaiah, Bloomfield.
Campbell, S. P., Tuscarora.
Diffenderfer, Amos, Millerstown.
Duncan, Joseph, Newport.
Etter, Eli, Newport.
Freeburn, Jesse, Newport.
Freeland, James, Howe.
Foreman, Joseph, Newport.
Frank, Lewis, Howe.

Gable, Samuel K., Millerstown.
Gingrich, Augustus, Tuscarora.
Gunderman, D. W., Howe.
Howell, Theophilus, Newport.
Harman, Wm. H., Greenwood.
Huggins, Geo. W., Buffalo.
Horting, Henry C., Howe.
Hughes, Stephen A., Newport.
Holtzapple, Michael, Millerstown.
Hopple, William, Newport.
Howanstine, And. J., Tuscarora.
Hain, Frederick, Howe.
Jacobs, Wm. S., Tuscarora.
Jacobs, James, Tuscarora.
Kipp, Peter, Newport.
Keely, Isaac, Newport.
Leas, Samuel R., Juniata.
Linn, John J., Tuscarora.
Lahr, Jerome B., Greenwood.
Liddick, Daniel, Howe.
Lightner, Scott W., Madison.
Loughman, Wm. H., Greenwood.
Mitchell, Joseph B., Greenwood.
Myers, George K., Millerstown.
Noll, Martin, Millerstown.
Omer, Joseph, Millerstown.
Rider, Josiah, Oliver.
Reiber, James, Spring.
Risher, Wm., Greenwood.
Shottsberger, Michael, Greenwood.
Shell, John, Millerstown.
Shade, Wm. H., Greenwood.
Sheaffer, W. M. D.
Smith, Josephus W.
Tschopp, A., Greenwood.
Tschopp, Cyrus, Greenwood.
Toland, John M., Penn.
Umholtz, W. H. W.
Van Newkirk, C. L., Penn.
Wright, James A., Greenwood.
Wagner, Joseph, Liverpool.
Watts, Samuel T., Juniata.
Wertz, William, Newport.
Williams, Stephen, Newport.
Whitekettle, Andrew, Juniata.
Yohe, John.
Yohn, Henry L.
Zimmerman, O. P., Tuscarora.

David Bistline and Joseph Duncan were killed at Fredericksburg. Many were wounded at both Fredericksburg and Chancellorsville.

CHAPLAIN, A PERRY COUNTIAN—140TH REGIMENT.

Rev. J. Linn Milligan, a sketch of whom appears elsewhere in this volume, was the chaplain of the 140th Regiment.

THREE-MONTH TERM—149TH REGIMENT, SOME PERRY COUNTIANS.

Patterned after the original Bucktail Regiment, the 149th wore "bucktails" as an insignia. It was organized in 1862 and was ordered to the front very suddenly to help repel the Confederate invasion. When the enemy retreated from Antietam the regiment was ordered to join Burnside's Army on the Rappahannock. It participated in the actions at Chancellorsville, at the very beginning and all through Gettysburg's three days, losing 205 killed and wounded and 131 missing—most of whom were dead or captured; also at the Wilderness, Laurel Hill, Spottsylvania, Bethesda Church, Petersburg, the Weldon Railroad, and a number of others. The Perry Countians:

Francis B. Jones, Capt., Duncannon.
John T. Miller, Duncannon.
John J. Boyer, Newport.
John Graham, Liverpool T.
John Morris, Penn.
Jacob A. Young, Penn.
Thomas B. Jones, Penn.
Thomas J. Evans, Duncannon.

Privates:

Coulter, David W., Greenwood.
Charles, Simon B., Liverpool T.

Clemson, W. E., Juniata.
Ehrhart, W. H., Tuscarora.
Jones, Joseph, Juniata.
Lefevre, D. P., Juniata.
Mutzebaugh, Daniel, Penn.
Miller, Alfred P.
Myers, O. G., Juniata.
Potter, Silas, Wheatfield.
Styles, Thomas, Rye.
Smee, John, Rye.
Sharp, Henry, Rye.

COLONEL A PERRY COUNTIAN—150TH REGIMENT.

This regiment was raised during the summer of '62 and mustered in at Camp Curtin. Its commander was Colonel Langhorne Wister, of Duncannon. It went into battle on the first day of July, '63, at Gettysburg. It lost many of its members there through being taken prisoner. The loss was 181 killed and wounded and seventy-two taken prisoners. It was in the actions at Laurel Hill, Spottsylvania, Bethesda Church, the Siege of Petersburg, the Weldon Railroad fight, as well as others.

CHAPLAIN A PERRY COUNTIAN—158TH REGIMENT.

The 158th Regiment had as their chaplain Rev. Daniel Hartman, of Duncannon, Perry County.

THREE-YEAR TERM—162D REGIMENT, COMPANY I.
(Seventeenth Pennsylvania Cavalry.)

The 162d Regiment of the Pennsylvania Line—ordinarily known as the Seventeenth Pennsylvania Cavalry—contained Company I, composed principally of Perry Countians. Capt. John B. McAllister, of Company I, upon the organization of the regiment, became its lieutenant colonel. It was recruited in the summer of '62, going to Washington November 25th. In the Chancellorsville campaign Companies C and I (the Perry Countians) were on escort duty with General Meade, and during the action their duty was the transmission of orders. At the commencement of the Battle of Gettysburg the division to which the Seventeenth Cavalry belonged held at bay the Confederates until the arrival of the First Corps. It later prevented flanking attacks. They were with General Sheridan during '64. General Devin's farewell order contained this beautiful tribute to the Seventeenth Cavalry: "In five successive campaigns, and in over three score engagements, you have nobly sustained your part. Of the many gallant regiments from your state, none has a brighter record, none has more freely shed its blood on every battlefield from Gettysburg to Appomattox." The roster of Company I:

Jno. B. McAllister, Capt., Bloomfield.
Andrew D. Vandling, Capt., Liverpool.
Isaac N. Grubb, Capt., Liverpool T.
Lewis W. Orwan, Centre.

George W. Orwan, Centre.
John M. Fry, Tuscarora.
William C. Long, Greenwood.
David R. Gussler, Centre.
Ephraim C. Long, Bloomfield.
David H. Lackey, Carroll.

Privates:

Arndt, John J., Liverpool.
Arndt, Abraham, Liverpool.
Brandt, Daniel, Greenwood.
Bitting, Henry, Liverpool T.
Black, George W., Bloomfield.
Berry, John, Bloomfield.
Bradley, Simeon, Liverpool.
Blain, Jasper, Bloomfield.
Best, William T., Bloomfield.
Cluck, Simon, Liverpool.
Campbell, James C., Bloomfield.
Drexler, Geo. S., Landisburg.
Drexler, John L., Landisburg.
Fry, John, Saville.
Fry, David, Saville.
Fry, William.
Foley, James, Liverpool.
Haas, Henry, Liverpool.
Hipple, Jeremiah, Bloomfield.
Henderson, Nathan, Bloomfield.
Kleckner, Daniel, Saville.
Kocher, Wm., Bloomfield.
Lamca, John, Greenwood.
Long, Jonas, Greenwood.
Long, Levi R., Greenwood.
Long, H. F., Saville.

Lesh, Wm. W., Juniata.
Meginness, ——, Bloomfield.
Maxwell, G. W.
Mengle, Thomas, Liverpool.
Paden, Andrew J., Saville.
Ritter, John, Liverpool.
Reed, Elias, Liverpool.
Rhoads, Amos, Liverpool.
Sharon, John, Liverpool.
Snyder, Silas, Liverpool.
Sweger, Levi, Liverpool.
Snyder, John J., Liverpool.
Scholl, Charles J., Sandy Hill.
Shafer, Edward, Juniata.
Smith, J. P., Juniata.
Stine, John, Juniata.
Swartz, John M., Bloomfield.
Stouffer, G. W., Carroll.
Stahl, Wm. C., Bloomfield.
Stouffer, John, Carroll.
Spriggle, Benj., Saville.
Swartz, Daniel, Bloomfield.
Sharon, Lawrence, Liverpool.
Vanaman, George, Greenwood.
Vanaman, Thomas, Greenwood.
Whitekettle, Chas., Juniata.
Wox, L. C., Marysville.
Wox, S. S., Carroll.

James C. Campbell was killed at White House, Virginia, and is buried in the National Cemetery at Yorktown, Virginia, in Section A. Daniel Brandt lost an arm at Opequan; Levi R. Long lost a leg at Falling Waters, being struck by a shell; Henry F. Long lost an arm at Cold Harbor, also being shot in the shoulder just previously. (Note: Mr. Long, now a retired Lutheran minister, is a near neighbor of the writer's.)

NINE-MONTH SERVICE—173D REGIMENT, COMPANY E.

During the fall of '62 the 173d Regiment of nine-month drafted men was organized at Camp Curtin, and in the latter part of November left for the field of action. During its entire time of service it did not get into any battles. Company E was from Perry County, its roster being:

Henry Charles, Capt., Buffalo.
Isaac D. Dunkle, Bloomfield.
Samuel Reen, Liverpool T.
S. Kirk Jacobs, Tuscarora.
Joseph Hammaker, Watts.
David P. Egolf, Tyrone.
Samuel R. P. Brady, Tyrone.
Henry M. Hoffman, Greenwood.
Simon S. Charles, Liverpool T.
Wm. Kipp, Greenwood.
Theodore O'Neil, Greenwood.
Robert Crane, Liverpool T.
Elias Clay, Centre.
Andrew Noye.
Jacob Potter, Buffalo.
Josiah Clay, Centre.
Alex. McConnel, Buffalo.
Julius Welner.

Privates:

Bressler, Charles, Oliver.
Brown, Christian.

Beasom, Henry, Greenwood.
Bealor, Wm. B., Greenwood.
Bair, Samuel, Buffalo.
Bucher, George, Tuscarora.
Baker, Abram, Greenwood.
Brenley, Benedict.
Beihl, Fred.
Bomisted, Joseph.
Brenley, Joseph.
Clemens, Peter, Greenwood.
Clemons, Geo. J., Greenwood.
Crater, Lewis.
Derr, Henry, Liverpool.
Ditman, Francis.
Dunkel, John.
Dressler, John.
Fortenbaugh, D. P.
Fry, Samuel, Greenwood.
Ferre, Cyrus.
Foulk, Philip.
Fisher, Ernest F.
Fleurie, Abram, Oliver.

Gougler, Absalom.
Gohn, Samuel.
Garnett, Andrew, New Buffalo.
Goudy, John.
Geiger, Philip.
Geiger, Jacob.
Hunter, Robert, Buffalo.
Hair, Joseph.
Hipple, John, Carroll.
Heckard, Lewis F., Liverpool T.
Hammer, Henry.
Heinsman, Daniel.
Jones, Theodore.
Jones, Ezekiel, Greenwood.
Jones, William.
Kinzer, William, Oliver.
Killinger, John, Greenwood.
Krumbaugh, Charles.
Leiby, Samuel, Oliver.
Liddick, Wm., Buffalo.
Long, John, Greenwood.
Lear, William.
Liddick, Samuel, Buffalo.
Lightner, Samuel.
Langan, Mathias.
Myers, William A., Centre.
Miller, Charles S.
Miller, Jacob.
McClintock, Benj.
Naher, Charles.

Parson, William, Watts.
Powell, Lewis, Tuscarora.
Propping, Fernando.
Percher, Jacob.
Pilger, Charles.
Roush, David, Greenwood.
Reed, Jacob.
Reisinger, Lewis, Liverpool.
Smiley, Henderson, Carroll.
Shearer, William, Duncannon.
Sweger, David, Centre.
Saucerman, Wm.
Scandling, Jacob.
Smith, Daniel, Juniata.
Stoner, Emanuel.
Shearer, John D., Duncannon.
Scott, John, Juniata.
Sheaffer, Reuben.
Sheaffer, Daniel F., Liverpool T.
Smith, Jonas, Juniata.
Smith, William, Juniata.
Smith, Jacob.
Trostle, Solomon.
Tobias, Reuben.
Ulsh, Joseph, Greenwood.
Williams, Wm.
Womelsdorf, George.
Warner, Samuel, Centre.
Young, Reuben.

THREE-YEAR SERVICE—187TH REGIMENT, QUOTA IN COMPANIES D AND K

The 187th Regiment contained contingents of soldiers from Perry County, in Companies D and K. Those of Company D were:

Henry H. Peck.
Henry H. Shearer, Tyrone.
Alexander Kennedy, Tyrone.
David Morrison.

Privates:

Allen, George N.
Burtnett, Wm. H., Landisburg.
Gensler, Peter.
Gensler, John F.
Gensler, Wm. P.
Kiner, William J., Tyrone.

Kennedy, Nathaniel, Tyrone.
Keck, Aaron, Tyrone.
Kiner, John I., Tyrone.
Morrison, Wm. T.
Nonemaker, Henry.
Sheaffer, Joseph.
Sheaffer, Wellington.
Shannafelser, Michael.
Sheriff, David.
Toomey, Henry.
Umholtz, Wm. W., Tyrone.
Warner, John.

COMPANY K.

Baltozer, Z. T.
Rhoads, Cornelius, Newport.

Minich, John W.
Sweger, Nicholas.

William P. Gensler was killed in front of Petersburg, Virginia, during the battle, and Henry Toomey was killed at the Weldon Railroad action and sleeps in the Poplar Grove National Cemetery in Virginia.

ONE-YEAR SERVICE—201ST REGIMENT.

The 201st Regiment was raised during the summer of '64 and organized at Camp Curtin, August 29th, under the command of Col. F. Asbury Awl. It contained a quota of Perry Countians recruited at Duncannon and vicinity. This regiment was broken up to detail the various companies at different points on provost duty, hospital duty, and as guards.

ONE-YEAR SERVICE—208TH REGIMENT, COMPANIES E, F, G, AND I.

The 208th Regiment included four companies, E. F. G., and I, of Perry Countians. It was organized at Camp Curtin, September 12, '64, and left Harrisburg the next day. It was assigned to the Army of the Potomac and during the winter was under fire at various times. After the Confederates captured Fort Steadman this regiment was engaged with the Federal troops in its recovery, losing forty-two killed and wounded, and taking 300 prisoners. It was engaged in the final assault on Petersburg.

COMPANY E.

F. M. McKeehan, Capt., Centre.
John T. Mehaffie, Saville.
Ephraim B. Wise, Juniata.
Joseph W. Gantt, Centre.
Joshua E. Van Camp, Miller.
David R. P. Bealor, Juniata.
William R. Dumm, Spring.
Daniel W. Lutman, Centre.
Darlintgon, Meredith, Centre.
John Raffensperger, Juniata.
William Dumm, Spring.
Joseph S. Wagner, Spring.
Samuel I. Shortess.
Wm. S. Mehaffie, Saville.
George Ramper, Saville.
Peter S. Albert, Juniata.
Harris A. Rohrabach.
Henry A. Albright.
David Adams.

Privates:

Albright, George.
Bitner, John, Carroll.
Bistline, George, Jackson.
Baker, John S.
Barrack, Fred'k, Tuscarora.
Bupp, John, Newport.
Burd, Ephraim, Juniata.
Burkpile, Jacob B., Centre.
Bryner, George M., Tyrone.
Best, William.
Barrack, Andrew J., Tuscarora.
Blain, Jasper, Juniata.
Billman, Daniel.
Boston, Thomas.
Clouser, Simon W., Centre.
Clemens, Adam, Greenwood.
Dehaven, Wm. H., Liverpool T.
Dice, John.
Davis, George E.
Foose, Jacob, Spring.
Foose, Isaiah C., Spring.
Foose, Frank, Spring.
Foose, Henry D., Spring.
Ferris, Henry.
Gantt, Isaiah M., Centre.
Garlin, John S., Madison.
Gregg, John.
High, Jacob.
Hirt, Joseph.
Heckart, Joseph.

Jackson, William.
Jacobs, Charles.
Jones, Thomas.
Kocher, George, Tyrone.
Kell, John W., Tyrone.
Kepner, William T., Saville.
Klinepeter, Darius I., Centre.
Kacy, William H., Spring.
Kennedy, William M., Tyrone.
Kinsloe, Edmund B., Centre.
Keilholtz, George.
Loy, John C., Jackson.
Lupfer, William.
Long, Robert W.
Martin, Samuel A.
Mercer, Manoah.
Miller, Jonathan, Centre.
Moore, James L., Centre.
Markle, Levi, Centre.
Markle, Robert, Centre.
Mickey, James, Carroll.
Magee, Richard, Carroll.
Mercer, John.
Mace, John.
Meginly, James L.
McCabe, Joseph P.
Nichols, Charles.
Power, William, Centre.
Persing, Wm. A. H.
Perry, William H.
Reamer, George W., Juniata.
Reapsome, John.
Ricedorff, Henry.
Rank, Harvey.
Robinson, William.
Snyder, Christian, Jackson.
Sullenberger, T. M., Jackson.
Shatto, Peter.
Swartz, Franklin, Jackson.
Spriggle, Jacob.
Shadel, Daniel.
Snyder, George.
Surrell, Robert.
Snyder, Henry.
Toomey, Jerome, Juniata.
Tressler, David P., Centre.
Turnbaugh, Jacob, Juniata.
Wertz, Daniel.
Warren, John S.
Zeigler, John.

George Rampfer, Henry D. Foose, and William H. Perry were killed at Petersburg, and Joseph Heckart, near the Appomattox River.

COMPANY F.

Gard C. Palm, Capt., Tyrone.
Henry Sheaffer, Toboyne.
Francis A. Campbell, Toboyne.
Thomas J. Sowers, Tyrone.
Martin H. Furman, Jackson.
Robert H. Campbell, Toboyne.
William Berrier, Jackson.
Hugh Smith.
Henry A. Wade.
Samuel G. Smith.
George Bistline, Madison.
George W. Reiber, Spring.
James Meminger, Saville.
John K. Stump, Tyrone.
John A. Newcomer, Tyrone.
David T. Ritter, Tyrone.
Samuel S. McKee, Madison.
Frederick Shull, Saville.
John A. Ettinger.
George H. Hahn, Jackson.

Privates:

Adams, Thomas A., Toboyne.
Armstrong, Wm. H., Newport.
Blackburn, Robert A., Toboyne.
Brickley, David B.
Burkel, Gottleib.
Bistline, Solomon, Madison.
Berrier, Thomas, Jackson.
Baltozer, Sylvester K.
Bender, Jacob R., Greenwood.
Bernheisel, S. W., Madison.
Berrier, Peter, Jackson.
Berrier, Henry, Jackson.
Bistline, Joseph, Madison.
Baltozer, William.
Bryner, John H., Tyrone.
Bryner, George S., Tyrone.
Collins, Joseph C.
Connor, Barnard A.
Daum, Fred.
Dillman, Reuben, Saville.
Droneberger, G. W.
Delancy, John, Juniata.
Ernest, Daniel, Madison.
English, James, Saville.
Emory, George.
Foose, James, Spring.
Finley, James A.
Fritz, Jacob, Centre.
Getz, John.
Gutshall, Jacob.
Garland, William, Madison.

Garber, William H., Madison.
Hoffman, Michael, Centre.
Hoffman, David, Centre.
Hull, William A.
Hollenbaugh, D. A., Madison.
Hollenbaugh, W. C., Madison.
Hohenshildt, A.T., Madison.
Henry, Daniel S., Madison.
Hench, John B., Madison.
Johnston, Samuel A., Toboyne.
Kistler, Lloyd K., Sandy Hill.
Kern, Simon, Jackson.
Kline, Charles W., Penn.
Lowe, Jacob S., Newport.
Morrow, Samuel R., Tyrone.
Messimer, Thomas, Jackson.
Mumper, Andrew J., Jackson.
Morrison, Wm. A., Toboyne.
Mathers, John H.
McElheney, Philip.
McElheney, S. W.
Peckard, Jonathan.
Rinesmith, Samuel, Jackson.
Reed, Robert.
Rhea, James D., Toboyne.
Reeder, William T.
Reeder, John.
Shaffer, Samuel F., Spring.
Shoff, George, Centre.
Sheibley, William, Spring.
Sheibley, George, Spring.
Shearer, Andrew, Jackson.
Smith, Samuel G., Blain.
Seager, William H., Jackson.
Swales, John.
Shumaker, Benj. F., Jackson.
Stroup, William, Madison.
Saylor, David E.
Shearer, Jacob, Saville.
Seibert, William D.
Shreffler, Andrew B., Toboyne.
Shope, Elias.
Shope, Henry.
Shields, Charles S.
Snyder, John G., Jackson.
Seager, Wm. H. R., Jackson.
Titzel, John H., Spring.
Waggoner, Henry, Madison.
Welsh, Samuel.
Wentzel, S.
Wilt, Daniel.
Walker, George E.
Zeigler, Philip.

Frederick Shull, of this company, was killed at Fort Steadman.

COMPANY G.

Benj. F. Miller, Capt., Newport.
William A. Zinn, Newport.
Wm. Fosselman, Juniata.

Lewis Beasom, Greenwood.
William A. Blain, Tuscarora.
Wm. S. Hostetter, Centre.

Thomas J. Latchford, Juniata.
Jere J. Billow, Carroll.
Nicholas Hogentogler. Greenwood.
D. B. Hohenshildt, Madison.
Isaiah W. Clouser, Centre.
Joseph S. Bucher, Tuscarora.
John B. Swartz, Saville.
L. H. C. Flickinger, Juniata.
Findley Rogers.
Daniel W. Gantt, Newport.
A. Worley Monroe, Liverpool.
John Howell, Greenwood.

Privates:

Acaley, John, Greenwood.
Arndt, Valentine, Liverpool T.
Byrem, Sylvester, Millerstown.
Baker, Peter S., Tuscarora.
Burrell, George W., Saville.
Bucher, Adam, Tuscarora.
Barnhart, Benj. F., Watts.
Clouser, William H.
Clouser, Cyrus S.
Clouser, Calvin H.
Charles, Henry C., Buffalo.
Cox, John H.
Comp, George L., Juniata.
Comp, Jacob S., Liverpool.
Dunn, Edward T. P.
Deitrick, Wesley, Liverpool.
Duffield, Samuel.
Fleck, Alex. M., Newport.
Fair, John.
Ferguson, Jesse M., Centre.
Flickinger, Wm. H., Juniata.
Fosselman, John, Juniata.
Fisher, Christopher.
Gardner, Ephraim F., Miller.
Gutshall, John.
Gantt, Watson I., Newport.
Hain, Isaac, Howe.
Hain, Jacob S., Howe.
Haines, Wendell.
Hoffman, Jacob.
Heinbach, William, Greenwood.
Hain, David W., Howe.
Johnson, William T.
Kochenderfer, J. B.

Kerlin, Peter.
Klinepeter, Jacob.
Kleffman, John I., Greenwood.
Lesh, John, Juniata.
Lesh, Baltzer, Juniata.
Long. Jacob M., Millerstown.
Latchford, James P., Tuscarora.
Maginnis, Samuel.
Mogel. Jacob.
Meredith, Henry C.
Myers, Daniel, Jr.
Miller, Shuman, Millerstown.
Miller, John, Millerstown.
Miller, Samuel G.
McLaughlin, Jacob.
Nace, Jesse S., Rye.
Newman, William.
Nipple, George F., Greenwood.
Nipple, James C., Greenwood.
Orner, Martin V., Greenwood.
Powell, Lewis W., Tuscarora.
Page, Adam J.
Price, Charles N.
Peterman, George.
Reeder, Thomas A., Centre.
Reichenbaugh, W. C.
Roush, Justice.
Rohm, Frank, Centre.
Reigle, William J., Greenwood.
Rider, Jacob R., Newport.
Sheaffer, Edward G.
Spahr, George A.
Sweger. George, Carroll.
Smith, John M.
Smith, Andrew C.
Smith, Abraham S.
Shoop, Christian, Buffalo.
Tschopp, Isaac, Greenwood.
Trego. George.
Troup, William H., Oliver.
Watts, Frederick.
Wright, John B., Greenwood.
Wrey, Daniel D.
Witherow, Samuel S., Centre.
Wagner, John W., Spring.
Weaver, Jonathan.
Weise, George W., Newport.
Yohn, David.

George W. Weise, of this company, was killed at Fort Steadman, Virginia.

COMPANY I.

Jas. H. Marshall. Capt., Bloomfield.
Isaac D. Dunkle, Bloomfield.
John D. Neilson, Bloomfield.
George K. Scholl, Liverpool.
John J. Monroe, Liverpool.
Samuel Keen.
Edwin D. Owen, Liverpool.
John F. Ayle, Centre.
Theodore Jones.
Abraham Kitner, Carroll.
Frank W. Gibson, Spring.

Benjamin Shaffer, Spring.
Rufus Potter, Buffalo.
Jacob Seiler, Buffalo.
Samuel Landis.
Henry F. Sweger, Centre.
Jacob P. Kerlin.
Vincent M. Gallen.

Privates:

Albright, Samuel, Buffalo.
Bruner, Owen, Wheatfield.

Behel, Samuel.
Bair, Samuel W., Buffalo.
Bair, Jeremiah, Buffalo.
Bair, Samuel W., II, Buffalo.
Bruner, Wm. H., Centre.
Bruner, George W., Penn.
Bair, Peter, Buffalo.
Clegg, James, Centre.
Clouser, John A., Bloomfield.
Clouser, Cornelius, Bloomfield.
Cless, Daniel, Bloomfield.
Clouser, Andrew J., Bloomfield.
Clouser, Simon S., Centre.
Carl, Abraham, Saville.
Duke, William, Juniata.
Dehiser, Wm. J., Juniata.
Derr, John T., Liverpool.
Dressler, George, Landisburg.
Dressler, Edward, Landisburg.
Dile, Abraham.
Donaldson, Wm. H.
Fetrow, Elias L., Bloomfield.
Gibney, James, Carroll.
Garlin, Abraham, Saville.
Gibney, Patrick.
Gohn, Samuel.
Gurdom, Ernest.
Grubb, Josiah, Liverpool.
Holmes, Benj.
Hench, John W., Madison.
Hunter, Levi, Liverpool.
Hilbert, Daniel, Buffalo.
Haines, Samuel.
Hammaker, Geo.
Hain, Jacob, Buffalo.
Hull, Jacob.
Hilbish, John A., Buffalo.
Howe, Abraham E., Buffalo.
Hunter, Robert, Buffalo.
Inch, William, Liverpool.
Kepperly, Samuel.

Kumler, William, New Buffalo.
Lickel, Christian.
Lenhart, George S., Liverpool.
Liddick, Samuel, Buffalo.
Lackey, William A., Carroll.
Miller, John H.
Miller, Joseph W.
Marshall, Henry, Howe.
Morris, William.
Motter, John P.
Motter, Daniel W.
Myers, George W.
Motter, John N.
Meck, Jacob B., Liverpool T.
McKenzie, William, Centre.
Potter, John, Buffalo.
Rice, John, Bloomfield.
Reubendall, Reuben, Buffalo.
Ritter, John L.
Ready, Joseph.
Swartz, George W., Watts.
Small, Benj. W.
Smith, Israel W.
Shortess, Alex., Juniata.
Sweger, Henry M.
Shearer, John.
Souder, George W., Spring.
Stoner, Emanuel.
Shaffer, John.
Shaffer, Daniel T.
Silks, John W., Buffalo.
Silks, John, Buffalo.
Shottsberger, John, Greenwood.
Shottsberger, Samuel, Greenwood.
Shottsberger, Henry, Greenwood.
Shoop, Noah, Watts.
Skivington, Isaiah, Bloomfield.
Spotts, Henry H.
Troutman, Emanuel, Greenwood.
Williams, William.
Zeigler, John A.

During 1862 and 1863 emergency troops and militia regiments were called to the colors to help repel the invasion of the Confederates into the North. Very many of these men had previously seen service during the war, in other units. The Sixth Regiment, called for that purpose, contained two companies partly from Perry County, D and E.

The Thirty-Sixth Regiment of ninety-day militia in '63 contained Companies B and I, partly from Perry County.

COMPANY D, FIRST BATTALION, 100-DAY MEN.

D. C. Orris, 1st Lieut., Saville.
George Flickinger, Saville.
And. J. Kochenderfer, Saville.

Privates:

Bender, Henry O., Saville.
Bender, Benj. F., Saville.
Flickinger, H. W., Saville.
Flickinger, Martin, Saville.
Graham, William H., Saville.

Gutshall, David, Saville.
Jacobs, Henry S., Saville.
Kerr, Irvin, Tuscarora.
Long, Peter, Saville.
Odell, William T., Tyrone.
Odell, John A., Tyrone.
Rice, David M., Saville.
Stambaugh, Wm. P., Saville.
Stambaugh, John A., Tyrone.

COMPANY E, SECOND BATTALION, 100-DAY MEN.

Joel F. Fredericks, Capt., Bloomfield.
John Jones, Juniata.
Samuel Briggs, Carroll.
George S. Lackey, Carroll.
Isaac B. Trostle.
James P. Laird, Bloomfield.
Israel Bair, Buffalo.
James E. Woods, Jackson.
Wilson D. Messimer, Bloomfield.
Carson S. Gotwalt, Bloomfield.
Charles B. Heinbach.

Privates:

Adams, John C., Tyrone.
Demaree, David R., Newport.
Dumm, David T., Spring.
Eby, Henry B., Toboyne.
Frank, John, Newport.
Grosh, A. Blain, Jackson.

Gibbons, Anthony, Spring.
Hollenbaugh, D. H., Madison.
Hench, Alex. M., Madison.
Hohenshildt, D. M., Madison.
Hoffman, Aaron, Madison.
Kochenderfer, Geo., Saville.
Miller, John.
Mickey, Silas H., Carroll.
Lightner, Andrew.
Musser, Isaiah D., Newport.
Murray, Charles, Bloomfield.
Musser, John S., Newport.
Noll, Samuel, Spring.
Noll, John M., Spring.
Rice, Benj., Spring.
Sheibley, Wm. W., Madison.
Sheibley, Wm. F., Madison.
Smith, David R., Spring.
Shuler, Philip, Jackson.
Waggoner, Alfred, Spring.

ONE-YEAR SERVICE—COMPANY A, FORTY-NINTH REGIMENT.

J. W. Eshelman, Corporal, Liverpool.

Privates:

Beigh, John R., Liverpool.
Bowers, John H., Liverpool T.
Brink, Bradford, Liverpool.
Brink, William, Liverpool.
Charles, Ira, Buffalo.
Dudley, John C., Liverpool.
Deitrick, Jacob R., Liverpool.
Funk, James, Liverpool.
Holman, Jacob, Liverpool.
Hamilton, Levi W., Liverpool.
Hunter, Isaiah, Liverpool.
Inhoff, Benj. H., Liverpool T.
Keiser, Jacob, Liverpool.
Knight, Cyrus, Liverpool T.
Kline, Jonas, Liverpool T.
Lebkickler, Joseph, Liverpool T.

Lebkickler, Geo. W., Liverpool T.
Long, William, Liverpool T.
Lutz, Isaac, Liverpool.
McLaughlin, G., Liverpool.
O'Neil, Jeremiah, Liverpool.
Reifsnyder, Lewis C., Liverpool.
Ritter, Wm. R., Liverpool.
Roush, Daniel, Liverpool.
Shull, Henry, Liverpool.
Snyder, Chas. C., Liverpool.
Sponenberger, Foster, Liverpool.
Sponenberger, Fred, Liverpool.
Shuman, Michael, Liverpool.
Sheesly, Geo., Liverpool.
Williamson, Cyrus, Liverpool.
Williamson, Ramsey, Liverpool.
Weirick, Henry H., Liverpool.
Zaring, John W., Liverpool.
Zeigler, Alfred C., Liverpool T.

This company was mustered in early in March, '65, and was mustered out on June 28, '65, their term of service being less than three months.

EIGHTY-THIRD REGIMENT, COMPANY I.

The following Perry Countians were enrolled at Harrisburg, in Company I, Eighty-Third Regiment, Pennsylvania Volunteer Infantry, during February, 1865, serving until the close of the war. They were mustered out in June, 1865.

John S. Campbell, Sgt., Newport.
Privates:
Gardner, James T., Newport.

Gantt, John C., Newport.
Hay, Thomas, Newport.
Woods, Samuel W., Newport.

PENNSYLVANIA INFANTRY, TWENTY-SIXTH REGIMENT, COMPANY C.

The late Geo. W. Campbell and Andrew J. Fickes were members of Company C, Pennsylvania Emergency Troops.

Other Soldiers.

Names not contained in any of the units, but known to be Perry County soldiers, are Benjamin Culler, Saville; Jacob Kleckner, who lost his right arm at Gettysburg; David Graham, killed in action; Frank Hench, killed at Gettysburg.

It is to be regretted that the home districts of the soldiers are not available, as official records never carried them, which accounts for the absence, no doubt, of many brave and good men who were in the service of their country. As previously stated, some of the names here mentioned are not Perry Countians, but where the unit was practically all from Perry, their names are included, in order to keep the rosters of such companies intact.

Even so great a Southerner as Henry Watterson, probably the greatest of all American editors, and long editor of the *Louisville Courier-Journal,* in his autobiography published in 1919, tells how he was swept into the army of secession, probably just as were hundreds of others. It follows:

"I could not wholly believe with either extreme. I had perpetrated no wrong, but in my small way had done my best for the Union and against secession. I would go back to my books and my literary ambitions and let the storm blow over. It could not last very long; the odds against the South were too great. Vain hope! As well expect a chip on the surface of the ocean to lie quiet as a lad of twenty-one in those days to keep out of one or the other camp. On reaching home I found myself alone. The boys were all gone to the front. The girls were—well, they were all crazy. My native country was about to be invaded. Propinquity. Sympathy. So, casting opinion to the winds, in I went on feeling. And that is how I became a rebel, a case of 'first endure and then embrace,' because I soon got to be a pretty good rebel and went the limit, changing my coat as it were, though not my better judgment, for with a gray jacket on my back and ready to do or die, I retained my belief that secession was treason, that disunion was the height of folly, and that the South was bound to go down in the unequal strife."

Along with Watterson there is in the Southland to-day an element and an overpowering one, who, with the North and West, are a unison in the sentiment expressed by the song:

> "Sail on, O Union, strong and great!
> Humanity with all its fears,
> With all its hopes of future years,
> Is hanging breathless on thy fate."

CHAPTER XXXII

THE SPANISH-AMERICAN WAR.

COL. A. K. McCLURE, in his "Recollections of Half a Century," says: "Soon after William McKinley entered the Presidential office he was confronted with the Cuban troubles which ultimately resulted in a war with Spain. I saw him many times during the progress of events which led up to the war, and he was often torn by conflicting desires. Like Lincoln, he was profoundly averse to war, and shuddered at the sacrifice of lives of his countrymen; but the wrongs of Cuba became so intolerable and aroused the country to such a measure of resentment that when the battleship Maine (which had gone there on a friendly errand) was blown up and the lives of hundreds of our brave sailors sacrificed there was no alternative but to accept the arbitrament of the sword in behalf of humanity and justice. He was reluctant until the last moment to accept war, but when it was no longer possible to avoid it with honor he entered into it with all the earnestness of his patriotic nature. After battles had been fought and victories won by both our army and navy he was earnestly for peace, and was largely instrumental himself in effecting the preliminary agreement that practically ended the war. But for the extraordinary efforts of himself, his cabinet and warm personal political supporters, the country would have been involved in interminable complications at the very outset of the war. It required all the political sagacity and moral power of the government to restrain Congress from involving us in the recognition of the Cuban Republic and making us accountable to the world for obligations entirely beyond the scope of our humane purposes or our national necessities."

This war of short duration, declared against Spain on April 20, 1898, was really the outcome of the horrible crimes committed by General Weyler in Cuba, the blowing up of the Maine having had a somewhat similar effect to the firing upon Fort Sumter prior to the War between the States. Perry County being a county of small population, had no military contingents of the National Guard within its confines, and accordingly had few soldiers in this war, as the army was almost wholly drawn from that source. From other contingents the following Perry County names are taken:

Barrack, Wm. H., served in Cuba.

Black, John, Tuscarora Township; Co. B, Nebraska Regiment. Died U. S. Hospital, Cavite, September 5, 1898.

Blain, Wm. A., Greenwood Township; Troop L, U. S. Cavalry. Enlisted at Reading, June 2, 1898.

Burd, John W., Buffalo Township; Co. D, Eighth Regt., P. V. I.

Fissel, Wm. H., Duncannon; Co. I, Fourth Regt., P. V. I.

Fosselman, John J., Tuscarora Township; C. G, Fifth Regt.

Frank, John R.; Co. C, Twelfth Regt.

Gettys, H. A., Marysville; Co. 8, Fourth Regt., P. V. I.

Gunderman, Edward C.; Ninth Infantry and Fifteenth Cavalry, Philippines.

Hain, Wm. J.; Sheridan Troop, Tyrone, Pa.

Jones, Harry E.; Co. I, Fourth Regt., P. V. I.

McNeely, John M.; Co. I, Fourth Regt., P. V. I.

Moyer, Chas. W.; Co. E, Twelfth Regiment.

Ney, Charles L.; Co. I, Fourth Regiment, P. V. I.

Pfafflin, Adolph R., Marysville; Co. I, Fourth Regt., P. V. I.

Patterson, Harry A., Marysville; Co. I, Fourth Regt., P. V. I.

Sellers, Harvey, Marysville; Co. I, Fourth Regt., P. V. I.

Shaffer, Elmer E., served in Philippines.

Shannon, Frank A.

Sharon, Austin C.; Co. I, First Regt., P. V. I.

Toland, Thomas E., Duncannon; Co. 1, Fourth Regt., P. V. I.

Wise, Walter E., Marysville; Co. I, Fourth Regt., P. V. I. Died in Brooklyn Naval Hospital, September 7, 1898.

Wolfe, Harvey F.; Co. I, Fourth P. V. I.

Wright, Jesse W.; Co. B, Twelfth Regt., Philippines.

CHAPTER XXXIII.

THE WORLD WAR, AND PERRY COUNTY.

"It's not the guns nor armament,
Nor funds that they can pay,
But the close coöperation
That makes them win the day.
It's not the individual
Nor the army as a whole,
But the everlasting teamwork
Of every bloomin' soul.
—*Kipling.*

NO human being coûld ever tell the stupendous story of this war. Much of it was a part of the annals of particular contingents, and, before there had been time to make any record, its men had again faced the enemy and paid the last great price. It was the most marvelous war of all ages. For over four years it swept through the continent of Europe and parts of Africa and Asia. Thirty nations and scores of different races were involved. Almost ten millions of men were slain in battle and thirty millions injured. Thousands were made blind and insane. No country on earth escaped the attendant losses and terrors of the war in one form or another. The high seas were ravaged and thousand of ships sent to the bottom. Millions of noncombatants, nurses, teachers, mothers and even little children—were slain or suffered death of starvation and disease. And then, when it was about over, that dreadful influenza, said by many to be one of the frightful war schemes, carried to their graves many thousands and left many other thousands with enfeebled systems.

America had stood aloof too long. In 1917, the world stood aghast. Was civilization to be overwhelmed? Then America plunged into the very vortex and was largely instrumental in grasping victory from defeat. From farm, mill and office two millions of Americans were rushed across the Atlantic, although a fiendish government had its submarines lurking beneath the waves to sink the liners and transports, just as they had sunk a passenger ship containing women and children some time before. To-day thousands of those boys are buried on foreign soil.

As long ago as 1899 it was no secret that Germany was preparing for war, and when Admiral Coghlan (then a captain), at a Union League dinner in New York, recited a pertinent poem, "Meinself und Gott," caricaturing the Kaiser, it caused a diplomatic flurry and even a conference between President McKinley and the German Ambassador. During all those years the great Krupp works were turning out huge cannon and other manufacturers were making smaller firearms in vast quantities. For what? "The day!" (When Germans met they always drank toasts to "Der tag.") That day finally came when the little Austrian Archduke was assassinated. Germany started its army to invade Belgium, although there was no trouble there, and that was the beginning of the most horrible holocaust of all ages. But that was not the first time the Teuton has shown his perfidy. It dates back to the early days of written history, 55 B. C., when Cæsar was on the banks of the Meuse and the Germans made an armistice with the Romans. Scarcely had the envoys left when the Germans fell upon the Roman brigade.

Perry County is only a small part of one of the forty-eight states, but the effect of the war on the nation was felt there just as everywhere else. During those memorable days of 1914, the average American little dreamed of the great effect the war would have on the United States and that eventually we would be drawn into it. German propaganda was at work, however, and the public press, the religious press, the forum and the pulpit of the nation were insidiously and unknowingly corrupted. A strain of American citizenship was organized with a hyphen name. War was levied on our industry and commerce. An effort was made to embroil our country in a war with Mexico and Japan, and this having failed, Americans were impudently warned off the great high seas, in an advertisement in the public press. A ship, disregarding the warning, was torpedoed, and hundreds of women and children, along with the men—all noncombatants—were drowned in midocean.

Perry County had been largely settled by a German population (many Wurtembergers), but not Prussianized Germans of the type that started the war, and there were mighty few sympathizers of the Prussian war machine, be it said to their credit. Government loan quotas were oversubscribed in the county, the quotas of troops went with regularity, and many a lad of German strain was in the ranks. Germany had long been held up as an example of efficiency, but America put them to shame. Germany had been preparing for forty years, and America was unprepared for war; yet in less than forty weeks she was operating a big railroad system on foreign soil, her merchant marine had grown to be the second largest in the world, she had dredged a foreign harbor and made docks for forty ships, and had a convoy system which was the marvel of the ages. The war had been in progress 1,452 days until America got to the front line, and in just 115 days the armistice was signed. German propaganda had kept us out of the war when we should have been in, but once in the Americans changed the German spelling of the word efficiency, to *in*efficiency.

Just as Col. A. K. McClure is quoted in the nation's affairs at various places in this book, let another former Perry Countian now be quoted. Charles William Super, Ph.D., LL.D., Ex-President of the Ohio University and noted author, studied at Tübingen, Germany, in 1869-71, and in 1882, 1896 and 1903 he again visited that country in research work. He has an intimate knowledge of Germany and its people, and until 1914 was an ardent pacifist. It is from such an authority, who even witnessed the bombardment of Strasburg in the Franco-Prussian War, that we would quote. The following is from his "Pan-Prussianism," 1918:

"I am not ashamed to confess that up to July, 1914, I was an ardent pacifist. Although I was not unaware of the spirit that reigned in Wilhelmstrasse, I could not believe it capable of the perfidy that it soon came to make a part of its settled policy. I was opposed to spending money on a great navy, because I was convinced that we had nothing to fear from any European or Asiatic power. I saw no use in fortifying the Panama Canal, because I believed that every government would pledge its word to regard it as passing through neutral territory and keep its pledge.

"Nevertheless, when the storm broke I was not for a moment in doubt as to its significance. For more than two years I was fully convinced that we were delaying participation in a conflict in which we were vitally interested,—on the issue of which our very existence as a nation probably depended. On the other hand, I realized that in a democracy the party in power can only act as far and as fast as it is supported by public opinion; and our public was utterly incredulous as to the aims and perfidious methods of the government that was responsible for the war. Our people had heard and read so much about the progress of Germany in the arts of peace, about its admirable educational system, and about its superior educational methods, that they mistook knowledge and power for enlightenment. * * *

"There is no crime in the penal code that the German soldiers, encouraged and abetted by their officers, have not committed. There is no prohibition laid down in the moral law that they have not disregarded. There is no deed of violence of which they are not guilty. They have raped, they have murdered in cold blood, they have looted, they have stolen or broken in pieces what they could not carry away. They have murdered without pity,—and slain without remorse,—women, children, old men and invalids. They have enslaved those they did not wish to kill, especially if they were women. From the lowest to the highest they have lied, they have perjured themselves without scruple, they have broken the most solemn promises, and have laughed at those who were credulous enough to trust their word. They have laid waste the invaded districts, they have ravished cities and villages, respecting neither crucifixes, nor priests, nor churches, nor hospitals, nor private property. They have made themselves drunk on stolen liquors, after which they demeaned themselves as men in that condition are wont to do, especially if there is no one to call them to account or to punish them for their villainies. They have shot innocent people by squadrons, and have executed individuals after a farcical trial. They have gloated over the sufferings of their victims and mocked at their agonizing cries for mercy. Their pastors have shouted pæans of victory over all these things and over worse,—if there could possibly be any worse,—as if they deserved praise rather than the bitterest execration. * * *

"In June, 1908, Wilhelm presided at a council held at Potsdam. * * *
He spoke at great length, saying among other things: 'At this solemn hour
I repeat this pledge before you, with the addition, however, that I shall not
rest or be satisfied until all the countries and territories that once were
German, or where great numbers of my former subjects now live have become a part of the great mother-country, acknowledging me as their supreme lord in war and peace. Even now I rule supreme in the United
States, where almost one-half of the population is either of German birth,
or of German descent, and where three million German voters do my bidding at the Presidential elections. No administration can remain in power
against the will of the German voters, who through that admirable organization, the German-American National League of the United States of
America, control the destinies of the vast republic beyond the seas.'

"In 1917 the Committee of Public Information in the United States reported the following activities of German agents, all or nearly all of the
participants being in the pay of the Imperial German Government:

"Destruction of lives and property in merchant vessels on the high seas.

"Irish revolutionary plots against Great Britain.

"Fomenting ill-feeling against the United States in Mexico.

"Subordination of American writers and lecturers.

"Financing of propaganda.

"Maintenance of a spy system under the guise of a commercial investigation bureau.

"Subsidizing a bureau for the purpose of stirring up labor troubles in
munition plants.

"The bomb industry and other related activities.

"When the international roll of dishonor is made up, German names will
be placed first, and there will be no one to challenge their primacy.

"From the very beginning of the conflict the Germans fired shells into
the most thickly settled parts of cities and towns, whether fortified or not;
and fortifications are never in cities. * * *   Men were tied to stakes and
burned alive. Mothers were shot with children in their arms and the children dealt with in the same way because they were orphans. Unarmed
youths were shot to prevent their becoming soldiers later on. Belgians of
all ages were dispatched with bullets because they were a filthy people.
Priests and nuns were special objects of ruffianism. * * *

"Another form of outrage upon women and children that was frequently
committed by the Prussians was to take refuge behind them. At one place
twenty-five women and children were compelled to walk beside a column
of the invaders to protect them against an enfilading fire. In numerous
places the German solders forced civilians of both sexes to walk before
them. At Nemy they drove five hundred men, women and children toward
the English, who of course, not being Germans, did not fire upon them.

"There could hardly be a greater contrast than that which exists between the English workingman and his German peer. The former feels
a class consciousness, a sense of power and dignity; he is firm, often to
the verge of obstinacy, while the latter is hardly more than a chattel."

Dr. Super is recognized as an authority everywhere. He goes
into the race characteristics of the Teuton, accounts for the status
of the German woman, for the looting propensity of the Prussian,
for the misconception of kultur against civilization that abides in
the Teutonic mind, and other phases in all their bearings. His
familiarity with Germany and its people and his skill as an accomplished reasoner, together with his ability as a ripe scholar, com-

mands attention. He is a former Perry Countian, and elsewhere in this book will be found a biographical sketch of him.

The registration board, which conducted the selective draft, was composed of D. L. Kistler, chairman; J. C. Hench, secretary, and Dr. A. R. Johnston. Later James W. McKee was secretary, and still later, Luke Baker. Attorney John C. Motter was chief clerk. The legal advisory board was composed of James W. Shull, James M. Barnett, and Wm. S. Seibert. The associate advisory board was composed of Wm. H. Sponsler, Luke Baker, Walter W. Rice, James W. McKee, James M. McKee, and Charles H. Smiley, attorneys-at-law; Samuel S. Willard, and Rev. Homer C. Knox. There were 1,616 men in the registration of June 5, 1917; 147 in the registration of June 5, 1918; forty-seven in the registration of August 24, 1918, and 2,366 in the registration of September 12, 1918, a total of 4,176. To thirty-nine camps and stations were entrained 474 drafted men, of whom fifty-two were rejected, thus leaving the number sworn into the service as 422. Owing to Perry County being an agricultural county many of the young men seek employment elsewhere. The high wages paid in the industrial plants during the war made this especially so, with the attendant result that the proportion of men sent from Perry County is much smaller than it would otherwise have been, as those men are credited to their place of residence at that time.

Proportionately Bloomfield Borough furnished by far the largest number of voluntary enlistments in the county, having had thirty-one from a possible forty. Marysville led the county in number, having had forty. The voluntary enlistments from all districts follow: Blain, 4; Bloomfield, 31; Buffalo, 3; Carroll, 7; Centre, 6; Duncannon, 26; Greenwood, 9; Howe, 0; Jackson, 5; Juniata, 8; Liverpool Borough, 16; Liverpool Township, 2; Madison, 9; Marysville, 40; Miller, 2; Millerstown, 17; New Buffalo, 4; Newport, 34; Oliver, 1; Penn, 10; Rye, 0; Saville, 6; Spring, 3; Toboyne, 3; Tuscarora, 3; Tyrone, 8; Watts, 7; Wheatfield, 3.

One of the incidents connected with the World War, in so far as Perry County is concerned, was the bringing of two French brides to its soil. Sergeant Montgomery Gearhart, of Millerstown, was united in wedlock to Miss Alice LeCointre, of Angiers, France, November 20, 1918. The other was reared in Soissons, Aisne, and was a prisoner of the Germans for fifteen days, who became the wife of Sergeant Robert Miller, having lost her father and only brother while fighting beneath the tri-colors of France.

Upon the ending of the World War the returned soldiers formed the American Legion, which has a number of Posts in Perry County. Its preamble is a masterpiece:

"For God and country we associate ourselves together for the following purposes: To uphold and defend the Constitution of the United States; to maintain law and order; to foster and perpetuate one hundred per cent Americanism; to preserve the memories and incidents of our association in the great war; to inculcate a sense of individual obligation to the state, community, and nation; *to combat autocracy, both of the classes and the masses;* to make right the master of might * * * to safeguard and transmit to posterity the principles of justice, freedom and democracy."

The American Expeditionary Forces, like the fighting forces of all our wars, have left their impress upon the period. They left part of their number to sleep on foreign soil, and the rest are scattered throughout the land. The *American Legion Weekly*, in a poem entitled "Requiem," gives a pen picture of them, which is worthy of being recorded, as a tribute to their spirit:

"It sprang from town and crossroads, when the call to battle came,
    And grinned and slung its pack upon its back;
It wrote red Chateau Thierry and the Argonne into fame,
    And swaggered, roaring down adventure's track.
It took a blasting, killing job, and damned it and went through,
    It faced six hells as part of every day;
In lousy barns and trenches, just before the whistle blew
    It sang of homes three thousand miles away.

"It knew the sleepless box-car nights, the sweat, the drawn fatigue,
    It lined itself with "willie" and hard bread;
Its hobnailed columns pounded France, for league on rain-swept league,
    Its nearest dream of Heaven was a bed.
Its days are done and ended now; its taps are sounding clear,
    One last long note, "Farewell"—and it is gone;
It lives in distant memory, but that memory is dear,
    The soul of it alone still carries on."

Were it possible to publish a cut of every Perry Countian who participated in the World War it would gladly be done, but that would fill a volume in itself. From among them we have chosen three who were from typical Perry County families, and from three different sections of the county: Lieut. Edward Moore, son of Dr. and Mrs. E. E. Moore, of New Bloomfield; Sergeant Paul Fleisher, son of Mr. and Mrs. Amos Fleisher, of Oliver Township, and James G. Zimmerman, son of the late L. C. and Mrs. Zimmerman, of Duncannon. These three young men came from among the best and most substantial families of Perry County and were educated young men of promise and character, and one likes to think of them as representative of the rank and file which left the county for camp and cantonment, brave, resolute, and sturdy. Their photos are selected, for I knew them best. James Zimmerman and Edward Moore I had known from their childhood, and Paul Fleisher, in young manhood, as a fellow student of a member

SOLDIERS OF THE WORLD WAR.*

BLAIN BOROUGH.

Dolby, Clarence. 47 Co., Group 4, W. T. D. C. O. K., 18 I. R. T., Camp Hancock, Ga.

Gutshall, Benj.

Gutshall, Geo. L., 3d Engineers, Canal Zone.

Kern, Edward, U. S. New Hampshire Band, Ft. Monroe, Va.

Knox, Paul, 112th Inf. Supply Co., France.

Knox, Stanley, 112th Inf. Supply Co., France.

Martin, Arthur, Exca. Hosp. No. 38, Ft. McHenry, Md.

Martin, George D., Marine Barracks, Hingham, Mass.

Martin, James (Sgt.), 314th Inf. N. A., France.

Shannon, John Miles, 307th Engineers, France.

Snyder, William, 336th Machine Gun Co., France.

Spotts, Carl, N. C. O. Training School, Camp Greenleaf, Tenn.

Wilt, Clarence R., 219th Aero Squadron, England.

Woods, Dr. H. W. (Captain), Convalescent Camp No. 3. France.

BLOOMFIELD BOROUGH.

Adams, Frank A., Officers' Reserve Corps, Camp Oglethorpe, Ga.

Adams, John P. (Captain), 7th Reg. M. G. Co., U. S. Marines, Cuba, U. S. Marine Corps since 1915.

Adams, Raymond, S. A. T. C., Univ. of Pa.

Askins, J. Stewart, 60th Pioneer Inf. Band.

Briner, Leon B., Quartermaster's Corps, Camp Upton, N. Y.

Bernheisel, Geo. H. (Captain), 102d Reg. Artillery; gassed Oct. 11, 1918; France.

Bucher, John B., 463d Aero Squadron, France and Germany.

Clouser, Duke P. (Sgt.), Infantry, Camp Taylor, Ky.

Clouser, John, Heavy Artillery, France.

Darlington, Jos. G., Sapper Troops, In transit, Nov. 11, 1918.

Darlington, Paul W. (Master Eng'r S. C.), Engineer Corps, France.

DeLancey, Chas., Infantry, France.

DeLancey, Harry, Infantry, France.

Fox, Paul N. (Sgt.), Motor Transport Corps, France.

Garber, Edgar M., Motor Transport Corps, France.

Harper, D. Neil, Flying Cadet Aero Service; died Feb. 11, 1918, from accidental machine gun wounds; San Antonio, Texas.

Johnston, John W., Cent. Medical Laboratory, England and France.

Kell, Frank E., Instruc. Co., Signal Corps, Leavenworth, Kansas.

Kell, George R. (1st Cl. Sgt.), 25th Reg. Engineers, France.

Keller, B. Frank, Trench Motor Battery, France.

Logan, Robert, Mechanic (?) Aviation, France.

Magee, John A. (2d Lt.), Aviation, Garden City, N. Y.

Masterson, Edw. M. (1st Lt.), 1st Philippine Inf.; Reg. Army since 1905; Ft. McKinley, P. I.

Miller, David, Quartermaster's Corps, Ice Plant Co. 301, France.

Miller, James, Motor Transport Aviation School, St. Paul, Minn.

---

*The list of soldiers was compiled by Dr. A. R. Johnston, of New Bloomfield, who credits the following with rendering valuable assistance: Ralph B. Kell, L. M. Wentzel, Dr. E. C. Kistler, W. E. Meck, John Asper, F. A. Johnston, Dr. J. A. Sheibley, H. W. Robinson, Ezra Bupp *Duncannon Record*, B. Stiles Duncan, Harry G. Martin, A. L. Long, D. A. Lahr, Harry L. Stephens, M. E. Flickinger, Jas. R. Wilson, Harry W. Morris, John D. Snyder, G. E. Beck, Robert Loy, *Marysville Journal*, Charles O. Houck, Walter Harper, A. R. Thompson, Thomas L. Smith, Rev. Wm. Dorwart, John S. Eby, James Bistline, Claude S. Fleisher, Linn C. Lightner, J. Claire Gray, Charles J. Swartz, Cyrus S. Bender, W. H. Gray, P. S. Dunbar, Ernest M. Stambaugh, Harry L. Soule, Russell Johnston, L. E. Donnally, Dr. W. T. Morrow, J. R. Lepperd, John F. Moreland, E. C. Dile, Fairlie M. DeLancey, and John Y. Wills.

Millington, Harold (Sgt.), died July 18, 1918, from wounds received in
Battle of Marne, France.
Millington, Margt. M. (Nurse), R. C. Nurse, Evacu. Hosp. No. 26, France
and Germany.
Moore. Edward L. (2d. Lt.), 39th Reg. Inf. Wounded in Argonne Bat-
tle, Sept. 28, 1918, and died in Evacuation Hospital No. 4, Sept. 30,
1918. Regular Army since September, 1916.
Myers, Henry G. (Sgt.), 314th Machine Gun Company, France.
Nickel, Ernest H., U. S. Marines, Washington, D. C.
Ramsay, Jas. M. B. (Mast. Sgt.), 28th Inf.; Regular Army since June,
1917; France and Belgium.
Seibert, W. W., S. A. T. C., State College, Pa.
Shearer, James M., 109th Inf., France.
Shearer, Louis G., M. G. O. T. Corps, Camp Hancock, Ga.
Shumaker, Wilbur, 7th Field Artillery; died Oct. 13, 1918, from wounds
received in Battle of Argonne, France.
Stein, Dr. M. I. (1st. Lt.), Medical Service, Camp Travis, Texas.
Stambaugh, Samuel, Infantry, Camp Lee, Va.
Swartz, Paul G. (Musician), 59th Inf. Wounded doing first aid on lines
at St. Martin, France; U. S. Regulars; France and Germany.
Sweger, Edward M., Infantry, Camp Upton, N. Y.
Sweger, Hobart M., Camp Hospital No. 40, England.

BUFFALO TOWNSHIP.

Fortney, John W., Field Hospital No. 39, France.
Johnson, Elmer, 128th Infantry; wounded; France.
Johnson, Lawrence, 330th Ambulance Co., France.
Killinger, Reuben, Camp Hancock, Ga.
Knuth, Fred W., Camp Meade, Md.
Miller, Harry A., 313th Mac. G. Batt; gassed and otherwise injured;
France.
Moretz, Ralph, Motor Transport Corps, France.
Nowark, Fred W. (Sgt.), R. R. Trans. Corps, 21st Div., France.
Rhoads. Harry E., 169th Inf. Killed in action, Nov. 7, 1918, France.
Rhoads, John W. (Sgt.), Quartermaster's Corps, Camp Eustis, Va.
Rhoads, Ralph M., Infantry, Camp Lee, Va.
Shriver, Charles, Camp Meade, Md.
Shuler, Chester E. (Sgt., Sen. Grade), Quartermaster's Corps, Camp Han-
cock, Ga.
Stephens, Miles M., 56th Pioneer Inf., Camp Wadsworth, S. C.

CARROLL TOWNSHIP.

Adams, Oscar, France.
Adams, William W.
Barrick, Guy, France.
Beam, Elmer Nelson, Artillery, France.
Beam, Herman, France.
Beam, Rue, France.
Bear. James, France.
Boyer. Richard S., 112th Inf. Wounded July 26, 1918, at Velse River,
France.
Dick, Cloyd O., Quartermaster's Corps, Camp Meade, Md.
Dundorf, Lloyd P., Camp Meade, Md.
Eberly, Norman M.
Eberly, William A., France.
Kerns, Roy W., Navy.
Kitner, Foster S., 20th Engineers, United States.
Long, Harry (Sgt.), Motor Mech., 3d Reg. Air S.
Lupfer, Harry C., Pioneer Inf., France.
McCallister, Archie. Pioneer Inf., France.
Meiss, Elwood, S. A. T. C.
Owen, John, France.
Sheaffer, Amos H., France.

Sheibley, C. Wilmot, Med. Corps, 112th Ohio Eng., France.
Sloop, John, Infantry. Killed in action, Sept. 30, 1918, France.
Sloop, Russell, 23d Infantry, France.
Smee, John H., Pioneer Infantry, France.
Smith, John, France.
Stone, Charles Wilson, 28th Infantry, France.
Stone, John H., France.
Sweger, James O., Ambulance Driver, France.
Weise, Floyd.
Yohn, Lawrence, Heavy Artillery, France.

CENTRE TOWNSHIP.

Bupp, John E., Aviation, Garden City, N. Y.
Foose, Charles W., Casual Battalion, Camp Merritt, N. Y.
Gantt, Bruce, Aviation, Kelly Field, Texas.
Gantt, Lloyd W., Infantry, France.
Heckendorn, Wm. M., died of disease, Camp Meade, Md.
Kepner, Arden B., Infantry, France.
Myers, Henry G., 314th M. G. C., Reg. Army, France.
Myers, Vernon, Camp Dix.
Rodemaker, Benj., 332d M. G. C.,; slight shrapnel wound; France and
    Italy.
Rodemaker, John F. T., 317th Supply Co., France.
Sheaffer, Horace, Quartermaster's Corps, France.
Smith, J. Roy, Navy.
Thebes, Henry, 60th Inf. Captured Oct. 15, 1918, at Metz, and held at
    Lemberg and Rastatt until Dec. 12, 1918; France and Germany.
Zeigler, John F., 3d Battalion, United tSates.

DUNCANNON.

Alander, Willis Wilmer, 77th Field Artillery, France.
Barringer, Arthur P., Machine Gun Tr. Camp, Camp Hancock, Ga.
Barringer, Francis, Aviation Mechanic, Camp Rockview, Cal.
Barringer, W. Van.
Black, Clyde E.
Bolden, James A.
Boyer, Elton W., Artillery Officer Tr. Camp, Camp Custer, Mich.
Boyer, George H. (Sgt., Sr. Grade). Quartermaster's Corps, Camp Mer-
    ritt. N. J.
Boyer, Wallace K. (Sgt.), Headqtrs., 3d Army, France; Ambulance Co.
    No. 342, Camp Grant, Ill.
Bucke, Samuel, Medical Department, Wash., D. C.
Collins, Elmer P., 314th Infantry, France.
Cretzinger, John I., 314th Infantry, France.
Dearolf, Abram (Master Engineer), 35th Engineers, France.
Derick, J. Homer, 40th Engineers, France.
Dunkle, Harry M., U. S. S. Winding-Gulf.
Ellis, F. B., Sig. Corps, Aviation Sec., France.
Fortenbaugh, Harrison Reid, 318th Field Hospital, France.
Foster, Walter, Washington, D. C.
Freeburn, C. A., 315th Tank Corps, Camp Cold and Camp Dix.
Fuller, W. E., France.
Hamilton, Elmer E. (Sgt.), Medical Dept., Gen. Hosp. 8, 30th Engineers,
    Otisville, N. Y.
Hamilton, G. C., 30th Engineers.
Hammaker, Charles, 107th M. G. B.
Hart, John L. (Sgt.), 77th Field Artillery, France.
Hart, John R., Flying Cadet, Mili. School of Aëronautics, Urbana, Ill.
Hart, Lane Scofield (1st Cl. Sgt.), Ambulance Co. 342. 68th Div., France.
Hart, Wm. B., Wagoner, Evac. Amb. Co. No.—. France.
Hays, W. Linn, 342d M. G. B., France.
Heckendorn, Wm. Roy, Ambulance Section, France.
Hockenberry, Berlin E., Aviation Corps, Lake Charles, La.

Jennings, Crist L., 101st Field Artillery, R. D., France.
Jennings, Ross S. (Sgt.), 11th Engineers, France.
Jennings, W. W. (Sgt.), 4th Div. P. O. D., France.
Kennedy, A. L., S. A. T. C., Bethlehem, Pa.
Kines, Norman W., 313th Field Artillery, France.
Kirkpatrick, Samuel Blake, 305th Infantry, France.
Klinepeter, Frank L. (Sgt.), 58th Infantry, France.
Knight, Lawrence, 20th Cavalry, Ft. Riley, Kan.
LaForm, Horace B., Headquarter's Department, Guatanamo, Cuba.
Lepperd, Floyd Charles, Chem. Div., Washington, D. C.
Light, Frank E., 1st N. H. Infantry.
Lightner, Herman, 112th Infantry. Died Jan. 14, 1919, from accident in France; France.
Loper, Joshua Gladden, 21st Engineers, France.
Lowe, Fred Thomas, 155th Dep. Brigade, Camp Lee, Va.
Lukens, Elton, 304th Am. Train, France.
Mikle, Oren, 107th Field Artillery, Camp Hancock, Ga.
Nolde, R. A., 112th Infantry.
Noss, Oscar Fritz (Lt. Col.), Construction Dept., Washington, D. C.
Noss, S. Russell, 110th M. G. Co., Camp Hancock, Ga.
Noye, David R., 15th Training Div.
Owen, William.
Poff, Harvey.
Poff, Joseph (Sgt.), Ambulance Co. 338, Russia.
Poff, Roy H., Ambulance Co. 362, Camp Lewis, Wash.
Quigley, Clinton Howard, 61st Engineers, France.
Raisner, Florian R.
Reynolds, Robert R., 154th Depot Brigade, Camp Meade, Md.
Richter, John Harper (Sgt.), Marines, Guatanamo, Cuba, Port au Prince, Haiti.
Rosborough, F. Wm., 310th Engineers, France.
Rosborough, John E., 323d Reg.F. A.
Sterner, Jacob, 109th Machine Gun. Killed in action.
Stewart, William A., Aux. Depot No. 312, Camp Sheridan, Ala.
Toland, Thomas E., France.
Wills, John Y., Ambulance Section, with French Army, France.
Wolpert, Earl N., Ambulance Co. 344; died of disease; Camp Clark, Tex.
Wright, Harry Clayton, Med. Dept., Camp Greenleaf, Ga.
Wright, Orville Harrison, Wagoner, 312th M. G. Co., France.
Zeigler, George Morris (Sgt.), 304th Eng. T., 79th Div., France.
Zerfing, George R.
Zimmerman, James G., F. A. Training School; died of disease; Camp Taylor, Ky.

GREENWOOD TOWNSHIP.

Anderson, Raymond S., 110th Inf. Wounded in Sergie Woods, July 28, 1918, France.
Anderson, Wilbur G., 110th Inf. Killed in action, Roucher's Woods, July, 29, 1918, France.
Barner, George E., Expert Rifleman, 332d Regiment. France and Italy
Beaver, Ralph G., M. Gun Off. Training Camp, Camp Hancock, Ga.
Bucher, Emery A., 314th Inf., Med. Dept., France.
Cameron, George J., Wagoner, 304th Ammunition Train, France.
Cauffman, Emery J., Medical Department, Overseas.
Cauffman, Wesley M., 349th Infantry, France.
Dillman, Earl, 322d Infantry, France.
Doughten, John J., United States.
Frey, Annabelle D. (Nurse), Base Hospital No. 57, France.
Grubb, Norman M., 43d Infantry, United States.
Hogentogler, John L., 314th Infantry, France.
Holman, Edward L. (1st Lt.), 152d Depot Brigade, United States.
Kramer, James L., 112th Infantry, France.
Markley, Norman S., Quartermaster's Detach., Camp Lee, Va.

Minium, Ezra H.
Sarver, Warren R., 110th Inf. Under constant shell fire from July 4,
 1918, until Sept. 27, 1918, when he was severely wounded; France.
Satzler, Roscoe L., 125th Infantry, France.
Snook, Ernest B., 112th Regiment, France.
Troutman, Horace, Orderly to Gen. Cloe, Quartermaster's Office, Haiti.
Ward. D. Earl, Wagoner, 314th Infantry, France.

HOWE TOWNSHIP.

Freeland, David F., Camp Greenleaf, Ft. McHenry.
Henderson, Elmer E., Co. G., 145th Infantry, France and Belgium.
Kirkpatrick, H. E., Camp Lee, Va.
Oren, Melvin, Co. E., 103d Art. Amu. Tr., France and Belgium.
Shull, Marlin, Evac. Camp, Co. 49, France and Germany.

JACKSON TOWNSHIP.

Berrier, Charles, 2d Bn. Inf. Replacm., England.
Britcher, Miles, 314th Infantry, France.
Gibbens, Maurice, United States.
Gibbens, William, United States.
Gutshall, David B., 1st Evac. Hospital, Camp Greenleaf, Ga.
Gutshall, Foster L. (2d Lt.), United States.
Hall, William F. (2d Lt.), United States.
Hockenberry, James, 155th Detroit Brigade, France.
Kunkle, Harry, Base Hospital, Camp Meade, Md.
Moreland, John F., 112th Inf. Severely wounded in action in shoulder,
 near Vesle River, Aug. 7, 1918, France.
Neidigh, Orth, Co. 3, Bn. 1, Camp Greenleaf, Ga.
Pryor, Hayes V.. 312th Cavalry, Ft. Sheridan.
Pryor, L. B., 3d U. S. Cavalry.
Pryor, Nellie F. (Nurse), Base Hospital No. 8, France.
Pryor, Sarah E. (Nurse), Gen. Hospital No. 2, Ft. McHenry, Md.
Pryor, S. C., 339th Field Art., Camp Dodge.
Rohm, Banks, 16th Bn. and I. R. C., France.
Shanafelter, Guy D., 23d Engineers, France.
Shumaker, Leslie, Tank Corps, Camp Colt, Pa.
Stahl, Clarence, Ammunition Train, France.
Sunday, Pierce (Sgt.), 112th Headquarters Inf., Camp Hancock, Ga.
Waldsmith, Earl G., 29th Infantry, Canal Zone.
Wilt, John Lloyd, 56th Pioneer Infantry, France.

JUNIATA TOWNSHIP.

Brown, Russell.
Flickinger, J. Clarence, United States.
Hench, Allen, Navy.
Latchford, Chester A.. Mechanic, 9th Inf., Reg. Army, France.
Latchford, John R. W., wounded in right arm at Soissons, July 18, 1918,
 France.
Leinaweaver, Harvey J., 106th Field Artillery, France.
Leinaweaver, Robert B., 121st Machine Gun B., France and Germany.
Leubergh, Lester.
Patton, Carl.
Patton, Ralph.
Reeder, James Albert.
Shotzberger, Norman.
Shotzberger, William.
Sheaffer. Graphus, Camp Hosp. 941, France.
Shumaker, Guy R., Evac. Hospital, No. 45, Camp Greenleaf, Ga.
Smith, Luther.
Smith, Chester.
Smith.
Staples, Oscar. died of diesase, United States.
Walker. Earl, France.

LANDISBURG BOROUGH.

Burtnett, Charles F., 15th Engineering Corps, France.
Burtnett, George P., Base Hospital No. 80, France.
Gibson, Robert, 50th Inf.; Med. Corps.
Keck, Oliver B., Medical Corps, Georgia.
Lightner, Bowman E., Aviation, France
Lightner, Hobson S., Coast Artillery, Philippine Islands.
Lightner, Noy I. (1st Cl. Sgt.), Signal Corps, United States.
Mumper, Frank L., 41st Div. Inf., France.
Wertz, Vernon A., 167th Reg., Co. C., France.

LIVERPOOL BOROUGH.

Barner, Emmett E. (2d Lt.), Construction Engineers, United States.
Boger, Dr. Geo. M. (1st Lt.), 1st Army Headquarters, France.
Brink, Ellismere (2d Lt.), 190th Aëro Squadron, United States.
Dehaven, J. Wesley (Sgt. Mjr.), 51st Coast Art. Corps. Killed in action, Oct. 17, 1918, France.
Hoffman, Russell, 110th Infantry, United States.
House, Jas. G., 5th Un. Marines, France.
Kurtz, Edward M., 103d Ammunition Train, France.
Kurtz, Marshal L., 504th Laundry Co., France.
Long, Harvey, Field Hospital No. 29, France.
Lutz, Elmer E., 6th Military Police Co., France.
Lutz, Geo. T. (Sgt.), 3d Motor Mechanics, France.
McKinn, Robert R., 316th Infantry, France.
Morris, Harry W., Wagoner, 55th Sanitary Squadron, France.
Mottern, Chas., M. Engineer. 6th Engineers, France.
Murray, Wm. H., Bugler, 2d Air Park Co., France.
Ritter, Deckard, U. S. S. Wyoming, foreign waters.
Seiler, Norman, 155th Depot Brigade, United States.
Shumaker, Wm. M., 154th Depot Brigade, United States.
Snyder, Eldon W., 2d Air Service Mechanic, France.
Williamson, Ralph (Sgt.), Quartermaster's Dept., West Point, U. S.
Wilt, Norman J., 304th Signal Battalion, France.
Zellers, Park L., 14th Field Artillery, France.

LIVERPOOL TOWNSHIP.

Hoffman, G. Cleveland, 314th Infantry, Co. C., France.
Long, Herman, 372d Aëro Squadron, France.
Long, J. Russell, 110th Infantry, France.
Mangle, Ross, 533d Ambulance Co., Base Hospital No. 71. In hospital four months on account of injuries received in fall from ambulance train, France.
Sweezy, Josiah, 314th Infantry, France.
Watts, Guy M., 11th Field Artillery, France.

MADISON TOWNSHIP.

Baltozer, Benjamin B., Machine Gun Bat., Quantico, Va.
Baltozer, Jacob, Officers' Training Camp, Atlanta, Ga.
Bechtel, Albert.
Brickner, Cloyd C., 33d Infantry, Canal Zone.
Cooney, Andrew, Infantry, Camp Meade, Md.
Cooney, Cloyd W., Camp Meade, Md.
DeLancey, Alford, United States.
Dillman, Jesse, Cook, 314th Regiment, Camp Meade, Md., and France.
Flickinger, Frank A., 72d Infantry, Camp Meade, Md.
Flickinger, George, 155th Depot Brigade, France.
Foose, Frank E., Camp Dix.
Foose, George, 3d Infantry, Canal Zone.
Foose, John, Panama.
Foose, Lee, Oversea.
Fritz, Frank, France.
Gutshall, Harry, 20th Engineers. Died of disease, Washington, D. C.

Gutshall, Harry R, 314th Regiment, France.
Heckendorn, Miles, United States.
Hench, John, France.
Hench, Roy, died of disease, France.
Hench, Thomas, France.
Hess, John Albert, 56th Pioneer Infantry, France and Germany.
Hess, Roy Lee, 56th Pioneer Infantry, France and Germany.
Hockenberry, Robert, United States.
Hollenbaugh, Roy, 363d Regiment, France.
Irvin, W. L., Sharpshooter, 314th Infantry, France.
Johnson, John W., 304th Engineers, France.
Junkin, Harry B., 155th Depot Brigade, Camp Lee, Va.
Lightner, Herman, Camp Meade, Md.
Lyons, David R., 363d Inf., 91st Div., France and Belgium.
Lyons, Jerry, 314th Inf., 79th Div., France.
Metz, Jesse R., 103d Ammunition Train, Oversea.
Morrison, Wm., 146th Infantry; wounded in hip; France.
Mort, James K., 119th Infantry, France.
Motzer, John, 314th Infantry. Died of disease; United States.
Moyer, Herbert, 363d Inf., 91st Div., France.
Moyer, William.
Nesbit, Earl A., 162d Infantry, France.
Reapsome, James, 363d Inf., 91st Div., Oversea.
Reed, Lee, 7th Division, France.
Rowe, Chester, Wagoner, 314th Infantry, France.
Rowe, William A.
Scott, Merle.
Sheaffer, Roy, Hdq. Co., 112th Inf., 28th Div., France.
Seilhamer, Luther, Oversea.
Shope, Samuel, 155th Depot Brigade, Camp Lee, Va.
Smith, Charles R., 155th Depot Brigade, Camp Lee, Va.
Smith, K. P., 56th Pioneer Infantry. France and Germany.
Smith, Ralph K., Infantry, 41st Division, France.
Snyder, Arthur, United States.
Snyder, Lenas, Oversea.
Stroup, W. R., 112th Inf. Gassed at Fismes, Aug. 21, 1918, France.
Wentz, Samuel, Army Training Detach., Cambridge Springs.
Weibley, Shelburn, United States.
Yohn, James, 314th Field Artillery, France.
Yohn, Joseph, 20th Field Artillery Supply Co., France.
Yohn, Jos. A. H., 20th Field Artillery, Camp Stanley.
Yohn, Russell Stroup, France.
Zimmerman, George (1st Lt.), 318 Field Artillery, Camp Jackson.

MARYSVILLE.

Anspach, Paul (Sgt.), 3 Cavalry, Camp Clark, Tex.
Bare, Dewey O., S. A. T. C., Myerstown, Pa.
Bare, Earl H., Bugler, Engineers, France.
Barshinger, Blain, Infantry. Died of pneumonia, Oct. 15, 1918, France.
Beers, Walter B., Bugler. Engineers, France.
Benfer, James, S. A. T. C., State College.
Bitting, Berkley, Gunner's Mate, U. S. S. Louisiana.
Bitting, Laurie (Sgt.), 78th Field Artillery, Egypt and Palestine.
Bitting, Thomas B., Signal Service, France.
Bratton, Harry, S. A. T. C., Lancaster, Pa.
Brightbill, Ellard, Cavalry, Passadena, Cal.
Brightbill, James, Field Artillery. Died Oct. 23, 1918, of pneumonia, France.
Carnes, William (Captain), Quartermaster's Corps, Newport News, Va.
Clendenin, Martin J., Quartermaster's Corps, Camp Lee. Va.
Cunningham, Wm. (Sgt.), Field Artillery, France.
Daum, Andrew, 110th Infantry, Camp Lee, Va.
Davis, J. D., 314th Machine Gun Co., France.

Deckard, Harry M., Gen. Hospital 36, Detroit, Mich.
Dice, Niles F. (Sgt.), 5th Field Artillery, France.
Dick, Frank T., 313th Field Artillery, France.
Dissinger, V. T., Ammunition Train, Camp Meade, Md.
Ellenberger, Paul (Sgt.), Officers' Training Camp, Waco, Texas.
Eppley, Roger, 67th Reg. Trans. Corps., France.
Eppley, S. Arthur, C. O. T. S., Camp Lee, Va.
Fenicle, Harry, Infantry, Camp Freemont.
Fenicle, Russell, S. A. T. C., Pittsburgh.
Fortenbaugh, Reid, 318th Field Hospital, France.
Gandy, William H., 3d Regiment, France.
Gault, Harry, Base Hospital 61, France.
Gault, Miss Jennie (Nurse), Red Cross Nurse, France.
Hain, John L. (Sgt.), 155th Depot Brigade, Camp Lee, Va.
Hammaker, Joseph, 304th Engineers, France.
Hess, George A. (Sgt.), 19th Engineers, France.
Hipple, Herman H., 155th Depot Brigade, Camp Lee, Va.
Jones, K. C., 314th Infantry, Camp Meade, Md.
Keller, Wm. T., U. S. Marines, France.
Kennedy, Cassius M., S. A. T. C., Myerstown, Pa.
Kennedy, Lester, Squadron E, Selifige Field, Mich.
Kline, Frank (Sgt.), 303d Reg. U. S. Engineers, France.
Kocher, L. K., Quartermaster's Corps, Camp Merritt, N. Y.
Leonard, Jesse F., 5th Co. C., M. G. O. T. S., Camp Hancock, Ga.
Lick, Alton W. (2d Lt.), 31st Field Artillery, Camp Meade, Md.
Lightner, Joseph K., S. A. T. C., State College, Pa.
Lightner, Linn C., 6th Co., Del. C. A. C., Ft. Du Pont, Del.
Longanecker, Benjamin, 3d Class Quartermaster, U. S. S. Wisconsin.
Luckenbaugh, John C., Camp Wheeler, Ga.
Martin, Miss Blanche, U. S. Debark. Hos. No. 3, New York City.
McConnell, Bryan C., Camp Lee, Va.
Mendinghall, A. M., 5th Div. Ammunition Train, France.
Miller, Harry, 6th Reg. C. & C., France.
Miller, Robert, Motor Truck Co. 105, France.
Mutch, Harry, 25th Aëro Squadron, France.
Mutch, Haven, 1st Inf. M. G. Co., Camp Lewis, Wash.
Naylor, George R., Quartermaster's Corps, France.
Neff, Edward N., Embarkation Hospital, Camp Stuart, Va.
Palmer, Robert (2d Lt.), 4th Officers' Co.. I. R. T. T., Camp Grant. Ill.
Palmer, Vernon, 15th Engineers, France.
Palmer, W. Foster, 5th Field Artillery. 1st Div., France.
Picerilli, Antonio, 314th Infantry, France.
Pierson, Frank A., Mechanic, 314th Infantry, France.
Pinci, Guiseppo, 314th Infantry, France.
Radabaugh, Wm. R., Quartermaster's Corps, Camp Gatun, Canal Zone.
Reynolds, H. M., Camp Hospital 35, England.
Rhinehart, John, Field Hospital 23, France.
Rice, Joseph (2d Lt.), Hgd. 3d Bat. Der Camp, Camp Upton, N. Y.
Rider, Bruce, S. A. T. C., Carlisle, Pa.
Rinehart; Burt, Camp Raritan, N. Y.
Roberts, Edgar, Pittsburgh S. A. T. C., Pittsburgh, Pa.
Robinson, E. W., Camp Wadsworth, S. C.
Sellers, Miss Nellie, U. S. Navy, Yeowoman.
Shearer, John, S. A. T. C., State College, Pa.
Shumaker, Charles, 1st Class Gunner's Mate, Submarine K-1.
Shumaker, Dawson, Navy, Seattle, Wash.
Smith, Edgar S., 304th Engineers, France.
Smith, Ralph A., 107th Field Signal Bn., France.
Snyder, Dr. C. R. (Captain), Med. Det. 5th Amm. Train, France.
Sommers, Jesse, Petersburg, Va.
Speck, Russell, Navy, U. S. S. Louisiana.
Spiedel, Howard, killed in action, May 23, 1918, France.
Stouffer, Paul, 314th Infantry, Camp Meade, Md.

Swartz, Ray, 311th Tank Corps, France.
Sweger, Charles, 303d Center Tank Corps, France.
Troy, John D., 13th Balloon Co., France.
Vitullo, Edward, 35th Engineers, France.
Wallace, John T. R., 155th Depot Brigade, Camp Lee, Va.
Weaver, John, 23d Machine Gun Battalion, Camp Freemont, Cal.
Weaver, John M., U. S. Marine Corps, San Juan, D. R.
West, Mrs. Florence Miller, Red Cross Nurse, Philadelphia, Pa.
Westfall, Harry, Hoboken, N. J.
White, Miss Grace, Red Cross Nurse, France.
Whitmyer, Ambrose, Camp Lee, Va.
Whitmyer, Thomas, Camp Jackson, S. C.
Wileman, L. Edison, S. A. T. C., State College, Pa.
Wise, Miss Elsie E., Red Cross Nurse, France.
Wise, M. L. (Sgt.), Kelly Field, Texas.
Wolf, Elmer E., Co. L, 358th Infantry, France.
Zimmerman, Albert, M. O. T. C., France.
Zimmerman, George, British waters, Tor. B. Cummings.
Zimmerman, Elmer, U. S. S. Dixie, Navy, France.

MILLER TOWNSHIP.

Baker, Albert, Infantry, France.
Baker, Edward, Camp Lee, Va.
Baker, Walter, Camp Meade, Md.
Campbell, Charles, Aviation, Texas.
Campbell, Harry F., Artillery, Camp Meade, Md.
Campbell, Joseph, Hospital, Baltimore, Md.
Hammaker, Harry, Camp Meade, Md.
Harper, Walter, Motor Transport., Camp Jessup, Ga.
Henderson, Elmer, France.
Kraft, Austin, Military Police, France.
Potter, Paul, Camp Meade, Md.
Roush, Nevin, Infantry, France.
Smee, Raymond, Infantry, France.

MILLERSTOWN.

Allen, Lee T., Aëro Photo. Service, United States.
Brown, Israel, 320 Supply Train, Camp Meade, Md.
Coffman, George, 16th Infantry. Wounded July 19, 1918, on Alsace-Marne
    Front; gassed Oct. 2, 1918, on Meuse-Argonne Front; France and
    Germany.
Diffenderfer, Guy, 20th M. G. Bat., foreign service.
Fahnestock, Wm. H., Camp Lee, Va.
Fry, Emory R., 355th Bat. Tank Corps, Oversea.
Garman, Robert H., 363d Inf. Died Feb. 25, 1919, from wounds; foreign
    service.
Gearhart, Mont. (Sgt.), Med. Dept., la Marne, foreign service.
Hall, Roscoe W. (Major), Medical Dept.; two stars and four gold stripes;
    France, England, and Scotland.
Hetrick, Esther S. (Nurse), Mussel Shoals, Ala., U. S.
Holman, A. L. (1st Lt.), Med. Corps, United States.
Knight, Edward S., 44th C. A. C. Killed Sept. 27, 1918. France.
Knight, Lawrence L., 78th Field Artillery, foreign service.
Lahr, J. Banks, S. A. T. C., United States.
Leonard, Thomas P. (Sgt.), 394th Engineers, France.
Liddick, Charles W., four stars on service ribbon; foreign service.
Liddick, H. J., 155th Depot Brigade, Camp Lee, Va.
Miller, Earl H., 23d Engineers, France.
Newman, George D. (Drill Sgt.), 112th Infantry, Camp Hancock, Ga.
Newman, W. V., 869th Transportation; three service stripes; France.
Powell, D. S., 314th Infantry, France.
Rhoades, Simon L., Wagoner, 304th Engineer's Train, France.
Rounsley, S. Nelson, Base Hospital 34, France.

Roush, John W., 301st Infantry, foreign service, France.
Rowe, Raymond A., Aviation, foreign service.
Shenk, Robert F., 108th Field Artillery, France.
Stewart, Percy E., Infantry, United States.
Swartz, Casper W., 314th Infantry, France.
Taylor, W. Rodney, Med. Department, United States.
Ulsh, C. Kenneth (2d Lt.), Infantry, United States.
Ulsh, Edgar A., 116th Infantry, France.
Ulsh, James E., 23d Engineers, France.
Wagner, Harry E., 306th Field Artillery; on firing line 108 days, with five
    off; France.
Yohn, George G., 58th Infantry, United States.

NEW BUFFALO.

Bair, Clarence.
Bixler, Thomas J.
Bowman, Benjamin T.
Freet, Charles H.
Howe, Miles, 112th Infantry, Camp Hancock, Ga.
Liddick, Noble C., 304th Engineers, France.
McMorris, Ralph W., Field Hospital No. 29, Camp Logan, Texas.
Noblet, Thomas L., 314th Infantry, France.

NEWPORT.

Armstrong, H. H. (Lt. Jr. Grade), Ordinance, Navy, United States.
Beasom, Charles A., 145th Infantry, France and Belgium.
Bassett, Charles P., Wagoner, 1st Engineers, France and Germany.
Beatty, Earl, Musician, Y. M. C. A., France.
Bechtel, Alfred, 304th Remount Sta., United States.
Bitner, Charles D., 118th Infantry, France.
Bosserman, Charles (Sgt.), Med. Corps, United States.
Bowerson, Wm. M., 155th Depot Brigade, United States.
Burkepile, Roy, 314th Infantry, France. ˋ
Butz, Jesse E., 314th Infantry; wounded in action; France.
Clay, C. E., 45th Balloon Co.; gassed; France.
Cooney, Cloyd W., Wagoner, 304th Engineers, France and Germany.
Davis, John F., 808th Aëro Squadron.
DeLancey, Fairlie M., 103d Signal Battalion; wounded in action; France
Demaree, Frank (S. M., 1st class), U. S. N. Aviation, France.
Demaree, Harry S. (S. M. 1st class), U. S. N. Aviation, France.
Demaree, D. Ralph (1st Lt.), Quartermaster's Corps, France and England.
Doner, Clyde, S. A. T. C., United States.
Dorwart, Frederick G. (Captain), Aviation Flyer, United States.
Dorwart, George M. (2d Lt.), 15th Machine Gun Bat; severely wounded;
    France.
Drake, Charles A. (Captain), 3d Infantry; Victory Service Ribbon, three
    stars; France and Germany.
Dudley, Harvey E., Bugler, 155th Depot Brigade, United States.
Dunn, Samuel M., Ordinance, 1st Battalion, United States.
Eby, Chas. McH. (Lt. Col. Adj.), 160th Brigade, France.
Evans, Philip A., 9th Infantry, Germany.
Fickes, Edgar B., 1st Prov. Guard, Train Battalion, United States.
Fickes, Stanley G. (Lt.), Fld. Trg. Depot, United States.
Flickinger, Herbert M., Gunner, Navy, France waters.
Flickinger, Ralph, 346th Transport, France.
Fry, George R. (Color Sgt.), C. O. T. S., United States.
Fulton, David, 41st Balloon Co., United States.
Fulton, Orville, C. O. T. S., United States.
Gantt, Paul T., 103d Sanitary Train, France.
Gunderman, J. Lawrence, Y. M. C. A., France.
Gutshall, Roy, 103d Engineers; gassed; France.
Heckendorn, Miles, 147th Engineers, United States.
Hench, Rodney, S. A. T. C., United States.

Hersh, James E.
Hockenberry, Merle.
Hockenberry, James K.
Hoke, Edward E., Battery Mechanic, United States.
Ickes, David C. (Sgt.), 14th Grand Div. K. T. C.; gassed; France and
  Germany.
Jones, Clyde C., 153d Depot Brigade, United States.
Kapp., John 55th Infantry, France.
Kauffman, Gustave C., 60th Infantry, France and Germany.
Keen, James G. (Sgt.), Base Hospital No. 60, France.
Kell, Russell, S. A. T. C., United States.
Kell, Warren E. (Sgt.), 4th Motor Supply Train, France and Germany.
Kipp, Miss Bird (Nurse), France.
Kuhn, Oscar S. (Sgt.), S. A. T. C. Aviation, United States.
Lahr, Max G., S. A. T. C., United States.
Leiter, Herman L. (1st Cl. Sgt.), Hospital Train 56, France.
Light, Horace, D. M. E. & E. S., France.
Manning, Frank (S. M., 1st Class), U. S. N. Aviation, United States.
Manning, Cloyd (1st Cl. Sgt.), 1st U. S. Engineers; gassed; France and
  Germany.
Markel, Leslie, S. A. T. C., United States.
McCulloch, D. H. (Sr. Lt.), Naval Aviation, United States.
McNaughton, Charles (Sgt.), 1st Engineers, France and Germany.
Miller, Herbert, 102d Infantry; wounded and gassed; captured by Huns;
  France.
Murtiff, Carl, C. W. S., United States.
Oren, Joe B., 42d Coast Artillery, France.
Oren, John R., 51st Howitzer Reg., France.
Oren, Melvin M., Cook, 103d A. T., France and Belgium.
Page, Lawrence, 37th Artillery, United States.
Page, Willard, 14th Balloon Co., France and Germany.
Peterman, Albert, 211th F. S. Bn., United States.
Reeder, C. Landis, Marines, United States.
Reeder, Louis E. (Sgt.), Infantry, unassigned, United States.
Rice, William, 327th Fire and Guard, United States.
Rush, Harry M., 9th Infantry, France.
Sanderson, Samuel P., 54th Infantry, France.
Shreffler, David E. (Sgt.), Med. Corps, United States.
Shuman, Frank (Sgt.), Intel. Dep. Amer. Embassy, France.
Smith, Chester.
Smith, Floyd H., C. W. S., United States.
Smith, Rodney T., C. A. C., United States.
Smith, Roy B., Fireman, Naval Reserve, England and France.
Smith, Thomas L. (Band Sgt.), 314th Inf., Hq. Co., France.
Soule, Edwin K., S. A. T. C., United States.
Soule, William H., unassigned, United States.
Sunday, J. Layton (Lt.), 32d C. A. C., United States.
Swab, Harry, 336th Bn. Tank, France, Germany, and England.
Sweger, Thomas W., 60th Infantry, France.
Wagner, Charles, 24th Spruce Squadron, United States.
Wagner, J. K., 8th Field Artillery, France.
Wagner, Harry K.
Wagner, Roy A., 314th Infantry, Co. B., France.
Wertz, H. Ray (2d. Lt.), 101st Div. Inf. Repl., United States.
White, Cloyd K., 134th Spruce Squadron, United States.
White, Earl D., 9th Corps, Headquarters T., France.
Wilson, Paul A., S. A. T. C., United States.
Wright, Charles W., 304th Engineers, France.
Wright, J. Fred (Sgt.), 1st Engineers, France and Germany.
Wright, Miss Mary (R. C. Nurse), Base Hospital No. 36, France.
Wright, Russell, 3d Balloon Co., France and Germany.
Zeiders, Harry, 43d Balloon Co., France.

OLIVER TOWNSHIP.

Acker, Lee W., 112th Field Artillery; gassed; France.
Campbell, Arthur L. (Sgt.), Medical Department, Ft. McHenry, Md.
Campbell, Harry.
Carl, John W., 110th Infantry. Captured July 15, 1918. 4 months; France.
Clay, Charles E., 45th Infantry, France.
Claybaugh, Ed., 51st Reg., Bat. E., France.
Crist, Charles B., 103d Infantry, France.
Dietz, Aldie A., 145th Infantry, France.
Dudley, Harvey E., 155th Infantry, Camp Lee, Va.
Fealtman, Harvey A., 103d Infantry, France.
Fisher, Bradford W.
Fisher, Raymond D.
Fleisher, Paul E. (Sgt.), Ordinance Dept. Died of disease, Jan. 23, 1919,
    at Hoboken; France.
George, David H.
Henry, Floyd H.
Hohenshildt, Irvin E., 315th Field Artillery, France.
Hohenshildt, Ralph A., 304th Infantry. Wounded and gassed; France.
Jeffries, E. J.
Jury, Albert J.
Kennedy, Loy, Camp Lee, Va.
Marshal, Richard.
Myers, Chester M., 56th Engineers, France.
Reamer, John, United States.
Rush, Harry, 9th Infantry, France.
Sharp, Paul W.
Wright, Frederick C.

PENN TOWNSHIP.

Achenbach, George W., 35th Engineers.
Achenbach, Howard (Sgt.), Quartermaster's Dept., Camp Meade, Md.
Barocini, John, 314th Infantry, Camp Green, N. C.
Bolden, Loy Arnold (Sgt.), 110th Infantry, France.
Crist, Charles, 103d Engineers.
Grabill, Benjamin Boyer, 4th Div. M. S. T.
Graff, John R., 54th C. A. C., France.
Griffith, Joseph, 304th Engineers, France.
Gross, John M., Med. Dep., 310th Engineers, N. Russia.
Gross, Lake, Aëro Squad, Kelly Field, Texas.
Haas, J. Earl, 314th Infantry, France.
Harris, Wm., Coast Artillery, Ft. Totten, N. Y.
Hetrick, Lloyd L., 314th Infantry, France.
Hockenberry, Wilbert, 314th Infantry, France.
Koons, Wm. Elbert, 29th Infantry, Canal Zone.
Leonard, George, Replacement Died Oct. 14, 1918; Camp Oglethorpe.
Lightner, Robert E., 39th Infantry, France.
Maguire, W. R., 6th U. S. Engineers, France.
Maxwell, Calvin J., Coast Artillery Corps, France.
Maxwell, Clarence F., Field Artillery, France.
Maxwell, W. C., Field Artillery, France.
May, William Ferris, 304th Ammunition Train, France.
McCann, Blake, 4th Infantry, France.
McCann, John, Remount Dept., 4th Infantry, Camp Meade, Md.
Messimer, Walter L., Medical Dept., Camp Custer, Mich.
Owen, Abram S., Aëro Squadron, San Antonio, Texas.
Pressler, Edward G.
Pressler, Robert D., 304th Ammunition Train, France.
Pressler, Wm. E., M. G. Corps, France.
Raub, Oscar M., Camp Meade, Md.
Snyder, Cloyd Englehart (2d Lt.), 5th U. S. Infantry, Canal Zone.
Snyder, Eldon Wert, 2d Reg. M. M. S. C., France.
Toland, Charles F., France.

Troutman, Norman R., 35th Engineers, France.
Wahl, Clarence. Cook, 314th Infantry, France.
Weaver, Charles F., Hoboken, N. J.

RYE TOWNSHIP.

Bailey, David, Navy.
Bell, Hugh A., S. A. T. C., Pittsburgh, Pa.
Bomgardner, Joseph, Asst. Postmaster, Angel Island, Cal.
Broomhead, Earl, 5th Co. Cavalry, Ft. Bliss, Texas.
Heishley, Newton C., Utility Detachment, Camp Eustis, Va.
Hill, George W., 15th Co., 4th Bat., 155th D. B., France.
Knaub, John A., 44th Co., France.
Menges, Paul, 149th Co., 12th Reg. H. A., St. Croix, Virgin Island.
Miller, Harvey, Bat. C., 6th Reg. C. & C., France.
Myers, Dr. C. W. E. (1st Lt.), Medical Corps, France.
Rodgers, John (Sgt.), N. G. Governor's Troops, France.
Snyder, John, Camp Greenleaf, Ga.
White, Charles A., Auto Mechanic, Pittsburgh, Pa.
White, Walter (Sgt.), Co. H., 314th Infantry, France.

SAVILLE TOWNSHIP.

Balmer, Earl, United States.
Barns, J. Arthur, Quartermaster-at-Large, Army of Occupation.
Bender, John, Co. C., 314th Infantry, France.
Bender, William, France.
Bixler, Frank R., 314th Infantry, Camp Meade, Md.
Brandt, Robert, Yoeman, U. S. Navy, U. S. S. Thetis.
Campbell, Joseph C., Horseshoer, 314th Infantry, France.
Clouser, Silas C.
Fry, Sherman, D., 155th Depot Brigade, United States.
Jacobs, William, United States.
Kiner, Frank S., United States.
Kline, Roy M., 1st Aëro Regiment, France.
Moyer, Charles, 156th Depot Brigade, United States.
Moyer Edward.
Moyer, George.
Moyer, James O., 28th Division. Shot through the right foot; France.
Moyer, Oscar, 28th Division, France.
- Orris, Lee, 153d Depot Brigade, United States.
Paden, Clarence E., Marine Service, United States.
Patterson, D. Ross, 110th Regiment, France.
Patterson, Harry, 108th Field Artillery, Nat. G. Governor's Troops, Mex.
    Border and France.
Raffensberger, Charles I., United States.
Reisinger, Charles W., 161st Infantry, France.
Reisinger, Jos. J., United States.
Reisinger, Ralph, Hdq. Co., 41st Infantry, United States.
Smith, J. Hartman, S. A. T. C., Co. F., Pittsburgh, Pa.
Smith, Paul R. (Sgt.), 28th Co. C. O. T. S., United States.
Smith, Walter A., Co. H., 110th Infantry. Killed in action, Aug. 21, 1918;
    France.
Snyder, Walker, 1st Pros. Co., 98th Division, United States.
Titzel, Frank, killed in action; France.
Utley, Ralph, Mechanic, Hdq. 304th Engineers, France.
Wax, Tolbert.
Wilson, Charles W., Co. H., 327th Infantry, France.

SPRING TOWNSHIP.

Baker, Charles.
Baker, Edward L., 55th Engineers, France.
Bender, Cyrus S., Wagoner, 314th Infantry, France.
Billman, Rev. A. M. (1st Lt., Chap.), Tank Corps, Camp Dix, N. J.
Bistline, Alvin L., Infantry, France.
Clelan, Samuel, Transportation Corps.

Cooper, Joseph (Sgt.), Ambulance Driver.
Dunkelberger, G. C., Hospital Train 68, France and Germany.
Fleisher, Raymond, 116th Supply Train, France.
Foose, Charles E., Infantry, on the sea Nov. 11, 1918.
Foose, Harry D., Bugler, France and Germany.
Garlin, Charles E., Camp Lee, Va.
Goodling, Benner (Sgt.), France.
Jacobs, Charles E., 14th Infantry, Camp Grant, Ill.
Jacobs, Frank, Camp Lee, Va.
Jacobs, Wm. F., Co. M., 6th Bn., United States.
Kennedy, Arthur L., 321st Field Artillery, France.
Kennedy, Earl, Infantry, France.
Kretzing, Walter Guy, 1st Platoon, 30th Co., Ft. Thomas, Ky.
Logan, Daniel W.
Mayer, Edward S., 13th Eng. Corps, Virginia.
Nary, Thomas J., 313th Infantry, France.
Reapsome, Ralph G., 39th Infantry, France.
Schey, Lawrence E., 601st Engineers, France.
Sheaffer, Ray, gassed; France.
Smith, Charles E., Infantry, 41st Division, France.
Stambaugh, M. E. (Sgt.), Teacher Reconstruction School, Ft. Sheridan, Ill.
Sundy, Ralph G., Machine Gun, France and Germany.
Weldon, Walter C., 314th Infantry, France.
Wentzel, George A., Med. Corps, Camp Lee, Va.

Toboyne Township.

Adams, Wilmot J., Ordinance Supply Division, Camp Hancock, Ga.
Anderson, Thomas, 3d Co., I. R. C., France and Germany.
Beaston, Roy, Field Hospital No. 14.
Burkett, Curts, 363d Infantry, France.
Gutshall, Harry, 101st Engineers. Died of disease; France.
Henry, Ralph, 1st Div., Field Artillery, Bat. D., France and Germany.
Hockenberry, Bruce.
Hockenberry, Roy.
Kessler, Clarence, United States.
Kessler, Roy, Oversea.
Mumper, Wilmer, Mechanic, Bat. E., 74th Artillery, C. A. C., France.
Stephens, Dean, Co. D., 407th Tel. Bn. S. C., France.

Tuscarora Township.

Aughe, V. L., 60th Infantry, France.
Black, Jonathan R. (Sgt.), 1st Field Signal Bat., Germany.
Black, Andrew S., 318th Field Artillery, Germany.
Burkepile, Calvin.
Burkepile, Harry.
Dimm, Wm. R., Co. Mechanic, United States.
Fosselman, Sherman L., Motor Transport Corps, United States.
Kretzing, Ard.
Kretzing, Jacob A., Engineers, France.
Jones, J. Russell, Expert Rifleman, U. S. Marines, France.
McNaughton, Ralph, 325th Infantry, France.
Mitchell, Lewis M., 155th Depot Brigade, United States.
Powell, Clarence R., Ammunition Train, France.
Reynolds, Lee, killed.

Tyrone Township.

Beard, Mabel S. (Nurse), Base Hospital 107, France.
Beard, Ralph B. (2d Lt.), Aviation, Camp Dick, Texas.
Bernheisel, Newton E., Engineers, Oversea.
Bernheisel, William, Supply Train, Oversea.
Bistline, Miles, Marine Corps, United States.
Briner, Dewey, Aërial Squadron, England.
Crawford, Luther E., 5th Reg., T. A. R. D., France.
Emlet, Chester (Sgt.), Motor Transport Train, Oversea.

Emlet, Earl, Motor Transport Train, United States.
Himes, G. Robert (Chaplain), Oversea.
Ickes, Kepner R., Camp Lee, Va.
Kline, Lewis, Med. Corps, Oversea.
Lightner, Forest M., Camp Dix.
Lightner, Herman, Quartermaster, Camp Meade, Md.
Lightner, Morris Wm., Med. Dept., Ft. McHenry.
Lightner, Noy I., 320th Field Signal Bat., California.
Lightner, Robt. E., Infantry, France.
Noll, John Harold (Sgt.), 79th Division. Wounded in leg; France.
Power, Frank, United States.
Reeder, Anderson B., Supply Train, Oversea.
Rice, Carl.
Ritter, George (Sgt.), Shell shock, Oversea.
Sherman, Jas. W., Med. Corps, Camp Dix.
Stum, James G., Infantry, Oversea.
Stum, Wm. R., Infantry, Oversea.
Weller, Samuel, M. Gun, Philippine Islands.

WATTS TOWNSHIP.

Arney, Harry Z., S. A. T. C., Carlisle, Pa.
Dorman, Russell, Patrol S. S. Blakely, Navy.
Dorman, John.
Gunder, Jacob.
Hammaker, Nelson, 39th Infantry, France.
Hoehn, John R., 17th Field Artillery, France.
Huggins, William M., Infantry, France.
Humphrey, Herbert, Engineers, France.
Humphrey, Samuel, Engineers, France.
Kulp, Ray (Sgt.), 9th Division, Camp Sheridan.
Liddick, Sheridan, 321st Field Artillery.
Louden, Benson, 314th Infantry. Killed in action; France.
Louden, George, 314th Infantry.
Lowe, Albert Jacob, P. O. W. E. Co. 71, France.
Lowe, John Drothy, 8th Field Artillery, France.
Lowe, Julius Columbus, Co. C., 5th Bn., Ft. B. Harrison.
Lowe, Norman Enos, Co. C., 314th Infantry, Camp Meade, Md.
Lowe, Roy D., Camp Meade, Md.
Miller, Alfred Byron, S. A. T. C., State College, Pa.
Smith, Charles Robert, Med. Corps, New York City.
Steele, Ralph Charles, 20th Engineers, Camp Forest, Ga.
Thompson, Robert M., 2nd Cl. Seaman, Navy, Hampton Roads, Va.
Whitney, Fred, 103d Infantry, Camp Hancock, Ga.

WHEATFIELD TOWNSHIP.

Bornman, Daniel, Camp Meade, Md.
Charles, John Paul, Military Police, France.
Durham, John, Oversea.
Durham, Lloyd, France.
Gilbert, John, France.
Huss, Otto D., 6th Div., Motor Supply Train, France.
Lepperd, Robert Earl, S. A. T. C., Lewisburg, Pa.
Losh, George, Med. Dep., Camp Meade, Md.
Losh, Isaac, Cook, Quartermaster's Corps, Camp Meade, Md.
McPherson, Benjamin Davis, 10th Engineers, France.
Peters, C. W., France.
Potter, Dexter, Teamster, 39th Infantry, France.
Rodemaker, William Elbridge, Camp Lee, Va.
Shearer, James Franklin, 310th M. Gun Bn., France.
Wallace, Andrew Loy, 110th Infantry, France.
Weldon, Samuel, 2d Cl. Engineer, Navy, North Sea.
Zeigler, George Russell, 304th Engineers. Died of disease; France.
Zeigler, James Smiley, 304th Engineers, France.

CHAPTER XXXIV.

PERRY COUNTY'S NOTED MEN, AND PROMINENT
DESCENDANTS ABROAD.

CONSIDERING its comparatively small size and population, the territory which comprises Perry County is remarkable as the birthplace of many noted and illustrious men, or their forbears, since that wintry day, February 3, 1755, when the land office for the settlement of these lands was opened at Lancaster, in the Province of Pennsylvania. Of the period since then, it was a part of Cumberland for sixty-six years and a separate county for over one hundred, during both of which periods there have sprung from the pioneers and their descendants men and women whose names have been written high in the annals of the state and nation. Almost in the very beginning among those early warrantees of lands appeared the Blaines, one of whom, Ephraim Blaine, became Commissary General of the Continental Army, the right-hand man and associate of General Washington. His wonderful organizing ability did much to advance the cause of freedom. Of a later generation came James G. Blaine, whose name will stand with those of Clay and Webster, as among the most illustrious American statesmen.

Only a few decades from the pioneers came one whose name is honored wherever law and justice are known, not only in his own country, but abroad. Chief Justice of his own state for many years when it was in the making, when settlements were still being made on the original public lands and when the great public works were being built, John Bannister Gibson stands in the forefront of American jurists. Henry Calvin Thatcher, a native Perry Countian of a later generation, became the first Chief Justice of that mighty empire of the West, Colorado, and his two brothers, Mahlon D. and John D. Thatcher, became great powers in the financial world, amassing fortunes running into the millions. Daniel Gannt, another native, became Chief Justice of the State of Nebraska. Twice in our own great Commonwealth of Pennsylvania have Perry County natives been occupants of the gubernatorial chair, as well as in the States of California and Minnesota, and the names of the Bigler brothers, Miller and Beaver, are a part of the annals of their native and adopted states. While the elder Bigler was the governor of Pennsylvania, his brother was occupying the governor's chair in far away California, the only time in America when brothers have been governors at the

604

same time. *Warren G. Harding, the President of the United States at this time, is a descendant of pioneers who dwelt on Perry County soil, through the Stephens family lineage. Having mentioned the names Blaine and Beaver in the preceding sentences recalls that on two other occasions Perry County almost had the honor of seeing a native or a descendant of a native occupy the Presidential chair of the United States. The turning of but one thousand votes in the State of New York, in 1884, would have placed James G. Blaine there, and at the National Republican Convention of 1880, when James A. Garfield was nominated, thus breaking the Grant-Blaine deadlock, the nomination for the Vice-Presidency was tendered to James A. Beaver, who declined, stating that he had consented to run for Governor of Pennsylvania. Had he accepted that nomination he would have been installed as President when the assassin's bullet had put an end to the career of the great and good Garfield.

While far the greater part of the actual work was being done on this volume the occupant of the second highest office in the land, the Vice-Presidency of the United States, was the son of a native Perry Countian, the mother of Thomas R. Marshall having been born at Ickesburg; and when the Southern Confederacy was formed the second officer of that government, Alexander H. Stephens, was likewise the son of a Perry Countian, his father having been born at Duncannon. Of these men and scores of others the following pages will go briefly into detail.

Twice have natives of Perry County been found upon the rolls of the greatest legislative body in the world—the United States Senate, William Bigler during the Buchanan administration, and Chester I. Long during the administration of Theodore Roosevelt, the first representing his own great State of Pennsylvania, and the latter, that red blooded, virile commonwealth of the West, Kansas. Both men made enviable records. The name of Alexander K. McClure, a Perry Countian, will ever stand in the very first rank of editors and newspapermen of this great country, along with those of Horace Greely, Charles A. Dana and Henry

---

*In the Evarts-Peck History of the Susquehanna and Juniata Valleys, the statement is made that the Robert Polleck, who warranted lands in what is now Jackson Township in 1755, was the grandfather of President Polk. Evidently somebody palmed off some spurious information upon the late J. R. Flickinger, who wrote the chapter on Jackson Township. In all of Prof. Flickinger's writings this is the only statement, as near as we know, which is not borne out by facts. He says: "Robert Polleck was the grandfather of President Polk, which is, in fact, the same name, as will become evident to any one pronouncing both names so as to sound every letter." President Polk's grandfather was Ezekiel Polk, a member of Congress from North Caroiina, and his father was Samuel K. Polk. Perry County has enough prominent men without laying a claim to a single one not a native or descendant.

Watterson. He was the close friend and confidant of the immortal Lincoln in those trying days of the Sectional War.

A native Perry County girl, born Marie Stewart, but known in the theatrical world as "Marie Doro," has attained a national reputation as an actress both upon the speaking stage and in the silent drama. Another, Dr. Elizabeth Reifsnyder, spent much of her life in China, where she is largely responsible for the building of a great hospital and where she was in charge—between the battle lines—even during the Chinese rebellion.

Notwithstanding that Perry County, and Pennsylvania generally, have sent to the great West and elsewhere many of their natives to help upbuild other communities, yet Pennsylvania is one of the states that keeps at home a very large proportion of its energetic men and women. According to "Who's Who," of 1,878 men and women born in Pennsylvania, 1,608 have made their home state their place of residence. As a comparison: of those born in the neighboring State of Ohio, about fifty per cent are no longer residents.

Philosophers tell us that the trinity controlling the future is heredity, training and environment. Since such is the fact great credit seems due the past generations, even from the time of the pioneer, for their manhood and womanhood, the home and family life which they lived where that training was bent in the right direction, and the environment which they chose and helped make among the hills and valleys which now form the county of Perry.

Perry County has ever been noted, not only for the number of illustrious men who have gone forth to larger fields, but for the number of worthy and successful professional men and educators, who have claimed it as their home; and to issue this book without paying especial attention to that reputation and those who have helped make it would be to make it defective. A noted theologian has advanced a reason for this reputation relating to the professions. According to his method of reasoning the fact that the soil is not so fertile as in some places makes the price of farm land less and enables more people to own their farms than in several near-by counties, thus fixing them to the soil instead of becoming a moving or roving tenantry, which gave them a better chance to become educated. A famous educator offered a reason along the same line when he said, "The people of your county did not keep their children home to 'strip tobacco' but sent them to school." The writer does not pretend to know the reason, but does know that unlike a number of near-by counties Perry has had no normal schools and colleges within its borders to which the rising generation could be sent at little expense, but from the product of these "poor" farms has educated a greater proportion of its youth than has been done in many other counties. Of one thing we are sure, and that is that practically all of these men and women who have gone forth and brought success upon their homeland have had good and very many of them Godly mothers, whose impress for good and right living has been wrought into their very fiber. In a letter lying before me, from the pen of a noted theologian, is this outstanding sentence: "I think it would be difficult to find anywhere else such interest and attractiveness in home life." Those words were written by a man whose duties bring him into the homes of hundreds each year, and often in widely separated parts of the country. Himself a Perry Countian, born and bred in one of these homes, he attributes all his success to a Godly mother. During the past decade the press ofttimes teemed of "the Fatherland," referring to a land across the sea. The writer always likes to think of America as "the Motherland,". and of Perry County as the home of the best of mothers—your mother and mine. To them, who went down to the very brink of eternity for us, who spent many weary and wakeful hours during the stilly night, who nursed us through the ills of childhood and mayhap later years, in whose hearts we are ever their boy or their girl—to them, lies much of the credit for the success attained by the men and women, sketches of whose lives occupy many of the following pages. Many of them were what would be termed old-fashioned mothers, not women of the period, perchance enameled and painted, whose bejeweled hands never felt the clasp of baby fingers; but dear, old-fashioned, sweet-voiced, loving mothers whose dear hands were often worn with toil in the rearing of their little children. I like that word old-fashioned, and especially as applied to mothers, for it is the old-fashioned mother of even to-day that makes the American home the foundation of the Republic. With few exceptions the sketches which follow, of the professional men, are of those who have gone abroad, as the field for advancement at home is necessarily limited by the small area and population.

One may estimate justly and try to record a perspective of the life and character of a person and yet fail to convey it to the reader as it appears to himself. Traits which to some of us seem most significant to others appear trifling and almost negligible. With any little vices which any of the characters may have possessed this book is unconcerned. The cynic will no doubt be able to dig from the depths of a perverted nature or from unfounded fact and rumor something to appease his or her appetite and allay within a curious desire to pull from a pedestal those whose greatness is acknowledged or whose success is marked. To those we can only quote the biblical injunction, "Let he who is without sin cast the first stone," and recall that even the Great Master in choosing his disciples did not have an entire twelve without fault.

In the sketches of these men membership in lodges is rarely mentioned, as no special distinction attaches thereto, save in so far as advancement to office of unusual note is concerned, neither is church membership dwelt upon, as that is but the duty of every one, but where men have done unusual things or great work along religious lines it is recorded, as it should be.

Some persons of note will be missed, unintentionally, probably from having no knowledge of them whatsoever or from failure to receive replies to letters, many hundreds of which were written, to points all over the Union. No attempt has been made to be conclusive in the biographical articles in the book, as the size of the volume has barred any such attempt, but the mere statement that certain men were born within the borders of Perry County or its territory would only be a chronological table of uncertain value. Accordingly the author has often read many volumes and from the mass of material has tried, in each biographical sketch, to portray the character, the most marked characteristics, and briefly, the story of the life of its subject.

Doubtless many readers will think that some very important characters have been overlooked in the preparation of these sketches, and possibly some will feel that a few names have been inserted which have small claim to distinction. While all have a right to their opinions, yet the author feels that each name here has in some way or another brought credit upon his native county and a careful perusal and consideration of the data, we believe, will convince the reader also of that fact.

Of the Perry Countians who remained at home these pages tell the story, not in any one place, but throughout the book. Take a given family, and in the history of a certain township you will find where the pioneer located his land, mayhap where one of his people had "an argument" with the Indians. Later his descendants may be found building a mill or in other matter of import. The grandson, perchance, was one of those enthusiasts who helped secure countyhood. In another generation the family may have attained county office, and among the names of the noted and successful Perry Countians who went abroad will doubtless be found those of still later generations. The story of those "to the manor born," who remained in the county, is already written in the county press. They are known to have been a red-blooded, virile people, else there would have been no occasion for this work, telling of their history and of the biographies of their descendants and kin. In the *People's Advocate and Press*" of New Bloomfield (1902) Rev. J. Dill Calhoun, a Perry Countian, writing from Illinois, said: "I have always maintained and do hereby affirm that 'Old Perry' has ever had within its borders a superior class of men in every legitimate vocation of life, and several visits to the haunts

Harding, who was born in Pennsylvania in March, 1802, and was united in marriage to Joshua Crawford, of Baltimore, in 1821. They located in Washington County, Pennsylvania. Joshua Crawford's daughter, Mary Ann, was united in marriage to Charles Alexander Harding, the father of Dr. George T. Harding, father of the President. Sophia Stevens' lineage is traced to the family of Capt. Alexander Stevens, who was the grandfather of Alexander H. Stephens, Vice-President of the Confederacy, and who resided near Duncannon, where he married Catherine Baskins.

The President on the father's side is a descendant of the noted Harding family of the Wyoming Valley, in Pennsylvania, where some members of the clan were among those massacred by the Indians, and others were patriots in the Revolution. He was born near Blooming Grove, Ohio. His family's start was rather humble and he was the first-born of eight children. At fourteen he matriculated at the Ohio Central College, at Iberia, no longer in existence, but had to stop a number of times to earn money to continue his studies. He drove team, helped grade a roadbed, painted buildings, and did other odd jobs. At college he was editor of the student publication, through which he was brought into contact with the printing business, at which his odd moments were employed. In 1884 Dr. Harding located at Marion, and some time later Warren G. Harding became the editor and publisher of the *Marion Star,* then a struggling paper. He placed it on a firm footing and it is to-day known as one of the substantial small city dailies of that great state. The President is still the principal owner, and can handle any position on the paper. After it was on firm footing he organized a stock company, and he and his employees own it. Entering politics he twice represented the Thirteenth District in the Ohio State Senate. From 1904 to 1906 he was lieutenant governor, and in 1910 was the Republican nominee for governor, but was defeated. In 1914 he was elected to the United States Senate by 100,000 majority, over 73,000 above the rest of the ticket. When the National Republican Convention met at Chicago in 1919 he stood fourth in the balloting for the Presidential nomination. A prolonged deadlock of the first three candidates made him the logical nominee and at the succeeding election, with Calvin Coolidge for Vice-President, he carried the entire country, save the "Solid South," from which he, however, captured Tennessee. Before becoming President he made three trips to Europe to study their systems of government. On entering the political arena he was associated with such men as McKinley, Foraker, Sherman, Taft, and Roosevelt. His strong point is mirrored in the single familiar expression, "Back to normalcy." Of the McKinley type he believes in the things which have been tried and proven, rather than the various "isms" oft clamored for by the populace. Early in 1922 he called a conference of the nations to meet at Washington to consider the reduction of armament and if, in the years to come, that shall have borne fruit it will possibly be the outstanding feature of his administration.

The efforts of Mr. Harding while a member of the United States Senate to safeguard national sovereignty and independence were largely instrumental in placing him in the President's chair, as there are many millions who still believe that the Monroe Doctrine, later so nobly upheld by President Cleveland, is a vital, living force, and that it should ever remain so. He early advocated preparedness and sponsored the bill for preparedness which had the endorsement of Col. Roosevelt, former President of the United States. His knowledge of economics and finance is generally conceded to be greater than that of any of his predecessors.

THOMAS RILEY MARSHALL, VICE-PRESIDENT OF THE U. S.

During the greater part of the period in which this book was written and compiled, or until March 4, of last year, the occupant of the second highest office in the land, the Vice-Presidency of the United States, was Thomas Riley Marshall, whose mother, *Martha E. Patterson, was born at Ickesburg, Perry County, March 5, 1829, being the daughter of Thomas and Susanna (Linn) Patterson, who subsequently moved to Richland County, Ohio, in 1832, where both soon died. Susanna Linn was the daughter of John Linn, who died on the old Linn farm, near Saville, in 1837, and the granddaughter of Rev. John Linn, pioneer pastor who passed away in 1820, the very year of the county's erection. On the Patterson side his mother was a descendant of Charles Carroll, of Carrollton, a signer of the Declaration of Independence. On his father's side the Vice-President is a scion of the Virginia family of Marshalls, being a grandnephew of the celebrated Chief Justice Marshall. The Linn lineage is numerous in Perry County, and is one of the substantial strains descended from the pioneers.

There are certain things about Mr. Marshall's election to and occupancy of the Vice-Presidency which stand out. He shares with John Adams and Daniel Tompkins the distinction of being elected on the ticket of the same party, with the same head, to succeed himself. Washington and Adams were twice elected, as were James Monroe and Daniel Tompkins, and not again did that condition occur until the case of Wilson and Marshall. When President Wilson was incapacitated from performing the duties of the Presidency, and there appeared no constitutional provision covering such a condition, a less tactful man in the Vice-Presidency

---

*Verified by a letter from Vice-President Marshall, in possession of the author, and by the records at the Perry County recorder's office.

membership. That fraternity, by the way, was founded by Chief Justice Marshall. Mr. Marshall took up the study of law at Fort Wayne, and on his twenty-first birthday was admitted to the bar. He located at Columbia City, Indiana, and in a short time was known all over northern Indiana. In a few years he was known over the entire state, as one of its most able attorneys. Then came his entry into matrimony. While acting as a special judge in the circuit court at Angola, Indiana, he met Miss Lois Kinsey, who was assisting her father, the court clerk, and later she became Mrs. Marshall.

In 1908 the Democrats of Indiana were in a quandary as to whom to nominate for the governorship. Some person suggested that they name some prominent lawyer. He had not been a candidate, yet "Tom" Marshall was the one man to whom all turned, and he was nominated. He took the stump and with him went Mrs. Marshall, who was of great assistance to him. As governor of Indiana Mr. Marshall showed himself to be opposed to the centralization of government. He is a Democrat of the old school. When he was elected governor he carried the state by 15,000 majority, while the Democratic candidate for President lost it by 10,000. Indiana thought so much of him that he was their first choice for President at the Baltimore convention, which accorded him second place on the ticket. His election then, and nomination and reëlection four years later are matters of history, with which all are familiar.

Throughout both terms of his service Vice-President Marshall was a prudent, self-determined, open-minded man, with a lofty purpose which commanded the respect and admiration of the Senate, of all branches of the Federal government, and of the nation. On his retirement Senator Lodge and Senator Underwood, representing two different political faiths, paid him a most remarkable tribute. Mr. Marshall filled the Vice-Presidency with an unusual dignity at a most trying time.

ALEXANDER H. STEPHENS, VICE-PRESIDENT OF THE CONFEDERATE STATES.

That the second highest officer of the Confederate States of America, the section which seceded from the Union in 1861, was a descendant of a family from Perry County, that staunch and loyal district which stood with Lincoln throughout the war, seems strange indeed, yet it is true, Alexander H. Stephens on the paternal side being a descendant of the Baskins family, one of the pioneer families of the county, and his own father having been born near Duncannon. And furthermore, Mr. Stephens was not ignorant of the fact of his Northern ancestry, but on one occasion came North to visit his relatives near Newport, traveling by packet boat,

Uncle James asked, 'Well, Alexander, what business are you pursuing?' He replied, 'I am a lawyer.' Instantly the whole table was silent. The old gentleman threw down his knife and fork and looked at his nephew with a sort of horrified amazement, as if he had said he was a highwayman or a pirate. 'What's the matter, Uncle James?' 'Did you say you were a lawyer?' 'Yes.' 'A lawyer?' 'What of that?' With an expression of complete despair he asked, 'Alexander, don't you have to tell lies?' His nephew, greatly amused, replied, 'No, sir; the business of a lawyer is neither to tell lies nor to defend lies, but to protect and maintain right, truth, and justice; to defend the weak against the strong; to expose fraud, perjuries, lies, and wrongs of all sorts. The business of a lawyer is the highest and noblest of any on earth connected with the duties of life.' This seemed to calm the old gentleman's fears."

The story of the meeting of the winsome Catherine Baskins and Alexander Stephens, the elder, and the grandfather of the Vice-President, reads like fiction. He came to Pennsylvania in 1746. He was a soldier under Braddock, had settled near James Baskins, in 1766, and, while crossing the Baskins' ferry at the mouth of the Juniata, got a glimpse of the ferryman's fair daughter and became infatuated. When military duty no longer claimed his attention he came back and again resided near the Baskins' ferry. He wooed and won the fair maiden and tradition says "not with the consent of her father, who refused to sanction the marriage and who disinherited her for that reason." And here is where tradition is at least partly wrong. The will of James Baskins, of Rye Township, dated January 30, 1788, recorded at the Carlisle Courthouse in Book E, page 117, and proven February 11, 1788, gives "five pounds" to each of his daughters, Elizabeth McCay, Catherine Stephens, Sarah Dougherty, and Jane Jones. The residue of his estate he willed to his son, Mitchell Baskins. His executors were Frederick and David Watts and Mitchell Baskins. The inventory, included ferrying flat, canoe, etc. The will shows that Catherine was treated in the same identical way as were her sisters, notwithstanding that all biographical works state otherwise. The reason for the nominal bequests to the daughters was probably due to the fact that they were all married and well cared for. Furthermore, James Baskins was not a wealthy man in the general acceptation of that term. Nevertheless, the young people were wed and located about five miles up the river.

In the meantime the Revolution came on apace and Stephens became a captain in the Continental Army, serving throughout the war. When the war was over he came back and with his wife settled in the vicinity of Duncannon, where in 1782, Andrew Baskins Stephens, the father of Alexander H. Stephens, was born. The Stephens family moved to Georgia in 1794, when Andrew was twelve years old; another son, James Stephens, going along, but later returning to Perry County and settling in Juniata Township, where he owned three hundred acres of land in 1820, the year of

Perry County's organization. There was a considerable migration to Georgia about this time by Scotch-Irish Presbyterians from Cumberland County, owing to the State of Georgia adopting a land policy which offered free homes to settlers.

Andrew Stephens married Margaret Grier, of Wilkes County, Georgia, July 12, 1806, and from this union of Puritan and Cavalier, was born Alexander H. Stephens, later Vice-President of the Confederate States, statesman, Congressman, and Governor of Georgia. Andrew Baskins Stephens, whether or not timid about getting parental sanction for the marriage, on May 17, of that year, made his request to her father for her hand, in writing, a single sentence stating, "The use of this written communication does not wholly originate in pusilanimity or in other sources that may be deemed timid, but in the intention to afford you requisite intelligence; and thereby to furnish you matter sufficient for absolute conclusion." In a further sealed enclosure, only to be opened in case his suit was looked upon favorably, he goes into details as to his birthplace, family, prospects, etc., a part of which follows and inseparably connects his parentage with Perry County:

"I was born in the State of Pennsylvania, in Cumberland County (in the part which is now Perry), in the year 1782, of poor parentage; by father's side particularly on account of my grandmother being a widow. Whether necessity, or the idea of promotion, or the tyranny of a domineering stepfather, induced my father at an early age to become a resident among the northern Shawnee Indians, I cannot tell, but he passed a considerable part of his youth with that copper-faced tribe; insomuch that his fortunes and accomplishments were by no means accepted by my mother's family. However, by an unwearied diligence he surmounted many inconveniences and became rather respected in the American Revolution. His manner of life since my remembrance has been regular and not uneconomical. He is now on the borders of eighty and possessed of more sprightliness than many of fifty. My mother was the eldest daughter of James Baskins, who in his life, kept a ferry above Harris's on the Susquehanna River. Her life was exemplary, and the Christian manner of her death a joy to every dutiful child that survived her. She had ten children, two of whom died at an early age; the others are widely scattered. My older sister and myself (the oldest and the youngest) with our father are the only remains of a once flourishing family. One sister, within three miles of us, is the only other known relative I have in the state. I never heard of felony being committed by any of my relations, but a considerable degree of dissipation. And as to achievements, I always leave them to be spoken of by better judges than myself."

Mr. Grier gave his consent, with the added rejoinder, that "the sentiments of her mother are such that she has no objection to offer, but that she is unfriendly to long courtships."

Andrew Stephens had a strong desire to again visit his Northern relatives, and did so in 1813, writing a letter to his sister from "Penton, Penna.," under date of April 28th. In it among other things he says: "I am now under old Cousin Hugh Stephens' roof.

* * * The Monday just two weeks after I left home I slept in Pennsylvania. * * * Brother (James Stephens) has a pretty promising family and a wife inferior to none. Indeed, Polly, I can and do call her sister. * * * I left brother's yesterday morning; on my way here I saw Aunt Baskins, Uncle Mitchell's widow, and family, who are living about two miles from grandfather's old ferry. Aunt was very glad to see me and appeared to live comfortably well. I love her nightily. She told me that uncle had entirely quit the use of spirits several years before his death. * * * Saw Cousin Hezekiah Martin." The letter is of much length, and of a personal nature.

Andrew Baskins Stephens, like his father, Capt. Alexander Stephens, was a learned man and a school teacher. The author has had the privilege of reading many of their personal and family letters and they show not only the earmarks of intelligence, but throughout are marked for their moral and even religious teachings. From a letter dated Wilkes County, Georgia, May 4, 1823, from Andrew B. Stephens, to his brother, James Stephens, in Perry County, the following paragraph is taken:

"When we hear of your children we want to hear that they are promising; we want and wish them to be so. We want and wish them to be patterns of obedience particularly to their mother, industrious and candid, ever scorning a mean or ungenerous act; striving as much as in them lieth to be peaceable, friendly and obliging, never fretting and finding faults of others to the neglect of their own, but by the faults of others correct their own; by so doing and living in obedience to the commands and precepts of their parents and senior superiors they will become honorable to themselves, useful to society, and a pleasing prospect to their friends and relations in every corner of the world."

The following is from Howard Carroll's "Twelve Americans":

"His grandfather, Alexander Stephens, was one of the Jacobites, who fled from England to America after the disastrous sequel to the ill-starred attempt of 'the Forty-Five.' Filled with a spirit of adventure, young and strong, he at first made his home with the Shawnee Indians in Pennsylvania. He took part in the French and Indian War, serving under Washington, and was present at Braddock's defeat. Subsequently in his wanderings he came to the ferry at the junction of the Juniata and Susquehanna Rivers, and there fell in love with the daughter of the ferry proprietor, a rich man named Boskins (Baskins). The maid looked favorably upon the young adventurer's suit; but the rich father, as rich fathers will, objected. Still the love-making went on, and in the end the young people, braving the father's displeasure, were married. The latter, true to his threat, disinherited her. Some time after this, the war for Independence having been declared, Stephens took service with the patriots. He was a good soldier and at the close of hostilities returned with the rank of captain. Unfortunately his estate was not in keeping with his rank, and to better his fortune he moved from Pennsylvania to Georgia."

That Alexander H. Stephens, the grandson, whose father was a native of Perry County territory, was a gifted man, a man of letters, a statesman and an historic personage, is verified by the fact

that in the Library of the City of New York the author of this
book found access to no less than forty-two distinct volumes devoted to or written by him. He was born in Wilkes County,
Georgia (in the part that is now Taliaferro County), on February
11, 1812. His mother died when he was a mere child and his father married again, the noted Linton Stephens being a child of
this second marriage. He was interested in securing an education
through the Presbyterian Church, which looked upon him favorably for the ministry, and provided means. He taught school for
a time and then read law and was admitted to the bar of his native county. He was offered a large salary to locate elsewhere, but
preferred to practice among his own people for a few hundred
dollars a year. He entered Franklin College (now the State University) in 1828, at the age of sixteen. He graduated with the
highest honors in 1832, as did his brother, Judge Linton Stephens,
at a later period. He was admitted to the bar in 1834. In 1836
he was elected to the lower branch of the Georgia Legislature, and
was later promoted to the State Senate. He was elected to the
United States Congress as a Whig in 1843, and served from the
Twenty-Ninth to the Thirty-Fifth Congresses, inclusive, and from
the Forty-Third to the Forty-Seventh Congresses, inclusive, retiring voluntarily in 1859. When the Sectional War was over he was
elected to the United States Senate by the State of Georgia in 1866,
but was not seated, as all of the disaffected section had not yet
been restored to the Union.

Human nature is interspersed with contradictions, which lend
charm to life, and this man, Alexander H. Stephens—his physical
appearance, his character and his career—is a study in that line.
While he was almost an invalid all of his busy life, yet, like Theodore Roosevelt, who was a delicate lad, he neither accepted that
condition of things or submitted to it. We quote from Gamaliel
Bradford's "Confederate Portraits": "Such a wretched frame for
such a fierce vitality might easily have made another Leopardi,
veiling all the light of heaven in black pessimism, cursing man and
nature and God with cold irony for the vile mistake of his creation.
Stephens fights his ills, makes head against them, never lets himself be really prostrated by physical torture or mental agony." He
once wrote, in a fit of despondence, "I have in my life been one of
the most miserable beings that walked the earth," and yet he rose
to eminence and to fame.

No man was more bitterly opposed to secession and to war than
he was. History records few finer things than Stephens' manly
stand against the tide of secession in his state, and certainly no
Southerner made a harder or more nearly successful fight to prevent the withdrawal of his state from the Union. When he delivered his famous anti-secession speech his friend, Robert Toombs,

although opposed to it, heartily applauded. When criticized for the action, he replied, "I always try to behave myself at a funeral." On one occasion he remarked, "I believe the state will go for secession, but I have a repugnance to the idea." Yet when Georgia did secede it was either necessary for him to go along with the tide or leave his home and state, an outcast from among his people. His view was that Georgia was his home and his state, and his allegiance was to Georgia. If Georgia remained in the Union then his allegiance was to the Union through his citizenship in Georgia, but when Georgia seceded then his citizenship likewise automatically removed him from the Union. Like Lee, Stephens went with his state; like Lee, he had opposed secession to the last, and like Lee, he became one of the really big men of the Confederacy. In fact, there were but three men considered at all for the Presidency of the seceded states, and Alexander H. Stephens was one. He was not chosen to that office but was made Vice-President of them on February 9, 1861, and championed the cause of the Confederacy, and yet he persistently opposed the conduct of that government from the beginning to the end. He opposed Davis on the important matters of finance and cotton and was opposed to conscription and martial law. He closed some rather severe remarks about President Davis thus: "It is certainly not my object to detract from Mr. Davis, but the truth is that as a statesman he was not colossal." After the government was organized at Montgomery it was reported that Davis said it was "now a question of brains," on which Stephens commented. "I thought the remark a very good one."

While in Congress he advocated the annexation of Texas but opposed that of Mexico. He ardently supported the compromise measures of 1850 and advocated the passage of the Kansas-Nebraska bill. He was Vice-President of the Confederacy until it fell. He was the South's representative to the conference with Lincoln and Seward at Hampton Roads on February 3, 1865, to consider terms of peace. A little incident of the Hampton Roads Conference shows the bigness of Mr. Lincoln. When the conference was over that had resulted in nothing. Lincoln and Stephens renewed a personal friendship that had begun in Congress before the war. After discussing many things, and just as they were parting Mr. Lincoln said, "Well, Stephens, is there anything of a personal nature I can do for you?" Mr. Stephens said, "Mr. Lincoln, I have a nephew who is a prisoner at Johnson's Island and we have heard nothing from him in a long time, and if you can do anything for him I shall appreciate it." Mr. Lincoln immediately was interested, wanted to know his name, etc., and took the information down in a note book which he carried, telling Mr. Stephens he would do what he could.

On February 5, 1865, Lieut. John A. Stephens, a Confederate prisoner at Johnson's Island, was ordered to report to headquarters. There he was told to pack up what he had and be ready at once to go to Washington, that orders had come that morning for him to be sent to the President of the United States. Young Stephens was dumbfounded, for he could not imagine why he should be ordered to Washington, unless it was to be tried, hung or something of an awful nature. But bidding his friends goodbye, he reported for the trip. It was a bitter cold day and he was driven across Lake Erie in a sleigh drawn by two mules. Reaching Sandusky he took the train and made his way to Washington. Upon reaching the Union capital he made his way at once to the White House to see the President. He sent in his name on a slip of paper, and after waiting some time was finally ushered into an inner office into the presence of Abraham Lincoln.

Mr. Lincoln was lying at full length upon an office table talking to Mr. Seward, Secretary of State, when Lieut. Stephens went in. He immediately got up and took both of Stephens' hands, giving him a very cordial welcome, and introducing him to Mr. Seward. He told him that he had seen his uncle at Hampton Roads and that he was well and that Mr. Stephens had asked him to send him to him and that he was going to do so. He told him to have the freedom of Washington as long as he wanted it and that when he got ready to go South to come to him and that he would give him his passes through the Union lines.

Young Stephens stayed in Washington several days and then reported to Mr. Lincoln to get his papers and to say good-bye. Mr. Lincoln turned to his desk and penned the following letter:

EXECUTIVE MANSION, WASHINGTON, D. C.,
February 10, 1865.

HON. ALEXANDER H. STEPHENS,
    Crawfordville, Ga.

My Dear Sir: According to our agreement your nephew, Lieut. Stephens, goes to you bearing this note. Please in return to select and send to me that officer of the same rank imprisoned at Richmond whose physical condition most urgently requires his release.   Respectfully,
                                                              A. LINCOLN.

Young Stephens was passed through the Union lines, joined the Confederate Army once more and, after the surrender, made his way to Georgia. When the letter from Mr. Lincoln was delivered to Mr. Stephens, Mr. Lincoln had been dead for some time.

Before the secession Mr. Stephens argued for the abolition of his own seat in Congress. He told the South that their agitators had done more than anything else to bring on the war. He wrote: "If they (the secession leaders) without cause destroy the present government, the best government in the world, what hope would I have that they would not bring untold hardships upon the people in their efforts to give us one of their own modeling." At the same time he was an ardent advocate of slavery, believing that slavery presented the most satisfactory solution of the difficult relations between whites and blacks, and that it was the duty of the superior race to protect and care for the inferior. Of all the eulogies of Stephens that of Abraham Lincoln is reproduced here as the most impressive. He wrote: "I just take up my pen to say that Mr. Stephens, of Georgia, a little, slim, pale-faced, consumptive man, has just concluded the very best speech of an hour's length I have ever heard. My old withered dry eyes are full of tears yet." Again we quote from Bradford's "Confederate Portraits": "He was probably one of the most logical, clear-headed, determined defenders of slavery and of the thorough subordination of black to white, yet few men have been more sensitively humane, more tenderly sympathetic with suffering in either white or black. The negroes loved him, and on one occasion after the war three thousand freedmen gathered on his lawn and serenaded him with passionate admiration and devotion." The eulogy of a slave would well serve for an epitaph for Stephens. It was: "Mars' Alex is kind to folks that nobody else will be kind to; he is kinder to dogs than mos' folks is to folks." Immediately after the war he was imprisoned as a secessionist in Fort Warren, at Boston, for six months, and from his diary we glean: "How strange it seems to me that I should thus suffer, I who did everything in my power to prevent (the war). * * * On the fourth of September, 1848, I was near losing my life for resenting the charge of being a traitor to the South, and now I am here, a prisoner under charge, I suppose, of being a traitor to the Union. In all, I have done nothing but what I thought was right."

There is a letter in existence in which Stephens discusses the possibilities, if the Confederate Government should fall upon his shoulders, in the event of the death of Davis. In it the clear appreciation of the abstract end to be attained is no finer than the full recognition of the immense difficulties and what he terms his own unfitness to encounter them.

Alexander Stephens never married, yet he loved children. He had two love affairs. The first he passed owing to poverty and ill-health. In the second instance he was already in Congress and well-to-do. The lady was not unwilling, but he took the lonesome way, claiming that a woman's due is a husband to lean upon instead of one whom she must nurse. He helped educate many young men. Cheerfulness, kindliness and sympathy won for him hosts of friends, as they will for any who practice them. In college, though poor, he was generally beloved. Of his official life in Washington it was the same. John Quincy Adams is said to have greeted him with verses more notable for feeling than for genius. Members of all parties treated him with respect. When voluntarily retiring from the United States Congress in 1859—although the smouldering embers of disunion were almost being fanned to a flame—he received the unusual honor of a dinner tendered by a list of members of both houses of Congress, without party distinction, headed by the Speaker of the House and the Vice-President.

Of his father he wrote: "Never was human anguish greater than that which I felt upon the death of my father. It seemed impossible to me that I could live without him; and the whole world for me was filled with the blackness of despair. * * * Whenever I was about to do something that I had never done before, the first thought that occurred to me was, what would my father think of this? * * * The principles and precepts he taught me have been my guiding star through life." And that father imbibed those principles early in life, while a resident of the vicinity of Duncannon. In the published works of Stephens one is impressed with the qualities of gentleness and courtesy. He disagrees with many. He condemns none. Even of Davis, whose policy he thought absolutely wrong, he has no unkind word. He says, "I doubt not that all—the President, the Cabinet and Congress—did the best they could from their own conviction of what was best to be done at the time." How many of us are willing to give like credit in our day? One of Lincoln's last efforts to avert the great struggle was through correspondence with Stephens, and of the prominent men on both sides that tolerant spirit was most shown by Lincoln, Lee and Stephens, in the order named. Stephens wrote on one occasion: "It may be that if the course which I thought would or could then save it (the Confederate Government), or would or could have saved it at any time, had been adopted, it would have come as far short of success as the one which was pursued; and it may be, that the one which was taken on that occasion, as well as on all the other occasions on which I did not agree, was the very best that could have been taken."

When he had thoroughly investigated a subject he was not easily swerved. During his celebrated speech in Congress in answer to Congressman Campbell, of Ohio, the latter interjected, "You are wrong in that." Quick as a flash Stephens retorted, "I am never wrong upon a matter I have given as close attention to as I have given to this." On an occasion Judge Cone, a powerful man, called Stephens a traitor. Stephens characterized it as a lie and threatened to slap Cone's face. They later met and Cone demanded a withdrawal. Stephens refused and struck. Whereupon Cone drew a knife, slashed him a number of times, got him down and shouted, "Retract or I'll cut your throat." "Never," said Stephens, "cut if you like." He caught the descending knife blade in his bare hand and had it horribly mutilated, the hospital attendants finding eighteen knife thrusts in his body and arms. The man, in the face of death, would not say he was wrong when he believed he was right.

It is said of Stephens that he devoted a portion of every day to a communion with God in prayer. In old age, in sickness, and in prison he summed the matter in a few words, thus: "That the Lord is a stronghold in the day of trouble I know. But for his sustaining grace, I should have been crushed in body and soul long ere this." And yet, he once made this most singular tirade against the ministry: "If I am ever to be tried for anything, may heaven deliver me from a jury of preachers! * * * Their most striking defect is a want of that charity which they, above all men, should not only preach but practice." That type of theologian happily has almost gone.

Omitting his part in secession, he has left a creditable record as a statesman, an orator and an author. Until 1855 he generally acted with the Whigs, although not in accord with them. From 1871 to 1873 he was editor of the *Atlanta Sun*. He was the author of a number of books, the most notable being "A Constitutional View of the War Between the States," in two volumes. He here gives probably the ablest statement that has ever been given of the South's doctrine of State Rights.

Even in his later years Stephens was allowed no respite from public service. In 1873 he was elected to fill an unexpired term in Congress as the representative of his old district—this after an intervening period of thirty years from his first entry into that body. He was reëlected each term until 1882, when he was elected Governor of Georgia by a large majority. He died in the governor's mansion, March 4, 1883, while in the midst of his term.

When old Dr. Massey, a friend of Stephens', heard of the death of President Lincoln he was a passenger on the train going towards Crawfordsville, where he got off and at once went to the home of Alexander H. Stephens and told him the news. According to Dr. Massey, Stephens burst into tears and said, "That is the greatest blow the South has had since Lee's surrender." Dr. Massey added that it took him eight years to see it that way.

In 1912 an old will was found among the papers of Alexander H. Stephens. While the name of the signer is torn off in the beginning of the document, and the first name of the signature itself cannot be made out, the will is evidently that of Alexander Stephens 1, the Jacobite who came to America about 1746. All of his children are mentioned in the will except Nehemiah Stephens, and it is probable that he is the one referred to when "my dutiful son ———" is mentioned, the latter part of the line being so faded and torn that nothing else can be made out. The will is

principally of interest in that the tomb of Alexander Stephens I,
records that he died March 15, 1813, while the will is dated November 29, 1813, later than his recorded death. The year of his‘
death was no doubt 1814, as, when his son Andrew Stephens visited what is now Perry County in 1813, in a letter dated "Penton,
Pennsylvania, April 28," to his sister, Mary Jones, he sends a
message to his father, Alexander Stephens. In the letter he also
speaks of leaving hime but two weeks before. The children to
whom bequests are given are named in the following order: Sarah
Coulter, James Stephens, Mary Jones, Catharine Hudgins (paper
torn at next name, probably Nehemiah, as stated above), and Andrew B. He names Andrew B. Stephens and Mary Jones as
executors. The will makes small bequests save for "an undivided
tract of land I am entitled unto, being a bounty of 2,000 acres, and
two claims, one for (paper torn here) from the Indians, and the
other on his Britannic Majesty.

Andrew B. Stephens, father of Alexander H. Stephens, later
left a widower, married Matilda Somerville Lindsay. The children of his first marriage were Alexander Hamilton, Aaron Grier,
and Mary; and those of the second marriage, Andrew and Benjamin, who died in childhood; Linton H., John Lindsay, and
Catharine Baskins. On May 7, 1826, pneumonia caused the death
of Andrew Baskins Stephens, and just one week later the same
disease was fatal to his wife.

Alexander H. Stephens was not the only one of Andrew B.
Stephens' progeny who attained greatness. Judge Linton Stephens, his half brother, was one of the most brilliant judges that ever
sat on the Supreme Court of Georgia, and was lieutenant colonel
of the Fifteenth Georgia Regiment. Some authorities think his
ability as great as that of Alexander H. John Lindsay Stephens,
another half brother, who died young, was one of the leading lawyer of the state, and one of Judge Alexander W. Stephens'
grandsons is now a judge of the Court of Appeals of Georgia,
while another, Dr. Robert Grier Stephens, of Atlanta, is one of
the leading physicians of that city. He is married to Lucy Evans,
a daughter of General Clement A. Evans, of Atlanta. A granddaughter (niece of Alexander H. Stephens), Mary Emma Holden,
is the wife of Judge Horace M. Holden, who presided over the
Northern Circuit of Georgia for seven years and was on the Supreme bench for four years, when he resigned and moved to
Athens, so that he might be near his children. He is one of the
most prominent lawyers of the state. Mrs. Holden is much interested in educational and philanthropic work and is a moving factor
in having a classical school located at Crawfordsville, where rest
the remains of Alexander H. Stephens, at "Liberty Hall," his old
home, which was purchased by the Stephens Monumental Asso-.

ciation, who also erected a monument there to his memory, unveiled by Mrs. Holden in 1893, just a week prior to her marriage to Mr. Holden, then a young lawyer of Crawfordsville, who was master of ceremonies. A third object of the Stephens Monumental Association was the erection of this school. The remains of Judge Linton Stephens, who died in 1872, were also removed to this historical location in 1914.

While Alexander H. Stephens was confined in Fort Warren, a political prisoner, after the war, his brother, later Judge Linton Stephens, visited him and met Miss Mary Salter, of Boston, whom he shortly married. She was of the Catholic faith, and her brother married her stepdaughter, Rebecca Stephens, and Father John Salter, president of the Jesuit College of Macon, Georgia, is their son.

When the call to arms came in the great World War, a number of the descendants of that old Jacobite, Alexander Stephens I, fought with the allies in France, one being a son of Mrs. Holden. During that same trying period Willis E. Ruffner (a descendant of James, who returned to Perry County), of Greensburg, Pennsylvania, was vice-consul in Italy. There are many descendants of James Baskins and a considerable number of those of Alexander Stephens I, residing in Perry and surrounding counties. In the letter of Andrew B. Stephens, from which quotation is made, he mentions "old Cousin Hugh Stephens," which shows that Alexander I, had at least one brother.

While at college Alexander Stephens' roommate was Dr. Crawford W. Long, who later became the noted discoverer of anæsthesia. The State of Georgia has designated that Stephens and Long shall represent that commonwealth in the Hall of Fame at Washington, and thus the sons of two sons of old "Mother Cumberland," one from south of the Kittatinny, and one from the section which became Perry, to the north, are accorded a great honor.

THE BLAINE FAMILY.

The family from which sprang James G. Blaine, the statesman, was one of the pioneer families of the territory comprising Perry County. Several members of the family were officers in the Revolutionary War, and one, Ephraim Blaine, financed the military operations of the colonies. Ephraim Blaine was a boy in what was then Toboyne Township, but in that part of the township which later became Jackson. Before the war had progressed very far he was a general. His brother, William Blaine, who owned the Solomon Bower farm, was a captain in Colonel Frederick Watts' battalion, having charge of the Fourth Company. Another brother, James Blaine, was the first lieutenant.

40

three, sons, who on attaining their majority, also located claims among these rich and fertile acres. All that portion of the Borough of Blain—the town dropping the final "e"—once belonged to the first James Blaine, mentioned above. Also both of the former Samuel Woods' farms, the Stokes' mill property, and part of the holdings of James Woods. As late as March 24, 1777, a deed from James Blaine and Isabella, his wife, residents of Toboyne Township, conveys to William Blaine, one of their sons, four hundred acres in Toboyne. As James Blaine was one of the substantial men of the province, also having a property at Philadelphia, tradition alone would tell us that he would be at Philadelphia— then the heart of the colonies—using every power at his command to preserve their liberties.

As the lands which now comprise Perry County were at that time a part of Cumberland, the will of James Blaine is found recorded at the courthouse at Carlisle, and that will establishes the fact that the elder Blaine resided in Toboyne Township (now Jackson) in 1792, and that he in all probability died there. After the death of his first wife, Isabella, he had married Elizabeth Scadden (Carskaden), the daughter of a neighbor in Toboyne, and the will, dated August 11, 1792, names as the executors of the estate, "my beloved son, Ephraim, and my beloved wife, Elizabeth." In the very beginning of the will he states his residence as "of Toboyne Township." It was proven May 19, 1794, shortly after his death. An extract from the will contains the provision:

"The house and garden I now possess be reserved and given to my widow and children begotten by me with her, together with sufficient pasturage for one horse and one cow, summer and winter, during her life, and that the plantation owned by me let out to rent by my executors, the rents and profits arising from same to be given to my widow and children to raise and educate them till the children come of age.

"I give and bequeath to my beloved wife, Elizabeth Blaine, one horse beast and the choice of any one of my cows, together with the one-third of the rents and profits arising and coming from my real estate, during her natural life," etc.

A plantation was willed "to my beloved son, James Scadden Blaine," with the provision that he pay certain sums to his sister, Margaret Blaine. To Alexander Blaine, Eleanor Lyons, Agnes McMurray, Mary Davison and Isabella Mitchell he willed five shillings each. (Book E, p. 330, Register of Wills, Courthouse, Carlisle.)

Evidently these were grown to manhood and womanhood and were well taken care of through marriage and otherwise. The custom of willing five shillings to married daughters at that period seems to have been somewhat general, the property going to the sons and ofttimes the larger portion to the first-born son.

About 1745 James Blaine and Isabella, his wife, took their little son Ephraim and journeyed from Londonderry, Ireland, to America, tarrying in Lancaster County, near Donegal, "on their way to the western world," which for them proved to be Toboyne Township. They stopped in Carlisle long enough to become well known and then took up a tract of land in Toboyne Township, then on the frontiers and in what is now a part of Perry County, and described as "on the south side of the blue Juniata." They assumed a leading part in the affairs of the province as long as it continued a province, an active interest in the state when it became a state, and in the nation when the nation was born.

Successful in every way, happy in his home, the father of nine children who survived him, his first recorded grief was the death of his wife, Isabella. He subsequently married Elizabeth, daughter of George Carskaden, of Toboyne Township. Of the nine children, the little Irishman, the oldest, was sent to Rev. Dr. Allison's school in Philadelphia. There is a logical reason for sending young Blaine there, inasmuch as Dr. Allison himself was from Ireland (Donegal) and had a farm in Toboyne Township, adjoining the Blaine home.

On graduating at Dr. Allison's school in Philadelphia, Ephraim Blaine, his son, became a commissary sergeant with the proprietary government. Then, when the Indian treaty of 1765 was signed he did as many of our World War heroes did so recently, married "the girl he left behind," Rebecca Galbraith, descended of a staunch stock and a resident of Carlisle, whom he probably learned to know while residing there as a boy while on their way to take up lands in the province. The lure of this beautiful girl is responsible for his subsequent location there, no doubt, where he later became sheriff (1772). Of course men from what is now Perry County were also officials of Cumberland at that time, it being an integral part thereof. His father was one of his sureties, and as the Executive Council, composed of five good men and true, attested to the recorder of Cumberland County that they did approve of Robert Callender and James Blaine as sufficient sureties, it follows that they were substantial men.

This man Callender was a very wealthy man, an Indian trader, and in a single encounter, while convoying a train of eighty-one pack-horse loads of goods, sixty-three were destroyed, the value of which was three thousand pounds. In vain he protested that they were not for the hostile Indians, but were for the Illinois, to be stored at Fort Pitt. He was charged with intending "to steal up the goods" before the trade was legally opened. He stood on good footing with young Blaine and his father, as the three combined to be "held and firmly bound unto our sovereign Lord, George, the Third, by the grace of God of Great Britain, France and Ireland,

King, Defender of the Faith," &c., in the sum of two thousand pounds lawful money of Pennsylvania to be paid to our sovereign Lord the King, his heirs and successors, to which payment well and truly to be made we bind ourselves, our heirs, executors and administrators and every one of them jointly and severally firmly by these presents, sealed with our seals and dated the fourteenth day of October, in the eleventh year of his majesty's reign, before John Agnew, Esq., one of his majesty's justices of the peace for the county of Cumberland aforesaid." A pound of Pennsylvania currency at that time was worth two and two-thirds dollars. Prior to being made sheriff Ephraim Blaine was also an Indian trader for a few years. When a posse rescued Frederick Stump from the Carlisle jail, as noted in our Indian chapters, Mr. Blaine was one who rallied to the aid of the sheriff.

When the war with the mother country broke out he was commissioned a lieutenant, later promoted to Colonel, and by a resolution of the Continental Congress was made chief of the commissary department. He was then about thirty-five years of age. It was he, the Toboyne Township boy, who organized the farmers and the millers and kept Valley Forge from starving while the Tories in the great city were dancing and engaged in merrymaking. In fact, many of the farmers were sending their wheat to Philadelphia to the dancing Tories instead of to the starving soldiers at Valley Forge. Practically everybody knows of the starving Continental Army at Valley Forge, but everybody does not know that hogsheads of shoes, stockings and clothing lay at different points awaiting teams and money to pay teamsters. The dearth of money is best realized when it is known that the colonies had voted eight million dollars for a year's war expenses, and at the end of five months had actually only furnished twenty thousand dollars.

But Ephraim Blaine, this boy who had come out of Toboyne Township, now a part of Perry County, already a man of affairs, having money of his own, his people having money and having a wide acquaintance among the well-to-do, raised the money privately to keep the war going, and at one time—in January, 1780—the Supreme Executive Council drew a warrant in his favor for one million dollars to reimburse him in part for advances and means which he had provided.

That the Continental Congress evidently appreciated what he did and was doing is evidenced by an act of 1780 granting him "a salary at the rate of $40,000 by the year until the further order of Congress, also six rations a day and forage for four horses," for he was then a general, having been promoted to that position April 6, 1777. Later he spent his winters in Philadelphia, where his friend, George Washington, first President of the United

States, resided, it being then the social centre of the new country, as the sessions of the Congress were held there.

Duels were yet in vogue in those days, and in the duel between John Duncan and James Lamberton in 1793, Ephraim Blaine was chosen as a second, and when the two met on the field of honor Duncan was killed. He was a brother of Judge Duncan, and years after Lamberton's grandson, Robert A. Lamberton, became president of Lehigh University.

Rebecca Galbraith, the wife of Ephraim Blaine, died in 1795. They had two sons, James and Robert, they being of the third generation of Blaines in America. James married Margaret Lyon, his cousin, whose father, Samuel Lyon, had taken up two hundred and seventy-three acres of land in Tuscarora. (This Lyon family should not be confused with that of the late Judge Lyons, of the Perry-Juniata judicial district.) James was sent abroad twice when a young man, being under voting age. It is recorded that John Bannister Gibson, the illustrious Chief Justice of the Supreme Court of Pennsylvania (of whom more elsewhere in this book), after Blaine's death, wrote of him: "James Blaine, at the time of his return from Europe, was considered to be among the most accomplished and finest looking gentlemen in Philadelphia, then the centre of fashion, elegance and learning on this continent." His reputation as a model gentleman was honestly sustained throughout life.

Ephraim Blaine died in 1804, but seven years previous he had married Sarah Elizabeth Postlethwaite Duncan, widow of his friend, who was killed in the duel previously mentioned, and who gave birth to a son who was also named Ephraim. His two sons by his first wife each had a son also named Ephraim, but the line of descent of James G. Blaine is from Ephraim Lyon (his mother's maiden name), the son of James, he being of the fourth generation in America. At one time there were four Ephraim Blaines at Washington College, all related.

Ephraim L. Blaine went to Washington College and studied law with David Watts, late judge, whose son later was United States minister to Austria. The father, James Blaine, had in the meantime settled at Sewickley, and there his son Ephraim L. met and paid court to Maria Gillespie, whom he married. They moved to Brownsville, to a house which his father had previously erected, and there, in the first stone house west of the Monongahela River, James Gillespie Blaine was born.

He graduated at Washington College in 1847, and was called to Maine to edit the first Whig newspaper, and made Maine his permanent home. He was elected to the Maine Legislature and was a delegate to the second National Republican Convention, which nominated Lincoln. He was elected to Congress in 1862 and served over twenty years, being speaker part of the time. He entered the sixth National Republican Convention at Cincinnati in 1876, with 285 votes for President of the United States, the second highest being Oliver P. Morton with 125, but Rutherford B. Hayes won on the seventh ballot with 384 votes. Hayes entered the balloting with 61 votes, while 378 were necessary for a choice. Hayes became President.

At the seventh National Convention at Chicago, in 1880, James G. Blaine entered with 284, while U. S. Grant had 304. James A. Garfield broke the Grant-Blaine deadlock in the thirty-sixth ballot with 399 votes. Garfield had no votes on the first ballot, and only two on the second. Necessary to a choice, 378 Garfield was elected.

At the eighth National Convention at Chicago, in 1884, Mr. Blaine entered with 334½ votes, Chester A. Arthur being second with 278. Blaine was nominated on the fourth ballot with 541 votes. Necessary to a choice, 410. He was defeated at the general elections by Grover Cleveland, through the disaffection of Senator Roscoe Conkling, of New York, thus losing that state by a very small majority.

At the ninth National Convention at Chicago, in 1888, he polled almost a half-hundred votes for a half-dozen ballots, although not a candidate. Benjamin Harrison was nominated and elected.

At the tenth National Convention, in 1892, he received 182 votes, Benjamin Harrison being nominated, but was defeated by Grover Cleveland at the polls.

No other man in American history carried a following so long or was voted for in so many national conventions. He was balloted for at five national conventions. He was twice Secretary of State (under Presidents Jas. A. Garfield and Benjamin Harrison), and was the greatest statesman since the days of Clay and Webster.

James G. Blaine, like William J. Bryan of our day, was a noted orator, which statement recalls a paragraph from the works of that famous Perry Countian, Col. A. K. McClure, in which he says: "It is a notable fact in political history that no preëminent political orator ever succeeded to the Presidency."

Concisely stated, the Blaine generations in America which sprang from the original settler in what is now Perry County, are:

1. James Blaine, who patented land in Toboyne Township.

2. Ephraim Blaine, who was also from Toboyne Township, and became Commissary General in the Revolution.

3. James Blaine.

4. Ephraim Lyon Blaine, an attorney.

5. James Gillespie Blaine, nominated for the Presidency, Congressman, Secretary of State, statesman.

As part of the Borough of Blain (the final "e" being dropped) was located on lands originally warranted by the Blaines, the town was called Blain. Under the chapters devoted to Jackson and Toboyne Townships are facts in reference to those early land locations.

The Stokes' mill property, at Blain, was originally the Blaine mill, and in the year of the county's erection, in 1820, on April 20, it passed from James S. Blaine to David Moreland. It was built by James Blaine, the head of the Blaine clan, and helped supply food to the Continental Army.

James Blaine, the ancestor of this famous family, was one of the men who warranted lands on February 3, 1755, the very first day of the allotment of lands which now comprise Perry County. He located 100 acres that day, its location adjoining John Carrothers. It lies south of Laurel Run and north of the spur of which Pilot Hill is the terminus, in Tyrone Township, not far from Landisburg. There is no evidence that he ever resided there. By referring to the chapters on Jackson Township and Toboyne Township more will be learned of their early holdings, as it was there that they resided.

The Blaine line of descent, as stated in your letter, is correct.—JOHN EWING BLAINE.—From a letter to the author. Mr. Blaine is the author of the genealogy of "The Blaine Family."

NOTE.—Many letters of Ephraim Blaine are to be found filed in the Congressional Library at Washington, D. C.

CHESTER I. LONG, UNITED STATES SENATOR.

Perry County territory has been the birthplace of two men who have become members of the United States Senate, part of the greatest lawmaking body of the world. The first was William Bigler, former governor of Pennsylvania, who represented his native state from 1855 to 1861, and Chester I. Long, who represented the great agricultural state of Kansas from 1903 to 1909. Senator Long is a scion of a noted family of that name living east of the Juniata. The branch of the family to which Senator Long belongs is traced to Isaac Long, who came to America early in 1700 and purchased one thousand acres of land from John, Thomas and Richard Penn, at a point about six miles north of Lancaster, in Manheim Township, Lancaster County, probably called after Mannheim, the principal city of Baden, from whence he came. His ancestor fled from England during the religious persecution under Queen Mary about the middle of the Sixteenth Century, and located near Baden. He had evidently lived in Switzerland for a time, as it is from that country that records show his emigration. The lands have long since been subdivided, but the Jacob R. Landis farm is a part of the area. Isaac Long had six sons, Isaac,

and his grandson, Abraham G. Long, then two years old, who became the father of Senator Long.

It was at the home of Isaac Long, the son of Isaac, the emigrant, that the United Brethren Church was organized, but, according to a letter from A. W. Drury, who in 1883 traveled Lancaster County, making a close study of its early history while writing the Life of Otterbein, the founder of that faith, "Isaac Long had two daughters, one of whom was married to Henry Landis." If Isaac Long had sons, I am sure I would have had a note to that effect." Accordingly the line of descent must have been from a brother of Isaac, and probably from Christian, as David, who came to Perry County and became the head of the clan there, had named his son Christian (probably after the grandfather, a custom of the period). When David Long removed to Perry County, he settled on the old Spahr farm, in Greenwood Township. He was successful, and gave a farm to each of his sons. His wife was Catherine Hershey, of Lancaster County, who preceded him in death.

The oldest son of Abraham G. Long, and brother of the future senator, was Ephraim C. Long, born in Greenwood Township, June 28, 1837. He died in Liverpool, August 17, 1887. He had studied law in the office of Benjamin McIntire, at New Bloomfield, and was admitted to the bar in January, 1862, and was elected district attorney that fall. He was a member of the 162d Regiment (Seventeenth Cavalry) during the Civil War. He started in the practice of the law with great success, but lost his health during service with the Union army and was not able to continue practice thereafter.

Senator Chester I. Long was born in Greenwood Township, on the farm of his father, on October 12, 1860, being the son of Abraham G. and Mary Cauffman Long, who migrated to Daviess County, Missouri, in 1865. He got his early education in the common schools and taught in the country schools. In 1879 he entered the Paola (Kansas) Normal School, from which he graduated.

As early as 1880 he made a reputation as an effective speaker for the Republicans in the national campaign. In 1883 he went to Topeka, Kansas, where he read law, being admitted to the bar in 1885, in the fall of that year locating at Medicine Lodge, Kansas. In the fall of 1889 he was elected to the State Senate of Kansas and immediately took rank as a leader, which was largely responsible for his campaign for Congress in 1892, against Jerry Simpson, one of the able men who was carried into power on the tide of Populism, and referred to later as "Sockless Simpson." In that contest Mr. Simpson won. In 1894 the two men were again opponents, and Mr. Long won. In 1896 the conditions were reversed and Mr. Simpson again was elected, only to have Mr. Long, in 1898, again wrest the office from him. Mr. Long was his own successor in 1900 and 1902, thus having served in the Fifty-Fourth, Fifty-Sixth and Fifty-Seventh Congresses. Both men were residents of Medicine Lodge at the time, and no other congressional fight in the Union attracted more attention. In 1903 Mr. Long resigned as a member of Congress, after he was elected to the United States Senate, serving until 1909. When elected to that office, January 27, 1903, Senator Long was but forty-two years of age.

At the time of the historic legislative war in Kansas, in 1893, Mr. Long was one of the attorneys for the Republican House of Representatives, and in that connection prepared a brief from which extensive quotations were made by Chief Justice Horton, of the Supreme Court, in making his decision in the case. While a congressman his speech on the Porto Rico tariff bill made for him a national reputation. He proved also an effective and uncompromising advocate of reciprocity with Cuba.

Shortly after the election of Senator Long to the United States Senate, a native Perry Countian wrote to Governor W. J. Bailey, of Kansas, for information in reference to him. From the reply of Governor Bailey, the following is taken:

"Chester I. Long was educated in Paola, Kansas, and came into political prominence after having moved west by running against Jerry Simpson for Congress. In his campaigns against Simpson, he evinced a clear head, a high character, and an ability to take care of himself.

"In Congress he soon became recognized as a growing and a prominent member. Matters growing out of the Spanish-American War raising national and international questions, new and momentous, brought Long to the front as a student of untiring zeal, a politician of practical skill, and a statesman of comprehensive grasp. There is no doubt that the President counted him one of his trusted advisers and appreciated his hearty efforts to carry forward the purposes so near to the heart of the executive. He is now elevated to a place in the Senate where he will be a new member in title only, being already thoroughly familiar with the questions, the men and the forms with which he will have to deal. In Kansas Senator Long ranks as a clean, dignified gentleman of high ability, who has earned his promotion by the splendid work he has done for his country, his party, and his state. The state knows him and is proud of him."

Senator Long was married while a member of Congress, to Miss Anna Bache, with whom he attended school at Paola. They lived together for almost twenty-five years, until her death in 1919. Their married life was unusually happy. They had two daughters, Agnes and Margaret, both of whom have been graduated from the University of Chicago.

After the expiration of his term in the Senate, Senator Long moved to Wichita, where he has since resided and practiced law. He has a large and lucrative practice in the state and Federal

courts, being a member of the firm of Long, Houston, Cowan &
Depew. He is a member of the General Council of the American
Bar Association and one of the Board of Editors of its Journal.
He is also president of the Kansas State Bar Association, chair-
man of the Commission to Revise the General Statutes of Kansas,
and a member of the American Society of International Law.

The story of the migration of David Long is told in the sketch
elsewhere pertaining to Theodore K. Long, founder of the Carson
Long Institute, as he was the ancestor of both.

GOVERNOR WILLIAM BIGLER.

It is no small thing for a barefoot Perry County boy to become
Governor of Pennsylvania, yet William Bigler, the twelfth man to
fill that important position, was born in the famous old *Gibson
mansion, in what is now Spring Township, Perry County, on
†December 31, 1813. His father, Jacob Bigler, was the miller at
Gibson's mill, and his mother's maiden name was ‡Susan Dock, a
sister of Judge Dock, of Dauphin County. They were of German
descent and were educated in both tongues, not an unusual thing in
those days.

When he was yet a boy, his parents in the hope of bettering their
fortune, moved to Mercer County, purchasing a large tract of
woodland. The title proved defective and they found themselves
left with only a small farm. The matter of providing even the

---

*At the memorial session of the Pennsylvania State Senate, March 11,
1881, Charles H. Smiley, then State Senator from Perry County, in his
eulogy, mentioned the birthplace of the Bigler brothers, Chief Justice Gibson, General George Gibson, Commissary General of the United States,
and Congressman Bernheisel, who adopted the Mormon faith and became
the representative of that people in Congress, as having taken place in
the same room, in the old Gibson mansion, at Gibson's Mill. This has been
widely quoted, yet it had an earlier publication, as it appeared on page 259
of Wright's History in 1873. Landisburg citizens have claimed that the
Biglers, or at least Governor John Bigler, was born in that town. The
facts are these: Jacob Bigler, the father, rented the Rice mill, near Landisburg, in 1795, and did not rent the Gibson mill until 1809, from which
the deduction is made that John Bigler, the Governor of California, whose
birth occurred in 1805, was born at Landisburg, where Jacob Bigler resided until renting the Gibson mill. That William Bigler, born in 1813,
was not born at Landisburg, but at the Gibson mill, is also no doubt the
truth, as his father rented the Gibson mill in 1809, after the death of Ann
West Gibson, the mother of the Chief Justice, at which time her other
son, Francis, located in Carlisle, where he remained for many years, later
returning to the old home. In an autobiography of the late Judge Dock
he states that in 1813 he visited his sister Susan, married to Jacob Bigler,
at their home on Sherman's Creek. The late William M. Henderson, during
his life, made the statement in writing that one was born at Landisburg
and one at Gibson's mill, as his parents had moved near the Gibson mill
as early as 1803 or 1804, and the families were friends.

†Date sometimes given as January 1, 1814.

‡Susan Dock Bigler, the widowed mother, lived to see her two sons become famous, and when she died, March 16, 1854, they were both in office,
as governors of widely separated commonwealths.

"war governor" of Pennsylvania, he went to Clearfield and began, not without misgivings, however, the publication of the *Clearfield Democrat,* a political paper. It is said of him that he "had no money, but possessed about everything else requisite to the publication of a paper." Aided by friends he secured a second-hand press and some old type, and as he later said, "started an eight-by-ten Jackson paper to counteract the influence of a seven-by-nine Whig paper." He did all the work, both editorial and mechanical. He was very courteous and was a veritable backwoodsman—a crack shot and a good hunter, political accomplishments of that period.

In 1836 he married a daughter of Alexander B. Reed, of Clearfield, sold his paper and went into partnership with Mr. Reed in the mercantile line. His industry soon placed him as a leader in that line and in the lumber business, which he also conducted. From 1845 to 1850 he was the leading lumber producer in Pennsylvania, and at that time lumbering was probably the leading industry in the state.

In 1841 he was nominated for state senator from the district comprised of the counties of Armstrong, Indiana, Cambria and Clearfield, and elected by three thousand majority. Though opposed by a regularly nominated candidate of the Whigs he polled every vote in Clearfield County, save one—an unheard-of result in politics. Sessions of the State Senate at that time were devoted to matters of unusual importance. The United States Bank and the Bank of Pennsylvania, with the funds of the state on deposit, had failed and had prevented payment of the interest on the public debt, then an enormous sum. Inevitable discontent and murmurings of repudiation of the public debt followed and Senator Bigler was the active leader of those who stood by the integrity of the commonwealth. His principal address upon the resumption of specie payments created such a favorable impression that Senator John Strohm, of Lancaster, said: "Young man, that speech will make you Governor of Pennsylvania, if you behave yourself well hereafter."

In 1843 he was elected speaker of the senate, the presiding officer being known by that title until the adoption of the Constitution of 1873, and was reëlected, having been returned to the senate in 1844. During his second term in the senate the question of railroad communication between Philadelphia and Pittsburgh was the absorbing topic in legislative halls. Capitalists from Philadelphia applied for a charter to construct a road between the two cities wholly in Pennsylvania territory. Pittsburgh, however, contended that a direct route across the Alleghenies was impractical and insisted on granting the Baltimore & Ohio Railroad Company the right to extend their right of way through western counties of the state to their city, claiming that for all time the only railroad communication between eastern and western Pennsylvania would be through the states of Delaware, Maryland and West Virginia. Senator Bigler's district was divided, but he pleaded for the road through the state. He did not believe the route to be impractical and had great faith in promised improvements in motive power, in which he has long since been justified. The matter was settled by a proposition which he himself advanced, that if a bona fide subscription of three million dollars was not made and paid towards the construction of the Pennsylvania Central Railroad on or before the first of the ensuing June then the act granting the right of way to the Baltimore & Ohio Company should become effective, but otherwise be null and void.

In 1848 his name was placed in nomination for governor, but he was defeated for the nomination by Morris Longstreth, then a canal commissioner, who was defeated by William F. Johnston at the polls. In 1849 he was appointed a revenue commissioner, whose duty it was to adjust the tax rate of different sections of the state. In 1851 he was given the Democratic nomination by acclamation and defeated Governor Johnston for reëlection at the polls. Not only were great questions of state then involved, but the Fugitive Slave Law and the question of slavery in the territories were leading topics. He was then but thirty-eight years old and was, until the election of Governor Pattison in 1883, the youngest governor of Pennsylvania ever elected. A curious coincidence was that his brother John was chosen Governor of California at the same time. His biography appears in the next few pages.

Governor Bigler's administration was characterized by the old-time virtues, insisting on rigid economy and strict accountability in the use of public monies. He took a decided stand against the pernicious practice of putting good and bad legislation in the same bill for the purpose of getting the bad measures enacted into law, and it was through his insistence that a bill was passed forbidding the passage of an act which did not fully state in its title the subject matter and which contained more than one subject. This was afterwards incorporated into the Constitution of 1874, as Section 3 of Article 3.

He was in March, 1854, again unanimously nominated, but a new party, the Native Americans, in conjunction with the Whigs, defeated him, electing James Pollock. In January, 1855, he was elected president of the Philadelphia & Erie Railroad Company, and later the same year was elected United States Senator from Pennsylvania, serving for six years. He was there while the war clouds of secession and rebellion gathered and burst in all their fury, spreading ruin throughout the land. In February, 1861, upon the senate floor he said, "as for secession, I am utterly against it. I deny the right and abhor the consequences." When Abraham Lincoln was elected President of the United States, Senator Bigler was untiring in his zeal to help adjust national difficulties, acting with Mr. Crittenden in efforts to secure a compromise. He held that the Southern states had no reasonable plea for resorting to violence until all peaceful means for adjustment had been exhausted. He was a member of the Committee of Thirteen to which were referred the famous compromise propositions and advocated their submission to a vote of the people of the several states, which was rejected, but which, it is contended by many, would have crushed secession.

He was a member of the National Democratic Convention at Charleston in 1860, and was against the nomination of Douglas. In 1864 he was temporary chairman of the National Convention which nominated George B. McClellan, whom he favored. He was a candidate for Congress in 1864, but was defeated.

In 1875 his name was placed in nomination for the governorship again, and for ten ballots he led all the candidates. His name was withdrawn and Cyrus L. Pershing, of Schuylkill, was nominated, but was defeated by John F. Hartranft at the polls. In 1876 he manifested much interest in the Presidential election, and when the result was seen to hinge on the disputed votes of certain Southern states, he, with Ex-Governor Andrew G. Curtin and Samuel J. Randall, for years a Pennsylvania Congressman, were sent to New Orleans to see that the canvass was fair. He was financial agent of the Centennial of 1876, the first national exhibition of any import.

Governor Bigler died at Clearfield, August 9, 1880. He was the father of five sons. His career was marked by honesty and ability. He was one of the statesmen of his day, and whether in official position or following the pursuits of private life his actions were distinguished for their honesty and good intent. When secession threatened, amid strife, contention and hesitation, his allegiance was unfaltering and he could realize no other destiny than that which has resulted, showing the firm foundation and stability of our government—an undivided Union.

His characteristics were marked: Of sturdy character, not brilliant perhaps, but honest, intelligent and faithful to every trust. On June 5, 1858, when he was a United States Senator, a writer in *Harper's Weekly* said: "He is less seen and more felt than any gentleman on the administration side of the senate." His messages and public papers were always expressed in excellent English and his arguments were logical and convincing. A colleague said of him: "His greatest glory was not his ability, his statesmanship, nor the high and honorable positions which he held. They are worthy of high honor, it is true; but they fade before the brighter, stronger claims of his generous, sympathetic, unselfish nature, manifested in a long life of kindness to his fellow man."

It was the lot of Governor Bigler to figure in three distinct eras of Pennsylvania history: In the period of our canal system, when the revulsion of 1841 had impaired the public credit, with the project uncompleted further impairing it; later, when the railroads were threading their way and seeking to use the national highways, and still later when the railroads were built and were attempting to control legislation.

For many years he was a ruling elder of the Presbyterian Church, and after retiring from active life he said in an address that he had "a higher and nobler enjoyment in discharging his religious duties than he ever experienced amidst the honors of official life." At the eulogistic services held by the Pennsylvania Legislature, after his death, a speaker said: "If I were a teacher and some ambitious pupil whose ideas were looking forth to future fame in the service of the republic, were to ask me, 'What governor's life should I study to prepare me for the contest?' I would answer, 'William Bigler's, for none fought the battle of life more successfully.'"

That great editor, Col. A. K. McClure, a personal acquaintance, in "Old-Time Notes of Pennsylvania," said of William Bigler:

"William Bigler became governor in January, 1852, when the conditions of trade and industry were greatly improved, giving him unusual opportunity to make a successful administration, and no governor in the history of the state could have more intelligently directed the government to the best interests of the people.

"He was born not far from the little community of Shermansdale, now Perry County, close to the home of my boyhood. It was a very primitive and sparsely settled section, but the eyes of the people always brightened when they spoke of the distinguished public men it had furnished to the country in Chief Justice John Bannister Gibson, Governor William Bigler, of Pennsylvania, and Governor John Bigler, of California, all of whom were in office at one time.

"William Bigler was elected Governor of Pennsylvania in 1851, and on the same ticket with him was John Bannister Gibson, then Chief Justice of the state, who was continued on the elective supreme court, and just one month before the election of Bigler and Gibson in Pennsylvania, John Bigler was elected Governor of California. John Bigler became foreign minister after serving two terms as governor, and William Bigler became United States Senator. It was certainly a remarkable development of the greatness achieved by these barefooted boys of Sherman's Valley.

"Pennsylvania has had governors of stronger intellectual force than Bigler, but I never knew a public man who had better command of all his faculties or could apply them to more profitable uses. He was a man of very clear conception and unusually sound judgment, with a severe conscientiousness that made him heroic in defense of the right. He was a man of unusually fine presence, of a most amiable and genial disposition, and delightful in companionship, but no influence or interest could swerve him from his convictions of duty in official trust.

41

"He was a careful student, an intelligent observer of men and events, and thoroughly mastered every question that confronted him in the discharge of his political duties. He was not an aggressive man in the general acceptation of the term, but his conservatism never restrained him in aiding legitimate progress, and no cleaner man ever filled the executive chair of Pennsylvania.

"He was a thorough forester, loved the woods, and soon learned to put something approaching a fair value upon the vast amount of fine lumber in that region. In a few years he became one of the largest lumber merchants of the West Branch, and I well remember the admiration he aroused among his political friends, when he was a member of the senate and a prospective candidate for governor, by making the entire journey from Clearfield to Harrisburg on one of his own rafts. He was well equipped for the practical duties of the gubernatorial chair. He was a thoroughly good judge of men and as thoroughly familiar with every public question relating to the interests of the state.

"Governor Bigler did more than any other one man in his day to save Pennsylvania from the scourge of an inflated wildcat currency. Pennsylvania had entirely recovered from the terrible financial depression of 1841 when repudiation was narrowly escaped. Commerce, industry and trade were generally quickened, and the discovery of gold in California, although then in its infancy, seemed to be furnishing an amount of the precious metal that must diffuse wealth into every channel of business enterprise. The few millions of gold that California produced in 1851 were regarded as tenfold more important than all the twentyfold of gold and silver now produced in the West. The feeling was very general that a tide of prosperity was approaching, and a deluge of applications for bank charters came upon the legislature during Bigler's first year.

"The legislators were fully in sympathy with the prospective tide of wealth that was dazzling the people, and they passed bank charters by the score, and all without any individual liability or security for depositors beyond the capital stock. In a single message Governor Bigler vetoed eleven bank charters, and during the session he sent to the senate or house thirty messages vetoing bank bills. He was thoroughly familiar with the industrial interests of the state and knew how easily the people would be tempted from the ordinary channels of industry by hope of suddenly acquired wealth, without pausing to consider that the floodtide of irresponsible banks, practically without limit as to the issue of currency, would produce a most unhealthy inflation that could end only in terrible disaster.

"He was the first governor who made an appeal to the legislature to halt what was known as log-rolling or omnibus legislation, by which a bank charter could be made an amendment to the bill for the removal of a local schoolhouse, and insisted that he should have the right to consider every different feature of legislation upon its own merits. He proposed also in the same message two amendments, which have since been adopted in our Constitution, relating to legislation, requiring each bill to contain but a single subject, and to be passed by a majority vote of each house on a call of ayes and nays.

"Bigler had served three terms in the senate, elected each time practically without a contest, and although he peremptorily declined at the end of his second term, and sent delegates from his county in favor of another candidate, the delegates from the other counties of the district gave a unanimous vote for him and he was compelled to continue legislative service. The prominent position he occupied in the senate had thoroughly familiarized him with all matters relating to state government, and, next to Governor Johnston, I doubt whether any man ever filled the position who was more thoroughly equipped for shaping legislation and administering the state government. His administration commanded not only the respect, but the hearty approval of his party, and even his political opponents, however earnestly they may have differed with him, held in high esteem his ability and integrity, and when he was nominated for reëlection in 1854 by the unanimous vote of the convention, given with the heartiest enthusiasm, there did not seem to be a cloud on the Democratic horizon even as large as a man's hand to threaten him with the tempest that swept him out of office by nearly 40,000 majority.

"The repeal of the Missouri Compromise by a Democratic Congress aroused the anti-slavery sentiment that largely pervaded the Democratic ranks in every section of the state and brought out the first distinct murmurs of revolt, and the sudden organization of the American or 'Know Nothing' party, with the Whig party practically on the verge of its death throes, found a wide field with loose aggregations of both Whigs and Democrats, and these elements were adroitly combined against Bigler in favors of James Pollock, who succeeded him.

"It was a most humiliating defeat, and at the time seemed to bring hopeless destruction to his political career, but his defeat for governor made him United States Senator and one of the great national leaders of his party during the Buchanan administration. Bigler's career in the senate showed that he was equal to the mastery of the gravest national problems, and his sound judgment and conservative aims gave him great power to aid in the election of James Buchanan, his favorite candidate for the Presidency. His personal devotion to Buchanan made him resolve all doubts in favor of supporting the President in his battle with Douglas, and that led to his support of the sadly mistaken policy of the administration in the Kansas-Nebraska disputes, although Senator Bigler always sought to temper the desperate policy of his associate leaders. He visited Kansas personally, and in perfect good faith appealed to the Free State men to come to the front, as they seemed to have the majority, but they had been overwhelmed by the hordes from Missouri, and they refused to accept his advice.

"Taking his career as a whole in the senate, it was eminently creditable, and after his retirement he continued to exhibit the liveliest interest in all public affairs. He was one of the leading men in the direction of the Centennial Exposition, and labored most earnestly and unselfishly to promote its success. Although he never made public utterance on the subject, nothing would have gratified him so much as to have been recalled to the gubernatorial chair of the state. In 1875, when the Democratic convention was in session in Erie, and had what seemed to be an almost hopeless wrestle with a number of candidates, he was hopeful and anxious that he might be accepted as a compromise between disputing factions. He was in my editorial office waiting for dispatches from the Erie convention, and when I handed him the dispatch announcing the nomination of Judge Pershing, he accepted it gracefully, and I doubt whether any other saw the expression of disappointment that he did not conceal from me when he felt that his last opportunity had failed."

The Senate of Pennsylvania, on April 27, 1881, held a memorial session, at which a number of eulogies were delivered in honor of Governor Bigler, long a member of that body, and whose death had but recently occurred. Lieutenant Governor Stone presided, and among those who spoke was Senator Charles H. Smiley, then representing the district which included Perry, the native home of the deceased governor, and whose birthplace was within a very few miles of his.

GOVERNOR JOHN BIGLER, OF CALIFORNIA.

In no other instance in the annals of American history have brothers served as governors of different states at the same time, yet the talented Bigler family of Perry County was not content with furnishing its own state with one of its very best governors, but gave to that empire of the Pacific slope, California, its third governor, and the very first one to be elected by the people—John Bigler. When California became a state on September 9, 1850, Peter H. Burnett was governor, and thus became the first governor of the new state. Later he resigned and his unexpired term was filled by the lieutenant governor, John McDougal, who was the second governor. Thus John Bigler, the lad born on Perry County soil, became, as stated, the first governor to be elected by franchise in the new state.

John Bigler was born at Landisburg, where his father then milled, January 8, 1805, and when still in his boyhood his parents moved to Mercer County, Pennsylvania, hoping to better their financial condition, purchasing a large tract of timber lands. Through a defective title they shortly found themselves bereft of all save a small farm, and it required the entire time and much hard labor by the elder Bigler to make ends meet. This constant toil was more than he could stand at that period of his life, and his death followed. He left a widow and children to battle with the pioneer conditions of a newly settled country. Jacob Bigler, the father of John, had later been a miller at Gibson's mill, in Perry County, and his mother was Susan Dock, a sister of Judge Dock, of Harrisburg, Dauphin County, Pennsylvania.

The death of the father curtailed the education which the parents had planned for the children, so John Bigler learned the printing trade and became the editor of the *Centre Democrat*, published at Bellefonte, before 1830, and when less than twenty-five years old. He continued its publication for some years and in the meantime studied law and was admitted to the bar in 1840. It was during this period, from 1830 to 1833, that his brother William, who was to become governor of his native state, learned the printing trade with him.

In 1849, having in the meantime married, and became the father of a daughter, he took his family overland to California, and settled at Sacramento. At first he turned his attention to anything to gain a livelihood, doing odd jobs, unloading steamships, cutting wood and even as an auctioneer. He was quick-witted, good-natured, fond of company, fluent of speech, but rough and ready

protempore of the house by a vote of seventeen to two, and on February 17, but a short while thereafter, when the speaker resigned, he was elected to the position. At the autumn election of 1850 he was returned to the legislature, and at the succeeding session was almost unanimously elected as speaker, which shows that he was not only an excellent presiding officer, well versed in parliamentary rules, but also a popular man. It was in the course of his service as speaker that he joined forces with David C. Broderick, then a political power in California, each being of great value to the other. It was largely owing to this combination that he was nominated for governor of California, shortly after the sessions of the legislature closed.

At the fall election he was elected to the highest office in the state, and on January 8, 1852, in the presence of the two houses of the legislature, he was sworn into office as governor of the "Golden State," the thirty-first one to attain statehood and a veritable empire whose shores are washed by the Pacific Ocean for a distance as great as the states on the Atlantic slope from Massachusetts to Georgia.

In his inaugural address, among many other things, he said that no state could prosper so long as its counsellors were governed by schemes of speculation and private aggrandizement, and no community could flourish under the influence of a wild, vacillating and unsettled policy. California had been, perhaps, more unfortunate in this respect than any of the other states of the Union. It should be his purpose, so far as the executive arm could reach the evil, to apply the remedy. It was better, he continued, to adhere to the principles and systems exemplified in the practice of the other states, which had been sustained by time and were tested by experience, than to follow after ideal and imaginary good. In these modern days of idealism and various other isms that homely statement shines forth like prophecy. It might well be adopted by many of our modern statesmen. He said the highways which had been successfully trodden in other states might be safely and prudently pursued by California. So long as American precedents were adopted and adhered to there would be no need to blush on account of the adoption of laws elsewhere successful. He was a believer in the wisdom of the aphorism "that the fewer and plainer the laws by which a people are governed, the better." There was much truth in the remark "that danger to popular government is to be apprehended from being governed too much." Few laws, well directed, would effect more good than numberless statutes, restraining, fettering and interfering with private enterprise. The greatest liberty consistent with good government was the true principal of republicanism and would contribute most to the development of the resources and energies of a people, he said.

The capitol had been located at Vallejo, but that community had failed to fulfill its part of the conditions, and as John Bigler was a resident of Sacramento, it was largely through his influence that the capitol was permanently located there, as he represented that district in the assembly from the first, and while governor had a powerful influence.

Shortly prior to his term as governor—in 1848—the first Chinamen came to California, welcomed at first, but soon found to be a menace as the ever increasing number of them was becoming a problem to the state, as it later became to the nation, resulting in the eventual passage of the Chinese Exclusion Act. As early as 1849 they were already barred from some mining camps. After much attention given to legislation by the two houses Governor Bigler gave impetus to the anti-Chinese movement by transmitting a special message to the legislature calling attention to the immediate necessity of exclusive legislation to check immigration. The message contained much sound logic and, while legislation failed to pass then, it has long since shown its practicability.

At that time there was much overland traffic to the mining lands of California, and a commission had been appointed and had opened relief posts which the legislature had provided for by the appropriation of a sum not to exceed $25,000. The sum was exceeded by the commission and became a matter of scandal, there being, as usual, two sides to the story. The one side claimed three thousand persons had been relieved, and the other contended it smacked more of political jobbery than of benevolence. The matter finally resulted in a duel. There was considerable fault found with Bigler's stand on this matter. Edward Gilbert, one of California's first congressmen and editor of an Alta newspaper, made some caustic comment which aroused the ire of James W. Denver, a state senator whom Bigler had appointed at the head of the commission, and his personal friend and business associate. Denver replied in a bitter communication which reflected on Gilbert's character. Gilbert immediately challenged Denver to a duel. Denver accepted and named the rifle as the weapon, as he was an expert rifleman. The duel, which was the first one between men of prominence in the state, took place in Oak Grove, near Sacramento, on August 2, 1852. Placed forty paces apart both missed at the first shot, whether intentionally or not will never be known. At the second shot the congressman (Gilbert) fell, being shot through the body. While Gilbert was a popular man no prosecution was made against his slayer, but on the other hand Governor Bigler appointed him as secretary of state six months later when a vacancy occurred by resignation. This act seems not to have been unpopular, either.

At the Democratic State Convention of 1853 his political partner, David C. Broderick, was in complete control, and Governor Bigler was renominated and, at the fall election, was reëlected. Until the present century he was the only governor to be reëlected, which shows that his administration of the affairs of the state must have been very satisfactory to the electorate.

In another respect than that of both becoming governors did the actions of these two brothers parallel. When William Bigler was a state senator of Pennsylvania it was he that stood for putting through the legislation for the building of the Pennsylvania Central railway over the Allegheny Mountains, which many claimed to be impractical, but over which line the Pennsylvania Railroad with four tracks of steel now connect New York City and Pittsburgh. When he was a member of the General Assembly of California in 1850, which was its initial session, on March 11, John Bigler introduced a joint resolution instructing the United States senators and requesting the representatives in Congress to urge the importance of authorizing as soon as practicable, the construction of a national railroad from the Pacific Ocean to the Mississippi River. Later, when he was governor, in a message to the legislature he proposed the establishment of military and post roads across the plains, to connect California with the Atlantic states. It was brought up, but as California had no jurisdiction without its own bounds, the national government was appealed to by resolution to build three military and post roads across the continent. The result was that the national government took up the matter and in a short time the Atlantic and the Pacific were connected by military and post roads, which eventually grew to the great transcontinental railway lines of our time.

It was during his administration that the great and famous San Quenten prison was established in California, which to this day is a noted place of confinement for evildoers in state as well as ordinary civil affairs and transactions. While a member of the assembly he was one of the men who helped establish a free school system, primarily patterned after the one from his native state.

In 1855 Governor Bigler was again renominated, but was defeated by John Neely Johnson, the nominee of the ascendant "Know Nothing" party. This was a party formed to combat foreign immigration and was a secret alliance. It got its name through that secret method, as any one who belonged to it, when pressed for information invariably said that he knew nothing. With the ascendancy of the "Know Nothings" Governor Bigler's political partner, David C. Broderick, lost his prestige for a time.

Through the efforts of his brother, United States Senator William Bigler, the former Pennsylvania governor, he was appointed United States Minister to Chili by President James Buchanan, in

1857, and served until the advent of Abraham Lincoln, in 1861. He returned to California and was nominated for Congress, but was defeated. In 1867 President Johnson appointed him a commissioner on the board to pass upon the construction of the Central Pacific Railroad. In 1868 he established the State Capital Reporter at Sacramento, where he died in November 29. 1871, leaving a wife and daughter. He and his wife and daughter are buried at Sacramento, where the State of California has erected a monument to his memory.

Physically Governor Bigler was comparatively short and inclined to be corpulent. He was good-natured, jolly, and what is known in modern parlance as "a good mixer," which no doubt accounts in a very large way for his political success for many years.

GOVERNOR STEPHEN MILLER, OF MINNESOTA.

Perry County also has the distinction of having furnished the third governor of Minnesota, the thirty-second state to be admitted into the Union, which attained statehood in 1858. The lands patented by George West, in Carroll Township, Perry County, on March 12, 1793, passed to Melchoir Miller, grandfather of Governor Miller, who emigrated from Germany in 1785. *His son David, who became Governor Miller's father, inherited his share of the estate, two other heirs being his sister, Mrs. Henry Lackey, and his brother, Daniel, who had a son, John T. Miller, who was elected sheriff of Perry County in 1865. Accordingly many persons who were born in Perry County, or who can trace their lineage there, are kin to Governor Miller.

Stephen Miller was born on his father's farm, now the G. W. Keller farm, in Carroll Township, Perry County, January 7, 1816, where he grew to young manhood. His mother was †Rosanna (Darkess) Miller (sometimes called Rosa). Some histories name his mother as Barbara Miller, designated "a widow," teaching school at Daniel Cowen's, fourteen miles west of Marysville, in Rye Township, which is not correct. He attended the local schools and was an expert penman.

He early devoted his attention to the milling business, and in 1837—the year he became of age—he engaged in the shipping and

---

*The will of Melchoir Miller, dated January 5, 1824, was probated at Landisburg, then the county seat, March 31, 1824. It names his children as Elizabeth, Rosanna, David, Anne, Susanna, and Daniel. It also designates Rosanna Miller as his wife. Rosanna was also the name of David's wife, who became the governor's mother.

†Mrs. Elizabeth Miller, residing with her daughter, Mrs. Chas. Etter, 208 Pine Street, Harrisburg, and who is in her ninety-third year, spent much time with the governor's mother, whom she knew as "Aunt Rosa," being a niece by marriage, which substantiates the fact that that was her given name.

in the temperance cause, and procuring a large canvas tent, he visited many parts of Pennsylvania as a lecturer, meeting with great success. His health becoming impaired, he thought a change of climate would be beneficial, and moved to Minnesota, settling at St. Could, where he entered business. It was soon perceived that the town had gained more than a merchant; that it had a man of alert mind, positive convictions and wisdom, and whose aid in the directing of public affairs would be invaluable. His evidencing an interest in politics had an almost immediate effect, and in 1860 he was sent as a delegate to the National Republican Convention which nominated Lincoln for the Presidency. He was also placed at the head of the Republican electoral ticket of the state that year. He was prominently brought before the people of his chosen state by holding joint discussions or debates with General Christopher C. Andrews, a Douglas elector, in the principal towns and cities. Then the pent-up slavery agitation of almost a century came to a crisis and Governor Ramsey, with whom he had early formed a friendship while yet in Pennsylvania, was instrumental in having him made Lieutenant Colonel of the First Minnesota Infantry, his commission being dated April 29, 1861. This friendship was not alone responsible for this assignment, for Stephen Miller had shown more activity in raising recruits than any man in Minnesota, and undoubtedly had great personal merits.

Of his meritorious military record let us give the words of "Minnesota in Three Centuries," edited by a historical commission of that state, which says:

"Colonel Miller's military career is resplendent with chivalrous actions and acts of bravery. He commanded the right wing of his regiment at the first Battle of Bull Run. He was in personal command of the regiment during many battles of the Army of the Potomac of Eastern Virginia. He was engaged with the enemy at Yorktown, West Point, in the two Battles of Fair Oaks, at Peach Orchard, Savage Station, White Oak Swamp, Nelson's Farm and Malvern Hill. He was on the rear guard on the retreat to Harrison's Landing and held in reserve at the Battle of South Mountain. On August 24, 1862, he was commissioned Colonel of the Seventh Minnesota Infantry, and was transferred to that regiment just before the Battle of Antietam. On account of an accidental fall from his horse, the result of which was serious, he was obliged to rest awhile at home before taking command of his new regiment. Therefore he was not in personal command during the two Indian campaigns in which his regiment took part. He, however, assumed command at Camp Release. He was subsequently the commander at Camp Lincoln, near Mankato, and had charge of the three hundred Sioux Indians, also was entrusted in December, 1862, with the execution of the thirty-eight that paid the penalty for their crimes."

Colonel Miller received his appointment as a Brigadier General of Volunteers, October 26, 1863, but resigned that position to assume the office of governor.

At the Republican State Convention held in 1863, General Miller—still a Colonel at that time—was nominated for the office of governor, and at the fall election was elected, receiving 19,628 votes to 12,739 cast for his opponent, Henry T. Welles, the Democratic candidate. He was inaugurated on January 11, 1864, and served one term, which expired January 18, 1866, not being a candidate to succeed himself. In his inaugural address he expressed profound gratitude to the Deity; dwelt upon the improvement of the schools and university; showed a thorough knowledge of the matter of railroads, in his judgment there being nothing more certain than the construction of a northern line of railroad to the Pacific Ocean—a fact long since realized; commended the citizens on the improved condition of Indian affairs, and complimented them on the glorious record they were making in helping keep inviolate the Union.

In 1871 he removed from St. Cloud to Worthington, where he was connected with the St. Paul & Sioux City Railroad Company, as general superintendent of their large land interests in southern Minnesota. In 1872 he was elected and represented his district, the six southwestern counties, in the state legislature.

Again let us quote from the pages of "Minnesota in Three Centuries": "Governor Miller was a rough and ready speaker, with remarkable wit, originality of style, and a somewhat brusque manner on the rostrum. No man's private character stood higher in all respects, with amiable domestic affections and strongly religious convictions. He was a man of moderate means, never a money-maker, and his last days were somewhat clouded by comparative poverty, but his rugged honesty and manly principles were never questioned." He died at Worthington, Minnesota, August 18, 1881.

In 1839 Stephen D. Miller had been united in marriage to Miss Margaret Funk, of Dauphin County, Pennsylvania, becoming the father of four children. Of these Wesley F. Miller, a lieutenant in the Union Army, fell at Gettysburg on July 2, 1863, while bravely fighting; Stephen C., a second son, was a captain in the commissary department, and Robert D. resided in Pennsylvania. A daughter died in infancy.

The execution of the thirty-eight Indians responsible for an uprising, of which Governor Miller, then a Colonel, was in charge, was probably the greatest number of human beings ever executed at one time in the United States. The scaffold from which they were all hanged at the same moment was erected in the open and was surrounded at some distance by a column of infantry, at a further distance by another column of infantry, and at a still greater distance by a column of cavalry. Outside of this cordon of military protection was the populace, prairie schooners, "dead" wagons, etc.—a scene never to be forgotten. A military commission had convicted 303, but President Lincoln commuted the death sentences of 264, and one proved an alibi.

Governor Miller was a man of considerable literary ability and was the author of a number of poems, many of which were of a serious or meditative nature. In 1864 there appeared from the press of a Chicago publisher, a volume entitled "The Poets and Poetry of Minnesota," by Mrs. J. W. Arnold. She dedicated the volume "to the Honorable Stephen Miller, Governor of Minnesota, the Soldier, the Patriot, the True Friend." Speaking of his poetical works the author said: "His verses are remarkable for the beauty and truth with which they express the reflections of the general mind, and emotions of the heart. Their tone is grave and high, but not gloomy nor morbid. The edges of the cloud of life are turned to gold by faith and hope. Making him, therefore, the Chaucer of our 'goodly companie,' he must lead the van of 'The Poets and Poetry of Minnesota.'" Accordingly, nine poems from the pen of Governor Miller, with a sketch of his life, occupy the first few pages of the volume. From them we have selected the following poem for the history of his native county:

SOW IN TEARS AND REAP WITH JOY.

Thine is the lot, 'mid stormy scenes,
  To sow the seed in tears,
And watch—with disappointment, oft—
  For fruit in following years.
Perchance it by the wayside falls,
  Where friendless birds devour;
Or blooms upon the stony ground.
  To wither in an hour;
Or thorns may choke the tender blade,
  And prospects pass away;
And toil, the hope of months and years,
  May perish in a day.

But, written in the book of God,
  Behold the great command:
"At morn and eve dispense the seed,
  Nor once withhold thy hand."
When bird, and storm, and thorn shall die.
  And stones and earth decay,
"*Some* shall bring forth a hundredfold"
  On that great gleaning day.
Then scatter seed, and deeds, and tears
  Where'er thy feet may roam.
So shall thou shout, with angel bands,
  A blessed harvest home.

The remains of Melchoir Miller, the ancestor, rest in the churchyard at Snyder's Church, in Wheatfield Township. The governor's mother Rosanna Miller, lived to be well up in years, and resided in Duncannon for a long time prior to her death, in the house located where Abraham Spence long had a jewelry store, now owned by Thomas Hunter. She is still remembered by some of the older people there, who recall the visits of her noted son.

GOVERNOR JAMES A. BEAVER.

Thirty-three miles west of Harrisburg, the State Capital of Pennsylvania, is Millerstown Borough, Perry County, plainly in sight of passengers from the opposite side of the Juniata River, as they travel via the Pennsylvania Railroad—that great transcontinental artery of traffic which crosses half the continent. It was there that James A. Beaver, later to be Brigadier General of the United States Army and the twentieth governor of Pennsylvania, was born, the James G. Brandt property, very recently purchased by Lewis G. Ulsh, now occupying the site of his birthplace.

He came of staunch stock, of the Huguenots of France, but of the German strain of that frontier province of Elsass (Alsace)— on the paternal side, and of the famous Addams family, which gave to the Union a commander of one of the two Pennsylvania brigades rendezvoused at York during the Revolution (Colonel John Addams), and a member of the Nineteenth and Twentieth Congresses of the United States (William Addams).

George Beaver, the progenitor of the Beaver clan in America, about 1740, for a faith condemned in France at that time, left Elsass (Alsace) shortly after that province was torn from Germany by France, to be restored by conquest in 1871, and again to be returned to France at the conclusion of the great World War in 1918. He settled in Chester County and became a farmer. Of the second generation his son George fought in the Revolution, and later settled in Franklin County, marrying a Miss Keifer, where his son, Peter Beaver, grandfather of the governor, was born. Peter Beaver was of the third generation and established himself as a tanner in Lebanon County, later becoming a merchant. He was also a local Methodist minister and preached over Berks, Lebanon and Dauphin Counties, being ordained at Elkton, Maryland, in 1809, by Bishop Asbury. He married a Miss Gilbert, of the substantial family of that name, many of whose descendants now live near Millersburg, Dauphin County. He died August 25, 1849, in Pfoutz Valley.

The father of the governor, Jacob Beaver, was born in Lebanon County, in 1805 (of the fourth generation in America), was one of six brothers, all of more or less importance; two of them, George Beaver and Jesse Beaver, were representatives in the State Legislature. Thomas Beaver, another brother, was a pioneer wholesale merchant in Philadelphia, and later became an iron master at Danville, Pa. It was the grandfather, Peter Beaver, who

governor. Her father, Abraham Addams, a merchant, had come from Berks County to what is now Perry County, in 1811, and purchased a tract of land, upon part of which Millerstown is now located. The stone farmhouse on this farm was built by him in 1817, and in it the mother of the future governor was born, January 30, 1812.

One of a family of two sons and two daughters, James A. Beaver was the third child and the first son, having been born on October 21, 1837, just three years before his father died, August 17, 1840, leaving four small children and their young mother, who was a good woman, of noble character and great intelligence, and who, March 4, 1844, was united in marriage to Rev. S. H. McDonald, a Presbyterian clergyman. During the first seven or eight years James A. Beaver knew no authority but that of this noble and godly woman. In April, 1846, the family removed to Belleville, Mifflin County. Most of the year of 1849 young Beaver was back in Millerstown, where he attended school. He was a gentlemanly, high-principled boy, peaceably inclined, yet a boy who would stand no affront. His grandfather died at the close of that year and he returned to the Presbyterian manse at Belleville. This again brought him into daily contact with the counsel and encouragement of his mother and under the influence of an exemplary Christian stepfather. For a period of over three years he studied under their guidance.

In 1852 he entered the Pine Grove Mills Academy. His progress was so rapid that before he was seventeen he was able to enter the junior class of Jefferson College (consolidated with Washington in 1869) at Canonsburg, Pa., where he graduated in 1856, before he was nineteen years old. The Class of '56, by the way, had exactly fifty-six graduates, of whom twenty-four entered the ministry, seventeen studied law, three medicine, and seven became teachers. A fellow classmate, Rev. Dr. James A. Reed, in a historical sketch of the class once wrote: "James A. Beaver, better known in his college days as 'Jim Beaver,' was a little bit of an enthusiastic fellow, full of fun and pun and pluck and frolic, who never did anything bad and always looked glad. James has been growing bigger and bigger ever since he was born."

Leaving college he settled at Bellefonte and entered the law offices of H. N. McAllister, who died while a member of the convention which framed the present Constitution of Pennsylvania. He was admitted to the bar when barely of voting age. Recognizing his ability his preceptor took him into partnership.

While preparing himself for the bar young Beaver had joined the Bellefonte Fencibles, whose captain was Andrew G. Curtin, soon to become Pennsylvania's great war governor. The reader will note that the two governors of Pennsylvania born in Perry

County—Bigler, the Democrat, and Beaver, the Republican—were both closely associated with Andrew G. Curtin, the three men being elected to the highest office in the commonwealth, their administrations and intervening ones covering a period of thirty-nine years. Beaver took such an interest in this military company that he was made a second lieutenant, a vacancy occurring.

The slavery agitation was at its height, and murmurings of secession were wafted across the Mason and Dixon line. Young Beaver's friend, the captain of the fencibles, had been swept into the governor's chair on the very question of an inseparable Union. From him the young second lieutenant had a promise that if troops were needed to save the Union this should be the first company called from Pennsylvania. A week before Governor Curtin took the chair Beaver wrote to his mother a significant letter:

"BELLEFONTE, January 11, 1861.

"*My Dear Mother:* The fencibles decided a day or two since to attend the inauguration of Governor Curtin on the 15th. So my hopes of staying at home and escaping the crowds, long marches and tiresome standups are pretty much blasted. You will see in your *Press* of this week, under 'Extraordinary War Preparations,' that we may have a longer march than to Harrisburg. Governor Curtin assures me that if a requisition is made upon this state ours will be the first company called out. Necessity for soldiers, however, is growing less and less, so that our chances for active service or a life of inglorious ease at Washington are not very flattering.

"Since writing the above I have been to the telegraph office. A dispatch from Washington says that hostilities have actually begun. The South Carolinians fired upon the 'Star of the West,' which contained supplies for Major Anderson. If this is true, which God forbid, war has actually commenced. Where will be the end? The nation must be preserved. And who can mistake his duty in this emergency? I have prayed for direction, guidance and clear revelations of duty, and I cannot now doubt where the path of duty lies. If required, I will march in it, trusting God for the result. There are few men situated as I am. No person dependent upon me, and a business which I will leave in able hands. If we have a nationality, it must be continued, supported, upheld. If we are ordered to Washington or elsewhere, I will see you before we go. God bless you, my mother.   Your son,

"JAMES A. BEAVER."

The firing on Fort Sumter was of no immediate benefit to the South, while in the North it had the immediate effect of arousing loyalty. President Abraham Lincoln issued his call for 75,000 volunteers to defend the nation, and the ink was hardly dry on the call before the fencibles were on the way, with Beaver now a first lieutenant. In the prevailing excitement of leaving he found time to write to his mother this calm, characteristic letter:

"BELLEFONTE, PA., April 17, 1861

"*My Own Dear Mother:* Oh, how I long to see you, if for but one brief moment! This boon denied me I must trust to a lame medium the expressions of my feelings. You have doubtless anticipated the action I have taken in the present alarming condition of our national affairs, and

42

I hope I know my mother too well to suppose that she would counsel any other course than the one which I have taken. I can almost imagine that I hear you saying, 'My son, do your duty,' and I hope that no other feeling than that of duty urges me on. If I know my own heart, duty—my duty first and above all to God, my duty to humanity, my duty to my country and my duty to posterity—all point in one and the same direction. Need I say that that direction points to the defense of our nation in this hour of her peril? We march to-morrow for Harrisburg; remain there until ordered into actual service, thence to whatever part may be assigned us. I have little fear of any hostilities between the different sections of our country for the present. Should the worst we fear come upon us, however, and in the providence of God my life be yielded up in the service, I feel and know that the sacrifice would be small when compared with the sacrifices, trials, and anxieties which you have made and undergone for me; and my mother, can I better repay them than by going straight forward in the path of duty? In reviewing my life, oh, how much is there that I would blot from memory's pages—how much for which I would atone at any cost! It may perhaps be as well than I am not able to see you *now*. It will spare us both some pain, but rob me of much pleasure.

"Affectionately your son,

"JAMES A. BEAVER."

His mother's response to this letter commended his prompt action and cheered him with her blessing. The fencibles proceeded to Harrisburg and were quartered at Camp Curtin. On April 21 the second regiment of Pennsylvania volunteers was organized and the fencibles became Company H. On the evening of the same day this regiment was despatched by rail for Washington. Arriving at Cockeysville, Maryland, the next morning, the Confederates, as the rebellious South termed themselves, had destroyed the railroad bridge, barring further passage, and necessitating the protection of railroad property by force. It was Sunday, and after a busy day, Lieutenant Beaver wrote to his mother: "The whole country round about is in commotion and the authorities seem determined to prevent the passage of more troops through Baltimore. This has been anything but a quiet, pleasant, Christian Sabbath, which like other blessings, is never fully appreciated until we are deprived of it. I hope that I am prepared to meet calmly anything which Providence may have in store for me."

After an encampment of forty-eight hours the regiment was ordered back to York and a military training camp established, known in that day as a camp of instruction. Observing all restraint gone with the call to arms, Beaver wrote his sister: "Of one thing I am more than ever convinced, that the army is terribly demoralizing to those who place confidence in their own strength Oh! how many will stumble and fall in this trying ordeal?" While in camp at York a special order came detaching him from his company and making him adjutant of the seventh regiment. The men of the company were opposed to the change, and, wanting to remain with them, he hurried to Harrisburg "to endeavor to be excused from having the promotion thrust upon him," as he put it. This request was granted and he went with his company to Chambersburg, where they remained from June 1st to June 16th, after which they encamped at Funkstown, near Hagerstown. In a letter from that place to his mother he made this prediction: "The only real result of this rebellion will be to establish this government upon a foundation which cannot be moved by the too violent uprising of factions and designing demagogues, and in view of it, I doubt not that this movement on the part of the South will demonstrate itself to be the most important and fortunate in its results which could possibly have happened. The government will have proved itself self-sustaining."

The call having only been for three-months' men, the time soon sped, and on July 26th the regiment was sent by rail to Harrisburg and mustered out. Lieutenant Beaver was barely out of the service before he was preparing to go back. With two other men he raised another regiment—the Forty-Fifth—from Centre, Lancaster, Mifflin, Tioga, and Wayne Counties, and on October 18th it was mustered in and Lieutenant Beaver became Lieutenant Colonel Beaver. Of the succeeding movements of this regiment much could be written, but the object of this chapter is to give a pen picture of James A. Beaver, the boy, the man, the officer, and the governor.

In December, 1861, we find him in command at Bay Point, South Carolina, an island on the one side of which were great quantities of cluster oysters, covered only during high tide, and consequently poisonous. A soldier ate some, against orders, and was found dead in his bunk on a Sunday morning. Under a palmetto tree a grave was prepared and at sunset the first military funeral of a member of the regiment occurred. As the soldiers surrounded the grave, the surf rolling on the beach, and the wind sighing through the palmettoes gave the occasion an added solemnity. The coffin was lowered and the officer in immediate command was about to call on the sergeant to offer prayer when the stern yet musical voice of Colonel Beaver said, "Let us pray!" A fellow officer further described the scene: "We stood awed and enraptured as we listened to his prayer. Never before or since has it been my privilege to listen to such a prayer. Colonel Beaver had been a strict disciplinarian and was liked by his command, as officers generally were in the volunteer service. But that evening he captured every heart present. The boys made up their minds that he was a good man, and they have never had reason to change the opinion formed at the grave of our comrade, under the palmettoes of South Carolina."

The fortunes of war brought back to Virginia Lieut. Colonel Beaver and his men. Here he had eight companies guarding railroads, a duty which he rather despised, as he longed for active, even hazardous service, which without his knowledge was already on its way. President Lincoln had called for 600,000 volunteers for the period of the war, and, as ever, Pennsylvania was leading in the response. Beaver was promoted to colonel and given charge of a regiment composed almost entirely of Centre Countians, men from his adopted home, at the request of both the men and officers. On September 6, 1862, he took command at Harrisburg, and badly as he wanted to see his mother, the necessities of war forbade. In three days he had his regiment—the One Hundred and Forty-Eighth Pennsylvania Volunteers — organized, equipped, and on the march.

Lee's army was in Maryland threatening Pennsylvania, his cavalry endeavoring to cut the lines of railway communication. The new regiment was assigned the duty of guarding a twelve-mile section of the Northern Central Railroad. Onward came the scourge of war to the North, and with Lee's army in Maryland and the Union forces approaching, Antietam was soon to see that bloody battle in which 200,000 men engaged and 30,000 were killed upon the field. Colonel Beaver's regiment was still guarding this great artery of communication southward and within sound of the guns when the Battle of Antietam was fought. There, in a desperate charge for the famous stone bridge, Hartranft's regiment suffered severely, and among the brave young officers to die was another lad born in Perry County, Colonel Beaver's only brother, Lieut. J. Gilbert Beaver, who was killed instantly at the head of his company. Colonel Beaver remained with the 148th along the Northern Central until December 10, 1862, training the new regiment so thoroughly during the first three months of its service that veteran officers in passing mistook it for a camp of regulars. The regiment was then ordered to the front, but before it could join the Army of the Potomac the disastrous Battle of Fredericksburg had been fought. Lee had driven Burnside back across the Rappahannock, making the reorganization of the army almost a necessity. It was at this time that Colonel Beaver arrived at the front with his regiment and reported for duty to General Winfield Scott Hancock. He was not yet twenty-four years of age. With the pale, beardless face of a boy he resembled a student more than a warrior, yet his soldierly bearing and instincts made an instant impression as he said, "General, while I would not presume so much as to suggest the disposition that is to be made of my regiment, I should be glad if it could be placed in a brigade of your division where the men can see a daily exemplification of the good results of the soldierly discipline I have endeavored to teach."

The great soldier replied: "Colonel, I regret to say that we have no such brigades. I only wish we had." But it was not long before he observed that his wish was realized so far at least as the regiment of the young officer was concerned.

Before the army was again ready to do battle General Joe Hooker, then in command, said of him, "It will not be long before he will be a Major General." Three times he refused command of a brigade, and when he finally did accept, it was the brigade in which was incorporated his own regiment. At the approach of spring, a few days before the army moved, he wrote to his mother:

"I do not despair of my country's future. God is indeed trying us with fire, but it is the fire which purifies, and if the nation comes out of the crucible refined, purified, sanctified, what are thousands of lives and millions of treasure compared with the new birth. Oh, mother, if my life can atone for any national evil; if I were satisfied that the result of this struggle is to be union, purity, liberty, how gladly I would resign life! What is life that it should weigh in the balance against such vast stupendous results? What is death that we should shudder, when behind it there arises such an effulgence of brightness and glory? I have no fear for the result in God's own good time and in his own right way—I am therefore resigned. It seems like doubting God to hesitate for an instant. I never doubt. I have therefore no anxious thoughts as to the future. Whatever that future is will be right; God does not go backward. Forward is the watchword of the creation of the universe—of nations as well as of armies. What a privilege to live when progress, civilization and universal liberty are making such colossal strides; when ignorance, superstition, slavery and wrong shrink back to their native darkness before the rising day."

As these words were being written General Hooker was preparing to cross the Rappahannock, and in a few days Colonel Beaver's regiment crossed the river and soon moved forward into the tangled thicket of Chancellorsville. The wood protected a needed fording of the river. Colonel Beaver led his regiment into the woods only to find them occupied by the enemy. The fight had barely opened when an enfilading fire caught the regiment from the Confederate advance and Colonel Beaver fell, a great hole torn in his uniform; a gutta-percha pencil, however, had turned the course of the bullet and it had gone only through the fleshy parts of his abdomen. From the hospital he was taken home to Bellefonte, but in July he was back at Harrisburg to report for duty, his wound still open.

President Lincoln had called for 120,000 emergency men to defend Pennsylvania and drive out Lee's army. Beaver, on reporting at Harrisburg at this time to rejoin his regiment, was refused sanction to do so by the surgeons. He was then given command of Camp Curtin, of which he said: "It was a position of much vexatious toil. The force was immense and untamed. I never saw anything equal to it."

Sharing the wider fortunes of the army throughout that disastrous campaign the regiment was thrice called to decisive service when the fate of the entire army was at stake. It had been shelled all day while defending the apex of Hooker's position during the cannonade which concealed the swift march of Stonewall Jackson around the Federal position. Suddenly it was called out of its entrenchments, where it was expecting an attack from the front to stem in the open field the advance of Jackson's men who had gained the rear of the Federal army and were threatening its communications with the river.

At a crucial stage of the subsequent fighting General Hooker, himself, called on Colonel Beaver and his regiment to hold an essential position. "There is your work, Colonel; occupy that wood," said Hooker, pointing up a slope that lay outside the Union lines. "Wait for nothing," he added, "Everything depends on holding those woods." Colonel Beaver distinguished himself on every occasion, but particularly at the Battle of the Po, May 10th, and Spottsylvania, May 12th, for which he was assigned to the command of the Third Brigade, but asked to be allowed to decline this advancement. Asked why, rather sternly, and when he would accept promotion, he replied, "When the losses of the war leave me the ranking officer of the brigade in which my regiment is serving."

To penetrate the Confederacy as far as the James River had cost thousands of lives and millions of money, but finally, by the middle of June, 1864, General Ulysses S. Grant had successfully pushed his way fifty-five miles across the peninsula, in the face of the enemy. Grant's audacious and successful move from Cold Harbor across the James was so bold and unexpected that Lee did not oppose it. Prior to these events Grant had been feeling the Confederate lines. General Smith had swung his troops toward Richmond, around Petersburg, but had failed to follow the advantage gained, the Confederates meanwhile strengthening their positions. Learning of this about noon of June 16th, General Grant decided to retrieve, if possible, the lost advantage by a general assault on the enemy's lines. General W. M. Mintzer, who was the Lieut. Colonel of the Forty-Third Pennsylvania, one of the regiments of the brigade which Colonel Beaver then commanded, gave this graphic account of his part in the assault:

"It was about four o'clock, I think, when we gathered about General Beaver and heard from him that we were to charge the redoubts in front of us at six o'clock. He explained the plan of attack and its perils. He designated the officers who were to succeed to the command if he fell. There was an open plain between our position and the earthworks of the enemy, which was swept by their guns, and over this cleared field we were to charge for several hundred yards. Not long after we had received our instructions General Beaver began forming the brigade behind our works. Knapsacks were piled up and everything left that would embarrass the men in the dash upon the enemy. After the line was formed we had remained in suspense but a short time, when General Beaver moved down to near the center of the brigade and ordered the advance. He was first over our works, and I shall never forget him as he looked that beautiful June afternoon, when he turned toward us, removed his sword from its scabbard, and shouted for the charge in clear, ringing tones. He was the picture of a soldier and he had the confidence of the command as few men had. The men followed him with a shout, and over the plain they swept, under his lead, amidst a perfect shower of shot and shell. When we were well on toward the Confederate works and the charge was at its height, with every prospect of victory, I saw a shell strike beneath General Beavers feet, bury itself in the ground, and explode. It threw him into the air, I and all of us then supposed, dead. He was quickly picked up by some of the men and carried to the rear with a severe wound in his side. Deprived of his inspiring leadership, despite the efforts of the officers, the brigade fell into confusion and retired. There was no one to succeed him in whose judgment and bravery the men and officers had the confidence necessary to rally a force to face a seemingly forlorn hope. But for his removal the fort would have been taken."

During the interim between the two wounds here spoken of, he had also been wounded by a spent ball, which a note book stopped. After this, his third wound, he was soon back, impatient to rejoin his command, but General Hancock refused to permit it and furloughed him again. Before his second furlough had expired he was again back to take command of his brigade in the desperate engagement which cost him the loss of a leg and almost his life. It was at the Battle of Ream's Station, where General Hancock with two divisions of his corps, against which the Confederates sent more than three times his number, was tearing up the Weldon Railroad. It was an important line of communication from Petersburg to Wilmington, North Carolina, with connections to the South Atlantic coast—an essential feeder to the enemy's position. When Colonel Beaver reported for duty the battle was imminent. General Hancock welcomed him eagerly, pointed out the position of his brigade, and instructed him to go over and take command. He had just done so and was reviewing his front and watching the Confederate advance, when he suddenly dropped, and his right leg lay at right angle from him, as he fell. Almost at the same instant the small force of cavalry in front was driven back by overwhelming numbers, and he was almost trampled to death. Lying there he waved his cap to attract attention, and the horsemen seeing, not only did not injure him, but hastily bore him to the rear. He had not been back in battle thirty minutes until he lost his leg. It was many days before he was able to return home to Bellefonte, and then, on November 10, 1864, came his appointment by President Lincoln as a Brigadier General of Volunteers, by brevet, "for highly meritorious and distinguished conduct throughout the campaign, particularly for valuable services at Cold Harbor, while commanding a brigade."

This description of General Beaver's military record is given principally to show the type of men born in Perry County, who went forth in '61 and later to serve their country—for there were hundreds and hundreds of brave men—and to give the reader a knowledge of his character, his manhood, his love for his mother, and all those good traits which eventually landed him in the governor's chair—the second Perry Countian to attain that coveted position, Governor William Bigler, as before stated, having been the other.

During his absence the law firm of McAllister & Beaver had continued to prosper, and the senior partner eagerly awaited General Beaver's return. All the energy he had displayed as a soldier he now threw into the law, and as he was a man of character, great mentality and the highest integrity he was in every respect successful. He stood for right in his community and labored for the upbuilding of his adopted town and county. He was no candidate for the nomination, but was drafted by the party of his choice—the Republicans—as the nominee for the State Legislature. He declined, but at the earnest solicitation of Governor Curtin, he acquiesced, but was defeated at the general election, Centre County being then strongly Democratic.

In December, 1865, he married Miss Mary McAllister, a daughter of his law partner and former preceptor, a refined and educated woman of character, who survives him and resides at Bellefonte.

During subsequent Presidential campaigns General Beaver was called into other states, where his eloquence and logic were invaluable. He continually refused to be a candidate for Congress. He filled so many positions of honor and trust, at various times, that it would take pages to name them all. He was the logical choice of his congressional district for delegate to the Republican National Convention of 1880. When the county convention met the sentiment for James G. Blaine was as five to one, and a committee was sent to him to ascertain his views. "I am for General Grant. If I am chosen I will not go back on my old commander, as long as he is a candidate before the convention." The reply was carried back to the convention, but he was endorsed nevertheless and the delegates to the state convention were instructed to have him made the delegate. At the same time those authorized to speak for Beaver reiterated the fact that he would support Grant, but yet the convention named him. He was chosen chairman of the Pennsylvania delegation at Chicago, and by his fairness held the respect of both the contending forces. After the deadlock and the subsequent nomination of James A. Garfield he was made the choice of the Pennsylvania delegation for the Vice-Presidency. The delegations of Ohio, Tennessee and some other states supported him, but the nomination went to Chester Allen Arthur, Beaver declining, with the statement that his friends in Pennsylvania wanted him to run for governor and he would accede to their wishes. And thus the second scion of Perry County missed the Presidency (James G. Blaine being the other).

When the Republican State Convention met in Harrisburg, in 1882, General Beaver was its choice for governor, but an Independent and Greenback ticket appearing in the field, split the Republican vote, and he was defeated by Robert E. Pattison at the general elections. This independent movement was not directed against Beaver, but against the Camerons, then in the saddle in Pennsylvania politics. It was led by John Stewart, later a judge of the Supreme Court of Pennsylvania, and deflected enough votes to cause Beaver's defeat. In 1886 he was again nominated and was elected over his opponent, Chauncey F. Black, by a plurality of 42,000 votes. He was inaugurated January 18, 1887. His administration had no great outstanding features, but was noted for the character of the measures, which largely bore on the betterment of life. Among them were approval of high license legislation and laws curbing the liquor traffic, the encouragement of industrial education, refusal to employ military force for the execution of civil process, save as a last resort; reduction of state debt by three million, better road legislation, and laws for the protection of men, women and children in manufacturing establishments.

It was during his term that the great Johnstown flood occurred, and he, with the backing of prominent citizens and banks, immediately borrowed $400,000 for the immediate relief of the sufferers. He was chairman of the Flood Commission, which received and dispensed over $6,000,000.

Although declining service in the United States Army he continued his interest in the Pennsylvania National Guard, and in 1872 Governor Geary, in its reorganization, appointed him Brigadier General, a position he held until he himself was elected governor. He was in command during the big strike and riots of 1877. While governor he appeared at the head of the National Guard during the Constitutional Convention Celebration of 1887. He was Chief Marshal of President Benjamin Harrison's inaugural parade of 1889, and during the same year led the National Guard at the Centennial Celebration of Washington's inauguration as first President of the United States, in New York. Although he had lost a leg he was a good horseman. At the first real reunion of the Union and Confederate Armies at Gettysburg, in 1888, he delivered the address of welcome to his old enemy-at-arms.

During 1895 the Pennsylvania Legislature passed an act creating the Superior Court, and General Beaver was one of the seven judges appointed. At the succeeding election in November he was elected to a ten-year term in the office, and in 1905 was reëlected, holding the office at the time of his death.

In 1871 he was made a trustee of Washington and Jefferson College, and for many years he was president of the Alumni Association. In 1873 he became a trustee of the Pennsylvania State College, on which board he served for forty-one years. Even before 1873 he was much interested in State College, but as Hugh N. McAllister, his law partner and father-in-law, to whom was largely due the credit for its inception, was already on the board it was not deemed advisable that both be trustees. In 1874 General Beaver was elected president of the board, and by reëlections held the position until he became ex-officio member by being elected governor. He was for thirty years president of the board, and as such was intimately related to the progress of the college and to the life of the students until his death.

He was a consistent churchman of the Presbyterian faith, and at the centenary meeting of the General Assembly he presided as vice-moderator, the first layman to hold that position, which he also held again on a later occasion. He was deeply interested in all phases of the work of the Young Men's Christian Association and was a frequent speaker at the state and national conventions. He helped to organize the State Committee for Pennsylvania in 1869, and was a member of that committee without interruption, for the rest of his life.

Governor Beaver died January 31, 1914, at his home in Bellefonte, mourned by county, state, and nation. He was the father of five children: Nelson, dying in early life; James, aged three, soon after the inauguration of his father as Governor of Pennsylvania, and Hugh, prominent in Y. M. C. A. work, in young manhood, in 1898. Two sons, Gilbert, of New York, and Thomas, recently elected to the legislature from Bellefonte, survive. Mrs. James A. Beaver also survives, as does the governor's half sisters, *Mrs. Anna McDonald Eckels, of Millerstown, and Miss Catharine McDonald, of Lewisburg.

CHIEF JUSTICE JOHN BANNISTER GIBSON.

Perry County soil has been the birthplace and the early home of three different men who have became the chief justices of three different states of the Union. Chief Justice John Bannister Gibson, of the Supreme Court of Pennsylvania, was one of the greatest to serve in that high office, and many authorities place him

NOTE.—While compiling this work the author interviewed Mr. D. M. Rickabaugh, a schoolmate of General Beaver's, residing at Millerstown, who was eighty-seven years of age last July (1920), and an intimate, lifelong friend. Mr. Rickabaugh has since passed away.

*Mrs. Eckels died in 1921.

north of the mountain, and his greatest distinction was service as register and recorder of Cumberland County for a term. The second son, George, became Commissary General of the United States Army, his biography appearing elsewhere in this book. A third son, William Chesney, became a miller, later going to sea. The fourth son, John Bannister Gibson, born November 8, 1780, is the subject of this sketch. A daughter died in infancy. The father, George Gibson II, removed to Sherman's Valley, in 1773, the year following his marriage. At the close of Lord Dunmore's war, in 1774, he returned to his home at Westover Mills (the Gibson mill), but at the call to arms of the Continental Army he hastened to Pittsburgh and recruited a company of one hundred men for service, the first company organized for that army west of the Alleghenies. No fifer could be found, and Captain Gibson became his own fifer. Composed of the roughest of frontiersmen, never subjected to discipline, they foraged regardless of orders or of trouble, and so became jocularly known as "Gibson's Lambs." Needing powder badly, Gibson was detailed to go to New Orleans and negotiate with the Spanish government for a supply. He traversed the wilderness then existing between Pittsburgh and New Orleans and in due time arrived with a supply loaded upon flats. Offered a monetary reward or promotion for his success, he chose the latter, and was made a colonel, serving as such throughout the Revolution. To Colonel Gibson, when Cornwallis surrendered his army at Yorktown, General Washington gave command of the surrendered troops, save the commissioned officers, to be sent to York, Pennsylvania, as prisoners of war. The statement that he never returned to the county's territory to reside is erroneous, as he did so in 1782, at the conclusion of the treaty of peace, and lived largely the life of a country gentleman until early in 1791, when Congress voted two thousand men—two regiments, from Virginia and Pennsylvania—to assist General Arthur St. Clair in an expedition against the Indians, renegades and British at Detroit, from where they harassed the residents of the Ohio Valley. George Gibson was appointed lieutenant colonel and field commander of the Pennsylvania regiment. This was the first considerable military undertaking of the new nation. Early on the morning of November 4, 1791, the troops were surrounded by the redskins, on the banks of the Wabash, and, early in the engagement, Colonel Gibson fell, wounded in the head. Bandaging it he again entered the fight, thus being a conspicuous target. He was again wounded, and for the third time, in the wrist, which disabled him. He was carried to a stockade, thirty miles back, and there, a few days later, he died; and there his body rests. The township, in Mercer County, Ohio, in which the battle was fought, is named Gibson, in his honor. At no other place, save the Custer massacre at the Little Big Horn, were American troops handled so severely. Of 1,400 men actually engaged, 593 privates were killed and 252 privates and thirty-one officers wounded. As a young man Colonel Gibson had engaged in the trade with the West Indies, and also as a trader, trafficking with the Indians at Fort Pitt. At the opening of the Revolution Francis West, of the Cumberland side of the mountain, his father-in-law, was a sympathizer of the mother country, and an extremely bitter feeling existed between them, Colonel Gibson being an ardent Federalist.

Unfortunately the mother, Ann West Gibson, did not live to see her son's elevation to high position. She died in 1809, and her son Francis leased the mill to Jacob Bigler (father of the two governors), and removed to Carlisle, where he remained for many years, later returning there, where he died March 18, 1856, aged 82 years.

When the county was created in 1820, George Gibson's heirs were assessed with 450 acres of land, a sawmill and a gristmill. Francis West, the maternal grandfather of Chief Justice Gibson, was the owner of five slaves which he disposed of in his will at the time of his death in 1784. As stated, he was judge of the Cumberland County courts, and is said to have been a brilliant man. His daughter Ann, who became the mother of the future jurist, was also a brilliant woman, and during the first ten years of her married life, besides rearing her family of little children, found time to build the old Westover mill, named after the family estate in England, now and long since known as the Gibson mill.

John Bannister Gibson's boyhood home, which occupied a site near the mill, was located in the wooded section of present Spring Township, near the Carroll Township line, almost on the banks of Sherman's Creek, with the towering peak of Mt. Pisgah immediately facing it, and below a mighty boulder jutting to the very edge of the waters of the creek, and known to this day as Gibson's Rock. Amid this wild and picturesque section he first beheld the light of day and heard the clatter of the mill and the swish of the waters.

John Bannister Gibson was born November 1, 1780. He was named after the celebrated Virginia soldier and statesman, *John Banister, a member of the Continental Congress, a signer of the Articles of Confederation, and an officer in the Virginia line during the Revolution—a friend of Colonel Gibson. His boyhood was similar to that of the boys of the period, save that he was early sent to Dickinson College. Absence of his father in the Continental Army placed entire responsibility upon his mother,

---

*In his early life Justice Gibson did not use his full name, and in later years spelled the Banister thus, Bannister, although the man after whom he was named spelled his name with a single "n."

Ann West Gibson, an educated and talented woman, to whom he
was indebted for much of his early education. With the determination that her sons should not degenerate she built a schoolhouse near the homestead and there, herself, became the teacher.
His preparatory education was received at the preparatory school
attached to Dickinson College, where he later graduated. The
exact date of his graduation is in doubt. He began to attend college in 1795 or 1796. In the Union Philosophical Society of the
college his name first appears in 1797, but in later published records of the students of the college his name appears in the Class
of 1798. Biographical sketches generally place the date of his
graduation as 1800. He was classed as an irregular student, his
terms not being consecutive. His graduation occurred during the
presidency of Charles Nesbit, D.D. He read law with that brilliant jurist, Thomas Duncan, later an associate justice on the supreme bench. He was admitted to the Carlisle bar in 1803 and
located at Carlisle, but soon left to locate in Beaver County. From
there he went to Hagerstown, but by 1805 was back in Carlisle,
resuming his practice there. In 1810 he was elected by the (then)
Republican party as a representative to the General Assembly of
Pennsylvania, being reëlected the following year. Judges were
then appointive and the governor of Pennsylvania, Simon Snyder,
was married to a cousin of Mr. Gibson, which accounts for his
first step up the ladder, probably, but his rise was one of attain-
ment altogether. His appointment was made in 1813, as judge of
the Eleventh Judicial District, in the northern part of the state.

When Gibson was a student at college he drew the attention of
Judge Hugh H. Brackenridge, who noticed the "country boy" and
invited him to use his fine library. Through his long life he often
mentioned this act, which created a lifetime friendship. A strange
coincidence is that Judge Brackenridge, Mr. Gibson and his preceptor, Thomas Duncan, all came to be justices of the Supreme
Court of the state. All did not sit together, however, as Gibson's
appointment came immediately after the death of Brackenridge.
At the time of being made a justice of the Supreme Court John
Bannister Gibson was a common pleas judge of the newly created
Eleventh District. He was appointed June 27, 1816, the day following the death of Judge Brackenridge, by Governor Snyder.
Appointments were during good behavior, which practically meant
for life. During the fall of 1812 Mr. Gibson had been united in
marriage to Sarah Galbraith, a daughter of a retired Revolutionary
officer. On his appointment to the supreme bench, they moved to
Carlisle, where they continued to reside, although the sessions of
court called him afar.

Of Gibson's mother it is said that she was a devout member of
the Church of England (Episcopal), and attended the services of

St. John's Church at Carlisle, fifteen miles distant, across the Kittatinny Mountain, either afoot or horseback. The justice later, when
at home at Carlisle, was a faithful attendant of this church. On
an occasion she invited the bishop of her church to come over and
baptize her boys. When he arrived they were gunning, and he
retired before their return, as it grew late. During the night a
slight snow fell, and the boys were off hunting before his reverence
arose, and he never did get to see them.

From the pen of the late Benjamin F. Junkin, himself an authority of note on legal matters, we quote:

"Thus, as he started in 1816, his opinions for over thirty-six years, to
1853, when he died, are models of perspicuity, sententiousness and accurate
diction. He had ceased to be chief justice in 1851, and the last opinion
delivered by him was filed January 6, 1853, in the case of Beatty vs. Wray,
reported in 7th Harris, page 517, determining 'that a surviving partner is
not entitled to compensation for winding up the partnership business,' and
after that his voice was heard no more. In his last opinion he said, 'At
the formation of a partnership, its dissolution by death is rarely contemplated. It is an unwelcome subject, for no man who enters on a speculation can bear to think he may not live to finish it,' and whoever will read
that last opinion and shut his eyes to the date of its delivery, will not be
able to distinguish his clear and vigorous language, citations of authorities and surprising grasp of the questions involved from one of his famous
efforts of twenty years before.

"There was that about Gibson's opinions which cannot be described.
While he entered learnedly into the question, with amplifications, his language was so terse, his words so few, the structure of his sentences so
harmonious, so replete with elegance of diction, that the conclusion was
reached, the point decided, and the judgment convinced ere the charm was
broken. He described a negotiable note in four words, 'a carrier without
luggage.'

"If we of Perry are proud of his achievements and wonderful powers,
other places have not withheld their admiration. As a jurist he had a
world-wide renown, wherever his language is spoken. It was difficult to
tell when he read and how he obtained his legal learning, but we have
seen him consulting books in the State Library very often."

While many of our readers will remember Judge Junkin, yet he
was already a member of the bar while Judge Gibson was on the
supreme bench and was a personal acquaintance, thus showing how
closely we follow the period of the celebrated jurist.

While James X. McLanahan was in the United States Congress
as the representative of the district of which Perry was a part,
he was abroad and sat in the court of Westminster, where the
twelve judges of England were hearing a case. A lawyer was
reading an opinion to the court without stating whose it was, when
the chief justice remarked, "That is an opinion by Chief Justice
Gibson, of Pennsylvania." The lawyer admitted it was, when the
chief justice replied, "His opinions have great weight with this
court." The congressman related the story to Chief Justice Gibson, in the presence of Judge Junkin, on an occasion, to which he

replied, a tear stealing down his cheek, "A prophet is not without honor, save in his own country."

It was Chief Justice John Bannister Gibson that rendered the important decision which settled for all time that the powers of the legislature are not judicial, but constructive. In the case of De Chastellux vs. Fairchild (15 Pa. 18), decided in 1850. The legislature attempted to order a new trial in an adjudicated case. Justice Gibson said:

"If anything is self-evident in the structure of our government, it is, that the legislature has no power to order a new trial, or to direct the court to order it, either before or after judgment. * * * The power of the legislature is not judicial. * * * It is limited to the making of laws; not to the exposition or execution of them."

In appearance Chief Justice Gibson was a powerful, broad-shouldered, tall man (over six feet): His face was handsome, intellectual and benevolent, with a florid complexion, and the oil painting of him which hangs in the Supreme Court room was pronounced by no less an authority than Judge Junkin as being "not recognizable, having, in fact, more the look and expression of the driver of a broad-wheeled wagon in the days when a six-horse team drew eighty hundred with a wheel locked, over the pike from Philadelphia to Pittsburgh." He was slow in gait, unheedful of surroundings, careless of personal appearance, and attracted attention. He was a connoisseur in music and painting, and was an adept on the violin. When Ole Bull played in Philadelphia, Gibson and another supreme judge attended, the other not being skilled along musical lines. While the audience was being held spellbound by the marvelous performance of the prodigy, the other judge turned to Gibson and remarked, "Let us go home; that fool will never get done tuning his fiddle." Gibson replied, "Why, you uncultivated heathen! That's the most enchanting music I ever heard."

Until 1826 the Supreme Court consisted of but three judges; during that year it was increased to five. In 1827, upon the death of Chief Justice Tilghman, Gibson was appointed chief justice, and so remained until 1851, when the new Constitution's provisions required that the five men elected to that august body should "draw cuts," the one drawing the shortest term (three years) to be chief justice, and the one drawing the longest term (six years) to be his successor. Through that law the state was deprived of his wonderful ability in that important position, but had he lived he would have again became chief justice in 1854, as he drew the long term of six years. When the amended Constitution was adopted, in 1838, he immediately resigned as chief justice. Although party excitement ran high, Governor Ritner, a Whig, ignored it, and reappointed him. In 1851, of the five justices he was the only one to be renominated.

Chief Justice Gibson discharged his duties until the illness which culminated in his death, on May 3, 1853. He sat in the Supreme Court with twenty-six different justices, none of whom, it is said, owed their position to him, save Judge Duncan, whose appointment he advocated. He was for twenty-four years chief justice and for thirteen years an associate justice. From 1824 to 1828 he was president of the Board of Trustees of Dickinson College. In the year following his elevation to the chief justiceship, the friends of General Andrew Jackson placed his name at the head of the Pennsylvania electoral ticket, with the result that the ticket received in the state an almost unprecedented majority.

Judge Gibson was a lover of the theater, and he and Judge Rogers, an associate justice, placed a marble slab upon the grave of the celebrated actor, Joseph Jefferson, who died in Harrisburg in 1832, and whose body rests in a Harrisburg cemetery, the epitaph being written by Judge Gibson. He also wrote the inscription for the monument of his preceptor, Judge Duncan, at Carlisle, and drew the design as well as wrote the inscription for that of Dr. Charles Nesbit, D.D., whose attachment for the American cause made him an exile from his native land.

As a boy he showed considerable skill as an artist, and two paintings by him still exist, having been presented by his nephew, Frank W. Gibson, to the Allegheny County law library at Pittsburgh. One represents Pulaski on horseback, and the other is his own likeness, painted on a poplar board. The latter was painted under unusual circumstances. While a law student at Carlisle he visited his mother at the parental home at Westover Mills, along Sherman's Creek, with the intention of going deer hunting. During his entire holiday it rained, and, kept within doors, he painted the picture for amusement.

Chief Justice Gibson was elected Grand Master of the Grand Lodge, Free and Accepted Masons of Pennsylvania, on December 27, 1823, being possibly the only man born within the limits of what is now Perry County to fill that high office.

Interested largely in geology he wrote several contributions along that line, which showed him to be an authority upon that subject. While acting in the capacity of judge in the Eleventh District and residing in Luzerne County, his method of relaxation was studying the coal formations and visiting the old Indian fortifications. The statement sometimes made that Mrs. Gibson claimed that the first anthracite coal fires were built in her home, is doubtless without foundation, as Judge Gibson was appointed as judge there in 1813, while coal had been discovered in the Wyoming Valley in 1787, a quarter of a century previous.

Justice Black said of him: "Abroad he has for very many years been thought the great glory of his native state." In addressing

43

the students of the University of Pennsylvania, in 1904, Governor
Samuel Pennypacker, himself a learned judge, said: "Be earnest
and thorough. If your field be the law, follow the example and
study the work of Gibson and Sharwood." To no other man is
America indebted so much as to Gibson for his interpretation of
the English common law and its adaptation to our needs for his
upbuilding of our system of equity and for his interpretation of
the Constitution. In the formative period of Pennsylvania law
he refused to slavishly follow outgrown conditions, when justice
and right pointed otherwise. At the time of his death he had been
longer in office than any contemporary judge in the world. His
opinions were an unbroken chain of logic. For vigor, clearness
and precision of thought they had no equals. At the May term of
the Middle District, in 1853, in memorializing his decease, Chief
Justice Black, among other things, paid this fine compliment to
Justice Gibson:

"He was inflexibly honest. The judicial ermine was as unspotted when
he laid it aside for the habiliments of the grave, as it was when he first
assumed it. I do not mean to award him merely that commonplace integrity which it is no honor to have, but simply a disgrace to want. He was
not only incorruptible, but scrupulously, delicately, conscientiously free
from all wilful wrong, either in thought, word or deed."

Ex-Governor Samuel Pennypacker, whose fame, both as a jurist
and historian, far excels that of his ability as governor, in his book,
"Pennsylvania, the Keystone," says of Chief Justice Gibson:

"What John Marshall was to the law of the United States, John Bannister Gibson, born in Perry County in 1780, was to the law of Pennsylvania. During the formative period, when principles were being established, he was the chief justice, and his was the directing mind, and among
lawyers he ranks higher than such famous men as Story. He established
the doctrine, now universal in America, that on the sale of goods the keeping of possession by the man who sells is a fraud as against creditors. He
had been a member of the General Assembly, had written some verse,
dabbled in art, and was regarded as an adept on the violin."

On an occasion Chief Justice Gibson and Daniel Webster attended a banquet in Boston. Mr. Webster left first and inadvert-
ently took Mr. Gibson's hat. Unaware of that fact Judge Gibson
put on Mr. Webster's hat and never discovered it until the next
day, as it was a perfect fit. Each of these men had exceedingly
large heads, about twenty-four inches in circumference, but Judge
Gibson's was slightly the larger.

There existed a warm friendship between the supreme justice
and his brothers, Francis and George, and throughout their long
lives they lived in perfect accord. George, long Commissary General of the United States Army, annually took the month of October as his vacation, and much of it the brothers whiled away together. General Gibson was a personal friend of General Jackson,

later President, who was a great admirer of the chief justice, and on several occasions wanted to make him a supreme justice of the United States, but was overruled by political combinations. Had another vacancy occurred in that august body during the Jackson administration there is little doubt that it would have gone to Gibson.

The chief justice was the father of eight children, as follows: Anne Sarah, John Bannister, and Francis West, who died in childhood; Margaretta, married to Col. Charles McClure, who represented the Cumberland district in the United States Congress and was secretary of the commonwealth during the term of Governor Porter; Anna Barbara, married to W. Milnor Roberts, once chief engineer of the state public works, whose name was associated with such projects as the Portage Road, the Harrisburg and Lancaster Railroad, and the Cumberland Valley Railroad; John Bannister II, a lieutenant in the First Artillery, U. S. A., at the breaking out of the Mexican War, brevetted for bravery; George, colonel of the Fifth Infantry, U. S. A.; and Sallie, married in 1851 to Capt. R. H. Anderson, of the Second Dragoons, U. S. A., a Southerner, and the last one of the thirty-three officers from South Carolina to resign from the United States Army in 1861, prior to the war between the States.

In these days of inflated salaries, it may be of interest to note that the highest salary ever paid the chief justice of Pennsylvania was two thousand dollars per annum. When the old historic State Capitol, the one replaced by the present building, was erected, Justice Gibson was one of the building commission appointed to oversee its construction.

Col. A. K. McClure, native Perry Countian, noted editor and author, in his book, "Lincoln and Men of War Times," says:

"Chief Justice Gibson is one of the most notable characters of Pennsylvania, and no one character is so carefully and so kindly studied by the legal profession of the state as is that of the great jurist. He stands in the annals of the commonwealth head and shoulders above his fellow great jurists, and his decisions are not only quoted in his state and country by judicial tribunals, but they have been quoted and commended in the courts of England. I did not know our great chief justice personally until within five years of his death, as he was chief justice of Pennsylvania a year before I was born. His name was a household word in the community of my boyhood, as his place of birth was only a very few miles from my own home. His name was referred to with a pride that is natural in a primitive rural community when one of their own number has reached the highest distinction in the state, and among my early recollections I recall the chief justice's brother, Frank Gibson, as the man who played the fiddle for nearly or quite all the dances, corn huskings and butter boilings of the neighborhood. The chief justice, like his brother, was passionately fond of the violin, and even until the latest years of his life he would retire to his room alone and enjoy his own music on his favorite instrument.

"His magnificently chiseled face ever arrested the attention of even the most casual observer. I had few opportunities in my brief acquaintance with him of seeing him alone, but I sought every opportunity to do so because he was one of the most delightful conversationalists, and being from the same community that had given him birth he loved to talk about his own people and his neighbors for whom he cherished the liveliest affection. The only attempt he ever made at poetry was when late in life he visited the dilapidated home of his birth after an absence of many years. It is not a great poem, but it shows the simple tastes of the great jurist, and the heartstrings of love which went out to his old home surroundings. It might be said of Gibson's poem as Horace Greely said in reviewing the poems of John Quincy Adams, that they show 'what middling things a great man may do." I quote the first and last of the six stanzas:

> " 'The home of my youth stands in silence and sadness,
> None that tasted its simple enjoyments are there;
> No longer its walls ring with glee and with gladness,
> No train of blythe melody breaks on the ear.

> " 'But time ne'er retraces the footsteps he measures;
> In fancy alone with the past we can dwell;
> Then take my last blessing, lov'd scene of young pleasures,
> Dear home of my childhood—forever farewell."

WHERE GIBSON SLEEPS.

In the graveyard at Carlisle, Pennsylvania, over the Gibson plot, is a stone on which appear inscriptions from the pen of that distinguished Pennsylvanian, Jeremiah S. Black, himself a jurist of note. On the face appears:

> John Bannister Gibson, LL.D.,
> For many years Chief Justice of Pennsylvania,
> Born Nov. 8, 1780,
> Died May 2, 1853,
> Also his wife, Sarah W. Gibson,
> Born Jan. 25, 1791,
> Died Jan. 25, 1861.

The inscription on the right:

> In the various Knowledge
> Which forms the perfect Scholar,
> He had no superior.
> Independent, Upright and Able,
> He had all the highest qualities
> of a great Judge.
> In the difficult Science of Jurisprudence,
> He mastered every Department,
> Discussed almost every question and
> Touched no subject which he did not adorn.
> He won in early manhood
> And retained to the close of a long life
> The affection of his brethren on the Bench,
> The respect of the Bar
> And the confidence of the people.

tled at Sandwich, Massachusetts, about 1630. Daniel Gantt was of
the sixth generation in America, the line of descent having been as
follows: first generation, Peter; second, Hanninah, who removed
to Shrewsbury, New Jersey, and was wed to Dorothy Butler;
third, Hanninah, Jr.; fourth, Joseph; fifth, Joseph, Jr. (who came
from New Jersey and settled on Middle Ridge); sixth, Daniel.

Chief Justice Gantt was educated in the schools of the period,
not yet the time of free public schools, having attended the log
cabin school located on his father's farm. He arrived at school
age in the very year in which the county was organized. He
studied surveying in 1832-33 at New Bloomfield. He studied law
at New Bloomfield, in the office of Joseph Casey, who had been
admitted to the bar in 1839, and at the August court of 1843 he
was admitted to the Perry County bar. During his practice at
New Bloomfield Mitchell Stever read law with him and was admitted to the bar in 1844. He located at Omaha, Nebraska, in
1857, and at once gained distinction in his chosen profession. In
1862 President Lincoln appointed him U. S. district attorney, and
he held that office until his election to the Nebraska Legislature,
two years later. He removed to Nebraska City in 1868, and in
1872 was elected judge of the First Judicial District, for the term
beginning January 16, 1873. Under the provisions of the Constitution then in force he sat also as an associate justice of the Supreme Court. On the expiration of his term, in 1875, he was
elected to the supreme bench, and three years later became chief
justice. He died May 29, 1878.

He was twice married, first, in 1843, to Agnes T. Fulton (sometimes stated Nancy T.), kin to Robert Fulton, the famous inventor
of the steamboat, by whom he had three sons and four daughters.
In 1858 he was married to Harriet Cooper. Chief Justice Gantt
was an uncle of Daniel Gantt, of Newport, and by marriage, of
H. R. Patterson, retired passenger conductor of Harrisburg, formerly of Perry County, who visited him while he was on the supreme bench. While a young man, reading law, to meet expenses
he taught a subscription school in Buffalo Township, and recorded
in his diary, in the possession of his heirs, near Lincoln, Nebraska,
are the facts showing that when the free school act was passed,
the first school in Pennsylvania to be opened in accordance with
that act was the one he taught, described as "at Col. Thompson's,"
which opened September 10, 1834. This location was in that part
of Buffalo Township which has since become Watts. According to
further entry in the diary Buffalo Township was the first district
in the state to adopt the free school law.

Citizens of the community interested in its passage were in
Harrisburg, and upon learning of its passage, rode home during

the night bearing the news. The following morning Mr. Gantt declared his school a free school.

While an attorney at New Bloomfield Justice Gantt took great interest in the community and civic life. His name is found as chairman of the premium committee of the first agricultural fair at that place, in 1852. Several years later he was its secretary. He was one of the men who purchased the grounds and laid out the present New Bloomfield cemetery in 1854. When a public meeting was held in 1856 declaring for "Free Kansas and no Popery" he was on the committee on resolutions. He was an important factor in the lyceum there in 1842-43, and for years thereafter. In 1844 he was the secretary. One of his educational addresses was so highly thought of that a committee publicly requested its reproduction in the county press, which was complied with. As long as he remained in the county his name was prominently connected with both the agricultural fair and the lyceums, as well as with all educational projects. When a society called the Sons of Temperance organized a branch in New Bloomfield in 1846, Mr. Gantt became its president. He was much interested in politics, and in 1850 was a senatorial conferee to the Republican conference. The success of Justice Gantt is all the more marked when it is remembered that when a lad of ten he cut his left knee so badly that he was confined to the house for six months and emerged with a crippled limb which he carried through life. Justice Gantt died at Nebraska City, May 29, 1878.

Immediately upon the opening of the July term of the Supreme Court of Nebraska, in 1878, after the death of Chief Justice Gantt, official notice was taken of his death, and something of the man may be learned from the opinion of the learned members of the court. Justice Marquett, opening the ceremonies, spoke of him as "The man who for near a quarter of a century has been with us as lawyer and judge, and who had not failed to attain the highest judicial honors of our state, commanding the greatest confidence of the community, and the affections of a large circle of friends, by a blameless and honorable life."

Upon presenting the resolutions of the State Bar Association, from among Justice Marquett's further remarks, are the following extracts:

"On the twenty-ninth day of May, 1878, Chief Justice Daniel Gantt died. He had lived in our midst for over twenty years, and during all that time, by a blameless life, he made many friends—but few enemies. A few days before his death I heard him say, in answer to the inquiry of another whether he did not think a recent decision of his would not in certain quarters elicit opposition: 'I care not for that, for I think I founded my decision upon correct principles.' To my mind this was the highest exhibition of manhood. This alone places him on a higher plane, which few men ever reach, in an atmosphere purer than men usually breathe. The 'old man' would rather be right than popular.

"But Daniel Gantt's eulogy is not to be pronounced by me. His best eulogy is found in the records of this court, and in his decisions, many of which are master productions. His was not the mind to find justice in an isolated case where justice appeared, but which was in reality a whitened sepulcher, and when once established as a precedent would lead to a long course of injustice. His mind dived deep and sought for golden lodes of truth far-reaching, opening up long pathways in which the future jurist might walk and find justice. He was my friend for twenty years without shade of differing."

George H. Roberts, Attorney General of Nebraska, as a part of his remarks, included this tribute to 'Justice Gantt, in reference to treatment of the younger members of the bar:

"Others have known the late chief justice longer, and more intimately than I, but no one appreciated more fully his kindness, his innate nobility of soul, his gentleness, his charity, his worth. To the younger members of the bar he was at once an elder brother, counselor, and friend. Here a word of caution, or reproof, so gently given that it left no sting behind; and again words of encouragement and cheer—so dear and highly prized by those struggling in the rear ranks for place and recognition at the front. The pure bright gold of his heart and mind will abide forever, written with a pen of steel upon the foundations of the jurisprudence of a great young commonwealth."

Of his professional characteristics, Attorney E. Wakely said:

"He was a conspicuously upright citizen, and a just, conscientious man. In his profession, without claim to brilliancy of genius, or eloquence of advocacy, and over modest in the estimate of his own powers, he had learning, industry, patience, solidity of judgment, and never-questioned integrity. These are aids which litigants learn to value and rely on, when sometimes, more captivating qualities have charmed the court, but lost the cause. On the bench he had never failing courtesy, equanimity, fairness, and love of justice, without ever an alloy or partiality, resentment or asperity. The opinions he has left here testify to his clearness of judgment, his research, his apprehension of legal principles, and his aptitude in applying them to the facts of the cause."

Chief Justice Maxwell, the successor of Chief Justice Gantt, in the course of his remarks said:

"In October, 1872, Judge Gantt and myself were elected Judges of this court. As the Judges at that time were also judges of the District Courts, nearly the entire business before the Supreme Court consisted of cases decided by local judges, a considerable number being up for review from Judge Gantt's district. He at no time manifested the slightest anxiety about the conclusions to be reached by the court in a case appealed from his decision. During the time that he acted as one of the Judges of the District Court his labors were constant and unremitting, and frequently burdensome. Throughout his career as Judge he seemed to be actuated by one motive, namely, to ascertain what the law was upon any question presented, and having arrived at a conclusion in that regard, he fearlessly declared it. His success as a lawyer and Judge was largely due—as it must be in all cases of real success in the legal profession—to a thorough mastery of legal principles, untiring industry, and unswerving integrity."

Chief Justice Henry Calvin Thatcher was the third son of Henry and Lydia Ann (Albert) Thatcher, and was born in New Buffalo, Perry County, April 21, 1842. After receiving the education afforded by the schools of the period, through the desire of his parents to see their children educated, he was enabled to attend Franklin & Marshall College at Lancaster, from which institution he graduated in 1864, taking the honors of his class. Choosing the law for his career he began reading law at Altoona, Pennsylvania, and at the same time he edited the educational columns of the *Hollidaysburg Standard*. In the spring of 1866 he was graduated from the Law Department of Albany University, of New York, and in the fall of the same year he went to Colorrado, located at Pueblo, and began the practice of law. There were no railroads then west of the Mississippi and the future justice made the pilgrimage by ox-team across the plains. It was a long and tedious journey.

His first public service was in 1869, when President Grant appointed him United States Attorney for the State of Colorado. After serving in that capacity for a little over a year he resigned. When Colorado gained statehood he was made a member of the Constitutional Convention from his district, upon a non-partisan ticket, with scarcely a dissenting vote. In 1876 he received the Republican nomination for the Supreme Court, and was elected to that high office. In drawing lots for terms, Judge Thatcher drew the short term of three years, and by the law's provision thus became the chief justice. He proved himself the peer of the most able members who have ever sat in the court of last resort, his decisions being marked by a masterful grasp of the most intricate problems presented for solution. In large measure he left the impress of his individuality and ability upon the history of the state, especially in connection with the framing and execution of the laws.

With his retirement from office he resumed the practice of law in Pueblo, becoming senior partner in the firm of Thatcher & Gast. That relation was maintained to the time of his death, which occurred in San Francisco, California, whither he had gone for the benefit of his health. Save for the three years when he was chief justice, he was in active practice in his adopted state from the time of his location there until his death, on March 20, 1884.

From a three volume History of Colorado, by *Wilbur Fiske Stone, himself an attorney of Pueblo and one of its first settlers, and who only recently passed away, we gain a pen picture of the life and characters of Chief Justice Thatcher. Speaking of him, Chief Justice Beck, of the Colorado Supreme Court,

*Judge Stone is credited with being a versatile writer, perfectly reliable, and better posted on men and affairs in Colorado than any other.

said, among other things: "* * * His was a busy life, and he accomplished much in the period allotted to him here. Endowed by nature with a comprehensive mind, which had been well cultured and disciplined by his mental exercise, gifted with a good judgment and a strong practical sense, he had risen to a leading position at the bar, and the force of his character and attainments has left an impress upon the fundamental law and upon the jurisprudence of the state. He gave valuable assistance in framing the one and in shaping the other, as the records of the constitutional convention and the opinions of the Supreme Court bear conclusive testimony. * * *" Judge Elbert thus portrayed him in part: "It was my good fortune to know Judge Thatcher intimately and well. For three years we came and went together in the discharge of our judicial duties. Purity in public life and purity in political methods found in him a zealous advocate. He was a most excellent judge. * * * His investigations were most thorough, and no fact connected with the case he was considering escaped his attention. Judge Thatcher never wrote a slovenly opinion. He knew distinctly and clearly the conclusions he had reached and the process of reasoning by which he had reached them, and his statement and his argument was always clear, accurate and logical. His mind was analytical and he treated the intricate mazes of a difficult legal question with a steady step and clear eye that made him a valuable member of any court. Above all he was pure and incorruptible, presenting a judicial character the purity of which was as the snow, and the integrity of which was as the granite. * * * Of the value of such a life there is no measure. * * * "

At a memorial meeting held by the members of the bar Judge T. T. Player, said in part: "* * * His epitaph might fairly be written in the one word 'excellent.' He was an excellent lawyer, an excellent citizen, and, above all, an excellent man. Judge Thatcher was essentially a modest and somewhat reserved man, and it is more true of him than of anyone else whom I ever knew, that his good qualities grew upon you day by day. * * * " Attorney E. J. Maxwell's tribute in part: " * * * It was not because of his greatness as a lawyer, not by reason of his having been chief justice of the State, not because of personal popularity, it was the grandeur of his character alone which had impressed itself on this community—character alone, which, notwithstanding the slurs of the cynical and the skeptic, the world admires and venerates for itself alone." Of him Mr. Richmond, another member of the bar, said: " * * * He was recognized from the first as an able lawyer and an upright man, and among his professional brethren as one thoroughly conversant with the ethics of his profession. It always seemed to me that he recognized the fact that no man could be truly a great lawyer who was not in every sense of the word a good man. He did not seek to shine with meteoric splendor, but hoped to achieve renown in the profession by studious habits and sterling integrity, believing that integrity and honor, with assiduity, would bring him fame in his profession and financial independence. He would not swerve from truth or fairness in any particular, and from the first to the day of his death he was able to stand the severest scrutiny of the public."

It was altogether natural that, when Henry Calvin Thatcher had completed his law course at the Albany Law School and located at Pueblo, he should become the attorney and counselor of his brothers in their growing and diversified interests, and so continue until his death eighteen years later. In this new relation the utmost harmony prevailed, each treating the other with the highest courtesy, consideration and kindness in all their business relations, thus adding strength and stability to their business growth.

In 1869 Judge Thatcher was married, his first wife being Miss Ella Snyder. One son, William Nevin, was born to them, December 3, 1870, but died in Chester, England, June 14, 1891, and there rest his remains. He had graduated and gone abroad with a party of college friends, when attacked with appendicitis. Two daughters passed away in infancy, and the mother in 1878. In 1879 Mr. Thatcher was again married, the bride being Sallie B. Ashcom, of Everett, Pennsylvania. Their only child, Coolidge, died in infancy.

*The Noted Thatcher Family.

Various Perry County families, notably the Blaine, Bigler, and Stephens' families, have had more than one noted descendant, but the Thatcher family not only had one, but three brothers of the same family who attained a preëminent place in their adopted State, as well as in that great section lying west of the Mississippi. Surely to the parents should go much of the credit for the foundation upon which these men builded. Their father, Henry Thatcher, was born in New Jersey, June 19, 1807, his father having come from the New England States, of Revolutionary stock.

---

*Mr. Wm. T. Albert, a cousin of the noted brothers, and less than six months the junior of the celebrated chief justice, has been associated with the Thatcher interests many years and has known them all his life. He and one other performed all the bank duties for several years. The force now comprises thirty-five men. Now in his eightieth year he is still daily at his post in the First National Bank of Pueblo. He was also personally acquainted with Judge Wilbur Fiske Stone, author of a History of Colorado, in three volumes, from whom we quote, and as late as August, 1920, shortly before the death of Judge Stone, had an interview of several hours at his office in Denver. Mr. Albert has kindly read the sketches of these noted brothers which appear in this book, and pronounces them to be correct. That of Chief Justice Thatcher appears with the sketches of the other chief justices, Gibson and Gantt, immediately preceding this page.

When a young man he came to Perry County, where he was a blacksmith upon the Pennsylvania Canal. He attended school and later became a teacher during his younger manhood. On the maternal side they are descended from William Albert, whose birthplace was in Switzerland and who came to America and settled in Northamptontown (now Allentown) during the period between 1720 and 1735. He had three sons, two of whom, Abraham and William, were Revolutionery soldiers. John Albert, the only son of Abraham, located in Adams County and married Charlotte Catharine Hykes, a daughter of George Hykes (of Swiss descent), locating later in Perry, where was born Lydia Ann, the mother of these noted boys. She was the eleventh child of a family of thirteen children, eight daughters and five sons, and was born March 8, 1814.

Before locating in Perry county John Albert had resided in Adams County until soon after 1800. He then located upon a farm near Alinda, where he not only carried on farming, but during the winters manufactured "grandfather's clocks," having learned clock-making in Allentown. He was a justice of the peace and a highly respected citizen. Throughout Perry, Cumberland and Adams Counties, especially in some of the older homes, are to be found these highly prized grandfathers' clocks. During recent years, when offered for sale, they have often brought fancy prices. That many of them were made in Perry County may be news to many, but is a fact. John Albert was an expert clock-maker in his day, and his clocks indicated seconds, minutes, hours, date of the month and phase of the moon. His death occurred in 1834, the result of accidently inhaling poison fumes from molten brass, while about to cast wheels for clocks. He was aged 61 years and left a wife, four sons and eight daughters.

When Henry Thatcher taught school in Tyrone township three terms were at the school near the Benjamin Smith farm near Alinda. He boarded at Smith's and there he first met Lydia Ann Albert, his future wife, she being a sister of Mrs. Smith, first born of John Albert. On September 24, 1835, she was joined in wedlock to Henry Thatcher, the young school teacher. They immediately went to New Buffalo, then a thriving shipping point on the new Pennsylvania Canal, and entered the mercantile business. They were successful from the beginning and continued business there until 1847, when the rapid strides of the town of Newport caused them to change locations. The change also brought them closer to their people, who largely traded at Newport. In 1857 they again changed locations, moving to Martinsburg, Blair County, Pennsylvania. They were the parents of six children, John Albert, Elvina (died at the age of fifteen), Mahlon D., Henry Calvin, Sarah Catharine (Mrs. Frank G. Bloom, living at Trinidad, Colorado), and Mary Caroline (Mrs. Marshall H. Everhart, living at Martinsburg, Pennsylvania).

Mr. Thatcher was a good business man, and the aged people of Perry County still speak of Thatcher's store at Newport. That he had ability in selecting his help is verified by the fact that one of his early clerks was Rev. T. P. Bucher, who became the second county superintendent of schools of Perry County, largely through the good reputation he had attained as Mr. Thatcher's clerk. (See "The County Superintendency.") The parents of this noted family were very strict with their children along moral and religious lines and they were baptized in the faith of the German Reformed Church. Their mother and her sisters, in fact, the whole family, are traditionally noted for their kindness, even temperament and motherly ideals.

The plains, when the Thatcher sons first located in Colorado, were dangerous. Frank G. Bloom, vice-president of the First National Bank of Trinidad, Colorado, and associated with and in charge of the Thatcher cattle and land interests in southern Colorado and northern New Mexico, was employed by Henry Thatcher at his store in Martinsburg in 1861. For almost a year prior to 1865 he was in correspondence with M. D. Thatcher about locating in Colorado in the fall of that year. The Indians were then on the warpath, and during that fall they burned every stage station, save three, for a distance of 450 miles along the Platte River. Their mode of attack was to fire the haystacks connected with the stations, and when the stage employees would rush out they would be shot. Mr. Bloom left the following spring and saw lying by the trail the oxteams, with their yokes yet upon their frames, but the wooden parts of the wagons all burned. Flour was emptied over the prairies so that the redskins could take the sacks for shirts. On his way west his outfit was held up at Fort Kearney, Nebraska, until fifty wagons came up. There they elected a captain who had charge of the train until the arrival at Denver. The outfit was loaded with green apples, the wagons first being faced with chaff and burlap, and the apples packed in bran. At Denver the apples sold for twenty-eight cents per pound. Mr. Bloom landed in Denver April 15, 1866. During the following October he was sent by the Thatcher Brothers to Four-Mile Creek, near Canon City, to start a store. He was there ten months and sold $20,000 worth of goods without any help. In 1867 he located at Trinidad, and in 1869 returned to Pennsylvania and was united in marriage to Miss Sarah Catharine, a daughter of Henry Thatcher, the Martinsburg merchant. On their arrival at Kansas City the trains only ran by daylight on account of the danger of Indian attacks. There were then no sleepers. On the train with Mr. Bloom and his bride, were General Custer and his wife. A curtain of blankets was rigged up and stretched across the car at nights, the ladies occupying the one apartment and the men the other, as they remained in the cars from Sheridan, Kansas, to Pueblo and Trinidad. In that same year Mr. Bloom became associated with the Thatchers in a business way.

Throughout all their dealings the Thatcher Brothers were never interested in shady dealings nor in grafting. It is said of them that during their long business career they never foreclosed a mortgage. What was the basis for the marvelous success attained by these three brothers, in their several spheres of activity and influence? An illustration may help answer. When John A. Thatcher, after crossing the plains, arrived in Denver, in 1862, and failed to secure immediate employment, he became uneasy and restless. When his new-found friend from Pennsylvania suggested that he remain at the store, that his partner would be down from the tannery, about thirty miles away, and might be able to give him work for awhile, at the tannery, he replied, "You bet your life I will not go away." He there showed his desire not to be idle, and his willingness to do anything honorable his hands found to do. The habits of his youth, formed in his father's store in Perry County, thus seemed the bulwark of his life at that critical time.

When M. D. Thatcher, after leaving Perry County, resided with his parents at Martinsburg, he was in full communion with his church and took an active part in Sunday school work, being librarian and treasurer of the latter. He systematized the methods and being a fine penman kept everything connected with the library in perfect order, carefully, neatly and accurately, up to the time of his going West. He showed that nothing was too small to do and that what was worth doing was worth doing well. His companions remember that when a school boy he would promptly and voluntarily return from school to his father's store and clear the counter of the miscellaneous mixture of dry goods usually found at the close of a busy day with customers. He there laid the foundation for his future career, doing all business throughout his busy life with the same careful accuracy and dispatch as was the habit of his youth.

When the last of these two brothers, associated so closely all their lives, had passed away, Alva Adams, their friend and former governor of Colorado, wrote thus to his friend, C. S. Morey:

"Although two and one-half years lay between the deaths of John A. Thatcher and Mahlon D. Thatcher, our tribute of appreciation and regret cannot be paid the one without including the other. The varied talents of the two men supplemented each other. Their business career was an example of the power of personal and financial confidence and harmony. Neither selfishness, envy, nor ambition ever broke the current of a common kinship. David and Jonathan were not finer friends than these two brothers. They were the joint architects of a great career. They built up a business fabric of surpassing splendor and influence. Under the guidance of their strong hand and brain, the firm, 'Thatcher Brothers' became a citadel of commercial and financial stability—it is one of the institutions of the nation. Thatcher—integrity, stability, have been synonymous terms in our business world. This reputation should be prized as a richer her-- itage than their estate of gold. 'Empire Builder' is one of the stock phrases in Western obituary and history—John A. Thatcher and M. D. Thatcher were state and empire builders in the truest sense. For half a century, Thatcher Brothers have been without a rival in business leadership and success. This distinction came from faith in Colorado and Pueblo coupled with a financial genius of a high order.

"As young men, the Thatcher Brothers had a splendid dream of the ultimate destiny of this new land, and they lived to see that dream come true. They had vision—courage and confidence. Chance had little part in their success—hard work, good sense and probity were their masters of achievement. They never read the ribbon of a stock ticker. Scheming and speculation were not in their business methods. They followed only legitimate channels of finance. They dealt in millions and every dollar was clean. For fifty years, these men walked the streets of Pueblo—their conduct and business open to every citizen—no stain ever touched their name or their business character. In their banking career, thousands became their debtor; not one of the thousands can say that he was ever oppressed by Thatcher Brothers. They never turned from misfortunes of the worthy. To aid honest men, they often went beyond the limitations of legitimate banking. Not a few business men owe their solvency to the liberality and tolerance of this ideal banking firm. Though absorbed with great interests, they were not exclusive. To all the door of their office as well as the door of their home was open. To gossip and harshness they were strangers. They were careful of themselves as they were of their business. No criticism— no bitterness ever fell from their lips. With all their power, they were modest and unassuming. In their home life, they were gentle, kindly and considerate.

"In the marts of commerce, their word was a bond from New York to the Pacific Coast. Their fortune was not hoarded, but has been invested in scores of great enterprises which have developed the West and helped to make Colorado a happy and prosperous home for a million people.

"All in all, Thatcher Brothers were ideal bankers—ideal husbands and fathers, and valued citizens.

"Not in the history of the Commerce Club has it been called upon to mourn the death of two members who have been so potential in the affairs of Pueblo and Colorado."

JOHN A. THATCHER, PIONEER, MERCHANT, AND BANKER.

The oldest member of the famous Thatcher family, John A. Thatcher, was born in New Buffalo, Perry County, Pennsylvania, on August 25, 1836, the son of Henry and Lydia Ann (Albert) Thatcher. The other children were Elvina, Mahlon D., Mrs. Frank G. Bloom, now of Trinidad, Colorado; Mrs. M. H. Everhart, now of Martinsburg, Blair County, Pennsylvania; Henry Calvin, who was the first chief justice of Colorado, and Dora. John A. attended school in New Buffalo until 1847, when his father, who was a merchant, moved to Newport, on the Pennsylvania Railroad, as a better business location and, later, April 1, 1855, moved to

County, and in 1857, went to Holt County, Missouri, where he
clerked for five years, becoming more familiar with the details of
mercantile life.

Oregon, the county seat of Holt County, and Forest City, on the
Missouri River, were flourishing places, during the opening up
and settlement of Kansas, and did a big business. The outbreaking of the Sectional War brought troublesome times, on the border, and Holt County became subject to raids from organized
bands of thieves and desperadoes who infested the Missouri River
territory. In 1862 conditions became so bad that Mr. Thatcher
decided to make a change, and follow the advice of some friends
who had preceded him. He and another acquaintance bought a
team, and loading the wagon with merchandise, set out across the
plains for Colorado. Starting from Nebraska City, Nebraska,
they arrived at Denver, September 15, 1862, where he remained
until December. At this time, James H. Voorhees, who had a
partner with him in business in Denver, proposed to John A.
Thatcher, that he would furnish a load of goods, share the profits
with him, if he would take them to Pueblo and open a store there.
As he was anxious to be at work the proposal was accepted.

They loaded a wagon with an assortment of goods, reaching
Pueblo (120 miles distant) in eight days. The driver, a Frenchman, was kept on the road to and from Denver all winter. In the
spring, Mr. Voorhees wrote John A. Thatcher to bring back to
Denver the remainder of goods on hand. At this point, the Denver partnership was dissolved; and later, Mr. Voorhees asked Mr.
Thatcher to join him in business in Denver. After considering
the matter a short time, he decided to join him, with the understanding that he could withdraw at any time, by taking his share
of goods. In a month or two he withdrew, taking his share of
goods which he took with an ox team to Pueblo, August 14, 1863.
About this time he received savings which he had loaned (when
clerking in Missouri) to an uncle named Snyder, who lived across
the river, in Doniphan County, Kansas. This was the beginning
of his own business, and the establishing of the first general store
at Pueblo, located at Second Street and Santa Fe Avenue. His
first counter consisted of two barrels with several boards or planks
laid from one to the other. Later, the store was moved farther
north on the corner of Fourth Street and Santa Fe Avenue, into a
two-story adobe building. During the spring and summer of 1864
he kept writing to his brother, Mahlon D., who had joined his
father in business, on Jan. 1, 1864, for a period of five years, to
come West. By September of that year, Mahlon D. Thatcher
decided to withdraw from his father's business and terminate the
partnership, in Martinsburg, December 31st. The father released
the son, and receiving $2,900 for his interest in the business,

other points in southern Colorado. They were also incorporators of the Grand Opera House Block, in Pueblo, Colorado, and owned great herds of cattle and vast acreages in southern Colorado and northern New Mexico.

John A. Thatcher did not care for politics, belonged to no clubs or lodges, and yet was a most companionable man. He was a member of the Pioneers Association of Southern Colorado, of the Sons of Colorado, and of the Pennsylvania Society of Colorado, having been honorary president of the latter at the time of his death. He gave liberally to all projects. He was shrewd, able, frugal, and thrifty, the corner stone upon which the Thatcher millions have been built. He was a home and family man, and built a home named "Rosemount," which, with the grounds occupies a city block, and is one of the most beautiful residences in the city. To the author's personal knowledge, John A. Thatcher was generous with friends of his youth, who had not been as successful as he, and funds from his hands reached places where they were badly needed.

Following a trip to Nevada and California, in June, 1913, he was taken ill, and on August 14th, exactly fifty years after the date of his arrival in Pueblo, passed away. Had he lived a few months longer, he would have seen the completion and occupancy of the new bank building, which is one of the finest in the state.

"The Thatcher Family," on the preceding pages, contains much in reference to John A. Thatcher.

MAHLON D. THATCHER, FINANCIER AND BANKER.

That there should be bred in Perry County, men who have amassed millions, may seem strange to some, especially those who oft use derisive terms in speaking of the county, but, nevertheless, it is true; and, when Mahlon D. Thatcher, leading financier of the State of Colorado, closed his eyes at his home in Pueblo, Colorado, on Washington's birthday, in 1916, there passed from the nation one of the most remarkable financiers of all time, having attained wealth reaching into millions. He was a power in the financial world, not only in his state, but of the nation. A younger brother, Henry Calvin Thatcher, became the first chief justice of the State of Colorado, and, in the State Capitol at Denver, stands a bust of this noted jurist.

Of Mahlon D. Thatcher, Hall's "History of Colorado" has this to say:

"His influence among the capitalized forces and productive interests of the commonwealth is coextensive with the great financial triumphs he has achieved. Intimate personal acquaintance with these brothers ripens into deep admiration of the qualities that have produced the results we have briefly enumerated. They have had no part in politics, except to exercise the duties of good citizenship; have not aspired to, nor held office. Busi-

then joined his father in the store, and later was admitted into the firm.

In 1865, Mahlon D. Thatcher went to Pueblo and joined his brother, John A., in the mercantile business, conducting it under the name of "Thatcher Brothers, Merchants." Their store, then on the east side of Santa Fe Avenue, at Fourth, was successful from the start, and soon became the headquarters for the cattlemen and mining men who stopped there, as they dealt in everything. The Thatcher Brothers' safe became their bank, being freely used, and it is told that often many thousands of dollars were left with them following a deal in cattle or a prospector's success. This accommodation on their part became so extensive that they saw the advisability of starting a bank, as "Thatcher Brothers, Bankers."

In 1871, John A. and Mahlon D. Thatcher moved the banking business into a new brick building built for that purpose, opening with a capital of $50,000.00. Mahlon D. Thatcher, the younger of the brothers, later, the same year, went to Washington, D. C., and obtained the charter for the First National Bank of Pueblo, with a capital of $50,000.00. From that time he became the controlling force of that institution. Such was their entry into the banking world. When Mahlon D. Thatcher died, in 1916, he was president of the First National Bank of Pueblo, and chairman of the board of directors of the First National Bank of Denver, president of the International Trust Company of Denver; of the First National Bank of Trinidad, Colorado, and of the Minnequa Bank of Pueblo. He was vice-president of the Pueblo Savings Bank, of the Central California Electric Corporation, and of the Standard Fire Brick Company. He was treasurer of the Great Western Sugar Company, a director in the American Smelting and Refining Company, the Cement Securities Company, and the Nevada-California Electric Corporation. He also, held large interests in the First National Bank of Florence; the First National Bank of Silverton; the Bent County Bank of Las Ammas; the American National Bank of Alamosa; the Miners' and Merchants' Bank of Ouray, and the Montrose National Bank. He was secretary-treasurer of the Pueblo Union Depot and Railway Company, and one of its organizers. He was actively interested in thirty-seven banks at the time of his death. His fortune has been variously estimated at from five to ten millions of dollars.

It is said that all the concerns in which Mr. Thatcher was interested were clean and above-board, and that the men under whose charge they forged to the front were carefully selected by him. His rise in the financial world was never spectacular, but of a steady growth, year by year. From the time of his locating in Pueblo, until his death, he never had a rival for the enviable position which he held in the financial world, so highly was he esteemed in the community. It was largely through the influence of Mr. Thatcher, supported by Pueblo people, that the Atchison, Topeka, and Santa Fe Railway Company built its lines into Pueblo. He, also, influenced the building of the first smelting plant in Pueblo, called the "Pueblo Smelter," and the Boston syndicate of stockholders asked his counsel and he became treasurer for them. When illness foretold his passing, his son, M. D. Thatcher, trained in the methods of his father, stepped into his place in the various organizations in which he was interested, performing his duties so like the father that they moved along in their characteristic manner.

Mahlon D. Thatcher was united in marriage, August 1, 1876, to Miss Luna A. Jordan, who survives him, residing in Pueblo. A son and three daughters also survive him. The son, Mahlon D., Jr., is spoken of above; the daughters are Mrs. Robert C. Wheeler, and Mrs. William Waller, Jr., both of Chicago, and Mrs. Robert L. Huntzinger, of New York; there are also still living two sisters, Mrs. M. C. Everhart, of Martinsburg, Pennsylvania, and Mrs. F. J. Bloom, of Trinidad, Colorado.

Mr. Thatcher had many charities to which he was deeply attached, and, when he died, both rich and poor in Pueblo felt that a very dear and helpful one had gone. During his life, Mahlon D. Thatcher had the reputation of being able to raise more money for any legitimate enterprise than any man between Chicago and San Francisco. The Thatchers did business, and the younger generation still do, with clients in every state in the Union. Throughout all their dealings the Thatcher Brothers were never interested in shady dealings nor in grafting. It is said of them that, during their long business career, they never foreclosed a mortgage. As times of great crises come in the lives of every individual, so they came also to these men of sterling worth and integrity, at various times and under trying conditions, during the fifty years of their activity in Pueblo. Two of these may be mentioned in this connection which stand out more prominently than all the others; the first occurring in the winter of 1878-79. Beautiful and mild weather prevailed during the fall months of 1878, until December; soon after the first of that month, a gentle rain set in; the atmosphere soon grew colder, the rain turning to snow, which continued falling, without cessation, for about three days and nights, until from three to four feet of snow covered the eastern slopes and plains of the whole of the Rocky Mountain region, New Mexico, on the south, Wyoming on the north, as well as the whole of Colorado. After the snow ceased falling, it grew intensely cold, the sun shining brightly, but perfectly clear. There occurred but one slight thaw for a day or so; the weather remaining cold until after the middle of February, 1879, entailing exceedingly heavy losses to all cattle and sheep men in the Western country; in fact, most men engaged in the stock business at that time lost about all they had. The winter referred to was especially severe all over the United States.

The second disaster which proved to be nation-wide was the financial panic of 1893, which brought very disturbed conditions throughout the whole United States, but especially severe in the middle and Western states. Many banks failed and never opened again. These conditions followed the demonitization of silver by the Congress of the United States. Colorado having previously attained the distinction of being one of the best producing precious metal mining states in the Union, received the worst blow it has had in its existence as a state, and to this date, has never recovered its former prestige in this respect, but has fallen very far below its previous activity and production. On July 5, 1893, most people became excited about the safety of the banks, and "runs" were made simultaneously on all the banks, eight in the city. Three or four were closed by noon on that day. The morning of the 6th, the "runs" continued on the banks which were brave enough to open, the Pueblo National, Pueblo Savings Bank, and the Western National, with the aid of the First National, until about noon, when it suddenly subsided and business resumed its wonted aspect. These two critical periods in the career of the Thatcher Brothers, only proved, beyond a doubt, the solidity of their financial building and made no difference in their attitude to associates and fellow citizens; they outwardly manifesting the same equanimity of temperament as characterized their success in other years; never a word of complaint or rehearsal of losses, and it is doubtful if any one outside themselves ever knew what they were.

Once Mr. Thatcher was urged to accept the mayoralty of the city, being elected, but he resigned before one year of his term expired. To-day, with M. D. Thatcher, Jr., as president; Mr. A. S. Booth, as vice-president, and Raymond C. Thatcher, as chairman of the board of directors, the First National Bank of Pueblo, organized by the fathers, half a century ago, is moving along with the undiminished confidence enjoyed by the elder Thatchers.

George J. Dunbaugh, a prominent Chicago manufacturer, among other things, writes of him:

"Have known M. D. Thatcher since 1870. Every one knew him as a man of sterling worth. His probity in every way was unquestioned. If he had confidence in a man he would go very much further than any capitalist I have ever known in furnishing him with financial backing. He was never autocratic in any way. He was most democratic in his manners, the door of his office being open to all, and he would see every one. He was always pleasant and genial and the most pleasant man I ever knew. He was a man of clear thought and a remarkably good judge of human nature. He recognized the frailties of man and made allowance for them. He once told me that he feared gambling more than any other vice; he said a drinking man cannot long conceal his failing, but a gambler may lose everything in a single night, and he could not have any confidence in a man who gambled.

"Mr. Thatcher was essentially a home loving man. He had a most beautiful home, and his family and his home meant more to him than anything in the world. No one who has met him in his home life could fail to realize this, and it was in his home that one appreciated his splendid character and his high ideals.

"He was a great power in the financial world, being known throughout the United States as one of the great financiers. He was always consulted in matters of finance, especially in the great West, where nothing of moment was ever done without consulting him. During the World War, when it was thought that the United States might become embroiled, he was one of the great financiers of our land who were assembled to plan the financial end."

The statement that he was one of the great financiers called on to plan the finances in case America became involved in the war is correct and is a matter of government record.

When well established in business and the opportune time had come, M. D. Thatcher, about 1880, built his first permanent home in Pueblo, on the crest of the ridge jutting down from the north toward the center of the city; this ridge (evidently the west limit of the Fountain Valley), overlooking the latter from Greenwood Street, also sloping southward and from Sixteenth Street overlooking the beautiful Arkansas Valley and River. The block of ground and home are called "Hill Crest," and it is still one of the most substantial and beautiful homes in the state, surrounded with grounds which are artistically laid out, with walks and driveways, planted with rare trees, plants and flowers from other climes. This home is still occupied by Mrs. Thatcher, to whom, also, was left an equally beautiful summer home at Harbor Point, on Lake Michigan, where she spends the summer months, as she and her husband formerly did. Mrs. Thatcher, by the way, is not idle, but much interested in welfare and charitable work, according to official reports along those lines. During the past year she was engaged in helping raise the funds to purchase a $40,000 home for the Young Women's Christian Association.

Through Paul Appenzellar, a noted New York banker who was born in one of Perry's neighboring counties, we have been able to secure some personal impressions of M. D. Thatcher. From his letter the following is taken:

"In Measure for Measure" the Duke, in bestowing some special honor on one of his deputies, addresses him thus:

> "There is a kind of character in thy life,
> That to the observer doth thy history
> Fully unfold."

To me, who knew Mahlon D. Thatcher only during the last twelve years of his life, there is a peculiar fitness in the application of this quotation. His unruffled, dispassionate temperament; his deep instinct for order, simplicity, accuracy; his passion for fairness and honesty told well the story of his life.

My association with Mr. Thatcher began through the business relationship of broker and customer. He came to my office to pay for some bonds which had been purchased for his account by one of the banks in New York where his account was handled. The business finished, he asked me if I was not from Pennsylvania, suspecting this from my inflection, and his reserve disappeared when he learned that my old home and birthplace was in a county adjoining the Perry County of which later he was to tell me so many stories. From the beginning our friendship grew until we formed the habit of spending a week-end together on each of his visits. Except for visits in the winter months we (my wife, Mr. Thatcher and I) would spend the Saturday-Sunday period in visits by automobile to some of the near-by resorts. The mention of these trips serves to recall one of his peculiarities—his unwillingness to accept any favor, or to permit himself to be placed in a position where he might feel under some obligation. He would go on none of these trips as my guest. He would go only if I agreed that we should share the expenses. This was final, and not open for argument. I asked him one day how he should feel if I should come to Pueblo and insist on sharing the expenses of the week-end trip which I well knew he would immediately plan for my pleasure. This was indeed a searching question, but his only reply was a smiling, "Let me do as I like to do in this matter even though you say it's absurd."

"Not apt for speech, nor quickly stirred
    Unless when heart to heart replied;
A bearing equally remov'd
    From vain display or sullen pride."

Mr. Thatcher's taciturnity undoubtedly led many who knew him casually to consider him as cold. He loved a fact but cared little for an opinion. He asked few questions when considering a proposition placed before him for his consideration as an investment.

If any attempt was made to hasten his decision, the answer was an immediate "No," and the subject was not reopened. His business judgment was so highly regarded in my own office that I used often to tell him that I had a proposition I wished to "try on the dog," meaning that I and my partners wished to see if on the data as presented to him by me, his approval of the venture could be won. If it was or was not, our own opinion was influenced decidedly for or against the proposition.

His pride in the remarkable record of the First National Bank of Pueblo, was certainly the only "vanity" I ever knew him to display. Its daily statement came to him when on his Eastern trips, and he would often hand me one of these reports. My almost invariable comment would be, "You have too much cash, why don't you buy a million more commercial paper?" The facts were that he did carry a far larger percentage of his deposits in cash and in reserve banks than any other bank in the whole United States, as far as I could determine. I doubt if he would have followed, or approved, such a policy in any other of the many banks in which he had a substantial stock interest; but the First National Bank of Pueblo wasn't to be judged as other banks—it had traditions which to him were sacred, and there were no minority stockholders pushing a management for larger earnings and larger dividends.

His visits to New York City usually were made at the time of the quarterly meetings of the board of directors of the American Smelting &

Refining Co., of which board he was a member. On these visits he would invest large sums in bonds and commercial paper for the account of the various banks in which he was interested and likewise for his personal account.

Those to whom M. D. Thatcher gave his friendship were, at least in the East, a highly favored few. With them he was a cordial companion, and to them his unexpected death brought a realization of a great loss.

GENERAL FREDERICK WATTS.

About 1760 Frederick Watts came to America with his family and settled upon a tract of 331 acres, now in Wheatfield Township, Perry County, which he warranted June 4, 1762. He was a Welshman, and was born June 1, 1719, and about 1749 took in wedlock Jane Murray, a niece of David Murray, who was Marquis of Tullibardine, a partisan of Charles Edward, the pretender, who after the Battle of Culloden fled to France.

The oncoming Revolution in America found him a patriot of the most advanced type, and as the Perry County territory was then a part of Cumberland, he was chosen as one of the eight men sent to Philadelphia, in June, 1776, to a convention, which was the first of a series of conferences which resulted in the Declaration of Independence. He was interested in the organization of the county's battalion and was made lieutenant colonel of the First Battalion, representing the same at the military convention held July 4, 1776, at Lancaster.

At the surrender of Fort Washington, November 16, 1776, he was in command of the "Flying Camp" of the First Battalion, and was captured, but soon after exchanged. April 1, 1778, he was commissioned as a justice of the peace of Cumberland County. In 1779 he was chosen as one of its representatives in the General Assembly. Following this he was appointed a sublieutenant of Cumberland County, April 18, 1780; brigadier general of Pennsylvania Militia, May 27, 1782; served as a member of the Supreme Executive Council of the Colony from October 20, 1787, until its abolition by the Constitution of 1790, which was the real governing body of the colonies during that trying period, being at the same time a member of the Board of Property.

Seven children blessed the Watts family, and on account of some of them becoming connected with the county's life and attaining more or less prominence, even in later generations, they are here mentioned. They were Margery, Catharine, Margaret, Elizabeth, Mary, Sarah, and David. Of these Elizabeth married Thomas Hulings, a son of Marcus Hulings, the pioneer, and became the mother of David W. Hulings, for a long time a prominent attorney of Lewistown, Pennsylvania, and Rebecca Hulings Duncan, whose husband was Robt. C. Duncan, a son of Supreme Court Justice Thomas Duncan. Mrs. Duncan was the grandmother of

P. F. Duncan, cashier of the Duncannon National Bank. Margaret was wed to George Smiley, of Shermansdale, thus bringing together the strains of two famous families. David Watts, the youngest and the only boy, studied law at Carlisle, married Juliana, a daughter of General Robert Miller, and became one of the leading attorneys of the state. He was interested in the early furnace industry of Perry County with William Power. His son, Judge Frederick Watts, of Carlisle. was of the third generation to attain prominence.

GENERAL GEORGE GIBSON.

George Gibson, who, by the way, was a brother of Chief Justice John Bannister Gibson, whose biography appears in the preceding pages, was born in Spring Township, at Westover, the name given the tract of land where the Gibson mill stands, when it was warranted, after the ancestral home in England. In his early life he traveled over a large part of the world, and when the War of 1812 broke out he was appointed a lieutenant and served throughout the war against the country from whence his ancestry had migrated. He was also an officer in the field during the Seminole War in Florida, serving with Andrew Jackson, who was his personal friend thereafter. Andrew Jackson, during his Presidential term, appointed him as Commissary General of the United States Army, his commission being dated April 18, 1818, and he served with credit and distinction. His remains lie buried in the Congressional Cemetery at Washington, D. C., where he died September 21, 1861, while still serving in the capacity of Commissary General. His rank at that time was Brevet Major General of the U. S. A.

COLONEL ALEXANDER K. McCLURE.

Perry County, in its first decade, was the birthplace of a lad who became one of the greatest editors in the United States, being classed with men of the caliber of Charles A. Dana and Henry Watterson. With Medill, McCullogh and McLean he was of the group of Celt-American editors. Alexander Kelly McClure was born in Madison Township on January 9, 1828. He was the son Alexander and Isabella (Anderson) McClure, and was born on the farm warranted by James Wilson, whose wife was killed there by the Indians in 1756, while passing from their home to Fort Robinson, for protection. Its location is but a small distance from the old Indian trail to the West, and close to Centre Church. Here, amid these historic surroundings, he spent his boyhood in the manner of the period, helping with the farm labor and attending a few months of school in the winters. It is recorded that he and his brother attended alternate weeks, one being needed at home.

During 1843, when fifteen years of age, he was apprenticed to James Marshall, then a New Bloomfield tanner, to learn the trade,

Hardly had he finished his trade when the Whigs of Juniata County were interested in having a paper started for them at Mifflintown. Reluctantly, upon the advice of Judge Baker, he bought a hand press and some type with a loan of about five hundred dollars which he secured from his father, and in the fall of 1846 started the *Sentinel* in that town, a paper which exists to this day. He was then only eighteen years of age. He mastered the mechanical end, and before a year had gone by he did all the work on the paper, with the help of a single apprentice. Young McClure had inherited a liking for politics, especially from his mother's family, and it had been nurtured in the atmosphere surrounding Judge Baker and the *Perry Freeman* office. Before he was of age he was a congressional conferee as a supporter of Andrew G. Curtin, who later became the great war governor of Pennsylvania. Curtin was defeated, but the friendship between him and McClure lasted through all the changes of politics in state and nation. Simon Cameron was a leader of a Democratic faction known as state improvement men, and about this time young McClure began fighting him.

During the campaign of 1848, when Governor William F. Johnson was the Whig nominee, McClure supported him editorially, the strength of his editorials attracting attention over the state. He also appeared on the stump, and when the new governor was inaugurated one of his first acts was to appoint McClure an aid on his staff, with the rank and title of Colonel. His commission was dated on the very day he became of voting age. Through Curtin, in 1850, he was appointed deputy United States Marshal of Juniata County, to take the census. As soon as he completed that task he sold the *Sentinel* for twelve hundred dollars, which, with the money he received as deputy marshal he invested in a half interest in the *Chambersburg Repository*. In 1853 the Whigs, then in a hopeless minority, nominated him for auditor general of Pennsylvania by acclamation, for which he was defeated. He was then but twenty-five years of age.

In 1855, at the formation of the Republican party, the *Chambersburg Repository* was the foremost paper in Pennsylvania to support it and to hammer the slavery traffic. McClure was one of the men who met at Pittsburgh to form the party in the state. He was opposed to the Know Nothing party of that day, and when the Whigs of Franklin County and the Know Nothings formed a coalition he sold his interest in the paper at once. In the meantime he had been reading law with William McClelland and was shortly admitted to the bar, becoming his preceptor's law partner. Governor Pollock appointed him superintendent of public printing, the first man to fill that position, being commissioned February 7, 1855. He resigned in a short time and was appointed superintendent of the Erie & Northeastern Railroad Company, and brought order out of chaos in the Erie riot trouble.

He was a delegate from Pennsylvania to the convention which gave birth to the Republican party, which nominated John C. Freemont for President in 1856. In 1857 he was nominated by the Franklin County Republicans for member of the General Assembly and elected by a large majority. In 1858 he was reëlected by a still greater majority. In 1859 he was nominated for the State Senate, and was elected after a hard-fought contest. In 1860, when the fate of the nation was in the balance, he was state chairman of the Republican party and saw Pennsylvania cast its vote for Abraham Lincoln. When the senate organized he was the most noted figure upon the floor, and when Fort Sumter was fired on by the Confederates he urged an immediate war policy and preparations for a long and bloody conflict. He was chairman of the Committee of Military Affairs, introduced war measures of great importance, and in consequence was closely associated with both Governor Curtin and President Lincoln. During the early part of the war and many times later the President saw Mr. McClure almost daily, so closely were they associated in the saving of the Union.

Upon the expiration of his term in the senate, in 1862, McClure was appointed assistant Adjutant General of the United States Army, and had charge of the draft in Pennsylvania, his appointment coming through unusual circumstances. Working night and day at Harrisburg McClure saw recruits to the number of a thousand a day come to Harrisburg, only to fret there in idleness against the "red tape" which held them instead of sending forth a regiment a day. The military commanders sent out only two companies each day, leaving the mass to be fed by army contractors. McClure wrote to President Lincoln, "You must send a mustering officer to Harrisburg who will do as I say: I cannot stay there longer under existing conditions." Lincoln sent for Adjutant General Thomas and asked the highest rank of military officer at Harrisburg. Thomas informed him "Captain, sir." The President retorted, "Bring me a commission for an assistant Adjutant General of the United States, with the rank of Major." And so the Perry County lad—now a man of affairs—was mustered in, and from then on a regiment a day of boys in blue left Harrisburg for the front and the preservation of the Union.

When the state's quota was filled he resigned and returned to his law offices at Chambersburg. His inclination was towards journalism, however, and in 1862 he purchased the *Chambersburg Repository*, in which he formerly owned a half interest, and returned to his favorite profession. In 1864 he was a delegate-at-large to the Republican State Convention, and at the following election was again elected to the General Assembly. When the Confederates invaded Chambersburg in July, 1864, all his property was destroyed. In 1868 he was not only a delegate, but at the head of the Pennsylvania delegation, to the Republican convention which nominated General U. S. Grant for the Presidency. He had campaigned in Connecticut, Rhode Island, Massachusetts, and Pennsylvania. After the election he decided to abandon politics and moved to Philadelphia to practice law.

In 1872 he aligned himself with the Greenback party and was state chairman of the Liberal Republican committee. He was again elected to the State Senate, this time from a Philadelphia district and on an Independent ticket. He was excluded from his seat by false returns, but contested the matter with his usual energy and success, obtaining his seat March 27th.

He was nominated for mayor of Philadelphia in 1874, but was defeated. He was chairman of the Pennsylvania delegation to the Cincinnati convention, which nominated Horace Greely for President.

In 1875, in conjunction with Frank McLaughlin, a noted printer and publisher, his brother John, and Philip Collins, a company was formed and began publishing the *Philadelphia Times,* at first an independent newspaper, but later Democratic in politics. McClure's interest was taken care of in the beginning by Governor Curtin, Charles A. Dana, Andrew H. Dill, and Colonel Scott. In 1892 the paper was burned out. It was in operation for twenty-six years, all of which time McClure was at its head, editorially, when it was sold to and combined with the *Public Ledger.* During that time it paid its owners in cash dividends their entire capital five times over, and the sale of the property was at an additional premium of $275 per share. In 1896 fellow newspaper workers arranged a banquet to celebrate Col. McClure's fiftieth anniversary in the newspaper business, and gathered about the festal board were the leaders of the nation.

Col. McClure was a man of fine physique and was over six feet tall. He was of Scotch-Irish ancestry, had a kindly face and always led a busy life, working hard in any capacity. He was a noted speaker and never lacked an audience. He was first married to Matilda S. Grey, February 10, 1852. They had one child, William Anderson McClure, who died in 1911. He was married a second time, and his widow, Mrs. Cora (Gratz) McClure, still lives at 1828 Spruce Street, Philadelphia. Colonel McClure died June 6, 1909.

No citizen of the republic has had as close an acquaintance with so many men who have filled the Presidency of the United States as had Col. McClure. He knew personally Presidents Fillmore, Pierce, Buchanan, Lincoln, Johnson, Grant, Hayes, Garfield, Ar-

west of the Mississippi, a monument to the dreams of his boyhood
in his Perry County home.

Luther Melancthon Bernheisel, at the time of his death was
president of the Bernheisel Construction Company of Chicago.
He was born on April 30, 1845, the son of Solomon and Hannah
(Dunkelberger) Bernheisel, at Green Park, Tyrone Township.
Either as an employee or as contractor Mr. Bernheisel was identified with many of the great steel structural installations throughout the country.   One of his earliest pieces of construction was
the supervision of the building of the Third Avenue elevated railway in New York City.   Another was the supervision of the construction of the bridge across the Hudson at Poughkeepsie, New
York.   Many of the steel "skyscrapers" in Chicago were erected
under his supervision, and many of the great steel railway bridges
that span the rivers of the Middle West were also erected under
his supervision, or through the Bernheisel Construction Company.
He was the organizer and became the president of the Bernheisel
Construction Company.

Mr. Bernheisel was a man of means, accumulated by his own
industry and ability.   He took a keen interest in social and civil
life, and for over a dozen years was identified with the Board of
Education of Evanston, Illinois.   He died May 22, 1920, leaving
the following children: Mrs. Fanny Bernheisel Quilling, of Meno-
monie, Wisconsin; Mrs. Helen Bernheisel Hier, of Denver, Colorado, and L. M. Bernheisel, of Chicago, Illinois.   He is also survived by Mrs. Bernheisel.

ELIHU C. IRVIN, NOTED PRESIDENT OF INSURANCE COMPANIES.

Of the Perry County teachers who have gone forth to larger
fields in the business world, Elihu C. Irvin, president of the Fire
Association of Philadelphia, ranks among the very first.   He was
born at Petersburg (now Duncannon), on May 22, 1839.   His
education was gotten at the local schools and at the New Bloomfield Academy, where he was prepared for college, graduating in
1859.   Just as he was about to enter college, business reverses of
his father necessitated his becoming a wage-earner, and he began
by teaching school, being teacher of the Duncannon High School
for several terms.   During the War between the States he had
charge of the Duncannon nail works.   In 1870 he removed to Harrisburg, where he represented the Germania Insurance Company
for five years, his territory being Pennsylvania and New Jersey.
In 1875 he became associated with the Phœnix of Hartford, locating in Philadelphia, with a territory from Lake Erie to the Gulf of
Mexico, remaining with them almost ten years.   In this work he
had become most proficient and was already recognized as an expert in fire insurance.

in 1921 he took over the Reliance Insurance Company and became its president, and is now president of the three companies. In addition to his duties as president of the Fire Association, Mr. Irvin is a director of the First National Bank, of the Chamber of Commerce, and of the Union League.

The Fire Association, of which he is president, occupies its own seven-story marble building, located at Fourth and Walnut Streets, in the very heart of the city. On the first floor of that building is a bronze tablet, placed there by the association, which is one of the finest tributes to Mr. Irvin's ability as an executive, and bears this inscription:

> This building
> Erected during the Presidency
> of
> Elihu C. Irvin
> is a tribute to
> His Ability and Untiring Devotion
> to the Interests of the
> Fire Association of Philadelphia.
> 1817   1912

Seated in his private office in 1919, when interviewed by the author of this book, Mr. Irvin said: "I have always wanted to return to Perry County—to Duncannon, where I was born, with its grand mountains and its charming river—to reside in retirement, but I am too busy," and he spoke the truth; for in that very year he had organized the Victory Insurance Company, asking for subscriptions to the amount of $1,000,000, and the stock had been oversubscribed by $700,000. Having taken over the Reliance Insurance Company, the plan is for the three associations to be run jointly. Mr. Irvin has gained his high position through vision and the motto, "Let well enough alone." His benefactions for young men and along religious lines have been manifold. He is of the Presbyterian faith. Through constant industry he has seen his company go from modest offices to more pretentious ones, and finally into the magnificent building now occupied by them, and its capital doubled. He is now (1922) over four score years of age, but retains the vigor of his fiftieth year.

"Marie Doro," Dramatic Star.

A Perry Countian by birth, but known throughout the nation, "Marie Doro" stands in the front rank of her profession as a dramatic star, both on the speaking and silent stage. She has appeared upon the stage not only in the leading cities of America but of the continent as well and had the great distinction of appearing "by royal command," the first American actress to be so honored. Her life story is one of succeeding successes, the climax to ambition and ability.

were then already known in the theatrical world two Mary Stewarts and one Marie Stewart, in order to avoid confusion in names, she adopted as her professional or stage name, Marie Doro, as being plain, short, easy to remember, and not likely to be confused with another.

She made her first appearance on the stage with Criterion Stock Company in St. Paul, Minnesota, June 9, 1901, as Katharine, in "Aristocracy," and with that company she assumed important rôles. In 1901-02, under the management of David Belasco, she appeared on tour in "Naughty Anthony." December 29, 1902, she appeared as Rosalba Peppercorn, in "The Billionaire," with Jerome Sykes, at Daly's theater, New York, and then on tour. In the summer of 1903 she appeared in "A Runaway Girl" and "The Circus Girl," with Duff Opera Company, in San Francisco. On November 2, 1903, she began her season at the Herald Square theater, New York, as Nancy Lowly, in "The Girl from Kay's," under management of the late Charles Frohman.

She entered dramatic work January 4, 1904, at the Empire theater, New York, appearing as Lady Millicent, in "Little Mary," and subsequently played as Lady Catharine Losenby, with William Gillette, in "The Admirable Crichton," on tour. On October 24, 1904, she began her engagement as Dora, in "Granny," with the late Mrs. G. H. Gilbert, and at the Savoy theater, New York, January 31, 1905, appeared in the title rôle of "Friquet."

Her first appearance on the London, England, stage, was at the Comedy theater, May 3, 1905, as Lucy Sheridan, in "The Dictator," with William Collier. She was seen next at the Duke of York's theater, London, September 13, 1905, in the title rôle of "Clarice," with William Gillette, and on October 17, 1905, she began playing the part of Alice Faulkner, in "Sherlock Holmes." On November 8, 1905, she played as Caroline Mitford, in "Secret Service." Returning to the United States, she reënacted the rôle of "Clarice," with William Gillette, at Garrick theater, New York, October 16, 1906. On October 7, 1907, in Boston, Massachusetts, she was promoted to the rank of "star," when she appeared as Carlotta, in "The Morals of Marcus," appearing in the Criterion theater, New York, November 18, 1907, in the same part. In Boston, September, 1908, she played Benjamin Monnier, in "The Richest Girl," appearing at the Criterion theater, New York, March 1, 1909, in the same part. On August 9, 1909, she appeared at the Lyceum theater, New York, as Carlotta, in "The Morals of Marcus." She played Adelina, in "The Climax," in Jersey City, January 5, 1910, and appeared in the same rôle at the Comedy theater, London, England, February 26, 1910. On October 26, 1910, she played Emeline Twimbly, in "Electricity," at Lyceum theater, New York.

During the spring of 1911 she went abroad for a period of rest and, returning to the United States, began a four weeks' engagement, February 26, 1912, in the title rôle of "Oliver Twist," in an all-star engagement. The engagement was extended, closing May 4th at the New Amsterdam theater, New York. On May 6, 1912, she appeared at the Lyric theater, New York, in the title rôle of "Patience," in a four-week revival of that opera. She went abroad and, on August 27, 1913, appeared in "The Scarlet Band," at the Comedy theater, London. Later she appeared in an extended engagement in "Diplomacy," at Wyndham's theater, London.

On February 1, 1914, by royal command, she played in "Diplomacy," in Waterloo chamber, Windsor Castle, before their majesties, the King and Queen, and an audience of one hundred and eighty celebrities, the other principals in the play with Miss Doro being Gerald Du Maurier, Lady Tree, Eli Jeffry, and Norman Forbes. At the conclusion of the play those named were presented to their majesties, and Miss Doro enjoys the unique distinction of being the first American actress to play before the King and Queen by royal command. The World War becoming imminent she hastily sailed for the United States, July 31, 1914, catching the German steamer, "Kaiser Wilhelm II," at Cherbourg, France, just a day before the declaration of war.

She began her season as Dora, in "Diplomacy," at the Empire theater, New York, in November, 1914, then on tour, appearing February 8, 1915, at Blackstone theater, Chicago, and at the conclusion of that engagement turned her attention to the silent drama. Her first picture, "Morals of Marcus," was produced by the Famous Players' Company. Then followed "The White Pearl," by the Triangle Company; "The Wood Nymph," and others.

She returned to the speaking stage November 5, 1917, in the title rôle of "Barbara," at the Plymouth theater, New York, but on February 8, 1919, after a few weeks' rest from moving picture work, which she had again entered, she sailed for Europe, pursuing a new engagement to play in the silent drama. During the greater part of her time, since then to July, 1920, her work before the camera has been done in Rome, Naples and Sicily, Italy, although her first European picture, "Twelve-Ten," was made in London and Paris, as was her next picture, "Midnight Gambols." She returned to America in 1921 and again assumed rôles on the speaking stage.

During 1917 Marie Doro was united in marriage to Elliott Dexter, who is also engaged in moving picture work, and is accordingly known in private life as Mrs. Marie Doro Dexter. Her salary during the past few years has far exceeded that of the President of the United States.

ROBERT NEILSON STEPHENS, AUTHOR, NOVELIST.

Perry County has been the home of a number of men who later became authors of note. Col. McClure's historical volumes and Dr. Super's works along educational and allied lines are widely read. Another whose fame was country-wide was Robert Neilson Stephens. He was descended from Alexander Stephens, the Jacobite who settled near the Juniata's mouth, and who was also the ancestor of Alexander H. Stephens, the Vice-President of the Confederacy. The head of the clan had two sons, James and Andrew, born near Duncannon, both of whom accompanied him to Georgia, where he settled, that state having passed a free land law in 1795 to induce settlement. James came back North and settled on the south side of Hominy Ridge, having married Elizabeth Garrett, of near Milford. He had several sons, one being named Robert. Prof. James A. Stephens was a son of Robert, and in turn became the father of Robert Neilson Stephens, the noted author, whose mother was Rebecca (Neilson) Stephens.

He was born July 22, 1867, in New Bloomfield, his father having been principal of the Bloomfield Academy on several occasions. With his family he was later taken to Huntingdon, where he graduated from the High School. His father's death, in 1876, put the little family in straightened financial circumstances, and he was only enabled to even finish school through his mother becoming a teacher, after his father's death. He then worked for $3.50 a week in the stationery store connected with the J. C. Blair manufactory. He was a delicate youth and books were his steadfast companions. Yet he chafed in the bookstore. He learned stenography and through W. B. Wilson, an old friend of his father, John Scott, solicitor general of the Pennsylvania Railroad, gave him a position in the Philadelphia offices of the Pennsylvania Railroad Company. As soon as he was settled there he sent for his mother and brother.

The *Philadelphia Press* was then a virtual cradle of authors, and in a short time he secured a position on that paper, and was assigned to write theatrical notices. In a year he had advanced to the post of dramatic editor. In 1889 he married Maud Helfenstein, of Chicago. In 1893 he became general agent for a firm of theatrical agents, part of his duty being to write plays for popular priced houses. He is said to have been the creator of the picturesque "Steve Brodie." His first melodrama was entitled "On the Bowery." He wrote "An Enemy to the King," which was his first ambitious production, 1895-96. With the noted E. H. Southern playing it he accompanied his wife the first night, but reluctantly, and remained without the theater. The call for his appearance was led by DeWolf Hopper and Richard Harding Davis.

Some time later Mr. Southern appeared in Boston in the same play, and L. C. Page, the Boston publisher, was in the audience. He recognized in it the elements which constitute a semi-historical romance, and foreseeing the extensive demand for that type of fiction, sought Mr. Stephens and proposed that he should make a book of the play. Inside of twenty-four hours the contract was signed. It was published in 1897, and he then abandoned "hack work."

His health began to decline with his entry to fame and fortune, for this book had started him on the way to both. He was once met by a friend who remarked that he appeared to be in ill health. His reply was, "I would rather be ill and well-to-do, as I am, than poor and in good health, as I was for many years. I have had my sorrows, but hardly a sorrow that was not aggravated, if not caused by poverty, or that very moderate wealth would not have ameliorated or prevented. The difference between pecuniary ease and poverty is oftentimes simply as the difference between heaven and hell."

Two other plays which gave him fame were "The Continental Dragoon," in 1898, and "The Ragged Regiment." With 1898 his other books began appearing. They were: "The Road to Paris," "A Gentleman Player," "Capt. Ravenshaw," "Clementina's Highwayman," "The Bright Face of Danger," "Tales From Bohemia," "The Mystery of Murray Davenport," and "Philip Winwood," the latter appearing in England, the United States and Canada simultaneously. There is something about Robert Neilson Stephens as a writer that makes one think of that other noted Scot, Robert Louis Stevenson, in his Samoan home—a certain resemblance, the same delicacy, and the same suggestion of indomitable intellectuality. His publisher, L. C. Page, said of him: "He is unsurpassed among the novelists of the day for mastery of bygone periods."

He is also quoted by his publisher as saying: "When a man makes any kind of a success, however small, he finds that his old friends resolve themselves into three classes. The first class turn sullen, and show their envy in many mean ways. The second class wax more friendly than ever, and come showering their attentions. The third class show a reasonable pleasure at your success, and remain just as they were before. God bless the last kind! God mend the second! and God pity the first!" He died in 1906.

CARLTON LEWIS BRETZ, PROMINENT RAILROAD MAN.

From among the Pennsylvania Railroad employes of Perry County one reached virtually the top in railroading. That man was Carlton Lewis Bretz, who was born in Newport, March 28, 1847. When a young fellow in his teens force of circumstances led him into the railroad business, but that was his proper sphere.

made trainmaster of the Lewistown Division. Two years later he was transferred to the Bedford Division as trainmaster, where he remained until 1888. The West Virginia Central and Pittsburgh Railroad was then under construction, and Mr. Bretz's thorough knowledge of railroading came to the attention of Senator Henry Gassaway Davis and associates, who were building it, and they offered him the position of general manager, which he held from 1888 to 1906, when the Gould interests got possession of that line. To him was then tendered the general managership of the Western Maryland, but it necessitated his removal to Baltimore, and as he was bound to Cumberland, Maryland, by home and financial interests, he declined. It is said of Mr. Bretz that from two streaks of rust insecurely spiked to derelict ties he saw and helped develop a railroad so perfectly equipped that it commanded a purchase price of approximately eighteen millions of dollars.

In a short time after his retirement as general manager, the Consolidated Coal Company tendered him the position of general manager of the Cumberland and Pennsylvania Railroad, which he filled until his death, September 30, 1910. This road had its beginning in 1844, with the construction of the Mt. Savage and Cumberland Railroad. It is essentially a coal road. Mr. Bretz also came into control of the Cumberland and Westernport Electric Railway, running from Cumberland through the Georges Creek mining region to Westernport, about 1908, and brought it to a high state of efficiency. He was president of this company at the time of his death.

He was a member of the Republican party, and was strongly urged, on several occasions, to be a candidate for Congress, and on one occasion refused the proffered State Controllership of Maryland. He was one of the most prominent citizens of western Maryland. He always stood high in the estimation of his men and never had a strike. Two labor organizations bear his name, the one after his wife being the Mrs. C. L. Bretz Auxiliary to the Railroad Trainmen, and the other the C. L. Bretz Division, Brotherhood of Railroad Trainmen. He was survived by his wife, who was Miss Matilda H. Hartley, daughter of the late William Hartley, of Bedford, a retired capitalist who amassed a fortune and acquired widespread prominence in the oil industry of western Pennsylvania.

He represented Senator Henry Gassaway Davis' West Virginia Central at a meeting of the Railway Congress of the World in London, England, in 1895, and was among those entertained by Queen Victoria at Windsor Castle. In 1900 he represented the same road at another session of the World's Congress, at Paris, and was entertained at Versailles, and in 1900 when it met at Washington, D. C.

Mr. Bretz, in railroad circles and in the home of his adoption, Cumberland—in fact, in all western Maryland—was known as a builder in every line as well as a thorough railroad man. He was quiet and unassuming, of a pleasing disposition, and his name will ever stand, in railroad annals, as an example of the self-made man. Of the hundreds of Perry Countians who have "made good" in the railroad world the name of Carlton Lewis Bretz stands at the top.

ELIZABETH REIFSNYDER, M.D.

Until recently, Dr. Elizabeth Reifsnyder was the only woman physician native to Perry County, but a very notable one, and one whose name was known afar. Furthermore, she graduated in medicine at that earlier period when it was an unusual thing for a woman to enter that profession, and her life work has placed her in the very first rank, not only of Perry County women, but of womanhood everywhere. Elizabeth Reifsnyder was born in Liverpool, January 17, 1858, the daughter of John and Nancy Musselman Reifsnyder. Her early life was that of the average girl in a country town, but she improved her time in the Liverpool schools, and entered the Millersville State Normal School, where she graduated. She then entered the Woman's Medical College at Philadelphia, where she graduated in 1881, when but twenty-three years of age. She served as an interne for one year, and left for China in 1883, where most of her life was spent, and where she opened the first hospital in China. It was opened under the auspices of the Women's Union Mission of America, and was interdenominational. It was known as the Margaret Williamson Hospital. The work was begun in a temporary building, and the hospital built from plans drawn by Dr. Reifsnyder herself.. She built up the organization as well, and it is principally to her that the greatest hospital in the Far East is to be credited. She interested not only friends in America, but the more wealthy Chinese who were her patients, and through their contributions was enabled to see that none were turned away. She was also a noted surgeon. Among her patients was Mrs. Wu Ting Fang, wife of the famed Chinese Ambassador to the United States. When the twenty-fifth anniversary was celebrated, press dispatches told that 800,000 had already been treated there, and that during the preceding year there had been treated 820 persons, with 56,700 others as office patients.

Dr. Reifsnyder left China about 1914 to come home for a visit, but owing to her health was never able to return. She left there a large sum of money which she had received for services, and with these funds the organization has erected a maternity building, the first one in China, and named it in her honor, the Elizabeth Reifsnyder Hospital. It will be marked by a bronze tablet telling of

attended the public schools and prepared for college under the instruction of her father and brothers, taking the final year at the Wellesley-Walton Preparatory School in Philadelphia. She graduated from Smith College with the degree of B.A and Phi Beta Kappa honors in 1900, and received the Ph.D. degree from the University of Pennsylvania in 1909, the first Perry County woman to attain that honor. She was instructor and professor of English at Hood College, Maryland, from 1900 to 1906, and professor of English at Cornell College, Mt. Vernon, Iowa, 1909-10. She then became dean of Milwaukee-Downer College, at Milwaukee, Wisconsin, where she remained until 1921, when she was appointed dean of Wheaton College, Norton, Massachusetts.

Mina Kerr is the author of "The Influence of Ben Johnson on English Comedy," and also of many articles in educational and religious magazines. She has twice visited Europe, has traveled in Alaska, many parts of Canada, the Hawaiian Islands and throughout the United States, to further her education. She is a well-known and able speaker along religious, educational and Americanization lines. During November, 1921, when a banquet was held in Boston in honor of Judith Winsor Smith, the surviving member of the group of early suffragists, including Susan B. Anthony, Julia Ward Howe, Lucy Stone and Elizabeth Cady Stanton, Mina Kerr was the principal speaker of the occasion. From 1918 to 1920 she was president of the Milwaukee Branch of the American Association of University Women, during which time a College Women's Club House was established by this association. During 1920-22 she was president of the National Association of Deans of Women, a department of the National Educational Association. Wheaton College, of which she is now dean, is a college for women just outside of Boston, chartered as a college in 1912, and already numbering over three hundred students. She is a member of various boards and committees of Boston Branch of the American Association of University Women, and of various bodies devoted to community and civic betterment. Every summer of her life so far, save three years when she was traveling abroad, she has returned to Perry County, for, although she has traveled afar, she still finds it "one of the most beautiful places on earth."

DAVID LOY TRESSLER, COLLEGE PRESIDENT.

Throughout the United States there are many small colleges, the value of whose usefulness as a whole is greater by far than those of the great universities. One of these—Carthage College—is located in the beautiful town of Carthage, Illinois, and the first president of that institution, Rev. David Loy Tressler, Ph.D., was a Perry Countian. In the sketches in this book devoted to the

of the Loysville Academy. During the summer of 1862 he organized a company which later became part of the 133d Pennsylvania Volunteer Infantry, and among those enrolled were most of the students of the little institution. He was made its captain, participating in the Battles of South Mountain, Antietam, and Fredericksburg, receiving two severe wounds in the latter engagement, but being again with his company in the Chancellorsville engagement. He was tendered a colonel's commission, at the expiration of his term of service, but declined. In 1864 he was admitted to the bar and practiced five years. His preceptor was the late Benj. McIntire, of New Bloomfield, to whose daughter, Ada Josephine, he was united in marriage in 1865. In 1870 he located in Mendota, Illinois, and in the autumn, entered the ministry of the Evangelical Lutheran Church at Lena, Illinois. He filled that position until 1872, when he accepted a professorship in Carthage College, a new institution, and a year later was made its first president, and subsequently its treasurer, both of which positions he held until his death.

Upon his retirement from military service the boys, whom he had instructed at Loysville and whom he had led in the field of battle, presented him with an expensive gold watch, as a token of esteem. While his period in the law occupied a bare five years, yet the press of the day spoke of him as a brilliant young lawyer. Made president of Carthage College, his friends showered him with congratulations. In replying to a letter from his family, on hearing of his promotion, he aptly put some thoughts, from which the following are extracts: "Condolence (rather than congratulations) is more befitting the occasion. * * * Trials, self-denial, heartaches and ills that careless observers dream not of, are the lot of a college president. * * * It is a mighty work to found a college, and half the work devolves upon the president. * * * I tremble in the presence of the greatness of the work." In leaving the legal profession he said to a loved one: "If I wish to be rich in this world's goods, I will remain in the legal profession— if rich in the next world, I will enter the ministry."

Carthage did not have a Lutheran church, and into the project of building a church there he put his entire energy, with the result that the Lutheran church then built was the largest and best church edifice in the county. To it he was a most liberal contributor, and at the time of his death also its beloved pastor. During the closing month of 1879 a new bell was placed in the belfry, and its dedication culminated when it "rang out the old, rang in the new" year. On that occasion Dr. Tressler remarked, "For which of us shall this bell first toll a funeral knell?" probably little thinking that he should be that one.

46

His death occurred February 20, 1880. He was a martyr to the cause in which he was enlisted, as his death will testify. His fatal illness began on February 2d. On February 1st (Sunday) he filled a preaching appointment twenty miles from the college. The roads being too muddy to make the journey by carriage, he went on horseback. So fatigued was he, upon his return, that he could not dismount without assistance.

At the obsequies of Rev. Tressler, Rev. Willis G. Craig, D.D., a Presbyterian pastor, among other things said: "You have taken this region for Christian culture with an honored grave." In the funeral procession were Company G, Illinois National Guard, with reversed arms; the faculty, the alumni, and the student body of Carthage College.

Dr. Tressler was a man of fine physique, slightly above medium height, with square shoulders, erect posture, an open face and a commanding presence. With a sunny disposition and a kind word he was every man's friend. Endowed with a splendid mind and a remarkable memory, with accurate judgment and large sympathy, he was a man among men. Successful as a teacher, as an officer in the U. S. Army, as an attorney, as a theologian, and as a college president, all in a span of but forty-one years, this native Perry Countian stands in the very front rank of those who have gone forth and writ their names high.

Dr. and Mrs. Tressler were the parents of five children, two of whom, Annie McIntire and John Arthur, died in early life. Mary Loyetta Tressler, born at New Bloomfield, Perry County, married Prof. Cyrus B. Newcomer, of Carthage College. She is much interested in the work of Carthage College, having been active in responsible positions in the carrying on of the work which her father so nobly commenced. She is a member of the school board, president of the Alumni Association of Carthage College, member of the General Literature Committee of the Women's Missionary Society of the United Lutheran Church, as well as being interested in organizations of civic betterment. Elizabeth Agnes Tressler, born at Newport, Perry County, married James Sumner Maloney, of Rockford, Illinois, where she is much interested in things religious and civic affairs. She is president of the Y. W. C. A. of the city of Rockford and teacher of a large organized Sunday school class in Trinity Lutheran Church. Charles J. Tressler is the alumni representative on the board of trustees of Carthage College. He is an attorney, and after nineteen years with Swift & Company of Chicago—ten of which he was assistant general attorney of the firm, united to form the partnership of McCabe & Tressler, attorneys, specializing in law along the lines relating to food. The firm has offices in Chicago and Washington City. Mr. Tressler was married to Miss Bess Ringheim, a Carthage

birth occurred at Pottsville his parents migrated here when he was a mere child, and Perry County he has always claimed as his home county. Likewise, Perry Countians always refer to Prof. Super as one of their boys. Receiving the rudiments of his education in the local schools, he attended Prof. John B. Strain's Duane Academy in the schoolhouse which stood on the grounds now occupied by St. Samuel's Church, and a term at the private school conducted by Silas Wright at Millerstown. He taught in Oliver Township and, during one term at college, he taught a private school during the winter of 1865-66, at Hunterstown, near Gettysburg. In the fall of 1866 he tried to resuscitate the old academy at Markelville, but did not succeed, and during the winter migrated to Canfield, Ohio, where he taught, also teaching at Lordstown. Later he conducted private schools at Milford and Frederica, Delaware, in connection with Rev. E. W. Caylord. Returning to Millerstown he became a member of the faculty of Prof. Wright's school for a term, and then went to Europe to pursue further studies. He had attended Dickinson College, and graduated in 1866, with the B.A. degree. He studied at Tubingen, Germany, in 1869-71, and received his Ph.D. degree from Illinois Wesleyan in 1874. In 1883 Syracuse University conferred on him the A.M. degree, and in 1894 Dickinson College made him an LL.D. He was married to Mary Louise Cewell, of Canfield, Ohio, in 1867. She died in 1913.

Prof. Super was Professor of Modern Languages in Wesleyan College at Cincinnati, 1872-78. While there he taught Greek, Latin, Hebrew, French, Spanish, Italian, and German at different times. During 1878-79 he read law, but preferred the educational field, and in 1882-1907 we find him Professor of Greek at the Ohio University. During 1883-84 he was the acting president of that institution, and from 1884 to 1901 he was its president. In 1907 he resigned his position as Dean of the Department of Literal Arts in the college and devoted his time to business and literary work. From 1887 to 1893 he was joint editor of the *Journal of Pedagogy*. Furthering his research work he visited Europe in 1882, 1896 and 1903. He is the author of a large number of books, including Weil's Order of Words of Ancient Languages, compared with those of Modern Languages translated from the French, 1887; History of the German Language, 1893; Between Heathenism and Christianity, 1899; Wisdom and Will in Education, 1907; A Study of a Rural Community, 1911; German Idealism and Prussian Militarism, 1916; Pan-Prussianism, 1918; Prohibition and Democracy, 1920. He has also written reviews of books in Greek, Latin, German, French, Italian, and Spanish. He is a contributor to about twenty educational and philosophical publications in the English and German languages.

The works of Dr. Super are noted for their broadness and thoroughness. Judging them all as excellent, the following opinion of Bibliotheca Sacra, in reference to his "Pan-Prussianism" is here reprinted:

"So far as we know, nothing has appeared in print which gives so complete and unanswerable verdict in condemnation of Prussian principles, aims, and activities as is done in Pan-Prussianism. This is more significant in that the author is of German descent, studied two years in a German university, has traveled much in Germany, and maintained an intimate friendship with a large number of German literati during his whole life. Up to 1914 Dr. Super was an 'ardent pacifist' and could not believe that the spirit that reigned in Wilhelmstrasse was 'capable of the perfidy that it soon came to make a part of its settled policy.' But his views rapidly changed as he watched 'the gradual deterioration of the German people, and the systematic way in which it was being corrupted by professors and clergy' (p. 305). The volume is specially valuable as dealing not with vague generalities but with specific facts. It also gives a large amount of biographical information concerning the leaders of German thought. The book deserves the widest attention."

The Ohio University, of which Dr. Super was long president, is the oldest institution of college rank northwest of the Ohio River, and was provided for before Ohio became a state. Owing to adverse legislation in 1843 its income was seriously reduced, and for years it "had a hard row to hoe." The well-known Dr. W. H. McGuffey was president at this time, but resigned shortly afterwards. In 1876 the matter began to be righted, and in 1884 another forward stride was made. In 1896 the Ohio Legislature passed an act placing the institution upon permanent footing financially. This law now yields an annual income of $65,000, which represents an endowment of about one and a third millions at five per cent. During the college year 1919-20 the college had more than a thousand students, about twenty buildings, and an income of $330,000. During Dr. Super's connection with the University the system of state aid to higher education was completely revised, and records show much of the credit to be due him for the consummation of this large task, and it was during his presidency that the Ohio Legislature made the first appropriation in the history of the state for the establishment of a normal department in any institution. During the same period the University, the first in Ohio to recognize the fact that business has a legitimate place in any scheme of higher education, established a department of commerce, which almost all universities now have. In the face of much discouragement and much opposition he also established a department of music, which has grown so that the services of no less than ten teachers are now required for that department alone. Drawing and painting was also added to the course of study. While Dr. Super was president he was at the same time professor of Greek, assistant in Modern Languages, and ever alert in any capacity to advance the institution.

Dr. Super resides in Athens, Ohio, the seat of the university over which he so successfully presided. One of his surviving sons spent about five years in Europe after receiving degrees from the University in 1895-96, in the study of languages. Part of this time he had charge of an exhibit at the Paris Exhibition, in 1900. For several years he has been professor of modern languages—mainly French and German—in Hamilton College at Clinton, New York. He is unmarried and was named Ralph Clewell, after his mother's family, which is largely represented in eastern Pennsylvania.

The first Phi Beta Kappa chapter in Pennsylvania was organized at Dickinson College, Carlisle, about 1887, and a few honorary members—less than a half dozen—elected to membership, among that number being Dr. Super, and his brother, Prof. Ovando B. Super, both former Perry Countians.

Jesse Miller, Congressman, Sec'y of the Commonwealth.

Jesse Miller was another of Perry County's noted men. His public life was coincident with that of the early years of the county's history, for he was clerk to the first board of county commissioners (1820-23), at an annual salary of $50. His birth occurred near Landisburg in 1800, and when he assumed his first office he was still under voting age. But he was ambitious, and in the *Perry Forester*—Perry County's first newspaper—on June 26, 1823, was this announcement:

"Encouraged by many of you I am induced to offer myself as a candidate for the office of sheriff at the ensuing general election. Should you deem me worthy of the office, I will perform the duties thereof with fidelity."   (Signed) Jesse Miller.

He won the election and became sheriff at twenty-three, the youngest man who has ever filled that office. His education was that furnished by the subscription schools, but he was a widely read man, and while serving as sheriff was elected Member of Assembly to succeed Jacob Huggins, thus becoming the fourth man to represent Perry County in that body (1826-27), when but twenty-six years of age. In the fall of 1829 he was elected State Senator, serving from 1830 to 1834. At the fall election of 1834 he was elected to the United States Congress from the district comprising Cumberland, Perry and Juniata Counties. This was during the Jackson administration, and Congress did not convene until December 30, 1835. He resigned October 30, 1836, to become the first auditor of the United States Treasury, a newly created position. The Van Buren administration had in the meantime

cial way, he removed to Perry County. The village which grew around the furnace came to be known as Baileysburg, taking his name, and to this day the station on the Pennsylvania Railroad at that point is known as Bailey.

During the term of 1851-53 he represented Perry and Cumberland Counties in the State Senate. In 1854, the legislature, which then possessed that power, elected him as state treasurer. He then took up the study of law, although well advanced in years, and was admitted to the bar in 1860, being then fifty years old. The same year he was elected to Congress. During his term in Congress he was a war Democrat and was proud of the fact that he had voted for the Constitutional Amendment prohibiting slavery. He was elected as a delegate from his senatorial district by the Republicans to the Constitutional Convention in 1872. He died August 26, 1885, and his remains rest in the beautiful cemetery at the county seat of his adopted county. On his monument is inscribed:

> "As a Member of Congress he voted for the Joint Resolution, submitting to the people of the United States the amendment to the Constitution prohibiting slavery."

WILLIAM H. MILLER, MEMBER OF CONGRESS.

William H. Miller was born at Landisburg, February 28, 1829, and was a son of Jesse Miller, also a Member of Congress, and once Secretary of the Commonwealth. He had an early desire for knowledge and a bright intellect. He graduated at Franklin & Marshall College and read law with Hermanus Alricks, of Harrisburg, being admitted to the bar in 1846. From 1854 to 1863 he was prothonotary of the Supreme Court of Pennsylvania. He was connected with the Harrisburg *Patriot,* and in 1862 was elected to the Thirty-Eighth Congress of the United States, from the district composed of Dauphin, Northumberland, Snyder, Union and Juniata, serving 1863-65. He died in his forty-second year. His widow, Ellen (Ward) Miller, and son, Jesse, survived. He had at that time the largest private library in the state, which his widow presented to Lafayette College.

GEN. J. HALE SYPHER, MEMBER OF CONGRESS.

The Sypher family was of Teutonic origin, and came to America in the early part of the Seventeenth Century, settling near Chester. Subsequently the family located in Pfoutz Valley, Perry County, where J. Hale Sypher was born July 22, 1837. He attended the local schools and was educated in Alfred University, New York State, in 1859. When the Sectional War came on he enlisted as a private in the First Ohio Light Artillery. He fought at Philippi and in other West Virginia engagements. He was promoted through all the grades, becoming colonel of the Eleventh U. S. Heavy Artillery in August, 1864. March 13, 1865, he was brevetted Major General of Volunteers. He was mustered out October 2, 1865.

During 1866 he practiced law in New Orleans. He also engaged in the cultivation of cotton and sugar cane. He represented Louisiana as a delegate in the National Republican Convention of 1868, and was elected by the Republicans to the Fortieth Congress from New Orleans, taking his seat July 18, 1868. He was reelected to the Forty-First, Forty-Second, and Forty-Third Congresses, serving from 1868 to 1875, and successfully contesting his seat in the Forty-First Congress with another claimant. In Congress he was a warm supporter of measures to improve the navigation of the Mississippi River. After the completion of his last term he removed to Washington, D. C., where he practiced law. He died in Baltimore, May 9, 1905.

Benjamin K. Focht, Member of Congress, Editor.

The present congressman from the Eighteenth District, to which Perry County belongs, and which is in size the largest district of Pennsylvania, is Benjamin K. Focht, a Perry Countian by birth. His district is so extensive that it is larger than several of the smaller states. While Congressman Focht is a native of Perry, his present home is at Lewisburg, Union County, from which he has been elected many times. His father was Rev. David H. Focht, pastor of the Lutheran churches at New Bloomfield and Newport for a number of years prior to the Sectional War, and to whom posterity is indebted for that valuable small volume, "The Churches Between the Mountains," which is devoted principally to the Lutheran churches. Rev. Focht was an able advocate of the Union cause, and when the state was invaded by the Southern army, he went to the Kittatinny or Blue Mountain to help form a line of resistance. Through unusual exposure there his death followed.

After the death of the father of Benjamin K. Focht, his mother removed with the little family to Lewisburg, where he grew up and has since resided. He was born at New Bloomfield, March 12, 1863, the very year of the invasion. He attended the public schools, Bucknell College, State College, and Susquehanna University at Selinsgrove. In January, 1882, he started the Lewisburg *Saturday News,* which is to this day a paper which has an individuality distinctly its own. But two men now in business in Lewisburg were then in business there. Mr. Focht has published the *News* continuously since then, and has been longer continuously an editor and publisher than any individual from Erie to Harrisburg. He served in various local offices, and in 1892, 1894 and 1896 was elected to the General Assembly of Pennsylvania. In 1900 he was

falo. Following that he attended the Central State Normal School at Lock Haven, graduating in 1889. Hearing the call to outdoor life he went to the lumber camps of Elk County, where he became a bark peeler, at the same time taking a business course by mail. His next position was conducting a store and keeping a set of books for a lumber firm. His greatest stride forward, until that time, was then made, when he became head of the shipping department of the New York and Pennsylvania Company, one of the largest paper mills in the world. He became a contractor for the same company, employing a large number of men during the past two decades.

There is usually a reason for the elevation of a man, politically, especially not a native, and it is not hard to find in the case of Harris J. Bixler. Johnsonburg was a fast growing, prosperous town, and naturally drew to it men and women of all types. Its earlier days were those of many a lumbering town. Mr. Bixler stood for a clean moral community, and on that single plank was nominated for chief burgess, by the Republicans, and elected, the entire better element supporting him. To this day he is named as the man who made the town morally clean. He also served on the board of education, having been its president. For a period of twenty-two years he served in all of the various city offices, beginning with auditor, and always made good. Naturally, the larger field of county offices were the next stepping stones, and he was elected sheriff of Elk County, and later county treasurer, in both cases almost unanimously. In addition he was also chairman of the Board of Reviewers and a member of the State Republican Committee. In 1920 he received the Republican nomination of the Twenty-Eighth Congressional District, and it was later followed by the Democratic nomination. He was elected in November and took his seat in 1921. Mr. Bixler is also identified with a number of corporations in his territory and is a director in the Johnsonburg National Bank. He was in office as sheriff during the drafts for the U. S. Army during the World War, and used the same painstaking thoroughness and conscientious scruples that have characterized his whole life, and landed him in the lawmaking halls of the nation.

In 1898 he was married to Miss Jennie Pray, of Penfield, Clearfield County. Mr. Bixler has erected one of the finest homes in Elk County, at Johnsonburg, where he resides.

John Milton Bernheisel, Delegate to Congress.

John Milton Bernheisel was born near Blain, June 23, 1799, the son of Samuel and Susan (Bower) Bernheisel. He attended the subscription schools of the period, and graduated from the medical department of the University of Pennsylvania in 1827. He moved from Pennsylvania to Utah, where he located, and became a member of the Mormon Church. He arose to a commanding position among that people, and was elected as Delegate to Congress, for Utah was then still a territory. He was elected to the three succeeding Congresses, serving from March 4, 1851, to March 3, 1859. After one term he was again elected and served as delegate in the Thirty-Seventh Congress, March 4, 1861, to March 3, 1863. He then returned to private life and to the practice of medicine, continuing until his death, September 29, 1881. During his service in Congress, according to the files of the *Perry Freeman,* he visited his mother, still living in Perry County.

ARCHIBALD LOUDON, HISTORIAN.

To a boy reared in what is now Perry County, Pennsylvanians are indebted for the portrayal of much of its early history. That boy was Archibald Loudon, a son of James Loudon, and he was the author of Loudon's Narratives, copyrighted in 1808 and published in 1811, and now so rare that copies of it never bring less than twenty-five dollars for the two volumes. At one sale in a great city they brought almost $500. By referring to our chapter on Tuscarora Township it will be seen that different members of the Loudon family warranted large tracts of land there. Among these was Archibald, who warranted 296 acres, October 16, 1784, the others dating almost twenty years earlier, among them being that of his father in 1767. He was a boy and not old enough to warrant lands when the others did.

Reared here, then a veritable outpost of civilization, he knew whereof he wrote, and in at least one of his descriptions he tells of his boyhood and of living in Raccoon Valley, near the foot of Tuscarora Mountain, surely proof enough that he was a resident. The article is here reproduced:

"The editor of this work well remembers when he was a boy that shortly after what was called the second Indian War, I think in the year 1765, then living in Raccoon Valley, near the foot of Tuscarora Mountain. On Saturday we had a report that the Indians had begun to murder the white people and on Sunday in the forenoon as we children were outside of the house we espied three Indians coming across the meadow a few rods from us; we ran into the house and informed our parents, who were considerably alarmed at their approach; the Indians, however, set their guns down outside the house and came in, when they were invited to take seats, which they did; after taking dinner they sat a considerable time. Logan could speak tolerable English; the other two spoke nothing while there but Indian, or something that we could not understand.

"They appeared to be making observations on the large wooden chimney, looking up it and laughing, this we supposed to be from a man on the Juniata, not far distant making his escape up the chimney when their house was attacked by the Indians. One of my sisters, a child three or four years old, having very white curly hair; they took hold of her hair between their fingers and thumb, stretching it up and laughing; this we conjectured they were saying would make a nice scalp, or that they had seen such; otherwise they behaved with civility.

"After some time when they saw we had no hostile intentions, I took a Bible and read two or three chapters in the Book of Judges, respecting Samson and the Philistines. Logan paid great attention to what I read. My father, upon observing this, took occasion to mention to him what a great benefit it would be to the Indians to learn to read. 'O,' said Logan, 'a great many people (meaning the Indians) on the Mohawk River, can read the Buch that speaks of God.'

"After remaining with us about two hours, they took their departure and crossed the Tuscarora Mountain to Captain Patterson's, two miles below where Mifflintown now stands. In a few days after, we were informed it was Captain John Logan, an Indian Chief. He was a remarkable tall man, considerably above six feet high, strong and well proportioned, of a brave, open, manly countenance, as straight as an arrow, and to appearance, would not be afraid to meet any man."

Archibald Loudon's youngest daughter, Margery B., was united in marriage to Dr. Isaac Wayne Snowden, a son of Rev. Nathaniel Randolph Snowden, a Presbyterian divine, and the father of Colonel A. Loudon Snowden, for many years superintendent of the United States Mint at Philadelphia. Dr. Snowden practiced medicine at Millerstown from 1830 to 1834. Archibald Loudon had located at Carlisle in later life, where he was postmaster for many years. He was also a book publisher there.

The Loudon transplanting from Scotland to the forests of Provincial Pennsylvania read like legend, but are facts. Matthew and James Loudon came from Scotland, about 1760, the son Archibald being born to James and wife while at sea. They settled in Sherman's Valley, but were driven out by the Indians and took up lands near Hogestown, Cumberland County, where they settled. After the Indian troubles subsided James went back to what is now Tuscarora Township, Perry County, and lived there and reared his family there. James Loudon died September 22, 1783, and his remains rest on the old Bull's Hill graveyard, in Tuscarora Township, where the oldest stone marks his grave. This old burial place is named after the famous Bull family, from whom came Capt. Bull, famous in the Second War with Great Britain.

Archibald Loudon's death occurred August 12, 1840, at Carlisle, in his 86th year. A notice of his death in the *Perry Freeman* of August 27th chronicles the fact and says that he was editor of the *Cumberland Register* for a time. His life covered the period when these lands progressed from savagery to civilization, and he lived under the Provincial, Colonial, and United States governments. He enlisted as a private in the Fourth Company of Col. Frederick Watts' battalion during the Revolution and was made an ensign of the Third Company. He was also a soldier in the Whiskey Rebellion.

George Robinson, Pioneer.

Thomas Robinson and his son Philip were among the first residents of the Cumberland Valley, of Scotch-Irish descent. George Robinson, Philip's second son, took up land in what is now Perry County, near Centre Church, of which he was one of the original members. Fort Robinson, mentioned in Provincial annals, was located on his farm. He was a justice of the peace, his commission issuing from George III. He was a captain in the Revolution. He remained in Sherman's Valley until 1797, when he removed to Kentucky, near Georgetown, where several of his sons had preceded him. There he resided until his death in 1814, at the age of eighty-seven. He was a ruling elder of the Presbyterian Church there. A grandson, James F. Robinson, became governor of Kentucky and remembered him well, describing him thus: "He was six feet tall, perfect in build, remarkably athletic and strong, fine large head, light hair, beautiful large blue eyes, large and well-developed forehead, with a benevolent and intellectual countenance. He was remarkable for his love of reading, especially that of the higher and more difficult kinds, works on law, ethics, and mental and moral philosophy. His library contains such works as Locke on Government, Blackstone's Commentaries, Stewart's Philosophy, the Spectator, etc. Among his acquaintances he was distinguished for his safe and sound judgment. He was a general counselor, a kind of oracle to all around, a Christian gentleman in truth whose memory was cherished by all who knew him, and was handed down as that of one of the worthies of his day." His tombstone in Kentucky bears this legend:

"Of softest manner, unaffected mind,
Lover of peace and friend of human kind,
Go, live! for Heaven's eternal rest is thine,
Go, and exalt this mortal to divine."

His descendants are widely scattered. As stated, a grandson became governor of Kentucky. A great-grandson, Rev. Thomas H. Robinson, D.D., was pastor of Market Square Presbyterian Church at Harrisburg for thirty years, from 1854 to 1884, when he became a member of the faculty of the Western Theological Seminary at Allegheny City, Pennsylvania. Jonathan Robinson, a son of George, who was the advance agent of the Robinson clan from Perry County who migrated to Kentucky, was married to Jane Black, and they became the parents of Governor James F. Robinson, of Kentucky, who was governor when the Southern states seceded, and largely through him it refused to join the movement.

Rev. John Linn.

Rev. John Linn was one of those early divines whose impress has been left upon the life of the county, although his ministry ceased with his death, which occurred in the year of the county's formation, 1820. He was born in Adams County in 1749, and professed religion when a mere boy. He graduated from Nassau Hall in 1773 and studied theology with Dr. Cooper, pastor of Middle Spring Church, in Cumberland County. Donegal Presbytery licensed him to preach in December, 1776, and about a year later he received and accepted a call to the churches of that faith—then the only ones—in Sherman's Valley. Here he labored and spent the balance of his life, faithfully and efficiently, being seventy-two years of age when death came in 1820.

Soon after settling here he married Mary Gettys, a daughter of the founder of Gettysburg. They became the parents of four sons and two daughters, one of the sons being Rev. James Linn, D.D., also a Presbyterian divine, who long served the church at Bellefonte and others.

Rev. Mr. Linn was, according to an account by Rev. Baird, about five feet, ten inches in height, portly, symmetrical in form, muscular and active in his bodily movements. He had a strong constitution and wonderful powers of endurance, an uncommon fine specimen of a man, generally so regarded by all. His pastorate of forty-four years is one of the very longest of any minister who has carried the Word to the territory which comprises Perry County. He had a jovial disposition, was cheerful and could easily acclimate himself to folks of different character and who lived under the various conditions of life. Characteristic of him was sobriety of mind rather than versatility, reflection rather than imagination. Accustomed to writing out his sermons at full length he would deliver them from memory, save on hot summer Sabbath mornings he would discourse on some particular story from the New Testament. His voice was remarkably clear, his expression solemn and impressive. Sermons which he wrote showed him to be a correct writer, instructive and methodical. Uncommonly devoted to his flock he did a wonderful amount of pastoral work. Christian dignity, even in his own family, tenderness and fidelity were marked traits in this first messenger from the Master to cast his lot among a new people, in a new country, then in the making. Like many other ministers of the period his salary was inadequate to support a growing family, and it was augmented by the ownership of a farm which he not only managed, but in rushed seasons helped till and harvest.

Rev. Linn has the distinction of having one of his blood, a direct descendant, occupying the second position in the nation at the time this is written (1920). Vice-President Marshall's mother was no other than Susannah Linn, a granddaughter. His descendants are the Linns, of Chambersburg, Williamsport, Philadelphia, Springfield, Ohio, and many other places.

superintendent of schools of Perry County. He refused a reëlection and began the study of law in the office of the late Ex-Senator Charles H. Smiley. The following year, 1886, he was elected to the lower house of the Pennsylvania Legislature, serving with distinction. On December 18, 1888, he married Caroline Milligan Rice, a daughter of William and Caroline (Milligan) Rice, who became his associate in business activities and in the work of the Presbyterian Church, in which he was much interested. He had gone to Colorado for his health during the previous year, and upon his marriage located there.

In 1889 the governor of Colorado appointed him a trustee of their proposed first State Normal School at Greely. This enabled him to perform a leading part in the organization of Colorado's first Teachers' College. In 1890 he was elected to the Legislature of Colorado, and served as chairman of the Committee on Appropriations and occasionally as speaker of the house. In 1893, declining a nomination to the State Senate of Colorado, he returned to Pennsylvania, his native state, and, while filling the chair of History in the State Normal at Westchester, took a postgraduate course in the University of Pennsylvania, and that institution conferred upon him the degree, Doctor of Science.

In 1896 he was chosen principal of the State Normal at Edinboro, Pennsylvania, an institution whose prospect of usefulness at that time had been practically ruined by prolonged factional quarreling. His success in effecting harmony and restoring confidence, soon proved him to be an educator and administrator of unusual sagacity and executive ability. Three years later, as a recognition of his marked efficiency as an educator he was elected principal of the Central State Normal at Lock Haven, Pa. He justified his selection, by building up the school and making it one of the most noted and prosperous educational institutions in the state. After twelve years of faithful and efficient service, during which he secured for that institution the highest standard of excellence, he died quite suddenly from a severe attack of gastritis, February 17, 1912. He was buried at New Bloomfield. His age was fifty-eight.

He was a highly esteemed member of the Lock Haven Board of Trade. His last public address was at their annual banquet a few days previous to his decease, and he commended to their favorable consideration the commission form of government for cities. He was a member of the American Historical Society, the American Academy of Political and Social Science, and the State and National Educational Associations. In 1902 he was elected president of the State Educational Association, being one of three native Perry Countians to gain such distinction. He was the author of a popular textbook on civics and of many papers on historical and economic subjects. His performance of every trust was character-

ized by integrity of character and nobility of purpose. His helpfulness to individual students was a vital characteristic of his work.
He held the degrees of A.B., A.M., (Princeton) and D.Sc. (Bucknell). He taught pedagogy, psychology and history of education
while principal of the State Normal School.

The following tribute, part of an article from the *Lock Haven
Bulletin,* at the time of his death, is from the pen of one who necessarily knew him and knew of his work:

"Very prominent among his many remarkable traits of character, was
his love of truth and right. This characteristic linked with his kind sympathetic helpfulness to all, have made him a man, the superior of whom
the Central State Normal can never hope to have.

"Aside from his culture and high intellectual attainments, he possessed
those rare traits of character which exert an inspiring influence over man-
kind; cheering the disconsolate, encouraging the downhearted, and helping them to feel that life is indeed worth living. He was an attractive
speaker, a leader of men who had the happy faculty of drawing people to
him irresistibly, because he was the personification of frankness and goodness and carefully followed the teachings of the meek and lowly Master.
The world has been made better by his life of service in the cause of education, and while others may rise to take his place, the lofty influence of
his noble life will continue to be manifested, in the lives of those who
were associated with him."

Dr. Flickinger was survived by his wife, who became custodian
of the public library at Dalton, Massachusetts, a position which she
still holds; and an only daughter, Jean, born at Pueblo, Colorado,
who completed the Normal course at Lock Haven and graduated
from Vassar, in 1916. She enlisted as a Red Cross worker in
January, 1919, to work among the homeless refugees along the
battle line in France, under the auspices of the Friends' Reconstruction Bureau, and was assigned to the superintendency of that
work along the Marne and the Meuse.

While it has not been within the scope of this book to include
any genealogy, save that connected directly with prominent natives, yet a sketch of Henry Flickinger, the ancestor of the many
Flickinger families follows, as an example of but one of the many
noted families who have left their marks along the line of good
citizenship of this and other counties and of this and other states.
Among such families might be mentioned those whose names appear in this work along historical lines and their ancestry, as well
as other families of prominence. Several works of that character, of
two and three volumes, comprising the counties of the Juniata Valley, and in one case also Snyder and Union Counties, are among
our prized possessions, but there is a place for a real Perry County
genealogy, in one volume, covering the families of prominence and
of historical significance within its confines and those which once
dwelt there. The author of this volume stands ready to aid any

person who will attempt to publish such work and who has the perseverance to pursue it to completion. Much data can yet be secured that in another generation will have passed away.

HENRY FLICKINGER.

Henry Flickinger, of Ickesburg was the worthy ancestor of the Flickinger families of Perry and Juniata Counties. Henry was the son of Peter Flickinger, 1730-1807, the immigrant, who was enrolled at Rotterdam, in Holland, as coming from the Palatinate in Germany and, sailing on the Edinburg, James Russell, captain, arrived at Philadelphia, September 14, 1753. Peter Flickinger, according to the best information available, was a farmer and, passing up the valley of the Schuylkill River, tarried awhile at Pottstown, but soon afterward located on the frontier in the vicinity of Reading, Berks County. Here he married Mollie Derr. Later he moved to East Buffalo Township (near Lewisburg), Northumberland, now Union County, raised a family of seven or eight children, and died at 77, in 1807. His wife died at the home of his son, Henry, at Ickesburg, four years later, and was taken for burial to the grave of her husband.

Henry Flickinger was a native of Berks County, and was born January 10, 1765. In his youth he made good use of his limited school privileges and learned the art of making shoes, that he might have steady employment during the winter months. About 1796, meeting Thomas Strock, of Perry County, he accompanied him and worked for him three years on the Strock farm, a few miles southwest of Ickesburg. In May, 1798, he married Margaret Yohn, a native of Montgomery County, and the next year located on a farm near Ickesburg. In 1833 he became a resident of Ickesburg and, assisted by Peter, his oldest son, devoted his entire time to shoemaking. Henry died November 10, 1853, in his eighty-ninth year; and Margaret, his wife, died at 74, on April 27th of the same year. Both were life-long, loyal and faithful members of the Lutheran Church, and were buried at Eshcol.

Henry Flickinger early in life formed the habit of reading useful books, and had a well-stored memory. He supplied his home, in that early day in which he lived, with a library that included some excellent works on history, biography, natural history, a German Bible, and Scott's complete commentary on the Bible. In his effort to surround his home and family with the best moral and religious influences, he was heartily seconded by his noble wife.

It is interesting to note the remarkable result. They raised a family of fourteen children. All of these growing to manhood and womanhood, became active members and highly esteemed workers in the Lutheran, Reformed, Methodist, and Presbyterian Churches. Such a beautiful record of the beneficent influence of moral and religious training in the home, in point of numbers and widely extended influence, has not likely been surpassed by many Pennsylvania families.

Large families and long lives are two other noteworthy characteristics of Henry and wife, their children and grandchildren. Their large families and great ages indicate an inheritance of physical vigor, that presages a lifelong period of usefulness.

The children of Henry and Margaret Yohn Flickinger married and located as follows:

1. Peter md. Margaret Ritter, lived in Perry Co.
2. Mary M. md. William Shreffler, lived at Peoria, Ill.
3. Bandina md. Henry Long, lived in Perry Co.
4. John md. Elizabeth Bixler, lived in Perry Co.
5. Nicholas md. Rebecca Rice, lived in Ohio.

6. David md. Rebecca Bousum, lived in Perry Co.
7. Elizabeth md. Jacob Reisinger, lived in Perry Co.
8. Margaret md. Erasmus Yocum, lived in Huntingdon Co.
9. Henry md. Elizabeth Reisinger, and later Betsy Paden, lived in Perry Co.
10. Isaac md. Mary Blain, lived in Juniata Co.
11. Daniel W. md. Julia Ann Saylor, lived in Juniata Co.
12. Lydia Ann md. Jeremiah Fuller, lived in Perry Co.
13. Joseph md. Nancy Campbell, lived in Perry Co.
14. George md. Susan Jacobs, lived in Perry Co.

Public service has been rendered by this family as follows: John Flickinger served three years as a director of the poor of Perry County, superintended the erection of the county almshouse, and was an honored official of the Methodist Church. Dr. Junius R., his son, served a term as county superintendent, two terms in state legislatures—one in each of two different states, and fifteen years as principal of two state teachers' institutions. Major Daniel W. Flickinger, enlisting at Ickesburg with three other brothers, as a member of the Green Mountain Riflemen, was soon promoted and served several years as a major for training the militia of Perry County. Later he served three years as a commissioner in Juniata County. Rev. Robert E., his son, became a Presbyterian minister and author of several historical books. Joseph Flickinger served three years as a director of the Perry County Almshouse, and Levi Hiram, his son, served three years as auditor, and four years as treasurer of Perry County. Prof. H. W. Flickinger, a son of Peter, in recognition of his genius and skill as a pen artist and lifelong service as an instructor, has been accorded the honor of being one of the best and most popular penmen of this country.

Lemuel E. McGinnes, Supt. Steelton Schools.

The schools of Steelton, Pennsylvania, have for several decades stood at the top in educational circles. They were largely made so through the planning and supervision of Lemuel E. McGinnes, whose life was dedicated to the training and instruction of the rising generations. He descended from a line of Scotch-Irish ancestry. James McGinnes, his paternal grandfather, came to America from the north of Ireland, in 1790, settling in Greenwood Township—in the part which is now Buffalo Township. His maternal great-great-grandfather was John Ditty, who settled in Lykens Valley, three miles northeast of Millersburg, in 1770. His father was John Cochran McGinnes, a native of Perry County, born in 1812. His vocation was that of a teacher. He died in 1887. His mother was Sarah Ann Ditty, born in 1828, and who died in 1910.

Lemuel E. McGinnes was born in Buck's Valley, Buffalo Township, May 15, 1853. His early life was like that of the average farmer's son, attending the public schools while they were in session and helping on the farm at other times. He early decided to follow the teaching profession, and enrolled at the summer normal school of Silas Wright at Millerstown, and from that early tutor drew much inspiration. He began teaching in 1872, and taught

1919. In 1918 he was appointed on the State Board of Education by Governor Martin G. Brumbaugh, himself a noted educator. As an instructor at teachers' institutes, L. E. McGinnes was a noted figure, and appeared in more than half of the counties of Pennsylvania, and in the states of Delaware and Indiana.

Mr. McGinnes was backed by all the larger interests of Steelton, including the Pennsylvania Steel Works, whose interest in education was marked. On three occasions, to the writer's knowledge, he turned down proffered positions elsewhere—the superintendency of the New Brunswick (N. J.) schools, in 1919; the principalship of the Millersville State Normal School, in 1912, and the position of Deputy Supt. of Public Instruction of Pennsylvania, in 1918.

It was the writer's privilege to know Mr. McGinnes since his early boyhood, our fathers' farms being within a half-mile of each other, and in all that territory of Perry County lying between the rivers he was held up as an example to the rising generation, and it is still so. Largely through his kindly encouragement at the very beginning of the undertaking, has the writing and compiling of this book been possible.

At a meeting of the Pennsylvania Educational Association, in Philadelphia, December 31, 1919, a memorial to Mr. McGinnes was read by Mr. Chas. S. Davis, a former president of the association. For thirty-six years Mr. Davis was associated with Mr. McGinnes, first as a teacher, and for thirty-one years as high school principal, a record of association in school work probably unparalleled in the state. Dr. J. P. McCaskey, a long-time friend of these two men, says, in the *Pennsylvania School Journal:* "Mr. Chas. S. Davis is elected to succeed Mr. McGinnes. They were close personal friends, and the tribute of Mr. Davis to Mr. McGinnes was worthy of the men and the occasion." Mr. Davis said in part:

"Born in Buck's Valley, Perry County, May 15, 1853, educated in the rural schools, Juniata Valley Normal School (at Millerstown), and later at the University of Pennsylvania, but most largely by studious habits, by attentive listening, and by close observation. A diary covering forty years contains an outline or brief résumé of every important lecture or address he ever heard, mention of every prominent person he ever met, and descriptions of places visited, together with many of his thoughts and ideals and inspirations.

"In the Pennsylvania State Educational Association he served as vice-president in 1894, president of the Department of City and Borough Superintendents in 1897, and president of the association in 1906. As a trustee of the Bloomsburg State Normal School and as a member of the State Board of Education he won a high place because of his grasp of the situations and because of his realization of what was needed to improve conditions and to place the cause of education on a higher plane. His power of initiative was one of his strongest characteristics. His attitude was essentially constructive."

From an editorial in the *Harrisburg Telegraph* the following tribute is taken:

"The public schools of Pennsylvania lose a great champion in the death of Prof. L. E. McGinnes. While his success in conducting the schools of Steelton marked him as a superintendent of more than ordinary ability, his reputation as an educator was not confined to his home town. As member of the State Board of Education he was a great factor in the development of the educational system of the state along modern and efficient lines, and as president of the Pennsylvania State Educational Association he became known the country over as a deep thinker and tireless worker in the great work of lifting the public schools of the nation to new and higher planes of usefulness. A lover of children, an executive of high type, an able teacher, and a staunch believer in the principles of Americanism and the future of the country, he was a mighty force for good not only in his home community but wherever his powerful personality made itself felt. His place will not be easily filled."

The Harrisburg *Patriot's* editorial columns contained this tribute among other things:

"Prof. L. E. McGinnes' death is one of those which shock and sadden a community. Though a resident of Steelton for many years, he was accepted by Harrisburgers as one of their own upstanding men, worthy of the honors and esteem that his fellow citizens gave him.

"For many years the excellence of the Steelton public school system has long been acknowledged. It was much ahead of districts of like size. Its graduates disclosed an educational finish that did not rub off readily. In colleges, where so many of them were inspired to go, these high school alumni were ever creditable to the teaching force and the system which produced them. For much of this Superintendent McGinnes was responsible. As educator, churchman, public-spirited citizen, he contributed much to his community, a rare product of the life of this part of Pennsylvania of which this city is the hub. Perry Countians can be proud of his nativity as Harrisburg and Steelton are proud of his residence. His going away seemed much too soon."

The Harrisburg *Evening News* said editorially:

"Only a man who deserved it could have had funeral honors as were paid Prof. L. E. McGinnes yesterday at his home in Steelton. Prof. McGinnes' personality and achievement had become such a part of Steelton that his death seemed to affect the life of the borough and the entire community,—a community, too, that extended in this case to Harrisburg and beyond.

"Upon the countenance of those who mourned at the bier yesterday or followed the cortege to the cemetery there was written the lines of deep-seated grief, personal and communal. It was a real honor paid to a man who richly deserved it, who gave so much of his life to community betterment and whose departure will long be regretted."

Early in his life Mr. McGinnes united with the Presbyterian Church at Duncannon and served as the superintendent of the Sunday school for several years. In the Steelton Presbyterian Church he was a ruling elder from the time of its organization, and was the first and only superintendent of the Sunday school in the thirty-seven years of its existence prior to his death. He was selected as commissioner from the Presbytery of Carlisle to the

Synod of Pennsylvania and West Virginia at a meeting held in Erie, in October, 1899, and to the Synod of Pennsylvania at the meeting at Beaver, in October, 1918. He served as commissioner from the Carlisle Presbytery to the meeting of the General Assembly of the Presbyterian Church, at Atlantic City, in 1916. He once served as moderator of Carlisle Presbytery.

Mr. McGinnes was married to Miss Ida Wilson, of Perry County, in 1879, and to them one child, Miss Sarah Ellen McGinnes, was born. His wife and Miss McGinnes, who is a member of the faculty of the Steelton High School, survive.

William Nelson Ehrhart, Educator and Supt. of Schools.

William Nelson Ehrhart, A.M., Ph.D., was born near Newport, Perry County, February 15, 1848, his parents being John and Eleonora (Super) Ehrhart, of whose family a son and four daughters are living. He secured his elementary education in the neighboring public school and completed the course of study at the Juniata Valley Academy. He was a member of the first graduating class of the Bloomsburg State Normal School, later taking the Scientific course and graduating from the Millersville State Normal School. Upon completing the prescribed four years' course of study, Taylor University, at Indianapolis, conferred upon him the A.M. and Ph.D. degrees.

Almost his whole professional life was spent in Schuylkill County, where he had endeared himself to the people and was so successful that his reputation stands second to none among educators in that populous county. His first position there was as principal of the Llewellyn schools for two years, followed by nine years as principal of the High School at Tamaqua. His work there attracted attention by reason of its marked efficiency, and he was elected principal of the High School at Shenandoah in 1884, where he raised the school's standard to first-class. Nine years later, in 1893, he resigned and removed to Pottsville to enter business, but his mind was ever turned toward the schoolroom, and in 1895 he accepted the principalship of the Mahanoy City High School, and a year later was made superintendent of schools of Mahanoy City, a position which he filled with credit for eighteen years, or until within a year of his death, when illness required that he relinquish the position. So highly was he esteemed that to-day there hangs in the High School at Mahanoy City a painting of him by a celebrated artist—bearing the inscription, "From the City Teachers. Prof. W. N. Ehrhart, 1895-1914."

Prof. Ehrhart was one of the best mathematicians of eastern Pennsylvania. Much of the success of the libraries at both Shenandoah and Mahanoy City is due to his labor. He was a leader of the Schuylkill County Educational Association from its incep-

emy. It has been said that the training of a newspaper office is tantamount to a liberal education, and this was a further supplement, for Edward Hackett learned the printing trade in the office of the *Perry County Democrat.* Upon finishing his trade he was employed in the newspaper offices of Philadelphia, Pittsburgh and other eastern cities. At the age of twenty-three he located at Bluffton, Indiana, where he purchased a half interest in the *Bluffton Banner,* becoming sole owner in a short time. In 1880, seeking a larger field, Mr. Hackett purchased the plant and business of the *Fort Wayne Sentinel,* moving to that place. Here he found adequate scope for his genius, and the *Fort Wayne Sentinel,* under his editorship, became one of the most prosperous and influential dailies in the State of Indiana. Here he also started the *American Farmer,* which for several years was printed in the *Sentinel* office, and later sold to a big publishing company. For a number of years he was also the owner of the *Indianapolis Sentinel,* which reached its greatest success under his control. During his life he was one of the most prominent and influential figures in Indiana journalism. He was dominated with an exalted integrity of purpose and high ideals which make for enlightened and useful citizenship.

As a young man Mr. Hackett was wed to Miss Mary A. Melsheimer, of Bluffton, Indiana, who died in 1898. Of their children the first born died in infancy; the second, Martha, is a talented physician and surgeon, and has charge of the hospital founded by her father at Canton, China; and Helen, the youngest, is the wife of John C. Johnson, of Los Angeles, California. Mr. Hackett was married a second time, on October 16, 1900, to Miss Susie Emma Reed. To this union were born three children, Catherine Reed, Edward A. K., Jr., and Wayne. Mr. Hackett died August 28, 1916.

Some years prior to his death Mr. Hackett established the Hackett Medical College at Canton, China, placing his eldest daughter, Dr. Martha Hackett, in charge. Mr. Hackett was earnest in the support of all moral agencies, including the cause of temperance, and was actively identified with the Winona Assembly and Summer Schools Association, at Winona Lake, Indiana. He was an earnest member of the First Presbyterian Church at Fort Wayne, and superintendent of the Sunday school for years. He also was one of the founders of the Fort Wayne Mission, the Y. M. C. A., and the Y. W. C. A., to all of which he gave liberally. Sincere, honest, enthusiastic, with strong moral views, Edward A. K. Hackett's name will long leave its impress in his adopted state.

THEODORE K. LONG, FOUNDER OF CARSON LONG INSTITUTE.

That a Perry Countian should come back after having made a success elsewhere and assume the task of rebuilding an academy which he had attended in boyhood, but which seemed to be drifting,

Jr., the author states that the Longs are of French origin, while in several later publications the authors invariably give the ancestry as German. It is altogether probable that all these accounts are reconcilable and correct. During the early religious wars in Europe it was not uncommon for families to migrate from one country to another. The Longs were devout Protestants and they doubtless felt it greatly to their advantage to move from time to time as governmental conditions changed from Protestant to Roman Catholic, or vice versa. When the Longs came to America they were Lutherans, and when the United Brethren Church was organized later in Lancaster County, they were among its most enthusiastic supporters. David Long was educated for the U. B. ministry, and though he devoted most of his time to farming, he frequently officiated in the pulpit of the United Brethren Church. When he came to Pfoutz Valley (then in Cumberland County) he moved his family, his household goods, farming implements and money chests containing the purchase money for his new home in silver dollars, all in three Conestoga wagons, each wagon drawn by four horses. The caravan moved up along the west bank of the Juniata River to a point about two miles above Newport, immediately opposite what is known as the Patterson farm, where the river was forded and the wagons then followed up along the east bank of the river until they came to the Cocolamus Creek. Here they bore off to the right and crossed Wildcat Ridge into Pfoutz Valley. At that time there were no bridges across the Juniata or the Cocolamus and there was no road leading from Millerstown to Pfoutz Valley.

Theodore Kepner Long was born on the old farm acquired in 1814 by David Long, and his early life was much like that of the average farm boy. He attended the local schools, the Millerstown High School, and the Juniata Valley Normal School (Prof. Wright's) at Millerstown. He also attended the New Bloomfield Academy and the State Normal School at Millersville, after which he specialized at Yale and was graduated from the Law Department in 1878. He was admitted to the bars of Dauphin and Perry Counties in 1878, but located in Mandan, North Dakota, where he edited the *Mandan Daily Pioneer* in 1882. In 1883 he compiled Long's Legislative Handbook of Dakota. In 1884 he began the practice of law, and in 1885 was made territorial district attorney for the district west of the Missouri River, in North Dakota. In 1849 he settled in Chicago. He was the attorney for the Illinois Life Insurance Company at its formation in 1899, and continued to act as its general counsel until 1908. He assisted at the organization of the Western Trust and Savings Bank in 1903, and was the bank's attorney until 1908. He retired from active law practice in 1908 and later was elected alderman of the Sixth Ward of Chicago, serving from 1909 to 1915.

As alderman Mr. Long originated measures in the city council for the reclamation of the shores of Lake Michigan for a city park and bathing beach and general playground purposes, which remain a benefaction to the public forever. He was the originator of Chicago's lighting system which utilizes the electric energy of the Sanitary District and Drainage Canal to supply light for the city. He also planned the general scheme for the location and development of Chicago's bathing beaches along the lake shore.

Mr. Long was united in marriage to Miss Kate Carson, at Eau Claire, Wisconsin, November 25, 1885.

During a vacation in 1914 Mr. Long came East, with a view of gratifying a lifetime desire of giving some benefaction to his native county, and while summering at Millerstown he drove to New Bloomfield to look over old-time scenes. His attention was drawn to what he terms the "shabby" appearance of the old academy and surroundings, and there, in his mind was born the Carson Long Institute, a change of name which he made in memory of a beloved son, drowned in the prime of his young manhood. He bought the academy grounds, and what he has since done is best told in the chapter in this book entitled "Carson Long Institute, Formerly New Bloomfield Academy."

The reader is referred to the sketch relating to Chester I. Long, former United States Senator from Kansas, as David Long was their common ancestor.

JUDGE HUGH HART CUMMINS.

Hugh Hart Cummins was born at Liverpool, May 25, 1841, the son of Dr. William and Mary (Hart) Cummins. Dr. Cummins, the father, a graduate of Jefferson Medical College, had located at Liverpool about 1830 for the practice of his profession, remaining there until his death in 1846. Hugh Hart, after attending the public schools, taught before his arrival at voting age. He attended York Commercial College, and in 1862 located at Williamsport, and entered the law offices of George White, an able attorney, as a student. While studying, he supported himself by clerical work in the county offices. He was admitted to the bar in 1864. From the very beginning he was noted for his high moral courage. Politically he was a Democrat, yet he received the nomination for Judge of the Courts of Lycoming County by a coalition of the Republicans and the independent Democrats in 1878, who believed that the judicial election should be non-partisan. He was elected, and began his term January 6, 1879, serving the entire term of ten years. On leaving the bench, he resumed the practice of law. When the great flood of 1889 swept Williamsport, the receding of the waters marked Judge Cummins' entry in the work of relief for the sufferers. This attracted the attention of Governor Beaver, and he was named one of a commission of nine prominent business and professional men to superintend the distribution of relief funds to the suffering Johnstown flood victims. The commission chose him chairman, and he at once located at Johnstown to carry out the relief work, but fell ill with diabetes and died August 11, 1889, at the Cresson Springs Hotel, where he had been removed during his illness. He is said to have been one of the most able judges of the Lycoming County courts.

According to the best records obtainable Judge Cummins was the first Perry Countian to take a business college course.

SHERIDAN E. FRY, JUDGE OF THE MUNICIPAL COURT, CHICAGO.

In that great metropolis of the West, enterprising and ever growing Chicago, another Perry Countian is to be found, a judge of the Municipal Court of Chicago. That man is Sheridan E. Fry, born at Donnally's Mills, February 25, 1867, his birthplace being near the place known as "Peace Union." His father was John M. Fry, born June 3, 1840, near New Bloomfield, the son of Abraham and Statira (Marshall) Fry, and his mother was Eliza Agnes Bucher, who was born in Adams County, but moved with her family during her early girlhood to Donnally's Mills, where her father followed his trade as a miller. His parents, John M. Fry and Eliza Agnes Bucher were married at New Bloomfield, May 16, 1866, and lived together to celebrate their golden wedding. Mrs. Fry died November 20, 1917, at Seward, Winnebago County, Illinois, where Mr. Fry still resides, though past eighty. He enlisted in the U. S. Army at Newport, September 16, 1862, and was mustered out June 16, 1865, having been engaged in thirty-four actions, among them Chancellorsville and Gettysburg. After the war he taught school in Perry County. In 1881, with his family he moved to Winnebago County, Illinois, and it was thus that the future Judge Fry became a citizen of Illinois. Their six children are Sheridan E., Chicago; Emory C., Sioux City, Iowa; George H., Mrs. Samuel Cuthbertson, and John A., of Seward, Illinois.

During his residence in Perry County Judge Fry was an attendant of the schools of Tuscarora Township, and in Illinois he worked upon the farm during the summer and attended the schools during the winter. He later attended the Illinois Normal School at Dixon, Illinois, and Wheaton College, at Wheaton, Illinois. In 1895 he graduated from the Northwestern University Law School of Chicago, with the degree of Bachelor of Laws. He was admitted to practice in the courts of Illinois during the same month, and later in the United States courts.

He practiced law for ten years and was then appointed by Judge Carter, of Cook County, as his assistant. Judge Carter was later elected to the Supreme Court of Illinois, and Judge Fry continued

County about 1760, and in warranting the farm which became the
birthplace of David Watts, they built a cabin and moved there—
to the very verge of civilization. Owing to the father's absence
as an officer in the patriot army and later as a member of the
Executive Council the training of the boy largely devolved upon
the mother, a gifted and educated woman. He was the first person
born within the limits of what is now Perry County to graduate
from a college—Dickinson College, founded in 1783, where he was
educated and graduated with the first class.

Entering the law offices of William Lewis, of Philadelphia, he
read law and was admitted to the bar, beginning practice at Carlisle, where he soon had a large patronage. He joined the troops
to suppress the "Whiskey Insurrection," four thousand of which
were reviewed by General Washington at Carlisle (then the county
seat of Perry County territory), in 1794. His courage and energy
soon placed him at the head of the Cumberland County bar, the
acknowledged equal of Thomas Duncan, for years the recognized
leader of the profession. They were men of extensive and varied
acquirements in professional and general literature, being distinguished for learning, integrity and manners. He died September
25, 1819, in the midst of a mature life, his death being hastened
by exposure while traveling over the legal circuit on horseback, the
mode of travel of the period. A printed volume of his arguments
is included in the State Reports of Pennsylvania.

In September, 1796, he was united in marriage to Julia Anna
Miller, and was the father of twelve children. The family was
reared in the faith of the parents, that of the Episcopal Church.

An anecdote connected with the early courts at Carlisle, in which
figured Thomas Duncan, later a justice of the Supreme Court, and
David Watts, the leaders of the bar, follows:

At court Mr. Duncan was distinguished by quickness, acute dis-
cernment, accurate knowledge, and every-ready repartee. His
rival was David Watts, bright, gifted and well read. Mr. Watts
was a large man, of athletic proportions, while Mr. Duncan was
of small stature and light weight. During a discussion of a legal
question in court Mr. Watts, in the heat of the argument, made a
personal allusion to Mr. Duncan's small stature, and said he "could
put him in his pocket." "Very well," retorted Mr. Duncan, "then
you will have more law in your pocket than you have in your
head."

REV. AND MRS. JOHN ROGERS PEALE, MARTYRED MISSIONARIES.

Martyrs to the cause of Christianity, being slain in far-away
China, the names of John Rogers Peale and Mrs. Peale are held
in veneration not only by their own county and their own denomination—the Presbyterian—but by a far wider zone. They were

mob burned the school building, the hospital, and the residence of the minister. The horrible affair happened at Lien Chow, China, a city of twenty thousand inhabitants, about two hundred miles inland from Canton. John Rogers Peale was from his early years a member of the New Bloomfield Presbyterian Church, and his education and preparation for the mission field lacked nothing.

On the walls of the New Bloomfield Presbyterian Church, in which he was nurtured, there was placed a handsome bronze tablet in 1906, on which is the inscription:

In Loving Memory of
Rev. and Mrs. John Rogers Peale,
Who Were Martyred at Lien Chow, China,
October 28, 1905.

"I am ready not to be bound only, but also to die
at Jerusalem for the name of the Lord Jesus."

Rev. John Kistler and Catharine McCoy Kistler, Pioneer Missionaries.

Although Rev. Morris Officer had founded the Muhlenberg Mission, the first one in Liberia, on the west coast of Africa, Rev. John Kistler was the first active missionary in that field, sailing late in May, 1863, and serving there until March, 1867, when, broken in health, he returned to his native land. He had married Catharine McCoy, of Duncannon, who succumbed September 20, 1866, to the then dreaded African fever, and her remains were laid to rest, the first in the mission cemetery in that far-off land. Catharine McCoy was born in Penn Township, and was nurtured in the Duncannon Presbyterian Church. She was the daughter of David and Mary McCoy. Rev. Kistler was a Perry Countian, the son of John and Salome (Tressler) Kistler, of near Loysville, where he was born November 12, 1834. He attended the Loysville school and the Loysville Academy, and later the old Markelville Academy, then conducted by his uncle, Rev. George Rea, a Presbyterian clergyman. In 1859 he completed the work of both the freshman and sophomore years at Gettysburg College. In 1860 he matriculated at the Susquehanna Missionary Institute, now Susquehanna University, at Selinsgrove, Pennsylvania, from which he graduated in 1862, as the valedictorian of his class. He was licensed to preach and ordained by the Central Pennsylvania Synod, which met at Newport in May, 1863, after which he sailed as a missionary as stated, the journey consuming seventy-eight days on the ocean. On his return from the mission field, he became superintendent of the Soldiers' Orphans' Home at Loysville, in September, 1867, remaining for two years. In 1869 he became pastor of the Water Street Lutheran Church in Huntingdon County, remaining for eight years. In the meantime he organized the First English Lutheran Church of Tyrone, Pennsylvania, the pastorate of which, in connection with the Sinking Valley Lutheran Church, he also served for six years. During those years he organized the Lutheran Church at Bellwood, Pennsylvania. In November, 1877, he became pastor of the Upper Strasburg Church in Franklin County, which he served for six and a half years while living at Orrstown. In 1844 he became pastor of the Lower Frankford charge, in Cumberland County, with headquarters at Carlisle, but at the end of three years, owing to asthmatic troubles contracted in Africa, he relinquished his work in the pulpit and devoted his time to the sale and distribution of Bibles. This work brought him much to the new and developing town of Riverton, now Lemoyne, in lower Cumberland County, and he organized the Lutheran Church there in 1895, and became its pastor, building a comfortable brick chapel, but at the expiration of three years again relinquished pastoral work, owing to a return of the same trouble. After that he did periodical work for the different conferences and synods of his church.

The writer enjoyed his acquaintance and knew him to be a man of strong convictions and unswerving faith, a pioneer in the temperance cause. He died at Carlisle, where he resided, September 2, 1910, being survived by his second wife, who was Sarah Swoyer, of Newville, and their three children., Mrs. Glenn V. Brown, Freda and Charles Reuel; also Harry L., a son by the first marriage.

EMMA MARGARET SMILEY, MISSIONARY.

Emma Margaret Smiley, daughter of Wilson and Sarah (Henderson) Smiley, was born at Shermansdale, on November 25, 1861. She was educated in the local schools, the McCaskey Select School at Shermansdale, and at the New Bloomfield Academy, followed by a course at the International University at Lebanon, Ohio, where she graduated in the scientific course, getting her B.A. degree. She was one of Perry County's efficient teachers of a period which had an unusual number of good teachers. She taught eleven terms. In 1892 an opening to enter the missionary field appeared. To prepare for that work, the following year she attended the school of the Christian and Mission Alliance in New York City (now located at Nyack, New York), under whose auspices she entered the missionary field. She sailed September 8, 1894, arriving at Bombay, India, six weeks later. She mastered the language in about two years and was stationed at Kaira, Guzerat, India. In 1897 a famine in other provinces of India caused many of the almost starved children to go to Kaira, where Miss Smiley was in charge of the mission. Their swollen abdomens, emaciated faces and listless demeanor were sad to behold. Originally the orphanage had but a few children, but this famine increased the population to over four hundred. During a famine in 1900 Miss Smiley's health broke down and she was granted a furlough, but the eve before her intended departure for the States she was stricken with cerebral hemorrhage and a few hours later, on June 12th, she passed to her reward. Her body was interred in the cemetery at Bombay, India, where a marker shows her grave. Emma Margaret Smiley's life was not in vain, for there is record that many of those poor, starved children have become Christian men and women.

Rev. John Linn Milligan.

No other American served as chaplain of such a pretentious penal institution as the Western penitentiary at Pittsburgh for such a long period—forty years—as did Rev. John Linn Milligan, native Perry Countian, named after that famous pioneer divine, Rev. John Linn, his ancestor. No other left his impress on such a long line of unfortunates as they again faced the world to begin life anew, or as they silently passed to eternity from prison cells.

John Linn Milligan was the first-born of James and Eleanor (Linn) Milligan, having been born in Ickesburg, July 31, 1837. He was educated in the local schools, the academies at New Bloomfield and Tuscarora (Juniata County), Washington College and Princeton Theological Seminary, graduating from the college in 1860 and from the seminary in 1863. In 1861 the famous Christian Commission, which did such heroic and excellent work during the War between the States, was appointed, and the second name on the Commission was that of John Linn Milligan. It was an organization formed at the call of the Young Men's Christian Association, of New York City, for the purpose of looking after the spiritual and temporal welfare of Union soldiers. Thousands of ministers and the most active laymen of the North worked personally under its direction, on the battlefield, on the march, and in camp and hospital.

Just home from graduation at the seminary, when Lee's army came north and when troops were rapidly being raised to meet the emergency, he enlisted in Company I of the 36th Regiment Penna. Volunteers, and was made captain of his company on July 10, 1863. Soon after the expiration of this three-month term of service, in November, 1863, he was appointed chaplain of the 140th Pennsylvania Volunteers, with which he remained until the war's end, being mustered out May 31, 1865. He came home with his faithful saddle horse, "Appomattox." On many a battlefield he aided the wounded and dying, while exposed to shot and shell. Soon after being mustered out he became pastor of the First Presbyterian Church at Horicon, Wisconsin, where he remained until February 3, 1869, when he was appointed chaplain of the Western penitentiary of Pennsylvania, located at Allegheny City, now a

part of Pittsburgh. He continued there until June, 1909, when he
was made chaplain emeritus, owing to his incapacity to fill the
duties on account of ill health.

The National Prison Association was organized in 1870, and
Mr. Milligan was a charter member and the secretary for eighteen
years. In 1908 he was its president. He was a charter member of
the Allegheny Prison Society and, after the death of the late Wil-.
liam Thaw, was its president until his death. He was six times the
representative of the United States government at the International Prison Congress, having attended the sessions at London,
Stockholm, Paris, St. Petersburg, Rome and Budapest. He was
stated clerk of the Allegheny Presbytery for thirty-seven years
and, upon its consolidation with the Pittsburgh Presbytery in 1906,
was elected its first moderator. The Presbytery presented him a
handsome loving cup, bearing the names of all its ministers and
their churches. His name will ever stand. foremost—the most
aggressive advocate of prison reform in the United States, and a
pioneer along more humane lines of punishment. Much of his
time was spent in inducing those who had led clean lives to take
an interest in those who had fallen by the way.

He will be remembered as the brother of the late Thomas H.
Milligan, who so long conducted a hardware business at Newport.
He died, aged 72 years, on July 12, 1909, at the home of Mrs. J.
H. Irwin, a sister, at Newport, from the result of an apoplectic
stroke, received in his pulpit at the penitentiary on Sunday, January 17, 1909. Mrs. H. O. Orris, another sister, also resides at
Newport. Among the tributes at his graveside was a wreath of
galix leaves, palms and carnations from the prisoners of the Western penitentiary, whom he loved and who loved him—in itself a
mighty sermon.

Rev. James Linn, D.D.

In the Presbyterian Church at Bellefonte, Pennsylvania, a grateful congregation has erected to the memory of a native Perry
Countian, long their faithful pastor, a tablet bearing this inscription :

In Memory of
Rev. James Linn, D.D.,
58 Years Pastor of this Church,
Born September 4, 1783.
Died February 23, 1868.
Faithful—Wise—Meek—Patient
Pure—Devout.

Rev. James Linn, son of Rev. John Linn, pioneer pastor of
Centre Church, in Perry County, and Mary (Gettys) Linn, was
born September 4, 1783. Of all the many ministers born within
the limits of what is now Perry County he occupies a distinctive

place, for during the fifty-eight years of his ministry he was the pastor of but one charge, the longest pastorate of any. James Linn attended the subscription schools of the period, and had the advantage of instruction in the home. He entered Dickinson College and graduated in the class of 1805. He then began the study of theology with Rev. Williams, of Newville, and on September 27, 1808, was licensed to preach by the Carlisle Presbytery. In later years he spoke of the membership of Carlisle Presbytery as "a noble band of venerable men, and men of talents." In the spring of 1809 he was sent to Spruce Creek and Sinking Valley as a supply for a few times, and then to Bellefonte, which had just become vacant. Lick Run was attached to the Bellefonte appointment. He filled in as a supply for but a few Sundays, when the two churches gave him a call, each to have half of his services and each to pay half his salary. He was released from Lick Run in 1839, as the Bellefonte church had grown from a membership of fifty to five times that number. When he went there the meetings were held in the courthouse, as there was no church, and there he was ordained. During the early years of his ministry he taught in the Bellefonte Academy, and for many years thereafter was president of its board of trustees. In 1859 the congregation celebrated the fiftieth anniversary of his pastorate, and two years later it was noticed that his strength was failing, but his people refused to give him up, and secured an assistant pastor for him. He passed away February 23, 1868. As his strength failed him he dwelt much among the earlier scenes in what is now Perry County and longed for a drink "from the old spring by his father's church" at Centre.

He was twice married. One of his children was Judge Samuel Linn, born February 20, 1820, and elected president judge of the Centre-Clearfield-Clinton District in 1859. Rev. Linn was given the D.D. degree by Dickinson. He was a man of strong individuality and sound judgment, with a rare vein of humor and a cheerful disposition.

REV. THOMAS CREIGH, D.D.

Elsewhere in this book appears the statement that Dr. John Creigh, a practicing physician of Landisburg from 1799 to 1819, moved from that town to Carlisle to educate his children. Rev. Thomas Creigh was one of the children, and was born in Landisburg, September 9, 1808, his mother having been Eleanor (Dunbar) Creigh. The family were of German origin, and the name signifies war or warrior. The ancestry had left Germany during the reign of James I and settled in Ireland. John Creigh, the first of the clan in America, settled in Cumberland County and was one of the delegates from Cumberland County to the historic meeting in Carpenter's Hall in Philadelphia, from June 18, 1776, to June

25, 1776, which unanimously declared that the Province of Pennsylvania was from thenceforth a free and independent colony.

Thomas was the seventh child of a family of six sons and four daughters, two others being the noted John D. Creigh, of California, and Dr. Alfred Creigh, of Washington, Pennsylvania. Landisburg at that time having no Presbyterian church the family worshiped at Centre Church. The first eleven years of his life were spent in Landisburg, a quiet, sober-minded youth, with a gentle, reserved, serious disposition which adhered to him throughout life. He graduated from Dickinson College in 1828. During his college course he was greatly perplexed over the matter of personal salvation, but with its completion joined the Presbyterian Church. He had kept a diary, and in it had promised that if God made him a child of His grace he would consecrate himself to His service. Accordingly, he read under Rev. George Duffield, D.D., and spent two years at Princeton Theological Seminary. On April 12, 1831, he was licensed to preach. He was unanimously called to succeed Rev. David Elliot, another Perry Countian, as pastor of the Upper West Conococheague Church at Mercersburg, and was installed November 17, 1831, being then in but his twenty-third year. This church, then one hundred and six years old, had but four regularly ordained ministers during that time. For forty-eight and one-half years he was the messenger of God unto that people, being their pastor at his death, April 21, 1880. Within four months after, his installation one hundred and seven persons had united with the church on profession of faith. He was a man of fine proportions, of the ordinary stature. He was affable, courteous, dignified and unassuming. His preaching was evangelical, orthodox and scriptural; a man of strong faith, much given to prayer and noted for habitual prudence and the purity of his life. He is spoken of "as the Apostle John in the good fellowship of the Presbytery."

He was twice married, his first wife having been Miss Anna Hunter Jacobs, of Churchtown, Lancaster County, and the second, Miss Jane McClelland Grubb, of Mercersburg. Lafayette College honored him with the degree of Doctor of Divinity in 1853.

DAVID ELLIOT, D.D., LL.D.

In the chapters relating to Saville Township and in the narrative of Robert Robinson mention is made of an Elliot family, one of whose descendants became a divine of note and for long years held a professorship in the Theological Seminary at Allegheny City. David Elliot was born near what is now Ickesburg, on February 6, 1787, on what later was the Boden farm. When sixteen years old he began attending a classical school in Tuscarora Valley conducted by Rev. John Coulter. In 1804 he transferred to a classical school at Mifflintown, staying with Rev. Matthew Brown, where he finished his Greek and Latin. In 1805 he became a junior instructor in Washington College, through the intercession of Rev. Brown, who had resigned his pastorate to become a professor in the same institution and who later became its president. In 1806 he matriculated as a student of Dickinson College and graduated in 1808. In 1811 he was licensed to preach by the Presbytery at Carlisle, and in 1812 received a call to the Upper West Conococheague Church at Mercersburg, where he remained until 1829. He was then called to Washington, Pennsylvania, where he was pastor until 1836. Washington College had been for years almost dormant, and to Rev. Elliot is due principally its rehabilitation: In 1835 the degree of D.D. was conferred on him by Jefferson College at Canonsburg, and in 1847 the degree of LL.D., by Washington College. In 1836, at the call of the General Assembly of the Presbyterian Church, he accepted a professorship at the Western Theological Seminary at Allegheny City, where he remained for thirty-four years, until 1870. He was then elected a professor emeritus, serving until his death in 1874.

At a most trying time in 1838 he was moderator of the General Assembly of the Presbyterian Church. Dr. J. I. Brownson, in an address on his life, mentions the opinion of Chief Justice John Bannister Gibson (another Perry Countian) in connection with litigation which reached the Supreme Court. It follows:

"Never did a Presbyterian moderator occupy the chair in so momentous and trying a crisis. Yet there he sat, calm above the tumult, meeting each emergency with instant decision, and yet with an accuracy which, in every instance, received the sanction of the Supreme Court of Pennsylvania, as expressed in the opinion rendered by one of the ablest judges of this or any other state,—the late Chief Justice John Bannister Gibson.

"That eminent jurist, after a most exhaustive review of the proceedings, —of which the moderator's decisions were often the most vital,—as well as the pleadings, arguments of counsel and the adverse judgments of the Court of Nisi Prius, vindicated each of these decisions separately, as well as all of them conjointly.

"It was just after this searching review that the distinguished chief justice is reported to have said, in conversation with a gentleman of the bar, that Pennsylvania had only missed having the best lawyer in the state, in the person of Dr. Elliot, by his becoming a minister of the gospel."

His father was Thomas Elliot, who at the close of the French and Indian War had settled on 400 acres of land in the vicinity of Ickesburg, the prior right of which he purchased for $800. He was one of five children, three being sons, of a second marriage. His was a case where the qualities of a religious and pious father and mother were transmitted to a son, his mother having taught him his prayers, his catechetical lesson, and his secular lessons almost as soon as he could talk. When he became six he went to such local schools as were available and where the books in use were Dillworth's spelling book, the Bible, and Gough's arithmetic. After graduating in 1808 his pastor, Rev. John Linn, became his preceptor in theology for two years. His third and last year was with Rev. Joshua Williams, D.D., of Newville. He was married May 14, 1812, to Ann, daughter of Edward West, then a resident of Landisburg.

Not the least of his works was the organization of the Franklin County Bible Society in 1815, which was one of the societies which a year later organized the American Bible Society in New York City.

Dr. Elliot is recognized as having been one of the leading theologians of the nation. To him, more than to any other, is due the credit of the success of the Western Theological Seminary, at Allegheny City, now a part of Pittsburgh. Almost a thousand men went forth, during his incumbency, as ministers of the gospel in this and foreign lands. The institution is a monument to his industry and devotion. He was its head for thirty-eight years. "He went there in his full prime," said Dr. Jacobus, "fifty years old— ripe in experience and rich in resources for his generation."

In his ministry Rev. Elliot went systematically to his work. With a faithful preaching of the word he joined regular pastoral visitation. Dr. Creigh said of him: "His people were devotedly attached to him. He was to them all they desired, both as preacher and pastor. As a preacher he was instructive and edifying; as a pastor he was sympathizing and laborious; as a friend he was sociable and reliable, and as a man he was godly and exemplary in all his conduct."

D. F. GARLAND, D.D., NOTED WELFARE WORKER.

When Will H. Hays, the recent Postmaster General of the United States, entered office under the Harding administration, he found conditions such that he immediately decided to organize a Welfare Department within the province of his bureau. He called, according to the public press, the two most expert men in that line in the United States, to his aid, and the first named was D. Frank Garland, D.D., a native Perry Countian, and known to many of its people.

Daniel Frank Garland was born July 10, 1864, in Madison Township, near Andersonburg, the son of Daniel Minich and Elizabeth (Kistler) Garland. Until sixteen he attended school near Bixler's Mill each winter, the term being then five months. He attended the New Bloomfield Academy during the spring term of 1880, and both the winter and spring terms of 1880-81. He taught two terms in Perry County. He entered Pennsylvania College at Gettysburg, September, 1884, and graduated with second honors, 1888, having been valedictorian of his class. During

the associated charities. The health department alone had a staff which included thirteen dairy and sanitary inspectors. The legal aid department took up the small troubles of householders too poor to employ attorneys, and the department of parks had charge of 520 acres of parks and recreation grounds. When Dr. Garland was chosen to fill this position of such great responsibility he was not unknown elsewhere, for his services as a minister, of the Lutheran Church, as a vigorous writer and forceful and eloquent lecturer had long attracted attention. From the first he seems to have dedicated his life to others, maintaining high ideals of man's duty to man and upholding these with all his physical strength and mental vigor. He labored in his chosen profession unselfishly and zealously, and when he saw a wider field and had a call to teach temporal truth, in order to bring about a better social condition of life, he did not hesitate to accept.

Study, investigation, travel and personal experience have well equipped Dr. Garland for his task. In 1912 he returned from Europe, where he had made a study of municipal government and welfare, and many of the admirable things observed in other municipalities were incorporated into the welfare work at Dayton. For many years he has made welfare work a study and has lectured to large, intelligent and enthusiastic audiences, among his subjects being city government, garden cities in Europe, food conservation, the World War, and welfare work in American cities. When he resigned his pastorate in 1914, which he had held for fifteen years, to accept the new task of welfare supervision, he stated the need of that work in these words: "We have reached a new era in public welfare. Public welfare work has come to be extended beyond the fondest dreams of social workers of a generation ago. The ultimate object of this enlarged field of social service is to restore to the people, efficient and effective citizenship." In the light of much knowledge and in protest against inequalities and iniquities that have brought misery to the helpless, Dr. Garland accepted a new conception of government that would concern itself with the special problems of human life, of community efficiency and community betterment, and with that conception let us again quote from a public address by him: "The city of Dayton, under the commission-manager plan of government, has laid the foundation for and is working toward the realization of this new conception of the obligation of the city to all her citizens. Under the present plan the Department of Public Welfare includes in the scope of its activities the public health, public recreation, public parks, correctional and reformatory institutions, outdoor relief, legal aid, municipal employment, a municipal lodging house, and a study of and research into causes of poverty, delinquency, crime, disease, and other social problems. Dayton is limited in revenues and therefore cannot assume as yet the entire community burden. However, the Department of Public Welfare, through a coöperative scheme of organization, has brought under one centralized control all public health, nursing and recreation functions of the entire city. These agencies are administered from its offices."

Upon Dr. Garland's retirement from the ministry on December 31, 1913, he was director of the Dayton Welfare Department from January 1, 1914, until December 31, 1920, when he became director of the Welfare Department of the National Cash Register Company of Dayton. During the first three months he was sent on a mission to Europe to study international relations and the working of the League of Nations.

Dr. Garland's reputation as a speaker is country-wide. Our own *Harrisburg Telegraph* said of him, January 5, 1916: "There have been many speakers before the Harrisburg Chamber of Commerce, including United States Senators, great architects, publicists and others, but none of these made a deeper impression upon the representatives of our business community than Dr. D. F. Garland, of Dayton, on the subject, 'The New Conception of the City,' etc." Elbert Hubbard's noted magazine, July, 1914, said of him: "I do not know his denomination and I am not interested in it. The man himself is bigger than party, bigger than sect. He is a humanitarian. His particular work is largely social. He knows the people, knows what they are doing, and his heart is full of desire to bless and benefit."

Dr. Garland occupies a position of prominence on many charitable and philanthropic boards, including: Dayton Tuberculosis Society, Greater Dayton Association, Federation for Charity and Philanthropy, Provident Collateral Loan Company, Community Chest Association, Barney Community Centre, Mary Scott Home, Feghtly Home for Widows, Associated Charities, and others. He was president of the Bureau of Municipal Research, 1912-16, and is a member of the Ohio State Commission on Health and Old Age Insurance. He is a trustee of the Tuberculosis Hospital of Montgomery and Preble Counties, and vice-president of the Lutheran Home for Aged Women. There is no doubt that Dr. Garland stands first in welfare work among those who have gone out from his home county and state, and it is to be questioned if he does not occupy the same place in the nation.

S. STANDHOPE ORRIS, PH.D., L.H.D.

S. Standhope Orris, Ph.D., L.H.D., son of Adam and Catherine (Shull) Orris, was born February 19, 1832, in Saville Township, near Ickesburg. He attended the public schools. He made a public confession of his faith in the Presbyterian Church of Lower Tuscarora, Pa., at the age of eighteen. His preparatory studies were pursued in the Tuscarora Academy at Academia, Pa., and he graduated with honors from Princeton College in 1862. Entering the seminary at Princeton in the fall of the same year, he took the full three years' course there, graduating in 1865. He was licensed by the Presbytery of Huntingdon, June 20, 1865. For a year after his licensure he was tutor of Latin in Princeton College. He was ordained by the Presbytery of Huntingdon, May 30, 1866, being at the same time installed pastor of the Spruce Creek (Pa.) Church. This relation was dissolved June 8, 1869. He spent the following year in study in Germany. Returning to this country he assumed charge of a mission chapel connected with the Collegiate Reformed Church of New York City, which he served for one year. He was professor of the Greek Language and Literature in Marietta College, Ohio, from 1873, to 1877, when he was called as an associate professor to a similar chair at Princeton. In the following year he was made professor. Later this chair was named the Ewing Professorship of Greek Language and Literature, and its occupant was also called instructor in Greek Philosophy. This chair he occupied until 1902, when the state of his health compelled him reluctantly to resign. He was made professor emeritus. He received the degree of Ph.D. from Princeton in 1875, and that of L.H.D. from Lafayette College in 1889. Dr. Orris was director of the American Classical School at Athens, Greece, during the academic year 1889-90. He was a lifelong student of Plato, and left a manuscript on the Plantonic and Aristotelian Philosophy and its bearing on Christianity and the Christian religion, which it is expected will be published. While traveling in China in 1903, he was stricken with paralysis in the city of Hong Kong. Upon his recovery from this stroke he returned to America and took up his residence at Harrisburg, Pennsylvania. There he suffered from a second stroke of paralysis in 1904. He died December 17, 1905, at Harrisburg, of paralysis, in the seventy-fourth year of his age. He had never married.

ANNA FRŒHLICH, NOTED TEACHER.

At a time when practically all principals of schools were men, the Duncannon (Pa.) school board elected Miss Anna Frœhlich as principal. That was in 1885, before which time very, very few women had ever risen to that distinction, as in those days positions of that character were invariably filled by men. Miss Frœhlich is a noted teacher even to-day. She is the daughter of Henry and Mary (Hecker) Frœhlich, and was born in Duncannon and reared in a country home, in Penn Township, a mile west of that town. She attended the Mt. Pleasant school and the Millersville State Normal School, where she completed the elementary course in 1882, and the scientific course in 1900. She then taught in the

further by summer courses at Columbia University and by a summer tour of Europe. She is now connected with the Training Department of the State Normal School at Millersville.

In 1818 Miss Frœhlich published "A Long Road Home," being fragments of history, genealogy and biography from among the families of her girlhood, but which in reality is a tribute to her parentage and her old home. It is to be regretted that more Perry Countians have not seen fit to issue small volumes along the same lines. The volume in possession of the writer is highly prized.

OVANDO BYRON SUPER.

Ovando Byron Super was born March 2, 1848, near Milford (later Juniata, now Wila P. O.), in Juniata Township. He was the son of Henry and Mary (Diener) Super. He attended local schools and elsewhere, but his preparation for college was mainly personal, a rare feat. He entered Dickinson College in 1871 and completed the course in two years, standing near the head of his class. He received the A.B. degree in 1873, and the A.M. degree in 1879 from his alma mater. He was granted the degree of Ph.D. by Boston University in 1883. For three years he was professor of Modern Languages in Delaware College at Newark, Delaware. He studied at Leipzig and Paris during the years 1876-78. He was instructor in modern languages in Williamsport Dickinson Seminary for two years, and at Denver University from 1880 to 1884. He was professor of Modern Languages at Dickinson College from 1884 to 1900, and professor of Romance Languages from 1900 until his retirement on a Carnegie pension in 1913. He edited the *Alumni Record* of Dickinson College and also about a dozen textbooks in German and French. In July, 1880, he married Emma Murray Lefferts, of New York City. He has three daughters. He resides at San Diego, California.

HENRY W. FLICKINGER, EXPERT PENMAN.

Henry W. Flickinger, the most expert penman native of Perry County, and one of the most prominent penmen in the United States, was born near Ickesburg, Saville Township, August 30, 1845, the son of Peter and Margaret (Ritter) Flickinger. He attended the public schools of his vicinity. Then came the Sectional War, with its attendant call to duty, and on July 18, 1864, he enlisted in Company D, First Battalion, to serve "100 days." He became fifer of the company and captain's clerk. He again enlisted, March 24, 1865, in Company F, 104th Regiment, Pennsylvania Volunteers, to serve one year. He was sent to Camp Cadwallader, Philadelphia, and detailed as a clerk in the registering office. He was honorably discharged July 20, 1865, the war having terminated. After a brief stay at home he matriculated at Eastman

trated by drawings of the founders and others, lettering and script, surrounded by an oval border of oak and ivy leaves, executed entirely with the pen. It was enclosed in a frame about 5x8 feet, and was valued at $4,000. It is now the property of the American Book Company of New York. Since that time Prof. Flickinger has taught in the Pierce School, College of Commerce, Temple College, Central High School, Catholic High School, besides being the author of various copy books. The Barnes Copy Books and One Hundred Writing Lessons are his work. He also wrote a series of copy books in French, for a Montreal publisher, and a series for the B. D. Berry Company, largely used in the Middle West. At a National Convention of the Teachers' Association, Prof. Flickinger was presented with a loving cup, and when a member of the Union League of Philadelphia entertained noted penmen he was the guest of honor. For about ten years he has made his home in Glenolden, Pennsylvania, a suburb of Philadelphia. He has written a number of sacred songs, published by the late Charles M. Alexander, the noted evangelist.

Another noted Perry County penman is J. C. Miller, born at Sandy Hill, January 15, 1849, the son of Andrew and Judith Ann (Ritter) Miller, at present living retired at New Bloomfield. He attended the local schools and Lancaster Business College, where he graduated. He also took a course at the Iron City Business College. He taught in business colleges at Lancaster, Chambersburg, Wilmington, Roanoke, Lynchburg, Elmira and Mansfield. Mr. Miller is an expert ornamental penman and alto-relief artist. In early life he also taught in the public schools.

Lelia Dromgold Emig.

Lelia Dromgold Emig is the author and compiler of the Hench and Dromgold Records, which in reality is a genealogy of the original families of Nicholas Ickes, Johannes Hench, Zachariah Rice, John Hartman, Thomas Dromgold and kindred families who had settled in Chester County prior to the Revolution, in which they fought. Through defective titles these pioneers lost their lands, and it was thus that Perry County became the haven of those goodly men and women whose impress is still felt in the community, and whose descendants have filled positions of note and trust, and are to-day a substantial part of the citizenship of Perry County.

Lelia Dromgold Emig was born near Saville, Saville Township, January 21, 1872, the daughter of Walker A. and Martha Ellen (Shull) Dromgold. When she was nine years of age her mother died. She had attended the public schools here, but two years after her mother's death, with a brother, she went to York, Pennsylvania, where her father, of the firm of Hench & Dromgold, was engaged in the manufacturing business. There she continued her

lutionary days. She also organized a Society of Children of the American Revolution, which was named by Mrs. Wm. Howard Taft, while mistress of the White House. This society from its membership produced fifty who served in the World War.

It was through the interest created by the Hench and Dromgold Reunions held in Perry County that Mrs. Emig became enthusiastic in genealogical work, and in 1915 she compiled and published her work on the Hench, Dromgold and allied families, as stated above. Her material for her new work, "The Johannas Hench Family," is well under way. Mrs. Emig is a descendant of not only all five of the family heads which comprise her former volume, and can trace her ancestry to Messrs. Hench, Hartman, Rice, Ickes, Loy, Foose, Donnally, Yohn and Shull, all Revolutionary patriots. During the World War her daughters all served the government. Gladys and Lelia were among the first women to enroll as Yeomen of the First Class in the Navy, and Evelyn was in the office of the Adjutant General. Her husband, Capt. Emig, served for seventeen months in the Aviation Department of the Signal Corps.

INVENTOR AND MANUFACTURERS, S. NEVIN HENCH AND WALKER A. DROMGOLD.

In York, Pennsylvania, there stands a large manufacturing plant, that of the Hench-Dromgold Company, which is a monument to the ingenuity, energy and industry of two native Perry Countians, S. Nevin Hench and Walker A. Dromgold. There farm implements are manufactured upon a large scale, and where farm implements are used the firm name of Hench & Dromgold is known and stands for stability. George W. Hench was the father of S. Nevin Hench, whose ancestry had by purchase accumulated holdings of about seven hundred acres of land in the vicinity of Ickesburg, in Saville Township, Perry County, at the close of the Revolution. The cultivation of many of these broad acres devolved upon the boys of the family, and S. Nevin, being of an inventive turn of mind, began experimenting on implements which would lighten their labors. There, in his grandfather's old blacksmith shop, at Saville, in 1873, S. Nevin Hench, the boy in his teens, invented and made during rainy days, the first pivot-axle riding cultivator. The succeeding year he built two machines for neighbors. In 1877, he and Walker A. Dromgold formed a partnership and manufactured eight machines. In 1878, they had 125 machines manufactured under contract at York, and the following year, in a modest little factory of their own, they began manufacturing on a more extensive scale. That was the real beginning of one of York's leading industries. After twelve years' occupation of that modest plant, in 1890, they erected a large manufacturing plant in

the public schools and then followed the carpenter trade for a time. He was married April 23, 1871, to Martha Ellen Shull, daughter of William and Elizabeth (Rice) Shull, and spent a few years farming in Juniata County, later returning to the Dromgold homestead, where, in 1881, Mrs. Dromgold died. He had previously associated himself in the business partnership with his cousin, S. Nevin Hench, and in 1882 moved to York, where they had erected a small plant. They were in partnership until the death of Mr. Hench, in 1910. Mr. Dromgold yet resides in York, Pennsylvania, and at this time is interested in a project to build twenty dams in the Susquehanna River, between Harrisburg and the bay, thus making the river navigable and furnishing power to many great industries.

Edgar Newton Lupfer, Prominent Manufacturer.

Edgar Newton Lupfer, president and general manager of the Springfield (Ohio) Metallic Casket Company, was born February 28, 1856, on the Lupfer farm, adjoining on the west the original site of New Bloomfield, and a part of it now covered by half of that borough. He is the eldest son of the late William and Hannah M. (Billow) Lupfer, his mother being from the vicinity of Dellville, in Wheatfield Township. Jacob Lupfer came to Perry County in 1778, from Montgomery County, where he had dwelt three years, after coming from Wittenberg, Saxony. He was the ancestor of the Lupfers and purchased the lands lying next to the Barnett tract, which passed from his great-grandson, William Lupfer, to W. A. Sponsler, in 1875. This property was later owned by John Adams, and in 1921 came into the possession of Robert E. McPherson. There is a legend that this entire tract was once purchased from the Indians for a string of beads and a bull calf. Unlike so many names, the name Lupfer is spelled just as it was signed by Jacob Lupfer on the passenger list of the ship "Phœnix," which sailed from Rotterdam and landed at the port of Philadelphia, November 22, 1752. On that farm were born four generations of Lupfers,—Casper Lupfer, his son David Lupfer, his grandson, William Lupfer, the father of Edgar Newton Lupfer, who was also born there. Casper Lupfer was a public-spirited citizen and deeded in perpetuity two tracts of land, lying side by side, to the rear of the Lutheran and Reformed Churches, as a burial ground, and in that belonging to the Reformed Church, he sleeps.

In the spring of 1861, William Lupfer, his wife and family of four children, removed from Perry County to Shelby, Ohio, and engaged in the dry goods business, a year later engaging in the same business in Shiloh, Ohio. In 1870 he sold that business and moved back to Perry County, purchasing from the heirs of his father, David Lupfer, who had died that spring, the Lupfer farm. In the fall of 1876, the family again removed, to Springfield, Ohio, the city in which the son, Edgar Newton Lupfer, has become so successful.

His earlier schooling was augmented by attending the High School at Shiloh, Ohio, until fourteen, and the New Bloomfield Academy from 1870 to 1873, when he entered the office of the *New Bloomfield Times,* of which Frank Mortimer was then editor, to learn the printing trade. Serving his three-year apprenticeship he worked but four and a half days as a journeyman printer, but is said to have "never regretted his experience in a printing office, as it stood him well in hand in after life." On removing to Ohio at the termination of his apprenticeship, his father induced him to drop the desire to follow his trade and to join him in conducting a grocery store. In 1884 he was appointed general agent of the Superior Grain Drill Company (now the American Seeding Machine Company), of Springfield, having his headquarters at Harrisburg, and supervising ninety-two agencies in eastern Pennsylvania, Delaware and Maryland. He was married in the fall of 1884 to Elizabeth Ann Baker, and in the spring of 1885 returned to Springfield, which he regarded as his home, and purchased an interest in a new firm, then started only about a year, to manufacture a new patented metallic casket. In 1886 the company was incorporated with Mr. Lupfer as secretary. The president was Ross Mitchell, who was born in Landisburg, Perry County, and who went with his parents to Springfield when quite a boy. He became very wealthy and successful, and was a member of the firm of Warder, Mitchell & Co. of Springfield, manufacturers of harvesting machinery, which firm later became the Warder, Bushnell & Glessner Co., and then the International Harvester Co. Mr. Mitchell became one of the largest landowners in and around Springfield, Ohio. He lived to the age of ninety-three years, highly respected, a successful son of old Perry County.

Elected as its secretary at its incorporation, Mr. Lupfer two years later, in 1888, was made secretary and general manager, which position he held until October 16, 1917, when he succeeded Charles E. Patric as president, being continued as general manager as well. During his connection of thirty-five years with the Springfield Metallic Casket Company, Mr. Lupfer has seen it grow from a small concern with a small line of goods to a large corporation with an extensive variety of funeral supplies, with a demand from coast to coast, and even in foreign lands.

Mrs. Lupfer died March 23, 1916, leaving one son, Robert Newton Lupfer, secretary of the Elwood Myers Company of Springfield. Mr. Lupfer on January 11, 1919, married Miss Minnie L. Bergman, of Madison, Wisconsin.

Mr. Lupfer has, by his ambition and foresight in managing, brought his company, the Springfield Metallic Casket Company, not only to a position of leadership among the powerful corporations of Springfield, itself a great manufacturing city, but, as well, to be one of the strongest, if not the strongest concern in its line in the world.

Col. George E. Kemp, Postmaster at Philadelphia.

Benjamin Franklin was the first postmaster of Philadelphia, and the twenty-seventh is Colonel George Edward Kemp, almost all of his early life a resident of Perry County, and the first one of the entire list of postmasters of that historic city to rise from the ranks. He assumed office January 1, 1922. As in other phases of his life, Colonel Kemp has started at the bottom rung and climbed to the top. Entering the employ of the post office department as a clerk on July 28, 1890, through a civil service examination he was assigned as a stamper, being promoted to state distributor on October 15th following. December 1, 1891, he was made distributor of New York and New Jersey mails, and November 27, 1898, receiver of second-class matter. On September 1, 1905, he was appointed superintendent of the West Philadelphia Postal Station, where he remained, save while serving his state and country in military duty, until his recent elevation to the postmastership —one of the big postal jobs of the country.

George Edward Kemp was born in Philadelphia, March 9, 1866, but his mother died before he was six years old, and his father left shortly after for New Orleans, no word or trace of him having been had since 1871. He accordingly became a member of the family of George and Martha Kemp, his grandparents, natives of England, who purchased and moved to what was then the Woods farm in Oliver Township, now the Wagner farm, near the Newport fair grounds. There he was taken in December, 1866, when but nine months old, and Perry County is the place to which he always refers as home. Roaming these rural hills as a boy he obtained the vigorous constitution which permitted him to go to the battlefields of France, when most men of his age were rejected. From hunting game in the "wilds of Purgatory" (a name oft applied to a heavily wooded section of Oliver Township), he obtained his love for rifle and pistol shooting that has made him one of the most noted rifle and pistol shots in Pennsylvania. He obtained his education in Evergreen school, in Oliver Township, under the tutorage of Alfred M. Gantt, Joseph M. Eshelman, Miss Flora Gantt, Peter Smith, John R. Smith, Irvin Smith, and S. E. Burke Kinsloe. There from studying history and from listening to stories of the Perry County soldiers who fought in the Sectional War, he was inspired to become a soldier, and at

with F. Valderchen. He became a journeyman, on his twenty-first birthday, but, steam having taken the place of sails, he entered the postal service as told above.

Colonel Kemp's military record is one of which any man would be proud. He became a private in Company A, Third Infantry, of the Pennsylvania National Guard, August 6, 1886, being promoted to corporal, June 22, 1888. On May 20, 1889, he was made second lieutenant, and on June 13, 1890, first lieutenant. On April 6, 1898, he was promoted to captain, and on July 11, 1903, to major. On July 24, 1915, he was made lieutenant colonel, and on July 1, 1916, colonel. On April 1, 1921, he was appointed inspector general, with the rank of colonel.

In the Spanish-American War he served as captain of Co. A, Third Penna. Volunteers, enlisting May 10, 1898, and being mustered out October 22d. When the Mexican border trouble came along in 1916 he was colonel of the Third Penna. Infantry and U. S. National Guard from July 1, 1916, to October 18th.

During the World War, he was mustered into the U. S. service March 28, 1917, as colonel of the Third Penna. Infantry, being assigned to guarding railroads and industries, with headquarters at Altoona. On August 5, 1917, he was drafted into the U. S. Army, and assigned to command the 110th U. S. Infantry from September 30th to December 30th. From January 3d to April 3d, he attended the Brigade and Field Officers' School at Fort Sam Houston, Texas. He commanded the Fifty-Fifth Infantry Brigade April 5th to July 4, 1918, sailing on S. S. Carmania, May 3d, in command of troops. He landed at Liverpool, May 17th, and at Calais, France, May 18th. From July 5th to July 29th, he was in command of the 110th U. S. Infantry, his former command, and from August 3d to August 8th, he had command of the U. S. troops at Nantes, France. From August 9th to November 30th, he was in command of Camp No. 1, Base No. 1, St. Nazaire, France, and from December 1, 1918, to July 10, 1919, he was administration officer at Embarkation Camp, No. 1, St. Nazaire, France. He sailed July 12, 1919, in command of U. S. S. Callao, and landed at Norfolk, Virginia, July 24, 1919, being mustered out at Camp Dix, New Jersey, August 27, 1919.

Colonel Kemp was in the Champagne-Marne Defensive, July 14 to July 18, 1918, and in the Ainse-Marne Offensive, July 18 to July 29, 1918.

By General John J. Pershing, Commander-in-Chief of the U. S. Army, a merited citation was awarded April 19, 1919. It follows:

"Colonel George E. Kemp, Infantry, U. S. Army, for exceptionally meritorious and conspicuous services at St. Nazaire, France, American Expeditionary Forces. In testimony thereof, and as an expression of appreciation of these services, I award him this citation."

JOHN J. PERSHING,
Commander-in-Chief.

While in London, England, on June 1, 1919, Col. Kemp visited St. Matthew Church, Bethel-Green, and found there the marriage record of his great-grandparents, William Kemp and Frances Ball, married August 20, 1782. He then visited Christ Church, on Newgate Street, where many notable persons are buried, including three former Queens of England, and there found the marriage record of his grandparents, George Kemp and Martha Twig, married December 24, 1820, instantly recognizing the signature of the grandfather who had reared him. The following day, at the old Parish Church, at Sheffield, England, he found the baptismal certificate of his grandmother, "Martha, daughter of Joshua and Sarah Twig, Cutler, baptized August 1, 1802."

David Billow, First Layman to Become President of Wittenberg College Board.

David Billow was another native Perry Countian who attained honor in his adopted state. He was the first layman to be elected as president of the Board of Directors of Wittenberg College at Springfield, Ohio. David Billow, a son of John George and Susannah (Ensminger) Billow, was born October 11, 1828, near Dellville, Perry County, where he spent his early life on a farm on the banks of Sherman's Creek, which his parents had purchased while still wooded and had "cleared." His education was secured in the rude log schoolhouse of the period, by trudging several miles to school. His principal literature was the Bible, the Lutheran catechism, a Bible concordance and Pilgrim's Progress, but through this study he secured a thorough knowledge of the Bible. Throughout his life he marked texts upon which he heard discourses and, with a wonderful memory, was able to repeat the gist of the various discourses, with much of it verbatim.

His health broken through overwork, he and a brother-in-law, Wm. Lupfer, engaged in general merchandising at Dellville for several years. A number of members of his family had moved to Crawford County, Ohio, and he also went to Ohio, locating at Shelby, Richland County, where he remained for twenty years. He followed the mercantile business there. He was also a loyal Unionist and foe of the liquor traffic, when that course was not always easy. He was a student in all things of an educational and religious nature, and naturally became a leader. For a number of years, 1872 to 1876, he was on the Board of Directors of Wittenberg College, located at Springfield. During this period he served several years as secretary and one year as president of the board, the first layman to fill that position. On February 26, 1852, he was married to Miss Susan Tressler, a daughter of David and Mary Catharine (Bernheisel) Tressler.

Assembly. From his first entry into that body he was noted as one of the influential figures. During the Thirty-fourth session he was a leader in the movement which finally landed General John A. Logan in the United States Senate. At the previous term it was proposed to erect a monument in Chicago to Col. James A. Mulligan, which was largely opposed because he only ranked as a colonel. Its defeat seemed certain, when Dr. Calhoun addressed the house, stating that he saw that intrepid officer fall when he received a mortal wound on July 24, 1864, in the action at Kernstown, Virginia; that several brave men attempting to keep the flag on the line of battle were shot down and that Col. Mulligan said to those about to assist him, "Lay me down and save the flag." The result was that not a single vote was cast against the bill.

On the expiration of his third term he removed to Decatur, Illinois, where he established the *Daily Dispatch*. Later he bought the *Decatur Herald* and consolidated the papers as the *Herald-Dispatch*. He is not only the owner and publisher, but as the editor-in-chief is still at the helm. His plant is one of the finest and his paper one of the most influential in central Illinois. Early during the administration of President McKinley he was appointed postmaster at Decatur and held the office under the Roosevelt and Taft administrations, a total of sixteen years. In May, 1918, he was elected as Department Commander of the State of Illinois by the Grand Army of the Republic, an organization to which he had belonged almost from its inception. He was married in 1868 to Miss Blanche Dedrick, of Seneca, Illinois, five children being born to the family. Mrs. Calhoun died in the fall of 1918. A large class of men in the First Methodist Church of Decatur is taught by Dr. Calhoun, and his pastor states that he is the best teacher of men among his acquaintances.

James McCartney, Attorney-General of Illinois.

James McCartney, son of Irvine and Margaret McCartney, was born in Raccoon Valley, in 1842, but with his people left for Mercer County, Pennsylvania, when he was eight years old, later moving to Illinois. He was admitted to the bar in 1861 and located at Galva, Henry County, Illinois. He was a member of General Henderson's 112th Illinois Volunteers, becoming a captain during the war. He had first belonged to the Seventeenth Illinois Volunteers. In 1880 the Republicans nominated him for attorney-general of the state, and he was elected and served a full four-year term, 1881-1885. After that he practiced law in Chicago, Illinois, until his death in 1913. (One informant says 1911.) He was an able lawyer and his term is said by the late General Henderson, under whom he served in the war, to have been marked by efficiency and industry.

His sister, Miss Lucy McCartney, also a Perry Countian, married Rev. P. A. Cool, D.D., who was later president of Wiley University at Marshall, Texas, and of the George R. Smith College of Sedalia, Missouri. Their son became a prominent pastor in New York City, and died in 1917, while serving an important pastorate at Buffalo, New York.

Assistant State Librarian and Deputy Attorney General.

Joseph M. McClure was born at Green Park, Tyrone Township, Perry County, December 28, 1838, the sixth of ten children of James and Rachel Oliver (Patterson) McClure. He attended the local schools and then learned the tanning trade. Studying in his spare moments he became a teacher in the higher departments of a graded school at twenty. The next year he entered Tuscarora Academy, in Juniata, County, and in 1862 entered Yale College, where he graduated in 1866. He studied law with Ezra Doty at Mifflintown, but completed his studies with the late Justice John Stewart and the noted A. K. McClure, at Chambersburg. He was admitted to the bar in 1867, began practice in Dauphin County in 1868, and was made assistant State Librarian in 1869. In the fall of the same year he was appointed Deputy Attorney General of Pennsylvania. In 1873 he edited an English and German weekly at Doylestown; in 1874 he resumed the practice of law, locating at Allentown, and in 1879 changed his location to Bradford. He was nominated by the Democratic party for president judge of the Potter-McKean District in 1892, but failed of election. As Deputy Attorney General of the commonwealth he detected the defalcations of George O. Evans, agent to collect the war claims of the state from the United States, amounting to $300,000. Evans fled the state, but returned and was imprisoned and judgment recorded against him for $185,000. Mr. McClure died October 20, 1908.

Douglass Family, Contractors.

The Douglass family, of Perry County, has had a varied experience in the contracting business. The first one to enter the business was William A. Douglass, born in Cumberland County in 1826, but who made his home in Perry practically all of his life. He was identified with the construction of the Pennsylvania Railroad at various points before entering the contracting business, including Millerstown, Huntingdon, and the Portage tunnel, being a superintendent there at its building. Following that he was superintendent of construction of fortifications with the Engineer Corps of the Northern army during the Sectional War, and at its close served in the same capacity in the reconstruction of the old Orange and Alexandria Railway, now part of the Southern Railway. He was also engaged in a similar capacity at the construction of the Hoosac tunnel and in general charge of the building of a seven-mile canal at Keokuk, Iowa, and the deepening the bed of the Mississippi. There he brought to success a project on which his predecessors had failed, and General Wilson, then chief engineer for the government, told him that a man of his ability should be working for himself instead of others and helped him secure his first contract. His contracting experience covered a period of seventeen years, from 1870 to 1887, inclusive. During that time he constructed 179 miles of railroad at a cost of approximately $7,000,000. The most important of these contracts was on the New York, Ontaria & Western, the New York, West Shore & Buffalo, and the Colorado Midland Railways, these three contracts amounting to over $5,000,000.

Mr. Douglass died April 3, 1887. He had been married in 1851 to Catharine C. Mitchell, a daughter of John Mitchell, of Greenwood Township, to whom were born three sons, John M., Samuel F., and William M., the latter two surviving and later succeeding their father in the contracting business, operating as Douglass Brothers, and having associated with them Dr. James B. Eby, of Newport, as a silent partner. Their various contracts with the Baltimore & Ohio Railroad and the Tidewater Railways approximated around $1,500,000.

MORE NOTED PROFESSIONAL MEN AND WOMEN.

The extent to which these biographies have grown and the necessity of keeping within the number of pages for a single volume necessitates the use of smaller type for the remainder, but has no other significance, as many of those following are no doubt the peers of many of those previously named, all having attained success in some particular field. For the same reason only the more important or outstanding facts are given, save in rare cases. A few pages farther on the list has been placed alphabetically, as it will facilitate the finding of names more quickly when reference is to be made, the placing of the names here also having no other significance. Some of these men have been dead for almost a century, and their records are brief, owing to the lapse of time. Undoubtedly many have been missed, but the foregoing and following lists will serve as a basis upon which to build. In fact, until such time as a Perry County Historical Society shall be organized, the author of this book will gladly receive information as to others, or any vital facts as to those here mentioned, which will be filed and turned over to such society, if organized. The only request in such cases is that a separate sheet of paper be used bearing on that subject alone, so that the original may be turned over.

this he served five years at Wenona, and the succeeding five at Lacon, the county seat of Marshall County. He served six years at Washington, Illinois, and is now at Metamora, in the first year of his pastorate, serving a federated church (Lutheran-Methodist-Presbyterian-Congregationalist-Baptist). Three beautiful churches and two fine parsonages have been erected as a result of his labors. Evangelistic in his methods, Rev. Calhoun has added hundreds to the rolls of several of his churches and many to each of them, and his courteous demeanor and kindly disposition have had a marked effect upon many nonattendants in these Illinois communities. He is a clear, logical thinker, and as a public speaker has had few equals in his state, being constantly called upon to deliver addresses at public functions. In 1911, with James A. Beaver, a former governor of Pennsylvania, he appeared upon the platform and delivered an address at the Old Home Week of his boyhood home at Blain, Pennsylvania, a never-to-be-forgotten occasion. Both were native Perry Countians and had brought credit upon it.

Several decades ago Rev. Calhoun wrote for the *People's Advocate and Press* of New Bloomfield, a series of articles on Perry Countians in the West, which contained much of historical value and to which we are indebted for many suggestions. He has also been called to his native state on other occasions. He has been secretary of his conference for more than twenty years, and is president of the ministerial association of his town, a city with seven churches, the pride of the community. Personally, the writer believes that Rev. Calhoun's success in the ministry is largely the result of his keeping in touch with the rising generation, which he has done in both school and church work, and even in the great every-day-world, where he has found time to say a kind word in passing or to write a cheering letter to a lonesome soul.

The Illinois General Assembly, at its sessions of 1920-21, selected Rev. Calhoun as one of its chaplains. Unlike many states, Illinois has adopted the plan of having a chaplain from each senatorial district, each serving for a stated period. Rev. Calhoun was chosen from the Thirtieth District, representing five counties of central Illinois.

While at work on this book, the author had the pleasure of getting personally acquainted with Rev. Calhoun, and found that, true to form, the succeeding generation are educationally inclined, and while not born Perry Countians, a word of them. Six children have been born to the family and, like their parents, all were teachers in the public schools. They are all married. William S. has taught for ten years in Knox and Henry Counties; John Paul is superintendent of schools at Morton, and Glenn H. is superintendent of schools at Lexington—they having completed their education at Hedding College. Harold Verne, a State Normal graduate, is superintendent of schools at Mackinaw. The daughters, Katharine Nellie (wife of Dr. L. M. Magill, of Lexington, Ill.), and Florence Grace (wife of B. Orin Ball, cashier of the First National Bank of Kewanee, Ill.), both graduated from St. Mary's Ladies' College, an Episcopal institution at Knoxville, Illinois. To his wife Rev. Calhoun is inclined to give much credit for his success, she being an efficient and capable religious worker, a power in missionary work among his people.

Rev. Calhoun has a characteristic that is quite common to those born among the charming scenery of Perry County, save that with him it amounts almost to a passion, and while his life has been largely spent in religious work in the State of Illinois—the value of which can never even be estimated—his heart has roamed the hills and valleys of his native county during all the years and he has made many pilgrimages back to the haunts of childhood.

50

SMITH, REV. MARTIN ALBERT. Rev. Martin Albert Smith was born on a farm, three miles west of Bloomfield, November 22, 1822. He was the son of Benjamin Smith (who, with his father, Adam Smith, emigrated from Alsace, in 1848,) and Elizabeth (Albert) Smith. His father having purchased a farm in Tyrone Township in the part that is now Spring Township, with his parents he moved there in 1829. He attended the local schools, then taught by William Power, Henry Thatcher (father of the noted Thatcher boys), and George R. Wolfe, who also married a sister of Mrs. Smith and Mrs. Thatcher. There he got his preliminary education in English, and in his home, from his parents, he learned to read German. During 1840-41 he taught Markel's school, near his home, attending the New Bloomfield Academy the following season. He then taught several seasons at Hogestown, Cumberland County, where the late noted A. Loudon Snowden was one of his pupils, attending summer sessions of the academy in the meantime. In 1843 he attended a course of catechetical lectures at the Loysville Lebanon Church, conducted by Rev. C. H. Leinbach, the Reformed pastor, which changed the future course of his life. This class numbered about seventy from the congregations of Lebanon, St. Peters' and Rudolph's. In the words of Mr. Smith, "As a catechist, Rev. Leinbach had few equals in the Reformed Church; more than once I saw tears flowing down his cheeks while expostulating." He attended Sunday school at Landisburg, as there was none then at St. Peter's Church, near his home. In the fall of 1843 he entered the freshman class of Marshall College, at Mercersburg. Conveyed in a covered wagon, by his brother, he and a cousin, Charles H. Albert, with their room furniture, bedding and stove, arrived at the primitive college town. Most of the students came in the same way—the custom of the period. Part of the time students would board themselves, and the cost would be as low as thirty cents a week. Corn was then thirty cents per bushel, and other products accordingly low in price. During two winters of his college career Mr. Smith taught school, as the terms were then short, and still kept up in his work. He graduated in 1847. During his senior year he had also taken some of his theological work, and in 1849 he graduated at the Theological Seminary at Mercersburg. He was licensed to preach on May 14, 1849. That summer he supplied the charge at Nittany Valley, and during the following winter taught in the York Institute. In the fall of 1850 he traveled by train and overland to Clarion, where he was installed as pastor of the Reformed Mission. Remittent fever caused him to relinquish it, and he started to return home overland on horseback. He stopped with a friend at Boalsburg, and about that time the charge there was divided, and later, in 1852, he became the first pastor of the new Aaronsburg charge, with five churches, at a salary of $350 per year. He also preached for the Presbyterians at Spring Mills for two years of this period. Two churches were built during this pastorate, which lated until December, 1856. He was married March 21, 1854, to Miss Mary Jane Myers, of the Nittany Valley charge, first served by him. He assumed the Hummelstown charge in December, 1856. It consisted of five congregations. Going into other congregations in eastern Pennsylvania he raised enough money to pay the considerable indebtedness of the church at Hummelstown, where he remained until 1866. In December of that year he began his ministry at Dryland and Bath, Pennsylvania, to which Nazareth was later added. At Bath a fine church was erected during his pastorate, and it became a separate pastorate about 1885, Rev. Smith remaining with Nazareth and Dryland. During December, 1890, he resigned the charge, and on March 13, 1891, he passed away. Prior to the organization of the Potomac Synod he was president of the old Synod of the United States. During his forty years' ministry he preached almost eight thousand sermons. Of his children, one, Charles M. Smith, is a prominent retired minister, residing at Middletown, Maryland, and another, Calvin, was long an editor and publisher at Pen Argyl. A third, George, is a druggist at Patterson, N. J.

———

ADAMS, JACOB LINCOLN. Jacob Lincoln Adams was born in Bucks Valley, Buffalo Township, the first-born of Frank and Catherine (Buck) Adams' children. When about nine years old his father died, and with four other children he was left an orphan. His mother married again and moved to near Wichita, Kansas, where he attended the public schools. His mother died when he was about twenty, thus breaking up the family. He first worked on a cattle range. About 1885 he began teaching at Geneva, Nebraska, and continued for fifteen years in the Fillmore County schools He was then elected county superintendent, which position he held until his death. He stood high in his profession.

ADAMS, JOHN QUINCY. John Quincy Adams, son of Nathaniel and Elizabeth Adams, was born in New Bloomfield, August 27, 1892. He was educated in the local schools and graduated from the Central State Normal School, Lock Haven, in 1913, where he was teacher of physical training the next year. In 1914-16 he was principal of the Consolidated High School at Corvallis, Montana. In 1917 he was appointed deputy clerk of the District Court of Ravalli County, Montana, and in 1920 was elected as clerk of the court.

ADAMS, WILMOT J. Wilmot J. Adams was born February 7, 1889, in Toboyne Township, the son of Robert Cochran and Sarah Jane (Yhost) Adams. He graduated at Millersville and took a course in the University of Pennsylvania. He teaches science and mathematics in the West Philadelphia High School.

ALBERT, WM. T. Wm. T. Albert was born in Landisburg, October 14, 1842, a son of Abraham and Lydia Albert. He attended the public schools and also Mt. Dempsey Academy there. He taught several terms, and was then engaged as clerk in John A. Linn's store, later teaching again and also employed as a clerk in the store of his uncle, Henry Thatcher, at Martinsburg, Pa., from 1864 to 1867. From then until 1871 he taught in Bethany Orphans' Home, at Womelsdorf. In 1871, he located at Pueblo, Colorado, where he has since been with the Thatcher Brothers' bank, save for a period of seven or eight years when, with a brother, he was engaged in managing the business of the Pueblo Transfer Co., which they owned, and a later period of years. From his first Sunday in Pueblo, April 30, 1871, Mr. Albert has been identified with the Protestant Episcopal Church. Mr. Albert's grandfather, John Albert, was a clockmaker at Landisburg.

ALEXANDER, SAMUEL E. Samuel Edmiston Alexander, son of John and Margaret (Clark) Alexander, was born in what is now Madison Township, January 17, 1785. Later in life he was an associate judge and county commissioner of Mifflin County, where his people had located during his earlier years. Of his fifteen children, John Edmiston Alexander became the founder of Hightstown Classical Institute in New Jersey.

ALEXANDER, WILLIAM. William Alexander and his twin sister, Emily, were born in what is now Madison Township, December 25, 1777. He was a son of Hugh Alexander and his second wife, Mrs. Lettice Thompson. Early in life he removed to Centre County, where he later became sheriff. His father was a member of the Constitutional Convention which adopted the first Constitution of Pennsylvania, and of the first Colonial Assembly.

ALLEN, ROY R. Roy R. Allen, son of Dr. William J. and Flora R. Allen, was born at New Germantown, February 27, 1887, where he attended the local schools. He also attended Gettysburg Academy and graduated from Harvard University in 1912. He attended three summer sessions at Columbia University. He was instructor of mathematics at New Castle, Pa., and vice-principal of the Meriden (Conn.) High School, 1914-19. From 1919 he has been vice-principal of the Tourtellotte Memorial High School, North Grosvenordale, Conn.

ANDERSON, ALEX. A. Alexander A. Anderson, son of William and Margaret (McCord) Anderson, was born in what is now Madison Township, in 1786. He graduated at Washington College, practiced law at the Mifflin County bar, and was twice a member of the Pennsylvania Legislature. He died in April, 1823.

ANDERSON, DR. B. H. Dr. Benjamin Hooke Anderson was born at Andersonburg, April 19, 1867, the son of Alexander B. and Mary Ann (Lackey) Anderson. He was educated in the common schools, the Bloomfield Academy, and at the Medico-Chirurgical College at Philadelphia, where he graduated in 1899. He is located at Wilkinsburg, Pa., and is a physician of the Pennsylvania Railroad Medical Department.

ANTHONY, B. F. Rev. B. F. Anthony was born May 30, 1844, at Juniata Furnace, Perry County. His educational advantages were limited to the public schools and private study. He died at East Berlin, May 23, 1886. He was licensed to preach by the Evangelical Church in 1875, and served on the Middleburg Circuit one year as a junior pastor, and as pastor on the circuits at McClure, Hagerstown, Lewisburg, Jarettsville and Dillsburg.

ARNOLD, JOHN H. John H. Arnold was born in Perry County and was educated in the public schools. He read law with Benjamin and C. J. T. McIntire, was admitted to the bar and located at Middleburg, Snyder County, in 1860. He was district attorney of Snyder County from 1876 to 1879.

ARNOLD, DR. GEO. D. Dr. George D. Arnold was born January 1, 1847, in Tyrone Township, near Loysville, the son of Jonathan and Mary (Ernest) Arnold. He was educated in the Loysville school and at Loysville Academy. At the age of seventeen he entered Susquehanna University at Selinsgrove, and a year later entered the University of Michigan, at Ann Harbor, as a medical student. He later transferred to the University of Pennsylvania, where he graduated in 1869 from the medical department. In 1887 he was appointed medical examiner of the relief department of the Pennsylvania Railroad, being stationed at Tyrone, Pa. He later moved to Cleveland, Ohio, becoming chief examiner of the Pennsylvania Lines west of Pittsburgh. He remained there until 1919, when he was retired on account of age. He removed to Mexico, Juniata County, to live in retirement among friends, but died June 14, 1920.

ARNOLD, DR. J. L. Dr. J. Loy Arnold, son of John S. and Ella (McKenzie) Arnold, was born at Millerstown, August 14, 1887. He attended the public schools, graduating in 1907 from the Harrisburg High School. He then entered Jefferson Medical College, from which he graduated in 1911. After serving as an interne for a year at the Allegheny Hospital he located in his home city—Harrisburg—where he has since practiced. During the World War he was a lieutenant in the Medical Corps, and was located at Fort Oglethorpe, Camp Forest, at the hospital for returned soldiers at Lakewood, New Jersey, and at Camp Grant, Illinois.

ARNOLD, JOSEPH M. Joseph Mitchell Arnold was born at New Buffalo, December 14, 1863, the son of Jacob L. and Elizabeth (Mitchell) Arnold. He attended the local schools and the New Bloomfield Academy. He prepared for college at Dickinson Seminary, and graduated at Lafayette College in 1887. He has since taken postgraduate work at the Uni-

ARNOLD, IRA E. Ira E. Arnold was born in Madison Township, December 27, 1885, the son of James S. and Clara J. (Ernest) Arnold. He attended the public schools and the Blain Summer School, also the New Bloomfield Academy. He taught a number of years in Perry County. In 1910 he took a clerical position with the Pennsylvania Railroad Company in Cleveland, Ohio, and while filling it for a period of three years he attended the Academy of Baldwin University, graduating in 1912. He also graduated from the Law School in 1913, in which year he was admitted to the bar in the State of Ohio. He began practice at once and specializes along the lines of common carrier law.

BAILEY, JACOB. Jacob Bailey was born in Miller Township, September 5, 1847, the son of Congressman Joseph Bailey and Mrs. Bailey. He studied law under C. J. T. McIntire and was admitted to the bar in October, 1870. After his marriage to Harriett Power, of New Bloomfield, he moved to Hastings, Nebraska, where he served four years as probate judge of Adams County. In 1905 he moved to Spokane, Washington, and became the senior member of the legal firm of Bailey & Brown. He died March 11, 1919.

BAKER, PAULINE. Pauline Baker, daughter of John D. (Jr.) and Clara M. (Baker) Baker, was born October 10, 1894, in Tuscarora Township, where she attended the local schools. She graduated at the Cumberland Valley State Normal School in 1913, at the University of Pittsburgh in 1919, and in the medical course at the same institution, in 1921, being the second woman physician from Perry County soil, and the first for many years. The other was Dr. Elizabeth Reifsnyder, of Liverpool.

BARNETT, ARTHUR E. Arthur Elliott Barnett, son of Chas. A. and Mary (McClure) Barnett, was born in New Bloomfield, October 15, 1875. He attended the public schools and the New Bloomfield Academy. He read law in the office of his father and was admitted to the bar in 1897. He practiced in New Bloomfield for two years, and in 1899 located at Beaver, Pa., where a year later he entered into partnership with John M. Buchanan, practicing until his death, which occurred on May 13, 1911.

BARNETT, DR. R. T. Dr. Robert T. Barnett was born in New Bloomfield, September 1, 1873, the son of George Smiley and Jane Rebecca (Ramsey) Barnett. He attended the public schools and the New Bloomfield Academy. He graduated from the medical department of the University of Pennsylvania in 1895. He practiced for a time in Duncannon, Pa., after which he located in Lewistown, Pa., where he is an associate surgeon at the Lewistown Hospital.

BEACHAM, H. H. H. H. Beacham, while born near Mifflin, Juniata County, was brought to Millerstown by the removal of his parents to that town when he was six months old. He was the son of James and Phœbe Beacham, and was born Oct. 23, 1875. He attended the public schools, the Cumberland Valley State Normal School, the Susquehanna University. He taught in Tuscarora and Greenwood Townships, Millerstown Borough, and in the boroughs of Jeannette and Juniata. For the past twelve years he has been supervising principal in the Altoona schools.

BEALOR, DR. JOHN WEIBLEY. John Weibley Bealor, M.D., was born March 18, 1853, near Markelville, the son of Benjamin Franklin and Elizabeth (Weibley) Bealor. He was educated in the local schools and graduated from the College of Physicians and Surgeons, at Baltimore, now the University of Maryland, on May 15, 1875. He located at Shamokin, Pennsylvania, where he practiced until his death, which occurred December 18, 1914.

BEALOR, G. A. Gustavus Adolphus Bealor, son of Benjamin Franklin and Elizabeth (Weibley) Bealor, was born at Markelville. He graduated at the National College of Law at Washington, D. C., and from the State University of Law, at Nashville, Tennessee. He practices at Huntingdon, West Virginia.

BEAVER, THOS. K. Thomas K. Beaver was born in Pfoutz Valley, in Liverpool Township, January 8, 1864, the son of Samuel L. and Mary (Kipp) Beaver. He attended the common schools of Liverpool and Greenwood Townships, Silas Wright's Summer Normal at Millerstown, and the Central State Normal School at Lock Haven. He then farmed for some years, and then, with his brother William A., entered mercantile business at Academia, Juniata County. In 1891 the latter withdrew, and since then Mr. Beaver has conducted the business. He is also the postmaster there. He represented Juniata County in the General Assembly of Pennsylvania during 1901-02.

BEAVER, PETER AND THOMAS B. These brothers were born at Millerstown (1802 and 1814), the sons of Rev. Peter and Elizabeth (Gilbert) Beaver. They were educated in the schools of the period, and in 1853-54, with several partners, erected the Union furnace, in Union County, under the firm name of Beaver, Geddes, Marsh & Co. Until about 1873 they received their ore from Millerstown. As early as 1834 Peter Beaver was in business at Millerstown. Thomas Beaver worked on a farm for $2.50 per month, then clerked in a store until 1833, when, with a partner he entered the mercantile business at Lewisburg. Two years later he returned to Perry County. In 1857 he moved to Danville and took charge of the Montour Iron Works, in which he had a large interest. He owned much property, his mansion at the foot of Baldhead Mountain having been one of the best homes in Montour County. In 1886 he donated to the town of Danville, as a memorial to himself and wife, a handsome gray stone library and Y. M. C. A. building, erected at a cost of $195,000. He also left an endowment of $50,000.

BEITZEL, A. J. Andrew J. Beitzel was born August 15, 1852, in Spring Township, the son of Jesse and Nancy (Bear) Beitzel. He attended the public schools and Mt. Dempsey Academy at Landisburg. He then entered the Cumberland Valley State Normal School, graduating in 1877. Mr. Beitzel conducted a teachers' summer school at Boiling Springs one term, and had two assistants, having had an enrollment of ninety-two. He also was principal at Newville, and supervisory principal at Mechanicsburg. He was once a teacher in the Cumberland Valley State Normal School. In 1887 he was elected as county superintendent of the Cumberland County schools, serving three terms, or nine years. During that time Franklin and Marshall College awarded him the A.M. degree. During the past twelve years he has been teacher of English in the Central High School at Harrisburg. Mr. Beitzel married Miss Mary S. Frownfelter, who was a fellow student in both the common schools and at Mt. Dempsey Academy. A daughter, Mildred, is the wife of Dr. Merwin G. Filler, Dean of Dickinson College.

BENFER, HENRY A. Henry A. Benfer, D.D., was born at Marysville in 1861, the second son of David and Matilda (Drees) Benfer. He was educated in the public schools and in the Union Theological Seminary, completing a divinity course in Oskalooska College, Iowa, from whom he received his degree, D.D. Rev. Benfer was ordained as a minister in the United Evangelical Church and has served pastorates in Williamsport, Lock Haven, Carlisle, York, and Baltimore. For eight years he was district superintendent, which is the highest office in the gift of the conference. He represented the conference three times as delegate to the General Conference, the highest legislative body of the church. He served for sixteen years on the Board of Examiners and served as trustee for the United Evangelical Church Home. He is now president of the Board of Conference Trustees, director of the Deaconess Board, and pastor of one of the largest congregations in Pennsylvania, being located at Red Lion, Pennsylvania.

BERGSTRESSER, REV. HENRY. Rev. Henry Bergstresser was born at Liverpool, January 19, 1831, and grew to manhood near New Bloomfield. In 1853 he settled in Richland County, Ohio, and two years later located at Newark, Licking County, Ohio, which he represented in the Ohio State Legislature. He subsequently joined the Ohio Conference of the Methodist Church, and began preaching in October, 1860.

BERNHEISEL, AUSTIN. Austin Bernheisel was born at Green Park, November 10, 1867, the son of Martin J. and Catherine A. (Heim) Bernheisel. He attended the country schools and learned the printing trade. For the past twenty-five years he has been editor and publisher of the *Neosho Valley Times*, published at Hartford, Kansas, and is a director in the Farmers' State Bank of that town, as well as an agriculturist.

BERNHEISEL, PETER. Peter Bernheisel was born August 18, 1806. His early education was secured in the subscription schools of the period. He learned the trade of carpenter and builder at Carlisle, and in 1830 located at Harrisburg, where he conducted a contracting business until 1859. During this time he built the county jail and the Market Square Presbyterian Church.

BILLMAN, REV. A. M. Rev. A. M. Billman, while born near McCrea, Cumberland County, was brought back by his mother to her girlhood home in Spring Township, six months after his birth, in the spring of 1890, his father having died two months before he was born. He was the son of Arasman M. and Sarah Ellen (Souder) Billman, and was born November 15, 1889. He attended the public schools of Spring and Tyrone Townships and attended Mercersburg Academy for three years, graduating in 1908. He graduated from Ursinus College in 1912 with the degree A.B. In 1918 he graduated from the Union Theological Seminary of New York City, and received the M.A. degree from Columbia University in 1920. He taught for three years, 1912-15, in the Syrian Protestant College at Beirut, Syria, traveling during the summer vacations in Egypt, Palestine, Russia, and most of Central Europe. He was a chaplain in the U. S. Army in 1918, being with the Tank Corps, and saw service in Camps Taylor, Colt and Dix. During his student days he had been assistant pastor of Christ Presbyterian Church and Madison Avenue Baptist Church, in New York City. During one year, 1919-20, he was with the Interchurch World Movement in New York City. In 1920 he became pastor of the First Reformed Church at McKeesport, Pennsylvania, which is his present location.

BILLOW, REV. HARRY J. Rev. Harry Jacob Billow, son of William H. and Ellen Rebekah (Kumler) Billow, was born in Buck's Valley, Buffalo Township, February 19, 1888. During his childhood his parents moved to Herndon, Northumberland County, where he got his early education in the public schools. He then taught school in that vicinity four years, from 1906 to 1911. In the fall of 1911 he entered Allentown Preparatory School, graduating in the spring of 1912. He then entered Muhlenberg College, graduating in 1916 with the A.B. degree. He entered the Lutheran Theological School in Philadelphia, and graduated in 1919. He was ordained to the gospel ministry June 5, 1919, and in a few weeks was elected pastor of the Lutheran Church at Turbotville, Pa., where he is still located.

BISTLINE, J. B. J. B. Bistline was born April 10, 1862, the son of Benjamin and Jane (Nesbit) Bistline, of Andersonburg. He was educated in the public schools and in Captain G. C. Palm's Select School at Blain. He taught school in Madison Township for two years, and in 1881 left for

BLAINE, EPHRAIM W. M.   Ephraim W. M. Blaine was born in 1804, on the Anthony Black farm, in Jackson Township. The family migrated to Northeast, Erie County, many years ago. Mr. Blaine was elected sheriff of Erie County in 1840. His brother, Alexander Blaine, represented Cumberland County in the State Legislature.

BOOK, WM. I.   William I. Book was born at Blain, June 9, 1875, the son of Edmund D. and Elizabeth (Long) Book. He attended the local schools, and graduated from Juniata College in 1897, and from the University of Pennsylvania in 1913. He was supervising principal at Stonerstown and Saxton, Bedford County, 1897-99, and at Duncannon, 1899-1900. From 1901 to 1909 he was principal of the Gettysburg schools. In 1909 he became instructor in Physics at the University of Pennsylvania. Since 1920 he has been Professor of Physics at the same institution. In 1913 he was awarded the Ph.D. degree.

BOSSERMAN, REV. C. O.   Rev. C. O. Bosserman was born in Newport, August 25, 1869, the son of William Henry and Mary Minerva (Miller) Bosserman. He attended the Newport schools, graduating in 1885. He graduated from the New Bloomfield Academy in 1887, from Princeton College in 1891, and from the Princeton Seminary in 1894. He was pastor of the Covenant Presbyterian Church in Harrisburg, 1894-1908, pastor of the Shippensburg Presbyterian Church, 1908-15, since which time he has been pastor of the Cape May, N. J., Presbyterian Church.

BOWER, DR. PETER.   Dr. Peter Bower was born in Landisburg, December 4, 1825, a son of Peter and Mary (Sheibley) Bower. He was educated in the public schools and located at Thomasville, Ga., where he spent most of his life. He served as a surgeon in the Confederate Army during the War between the States, and died December 19, 1897.

BOWERS, B. J.   Ben. J. Bowers was born in Saville Township, February 3, 1864, the son of David B. and Diana (Hopple) Bowers. He attended the public schools of Saville and Tyrone Townships, Tressler Orphans' Home as a pay student, and the New Bloomfield Academy a number of terms. He graduated from the Cumberland Valley State Normal School in 1892. He taught two terms in Dauphin County, and from 1894 to 1899 taught in Mill Hall, where he organized the high school and graduated the first class. He later taught in the schools of Clearfield and McKean Counties. In 1910 he became principal of the Washington School Building in Johnstown, where he is now a supervising principal over two districts. For nine years he also taught in the night school in Johnstown. He has taken several university extension courses.

BOYER, SAMUEL J.   Samuel J. Boyer, M.D., was born at Markelville in 1856, and educated at the New Bloomfield Academy. He read medicine with Dr. J. E. VanCamp, and graduated from the College of Physicians and Surgeons, at Baltimore, in 1881. Practiced with his preceptor for seven years, also in Illinois and at Elliottsburg. In 1884 he located at Siglerville, Mifflin County.

BOYER, REV. HARRY.   Rev. Harry Boyer was born at Duncannon, January 28, 1870, the son of John B. and Annie (DeHaven) Boyer. He attended the local schools and graduated from Lebanon Valley College in 1887. He entered the ministry of the U. B. Church and served the following charges: Dover, York County, 1897-1901; Spry, York County, 1901-07; Shermansdale, 1907-15, and since then at Oakville, Cumberland County. Rev. Boyer has been one of the examiners for the reading course of the U. B. Conference for fifteen years.

BRANDT, ANTHONY.   Anthony Marion Brandt, son of Isaac and Caroline (Emerick) Brandt, was born at Millerstown, April 8, 1844. His father was a railroad contractor, and died when the boy was but five years old. He was educated in the public schools. was a page in the Pennsylvania Legislature as a boy, learned harness making in Philadelphia, and located in the West, at Clinton, Iowa, in 1866. He was in the livestock business at Bellevue, Iowa, for twenty-six years, at the same time conducting a farm and livery business for ten years. He purchased the *Bellevue Herald* in 1887, and from then to his death was its editor. He died April 16, 1921, a leader among the editors of the country press of his adopted state.

BRETZ, F. K.   F. K. Bretz was born at Newport. August 4, 1872, the son of Mahlon T. and Emma P. (Kirby) Bretz. He was educated in the public schools and graduated from Lafayette College in 1893. In 1888 he was a telegraph operator on the P. R. R., and 1888-89 was private secretary to the general manager of the W. Va. C. & P. Ry. at Cumberland, Md. During his college vacations he was with the engineering department of the same road. During 1893-94 he was secretary to the general counsel, and from 1894 to 1902 was general manager of the Dry Fork Railroad, at Hendricks, W. Va. During the period from 1902 to 1919 he was general manager of the Morgantown and Kingwood Railroad, being vice-president of the same from 1909 to 1919. He was elected to the Phi Beta Kappa, of Lafayette College.

BRINER, GEO. M.   Geo. M. Briner was born in New Bloomfield, January 11, 1883, the son of George S. and Susan B. (Moose) Briner. He attended the public schools and graduated from the Shippensburg Normal in 1901, from Dickinson College in 1907. From 1907 to 1917 he was a member of the faculty of the Carlisle High School, being principal from 1910 to 1917. He now represents a publishing house, and resides in Carlisle.

BRINER, W. GRIER.   William Grier Briner was born in New Bloomfield, July 21, 1885, a son of George S. and Susan B. (Moose) Briner. He attended the public schools and graduated from the Carlisle High School in 1905, and Dickinson College in 1909. He was vice-principal of the Emporium High School from 1909 until 1911, and its principal from then until 1914. During 1914-15 he was principal at Greencastle, Pa., and 1915-18, supervising principal of the State College schools, since which time he has followed other vocations, residing at Newark, N. J.

BRINER, J. FRANK.   J. Frank Briner was born in Newport, October 30, 1887, the son of George S. and Susan B. (Moose) Briner. He attended the public schools and graduated from the Carlisle High School in 1906, since which time he has been connected with the Farmers Trust Company of Carlisle, being its assistant secretary.

BRINER, CHAS. S.   Chas. S. Briner was born in Newport, December 6, 1889, the son of George S. and Susan B. (Moose) Briner. He attended the public schools and graduated from the Carlisle High School in 1907, and from Dickinson College in 1911. He was instructor in Latin and Greek in the Wilmington Conference Academy at Dover, Delaware, from 1911 to 1913, and in the same branches in the Montclair (N. J.) Academy from 1913 to 1916, since which time he has followed other vocations.

BRYNER, IRA L.   Ira L. Bryner, the son of George M. and Frances (Peck) Bryner, was born at Cisna Run, May 29, 1867. He was educated in the public schools, the Millersville State Normal School, and graduated from Ursinus College in 1892. He took postgraduate work at Worcester University, studied law and was admitted to the Cumberland County bar in 1902. Prior to this he was an instructor for four years in the Shippensburg Normal School and had also taught in Perry and Lancaster Counties. He was county superintendent of the schools of Cumberland County for six years. In 1902 he located in Pasadena, California, being interested in banking and the development of the oil fields of California and Wyoming.

While Mr. Bryner was county superintendent of the Cumberland Valley schools, his brother, Ezra H. Bryner, was county superintendent of the schools of Perry County, probably the first instance in the state where brothers were superintendents of adjoining counties at the same time.

BRYNER, E. H. E. H. Bryner, son of George M. and Frances (Peck) Bryner, was born at Elliottsburg, February 13, 1864. He attended the public schools and graduated from the Millersville State Normal School in 1890, prior to which time he had been teaching in Perry and Lancaster Counties. After his graduation he taught in Lancaster County, and prior to September, 1896, was principal of the Newport schools for three years. At that time he was appointed county superintendent of schools to succeed Prof. Joseph M. Arnold, who resigned. In 1899 and 1902 Mr. Bryner was elected to the county superintendency, but resigned in October, 1905, to accept a position in New York City, where he died in November, 1909.

BRYNER, DR. J. H. Dr. J. H. Bryner was born at Andersonburg, February 18, 1864, the son of John H. and Margaret (Rice) Bryner. He attended the common schools, the New Bloomfield Academy, the University of Pennsylvania, and the Columbus Medical College, graduating from the latter in 1882. Dr. Bryner began practice at New Germantown, but after a few years removed to Ickesburg, where he was long located. He is now located at Quentin, Lebanon County, Pa.

BRUNNER, DR. M. W. Dr. M. W. Brunner, son of William and Sarah (Brindle) Brunner, was born in Centre Township, on November 7, 1872. He attended the public schools and the New Bloomfield Academy. He graduated from the Cumberland Valley State Normal School in 1885, and from the Lebanon Valley College in 1901. He graduated from Philadelphia College of Osteopathy in 1904, and since that time has practiced his profession at Lebanon, Pennsylvania.

BUCKE, W. FOWLER. W. Fowler Bucke was born in Hunter's Valley, Buffalo Township, September 29, 1866, the son of Samuel E. and Nancy Jane (Fortney) Bucke. He attended the public schools and select school at Liverpool. He entered the Bloomsburg State Normal School in 1886 and passed to the senior class at the end of the spring term, graduating in 1887. He entered Dickinson College in the fall of 1892, graduating in 1895, receiving the A.M. degree in 1898. In 1895 he began non-resident work at the University of Wooster, Ohio, and completed the course for Ph.D. in June, 1902. He was then appointed Scholar in Clark University, at Worcester, Massachusetts, and subsequently Fellow, specializing in psychology and education, receiving the degree of Doctor of Philosophy from Clark in June, 1904.

He taught in the schools of Huntingdon, Perry, and Juniata Counties from 1884 to 1889. In 1889 he opened a school for teachers at Thompsontown. After graduating from college he was called to head the Department of Mathematics in the Centenary Collegiate Institute at Hackettstown, N. J. He remained here three years, leaving to become principal of the Newcastle (Pa.) High School, remaining there four years. He was the first principal of the Technical High School of Harrisburg, before going to the head of the Department of Education in the State Normal School at Geneseo, N. Y., in the fall of 1905. Due to the illness of the principal of this institution, he has been acting principal since November, 1920. There he organized the training school and developed courses in observation, psychology, history of education, etc. In the fall of 1920 an act of the legislature established the Craig Colony School of Educational Therapy, in which he is a director in addition to his other duties. This institution correlates with the Normal School in the development of defective children. He is a noted speaker along educational lines in the

Central Eastern States. In G. Stanley Hall's work on Adolescence he is quoted for original work in that line.

BUCKE, REV. J. E. A. Rev. J. E. A. Bucke was born in Hunter's Valley, Buffalo Township, November 3, 1875, the son of Samuel Elias and Nancy Jane (Fortney) Bucke. He attended the Mt. Patrick school, with the exception of one term when his family resided at Montgomery's Ferry. At the former school his father was his teacher at all times. He graduated from the Lock Haven State Normal School in 1897, prior to which time he had taught school in his home township. Following his graduation he taught in Liverpool, and was principal of the Ramey (Pennsylvania) schools for two terms.

When a lad of seventeen he had gone to Harrisburg to work in a shoe factory, where he joined the Stevens Memorial Methodist Episcopal Church, which later licensed him to preach, a year before his graduation at the State Normal School, the quarterly conference granting him a local preacher's license. Although he had been elected for the third term as principal of the Ramey schools, he resigned to enter Drew Theological Seminary at Madison, N. J., in September, 1900, from which he graduated in 1903. While a student, 1901-03, he served the New Germantown (N. J.) Methodist Church as pastor. As he was already married this helped supplement the funds needed for the support of his family and the securing of a college education at the same time. After his graduation he joined the Central Pennsylvania Conference of the Methodist Church at the spring session of 1903, and has since served the following charges: Buckhorn, Columbia Co., 1903-05; Sunbury, Catawissa Avenue (which he organized), 1905-12; Newberry, Williamsport, 1912-20; St. Paul's, Hazleton, 1920-21. In 1921 he was elevated to the position of district superintendent of the Central Pennsylvania Conference, probably the youngest man ever selected to fill that honorable position, the most important of the conference.

BUCK, HARVEY E. Harvey E. Buck was born December 17, 1869, in Buck's Valley, Buffalo Township, the son of Jacob Resler and Esther (Albright) Buck. He attended the local schools, later becoming a teacher in his home township. In 1890 he located in Philadelphia, having a position on the street cars. In the fall of 1892 he opened a grocery there, the following year he and his father entering into a partnership in the grocery and meat business, and later, in 1896, taking his brother, Jacob U. Buck, into the firm. This continued until 1900, when the brothers begin gradually entering the cake business, and in 1902 the partnership was dissolved and they engaged entirely in the cake business, being the establishers and sole proprietors of the Enterprise Cake Company, which continued in business until the death of the younger brother, Jacob U. Buck, in 1916. The business was then conducted by Harvey E. Buck until his death on October 11, 1918. This firm had become one of the leading wholesale cake firms of the City of Philadelphia, and employed a large number of delivery wagons in the distribution of their product.

BURD, W. H. W. H. Burd was born at Donally's Mills, April 8, 1873, the son of Ananias and Sarah E. (Long) Burd. He attended the local schools in which he later taught. He graduated from the Cumberland Valley State Normal School in 1892, and from Lebanon Valley College in 1901, since which time he has taken postgraduate work at Harvard College and the University of Pennsylvania. At present he is principal of the Central Junior High School at Altoona, and a member of the Executive Committee of the Pennsylvania State Educational Association.

BURKHOLDER, A. K. A. K. Burkholder was born in Juniata Township, and was educated at the Markelville Academy. He read law in the office of B. McIntire at New Bloomfield. After being admitted to the bar he located in Ohio, becoming a captain of volunteers in the Northern army. After his term of service expired he located in Missouri, where he later served as a president judge of the courts of a district.

BURNS, REV. CHAS. E. Rev. Charles Edward Burns was born in Duncannon, August 13, 1846, the son of Ephraim and Eleanor (Maxwell) Burns. He attended the local schools and academy and graduated from Lafayette College and the Union Seminary in New York City. He began his work in the Presbyterian ministry in October, 1876, at Beemerville, New Jersey. He was pastor of the Manayunk Church for twenty-five years, later being located at Bristol, Pennsylvania, where he died in November, 1918.

CALHOUN, REV. W. SCOTT. Rev. W. Scott Calhoun was born July 16, 1846, near Cisna's Run, Madison Township, the son of John and Catharine (Kiner) Calhoun, one of a family which has become distinguished in the annals of Illinois, being a brother of Rev. J. D. Calhoun and Wm. F. Calhoun, once speaker of the Illinois Assembly, brief biographies of whom appear elsewhere. After the death of his father in 1858 the family removed to Blain, and in 1866 migrated to Illinois, locating in LaSalle County. Being refused enlistment on account of his youth he served in a civil capacity at Washington for a period during the war. Upon his return for a time he attended Sherman's Valley Institute at Andersonburg. He taught for several terms in Perry County and for a time in Illinois. Learning photography he followed that occupation for several years.

He was converted in 1875, and the following September was ordained to preach by the M. E. Conference of Illinois. He served the pastorates of such towns as Newcomb, Marshall, South Champaign, Newman, Perry, Pittsfield, Barry, Alanta, Beardstown, Tuscola, Monticello, Saybrook and Potomac, Illinois. While at Tuscola a new edifice costing $19,000 was built. While he was pastor at Perry (1883-84) a member of his church was Miss Mame Baird. In 1884 she was united in marriage to William Jennings Bryan, then a struggling young lawyer. Rev. and Mrs. Calhoun attended the wedding and heard the new wife express her ambition "that Will might go to Congress," little dreaming that he should lead his party three times as a candidate for the Presidency of the United States. It was the opinion of Rev. Calhoun that never were two more honest men than Wm. McKinley and Wm. J. Bryan opponents in a political contest.

Married in 1878 to Miss Anna Brown, of Ohio, four children were born to the family. During his lifetime Rev. Calhoun made a pilgrimage back to Perry County almost bi-annually. He died at Tuscola, Illinois, September 10, 1917, where he made his home after retiring from the ministry, after the close of his pastorate at Potomac, in 1905, his death occurring in a physician's office, from heart failure.

Rev. Calhoun had a remarkable family, all three of his children graduating at Wesleyan University at Bloomington, Illinois. His son, G. M. Calhoun, is the Methodist pastor at Stevens Point, Wisconsin, one of the most important churches in that state and the location of the State Normal School. Another son, W. W. Calhoun, has for years been on the staff of the *Cincinnati Post*, and the only daughter married H. Verne Swartz, a successful young attorney of Chicago. Mrs. Calhoun resides at Long Beach, California.

CAMPBELL, DR. OLIVER HOWARD. Dr. Oliver Howard Campbell was born at New Germantown, July 26, 1871, the son of James Robinson and Mary Eliza (Douglass) Campbell. He attended the local schools and the College University of Kansas, graduating from the Medical Department of Washington University at St. Louis, Mo., in 1899. He is a member of the staff of the city hospital at St. Louis, Mo.; of the St.

Louis Hospital, and the Missouri Baptist Sanitarium. During the World War he was a lieutenant colonel and was stationed at the Base Hospital at Camp McArthur, and at Toul, France.

CHARLES, J. O. J. O. Charles, son of Edward T. and Emma (Sheaffer) Charles, was born in Penn Township, in 1899. His family moved to Wheatfield Township, where he attended the public schools. He attended the New Bloomfield Academy, Cumberland Valley State Normal School, and Muhlenburg College, at Allentown. He taught school in Wheatfield Township, and since graduating was first assistant principal in the State High School at Creswell, N. C., principal of the Millerstown schools, prefect at Girard College. and principal of the public schools at Macungie and Emaus, Pa.

CISNA, DR. WM. R. Dr. Wm. R. Cisna was born at Chambersburg, December 8, 1837, but moved to Cisna's Run, Perry County, with his people when but a mere lad, in 1845. His parents were William and Anna (Everidge) Cisna. He attended the local schools and worked on the farm. He prepared for college at Mt. Dempsey Academy, and in 1863 graduated from Dickinson College. In 1865 he received his medical diploma from the University of Pennsylvania. At the closing of the Sectional War he was a surgeon in the U. S. Army. He was transferred to Texas, where General Kirby Smith's troops were still fighting, and made chief medical officer. He was brevetted major for meritorious conduct in the field. On his return he first located at Landisburg, but in 1866 located at Ickesburg. In 1889 he was appointed medical examiner of all the Pennsylvania Lines west of Pittsburgh, with headquarters in Chicago. There he served for over twenty-five years, when he returned to Perry County. He died in 1920.

CLARK, ARTHUR B. Arthur B. Clark was born at New Bloomfield, June 16, 1872, the son of James B. and Margaret Jane (McFarland) Clark. He attended the public schools and learned the printing trade. In 1893 he located at Altoona, being employed on the *Morning Tribune* (for six or seven years). On his arrival there he began attending night school. He later became advertising manager of the Altoona *Evening Gazette,* subsequently being elected a director and treasurer, and in 1912 was elected general manager of the company. In February, 1905, he was elected city treasurer of Altoona on the Democratic ticket, being the only Democrat to win out. In 1908 he was reëlected, carrying every voting precinct in the city, something that had never been accomplished by any other candidate. In 1914 he was nominated by the Democrats of Pennsylvania for Congressman-at-large, but failed of election, as the entire Republican ticket swept the state, but led the entire Democratic ticket by more than 8,000 votes.

CLARK, REV. JOSEPH. Rev. Joseph Clark was an early minister. He was licensed to preach by the Carlisle Presbytery, June 11, 1851, and ordained in 1852. He was pastor of the Falling Springs Church, at Chambersburg. from 1852 to 1857. He died June 9, 1865.

CLEGG, JOHN. John Clegg was born at New Bloomfield, the son of C. T. and Jennie (Stultz) Clegg. He attended the public schools and learned the printing trade. In 1902 he became associate editor of the *Everett* (Pa.) *Press,* and in September, 1914, purchased the plant of the *Everett Press* and became its editor and publisher. It is one of the best country newspapers in the state.

CLOUSER, EMMA. Emma Clouser (Mrs. Andujar) was born at New Bloomfield, November 6, 1857. She attended the local schools and took a great interest in church work. She was united in marriage to Rev. Andujar, then pastor of the New Bloomfield Methodist Church. Shortly after

51

their marriage, Rev. and Mrs. Andujar were sent to San Juan, Porto Rico, in June, 1901. There she entered the work of a missionary with enthusiasm and success, but during a severe electrical storm was struck by a bolt of lightning and was killed, her death occurring September 28, 1902. With her husband she had charge of the Methodist Missions of the entire Island.

COCHRAN, DR. THOS. P. Dr. Thomas P. Cochran was born in Pfoutz Valley, near Millerstown, October 25, 1866, the son of Robert Patterson and Anna Mary (McFarlane) Cochran. He attended the public schools, the New Bloomfield Academy, Blair Hall, at Blairstown, N. J., and graduated from Jefferson Medical College in 1893. He practiced his profession in Millerstown until 1897, when he located at Pittsburgh. He has been on the staff of St. Joseph's Hospital since its organization in 1904, and has been president of the staff since 1905. In 1901 he helped organize the Lyman Building and Loan Association with a capital of $5,-000,000, and was selected its president, a position which he still holds. He is also president of the St. Clair Incline Plane Company, and a member of the board of directors of the Hill Top Savings and Trust Company.

COCHRAN, REV. WILLIAM P. Rev. William P. Cochran was born in Millerstown in 1803, where he attended the subscription schools. He graduated from Dickinson College in 1824, and from Princeton in 1827. He went to Missouri in 1831 as a home missionary, where he remained until 1862-68, when he was pastor of the Millerstown Presbyterian Church. He returned to Missouri in the spring of 1868. While in Missouri he was the owner of a plantation which he conducted in connection with his ministry. During his stay in Pennsylvania he organized the Presbyterian congregation at Newport. He died in Missouri, in 1886.

COMP, REV. GEO. L. Rev. Geo. Leiby Comp, the son of Andrew and Margery (Miller) Comp, was born near Walnut Grove, Juniata Township, February 28, 1848. He attended the local schools, and when fifteen years old ran away from home to enter the Union Army. His father brought him back, but he later enlisted as a member of the Emergency Corps and reached Gettysburg after the battle was fought, but assisted in restoring the field from the havoc of war. In 1864 he reënlisted in Company G, 208th Regiment, Pennsylvania Volunteers, and served to the end of the war. He then farmed on the Comp homestead until 1889, when he entered the ministry of the Methodist Episcopal Church, serving appointments at Alum Bank, Reedsville, Ennisville, Warriors Mark, Hopewell, Petersburg, Duncannon, Barnesboro, and Coalport. On account of his health he retired from the ministry in 1914. He died at Newport, November 2, 1916.

CROW, REV. H. I. Rev. H. I. Crow was born in Hunter's Valley, Buffalo Township, February 2, 1865, the son of Abraham and Mary (Bair) Crow. He attended the public schools and the New Bloomfield Academy for several terms. He graduated at the Bloomsburg State Normal School in 1888, and from the Reformed Theological Seminary at Lancaster, in 1895. Prior to entering the ministry he had taught in Perry and Dauphin Counties, being four years in Marysville, the last two of which he was principal of schools. He was ordained to the ministry of the Reformed Church in 1895, and served the New Hamburg (Mercer Co.) Church until 1900. He was on the Nittany Valley charge from 1900 to 1908, at Hublersburg (owing to a division of the former charge) from 1908 to 1911. Since that time he has been pastor of the Bethany congregation at Bethlehem, Pa. Mr. Crow is president of the East Pennsylvania Classis of the Eastern Synod, which is the oldest classis in the United States. He was also president of each of the other classis of which he was a member, and was a delegate of the General Synod of the United States.

CROW, REV. H. E. Rev. H. E. Crow was born August 27, 1871, in Hunter's Valley, Buffalo Township, the son of Abraham and Mary (Bair) Crow. He was educated in the public schools and graduated from the Bloomsburg State Normal School in 1893. Prior to his graduation he had taught in Perry and Clearfield Counties. After graduating he taught in Liverpool and Downingtown, Pa. He prepared for college at Centenary Collegiate Institute at Hackettstown, N. J., graduating in the class of 1897. In 1901 he graduated from Dickinson College, and in March of that year was admitted to the Central Pennsylvania Conference of the Methodist Episcopal Church, and has since been pastor of charges at Greencastle, Vira, South Williamsport, Wilburton, Laurelton, Conyngham (1911-18), and since 1918 has been at Dillsburg, Pa.

DARLINGTON, DR. E. E. Dr. E. E. Darlington was born at New Bloomfield, March 24, 1874, the son of John and Mary Elizabeth (Arnold) Darlington. He was educated in the public schools and the Bloomfield Academy, graduating from the Maryland Medical College in 1900. He practiced seven years at Gordon, Pa., after which he located at Harrisburg, where he now practices.

DAVIS, CHAS. S. Charles S. Davis was born in New Bloomfield, November 14, 1864, the son of James Reynolds and Margaret (Dougherty) Davis. His father later located at Liverpool, and there Mr. Davis attended the public schools. He taught school at Thompsontown, and graduated at the Central State Normal School at Lock Haven in 1883. He began teaching in Steelton in 1883, and in the Steelton High School in 1885, being its principal from 1888 to 1919, when, on the death of L. E. McGinnes, superintendent of schools, he was elected to that position. The record of Mr. Davis and Mr. McGinnes for joint service in the educational field in Pennsylvania probably stands first for length. In 1910 Mr. Davis was president of the high school department of the State Teachers' Association, and in 1917 was elected president of the State Educational Association. He was one of the original enthusiasts of clean sport, and in 1913 he was chairman of the committee that drafted a constitution for control of Pennsylvania high school athletics, and was the first president of the State Board of Athletic Control under this constitution, thus helping to place high school athletics in Pennsylvania on a higher plane. He is interested in community and municipal affairs, holding office in the Municipal League, the Park and Playground Commission, and on the Shade Tree Commission of Steelton.

DEACH, REV. SAMUEL R. Rev. Samuel R. Deach was born near New Germantown in 1838. He was a captain in the Union Army in the Sectional War. He had been licensed to preach in 1860, and at the end of his term of service, in 1864, he became pastor of the Dwight and Odell charge of the M. E. Church in Illinois. He served in the ministry for thirteen years, when pulmonary trouble caused his retirement. He was regarded as a zealous and able preacher, one of the best in his conference. His mother was a daughter of Peter Sheibley. He died May 4, 1882.

DEACH, REV. JACOB N. Rev. Jacob N. Deach was born June 16, 1846, near New Germantown, his mother being a daughter of Peter Sheibley and his father dying when he was very young. He was educated at the Cumberland Valley Institute at Mechanicsburg and at the New Bloomfield Academy and taught for several years. He then joined the Central Illinois Conference of the Methodist Church and for sixteen years engaged in the ministry, when a throat affection resulted in his retirement. He is spoken of as an able and pursuasive divine. He had entered the army on a three-year enlistment, but was discharged on account of his health. He lives in retirement in the State of California, where his son

Ivan, a brilliant educator, is a member of the faculty of Leland Stanford University.

DECKARD, DR. J. W. Dr. John Wesley Deckard was born in Howe Township, December 27, 1850, the son of David and Barbara (Stence) Deckard. He attended the public schools and the Summer Normal School of Prof. Silas Wright, at Millerstown. He then taught in Buffalo and Howe Townships. His summers were occupied in studying medicine, with Dr. Samuel Stites, of Millerstown, as preceptor. He then entered the Ohio Medical College at Cincinnati, graduating in medicine and surgery in 1874. He located at Richfield, Juniata County, where he has been engaged in practice ever since. He was a member of the school board for twenty-two consecutive years, and is now president of the Juniata County Medical Society.

DECKARD, DR. PARK A. Dr. Park A. Deckard was born at Liverpool, September 12, 1881, the son of Elmer E. and Mary (Lutz) Deckard. He graduated from the Liverpool High School in 1898, from the Central State Normal School in 1900, from Pierce Business School in 1903, and from the Medico-Chirurgical College and the University of Pennsylvania, in 1908. In 1914 he took a postgraduate course in the New York School of Medicine. He has practiced at Harrisburg, Pa., since his graduation, in 1908, and has been electro therapeutist at Harrisburg Hospital since 1912. Dr. Deckard was president of the Harrisburg Medical Club in 1915, secretary-treasurer of the Harrisburg Academy of Medicine, 1918 to 1920, and president of the Harrisburg Academy of Medicine in 1921. He was also a member of the Medical Advisory Board of this district during the World War.

DEMAREE, HARRY S. Harry S. Demaree was born at Newport, the son of B. F. and Jennie M. (Stambaugh) Demaree. He graduated from the Newport High School and attended Franklin and Marshall College and Lehigh University. He later entered the United States Bureau of Standards, and was transferred from there to the Patent Office. While at the latter place he took up the study of law at Washington University, graduating in 1917. In the World War he was located at the Pontiac Naval Air Station, near Bordeaux, France. Returning home he reëntered the Patent Office, took a law examination, and was admitted to the bar at Washington, D. C. In August, 1920, he became associated with a large electrical company in Chicago as patent attorney.

DERICKSON, S. H. S. Hoffman Derickson was born in Greenwood Township, April 9, 1879, the son of Henry Benner and Elizabeth Naomi (Hoffman) Derickson. He attended the public schools and the Newport High School. He graduated from Lebanon Valley College in 1902, and attended Johns Hopkins University in 1903, Bermuda Biological Laboratory, Cinchona Botanical Laboratory, and the Brooklyn Institute of Arts and Sciences. He has been professor of Biology at Lebanon Valley College since 1904. In 1903 he was the land zoologist with the Bahama Expedition of the Baltimore Geographical Society, and in 1908 was director of the field expedition for the collection of Eocene fossils for Vassar College. In 1920 he was made treasurer of Lebanon Valley College.

DERICK, GEO. W. Geo. W. Derick was born at Newport, November 30, 1863, the son of Geo. and Sarah (Burd) Derick. His family removed to New Bloomfield in 1869, where he attended the public schools and New Bloomfield Academy. In 1881 he graduated from Allen's Business College, Elmira, N. Y., learned telegraphy, and entered the employ of the H. & B. T. M. R. R. Co., remaining in various capacities for fifteen years. He became interested in politics and held all the Republican party offices of Bedford County. In 1905 he was elected prothonotary and clerk of the courts. In 1904 he started the First National Bank of Saxton, Pennsylvania. In 1905 he became a partner in the Everett (Pa.) Bank, and in 1909 he became cashier of that institution. During the war he was chairman of the Bankers' Liberty Loan Committee, Bedford County, and took a leading part in other World War activities.

DICE, REV. L. M. Rev. L. M. Dice was born at Marysville, February 10, 1870, the son of Levi and Mary J. (Ilgenfritz) Dice. He attended the public schools and graduated from Central Pennsylvania College in 1894. He entered the ministry of the United Evangelical Church in 1896, filling several important churches and being active in the work of the conference and the denomination. He is an officer of the management of the United Evangelical Home at Lewisburg.

DICK, REV. J. M. Rye Township was the birthplace of the late Rev. J. M. Dick, he having been born May 3, 1853. His parents were Israel and Elizabeth Dick. He attended the Juniata Valley Normal School at Millerstown, conducted by Prof. Silas Wright, taught school several terms, and was then ordained a minister of the gospel in the Church of the Evangelical Association. From 1880 to 1893 he served various congregations of that faith, when, owing to a schism he transferred to the Congregational Church, serving a number of pastorates until 1903. He then became a Sunday school organizer and missionary of the Congregational Church for the western section of the State of Washington, serving until his death, which occurred February 5, 1920, at the Swedish Hospital, in Seattle, Washington, where he had dwelt for many years. His early work was in Pennsylvania, but in 1887, he removed to the State of Washington, which was the scene of his later success. His marked Christian character and kindliness made him a notable man in the religious annals of his adopted state. His Pennsylvania pastorates were at Liverpool, Perry County, and at Lock Haven, Pa.

DIFFENDAFER, A. P. Alton P. Diffendafer was born at Millerstown, December 16, 1870, the son of Thomas and Johanna (Graham) Diffendafer. He attended the public schools, graduating at Millerstown in 1887, and from the Lock Haven State Normal School in 1888. He is also a graduate of the Chautauqua Institution, Chautauqua, New York. He taught at Millerstown, and in 1891 was elected principal of the Nanticoke High School, later being elevated to the position of superintendent of the Nanticoke schools, which he still holds.

DRAKE, CAPT. C. ARTHUR. C. Arthur Drake was born at Avon, Illinois, May 20, 1894, and was brought to Perry County by his mother, Myrtha (Campbell) Drake, on July 3d of the same year, and was reared in the home of his grandfather, John S. Campbell. He attended Evergreen school, in Oliver Township, completing the course at fourteen. He then entered Grove City College, but when Dr. J. R. Flickinger took charge of the Central State Normal School he matriculated there, at the suggestion of his grandfather, who had been a co-worker of Dr. Flickinger's in the Perry County schools. He graduated at Lock Haven when but eighteen. He then taught at Homestead as headmaster of the Schwab Industrial School, and later graduated from the University of Illinois, at Champaign, where he had four years of military training. He enlisted and saw service on the Mexican Border, and in the World War rapidly rose to the rank of captain, having been connected with General Pershing's Headquarters Company. Upon the completion of the World War he was sent to Hawaii by the government upon an educational mission.

DROMGOLD, DR. S. T. Dr. S. T. Dromgold, son of John and Bandinah (Hench) Dromgold, was born in Saville Township, March 26, 1852. He attended the common schools, Airy View Academy, and the Bloomfield

EVERHART, DR. EDGAR S. Dr. Edgar S. Everhart was born at Millerstown in 1879, the son of William and Mary (Goodman) Everhart. He attended the public schools and Phillips Exeter Academy. He graduated from Dickinson College in 1903, and from the University of Pennsylvania in 1907. He entered medical practice at Lemoyne, Pa., where he was in active practice until the World War. He then entered the Medical Corps of the United States Army as first lieutenant, later being assigned as Junior Medical Officer of the 308th Infantry, at Camp Upton, New York. March 1, 1918, he was assigned as surgeon of the 302d Ammunition Train, and landed in France on May 4th. From July 15th to November 11th he was in the Oise-Ainse offensive and the Argonne-Meuse offensive engagements, On October 16th he was transferred as the commanding officer of the 307th Field Hospital, Seventy-Seventh Division. He was promoted to the rank of captain, April 13, 1918, and on November 26th was promoted to the rank of major. He is at present with the Pennsylvania State Department of Health.

EVERHART, DR. JAMES K. Dr. James K. Everhart was born at Millerstown, June 15, 1878, the son of William and Mary E. (Goodman) Everhart. He attended the public schools and Millersville State Normal School. In 1902 he graduated from the University of Pennsylvania. During 1902-03 he was an interne at Germantown Hospital, Philadelphia. He located at Millerstown in 1903, and practiced there for over a year, when he located at Pittsburgh, where he has since practiced. He is assistant professor in Diseases of Children at the University of Pittsburgh at this time.

FAHNESTOCK, S. B. S. B. Fahnestock, the ninth county superintendent of schools of Perry County, was born in Oliver Township, March 3, 1848, the son of Daniel and Nancy (McNaughton) Fahnestock. He was educated in the local schools, at Juniata College, and the Millersville State Normal School. He was principal of schools at Duncannon, Newport, Millerstown, and Williamstown, Dauphin County. He served as county superintendent of schools during 1878-80, inclusive. After retiring he became connected with the Surgeon General's office at Washington, D. C., in 1885, which position he held until his death on October 14, 1887. He was notable as a Bible student.

FERGUSON, JOHN F. Although born at Pittsburgh, February 12, 1890, John F. Ferguson was early brought, with two sisters, to New Bloomfield, where he was reared in the family of Mr. and Mrs. Luke Baker, his uncle and aunt. His father was John Ferguson, and his mother Cecilia (Clancy) Ferguson. He attended the public schools, graduating from the New Bloomfield High School, and the International Correspondence Schools of Scranton. He is at present public accountant and treasurer, tax collector, and public administrator of Shoshone County, Idaho.

FERGUSON, JOHN F. John Frazier Ferguson was born in Centre Township, February 6, 1870, the son of Jesse Miller and Mary Ellen (Orwan) Ferguson. He attended the public schools, the New Bloomfield Academy, the Cumberland Valley State Normal School, Columbia University, State College, and took extension courses during the last nine years from the University of Pittsburgh, the University of Pennsylvania, and Lehigh University. He is a supervisory principal of the Harrisburg public schools.

FLICKINGER, DR. W. H. Dr. William H. Flickinger was born at Loysville, May 10, 1886, the son of Newton F. and Minnie (Oxenford) Flickinger. He attended the public schools and the University of Maryland, graduating from the Medical College of Virginia in 1917. In earlier years he had taught in the public schools of Jackson Township. He is a

Markelville Academy and also at college he taught in the interim to help pay his way to an education. In 1864 and 1865 he was in charge of the academy at Aaronsburg, Pennsylvania. During 1866-67 he taught at Lima, Ohio, and in 1868-69 was superintendent of schools at Miamisburg, Ohio. In 1869-70 he was at the head of the Boys' High School at Harrisburg, Pennsylvania, and in 1870 was elected superintendent of the schools of the City of Harrisburg. His selection came through his stand for system and order in the schools. Under his supervision a course of study was adopted and the schools of the state capital forged to the front. He remained at the head of the city schools until his death in 1905. He was one of the founders of the public library and long chairman of the Bible Society. In 1868 he was united in marriage to Elizabeth Eleanor Kuhn, a daughter of Rev. Samuel Kuhn.

FOSSELMAN, REV. M. F. Rev. Millard F. Fosselman was born in Juniata Township, October 4, 1856, the son of John and Susan (Dum) Fosselman. He attended the public schools and Union Seminary at New Berlin, Pennsylvania, from 1878 to 1881. He entered the ministry of the Evangelical Association, now the United Evangelical Church, in the year 1881. He served forty years in the ministry, eight of which he was presiding elder, the highest position within the gift of his conference. He is now located at Williamsport.

FOSSELMAN, JOHN JONES. One of four children of William and Rebecca (Jones) Fosselman, John Jones Fosselman was born in Donally's Mills, Tuscarora Township, October 18, 1879. He attended the local schools and taught at seventeen. He attended the New Bloomfield Academy and Indiana State Normal School, where he graduated in 1898. Immediately afterwards he enlisted in the Spanish-American War. In 1900 he was appointed a clerk in the U. S. Pension Bureau at Washington. In 1901-02 he attended Lafayette College at Easton, where he took a scientific course. In 1903 he became a clerk in the U. S. Bureau of Education at Washington and matriculated at George Washington University, from which he later received his A.B. and LL.B. degrees. In 1906 he was appointed fourth assistant examiner in the United States Patent Office. On January 25, 1910, he was admitted to the bar of the District of Columbia. In 1912 he received the degree M.L.P. (Master of Patent Law) from the National University, having passed at the head of his class. In 1913 he was admitted to the bar of the U. S. Supreme Court. January 1, 1918, he was made first assistant examiner of the Patent Office, after having been successively promoted to second and third assistant. He was a member of the Pennsylvania Society of the District of Columbia and a student and champion of Esperanto, the universal language.

FOYE, EDWARD M. Edward M. Foye was born at New Bloomfield, January 16, 1870, the son of Charles and Zorah (Boyles) Foye. He was educated in the public schools and learned the printing trade in the office of the *Duncannon* (Pa.) *Record*. Locating in Erie County, he edited and published the *Northeast Advertiser* for ten years. In the meantime he studied law at Erie, was admitted to the bar and practiced many years. He is the author of several legal publications which had a large sale. Mr. Foye is now an extensive fruit grower on the shores of Lake Erie.

FRANK, REV. A. L. Rev. A. L. Frank was born in Howe Township, near Newport, November 22, 1865, the third son of Lewis and Susan (Rathfon) Frank. He attended the public schools, the night school conducted by Silas Wright, and the Bloomfield Academy for a number of spring terms. He began teaching in 1885, and continued until 1898, in the townships of Howe and Miller, New Buffalo High, East Newport High, Evergreen High, Marysville Grammar, and Baskinsville High Schools.

Entering the ministry of the Methodist Episcopal Church, he served pastorates at Thompsontown, Hustontown, Frankstown, Shawville, New Washington, Stormstown, Mahaffey, Mt. Holly Springs, Coalport, Hopewell and Weatherly, where he is now located.

FUNK, REV. J. J. Rev. James Julius Funk was born May 21, 1869, at Liverpool. At nine years of age he began to follow the life of a canal boatman on the old Pennsylvania Canal during the summer, attending the public schools in the winter. He later lived near Montgomery's Ferry, and attended school there. He taught school in Watts Township, and in 1891 was converted at a revival meeting at the Hill Church. In 1899 he entered the ministry of the United Brethren Church, serving the following charges in the Allegheny Conference of Western Pennsylvania: Industry, Ligonier, Woodland, Westmoreland, and the Homestead Avenue Church at Johnstown, where he has been for the past eight years. He was ordained in 1901 by Bishop Kephart. During his present pastorate his congregation has erected a handsome and expensive church and parsonage. In 1917 he served as a delegate to the General Conference of the U. B. Church in the United States, which met at Wichita, Kansas.

GABLE, J. H. J. H. Gable was born near New Germantown, the son of John and Elizabeth (Eby) Gable. His mother was a daughter of Elder John Eby, long one of western Perry's prominent citizens. Mr. Gable was the second of twelve children, all of whom are living and who were reared without ever calling a physician—a most remarkable occurrence. When a lad he was taken West with the family. In Illinois he learned telegraphy, serving almost ten years at that occupation. For thirty years he was the traveling passenger agent of the Chicago & Northwestern Railway System, a position requiring tact and diplomacy. He was retired at his own request, and resides at Lincoln, Nebraska.

GANTT, T. FULTON. T. Fulton Gantt was born at New Bloomfield, January 31, 1849, the son of Daniel Gantt (later Chief Justice of Nebraska) and Agnes T. (Fulton) Gantt. In 1857 the father moved to Nebraska and, with him went the little son. Upon the death of his mother he returned to Pennsylvania, but in 1863 again went to Nebraska. In 1867 he completed the machinist trade in the railroad shops at North Platte, Nebraska. After finishing his trade he went to Nebraska and studied law with his father. He was admitted to the bar in 1870, and located at North Platte. Later he practiced at Deadwood, S. D. From 1877 to 1888 he was connected with the U. S. Government at Washington, D. C. He then returned to North Platte, Nebraska, where he practiced law until his death in August, 1897. Like his father, he was an exemplary man.

GANTT, AMOS E. Amos E. Gantt was born October 4, 1853, in New Bloomfield, the son of Daniel Gantt (later Chief Justice of Nebraska) and Agnes T. (Fulton) Gantt. His family moved to Nebraska in 1857, where he was educated in the public schools, with several years at the State University. He read law with his father, and at the age of twenty-one was admitted to the bar. He entered the newspaper business, and from 1876 to 1879 published a paper at North Platte, Nebraska. In 1879 he settled in Falls City, Nebraska, and practiced law there until his death in March, 1914. He served as district attorney in 1891-92. Like his illustrious father, he was held in high esteem.

GANTT, WILLIAM E. William E. Gantt, son of Joseph and Mary A. (McGowan) Gantt, was born in Centre Township, April 29, 1845. He was educated in the common schools, and when eighteen enlisted in the Signal Corps of the Union Army. After the Civil War he taught school in Perry County and then went West as a surveyor, being located at Sioux City, Iowa, for a time. He read law at Elk Point, South Dakota. On being admitted to the bar he opened a law office at Ponca, Nebraska, where he remained until 1899, when he removed to Sioux City. He later located at California, where he died in 1920.

GARDNER, REV. J. CHAS. Rev. J. Charles Gardner was born at Benvenue, Duncan's Island, on June 24, 1858, being the son of Ephraim Finley and Catrinah Jane (Kenee) Gardner. He was educated in the public schools and in Silas Wright's Academy, at Millerstown. He graduated from the U. B. Theological Seminary at Dayton, Ohio, in 1894, since which time he has preached at Baltimore, Md.; Dayton, Ohio; Shippensburg, Shiremanstown, Newburg, Red Lion, Gettysburg, Greencastle and Duncannon. For the last six years he has been located at Williamsport, Md. Six churches and three parsonages have been built by the congregations over which he was in charge.

GARMAN, REV. SHERIDAN G. Rev. Sheridan G. Garman was born in August, 1866, before his father, Rev. John Garman, located in Perry County, but came with him as a child, and always counted Perry County his home. His mother was Margaret (Ferguson) Garman. He received his education in the public schools and taught several terms in Perry County, before entering Lebanon Valley College, where he graduated. He then entered the ministry and preached at York, Pennsylvania, for over a year, but left to enter Bonbrake Theological Seminary at Dayton, Ohio, from which he graduated in 1901. Resuming the ministry, this time in the State of Wisconsin, he preached for several years. He then transferred to the Galesburg Conference, and in 1910 was elected presiding elder and conference treasurer. He died during November, 1901, his wife living but one year longer.

GELBACH, W. H. William H. Gelbach was born in Penn Township, October 9, 1866, the son of Henry and Louisa (Bowser) Gelbach. He attended the public schools, the Keystone State Normal School, and Rochester Business University in New York. He taught in the Perry County public schools for seven years, and quit teaching to become the cashier of the Second National Bank of Mechanicsburg, Pa. For the last eighteen years he has been cashier of the Citizens National Bank of Waynesboro, which has erected one of the finest banking buildings in southern Pennsylvania. He suggested a plan for using Liberty Bonds for circulation—bank currency. which appeared in the Congressional Record.

GIBSON, GEORGE E. George E. Gibson, son of Francis West and Tabitha (Kennedy) Gibson, was born on the Gibson homestead, near Falling Springs, September 27, 1860. He attended the public schools and learned printing under the tutelage of J. L. McCaskey, in the *Duncannon Record* office. He located at Erie, where he was employed as a compositor on the Erie *Daily Times*. He then studied law at Normal University in Ohio, and was admitted to the Erie bar in 1884. He died January 28, 1916. Mr. Gibson was a man of a kindly and philosophical disposition and absolute integrity, and is reputed to have been a good lawyer.

GIBSON, REUBEN. Reuben Gibson, known as R. Bannister Gibson by reason of having been jokingly referred to as "Bannister" on account of his last name being Gibson, adopted that name when he began the practice of law. He was born May 19, 1862, at the Gibson home, near Falling Springs. He attended the public schools and New Bloomfield Academy. He then taught a number of terms in the public schools and graduated from Dickinson Law School in 1894, being admitted to the Perry County bar the same year. After practicing a number of years he located elsewhere.

GRUBB, DR. I. N. Dr. Isaac Newton Grubb was born August 25, 1845, in Perry Valley, the son of Henry and Margaret (Charles) Grubb. He

burg Academy in 1905, and from Dickinson College in 1908. He graduated
from Johns Hopkins Medical School in 1912. He was connected with the
Johns Hopkins Hospital from 1915 to 1919. He entered the United States
Medical Corps during the World War as captain and was promoted to
major. He saw service with the British in various shell shock hospitals
in France and in the First Army of the A. E. F. In 1919 he became senior
assistant physician at St. Elizabeth's Hospital in Washington, D. C.

HALL, WM. F. William F. Hall was born in Jackson Township, adjoining Blain, on January 19, 1892, the son of Harry M. and Florence V.
(Shreffler) Hall. He attended the public schools of Jackson Township
and graduated from Millersville Normal School in 1913. He taught in
the schools of Jackson Township and Duncannon, and was supervisory
principal of the Christiana schools, 1914-15. He graduated from Pennsylvania State College in 1920. He served in the World War, being commissioned a second lieutenant in the U. S. Infantry, on August 20, 1918.
In 1920 he was director of the Vocational High School at Newtown Square,
and in 1921 he was director of the Petersburg Community Vocational
School, since which time he has been associated with the rural life department of the Pennsylvania State College, as head of the farm shop work.

HAMILTON, F. A. F. A. Hamilton was born in Liverpool, February
18, 1873, the son of John J. and Susan A. (Myers) Hamilton. He was
educated in the local schools, graduating from the Liverpool High School
in 1888. He attended the Bryant & Stratton Business College in Philadelphia, and graduated from the Millersville Normal School in 1898. In 1916
he attended State College, taking special work. He taught school in Liverpool Township, was principal of the Liverpool schools for nine years, and
principal of the Bellwood schools for fourteen years, still holding that
position.

HARKINS, REV. JOHN F. Rev. John F. Harkins was born in Jackson Township, February 21, 1891, the son of Simon Edward and Mary
Elizabeth (Stambaugh) Harkins. He attended the Blain schools and Susquehanna University, from which he graduated in 1915. He finished his
theological course at the same institution in 1918, since which time he has
been pastor of Grace Lutheran Church at State College. During 1919-20
he was president of the Northern Conference of the Central Pennsylvania
Synod.

HART, REV. L. I. Rev. L. I. Hart was born near New Germantown,
October 16, 1871, the very year of his father's death, who left six small
children. His father was Levi J. Hart, and his mother Mary Elizabeth
(Cogley) Hart. He attended the Loysville Soldiers' Orphans' Home four
years, Juniata College one year, and Williamsport Dickinson Seminary
four years. On August 26, 1901, he joined the Colorado Conference of
the Methodist Episcopal Church. In 1903 he transferred to the Ohio Conference, in 1914 to the Northeast Ohio Conference, and in 1916, again to
the Ohio Conference. In 1921 he retired to enter business, and is now
assistant to the president of the Cleveland Discount Company, the largest
first mortgage concern in the United States. During his ministry he served
pastorates at Beuna Vista, Mosca and Del Norte, in Colorado, and at
Crown City, Chatham, Neil Avenue in Columbus, Manly, Portsmouth and
Galion, in Ohio.

HARTMAN, REV. H. H. Rev. Harry H. Hartman was born in Saville Township, October 25, 1868, the son of John and Catherine Matilda
(Brandt) Hartman. He was educated in the public schools and the Cumberland Valley State Normal School. He completed the academic course at
Ursinus and entered the college in 1890, graduating in 1894. He completed
his theological course at Ursinus in 1897, and was ordained to the min-

istry of the Reformed Church in May. He served as pastor at East Vincent, in 1897-98; of the Woodcock Valley charge in Huntingdon County, 1898-1902; of Memorial charge, Dayton, Ohio, 1902-13, and of Bethany Tabernacle charge, Philadelphia, from 1913 to 1921. He was president of Miami Classis in 1904 and served as a member of the Board of Publication of the Ohio Synod in 1904-10. He served as a member of the Board of Visitors of the Central Theological Seminary 1910-13, and was president of Philadelphia Classis in 1920.

HARTZELL, REV. C. V. Rev. Chas. V. Hartzell was born at Newport, March 9, 1856, the son of John and Augusta (Giebel) Hartzell. He attended the public schools of Newport, Williamsport Dickinson Seminary, where he graduated in 1879, and Drew Theological Seminary at Madison, New Jersey, taking a postgraduate course at the latter place. For several years before entering Dickinson Seminary he was employed as a telegraph operator on the Middle Division of the Pennsylvania Railroad, being stationed at Newport, Marysville, Mifflin, Huntingdon, Tyrone and Altoona. He resigned this position to become agent of the East Broad Top Railroad, at Robertsdale, on the opening of that road. He resigned this position in 1875 to enter Dickinson Seminary. In 1879 he entered the ministry of the Methodist Episcopal Church, serving continuously until March, 1921, when he voluntarily retired, locating at Muncy, Pennsylvania. Among the churches he served were Millerstown, Huntingdon, Hollidaysburg, Waynesboro, Harrisburg, and York. From March, 1903, to January, 1913, he was chief clerk of State Department of Factory Inspection, and from January 6, 1913, to June 3 of the same year, he was chief factory inspector, being the last person to hold that office. During his years of employment by the state he served pastoral charges at a merely nominal salary. In 1904 the Ohio Northern University conferred the D.D. degree upon him.

HEIM, REV. G. R. Rev. G. Robert Heim was born on the old Heim farm, near Loysville, April 13, 1883, the son of George W. and Mary V. (Shuman) Heim. He attended the public schools until seventeen, and graduated from the Millersville State Normal School in 1905. He graduated from Gettysburg College in 1913, and from the Gettysburg Theological Seminary in 1916. Prior to this he had taught school seven years in ungraded, summer normal and high schools. He organized the first Township High School in Perry County, at Lower Duncannon, in Penn Township. This school was later merged with the Duncannon High School. Entering the ministry in 1916, he was pastor of the Lutheran Church of Our Saviour at Coatesville. On March 2, 1918, he entered the U. S. Army as a chaplain, serving fifteen months, of which one year was in France. He was assigned to the Eightieth Division, and was on active duty, including participation in the great Meuse-Argonne offensive. Soon after his discharge he assumed charge of the Lutheran pastorage at Blain, where he is now located.

HEISLEY, REV. L. H. Rev. L. H. Heisley was born in Rye Township, near Marysville, January 3, 1894, the son of William and Annie Rebecca (Fisher) Heisley. He attended the public schools and Albright Academy at Myerstown, where he graduated in 1914. He was a student at Albright College, the Moody Bible Institute, and McCormick Theological Seminary of Chicago. He was pastor of the North Ashland Avenue United Evangelical Church of Chicago during 1916 and 1917. He was pastor of the church at Manhattan, Illinois, during 1918, and in 1919 became pastor of the Cragin Congregational Church of Chicago, which position he fills at this time.

HENCH, ATKINSON L. Atkinson L. Hench, oldest son of George and Mary (Hackett) Hench, was born in Saville Township, January 24,

1838. He attended Big Spring Academy, walking home to Centre over the week ends, one of many young men then attending academies and colleges who did that. He then entered his father's tannery and later was the owner of an interest in it, which he resold to his father, and in 1872 located at Pleasantville, Bedford County, where he built a tannery. He became one of Bedford County's representative citizens and was twice elected to the General Assembly of Pennsylvania.

HENCH, REV. SILAS M. Another Perry Countian who carried the Christian message to distant peoples was Rev. Silas M. Hench, born in Northeast Madison Township, November 1, 1851. His parents were George W. and Frances Rice Hench. His schooling started in the district schools, continued at Markelville Academy and at Airy View Academy at Port Royal, Pa., where he prepared for college. Was valedictorian of his class at Ursinus College in 1877, and in 1879 graduated from the Theological School of the same college. Entered the ministry at Walkersville, Maryland, the same year and remained in that pastorate twenty-eight and one-half years, a rare record indeed. During the greater part of this period he resided in Frederick, Maryland. Served many religious offices of distinction while there, the principal one being that of the presidency of Maryland Classis of the Reformed Church. During this pastorate one new congregation was organized, the parent one became two self-supporting ones, and four new church buildings were erected. His second and last pastorate was the charge at Cavetown, Washington County, Maryland, from October 1, 1909, to November 1, 1916. He then retired from active service, and at Trappe, Montgomery County, Pennsylvania, he lives in retirement.

HENCH, JACOB BIXLER. Jacob Bixler Hench, the son of Atcheson L. and Alice (Bixler) Hench, was born at Center, Madison Township, February 21, 1863. He attended the common schools of Perry and Bedford Counties, Shellsburg High School, and graduated from Lafayette College. He taught in the Freemount Seminary at Norristown, in Blair Presbyterian Academy, at Blairstown, N. J.; Dearborn-Morgan School, Orange, N. J., and at Shady Side Academy at Pittsburgh. He then became the founder and is the present principal and owner of the University School, Pittsburgh, Pa. He is secretary of the Pittsburgh Society of the Archæological Institute of America, the Academy of Science and Art of Pittsburgh, and of the Presbyterian Union of Pittsburgh.

HENCH, REV. C. R. Rev. C. R. Hench was born at Eshcol, Saville Township, June 12, 1875, the son of Ross and Mary (Bixler) Hench. He attended the public schools, two summer terms under Prof. W. E. Baker, at Eshcol, and the Rochester Business Institute. He graduated from the Theological Department of Temple University, Philadelphia, in 1904. Before entering the ministry he was a bookkeeper at the League Island Navy Yard. His first pastorate was the Rosedale Baptist Church at Camden, N. J., 1907 to 1910. In 1910-11 he was pastor of the Baptist Church at Powell, Wyoming. From 1913 to 1918 he was again pastor of Rosedale Baptist Church at Camden. During the World War, from April, 1918, to August, 1919, he was in Y. M. C. A. work in France and Belgium.

HENCH, REV. S. L. Rev. S. L. Hench was born September 29, 1885, at Kistler, Perry County, the son of William Monroe and Matilda Emaline (Ernest) Hench. He attended the public schools until seventeen, and then taught one term. He attended the New Bloomfield Academy and Albright College, where he graduated in 1910. In 1913 he graduated from the Lutheran Seminary at Gettysburg. He has been pastor of Christ Lutheran Church, Dallastown, for the past seven years. He has been president of the York County Conference and a delegate to the United Lutheran Church Convention in Washington, D. C. For over two years, during war times, he was a teacher in the Dallastown High School.

HENCH, REV. THOMAS H. Rev. Thomas H. Hench was born April 5, 1840, at Centre, Madison Township, the son of George and Mary (Hackett) Hench. He attended the public schools and prepared for college at Loysville Academy, 1855-58. He graduated from Princeton College in 1861, and from the Theological Seminary in 1866. He was made a D.D. by Hanover College, Indiana, in 1894. He was a Presbyterian pastor and a noted one for over fifty years. He resides at Carthage, Missouri, in retirement.

HIPPLE, WESLEY. Wesley Hipple was born in Rye Township, and later became a successful ward principal in the city schools of Harrisburg, a position which he held until his death, in 1910.

HOBACH, DR. JOHN U. Dr. John U. Hobach was born at Green Park, Tyrone Township, the son of George and Catharine (Bernheisel) Hobach. He attended the public schools, graduated from Franklin and Marshall College in 1878, and the University of Pennsylvania in 1884. He has long been connected with the Penn Mutual Life Insurance Company of Philadelphia, as medical examiner.

HOLLENBAUGH, REV. J. A. Rev. J. A. Hollenbaugh was born at Blain, March 5, 1852, the son of Samuel and Mary (Rowe) Hollenbaugh. He attended the public school at Stony Point, the Select School at Blain, and entered Union Seminary at New Berlin (Now Albright College, Myerstown), in 1873. He entered the ministry of the Evangelical Church, and preached for forty-four years. He was presiding elder of the Williamsport District of the Central Pennsylvania Conference for four years and of the Carlisle District for four years. He served six years in the Oregon Conference, and at the following places in Pennsylvania: Lewisburg, Lock Haven, Williamsport (two churches), Altoona and Lewisburg, also at Baltimore, Md., always staying the limit of time. He was thrice delegate to the General Conference of his church. He was retired in March, 1921, and resides at Lewisburg.

HULINGS, DAVID W. David W. Hulings, a Perry Countian, graduated at Dickinson College, read law in the offices of his uncle, David Watts, and located at Lewistown in 1818; same year appointed deputy attorney-general for Mifflin County. About 1830 became the owner of Hope furnace, which he operated for many years. Later ceased the practice of law.

HULINGS, FRED'K. WATTS. Frederick Watts Hulings, son of Thomas and Elizabeth (Watts) Hulings, was born in Buffalo (now Watts) Township, March 9, 1792. He settled in Tennessee, where he became speaker of the House of Representatives. He cast his lot with the Confederacy and became a captain in the Southern Army. While attempting to board a train during the war he was severely wounded, from the effects of which he died.

HULL, DR. G. L. Dr. G. L. Hull, principal of Banks Business College, at Philadelphia, was born at Markelville, Perry County.

ICKES, DR. JONAS. Dr. Jonas Ickes, a son of Nicholas Ickes, is spoken of in the Bloomfield Borough chapter, elsewhere in this book. He first practiced medicine several years at Ickesburg, then from the farm of Rev. Joseph Brady, one mile west of Duncannon, whose daughter he had married. In 1825 he located at Bloomfield, and in 1856 moved to Monmouth, Illinois, and later to other sections of the state. His wife died in

1868. In 1879 he returned to Monmouth to reside with his daughter, Susan Ickes Harding. Later he lost his sight, and his hearing was also greatly impaired. Susan Ickes Harding had married Gen. A. C. Harding, in 1835, and resided at Monmouth. During her life she was a great friend of the Collegiate Institute at Geneseo, Illinois, and presented two buildings to that institution, one a dormitory and the other known as Harding Hall.

IRVINE, REV. J. E. Rev. J. E. Irvine was born in Saville Township, the son of John and Eleanor (Elliot) Irvine. He was educated in the public schools and the Juniata Valley Normal School of Prof. Wright, beginning teaching at the age of sixteen. He later attended the Culpepper Classical Academy, and then entered Washington and Jefferson College, at Washington, Pa., where he graduated in 1883. He then taught in Buffalo (Washington Co.) Academy for one year, after which he entered the Western Theological Seminary, at Pittsburgh, graduating in 1887. He was ordained into the ministry of the Presbyterian Church in 1888, and served as pastor at Fredonia and Cool Spring for two years. He became pastor of the Third Presbyterian Church of Altoona, in 1889, and remained until 1917. Was awarded the Ph.D. degree by the University of Wooster in 1898. In 1917 he became the pastor of the Williamsburg (Blair Co.) Presbyterian Church. He is the stated clerk of Huntingdon Presbytery since 1905.

IRVINE, REV. S. L. Rev. Samuel Linn Irvine, son of John and Mary (Elliott) Irvine, was born at Ickesburg, June 13, 1862. He attended the public schools, graduating from Roanoke College, located at Salem, Virginia, in 1886, as valedictorian of his class. In 1889 he graduated from Princeton Theological Seminary. He entered the ministry of the Presbyterian Church in the same year and was pastor of the Cooperstown, Sunville and Sugar Creek Memorial churches. in Venango County, Pa., from 1889 to 1894; the Lower Brandywine Presbyterian Church at Wilmington, Delaware, from 1889 to 1903; the Hobart, Oklahoma, Church, 1903-04; Sapulpa (I. T.), Oklahoma, 1904-06, and Highland Church, located at Street, Maryland, from 1906 to the present time (1922).

JACKMAN, WM. J. William James Jackman, son of James and Eliza Louisa (Mitchell) Jackman, was born at Liverpool, September 20, 1837. He attended the public schools and William Mitchell's Select School at Dauphin, and the New Bloomfield Academy. He then learned printing, and in 1856 again attended the New Bloomfield Academy, after which he taught several terms in Perry County. He worked throughout the West as a journeyman printer, enlisted in the First Pennsylvania Cavalry, in July, 1861, and after the war purchased the *Juniata True Democrat*, at Mifflintown, which had been owned by Dr. E. Darwin Crawford, forming a partnership with Mr. Grier. In October, 1867, he and Amos Bonsall, owner of the *Register*, formed a partnership and merged the papers into the *Democrat and Register*. Mr. Bonsall died in 1888, and Mr. Jackman became sole proprietor, publishing the paper until his death, November 5, 1900.

JACKSON, J. ROY. J. Roy Jackson was born at New Buffalo, May 3, 1886, the son of J. Benson and Caroline (Bair) Jackson. He attended the public schools, graduated from the Cumberland Valley State Normal School in 1908, and from Dickinson College in 1914. During 1920 he did graduate work at the University of Pittsburgh, and in 1921, at State College. He was at the head of the Department of Science in the Coraopolis High School, supervising principal of the Battles Memorial School at Girard (1916-19), and principal of the New Brighton High School since 1919.

52

JACKSON, W. B.   William B. Jackson was born at New Buffalo, October 3, 1880, the son of J. Benson and Caroline (Bair) Jackson. He attended the public schools and Dickinson Preparatory School at Carlisle. He graduated from Dickinson College in 1903, attended three summer sessions of the University of Pennsylvania, and traveled three months in Germany. He was the principal of the Township High School at Madeira, Pa., assistant principal of the Lewistown Schools, instructor of languages at Wenonah Military Academy (Wenonah, N. J.), instructor of languages at the Harrisburg (Pa.) Academy, and assistant principal of the Duncannon schools. He spent ten months in France with the A. E. F. as a Y. M. C. A. secretary, since which time he has been instructor of languages in the Friends' Central School at Fifteenth and Race Streets, Philadelphia.

JACKSON, WM. STEELL.   William Steell Jackson, son of Joseph E. and Isabelle (Steell) Jackson, was born at Duncannon, March 11, 1871. He attended the public schools and prepared for college at Blairstown, New Jersey. He then learned the machinist's trade at Steelton. He graduated in the electrical engineering course at Lehigh University and took law courses at the National University, Washington, and Columbian (now George Washington) University. He then spent five years as an assistant examiner in the Patent Office at Washington, D. C. He located at Philadelphia, where he has since practiced law, specializing on patents

JOHNSTON, DR. R. W.   Dr. Russell W. Johnston was born at New Bloomfield, December 12, 1888, the son of Alexander Russell and Laura Theresa (Willhide) Johnston. He attended the public schools and graduated from the New Bloomfield Academy in 1904. He graduated from the College Preparatory Department of the Lock Haven State Normal School in 1905, attended Princeton University for one year, and graduated from the Jefferson Medical College in 1910. He served as an interne in the hospital of the Protestant Episcopal Church at Philadelphia, from June, 1910, to November, 1912. With the exception of a period of four months of military service as a first lieutenant in the Medical Corps of the U. S. Army, he has since practiced medicine at Selinsgrove. He is an assistant surgeon on the staff of the Mary Ann Packer Hospital at Sunbury.

JOHNSTON, REV. ROBERT.   Rev. Robert Johnston was born in the Sherman's Valley about the time of the Revolutionary War. In 1792 his father removed to western Pennsylvania and settled on a farm near Canonsburg, Washington County. This enabled Robert to secure a collegiate education and enter the ministry. The families on both sides were Presbyterians, of Scotch-Irish descent.

JOHNSTON, REV. EDWARD.   Rev. Edward Johnston, a brother of Rev. Robert, named above, was born in the Sherman's Valley about the time of the Revolutionary War. His father removed to western Pennsylvania in 1792 and settled on a farm near Canonsburg, thus enabling Edward to secure a college education and enter the ministry. He was a descendant of Scotch-Irish Presbyterians on both the paternal and maternal sides.

JONES, CHAS. A.   Charles Alvin Jones was born at Newport, August 27, 1887, the son of Alvin and Mary Elizabeth (Sheats) Jones. He attended the public schools, Mercersburg Academy, and Williams College at Williamstown, Mass. He graduated from Dickinson Law School in 1910 with the LL.B. degree, since which time he has been a members of the Allegheny County bar, having served on the executive committee of the same for two terms.

KELL, C. J.   C. J. Kell was born at Blain, May 8, 1892, the son of Reuben H. and Annie M. (Baker) Kell. He was educated in the public schools and attended Conway Hall Preparatory School at Carlisle, graduating from State College in 1916, in the agricultural course. He was supervisor of agriculture in the Falls Township Vocational School, at Mill City, Pa., 1916-17, and director of the Vocational School at Newfoundland, Pa., 1918-19, since which time he has been county supervisor of agriculture of Westmoreland County, with headquarters at Greensburg, Pa.

KELL, REV. B. H. Rev. Benjamin Harrison Kell, son of Amos Frank and Elizabeth Jane (Kuhn) Kell, was born near Ickesburg, in Saville Township, August 22, 1889. He attended the common schools and New Bloomfield Academy. He was graduated from Ursinus College in 1914, with a B.A. degree, and from McCormick Theological Seminary in Chicago, in 1917, with the degree of B.D. He also graduated from the University of Chicago in 1917. He was licensed by the Chicago Presbytery and ordained to the gospel ministry in 1917. He was a chaplain in the United States Army during the World War, 1918. He was the pastor of the First Presbyterian Church at Hazleton, Idaho, 1918-20, since which time he has been pastor of the Milwaukee (Wis.) Berean Presbyterian Church.

KELL, DR. E. A. Dr. Elmer Andrew Kell was born in Loysville, January 20, 1879, the son of Peter J. and Sarah E. (Long) Kell. He attended the public schools and the New Bloomfield Academy, graduating there in 1895. He taught school one term and then entered Baltimore Medical College, from which he graduated in 1900. He served one year as interne at the Maryland General Hospital at Baltimore. He then became medical examiner in the relief department of the Pennsylvania Railroad at Baltimore, where he remained until 1910. He was in active practice at Pottstown (Pa.) from 1910 to 1915. In November, 1915, he began practice at Rawlins, Wyoming. Taking an interest in Republican politics, he was elected mayor of Rawlins in 1921 by that party, on a law and order platform.

KELL, DR. RALPH C. Dr. Ralph C. Kell was born November 11, 1882, at Elliottsburg, the son of Emanuel and Jemima (Foose) Kell. He attended the public schools and graduated from the New Bloomfield Academy. He entered Jefferson Medical College, from which he graduated in 1905. He was resident physician of the Phœnixville Hospital for a year. From 1906 to 1909 he was at Waverly, Massachusetts, as assistant physician at the McLean Hospital, doing special work in mental diseases. In 1909 he was with the Worcester State Insane Hospital, and from 1910 to 1912 he was superintendent of the Chester County Hospital for the Insane. In 1913 he entered the services of the relief department of the Pennsylvania Railroad as a medical examiner.

KELL, PHILIP S. Philip S. Kell, son of Joseph and Margaret (Hench) Kell, was born October 22, 1850, in Saville Township. He attended the usual four months' school sessions of that period until he was eighteen. In February, 1869, having a desire to see the great West he went to Wilton Junction, Iowa, where he attended a Western Baptist School, affording an academic course, making his home with his sister, who lived there. He taught several years and then located at Des Moines, engaging in the newspaper business. He began at the bottom, setting type, and passed through all departments until he became general manager. In 1890 he founded the *Spirit of the West*, a weekly journal devoted to the promotion of country, district and state agricultural fairs, pedigreed stock, etc. He owned and controlled this for twenty-five years, but sold it in 1915 and moved to California. He was nominated for Congress by the Democrat Congressional Convention of the Seventh Iowa District in 1888, but declined the nomination.

KELL, RALPH L. Ralph L. Kell was born at Loysville, September 8, 1881, the son of Peter J. and Sarah E. (Long) Kell. He attended the public schools at Loysville and the New Bloomfield Academy, where he graduated in 1901. He graduated from State College in 1905 in civil engineering. He was assistant supervisor for the Pennsylvania Railroad, being located at Millville (N. J.), Freeport, Altoona, and Chester (Pa.). Since that time he has held positions with prominent engineering firms and with the State Water Supply Commission of Pennsylvania. He is now connected with a prominent engineering firm at Lancaster.

KELLER, REV. B. F. Rev. B. F. Keller is another of those persons generally known as Perry Countians, but who was born elsewhere. Rev. Keller was born of Perry County parents, then residing at East Prospect, York County, on March 4, 1851. Before he was six his parents moved back to the county. He was a son of Emanuel and Elizabeth (Barshinger) Keller. He attended the public schools and Union Seminary at New Berlin. He entered the ministry of the Evangelical Church, in March, 1875. He has served as pastor at Jersey Shore, Bendersville, Liverpool, Tunkhannock, and many others of like import.

KERN, O. B. Oliver B. Kern was born at Blain, Pa., September 29, 1871, the son of David N. and Ellen M. Kern. He attended the Blain public schools, and during the winter of 1887-88 took private lessons with the late J. C. Preisler at Landisburg. He graduated from Millersville Normal School in 1893, and from Franklin and Marshall College in 1899. He spent a year at the Teachers' College, Columbia, Missouri, 1903-04. He taught in Perry and Lancaster Counties for a number of years, and from 1900 to 1902 he was principal of the San Juan (Porto Rico) graded and high schools. He was principal of the Reynoldsville High School 1902-03, and a supervising principal in the schools of Camden, N. J., since May, 1904.

KERR, MISS AMANDA. Miss Amanda Kerr was born at Marsh Run, Tuscarora Township, Perry County, April 16, 1875, the daughter of Thompson and Margaretta (Fry) Kerr. She attended "the little red schoolhouse" known as Kerr's, and graduated from the Cumberland Valley State Normal School in 1899. Before graduation she had taught four years in Perry County, and after that she taught six near Easton, Pa. In 1905 she entered the mission field and sailed for India, where she first taught in the schools for Mohammedans and Hindus at Saharanspur. Later she had charge of the Christian Boarding School at Jagroon. In 1915 she enjoyed a furlough, since which time she has been in charge of the Orphanage and Boarding School at Hoshiarspur, where she has more than a hundred "brownies" to mother. Miss Kerr's work in the mission field has been a notable one.

KERR, SAMUEL W. Samuel W. Kerr was born at Landisburg, the son of Lewis Barnett and Elizabeth (Postlethwaite) Kerr, December 5, 1867. He attended the public schools of Madison and Saville Townships, and graduated from Franklin and Marshall College in 1892. He then accepted the principalship of the Clarion Collegiate Institute at Rimersburg, Pennsylvania, which he filled for several years. He taught one year in Franklin and Marshall College, and then, with Prof. Ambrose Cort, established the Reading Classical School at Reading, Pennsylvania, with which he was associated for almost ten years. He then was selected to the faculty of the Boys' High School, at Reading, Pennsylvania, and still fills that position.

KERR, REV. DAVID W. Rev. David W. Kerr, son of Lewis Barnett and Elizabeth (Postlethwaite) Kerr, was born in Tuscarora Township, February 6, 1864. In 1886 he graduated from the Cumberland Valley State Normal School and taught two years as principal at Dauphin, Pennsylvania, having previously taught three years in Saville Township, Perry

County. In 1888 he entered Mercersburg College, spending two years there. He then entered the Theological Seminary of the Reformed Church at Lancaster, where he graduated in 1893. He entered the ministry of the Reformed Church and has since been pastor of the churches at Worthville, Grove City, New Hamburg and Apollo, Pennsylvania. In 1914 he located at Fayette, New York, where he had charge of a unique work along the line of church federation, having been the pastor of the Reformed and Lutheran congregations. There each church maintained its organization as well as its relations to its denomination, but both worship under the ministry of one pastor. The church buildings were used on alternate Sundays. In January, 1921, he assumed charge of the Reformed Church at Orangeville, Pa., where he is now located.

KERR, REV. F. L. Rev. Frank L. Kerr, son of Lewis Barnett and Elizabeth (Postlethwaite) Kerr, was born at Landisburg, September 14, 1869. He was educated in the public schools and later taught in Saville Township. He graduated at Franklin and Marshall College and in 1894 entered the ministry of the Reformed Church. He has served in the following pastorates: Penbrook, Meadville, Newport, Pitcairn, Phœnixville, and New Kensington, where he is now located.

KINER, HENRY L. Henry L. Kiner was born February 1, 1851, the son of William and Margaret (Calhoun) Kiner. While very young, he went with his parents to Illinois, where he became proprietor of the *Geneseo News*, a position which he filled for thirty years. He was mayor of Geneseo, and was a gifted newspaper man. His last work was the writing of a History of Henry County, Illinois. Of his two sons, one is an attorney in Chicago, and another a civil engineer. Mr. Kiner died March 11, 1920, in a hospital in Moline, Illinois, where he had made his home in later years.

KINTER, DR. JOHN H. G. Dr. John H. G. Kinter was born at Millerstown, June 5, 1880, the son of John H. G. and Ann E. (Smith) Kinter. He attended the public schools and graduated from Lafayette College in 1905, and from Jefferson Medical College in 1907. He then located at Chambersburg and is now county medical director and coroner of Franklin County.

KISTLER, LLOYD K. Lloyd K. Kistler was born at Loysville, September 16, 1847, the son of David and Susanna (Rice) Kistler. He was educated at the common schools and the New Bloomfield Academy. He taught in Perry County and in the State of Iowa and Kansas. He served in the 208th Regiment, Pennsylvania Volunteer Infantry, during the Sectional War. He homesteaded a quarter-section near Waterville, Kansas, in 1869. He has written a number of pamphlets upon economic and social lines.

KISTLER, REV. J. L. Rev. John Luther Kistler, son of David and Susanna (Rice) Kistler, was born at Ickesburg, Pa., September 25, 1849. He attended the public schools and graduated from Gettysburg College in 1872. He taught at Susquehanna University in 1874-75. He then went to Hartwick Seminary, Otsego Co., N. Y., in 1876, where he was professor of Greek and Mathematics, resigning in 1920. He received the degrees Sc.D. and D.D. from Gettysburg College.

KISTLER, MARY J. Mary J. Kistler was born at Blain, the daughter of John A. and Caroline V. (Sheibley) Kistler. She attended the public schools and the New Bloomfield Academy, graduating from the Edinboro State Normal School in 1896. She has taught in the schools of Pennsylvania, Massachusetts, and Connecticut, and is now a deaconess in the St. James' Methodist Episcopal Church at New York City, superintendent of the New York Deaconess Home, and superintendent of the New York Deaconess Association.

KISTLER, CLARK B. Clark B. Kistler was born May 22, 1885, at Elliottsburg, the son of Clayton J. and Ellen (Shearer) Kistler. He attended the public schools and the New Bloomfield Academy, graduating from Pennsylvania College in 1909. He did special work at the University of Pittsburgh since then. He taught in the schools of Perry County and in the High School at Connellsville, Pa. In 1913 he taught in the Department of History in the Pittsburgh High School, and in 1915 began teaching Mathematics in Carnegie Institute of Technology.

KISTLER, MISS SUE R. Miss Sue Rice Kistler is another of Perry County's missionaries of note. She is a daughter of David and Susan (Rice) Kistler, and was born October 25, 1863.

KLINE, IRVIN E. Irvin E. Kline was born near Blain, November 22, 1874, the son of William A. and Catherine (Mumper) Kline. He attended the public schools at Blain, graduated from the Lock Haven State Normal School in 1896, and from Dickinson College in 1901. He was a graduate student at Columbia University, New York City, during the summer sessions of 1904-06-07. He taught at Dickinson College Preparatory School, Blair Hall (Blairstown, N. J.), and in the Atlantic City High School, where he is located at present.

KLINE, G. ALFRED. G. Alfred Kline was born near Blain, July 27, 1880, the son of William A. and Catherine (Mumper) Kline. He attended the Blain schools, Shippensburg Normal School, Conway Hall, at Carlisle, and graduated from Dickinson College in 1907. He did postgraduate work there in 1907-08. He did graduate work at the University of Pennsylvania, specializing in Mathematics and Science. Before going to college he taught several years in Perry County. He had charge of Mathematics in Conway Hall three years after graduation, the last two of which he was vice-headmaster. In the fall of 1910 he went to Philadelphia, and has been in the Mathematical Department of the South Philadelphia High School the past eight years. He has also been teaching higher mathematics in the evening schools at Drexel Institute.

KOCHENDERFER, REV. H. W. Rev. H. W. Kochenderfer was born near Saville, in Saville Township, March 19, 1875, the son of Thomas F. and Caroline (Adams) Kochenderfer. He attended the public schools and Prof. W. E. Baker's select school at Eshcol. He prepared for college at Ursinus Academy and graduated from college and the School of Theology. He also attended Ludlamb's School of Dramatic Art, and the University of Pennsylvania, where he received the M.A. degree. He had taught school in Saville Township and in Ursinus Academy. He served four years as pastor of the Royersford Reformed Church, was located at Altoona for two years, and at Linfield for ten years, teaching during the same time at the Central High School of Philadelphia.

KRETZING, REV. JOHN. Rev. John Kretzing was born March 7, 1840, in Juniata Township, the son of John and Susan (Ernest) Kretzing. He attended the local schools and an advanced school at Chambersburg. as well as Selinsgrove Institute. He entered the ministry and served pastorates at Littlestown. Newport, Brodhead's Mill, and other places. He died about 1894.

LANE, ALBERT M. Albert M. Lane was born at Duncannon, July 31, 1878, the son of Austin Luther and Rebecca (Moore) Lane. He attended the public schools and graduated from the Duncannon High School in 1894. He entered Lafayette College and graduated in the class of 1905. The college retained his services upon his graduation and he has been with them ever since, being now bursar and acting treasurer of the college, as well as superintendent of the buildings and grounds.

LATCHFORD, DR. O. L. Dr. Orwan Luther Latchford, only son of Philip Leonard and Elizabeth E. (Orwan) Latchford, was born at Markelville, March 15, 1874. He attended the public schools and Prof. W. E. Baker's select school at Eshcol, from 1890 to 1893. He taught during 1893 and 1894. He then entered the drug business with John W. Cotterel, at Harrisburg, where he was located for two years. He graduated from the Philadelphia College of Pharmacy in 1898. From 1898 until 1899 he occupied positions as head pharmacist. He entered Medico-Chirurgical College in 1899, and graduated in 1903. He then began the practice of medicine at 1319 Girard Avenue, Philadelphia, with office also at Fifth and Chestnut Streets, and has been in continuous practice there since that date. He entered the Philadelphia Polyclinic and College for Graduates in Medicine, in the Department of Eye Diseases, in 1907, and was clinical assistant instructor in diseases of the eye, and acting chief of the clinic until 1912. In 1908 he was a special student at Jefferson Medical College, taking diseases of the nose and throat. During the same year he was clinical assistant on diseases of the nose and throat at Lebanon Hospital, Philadelphia. He was once a member of the associate staff of Northwestern General Hospital. In 1921 he helped organize the Broad Street Trust Company with a capital of $250,000, and was elected one of its directors.

LEONARD, JOHN M. John Moore Leonard, son of Edward Burchard and Julia (Rumple) Leonard, was born in Landisburg, where his father practiced law. He attended the local schools and graduated from Dickinson College, later studying at the University of Berlin. He was professor of Greek for years at the University of Cincinnati, where he died in 1894. Prof. Leonard had the unique distinction of having been an instructor of the noted President, William McKinley.

LIGGETT, MARTIN L. Martin L. Liggett was born at Ickesburg, November 10, 1839. He was educated in the public schools and the Academy at Academia, Juniata County. He graduated at Princeton and read law in Berks County and at Chillicothe, Missouri. He practiced seven years in Williamsport, but failing health caused him to return and locate at Newport, where he died a year later, on December 30, 1883.

LINDAMAN, DR. R. H. Dr. R. H. Lindaman was born at Blain, March 20, 1881, the son of Rev. F. S. and Amelia Josephine (Rice) Lindaman. He left the county as a lad. He attended the schools of Adams County, later studying medicine. He practices at Littlestown, Adams County.

LINN, JOHN ACHESON. John Acheson Linn was born in Landisburg, January 24, 1820, a grandson of Rev. John Linn, the pioneer pastor of old Center Church for forty years. He was a son of Samuel and Mary (Diven) Linn. He attended the Landisburg schools and later engaged in mercantile business there until 1860, when he removed to Philadelphia and became a member of the noted grocery firm of Coyle, Laughlin & Co., Mr. Coyle being married to his sister, with whom he made his home. He was an active and honorable business man, an active church man, and passed away January 14, 1901, at the home of his daughter, Mrs. William Patton, whose husband is first assistant to the president of the Pennsylvania Railroad at Philadelphia.

LONG, REV. HENRY F. Rev. Henry F. Long, son of Isaac and Elizabeth (Smith) Long, was born in Saville Township, September 3, 1841. He was educated in the public schools. The Sectional War attracted him to the colors. He enlisted in Company 8, Seventeenth Regiment, Pennsylvania Cavalry, and served until May 31, 1864, when he was shot through the shoulder at the Battle of Cold Harbor, and the next day lost his left arm through amputation as the result. Returning home, he entered the Eshcol Select School and the Markelville Academy. He taught a term and attended the academies at Greason, Cumberland County, and at New Bloomfield. He then spent six years at the Missionary Institute (now Susquehanna University) at Selinsgrove, graduating in 1873. He served charges at Arndtsville, Pine Grove Mills, Spring Hill, Illinois, and Bunker Hill, Kansas. At Bunker Hill, through the efforts of Mr. Long and his wife, with Eastern friends, Zion Lutheran Church—the first church in the town, was built. In 1883 he returned to Perry County and became pastor at Duncannon, later being located at Sharpsburg, Shippensburg, and also in Fitzgerald, Georgia, where a new church was built during his pastorate. He retired in 1901 from the regular ministry.

LOSH, SAMUEL S. Samuel Stephen Losh, pianist and baritone, was born at Lebo, Tyrone Township, October 4, 1884, the son of Charles S. and Alice (Wagner) Losh. He attended the schools of Perry County and Hagerstown, Md., graduating from the Hagerstown High School in 1902. He also attended Leipsic Conservatory. He has been director of music at Catawba College, N. C., the Texas Christian University, and army song leader at Camp Bowie. He is director of municipal grand opera at Fort Worth, Texas, and was one of the forerunners in the development of community music in the United States, having led mass singing from coast to coast. He is widely known as a pianist, singer, conductor and lecturer.

LUPFER, ALEXANDER McCLURE. Alexander McClure Lupfer was born at Blain, September 17, 1855, the son of Samuel and Matilda (McClure) Lupfer. His early education was gotten principally in the schools of Newville, where his parents moved shortly after his birth. He attended Millersville State Normal School, where he prepared for college. He graduated in the civil engineering department of Lafayette College in 1880. The following year he went West and became one of the famous engineers who blazed the trails of the great transcontinental railways. He is recognized as one of the great locating and construction engineers of the great Northwest. He constructed lines in Pennsylvania, Minnesota, North Dakota, Montana, Washington, Idaho, Oregon, and British Columbia. For practically thirty years he was one of James J. Hill's chief engineers on the Great Northern Railway. He died February 3, 1920.

LUPFER, DR. GEORGE W. George W. Lupfer, M.D., was a son of Jesse K. and Sarah (Ricedorf) Lupfer, born at Markelville, November 15, 1856. He was the eldest of a family of twelve children. He attended local schools until fifteen, then the New Bloomfield Academy, and three terms at Millersville. He taught two terms in Perry and two in Northumberland County. He worked with his father at carpentering to secure funds for his education. He read medicine with Dr. J. D. Shull, of Williamsport, and graduated from College of Physicians and Surgeons at Baltimore in 1881. His preceptor had in the meantime removed to Markelville, and with him he practiced for a year and a half. He then located at Neff's Mills, being postmaster there during a term starting in 1893. After assisting a physician perform an operation at Petersburg, Huntingdon County, November 2, 1905, he started home in his carriage. About a mile and a half east of that town he was observed in a reclining position, with his hat off and the horse driverless. Kind hands conveyed him into the neighboring farmhouse, and in a few minutes he expired.

LUPFER, EDWARD P. Edward P. Lupfer was born at Toboyne Tannery, Perry County, October 22, 1868, the son of Samuel and Matilda (McClure) Lupfer. He attended school at Beavertown, Pa., where his family resided later, and at Newton, Kansas, where he graduated from the

High School in 1889. From 1892 to 1894 he was at the University of Kansas at Lawrence. Since that time he has been assistant engineer in charge of heavy mountain construction on the Rio Grande Western, assistant engineer of construction on the western extension of the Great Northern Railway in Montana, Idaho and Washington; assistant engineer of construction on the Rio Grande Western in Utah; transit man on location of a route of the Great Northern Railway; assistant engineer of the Middle Division of the Great Northern Railway; division engineer of the Eastern Minnesota Railway; locating engineer on mountain work on the Great Northern Railway in Northern Washington; locating engineer on the West Branch Valley Railroad in Pennsylvania; resident engineer of the Pennsylvania Division of the New York Central; locating engineer of the Buffalo & Susquehanna Railway in New York, and later division engineer and assistant chief engineer of the same line. In May 1907, he entered private construction work and contracting at Buffalo, New York, under the firm name of Lupfer & Remick, in which he still continues. This firm makes a specialty of heavy bridge building and filtration plant work.

LUTZ, ALBERT J. Albert J. Lutz, the son of Isaac and Sarah (Inch) Lutz, was born in Liverpool, May 9, 1863. He attended the Liverpool schools and graduated at the Lock Haven State Normal School. He then followed teaching for a number of years, having been principal at various places, and ranking high in the profession. He was a writer of no mean ability and contributed to the press both prose and verse. Upon the founding of the Mont Alto camp for tubercular patients in the South Mountains he founded and edited a little magazine called *Spunk*, which gave him a nation-wide reputation as an optimist. Later returning to Liverpool he entered the furniture business with his father, but March 11, 1912, died in the prime of his manhood.

MacCLUER, REV. DONALD W. M. Rev. Donald W. M. MacCluer was born May 28, 1885, at Springfield, Ohio, but spent all of his early life in Perry County. He was the son of William M. and Mary C. (Rice) MacCluer. He attended the Centre Township schools and graduated from the New Bloomfield Academy in 1902. He graduated from Mercersburg Academy in 1904, Washington and Lee University, Virginia, in 1907, and from Auburn Theological Seminary in 1910. From September, 1910, to September, 1911, he was a missionary in charge of the educational work of the Presbyterian Church in Chieng Rai Province, Siam. He was invalided home with jungle fever. He was pastor of the Third Presbyterian Church at Niagara Falls, 1911-13; pastor of the First Presbyterian Church at Cold Water, Michigan, 1913-19; assistant pastor of the Central Presbyterian Church, at St. Louis, Missouri, 1919-20, and pastor of the Rose City Park Presbyterian Church, at Portland, Oregon, since July 1, 1920, the membership of which is 663. During the war he was camp pastor for the National Service Commission, being stationed at Fort Leavenworth, Kansas.

McGUIRE, REV. F. W. Rev. Frank W. McGuire was born October 11, 1863, in Wheatfield Township, the son of Robert and Harriet Henrietta (Greenbaum) McGuire. He attended the local schools, the Duncannon High School, the Bloomfield Academy, and entered Washington and Jefferson College as a freshman, quitting owing to his health. In October, 1887, he was ordained a minister of the gospel by the Church of God. He has since served at Smithville, Matamoras, Elizabethtown, Churchtown, Newville, Shiremanstown, Landisville, Saxton, Lisburn, and Roherstown, where he is now located. For twenty-five years he has been president of the Board of Extension of the East Pennsylvania Eldership, and for almost that long a member of the Board of Missions. At present he is ex-executive controller and a member of the standing committee. He has

teen he taught, and at nineteen he secured a position in a large printing house in Philadelphia. He was converted at the age of sixteen, and from then on his object was to enter the ministry. He took a theological course in Philadelphia, and at the age of twenty-one was ordained to preach. He was reared a Presbyterian, but changing his views about baptism in his twenty-seventh year, he transferred his allegiance to the Baptist denomination. He visited the Holy Land in 1900 and spent four months in study of Biblical locations. He served pastorates in Pennsylvania at Port Providence, Tyrone, Altoona, New Brighton and Sharon; in Indiana at Kokomo, Lebanon and Indianapolis, and in Illinois, at Vermont and Canton. He also served once at Fredonia, Kansas. Rev. McKee was married to Miss Luella Wickey, a daughter of Rev. L. A. Wickey, of Eshcol, Perry County, who survives him. Three daughters and a son composed the family. He was a director of the Graham Hospital of Canton, Illinois, where he died of apoplexy, August 13, 1921, being then the beloved pastor of the First Baptist Church of Canton. He is spoken of as a man of broad vision, positive convictions, and of a kindly and loving disposition.

McKEE, REV. J. KERN. Rev. J. Kern McKee, son of Samuel and Margaret (Kern) McKee, was born at Andersonburg, August 22, 1872. He attended the local schools and preparatory school at Blain. He graduated from Ursinus College in 1898, and from the Ursinus School of Theology in 1901. He has been pastor of the following Reformed churches: Red Lion, 1901-06; Christ's, Pittsburgh, Pa., 1906-07; Zion, York, Pa., 1907 to date. During his pastorate two fine churches have been built, Zion Church, at York, having cost $120,000. This church has over nine hundred members.

McKEE, JOHN M. John M. McKee was born at New Bloomfield, March 1, 1851, the son of Wilson and Martha (Milligan) McKee. He was educated in the public schools and the New Bloomfield Academy. He learned the machinist trade in Harrisburg, later working in Sunbury and Renovo. In 1880 he went to Colorado, where he prospected in the mountains, finally settling in Pueblo, where he was made master mechanic in the railroad shops. He served four years as deputy revenue collector in that district. At the outbreak of the Spanish-American War he enlisted in Co. E, First Regiment, Colorado Volunteers, and served in the Philippines two years. On his return while lying sick in San Francisco he was elected treasurer of Pueblo County, in which office he served two terms. Subsequently he was selected sheriff of his county, and died during his second term in that office, April 19, 1918.

McKEE, THOMAS L. Thomas L. McKee was born at New Bloomfield, October 17, 1854, the son of Wilson and Martha (Milligan) McKee. He was educated in the public schools and the New Bloomfield Academy, learning the printing trade in Harrisburg. In 1880 he published *The Voice*, a weekly, in Martinsburg, Blair County, Pennsylvania. Later he went to Colorado, where he became editor and manager of the *North Park Miner*. From there he went to Laramie, Wyoming, and bought a half interest in Bill Nye's *Daily Boomerang*, afterward the *Laramie Republican*. While in Laramie he served two terms as county treasurer, and was also internal revenue collector for the State of Wyoming. In 1905 he went to Aberdeen, South Dakota, and was one of the founders of the *Aberdeen American*. He died in St. Luke's Hospital, in Aberdeen, February 6, 1920.

McKEEHAN, REV. H. D. Rev. Hobart D. McKeehan, son of L. Scott and Ella (Mahaffey) McKeehan, was born at Mannsville, April 26, 1897. He was educated in the public schools, the New Bloomfield Academy, Franklin and Marshall Academy, and the Universities of Chicago and Valparaiso. He graduated from the Theological Seminary of the Reformed Church at

Lancaster with the B.D. degree, and the Lincoln and Jefferson University at Chicago conferred upon him the degree of B.D., and S.T.M. For two years he was president of the Historical Research Association at Valparaiso University, and is the author of a treatise on "The Influence of Calvinism Upon John Knox and the Scottish Reformation." In 1918 he was acting minister to Bethel Church at High Point, N. C. The following year he became pastor of St. Paul's Reformed Church at Dallastown, Pennsylvania, where he is still located.

McKENZIE, REV. DAVID LEMUEL. Rev. David Lemuel McKenzie, son of John and Nancy Agnes (Smiley) McKenzie, was born November 11, 1838, in Wheatfield Township. He was a minister of the Lutheran Church from 1871 to the time of his death, in 1906. He was married to Mary Louise, a daughter of Rev. C. F. Stover, of Mechanicsburg. During the war he served in the 138th Infantry, and was later appointed a lieutenant. Among charges he served were Frostburg, Maryland; Rhinebeck, New York; Sioux City, Iowa, and Indianapolis, Indiana. He died about 1901, while serving as pastor of the Lutheran Church at Lykens, Pa.

McMILLEN, REV. HOMER GEORGE. Rev. Homer George McMillen was born February 24, 1883, near Sandy Hill, the oldest son of Albon and Martha Jane (Milligan) McMillen. He attended the local schools, and in his teens spent two years at the New Bloomfield Academy and Smith Collegiate School, at which he graduated. He graduated from Washington and Jefferson College in 1907, and from the Western Theological Seminary in 1910. In 1909, while yet a student at the seminary, he was licensed to preach the gospel by the Presbytery of Carlisle. In 1910 he accepted the pastorate of Cove Presbyterian Church, at Holliday's Cove, W. Va., where he was ordained and installed, and where, in 1913, under his supervision was erected a fine church building at a cost of $60,000. He was later given an assistant pastor and stenographer. This church worked much among the foreign element. Rev. McMillen remained there until the end of 1921, when he became pastor of the First Presbyterian Church at St. Clairsville, Ohio, where he is now located. While in West Virginia he was moderator of the Presbytery of Wheeling, and also treasurer of the Presbytery for a number of years. He has attended the last six General Assembly meetings of the Presbyterian Church, representing his Presbytery in a special way. By referring to the description of Sunday school work in Perry County, elsewhere in this book, it will be noted that Rev. McMillen had a large part in the forward movement of this work.

McMORRIS, REV. JOHN W. Rev. John W. McMorris, son of John W. and Mary J. (Bair) McMorris, was born at New Buffalo, December 15, 1886. He attended the local schools, Harrisburg Academy, and graduated at Ohio Wesleyan University. He then attended the Northwestern University at Chicago, for a year, after which he graduated from the Boston Theological Seminary. He entered the Methodist ministry in 1920, at Hustontown, and is now located at Millerstown.

MAGEE, A. J. A. J. Magee, son of James and Matilda (Mumper) Magee, was born near New Germantown, October 24, 1856. He attended the local schools and worked on the farm until he was sixteen. He then attended the Blain Summer School several summers, teaching during the winters. He taught Shenandoah (near Ickesburg), Manassa (near Blain), and the Church Hill school at Blain. He went West in 1878 and worked upon farms and taught near Woodhull, at Alpha and New Windsor. At Port Byron, Wyanet, Cambridge and Buda he was principal, being at the latter place nine years. After locating in Illinois Mr. Magee, during his vacations, attended Heading College, Dixon College, Valparaiso (Ind.) Normal and the University of Illinois. He was regarded as one of the most successful teachers of western Illinois. In 1902 Mr. Magee quit teaching and moved to Iowa, where he purchased a farm, later residing in Kansas and at Des Moines, Iowa, where good schools were an enticement for his children. Asthma had been the cause of his retirement from his favorite vocation, and, as it still troubled him, the family located at Sanford, in the famous San Luis Valley of Colorado, in 1909, on a quarter section of irrigated land. His wife was Annie L., daughter of G. W. Garber, of Blain.

MAGEE, HENRY C. Henry C. Magee was born in Carroll Township, February 6, 1848, the son of Richard L. and Margaret (Black) Magee. He attended the public schools and graduated from the Bloomsburg State Normal School in 1870. He was principal of the public schools of Plymouth, Luzerne County, from 1871 to 1875, of which town he was also mayor for two years later on. He read law in the meantime, and in August, 1875, he was admitted to the Perry County bar, and later to the bar of Luzerne County, where he located for practice. He served two terms in the State Legislature as a representative from that county, 1881-82.

MANNING, DR. J. CHARLES. Dr. Charles J. Manning, although born at Little Washington, Lancaster County, was brought to Perry County by his parents so early in life that he is recognized as a Perry Countian. He was born January 9, 1860, the son of Jacob and Elizabeth (Kendig) Manning. He was educated in the public schools of Newport and taught five years in Perry County. In 1884 he started reading medicine with Dr. J. D. Shaw, of Markelville. He attended the College of Physicians and Surgeons at Baltimore one year, and in 1887 entered Jefferson Medical College at Philadelphia, where he graduated two years later. He practiced at Markelville until 1893, when he located in Harrisburg, where he now practices.

MEMINGER, REV. SAMUEL E. Rev. Samuel E. Meminger was born November 21, 1852, at Sandy Hill, Madison Township, the son of John Fell and Sidney E. (Behel) Meminger. He was educated in the public schools, and in March, 1883, was admitted to the Central Pennsylvania Conference of the Methodist Episcopal Church. In 1889 he located in Oregon, where he followed the calling for twenty-five years. He is now retired and resides at Roseburg, Oregon.

MEMINGER, REV. WM. M. Rev. Wm. M. Meminger was born in Liberty Valley, Perry County, March 16, 1822, the son of Theodore and Susan (McKean) Meminger. He attended the subscription schools, the Academy at Academia and Dickinson College. He was licensed to preach by the Quarterly Conference of Mifflin Circuit in 1843, when but twenty-one years of age. In 1845 he was admitted to the Baltimore Annual Conference, being ordained as a deacon in 1847 and as an elder in 1849. During his ministry he was a member of the Baltimore Conference, the East Baltimore Conference, and the Central Pennsylvania Conference, and served charges in Virginia, Maryland and Pennsylvania. He died January 5, 1888.

MICHENER, A. R. Albert R. Michener was born in Marysville, December 6, 1892, the son of Philip Milton and Sarah W. (Roberts) Michener. He obtained his early education in the Marysville schools, and upon the death of his parents in 1913, he gave up college preparatory work and entered the circulation department of the *Harrisburg Telegraph*, where he had spent several vacation periods. After a few months he entered the editorial department as a reporter. In 1910 he was appointed circulation manager of the *Telegraph*, a position which he still holds, being the youngest Perry Countian to obtain such a responsible position in the newspaper field, and probably the youngest in the state. He is president of the Interstate

Circulation Managers' Association, an association composed of circulation managers of the more important dailies in Pennsylvania, Delaware, Maryland, West Virginia, and the District of Columbia. He has also been chairman of several committees of the International Circulation Managers' Association, including the important committee on postal affairs. During the war he was selected by the Commission on Training Camp Activities to become a member of a committee to arrange plans for the distribution of home newspapers in training camps here and abroad, at the request of the War Department.

MILLER, CHAS. R. Chas. Reed Miller was born in Duncannon, April 14, 1864, the son of Thomas Dromgold and Sarah (Reed) Miller. He attended the public schools, graduated from New Bloomfield Academy, from Dickinson College in 1887, and from the University of Pennsylvania in 1885. Specializing in modern languages, he made three trips to Europe, studying in Berlin and Leipsic. For six years he was an instructor at the Brooklyn Polytechnic Institute, and for the next six years at Lehigh University. Owing to the state of his health he retired to a farm in Rye Township, later removing to Harrisburg, where he died early in 1920.

MILLER, CURT W. Curt W. Miller, son of Isaac Pfoutz and Margaret Ellen Miller, was born in Pfoutz Valley, October 4, 1863. When he was four years old, his people removed to Loysville. He attended the public schools and later learned the printing trade in the office of the *Perry County Times*. He located in the territory of Arizona, in 1883. He served as chief clerk of the House of Representatives of the twenty-first and twenty-second sessions of the Territorial Legislature, 1901-03. He served two years as secretary of the Board of Education of the Tempe Normal School of Arizona, and one term as postmaster of Tempe. For eight years he was a captain of the National Guards of Arizona, and since February, 1916, has been chairman of the Board of Pardons and Paroles of the State of Arizona. Since 1887 he has been editor and manager of the *Tempe News*.

MINICH, REV. ROY L. Rev. Roy L. Minich, son of Ezekiel and Mary E. (Kell) Minich, was born at Blain, November 15, 1889. He attended the public schools, graduated from Mercersburg Academy in 1911, from Ursinus College in 1915, with the A.B. degree, and from Union Theological Seminary in 1918. He did graduate work at Columbia University during 1915, and was physical director of the Y. M. C. A. From 1916 to 1918 he was pastor of the Borough Park Church, at Brooklyn, N. Y. During that year he became a chaplain in the U. S. Army, and was assigned to Camp Upton as battalion athletic officer. Upon the termination of the war he became pastor of Christ Church at Woodhaven, Long Island. Rev. Minich married Gertrude DeWitt Talmage, August 27, 1918, who is a granddaughter of Rev. T. DeWitt Talmage, her father being the late F. DeWitt Talmage.

MITCHELL, DR. G. W. Dr. Geo. W. Mitchell was born January 4, 1834, in Greenwood Township, the son of William and Alice (McBlair) Mitchell. His parents moved to Juniata Township when he was six years old and he attended the public schools of that township. He also attended the New Bloomfield Academy and Dickinson College, intending to complete the course in the latter place, but went to Kansas in 1856, at the time of the slavery agitation. He taught school in Missouri for several terms and then returned to Perry County with the intention of studying medicine. He read medicine with Dr. Brown, of Newport, and then entered Jefferson Medical College, where he graduated in the class of 1860. He practiced at Newport until 1861, and then removed to Andersonburg, where he enjoyed a large practice until 1902, with the exception of the war period, when he served as surgeon of the 119th Pennsylvania Volunteers, from February 8, 1863, to the close of the war. He was at Chancellorsville, Gettysburg, and all the principal battles of the Army of the Potomac. In connection with his practice, he owned and supervised the cultivation of a large farm. He died February 5, 1917, at Denver, Colorado.

MITCHELL, WILLIAM. William Mitchell was born at Newport, the son of Dr. George W. and Ellen C. (Carpenter) Mitchell. His parents having located at Andersonburg, he attended the public schools there, and later the New Bloomfield Academy, and Lafayette College for three years. He located in Nebraska in 1887, since which time he has been engaged in the practice of law at Alliance, in that state.

MITCHELL, G. W. George Willis Mitchell, son of Charles and Thiana Mitchell, was born in Greenwood Township, July 26, 1870. He attended the public schools, and the Newport High School, walking five miles each way daily to attend the latter, from which he graduated before he was seventeen. He then began teaching in Greenwood and Liverpool Townships. In the meantime he had attended Williamsport Dickinson Seminary one spring term, and in April, 1890, he entered the Dickinson Preparatory School, graduating from Dickinson College in 1895. He was elected a member of the Phi Betta Kappa. He was then principal at Pemberton and Point Pleasant, N. J., and at Lewes, Del., for eight years. He was principal at Marionville for three years, and in 1908 became principal of the Johnsonburg (Pa.) schools, remaining for ten years, after which he located in Philadelphia, taking up the insurance business.

MOTZER, REV. DANIEL. Rev. Daniel Motzer, son of Daniel and Susan (Hench) Motzer, was born in September, 1817. He attended the subscription schools, and later graduated at the Jefferson College, at Canonsburg, Pa. He entered the M. E. ministry, and served until his death, in 1864.

MYERS, WALTER. Walter Myers was born in Rye Township, the son of George R. and Harriet (Heishley) Myers. He was educated in the public schools of Rye Township, New Bloomfield Academy (now Carson Long Institute), at Yale University, and the University of Indiana. In 1905 and 1906 he was instructor in social science and economics in the University of Indiana. In 1907, he was admitted to the bar of Indianapolis, where he has since practiced law. He was one of the counsel for the committee that drafted the first presentation of what became the Federal Reserve Act. During the last administration, he declined appointment as one of the assistant attorneys general of the United States and also to the Federal Trade Commission. During the World War, he served as an officer in the Chemical Warfare Service. Mr. Myers is city attorney of Indianapolis, as well as the attorney for several noted organizations.

MYERS, DR. CHAS. W. Dr. Charles W. Myers was born in Rye Township, December 16, 1890, the son of George R and Harriet (Heishley) Myers. He attended the public schools, the Landisburg Training School for Teachers, and the New Bloomfield Academy. He taught school in Rye Township from 1908 to 1911. He then entered the University of Maryland and graduated from its School of Medicine in 1915. He was an interne in the Maryland General Hospital until 1917, when he became surgeon for the Davis Coal & Coke Co., at Thomas, W. Va. On April 18, 1918, being called into active duty in the U. S. Army, he entered the training camp at Fort Oglethorpe, Ga. On June 7th he sailed from Hoboken, and was immediately ordered to the Ninth United States Infantry of the Second Division Regular Army at Chateau Thiery. He joined this organization on July 1st, and on July 2d, less than twenty-four hours after his arrival in the front lines, was awarded the distinguished service cross.

He continued as surgeon of the Second Battalion, Ninth Infantry, through the remainder of the war, taking part in five major operations accredited to the Second Division. He was awarded the Croix de Guerre with Palm for activities in the Champagne Sector, and the Croix de Guerre with Star for later activities in the Argonne Forest. Upon the signing of the armistice he accompanied the victorious army into Germany, being stationed near Coblenz until May, 1919, at that time securing his transfer to an organization which was homeward bound. He was discharged from the army at Camp Zachary Taylor, in Kentucky, July 2, 1919. He was then commissioned to the United States Public Health Service as past assistant surgeon and stationed at Indianapolis with the Bureau of War Risk Insurance, or the United States Veteran Bureau for the care and treatment of ex-service men. He is now (December, 1921) still located there, and is an associate physician in gynecology to the Indianapolis City Hospital and a member of the staff of the Methodist Episcopal Hospital at Indianapolis.

NEILSON, REV. S. B. Rev. Samuel Black Neilson was born in New Bloomfield, August 19, 1853, the son of Robert and Sarah A. (Gallatin) Neilson. He attended the local schools and the New Bloomfield Academy. He graduated from Lafayette College in 1876, and from the Union Theological Seminary in New York, in 1879. He was elected the same spring to the pastorate of the Waterloo (Nebraska) Presbyterian Church, remaining until 1884. He had been married in 1883 to Miss Ella R. Trout, of Omaha. He spent one year in Nevada, and in 1886 became the pastor of the Presbyterian Church at Falls City, Nebraska, remaining until 1891. He then spent two years as pastor of the Frankfort (Kansas) Church, returning to Perry County, where he remained four years, caring for his aged mother. From 1897 to 1900 he was pastor of the Winamac (Indiana) Presbyterian Church. Locating at Glenwood, Iowa, he expected to make his permanent home on a small fruit farm, but, on a visit to Colorado a position was offered him with the Union Pacific Railroad Company, by whom he was employed until his death, January 14, 1920.

NIPPLE, DR. D. CLARK. Dr. D. Clark Nipple was born in Greenwood Township, August 1, 1852, the son of Henry and Mary (Orner) Nipple. He attended the public schools and at sixteen became a teacher, teaching in Perry, Juniata and Snyder Counties for seven years. During the summers he attended the Freeburg Academy one term and the Millersville State Normal School two terms. For two years he read medicine with Dr. J. A. Leinaweaver at Millerstown, earning his living by clerking in the drug store of his tutor. He then attended Jefferson Medical College for a term and the Ohio Medical College at Cincinnati for two terms, graduating from the latter in 1877. He then practiced for a short time at Fremont, Snyder County, and with his brother at Freeburg, Snyder County, until 1882, when he located at Newton Hamilton, succeeding to the practice of Dr. J. T. Mahon.

NIPPLE, DR. H. M. Dr. Henry M. Nipple was born in Greenwood Township, the son of Henry and Mary (Orner) Nipple. He attended the public schools, later graduating from Jefferson Medical College at Philadelphia. He located at Freeburg, Snyder County, where he practiced medicine for many years. He was one of the organizers of the Snyder County Medical Society.

NIPPLE, DR. J. O. Dr. John O. Nipple was born in Greenwood Township, the son of Henry and Mary (Orner) Nipple. After attending the public schools he graduated from Jefferson Medical College in 1873, and practiced at Port Trevorton for many years.

NIPLE, DR. D. M. Dr. D. M. Niple was born at Ickesburg, May 24, 1879, the son of J. C. and Fietta J. (Adams) Niple. He attended the local schools, the Mifflintown Academy, and the Cumberland Valley State Normal School, where he graduated in 1900. In 1906 he graduated from Jefferson Medical College, and during 1906-07 he served as resident physician at the Williamsport Hospital. In September, 1907, he located at Turbotville, where he still practices.

NOEL, W. A. W. A. Noel was born at New Germantown, March 3, 1887, the son of W. A. and Elizabeth (Hollenbaugh) Noel. He attended local schools, graduating from Conway Hall, at Carlisle, in 1910, and from the Mechanical Engineering Department of State College in 1914. For a number of years he was draftsman and was engaged in research work in Pensylvania. He was on the engineering faculty of the Kansas State Agricultural College at Manhattan, Kansas. Later he was an efficiency engineer with the Savage Arms Company, on the Lewis Automatic Machine Gun. He was with the imperial ministry of munitions at Ontario, Canada, as chief examiner, and during the war was in charge of the Pacific Coast district work in grain dust explosion investigations and fire prevention in flour mills and grain elevators. He was also in charge of the Middle West district investigation for the prevention of fires and explosions in threshing machines, all of which had to do with the conservation of food during the war. He is connected at present with the Department of Agriculture at Washington.

NOLL, CHAS. F. Charles F. Noll was born at Green Park, July 22, 1878, the son of Jonas and Rosanna (Hostetter) Noll. He attended the public schools and the New Bloomfield Academy, graduating from the Cumberland Valley State Normal School in 1900, and from State College in 1906. He received the degree of M.S. from Cornell University in 1911. He is connected with the Pennsylvania State College as Professor of Experimental Agronomy.

NOLL, WALTER L. Walter L. Noll was born at Green Park, January 15, 1883, the son of Jonas and Rosanna (Hostetter) Noll. He attended the public schools and graduated from the Shippensburg Normal School in 1902, and from Bucknell University in 1908. He has also done some postgraduate work at Columbia University. He has always been a teacher, and in the last ten years has been instructor in science in the Barringer High School at Newark, N. J.

ORNER, REV. T. P. Rev. Theodore Porter Orner was born December 22, 1839, the son of Joel and Mary C. (Kepner) Orner. He attended the local schools, and the Loysville Academy, after which he entered the ministry of the United Brethren Church. In 1884 he located in Altoona as pastor of the First United Brethren Church. After four years of that service he was assigned the duty of organizing a new congregation in Altoona, and thus became the founder of the Second United Brethren Church. He served for two years as pastor there, and then was made presiding elder of the Allegheny Conference. After that he served charges at Pitcairn, at Tyrone, and on two different occasions was returned to the First Church at Altoona, where he was retired as pastor emeritus. He died in Altoona, in October, 1920.

OWEN, REV. REUBEN. Rev. Reuben Owen was born in Wheatfield Township, the son of Benjamin and Mary (McBride) Owen. Educated in the schools of the period, he studied for the ministry and entered the Eastern Pennsylvania Conference of the Methodist Church, serving various appointments in the vicinity of Schuylkill County.

OWEN, REV. GEO. D. Rev. Geo. D. Owen was born in Centre Township, in 1883, the son of George D. and Sarah (MacFarland) Owen. He attended the New Bloomfield Academy and graduated from Lebanon Valley College in 1905, taking graduate work in Yale University for three

53

years, and graduating from the Divinity School with the degree of S.T.B. Rev. Owen was a "sky pilot" in South Dakota for two years, and since has held pastorates in Trumbell and Thomaston, Connecticut, and is now located at Pawtucket, R. I., where he is pastor of the Smithfield Avenue Congregational Church. During the war he was an official speaker in Connecticut for the Council of Defense, as well as educational and religious secretary for the Y. M. C. A. at Fort Terry. He was the state representative of the town of Thomaston and served in the legislature of Connecticut two years, 1918-20.

PATTERSON, DR. FRANK. Dr. Frank Patterson was born near Landisburg, December 20, 1877, the son of John S. and Ada K. (Lightner) Patterson. He attended the public schools and a private school at Landisburg, the Millersville Normal School, and Baltimore Medical College, graduating from the latter in 1902. Dr. Patterson is medical examiner for the Pennsylvania Railroad Company, with headquarters at Huntingdon, Pennsylvania.

PATTERSON, D. JAMES. D. James Patterson was born in Tyrone Township, August 6, 1876, the son of John S. and Ada K. (Lightner) Patterson. He attended the public schools and graduated from Millersville State Normal School in 1896, being an expert mathematician. He later taught at various places, among them the New Bloomfield Academy, and as a township superintendent in the Cambria County schools. During the World War he was with the 137th Engineers as an instructor. He died in 1921.

PEFFLEY, REV. W. E. Rev. W. E. Peffley was born at Marysville, March 31, 1876, the son of John and Susan B. (Kocher) Peffley. The father died when he was very young and his mother was later married to William A. Houdeshel. In early life Mr. Peffley was a clerk in Wise's store at Marysville for seven years. He attended the Marysville schools, also the schools of Baltimore, Maryland. He graduated from Central Pennsylvania College (now Albright College) in 1902, and from the Theological Department of Temple University in 1912. He entered the ministry in 1902, serving appointments at Millmont (Union Co.), York, Scranton, Juniata, and Lewistown. He was elected associate editor of the Sunday school literature of the Evangelical Church in 1916, and has since filled that position. He was elected general secretary of Sunday School and Christian Endeavor work in 1910, and has since served in that capacity. He was also elected as one of the two members of his denomination on the board of trustees of the United Society of Christian Endeavor. He is the author of the "Evangelical Teacher Training," a book which has a wide sale and large influence.

POTTER, J. W. John Wesley Potter was born in Howe Township January 27, 1882, the son of Samuel Astor and Agnes Minerva (Bair) Potter. He attended the Miller Township schools and Newport High School, and graduated from Williamsport Dickinson Seminary in 1904. He graduated from Dickinson College in 1913, having been chosen a commencement speaker on that occasion. He was the first Pennsylvania teacher to take up the study of agriculture, which he began at State College in 1914. He taught school in Perry County for a number of years, being assistant principal of the Newport High School, 1905-06. He was principal at Millerstown, 1907-08. During the intervening year he taught the Newton Township High School in Cumberland County. From 1908 to 1912 he was teacher of science and mathematics in the Carlisle High School, and from 1913 to 1918 he was teacher of science and mathematics in the Wilkes-Barre High School. He secured a leave of absence and became a curative workshop instructor in the United States Army Medical Department at

Large, November 20, 1918, being stationed at General Hospital No. 3, later becoming head of academic work in this hospital. He became principal of the Carlisle High School on September 19, 1919, which position he now fills.

POTTER, REV. ISAIAH. Rev. Isaiah Potter was born in Buffalo Township, January 7, 1819, the son of Jacob and Elizabeth (Buck) Potter. He attended the subscription schools and the New Bloomfield Academy. He was one of the early ministers of the United Brethren Church and served charges at Scottdale, Mapleton, Ligonier, Liverpool, Warrior's Mark, Port Matilda and other places. Of his seven children, Miles I. Potter, the youngest, is now president judge of the Seventeenth Judicial District, composed of Snyder and Union Counties. Albert W. Potter was for years an attorney in Selinsgrove, but about fifteen years ago was injured in a railroad wreck which crippled him for life. N. I. Potter was an attorney, but died at Selinsgrove in his twenty-ninth year. M. G. Potter was a minister of the Methodist Church until a few years ago, when he died at Pittsburgh. Of his other children, Silas M. Potter is in the Post Office Department at Washington; Elizabeth is the wife of Ira C. McCloskey, county superintendent of the schools of Clinton County, for the past five or six terms, and Emily I died in her twenty-first year at Scottdale, Pa., where her father was then stationed as a minister.

PORTER, JOHN B. John B. Porter was born in Perry County territory, near Liverpool, in 1800. He was educated in the subscription schools. He was an old-time scrivener at Liverpool and taught school several terms at Millerstown. He then removed to Juniata County, where he was elected as county superintendent in 1860. Upon the completion of his term, in 1863, he removed to Iowa, where he was soon elected as county superintendent of the schools of Louise County, serving two terms.

RAFFENSPERGER, REV. C. I. Rev. C. I. Raffensperger was born in Centre Township, October 12, 1872, the son of John and Catherine (Fry) Raffensperger. He attended the common schools and spent five terms at W. E. Baker's school in Eshcol. He graduated from the Cumberland Valley Normal School, and taught school for nine terms, eight of which were in Perry County. He enrolled as a non-resident student at Oskaloosa Bible School and continued for five years, completing both the English Bible course and the regular theological course. Four years later he was granted the D.D. degree by the institution. For twenty-one years he has been in the ministry of the gospel, having been located at Cearfoss, Md.; Newport, Hallam, and Mt. Holly Springs, Pennsylvania; Baltimore and Williamsport, Maryland, and Berwick, Pa., where he is now located. Rev. Raffensperger has served in many of the highest offces of his conference for terms of from seven to a dozen years.

REAMER, CHAS. W. Chas. W. Reamer was born near Markelville, February 8, 1871, the son of Geo. W. and Susan C. (Freeburn) Reamer. He attended the public schools there, and at Marysville, where his family moved in 1883. He studied telegraphy and was employed as a telegraph operator of the Pennsylvania Railroad, from 1887 to 1890, and by the Western Union and Postal Telegraph Companies in Pittsburgh, New York, Chicago and other cities from 1890 to 1898. During this time he took a law course and graduated from the Western University of Pennsylvania with the degree of LL.B. He was admitted to the bar of Allegheny County in 1898 and has practiced there since then. In 1911 he was appointed a member of the Board of Viewers of Allegheny County.

REEDER, DR. FRANK E. Dr. Frank E Reeder was born at New Bloomfield, April 9, 1883, the son of Jacob B. and Jemimah C. (Fry) Reeder. He attended the public schools, the New Bloomfield Academy, Mercersburg Academy, Lafayette College, which conferred upon him the

Ph.B. degree, and the University of Michigan, where he graduated in medicine and surgery. He is located at Flint, Michigan. During the World War he was a first lieutenant in the Medical Corps.

REEDER, GEO. W. George W. Reeder was born in Jackson Township, near Blain, the son of Solomon and Hannah (Smith) Reeder. He attended the common schools and Millersville State Normal School. He entered the teaching profession and made a success in the Middle West. He was principal of the Coquillard School at South Bend for over twenty years. He enlisted in the Sectional War at the age of seventeen. He died July 26, 1914.

REEN, REV. GEO. H. Rev. George H. Reen was born near Liverpool, January 17, 1867, the son of Samuel and Sarah (Hunter) Reen. His family removed to Newport, where he was educated in the public schools. He then went to Troy (Pa.) and prepared for Gettysburg College, under the late Daniel Fleisher, Ph.D. He graduated from Gettysburg College in 1890, at the head of his class. He graduated from the seminary in 1893, and was ordained to the Lutheran ministry. He was pastor of the St. Luke's Lutheran Church at Mansfield, Ohio, 1893-98, and of the First Lutheran Church at Columbia, Pa., 1898-1903. As a member of the Board of Home Missions he became greatly interested in St. Paul's Mission at St. Louis, Missouri, and in 1903 he became its pastor. The congregation formed there by him built a fine church building, towards which he and his wife contributed $3,600, which represented the profits of a boarding house which they themselves conducted during the St. Louis World's Fair during the year of 1904. Worn by his strenuous labors he fell a victim of disease, dying October 13, 1906, at the age of thirty-nine years. The Sunday following his funeral had been fixed as the time he should deliver his first sermon in the new church, just completed. That day the congregation voted to change its name to the "Reen Memorial Church of St. Louis," the name by which it is now known.

RHINESMITH, ARTHUR D. Arthur D. Rhinesmith was born near New Germantown, August 13, 1870, the son of Samuel and Adeline (Deach) Rhinesmith. He attended the Mt. Pleasant school, and later the school at Blain. In 1891 he located at Peoria, Illinois, becoming a hardware clerk. He later established a business in the Board of Trade building which has grown into a leading cafeteria. In 1919 he organized the Peoria Cafeteria Company, of which he is secretary. As his father had served in Captain Palm's military company in the War between the States he became active in the Sons of Veterans, and in 1913 was elected State Secretary of that order in Illinois. In 1914 he was elected State Commander. After his term as commander he was again elected State Secretary for a term of three years.

RHINESMITH. B. H. Blaine H. Rhinesmith was born at Blain, June 17, 1875, the son of Henry and Mary E. (Stambaugh) Rhinesmith. He attended the public schools and the State Normal Schools at Edinburgh and Lock Haven. He was principal of the schools at Caledonia, Pa., and of the Ridgeway Township High School. At present he is superintendent of the Ridgeway Township (Elk County) schools.

RHINESMITH, CHAS. W. Chas. W. Rhinesmith, eldest son of David M. and Sarah A. (Smith) Rhinesmith, was born at Blain, February 10, 1856. He attended the public schools, New Bloomfield Academy, and Eastman Business College, at Poughkeepsie, New York. He read law with the late Judge W. N. Seibert, and was admitted to the Perry County bar in 1882, after which he served three years as clerk to the county commissioners. He removed to Iowa in 1886, and located at Harlan, where he is engaged in the newspaper business. He served as postmaster at

Harlan under Presidents McKinley and Roosevelt. In 1904 he located at Charles City, Iowa, where he again engaged in the newspaper business.

RICE, DR. CHAS. S. Dr. Charles S. Rice was born at Ickesburg, December 23, 1865, the son of Samuel L. and Anna E. (Rowe) Rice. He attended the public schools and the select school in Newport, and the New Bloomfield Academy, as well as the Cumberland Valley State Normal School. He graduated from Jefferson Medical College, Philadelphia, in 1891, and in dentistry at Columbian University at Washington, in 1894. He is medical examiner in the Bureau of Pensions, at Washington.

RICE, REV. HARRIS G. Rev. Harris G. Rice was born at Ickesburg, October 1, 1853, the son of William and Caroline (Milligan) Rice. He attended the public schools, the New Bloomfield Academy, and graduated from Princeton College in 1876. He then taught school one year at Van Wert, Ohio, and in 1880 graduated from the Union Theological Seminary in New York. The same year he was ordained to the Presbyterian ministry, and has served charges at Jefferson and Albia, Iowa; Delphi and Monticelli, Indiana, and at Seven Mile, Osborn, and De Graff, Ohio. He has been stated clerk of the Fort Dodge and Logansport Presbyteries, and permanent clerk of Iowa and Indiana Synods. Of his six children, Rev. Chas. Herbert Rice is a missionary to India since 1911; another is an attorney, and one a physician.

RICE, REV. JOHN W. Rev. John W. Rice, son of George and Magdalena Ickes Rice, was born February 22, 1839, in Saville Township. He graduated at Pennsylvania College at Gettysburg, and from the Seminary there in 1864. He went to Africa as a missionary for some years. Later, after returning, he was located in Bedford County, Pennsylvania.

RICE, REV. VERNON S. Rev. Vernon Spurgeon Rice, son of Josiah and Margaret (Howell) Rice, was born near Saville. He was educated in the public schools and at Blain and the New Bloomfield Academy. He taught school for a time and graduated from Ursinus College in 1901, and from Ursinus Seminary in 1905. His pastorate began at the St. Vincent Reformed Church in Chester County. He died April 8, 1912.

ROBISON, PUERA BEATRICE. Puera Beatrice Robison was born at Liverpool, July 1, 1889, being the daughter of Samuel Alexander and Emma (Kerchner) Robison. She was educated in the Liverpool schools, Williamsport Dickinson Seminary, Carnegie College, Pennsylvania State College, Pennsylvania Business College, and Temple University. She taught in the schools of Buffalo and Liverpool Townships three years, and in Liverpool Borough eight years. She was supervisor of the Junior School and Bible instructor, also had charge of Americanization work in the Williamsport Dickinson Seminary, since 1918. She is also teacher of Junior Methods in the Williamsport School of Religious Education for the second year. For eight years she was corresponding secretary of the Perry County Sabbath School Association. In 1921 she was licensed to preach in the Methodist Episcopal Church, and is, as near as the writer knows, the first Perry County woman to be ordained to the ministry of the gospel.

RODDY, H. JUSTIN. H. Justin Roddy was born at Landisburg, May 25, 1856, the son of William H. Roddy, a teacher, and Susan C. (Waggoner) Roddy. His early education he received in the Landisburg schools and at Mt. Dempsey Academy. He taught in Perry County from 1875 to 1880, and graduated from the Millersville State Normal School in 1881. He taught in Lancaster County higher grade schools from 1881 to 1887, in which year he became a teacher of geography (physical, political, and commercial) in the State Normal School. In 1896 he took charge of the Department of Geography and Geology. In 1906 he was given the Ph.D degree. In 1908 he was put at the head of the Department of Natural Science. He was made a Fellow in the American Geographical Society in 1910, and of the Geographical Society of America in 1919. He was a contributor to Warren's "Birds of Pennsylvania," published by the state, and wrote a series of geographies for the public schools which has had a wide sale. He also wrote a geography of Lancaster County. He has made many original contributions of the geology of Lancaster County and assisted Professor Gilbert Van Ingen in a geological survey of Perry County. Professor Roddy edits the Educational Department of the *New Era,* a Lancaster daily.

RODDY, REV. JOSEPH STOCKTON. Rev. Joseph Stockton Roddy was born at Mt. Pleasant, Jackson Township, June 10. 1864, the son of George Black and Martha Eliza (Ege) Roddy. He attended the public schools of Jackson Township and Blain, also Capt. G. C. Palm's summer school. He then attended the George G. Meade Grammar School in Philadelphia, the New Bloomfield Academy, the Scott-Browne Phonographic School in New York City, and graduated from Princeton University and Princeton Theological Seminary. Entering the ministry he served these pastorates: Dexter-Earlham Churches in Iowa, Raymond-Bradley Churches (supply) in South Dakota, Olivet Church at Harrisburg, Pennsylvania; college and community pastor of Arch Street Presbyterian Church, Philadelphia; Olyphant, Pa.; Dutch Reformed Church at Churchville, Pa., and Gloucester City (N. J.) Presbyterian Church, where he is now stationed. Rev. Roddy is also chaplain of the First Regiment. Penna. National Guard.

While at Princeton Rev. Roddy was captain of the General Athletic Team, and in 1890 tied for first place in the Canadian one-half-mile championship. In 1891 he was a member of the American Athletic team which went to Europe, and there captured the world championship in the 1,500-meter run. The Manhattan Athletic Club elected him to life membership in consideration of winning these events. He has been a member of the General Assembly of the Presbyterian Church (1902) and moderator of the Des Moines (Iowa) and Carlisle (Pa.) Presbyteries. He has also taught in Dexter (Iowa) Normal College, been editor of the *Pennsylvania Endeavorer* and *M. A. C. Chronicle,* and has done much contributing to newspapers and religious journals along the line of Christian endeavor, sports, and community work.

RUPP, REV. J. C. Rev. J. C. Rupp, son of Geo. W. and Catherine (Leiter) Rupp, was born at Liverpool, January 3, 1874. He was educated in the Liverpool schools, Central State Normal School at Lock Haven, and Lebanon Valley College, from which he graduated in 1906 with the A.B. degree. He graduated from Western Theological Seminary, at Pittsburgh, in 1921. Prior to this he had taught school seven years in Perry County, while farming, and learned the printing trade in the office of the *Perry County Democrat.* He entered the ministry in 1906 and has since served charges at Bigler, Coalport, Wall, and Beaverdale, being located at Wall from 1913 to 1921. His present charge is at Beaverdale. While at Coalport he was assistant principal of the Beccaria Township High School, and while at Wall he was principal of schools for two years and clerk of the borough council for six years.

SANDERSON, GEO. W. George W. Sanderson, son of John and Sarah (Rice) Sanderson, was born at Ickesburg, October 31, 1844. He attended the public schools and the New Bloomfield Academy, during the principalship of Prof. James A. Stephens, teaching three terms in the country schools, and two in the Loysville Orphans' School. In the meantime Prof. Stephens had taken charge of the Huntingdon Academy, and Mr.

Sanderson attended it two terms. He then taught nine years in the Huntingdon schools and was principal at McConnellstown and Petersburg, after which he engaged in business at Huntingdon for thirty-nine years.

SANDERSON, T. C. T. C. Sanderson, son of John and Sarah (Rice) Sanderson, was born near Ickesburg. He attended the public schools and the Bloomfield Academy. He then taught for several terms, and attended Gettysburg College for a period. Entering railroad work, he was trainmaster of the Huntingdon and Broadtop Railroad for twenty-five years. He represented Huntingdon County in the General Assembly in 1901-02. He died in Harrisburg, February 7, 1902.

SCHOLL, T. J. T. J. Scholl, son of Alfred C. and Sarah A. (Rice) Scholl, was born in Landisburg, October 22, 1871. He attended the public schools, after which he took a course in Eastman Business College at Poughkeepsie, N. Y. He taught school three terms in Perry County, and in 1895 entered the First National Bank at Patton, Pennsylvania, as stenographer, later being elected cashier, a position which he filled for several years. He resigned to take up general auditing and examination work among banks and trust companies, subsequently entering the employ of the Second National Bank at Mechanicsburg. In 1913 he was promoted to cashier. Mr. Scholl is a member of the board of trustees of the Methodist Home for Children, near Mechanicsburg, as well as treasurer of the board of managers.

SCHROEDER, G. G. George G. Schroeder was born May 1, 1860, near Dry Sawmill, Liverpool Township, the son of Tillman and Kate (Kerstetter) Schroeder (sometimes spelled Schrawder). He attended the public schools of Liverpool Township and Borough, and spent four years in preparatory school and college in New York. He was an artificer in the United States Army for almost five years, testing oils and coals as fuels for the army and navy contracts. He has been assistant and chief engineer for probably fifteen large companies during the past twenty-eight years in Washington, New York, Chicago and elsewhere. Mr. Schroeder is also a patent attorney, being senior member of the firm of G. G. Schroeder & Company. He is also senior member of Schroeder & Armstrong, engineers. He is also an inventor, some of his inventions being of considerable value.

SEIBERT, DR. J. L. Dr. J. L. Seibert was not born in Perry County, but near Mifflinburg, on October 16, 1851, the son of Rev. Samuel W. and Eleanor K. (Neilson) Seibert. By reason of his parents' long residence in Perry County, where he attended school and the Bloomfield Academy, he is recognized usually as a Perry Countian. After teaching school for a number of years he graduated from the Medical Department of the University of Pennsylvania, in 1883. He then located at Bellefonte, where he has since practiced.

SHAEFER, DR. J. C. Dr. J. C. Shaefer was born at New Buffalo, in 1833, and was graduated at the Philadelphia Medical College. He practiced medicine at Millersburg, Berrysburg and Freeburg.

SHAVER, REV. JOSEPH B. Rev. Joseph B. Shaver was born near Bixler's Mills, Madison Township, December 3, 1844, the son of Rev. David and Nancy E. (Linn) Shaver. His father was a member of a commission which met in Harrisburg to equalize taxation over the state, and later Member of Assembly from Perry County. Joseph B. Shaver was educated in the public schools of the period, and under the instruction of a well-read father. When less than eighteen he enlisted in the Forty-Seventh Penna. Volunteer Infantry, and served in the Red River campaign, where he was wounded in the arm. After his discharge from the army he attended Williamsport Dickinson Seminary, and in 1867 traveled

Newport Circuit of the M. E. Church under the presiding elder. In 1868 he was ordained to preach, and served congregations at Gettysburg, New Cumberland, Greencastle, Thompsontown, Osceola, Bedford Circuit, Miles-burg, Hollidaysburg, Curwensville, First Church at Altoona, Hazleton, Danville, and Williamsport. He was a noted preacher of the Word from a Biblical standpoint, rather than from present day themes. He died at the home of his eldest daughter at Hazleton, November 17, 1903.

SHEAFFER, REV. W. J. Rev. W. J. Sheaffer was born in Sheaffer's Valley, near Landisburg, July 18, 1863, the son of John Baer and Emma Carrie (Spence) Sheaffer. He attended the public schools and graduated from Williamsport Dickinson Seminary in 1890, with the A.B. degree. He graduated from Illinois Wesleyan University and from Oskalooska College, postgraduate work, with A.M. and Ph.D. degree in 1914. He entered the ministry of the Methodist Episcopal Church in 1890. He is now pastor at Jersey Shore, Pa., and secretary of the directors of the Methodist Home for Aged at Tyrone, Pa.

SHEAFFER, DR. J. C. Dr. J. C. Sheaffer was born at New Buffalo in 1833, attended the local schools, and was graduated at the Philadelphia Medical College. He practiced at Millersburg, Berrysburg and Freeburg.

SHOEMAKER, HARRY W. Harry Watters Shoemaker, son of Benjamin and Penniah Shoemaker, was born in Perry County, his father once having operated Oak Grove furnace. The son became in turn an iron man and founded the Hartman Steel Company at Beaver Falls, Pa.

SHORTESS, REV. SAMUEL IRVINE. Rev. Samuel Irvine Shortess was born June 7, 1834, near New Bloomfield, the son of Thomas and Eleanor (Greer) Shortess. In his early years he learned carpentering. In 1864 he enlisted in Co. 3, 208th Regt., Pennsylvania Volunteers, and served in the Sectional War. He had been educated in the public schools, and in 1866 entered the ministry of the Evangelical Church, being ordained in 1867. After serving a number of congregations within the bounds of the Central Pennsylvania Conference, he retired from the active ministry in 1903, and continued to reside at Millersburg, his last charge, where he died in 1910.

SHORTESS, REV. J. D. Rev. John David Shortess was born near Markelville, March 22, 1860, the son of Rev. Samuel Irvine and Elizabeth (Kline) Shortess. He attended the public schools until his eighteenth year, when he entered the Union Seminary at New Berlin. During the winter of 1879-80 he taught school in Union County to help secure his education. In 1882 he graduated from the Theological Department of the Seminary, and during the same year was admitted to the Central Pennsylvania Conference, where, with 1922, he is closing his fortieth year of active work. He was elected by his conference in 1917 as presiding elder, and was stationed at Carlisle for the four-year term. Upon being reëlected, in 1911, he was stationed in the Lewisburg District. In 1914 the D.D. degree was conferred upon him by Oskaloosa College. For sixteen years he has been an active member of the board of trustees of Albright College at Myerstown, and is also a member of the board of trustees and treasurer of the Ministerial Aid Society of the Central Pennsylvania Conference. In 1915, he had a prominent part in the establishing of the United Evangelical Home for children and the aged at Lewisburg, Pa., and has since served as a trustee and on the executive board. At the last meeting of the Historical Society of the United Evangelical Church, he was elected president, to succeed Bishop U. F. Swengel. He has also represented his conference at three quadrennial sessions of the General Conference, the highest legislative body of his church. Of his four children, Samuel Irvine Shortess, A.B., is professor of Biology in Girard College, Philadelphia.

SHULL, B. M. Brinton McClellan Shull was born near Keystone, Perry County, January 17, 1873, the son of David and Leah (Yohe) Shull. He attended the Rye Township schoolst for two years, and graduated from the Marysville High School and the Cumberland Valley State Normal School. He received his A.B. degree from Milton University, Baltimore, Md., and has attended the summer sessions of other institutions. He taught in the schools of Dauphin County, and Penn Township, Perry County, also in the graded schools at Marysville, and in the Lower Duncannon High School. He has been grammar school principal, assistant principal, principal of schools, and supervising principal successively at Lehighton, Carbon County, having held his present position for fourteen years. The fine granite-faced high school building at Lehighton, Pennsylvania, is largely due to the work of Mr. Shull.

SHULL, DR. J. D. Dr. J. D. Shull was born at Markelville, Perry County, June 10, 1851, the son of Simon and Elizabeth (Fleisher) Shull. He attended the common schools, Markelville Academy (1871-72), Juniata Valley Normal School (1874), Medical College of Physicians and Surgeons at Baltimore (1881-82), and graduated from the University of Pennsylvania in 1887. He practiced medicine at Markelville for about ten years, since which time he has been medical examiner of the Pennsylvania Railroad at Baltimore, a period of over thirty-three years.

SHULTZ, REV. W. K. Rev. W. K. Shultz was born at Elliottsburg, in 1883, where his father, Rev. James F. Shultz, was pastor of the Evangelical Church. His mother was Mary E. Shultz. The son of a minister, his early schooling was in many different places. He spent three years at Central Pennsylvania College (now Albright College) at New Berlin, Pa., after which he entered the ministry of the United Evangelical Church. He taught in the public schools, edited the *Sullivan Review,* a Sullivan County weekly, and has been in the ministry for nineteen years, at present being pastor of Calvary United Evangelical Church at Newport, Perry County.

SHUMAKER, DR. L. M. Dr. Luther Melancthon Shumaker, son of Henry and Margaret (Kessler) Shumaker, was born April 6, 1856. He was educated in the public schools, the New Bloomfield Academy, and Gettysburg College. In 1882 he entered Carthage College, at Carthage, Illinois, but failing health brought him back to Perry County. He then taught school three years in Perry County and three years in the Wyoming Valley. In 1887 he entered Jefferson Medical College, where he graduated in 1889. He established an office at Elliottsburg, where for a decade he had a good practice. Seeking a larger field he then located in Harrisburg, where he was successful, and where he gave his life through overwork during the serious influenza epidemic early in 1919.

SHUMAKER, JOHN H., PH.D. John H. Shumaker, Ph.D., was born near Sandy Hill, Madison Township, in 1828. He was educated in the free schools, just opened when his schooling started, and at the Tuscarora Academy and Marshall College, from which he graduated in 1850. An ancestor of his had been tutor to the King of Prussia, and he early decided upon teaching as a profession. In 1851 he began teaching at Tuscarora Academy, where he remained as principal until 1868. From then until 1883 he was principal of the Chambersburg Academy, when he was elected as principal of Blair Presbyterial Academy at Blairstown, New Jersey. He was the first principal of this institution to receive a salary. He was so successful that it became necessary to enlarge the institution, the new girls' dormitory being added. He remained there until 1892. He returned to his home in Chambersburg, where a malignant disease cut short his life in 1894. He was a noted speaker and was frequently heard at normal, county and state meetings. He had pursued a course in theology and filled many vacant pulpits as an able supply.

SHUMAN, WILLIAM C. William Colhozeh Shuman was a Perry County lad from very early years, although born in Lancaster County in 1836. Orphaned in his first year, the youngest of fifteen children, he was reared among his kin here. In 1852, while a Miss Minnie Owen, of Croton Falls, New York—who later was married to Dr. David Fetter, of Landisburg—was conducting a select school in Ickesburg, she boarded with his people, and he thus got his first lessons in grammar—private lessons, as it was not then taught in the public schools. Securing a position in Auburn, New York, in a printing office, he worked there a year, but returned to Ickesburg and spent a year at Academia Academy (Juniata County), of which Prof. John H. Shumaker, of Perry County, was then principal. In 1856 he began teaching. He attended the academy of Rev. John B. Strain one term. In 1859 he attended Millersville, but again taught in Perry for several years. In 1862 he married Rebecca Fertig, of Millerstown, and then taught in Lancaster for several terms. In 1878 he removed to Chicago, where he taught in the Cook County Normal School five years, was principal of the Chicago grammar school for five years, and in charge of the evening schools for several years. While Prof. Shuman's name will ever stand high in the educational world, yet his successful compilation of the Genealogy of the George Shuman Family, a volume of over three hundred large pages, will ever stand as a monument to the energy and persistency with which he pursued that task for a period of twenty years during the declining years of an active life, after relinquishing school work. It is of this famous family that came Lieutenant Governor Shuman, of Illinois, but he was born and reared in Lancaster County. From it also came the names of Shuman's Mill, Shuman's Church, etc. Following a slight stroke he slept peacefully away, July 7, 1917.

Prof. and Mrs. Shuman were the parents of five children: Edwin L., a noted literary writer; Roy R., expert advertising man; Jesse J., engineering expert on steel; Lucy Estelle (Mrs. Chester B. Masslich), and Grace Ethel (Mrs. John Ernest Smiley). All are graduates of Northwestern University of Chicago.

Mrs. Shuman, nee Rebecca C. Fertig, of Millerstown, at the request of Miss Frances E. Willard, in 1890, undertook the mounting of the World's Polyglot Petition, a document which was to make a strong appeal to the governments of the world to abolish the manufacture of opium and alcohol. Miss Willard's "Around the World" workers had solicited signers of this petition in every country in the world and the islands of the sea. The names came in great rolls—sometimes in sheets, sometimes singly—and were mounted on canvass half a yard wide. Counting three names to the inch the petition was eight miles in length; but including the six millions attestations from societies of various organizations, the entire length of the petition would have been forty miles. Mrs. Shuman was educated in the Millerstown schools and in the select school of S. H. Galbraith at Blain.

SHUMAN, TIMOTHY BAXTER. Timothy Baxter Shuman was a son of Samuel and Susannah (Bixler) Shuman, born August 1, 1857, at Eshcol, the father being noted as the champion wrestler of Perry County, an athletic sport of much note in that period. He was educated in the local schools. When entering young manhood he went with his parents to Huntingdon County, where he taught school, later entering the business world. He was appointed register and recorded of Mifflin County, by Governor Pattison.

SHUMAN, LEWIS WAYNE. Lewis Wayne Shuman was a son of John and Rebecca Ann (Crane) Shuman. He was born near Ickesburg, October

4, 1855, educated in the local schools and attended the sessions of '73, '75 and '76 at the New Bloomfield Academy. He taught continuously from 1873 to 1883, three terms in Perry County, three at Earlville, Illinois, and four at Aurora, Nebraska. In the fall of 1883 he was elected clerk of the courts of Hamilton County, Nebraska, of which Aurora is the county seat. He was also a deputy in the county clerk's office, and in the fall of 1891 he was elected county clerk. In 1894 he was elected grand chancellor of the Knights of Pythias of the State of Nebraska. The same year he entered the real estate business, and later located at Long Beach, California, where he resides.

SHUMAN, WILLIAM CUMMINGS. William Cummings Shuman, a son of Michael and Elizabeth (Chesney) Shuman, was born in Liverpool, September 9, 1849, and there he received his early education. With his family he removed to Ohio in 1866. He has always been in business in Ohio, where, at Covington, he is known as the manufacturer of Milky Evaporated Sweet Corn, a table delicacy. One of his sons, Clinton Polleck Shuman, a graduate of the University of West Virginia, is superintendent of mails of the Philippine Islands.

SHUMAN, JOHN RUSHER. John Rusher Shuman was born November 17, 1826, at Liverpool, the son of George and Susannah (Rusher) Shuman. He was educated at the local schools and at Tuscarora Academy. He located at Covington, Ohio, in 1850, where for over fifty years he was identified with its growth. In 1871 he organized and became president of the Stillwater Valley Bank of Covington, holding that position until his death, which occurred September 14, 1906. Among his children is George George L. Shuman, head of the noted publishing firm of George L. Shuman & Company of Chicago.

SMILEY, REV. JAS. W. Rev. James W. Smiley was born near Shermansdale, April 12, 1824, the son of William and Anne (Wilson) Smiley. His father was a son of John Smiley, one of the original settlers of 1755. He entered the Methodist ministry and preached for a time in the South. His health failing he returned to Carlisle, and for years conducted a large clothing store in that town. He was for many years a trustee of Dickinson College. He died March 22, 1893.

SMILEY, REV. FRANKLIN. Rev. Franklin Smiley was born near Shermansdale, April 24, 1867, the son of James and Emily (Green) Smiley. He became a Presbyterian minister. He died March 15, 1892.

SMILEY, REV. L. C. Rev. L. C. Smiley was born near Shermansdale in 1869, the son of William A. and Martha A. (Adair) Smiley. His grandfather was a son of John Smiley, an original settler in 1755. He attended the public schools and the Union Biblical Seminary at Dayton, Ohio, where he graduated in 1898. He entered the ministry of the gospel and is now a member of the Presbytery of Carlisle, being their supply pastor. He resides at Lemoyne, Pa.

SMILEY, REV. J. E. Rev. J. E. Smiley was born near Shermansdale, February 10, 1848, the son of Andrew B. and Frances (Lenhart) Smiley. He attended the public schools, the Millerstown Normal School of Prof. Wright, and the Millersville State Normal School. He went to Ohio in 1872 and taught for a number of years. He finally located in Paulding County, Ohio, a new territory, and entered the mercantile and timber business. While there he was postmaster, railway agent, and express agent, the post office being named Smiley. In 1908 he began teaching in the Fairmount Bible School, at the same time taking the course himself and graduating in 1911. He continues to teach there but is also a licensed minister. He is treasurer of the Indiana Conference of the Wesleyan Methodist Church, having filled the position for the past twelve years.

He is now assistant to the president of the Fairmount Bible School, which is developing into Marion College, at Marion, Indiana, with a prospect of becoming a noted church school.

SMILEY, REV. JOHN M. Rev. John M. Smiley was born near Shermansdale, in 1822, the son of William and Anne (Wilson) Smiley. He was the grandson of one of the original settlers of 1755, being a brother of Rev. James W. Smiley. He entered the ministry of the United Brethren Church and served for many years. He died at Shippensburg, Pa.

SMILEY, REV. GEO. W. Rev. George Washington Smiley, who was born near Shermansdale, was a noted preacher and lecturer. His lecture on "Origin of the North American Indian," delivered many years ago at the courthouse at New Bloomfield, is still remembered by some of the older people who heard it. He was the son of Frederick Smiley, whose father was one of the original settlers of 1755. He graduated at Dickinson College at Carlisle. His mother was a Miss Berryhill. He preached in some of the Southern states, and died in Pottsville, Pa., but his remains were buried in the State of Kentucky.

SMILEY, DR. JAMES M. Dr. James Meredith Smiley, son of John and Sarah Eliza (McBride) Smiley, was born at Shermansdale, February 20, 1867. He attended the public schools, the New Bloomfield Academy, and the Cumberland Valley State Normal School, where he graduated in 1891. He taught several years, and then entered Jefferson Medical College, where he was three years a student, when overtaken by illness. He later finished the course at the University of the South at Suwanee, Tennessee, in 1900. He practiced at Nashville, Tennessee, for one year, and then returned to Pennsylvania, and formed a partnership with his brother, Howard M. They are now located at Yeagerstown, Pennsylvania.

SMILEY, DR. HOWARD M. Dr. Howard Miles Smiley, son of John and Sarah Eliza (McBride) Smiley, was born at Shermansdale, February 22, 1869. He attended the public schools, the New Bloomfield Academy and the Cumberland Valley State Normal School, where he graduated in 1893. He then attended Pennsylvania State College for a year, after which he matriculated at Jefferson Medical College, graduating in 1897. He practiced at Landisburg for six years, at Cincinnati, Ohio, for three years, and at Huntingdon, Pennsylvania, for a year, when an opening occurred at Yeagerstown, Pa., where he located and where he still practices, in connection with his brother, Dr. James M. Smiley, a partnership having been formed.

SMITH, REV. JOSHUA. Rev. Joshua Smith was born December 6, 1841, near Hagerstown, Md., of a Perry County mother. He was the son of William Alexander and Elizabeth (Kiner) Smith. At a very early age his family removed to Blain, where they lived until the close of the Civil War, when they located in Illinois. He was educated in public and select schools. In the War between the States he was a member of Co. A and first lieutenant of Co. K of the Twentieth Pennsylvania Volunteer Cavalry. He was on the staff of General Fitzhugh as assistant quartermaster of the Second Brigade of the First Cavalry Division of Sheridan's Army. He was also an assistant inspector general of the First Brigade, Second Division, on the staff of General Avery. He attended dental lectures and practiced dentistry in Chicago for thirty years. He took the theological course of the Rock River Conference of Illinois and was ordained an elder of the M. E. Church in 1885. He was superintendent of Marie Chapel, and pastor of the Marie M. E. Church, 1890-1905, and pastor of the Forty-Seventh Street Church, 1905-11, when he retired from the active ministry. In 1911 he founded the Burnside Settlement, a noted community charity of Chicago. He is the author of "From Gettysburg to Appomattox," and of

Christmas Gems and various other Sunday school literature, as well as several songs. He is also a lecturer of note on war topics.

SMITH, C. LESTER.   C. Lester Smith was born at Wila, Juniata Township, August 12, 1870, the son of William H. and Elizabeth (Crist) Smith.   He was educated in the public schools, Central State Normal School, where he graduated in 1894, and through postgraduate work at both Lock Haven and Columbia Teachers' College.   He was assistant principal at Mt. Carmel, and from there went to Altoona, where he has been a ward principal for twenty-seven years.

SNYDER, DR. J. W. O.   Dr. John Wesley Owen Snyder was born in 1835 in Wheatfield Township, the son of Rev. John G. and Peggy (Owen) Snyder.   Went with his family to Iowa when twenty years of age and prepared for college there.   After the Sectional War he graduated in medicine and surgery in a New York college and practiced at Pueblo, Colorado, where he died.   Of his children Almira J. married Henry Calvin Thatcher, a native Perry Countian who became the first chief justice of the State of Colorado, and Rev. Henry D. became a United Brethren minister.

SNYDER, REV. J. G.   Rev. John George Snyder was born in Perry County, and was educated in the public schools.   He entered the United Brethren ministry and served at various places, the longest being with Western U. B. College, where he was an instructor.

SNYDER, DR. GEO. GUY.   Dr. George Guy Snyder, son of George C. and Mary Elizabeth (Zaring) Snyder, was born at Liverpool, August 10, 1875.   He graduated in the Liverpool schools and at the Central State Normal School at Lock Haven, in 1893.   He then read medicine with Dr. E. Walt Snyder, and in 1899 graduated from Jefferson Medical College. He practiced in Marietta for a year, and then located at Harrisburg, where he has since practiced.   Dr. Snyder is now the county physician of Dauphin County.

SNYDER, WM. S.   William S. Snyder was born in Millerstown, October 11, 1870, the son of David A. and Margaret A. (Foster) Snyder.   He attended the public schools of Millerstown, graduating in the class of 1887. He then entered Millersville Normal School, graduating in the class of 1888.   He entered Dickinson College and graduated from that institution in 1894.   In earlier life he was a teacher and at one time principal of the public schools of Duncannon.   He later entered the legal profession, and is now a member of the firm of Olmsted, Snyder & Miller, one of the leading law firms of Harrisburg, Pennsylvania.

SOULE, BLANCHE.   Blanche Soule was born at New Bloomfield, August 28, 1874, the daughter of John W. and Margaret (Smith) Soule. She attended the local schools and graduated at the New Bloomfield Academy and Cumberland Valley State Normal School.   She taught in the public schools for five years, served as a trained nurse from six to eight years, and was head nurse at the Germantown Hospital for five years, being recognized as at the head of her profession.   She has always been interested in mission work, and in 1921 set sail for the Egyptian Soudan, 1,500 miles up the Nile, several hundred by caravan.   She will have charge of the dispensary in her new field, under the Presbyterian Board of Foreign Missions.

SOWERS, T. J.   T. J. Sowers was born near Landisburg, December 30, 1840, the son of David and Elizabeth (Reiber) Sowers.   He was educated in the common schools.   He was at Gettysburg with the Thirty-Sixth Pennsylvania Home Guards, and in 1864 joined the 208th Pennsylvania Regiment, serving until the end of the war.   In April, 1869, he moved to Ford County, Illinois, of which county he was elected treasurer in 1898, and in the House of Representatives for four years. He was on the building committee which supervised the building of the new courthouse of Hardin County, Ohio.

STAHL, C. L. C. L. Stahl was born October 8, 1879, at Newport, the son of William C. and Julia Ann (Horting) Stahl. His family later (in 1885) moved to Virginia, and he became a student in agriculture, specializing in dairying at the Virginia Polytechnic Institute, at Blacksburg, Virginia, in the class of 1907. He did special work at Purdue University, Lafayette, Indiana, 1908. He then entered the employ of Ex-United States Treasurer Carter Glass and others, having charge of their dairy farms in Virginia, and being manager of two creameries. He is at present dairy director of the Virginia State Dairy and Food Division at Richmond.

STAHL, HORATIO S. Horatio S. Stahl was born October 19, 1868, at Newport, the son of William C. and Julia Ann (Horting) Stahl. In 1885 his family removed to Virginia, where he graduated at the Virginia Polytechnic Institute, with the B.S. degree, as an honor student in various branches. He has since done research work in diseases of the peach, apple, corn, and potatoes. He is now professir of Biology in the Virginia Polytechnic Institute.

STEPHENS, PROF. JAS. A. Prof. James A. Stephens was born May 14, 1831, in Juniata Township, the son of Robert G. and Martha (Jones) Stephens. He was a noted educator in the days when academies flourished, and was twice principal of the Bloomfield Academy, as will be noted in the chapter on that subject, in this book. He was also principal of the Huntingdon Academy, where he died April 22, 1876. He had two sons, Robert Neilson and James, the former having been an author of considerable note, a sketch of his life appearing earlier in this book. The *Advocate* described him as "a man of ability, fine education, and an excellent teacher."

STEWART, RICHARD HENRY. Richard Henry Stewart was born in Duncannon, May 23, 1859, his parents being William Jones Stewart and Hannah (Henry) Stewart. He was educated at the public schools and at the New Bloomfield Academy, and read law with the late Charles A. Barnett. He was admitted to the bar, December, 1881, and served as district attorney from 1885 to 1888. At the conclusion of his term he located at Kansas City, Missouri, where he practiced law and acted as trust officer of a large trust company. In 1901 he located in New York City, where he is engaged in corporation law practice. Mr. Stewart bears the unique distinction of being the father of one of America's leading theatrical stars, "Marie Doro," whose biography appears earlier in this book in an extended form.

STINE, DR. H. A. Dr. H. A. Stine was born April 23, 1878, at Pillow, Dauphin County, but was brought to Perry by his parents' removal here, when he was a mere child, so is recognized as a Perry Countian. He is a son of Charles and Catherine (Row) Stine. He was educated in the Perry County schools and graduated at the Cumberland Valley State Normal School in 1902. He taught for a number of years, and then entered Baltimore Medical College, where he graduated in 1912. He located at Harrisburg, where he has since practiced.

STITES, DR. GEO. M. Dr. George M. Stites was born in Millerstown, March 11, 1860, the son of Dr. Samuel and Katharine (Matter) Stites. His father was descended from a long line of medical men on both sides. His mother's name was Rush, and she was of the famous Benjamin Rush family. On the father's side the first Stites came as a surgeon to the colonists in the time of Cromwell. Dr. William Stites, who practiced in Perry County for a few years, was a brother of his father. Dr. Stites

postgraduate course in the Polyclinic College at Philadelphia and again located in Harrisburg, where he remained until 1900, when he traveled Europe, visiting the principal hospitals in order to advance further in his profession. He returned to his Harrisburg practice, but in January, 1906, left on a trip South to regain his health, going to Cuba. Two days after his arrival there he died. Dr. Stites had another distinction. In 1870 he organized Newport Council, No. 107, Junior Order of United American Mechanics, and two years later was elected National Vice-Councilor, becoming National Councilor the succeeding year, so far as is known, the only Perry Countian to become the national head of a beneficial order.

STROUP, F. NEFF. F. Neff Stroup was born near Blain, in 1884, the son of George M. and Mary Ellen (Martin) Stroup. He attended the public schools of Jackson Township and graduated from the Millersville State Normal School in 1908, and at Dickinson College in 1913. In 1918 he graduated from Columbia University with the M.A. degree. He taught four years in Jackson Township, was principal of the Strasburg (Pa.) High School for two years, and assistant in mathematics at the Millersville State Normal School one year. For three years he was supervising principal of the schools of Spencerport, N. Y., and then became superintendent of schools at Palmyra, N. Y., where he served five years. He is now superintendent of public schools at Newark, N. Y.

SWEGER, DYSON. Dyson Sweger was born in Buckwheat Valley, September 21, 1882, the son of Aaron and Martha Ann (Campbell) Sweger. He received his early education in the public schools, in Prof. W. E. Baker's Summer School at Eshcol, and at the New Bloomfield Academy, graduating in 1904. He later attended the Lebanon Valley College while teaching in the Annville schools. After completing a term in the A. Grammar School, at Newport, in 1906, he went West and located at Los Angeles, where he was first connected with the Pacific Electric Company. In 1911 he entered the Department of Health, and in 1918, through competitive examination, was promoted to the position of Executive Secretary of the Housing Commission—a Bureau of the Health Department. Mr. Sweger has charge of all housing and hotel and tenement maintenance in the City of Los Angeles.

SWEGER, R. L. Roy L. Sweger was born at New Bloomfield, October 14, 1886, the son of Isaac and Annie (Briner) Sweger. He attended the public schools and later learned printing. He left Perry County in 1905 and worked as a printer in New Jersey, Connecticut, and at Philadelphia for about four years. In the fall of 1909 he returned to New Bloomfield and attended the academy until spring, when he went to Florida and located at Live Oak, as foreman of the *Suwance Democrat*. After two years he was made manager of this publication. He held this position four years, and then became manager of the *Gasden County Times* of Quincy, Florida. In 1918 he bought this plant, and has since owned and edited the paper. When Cary A. Hardee became governor of Florida it was after his name had been first announced by Mr. Sweger, who has since been made a member of the governor's staff, with the rank of lieutenant colonel.

SYPHER, J. R. Author and War Correspondent. Josiah Rhinehart Sypher was born in Greenwood Township, in 1832, being a brother of Gen. J. Hale Sypher, whose biography appears earlier in these pages. The Sypher family came to America during the early part of the Eighteenth Century, settling in Chester County. Subsequently a branch of the family located in Pfoutz Valley, where these sons were born. Josiah Rhinehart Sypher attended the public schools and then entered Union College at Schenectady, New York, where he graduated in 1858. He read law with

54

Thaddeus Stevens at Lancaster, and in 1862 was admitted to the Lancaster County bar. He had in the meantime been doing corresponding for city newspapers, and when the Sectional War came on he went to the front as war correspondent of the *New York Tribune*. After the war he opened up the first Philadelphia office for that paper, and later was made an associate editor for the same. After the war, in connection with his newspaper work, he wrote and compiled the "History of the Pennsylvania Reserves" (1865) and a "School History of Pennsylvania" (1868). In connection with E. A. Apgar he also wrote and published a School History of New Jersey. He was also a temperance worker and writer. For many years thereafter, or until his death in 1902, he practiced law in Philadelphia, specializing along the lines of copyrights, trade-marks and patents.

TAYLOR, DR. S. BANKS. Dr. S. Banks Taylor, son of George D. and Frances Taylor, was born in Tuscarora Township, March 14, 1868. His parents moved to Millerstown, where he attended the public schools, later graduating at the Central State Normal School at Lock Haven (1889) and at Jefferson Medical College (1895). After graduating at Lock Haven he taught until 1892. Upon graduating in medicine he located at Reading, Pennsylvania, where he is practicing at this time.

TOLAND, DR. L. L. Dr. L. L. Toland was born near Iroquois (Miller Township) in 1870. His people located in the West and he graduated at the Sterling High School, the Ada (Ohio) Normal School, and the Western Reserve Medical College, and Chicago Polyclinic Medical College. He has been a teacher, pharmacist, physician, and is now an obstetrical physician. He also served one year as interne at St. Clair Hospital at Cleveland.

TRESSLER, PROF. JOHN A. John Andrew Tressler was the oldest son of Col. John and Elizabeth (Loy) Tressler, and was born at Loysville. His early education was secured in the local schools. He graduated from Pennsylvania College at Gettysburg in 1848. He then became an instructor in the State University at Columbus, Ohio, reading law simultaneously. There he met and became a close friend of Stephen A. Douglas, later a national figure. He died September 12, 1851, while connected with the university.

TRESSLER, REV. JOHN WILLIAM. Rev. John William Tressler, a son of Colonel John and Elizabeth (Loy) Tressler, was born at Loysville. Educated in local schools and at Pennsylvania College at Gettysburg, where he graduated. He entered the Lutheran ministry, serving principally charges in western Pennsylvania. He became known as "the missionary preacher," being successful in building many churches. He died in Kittanning, Pennsylvania, in 1907. He was the father of two daughters and a son, Rev. Victor G. A. Tressler, D.D., who is to-day one of the leading figures in Lutheran circles in the United States.

Rev. Victor G. A. Tressler, after finishing his course at McCormick Seminary at Chicago, started a mission at San Jose, California, where, after a few years of hard work he built a church. His postgraduate work was at London, Paris and Berlin. After four years of study and travel Leipsic University conferred the Ph.D degree upon him. Returning to America he occupied prominent positions in several institutions, among which was Wittenberg Seminary, at Springfield, Ohio. In 1919, at the time of the consolidation of the Lutheran Churches of America, he was the president of General Synod of the Lutheran Church in America.

TRESSLER, DR. JOSIAH EZRA. Dr. Josiah Ezra Tressler, a son of Colonel John and Elizabeth (Loy) Tressler, was born at Loysville. He was educated in the local schools, and in 1866 graduated in medicine at the University of Pennsylvania, having previously attended Loysville

Academy and Muhlenberg Institute. He practiced his profession for some years in Illinois and then removed to Peabody, Kansas, where he engaged in the banking and brokerage business. He lives retired at "Luther Lawn," Peabody, Kansas. He is the only living son of Colonel John Tressler.

TROSTLE, WM. P. William P. Trostle was born near New Germantown, January 14, 1871, the son of Abraham M. and Susannah (Long) Trostle. He attended the public schools of Toboyne Township until 1889, and then taught in the same township until 1897. He took the normal course at Juniata College at Huntingdon, 1897-99, and the A.B. course 1899-1903. He later did postgraduate work in school administration. During 1903 and 1904 he was principal of the Second Ward schools of Huntingdon. During 1904-07 he was principal of the High School at Williamsburg, and 1907-18 he was the supervising principal of the Woodward District schools of Clearfield County. In 1918 he was elected county superintendent of the schools of Clearfield County, which position he has since filled. In college he was a noted debater.

TRUBY, REV. CHARLES. Rev. Charles Truby was born in Millerstown, November, 1867. After his completion of public school work he attended the New Bloomfield Academy and Princeton College, from which he graduated. He then entered McCormick Theological Seminary at Chicago, also graduating there. He served charges in Fowler, Winchester and Lafayette, Indiana, but is now located in New York City.

ULSH, DR. J. A. Dr. J. A. Ulsh was born in Greenwood Township, December 10, 1854, the son of George and Susannah (Cauffman) Ulsh. He attended the public schools and the Freeburg Academy (1870-71), and the Juniata Normal School at Millerstown (1872-73). He taught in the public schools of Greenwood and Liverpool Townships, and graduated in 1878 at the Medical College of Ohio, now the University of Cincinnati. He took postgraduate courses at Philadelphia Polyclinic and College of Graduates in Medicine, 1885 and 1893. He practiced medicine at Enders, Dauphin County, from 1878 to 1881, and at Elizabethville, 1881 to 1885, since which time he has been practicing in Lykens.

ULSH, RALPH. Ralph Ulsh was born near Millerstown, July 29, 1884, the son of James Morrow and Ada M. (Dimm) Ulsh. His people moving to Duncannon, he graduated from the high school there, from Franklin and Marshall Academy, and from Franklin and Marshall College (A.B.) in 1907. He was admitted to the bar in the State of New York in 1910, and practiced law at Elmira, New York, for about three years, and at Buffalo, New York, for about eight years.

VanCAMP, DR. J. E. Dr. Joshua Emanuel VanCamp was born at Bailey's, Miller Township, February 22, 1844, the son of William and Melvina (Hoffman) VanCamp. He attended the Loysville Academy in 1860, and went with Captain Tressler's company to serve in the Sectional War. Returning he attended Gettysburg College, 1865-66, and the University of Michigan, 1866-68, graduating in medicine from the latter place. As a young man he had clerked in Dr. Singer's store at Newport. Upon his graduation in medicine he located at Markelville, where he practiced from 1869 to 1871. He located at Plainfield, Cumberland County, in 1872. He located at Carlisle in 1899, where he practiced until his death in 1904. He was a member of the commission to erect the Hartranft memorial, which stands at the west entrance to the Pennsylvania State Capitol, and made the presentation speech to the state.

VanCAMP. DR. DAVID W. Dr. David W. VanCamp was born at Markelville, Perry County, educated in the public schools of Cumberland County, graduated from Gettysburg College as salutatorian in 1894, and from the Medical Department of the University of Pennsylvania in 1898.

During 1918-19 he was president of the Cumberland County Medical Society, and is on the staff of the Carlisle Hospital.

WAGNER, REV. JAS. M.   Rev. James M. Wagner was born in Tyrone Township, March 1, 1842, the son of George and Mary (Stambaugh) Wagner. He attended the local schools and the New Bloomfield Academy, and later entered the ministry of the Church of God. He was later retired and resides at Penbrook, Pa.

WAGNER, JOHN C.   John C. Wagner was born in Saville Township, March 10, 1872, the son of John W. and Sarah (Eby) Wagner. He attended the public schools, Millerstown High School, New Bloomfield Academy, and graduated from the Cumberland Valley State Normal School in 1892. Since that time he has done special work under various institutions. He taught in the townships of Miller and Howe, and was principal of the schools at Mt. Holly, 1892-97, and of Newport, 1897-1903. Since that time he has been superintendent of the schools of Carlisle, Pa. In 1905 Dickinson conferred the M.A. degree upon him. In 1917 he was elected treasurer of the Pennsylvania State Educational Association, in which position he still serves.

WAGNER, REV. SCOTT R.   Rev. Scott R. Wagner was born in Saville Township, August 16, 1874, the son of John W. and Sarah (Eby) Wagner. He attended the public schools, the New Bloomfield Academy, where he graduated in 1893, and Franklin and Marshall College, where he graduated in 1897. He then entered the Reformed Theological Seminary, and graduated in 1900. He served congregations in Allentown, Riegelsville, and Reading, Pa., and is now pastor of Zion Reformed Church at Hagerstown, Md. He received the degree of D.D. in 1918. He served as chaplain in the World War with the rank of first lieutenant, being stationed at Camp Zachary Taylor, in Kentucky, and Camp Jackson, in South Carolina.

WAGNER, REV. S. T.   Rev. Samuel T. Wagner was born in Spring Township, in 1846, the son of Samuel and Elizabeth (Tressler) Wagner. He attended the public schools, and graduated from Mercersburg College, of which Dr. E. E. Higbee was then president, in 1874, and in the postgraduate course in theology in 1878. Between the two courses he was principal of an academy in Iowa, 1874-75. He had also taught two terms in Perry County prior to that. He served several pastoral charges in Pennsylvania until 1905, and since then has had no regular appointment, being classed as retired. He has several times served as president of Classis, and one year as president of the Pittsburgh Synod. For fifteen years he was a member of the board of directors of St. Paul's Orphan Home, now located at Greenville, Pa. He resides at Alinda, Perry County.

WEIRICK, DR. CARL.   Dr. E. Carl Weirick was born at Liverpool, March 5, 1876, the son of John C. and Ada C. (Patton) Weirick. He attended the Liverpool schools, graduating from the high school in 1889, and from the Harrisburg High School in 1893. In 1904 he graduated from the University of Michigan, and located at Harrisburg, Pa. In 1905 he was appointed as surgeon of the Pennsylvania Railroad Company, which position he still holds, being located at Harrisburg.

WEISE, REV. CHAS F.   Rev. Charles F. Weise, son of Henry C. and Delila (Cook) Weise, was born at Milford, Juniata Township, December 2, 1867. He attended the public schools and the Bloomfield Academy. From 1883 to 1890 he was a telegraph operator in the employ of the P. R. R. During 1891-92 he was connected with the P. & R. in a similar capacity. He then entered the ministry of the Methodist Episcopal Church, and has been a member of the Central Pennsylvania Conference for twenty-five years. During 1912 he organized the First National Bank of Three Springs,

Pennsylvania, of which he was president for three years. In 1919 he organized the First National Bank of Port Royal, Pennsylvania, of which he is a director. He has been pastor of the Port Royal M. E. Church since April, 1917.

WEST, REV. WM. A. Rev. William A. West was the son of William ·and Susan (Loy) West, his grandfather having been Edward West, the pioneer who settled near Falling Springs, about four miles east of Landisburg. Rev. West was born at Landisburg, February 25, 1825. That spring the family removed to Warm Springs, Perry County, where they resided for ten years, then living a year in Landisburg. In 1836 they removed to New Bloomfield, where the future theologian attended the public schools. A year later. when the Bloomfield Academy opened its first term, he was one of the students, and there he prepared for college, teaching in the meantime, when yet not seventeen. He united with the Bloomfield Presbyterian Church in 1843. In 1844 he entered Marshall College, at Mercersburg, but lost a year by becoming organizer and first teacher in the Reformed Parochial School at Middletown, Maryland, and six months as a private tutor, to replenish his funds for his education. He graduated in 1849. He then entered the Western Theological Seminary at Allegheny, Pa. While at the seminary he taught latin and mathematics two hours daily at Caton Academy, in Pittsburgh, and during one vacation at the Plainfield Academy, near Carlisle. On April 14, 1852, he was licensed by the Presbytery of Carlisle, to preach the gospel. During the following winter he filled the Upper Path Valley pastorate for Rev. Wm. A. Graham, who was ill. When Rev. Graham resigned, he became the pastor, being installed in 1853. He remained there until 1873, when he went to Harrisburg to engage in mission work, under the joint care of the Market Square and Pine Street churches. During September of that year Rev. West organized Westminster Presbyterian Church, in the small, dingy lodge room over the Broad Street market house. The next year a small chapel was erected at Reily and Green Streets, and there he remained until 1890. Then, owing to throat trouble he had to leave a river atmosphere, and located at Carlisle, filling the pulpit of the Second Presbyterian Church for over a year, while the pastor was in Europe. He then returned to Path Valley, feeling that his ministry was at an end. However, he filled pulpits as stated supply, served a year at the Biddle Memorial Mission, in Carlisle. He was pastor of the Robert Kennedy Memorial Church at Welsh Run for five years. There, on February 6, 1898, Mrs. West passed away, and Rev. West then left there to become president of Metzgar College, at Carlisle. In 1900 he was called to the McConnellsburg and Green Hill churches, where he was pastor until his retirement, about 1905. He died in 1908. He was stated clerk of Carlisle Presbytery for many years.

WHITE, JAMES W. James W. White was born near Shermansdale, June 9, 1886, the son of James A. and Jennie S. (Smiley) White. He attended Lackey's school and later the New Bloomfield Academy. He took teachers' training instruction during two summers at Landisburg select school, teaching during the winter. He graduated from the Cumberland Valley State Normal School in 1910, and took postgraduate work at Columbia University in 1916, and at the Maryland University in 1919. He was principal of the Cold Spring Harbor (N. Y.) public schools for three years, and of the Darnestown (Md.) High School, seven years.

WHITE, THOS. J. Thomas J. White was born in Perry County, May 17, 1827. His parents early moved to Ohio, settling in Crawford County. He was elected to the General Assembly of Ohio.

WICKEY, H. J. H. J. Wickey, son of Rev. Lewis A. and Lydia A. (Wagner) Wickey, was born at Mont Alto, Pa., November 1, 1870, but was taken to Perry County when about six years old, and spent all of his early life there. He attended the village school at Eschol under Professor William E. Baker. In 1889 he taught his first term of school in Saville Township, teaching three years in Perry County. In 1893 he graduated from the Cumberland Valley State Normal School, and was elected principal of schools of Orbisonia, Huntingdon County, where he remained until 1896. He was then elected principal of the high school at Middletown. In 1899 he was advanced to the superintendency of the schools at Middletown, Pa., which position he is still filling.

WICKEY, J. GOULD. Rev. J. Gould Wickey, son of W. O. and Jennie A. (Hartman) Wickey, was born at Eshcol, where he attended Prof. W. A. Baker's school. His parents moved to Littlestown, Pa. He graduated from the Littlestown schools in 1907, Gettysburg College (1911), and the Theological Seminary there (1915), after which he entered Harvard and war awarded the D.D. degree in 1921. He won a year's scholarship at the University of Oxford, England. He returned to America, in 1920, and is now professor of philosophy at Concordia College, Moorhead, Minn., of which he is dean and where he teaches religious philosophy.

WOODS, REV. ROBERT W. Rev. Robert W. Woods was born at Blain, May 30, 1873, the son of William Wharton and Catherine Jane (Loy) Woods. William Wharton Woods was the descendant of General Anthony Wayne. Rev. Woods attended the public schools at Blain, and at an early age joined the Zion Lutheran Church. He attended the Blain schools, Gettysburg Academy, and graduated from the Pennsylvania College at Gettysburg in 1898. In 1901 he graduated from the seminary there. During the summer prior to his graduation he had worked up a charter membership for the organization of a new Lutheran church at Pittsburgh, to be known as the Lutheran Church of the Redeemer. On his graduation he was called as its first pastor, and is still connected with this church, although twenty years has elapsed, and he has received calls from elsewhere. He has taken into this church over 1,500 adults, and has had an average annual increase in salary of $100. He has served as the president of the Homewood Christian Committee for social betterment, and as secretary, treasurer, and president of the Lutheran Ministerial Association of Pittsburgh at different times. For eight years he was president of the Perry County Association of Pittsburgh. He is a member of the Committee on Jewish Mission Work of the United Lutheran Church, and has served as president of Pittsburgh Synod of the Evangelical Lutheran Church.

WRIGHT, DR. W. J. Dr. Winfred J. Wright was born in Millerstown, November 8, 1876, the son of Silas and Fannie E. (Calhoun) Wright. When about five years old, his parents removed to Greenwood Township, where he received his early education. During 1895-96 he taught in Pfoutz Valley, and from 1896 to 1898 attended the Mifflin Academy, where he graduated. In 1902 he graduated from the Medico-Chi. College at Philadelphia, and began the practice of medicine at Ickesburg. In March, 1903, he located at Duncannon, succeeding Dr. Robert T. Barnett. He remained here until August, 1909, when for less than a year he was located at Swarthmore, Delaware County. He then purchased the home and practice of a physician at Skippack, Montgomery County, where he has practiced successfully since. He was president of the Montgomery County Medical Society during 1918, and while in Perry County was president of the Perry County Medical Society.

ZEIGLER, REV. GEO. C. Rev. Geo. C. Zeigler was born in Howe Township, January 16, 1867, the son of Jacob A. and Hannah M. (Lahr) Zeigler. He began attending school there, but when eleven years old his parents removed to Mifflintown, where he finished his common school education. He attended several theological schools, beginning the ministry at the same time. Mr. Zeigler has been awarded the D.D. degree. He has served churches in Altoona, Williamsport, Berwick, and Bloomsburg, Pa.; Petersburg, Va.; Rocky Mountain, N.C., and is now at Wytheville, Va. He is also a lecturer, having appeared on the platform, both North and South. He is connected with the Christian Church (Disciples of Christ).

ZELLERS, PARK. Park Zellers was born at Liverpool, April 26, 1897, the son of John Adam and Caretta Louise (Lutz) Zellers. He attended the Liverpool schools, graduating in 1914. He graduated at the Central State Normal School in 1917. During 1917-18 he taught in Marysville. He was instructor in printing at the Edison Junior High School in Harrisburg, principal of schools at Liverpool (1920-21), and is now principal of schools at Mill Hall, Pa.

ZIMMERMAN, CHAS F. Charles F. Zimmerman, son of Lucian C. and Clara R. (Steele) Zimmerman, was born in Allen's Cove, Penn Township, June 21, 1878. He attended the Duncannon public schools. From 1895 to 1898 he attended Lafayette College. He then transferred to Princeton University, graduating in 1900, the next year taking a postgraduate course there. He was then with the First National Bank at Harrisburg as correspondence clerk for a time. When the Steelton Trust Company was organized in 1902 he was tendered a position there, and in 1906 became its treasurer. In 1912 he was elected treasurer of the Lebanon County Trust Company at Lebanon, Pennsylvania. He was chairman of Group Five of the Pennsylvania Bankers' Association, 1919-1921, and in 1921 was elected secretary of the State Bankers' Association. He is also chairman of the committee on education.

ZIMMERMAN, FRANK A. Frank A. Zimmerman was born in Allen's Cove, Penn Township, March 16, 1875. He is a son of Lucian C. and Clara R. (Steele) Zimmerman. He was an attendant of the Duncannon public schools from 1883 to 1893. His first position was with the Duncannon National Bank, from which place he went with the Citizens' National Bank at Waynesboro as cashier. After a number of years there he was elected treasurer of the Chambersburg Trust Company, with which he is still connected as vice-president, secretary and treasurer. This trust company, by the way, has a capital stock of $218,000, a surplus, profit and reserve fund of about $350,000, and is one of the best institutions in the Cumberland Valley. Mr. Zimmerman has been there eighteen years.

ZIMMERMAN, DR. G. L. Dr. G. L. Zimmerman was born in Madison Township, January 9, 1862, the son of William and Margaret (Bower) Zimmerman. He attended the public schools, Captain G. C. Palm's select school at Blain, Susquehanna University (then Missionary Institute) at Selinsgrove for three years, ending in 1886. He graduated in medicine at Jefferson Medical College in 1889 and located at Carlisle, where he has since practiced. He is a member of the staff of the Carlisle Hospital in the Department of Obstetrics. From 1904 to 1907 he was medical superintendent of the Cumberland County Hospital for Insane.

OTHER NOTED AND PROFESSIONAL MEN.

The task of compiling the list of these men and women seems endless, and must be relinquished so that the book may go to press. Other Perry Countians, briefly: Rev. W. N. Wright, pastor of the Marysville Church of God, whose work so far has been within the county; Rev. L. E. Henry, a pastor of the same denomination, residing at Penbrook; Rev. Daniel Motzer, a graduate of Canonsburg College, who died in 1864; Rev. Martin, a Spring Township native who became a D.D.; Rev. G. C. Hall, born at Blain, who graduated from Franklin and Marshall College in 1875, entered the Episcopal ministry, and served charges principally in New York State until about 1915, when he retired; Rev. John Adams, a Lutheran minister born in Spring or Carroll Township; Rev. Linden H. Rice, a Reformed pastor; Rev. Dison Hench, who passed away a few years ago; Isaac G. Black, lately of Duncannon, but long a resident of Philadelphia, where during the period after 1880 he taught for many years in Old Bethany (John Wanamaker's Church), a Sunday school class of over a hundred Pennsylvania University students; Dr. Lewis Smiley, who located in Philadelphia and became noted as a great Sunday school man and welfare worker as well as a physician of note; Albert Leonard Dorwart, a young student at State College, a fine spirited youth whose clean moral life and sunny disposition caused that great institution to issue "The Story of a Brief Life," a booklet of appreciation of his work; Robert E. Ferguson, a Perry County boy, who edited the *Bradford Herald* at Towanda, Pennsylvania, during the Sectional War period; Anna Thompson (Sutch) Stevens, wife of Rev. Stevens, and her sister, Frances Bates (Sutch) Friese, wife of Rev. Friese, whose long work in the Indian mission fields is of note; Milton C. Miller, an attorney at Wichita, Kansas, and the late J. Cal. McAlister, who died about 1917; Theo. K.' Holman, who is an attorney in Salt Lake City, and who held a prominent state office in Utah; Millard F. Clouser, a former checker expert of international fame, and long editor of the Chess and Checkers page of the *New York World;* Lew Ritter, long catcher of the Brooklyn National baseball team, and Robert Clark, with the Cleveland world series winners in 1921; H. W. Mc-Kenzie, of Walton, New York, an executive committeeman of the American Farm Bureau Foundation, which represents a million and a half of farmers in the northwestern region of the United States, he being one of three men on that committee from this large territory; Samuel Tressler, Washington, New Jersey; J. Cloyd Tressler, New Gardens, Long Island; Ed. S. Taylor, Mt. Carmel, Pa.; S. E. B. Kinsloe, from 1890 to 1900 a ward principal in the Philadelphia schools, and Helen Elizabeth Wilkinson, a graduate of the University of Pennsylvania, who held a similar position until her death in 1921; John Dum, once principal of the White Hill Orphans' School; E. C. Miller, half owner and treasurer of the Milligan Fruit Company at St. Louis, which handles several hundred carloads of fruit each season, and who attended the public schools of Pennsylvania, Ohio, Illinois and Missouri, teaching for some years; Jos. W. Billow, long a ward principal at Lewistown; Dr. Ben Hooke Ritter, who had located in Juniata County and became first president of the Juniata County Medical Society; Dr. John L. Ickes; Dr. Geo. A. Ickes, who practiced at Altoona, Pa.; Dr. Gilbert Conner, born at Landisburg, who practiced medicine in Michigan, where he died, and Dr. Fetter, born at Landisburg, who settled at Croton Falls, New York, about 1885; E. D. Bistline, works accountant with the Federal Shipbuilding Company; H. B. Raffensberger, holding a responsible government position at Chicago; Dr. C. A. Rinehart, of Philadelphia; Wm. Kinter, a Philadelphia attorney; E. R. Sponsler, a Harrisburg attorney; Rev. C. W. Winey, Pittsburgh; Rev. Melancthon Sohn, Rev. Eugene Raffensberger, Rev. Joseph W. Wagner, Rev. Elmer E. Hench, Rev. Harry Kleckner, Rev. C. J. Dick, Rev. B. F. Hall, Rev. D. L. Kepner, Rev. I. M. Pines, and Rev. B. A. Shively, the latter five being ministers of the Evangelical Church; Rev. G. W. Crist and Rev. John A. Flickinger, Lutheran ministers; Rev. Cassius E. Bixler, minister to Brazil, and Dr. Zenas J. Gray. The Young Men's Christian Associations throughout the world are directed by secretaries who are under the guidance of Paul Super, a native of Perry County.

One of the big lines of business of New York City is the Casket business, and there, as secretary of the Casket Manufacturers' Association, and also secretary of the Casket Manufacturers' Service Bureau, is another Perry Countian, J. W. Lukenbach, a native of Liverpool. Mr. Lukenbach's father, Wm. Lukenbach, was once a Newport photographer, and later moved to Liverpool, in 1863.

Two others often considered Perry Countians and whose associations were mostly in the vicinity of the county seat, are Henry C. Dern, late publisher of the *Altoona Tribune,* and Dr. J. Frank Raine, who has practiced medicine at Sykesville, Pa., since his graduation at the College of Physicians and Surgeons at Baltimore, in 1905. Both men learned the printing trade in New Bloomfield, but Mr. Dern was born in Carroll County, Maryland, and Dr. Raine, at West Fairview, Cumberland County.

Perry County has furnished many men who have filled and fill responsible banking positions in other states, the most noted having been M. D. Thatcher and John A. Thatcher, whose biographies appear elsewhere, and whose names as financiers were noted over half the continent. They, however, drifted from general business into the banking business. Others who have made a success abroad are George W. Derick, of the Everett (Pa.) Bank; Frank A. Zimmerman, W. H. Gelbach, Charles F. Zimmerman, Tolbert J. Scholl, Wm. K. Swartz, Chas. W. Bothwell, Wm. T. Albert, W. C. Boyles, T. Ward Rice, J. A. Garber, Edgar Ulsh, Warren Sellers and Max Taylor. Others are holding responsible banking positions. It is doubted if there is an inland town of its size in Pennsylvania which has sent out in the past few years so many bank cashiers as has Landisburg, through the Bank of Landisburg, of which James R. Wilson is cashier. The list includes: James M. Sheibley, Creigh Patterson, Mervin N. Lightner, J. Todd Stewart, Karl Rice, John F. Neely and Harry R. Patterson.

It is not inappropriate to cite here a fine illustration of the far-reaching influence of a Godly home, as found in the life and career of George McGinnes, who resided in Buffalo Township from 1787 to 1814. He came from Ireland and, on leaving what is now Perry County, located at Shippensburg. His people were Presbyterians, and he was brought up in the church at the mouth of the Juniata, the forerunner of the Duncannon Presbyterian Church, becoming an elder in early life. Two of his sons were educated for the Christian ministry at Jefferson College, Canonsburg, Pennsylvania. One of these sons, Rev. James Y. McGinnes, became the founder of Milnwood Academy at Shade Gap, Huntingdon County, where he preached, and where he died August 31, 1851. In 1840 he had married Elizabeth Criswell, of Franklin County. His only son, George Harold Criswell, expected to study for the ministry, but entered the Union Army in 1862 and died after the Battle of Chancellorsville. His mother had moved to Canonsburg, so that he might be educated in the institution where his father had graduated. She died there February 10, 1887. Four of their daughters married Presbyterian ministers, and two of them, now deceased, went as missionaries to India. A fifth, Miss Alice Y. McGinnes, of Wooster, Ohio, remained in this country to look after the education of the children of her two missionary sisters, and through her self-sacrificing devotion they have taken the places of their parents in the missionary fields of India. Of these sisters, Elizabeth McGinnes married Rev. J. V. Hughes; Mary McGinnes married Rev. Horatio W. Brown; Amanda B. married Rev. J. M. Goheen (Kohlapur, India), and Anna M. married Rev. J. J. Hall (Vengurle, India). The sons of the McGinnes sisters who became missionaries are Dr. R. H. H. Goheen (Vengurle, India), and John L. Goheen (Sangli, India). A daughter, Frances Goheen (now Mrs. Avison), of Pittsburgh, became a trained nurse.

THE BLOOD OF THE PIONEER.

Of the bravery, tact and resolution of the pioneers who settled the soil of Perry County volumes could be written and yet much remain untold. Throughout this book is recorded much of their early history, including the names and first settlements of many, whose mantle has fallen upon their descendants down through the generations and the years, who has crossed the Alleghenies, helped settle Ohio, Indiana and Illinois; braved the dangers of the plains, helping populate Wisconsin, Iowa and Minnesota—where they furnished a governor to the state; the Dakotas, Nebraska and Kansas—where a boy in Perry County became a United States Senator, and crossed the Rockies, contributing a share of the population on the way, to settle in the three great states bordering the Pacific—in all of which they or their descendants are to be found, a people unafraid, red blooded, and a credit to the land from whence they came. In other words, they have ever been in the van of civilization and have helped build a mighty empire. Charles Dickens is credited with having said that "the typical American would hesitate to enter Heaven unless assured that there he could still go farther west." That surely has been largely applicable to many generations of Perry Countians, and even to this day there is considerable migration.

The ancestry of many families of Washington County, Pennsylvania, can be traced to the Scotch-Irish emigrants from Perry County. In the State of Kentucky that is also true. George, Anthony and William Logan, sons of old Alexander Logan, the pioneer who lost his life while defending his home from the Indians in 1763, located in that state in 1786. James Anderson removed to Kentucky in 1802 and wed Mary Logan, a descendant of these Logans. In 1785 Jonathan Anderson, a son of George Anderson, visited Kentucky, selected several hundred acres of land there, returned to Perry County territory, and at once removed to Kentucky. Other members of the family followed, and in 1797 George Robinson and wife removed there, settling near the present town of Georgetown, Kentucky. Jonathan Robinson, the advance agent of the numerous Robinson families who then went to Kentucky, was a Revolutionary soldier from Perry County territory, and was married to Jane (Black) Robinson. They became the parents of James Fisher Robinson, the twenty-second governor of Kentucky, that staunch Unionist who helped retain Kentucky in the Union and who sent three of his own sons into the army. Governor Robinson was born in Scott County, Kentucky, October 4, 1800. He held a high place among Kentucky lawyers and died in 1892.

The Ellmakers, who were of the first to warrant lands in Greenwood Township, settled in Iowa, when that state was in the making, and a later generation to this day is among the residents of the productive Williamette Valley, Oregon.

When Kansas was being settled dozens of Perry Countians "took up" lands there of the public domain, and among them was Joseph W. Huggins, whose ancestors were among the first settlers of Perry County soil, and one of whom—Jacob Huggins—was a member of the first board of county commissioners and the Perry County representative in the State Legislature when the county seat controversy was settled by locating it at New Bloomfield. Mr. Huggins located on a quarter section in Ellsworth County, Kansas, and became one of the new state's successful farmers, owning and operating at one time land to the number of 1,280 acres. His sons and sons-in-law, eight in number, are almost all engaged in agriculture there on a large scale. From the same section (Buffalo and Howe Township) with Mr. Huggins went George W. Sneath, part of whose family remains in that state engaged in agriculture, and William Hetrick, both of whom died in 1919.

"Going West" before railroad travel was available was not the easy matter that it is to-day. In 1856 William Woods and William Owings left Jackson Township, in western Perry, for Iowa, with a covered wagon and two horses, leaving Blain on a Monday morning, and getting to Pittsburgh the following Sunday morning, for it must be remembered that the roads were not then what they are now. The state capitol at Des Moines was just then being built, and the Mormons, five or six thousand of whom they saw, were just migrating from the Middle West to the great Salt Lake, where they are now so impregnably entrenched.

John Bistline, who was born near Elliottsburg, went to Illinois in 1857, and was there early enough to help break up the virgin soil with an oxen team. Robert L. Woods, of Blain, landed at Ottawa, Illinois, in 1856, and remembered it as "a vast prairie country, sparsely settled, and beautiful to look upon."

William Kiner, of Sheaffer's Valley, in 1851 went to Illinois with his family and his son, Henry L. Kiner, two and one-half years old, also born in Perry County, became the editor of the Geneseo, Illinois, *News*, in 1874, and conducted it until 1904. His editorial work was noted throughout the state along moral lines and he came to be known as "Parson Kiner."

The post office and village at Smiley, Ohio, was named after J. E. Smiley, an early settler who was born in Perry County and whose biography appears under the chapter devoted to theologians, as Mr. Smiley has since entered the ministry. The post office has been superseded by rural delivery.

Wesley Shannon, a prominent citizen of Seattle, Washington, was among the Perry Countians who aided in the railroad construction of the great transcontinental lines, helping to "carry the chains" in the survey of the Northern Pacific, between Butte, Montana, and Seattle.

The counties of La Salle, Bureau, Dupage, Carroll, Henry, Ford and Knox, in the State of Illinois, contain a large percentage of former Perry Countians and their descendants, who are among their best citizens. The country surrounding Buda, Illinois, is a veritable garden spot, and is peopled largely by Perry Countians and their descendants. In one section surrounding Buda, Illinois, are the Stutzmans, Toomys, Gutshalls, Bittings, Morgans, Tresslers, and other Perry County families. Other Perry Countians than those already named who were pioneers there were Alfred B. Preisler, who left Sheaffer's Valley and located in Ottawa, Illinois, in 1871, later a prominent marble dealer of that city; George A. Kline, of Blain, who went West in 1866 and settled in La Salle County, Illinois, but later migrated to Grundy County, Iowa; Sylvester Toomey, now a prominent druggist at Buda, who left the county in 1878; Jacob P. Kiner, of Madison Township, who left for Ottawa, Illinois, in 1854; John L. Woods, of Blain, who went West in 1881, and is now proprietor of a dry goods store in Woodhull, Illinois; Henry Briner and his wife (Jane Stroup), of western Perry, who went West as newly-weds in 1855, settling in La Salle County, where he gained quite a competence; Benj. Kell, of Blain, who left for Carroll County, Illinois, in 1878, a mere child with his parents, later going to Sioux City, where a son, Ben, is one of the owners of a large engine and iron company; Andrew Bistline, of Madison Township, who went to Ogle County, Illinois, later migrating to Waterloo, Iowa, and then Ogden, Utah; Jonathan F. Bistline, of Blain, who left for Ford County, Illinois, in 1870, but later located at Finley, North Dakota; Daniel E. Burd, of Mannsville, who was confined in Libby prison during the war, and migrated to Mercer County, Illinois; Margaret Mumper, a daughter of Henry and Elizabeth Kiner Mumper, a Perry County girl, who wed Philip M. Shoop, and with him was among the early stand-bys of Hedding College, at a time when help was sorely needed, among their children being Rev. W. B. Shoop, D.D., pastor of the M. E. Church at Pekin, Illinois.

Willis Sylvester Long, who left Perry County in 1879, "without anything," as he says, and later owned a valuable quarter-section; David A. Grubb and Preston Grubb, who were successful agriculturalists near Ellsworth, Kansas; Blair Moul, who went West as a laborer, and by hard toil became the owner of a 200-acre farm, which he sold in war times for $60,000, giving each of his seven children a present of $6,000, and still retaining $18,000; David Billow and his wife, Susan (Tressler) Billow, who left Perry County in 1860 and settled in Shelby, Richland County, Ohio, where was born their son, C. O. Billow, the noted consulting engineer, now located in Chicago; William W. Sheibley, of New Germantown, who located in Shelby, Ohio, in 1873, but later moved to Tiffin, where he was a prominent real estate dealer; Henry Albert, bereft of a father during the Sectional War, who located a claim in California in 1877, and later became an orange grower at Alta Loma, California. He was president of the Orange Growers' Association there for four years and of the Chamber of Commerce for two years.

The counties of Ogle and Winnebago, Illinois, include the names of many Perry Countians and their descendants. Among them were Jacob Barrick, who went West in 1851, settling near Byron, where the Wrays, William and Samuel Tate and their mother, from Donally's Mills, also first located in 1856. William Linn left Perry Valley in 1852 with his wife and five children, and also located near Byron, one of the sons, David W., now over eighty years of age, still living on his farm near there. Robert Bull and his family settled in North Byron in 1851, as did John Hench and his family, some of these two families being sweethearts and later married. John Swartz Kosier, a venerable contractor of Byron, married one of the Misses Bull, who died many years ago, but he is still hale and hearty and ninety-one. The Meredith family settled in the Middle Creek region in 1852, Calvin being deceased, but David still resides near the old home on his farm, his sister Jennie living in Rockford. Adam Hamaker and Jacob Hetrick, from Perry Valley, settled near Byron, where their descendants still live. Ephraim Burd and his sister, Mrs. Elizabeth Kline, settled near Leaf River and now live at Byron. Two Millerstown teachers, Misses Ellen Jane and Caroline Wray, moved to Winnebago in 1871 and followed their professions. Both are now dead. Among the later emigrants to this territory were John M. Fry and family, from Donally's Mills, in 1880—the parents of Judge Fry, of Chicago; J. Ambrose Leonard and wife, from Donally's Mills, in 1885, settled at Byron and engaged in general contracting, removing to Rockford in 1904, and continuing the business there; Emerson Martin Leonard, from Donally's Mills, in 1886, located north of Byron; Cameron Wesley Leonard, from Donally's Mills, in 1900, and Margaret (Leonard) Kennedy, in 1890, are Rockford residents.

To all parts of the world go Perry Countians. To the Klondike went David Shearer, of Spring. To help build the Panama Canal went Benj. Kuller and sons, of near Landisburg; Charles F. Lomman, of Duncannon, and C. Deane, Roy and Russell Eppley, of Marysville, and others. C. Deane Eppley yet remains there in a supervisory position.

CHAPTER XXXV.

AGRICULTURE IN PERRY COUNTY.

PERRY County is largely an agricultural county, having principally engaged in the raising of the standard grains since its very first settlement; but it is now slowly drifting towards the raising of fruit and dairying. The fact that Perry County is the best watered county in the Commonwealth of Pennsylvania is probably the reason for the statement, by a noted lecturer of the State Agricultural Department, that there is no other county in the state where grazing and attendant dairying can be made more profitable. That its soils are excellent for fruit raising has been proven by the young and numerically small Fruit Growers' Association of Perry County, which was captured on four occasions the first prize for the finest exhibit of apples grown in Pennsylvania, which has captured it for three successive years (1918, 1919 and 1920), and which only failed in 1921 owing to an extensive late frost which ruined the entire crop, thus barring any exhibit whatever. The agriculturists of Perry County should more generally belong to this association and gradually work into the fruit business. The raising of fruit has been reduced to a science and no haphazard plans will bring success. The pioneers planted orchards from the very year of their entry, and with their primitive stills and stillhouses, they turned to profit the product of their trees, which was largely sold later in Baltimore, where their "applejack" and "peach brandy" commanded a fancy price. Already the product of the Perry County Fruit Growers' Association commands a fancy price in the choicest markets of our eastern cities, and the highly tinted fruit stands beside the choicest product of the orange groves of California and Florida.

The pioneer used a sickle, his son the scythe, his grandson the grain cradle, and another generation, the reaper, only to see it replaced by the self-binder of a later day. Even the mower is not many generations away, for, according to available data Capt. Andrew Loy, father of Ed. R. Loy, on the very farm on which stood Fort Robinson, and which is now owned by the latter, owned and used the first mower which was brought into Perry County. · It cut a wide swath and required four horses. The first reaper is believed to have been brought to the county by John Robinson, tanner and farmer, in 1849, he having been what is termed an advanced farmer. The first method of threshing wheat and rye was to tramp it out on the barn floors with horses, or to flail it out; and many persons little over middle life can recall such threshings in their early years. The primitive way of cleaning the wheat was to throw scoopfuls of grain and chaff into the air and let the wind blow away the chaff. Then came the horse-power and treadmill, with the windmill or fanning mill, and later the steam thresher and separator. While still "in my forties" I can recall all four methods of extracting the grain in the community in which I was reared. The flailing out of rye left the straw in fine shape for use as bands in the tying of corn fodder, then the method used. Along with the self-binder and the steam thresher and separator has come labor-saving machinery for almost every operation, and the many little homes which once nestled by the side of the farms, and even the tenant houses upon them, where dwelt those who helped in the farm operations, are largely gone, the result of the introduction of labor-saving machinery and the demand for labor from the mill and factory of the town and city. The former laborer is to-day often the skilled operative of the industrial plant.

Agriculture is the most important and most extensive single industry in America, for it is both a necessity for maintaining life and the basis of all commerce—of the big meat packing industry, the canning factory, the dairying industry, and all of their kind. The very life of the great transportation lines depends upon the handling of the products of the farm and the manufactured products dependent upon it. The life of the town and city are so intertwined with that of the farm that neither could long exist without the other. Were there no towns and cities where would the surplus products of the farms be sold? And were there no farms how long would life be sustained? In Pennsylvania the commonwealth conducts the great and noted State College, second to none in the nation, and also holds a number of farmers' institutes in every county. The national government, through the Department of Agriculture, furnishes bulletins and the result of tests upon every imaginable subject, and in almost all counties (including Perry) farm bureaus exist, with their farm agents (wrongly named) in charge, thus helping advance agricultural science. There is room for improvement in the production of Perry County. During 1920 there were 23,591 acres in corn, with an average yield of only 38.1 bushels per acre. The cash value of the crop was $808,935, according to the State Department of Agriculture. The wheat crop was harvested from 25,805 acres, with an average yield of only 15.4 bushels per acre. The cash value of the crop was $675,574.

One reason why the average crop per acre is as small as it is in Perry County is that one class of farmers have been hard taskmasters on the land. They have cropped the soil for years and have returned but little to the soil in the way of fertilizer. A noted Perry Countian still living, refers to that condition in these words: "As early as 1850 there were a number of fields in our vicinity that had been farmed to death. Some that were still cultivated yielded poor crops, while others had been abandoned and were covered with scrub pines in places growing so thick that any living being larger than a dog had hard work to get through."

While the soils of Perry County are not noted for their fertility yet there are several limestone sections in which the soil rivals any other in the state. In the vicinity of Blain, Landisburg, and Loysville, and in the famous Pfoutz Valley, farms bring from about ten thousand to almost twenty twenty thousand dollars on occasions when they come into the market, and they do not lie next door to any city or have a market at their very side. William Woods, of Blain, once owned five farms at one time valued at $125,000, and in recent years Jacob Loy, of Blain, owned seven at one time, all very valuable. From the public records at the county seat records of a number of sales at good prices are to be found. In 1915 Frank P. Lightner purchased 179 acres in Tyrone Township, from the heirs of Daniel E. Garber, for $16,017.52. In 1920 Elmer E. Rice purchased 286 acres in Saville Township, from John E. Lesh, for $16,000; Aurand A. Ickes, 185 acres in Centre Township, from Chas. L. Johnson, for $14,550; Dr. W. T. Morrow, the John S. Ritter farm near Loysville, from Samuel B. Shumaker, for $10,500; Ralph B. Adams, 190 acres near Bloomfield, from the H. C. Shearer estate, for $10,200; Charles D. Stahl, 240 acres (much of it woodland), in Madison Township, from Mr. and Mrs. Flickinger, for $14,800; Herman H. Smith, 138 acres, a mile west of Bloomfield, from Miles Ritter, for $14,000, and Wm. J. Hall, a Spring Township farm, from John S. Zimmerman, for $15,750. In 1921 N. Kurtz Bistline purchased 167 acres, located in Jackson Township and Blain Borough, from Sarah C. Loy, for $17,000; Charles L. Darlington purchased 181 acres in Spring Township, from Frank G. Dunkelberger and others, for $17,000, and John L. Bernheisel, 153 acres in Tyrone Township, from Thomas Bernheisel, for $16,000.

The spring sales of farmers who are retiring, of estates and of others are a noted institution, from the time of the pioneer. Chas. L. Johnson, an ex-sheriff, holds one annually, which has attained wide fame, and at which the proceeds often exceed $10,000. At these sales personal property of every nature is offered, as well as livestock and agricultural implements.

In 1914 the State of Pennsylvania through the Department of Agriculture, issued a publication called "The Soils of Pennsylvania," eighteen pages of which describe minutely the soils of the various townships and sections of Perry County, from which the following is taken:

"The soils of the county, leaving out of consideration the trap dykes, are derived from eighteen geological strata, differing sufficiently to be separately classified.

"The strata begins with the Trenton limestone, which outcrops in Horse Valley, and extends through the Utica shale, the Hudson River shale, the Medina and Oneida standstone, the Clinton shale, the Onondaga grey and red shale, the Lower Heidelberg limestone, the Oriskany sandstone, the Marcellus black shale, limestone and ore beds, the Hamilton lower shale, the Hamilton sandstone, the Hamilton upper shale, the Genesee shale, the Portage shale, the Chemung olive shale, the Catskill red sandstone and shale, the Pocono grey sandstone and the Mauch Chunk red shale. All these together, with the narrow trap dykes, enter into the composition of the soils throughout the various townships of the county."

With the exception of five states—Ohio, Indiana, Iowa, West Virginia and Kentucky—Pennsylavnia has more native-born farmers than any other state. In Perry County they are all native-born, not a foreigner and only one negro. In the state ninety-two and six-tenths per cent are native-born and of the white race, with not a single Japanese or Chinaman. The state has 202,252 farms. These figures are from the State Agricultural Department, which in turn compiled them from the Federal census of 1920. The last census credited the county with having 2,105 farms and with 5,683 families, from which the deduction is made that, while it is a rural and an argricultural county, yet but thirty-seven per cent of the families are engaged in agricultural pursuits. The 1910 census showed that seventy-five per cent of the Perry County farms were operated by owners, twenty-three per cent by tenants, and the remaining two per cent by managers. During 1920 the totals of the various products were as follows: wheat, 392,000 bushels; oats, 546,600 bushels; corn, 980,900 bushels; potatoes, 190,500 bushels, and hay, 51,700 tons. The tractor is just being introduced, but, owing to the physical formation of the county, will never become of general use. Speaking of motors recalls that the first steam tractor was sold to Andrew Keller, over forty years ago, by Jacob Sheibley, long an agricultural implement agent.

While the argricultural, animal and poultry production in recent years has attracted attention, yet as early as 1884 there was a considerable poultry plant located in East Newport (Oliver Township), with Hirsh & Fulton as proprietors. They had four hundred laying hens and a hatching and brooding house, using four incubators with a capacity of two hundred eggs each. While this plant would be considered very ordinary now, yet in that day it was one of the larger plants of central Pennsylvania.

As early as 1873 George A. Wagner embarked in the nursery business in Spring Township, and for a period of almost half a century has supplied fruit trees, vines and plants not only to the inhabitants of the county, but also to surrounding counties and even to states far distant. He was a pioneer in this line and the

55

Wagner nursery was known far and near. Trees from his nursery were among those which brought to the county for a number of years the prize of the state for raising the finest varieties of apples in the entire commonwealth.

Agriculture in the great Susquehanna Valley, of which Perry County is a part, originated not so far from Perry County's southern line, for that pioneer minister at "Paxtang" (now Harrisburg), told William Maclay that John Harris "was the first person to introduce a plough along the Susquehanna." The modern farmer often thinks that all his ills are of recent origin, but as early as 1823 *The Forester,* Perry County's first paper, in various issues was bemoaning the "Hessian fly," that destroyer of the wheat crop. On one occasion the statement was made that "if Gregg is elected governor he will exterminate the Hessian fly."

Perry County farmers who have migrated to the neighboring counties of Cumberland and Lancaster, and to the valley of the Ohio and the many states drained by the Mississippi, as well as farther west, have not only become successful farmers in their new homes, but hundreds have amassed fortunes. Not unlike the professional men who have gone forth, they have been a credit to their native county.

As showing what can be done with hillside lands, in 1890, J. C. Hench began the cultivation of berries and small fruit on eighteen acres of what was considered practically worthless land, in Wheatfield Township, at a point almost central to Duncannon, Newport and New Bloomfield, and became the largest berry producer of the county, often raising 500 bushels in a season and employing as many as twenty pickers at a time in the busy season. In those days berries retailed at three boxes for a quarter, or thirteen for $1.00, and yet Mr. Hench amassed a competence. Later in life, after he had largely curtailed the production of berries, he was elected a commissioner of Perry County on the Republican ticket.

In the dairying line the Dickinson, Gilbert & Keen Creamery, at Loysville, was the successful pioneer. It was later followed, in 1919, with a milk condensory at Elliottsburg, operated by the Hershey Creamery Company. During 1921 the Supplee-Jones Company opened a large shipping depot at Duncannon for forwarding dairy products to Philadelphia via fast express trains. It would appear that Perry County is but starting in the dairying businesss. Future years will tell.

To the efforts of a few men Perry County is indebted for standing first on at least four occasions as growing the finest apples in Pennsylvania. Among these men are William Stewart, Daniel Rice, and D. R. Kane, of Spring Township. Some years ago the Perry County Fruit Growers' Association was organized, and, largely through its efforts the growing of fruit was stimulated.

Exhibitions were made at the State Horticultural Shows, and, in 1914, when the exhibition was held at York, the county captured the first prize for the largest and best display of apples. William Stewart and Daniel Rice, of Spring Township, and the Samuel Sharon Fruit Farm, near Newport, were the exhibitors who staged this first successful exhibit. Then, again in 1919, 1920 and 1921—three successive years—at the State Horticultural Exhibition at Harrisburg, the award was made to the county for the largest and best display of apples. The principal exhibitors at this last show (1921) were William Stewart, Daniel Rice, Sharon & Jones, and D. R. Kane. In the United States Government Year Book New York State is accredited with being first in the Union in the production of apples, with Pennsylvania second, notwithstanding that so much is heard of Pacific slope fruit farms. It is no mean position to hold—standing first three consecutive years in the second apple growing state of the Union.

Along the county's northern tier, from Pfoutz Valley to Ickesburg, a number of baby chick hatcheries do a large business over the state, shipping by parcel post. J. A. Schiffer ships 2,000 a week during the season, from what he terms the Cyclone Hatchery. Mrs. John Ward operates the Buckeye Hatchery, with a dozen incubators. At Ickesburg Ira M. Johnson hatched and shipped over 50,000 last year. His plant consists of three mammoth incubators in which the eggs are turned automatically. These are mentioned to show that Perry County argiculture in the broad sense is varied.

As the county commissioners refused to employ a county farm agent, or to contribute towards the support of one, it was done independently, beginning with the organization of a County Farm Bureau, July 1, 1921. The officers of this association were: Edgar A. Stambaugh, president; Daniel Rice, vice-president; John Bernheisel, secretary, and E. R. Loy, treasurer. At the regular annual election, December 7, 1921, the following officers were elected: John M. Gantt, president; E. R. Loy, vice-president; John L. Bernheisel, secretary; D. A. Kline, treasurer.

Even the wood lot is receiving an attention once not accorded, for, according to the State Forestry Department, during the past year over five thousand such trees were planted on private lands in Perry County, that department furnishing the seedlings without cost. Of these trees over two thousand were white pine, 1,900 being Norway spruce.

During the past two years, largely through the efforts of Rev. L. E. Wilson, rural life institutes were held each fall at Roseglen, Wheatfield Township, at which home and church problems as well as agricultural matters were discussed. Noted speakers from abroad were there with their messages along these lines. These community meetings show the trend of the times towards civic betterment in the farming communities, and presage better conditions in any community. Rev. Wilson is pastor of the Duncannon M. E. Church, and is to be commended for filling a broader field in religious and community work.

Long before the present Perry County Agricultural Fair became a reality there was a county fair held at New Bloomfield. The first fair was held there on Wednesday, Thursday and Friday, October 13, 14 and 15, 1852. Finlaw McCown was the president of the County Agricultural Society at that time. Charles McIntire and Jacob Lupfer were the secretaries, and David Lupfer the treasurer. Daniel Gantt, later Chief Justice of Nebraska, was chairman of the premium committee. and Rev. Matthew B. Patterson was an exhibitor and won a prize. The last fair was probably held in 1859, as the local press contains nothing in reference to it after that. The dark clouds of Sectional War were then rising, which evidently was the reason for its abandonment. Jacob Billow was president of the association for the larger part of the period when the fairs were held there.

Then, in 1868, a notice calling for a fair to be held at "Everhartville," near Newport, was issued, being dated August 5th, and signed by Jesse L. Gantt, president; J. E. Singer, D. R. P. Bealor, C. L. Murray, and William Kough, Sr. The first fair at that location was held on October 6, 7 and 8, 1868, and there is record in the public press of its continuance until at least 1874, when the seventh fair was held.

The present Perry County Agricultural Society fair was instituted in 1885, with B. F. Junkin, president; Dr. James B. Eby, secretary, and J. H. Irwin, treasurer. The directors were J. B. Black, A. S. Whitekettle, J. M. Smith, T. H. Milligan, T. H. Butturf, and William Wertz. In 1911 the association was incorporated anew. The officers since the organization have been:

Presidents:	Secretaries:
1885-89—B. F. Junkin.	1885-90—James B. Eby.
1889 —Frank Mortimer.	1891-97—F. A. Fry.
1890-08—D. H. Sheibley.	1898-99—J. B. Eby.
1909-22—T. H. Butturf.	1900 —Chas. K. Diven.
	1901-20—J. C. F. Stephens.
	1921-22—M. L. Ritter.

J. C. F. Stephens was assistant secretary from the organization in 1885 until 1901, when he was elected secretary, his connection with the annual fair thus exceeding the periods served by any other. The fair grounds are located a mile north of Newport, on the old John Kough farm, opposite the Evergreen school building.

Agriculture in Perry County has been stimulated towards better things by the organization known as the Patrons of Husbandry, or more frequently termed The Grange. In many cases this organization is to the farming community just what the community centre is to the city and town. The meetings of the organization also include literary and other entertainment. Exhibitions made by these granges at the county fair have equaled those at exhibits of far greater note, save that the display was not so expensively garbed in modern receptacles and cartons. On May 23, 1919, a County Pomona Grange was organized at Green Park Grange Hall, with Wm. E. Raffensberger, master; J. Frank Newlin, lecturer, and E. A. Stambaugh, secretary. All members of the order in Perry County are entitled to become members in that organization. There is also a Junior Grange connected with the organization in Buck's Valley. The first organizations were formed about 1874 or 1875, but disbanded.

Of those granges now in existence the oldest is Perry Grange, No. 759, organized in Hunter's Valley, October 16, 1881, with J. W. Charles as master, and Jacob Charles, Jr., secretary. It meets at the homes of its members and now has a membership of but 16.

Pine Grove Grange, No. 1038, in Miller Township, was organized May 19, 1891, with H. B. Cumbler, master, and W. H. Evans, secretary. It meets at Pine Grove schoolhouse and has a membership of 78.

Oliver Grange, No. 1069, was organized in Oliver Township, August 2, 1892, with John W. S. Kough, master, and Philip Troup, secretary. It meets at Oak Hall schoolhouse and has a membership of 109.

Green Park Grange, No. 1615, was organized at Green Park, Tyrone Township, May 27, 1914, with E. A. Stambaugh, master; Carrie Stambaugh, lecturer, and Paul Noll, secretary. It meets in a fine hall which it has erected and has a membership of 229.

Ickesburg Grange, No. 1729, was organized March 29, 1917, at Ickesburg, Saville Township, with D. N. Hall, master; Miss Mary J. Gray, lecturer, and James O. Gray, secretary. It meets in P. O. S. of A. hall and has a membership of 81.

Buck's Valley Grange, No. 1745, was organized in Buck's Valley (part of Buffalo and Howe Townships), June 26, 1919, with Wm. E. Raffensberger, master; Miles Stephens, lecturer, and S. W. Billow, secretary. It meets in Grange Hall and has a membership of 172.

Community Grange, No. 1767, was organized in Juniata Township, July 6, 1918, with J. F. Newlin, master; John M. Gantt, lecturer, and H. H. Shumaker, secretary. It meets in its own grange hall and has a membership of 135 members.

Shermanata Grange, No. 1796, was organized in Penn Township, May 31, 1919, with E. T. Charles, master; Mrs. Lena Smith Snyder, lecturer, and C. L. Snyder, secretary. It meets in a fine new grange hall, erected in 1920, and has a membership of 192.

Perry Valley Grange, No. 1804, was organized in Perry Valley (parts of Greenwood and Liverpool Townships), July 29, 1919, with C. E. Reissinger, master; Brant Mangle, lecturer, and Herbert Sarver, secretary. It meets at Beaver's schoolhouse and has a membership of 117.

Shermansdale Grange, No. 1858, was organized at Shermansdale, Carroll Township, September 1, 1920, with Alfred P. Barnes, master; Edward C. Hall, lecturer, and H. C. Minich, secretary. It meets in Mechanics' Hall, at Shermansdale, and has 109 members.

CHAPTER XXXVI.

*THE TUSCARORA FOREST.

UNDER original natural conditions Pennsylvania was one of the best wooded states, if not the best, in the eastern half of the United States. Not only were forests dense and trees large and valuable, but the varieties were of a greater commercial value. For years the state stood first, then second. Few counties in the state excelled Perry, which had a reputation for prompt shipments of fine lumber. Its forests were well set with rock, chestnut and black oak, white and yellow pine, hemlock, locust, hickory, etc.

Even before 1700, when an act was passed by the Provincial Assembly putting a penalty of ten pounds for felling or removing a tree or other landmark, there was legislation on forestry in Pennsylvania. This, however, had principally to do with landmarks and was not intended to deal with the preservation of the forests in a general sense. While the nation and some of the states had viewed with alarm the stripping of the hills of timber, thus interfering with the water supply, very little was done in Pennsylvania until 1896, when Dr. J. T. Rothrock, Pennsylvania's first Commissioner of Forestry, recommended in his report the forming of state forests, in the following words:

"In view of the generally admitted effect of forests upon the water supply of our streams, I would strongly advise that as soon as the condition of the State Treasury will permit, an attempt should be made to obtain control of at least a portion of the timber areas on the watersheds of one or both branches of the Susquehanna, in Pennsylvania, by imitating the example of other states, and be placed in a position in the near future to influence the water supply by controlling the character and condition of the forests upon the watersheds. The experiment may be made by degrees, as the condition of the treasury may warrant, but a beginning cannot be made too soon, as the emergency becomes more pressing each year, and the difficulty of obtaining control of these areas is annually increasing."

The act first authorizing the purchase of lands was passed by the Legislature of 1897, the member of assembly from Perry County

---

*Forester H. E. Bryner is a son of Mr. and Mrs. A. K. Bryner, of Southwest Madison Township, where he was born May 16, 1883. He was an attendant at the New Bloomfield Academy, Shippensburg State Normal School, Ursinus Academy, Ursinus College, and the State Forestry Academy, where he graduated in 1908, being the first Perry County native to graduate in forestry. Mr. Bryner has since been promoted to the State Forestry Department at Harrisburg. We are indebted to him for much valuable information, as well as to various other officials of the Department of Forestry. D. B. McPherson, his successor, is also a native Perry Countian.

being J. Harper Seidel, and the state senator of the district of which Perry is a part being William Hertzler, of Juniata County —both of whom supported it—and it was signed by Governor Daniel H. Hastings on March 30, 1897. It applied to lands sold for taxes. Another bill signed on May 25, 1897, authorized the purchase of lands in large bodies. Under the provisions of the former act the first purchase of lands was made in Clinton County on June 13, 1898, by Dr. Rothrock, the Commissioner of Forestry.

While the attitude of the various governors of Pennsylvania is not exactly a matter of Perry County history, yet it is deemed of sufficient importance in connection with our two Divisions of State Forests to be briefly recorded. Governor John F. Hartranft, the first to consider it, called attention to the coming need of forestry legislation. Governor James A. Beaver urged it further and also had the State Board of Agriculture take it up, but nothing practical resulted. Governor Robert E. Pattison presided at a meeting to draw up the law to create three forest reservations of 40,000 acres each. It was defeated. During his administration the first forestry commissioners were appointed. When Governor Daniel H. Hastings was inaugurated in 1895, he helped the movement from the start. When the Department of Agriculture was created in that year the interests of forestry were provided for and a special division given charge of the work. Legislation was passed during his term, as previously stated, and at its close, in 1899, the state had already acquired 19,804 acres.

Governor William A. Stone found the way paved and promptly began the task of providing forest reservations for the people, to be their property and their outing grounds forever, and upon which timber could grow to restore the lumbering industry and to maintain the water supply. At his retirement in 1903 the state possessed over a half-million acres. On February 25, 1901, the bill creating the Department of Forestry became a law with the signature of Governor Stone. Governor Samuel W. Pennypacker, whose administration was marred by the capitol scandal, was greatly interested in the forestry movement, and in 1903 signed the law creating the State Forestry Academy. During his term 375,000 acres were added to the state lands. Most of the lands were by this time being bought from the owners and few from tax sales. Governor Pennypacker's great interest was no doubt responsible for the State Forestry Reservation Commission naming the newly created domain in Perry County the Pennypacker Reserve.

During the administration of Governor Edwin S. Stuart laws were enacted for the protection of roadside trees, enabling municipalities to acquire forest lands, authorizing the appointment of shade tree commissions by municipalities and first class townships, and providing that a fixed charge be made on state forest lands for school purposes. The administration of Governor John K. Tener saw legislation furthering the protection of shade and fruit trees along highways, and provided for taxing auxiliary forest reserves. During his administration the most of the work for the eradication of chestnut blight was undertaken, but unfortunately failed. During the administration of Governor Martin G. Brumbaugh a number of important forest laws became effective. Among them was a law permitting the Forestry Department to grow and distribute young forest trees to private owners of forest lands; a law creating within the Department of Forestry a Bureau of Forest Protection, which is regarded as the best of its kind in the United States, giving to the chief forest fire warden of the state power not equaled by any other forest officer anywhere; a law authorizing the purchase of surface rights for use as state forests, and allowing the state to lease for agricultural purposes those of its lands which are more useful for that purpose than for forestry. The present incumbent, Governor Wm. C. Sproul, is a consistent friend of forestry. His appointment of Gifford Pinchot as Commissioner of Forestry, and of Major Robert Y. Stewart later as deputy commissioner, and still later as commissioner to succeed Mr. Pinchot, was ample proof of that. Mr. Pinchot, after graduating from Yale, had studied forestry abroad, and became a pioneer in conserving American forests and natural resources, and was at the head of the Federal forest service during the Roosevelt administration of the Presidency. Major Stewart, after graduating at Dickinson, had entered the Yale Forestry School, and, after becoming a master forester, had held a number of the more important assignments in the Federal service and won a citation and a major's commission in the A. E. F., during the World War, where he was District Commander of the Forestry Troops in the Gien District. Among the acts which have become laws during his administration is one for the exchange or sale of forest lands, a law making a fixed charge on state lands for county purposes, a law providing for the condemnation of lands suitable for forest purposes, and a law permitting the Federal government to acquire lands from the state for national forestry purposes. The Legislature of 1921 appropriated $1,000,000 for forest protection, which has permitted the development of many necessary lines of forest work. No executive so far has taken a backward step.

Lumbering, as it was later carried on in Perry County, began about 1870, by winter cutting each year of only the finest specimens of valuable varieties. From the time of the pioneer water-power sawmills of the old "up-and-down" variety were set up along the streams to cut construction timbers from white oak and white pine, and some cutting was done chiefly to produce bark for the many small tanneries which dotted the county. At the time the only railroad in the county was over twenty miles distant from western Perry, and no great inroads were made on the timber until about 1880, when steam mills and circular saws came. From then until 1891 a large area was cut clear and much of the remainder thinned of its best growth. The construction of two railroads in the county—the Perry County line to Landisburg and Loysville, and the Newport & Sherman's Valley to New Germantown about 1890—brought the market nearer to the lumber, and for years it was a great source of income to those roads.

THE PENNYPACKER DIVISION OF THE TUSCARORA STATE FOREST.

By resolution of the State Forestry Reservation Commission adopted December 7, 1906, the forest located in southwestern Perry County was officially designated the Pennypacker Forest, "in honor of Governor Samuel W. Pennypacker, who has so worthily upheld the cause of forestry and during whose administration about 375,000 acres were added to the state reserves." Of the two divisions, the greater part of which is in Perry County, the Pennypacker was the first to be formed. The first lands purchased in Perry County were bought on October 11, 1906, from Harry W. Meetch, the tract comprising 2,962 acres, a part of which was over the line in Franklin County. The price paid was $2.75 per acre, and the transaction amounted to $8,147.72. This was the nucleus of the Pennypacker Forest.

*This forest lies in Perry, Franklin and Cumberland Counties. The greater part of the land is located in Jackson and Toboyne Townships, Perry County, and extends southward over the great ridges which traverse the western end of the county. There are 8,915 acres in Jackson and 17,200 acres in Toboyne Township. These ridges are, in order from north to south: Conococheague Mountain, Round Top, Little Round Top, Rising Mountain, Amberson Ridge, Bower Mountain, Sherman's Mountain, and the Kittatinny or Blue Mountain, the summit of the latter forming the boundary line between Perry and Cumberland Counties.

The main body of the land lies on the southwestern side of the county, extending from the Franklin County line eastward about twelve miles, and from the southern boundary northward to the north side of Bower Mountain, inclosing Henry's Valley and part of Sheaffer's Valley. This area incloses several tracts in Toboyne Township which are yet owned by individuals, while in Jackson Township there are a number of interior tracts situated in Henry's and Sheaffer's Valleys.

The area lying southwest of New Germantown is nearly all on the Round Top and Rising Mountain. It is very irregular in outline and almost separated from the area lying to the south, being connected in Fowler's Hollow by a narrow strip at each end.

*See shaded part of county map on page 6.

There are several large tracts lying within the outer boundary which are owned privately. They cover nearly all of Fowler's Hollow and a part of Amberson Ridge.

The portion lying in Franklin County, designated on many old maps as the "Elder Lands," is located on a continuation of the Rising Mountain, which divides Path Valley from Amberson Valley, and contains about 3,668 acres. In outline it is not unlike the shape of a wedge, being wide at the county line and tapering gradually to the west until it becomes very narrow at its western extremity. Although included in the Pennypacker Forest it is separated by a large tract which is owned by George B. Dum, P. F. Duncan, and William Wills (who compose the Oak Grove Lumber Company, having purchased from McCormick heirs, March 23, 1911).

Five mountain ranges traverse parts of Perry County, and three of the five ranges are of one geological character and physical formation. The body of land in which the state is interested here includes but two of the three ranges, which are similar in form and character. The first of these ranges includes Tuscarora Mountain, Conococheague Mountain, Round Top, Little Round Top, Rising Mountain, Amberson Ridge and Bower Mountain. All of these are merely longer or shorter zigzags of the one range, which encloses the western end of the county. The Kittatinny or Blue Mountain is the second range and similar in form and character to the others. The general trend of these mountains is from northeast to southwest.

Gunter Run is the only stream that rises on the Perry County part of the state forest, which flows westward. Rising at the watershed, it flows about one and a half miles through the forest and then crosses into Franklin County, continuing westward to near Forge Hill, where it turns to the south. It passes through a gap in the Blue Mountain and enters the Cumberland Valley north of Roxbury. Sherman's Creek, Brown's Run, Huston's Run and Laurel Run flow eastward, their waters reaching the Susquehanna at Duncannon via the first named stream.

There are considerable areas of cleared land scattered at various points through the forest which were once dotted with homes. There are few houses remaining, while crumbling walls and desolate orchards mark the sites of former firesides. A few of the remaining houses are in fair condition. Two are occupied by forest rangers and several others are rented. The abandonment of these lands was largely due to the fact that the soil was thin, being better adapted to the growing of trees than the production of crops, and with the passing of the industries, such as the tanneries and the sawmills, the inhabitants of these areas were unable to earn a living from the tilling of the soil alone because the timber in these regions contributed largely toward their existence. Many of these cleared areas have been planted with forest tree seedlings while in other places natural regeneration has practically reclothed the cleared areas.

Practically nothing remains of the original growth which once covered this land. From a few scattered trees of different species and one small stand of hemlock one can get a relative idea of what it once was. The entire area had been lumbered over and burned over with forest fires for probably twenty-five years before the purchase by the state. The present growth is almost all of mixed hard woods in which chestnut and rock oak predominate. On the lower slopes of the mountain and ridges, where the soil is deep and there is considerable vegetable mould, there is an abundant growth of rock oak, black oak, hickory, white oak, locust and red oak, while higher up the slopes toward the top are numerous areas almost bare. At such places there is a scanty undergrowth and some scattered rock oak, red oak, chestnut, birch, and a few pitch pine and hemlock.

The area southwest of New Germantown, from the summit of Sherman's Mountain to the Conococheague Mountain, was lumbered over about 1890 by the Perry Lumber Company. The upper slopes of the Round Top are sparsely covered with a mixture of hemlock, red oak, rock oak and birch, where most of the trees are overmature. On the lower slopes there are thrifty growths of chestnut, rock oak, hickory, locust, white oak and red oak. Hickory is plentiful on the southern slopes and grows in groups. It forms clean trunks and attains a good height. In the hollows and lowlands the growth is tall, and in addition to the species found on the lower slopes some birch, yellow poplar, ash, gum, basswood and hemlock are ocasionally found. Near the head of Patterson's Run is a small stand of virgin hemlock, the only stand of virgin timber in the forest.

The south side of Sherman's Mountain is covered with a good and almost even aged growth of rock oak, white oak, and hickory, being from eight to twelve inches in diameter. The trees are mostly straight and middling tall. The growth in Sheaffer's and Henry's Valleys consists principally of chestnut, rock oak, white oak, black oak, pin oak, red oak, hickory, yellow poplar, red maple, sugar maple, butternut, locust and hemlock. The slopes bordering on the south side of Laurel Run are covered with a mixture of white oak, hickory, rock oak, chestnut and black oak. White oak and hickory being the most abundant. Damage by snow and ice, November 16-20, 1920, amounted to thousands of dollars, and the loss is almost incalculable.

Pennypacker division at the present period is divided into four ranges, each in charge of a ranger who gives his entire time to the vocation. In surveying, many of the boundary marks were found to have been almost or completely obliterated, and there was difficulty in locating them, even in the case of the county line between Perry and Cumberland. Springs are numerous along the lower slopes and ridges of the mountains, the greater number being on the southern slopes, but the water on the northern ones being colder and apparently better. Telephone lines have been run to connect with the headquarters of the rangers. Old roads have been maintained and accessible for use while new ones have been made where necessary. In one year alone over 35,000 trees, principally red oak, were planted. Up to 1914 there had been 233,000 planted, of which 154,000 were white pine.

Owing to the transfer from narrow gauge to standard gauge cars at Newport the prices for lumber showed little profit after paying the present high prices for labor. During 1912 there were two forest fires, both in the month of December.

In 1912 a part of the forest was set apart as a game preserve. It was stocked with thirty deer, six males and twenty-four females, since which time there has been a constant increase, and they can be seen grazing in widely separated parts of the mountain.

The McClure Division, Tuscarora Forest.

The area comprising the McClure Division of the Tuscarora State Forest contains approximately 6,093 acres, the first purchase having been made on April 23, 1907, when 4,311 acres of land were bought from the Perry Lumber Company at a cost of $10,-098.36, or $2.25 per acre. It was named in honor of Col. A. K. McClure, a Perry Countian who attained national fame, and its location is in the extreme northwestern part of Perry County, in the townships of Toboyne, Jackson, and Northeast Madison, the main body being in Horse Valley, on the slopes of the Conococheague and Tuscarora Mountains. The region is one of deep, narrow valleys having the same general direction, and are nearly surrounded by great mountains and valley ridges, giving the country a rough contour and making access to the interior and the settlements within very difficult. This condition is causing the settlements to decrease and in a few years perhaps the greater portion of the land once cleared will have reverted to its original state.

The bordering land of this forest is to a great extent timbered for a short distance, where it meets the agricultural section with its well settled communities. It is irregular in shape, long and narrow, attaining its greatest width at the eastern end. There are no known minerals in this reservation, yet the state in its original grants exacted a proportion of such as will be noted in the chapter relating to Jackson township, elsewhere in this volume, where the specific reservation is copied from one of the original Blaine warrants for the farm lands now belonging to Clark Bower, member of the General Assembly. The main outlets of this reservation are to the north and west.

About the year 1900 a stock company was formed known as the Union Oil & Gas Company, supported in part by local capital, and extensive operations were carried on in the Tuscarora Valley, adjoining these state lands in an endeavor to locate oil and gas. Three wells were drilled, ranging from 1,000 to 2,600 feet, and natural gas seems to have been tapped, but not in sufficient quantity to warrant further operations. During the excitement lands for miles around were leased for oil and gas rights. Since then another corporation has been trying to locate beds of iron ore on an adjoining tract. The first mail route from Perry County to the West was through this reservation, entering between the Conococheague and the Tuscarora Mountains, and crossing to East Waterford.

The general supervision of a state forest is in charge of a forester. While the two divisions of the Tuscarora Forest were separate forests there were two foresters until the World War, when the McClure section was placed under H. E. Bryner, the forester of the Pennypacker Forest. J. L. Witherow had been the first forester of the McClure Forest. John H. Zeigler, of East Waterford, is now the ranger of that section. Mr. Bryner became forester September 1, 1908, and continued until 1922, when he was succeeded by D. B. McPherson. The forester, besides having general supervision, such as the laying out of roads, planting of trees, fighting of forest fires, etc., is also in charge of the fire wardens of the Tuscarora District.

The headquarters of the ranger are at what was known as the "Cole House," in Horse Valley. In that valley are mineral and magnesia springs.

There are four streams on the McClure division, Laurel Run, Blain Run, Kansas Creek, and Horse Valley Creek. Blain Run rises between the Conococheague Mountain and the Big Knob, and flows in a northwesterly direction, emptying into Kansas Creek near the west base of the Big Knob. Laurel Run rises at the head of Liberty Valley and flows eastward to near where Mohler's tannery stood, where it turns northwest and passes through the Honey Grove narrows, emptying into Tuscarora Creek near Honey Grove, in Juniata County.

The Ohio Oil Company has a right of way twenty feet wide, entering the forest near the Juniata County line, in the Waterford narrows. Two long-distance telephone lines cross from east to west. It has practically no virgin growth, except a few overmature chestnut and rock oak.

Such timber as arrives at maturity or is impaired by disease or fire is marketed from time to time, under the supervision of the district forester. During a single recent month, about 150,000 staves for nail kegs were manufactured and shipped. The staves were produced from chestnut timber that was dead or dying as a result of the chestnut blight. This stave-mill operation is located at the Hockenberry tract, in Horse Valley.

Forest fires sometimes become almost a tragedy in more ways than one. A few years ago when a fire was raging in that part of the Tuscarora Forest known as the Pennypacker Division, the wife of a recluse, whose cabin was in the woods, lay dead. The flames were within 200 feet of the house and were gradually forcing their way towards it. The forester had planned the removal of the body should it be necessary, but fortunately the fire was gotten under control in time.

In June, 1894, 1,500,000 acres of Pennsylvania woodland, most of which had been cut over, was advertised for sale for unpaid taxes. To the credit of Perry County, not a single acre was within its borders.

A few facts about general Perry County forestry may not be inappropriate here. In 1896, 545 acres were cut over, 150 of which were to be used for farming. The following product was marketed:

Feet (board measure) of white pine, ... 335,000
  "   "   "   " hemlock, ... 200,000
  "   "   "   " other woods, ... 2,552,000
Number of cords of bark peeled, ... 660

In 1902, 2,867 acres were cut over, none of which were to be utilized as farm lands. During that year the marketed product was as follows:

Feet (board measure) of white pine, ... 275,866
  "   "   "   " hemlock, ... 55,000
  "   "   "   " other woods, ... 3,131,000
Cordwood, ... 30,950
Pulp wood. 299
Number of cords of bark peeled, ... 1,507

In 1903, 1,459 acres were cut over, from which were taken the following product:

Feet (board measure) of white pine, ... 515,209
  "   "   "   " hemlock, ... 102,000
  "   "   "   " other woods, ... 1,605,425
Cordwood, ... 28,777
Pulp wood, ... 180
Number of cords of bark peeled, ... 844

In 1904, 2,338 acres were cut over, twenty-five of which were cleared for farming, with the following result:

Feet (board measure) of white pine, ... 321,279
  "   "   "   " hemlock. 20,000
  "   "   "   " other woods, ... 1,798,210
Cordwood, ... 34,093
Alcohol wood, ... 21,762
Number of cords of bark peeled, ... 402

In 1905, 910 acres were cut over, none to be cleared. The product was as follows:

Feet (board measure) of white pine. 160,000
  "   "   "   " hemlock, ... 10,000
  "   "   "   " other woods, ... 230,000
Cordwood, ... 8,343
Alcohol wood, ... 8,343
Number of cords of bark peeled, ... 10

In 1916, 1,121 acres were cut over, ninety-five being cleared for farm lands. The product:

Feet (board measure) of white pine, ... 1,242,000
  "   "   "   " hemlock, ... 175,000
  "   "   "   " other woods, ... 2,553,400
Cordwood, ... 8,554
Alcohol wood, ... 8,179
Number of cords of bark peeled, ... 446

In 1907, 1,223 acres were cut over, none to be utilized for farming. The product:

Feet (board measure) of white pine, ... 1,260,000
  "   "   "   " hemlock, ... 130,000
  "   "   "   " other woods, ... 1,995,000
Cordwood, ... 7,078
Alcohol wood, ... 6,978
Number of cords of bark peeled, ... 521

Forest fires sometimes play havoc and burn over large acreage in Pennsylvania. For the period of 1902 to 1911, inclusive, the acreage in Perry County burned each year was as follows:

1902—689 acres   1906—1,172 acres   1909—1,097 acres
1903—574   "   1907— 61   "   1910—1,840   "
1904—325   "   1908— 260   "   1911— 14   "
1905—331   "

Other products from the forests of Perry County are railroad ties, mine props, trolley poles, telegraph poles, etc., over three million mine props being shipped in a single year. Trees that grow best are white pine, white oak, rock oak, red oak, hickory, black walnut and locust. Gravel and limestone are best for walnut, chestnut, oak and locust; bottom lands surpass for hickory.

The rangers of Tuscarora Forest at this time are F. P. Sunday, residing in Henry's Valley; Leroy Koontz and H. N. Hart, residing in Toboyne Township proper, and John H. Zeigler, residing in Horse Valley.

In August, 1921, the entire state was divided into twenty-five districts and a forester placed in charge of each. On September 14, 1921, the State Forestry Commission approved the report of Col. Henry W. Shumaker, which recommended that each district be given a name which would also apply as the name of all state forest land within the district. The separate units in the district are designated divisions of the forest.

The Tuscarora District is so named because of the Tuscarora Indian path, which ran through the eastern part and the lofty Tuscarora Mountains, which bisect it. Perry County is included in the Tuscarora District, which also includes about one-half of Cumberland County, two-thirds of Juniata County, and a small portion of Franklin County. The total area of the district is 1,173 square miles.

The Tuscarora State Forest includes the Pennypacker and McClure Divisions. These divisions were so named because Col. Alexander K. McClure was an early editorial advocate of conservation and a native of this region. Governor Pennypacker was during his entire term of office an earnest advocate of improved forest methods. This district comprises 37,500 acres of state-owned forest land, of which 29,467 acres are in Perry County, 4,365 acres in Cumberland County, and 3,668 acres in Franklin County.

The Tuscarora State Forest is well covered with a mixed growth of hardwood forests, although very little remains of the original forests which once covered this land. There are many places of great natural beauty and the landscape is highly diversified. The forest contains many ideal spots for outing and recreation. In and adjoining the state forest are numerous trout streams which afford sport for the fishermen. Small game is plentiful in the forest and each year, especially during the hunting season, hundreds of people avail themselves of the opportunity to use the forest as an outing ground.

A number of mineral springs containing principally sulphur and magneisia, are found on the state forest in Horse Valley, Perry County, and in Doubling Gap, Cumberland County. Many persons visit these springs. The White Sulphur Springs Hotel, located on a privately owned tract within the boundaries of the forest in Doubling Gap, is a famous summer resort.

The first plantation of forest trees on the Tuscarora State Forest was made in 1908. Since that time extensive plantations have been in various parts of the forest, and 575,000 seedlings have been planted, largely white pine; also sixty-eight bushels of seed, consisting principally of black walnut and red oak.

During the past two years the Tuscarora State Forest has been practically free from the curse of forest fires. This condition is largely due to the fact that the people using the forest have shown their appreciation of it as an outing ground, by being careful with fire in the woods. Constant care with fire in the woods will not only insure a better playground for the people, but will also add to the beauty and value of the land by producing valuable forest crops for future generations.

Henry's Valley, now uninhabited save for the residence of F. P. Sunday, the forest ranger, is the location of an old cemetery, where many former residents are interred. The hemlock area southwest of New Germantown, proposed to be set aside as a tract of original timber or a recreation park, is fast deteriorating and almost inaccessible for access. If the State of Pennsylvania desires to spend any money for recreation park purposes it had better be in the vicinity of the Big Spring, above New Germantown, one of the headwaters of Sherman's Creek, or some other place easy of access.

CHAPTER XXXVII.

PERRY COUNTY FROM MANY VIEWPOINTS.

PERRY County is noted as a community where law and order prevail, and frequently the county jail is without a single occupant. Many times during recent years the grand jurors have not been called, as there were no criminal cases, and on several occasions during the past few years the traverse jury was not needed, as there was no litigation whatsoever. For years many men have refused to be elected to the office of justice of the peace, and others, when elected to that office, refuse to be commissioned, as the fees in many cases do not pay the cost of the necessary books. Only once has it been necessary in Perry County to inflict capital punishment, and in that case the victim was neither a native, nor the descendant of one, but had moved to the county less than two years before the commission of the crime.

This reputation for law and order in the county is no matter of mere whim or opinion, but is a matter of record for a .century. Pages could be filled with statements from the press and from court records, but that is unnecessary. However, the charge of Judge Reed to the grand jury, January 7, 1834, which was substantially as follows, is of interest:

"It is a matter of congratulation to find so small a number of criminal prosecutions in the sessions of this county. We are advised that only one or two cases have been returned, and those of a very unimportant character. It is usually so here. For a number of sessions past we have been able to dispose of all the sessions in a day, and often in a half-day. Jails and penitentiaries, no doubt, have their effect; but there is in public opinion a more sure and certain preventative of crime, than results from public punishments. Whenever reproach and opprobrium are attached indignation frowns upon the culprit when placed upon his trial—whenever the scorn of the community points its condemnation at the convict, and detestation as well as punishment follow a conviction—whenever a criminal finds that he goes abroad disgraced, after paying the forfeiture or suffering his punishment—then criminal courts are encouraged to proceed and the community have cause to rejoice in their success.

"But if the public look on with indifference, and no disgrace is added to the sentence of the law, the mere principle of fear will have but a limited effect. Public sentiment is generally exercised in this county; and it is mainly owing to that circumstance that our criminal list is so meagre. When we consider that the grand jurors are sworn to present truly, not only such cases as are given them in charge, but all others that they know to be presentable here—when from both sources but a case or two can be found at a term, we have good reason to rejoice."

Five years later, on assuming the judgeship, Samuel Hepburn, upon opening his first court here on April 1, 1839, in his address to the grand jury, noted the fact that there was not a single person in jail and complimented the county upon its morals. In fact, the small number of criminal cases has become a tradition. In 1853 again the jail was empty so much that it attracted the attention of the press of the state.

The public institutions of the county have been devoid of scandals, and when Bromley Wharton, representing the State Board of Charities, inspected the Perry County jail, in 1903, the few prisoners protested that they were given too much food considering their close confinement—a most unusual proceeding, especially for a penal institution.

The county's population has largely descended from pioneers, principally of the Scotch-Irish and German strain, as noted more fully in earlier pages, and has always been practically all Protestant in faith, so much so in fact that not a single Catholic church has ever been built within the county's borders. The population has also been practically all Gentile and of the white race, with the exception of a small colony of negroes which has inhabited the borough of Millerstown.

Although a small county having many rivers and creek bridges, it freed its toll roads over a half century ago, and its toll bridges about forty years ago, while several wealthy and populous near-by counties which boast of their rich soils, only recently freed their toll roads (and then at the partial expense of the state), and even yet have toll bridges, a relic of a departed age. A noted Perry Countian of a Middle Western state, commenting on this, writes: "I have tramped almost over this entire county (his adopted residence), and not infrequently have had difficulty in crossing streams over which there was neither bridge nor foot-log. As long ago as 1850 I had no such experience in Perry County; for, although not all the small streams in our neighborhood were bridged, the foot-log was never absent." He then quotes a beautiful little Perry County stream of but three miles in length, with the statement that it was then already spanned by eleven bridges or foot-logs.

Perry County sometimes has been referred to as "the hoop pole county," just as some counties are referred to as coal counties, and another as the tobacco county, but, while it has not always been applied with an affectionate motive, yet the title in itself is one of a historical character, as it shows that the county or the territory comprising it was settled during the pioneer period. In those days there were no bags and boxes used in marketing; everything was in barrels, and to this day we speak of a barrel of flour, yet much of the flour is not actually barreled in our day. The period has even left its language to posterity for all time. The grains that were not ground into flour and meal were distilled into liquors, for in those days drinking was general. There again the barrel was a necessity. To make barrels required hoops, and the modern steel and iron mills were not even dreamed of. Hoops were made of wood and the hickory, which grew in the wooded lands of Perry County territory was then, as it is to-day, of a superior quality. Expert woodmen even vouch for the fact that the hickory from the northern slopes of a mountain is superior to that grown on the southern slopes. Perusal of the various chapters of this book will show an additional source of supply of hoop poles in the number of early charcoal furnaces which operated in the territory, and a demand even at home for hoops by the large number of mills and distilleries which an industrious people had erected in the wake of the redmen at that early period. To keep these furnaces going large tracts of timber were cut over, and in a very few years the second growth was ready for the market as hoop poles. As there were no canals or railroads at that time, and as the Sterrett's Gap road was the most improved highway leaving the county territory, the continuous stream of wagons bearing the products to Carlisle, Columbia and other markets fastened the name to the county. There was a great demand for hoops by the manufacturers at Baltimore, Lancaster and other towns to the south and east, and it was a noted fact that orders from Perry County were filled more quickly than from elsewhere. There was, of course, a reason for this. The hickory close to these cities had been largely depleted and their orders had to come north to the Blue Mountain section, and the traffic by river led them up the Susquehanna. Once there the territory of Perry was the very first to which they came, and the promptness with which the orders were filled and the satisfactory product finally attached its name to the county. The mother country imported largely hogsheads, barrel staves and heads, hoop poles, etc., according to Adam Smith's "Wealth of Nations," as contained in the Harvard Classics, and paid a bounty for their importation from January 1, 1772, to January 1, 1781. This helped enlarge the demand, even at that early date, as the lower Susquehanna trade then entered the traffic.

An anecdote connected with this subject may not be inappropriate. Just prior to the Sectional War, Congressman B. F. Junkin was scheduled to speak in a northern tier county of Pennsylvania. Large bills proclaimed the coming of "Congressman B. F. Junkin, of Perry County." In the district a paper condoning slavery in an indirect way was being published, its editor belonging to the class usually termed "copperheads," and in that paper the residence of the congressman was quoted "from hoop pole Perry." In opening his address Congressman Junkin described the uses of hoop poles, remarking that "hoop poles are of use in supplying hoops for kegs to contains nails, for barrels to contain meats, flour, liquor, fish and many other products, and they are also a d— good thing to kill copperheads with."

During the compilation of this volume, reference was made to "the Pennant County," by persons in four widely separated sections of the Union. Three of these persons, descendants of Perry Countians, had never seen the county, save as pictured upon a map. Interrogated as to the name, a noted woman replied, "Did you never notice on the Pennsylvania map how it hangs there upon the dear old Susquehanna River of my ancestry just as a pennant floats from its staff?" And so it does! And how appropriate seems this name conferred upon it by descendants of the pioneers, for, in many ways is it not a "Pennant Perry"? Where is there another whose scenery excels its scenery? Where is there another so well watered? Where is there another which has captured the State prize for the finest apples for three successive years? Where is there another of like size and population with more noted sons and daughters who have attained fame? Where is there another, considering size and population, which has sent into the ministry and the teaching profession an equal number of successful men? And thus we might go on! So, here's to the name conferred by the descendants, "Perry, the Pennant County"; may it ever stand upon those other traditions of the pioneers which have made it worth while!

Almost with the coming of the pioneer and civilization came the first physician, which in this case was Dr. John Creigh, who located in Landisburg in 1799, twenty-one years before the formation of the county. Even to this day the territory covered by the county's physicians often requires a ten-mile drive to see a patient. In the earliest days of the new settlements, with no roads except paths, and almost the whole country yet in forests, with only a few scattered physicians in the entire territory, their practice led them to places far remote from their offices. The first practicing physicians were located at Landisburg, Millerstown, Ickesburg, Duncannon, Milford (near Newport) and Liverpool. Theirs was not an easy service, and their life was rather a hard lot. They were held in high esteem by their communities, a fact which generally applies to the profession to this day.

The Perry County Medical Society is one of the oldest in the State of Pennsylvania, having been organized in Millerstown on November 19, 1847. As the result of a call among the medical profession the following physicians met and formed the organization:

Dr. J. H. Case, Liverpool.
Dr. T. G. Morris, Liverpool.
Dr. John Wright. Liverpool.
Dr. A. C. Stees, Millerstown.

Dr. T. Stilwell, Millerstown.
Dr. B. F. Grosh, Andersonburg.
Dr. J. E. Singer, Newport.
Dr. P. Whiteside, Newport.

The first officers of the organization were: President, Dr. J. H. Case; vice-president, Dr. A. C. Stees; treasurer, Dr. J. E. Singer; secretaries, Dr. B. F. Grosh, Dr. T. Stilwell.

The constitution then framed and adopted, with little modification, is still the organic law of the association. The objects of the society were defined to be "the advancement of medical knowledge, the elevation of professional character, the protection of the interests of its members, and the promotion of all means to relieve suffering, to improve the public health and protect the life of the community." Incidentally, the real object, to promote a social and fraternal spirit among the fraternity, has been largely attained. Meetings are held several times each year.

While the great Sectional War was over in 1865, the Soldiers' Reunions, so familiar to a later generation, were not inaugurated at once, but ten years intervened before the first one was held, at Newport, on September 30, 1875. The chief marshal of the first parade was Capt. B. F. Miller. The aids were Major George A. Shuman, Capt. A. D. Vandling, Lieut. D. C. Orris and Sheriff J. W. Williamson. The procession included the following and marched over the principal streets of Newport:

Barnet Sheibley, survivor of the War of 1812, in carriage.
Dr. Isaac N. Shatto, of the Mexican War, in carriage.
Keystone Band, of Newville, Pa.
Company of Veterans, under Lieut. S. S. Auchmuty, of the Forty-Seventh Regiment Penna. Volunteers, and also a Mexican War veteran. (The Duncannon contingent.)
Morris Drum Corps, Liverpool; Wm. Morris, drum major, 8 drums.
Company of Veterans, commanded by Capt. H. C. Snyder, of Liverpool, late captain of Company B, Seventh Reserves. (Liverpool veterans.)
Germania Band, Newport; Wm. A. Zinn, leader, 16 pieces.
Company of Veterans, commanded by Capt. F. M. McKeehan, late captain of Company E, 208th Regiment. (Probably Newport and Bloomfield veterans.)
Duncannon Band, Joshua H. Gladden, leader.
Company of Veterans, commanded by Capt. Wm. H. Sheibley, Landisburg, late captain of Company G, 133 Regiment. (Upper Sherman's Valley contingent.)

Charles H. Smiley, a veteran and then a rising young attorney, later a state senator from his native district, was the orator of the day.

For the information of descendants of former or native Perry Countians it may be wise to state that the climate of Perry County is that variable one of the Northern Temperate zone, where the average summer heat is from seventy-five to ninety degrees, and where the temperature in winter sometimes reaches points below zero. Some winters are mild, with little snow, while others find snow lying from early December until the advent of April. Likewise some summers are hot and dry and others cool and rainy. However, generally speaking, the climate of Pennsylvania com-

pares very favorably with that of any other state, and Perry lies
not so far from its centre. The transition from the seaboard to
the mountain districts has the effect of breaking the keenness of
the winds. As the years have passed odd conditions of the weather
are worthy of notice. In 1821 it was so cool over the nation that
it even snowed in July on Capitol Hill, Washington, D. C., according to the press of that period. In 1827 cold weather gripped the
very harvest time with high winds and even frost. On June 22d
of that year there was a severe frost. The *Perry Forester* tells of
"trees being uprooted, fences leveled and great coats being worn
to put away hay." The winter following seems to have been the
opposite, as the issue of January 31, 1828, tells of a "black snake,
two feet long, being killed in Toboyne Township, yesterday." The
winter of 1847-48 was unusually severe, according to records. The
winter of 1875 was very mild, no snow falling after January. By
the end of April clover was in bloom, while wheat was in head and
potato stalks a foot high by the middle of May. Then, on May
13th a heavy frost froze the corn and potatoes and injured the
wheat on the lowlands. The winter of 1885 was a severe one.
A regular blizzard raged four days around Washington's birthday.
On that day, Mrs. Edward Miller, of Loysville, died, and before
her remains could be interred her husband too, passed away. They
occupy one grave in the old Centre churchyard. The winter of
1890 was so mild that farmers plowed during January. A. L.
Knisely, a reputable citizen of Buffalo Township, while plowing
found grasshoppers already jumping around. The early part of
1921 found gardens being dug at Blain as early as February 15th,
but a later frost ruined the apple, cherry and peach crop.

The diary of Jacob Young, deceased, which began with records
told him by people yet living, dates back to 1784. He refers to
the winter of 1888-89 being a remarkable one, stating "No snow
of any account fell until January 20th when we had first sleighing.
Farmers ploughed during December and first eighteen days of
January. Shrubbery put forth buds and some days were mild
and spring-like." He also refers to the summer of 1854 being
very dry. The present summer (1921) has been the hottest and
dryest since 1881, the year when President Garfield lay so long at
the point of death, according to local records.

The visitor to Perry County will find along the countryside
many clean little homes, which stand refreshingly in contrast to
the more stately mansions of the city. Most of them stand alone,
with here and there a cluster almost attaining the dignity of a village. Few of them will be found fashionably foolish or foolishly
fashionable, but in many of them will be found that which many
city houses often lack—a real home and family life, the bulwark of
the republic. Some will need paint, yet in the owner's desk in

place of a receipt from the painter there often is a receipt for board and tuition of a member of the family at a far-away normal school or college. At others the surroundings may appear unkempt, but, there perchance, is where the occupants are aged or where the great reaper has gathered the father or the mother, and the other, aged and unable to keep the old home as it had been, only awaits the summons to join the departed.

The one sad thing in connection with the last resting places of the dead is that, in some places, they are kept in such slovenly condition that they are a discredit to their towns and townships. This is not applicable to Perry County alone, but to many counties. Towns which take great pride in their public squares and main streets neglect their old cemeteries, and many of their citizens would not for a minute think of conducting a visitor in that direction. Whether there is legislation in any state covering these old burial places, the writer is unable to state, but believes there should be some method devised whereby they would be kept in at least as respectable shape as the surrounding fields, instead of becoming a breeding place for noxious weeds and underbrush. The very names on the tumbling tombstones tell of a past day and generation when the parents evidently read much of the Bible. They were mostly of a generation following the pioneers and later, and are the ancestors of the present race. Several towns have already restored these historic old resting places and others are about to do so, but in order to add permanency to the movements some particular organization, such as the civic clubs, should have the matter in charge. The principal reason for neglect has been unorganized effort—"what is everybody's business seems to be nobody's business."

The towns and boroughs of Perry County, during the past thirty years, have been intent upon getting modern water and lighting facilities. Prior to that time Blain Borough was the only town in Perry County with a water system. Since then Duncannon, Marysville, Millerstown, New Bloomfield and Newport have had water systems installed. Newport, Duncannon and Marysville had light plants, but they were privately owned, save in Duncannon, which is the only one still in existence of these three. The light plant installed for the Tressler Orphans' Home at Loysville, now (or will soon) lights up Blain, Loysville, Green Park and Landisburg. Newport, New Bloomfield, Millerstown and Liverpool are lighted by the Juniata Public Service Company, whose plant is located upon Wiconisco Creek, one-half mile from Millersburg, towards Lykens. The voltage is carried across the Susquehanna River from Halifax, on a 22,000-volt high tension line, carried by steel towers. It then runs along the Susquehanna River to Montgomery's Ferry, where the line divides. The Liverpool extension also lights Middleburg, Paxtonville, Beavertown, Beaver Springs and McClure, in Snyder County. The Newport extension also lights Thompsontown, Port Royal, Mexico, Mifflin and Mifflintown, in Juniata County. This corporation also lights Marysville, but leases the current from the United Electric Company at Lemoyne, Cumberland County. The Juniata Public Service Company was organized in 1916, and completed the Newport and Mifflin extension in 1916, and the Liverpool extension in 1917.

The assessments in different sections of Pennsylvania vary from full valuation to less than a third of the actual value. According to a statement in the public press those in Perry County are estimated at sixty per cent, but the assessment books show a wide variance.

During the year 1906 the chestnut blight struck that part of the state which includes Perry County, and thousands of trees, in fact, all of them, were victims. The chestnut crop, long a noted one, has dwindled to nothing. Many of these trees were older than the oldest inhabitant. The largest one, yet standing on the farm of the W. A. Smiley estate, in Carroll Township, is thirty-three and one-half feet in circumference. Its location is about three miles east of Shermansdale, on the Sherman's Creek road. Experts quote its age as between 400 and 500 years. Until the blight it bore large crops of chestnuts annually. Another large tree, west of New Germantown, a willow, measured twenty-four feet, nine inches.

Prior to the purchase of the lands by the state and the creation of the Tuscarora Forest, the farmers of western Perry, northern Franklin and Cumberland Counties turned their young cattle into the mountains for pasture and forage during the summer months, and along the lower hills and in the lowlands often grazed large droves. Since 1907, when the grazing was forbidden by the state, those who formerly pastured their cattle there, have annually held a reunion which dates back to 1913, when it was held at "Camp Meetch," near Laurel Run, on the road between New Germantown, Perry County, and Newburg, Cumberland County.

That there were a considerable number of unpatented lands in Perry County territory, even when the first third of the last century had elapsed, is evidenced by a settlement at the office of the Auditor General of Pennsylvania, dated March 28, 1833. The payments were to William Wilson, Esq., Deputy Surveyor of Perry County, from the commonwealth, aggregating $179.50, for surveying twelve tracts of unpatented lands at $9 each, five tracts at $6 each, eight tracts at $5 each, and one tract at $1.50. According to the public records at the State Capitol, the last lands in Perry County to be patented were on February 19, 1918, when C. A. Baker patented three tracts, containing, respectively, 84, 84, and 120 acres. The number of patents in the last fifty years have not been many. There are properties in Perry County for which there are no deeds, yet the title is as good as any title can be. The lands were warranted by the province, and have descended down through the generations without being sold. One such is the farm of C. A. Anderson, at Andersonburg, Jackson Township, whose father, Alexander Blaine Anderson, was a cousin of the late James G. Blaine, the grandfather, William Anderson, having married a daughter of James Blaine. The first wife of this old pioneer, William Anderson, gave birth to a daughter, who became the mother of the celebrated A. K. McClure.

Among the more prominent landowners the records show that a President of the United States once held title to Perry County soil. The lands owned by the Sterrett brothers, in the vicinity of Sterrett's Gap, passed to their descendants, and from them to William Ramsey, once congressman from the district. In a mortgage dated June 26, 1830, the Ramsey property, in Rye Township, included 850 acres, two fulling mills, a woolen facory, three dwelling houses, one wagonmaker's shop, stable, shed and part of tavern house and orchard at Sterrett's Gap. Through a mortgage President James Buchanan became owner, and in 1835 he is found on the assessment lists, being taxed for 150 acres and a fulling mill. This he sold to the Ramsey heirs. William Ramsey died, while absent on a foreign mission, and it became necessary to purchase the lands, following an execution for judgment. Thomas C. Lane was the purchaser, and his death followed. A special act of the legislature then made the Buchanan title secure.

During the past century many political parties existed in the United States, and, oddly enough, one of them, called "The Light of the World" party, held its national convention in Pfoutz Valley, April 23, 1868, and nominated Dr. Robert A. Simpson, then a practicing physician from Liverpool, for the Presidency. It was based upon religious principles, and its double motto read: "1st, Our God; 2d, Our Country." The convention is described as having been held by "laborers, farmers, mechanics, and ex-soldiers." H. J. Heckard presided. After leaving Liverpool Dr. Simpson located at York, where he practiced until his death, about 1904. People who knew him in York describe him as a top-notcher in the practice of medicine and a very learned and cultured gentleman. A daughter still resides there. Dr. Simpson's letter of acceptance is still in existence.

Probably the longest balloting contest of the old county conventions was that of the Republican nominating convention of August 12, 1895, when Charles L. Johnson, the youngest candidate for sheriff, won over nine other candidates. Seventeen ballots were taken, consuming over three hours.

Like many other counties of the state, Perry County does not have a hospital with its borders, the most of its cases being cared for at the Harrisburg Hospital. According to statistics of that institution during the past decade the following number of cases from Perry County have been treated there: 1912, 111 cases; 1913, 114 cases; 1914, 160 cases; 1915, 175 cases; 1916, 148 cases; 1917, 159 cases; 1918, 164 cases; 1919, 119 cases; 1920, 151 cases; 1921, 204 cases.

The State Health Department, however, since April, 1916, has had stationed in the county a trained nurse, who devotes her time to the public health and child welfare work. Miss Kate Bernheisel, of near Green Park, has filled the position since its beginning.

Almost everybody knows that the mother of Abraham Lincoln was Nancy Hanks, yet few know that there has long resided in Perry County a family in whose veins coursed the same blood as that of the ancestry of the immortal Lincoln, probably the greatest of all Presidents. Ephraim Hanks, of Loudon County, Virginia, was the father of three daughters, Leah, Rachel, and Nancy, and two sons. Nancy Hanks married Thomas Lincoln and became the mother of the future President. Leah and Rachel Hanks married brothers by the name of Akers, who moved to Bedford County, Pennsylvania, Rachel becoming the wife of Ephraim Akers, and their daughter, Sarah, married Charles McLaughlin, to whom was born the late Ephraim McLaughlin, of Toboyne Township. His mother, accordingly was a first cousin of President Lincoln. Mr. McLaughlin was a resident of Toboyne Township, until the time of his death, December 23, 1907, having lived there since 1848, when he purchased 176 acres of land, then belonging to Roland Brown, but having been the property of his grandfather, James Campbell. Like his grandfather and like Abraham Lincoln, he split rails to fence the lands as they were taken from the forests. At the time of his death he was 86 years of age. His daughter, Miss Luella McLaughlin, long a Perry County teacher, still resides there. When yet in the possession of James Campbell he gave the lands for the location of the schoolbuilding, and the one there now is the third to occupy the location.

At least one resident of Perry County was a direct descendant, though of the seventh generation, of that noble little band of Pilgrim Fathers which landed at Plymouth Rock, Massachusetts, in the midst of a blinding snowstorm, on a bleak December day, in 1620. It was Reuben Carver, who was employed at the Duncannon nail factory when that industry was flourishing, and who lived for many years at Duncannon. Among the little party landing at Plymouth Rock, was John Carver and his family, eight in number. He was elected the first governor of this pious band, but

died soon thereafter. It is told that as late as 1755 a grandson of
Governor Carver still lived in Massachusetts, aged 102 years.
Reuben Carver, the Duncannon descendant, died in 1885, and in
the Lutheran cemetery at Duncannon there is a Scotch granite
tombstone bearing this legend:

```
        Reuben W. Carver,
            Son of
         Jabish Carver,
   Who was the son of Jabez,
    Son of Jonathan, son of
   Nathaniel, son of Eleazer,
     Son of Gov. John Carver,
   Who landed at Plymouth Rock,
          Dec. 21, 1620,
    was born at Taunton, Mass.
           Oct. 3, 1807,
   and died at Duncannon, Pa.,
          Oct. 25, 1885,
    Aged 78 years and 22 days.
```

Susan McKean, a sister of Thomas McKean, one of the signers
of the Declaration of Independence, and second governor of Pennsylvania, was married to a Mr. Meminger, a pioneer Perry Countian who settled near the Saville-Madison Township line, whose
descendants reside in Perry and adjoining counties.

Representatives of many other famous families live and have
lived in Perry County. In the veins of some flows a strain of the
same blood as that of General Anthony Wayne, in others (the
Scotts) a strain of the same blood as coursed the veins of Francis
Scott Key.

Among long pastorates of the clergy in Perry County were Rev.
John Linn, 42 years; Rev. John William Heim, 35 years; Rev.
Jacob Scholl, 28 years; Rev. W. D. E. Scott, 32 years, and
Rev. W. R. H. Deatrich, 19 years.

The first prohibitory liquor law ever offered in the Pennsylvania
Legislature was offered by a Perry Countian, Rev. David Shaver,
who represented the county in the session of 1853. He was chairman of the Committee on Vice and Immorality, and in that capacity reported in favor of the adoption of a bill for a prohibitory
liquor law.

The Department of Labor and Industry of the State of Pennsylvania, in its Industrial Directory for 1920, the centenary of
Perry County's erection, states that the county's principal centers
of population are Newport, Duncannon, New Bloomfield and
Marysville," naming the towns in the order stated. There are no
large manufacturing plants within the county, the Duncannon Iron
& Steel Company's plant being the largest and employing the most
men. The number at that time was 528 men. The Juniata Foun-

dry and Furnace Company, of Newport, ranked second, with 80 employees. The Elk Tanning Company, of Newport, was a close third, with 77. Others following in order were the Oak Extract Company, at Newport, with 52; Standard Novelty Works, at Duncannon, with 35; Newport planing mill, with 14, and the C. A. Rippmann's Sons' tannery, at Millerstown, with 12.

In the textile lines the Romberger Hosiery Factory, at Newport, led with 32 males and 68 females, total 100. The J. Arthur Rife shirt factory, at Duncannon, was second, with 1 male and 53 females. Others were the Page shirt factory, at Millerstown, with 7 males and 43 females; Darlington & Clouser's hosiery plant, at New Bloomfield, with 8 males and 42 females; Newport shirt factory, with 2 males and 38 females; Mexico Shirt Company, at Millerstown, with 4 males and 23 females, and the Smith hosiery mill, at Newport, with 5 males and 10 females.

POPULATION OF PERRY COUNTY.

DISTRICTS.	1820	1830	1840	1850	1860	1870	1880	1890	1900	1910	1920
Blain	.....	.....	.....	.....	.....	.....	270	249	32(	326	310
Bloomfield	.....	.....	412	581	661	655	673	737	777	762	778
Buffalo	875	1,270	948	782	1,002	770	708	691	576	479	455
Carroll	.....	.....	1,100	1,169	1,294	1,425	1,417	1,283	1,213	1,053	997
Centre	.....	.....	982	944	1,070	1,121	1,120	1,283	1,213	1,053	824
Duncannon	.....	.....	.....	.....	.....	960	1,027	1,074	1,661	1,474	1,679
Greenwood	1,660	967	725	995	957	1,080	1,109	868	802	754	673
Howe	.....	.....	.....	.....	.....	410	398	383	338	322	299
Jackson	.....	.....	.....	885	1,058	1,103	1,004	955	981	756	623
Juniata	1,748	2,201	1,450	1,435	1,017	983	968	938	878	794	737
Landisburg	.....	.....	‡	416	363	369	336	318	300	252	185
Liverpool Boro.	.....	.....	451	606	.....	823	838	821	653	596	586
Liverpool Twp.	.....	1,104	763	956	1,072	859	825	751	678	628	538
Madison	.....	.....	1,299	1,292	1,534	1,577	1,699	1,584	1,568	1,344	1,169
Marysville	.....	.....	.....	.....	.....	863	1,206	1,115	1,463	1,693	1,877
Miller	.....	.....	.....	.....	761	438	379	356	586	417	305
Millerstown	.....	.....	371	889	.....	533	652	594	555	549	616
New Buffalo	.....	.....	.....	‡	.....	259	222	220	171	135	93
New Germantown*	.....	.....	.....	69	.....	.....	.....	.....	.....	.....	.....
Newport	.....	.....	423	517	649	945	1,399	1,417	1,734	2,009	1,972
Oliver	.....	.....	796	870	787	511	811	969	955	1,015	1,029
Penn	.....	.....	839	1,109	1,238	1,529	1,771	1,965	1,886	996	1,053
Petersburg†	.....	.....	.....	680	831	.....	.....	.....	.....	.....	.....
Rye	1,704	843	451	606	702	708	849	710	680	554	506
Saville	1,154	1,319	1,283	1,501	1,644	1,693	1,743	1,542	1,496	1,405	1,194
Spring	.....	.....	.....	1,282	1,442	1,492	1,538	1,340	1,280	1,179	1,003
Toboyne	1,965	2,310	1,442	707	940	914	853	851	812	702	544
Tuscarora	.....	.....	.....	.....	767	899	995	762	747	595	603
Tyrone	2,236	2,756	2,891	1,069	1,180	1,287	1,486	1,562	1,447	1,397	1,262
Watts	.....	.....	.....	460	413	725	451	396	407	377	320
Wheatfield	.....	1,487	617	678	749	780	790	779	712	661	645
Totals	11,342	14,257	17,096	20,088	22,793	25,447	27,52?	26,276	26,263	24,130	22,875

*New Germantown's existence as a borough was of short duration. Prior to the census of 1850 and thereafter its population is included in that of Toboyne township, within whose limits it is located.
†The name of Petersburg Borough was changed to Duncannon Borough in 1865.
‡Figures not given in United States Government reports.

When the county was established, in 1820, the center of population of the United States was in West Virginia, just west of the Maryland line. For the last three decades it has been in slightly varying positions in Indiana, being now eight miles southeast of Spencer. The trend of population is toward the great cities, or

more especially toward means of employment, which are to be
found cityward. When Perry County was formed from Cumberland, in 1820, the population was 13,162. Its growth was slow
and gradual until 1880, when it showed its largest population,
27,522. In the next ten years it dropped over a thousand. Between 1890 and 1900 it practically held its own, with a population
in 1900 of 26,263. Ten years later, in 1910, its population had
dwindled over two thousand, and was placed at 24,136. In 1920
it was 22,875. There are several reasons for this. One reason is
that families are of smaller size than in the far past. Another is
that labor-saving machinery has cut the requirements of the farmer
for help, and the tenant house on his farm and that of the laborer
on the adjoining small place are a thing of the past, thus materially
helping in the reduction of population in the townships. A third
reason is the general trend cityward in search of employment, and
still another reason is that the state has taken over thousands of
acres for a forest resrevation, considerable of which was once
populated. One of these sections, now devoted to forestry, is
Horse Valley, located between Conococheague and Tuscarora
Mountains, where once dwelt fifty or more families, and where
once resided such substantial families as the Beers, Cooks, Emerys,
Kellys, Lacys, Naugles, Scyocs, and others. It had two schools
and a church, but to-day there are only seventy residents of that
part of the valley lying in Perry County. Fifty to seventy-five
years ago Henry's Valley, that very narrow section between Bowers' Mountain and the Kittatinny or Blue Mountain, in western
Perry County, contained a hundred or more houses, a store, church,
schoolhouse, etc. The tanning industry was then at its height, and
the tannery people there owned from four to five thousand acres
of land. A neat graveyard then in use is hardly discernible, and
only two persons reside in the valley, practically all the lands having been added to the state forest. In what is Sheaffer's Valley,
which merges into Henry's Valley, above the Doubling Gap road,
once resided probably fifty families, yet to-day, including the Forest
Reserve farm, only two persons have their habitation there. The
location is in Tyrone Township. Then there is Liberty Valley, in
Madison Township. Its story too, is the tale of many other sections of Pennsylvania. Many years ago, before manufacturing
had become general, several thousand acres, now growing in pines,
had been cleared and was farmed in rye, the product being sold to
distilleries. There is a story that this valley was once so poor that
many could not pay their taxes, but with the advent of the mountain tannery once located there, the people became well-to-do.
With the tannery gone and no means of employment the population is not a third of what it once was, numbering only about
seventy-five.

Another valley, once tilled and the site of many homes, is the Sugar Run Valley, in Tuscarora Township, now almost returned to the virgin state, the remaining houses being small, and growing less in number each year.

At every prominent crossroads and village in the county there was once a blacksmith shop, at which frequently two men found employment, and whose families resided near by. To-day they are gone, with few exceptions. Old residents recollect the time when there were twenty such shops from New Germantown to Shermansdale, including the ones in those towns. To-day there are but four.

The story of the slow decrease of rural population in Perry County applies elsewhere. In 1890, according to the United States census, the rural and urban populations were about equally divided. In 1900, fifty-five per cent of the population was urban. By 1910 sixty per cent were dwelling in cities and towns, and the last census showed over sixty-four per cent.

During the decade between 1910 and 1920 all the districts of the county lost in population save the townships of Oliver, Penn and Tuscarora, and the boroughs of Bloomfield, Duncannon, Marysville and Millerstown. In all cases the townships which gained either surround or adjoin a borough which gained, which bears out the fact that people will drift townward.

The population of 1920 places Perry as one of sixteen Pennsylvania counties which has neither Indian, Chinese or Japanese inhabitants. Of its population of 22,875, the number of males is 11,465, and of females, 11,410. Of the total population only 156 are foreign-born. Of the total, 22,107 were born of native parentage, 263 of mixed parentage, and 249 of foreign parentage. The negro population is 80. The percentage of native white population is 98.5; foreign-born, 1.2, and negroes, .3. The number of families in the county was 5,683, residing in 5,530 dwellings.

The number of farms is decreasing, as it is all over Pennsylvania. In 1900 the state had 224,248 farms; in 1910, 219,256, and in 1920, 202,256. In 1900 Perry County had 2,286 farms; in 1910 the number had however, increased to 2,409, and in 1920 dropped to 2,105. The expanding Tuscarora State Forest is one of the reason for the decrease in Perry County farms, the high wages of industrial plants being another. The number of automobiles in Perry County during 1921 was 947, with 60 motor trucks, and 40 tractors.

A history of a number of counties in several volumes, published a few years ago, was evidently written at "long distance" and without much consideration for correctness. As an example of some of the statements the population of various places is quoted as follows: Andersonburg, 180; Bixler, 180; Cisna's Run, 95;

Donnally's Mills, 104; Eshcol, 95; Green Park, 178; Ickesburg, 430, and Loysville, 500. All wonderful exaggerations.

According to the last year's births and deaths as taken from the reports of the registrars of vital statistics for 1920, the births exceed the deaths to a large degree. During that year there were 559 births and 321 deaths. The deaths were over twenty-six per thousand of population.

District.	Registrar.	Births.	Deaths.
Bloomfield, Carroll and Centre, ...D. C. Kell, ...		59	37
Duncannon, Penn and Wheatfield, .W. Walter Branyan, .		97	59
Liverpool and Liverpool Twp., ...Dr. Wm. G. McMorris,		26	18
Saville Twp., ...H. A. Johnston, ...		25	16
Blain, Madison, Jackson and To-			
boyne, ...R. H. Kell, ...		70	40
Landisburg, Spring and Tyrone, ...D. B. Dromgold, ...		48	25
Marysville and Rye, ...Dr. E. Walt Snyder, .		59	32
New Buffalo and Watts, ...Amos A. Ober, ...		19	17
Newport, Miller, Oliver, Howe, Ju-			
niata, ...Frank H. Zinn, ...		90	47
Millerstown, Greenwood and Tus-			
carora, ...James Rounsley, ...		66	30
Totals, ...		559	321

Pennsylvania legislation frequently deals with its various counties upon a basis of population, and for that purpose passed a bill placing all the counties in eight different classes, according to population. Perry County is included in the Seventh Class, comprising counties of from 20,000 to 50,000 population.

With the four tracks of a great trunk line crossing the county, it is not strange that occasionally a great train wreck should happen within its borders, even on the best managed railroad in the world. Probably the worst one that has occurred happened at two o'clock a. m., of October 24, 1895, when an axle of a car on an east-bound freight train broke and threw several cars off the track and across the westbound passenger track of the Pennsylvania Railroad at Trimmer's Rock, below Newport, where there existed at that time a considerable bend in the road, since obviated. At that moment train No. 7, a fast westbound mail and passenger train from New York to Pittsburgh, had already entered the block not many rods away and crushed into the debris. The engineer had a bare instant to reverse his lever when the crash came and his engine toppled into the waters of the adjoining canal, carrying with it a working car in which mail was being distributed. Three other mail storage cars, out of a total of six, were demolished. The imprisoned mail distributors clambered from the broken cars just in time, for in a few minutes the cars took fire and were consumed. Daniel Wolfkiel, the engineer, aged 51, and Joseph W. Haines, the fireman, aged 27, were killed. Mr. Haines, who had been with the railroad company for eight years, met death within sight of his birthplace, Newport. Mr. Wolfkeil, the engineer, was from McVeytown, and had been a soldier in the War between the States. Ten postal clerks were injured, but escaped with their lives: C. A. Chamberlain, John Zerbe, and B. I. Brand, of Harrisburg; E. L. Colville, of Pittsburgh; A. E. Woodruff, of Lewistown; S. Groff, of Mount Joy; A. T. Rowan, of Trenton; George Gilmour, of Philadelphia; James Norris, of Hightstown, N. J., and John I. Campbell, of Gallitzin. Of those eight, Mr. Brand, Mr. Colville, Mr. Woodruff, Mr. Gilmour, and Mr. Campbell are yet in the service of the government, although a period of more than twenty-five years has elapsed.

From the time of the pioneers, when the Indians lurked about, ready to visit death upon the unsuspecting, there have been the usual accidental deaths by drowning in the two rivers and the canals, by grade crossing accidents on the railroads, by accidents in the manufacturing establishments, by hunting season errors, and by various other causes. Friends and those very near and dear to the writer have been left fatherless and have gone down the years mourning the demise of a loved one, lacking a father's care and support, and sometimes the home which they otherwise would have had. These things seem to be incidental to existence everywhere, and Perry County has probably had far fewer than larger communities wherein are located huge industrial plants.

Twice since the creation of the county have children strayed into the mountains never to return. The first instance was during July, 1871, when an eleven-year-old girl of the Crounce family, of Penn Township, became lost. Her remains were not found until in August, 1873, when they were discovered in the fastnesses of Cove Mountain, one and a half miles from Perdix Station. The other was the case of little Alice Arnold, who wandered away from her home in Tuscarora Township, May 22, 1911, and whose remains were found many months later in a thicket near the top of Tuscarora Mountain, three miles east of Ickesburg.

Fashions seem to pass in cycles. Wide comment in the public press since the advent of the World War as to the abbreviated dress of females seems to be the counterpart of "the thirties" of last century. The Perry Forester, of April 1, 1834, contained the following lines:

> "They've shortened their dresses a cubit or more,
> Now scant in the rear, and scanter before;
> Till at length they have got them so short and so small.
> That, by gracious, they seem like no garments at all."

The males of the period, too, were afflicted with vanity, as their tight trousers, green eyeglasses and small headgear bears evidence.

According to records and prints of the early and middle period of the past century the men generally dressed well, first in "pigeon tail" coats, and later in "Prince Alberts." The clothing in the

57

earlier period was tailor-made, and every village and town had its tailor shop.

During the first eighteen years of the existence of Perry County all the officers were Democrats. The first person, not a Democrat, to be successful at an election, was Joseph Shuler, who was elected sheriff upon the Whig ticket, in 1838.

During the first century of Perry County's existence but one Perry County woman was elected at the general elections to fill a public office. Until women were granted the franchise by the passage and adoption of the suffrage amendment in 1920, the only office to which they were eligible in the State of Pennsylvania was that of school director, and throughout the many counties very few were elected even to that office. When Hugh W. Bell, a school director of Rye Township, died early in 1907, the school board appointed his widow, Mrs. Effie I. Bell, to fill the vacancy, she assuming the duties in the spring of that year. Two years later Mrs. Bell was nominated by the Democrats and elected at the general election, serving a full term and being in office when the present county superintendent, Prof. Daniel L. Kline, was elected for his first term. She thus attained distinction in three different ways. She was the first and only woman in the county during its first century to hold public office by appointment; she was the first and only one to hold it by election, and she was the first and only one to attend a county convention and vote for the election of a county superintendent. Mrs. Bell is a daughter of H. F. and Katharine (Harter) Long, and was born April 11, 1866, at Millerstown. She taught ten years in Liverpool, Greenwood and Rye townships and Millerstown Borough. She was educated at Millersville State Normal School and with tutorage by Prof. Silas Wright. She was united in marriage in 1892 to Hugh W. Bell, a son of the late James Bell, of Rye Township. Left with five small children at his death, the youngest of whom was but six months old, she assumed the management of his mercantile business. Since the World War and the attendant scarcity of teachers, Mrs. Bell, like many other former Perry County teachers, has returned to the profession, and is teaching in the township (Rye) in which she once was a director. Two of her daughters teach— Effie O. Bell, the elder daughter, in Marysville, and Beatrice M. Bell, her second daughter, at Sandy, Utah.

It was planned to include a number of additional poems by Perry Countians in this volume, but the size to which it has grown bars their insertion, with the result that they will possibly later be issued in a separate volume. The more notable writers of verse from among the natives includes Chief Justice John Bannister Gibson, Governor Stephen Miller, G. Cary Tharpe, Dr. Zenas J. Gray, Rev. J. D. Calhoun, W. Walter Branyan, J. Albert Lutz, W. W.

Fuller and others. Mrs. Emma F. Carpenter, of Duncan's Island, was also a well-known writer of verse. The author of this volume will appreciate any information upon this subject.

In the greatest undertaking since the World War, in May, 1919, another Perry Countian figured, for while Lieut. David McCulloch was born in Juniata County he was brought here when a small boy and is recognized as a Perry Countian. When the attempt was made by the United States government to send three sea-planes across the Atlantic Ocean, the NC-3 had as one of its officers Lieut. McCulloch, who was one of the most expert air men in the government service. He had previously been in the employ of Rodman Wanamaker in his air activities and was instructor for the Italian government in aviation. During the World War he was chief of naval operations in aviation and had charge of the Liberty motor tests.

A real king visited Perry County in 1920, when the special train containing King Albert, of Belgium, was placed on the old railroad line in Newport, for several hours, awaiting the new day before proceeding to Harrisburg, where the royal party were entertained. Ex-Member of Assembly John S. Eby greeted the visitor and introduced him to a small party who had gathered to see the train bearing the noted ruler.

Perry County has also been the birthplace of some inventors, among the more noted being W. A. Dromgold, whose agricultural implements cover the land, and J. L. McCaskey, whose electric program clock system is installed in many of the schools and colleges of the country, and who invented a torpedo deflector during the World War. No list of these men and inventions are available, but that of George H. Leonard, of Landisburg, who died as recently as 1915, deserves to be recorded. Years ago he invented a "flying machine," not unlike the earlier models of the recent pioneer product of that line, but his expectation that it could be propelled by human power was wrong. He also invented and had patented a hat with ventilators and a process for tanning leather. He made little out of either, yet both are in use to-day under others' patents, but the hat patent has never made any person wealthy. The other is what is known to us as "patent leather." John H. Noviock, of Buffalo Township, invented the first potato separator, now in general use, and exhibited it at the Grangers' Picnic, a state-wide affair of two decades ago, with the result that some one took his idea, improved it, and made a snug fortune. Samuel Endslow, of Blain, years ago invented a fly trap which was among the very first of those machines, and which was built along the lines of those used by civic bodies and others in their campaign against the fly.

The lines of two long distance telephone companies cross the county from East to West, entering over the Kittatinny Mountain at Sterrett's Gap, and disappearing through the Tuscarora Forest and over the Tuscarora Mountain. From Dauphin County to Perry County, spanning the Susquehanna River, stretch four great cables of the American Union Telegraph Company, the length of the span being 5,000 feet, with a 460-foot dip, from the jutting ends of Berry's Mountain, through which the river breaks. This is the second longest cable span in the world. it is said, and the longest in the United States. Pipe lines carrying oil cross the county from the oil fields to the seaboard.

There is not within the county a public library, save in the schools, though in 1842 New Bloomfield opened a free library, known as the Young Men's Library, of which George A. Shuman was secretary and librarian in 1844. Some day some native Perry Countian who has become well-to-do will donate or will to one of the important centers of the county a public library and become the benefactor of unborn generations. There are many school libraries of no mean proportions, however. This early library at the county seat was refused further use of the public school building in 1854, after which time there appears to be no records of it.

The preserving of genealogical records and their compilation and publication in so far as Perry County is concerned, has been sadly neglected. Among the most extensive records are those of Mrs. Leila Dromgold Emig, now of Washington, D. C., and Dr. A. R. Johnston, of New Bloomfield. Mrs. Emig's volume, "Records of the Hench and Dromgold Reunion," first published in 1913, would better be "Records of the Hench and Dromgold Families," as it is a very complete and comprehensive book of almost two hundred pages. It was a painstaking task, but one which any one would be proud to have consummated. Dr. Johnston's volume of almost a hundred pages shows a like degree of patience and leaves to posterity a record of the Johnston clan, which is invaluable. In the beginning a number of pages are devoted to the early history of Sherman's Valley. A volume covering the Mahaffeys and allied families, very comprehensive also, was issued at the hands of Estelle Kinsport Davis and Mrs. Mary E. (Mahaffey) Carst, of Harrisburg, in 1914. In 1892 the "Family Record of the Ickes Family," from the pen of the late Susan A. (Ickes) Harding, of Monmouth, Illinois, wife of General Harding, left for future generations the record of that noted family. Mrs. Harding was a daughter of Dr. Jonas Ickes, who was an early practitioner at the new county seat, after the county's establishment.

Others are on the way. Mrs. Laura T. (Willhide) Johnston, of New Bloomfield, assisted by her son, Frank Johnston, is compiling the genealogy of the Sheibleys, her maternal ancestry which will put on record the line of that noted pioneer family. Harry G. Martin, of Millerstown, has the nucleus of the Wrights, a noted east-of-the-Juniata family, in good shape. Edward P. Lupfer, of Buffalo, New York, has valuable data pertaining to the Lupfer, McClure and Marshall families, from whom he is descended. Rev. R. E. Flickinger, a retired Presbyterian minister of Rockwell City, Iowa, has ready for the press "The Flickinger Ancestry," having devoted several years to pursuing the work. Mr. Flickinger is the author of many noted books. Mr. W. H. Graham, of Washington, D. C., is preparing a work on the Graham and Rhinesmith and related families. Mr. Graham is a former Perry County teacher and also taught in Washington and Idaho. George W. Ebert, of Indianapolis, Indiana, has gathered much data pertaining to the Dunkelberger, Adam Smith and Heim families. Wm. T. Albert, of Pueblo, has gathered much data of the Albert, Smith, Thatcher and allied families, to which the writer has had access in the preparation of this book. Dr. Percy Edward Deckard, of Williamsport, Pennsylvania, a son of Dr. J. W. Deckard, of Richfield, Juniata County, has almost completed a genealogy of the Deckard family, which will soon be published in book form. The little volume, "A Long Road Home," by Miss Anna Froelich, is also a good one, briefly covering various families connected with the Duncannon Reformed Church. Mrs. Rachel Jones, of a Southern branch, and P. F. Barner, of Altoona, are compiling the Barner genealogy, and W. A. Brunner, of Harrisburg, is busy along the same line with the Brunner family. J. A. Leonard, now of Cleveland, is at work on the Leonard records, and the late Prof. W. C. Shuman issued a fine genealogy of the Shuman family. These and many others, which it is hoped this book will inspire, will add much to the county's historical records, for all history is but a record of the doings of those who inhabit the territory.

A County Historical Society.

While Perry County has never had a historical society, yet there existed, during the winter of 1880-81, at the New Bloomfield Academy, a society known as the Philomathean Society of that institution, which did more during that year to preserve historical traditions than many historical societies have done in a decade. The Philomathean Literary Society of that institution was organized in the early days of the academy's existence. At a meeting on November 15, 1880, the society decided to add to its exercises the preparation and presentation of articles along local historical lines. To John A. Baker, then editor of the *Perry County Freeman*, who offered the use of his columns for articles which had the approval of the society, posterity is indebted for much of real historical value. On June 17, 1881, the society held its last meeting and thus passed an organization which during its short life did mòre to preserve much that is of historical value than any organization since the foundation of the county.

The presidents during its existence were: Prof. J. R. Flickinger, James W. McKee, W. H. Sponsler, Clarence W. Baker, A. B. Grosh, and C. W. Rhinesmith.

The historical committee was composed of W. H. Sponsler, Prof. J. R. Flickinger, Clarence W. Baker, J. C. Wallis, Rev. A. H. Spangler, and Rev. John Edgar. The duties of this committee grew to such proportions that they asked that it be increased, which was done by adding the names of Wilson Lupfer, J. W. Beers, A. B. Grosh, J. W. McKee, George Rouse, C. W. Rhinesmith, William Orr, and R. H. Stewart.

The members who were active in the gathering of data in this old society were: W. H. Sponsler, Clarence W. Baker, Prof. J. R. Flickinger, who, according to a statement of R. H. Stewart, now an attorney in New York City, were indefatigable and ardent in the work; Rev. John Edgar, Rev. A. H. Spangler, Wilson Lupfer, A. B. Grosh, J. W. Beers, Lewis Potter, J. C. Wallis, William Orr, C. W. Rhinesmith, George R. Barnett, Cloyd N. Rice, James W. Shull, Fillmore Maust, James W. McKee, William Mitchell, George A. Rouse, Joseph Arnold, William R. Pomeroy, L. E. Donnally, William R. Magee, J. L. Markel, and R. H. Stewart. There are many names on that list whose owners have appeared in legislative halls and who have been elevated to the bench.

The honorary membership, too, is here reproduced: Dr. William H. Egle, Harrisburg; Ed. C. Johnston, New Germantown; James Woods, Blain; William E. Baker, Eshcol; Frederick Watts, Carlisle; F. W. Gibson, Falling Springs; James L. Diven, Landisburg; W. A. Meminger, Donnally's Mills; A. L. Hench and Rev. J. J. Hamilton, Roseburg; William W. McClure, Green Park; John A. Wilson, Landisburg; A. K. McClure, Philadelphia; Dr. Alfred Creigh, Washington, Pa.; James B. Hackett, George S. Briner, John A. Baker, and William A. Sponsler, New Bloomfield.

It is to be hoped that a historical society may soon be organized; and that this book may, in a way, become of some little value as a basis for a systematic and thorough compilation of the county's historical, biographical, and genealogical records. However, if such a society is to be organized only to be a weak, inanimated one, merely holding an occasional session, the principal function being the election of officers, its organization would be futile. At this time (1921) there are thirty-five of the sixty-seven counties which do not have historical societies, and an effort will be made to put one in every county.

Perry County Societies Abroad.

It is not an unusual thing for the native sons of a state to organize a state society in their adopted state, such as the Pennsylvania Society of New York, but it is rather unusual for the native sons and daughters in other counties and states to organize a county society of their native county. What is being developed in many places and is known as a community spirit has always existed in Perry County and is so strongly inbred that Perry Countians at various places have organized Perry County societies, some of which hold an annual banquet, others an annual outing or picnic, and some both.

The Perry County Society of Chicago was organized September 6, 1913, in Lincoln Park. The following officers were elected and have been reëlected each succeeding year: President, Grant Womer; vice-president, Charles W. Singer; secretary, Mrs. H. B. Raffensperger; treasurer, Judge Sheridan E. Fry.

The Pennsylvania Society of Chicago, to which some of the Perry County people belong, is an older organization than the Perry County Society, but probably not much better supported, as the members of the Perry County organization are in closer sympathy with each other, being from the same county. It has two meetings a year, one in June and the other in February, besides having frequent surprise parties during the winter months in the homes of the different members. The latter feature has made the society very popular and contributes much to the happiness of the members in their adopted homes, in the largest metropolis of the Middle West. As an example of the community spirit connected with this society, when Mrs. Mary Schiller Miller, a talented and educated woman, died there during 1921, the society "said with flowers" what was in the hearts of the members. On other occasions it is the same.

The Perry County Society of Allegheny County was organized during the last decade, its principal feature being an annual picnic.

For many years there has been a Perry County Society of Blair County, which has held its outings at the parks there.

A movement is now on foot to organize a Perry County Society in Philadelphia, Dr. O. L. Latchford, a native Perry Countian, having the matter in charge.

On June 19, 1920, the Perry Countians residing in Lancaster County met and organized a Perry County Society, with the following officers: A. D. Garber, president; George S. Endslow, secretary, and S. H. Tressler, treasurer. At the same time they held a picnic.

The residents about Buda, Illinois, who are native Pennsylvanians, have an association and hold an annual picnic, but the larger part of the membership are native Perry Countians. At the election of 1920, both the president, W. H. Stutzman, and the vice-president, Chas. Moretz, were native Perry Countians, as were two of the speakers, Rev. J. D. Calhoun, and H. B. Raffensperger.

PICTURESQUE PERRY.

"Beyond the city's edge, where meadows lie
  And crooked fences are, and winding streams,
Where remnants of old orchards linger, I
  Have found the gateway to the land of dreams.
The sun, I think, shines with a friendlier glow
  Out there, where Nature still may have her way,
Than in the city streets, with all their show
  And artificial glitter and display."—*Selected.*

States and countries boast of their scenery, and why not a county? Especially Perry County, which, from a scenic standpoint, stands second to none in this grand old commonwealth! The scenery of many parts of the mountainous section of the state, particularly where the mountain ranges are either cut through or skirted by large streams, is noted abroad for its grandeur, wildness and beauty, and about Perry County it is at its best. The charm of Perry County lies in the beauty and variety of its scenery.

Especial mention should be given to the marvelous breaks through the mountains by the Susquehanna River at Liverpool, Mt. Patrick, Duncannon and Marysville, to that of the Juniata through the Tuscarora Mountains at Millerstown, to the Conococheague Mountain in western Perry, to the wonderful mountain scenery west of New Germantown, where the great Creator laid down a series of mountains in mighty folds as a dry goods clerk would lay ribbon upon a counter, to the beautiful view of Mt. Dempsey and its sister mountains at Landisburg, and to the meeting place of the two rivers—Juniata and Susquehanna—where they merge to go forward to the sea. Further descriptions of these mountains and rivers will be found in the chapters covering Mountain, River and State Forest.

Of "the land between the rivers" I would write, not as a stranger, for there I first beheld the light of day; just where the watershed breaks the drainage, some flowing past Buck's Church —that old landmark of Christian influence in the community—to join the Susquehanna at Montgomery's Ferry; others crossing the farm, passing by "Finton's corner," Finton's woods, pretty glen and deep ravine—on past the old James Barkey gristmill, now Seiders'—to become a part of the Juniata at the old historic Patterson place, a relay point of stagecoach days on the Allegheny turnpike. That boyhood farm, remote and uninviting as it might appear to others, is to me by associations tender as heartstrings the one spot hallowed by treasured recollections of father, mother, home and childhood—a quartette of words which contain almost all that is near and dear to the human heart. Of the five townships forming that part of Perry County lying at the junction of the two rivers this was the heart. To the north lay Berry's Mountain, steep, beautiful with foliage and in respective seasons either green, golden or a crystal white hulk, glistening in the winter sun. To the south lay the broad and not so steep Half-Falls Mountain, which, like the Berry Mountain, ends abruptly at both rivers.

THE LAND BETWEEN THE RIVERS.

BY G. CARY THARPE.

Let those who will as pilgrims go
 To climes across the ocean,—
I love the scenes which long ago
 Awaked my young emotion;
That bade my youthful thoughts arise,
 And manhood's high endeavors,—
My native home, that smiling lies,—
 The land between the rivers.

Though there no lordly castle throws,
 O'er moor, or plain its shadow;
From where the Susquehanna flows
 Through mountain gap and meadow,
To where the Juniata's tide
 Its tribute wave delivers;—
The streams that bound on either side,—
 The land between the rivers.

And spreads our river broad, a lake,
 With ceaseless currents fretting,
A thousand islands green that break
 The crystal of their setting;
And there the wild fowl gayly swim,
 And there the sunlight quivers,
Till evening veils, with mantle dim
 The land between the rivers.

The purple mists of early morn,
 With diadems of glory
Our rugged mountain crests adorn,
 Unknown to song and story;
And monarch-rob'd in golden light,
 They look, where sways and quivers,
The water lily's spotless white
 That grows beside the rivers.

And soft in beauty sweetly lie
 Our fertile vales extended,
Afar, where golden clouds on high,
 And gold-green earth is blended;

No eye can trace the faint drawn line
  Which hill and sky dissevers;
So close the heavens bend down to join
  The land between the rivers.

And there, in sunset's dying day,
  Through evening sapphire portals,
Bright forms angelic countless stray
  Unseen by eye of mortals;
Charmed from their fair celestial home,
  Where death ne'er comes nor severs,
To bless a second Eden's bloom
  In land between the rivers.

The Susquehanna River, described elsewhere in this book, and famous its entire length for its scenic beauty and picturesqueness, is at the same time one of the most legendary and historic streams of the Atlantic slope. Entering Perry County from the North, over the famous Susquehanna Trail, that great highway which replaces the first trail of the red men as they followed its shores, the tourist is impressed by the vista of gently sloping farm lands to the right, while on the opposite shore from Liverpool, ending abruptly at the river, is a huge mountain of great and mighty rocks heaved from the interior of the earth long geologic ages ago. A little farther down, at Mount Patrick, comes the first of the four celebrated Susquehanna water gaps of Perry County, through which ages ago the waters forced a passage, the others being at Duncannon, above Marysville, and at the Kittatinny Mountain, below Marysville. Almost from the waters' edge rise these rocky, wooded cliffs that stand like giant sentinels against the azure sky, seemingly guarding the winding river on its way toward the sea. These cliffs tower to great heights and their rugged ledges are gorgeous with the hues that shine through the trees which grow even between the crags and shelving rocks. Mount Patrick, several miles below Liverpool, is the local name of the jutting end of Berry's Mountain, which with Buffalo Mountain forms a cove (Hunter's Valley) which is the west end of the Wiconisco anthracite coal basin. (Claypole's Geology, pp. 10-11.) Crossing the Susquehanna at Mount Patrick, it runs eastward, turns, and returns as the Peters (or Cove) Mountain, at Duncannon. There again a cove is formed which is the pointed ellipse of the Dauphin County anthracite coal basin, the east end of which is in Carbon County, beyond the Lehigh River.

As early as 1806, Thomas Ashe, a traveler, thus records his impressions of the beautiful Susquehanna: "The breadth and beauty of the river, the heights and grandeur of its banks, the variety of scenery, the verdure of the forests, and the melody of the birds, all combined to fill my mind with vast and elevated thoughts."

From the "State Book of Pennsylvania," published by Thomas H. Burrowes, in 1851, we cull the following, which shows the importance of the junction of the Juniata and Susquehanna Rivers at that period:

"The point on the Susquehanna, called Duncan's Island, or Clark's Ferry, is remarkable in many respects. The mountain and river scenery of the vicinity is wild and beautiful. The Juniata and Susquehanna here meet, presenting in the boating season, even before the public works were constructed, a busy and interesting scene. But now that the state canals along the Susquehanna and the Juniata are in operation, and the Wiconisco Canal certain of being completed, there are few points at which so many of the elements of the prosperity of the state are presented at a single glance. Down the Susquehanna are seen gliding, either on her broad bosom or on the canal along her margin, the lumber, the anthracite coal, and the other valuable articles found on her headwaters. Along with these are the grain, the bituminous coal, and the lumber of the West Branch. The Juniata, with the celebrated iron that bears her name, the bituminous coal of the great Allegheny, and the agricultural produce of her own banks, pours out the rich produce of the western counties and states; while the Wiconisco Canal will add the available coal of the Lykens Valley.

"On the other hand, hundreds of boats freighted with merchandise for the North and the West may be seen ascending the canals to supply the farmers, the lumbermen, the miners, and the ironmen along their banks. It is while contemplating a scene like this that the Pennsylvanian learns to confide in the internal resources of his native state, and to disregard what is called the diversion of her business into other routes."

"The scenery along the Perry County bank of the Susquehanna and on the Juniata is grand and beautiful. At Duncan's Island and Liverpool, especially, the mountains and the river present views scarcely surpassed even by the storied localities of the Old World. The heights, it is true, are not crowned by ancient and picturesque ruins; neither are the streams the dividing lines between princes whose past struggles for power have associated with them the legends of chivalry. But they remain in all their native beauty and grandeur, unchanged, except so far as human ingenuity has applied their resources to the promotion of human happiness. They remain a type of what our country's history should be, with no change recorded, except for the common good; no monument erected except to virtue."

Even the vistas surrounding the towns and villages, and the very places themselves, present a panoramic scene of varied beauty. Of Liverpool, Charles W. Huggins, a Chicago business man, writes: "The most beautiful place in Pennsylvania!" Of Ickesburg, Prof. William C. Shuman, long a resident of the vicinity, wrote: "A bright little Heaven within my early memory!" Another spoke of "where the Cocolamus joins the Juniata (below Millerstown), the most beautiful country in the United States." The view from the top of the Tuscarora, at a point above Ickesburg, is beyond description. To the north lies Mifflintown, the beautiful county seat of Juniata County; through the valley winds the picturesque Juniata River; in the distance are the Black-log Mountains, while afar can be seen the ranges of the Shade Mountains. Looking southward the western part of Perry County nestles between ridges, while in the distance looms the long, straight Kittatinny Mountain of the Blue Ridge system.

One of the features of the beautiful scenery throughout Perry County is the wooded lands—the trees. Everywhere we have trees, trees, trees! True, the woodman has, here and there, for financial gain, destroyed the forests, but as a whole, the effect is slight, and Perry County is still a land of trees, even including the greater portion of a state forest. And what is more beautiful or has taken a longer time to form than a full-grown tree? Can man fashion a tree, or can one be bought in the market place? Is a tree naught but firewood, or telegraph poles, or ties? It is a fine thing that many think otherwise, and that not only in the wooded sections, but by the roadside, there stand large and beautiful specimens. On a Perry Couny farm, by the roadside, once stood a great oak, from which a large number of ties could have been made and a considerable return have been received, but the man who owned and tilled that farm never even considered it, although probably the funds so secured may oft have been needed. To him that tree was a landmark, one of those left when the land was claimed from the forest for cultivation, and no money value would he have thought of placing upon it. That man was the father of the author of this book, and when he passed away, that old oak still stood—a sentinel by the roadside.

From the birth of the new county of Perry its scenery must have been a marked feature, for the newly established weekly paper, the *Perry Forester*, placed at its head and long carried the following lines:

> "—Ye who love through woods and wilds to range,
>   Who see new charms in each successive change;
> Come roam with me Columbia's forests through,
>   Where scenes sublime shall meet your wondering view."

Spring, summer and fall in the mountains finds attraction from the earliest buds of the arbutus, through the laurel and rhododendron season until the last of the beautiful colored leaves have fallen from the trees. In the shady and cool recesses of the forest, winding trails, dating back even to the time of the red men, lead through mile after mile of oak, pine and hemlock, with the most beautiful ferns that are to be found anywhere, in many a ravine and glen.

And there is summertime, with the glamour, the romance, the indescribable charm of summer days! It is pleasant to recall from Harry Kemp's "Chatneys and Ballads":

"Tell all the world that summer's here again,
  With song and joy; tell them, that they may know
How, on the hillside, in the shining fields
  New clumps of violets and daisies grow.

"Tell all the world that summer's here again,
  That white clouds voyage through a sky so still,
With blue tranquility, it seems to hang
  One windless tapestry, from hill to hill."

Summertime in Perry County, from the time when innumerable daisies grace the sides of the highways of the countryside, until long stretches of goldenrod make your pathway a veritable dream, is but the introduction to that later period of the year—Indian Summer—when the lazily drifting and fleecy clouds o'erhead, combined with the warm sun rays of the passing autumn, make this a veritable land of dreams. And there is beauty, even in the winter, with its myriad snowflakes, its forests garmented in white and its mountains, great white hills, glistening in the winter sun. Then, there is the feeling so minutely sensed by the great John Greenleaf Whittier, in "Snow-Bound," with which many persons native to Perry County are familiar.

There is ever, also, the attraction of solitude known only to the very fastnesses of the forests, where for a time one may feel the vastness of the great out-door world, where, from the loftiest tree of the forest to the tender verdure clinging to the crevices in the rock, one may behold the handiwork of the great Creator.

"When lights are low, and the day has died,
  I sit and dream of the countryside.

"Where sky meets earth at the meadow's end,
  I dream of a clean and wind-swept space
Where each tall tree is a staunch old friend,
  And each frail bud turns a trusting face.

"A purling brook, with each purl a prayer,
  To the bending grass its secret tells;
While softly borne on the scented air,
  Comes the far-off chime of chapel bells.

"A tiny cottage I seem to see,
  In its quaint old garden set apart;
And a Sabbath calm steals over me,
  While peace dwells deep in my brooding heart."—*Selected*.

In many large eastern cities and, in fact, at many widely scattered points, are Perry Countians whose names are writ high in the world of commerce and letters, and whose faces are familiar in the great marts of trade. When they left Perry County during their earlier years many registered a purpose to some day return and there spend the declining years of their lives. With the passing years their children have grown to manhood and womanhood in their adopted homes, and when the time came for them to fulfill their cherished desires, they have found that it meant the leaving of their closest kin and the parting from friendships formed during a generation or two, to return to the home of their youth, only to find the scenes changed, with few, perhaps, remaining of those whom they knew in the old days. During the swiftly passing years many have fallen asleep and are resting in the cemetery upon the hill, while others, like themselves, have gone abroad and are scattered throughout many states.

The city, with its bright lights, its teeming humanity, and its many amusements, beckons to the country lad and lass, and illusioned ofttimes, they leave a good home, a comfortable wage, and God's bright sunlight and open air, the very foundation of their health, for the beckoning paradise—often a lonesome hall-room and a stuffy office, with its many cares and worries. There is something about the open life of the countryside, or even that of the small town, with their freedom, community spirit and neighborliness, which the city denizen never knows; and lucky is that boy or girl who is born where he or she can breathe pure air and revel in God's sunlight.

> "I sometimes catch my breath, remembering
>   A picture that I love:
> A shining river running by a town
>   With high, white cliffs above,
> And from the farthest heights a cedar tree
> Reaching forever its wide arms to me.
>
> "And I am often touched to brimming tears
>   Recalling some old place:
> Exquisite purple twilight down a street,
>   A maple's leafy grace,
> And like a far sweet star lit suddenly
> An open lighted window flames for me."
>   —*Grace Noll Crowell.*

CHAPTER XXXVIII.

PERRY COUNTY'S BOROUGHS, TOWNSHIPS AND VILLAGES.

WHEN the lands which now form Perry County were purchased by the Penns, from the Indians, in 1754, that part of the county lying west of the Juniata and generally termed Sherman's Valley, was formed into a single township, of Cumberland County, called Tyrone. That part of the county lying between the Juniata and Susquehanna Rivers was a part of Fermanagh Township, Cumberland County, from the latter part of 1754 or early in 1755, when that township was erected. Fermanagh Township then was of large extent, including all the lands of the new purchase lying between the Juniata and Susquehanna Rivers. It also included that part of Mifflin County lying south of the Juniata, to the Black Log Mountain, and parts of Snyder, Centre and Huntingdon Counties. That extensive and original township, Tyrone, is to-day subdivided into six boroughs and fifteen townships. As settlement continued and the population demanded smaller units of self-government Fermanagh Township, lying northeast of Sherman's Valley, also was subdivided, and all that part of Perry County, save the small section lying north and west of Cocolamus Creek, was made into a separate township, named Greenwood, in 1767. That section lying between Cocolamus Creek and the present Juniata boundary, from "the middle of the long narrows, to the head of Cocolamus Creek," remained a part of Fermanagh Township until the creation of Mifflin County (which included present Juniata County), on September 19, 1787, when it was thrown into Perry County. This original township lying east of the Juniata, named Greenwood, is to-day divided into five townships and three boroughs. When the new county of Perry was erected, in 1820, there were already five townships west of the Juniata—Tyrone, Toboyne, Rye, Juniata and Saville, having been formed in the order named. The part east of the river at that time comprised but two townships, Greenwood and Buffalo.

The author is indebted to hundreds for information, but especially so to the following for help on many occasions: J. Earl Sheaffer, New Bloomfield, for assistance in searching files; W. Walter Branyan, Local Editor of the *Record*, Duncannon, for the use of a number of privately owned cuts of scenery; H. B. Kell and Alton J. Shumaker, Blain; E. C. Dile, Landisburg; S. Maurice Shuler, Liverpool, and H. G. Martin, Millerstown.

By referring to the history of the various townships following
it will be seen that certain farms and parcels of property have been
an integral part of various different subdivisions.   Take the Duncannon Iron Company property as an example.   In 1755 it was
located in Tyrone Township, Cumberland County.   After 1766 it
was in Rye Township, Cumberland County.   After 1820 it was in
Rye Township, Perry County; after 1826, in Wheatfield Township, Perry County, and since 1840, in Penn Township, Perry
County.

While the facts relative to the formation of the various townships will be found in the chapters relating to their history, yet the
following tables, compiled by the author, may be of service.   For
the convenience of the reader a map showing the townships, as at
present constituted, can be found on page 6.   By reference to it
the following table will be more easily understood.

FORMATION OF TOWNSHIPS.

Township	Y'r	Formed From	Line of Descent, Etc.
Tyrone	1754	Original township .	Comprised all of Perry county lying west of Juniata.
Toboyne	1763	Tyrone	Originally included Jackson and Madison.
Rye	1766	Tyrone	Originally included Penn, Wheat-field, Miller, Oliver, Juniata, Tuscarora, and parts of Centre and Carroll. Also sites of New-port and Bloomfield.
Greenwood	1767	Fermanagh	Fermanagh was an original town-ship of the Purchase of 1754, in Cumberland county. Green-wood included that part of Perry east of Juniata river and south of Cocolamus creek. See Greenwood township chapter.
Juniata	1793	Rye	Originally contained all of Tusca-rora and Oliver, and parts of Miller and Centre. Also sites of Newport and Bloomfield.
Buffalo	1799	Greenwood	Originally included all of Howe and Watts, and site of New Buf-falo.
Saville	1817	Tyrone	Originally included a part of Cen-tre and a small strip of Madi-son.

The seven townships named above were townships of Cumberland County,
before Perry was formed, and became the original townships of the new County
of Perry.

Township	Y'r	Formed From	Line of Descent, Etc.
Liverpool T. ...	1823	Greenwood	Includes Liverpool borough.
Wheatfield	1826	Rye	Included all of Penn and parts of Miller, Centre and Carroll. Also site of Duncannon.
Centre†	1831	Saville, Juniata, Wheatfield and Tyrone	Originally contained parts of Oliver, Miller, Carroll and Spring.
Carroll	1834	Tyrone, Rye and Wheatfield	Originally contained part of Spring.
Madison	1836	Toboyne and a small strip from both Saville and Tyrone	Includes Sandy Hill District, sometimes termed N. E. Madison.
Oliver	1837	Juniata, Centre and Buffalo	Originally included part of Miller and all of *Howe. Also site of Newport.
Penn	1840	Wheatfield	Once part of Tyrone, then Rye, then Wheatfield.
Jackson	1844	Toboyne	First a part of Tyrone. Contains site of Blain.
Spring	1848	Tyrone and a strip of Centre	
Watts	1849	Buffalo	Once part of Greenwood. New Buffalo within its confines.
Miller	1852	Oliver and Wheatfield	
Tuscarora	1859	Greenwood and Juniata	*
Howe	1861	Oliver	Originally in Greenwood, then Buffalo, then *Oliver.

*In only two instances were lands from opposite sides of the Juniata combined in the same township. The first was in 1837, when that part of Buffalo which later became Howe was attached to Oliver and so remained for twenty-four years, when it became Howe Township. The other was when a petition was presented to the Court January 4, 1854, asking that the lines of Greenwood Township be altered, to include a portion of Juniata Township lying west of and along the Juniata River, in the Raccoon Valley. The petition was granted and it was a part of Greenwood Township until Tuscarora became a township, in 1859, when it became a part of Tuscarora.

Laying Out of Towns.

Town.	Y'r	Then Located In.	Township Adjoining Now.
Millerstown	1790	Greenwood	Greenwood.
Petersburg (now Duncannon)	1792	Rye ....:	Penn.
Landisburg	1793	Tyrone	Tyrone.
Reider's Ferry (now Newport)	1804	Juniata	Oliver.
Liverpool	1808	Greenwood	Liverpool.
New Germantown	1816	Toboyne	Toboyne.
Ickesburg	1816	Saville	Saville.
Baughmanstown (now New Buffalo)	1820	Buffalo	Watts.
Bloomfield	1823	Juniata	Centre.
Andesville (now Loysville) .	1840	Tyrone	Tyrone.
Blain	1846	Jackson	Jackson.
Haley (Marysville)	1861	Rye	Rye and Penn.

58

INCORPORATION OF BOROUGHS.

Name.	Y'r	Location When Formed.	Location Now—Other Data.
Bloomfield	*1831	Juniata	Centre, which dates to Aug. 4, 1831.
Landisburg	†1831	Tyrone	Tyrone. Temporary county seat.
Liverpool	1832	Liverpool	Liverpool.
Newport	1840	Oliver	Oliver.
Petersburg (Duncannon)	1844	Penn	Penn. Name changed to Duncannon and reincorporated in 1865.
New Buffalo	1848	Buffalo	Watts, which dates to 1849.
Millerstown	1849	Greenwood	Greenwood.
Haley (Marysville) .	1866	Rye	Rye, borders Penn also. Name changed to Marysville in 1867.
Blain	1877	Jackson	Jackson.

It is impossible, in a volume of this size, to include all of the warrants and patents for the lands which comprise Perry County, as that would take several volumes alone, but some of the earlier or more prominent are included. In the case of the history of the churches it has been almost impossible to get facts. Manuscript sent out to authorities was never returned, with the result that much of the work along that line had to be done twice. The records are not as complete for those reasons, as were anticipated in the beginning, but will form a foundation upon which to build. Some of the history of the early mills and industries has been lost forever, much of it appears under a chapter devoted to that topic, and some is in the following chapters. In fact, much of the general matter in this volume could have been included in the township chapters, but had a more general bearing as county history.

BLOOMFIELD BOROUGH—THE COUNTY SEAT.

The story of the long fight for the county seat and the manner of New Bloomfield's selection is dwelt upon at length in the chapter in this book devoted to "The Fight for the County Seat." There was no town there then; it was on a farm formerly belonging to Thomas Barnett, from whom the Barnett families hailing from New Bloomfield have descended. Thomas Barnett had purchased the warrant rights to it in 1784 from David Mitchell, who had made some improvements upon it. The tradition is that Mitchell had settled there in 1743, but that is wrong, as the lands were not purchased from the Indians until 1754, and Mitchell's name is never mentioned in the provincial records among the squatters who were driven from the county, and according to these records all persons who had then presumed to settle north of the Kittatinny or Blue Mountain were driven out. There is evidence, however, that Mitchell did come in during the latter

*March 14.
†December 23.

part of 1753, although the lands were not thrown open until February 3, 1755. a full account appearing on page 191 of this book. While David Mitchell resided there his son Robert, who later became one of the first board of county commissioners, was born. The patent in possession of the Barnett family shows that four pounds, fourteen shillings and three pence was the price, and according to the old English custom of naming estates it is named on the patent "Bloom Field." When the borough was incorporated it too was named Bloomfield, but the post office was named New Bloomfield, to distinguish it from an office named Bloomfield, already in existence. There is a pretty little story of the town's being laid out in the center of a clover field in full bloom, but the patent and other historical papers bear out the naming as stated·above.

Thomas Barnett, at the time he warranted the tract, lived at "The Cove," that section of Penn Township lying within "the horseshoe." It contained four hundred and eighteen acres. The warrant is dated December 19, 1785, and the patent, August 17, 1796. The title to the lands passed to a son, George Barnett, on May 10, 1804. On Monday, June 2, 1823, the commission appointed by Governor Heister, under the act of March 31, 1823, selected the site for the county seat upon the farm. The legislature confirmed the report, and on April 12, 1823, George Barnett, for a consideration of one dollar, sold to the county commissioners a tract of land on both sides of the road leading from Carlisle to Sunbury, comprising eight acres and one hundred and thirty-six perches, the tract being 564x684 feet in size. He also granted to the county the use forever of a spring, near the southwest boundary of the tract. free of all obstructions. To this day that spring is known as "the big spring." The deeds for surrounding properties contain the same clause granting the privilege of the use of this spring. Shortly thereafter the county commissioners employed Robert Kelly to plot the town. There were to be three streets running from east to west: Main Street, sixty-six feet wide; McClure Street, sixty feet wide, and High Street, fifty feet wide. There was to be one street north to south, known as Carlisle Street, sixty-six feet wide. It was plotted into sixty-four lots. At the intersection of Main and Carlisle Streets a public square was laid out, and four square lots abutting the public square were reserved for public use.

The courthouse was erected on the northeast corner plot in 1826, and the opposite corner was planned for a market house, which, however. has never been built, but instead there is a beautiful shaded lawn, well kept by the municipality, and frequently the scene of local gay festivities. The trees were donated by public spirited citizens, their cost being $1.00 each. Later the lots on the other two corners were sold by the commissioners. One is owned by the Sheibley Brothers, on part of which stands the publication offices of the *Peoples' Advocate and Press,* and on part of the other the famous old hostelry once known as the Perry House, but now as Rhinesmith's Hotel. The first jail was erected in 1825, on McClure Street. On June 23, 1824, the county commissioners offered twenty-six lots for sale at auction, nearly all of which were purchased, and deeded on August 3, 1824.

There were no buildings on the plot when it was taken over by the county, but adjoining it on the north was a church building known as the Union Church. The first building was a two-and-a-half-story house, constructed of sawed logs. It was at the southeast corner of Carlisle and McClure Streets, and was built by John Attick. The contract for building the jail was awarded to John Rice, who then went into business in the town and was so engaged until 1850. On May 13, 1824, George Barnett, for a consideration of sixty-eight cents, conveyed to the county commis-

sioners a tract of five acres of woodland, "situate on the north side of the road leading from the Dutch meetinghouse, in Juniata Township, to the Blue Ball tavern." Evidently the fuel proposition was being looked after.

In the sale of lots by the county commissioners, lot No. 1, at the northeast corner of the public square, was sold to Andrew Shuman. The statement sometimes made that "he owned the greater part of Bloomfield," is a gross error. The change of the county seat from Landisburg to New Bloomfield was accompanied by a change of location for a number of business men, among them being James Atchley and John Hipple, who kept taverns there; Robert H. McClelland, a merchant; Alexander Magee, publisher of the *Perry Forester,* and Charles B. Davis and John D. Creigh, attorneys. In the new county seat's early days Dr. Jonas Ickes, in 1826, built a tavern house, as they were then known, where the Mansion Hotel (until recently) stands. David Lupfer purchased the lot directly north of the courthouse, on Carlisle Street, and built a two-story brick tavern building which still stands. In 1830 it was licensed as a public house and run by him until 1854, after which it passed to others by lease until 1866, when George Derick purchased the building and conducted it until his death. For a time thereafter Mrs. Derick conducted it as a temperance house. It passed through the hands of various men until recently, when it came into possession of Theodore K. Long, owner of the Carson Long Institute, who remodeled it into a hall for the use of students, it being known as the "Eaglerook" Hall. The next lot north was bought by John Hipple, who had kept hotel in Landisburg from 1819 until 1826, when he was elected sheriff. At the conclusion of his term as sheriff he bought the Warm Springs property and kept a tavern there for several years. Captain William Power owned the next lot, corner of Carlisle and High Streets. Robert Kelly, for many years a school teacher and surveyor, bought the lot on which the First National Bank is now located.

Among the early business men and manufacturers were Dr. Jonas Ickes, who practiced medicine, kept the post office, a drug store, and a tavern— a sort of a small monopoly; Robert H. McClelland, a tavern and a store at different periods; David Deardorff, a tavern; William McCaskey, a tailor; Mrs. Jane Axe, millinery; Jeremiah Drexler, a tailor; John Dunbar, cabinetmaker; Thomas A. Godfrey, merchant; John Dubbs, a merchant; Thomas Black, a merchant, and George Arnold, a shoe shop, employing a dozen men, for there were no shoe factories then. John Gotwalt was a chairmaker; Adam M. Axe was a saddler and harness manufacturer, and Robert R. Guthrie, a silversmith. Among the early settlers were John Crist, a weaver; Henry Fritz, a mason; Andrew Moyer, a printer; Joseph Johnston, a wagonmaker; David Lupfer, a blacksmith, and James Marshall, a tanner.

Logically, the legal talent followed the courthouse. John D. Creigh, an attorney, bought lots on the northwest corner of the square and erected a brick house. Charles B. Davis, an attorney, was admitted in 1821 and died in 1829. Benjamin McIntire, an attorney admitted in 1825, located in the town soon after the transfer of the county seat and bought of Andrew Shuman lot No. 1, adjoining the courthouse, where he lived until the time of his death. Conrad Roth began keeping a tavern in 1831 and continued until his death, after which it was a temperance house until 1885.

On September 21, 1824, William McClure, who was a son of William McClure I, who located the lands on which the Perry County Home now stands, purchased two lots from George Barnett, upon which he erected a tannery. Mr. McClure owned and operated the tannery from 1825 until 1842, when he sold to Henry S. Forry, who also purchased the Marshall tannery and opened a store. Among others who later owned this tannery

were James McNeal, Wilson McKee, Joseph Page, Bucher & Simpson, and
Daniel Bucher, Sr., who in 1865 sold it to Samuel A. Peale. Mr. Peale
operated it until 1873, at which time the business was discontinued.

In 1830 James Marshall purchased a lot of ground from George Barnett,
on the south side of McClure Street, and erected a tannery. In 1851 it
was owned by John Bowers, who sold it to William Peale. After his death
in 1860, it was continued by his son, Samuel A. Peale, until 1866, when it
was destroyed by fire. It was in this tannery that young Alexander K.
McClure learned the tanning business, and later gave it up to become a
newspaper man, which for him was the opening door to national fame.

The following from the *Perry Forester* of April 30, 1829, is a pen picture of the new county seat:

"There are now 29 dwelling housess, 21 shops and offices, a courthouse and
jail, besides other out-houses in this town. There are 4 stores, 5 taverns, 1
printing office, 2 shoemaker shops, 2 tailor shops, 1 saddler, 4 cabinet makers,
1 hatter, 1 tinner, 2 blacksmith shops, 2 tanneries, 2 or 3 carpenters, more than
half a dozen lawyers and half as many doctors. The population of the town
is about 220. Little more than four years ago, the site upon which the town
stands was an inclosed cloverfield, without a solitary building upon it."

William Sponsler, a brewer by occupation, came over from Carlisle, and
in 1833 purchased from George Barnett a plot of ground on the east side
of Carlisle Street on which he erected a brew house, continuing in business
until 1843. For many years thereafter this same building was occupied by
a foundry. On the west side of Carlisle Street, in the southern section of
the town, Jeremiah Madden, who had been an associate judge from the
formation of the county until 1832, located a cooper shop, upon several
acres of land purchased of Barnett, where he plied his trade. Later it
was used as a foundry for a few years.

The old foundry building, recently turned into a garage, was opened
in 1852, being described by the erector as "at the south end of Carlisle
Street." An early chair factory at New Bloomfield, operated by Samuel
Dunbar, continuously employed three or four men. This was unusual, as
in those days there were few employees in business, most of it being done
by individuals in shops of their own.

As early as November 25, 1830, a meeting was held to organize for better protection against fires, which later resulted in the organization of the
"New Bloomfield Marine Fire Company," which purchased a hand engine
and other necessary paraphernalia. There have been a number of successors to this early company, which was short-lived.

Bloomfield was the first town in the county to be incorporated as a borough, that act being dated March 14, 1831, and preceding that of Landisburg by nine months. The preliminary meeting was held on November 25,
1830, to consider the necessity and arrange for petitioning the legislature
for a borough charter. This date is the same as the one which resulted in
the organization of the fire company, which leads us to believe that these
early citizens of the county seat were progressive. In fact, town meetings
would be a mighty good thing to-day in many places, for frequently the
one who holds office is not the logical man nor the one best fitted, but
rather a result of our political system. Alexander Magee was the first
burgess of the borough. The present town of Bloomfield also occupies a
part of the 294-acre tract warranted by Jacob Lupfer, August 4, 1787. Mr.
Lupfer was the ancestor of the numerous Lupfer families of succeeding
generations, a sturdy strain of whom inhabit not only Pennsylvania, but
many states of the Union. He was born in Germany, in 1721, emigrated to
America in 1752, settling in Berks County. He removed to Perry County
territory in 1776, settling on the claim which bordered his later possession

on the west and which was warranted by James Cowan, February 4, 1755, —the very first day of the opening of the land office for these lands. This latter tract is named in the patent as "Rye." The sites of the Lutheran and Reformed churches and the old graveyard were a part of this 294-acre tract. In the latter burial grounds rest five generations of Lupfers.

The big spring at New Bloomfield was excepted for general use of surrounding property owners, and the old deeds contain a clause which gives the purchasers the right to secure water at this spring. The town citizens some years ago had it improved with cement surroundings, but of recent years the water has been condemned, having been contaminated.

Prior to 1833 two additional plots were laid out in town lots, one by George Barnett, on the north side of High Street, and one by Matthew Shuman, bordering the western line.

The village, for it then was a mere handful of houses, was granted a post office under the John Quincy Adams administration, in May, 1825, with Dr. Jonas Ickes as postmaster. A list of the men who have held that position, with the dates of their assuming it:

Dr. Jonas Ickes, 1825.	†Dr. Isaac Lefevre.
Joseph Duncan, 1830.	Joseph Miller, 1861
Alexander Magee, 1835.	Mrs. Elizabeth Dickson, 1865.
Robert R. Guthrie, 1841.	Samuel Roath, 1869.
Samuel G. Morrison, 1845.	James B. Clark, 1885.
*Frances M. Watts.	H. C. Shearer, 1889.
Joseph M. Shatto.	Wm. Grier, 1897.
Robert R. Guthrie, 1849.	A. B. Grosh, 1901.
Isaac N. Shatto, 1853.	William Clegg, 1913.
†Jacob Fenstemacher.	

The barn on the Barnett farm, now owned by George R. Barnett, attorney, was erected in the very year in which the county was formed, and still stands. The late Frederick and Sarah Barnett, then children of five and nine, remembered the day of its raising and told of the occurrence and the large number of men there, as was the custom.

Like its sister town, Landisburg, the new county seat celebrated the fiftieth anniversary of American Independence, in 1826. Ralph Smiley presided and the Declaration of Independence was read by John Harper. Charles B. Power was the orator for the occasion. A dinner was served at the big spring by Dr. Jonas Ickes, then proprietor of the "Rising Sun Inn."

The New Bloomfield cemetery land was bought by Alex. C. Klink, John Campbell, Daniel Gantt (later Chief Justice of Colorado), and B. McIntire, and plotted in 1854, the lots being 14x16. It is well kept. In 1871 the southwest corner of the square was burned out, the principal building being that of Samuel Wiggins, occupied by him as a residence and by the *Peoples' Advocate and Press*. The fourth floor was finished for lodge purposes and all the town orders then met there, including the Masons, Odd Fellows, American Mechanics, Red Med and Good Templars. The *Democrat* was published for years from a building on the western end of the Wiggins plot, which was a present to Mrs. Wiggins from a relative, General Dowdell, of York. Other buildings burned in this fire were a hotel on Carlisle Street, a residence on the corner of Carlisle and Main, and a building in which there was a marble cutting establishment. In 1888 there was a fire which burned several residences on the west side of Carlisle Street, one of them being the home of the late Judge Junkin. It joined the section burned in the earlier fire.

---

*Filled unexpired term of Morrison, who resigned.
†Succeeded Shatto during Buchanan administration.

In 1893 the New Bloomfield Water Company was organized, with Dr. A. R. Johnston as president and principal in the movement, and the following year water was piped from the Garland springs, a point somewhat over a mile from town. The company supplies water for public and private purposes to the inhabitants. Its capital is $15,000. During 1898 the Newport Electric Company, of which Joshua S. Leiby was president, secured the franchise for lighting the streets and introducing electric lights into private residences and business places, the current being carried overland from the plant at Newport. Since then that company and its successors have furnished the borough's electric current.

Prior to the laying out of the county seat the physicians of Millerstown and Milford served the needs of this community. The first physician to locate in New Bloomfield, Dr. Jonas Ickes, moved there in 1825, the year before it became the county seat. He was born in Montgomery County, but his parents removed to Perry County when he was three years old. He began practice in Ickesburg in 1820, located in Duncannon in 1823. One of his daughters, Susan, was married to General Harding, an Illinois congressman. He practiced in New Bloomfield for thirty-one years. Dr. Vanderslice practiced here from 1827 to 1832, when he died of smallpox. Others for short periods were Dr. John H. Doling, 1830; Dr. T. L. Cathcart, 1830, and Dr. Joseph Speck, about 1836, he having previously been at Duncannon and returned. From 1840 until his death, in 1849, Dr. John M. Laird practiced in New Bloomfield, having been in Millerstown from the time of his graduation in 1824 until then. In 1845 or '46 Dr. Miller was located here. Prior to 1853 Dr. J. P. Kimball practiced here for a half-dozen years. Dr. Joseph Ickes was a son of Dr. Jonas Ickes. He practiced with his father here for a short time after his graduation in 1849, then located at Manheim, but moved to Duncan's Island, where he died in 1851. Dr. David F. Fetter located there in 1852, practiced for several years, and then located in New York. Dr. Isaac Lefevre succeeded him, removing from Loysville in 1855. Dr. Burkley practiced several years prior to 1862, when he located in Harrisburg. Dr. E. W. Baily located here in 1860, but did not remain long.

Dr. M. B. Strickler, who was a native of Cumberland County, graduated at the University of Pennsylvania in 1861. A year later he located at New Bloomfield. Dr. Thomas G. Morris, of Liverpool, practiced here during the period from 1865-67. After the War between the States Dr. David H. Sweeney was located here for a few years, removing to Clearfield. Dr. W. D. Ard, a native of Juniata County, graduated at the University of the City of New York in 1869, and the next year located in New Bloomfield, where he practiced until 1881, when he died, aged only thirty-five years. He was succeeded by Dr. O. P. Bollinger, who had previously practiced at Newport and Milford and who removed to the West in 1885. Dr. A. R. Johnston, a native son of Perry County, graduated from the Jefferson Medical College in 1881 and located in New Bloomfield in 1884. He also conducted a drug store here for a long period. He is still in active practice. Dr. E. E. Moore graduated from Jefferson Medical College in 1887 and located at his home town, where he still conducts probably as wide a practice as any physician in Perry County. Dr. M. I. Stein, University of Maryland, 1909, located here in 1915.

A few years after the founding of the town there was a schoolhouse on the Barnett farm, south of the mill race, on the road leading to Duncannon, which sufficed for a time. It was the first school west of the Susquehanna River. (See School chapter.) Later George Barnett donated a lot on High Street, east of the present Lutheran Church, which is in use to this day for school purposes. Upon this land a small brick schoolhouse was built, but the exact date is a matter of conjecture, yet there is documentary evidence that it was probably about 1829, as "the stockholders of the schoolhouse" met December 26th of that year, at the tavern house of David Deardorff, at "early candlelight to attend to important business." On March 7, 1831, Alexander Magee, James Hill and Joseph Marshall were elected to sit with John Rice and Isaac Keiser as trustees of the school. John Heineman taught one term in the tavern house of John Rice in the year 1830-31. He also taught in the new school building when completed. Teachers following were a man named Lowell, Samuel Black, Samuel Ramsey and John L. Amoreaux. As conditions required more room an addition was built to the north end, and later a building was erected on the south side of McClure Street. The two buildings were in use until 1870, when the present building was erected on the old site at a cost of nine thousand dollars.

The establishing of the New Bloomfield Academy, with its interesting history, and that of the Carson Long Institute, are a part of the annals of New Bloomfield Borough, but in this book belong more properly under the chapter devoted to Public Institutions and Academies, where it will be found. In 1837 this school was first opened in the corner room of the second story of the old Mansion House. In 1919 Theodore K. Long leased this building, which had been in use as a hostelry since 1831, and adapted it to office and dormitory uses for the Carson Long Institute, as the old academy is now known.

The organization of Adams Lodge, No. 319, Free and Accepted Masons, took place at New Bloomfield, under a warrant dated March 1, 1858. It was the successor of Golden Rule Lodge, No. 76, organized at Landisburg, on June 26, 1825, but which ceased holding meetings about 1833, it having been the oldest Masonic Lodge in the Juniata Valley. The first officers of the New Bloomfield Lodge were Irvine J. Crane, master; Charles J. T. McIntire, senior warden, and Alexander C. Kling, junior warden.

Probably the women's club longest in existence in Perry County is the Women's Club of New Bloomfield, affiliated with the State Federation of Pennsylvania Women, and classed as a literary club with departments. It was organized in the fall of 1890, under the title, "Chautauqua Literary and Scientific Circle," which name was only changed when joining the State Federation. in 1908, for uniformity's sake. It organized with eleven members. Early officers were Mrs. A. R. Johnston, president, and Miss Charlotte Barnett, secretary. As its name at first implied, it is devoted to literary work. One of the first acts of this club was the purchase of a piano for use in the courthouse, where practically all entertainments of a public nature—save religious—take place. Churches are allowed its use free for all charitable objects, but others are charged a small fee. The Women's Community Club was organized December 6, 1920, with Mrs. J. T. Alter, president; Mrs. A. R. Johnston. vice-president; Miss Elizabeth H. Roth. secretary, and Miss M. Zulu Swartz, treasurer. Its object is "to create good fellowship, and cultivate social, intellectual and civic interest. The Community Club meets every two weeks in the chapel of the Carson Long Institute and has held several public meetings in the courthouse, its finances being so far principally devoted to those charities which are world-wide and which since the great war have been so pressing.

The first Woman's Christian Temperance Union in New Bloomfield was organized in December, 1884. The first officers were: Mrs. Elizabeth W. Orr, president; Mrs. A. H. F. Fischer, vice-president: Mrs. Amanda Abrams, treasurer: Miss Charlotte Barnett, secretary. A bill requiring the teaching of physiology, with special reference to the effects of narcotics on the human body was at that time before the legislature, and the first work of the newly organized union was the securing of signers to petitions favoring the passage of the bill. The union continued its work, holding meetings at the homes of the members, and doing various kinds of work, among which was the presentation of remonstrances to the license court. The first remonstrance was presented in 1888. After some years of work, the union lapsed, but was reorganized during the winter of 1910-11.

New Bloomfield is not a manufacturing town, but has a planing mill and a hosiery mill. The hosiery mill was established in 1903, by W. H. Darlington and H. E. Clouser, trading as Darlington & Clouser. In 1917 Mr. Darlington purchased the other interest and now operates the plant.

With the stopping of the sale of intoxicants most of the hotels in the county went out of business, but this was not the case with Hotel Rhinesmith, in New Bloomfield. This was long known as the Perry House, but was purchased by the late D. M. Rhinesmith in 1889, and conducted by him from 1890 to 1895, when it was rebuilt by the present proprietor, H. B. Rhinesmith.

According to the report of the mercantile appraiser the following persons are engaged in business in Bloomfield Borough, the date following their names being the date when they began business:

General Stores, G. W. Garber. G. W. Keller.

Groceries. C. O. Davis (1918), Amos Sheaffer.

Notions, Clarence Askins (1911).

Lumber, Chas. L. Darlington (1912). Hoffman & Tressler.

Auto Supplies, D. Boyd Alter (1914).

Stoves and tinware, J. A. Spahr (1883), established by George Spahr in 1848. This is the oldest established business in Bloomfield.

Implements, B. F. Keller (1919).

Perry Mercantile Co. (James L. Butz), clothing; Thomas Bender, cigars; H. B. Rhinesmith, hotel; H. Earl Book, drugs; Frank Eckerd, meat market; W. J. Grenoble, jewelry (1917); Robert A. McClure, grain and feed (1920); Hoffman & McClure (1918), established by W. H. F. Garber in Nepwort in 1878, and in 1889 at Bloomfield; J. C. Motter, lumber; Nickel Furniture Co. (1920), established by Jacob Fenstemacher, whose successor was A. P. Nickel (1870); Harry Shellehamer, meat market; Charles Rouse, furniture, established by George A. Rouse & Bro. (1873); Harriet Nickel, millinery; W. H. Cupp & Son, vehicles; Bretz & Tressler, Sheller Bretz, Gutshall's Garage & Machine Co., garages.

The Old Union Church. On Saturday, June 19, 1798, the first church in New Bloomfield, the Old Union log church, was raised. It was erected jointly by the Lutheran and German Reformed congregations, and was 36x30 feet in size. Each parishioner who was able to do so brought one or more logs of white pine, oak or poplar, as his contribution towards its erection. Heavy crossbeams were inserted for the support of a gallery, but that was not added until twenty-two years later. Soon after its erection Andrew Shuman covered it with a substantial roof and thus it stood, it is said, doorless, windowless and without a floor, until 1802. It contained no stove and was used only in summer. The seats were of slabs and the preacher stook back of a rough wooden table. During the winter the meetings were held in private dwellings, when held at all, they being few and far between. The minister resided at Carlisle and the roads were only roads in name at that time.

The church was built on an acre and a half of land which Jacob Lupfer sold to them for twelve dollars. He had located it in 1787, according to the land office. It was surveyed for church purposes in 1802 and deeded to the two congregations, May 14, 1804. The graveyard was laid out soon thereafter and the first interment was that of Peter Moses. The site is the old High Street site in the borough, and at that time was surrounded by woods, the nearest homes being those of Thomas Barnett and David

Lupfer. Where the schoolhouse now stands was a frog pond, and between it and the big spring was a lowland covered with green briar and other underbrush.

In 1820 it was completed, seats being constructed on the board floor and a high pulpit similar in design to a wine glass was erected. The ceiling was arched, the gallery built and windows put in. It was plastered and the woodwork painted white, and was then called Christ's Church.

On October 4, 1857, Rev. D. H. Focht preached at the last service held in the old log church, and from his discourse are gathered many facts included in this article. As it had long been uncomfortable an effort had been begun in 1855 looking to the erection of a new church. The German Reformed and Lutheran churches then divided equally the ground and on it to-day are located well-kept brick churches in which each have their exclusive title. Even the timbers of the old edifice were equally and amicably divided. The new Lutheran Church was erected under the supervision of a building committee composed of Samuel Comp, Dr. Jonas Ickes, Henry Rice, John Beaver, Sr., and Jacob Stouffer. It was dedicated October 22, 1857, and cost three thousand dollars, a mere fraction of what the cost would be now. It was remodeled in 1885.

Christ's Lutheran Church. The Lutheran congregation had its beginning in the old log church as stated above, which came to known as Christ's Church in 1820, the year of the county's formation. Of some of the original Lutheran families to worship at the log church were the Comp and Shover families, who settled there about 1780; the Cless family, in 1785; the Clark, Fritz and Myers families, about 1790; the Westfall, Slough, Smith, Crist and Sweger families, between then and 1800, and the Roth family, in 1803. These were among those who formed the nucleus of this congregation. When a minister came they gathered from distances as far apart as twelve miles to hear the gospel. Private dwellings, barns, schoolhouses and the forests themselves were the scenes of their devotions. Tradition says (probably) Rev. John G. Butler, of Carlisle, came over occasionally to preach between 1780 and 1788.

About that time Rev. John T. Kuhl commenced visiting and preaching throughout the Sherman's Valley. In 1790 he located near Loysville, and between 1788 and 1795 he preached also to the scattered members of the little congregation at what is now New Bloomfield. Rev. John Herbst, of Carlisle, in 1796 began serving the congregations of Sherman's Valley, and to him is likely due the credit for organizing the congregation here. In 1801 Rev. Herbst resigned the Carlisle charge and then there was no regular pastor until 1809, when Rev. John Frederick Osterloh assumed charge of the congregations of Sherman's Valley, serving until 1816. In June, 1816, Rev. John William Heim, that famous old circuit rider, became the leader of the Lutherans of the valley and served New Bloomfield until his death in December, 1849. He preached once every four weeks, and only in the German language.

In September, 1842, the West Pennsylvania Synod of the Lutheran Church was held at New Bloomfield, and some of the ministers preached in the English language, with the result that some of the membership desired Mr. Heim to associate with himself a pastor who could use the English language, which he either would not or did not do. Rev. A. H. Lochman, then president of the Western Pennsylvania Synod, sent Rev. Levi T. Williams, who was stationed at Petersburg (Duncannon), to preach a trial sermon. He was also to preach in German, but finding friction with the German-speaking membership, induced Rev. Jacob Scholl, a German Reformed minister, to fill those appointments for him. Finding all efforts in vain to reconcile them it was decided to organize an entirely separate congregation of English Lutherans. It was effected Friday, June 14, 1844, the officers being Jacob Crist, Sr., and David Deardorff, elders, and H. C. Hickok, and George Attick, deacons. Their first services were held in the schoolhouse, but the Presbyterians then invited them to use their church edifice. Rev. Williams resigned in 1845. In 1848 the German Lutherans had again invited the English membership to use its building as a place of worship. Rev. Lloyd Knight, a resident, then became pastor until 1849. He was succeeded by Rev. Jacob Martin, under whose pastorate the two congregations became one.

In July, 1849, when he became pastor, the charge comprised New Bloomfield, Petersburg, Billow's (St. David's), Mt. Pisgah, Newport, Buffalo (near Ickesburg), and New Buffalo. With the close of 1849 Father Heim passed away and a convention of the Lutheran churches of Perry County met in New Bloomfield during February, 1850, and divided the field into three pastorates, called the Loysville, the New Bloomfield and the Petersburg charges. Rev. Martin was assigned to the New Bloomfield pastorate, which included the churches at Newport, Shuman's or St. Andrew's, St. John's, near Markelville, and Buffalo, near Ickesburg. As Rev. Martin could preach in both languages he was logically made the pastor of the New Bloomfield charge and thus also became the regular successor of Father Heim as the pastor of the German-speaking branch. He preached once every three weeks there, alternately in English and German. He resigned in June, 1853. Since that time the pastors of this congregation have been:

1854 —Rev. Adam T. Height.	1889-95—Rev. Chas. Fickinger.
1855-63—Rev. D. H. Focht.	1895-00—Rev. A. J. Rudisill.
1863-65—Rev. P. P. Lane.	1900-01—Rev. Geo. A. Greiss.
1866-68—Rev. G. F. Schaffer.	1901-05—Rev. Chas. M. Nicholas.
1869-72—Rev. S. A. Hedges.	1906-13—Rev. W. J. Wagner.
1873-78—Rev. R. Sheeder.	1913 —Rev. A. R. Longenecker.
1879-82—Rev. A. H. Spangler.	1914-20—Rev. Jno. W. Weeter.
1883-89—Rev. A. H. F. Fisher.	1921- —Rev. S. M. Kornman.

Trinity Reformed Church. Uniting with the Lutherans of the vicinity, as recorded on the foregoing page, the members of the Reformed faith in the vicinity helped build the Old Union church, a log structure, in 1798. All the Reformed people of Sherman's Valley then comprised one charge. Just who the first pastor of that faith at New Bloomfield was will forever be a mystery, but it is believed to have been Rev. Ulrich Heininger, an itinerant preacher of the word, who preached throughout the territory from 1789 to 1802. Succeeding ministers in the territory were: Rev. Samuel Dubbendorf, 1790-95; Rev. Anthony Hautz, 1798-1804; Rev. Jonathan Helfenstein, 1805-11; Rev. Albert Helfenstein, 1811-19. In 1819 Rev. Jacob Scholl was made pastor of the entire charge, which of course, included Trinity church. He continued in charge until his death, September 4, 1847.

In 1855, coincident with the similar effort of the Lutheran Church, a movement was started for the erection of a new church, not however until overtures had been made to the Lutheran congregation, with a view of building a new Union church. The Lutheran Synod, however, had frowned upon further building of union churches generally and so the effort failed. David Lupfer, John McKeehan, George W. Meck, Charles Boyles and Jacob Mogel were appointed a building committee. On September 20, 1857, the new church was dedicated.

As early as 1838 an effort was made to divide the Sherman's Valley charge into two, and a year later it was consummated. The matter of language was also producing friction in this denomination, similar to that of the Lutherans. After this division the New Bloomfield charge consisted of six congregations: Trinity, New Bloomfield; Christ's, Newport; St. John's, Markelville; St. Andrew's, Shuman's (now Eshcol); St. David's, Fio Forge; and Zion's, Fishing Creek. After Rev. Scholl's death, in 1847, Rev. Daniel Ganz was pastor until 1851, when Rev. Samuel Kuhn succeeded him, serving eleven and a half years. It was then decided to reduce the number of churches to four by uniting Zion's with St. David's, and St. Andrew's to the Blain charge. Succeeding pastors were:

1863-67—Rev. David W. Kelly.	1876-81—Rev. John Kretzing.
1867-70—Rev. Wm. F. Colliflower.	1881-00—Rev. W. R. H. Deatrich.
1871-75—Rev. James Crawford.	1901-21—Rev. J. T. Fox (still there).

During 1911 the church was remodeled, the repairs including memorial windows, etc.

Bloomfield Presbyterian Church. When the new town of Bloomfield was laid out the members of the Presbyterian faith residing in the vicinity had been attendants at either the Middle Ridge or Limestone Ridge, sometimes known as "Sam Fisher's Church," both of which were distant points. Among these were the Maddens, the Barnetts, the McKees, the Neilsons, and others. Just as Limestone Ridge had been abandoned, ten years before, being weakened by the organization of Landisburg and Buffalo, so did the organization of the New Bloomfield church and the subsequent withdrawal of many of the communicants to unite with it and the church at Millerstown, weaken and forecast the end of the old Middle Ridge Church. Rev. John Niblock, who was the pastor of the churches at the mouth of the Juniata, Sherman's Creek and Middle Ridge from 1826 to 1830, lived for a short time in Juniata Township, but chose to reside at the new county seat. Occasionally he conducted services in the courthouse, with the result that early in 1831, other data makes certain, a congregation was organized. While no such record is available, yet an advertisement of Benjamin McIntire, secretary of the trustees, dated April 21, 1831, invited proposals for building a brick church, 43x45, with a height of twenty-two feet, and including a gallery, at Carlisle and High Streets. Rev. Niblock died in August, 1831, at New Bloomfield, and the erection of the church lagged. The three churches over which Rev. Niblock presided were then without a pastor until 1833, when Rev. Matthew B. Patterson was sent by the Presbytery as a supply. David Lupfer had the contract, and early in the summer had completed the excavation and had the walls almost up when a continuous soaking rain, followed by a high wind, toppled them. The resultant delay retarded completion until 1835. It was in use until 1870, when it was succeeded by the present brick church, which was built at a cost of seven thousand dollars.

On October 2, 1833, the church asked Presbytery for recognition, and on November 30, 1833, it was perfected. Bloomfield, Ickesburg and Landisburg was formed into a charge, and Rev. John Dickey called December 23, 1834. He is described as a man of gentleness, but great firmness. Rev. Dickey remained until 1854, when he resigned. He died during the next year. Supplies then served for a time, and in 1857 the Bloomfield church united with those at Petersburg (Duncannon) and Sherman's Creek. Rev. William B. Craig served then from 1857 to 1867, when Bloomfield decided to become a separate charge and called a pastor. The pastors since then have been

1868-70—Rev. P. H. K. McComb.	1894-02—Rev. Frank T. Wheeler.
1870-83—Rev. John Edgar.	1902- —Rev. I. Potter Hays.
1884-92—Rev. Robert F. McClean.	

Since 1885 the Shermansdale (formerly Sherman's Creek Church) church has been served by the New Bloomfield pastors. In 1907 the church was improved by being frescoed and the replacing of the ten windows with memorial windows. At the same time Mr. Ward Rice, of Los Angeles, California, presented to the church a very fine pipe organ, as a memorial to his parents, William and Caroline Milligan Rice.

In connection with the membership of the old Middle Ridge Church, who desired transfer to the New Bloomfield Presbyterian Church, the fact might be noted that the original petition is in the possession of the session of the church here, and with it are several old envelopes addressed to Rev. Matthew B. Patterson, bearing the Mercersburg postmark. The following is a copy:

"We, the undersigned, members of the Middle Ridge church, wishing to join the church about to be organized at Bloomfield, respectfully ask for certificates of dismission for that purpose:

"Absalom Martin, Wm. M. McClure, Ann Martin, Sarah Roth, Mary Hill, James McKee, Jonas Ickes, Mary L. Ickes, Susan A. Ickes, Jeremiah Madden, James Madden, Susannah Madden, Matilda A. Madden, Joseph Duncan, B. McIntire, Sarah Beatty, Mary McKee, Phebe McClure.

"Joseph Johnston, George Barnett, Jane Barnett, Sarah Barnett, Mary Fritz. Eliza Power, G. W. Power, Mary Marshall, James Humes, Molly Humes, Julianna Humes, James McCafferty, Emilia McCafferty, Gowdy Boyd, Mary Scroggs, Mary Harshey, William Neilson, Rebecca Neilson."

From this church there entered the ministry Rev. William A. West, D.D., Rev. S. B. Neilson, Rev. Harris G. Rice, Rev. J. S. Roddy, Rev. Donald McCleur, who went to Siam as a missionary, but was obliged to return on account of his health, and the martyr missionary, John R. Peale.

Methodist Episcopal Church. The first services held by the Methodists in New Bloomfield was on June 18, 1829, in the courthouse, "at early candlelight," by Rev. Tarring. An organization was formed shortly afterwards and John Gotwalt, Adam M. Axe, Noah Hedden, Samuel Hedden and William McCroskey were named as trustees. On October 29, 1830, the trustees purchased a lot from George Barnett, on High Street, and in 1831 erected a church. Unlike many other churches, the Methodist Episcopal Church assigns its pastors through a conference committee, and frequent changes often occur. Accordingly the list of pastors is lengthy, as follows:

Rev. Daniel Hartman.	1867 —Rev. G. W. Izer.
Rev. Lanahan.	1868-70—Rev. George W. Bause.
Rev. Elisha Butler.	1869-70—Rev. William Schreiber.
Rev. David Shover.	1871 —Rev. E. Shoemaker.
Rev. Alexander McClay.	1872-74—Rev. A. W. Decker.
Rev. Parker.	Rev. L. F. Smith.
Rev. James Brady.	1875-76—Rev. George W. Dunlap.
Rev. Geo. A. Stephenson.	Rev. W. H. Bowen.
Rev. Cornelius.	Rev. J. H. S. Clark.
Rev. Enos.	1877-79—Rev. John H. Cleaver.
Dr. Coffin.	1880-82—Rev. James M. Johnston.
Rev. G. W. Elliot.	1883-84—Rev. J. A. McKendless
1848 —Rev. W. A. McKee.	1884-86—Rev. Thomas M. Griffith.
1851-52—Rev. J. W. Haughawout.	1886-89—Rev. R. H. Wharton.
1853 —Rev. David C. Castleman.	1889-93—Rev. R. H. Stine.
1855 —Rev. D. S. Monroe.	1893-95—Rev. J. K. Knisely.
1856 —Rev. Gideon H. Day.	1895-98—Rev. W. H. Stevens.
1857-58—Rev. Cambridge Graham.	1898-01—Rev. H. K. Ash.
Rev. W. H. Keith.	1901-02—Rev. T. S. Stansfield.
1859-60—Rev. J. Y. Rothrock.	1902-04—Rev. J. R. Shipe.
1860 —Rev. J. B. Mann.	1904-06—Rev. Walter G. Steele.
1861-62—Rev. M. S. Mendenhall.	1906-09—Rev. H. C. Burkholder
1862 —Rev M. K. Foster.	1909-13—Rev. E. C. Keboch.
1863-65—Rev. F. B. Riddle.	1913-15—Rev. W. G. McIlnay.
Rev. S. A. Creveling.	1915-19—Rev. H. C. Knox.
1866-67—Rev. Franklin Gerhart.	1919-20—Rev. Roy S. Cuddy.
Rev. J. C. Heagy.	1920- —Rev. L. L. Owens.

On December 4, 1910, a new church was dedicated, its location being a Main and Church Streets, its cost having been over $16,000. It is 50x90 feet in size, and is built of cement blocks. The trustees at the time of its building were: W. C. Lebo, J. A. McCroskey, J. J. Rice, P. S. Dunbar, George Kling, F. D. Parson, James M. Burd and W. H. Cupp. The building committee was Rev. E. C. Keboch, P. S. Dunbar, J. J. Rice and W. C. Lebo.

U. B. Church. The New Bloomfield United Brethren Church is the result of meetings having been held at Jericho schoolhouse, in Centre Township, for many years, by the Shermansdale pastor. The church, a well built brick structure, stands on Barnett Street, having been built in 1896. The building committee was composed of Andrew Clouser, George Kerr, Daniel Garlin, David Sweger, I. G. Brunner, John Owens and Rev. Barnhart. The Shermansdale pastors fill the pulpit. See Carroll Township.

BLAIN BOROUGH.

The borough of Blain nestles in the famous Sherman's Valley, near the western end of the county, the center of a veritable garden spot. It is a neat, well-kept town and the smallest borough in Pennsylvania to own its own water plant and electric street lighting system. Jacob Wentz was largely instrumental in the construction of the first water plant, which was built about 1869 or 1870, and was incorporated in 1877, when the borough water bonds were issued.

By an order of the Perry County court dated November 3, 1877, Blain Borough, the last of the townships and boroughs in the county to be organized, was incorporated. The order of the court gave the boundaries thus:

"Beginning at a post on the lands of James Woods, Esq.; thence by lands of D. Gutshall, James F. McNeal and Samuel Woods, north twenty-seven degrees west, two hundred and twenty-four perches to a post; thence by lands of William Hall and others, south fifty-one and a half degrees west, one hundred and sixty-six perches to a post; thence by lands of W. W. Woods and Isaac Buttorf, south twenty-six and a half degrees east, one hundred and eighty perches to a post; thence by lands of Isaac Buttorf and Isaac Stokes and James Woods, Esq., north sixty-seven degrees east, one hundred and sixty-four perches to a post and place of beginning. The annual borough election shall be held at the public schoolhouse in said borough on the third Tuesday in February, in accordance with and subject to all the provisions of the laws regulating municipal elections, and said borough shall be a separate election and school district: the court further decree and fix the first election for said borough for the election of the officers provided for by law, to be held at the public schoolhouse in said borough on the third Tuesday in February, A. D. 1878, between the hours of 7 o'clock a. m. and 7 p. m. of said day; and designate George H. Martin, Esq., to give notice of said election and the manner thereof; and the court further decree that Wilson Messimer be the judge and Samuel Woods and James B. Moreland be the inspectors of said elections."

Blain had its beginning in the early settlement which grew up about the mill erected by James Blaine in 1778, after whom the town took its name. The final "e" has been dropped, but from what date or why it is impossible to state. County newspaper files use the "e" in the town name in 1856 and during the intervening period from then to 1868. Early in the last century this mill came into the possession of William Douglas, although David Moreland is assessed with it in 1814. Douglas succeeeded in getting a post office located there named Douglas' Mills. This is the mill known as the Stokes' mill to the present generation. Anthony Black, named as an early schoolmaster, purchased the "McNeal" farm and the Stokes mill from David Moreland, successor to Douglas, and had the name

of the post office changed from Douglas' Mill to *Multicaulisville, in honor of the *moros multicaulis,* or Italian mulberry tree in which he was financially interested. According to Hazard's U. S. Register, 1839, there was a widespread speculation in these trees, the prices varying from ten cents to a dollar each. The number of trees changing hands in Pennsylvania alone amounted to over 300,000. The business seems to have been conducted somewhat upon the principle of many of the stock-selling schemes of the present day. Extensive preparations were made for the enterprise and many trees were planted, but in 1841 Mr. Black died. By 1842 most of the trees were dug up. As early as 1839, three years before his death, Hazard's Register exposed the whole business. He had been a merchant and was well-to-do. He called his store the "Multicaulisville Emporium," the sign being distinctly remembered by Wilson Morrison. The location was the Solomon Gutshall place.

Dr. William Hays purchased three acres from Francis Wayne Woods in 1846 and divided it into twelve lots, this being a part of the land warranted by James Blaine in 1765. Solomon Bower I, built a house and blacksmith shop early in the last century, and John Seager and William Sheibley built houses in 1846. When the lots were laid out in 1846, James and Francis Wayne Woods got the name of the post office changed to Blain. The present school building was erected as an Odd Fellows' hall in the early seventies, and was purchased a few years later and remodeled for a schoolhouse. Among the early merchants were Anthony Black, John Stockton, David Wentzell and A. B. Grosh. Mr. Grosh, in 1919, told of remembering when it had but three houses, upon his first visit in 1846, as a boy of six. The Blain hotel was a licensed house until 1884, and at various times after that before the county "went dry" it was licensed. Among the proprietors were John Sheibley, who later became sheriff, and D. M. Rhinesmith, who had previously been sheriff.

In 1852 Arnold Faughs built a tannery which he operated by steam. He sold to James F. McNeal in 1860. It gave employment to many men until September, 1878, when it was destroyed by fire. It was never rebuilt. Harry Hall now owns the farm on which it was located.

The first schoolhouse was on church hill, where the Presbyterian Church is located. Just when it was erected there is no way of knowing, but it was still standing in 1815. William Smiley was one of the early teachers, as was also Miss Gainor Harris, whom he married. As far as can be ascertained she was probably the first female teacher in the county. This building was replaced by a stone schoolhouse, which the older people can yet recall. There was another building near the "German meetinghouse" (the Lutheran and Reformed church) at which Mrs. Gainor Harris Smiley taught while her husband taught on church hill. S. G. Smith, yet living (1920) and now over eighty years of age, attended the stone building and recollects when the enrollment was as high as 116 pupils. The first building was a log one with but three windows, each having three window lights 8x10 inches in size. An act of the Pennsylvania Legislature, dated February 19, 1845, made the church hill schoolhouse the voting place for Jackson Township. See School chapter for facts about the Vocational School's beginning.

Postmasters at Blain have included William Douglas, Anthony Black, Capt. David Moreland, Thomas Seager, J. C. Rickard, Wilson Messimer, A. D. Garber and D. P. Stokes.

The oldest lodge there is Blain Lodge, No. 706, I. O. of O. F., chartered

---

*A. B. Grosh, born in 1846, who died during the past year, remembered seeing this name on a sign there in 1852.

April 25, 1870, with John M. Evril, noble grand, and W. D. Messimer, secretary.

The Blain business men, according to the report of the mercantile appraiser, are as follows, the date being the year of beginning the business:

General stores, J. C. Rickard, Smith & Stine, S. M. Woods, the latter being the former Garber stand—an old one.

D. W. Sheaffer (1898), groceries; S. L. Rickard (1873, saddlery; W. H. Book, flour and feed; Israel Lupfer, coal and feed; M. L. Wentzell, Wentzell & Stambaugh, lumber; W. H. Sheaffer, machinery; Paul Shreffler, meat market; S. I. Bistline, confectionery; Henry & Smith, hardware; H. B. Kell, jewelry; J. A. Snyder, confectionery; S. L. Bistline, cigars; C. R. Hench & Bro., George Stokes, oils; M. L. Smith, millinery; G. D. Flickinger, stoves. Isaac Stokes was in business from 1857 to 1907, when he was succeeded by David P. Stokes.

Dr. G. Milton Bradfield located at Blain in 1865, remaining a decade, and being succeeded by Dr. F. A. Gutshall, a graduate of the University of Pennsylvania, 1866, who had been located previously at New Germantown. Others to locate there were Dr. Chas. E. Gregg, a graduate of the Medico-Chi., '93, and Dr. H. W. Woods, a graduate of the Baltimore University School of Medicine, '98, and of Maryland Medical College, '99. Dr. F. C. Kistler has long been located there.

Zion Lutheran Church.   The Zion Lutheran Church, located in Blain, was erected jointly by the Lutheran and Reformed congregations. It was located on the original Abraham Mitchell tract, which James Adams owned in 1800. January 10, 1801, he deeded two acres for church and burial purposes to Henry Zimmerman, Adam Hubler, Christopher Bower, and Peter Brown, trustees, "for building a German meetinghouse." The price was twenty-five pounds Pennsylvania currency. In the possession of Clark Bower, Member of Assembly from Perry County, and himself a member of the Blain Lutheran Church, is the old agreement for the purchase of the cemetery plot. It follows:

Articles of an agreement made and concluded this 13th day of December, 1800, by and between James Adams, Junior, of Toboyne Township, Cumberland County, and Henry Simmerman, Adam Hoobler, Christopher Bower, and Peter Brown, "trustees for a certain piece of land undermentioned to build a meeting house on."

For two acres of land off the northeast corner of his land, adjoining James Morrison's land; "and said trustees do obligate ourselves to pay twenty-five pound specie upon the first day of January next." Adams "is to give privilege of a road from the Great Road to said land.

One of the witnesses is James Blaine.

Prior to this time Rev. John Herbst had been holding services at the homes of members. In the meantime Reverends Sanno and Osterloh preached here, there being no regular organization. In 1815 came Rev. John William Heim, who organized the Lutheran congregation and remained its pastor until 1849. The first officers were: John Seager, Henry Zimmerman, elders; Abraham Bower, Solomon Bower, John Stambaugh, deacons.

Not until 1816 was an effort made to erect the church. It was dedicated July, 1817, and named Zion Church. The building was of stone, with a high gallery at three sides, its dimensions being 40x50. It seated over six hundred. It had a cupola and bell, and an altar balustrade. The pulpit was a high one reached by a flight of steps, and had a sounding board suspended above. The building cost about five thousand dollars, which in that day was much money to be expended on a rural church, and was considered strictly modern. From the advent of Rev. Heim until its division from the Loysville charge in October, 1858, its pastors were the same as those of

Lebanon Church at Loysville: Rev. Frederick Ruthrauff, 1850-52; Rev. Reuben Weiser, 1853-55; Rev. Philip Willard, 1856-58.

In 1860 a parsonage was erected. In 1859 Rev. John T. Williams became pastor of the Blain charge, which included St. Paul's and the church at Buffalo Mills. He remained until 1865. His successors have been:

1865-67—Rev. W. I. Cutter.	1891-94—Rev. W. H. Dale.
1867-72—Rev. T. K. Secrist.	1894-03—Rev. J. B. Lau.
1872-73—Rev. R. H. Clark.	1903-05—Rev. J. W. Weeter.
1873-81—Rev. J. R. Frazer.	1906-07—Rev. R. T. Vorberg.
1882-83—Rev. M. L. Heisler.	1907-18—Rev. J. C. Reighard.
1883-90—Rev. I. P. Neff.	1919- —Rev. G. Robert Heim.

During the pastorate of Rev. W. D. Rodrick, of the Reformed Church, and of Rev. W. I. Cutter, of the Lutheran Church, in 1866, a large brick church was erected to take the place of the old one, being again built as a joint building for both congregations.

These two congregations—the Lutherans and Reformed—continued to worship in the same building until March, 1898, when the Lutherans purchased the interest of the Reformed people in the building and plot and erected a new church at a cost of $10,000, which was dedicated in March, 1899. A few years later a pipe organ was installed at a further cost of over $1,000.

In 1919 the old stone parsonage, built in 1860, was renovated and partially rebuilt. The firm old stone walls were left standing, only re-. pointed. The whole property was beautified and repaired at a cost of about $4,300. The present pastor, who occupies it, is a great-grandson of the original organizer of the congregation, Rev. John William Heim, who came on horseback and preached while his horse was being fed so that he could leave at once for his next church, having a large charge. The latter statement is made by Solomon Gutshall, born in 1839, who remembers the occurrence.

The shingles for this first Lutheran church at Blain were brought from Horse Valley, over the Conococheague Mountain, near New Germantown, on horseback and on the backs of men, Rev. Heim himself joining in the work. The singing and services were in German, and the collections were taken in a small receptacle attached to a long pole, the pews being deep.

Blain M. E. Church. About 1830, the Methodists of Blain were first organized, David Moreland and William Sheibley being principally interested. The first services were held in homes and schoolhouses. In 1855 a brick church was built on lands purchased of David M. Black, by the congregation. This church belonged to the New Bloomfield Circuit (where the pastors' names will be found) until 1877, when Blain was made a separate charge. The pastors of the Blain charge have been as follows:

1877-79—Rev. M. C. Piper.	1899 —Rev. W. C. Charlton.
1880-81—Rev. J. W. Ely.	1900-03—Rev. John T. Bell.
1882-83—Rev. J. L. Leilich.	1904 —Rev. W. W. Sholl.
1884-85—Rev. Jas. F. Pennington.	1905 —Rev. M. C. Flegal.
1886-87—Rev. W. W. Picken.	1906 —Rev. W. S. Rose.
1888 —Rev. J. Bruner Graham.	1907 —Rev. W. H. Norcross.
1889-90—Rev. J. S. Souser.	1908-13—Rev. G. P. Sarvis.
1891-92—Rev. J. R. Shipe.	1914-16—Rev. Thomas R. Gibson.
1893-95—Rev. J. S. Souser.	1916-17—Rev. G. H. Knox.
1896-98—Rev. L. D. Ott.	1918-22—Rev L. D. Wible.

The new church was erected in 1898, and the old one sold to L. M. Wentzel, who used it as a planing mill until it burned. The Blain Circuit also includes the churches at Fairview, New Germantown and Emory Chapel, in Madison Township.

Zion Reformed Church. The history of Zion Reformed Church, in so far as the original buildings are concerned, is identical with that of Zion Lutheran Church, immediately preceding. During its early days it was known as "Toboyne" or "Toboine" Church. The two congregations jointly built and worshiped in the same church from 1816 to 1898, almost a century. In that year the Lutherans bought the interest of the Reformed congregation, which purchased a lot and erected a fine brick church at a cost of $10,000. Just when the first meetings were held will probably never be known, but Rev. Groh's valuable historical sketch on "The Sherman's Valley Charge," places the date as 1790, and names Rev. Samuel Dubbendorff as the pastor from then to 1795. Other works give the date as 1798 or 1799, and name a Rev. Koutz as pastor, under whom the congregation was organized. Personally the writer believes the former to be authoritative, but, as the congregation was then unorganized, no records were kept. Meetings were held in houses and barns. It was a part of the Sherman's Valley charge until 1858, when, with Buffalo Church, in Saville Township, it became a separate charge. The record of pastors was as follows:

1790-95—Rev. Samuel Dubbendorff.	1868-72—Rev. Samuel E. Herring.
1798-04—Rev. Anthony Koutz.	1872-86—Rev. F. S. Lindaman.
1805-11—Rev. Jonathon Helfenstein.	1887-92—Rev. Silas L. Messinger.
1811-19—Rev. Albert Helfenstein.	1892-95—Rev. S. P. Stauffer.
1819-40—Rev. Jacob Scholl.	1896-02—Rev. T. C Strock.
1842-59—Rev. C. H. Leinbach.	1902-07—Rev. Charles A. Waltman.
1859-61—Rev. J. M. Mickley.	1907-14—Rev. P. H. Hoover.
1862-65—Rev. David E. Klopp.	1914-17—Rev. John W. Keener.
1866-68—Rev. W. D. C. Ridrick.	1917- —Rev. Edw. V. Strasbaugh.

For many years this congregation was the largest numerically of the entire Carlisle Classis of the Reformed Church.

BUFFALO TOWNSHIP.

Buffalo Township, named after the massive animal which once roamed its hills as they later did the plains of the great West, was the sixth township to be formed of territory which now comprises Perry County, being made a township in 1799, the same year that George Washington, the first President of the United States, breathed his last. This comparison is made here to show the fact that the history of the township is almost as old as that of the country itself.

Buffalo was formed from Greenwood and originally included all of Howe and Watts Townships. Upon petition of many inhabitants of Green-. wood Township who resided south of Buffalo Hill, to the Cumberland County courts, in October, 1799, setting forth that "the petitioners were subjected to many and great inconveniences, occasioned by the largeness and irregular shape of the said township of Greenwood, which comprehended all the country between the Juniata and Susquehanna Rivers, as far as twenty miles up each river; that the said tract of country was nearly equally divided by the said Buffalo Hill, which begins at the Juniata, about one mile below Wildcat Run, and continues to the Susquehanna, below the house of David Derickson, and praying the court that that part of said township of Greenwood, contained between the rivers Juniata and Susquehanna and lying south of Buffalo Hill, may be erected into a new township."

The order of the court granted the prayer of the petitioners forthwith and adjudged the same thereafter to be two townships, the division line to be Buffalo Hill, and the new township to be known as Buffalo Township. Its size was diminished by the creation of Watts Township, in 1849, and by that of Oliver Township, in 1837, when the present territory comprising Howe Township was made a part of Oliver.

Buffalo Township as at present constituted is bounded on the north by Greenwood and Liverpool Townships, on the east by the Susquehanna River, on the south by Watts Township, and on the west by a small stretch of the Juniata River and by Howe Township. It is composed of two valleys, Buck's and Hunter's, the former being two miles in width, and the latter being virtually a cove, tapering from considerable breadth at the east to almost a point at the west. The mountain separating the two valleys is known as Berry's Mountain.

The first settlers of that part of the township comprised in Buck's Valley were Reuben Earl, John Law, George Albright, Samuel Rankin and Martin Waln, who took up lands along the Susquehanna River. In the body of the valley were Jacob Buck, Henry Alspach and Nicholas Liddick. These eight settlers took up their lands probably before 1772, as they were surveyed June 1, 1772. The Henry Alspach place is still in the hands of a descendant, Joseph Deckard.

George Albright located on the farm long owned by John Bair, while president of the Peoples' Bank of Newport (now the First National), and now in possession of Harry Shutt. Other early settlers locating in the same vicinity were John Rutherford, who warranted 320 acres in January, 1768, southwest of Albright; John Purviance, to the south; west of this Andrew Berryhill, 165 acres in May, 1774; adjoining Berryhill Joseph Swift had 296 acres warranted at the same time; adjoining this place on the east and next to Berry's Mountain Zachariah Spangler and M. Copp had tracts of 174 acres; adjoining them on the east was George Fetterman's claim, which also adjoined George Albright's place.

George Albright, here spoken of, was a Revolutionary patriot, whose remains lie buried in the valley which he helped grasp from the primeval forest. See the chapter, "Perry County in the Revolutionary War."

John Taylor warranted 208 acres of land in August, 1789, located at a place locally known as "Girty's Notch," along the Susquehanna River at the township's southern boundary. There is a cave there, in the end of the mountain, where it juts out to the edge of the river and where tradition would have Simon Girty, the younger, hide while acting in the capacity of a spy for the Wyandotte Indians. Tradition in this case, however, is most probably only tradition, as the record of Girty in the vicinity of Ohio is well established. The author of this volume has seen fit to delve rather deeply into the career of this renegade, the result appearing earlier in the book, under the title, "Simon Girty, the Renegade."

In October, 1776, Samuel Rankin took up 200 acres of land, which stretched over a mile along the Susquehanna River and included the site of the present village of Montgomery's Ferry, which was a post office for many years until 1919, when it was finally discontinued, the business having practically all been diverted to the rural delivery service. North of the Rankin tract was Martin Waln's thirty acres, which extended to the base of Berry's Mountain, and which was warranted in May, 1772, but passed to Reuben Hains by survey two years later.

The George Barner farm at Mt. Patrick was known as the "Garden Tract," and was early owned by a man named Brubaker. Later it was in possession of Peter Ritner, a brother of Governor Ritner. It was afterwards sold at sheriff's sale to the Lyken's Valley Coal Company, who built a small railroad from the river shore to the canal basin, by which they transferred their coal from river flats to canal boats. George Blattenberger, who later became an associate judge of the county, owned it later for many years, having purchased it in 1841.

A special act of the Pennsylvania Legislature, dated March 7, 1856, provided "that a certain island lying in the Susquehanna River, in Upper

Paxton Township, Dauphin County, and known by the name of Crow's Island, be and the same is hereby declared to be attached to, and thereafter become a part of Perry County." Michael Crow, a well-to-do citizen, was an early citizen in Hunter's Valley, owning a tract of over 300 acres.

When the new county of Perry came into existence, in 1820, the assessment list of the township of Buffalo was as follows, Watts and Howe Townships still being a part of the township:

Michael Horting, 98 acres; Samuel Hominy, 77 acres; Jacob Huggins, 60 acres; Jacob Kumler, 270 acres; John Kline, 78 acres and sawmill; Michael Krouse, 250 acres, sawmill and ferry; John Kinch, 154 acres; Peter Liddick, 200 acres; John Low (weaver), 100 acres; Peter Liddick (weaver) 50 acres; John Lowden (carpenter), 84 acres; William Linton, 106 acres; Samuel Leedy; Jacob Livingston, 100 acres; Daniel Liddick, 148 acres; Christian and Daniel Livingston. 135 acres; John Liddick, 148 acres; William Montgomery, 282 acres, sawmill and ferry; Jacob Liddick, 60 acres; Robert Moody, 153 acres; Daniel McKinzy, 163 acres; ———— McKee, 100 acres; John McGinnes, 100 acres and distillery; Joseph Morris, 50 acres; Susannah Moore, 40 acres; James Person, 100 acres; James Porter, 97 acres; James Reed, 150 acres; Philip Reamer, 200 acres; Jacob Reamer, 70 acres; Philip Reamer, 100 acres; Philip Rodenbaugh, 36 acres; Joseph Steele, 200 acres; Abraham Steele (blacksmith), 10 acres; Paul Still, 200 acres; Henry Stevens, 170 acres; John Stevens, 56 acres; Christian Siders, 124 acres; Margaret Steele 338 acres; Andrew Trimmer, 112 acres; Robert Thompson, 210 acres; Samuel Thompson, 167 acres; Samuel Wright, 200 acres; Andrew Watts, 30 acres and grist mill; Michael Wiland, 80 acres, Henry Yungst, 90 acres; heirs of Jacob Buck, Jr., 100 acres; heirs of Jacob Buck, Sr., 113 acres; John Brady, 300 acres; heirs of Thomas Hulings, 445 acres and ferry; George Thomas, 300 acres; Samuel Albright, 156 acres; John Albright (weaver), 135 acres; Peter Arnold, 100 acres; George Arnold (carpenter), 35 acres; Peter Arnold. Jr., 3 lots and sawmill; Christian Alsdorf, 160 acres; George Albright, 100 acres; Frederick Albright; Robert Baskins' heirs. 60 acres and fulling mill; George Bauder, 85 acres; Jacob Bauder (blacksmith); John Bare, 40 acres; Jacob Bauder (weaver), 14 acres; Samuel Bare's heirs 60 acres; David Brubaker. 187 acres and sawmill; Robert Buchanan, 200 acres; Jacob Baughman, 77 acres; grist and sawmill, distillery and ferry; Henry Bowman, 160 acres; John Bowman, 260 acres; Jacob Bixler, 20 acres; Richard Baird, 100 acres, sawmill and distillery; John Boner (weaver), 80 acres; Thomas Boyd, (weaver), 14 acres; Malcolm Campbell, 200 acres; George Charles, 130 acres; Christian Charles, 140 acres; Jacob Charles, 100 acres; Richard Cochran, 109 acres; Frederick Diehl, 133 acres; Philip Deckard, 100 acres.

The Rankin tract, where Montgomery's Ferry is located, passed to Joseph Clark in December, 1776. His daughter married John Black, of Juniata Township, who subsequently acquired title, and in November, 1827, sold it (then 282 acres) for $4,822, to William Montgomery, whose name the village and community bears, although the ferry has been out of existence for generations. On the Dauphin County side this ferry was known as Morehead's, as the landing was made on lands belonging to a family of that name. Z. T. Shuler has long kept a general store at Montgomery's Ferry.

The first schoolhouse in Buffalo Township was a log one, built for that purpose in 1808, and located on the Richard Baird place, its location being at the forks of the road, near the Richard Callin residence. Mrs. William Kumler, born in 1842 (then Mary Buck), who is still living, remembers when this building still stood and was in use as a schoolhouse, she having attended there, when it was again used for a few terms after Centre schoolhouse burned. She describes it as being weatherboarded, but never plastered. Teachers at this school were George Baird, Benjamin Elliot, Mary McMullen and James Denniston, the latter being the last one. The building was abandoned for school purposes after 1824. In that year (1824) the first Sunday school in Buck's Valley, and the first one in the county east of the Juniata of which there is record, was organized. It was also one of the first few in the county.

In 1824 a log schoolhouse was built near where Buck's Church now stands. It was also used as a church. Teachers at this school were Joseph Foster, Ann McGinnes, Francis Laird, David Mitchell and Samuel Stephens. Another early schoolhouse was at Montgomery's Ferry.

A schoolhouse known as Centre early stood near where the present Centre schoolhouse stands, being built in 1850. It was subsequently moved about a mile east on lands of Jacob Bucke. It was used for school purposes until 1857, when it burned down. The Baird schoolhouse was then used for five or six terms, when another was built at the present site. It in turn was succeeded by the present building in 1879. Two other noted teachers of an early period were John C. McGinnes, Sr., and John Stephens, Sr.

The oldest schoolhouse in Hunter's Valley was erected on lands of Joseph Hunter (later the Abram Crow place). It was a roughly built log house covered with slab roof. It accommodated the children of all the families—probably a dozen—within a radius of two or three miles.

When the question of accepting or rejecting the free school act of 1834 came up at a public meeting on December 6, 1834, forty-six voted to reject it and one voted for it. On November 5, 1835, a meeting to examine teachers was held at Patterson's tavern (then Juniata Falls post office). Four directors, Joseph Foster, George Baird, George Arnold and William Howe, were present. In 1840 the schools were not in session, the funds being used for the erection of schoolbuildings.

It is with considerable pride that it is here recorded that the first free school in Pennsylvania, under the free school act, was opened in Buffalo Township, but it was in the part which is now Watts Township. In the chapter on "The Public Schools," elsewhere in this book, it will be noted that the late Chief Justice Daniel Gantt, of the State of Nebraska, is authority for that statement. He was the teacher and the school was located "at Thompson's Crossroads," near the present farm buildings of Allen R. Thompson.

When the assessment of 1820 was made there were four ferries assessed within the limits of Buffalo Township, which then included Watts and Howe. They were those of Michael Krouse (Crow), William Montgomery, Jacob Baughman and Thomas Hulings. Coming down the river they were, in order, Crow's Ferry, Montgomery's Ferry, New Buffalo and that at the Junction.

According to Claypole's Geology the ridge through central Buck's Valley, extending almost to Montgomery's Ferry, is but an extension of Middle Ridge, of Juniata Township.

A gristmill of the burr type was erected near the Juniata River by James Barkey. It later descended to a mill of the chopping type, and was long owned by Mrs. Jacob Seiders, still being in possession of her heirs.

Buck's Valley was so named for the first settler by that name, Jacob Buck, the head of the clan of that name. Hunters' Valley takes its name from the many persons of that name that resided there. In the early days when Scotch-Irish settled there, with attendant Presbyterianism, there dwelt there at least four James Hunters, who were thus distinguished: One who had a defect in his speech, wherein he repeated the letter "C" frequently, was known as "C Jimmie"; then there was "Oxen Jimmie," "Long Jimmie," and "Short Jimmie."

John Bair, later president of the People's Bank of Newport, when a young man built a hotel at Girty's Notch, where he proposed to entertain raftsmen and lumbermen. He conducted it for eight years.

Just when the Montgomery's Ferry Hotel was built is not known, but the date sometimes given, 1817, is evidently wrong, as it was built by William Montgomery, and he did not purchase the lands, as previously stated in this chapter, until 1827. He built the hotel and conducted it, as well as operated the ferry, but sold the hostelry and a considerable area of land to John A. Hilbish, in 1845. On his death, in 1872, the heirs, John A., Zachary T. and Sarah C., the latter the wife of Prof. William Moyer, of Freeburg, divided the property, the hotel going to the latter. It was kept by various proprietors, some of whose morals had a wide range, until 1913, when Elmer E. Stephens purchased the building, and may it ever be said to his credit, refused to lease it for the sale of liquor, although to do so would have meant considerable financial gain. Mr. Stephens also had previously purchased the other acreage from the other two Hilbish heirs. He and his family have since resided in the old road house and have conducted it as a public house, save that liquor has never been sold.

The village of Mt. Patrick, important in boating days, has dwindled to a mere shadow of its former self. In the old boating days David Deckard had erected a store and warehouse there, about 1848, and which he conducted until about 1910. He always employed a number of clerks, as there the boatmen replenished their needs while their boats were being passed through the canal locks. He dealt largely in grain, which they used in large quantities. From them he got his goods from the city for the trade of the countryside. The mill there, which is fully described in our chapter relating to Old Landmarks, Mills, etc., did a big business from much of the territory east of the Juniata, and there a blacksmith plied his trade with few idle moments. Mr. Deckard had erected there for his residence a fine home, which in 1913 was rented by Samuel F. Seal, who has conducted a road house there since, known as the "Mountain Springs Hotel." Mt. Patrick has had no licensed hotel since 1848.

Dr. Joseph Foster was located in Buffalo Township in 1834, but records fail to tell where and when he began practice, or the time of its termination.

According to the report of the mercantile appraiser the other business places of the township are as follows:

Z. T. Shuler, general store at Montgomery's Ferry, since 1883. Located in the store-stand built by John H. Noviock in 1865, and where he kept until 1873. Mr. Shuler was postmaster there from 1883 to 1920, when the office was discontinued.

H. C. Zaring, near Liverpool, groceries.

J. W. Knuth, Mountain Hall Park, 1910.

Centre Lutheran Church. Rev. D. H. Focht, in his "Churches Between the Mountains," says that "some of the earliest settlers of this beautiful and fertile valley were Lutherans." Prior to 1833 Rev. John W. Heim preached an occasional sermon to those at the eastern end of the valley. In 1833, Rev. C. G. Erlenmeyer took charge of the Liverpool Circuit, and until 1842 preached sometimes at Buck's schoolhouse. In 1842, Rev. Andrew Berg, in connection with Petersburg (Duncannon), Liverpool and other places, preached at Buck's schoolhouse regularly. On June 24, 1843, he confirmed a class of twelve persons there. Six months later he resigned and the membership had no preached word from their own church in many years. They naturally drifted to other denominations. Then Rev. William Weaver, from 1847 to 1851, preached occasionally at different places in the valley. Then, until 1859, they were again left without services, which had on all occasions been held in schoolhouses. Other Lutheran families had located in the western part of the valley, and Rev. D. H. Focht, of the Bloomfield charge, began visiting the valley. On May 7, 1859, Lewis Acker and John Gunderman, on behalf of those interested, met the other church councils at New Bloomfield and asked to be made a part of that charge. On June 5, 1859, Rev. Focht organized the congregation after his sermon in Huggins' schoolhouse, with twenty-one members. The officers elected were John Moretz, elder; Lewis Acker and Jacob Harris, deacons. Services were then held every three weeks at Huggins' schoolhouse, and occasionally at Patterson's (now the Lewis Steckley place). It required an occasional sermon in the German language. The meeting to consider building a church was held at the home of George W. Huggins, March 26, 1860. At that meeting were Lewis Acker, John Bowers, Adam Hetrick, George W. Huggins, Jacob F. Zeigler, Jacob Harris, Philip Peters, John Gunderman, Peter K. Lehr (Lahr) and Wm. H. Mowry. It was decided to locate it near the Buffalo-Howe Township line, and to call it Centre Lutheran Church. It was built on the corner of Mr. Harris' field (now B. B. M. Bair's), adjoining the private road, and the farm of John Potter, during 1860. The trustees were John Moretz, Lewis Acker and Jacob Harris. The contract was let to Philip Peters, for $550. It was dedicated October 21, 1860. The Bloomfield charge having been large, this church was transferred to the Millerstown charge in November, 1861. As that charge at best was a weak one, it later passed to the Newport charge, but, about 1880 to 1885, with the older members passing away, with removals and the more spirited United Brethren meetings close by, regular services were no longer held. A decade later an attempt to revive it was discontinued after a short time.

Centre Union Church. Prior to the building of this church the members of the Evangelical faith held services in Huggins' schoolhouse nearby, later holding them in the church. During almost half a century, however, the United Brethren denomination is the only one that has held services there. Among the Evangelical ministers who served the charge, were Rev. Harris, Rev. Young, Rev. Graham and Rev. S. W. Seibert. The U. B. pastors have been the same as those of the Liverpool church, which may be found in the chapter relating to that borough. The church was built in 1860, the trustees and building committee being John Bretz, John Hain and John Potter, to whom Geo. W. Bretz deeded the ground, for $25. Jacob Bretz was the builder. It is named Centre Union Church in the deed. It was destroyed by a probable incendiary fire on the night of February 21, 1902, and rebuilt in 1913. It was dedicated February 22, 1914. There was a certain something in the outline and construction of this old church which lingers through the years in the memory of those who were boys and girls in the community and attended there. A lady in a far western city, who was one of them, aptly put it thus: "If I could put on paper the picture I carry in my memory, I could give you a perfect reproduction in every detail; even to the wasps' nests, built along under the window frames, and the curly-cue cornice that adorned the deep roof's edge."

The rebuilding of the church, after a period of eleven years had elapsed since it burned, came about largely through the efforts of Mrs. Alice (Hain) Callin, whose people of several generations lie sleeping in that little churchyard, and who with a subscription paper raised practically all the money besides that received for the insurance on the old church, and that raised at its dedication. The trustees at the time of its building were Ruben Seiders, Ed. Deckard and G. B. M. Bair, who were also the building committee.

Buck's Union Church. The inhabitants of Buck's Valley, Buffalo Township, and present Watts Township, worshiped early in a primitive church situated on the top of Half-Falls Mountain, which runs parallel between the two communities. Tradition says it burned down in 1800. The log schoolhouse that once stood at the corner of the graveyard at Buck's Church, was later used by those who resided in Buck's Valley. In it Rev. William Behel, of the United Brethren denomination, held a protracted meeting in 1843. Largely through the results of that meeting was the building of Buck's Church, in 1848, the late Jacob Buck being one of the trustees and a member of the building committee. One result of this revival was the conversion of Isaiah Potter, the most able theologian the community produced, who later was one of the organizers of the Allegheny Conference of the U. B. Church. On January 7, 1848, the lands connected with the church were conveyed to Philip Deckard, Jacob Buck, John Potter and John Bair. The church was rebuilt in 1892, the trustees being J. R. Buck, Wm. Kumler, Josiah Bair and James B. Stephens. William Kumler, James B. Stephens, Isaiah E. Stephens, Lawrence L. Kumler and J. Wesley Bair, are named as incorporators of the cemetery. The Evangelical denomination used it for a time in the earlier years, but for almost half a century it has been used exclusively by the United Brethren, being a part of the Liverpool charge, the names of the pastors appearing under the chapter devoted to Liverpool.

New Jerusalem Church. The chapel of the New Jerusalem Church, near Montgomery's Ferry, was dedicated June 19, 1898. Its building came about through the efforts of Rev. John Edgar Smith, a missionary of that denomination.

Messiah Union Church. Messiah Union Church is located in Hunter's Valley, and was erected in 1865. Among those interested in its erection were Jacob Charles, John W. Charles, G. W. Kepner, Michael Seiler and Abraham Crow. The Lutherans, Evangelicals, Methodists and Reformed peoples held services there at different times. When it was remodeled, in 1883, it was done as a union church of the Lutherans, Evangelicals and Methodists. This was the first church built in the valley, being constructed of stone. Prior to its construction services were held in the schoolhouses. It is in regular use, and is supplied by the pastors from Liverpool. See Liverpool chapter.

CARROLL TOWNSHIP.

Carroll was the eleventh township to be formed, the petition being presented to the courts at the April session of 1834. The petition, signed by one hundred and sixty-eight citizens of the district, follows:

"The petition of divers inhabitants of the townships of Tyrone, Rye and Wheatfield, in the said county, humbly sheweth that your petitioners labor under great inconveniences for want of a new township, to be composed as follows, that is to say: Beginning at Sterrett's Gap; thence through Rye Township, along the great road leading to Clark's Ferry, to a certain field of Henry Souder's; thence to a sawmill belonging to the heirs of Robert Wallace in Wheatfield Township; thence along the great road leading to Bloomfield, until it intersects the division line of the townships of Wheatfield and Centre; thence along the said line to a corner of Centre Township; thence along said line to a point from whence a south course to the Cumberland line at Long's Gap; thence down the Cumberland line to the place of beginning."

Robert Elliott, James Black and John Johnston were appointed as viewers and presented their report to the court which confirmed it on November 5, 1834, naming it Carroll. It was formed in accordance with the report of the viewers and so remained until the creation of Spring Township, when it contributed a share of its territory towards the formation of that township. Carroll Township is bounded on the north by Centre, on the east by Wheatfield and Rye, on the south by Cumberland county, and on the west by Spring Township. Carroll is touched by no railroad, and is drained entirely by Sherman's Creek.

It was in what is now Carroll Township that the old Indian trail crossed Croghan's (now Sterrett's) Gap and wended its way westward along Sherman's Creek, past Gibson's Rock and across the county and Tuscarora Mountain to the West. The Crane's Gap road was a footpath across the

mountains at an early day, and in 1848 it was made into a road. About
a mile west of Crane's Gap was another known as Sharon's Gap, after the
man who originally warranted lands through which it was located. There
was a road there once, but it was abandoned long ago.

Among the pioneers who took up lands was William West, who, April 7,
1755, patented 322 acres, some of it lying in Spring Township, where it is
further described. On the maternal side Chief Justice John Bannister
Gibson was a descendant of the Wests. Among other early warrants for
land were those of Francis West, 79 acres in 1762; George Smiley, 212
acres, February 3, 1755; William Smiley, 241 acres, February 3, 1755, this
tract being bottom land, along Sherman's Creek, upon a part of which
Shermansdale is located; Thomas Smiley, an ensign in the Revolution who
was in New York when the British evacuated it, 424 acres, March 12,
1755, and March 21, 1768, 250 acres lying northeast of Shermansdale, part
of which was later the James Gibney tract; John Downey, 150 acres in
1769, he having previously, in 1766, taken up 400 acres; Robert Bunting,
562 acres in 1768; John Moore, 300 acres in 1794; John White, 110 acres
in 1788, and 100 in 1792; Thomas White, 150 acres in 1788, and 50 acres in
1792; Anne Campbell, 408 acres in two tracts in 1793; William Rogers,
120 acres in 1787; David Lindsay, 300 acres in 1786; James Sharon, 200
acres in 1769, and 150 acres in 1786; Rev. William Thompson, 152 acres in
1768; William Wallace, 369 acres in 1785; and in 1793 the following:
James Louther, 50 acres; Stephen Duncan, 311 acres; William Boyd, 105
acres, on which he later ran a nail factory; Andrew Porter, 300 acres;
John Lawshe, 200 acres; Enoch Lewis, 111 acres; Lewis at one time
owned almost 1,000 acres, and he and John Rinehart owned practically
all that district known as "Sandy Hollow"; Ephraim Blaine, of the famous
Blaine family, 200 acres, and Ralph Sterrett and brother, several tracts.
This is the family of Sterretts whose name was given to Croghan's Gap.
Thomas Sutch, Hugh Ferguson, Obadiah Garwood and Thomas Mehaffie
were other early pioneers who located lands.

On September 6, 1793, William Boyd, a blacksmith, warranted 105 acres
in the eastern part of the township. He was a brother of Rhoda Boyd,
who was an Indian captive for a period of eight years, and who later married Ensign Thomas Smiley. He erected several forges at Boyd's fording
and began the manufacture of nails. His iron was brought over the mountain from Carlisle on horseback. Here he slit it into rods and manufactured handmade nails, for which there was then a great demand. His sons,
Matthew, Goudie and William, were all interested in the business later on,
each working a fire, and so continued until after the creation of the new
county. The black ash—remnant of the charcoal forges—is well remembered by the present generations as showing the site.

George West patented a large tract on March 12, 1793, which passed to
Melchor Miller, whose son David became the father of Stephen Miller,
war-time governor of Minnesota. Another son, Daniel, was the father of
John T. Miller, sheriff of Perry County from 1865-68. On April 14, 1788,
Thomas White warranted 150 acres, and on May 7, 1792, fifty acres. Along
a mountain stream located on these lands the Whites built a sawmill and a
fulling mill about 1802. At the time of the erection of the county, in 1820,
John White, Sr., was assessed with 200 acres; John White, Jr., 200 acres
and a sawmill, and another son, James White, with 280 acres and a fulling
mill. The mill properties were later owned by James S. Sykes. Adam
Nace later owned the sawmill. Prior to 1820 Anthony Kimmel had purchased land on Fishing Creek, being assessed in that year with a grist and
sawmill. He died in 1823, and his son, Peter Kimmel, succeeded him, building also an oil mill, manufacturing linseed oil, in which he used large

quantities of flaxseed. About 1827 Jacob Stouffer purchased five acres of ground along Sherman's Creek, near where Shermansdale is located. and built a grist and sawmill. He sold it to Jacob Billow, from whom it took its name. Others who possessed it at different times were William Welsh, Samuel Rebert, Henry Brown, Jeremiah Smith and others. Jeremiah Smith purchased it in 1881 and rebuilt it. In 1899 he changed it into a roller process mill. A cider mill and sawmill are also operated in connection with the flouring business. This Jacob Stouffer was a practical mill man and before this, in fact, before the erection of the county—as he was then assessed with it—he had erected a gristmill, which later came to be known as the Loucks' mill, a sawmill and a distillery. He was also assessed with 200 acres of land in that year. He sold the mill property to William Ramsey. It later passed to Adam Fisher, John Grier, John Loucks (from whom it took its name),George Albright and others. Fred Albright was the last owner. Loucks' Mill was a post office until the establishment of the Shermansdale office.

Obadiah Garwood, in 1767, owned 125 acres of land, and June 12, 1770, he warranted others. It was probably on these lands that Robert Garwood built the mill with which he was assessed in 1782. T. M. Dromgold built a tannery in Carroll Township, where the Bloomfield road joins the Carlisle-Landisburg road, in 1874, and conducted business there for twenty years. Prior to the institution of rural delivery service there was a post office there for ten years, known as Dromgold, Mr. Dromgold being the postmaster.

The early tavern history is somewhat obscure. George Croghan is credited with having a tavern "about twenty miles west of Harris' Ferry," in various official documents. Tradition has it that he was located at Sterrett's Gap, which is approximately that distance. A man named Buller is also said to have kept there. The father of Dr. J. A. Sheibley, of Shermansdale, also once kept the hotel at the gap. At a very early date a man named Thomas Norton kept a tavern somewhere in the township. He lived in Ohio until the middle of last century, being then almost one hundred years of age. He remembered well the Gibsons, Wests and Smileys of the preceding century.

The Smileys were the largest owners of land in the township in the early days. They were prominent in the civil affairs of the district when it was a part of Cumberland County and have been since it became Perry County. William Smiley, who warranted lands February 3, 1755, was the father of Samuel, Thomas, John, George and William, all of whom took up or purchased lands in the vicinity. The elder Smiley came from Hopewell Township, Cumberland County, and earlier from a location along Swatara Creek.

Probably the first schoolhouse built in the township was Sutch's (Reiber's), located about two miles west of Shermansdale, its erection dating prior to 1780. Thomas Sutch had located this land about 1775. It was of logs and was also used as a place of worship. It was in use when the county was formed, and after being remodeled was in use until 1850, and stood until 1857. Wolf's school succeeded it. Another early school was known as Smiley's, and was built of logs. Its location was just across the road from the location where Wilson Smiley later built his blacksmith shop and foundry, being near Sherman's Creek and upon lands warranted by the Smileys. It had the usual clap-board roof of the pioneer schoolhouse, and on the sides of the building a log was omitted, making windows unnecessary. Greased paper was used to cover these openings, thus admitting the light. Back of the teacher's desk was a window frame with places for six eight-by-ten panes of glass, but greased paper was also used there. The seats were of slabs.

There was a school known as Shortess' school, on the banks of Fishing Creek, another known as Kimmel's, farther down the valley. Prior to the acceptance of the common school act of 1834 Samuel McCord had a select school in his spring house, the milk crocks standing along one side and the spring in a corner being covered over with a board platform, to keep the pupils from falling in. Carroll Township accepted the provisions of the act of 1834 in 1836, and reports show that $58.23 was received from the state. The schools were kept open two months and the salary was $11.00 per month. The following year the term was increased to five months. In 1843, by a vote, the free school system was set aside and only two schools were open, but the following year this action was gladly rescinded. Among the early teachers in Carroll Township were Matthew Adams, David G. Reed, James McCafferty, Hugh Porter, Henry T. Wilson and George R. Wolf.

When Hodgden Henderson married Nancy White, of Fishing Creek Valley, during the earlier period, they had a wedding party and went into the woods and built their home—a log house—in one day. The location is now the farm of John Steineberger, Jr. Many Perry Countians and former Perry Countians are descendants of this couple.

The early name for the gap through the mountain on the Carlisle road was Croghan's, after George Croghan, the trader. Later the property was warranted by the Sterretts, and their home was upon the mountain's crest, as a letter from Thomas Craighead, Jr., of White Hill, dated December 16, 1845, and printed in Rupp's History, will prove. It tells of having in his possession a copy of the Westminster Confession of Faith, which had descended to the fifth generation. "It properly belongs to my better-half," he says, "who, though of the 'blue-stocking order' is of *high* birth." He further adds that his wife was Mary Sterrett, who was born on the heights of the Blue Mountain, at Sterrett's Gap. When the Indian school was first established at Carlisle, the late Captain Pratt had an encampment of over 150 Indians on the mountain's crest, near the gap.

The mercantile appraiser's report shows the following business firms in Carroll Township. Figures following show date of entry into the business:

General stores, George T. Adams, A. R. Dromgold, H. L. Jones, George K. Shearer, Jacob Weldon.

O. F. Stouffer, hotel; J. N. Crum, groceries; J. C. Smith (1910), grain and feed.

In 1851 Dr. John W. Crooks located at Shermansdale and practiced several years. Then came Dr. Longsdorf, who succeeded him and who remained until 1856. In 1857 Dr. A. E. Linn located there and practiced for several years, coming from Loysville. After Dr. Linn left came Dr. Fuget, then Dr. Agnew. In 1879, the year of his graduation from the University of New York, Dr. James P. Sheeder located there, practicing for a number of years. Dr. J. A. Sheibley, University of Pennsylvania, '91, has been located there since that time. About the middle of the last century Dr. A. J. Herman, later of Carlisle, practiced on the Perry County side of Sterrett's Gap.

Shermansdale. The village of Shermansdale is located on lands warranted by William Smiley, February 3, 1755, and was originally known as "Smileytown." The post office known as Sterrett's Gap was removed to this location about 1850, and as there was already a post office named Smileytown, the name was changed to Shermansdale. Prior to that time the settlers in the community had received their mail at Loucks' Mill (later known as Albright's mill), located farther down the creek, being carried from Carlisle, a

The River Brethren were organized in Carroll and other townships about 1859, but built no churches, conducting worship in the homes of the membership.

A church once stood opposite the Jeremiah Smith mill dam, on an elevation about fifteen feet above the level of the dam, and about five hundred feet to the rear of its breast. It was known as the Methodist Protestant Church. It was built of logs, in 1838, on lands donated for that purpose by George Smiley, to Lawrence Hipple, John Kennedy, Thomas J. Stevens, William Murray and William McClintock. The building stood until 1868, although no services were held long prior to that. In that year it was sold to William A. Smiley, who dismantled it, selling the hard yellow pine pews to residents for use as benches. Rev. James W. Smiley preached there at times. Among the regular pastors were Reverends Jordan, Holmes, Wright, Swengler, Hamilton, Thompson and White, according to the Evarts-Peck History of the Susquehanna and Juniata Valleys.

Mt. Zion Union Church. As early as 1763. located immediately north of the Kittatinny Mountains, in the southeastern part of Carroll Township, were a number of families, some of which crossed the mountains to worship at Carlisle, traveling the rugged Indian trail. Among these families were the Foulks, Ensmingers, Reibers, Kimmels, Sloops, Fenicles, Hinkels and Billows. And from Carlisle occasionally came ministers, who preached in the various homes, until the Loysville Lutheran charge was organized, after which the minister of that congregation preached in this territory once every four weeks. On August 14, 1816, the Union Church in Carroll Township, was dedicated. It was of hewed logs and 35x40 feet in size. Its capacity was almost doubled, however, by a gallery around three sides. It had a highly elevated pulpit at the fourth side. The galleries were removed in 1854, and in 1878 it was rededicated, after improvements, as a Union (Reformed and Lutheran) Church. The organization of St. David's Church, in 1846, and of Mt. Pisgah, in 1839, drew largely upon the membership and the territory of this church. About 1870 regular services ceased to be held. The Reformed pastors were: Rev. Helfenstein, until 1847; Rev. Daniel Gans, 1849, and Rev. Samuel Kuhn, 1851-63. In 1863 this congregation united with St. David's, at Dellville. The Lutheran pastors were:

1780-88—Rev. John G. Butler.	1850-53—Rev. John P. Heister.
1788-96—Rev. Timothy Kuhl.	1854-58- -Rev. George A. Nixdorf.
1796-01—Rev. John Herbst.	1858-62—Rev. Wm. H. Diven.
1802-09—Rev. Frederick Sanno.	Rev. Kinsel, 6 months.
1809-15—Rev. F. Osterloh.	1863-64—Rev. Samuel Aughey.
1816-27—Rev. Benjamin Keller.	1865-66—Rev. M. L. Kuller.
1828—Rev. L. H. Meyer.	1867-70—Rev. J. E. Honeycutt.
1829-49—Rev. John W. Heim.	

Mount Pisgah Lutheran Church. The Mount Pisgah Lutheran Church was erected on the site of Sutch's schoolhouse, in Carroll Township, which was built some time between 1775 and 1780, and in which the early residents of that community first worshiped. It was located on the southeast side of Sherman's Creek, not far from what was known as Billow's mill. As the regular services of the other Lutheran churches in Sherman's Valley were in German, the residents of this community (who spoke English) attended the English church at Carlisle. Rev. John Ulrich, the Carlisle pastor, then organized the Mount Pisgah congregation, and names, in a letter, Richard Adams, Joseph Egolf and John Henderson as the most prominent and active members of that period. They were the first trustees, to whom the ground was deeded. Of Mr. Adams he said: "Richard Adams was a true Israelite—one of the excellent of the earth. He was loved and respected by all who knew him. No man in that section of the country had more influence as a Christian than he. In those days all looked up to him for counsel in spiritual matters. Others were indeed active, but they had not the influence he had, as he was the oldest of the English-speaking members of our church in the whole valley." Rev. Ulrich began preaching there once every four weeks, on Friday evenings and Saturday mornings, in 1838. The congregation was organized in 1839 with Richard Adams and John Henderson as elders, and Joseph Egolf and John Losh as deacons. Abraham Jacobs deeded the lands, on February 12, 1842, and on September 26. 1842, the church was dedicated. The pastors have been:

1838-42—Rev. John Ulrich.	1854-58—Rev. George A. Nixdorff.
1843 —Rev. Jacob **Kempfer.**	1858-62—Rev. Wm. H. Diven.
1844-45—Rev. Levi T. Williams.	1863 —Rev. Kinsel.
1845-49—Rev. Lloyd Knight.	1863-64—Rev. Samuel Aughey.
1849-50—Rev. Jacob Martin.	1865-66—Rev. M. L. Culler.
1850-53—Rev. John P. Heister.	1867-70—Rev. J. E. Honeycutt.

From that time on the church was without a pastor, and as a natural result the organization disintegrated, and the church has only been in occasional use. At the same location is one of the oldest burial grounds in the county, where sleep many of the pioneers.

Mt. Gilead Methodist Church. Before the congregation became an organization in 1838, the Methodists had held meetings for years at the home of Henry Lackey. They then began holding their services in Lackey's schoolhouse, which was built near-by. Until 1870 they continued to meet in the various schoolhouses. In that year they built a church and named it Mt. Gilead. The list of earlier pastors follows:

1836 —Rev. Geo. Bergstresser.	1859-60—Rev. J. Y. Rothrock.
1848 —Rev. W. A. McKee.	1861-62—Rev. H. S. Mendenhall.
1851-52—Rev. J. W. Houghawout.	1863-65—Rev. F. B. Riddle.
1853 —Rev. D. Casselman.	1866-67—Rev. Franklin Gerhart.
1854-55—Rev. Plummer Waters.	1868-70—Rev. Geo. W. Bouse.
1856 —Rev. Gideon H. Day.	1871-72—Rev. E. Shoemaker.
1857-58—Rev. Cambridge Graham.	

From 1871 the pastors were the same as those at New Bloomfield, to which charge it was attached.

Shermansdale U. B. Church. The earliest services by the people of the United Brethren faith in Carroll Township, were held at the home of Henry Young, by Rev. John Schneider (Snyder). In 1835, the first organization was made by Rev. Peter Harman, many being added by a revival in 1840. Work upon the first church was begun in 1841, and in June, 1842, it was occupied; its dedication, however, having been postponed until October 2, 1842. It was known as Young's Church. Then, in 1863, another location—Shermansdale—was deemed a fertile field, and services were started in the schoolhouse there, until 1878, when, during the ministry of Rev. G. W. Kiracofe, a church was built near the village, with a parsonage on the same lot. Until 1845 these people were served by Carlisle pastors, but at that time it was made a charge. A list of the ministers follows, in part:

Rev. John Schneider (until 1834 1831).	— Rev. Peter Hoffman.
	Rev. Ezekiel Boring.
Rev. Wm. Sholty (until 1831). 1835	—Rev. Jacob Ritter.
1832 —Rev. Jacob Schneider.	Rev. Jacob Shoop.
Rev. Andrew Ringer.	1836 —Rev. Jacob Ritter.
1833 —Rev. Jacob Schneider.	1837 —Rev. Frederick Gilbert, English pastor,
Rev. Francis Wilson.	

Rev. Daniel Funkhouser, German pastor.
1838 —Rev. Frederick Gilbert.
Rev. John G. Schneider.
1839-40—Rev. John Hirsh.

Rev. Enoch Hoffman.
1841 —Rev. Wm. Waggoner.
Rev. Jacob Sholes.
1842 —Rev. Alexander Owen.
Rev. Jacob Sholes.

From then on there appears to have been but one pastor, the ministry in two languages having drifted into English altogether. Prior to that one pastor spoke German, and one English.

1843 —Rev. Wm. Waggoner.
1844 —Rev. Simon Dressback.
1845 —Rev. James Bishop.
1846 —Rev. John Dickson.
1847 —Rev. Geo. W. Showman.
1848 —Rev. Geo. Schneider.
1849 —Rev. B Waggoner.
1850 —Rev. Augustus Bickley (Succeeded by Rev. J. F. Seiler).
1851-52—Rev. Wm Raber.
1853 —Rev. D. A. Tawney.
1854-55—Rev. Alex. Tripner.
1856-57—Rev. Wm. Humberger.
1858 —Rev. Isaac Coombs.
1859 —Rev. Hiram Fetterhoff.
1860 —Rev. James Bratton.
1861 —Rev. Jacob Wentz.
Rev. Hiram Schlichter.
1862 —Rev. Jacob Wentz.
1863-65—Rev. Henry Brown.
1866-67—Rev. Jacob Clem.

1868-69—Rev. Geo. W. Lightner.
1870-72—Rev. W. J. Beamer.
1873-74—Rev. D. R. Burkholder.
1875-76—Rev. John Garman.
1877-78—Rev. J. B. Jones.
1879-80—Rev. G. W. Kiracofe.
1881-83—Rev. A. R. Ayers.
1884-85—Rev. S. N. Moyer.
1886-87—Rev. Wm. Hesse.
1888-90—Rev. Wm. Quigley.
1891-93—Rev. J. W. Houseman.
1895 —Rev. J. D. Killain.
(Resigned, October.)
1895-97—Rev. D. Barnhart.
1898-01—Rev. T. Wagner.
1902-05—Rev. A. L. House.
1906-07—Rev. N. A. Kiracofe.
1908-15—Rev. Harry Boyer.
1916-18—Rev. R. R. Zeigler.
1919-20—Rev. Geo. A. Hiess.
1921 —Rev. H. P. Baker.

Sandy Hollow Church of God. About 1830 to 1833 residents of this faith residing in Carrol Township met at the house of John Soule, in Sandy Hollow, where they organized. For many years services were held in his home, but in 1850 a church was built on land donated by him. It was replaced by another church in 1878. Mr. Soule had two sons, Henry L. and Jacob B., and both entered the ministry. The church was not regularly organized until after 1840, in which year a revival was held. At its organization John Soule and George Kintner were chosen elders, and Peter Kintner, deacon. Rev. M. F. Snavely was then the pastor. The pastors of this congregation have been the same as those of the church at Landisburg, in which chapter they appear.

CENTRE TOWNSHIP.

Centre was the tenth township to be formed from the lands which embrace Perry County, Saville, Juniata, Wheatfield and Tyrone each contributing a share of the territory of the new township. It was at the November sessions of the Perry County courts, in 1830, that a petition asking the creation of a new township and signed by about ninety residents of the sections named above was presented. Robert Elliot, James Black and William Wilson were appointed viewers, and at the April sessions their report was presented, as follows:

"After being severally sworn and affirmed according to law, we proceeded to the discharge of the duties assigned us by the annexed order. That we did view the townships out of which the proposed new township is to be erected. That we made inquiry into the propriety of granting the prayers of the petitioners. That we have made a plot or draft of the several townships out of which the proposed new township is to be erected. That we are of opinion that a new township is necessary for the convenience of the inhabitants and that the prayer of the petitioners ought to be granted; that we have designated in the same plot or draft the boundaries of the new township prepared to be

60

erected by natural boundaries and courses and distances, all of which will fully appear by the annexed plot or draft."

The report has the signature of William Irvine, who was appointed in place of James Black (who was a member of the legislature and ineligible to serve), Robert Elliott and William Wilson. On August 4, 1831, the report was confirmed by the court and the township was named Centre, owing to its central location. Since its erection it has been reduced by contributing parts of Oliver, Miller, Carroll and Spring Townships. It is bounded on the north by Saville and Juniata, on the east by Oliver and Miller, on the south by Wheatfield, Carroll and Spring, and on the west by Spring and Saville. When the township was formed it had 361 taxables. New Bloomfield, the county seat, is located almost in the center of the township.

Among the first settlers, and probably the first, was William Stewart, who came from Newry, Ireland, in October, 1752, with his parents, Archibald and Margaret Stewart, and his brother John. The family came to Cumberland (now Perry) County and stopped in September, 1753, at Duncan's Island, where some pioneers had already located. Learning of some lands on Little Juniata Creek they found a bark cabin of a trader who dispensed "fire water" to the Indians in exchange for furs. Archibald Stewart became the owner by purchase. The passing of the father and mother is unrecorded, also anything further of the brother, John. They were driven off by the Indians, but returned, as there is evidence that William Stewart was active in the location and clearing of lands. In litigation early in the last century one tract is described as the "Bark Tavern" tract and contained 348 acres. While he had settled here a year before the Albany purchase, which location adjoined these lands, he did not warrant the claim until 1765. The original claim, when surveyed in 1769, contained 105 acres, instead of 150, as he had supposed.

The lands are described as "beginning at the mouth of Stewart's Branch of Little Juniata Creek, then northerly, to a gap in the Mahonoi Mountain, and not to cross said mountain, which line was agreed to by John Mitchell, who assisted Stewart in building a house on said tract some time in the fall of 1753." Stewart moved in with his family the next spring, cleared ground and raised a crop that season.

It is not known when the old "Bark Tavern" was built, but prior to 1820 Jacob Fritz was the innkeeper. On the formation of the county in that year he was appointed the first register and recorder of Perry County. Its successor, the new "Bark Tavern," was built in 1830, opposite the Andrew Comp stone house, on the Duncannon road. The Fritz property was advertised for sale by Israel and Richard Fritz, February 16, 1832, and then embraced 350 acres of land.

Naming of properties, according to the old English custom, was then in vogue. In 1755 James Dixson warranted fifty-five acres which later became the Neilson lands. The stone house on this property was built in 1767. In 1788 he warranted 220 acres, fifty-five acres which he named "Dixson's Park," and 220 acres shown on the title as "St. James." The Neilsons came into possession of most of these lands. William Neilson came from Chester County and kept a tavern a few years at Sterrett's Gap. He warranted 250 acres in 1786, and 241 acres in 1793. William Power warranted 225 acres in 1763, and two tracts of 597 acres in 1775. He was a saddler and also warranted other lands and purchased many. He was at one time the largest landowner in the county.

An early resident of the county was Thomas Barnett, who emigrated from Germany before 1767, in which year he was a resident of Rye Township, Cumberland (now Perry) County, and assessed with fifty acres of land, which was within the confines of what is now Penn Township, and in the part then known as Barnett's Cove, but since termed Allen's Cove, The Cove, etc. Until 1785 he warranted no lands, but then he warranted 400 acres in the Cove section (evidently under the right of George Allen), and in the same year 418 acres at and adjoining the present county seat, bordering the lands of William Long and Alexander Stewart. The right to the latter tract he purchased of David Mitchell, who had erected a house there. The stone house on this property was built in 1795. He had it patented in 1796 and named it "Bloomfield." Shortly after the purchase a sawmill and a gristmill were erected. Thomas Barnett died in 1814, leaving two sons, George and Frederick, the latter settling at The Cove, in Penn Township, where his descendants resided until recently. The other son, George Barnett, purchased the "Bloomfield" tract and married Jane Smiley, from whom descended three sons, Frederick, George and Charles A. The latter was president judge of the Perry-Juniata district from 1881 to 1891, and his son, James M. Barnett, was elected to the same position in the fall of 1919, and assumed the office on January 1, 1920, on the one hundredth anniversary of the county's formation. Of the descendants of George, two have entered the professions, George R. Barnett being an attorney with offices in New Bloomfield and Harrisburg, and Dr. Robert T. Barnett, practicing at Lewistown, Pa.

Matthew McBride warranted lands about 1780 and purchased others of Rev. Hugh Magill. He had a blacksmith shop, a distillery and a tilt hammer, manufacturing sickels. Rev. Hugh Magill warranted lands in 1758 and 1762. Matthew McBride, in 1774, took up two tracts. The tract adjoining the western border of New Bloomfield was warranted by James Cowen, on February 4, 1755, just one day after the opening of the land to settlers. In 1794 he warranted 294 acres. In 1762 John Darlington warranted 345 acres. In 1766 tracts of 107 and 193 acres were warranted to James McConaghy, but surveyed to William Power, Jr.

John and Margaret Clouser had settled and made improvements upon a tract but failed to patent it until after his death, when, in 1794, Margaret, the widow, took out the warrant in favor of his heirs. The Oliver Rice farm was warranted by Francis McCown, who was for years a justice of the peace. It was later owned by Finlaw McCown. Joseph Whelan warranted the 247-acre farm lying east, which later passed to the hands of Congressman Joseph Bailey, and was owned recently by Charles L. Johnson. The lands later owned by Andrew Comp, Wesley Soule and others was warranted in 1793 to Robert McClay. The warrant called for 436 acres. Other warrants were: John Parks, 50 acres in 1767; Adam Slack, 265 acres in 1784; Enoch Lewis, 110 acres in 1788; Joseph and Michael Marshall, 263 in 1769; Edward Irvin, 130 acres in 1773; John Moore, 284 acres in 1793, and Robert Hamilton, 330 acres in 1767.

The first gristmill was built upon the Barnett tract very early, being demolished in 1841. It stood a short distance west of the site of the present mill, where a mill was built in 1838, but destroyed by fire, March 30. 1840. It was rebuilt in 1841 and still stands.

There is record of a sawmill being located above the gristmill's present location as early as 1795. There was a mill known as the Lupfer mill, which was purchased by George Barnett and dismantled, the lumber being used in the erection of the Barnett barn in 1820.

Matthew McBride, a son of the first Matthew, who had located the land, sold a plot of twelve acres, in 1831, to Matthew Shuman, who erected a stone gristmill, later known as Clark's mill. The mill passed to Joseph Kline in 1833, to George Loy in 1836, and to Edwin and David Clark in 1839, from whom it took its name. The Clarks were in possession of the plant until 1884, when it passed to Leonard & Baker. William Shoaff owned it later, and sold it to Silas Baker, each of whom operated it. In 1916 it was purchased by William Zeigler, a Schwenksville merchant, who converted it into a cold storage plant.

About 1835 James McKee built a sawmill farther down the stream, and the ruins of another still farther down are remembered by old residents. These mills were built on a stream which flows into Little Buffalo Creek. In 1808 David Watts, of Carlisle, became part owner of a tract warranted to James McConaghy in 1766, and surveyed to William Power, Jr., and with others erected Juniata furnace. William Shoaff was later in possession, and the property is now owned by Ellis Shoaff. This mill was built by John McKeehan and James McGowan, about 1840. It has long been out of use as a gristmill.

Less than two miles east of Bloomfield there flows a number of streams which join and form Trout Run—one of many streams of that same name in Perry County. Upon that stream, in 1833, Absalom Martin erected a woolen, carding and fulling mill. In 1836 he sold to Jacob Billow, who operated it until 1838, when he sold to John Witherow and Thomas Patterson. Mr. Witherow rebuilt the mill on a larger scale and added a sawmill and cider press. The fulling mill was operated for many years. Farther down the stream Ralph Smiley had purchased forty acres of land from William Gardner, in 1823, and erected a gristmill. It was destroyed by fire, Sunday, March 21, 1830, with 1,500 bushels of wheat, 600 bushels of rye and corn, and about eighty barrels of flour. The mill had then been in operation less than two years. It was an old stone mill and was rebuilt by Daniel Gallatin, who purchased the property in 1833. As early as 1849 Atkinson, John and William Bergstresser milled there, selling to Samuel Comp, who in turn sold to Samuel Fravel. These two mills were in operation until 1890 to 1900, but the old race and dam alone remain at the former, and a crumbling stone wall alone remains of the latter. The Fravel mill burned down and the property is now owned by Phares D. Royer.

In 1891, D. P. Clark and J. M. Gilliland, trading as Clark & Gilliland, erected a steam mill a half mile west of New Bloomfield, and operated it until 1898, when it was sold to C. N. Reeder. During the same year it burned to the ground, but was rebuilt by Mr. Reeder. Later it went out of business and was dismantled and torn down.

Mannsville is a village situated at the northern boundary of the township, near the Saville Township line. It was first known by the name of Phœnixville. Daniel Swartz owned all the land in the vicinity, and in 1850 sold a small tract to Adam Doren, who erected and operated a tannery there for many years. He later sold it to John Bower, who continued the business until his death in 1870, when it ceased operation. William Burd opened the first store, and shortly after a post office was located there and named Mannsville.

On the Barnett farm, at New Bloomfield, the first schoolhouse of which there is any record, was located. It was south of the mill race and was built of logs. The site was in use until 1838. There is a tradition that the pupils were required to stand on a near-by rock as punishment. Among the early teachers were Messrs. Elliot, Ferguson and Robert Kelly. From 1832 to 1840 there was a building on the old McBride farm. Laurel Grove, a short distance away, replaced it. John, James and Joshua Triplett were teachers. George Barnett (a son of Thomas Barnett), on whose lands this building was located, not only erected the building but hired the teacher, paying therefor from his own private funds and allowing all the children of the community to attend. While it was the first free school in Perry

County, it still had a greater distinction, as it was the first public free school in the State of Pennsylvania, west of the Susquehanna River.

The lands long owned by Wesley Soule, Andrew Comp and others was warranted by Robert McClay, in March, 1793, the Soule tract being noted as the location of the "box huckleberry," one of the most rare species to be found in the United States. See "Features of Distinction," page 31.

Centre Township was the early location of both Juniata and Perry furnaces, their history appearing under the chapter devoted to "Old Landmarks, Mills and Industries." It was also the location of Ferguson post office, at the McKeehan place, in later years. Annie L. McKeehan, and later Ada C. McKeehan, were the postmistresses.

The business places in Centre Township, according to the report of the mercantile appraiser, are as follows, the year being the date of entering the business:

George R. Lightner (1919), established by Lightner Bros. (1913), Cornelius Clouser (1914), general stores; J. F. Rudy, groceries; George Eckerd, meat market; Myers Bros., cigars; Chas. S. Bruner, fertilizers; Tyson Reeder, wall paper; J. Arden Rice, George B. Coller, oils; Jacob S. Kitner, grocery.

There was once a United Brethren Church at Mannsville, which belonged to the Eshcol Circuit, long since out of existence. The church was sold on August 15, 1911, to the Maccabee Lodge, located in that village.

Mansville Lutheran Church. The residents of Mannsville and vicinity first attended church at Loysville and New Bloomfield, later at Eshcol, Markelville, and "Little Germany." The first services were held in the old log schoolhouse in 1856, in both German and English. During the same year this congregation was admitted as part of the New Bloomfield charge, to which it still belongs. The church was built in 1864, on lands of Daniel Swartz, donated for that purpose. The trustees at that time were Daniel Swartz, George Swartz and John Lepperd. The pastors have been the same as those at the New Bloomfield church and will be found in that chapter.

DUNCANNON BOROUGH.

Duncannon Borough is located on the western bank of the Susquehanna River, at the very farthest point westward of that noted river in its long course, for while it flows in a southwesterly direction that far, at the very heart of Duncannon its trend starts southeastward. Duncannon is a long town, extending all the way from the point where the Juniata's waters join those of the Susquehanna to Juniata Creek, which flows into the Susquehanna not many rods above where Sherman's Creek empties into the river. It is within the limits of Penn Township, to which it belonged until 1844, when it became the Borough of Petersburg. It was a part of Rye Township from 1766 until 1826, when Wheatfield was formed, which included it. When Penn Township was formed in 1840, it was a part of Penn until it became a borough. In 1865 the name was changed to Duncannon, it being incorporated as a borough under that name.

Here the Susquehanna's break through the mountains creates as marvelous mountain scenery as can be seen anywhere in the state. Southwest of the town is Duncannon Hill, a veritable mountain, yet cleared and once tilled, its grassy slopes being used for grazing to this day. The view from this hill includes the junction of the two rivers, the hundreds of acres of cultivated homelands, the water gaps both here and above Marysville, where the Susquehanna breaks through, the famous and historic Duncan's and Haldeman's Islands nestled in the rivers above, and the broad valley of the Susquehanna stretching away among the mountains.

The present town of Duncannon was long known as Petersburg (being incorporated as Petersburg Borough in 1844), and the adjoining village of

Lower Duncannon, lying between Juniata and Sherman's Creek, was known as Duncannon. Petersburg only extended to Ann Street, Dr. Ebert owning the field lying north of that. The original borough only extended from Juniata Creek to an alley, where the present electric light plant is located, but in 1900 it was extended to include the western end, which had been known as Baskinsville, and the Carver's Hill section, both of which bear the name of pioneers.

While these two outlying sections were made a part of the borough there are yet several outlying settlements which contain considerable population. These are Lower Duncannon, the settlement south of Sherman's Creek known as Boston, and another at some distance known as Stewartsville, named after William J. Stewart, a son of Richard Stewart, one of the first merchants of the town. The name Duncannon was derived by contracting the names of Duncan & Morgan, which firm operated the iron works. The changing of the name of the borough from Petersburg to Duncannon was done to avoid confusion in the mails and in other shipments, as there were towns and post offices named Petersburg in Somerset, Huntingdon and Adams Counties, the latter county having had two places known by that name.

The tract of land on which the original Borough of Duncannon was located was warranted by John Brown, on June 3, 1762, and contained 267 acres of land. It was purchased in 1777 by Robert McHassy, who died a few years afterwards, and his administrator, Samuel Goudy, gained possession. Marshall Stanly, assignee of John Brown, obtained judgment against Goudy, as administrator of McHassy, and the property was sold by the high sheriff of Cumberland County, to Samuel Postlethwaite. He sold it to Robert Armstrong in 1786, and in 1792 Armstrong sold a part to Christian Miller, who at once laid out lots and named it Petersburg. There was a driveway along the river shown on the plot as Water Street, now largely occupied by the Pennsylvania Railroad tracks. Lot No. 2 was purchased by James Beatty, on February 20, 1793, and is at this time in the possession of Frank Harper, who has resided there and used it as a business place for over thirty years. It is located on the plot and described as "the corner of Water and Cumberland Streets, extending back to Market," and lies to the left going from the new Pennsylvania Railroad station.

On December 20, 1792, Alexander McLaughlin purchased the lot owned in recent generations by Joseph Mayall, at the southeast corner of Market and Ann Streets. In 1823 Robert Stewart purchased it and conducted there for many years a general store. In 1795 the lot owners were Robert Armstrong, Christian Miller, Dr. McNaughton, William Beatty, James Beatty, Levi Owen, Isaac Jones, James Mehaffy, James Brown, Peter Kipp, Samuel Harvies, Philip Swisher, George Glass, John Elliot, Robert Wallace, Thomas Eccles, Thomas Tweedy and Alfred Snider.

Christian Miller, who laid out the town, died before 1820, when the county was created, and his wife and children moved to New Berlin, Union County. In that year the property holders were: Daniel Baker, a shoemaker; Robert Clark, David Carnes, heirs of Maximilian Haines; George Jones, a blacksmith; William Irwin, a merchant; James Kirkpatrick, John Leedy, heirs of Christian Miller; Nathan VanFossen and Samuel McKenzie, blacksmith. In addition to the above, in 1828, lots were owned by Samuel Alexander, Robert Bonner, heirs of Alexander Bonner; William Hunter, John Ashbel. Lewis Gryan, a hatter; David McCoy, Richard Stewart, a merchant; Philip Swisher, John Steel and Nathan VanFossen, the latter having several lots and a tanyard.

According to tradition, in 1830 there were only eight houses from the

successor would then have been the one which was in use until 1840. The next schoolhouse was erected upon the site of the present building and was in use until 1873, when it was moved to Ann Street and was remodeled for residential purposes. In that year the present building was erected. In 1857 Petersburg had three schools, two being designated as "high schools." The teachers were Lewis B. Kerr, with 32 pupils; Lydia A. Fenstymaker, 20, and Henry Hall, 25.

During the "early seventies" the Susquehanna Building and Loan Association was in existence at Duncannon. The late John Wister, president of the Duncannon Iron Company, was also its president. The section known as Baskinsville was laid out in 1869, by Dr. Joseph Swartz, John Shively and Wm. C. King. Geo. Kinter's store was blown up with powder, on March 8, 1852.

Duncannon has the unique experience of having had one of its streets extended by an act of the Pennsylvania Legislature. An act was passed on March 29, 1849, extending Ann Street, in the Borough of Petersburg, "so as to connect with the great road leading to New Bloomfield."

The western landing of Clark's ferry was in Duncannon, on lands warranted to Samuel Goudy, in 1766, consisting of 215 acres. Goudy lived upon it and later sold it to John Clark, whose father had established the ferry, and who later conducted it himself, as also did Robert Clark, of the third generation. The Indians had a fording here which they called "Queenaskowakee." John Clark built a tavern building (now occupied by Joseph Smith), and kept the first tavern there. It was later kept by his widow, by her son, Robert Clark, John Boden, Henry Lemon and William Wilson, in turn. Jacob Keiser was postmaster at one time when the Clark's Ferry post office was located in this stone tavern building, and a Mr. Keesberry was the first postmaster after the town became known as Petersburg. The large shade trees about Duncannon were largely planted by William Lindley, who came to the place with Fisher & Morgan, in 1834, and who died in 1881. He was a benefactor and trees planted by him still cast their shade upon the wayfarer and cool the brow of the toiler. One of the merchants of the middle of last century was George Kinter. On April 2, 1851, a boy who slept in his store was tied in the second story and the building set on fire by burglars who got away with over $500. On March 9, 1852, his store was blown up with powder. The first fire company in the town was the Spry Fire Company, which existed in "the early fifties."

The first news stand located in Perry County was opened in Duncannon in November, 1881, by Harry H. Sieg, now a justice of the peace. In those days only four Sunday papers came to Duncannon, two on order and two extras to be put on sale. During the Spanish-American War, seventeen years later, his standing order was for over a thousand copies.

Joseph M. Hawley, who died in 1889, was a prominent business man and left his mark on the community.

The oldest lodge in Duncannon is Evergreen Lodge, No. 205, I. O. of O. F., instituted October 10, 1846, with Wm. Stewart, noble grand; Wm. Allison, vice grand; Jos. D. Simpson, secretary, and John Shearer, treasurer.

The stone gristmill, owned by the Duncannon Flouring Mill Company, was begun in 1814, and put in operation July 4, 1817, by Ramsey, Clark & Boden. John Chisholm, a native of Scotland, did the building and for a number of years was the miller. About 1839 it came into possession of Amos Jones, and from him to Griffith Jones. Later it was owned and operated by Stewart, Young & Rife, and later by Stewart & Young. In 1885 it was purchased by George Morris, who in 1889 conveyed it to Joseph M. Hawley, John Sheibley, William Grier, and James Elliott. From them it passed to W. F. H. Garber, in 1895. In 1909 Mr. Garber sold a two-thirds interest to E. S. Heckendorn and W. G. Wagner. It is a three-story stone mill doing a good milling business.

In 1883, S. K. Sankey & Company erected the Duncannon planing mill, which has had a varied experience. William Bothwell was later associated with Mr. Sankey, and on his withdrawal it was operated by Sankey & Son. Their successors were Dr. R. H. Moffitt and William Bothwell, who in turn sold to the Duncannon Planing Mill Company, limited, of which E. B. Hartman was manager, the owners being non-residents. Since about 1900 the plant, now owned by Duncan & Wills, has lain dormant.

In 1894, through a newly formed Board of Trade, Duncannon citizens obligated themselves for the erection of a fine brick building to be used in the manufacturing of brass specialties, but it was operated less than a year by those for whom it was built. This building, ownership of which rested in the Duncannon Improvement Company, a limited partnership, of which P. F. Duncan was president, and W. A. Laird, secretary, was sold to the Standard Novelty Works, and became their main workshop. Several small knitting mills and another shirt factory were operated for short periods at various times, but have passed out of existence.

The Trout Run Water Company was incorporated August 20, 1894, by John Wister, president; W. L. Coover, secretary; P. F. Duncan, treasurer; George Pennell, William Wills and J. C. Hawley. The reservoir was constructed on the northern side of Cove Mountain, and on December 10, 1894, the first water passed through the pipes. Later, in 1907, an additional supply was piped into the reservoir from the Washington Fritz lands at "the Loop." The system is entirely by gravity and the water unexcelled. P. F. Duncan is president of the company, and B. Stiles Duncan, secretary.

The Good Intent Shirt Factory dates back to 1899, when citizens of Duncannon donated the ground and furnished an additional $500 towards securing the industry. Emanuel Jenkyn, of Tremont, was the projector and owner, and successfully managed the business until 1911, when it was purchased by J. Arthur Rife. In October, 1919, it was purchased by S. Rosenbloom, of Baltimore, Mr. Rife remaining as manager. This industry has been operated continuously with from forty to sixty employees.

The Standard Novelty Works, incorporated, began business in 1904, in the brick manufacturing plant, formerly the brass works, purchased from the Duncannon Improvement Company. The business began in a small way, with the manufacture of children's sleds, and while that still is the principal product, the line now includes porch swings, porch gates, magazine racks, roller coasters and other novelties. During the past year (1920) more children's sleds were made there than in any other plant in the world, and the substantially constructed little "Lightning Guider" makes happy the lives of children in every land where snow abounds. The capacity is from 1,600 to 1,800 sleds a day. The first officers of the Standard Novelty Works were: William Wills, president; C. A. Walter, secretary and manager, and P. F. Duncan, treasurer. The present officers are: William Wills, president; P. F. Duncan, secretary and treasurer, and C. H. Maneval, manager. A large additional building, used as a planing mill, was erected in 1910. The old Duncannon planing mill building is also about to become a part of the plant. About sixty persons find employment at this plant.

During 1920 William Wills presented to the borough a plot of ground on Carver's Hill for park purposes, and during 1921 P. F. Duncan donated the use of grounds in the upper end for the same purpose.

Duncannon people keep up two organizations having as their object relief in case of death. The first, known as the Duncannon Workingmen's Burial Association, was at first confined to employees of the Duncannon Iron Company, and came about through the "passing of the hat" in many instances after a death had visited a family. After its organization $50 was paid in case of death. In later years the G. A. R. Burial Association was organized along the same lines, paying the same amounts. These organizations have large memberships and are a distinct aid to the community. A Community League was organized in 1920.

The first physician of which there is record who located at Duncannon —then "Clark's Ferry"—was Dr. John W. Armstrong, who practiced from 1818 to 1824, when he changed his location to Liverpool, in whose list of physicians he is spoken of again. Dr. Armstrong's successor was Dr. Joseph Speck, who was a graduate of Dickinson College as well as a medical college. He practiced in Duncannon until 1834, when he moved to New Bloomfield, where he remained two years. He then moved back to Duncannon, and later went West. In May, 1834, Philip Ebert, of York County, according to records, located at "Clark's Ferry" (now Duncannon). He was a graduate of the University of Maryland. He practiced until 1865, when he removed to Runyan, Ohio. He was once an associate judge of Perry County. About 1850 Dr. A. J. Werner, of Reading, a graduate of the University of Pennsylvania, located and practiced until his death, in 1881, which occurred while on a professional call to the country, his body being found in his carriage. Dr. Joseph Swartz graduated at Jefferson Medical College in 1857, and located at Grier's Point, Perry County, where he succeeded Dr. Kaechline. In 1860 he located in Duncannon, and in the War between the States he was a surgeon of a Pennsylvania regiment. He conducted a drug store in connection with his medical practice. He was married to a daughter of Dr. Philip Ebert. He died in 1887. In 1860 Dr. W. W. Culver and Dr. Frederick Nockel were located in Duncannon, and in 1862 Dr. II. A. Boteler located and practiced a few years.

In 1859 Dr. N. C. McMorris graduated at the Pennsylvania Medical College and practiced on several different occasions at Duncannon. He died in 1905. Dr. Thomas L. Johnston, of Lebanon, graduated at the University of Pennsylvania in 1868, and after a brief practice elsewhere located in Duncannon in 1871, where he remained in practice until 1896. Dr. Alfred L. Shearer, a native of the county, graduated at the University of New York in 1883, and located in Duncannon, where he also conducted a drug store for many years in connection with his practice. He practiced here until 1905, when he located in Harrisburg. Dr. Harry D. Reutter, a son of Dr. George N. Reutter, graduated from Jefferson Medical College in 1884, and located in Duncannon, where he practiced until his death in 1915. Dr. H. W. McKenzie graduated from Dickinson College in 1886 and from Hahnemann College in 1889. He immediately located in Duncannon, his home town, and became the first homeopathic physician to practice in the county. Dr. Frank C. McMorris, University of Pennsylvania, '93, practiced for about ten years thereafter, until his health failed. Dr. B. F. Beale located here in 1905, succeeding to the practice of Dr. A. L. Shearer. He and Dr. McKenzie are the only physicians now, while several decades ago there were seven for a time.

Dr. Jerome Sunday, educated at the medical department of the University of Hudson, Ohio; Dr. Sylvanus H. Green; Dr. John U. Hobach, now of Philadelphia; Dr. Robert T. Barnett, who later located at Lewistown; Wr. Winfred J. Wright, who later located at Skippack, Pennsylvania, and several others practiced for a number of years.

Dr. Joseph B. D. Ickes practiced on Duncan's Island until his death in 1851. He also practiced in territory of Perry County contiguous to that island.

When the state passed a law, recently, authorizing boroughs to appoint Park and Shade Tree Commissions, Duncannon was the first borough to appoint one, the members of which were B. Stiles Duncan, Abram Dearolf and Joseph N. Wolpert.

The mercantile appraiser reports the following in business in Duncannon, the date following the name specifying the time of their beginning business in that line:

General stores, Samuel Sheller (1905), established by Samuel Sheller, Sr. (1852) ; George B. Noss, established by Samuel Noss; W. O. Miller, L. W. Miller, A. S. Hays (1890), Duncannon Merchandise Company, John S. Kennedy (1896), C. F. Mutzabaugh.

Groceries, Wm. E. Bender (1916), George E. Boyer (1905), C. A. Hunter, George Hemperly, W. D. Owens, F. E. Wase, E. F. White (1906), Oscar Wagner.

Notions, etc., Mrs. L. F. Gintzer, Mrs. E. G. Gladden, Mrs. N. M. Miller, Mrs. Carrie Fenstemacher (1914).

J. A. Martin, jewelry and saddlery (1906), established (1874) at New Bloomfield by J. A. Martin and removed to Duncannon (1893).

Alander & Bolden, Theodore Noye, meat markets.

Sylvester Sheller (1905), established by Samuel Sheller (1882), coal, grain and lumber.

C. N. Reed, coal and feed; C. F. Gelbach (1900), fertilizer and lime.

J. Y. Wills & Son (1890), George M. Zerfing (1917), hardware.

W. H. Zeigler (1904), Nickel Furniture Co. (1920), established by S. H. Moses (1853), furniture and undertaking.

Joseph E. Lestz, Wm. D. Kline Estate (1895), clothing.

D. W. Bell, W. H. Heffley, Chas. Mager, cigars.

Miscellaneous : E. S. Glass, bakery (1908) ; Charles J. Wagner, news stand; E. C. Smith, drugs (1913) ; Central Garage Company (John S. Kennedy and Robert E. Owen, 1917) ; Frank Snyder, marble works; Elmer S. Loy, jewelry ; Ed. Michener, restaurant ; M. J. Derick, musical instruments; O. S Ebersole & Co., feed ; Abram Roth, wallpaper ; Miss Ida Kline, millinery.

Frank Snyder, marble works, long operated by Lupfer & Flickinger, and later by F. E. Flickinger.

*Duncannon Presbyterian Church. Almost with the first settlers came Presbyterianism. The early records tell of the establishment of churches in the west end of the county, but are mute as to the very first efforts to establish a congregation at what is now Duncannon. In October, 1793, Presbytery appointed supplies for Sherman's Creek, Dick's Gap and "at the mouth of the Juniata," a Sabbath to be spent at each place. This is the first mention of the place, yet the fact that no mention of it is made as a new place signifies that it was already a place where services had been held and where a people awaited the gospel.

In conjunction with Middle Ridge and the Sherman's Creek Church the people of that faith residing here issued a call, March 10, 1803, to Rev. James Brady, of Carlisle, to become pastor. The services were then held in a stone house, above William Irwin's store. During the next year a log church, 25x30 feet in size, was built on the bluff, above Duncannon, on lands purchased of Cornelius Baskins—the location occupied by the Presbyterian cemetery. On October 3, 1804, Rev. Brady was installed as pastor of these three churches.

Rev. Brady located on a farm, where he opened an academy and in conjunction with his work for the Master gave attention to the great need for

*The author is indebted to the Duncannon Presbyterian Church for a number of the electrotypes used in this book.

education. He died April 24, 1821, and his remains are interred in the cemetery started by the church he loved. Shortly after this what was probably the first Sunday school in the county was started, the exact date being unknown. It has been stated as being in 1816, but no official record can be found substantiating that date. Mrs. Campbell and her daughter, Sarah and Julianna, and her sister, Miss Harriet Miller, of Carlisle, were the factors to whom posterity gives credit for its organization. It had about forty pupils, who walked, as the roads were few and the vehicles fewer. This school, however, must have failed to continue, as there is record of its reorganization by Mrs. William Irwin, the wife of a ruling elder of the church, in her home. Mrs. Irwin personally purchased all of the supplies, Bibles, Testaments, etc., in Harrisburg, making the trip in a small boat which was poled there and back by a man named John Harris, the ancestor of the Harris family which resided in the vicinity of Duncannon, until recently.

After Rev. Brady's death Rev. Cornelius Loughran filled the pulpit for a short time. November 1, 1826, Rev. John Niblock was called. He served until his death, August 30, 1830. His remains lie in the Middle Ridge graveyard. From January, 1831, until October, 1844, Rev. Matthew Patterson was pastor. He was a pioneer in the cause of temperance. In the meantime the town, then known as Petersburg, had grown from the small settlement to a village of considerable size, and a new church had been built on High Street and was dedicated in August, 1841. It was a frame church, 40x50 feet in size, and on the site of the present church. The Sunday school was held for a time in the old building on the heights, but was soon transferred to the new school building, where it met until the church was erected. Occasional services were also held in the old church until April 12, 1866, when a storm laid it in ruins.

From 1844 until 1847 the pulpit was filled by supplies, Rev. Charles B. McClay being installed in 1847 and serving during 1848-49. From 1849 to 1853 Rev. Hezekiah Hanson was a supply, and from then until 1856 the regular pastor, being installed as such. In 1856 Rev. William B. Craig was called, and remained until June, 1867. He also served the New Bloomfield church, which paid half his salary. He resided in New Bloomfield until 1863, when he purchased a farm near Duncannon and removed there. He conducted an academy at Duncannon, but its life was brief, owing to lack of support. Rev. Craig established a congregational library in the church during his pastorate. Rev. Craig was then a young man and lived for many years thereafter. When the writer was editor of the *Duncannon Record*, during the period from 1891 to the end of the century, Rev. Craig was a frequent visitor to his office, and while half a century of difference existed in their ages, a friendship sprang up which lasted until the death of Rev. Craig. The New Bloomfield church had become self-sustaining, and after the pastorate of Rev. Craig it became a separate pastorate. The successive ministers since then have been:

1868-73—Rev. Wm. B. Thompson.	1884-85—*
1874-77—Rev. George Robinson.	1886-99—Rev. O. B. McCurdy.
1877-80—Rev. W. W. Downey.	1901-08—Rev. J. N. Wagenhurst.
1881-84—Rev James W. Gilland.	1908-21—Rev. George H. Johnson.
	1921- — Rev. Raymond Wilson.

A new brick edifice was erected upon the same site at a cost of over $10,000, being dedicated April 27, 1888. In 1901 the old parsonage was sold and a new and commodious one erected on Market Street.

A local tradition connected with the building of this first church at its elevated location at the mouth of the Juniata appears faulty. The statement is made that it was built there so that Indians could be seen even

---

*During 1884-85 Rev. McClurkin filled the pulpit, but was not installed as pastor.

at far-away points. As it was not built until 1803 and as the Indians had gone even before the Revolution, that is hardly plausible. However, the graveyard may have been located there for that reason, as it dates farther back.

Duncannon Methodist Church. The farm one-fourth of a mile west of Duncannon, on the New Bloomfield road, long owned by William Morrison, and now by J. W. Mumper, was the scene of the first meetings of members of the Methodist faith. It was then owned by Abraham Young, who was a pioneer in the district, and who gave the use of his home for services, which date as far back as 1809. Methodism was then a comparatively new faith and attracted people from long distances. The congregation was known as Young's and was one of four appointments of the Juniata Circuit, the original Methodist charge of what is now Perry County. The others were Alexander Shortess' home, near Shermansdale; Liverpool and Pfoutz Valley. The preachers at that time and following were:

1809	—Rev. Michael Borge,	1820	—Rev. John Henry.
	Rev. Allen Green.	1821	—Rev. Israel Cook.
1810	—Rev. John Thomas.	1822	—Rev. Thomas Magee,
1811	—Rev. John Gill Watt.		Rev. N. B. Mills.
1812	—Rev. Nathan Lodge.	1823	—Rev. N. B. Mills,
1813-14	—Rev. John Thomas.		Rev. Jacob B. Shepherd.
1815	—Rev. David Stevens.	1824	—Rev. Thos. Magee,
1816	—Rev. Wm. Butler,		Rev. John Gier.
	Rev. Morris Hoes.	1825	—Rev. Jacob R. Shepherd,
1817	—Rev. John Everhart.		Rev. J. Wm. Pool.
1818	—Rev. James Moor.	1826	—Rev. Jacob R. Shepherd,
1819	—Rev. Robert Cadden.		Rev. Jonathan Munroe.

The adjoining farm to the north, long known as the Godcharles farm, now in the possession of Samuel B. Sheller, was then owned by Christian Young (a nephew of Abraham, in whose house the meetings had been conducted all these years). On a level plateau, at the top of the hill, Christian Young gave the ground for burial place and the erection of a meeting house. The pastors then were Rev. John Smith and Rev. Oliver Ege, who with the first official board, soon had a church erected. The members of this board were Christian Young, John L. Morgan, John Young, Sr., and Henry Branyan. The building, 20x20 in size, was dedicated in 1827. It faced the highway and had a rough, high pulpit and slab seats. The only thing left to show the site is the old burying ground, often sadly neglected, at the top of the hill.

At the time of the erection of this old church, long known as Young's Church, this congregation was a part of the Concord Circuit, which extended from Concord, Franklin County, through western Perry to the Juniata and along that river as far as Mifflintown.

This church was in use until 1840, when it was sold to the school board for use as a school building, being in use only a few years however. In the meantime Petersburg (Duncannon) had grown to be a considerable town, and it was decided to build the new church there. A lot was purchased from Jacob Clay for $100, its location being on the corner of High Street and an alley. It is the site of the church to this day. On New Year's Day, 1841, it was dedicated. The official board at the time of its building was composed of Jacob Bruner, Sr., Jonathan Beck, Henry Branyan, Abner VanFossen, and George Bruner. In order to help defray the expense of building two lots were cut from the church property and were sold to Robert Jones and John Glass.

In 1882 the present substantial brick parsonage, one of the finest homes in Duncannon to this day, was built. The Duncannon organization also owns Pennell's Church, in Wheatfield Township, in the history of which an account of that church appears. The appointment on Duncan's Island, the result of Rebecca Duncan's efforts towards having services held there, were supplied by the Duncannon charge. See Duncan's Island chapter. The pastors, since the building of Young's Church in 1827, have been as follows:

1827—Rev. John Smith,	1842—Rev. Joseph Parker,
Rev. Oliver Ege.	Rev. Charles McClay.
1828—Rev. John Smith,	1843—Rev. Wm. H. Enos,
Rev. John Forrish.	Rev. E. Teal.
1829—Rev. Jonathan Munroe,	1844—Rev. Wm. H. Enos,
Rev. Henry Tarring.	Rev. Wm. F. Pentz.
1830—Rev. Edward Allen,	1845—Rev. F. Dyson,
Rev. Allen Britten.	Rev. John Ewing.
1831—Rev. Thomas Taneyhill,	1846—Rev. F. Dyson,
Rev. Zachariah Jordan.	Rev. W. W. Meminger.
1832—Rev. David Thomas,	1847—Rev. Robert T. Nixon,
Rev. Daniel Hartman.	Rev. John Thrush.
1833—Rev. David Thomas,	1848—Rev. Geo. Berkstresser.
Rev. Wesley Howe.	Rev. Wm. Harden.
1834—Rev. Jacob McEnaly,	1849—Rev. Geo. Berkstresser,
Rev. John Wosborn.	Rev. John Lloyd.
1835—Rev. Thos. S. Harding,	1850—Rev. Oliver Ege,
Rev. Robert T. Nixon.	Rev. W. Champion.
1836—Rev. John Hodge,	1851—Rev. Oliver Ege,
Rev. Geo. Berkstresser.	Rev. James Beatty.
1837—Rev. David Shaver,	1852—Rev. Wesley Howe,
Rev. Jesse Stanbury.	Rev. David C. Wertz.
1838—Rev. David Shaver,	1853—Rev. Wesley Howe,
Rev. John M. Green.	Rev. H. C. Westwood.
1839—Rev. Peter McEnally,	1854—Rev. W. R. Mills,
Rev. John Lanahan.	Rev. Job Price.
1840—Rev. Peter McEnally,	1855—Rev. W. R. Mills,
Rev. Joseph S. Morris.	Rev. R. E. Wilson.
1841—Rev. Joseph Parker,	1856—Rev. G. Stevenson,
Rev. John McClay.	Rev. W. F. Keith.

In the meantime Duncannon and Newport had been formed into a charge, which was separated after 1856 and each made a separate pastorate. The pastors, from then:

1857-58—Rev. T. D. Gotwalt.	1888-89—Rev. J. A. DeMoyer.
1859-60—Rev. John Stine.	1890-94—Rev. George M. Hoke.
1861-62—Rev. Daniel Hartman.	1895-97—Rev. John B. Mann.
1863 —Rev. S. L. M. Conser.	1898-99—Rev. John Horning.
1864-65—Rev. James Brads.	1900-03—Rev. W. H. Stevens.
1866-68—Rev. A. W. Gibson.	1904-05—Rev. J. Emory Weeks.
1869-70—Rev. G. T. Gray.	1906 —Rev. Edgar R. Heckman.
1871-73—Rev. C. Graham.	1907 —Rev. Wilbur H. Norcross.
1874 —Rev. G. Leidy.	1908-09—Rev. George L. Comp.
1875-77—Rev. W. H. Keith.	1910-11—Rev. Ellsworth M. Aller.
1878-79—Rev. Wm. Rink.	1912-16—Rev. W. W. Sholl.
1880 —Rev. J. H. McCord.	1917 —Rev. H. L. Schuchart.
1881-82—Rev. J. Ellis Bell.	1918-19—Rev. Samuel Fox.
1883-85—Rev. B. F. Stevens.	1920-22—Rev. L. Elbert Wilson.
1886-87—Rev. J. T. Wilson.	

Christ's Lutheran Church. When the settlement below the mouth of the Juniata grew to some size and was called Petersburg, there had come into the community a number of families of the Lutheran faith. The nearest churches of the denomination were at New Buffalo and at Fishing Creek. To Dr. Philip Ebert is largely due the establishing of the church here.

He appeared at the sessions of the West Pennsylvania Synod, held in New Bloomfield in 1842, and presented the necessity of such a move. In November, 1842, Rev. Andrew Berg held the first Lutheran service in the Methodist Church, after which such services were conducted there every four weeks. At the close of the following month, December, 1842, an organization was effected by electing George Keim, elder, and Jonathan Michener and Dr. Philip Ebert, deacons. In the following January it had seventeen members, and admitted eighteen more in June. After this Rev. Berg resigned and was succeeded in October, 1843, by Rev. L. T. Williams. On November 10, 1844, the new church was dedicated, the building committee being Andrew Hantz, Dr. Philip Ebert and Edward Miller.

On October 1, 1845, Rev. Lloyd Knight succeeded to the pastorate, and was in turn succeeded by Rev. Jacob Martin, in July, 1849. In February, 1850, the Petersburg congregation with Mt. Pisgah and Mt. Zion, in Fishing Creek Valley; St. David's (formerly Billow's), at Dellville, and the church at New Buffalo were formed into one charge. Rev. Martin resigned in June, and Rev. John P. Heister became pastor of the new charge. A list of the later pastors follows:

1850-53—Rev John P. Heister.	1875-78—Rev. J. J. Kerr.
1854-58—Rev. George A. Nixdorff.	1879-82—Rev. G. W. Crist.
1858-62—Rev. W. H. Diven.	Rev. A. F. Yeager (supply).
1863 —Rev. ——— Kinsel.	1884-87—Rev. H. F. Long.
1863-64—Rev. S. Aughe.	1887-92—Rev. F. L. Bergstresser.
1865-66—Rev. M. L. Culler.	1892-93—Rev. G. W. Leisher.
1867-69—Rev. J. E. Honeycutt.	1894-05—Rev. W. C. Dunlap.
1870 —Rev. M. L. Heisler (supply).	1896-00—Rev. Jerome M. Guss.
1871-73—Rev. P. B. Sherk.	1900-02—Rev. George W. Engler.
1874 —Rev. S. E. Herring (supply).	1903-05—Rev. E. E. Dietterich.

Then, from 1900, for a period of several years the Marysville church was separated from the Duncannon church, each having its own pastor until October 1, 1905. After again uniting, as the Marysville charge, the pastors have been:

1905 —Rev. J. G. Langham.	1912-18—Rev. S. L. Rice.
1806-11—Rev. H. L. Gerstmyer.	1918- —Rev. J. C. Reighard.

The old church, a stone edifice, was torn away in 1885, and on the site was built the present white church, a frame structure, 34x55 feet in size. It was dedicated November 25th. The building committee was composed of S. H. Moses, John Shively and B. F. Wert, the latter also being the contractor. It is mounted by a large steeple, and its entire cost was but $2,600. That was a remarkably low figure for a church of such substantial construction and modern finish, even in those days. The church was incorporated as "Christ's Lutheran Church of Duncannon," on April 6, 1865.

Duncannon U. B. Church. The United Brethren Church at Duncannon was organized in 1845, and up to 1870 constituted a part of what is known as the Perry Circuit, and was served by the pastors serving that charge. In 1870 it was detached from Perry Circuit and with Marysville, Duncan's Island, and the Hill Church near New Buffalo, became a circuit, known as Duncannon Mission Charge. It remained that way one year, under Rev. G. W. Lightner. In 1871 Marysville church was detached from Duncannon, and attached to that at West Fairview. Duncannon, Duncan's Island and Hill Church continued in their relationship under the pastorate of Rev. G. W. Lightner, succeeded by Rev. J. R. Hutchinson, until 1874, when the Hill Church was detached and attached to the Allegheny Conference, it being in the bounds of the Allegheny Conference territory. The church in Duncannon, and the Duncan Island class remained in relationship as such until about the year 1886 or 1887, when the members of the latter class united with the church at Duncannon. From then on the church at Duncannon has been a station. The new church, built in 1903, is a brick structure of modern design, valued at $8,000 to $10,000. A new parsonage was recently purchased at a cost of $4,500. An incomplete record of the pastors follows:

1873-75—Rev. Jos. Hutchinson.	1903-05—Rev. Chas. J. Gardner.
1884-86—Rev. A. R. Ayres.	1905 —Rev. McDaniels (died).
1891 —Rev. Chas. J. Gardner.	1906-09—Rev. Oyer.
Rev. A. A. Long.	1909-11—Rev. Samuel G. Zeigler.
1891-94—Rev. J. A. Gohn.	1911-13—Rev. John I. Green.
1894-96—Rev. E. H. Hummelbaugh.	1913-17—Rev. Fillmore T. Kohler.
1896-99—Rev. John W. Owen.	1917-20—Rev. Marks.
1899 —Rev. Schlichter (died).	1920-21—Rev. W. L. Murray.
1900-03—Rev. J. E. Kleffman.	1921 —Rev. B. P. S. Busey.

German Reformed Church. The Duncannon Reformed Church is, in a way, an outgrowth of the St. David's congregation at Dellville. On May 16, 1858, it was organized, and the majority of the membership were those transferred from St. David's. The organization took place in the United Presbyterian Church, which had been erected in 1852, and which the congregation afterwards purchased. Lewis Harling and John Achenbach were the first trustees; Frederick Wahl, Sr., and George F. Moyer, elders, and Lewis Sommers and John Achenbach, deacons.

This church was in use until 1913, when it was sold to the Duncannon School Board and used for school purposes until it was destroyed by fire. The congregation erected a fine new church building on High Street, at a cost of $7,000, which was dedicated December 16, 1913. The building committee was composed of Rev. S. L. Flickinger, Dr. B. F. Beale, G. W. Reeder, W. A. Aughinbaugh, Charles F. Gelbach, L. F. Smith and W. G. Wagner.

The Duncannon, Marysville and Dellville churches comprise one pastorate, the list of pastors being under the Marysville chapter.

Duncannon Church of God. The first meetings of members of this faith were held in May, 1871, in the Lower Duncannon school building. Rev. J. M. Speece and Elder G. W. Selheimer conducted services alternately the first year. In 1872, under Elder J. Cooper, an organization was effected, Edgar Graybill and Henry Clay being chosen elders, and Christian Keene, John Keene, Wm. Mutzabaugh and Josiah Manning, deacons. A plot of ground fronting on Lincoln Street was purchased and the present church erected, being dedicated in January, 1873. The preachers who have served the church have been:

1874-76—Rev. John Hunter.	1898-01—Rev. J. Pease.
1876 —Rev. R. M. Pine.	1901-02—Rev. S. T. Stouffer.
1877-79—Rev. J. M. Grissinger,	1902-03—Rev. G. W. Getz.
Rev. I. M. Still.	1903-05—Rev. J. W. Miller.
1879-81—Rev. G. W. Coulter.	1905-07—Rev. J. W. Gable.
1881-82—Rev. C. I. Behney.	Rev. E. Myers, last half year
1882 —Rev. J. W. Grissinger.	of Gable's pastorate.
1883-85—Rev. J. W. Miller.	1908-09—Rev. G. H. Huston.
1886-87—Rev. O. E. Huston.	1909-11—Rev. L. C. Sollenberger.
1887-89—Rev. S. E. Herman.	1911-14—Rev. S. T. Stonesifer.
1890-92—Rev. J. T. Fleegal.	1914-17—Rev. W. N. Wright.
1892-93—Rev. J. F. Meixel.	1918-19—Rev. E. T. Sheets.
1893-95—Rev. F. Y. Weidenhammer.	1920-21—Rev. S. T. Stouffer.
1896-98—Rev. H. E. Reever.	1922- —Rev. C. W. Peters.

GREENWOOD TOWNSHIP.

Greenwood Township at one time comprised all of the present territory of Perry County lying east of the Juniata River, which includes its present territory as well as that of the townships of Liverpool, Buffalo, Howe and Watts. In 1763 Stephen Munce took out a warrant for land in Greenwood Township, but which is located in what is now Watts Township. He was made the first tax collector upon the erection of the township in 1767. Others on the assessment roll of that year were Joseph Greenwood, after whom the township was named, and John Foughts (Pfoutz). Joseph Greenwood is mentioned by Marcus Hulings, who owned Duncan's Island and who resided at the Dr. George N. Reutter farm—now known as Amity Hall, and the present owner being McClellan Cox—as one of his closest neighbors. John Foughts (Pfoutz) lived in Pfoutz Valley, which bears his name, most of which lies within the confines of Greenwood Township, as at present constituted. The name Pfoutz is now extinct here.

Greenwood was formed from a part of the territory of Fermanagh Township, an original township of Cumberland County, on March 25, 1767, being the fourth township formed of the territory now comprising Perry Couty. At the July sessions of the courts of that year the boundaries of Fermanagh Township were fixed as follows: "Beginning at the mouth of Cocolamus Creek, up the north side of the Juniata, and to terminate at the middle of the Long Narrows; thence (along the mountain) to the head of Cocolamus Creek; thence down the said creek to the place of beginning." Hence it will be noted by the above boundaries that that part of Greenwood Township north of the Cocolamus Creek, including the Borough of Millerstown, was in Fermanagh Township and so remained until the organization of Mifflin County (which included the present county of Juniata), on September 19, 1789.

At the same session of the Cumberland County courts in July, 1767, the boundaries of Greenwood Township were defined thus: "Beginning at McKee's path, on the Susquehanna River; thence down the said river to the mouth of the Juniata River; thence up the Juniata River to the mouth of the Cocolamus; thence up the same to the crossing of McKee's path; thence by the said path to the place of beginning." McKee's path, mentioned therein, began at the mouth of Mahantango Creek, a short distance below the residence of Thomas McKee, on the Susquehanna River. It followed the line of the present public road which runs through Greenwood Township, Juniata County, westward to the mouth of Delaware Run, at Thompsontown.

Then, when Mifflin County was organized, in 1789, the territory that lay between the present county line and McKee's path became a part of Greenwood Township, in Mifflin County (now Juniata), and the territory that lay between the present county line and Cocolamus Creek became a part of Greenwood Township, Perry County. In 1799 Buffalo Township was created and took off the territory now comprised in Buffalo, Howe and Watts Townships. In 1823 it was again divided by the erection of Liverpool Township. January 4, 1854, a petition was presented to the Perry County courts asking that the lines and boundaries of Greenwood Township be altered and a portion of Juniata (now in Tuscarora) Township, lying in the Raccoon Valley, bordering the river, become a part and so remained until the erection of Tuscarora Township, in 1859, when it became a part of that township.

As now constituted Greenwood Township is bounded on the north by Juniata County, on the east by Liverpool Township, on the south by Buffalo and Howe Townships, and on the west by the Juniata River. The township is composed of two valleys—Pfoutz and Perry—the former being of limestone soil, and the most fertile section of the county lying east of the Juniata River, and the equal of the best lying west of it. Perry Valley was once known as Wildcat Valley, but an organization formed in 1884, and known as the Farmers' Mutual Protection Association, was instrumental in having it changed to Perry Valley. This organization was formed for mutual improvement and to protect its members from the impositions of traveling agents who then infested the country. The valley is ten miles long and four miles in width.

Located in Perry Valley there is a small village known as Reward—formerly Liberty Hall—which was laid out in 1847 by John Reifsnyder, on lands of Samuel Grubb. The first store there was kept by Keck & Goodyear. In 1882 Mrs. C. A. Long opened a store. Reward was made a post office in 1883, and so remained until 1905, when rural delivery superceded it. The mail was first carried twice a week, later three times, and still later, daily. H. F. Long was in business there for over thirty years.

The assessment of 1768 contained the following names:

Thomas Allen, 50 acres; Peter Ash, 300; Robert Brightwell, 50; Nathaniel Barber, 100; Henry Bentley, 100; John Bingam, 200; Hawkins Boon, 200; William Collins, 200; Robert Crane, 150; Craft Coast, 100; Philip Donnally, 100; Thomas Desar, 200; Francis Ellis, 200; Andrew Every, 300; Richard Irwin, 150; William and Matthew English, 100; David English, 1,100; Joshua Elder, 100; John Pfoutz, 700; Joseph Greenwood, 500; John George, 300; Marcus Hewlin (Hulings), 400; Philip Hover, 300; Abraham Jones, 100; William Loudon, 100; Everhart Leedich (Liddick), 100; Stophel Munce, 200; William McLeavy, 100; James McCoy, 200; John McBride, 200; John Montgomery, 200; Alexander McKee, 300; Samuel Purviance, Jr., 300; Edward Physick, 100; George Ross, 350; John Sturgeon, 100; Jacob Secrist, 500; Andrew Ulsh, 100; Frederick Wahl, 100.

Of those on the above list the following were on the assessment list of Fermanagh Township, in 1763: Stophel Munce, Robert Brightwell, Joseph Greenwood, John McBride, William and Matthew English.

In the assessment of 1805 the following industries were listed: Joseph Bonar, tanyard; Daniel Lewis, forge; Catharine North, sawmill; John Sherman, grist and sawmill; Jacob Ultz (Ulsh), sawmill.

Prior to the organization of the new county (in 1814) the assessment list was as follows:

William Arbogast, 250 acres and distillery; Jacob Bonsal, 100 acres and tanyard; Peter Beaver, tanyard; Joseph Fry, Sr., 100 acres and distillery; Harter's estate, 400 acres and grist and sawmill; Henry Grubb, Sr., 150 acres and distillery; Henry Grubb, Jr., 150 acres and sawmill; George Hoffman, 140 acres and fulling mill; Jacob Long, 150 acres and sawmill; George Mitchell, 900 acres and sawmill; Jacob Myer, Sr., 50 acres and sawmill; John Rafter, Jr., 190 acres and sawmill; Michael Rowe, sawmill; Catharine Shoeman (Shuman), 180 acres, grist and sawmill; John Staily, Sr., grist and sawmill, and distillery; John Sweezey, 700 acres and sawmill; Jacob Ultz (Ulsh), 200 acres and sawmill; Adam Wilt, 100 acres and sawmill; Henry Wilt, 227 acres and distillery.

The fertile lands in Pfoutz Valley were evidently known of very early. The land office had no authority to grant warrants prior to February 3, 1755, yet there is record of a grant dated July 28, 1839, for five hundred acres, in this valley, to Thomas Kirton, of Speen, Bates County, Great Britain, evidently a personal acquaintance of some one connected with the proprietary government. There is no evidence, however, of his having taken possession of it, but a part called "Rose in the Garden" was surveyed in November, 1774, to John Pfoutz, assignee of Thomas Kirton, by William McClay, deputy surveyor. On the first day of the opening of the land office John Pfoutz had located 329 acres in the valley which bears his name, and the fifty acres mentioned above adjoined his claim. These lands remained in the Pfoutz family name until 1860, when they were sold as the property of the heirs of Isaac Pfoutz.

On the same date, February 3, 1755, John Pfoutz warranted 142 acres in what is now Liverpool Township, located along the Susquehanna River, below the Borough of Liverpool.

Fifty-six acres adjoining Pfoutz were warranted to William Patterson in 1773. Philip Shoover had 247 acres, the re-survey being dated 1810. Adjoining James Gallagher's (site of Millerstown) tract was John Mc-Bride's large tract, warranted in 1755 and 1767. Henry Ulsh warranted 150 acres in 1791 and 160 acres in 1795. John Jones warranted 300 acres in April, 1767.

Conrad Stigers took up a tract in 1790 containing 172 acres, part of which was owned by Henry Martin in the last generation, and is now owned by H. G. Martin. Joseph Elder warranted 147 acres in 1766, later known as the Joseph Wert farm. Christopher Ulsh warranted 200 acres in January, 1798. A survey called "Old Town," on the west side of the Cocolamus, was made to James Murray in 1765, but passed at once to John Pfoutz.

The stone bridge, on the William Penn highway, below the Everhart mill, was erected by the commissioners of Cumberland County in 1816, when the Perry County territory was still a part of its domain. The builders were Jacob Hoffman and Henry Lemon.

George Mitchell was a prominent early settler of Perry Valley, having purchased 1,500 acres of land between Buffalo Mountain and the Rope ferry. The father of eleven children, five sons married and remained in the township, viz: John, Isaac, David, Joseph and Samuel. With one exception their descendants occupy the old homesteads. George Mitchell died April 3, 1817, aged fifty-six, his remains being interred in the old Mitchell graveyard. He was of the old type of country gentlemen, and at the foot of his grave lies his faithful body servant, John Anderson, who accompanied him to this country, and who, tradition says, died of grief, August 2d, four months after the death of his master. George Mitchell was married to Mrs. Hannah Taylor-Wright, mother of Charles Wright, in Philadelphia, before locating in Greenwood, his wife thus becoming the ancestor of two noted families of the township.

There was once a powder mill on the Edward Rippman farm, above Everhart's mill. This property and that of Randolph Wright are parts of an original grant known as "The Hermitage," upon which also stood the Lewis forge, described in the chapter on "Old Landmarks, Mills and Industries." This tract was warranted February 13, 1796, to David Miller, and contained 180 acres.

Shrenk's gristmill, four miles east of Millerstown, on Cocolamus Creek, was built prior to 1805, by William Stahl, in whose name it is assessed in that year. It passed through many hands until 1876, when Henry Shrenk purchased it. After Mr. Shrenk's death it ceased to do business as a gristmill, but was turned into a planing mill. The owners are Mrs. Elizabeth and William A. Treaster.

Hart's gristmill was located over two miles from Millerstown, on a branch of the Cocolamus. It was erected by Frederick Harter, a resident of Millerstown. In the assessment of 1805 he is assessed with 400 acres of land, a gristmill and a sawmill. Michael Wenner purchased it and sold it to Joseph Hart, at whose death it descended to his only heir, Mrs. William Fitzgerald. She ran it for a time, employing a miller, but it eventually ceased operations.

A fulling mill is assessed to George Hoffman, in 1805, hence it must have been built prior to that time. It was subsequently owned by Beaver & Hoffman, Anthony Brandt and William J. Williams. Mr. Williams purchased it about 1865, built a dwelling house and put in new machinery. He sold the machinery in 1882 and discontinued business. He is still living.

The school connected with St. Michael's Church, in Pfoutz Valley, according to Prof. Wright, was the only one in the territory comprising present Greenwood Township prior to the free school law of 1834. It was also attended by children from Perry Valley. Wright's, at the site of Wright's Church, and Grubb's, were erected in 1836. John Wright, the father of Prof. Silas Wright, and Christian Heisey were teachers at Wright's school. Mrs. Henry Martin (then Lucrissa Ann Wright) was one of the attendants at this school, the first free school in the township, being interviewed by the writer in 1920. About 1855 schoolhouses were built near the present Randolph Wright farm, near J. R. Satzler's, and on the Jesse Bonsall farm, now Andrew McGowan's. This latter one was torn down in 1861, and one erected to replace it at Calvin Casner's. There was also a school building not far from Mitchell's Gap. A summer school was conducted about 1860 at the Wright schoolhouse. County Supt. Height's report of 1856 designates these buildings as Juniata, Kramer's, Brandt's, Bonsall's, Mitchell's and Rope Ferry.

According to the report of the mercantile appraiser there are but two business places in the township, the general stores of Jacob Markel and Howard E. Zaring (1919).

Reward U. B. Church. Before the building of the United Brethren Church there was a union church located at Reward, where all denominations were permitted to worship. The Church of God principally occupied this church, but the congregation dwindled and finally it was torn down. It stood on the opposite side of the street from the present church, which the United Brethren built and dedicated about 1850, on lands donated by Cyrus Douty. It was rebuilt in 1878, and again in 1893. The Liverpool pastors of the same faith preach there, as it is a part of that charge.

Wright's Church. This church replaces a schoolhouse which formerly stood at this site. It is a Presbyterian church and the services are held by the Presbyterian minister from Millerstown, the list of ministers being the same. (See Millerstown.) It received the name Wright's Church through a bequest of Charles Wright, Sr., of one acre of adjoining ground for a cemetery, which is plotted and well kept. It was built in 1890, and was dedicated May 24, 1891. The schoolhouse which the church replaced was bought from the township by Mr. Wright and any denomination privileged to use it. It was used at different times by the Lutherans, Evangelicals, Methodists and Presbyterians. That resulted in the building of this church.

Howe Township.

Howe Township was the last of the townships to be formed in Perry County, being made such in 1861. It is also one of the smallest townships in the county, its territory comprising less than ten square miles. It was originally a part of Greenwood Township, and when Buffalo Township was formed in 1799, it became a part. Then, in 1837, when Oliver was created it became a part of Oliver, where it remained until attaining the distinction of a separate township. In 1860 petitions were circulated asking that that part of Oliver Township lying east of the Juniata River be made a separate township. They were presented to the courts and at the April sessions, in 1861, the following decree was issued:

Decree of the court, in the matter of dividing Oliver Township: "And now, 6th of April, 1861, the court order and decree that the township of Oliver be divided into two parts agreeably to the report of the viewers. That part west of the river to retain the name of Oliver, and the part east of the river to be called Howe Township."

Howe Township is bounded on the north by Greenwood, on the east by Buffalo, and on the south and west by the Juniata River. Of the early settlers of the territory comprising Howe was Robert Brison, who warranted 200 acres of land almost opposite Newport, in June, 1762. When the new township was formed this claim was in possession of Christian and Abram Horting. Below this William McElroy took up 277 acres under warrant dated June, 1762. This tract was later owned by John Hopple and John Freeland, and is now in the possession of Samuel Sharon and Harry Freeland.

The next property below comprised 306 acres, and was warranted in June, 1768, by Thomas Elliott. It bordered the river, and the next in succession was William Howe's 300-acre tract, warranted in June, 1813, but not patented until 1839. It was after this Mr. Howe that the township was named. John Sweezy had made "an improvement" on this tract as early as 1791. Farther down the river Frederick Stoner took up a long narrow strip, over a mile in length, which he sold to Robert Brightwell between 1763 and 1767, who in turn sold it to Samuel Martin, who erected a gristmill and a sawmill on the upper end of it before 1769, as in his will, dated that year, they are bequeathed to his son Joseph. It then passed through several hands, as told in the chapter, "Old Landmarks, Mills, etc., under the caption, "The Martin Mill," until a part of it reached John Patterson, August 19, 1803, and his son John, July 25, 1863. There John Patterson ran a tavern and there was located a post office first known as Fahter's Falls, and later as Juniata Falls. That tavern was a noted stopping place and relay station during stagecoach days. In the past several decades this original tract has been in the possession of Lewis Steckley and Emanuel Kraft, the Steckley homestead occupying the site of the old tavern. The Kraft property is now in the possession of Charles Kraft.

North of the Stoner tract Samuel Martin took up 341 acres in November, 1768. Adjoining this property on the north was the claim of John Whitmore, containing 335 acres, and that of Abraham Whitmore, containing 319 acres, warranted in September, 1774. Among the lands lying along the Berry Mountain warrants were issued to Messrs. Awl, Welch, Wert, Dawson, Ritter, Gibson, Smith and Clay. Along the north township line, bordering the Juniata River, Jacob Awl and John Welch warranted 400 acres in February, 1794. Part of it was later the Alfred Wright farm. Next below this tract was one of 321 acres, warranted by John Sturgeon, in January, 1767. Below this and adjoining the Brison claim—opposite Newport—Andrew Lee warranted 124 acres in February, 1767.

At a meeting of the Oliver Township school board on September 7, 1839, the board decreed "that there shall be six schools on the district (this included Howe Township), provided a schoolroom can be got at A. Zeigler's, to commence about the first of December, and to continue three months, and that the salaries shall be eighteen dollars per month for each, except at Newport, which shall be twenty-two dollars." On December 21, 1839, the board met and decided to divide the township into seven districts, as follows: "That part of the district formerly belonging to Buffalo Township to be divided into two subdistricts by a line running from Beelen's ferry (below Fetterman's ferry) to Buffalo Mountain, leaving Jacob Harman to the lower or eastern subdistrict." In this lower district no school was held that year on account of erecting a schoolhouse, which absorbed all the funds available. The upper schoolhouse was called Kumbler's, and the lower one Howe's. The teachers were George Taylor and John C. Lindsay.

In May, 1843, the school board (that of Oliver Township, to which it belonged) "voted down" the free school system, but a year later, in March, 1844, at a general election the public voted it back by a vote of sixty-three to seven. The officers of the board who thereupon assumed the duty of enforcing the wishes of the voters were: John Allison, president; Henry Troup, secretary; William Kumbler, treasurer; William Howe, collector. The teachers that term were John Wright and Solomon Bingham. In 1846 it was agreed to divide that part of the township which now is Howe Township into three subdistricts and to have no school that year, or until the schoolhouses were completed. At the August meeting of the school board that year a contract to build a schoolhouse on lands of John Patterson was let to Philip Peters for $108. At the October meeting of the same year it was decided to build two others, one on lands of Jesse Oren, and one on lands of Abraham Howe. In 1846 the salaries of teachers in the schools were $16 per month, and in 1884 they were $25.60.

The lands which now comprise Howe Township once had the landings of three old-time ferries within their borders. At Newport Reider's ferry crossed the Juniata. Where the Red Hill road leaves the William Penn highway (not yet taken over), was Fetterman's ferry landing, and opposite Bailey's Station was the landing of Beelen's ferry.

Where the back Buck's Valley road turns from the river route, Jacob Miller built a pottery in 1847, which was operated by him and his kin until after the flood of 1889.

Three old-time taverns, "the Fahter Falls," at Lewis Steckley's; the "Fetterman's Ferry," at Wright's, where the Red Hill road diverges, and "The Red Hill," at the old Alfred Wright farm, now owned by C. S. Wright, did a big business during the old turnpike days, between 1822 and 1857, when it was abandoned as a turnpike. Before the days of free delivery of mail over rural routes, Lewis Acker, in 1867, established a store at his farm, almost against the Buffalo-Howe Township line, on the middle road. Later the post office known as Acker was established there and continued until the advent of rural delivery. The petition asked that it be named Oak Tree, but as there was an office by that name the government named it Acker. The store passed from him to his son, D. R. Acker, in 1887, and on his death, in 1889, to his widow, Mrs. Emma R. Acker, who still conducts it. Henry Stone opened a small store near by and during the two Cleveland administrations was postmaster. It has long since ceased to exist. Mrs. Acker and C. E. Kraft, designated as a flour and feed dealer, are the only two in the township named in the report of the mercantile appraiser.

Red Hill Church. The Church of God located a mile east of Newport, in Howe Township, is known as the Red Hill Church. It was erected in 1856, and is a frame building, its original size being 24x26 feet. It has since been remodeled and an addition erected. It is the only church located within the limits of Howe Township. Rev. Howard organized the congregation, and the leading persons in the organization were Jesse Oren, Samuel Glaze (who served as a local preacher for many years), George Varnes, Jacob Frank and others residing in the neighborhood. The pastors who have served this people have been the same as those which served the Pine Grove Church of God in Miller Township, to be found elsewhere in this book.

JACKSON TOWNSHIP.

At the November, 1843, sessions of the Perry County courts citizens of Toboyne Township petitioned for the appointment of commissioners or viewers to lay out a new township. At the August, 1844, sessions two of the three viewers, W. B. Anderson and Jacob Bernheisel, filed their favorable report and the court confirmed it and named the township Jackson, after the seventh President of the United States. This was the fifteenth township created. The viewers' report designated the boundaries as follows:

"Beginning at the county line on top of the Tuscarora mountain; thence south thirty degrees east, nine miles, one hundred and twenty perches through mountain land of Peter Shively, John Baker, David Kern, Jacob Kreamer, Peter Smith, John Long and others to the Cumberland County line; thence along said county line on the top of the Blue mountain to the Madison Township line; thence along the said township line to the top of the Tuscarora mountain and Juniata County line; thence along the county line and on top of Tuscarora mountain to the place of beginning."

Accordingly it extends from Juniata to Cumberland County, those counties being its northern and southern boundaries. On the west it joins Toboyne, and on the east, Madison. Much of the land in this township is like a garden spot, which accounts for those early pioneers warranting it as soon as the land office opened. The soil is underlaid with limestone. Of it the late Prof. J. R. Flickinger said: "The even crests of the Conococheague on the north and west, and Bowers' Mountain on the south, inclose as rich and prosperous a vale as can be found in the state," and be it remembered that Mr. Flickinger had traveled Pennsylvania extensively and knew whereof he spoke.

The early settlers, mostly Scotch-Irish, began coming in as soon as lands were made available by the land office; later the newcomers were mostly of German origin. Of course, the opening of the lands to settlement had been anticipated, as many of the warrants were taken out on the very day the land office opened, February 3, 1755. As the old Indian trail, which later became the pioneer highway, led through this part of the county, it is natural to suppose that those who came and went knew of these lands long before. Ross and James Mitchell each took up over 100 acres in 1755; Robert Pollock and Ludwig Laird each took up over 200. The Endslow mill is located on one of these tracts, the first mill being built prior to 1778, in which year it was assessed in the name of James Miller. Its history is covered in the chapter relating to "Old Landmarks, Mills and Industries." William Croncleton took up 145 acres in 1755; Abraham Mitchell, 244 acres in 1762; James Morrison, 194 acres in 1766, on which stands the northwestern section of Blain; the homestead now being in the possession of Harry Hall. Others who took up lands were Alexander Murray, Robert Murray, William Huston, John Montgomery, John and William Nesbit, William Forrest, Andrew Moore, John Whiting and Adam Boal, Peter Grove, John Rhea, Anthony Morrison, Ann Boal, Thomas Hamilton, Robert Miller, Allen Nesbit, Robert Adams, Alexander Rogers, George Kerscadden, William Harkness, and in Henry's Valley David Deihl, Philip Christian and others.

A chapter of this book is devoted to "The Famous Blaine Family," pertaining chiefly to the strain from which James G. Blaine, the statesman, sprung. These early Blaines took up much land in what was then Toboyne Township, but which is within the present limits of Jackson Township. Of the father's (James Blaine's) earliest holdings all the records are not available, but all that portion of Blain Borough lying west of Main Street and adjoining the part later taken from the Hall farm, once belonged to

and others. It is from Ephraim that the line of descent passes down to James G. Blaine. Alexander Blaine warranted 131 acres in 1766, which is now owned by Lewis Stambaugh. In 1793 he warranted an additional tract.

From the date of the township's birth, in 1844, until 1880, the elections were held in the schoolhouse on Church hill. They were then changed to the present location.

Robert Robinson, in his narrative, mentions the killing of a daughter of Robert Miller, just outside their fort, in harvest time, 1756. Robert Miller, who took up 300 acres of land in what is now Jackson Township, in 1766, is probably the same man.

The large steam tannery, in Henry's Valley, was erected about 1850, by I. J. McFarland. He sold it to James Marshall, who owned it for many years. In 1859 Samuel and Joseph M. Lupfer purchased it. They operated it for ten years, when they sold to Ahl Brothers. This firm operated it until 1877, when operations ceased. It is located about ten miles south of Blain. In 1814 Bailey Long is assessed with a gristmill, but by 1820 it had passed to Joseph Woods. The Endslow mill's history appears in the chapter devoted to "Old Landmarks, Mills and Industries." The erection of the Beaver tannery was before 1835, a description of which will be found on page 269. In 1857 a foundry was started by John Baltosser and Wm. Hollenbaugh, and was operated until 1863. It was located along Houston's Run, and manufactured stoves. Some of the stoves are still in use, thus showing skilled workmanship.

As early as 1790 there was an old schoolhouse back of the orchard on the George Trostle farm, now owned by Foster Dimm. It was still standing in 1810, and is spoken of as one of the most primitive in the county. William Shields, John Morrison and James McCulloch were among its teachers. On the Peter Brown farm, now owned by Thomas Adams, on the bank of Sherman's Creek, near the mouth of Brown's Run, stood an old log schoolhouse, part of the chimney yet remaining. This building was in use before 1820, when Perry County yet was a part of Cumberland. To it came pupils from above New Germantown and from points as far as the foot of Bowers' Mountain. There was another on the Black farm, at Mount Pleasant, dating back to before 1800, the lands being donated by George Black. This farm is now owned by George Anderson. The present building is at the same site. (See cut on page 322.) This school had over fifty pupils and two of the teachers were Anthony Black and a Mr. Johnston. Two of the schoolhouses of this township were named Bull Run and Manasses Gap. Their names came about through a contention as to the proper location for a school building, which was finally decided by building two buildings instead of one. This was about the time of the Second Battle of Bull Run, and as the one building was close to a natural gap in Chestnut Ridge at Manassas, a wag suggested that the buildings be named Manassas Gap and Bull Run, and the school board adopted the names. There is a small settlement south of Blain known as Beavertown.

According to the mercantile appraiser there are but two business places in Jackson Township, Ernest Eberhardt, general store, and S. W. Gutshall, oils.

Henry's Valley, although once well populated, never had a church, although there was a Lutheran organization there and regular services held in the schoolhouse for a long time. It was organized November 24, 1860. There were about forty members. Christian Henry and John Snyder were the first elders, and Henry Snyder and Daniel Henry, the first deacons. It was connected with the Blain charge. Before its organization Rev. J. Evans, of Newville; Rev. I. J. Stine and Rev. Philip Willard, of Loysville, preached occasionally. The old graveyard still remains, surrounded by the

Tuscarora State Forest, the signs of a former occupation gradually disappearing.

Church of the Brethren. This church was formerly known as the German Baptist Church. The building is known as the Three Springs Church, because of there being three springs near it, and the congregation is known as Perry Congregation. There is but one other congregation of this faith in Perry County, Mt. Olivet, in Oliver Township. The congregation at Three Springs was organized by Elders Peter Long and John Eby, both of whom located west of New Germantown, in 1843. The former came from Huntingdon County, and the latter from Cumberland. They became the first elders. About the same time Jacob Swartz moved from Juniata Township, where there were some people of the same faith, and became the first deacon. The first services were held in the homes of the members, and the communion services, which are known as Love Feasts were held in the barns, using the barn floors for that purpose, while the communicants sat on the mows. The first one was held at the barn of Elder Long, in September, 1843. They worshiped thus until schoolhouses became more plentiful, when the services were held in them, but the communion services was still held in barns until the church was built. The pastorate at that time embraced all the territory west of the Juniata River, and the different ministers, who served without pay, were chosen from among their own congregation by vote. They were Peter Long, John Eby, Jacob Spanogle, David Poole, Abraham Bowman, Jacob Harnish, Daniel P. Long, Isaac Eby, Edmund Book, Josiah Eby and David Roth. The elder is the highest office in the church. Edmund Book served from 1892 until his death in 1914. The present resident minister is David Roth, and Charles Steerman is the pastor. The pastors are paid a salary, but the resident ministers, very rarely, if ever, are paid. The church house was built in 1876 on land donated by Samuel Book. Later his son, Edmund Book, enlarged the grounds by donation. The building committee was Edmund Book, B. F. Shoemaker and Isaac Eby. Andrew Trostle was treasurer of the fund.

Manassas Union Church. Manassas Union Church is located on the Newville road, about two and a half miles south of Blain. After much consideration as to whether a union church should be built or not, a final community meeting was called for December 1, 1870, at Manassas schoolhouse. At this meeting all five denominations who had members living in the vicinity agreed to assume their share of the debt incurred in building a union church. The site chosen was near the old "still house" on lands then owned by David Rowe. The building committee was William A. Boyd (Lutheran), John Wilt (German Reformed), James A. Woods (Presbyterian), David Rowe (Methodist) and Barnet Roth (German Baptist). The committee began work at once, and the church was dedicated the following spring. The five denominations continued to worship there at intervals until 1901, when the building needed a new roof and other repairs. The Presbyterians, then having no members in that vicinity, donated their share to the other denominations, who repaired it.

Jackson Township surrounds Blain Borough, where most of its citizens worship.

JUNIATA TOWNSHIP.

Juniata Township, as originally formed, contained all of Tuscarora and Oliver Townships and parts of Miller and Centre. It was the fifth township to be formed in the territory now comprising Perry County. It was taken from Rye Township, which then extended clear across the county from the Cumberland to the Juniata County line.

At the present time its boundaries are as follows: On the north by Tuscarora, on the east of Oliver, on the south by Centre, and on the west by Saville. Through it flows Buffalo Creek, and on the south Little Buffalo Creek divides it from Centre Township, its lands being drained by both creeks. The most conspicuous physical feature of the township is Middle Ridge, whose gentle slopes are everywhere under cultivation and dotted with prosperous farm buildings and homes. Along its very top westward for many miles runs the Middle Ridge road.

Juniata Township was formed in 1793, or twenty-seven years before the creation of Perry County. At the January sessions of the Cumberland County courts, in 1793, two petitions were presented, signed by a large number of citizens of Rye Township, stating that they "labored under many and great disadvantages by reason of the great extent of said township, and praying the court that the said township may be divided by a line along the top of Mahanoy Mountain from the line of Tyrone Township to the Juniata River." The court granted the request of the petitioners and named the township Juniata, by reason of its bordering the Juniata River. Bloomfield Borough was taken from Juniata before Centre Township was formed.

In the western end of the township, extending into Saville, are lands early patented by the pioneers, one of 329 acres being granted to John D. Creigh, in August, 1791, who sold it to Jacob Miller in 1812. In 1788 Job Stretch owned the land of the Tressler farm; Robert Garrett, the lands on Buffalo Creek below Milford, later owned by B. F. Miller and George Campbell; James Keenan, near the old Middle Ridge Presbyterian Church, a farm on which he kept a small store, and Alexander Stuart, the farm known in the community as the James Stephens farm.

The village known as Milford was first known as Jonestown, and was laid out about 1814-1816. It then became Milford, later Juniata, and now Wila, the post office known as Juniata being discontinued for a very short time and then reëstablished with the name of Wila, as a suburb of Altoona, which had long wanted to use the name of Juniata, immediately preëmpted it when it was discontinued. Many consider the temporary closing of the post office at this point to have been a ruse to use the name Juniata elsewhere. The little village is romantically located on the banks of Buffalo Creek, two miles from Newport, on lands warranted to William Parkinson, in 1755. The tract comprised 161 acres, on which was located a sawmill and pond. To present and past generations this site is known as Toomey's mill. Edward Riggins was the owner of the Toomey gristmill at Milford, in 1841, when Emanuel Toomey entered it to learn the milling business. In after years he leased the mill for a three-year period, but never owned it. His son, Jerome Toomey, one of the best millers in the county in his day, purchased it in 1880, and operated it until 1896, when his son, Thomas L. Toomey, the present owner, purchased it. The founder of Milford was Joseph Jones, great-grandfather of D. Meredith and Alvin Jones, late of Newport; also of John A. Jones, a cavalryman under Fitzpatrick, and a law student at New Bloomfield, who was killed in action at Solemn Grove, North Carolina. The farm known as the Jacob Fleisher place was taken up by Job Stretch, who was loyal to the mother country in the Revolutionary War, and who suddenly left for Canada when things got "too warm."

Milford was one of the earliest settlements in the county. Prior to 1823 Dr. John Eckert was already practicing medicine there, he having died in that year. He was a German, said to have been very successful, and was probably the first physician located there. Then for ten years there is no record of there being any physician there. About 1834 Dr. John H. Doling moved from Newport to Milford, where he practiced until his death in 1857, excepting for a short period when he got the "gold fever" and went to California. Of powerful physique he has left a record for wonderful strength. Prior to 1841 for a few years Dr. Ward practiced there, and then removed to Carlisle. Before 1847 Dr. Philip Whitesides practiced there. In that·year he removed to Newport, where he practiced until 1856. The Drs. Simonton, who had practiced at Ickesburg, also practiced at Milford for a time prior to their removel to Illinois. In 1857 Dr. Joseph Eby settled there, but removed to Newport in 1860. During the early years of the War between the States Dr. Fetzer was located there. From then on, excepting for a short period in 1881, when Dr. O. P. Bollinger located there, Milford has ceased to be the location for a physician.

One of the oldest schoolhouses in this township as now constituted was on a line running from the upper part of Middle Ridge to Saville Township. Another was on the Jefferson Super farm, now owned by George H. Super, and was known as "the Eight-Square schoolhouse," by reason of its being built in octagon shape. Its location was two miles southeast of Donnally's Mills, where the road to Newport crosses the road to Markelville. The contract was let May 12, 1838, to Jacob Swartz, who built it for $140. The directors were to haul the sand and stone and Mr. Swartz was "to build of stone in a good and substantial manner of an eight-square figure, ten feet in the story, and each square to be ten feet in the inside, from corner to corner, to be eighteen inches in thickness, a twelve-light window in each square, to be well floored, and well nailed with brads." It was a noted meeting place, but was torn down almost a half-century ago. Lydia Stewart was the first teacher in 1839. Dr. Super, one of the two Perry County boys who became' college presidents, first went to school in this building. The farm on which it stood was warranted by Squire Monroe.

Less than a mile south of Milford, at the top of Middle Ridge, on the road leading from Carlisle to Sunbury, was an old tavern known as the "White Ball Tavern," which was kept by Philip Clouser in 1812. Clouser at that time owned a large tract of land adjoining. This hostelry was discontinued about 1840. South of it, on Little Buffalo Creek, John Koch (Kough) kept the "Blue Ball Tavern," which was a popular resort for "shooting matches." From the "Blue Ball" tavern a horn notified the "White Ball" tavern, during the Second War with Great Britain, that a mounted messenger or dispatch rider from Washington was passing, so that on his arrival at the top of the ridge a fresh mount was saddled and waiting. Springing from one horse to the other he proceeded to Reider's Ferry (now Newport), where a ferry flat awaited his arrival. There being no telegraph or telephone lines in those days, messages were relayed from the War Department at the National Capital to the army at Niagara by speedy horses. The route from what is now New Bloomfield seems an odd one to have taken, but it must be remembered that Newport and New Bloomfield were nonexistent and the highway connecting those towns was then not even dreamed of.

William Fosselman built a tannery near St. Samuel's Church, in 1866. Robert Stephens, who lived on Hominy Ridge, occupied a stone house and operated a tannery, but the trend citywards and the modern tanning operations on a huge scale have left the once busy place deserted and almost a ruin.

Juniata Township was the home of James Stephens, a brother of Andrew, who was the father of the noted Alexander H. Stephens, Vice-President of the Confederacy. Their father, Capt. Alexander Stephens, had taken the two boys, James and Andrew, along to Georgia, when he emigrated there in 1794, but James returned to Perry County and settled in Juniata Township, where he owned 300 acres of land in 1820, the year of the county's erection. He married Elizabeth Garrett and was the father

of nine children, and his brother, Andrew, in the South, was the father of
eight. The sons of James, tall, and erect, are remembered by many of
the present generation. They were full cousins of the noted Alexander H.,
but were loyal Northerners. The noted Southern commoner, when a young
man, visited his uncle, James Stephens, in Juniata Township, an account of
which appears in the chapter devoted to Alexander H. Stephens, elsewhere
in this book. Descendants of James Stephens yet reside in New Bloomfield. From James, who returned North, descended Prof. James A.
Stephens, a noted earlier educator, and his son, Robert Neilson Stephens,
the famous author.

Markelville. In February, 1763, the lands on which Markelville is located were warranted to Edward Elliott, and named in the warrant as
"Pretty Meadow." In April, 1769, the adjoining tract was warranted to
John Peden, who came from Lancaster County, and was named "Down
Patrick." The "Pretty Meadow" tract contained 120 acres, and the "Down
Patrick" 142 acres. The "Pretty Meadow" tract was sold to William Wallace, an innkeeper of Carlisle, in 1782, and he came into possession of the
other tract through the will of his sister, Martha Peden. In John Peden's
will, dated August 1, 1775, is this clause: "And J allow, in case my child
dies, that my wife, Martha, shall have that plantation lying in Sherman's
Valley, known as 'Down Patrick,' she to pay twenty pounds to the other
executor, to be put to use for the support of a minister in Donegal." By
her will, dated a year later, it passed to the innkeeper. There is no record
of any improvements until 1775, when part of it was under cultivation by
some squatters who had been driven off by hostile Indians. Not until 1776
or 1777 did Elliot and Peden clear and cultivate land there. Tradition says
these lands were settled earlier but there records do not bear it out.

Wallace transferred the lands to James McNamara in 1793, and he
erected the first house in the place, and later a mill, and it came to be
known as "McNamara's Mill." McNamara sold the tract to Valentine
Smith, from whom his son, John Smith, acquired twenty-two acres, including the grist and sawmill, and the lands upon which Markelville is
located. From Smith it passed to John Weary, and from him to William
Bosserman, in 1834. It then came to be known as Bosserman's Mill, and
a post office was established bearing that name. Then the property was
sold in two parcels, the lands principally going to John Leiby, who, in 1853
sold to George Markle, whose building operations and public spirit gave
his name to the town. The mill, on the other hand, passed to George
Leonard, who, in 1868, sold to David Bixler. The next owners were A.
S. Whitekettle, whose title dates to 1886; Henry K. Frymoyer, 1894;
Yearick & Dock, 1898, Mr. Yearick later becoming sole owner; Gordon
Brothers, 1900; J. T. Alter, 1909, selling almost at once to Linn H. Boyer;
Wm. A. Patton, 1911, and Lloyd D. Stambaugh, the present owner, in 1915.

Jonas Lesh kept the first store there. Other early storekeepers were
Thomas Black, Peter Ouran, William Bosserman, George Leiby, George
Markel, Jr., Daniel Sutman, and later A. S. Whitekettle and Miller E.
Flickinger. The present Markelville includes the site of "Little Vienna,"
which was patented by Alexander Myers in 1809, and contained 365 acres.
In 1815 he planned and laid out the "future city" on lands just south of
the Lutheran Church. In March of that year he had public auction of lots
and succeeded in selling eighteen, each of which contained thirty-one
perches. But three houses were built upon them, as follows: One by a
tailor named John Smith, another by George Folk, and the third by Isaac
Frantz. A right-of-way was reserved to Buffalo Creek for the residents
and a public road provided, but with the death of Myers also died the
dream of the great city to be located there.

The Markelville Academy was opened in 1855, but its history is more property part of the chapter on Public Institutions, elsewhere in this book.

Markelville has been the location of a number of physicians. Among them were Dr. J. E. VanCamp, 1869-71; Dr. J. D. Shull, 1887-96; Dr. Geo. W. Lupfer, after 1881, and Dr. Chas. J. Manning, after 1889.

According to the report of the mercantile appraiser the following are the business firms of Juniata Township, the year following names being the date of beginning business:

M. E. Flickinger (1898), general store and postmaster at Markelville. Opened by Geo. Markel (1856), whose successor was A. S. Whitekettle.

C. A. Scott and A. F. Walkmeyer, general stores.

L. D. Stambaugh and T. L. Toomey, grain, flour and feed.

Middle Ridge Presbyterian Church. Among the earlier churches located in Juniata Township, Middle Ridge Church stood first. Many yet living can remember its individual pews, with gates hung on forged hinges with brass screws. It stood on the Adam Sheaffer farm (formerly W. E. Raffensberger's), in the Middle Ridge road, and was used by the Reformed Presbyterians, known as "the seceders," after it had been abandoned by the Presbyterians. A full description appears under the chapter, "The Earliest Churches."

Sulphur Springs Church. This is now Rodenbaugh's Church, earlier known as Kough's Church, located near the former Henry Fickes farm, close to Little Buffalo Creek, opposite Shoaff's mill. It is now known locally as the Sulphur Springs Church. Its erection must have been prior to 1824, as in that year New Bloomfield's location is named as "on the road leading from the Dutch Meeting House in Juniata Township."

Markelville Churches. The residents of this territory ·practically all attended the Middle Ridge Presbyterian Church until about 1840, when Marx Bealor deeded a half-acre of ground to the Lutheran and German Presbyterian congregations. They erected a union church the same year. German Lutherans in the community included the Beistleins, Lenigs, Swartzs, Smiths, Crists, Burrells and others. This church was sometimes known as Bealor's Church. In 1839 Rev. John William Heim began holding services at the hill schoolhouse, near Bosserman's mill. Simultaneously a Sunday school was organized. This was the nucleus of this church. Daniel Swartz and John Bealor were the building committee. It was a log building 30x35 feet in size, had high galleries on three sides, supported by heavy posts and crossbeams, a high pulpit and high seats. Of it Rev. D. H. Focht said: "It seems to have been adapted to make preaching go hard." The first officers were John Beistlein, elder, and Daniel Swartz, deacon. It was dedicated in 1841, and was named St. John's Church. Rev. Heim preached every four weeks in German until his death in December, 1849. He was succeeded by Rev. Jacob Martin, who preached every third time in English, which enraged the German-speaking members, who even refused to attend the sacramental service. He resigned in March, 1852, and was followed by Rev. William Gerhardt, who served until June, 1853. Rev. A. R. Height followed in March, 1854. He became the first superintendent of schools of Perry County the same year.

On June 1, 1855, this church became a part of the New Bloomfield charge, and on the same date Rev. D. H. Focht became the pastor. The ministers from then on have been the same. See chapter on New Bloomfield. The new brick church was built in 1882. It is 40x60 feet in size. The building committee was composed of Joseph Flickinger, Thomas Lenig, Samuel Carl and A. S. Whitekettle. The Reformed Church was built about 1888. It is served by the New Bloomfield pastors.

*St. Samuel's Lutheran Church.** The early history of this church seems to be somewhat obscured. Rev. Focht, in his Churches Between the Mountains, tells of the organization of a congregation at Millerstown in March, 1850, by Rev. William Weaver, with "upwards of forty persons." He also tells of a Mr. John Kinter donating a plot for the erection of a church "near Millerstown" and of the laying of the corner stone on September 26, 1861. His book was printed in 1862, and in it he says: "It is expected the new church will be ready in August of this year." It appears to have been built upon the lands of William Rice, in Tuscarora Township, about two miles from Millerstown. Rev. J. J. Kerr was instrumental in having it torn down and removed from that location to lands of Andrew T. Brown, in Juniata Township, later owned by Isaiah Mitchell, and now by Harvey Ulsh. Since it has been located in Juniata Township the Newport Lutheran pastors have supplied it. See Newport chapter.

Walnut Grove Methodist Church. Prior to the building of the Walnut Grove Methodist Church the meetings or services were held in the school building, which was later destroyed by fire. Rev. John B. Mann was one of the first pastors. The church was built in 1880-81, being dedicated in the spring of 1881. It was remodeled in 1911. Its membership is about 120, with a Sunday school of over 100 members. It is a part of the New Bloomfield charge, where the pastors' names appear.

Milford United Evangelical Church. The Milford United Evangelical Church is located at Milford (Wila). The first services in this vicinity were held at the home of Henry Toomey (now Mr. Kinzer's), about one mile west of Milford, in or near 1840. In 1844 a church was built, of which George Houtz, Frederic Dum and Daniel Lesh were trustees. While they were raising the frame a storm blew it down, so the size was made somewhat smaller (35x40), so that the same lumber could be used. It was at first a pebble dashed church, but about 1885 was weatherboarded and new windows and shutters placed thereon. Samuel Tressler, Peter E. Smith and John Fosselman were then trustees. In 1902 modern pews replaced the old seats. In 1913 a belfry and bell were added. It has always been a part of the Perry Circuit, the ministers being the same as those found under the Elliottsburg church in the chapter relating to Spring Township.

LANDISBURG BOROUGH.

Landisburg is ten miles southwest of New Bloomfield, the county seat, and fourteen miles from Carlisle. By air line it is within twenty-five miles of the State Capital. It is located near the eastern line of Tyrone Township, not far from Spring, and opposite Mount Dempsey, a magnificent mountain peak, a spur of the Blue or Kittatinny Mountain, which stands there in all its grandeur through the ages, a piece of God's handiwork.

Landisburg was designated as the first county seat of Perry County, pending a choice by the citizens, and remained so from the date of the formation of the county until the beginning of 1827, when it was changed to New Bloomfield. As that matter is covered fully in the chapter entitled "Perry County Established," it is not repeated here.

These business men were located at Landisburg when it was the county seat: H. W. Peterson and Alexander Magee, who published the *Perry Forester,* the first paper published in Perry County, a more extensive account appearing under the chapter devoted to "The Press"; Samuel Maus, watchmaker; Robert H. McClellan, general store; Alexander & Hays, harnessmakers; John D. Creigh, Charles B. Davis and F. M. Wadsworth, attorneys; Valentine Miller and William Dalton, apothecaries.

---

*To Levi Smith, aged 81 in 1920, the author is indebted for facts in reference to this church.

Long before Perry County was created, in fact, in 1793, what is now the Borough of Landisburg was laid out in lots by Abraham Landis, a resident of Cocalico Township, Lancaster County, who had on May 25, 1787, taken out a warrant for 116 acres of land lying along Montour's Run. Landisburg was a part of the tract. A man named John McClure made the survey. The size of the lots was 60x150, and they were disposed of by lottery. Originally each lot was subject to a "quit rent" of seven shillings and six pence, with a requirement to build a two-story house within three years. The earliest deed on record was made to George Wolf, a wheelwright, and was dated December 1, 1795. The town was incorporated as a borough on December 23, 1831. Some of the original houses, over one hundred years old, still stand.

On the town plot of 1793 a lot was set aside for school purposes, on which a log schoolhouse was built, which was continued in use until 1837, when it was replaced with a stone building, which was in use until 1894. A large frame building was then erected, but it was destroyed by fire in 1919. Since that time the school board has purchased the former Presbyterian and Methodist church buildings and transformed them into school buildings. In 1831, in response to a petition of the people, an act was passed by the state legislature, providing for the appointment of trustees of the public schoolhouse of the town of Landisburg, and empowering these trustees to examine teachers for said school, to visit same once a month, and to dismiss the teacher for misconduct, want of capacity, or negligence. John McClure, a surveyor, was an early teacher, teaching at various times and being the first teacher in the new school building in 1837. Jonathan Ross and Alexander Roddy were teachers in the first building, and a Mr. Anderson and Edward Dromgold among those in its successor. In November, 1827, James B. Cooper began a night school, but how long continued we can find no record. In 1835 W. P. Johnson had a select school. The first school was managed by a board of trustees chosen by the citizens in accordance with the act of 1831, for Landisburg Borough. John Kibler, Henry Fetter and John Diven were made trustees of the school. The public school act of 1834 was accepted in 1836, and the board of trustees gave way to a board of directors.

Mount Dempsey Academy was located here, an account of which appears in the chapter headed "Public Institutions and Academies."

James Diven purchased lot 20, on which he erected a dwelling. The Diven tannery was located on lots purchased by J. Scroggs and John Bigler, Scroggs building it and selling it to the younger James Diven, who died in 1816. It was then rented by the heirs until 1840, when it was purchased by James A. Diven, a son and one of the heirs. In 1853 it passed to John D. Diven, who died in 1872. The tannery was then sold to William W. McClure, who in 1880 sold to D. Moffitt & Co., of New York.

In 1831 another tannery was erected upon lot No. 1 by James Diven. Upon his death, in 1840, the tannery passed to Parkinson Hench and Samuel Black, who were in possession until 1859, when William B. Diven, a son of the former owner, purchased it. In 1867 he sold to James Murray, who operated it until 1870, when it came into possession of the Perry County Bank, who in turn sold it to R. H. Middleton & Co. Peter A. Ahl & Co. purchased it from them.

Albert Nesbit had a small tannery at the rear of the old courthouse lot, which he operated from 1818 to 1829.

The first tavern was kept by Jacob Bigler, at Carlisle and Water Streets, and was known as the Bigler House. In 1820 David Heckendorn was the proprietor. The next tavern was on High Street, on lot 73, which in 1807 passed from James Wilson to Christian Bigler, then Jacob Fritz, who

62

built a log tavern and kept it a few years, when he sold it to Abram Fulweiler. Mr. Fulweiler built an addition and added a store, which he kept
until 1825, when he built a stone house on Main Street and moved there.
The third tavern was on lot 48, later owned by John A. Wilson, before
the county was organized. In 1820 it was kept by John Creigh. Another
tavern was in the James L. Diven building, which was used by John
Wingert as a store until 1803. It was then equipped for a tavern and
first kept by Michael Sypher. Thomas Craighead kept it during the period
when the town was the county seat. In 1821 one tavern was known as
"The Spread Eagle."

Jacob Fritz built the building now known as Hotel Dempsey, operated by Robert Shuman (1920). In 1820 it was kept by John Hackett. In
the following years it was kept by a variety of proprietors, until 1834,
when Jacob Evinger purchased and ran it until his death in 1845. Major
George A. Shuman, father of Robert Shuman, kept it for many years
after 1868. On lot 47 there was once a hotel run by James Atchley, and
on lot 45 one run by John Hipple, who became sheriff.

In 1811, Henry Wingert, a hatmaker, located in the town and built on
lot 33 a house, later owned by his son, Dr. J. F. Wingert. During Wingert's time he purchased a lot which he paid for entirely with hats of his
own manufacture.

The first Masonic lodge in the county, as well as in the Juniata Valley,
was organized at Landisburg, Monday, June 26, 1825, and was known as
Golden Rule Lodge, No. 208. Its first officers were: Robert H. McClellan,
worthy master; Jacob Stroop, senior warden, and John Dunbar Creigh,
junior warden. It was disbanded about 1833. The day of its organization
there was a parade led by detachments from the two volunteer military
companies.

The oldest lodge in Landisburg is Mt. Dempsey Lodge, No. 707, I. O.
of O. F., which was organized April 20, 1846, with Wm. R. Fetter, noble
grand; David A. Clugston, secretary, and Frederick Sheaffer, treasurer.
During the same year the lodge purchased the Stambaugh building, on
Main Street, and fitted up the top story as a hall, selling the lot and the
first story, a rather unusual transaction. They met there until 1863, when
they purchased the Landisburg Hotel building, where they still meet.

The Landisburg Civic Club was organized during August, 1920, with
Mrs. A. L. Dum, president; Alice Cooper, secretary, and Mrs. James R.
Wilson, treasurer.

About 1829 a fire company was established and a hand engine purchased,
but the life of the company was short and the engine was finally sold. On
August 16 and 17, 1821, a fair and stock show was held in Landisburg,
which was the first attempt to hold a public exhibition of that character
in the county.

Landisburg celebrated officially the fiftieth anniversary of American
Independence. On July 4, 1826, the Landisburg Artillery Corps, under
Captain Henry Fetter, the Landisburg Guards, under Captain Robert Mc-
Clellan, and the citizens formed in Centre Square and marched to the
courthouse, where an address was delivered by James Butterfield, after
which all marched to the farm of William Power, where a dinner was
served and toasts drank.

When the first post office was established in Landisburg is a matter of
conjecture, but in 1820 Samuel Anderson was postmaster. He died in 1823,
and Henry Fetter was appointed. A list of postmasters since that time, with
the dates of their induction, follows: Jonas Butterfield, 1825; John Kibler, 1826; Francis Kelly, 1828; John Burtnett, 1834; William Blaine, 1841;
Jesse Hipple, 1844; George Shaffer, 1848; John Burtnett, 1852; Mary

Sheibley, 1861; Mary Hutchinson, 1866; R. H. Preisler, 1868; Nancy Connor, 1877; James C. Preisler, 1885; Dr. J. F. Wingert, 1889; Wm. B. Burtnett, 1893; Katharine Eaton, 1898; A. H. Billman, 1913; Nora Lightner, 1920.

In 1821 Joseph H. Kennedy operated a nail factory, manufacturing nails by hand. It was located on Water Street, in the rear part of a building started in 1794, but not completed until 1809, now the property of Mrs. Robert Shuman. The front part of the building is of stone, but the rear, which was used in the manufacture of nails, was built of logs.

Dr. John Creigh was the first physician to locate on what is now Perry County soil. He was a son of Judge John Creigh, of Carlisle, born in 1773. He graduated at Dickinson College in 1792, and completed his medical course at the University of Pennsylvania in 1795. He first practiced at Pittsburgh, then at Lewistown, and located at Landisburg in 1799. He practiced there until 1819, when he removed to Carlisle to educate his children. He died in 1848. He was rated as very successful. Dr. John Parshall succeeded him and remained until 1825. Dr. James T. Oliver, of Silver Springs, Cumberland County, practiced five years, and then returned to his home location. Dr. Samuel A. Moore, who studied with Dr. Ely, of Shippensburg, had a large practice from 1825 to 1843. Dr. Samuel Edwards located in Landisburg in 1838. After practicing here for six years he moved to Newport, and later to Blain, after which he moved out of the county. Dr. David A. Clugston came to Landisburg from Franklin County in 1841, practiced here for eleven years, then removed to Duncannon, and later went West. Dr. James Galbraith, who was born in York County in 1799, but who had gone to Ohio with his parents when a mere boy, graduated at Jefferson Medical College in 1826. He located in Landisburg in 1843 and practiced there until his death in 1872. He was reputed to be a good physician and a broad-minded man.

Dr. William Niblock, a native of Ireland, graduated at the University of Glasgow, in 1813. He migrated to this country in 1821, and settled in Landisburg in 1827, where he practiced until his death in 1859. His son, William G. Niblock, read medicine with his father and graduated at the Jefferson Medical College in 1847. He practiced in Landisburg for five years, when he died. Both Niblocks were learned men and good doctors. Dr. John F. Wingert was a native of Landisburg, and read medicine with Dr. David A. Clugston. He practiced from 1851 to 1872, when he retired from practice.

Dr. David B. Milliken, who was born in Juniata County in 1833, graduated from the University of the City of New York in 1854, and at once located in Landisburg, where he practiced until his death in 1918. He was a successful physician, a shrewd business man, and at one time represented the county in the state legislature. Dr. James P. Sheibley, a son of Bernard Sheibley, was a native of Landisburg, and graduated at the University of Pennsylvania in 1868. He located in Landisburg in 1870, where he practiced until 1905. Dr. H. M. Smiley practiced here for a short time. Dr. W. J. Allen, after leaving Blain, practiced here several years before his death.

According to the report of the mercantile appraiser the following business houses are located in Landisburg, the date following being the time of entering the business:

General stores, J. L. Garman, in the old James Diven stand (1905 till his death, 1921), Chas. H. Delancey, D. W. Wertz.

Charles Burtnett (1898), furniture; J. M. Kennedy. clothing; Z. E Rice (1889), jewelry; S. L. Patterson, meat market; E. S. Rice, Mt. Dempsey garage (1918), oil; Nancy Clouse, confections; D. B. Dromgold, machinery.

Landisburg Presbyterian Church. Prior to the organization of Perry County the members of the Presbyterian faith residing about Landisburg attended Limestone Ridge, sometimes known as Sam Fisher's Church, and Centre Church. With the organization of the new county and Landisburg becoming the county seat, it was naturally supposed that the population would increase and that it would be a good location for a church. Rev. John Linn had died a short time before, and Rev. Nathan Harned, who was supplying his pulpits, quickly arrived at such conclusion, and thirty-two persons withdrew from Limestone Ridge and Centre and formed a new congregation at Landisburg, in 1823, Limestone Ridge furnishing far the larger number. At the same time Buffalo Church, near Ickesburg, was organized, and that part of the membership of Limestone Ridge which did not go to the new charge at Landisburg went to Centre and Buffalo, thus abandoning Limestone Ridge for a location considered more favorable. It might practically be said that the Landisburg church was the successor of Limestone Ridge.

In several historical works the statement is made that "Rev. James M. McClintock was installed as pastor and continued until 1834, when Rev. John Dickey became pastor of the New Bloomfield charge." According to the records of Presbytery taken from the Centennial Memorial, that is wrong, as will be seen in the list of ministers following. The congregation worshiped at first in the building used as a courthouse during the time Landisburg was the county seat. In 1829 the congregation erected a substantial frame building on Main Street.

Rev. James M. Olmstead became pastor in 1825, and remained until 1832. In 1834 Rev. John Dickey became pastor at New Bloomfield, and the churches at Landisburg and Ickesburg were added to that pastorate. He preached here until 1854, when Centre, Upper and Landisburg churches called Rev. Lewis Williams, who served until his death in 1857. He was succeeded by John H. Clark, 1857-62, followed by Rev. James S. Ramsey, D.D., 1864-67.

Blain then withdrew and united with Ickesburg. Centre and Landisburg then called Robert McPherson. He preached at Landisburg from 1869-76. From 1878 to 1880 Rev. Silas A. Davenport served; 1883-84, Rev. J. C. Garver, and 1884-85, Rev. John H. Cooper. Then from 1887 to 1895 Rev. Wm. M. Burchfield was pastor of the four churches, Landisburg, Blain, Centre and Buffalo (near Ickesburg). In the latter year the charge was again divided, Rev. Burchfield remaining at Centre. Landisburg was then served by the following: 1896-97, Rev. Hugh G. Moody; 1898-1902, Rev. A. F. Lott; 1904-1909, Rev. Will H. Dyer.

Following Rev. Dyer's pastorate the Landisburg church was again united with the pastorate at Centre, and Rev. George H. Miksch was the pastor until the beginning of 1914.

The first services of this people were held in the building used as a courthouse, when the county seat was temporarily at Landisburg. In 1830 a frame church was built, the trustees being Samuel Linn, Jacob Stambaugh and William Cook. The membership having largely died or migrated the residue transferred their membership elsewhere, and during the summer of 1920 the church property was sold to the school board and is now used for high school purposes.

The Church of God. The organization of this church almost parallels the organization of the new county. The founder of this faith, Rev. John Winebrenner, visited Landisburg and preached April 10, 1821, which is the earliest record. During 1828 services were held by Henry Wingert, of Landisburg, who began preaching as a teaching elder, serving until 1832, when the congregation was organized under supervision of the East Pennsylvania Eldership. Until 1836 the services were held in the old log school-house, Elder Wingert then building a small log bethel adjoining his residence on Main Street. In 1832 a lot was purchased on a corner, fronting on Water Street, and a brick church erected, which was in use until 1873, when the present brick church took its place.

The elders who have officiated since then, from incomplete records, so that no dates can be given before 1855, follow:

Edward West,	Michael Snavely,	Solomon Bigham,
David Kyle,	Carlton Price,	A. Fenton,
John B. Porter,	William Mulnex,	Josiah Hurley,
Wm. McFadden,	Joseph Hazlett,	Wilson Coulter,
William Mooney,	A. Swartz,	Henry Clay,
Geo. McCartney,	William Miller,	J. F. Weishampel,
Joseph Bumbarger,	Thomas Desbaree,	Thomas Steel.

1855-56—Samuel Crawford.
1856-57—Wiliam Johnston
1857-59—Simon Fleegal.
1859-61—J. C. Seabrooks.
1861-63—B. F. Beck.
1863-64—J. F. Weishample.
1864-66—A. J. Fenton.
    Solomon Bingham.
1866-67—D. Rockafellow.
1867-69—H. E. Reever.
    S. S. Richmond.
1869-70—S. S. Richmond.
    J. M. Speece.
1870-74—G. W. Seilhamer.
1874-75—W. L Jones.
1875-77—W. P. Winbigler.
1877-79—F. L. Nicodemus.
1879-80—J. A. McDannald.
    W. Sanborn.

1880-83—J. F. Meixel.
1883-85—J T. Fleegal.
1885-87—W. J. Grissinger.
1887-89—Jesse Berkstresser.
1889-94—William Palmer.
1894-97—S. C. Stonesifer.
1897-99—J. A Staub.
1899-00—J. C. Pease.
1900-03—F. Y. Weidenhammer.
1903-05—J. H. Esterline.
1905-08—W. S. Sturgen.
1908-09—H. P. Aston.
1909-10—H W. Long.
1910-12—G. B. M. Reidell.
1912-14—J. O. Weigle.
1914-17—J. W. Gable.
1917-20—E. E. Fackler.
1921- —W. F. Johnson.

The Landisburg Church of God is one of seven churches which comprise the charge. The others are Little Germany, Sandy Hollow, Sheaffer's Valley, Kennedy's Valley, Oak Grove and Centre Square, the latter in Toboyne Township.

Trinity Reformed Church. The organization of Trinity Reformed Church in Landisburg, came about through a portion of the membership of Lebanon Church at Loysville desiring a church in closer proximity to their homes. It was organized in 1850, Rev. Charles H. Leinbach becoming pastor. Prior to its organization Rev. Jacob Scholl had preached here occasionally, he having charge of the churches of that faith in Sherman's Valley. A lot was purchased on Carlisle Street and the present brick church erected. Its pastors have been:

1850-59—Rev. C. H. Leinbach.
1860-64—Rev. Henry Musser.
1865-67—Rev. James A. Shultz.
1868-72—Rev. T. F. Hoffmeier.
1872-73—Rev. D. L. Steckel.
1874-80—Rev. W. H. Herbert.
1880-84—Rev. H. T. Spangler.
1884-88—Rev. M. H. Groh.
1888-91—Rev. A. B. Stoner.

1891-99—Rev. Geo. House.
1899-01—Rev. C. H. Brandt.
1901-03—Rev. G. W. Shellenberger.
1904-11—Rev. Roy Leinbaugh.
1911-14—Rev. T. H. Materness.
1915-17—Rev. A. N. Brubaker.
1918-20—Rev. Seward Kresge.
1920- —Rev. O. W. Moyer.

It was located upon a plot of ground offered gratuitously by Henry Fetter. The local members built the first story masonry and let the contract for finishing the building to Henry Myers, of Carlisle, for $1,500, brick to be furnished. The lower story was divided into two parts, in one of which Mt. Dempsey Academy was conducted from 1856 to 1864, when it closed. The other became the Sunday school room. The building committee was composed of Henry Snyder, Rev. C. H. Leinbach, George Wetzel, George Wagner and Jeremiah Rice. The corner stone was laid at a height of ten feet from the ground. It was dedicated April 17, 1853. The first officers were George Wetzel and Jesse Hipple, elders; A. B. Albert and David Rhodes, deacons, and John Burtnett and Jeremiah Rice, trustees. St. Peter's, Landisburg and Elliottsburg constitute one charge, hence the same ministers.

M. E. Church. First services of this denomination were held in Landisburg prior to 1831, by Rev. Sheperd, Rev. Tannehill, Rev. Finicle and others. In that year an organization was effected and the Landisburg church built. It has always been a part of the New Bloomfield charge, but the membership gradually dwindled away until 1921, when the church building was sold to the Landisburg school board for $400. The pastors will be found under the chapter relating to New Bloomfield.

LIVERPOOL BOROUGH.

The plot on which Liverpool was originally laid out was warranted by John Staily. On October 25, 1808, he and his wife (Eve) gave deed to John Huggins for 121 acres, reserving therefrom one and a half acres for a graveyard. John Huggins had it surveyed and plotted by Peter Williamson. This old plot shows it as extending from Strawberry Street to North Alley. It was incorporated by an act of the legislature of May 4, 1832. The Huggins and Staily families, who were relatives, were very numerous then.

Adjoining it, in 1818, the town of Northern Liberties was laid out by Samuel Haas. When it was decided to embrace the new town with Liverpool a new plot was made by Dr. J. H. Case and William Mitchell, the latter at the time being a school teacher there. Northern Liberties began at North Alley—the northern limit of Liverpool—and extended north along the river to the property of Dr. Case. This section, until then known as Northern Liberties, was included in the Borough of Liverpool when incorporated in 1832. The limits were later on extended still further north to include an outlying section known as Perryville, and south to include the Lenhart sawmill and village surrounding it, and west to include the steam flouring mill. The part of the borough known as Perryville was on the George Wilt farm, which passed to Anthony Rhoades in 1812.

On the same day in which he got his deed from Staily, John Huggins sold his first lot—number 4—to Jacob Snyder. In all his deeds he reserved "to himself, his heirs, and assigns forever, all ferries and ferry rights, now made or hereafter to be made or erected, which shall remain in the undisputed possession of the said John Huggins, his heirs and assigns, anything in this present plot, poll or plan of said town, to the contrary, in anywise notwithstanding." John Huggins, having reserved all rights to the ferries, on March 24, 1824, sold half, or the west side of the Liverpool ferry to Richard and Robert B. Rodgers, who had leased it as early as December, 1819. They sold it in 1834 to Daniel Bogar, and he in turn sold it to Isaac Meek, in 1838. The old tavern at the west end of the ferry was first kept by John K. Boyer.

The Calder & Wilson stage line, later the Calder, Copp & Company line, came up the east side of the river and crossed this ferry, continuing on to Selinsgrove. This was a mail route. The first mail was carried on horseback, then with a two-horse stage, and later with a four-horse stage.

When the town of Liverpool was laid out there was in the river an island extending its entire length, with a channel about fifty feet wide between it and the shore. It was then farmed and a considerable part of it

John Roush erected a gristmill, which was long run by Rowe and Williamson. It burned in 1912 and was never rebuilt.

Pioneer business men were Thomas Gallagher, who kept a store and later became a contractor on the canal; George Tharp, before 1820; a man named Dupes; Henry Walters, who afterwards became cashier of the Harrisburg National Bank; James Jackman and Henry W. Shuman. John Huggins erected a large house and kept the first tavern, which occupied the site of the hotel later kept by Robert Wallis, and now in the possession of Blanton Blattenberger. It burned and he then erected one on the opposite corner, where he lived until 1824. Richard Knight kept the first tavern in the stone house which was replaced by the present brick building known as Hotel Mitchell, it having been built by David Owens, who owned the property at one time and ran the hotel for some years.

Liverpool early had a fire engine, it having been purchased about 1835. It was in use until 1873, when it was destroyed in a ravaging fire, which reduced to ashes six residences, two belonging to the John Huggins' heirs, one to John Reifsnyder and including the stores of G. Cary Tharp and D. Wagner. Twenty-two years later another devastating fire destroyed the Wallis Hotel, Winters' drug store, Jesse Coffman's tinshop, and dwellings belonging to Lewis Grubb, J. W. Williamson and Mrs. Cummins.

The first schoolhouse was built on the one-and-a-half-acre lot reserved by Staily when he sold to Huggins. It was a log building, afterwards being weatherboarded and was about twenty-five feet square. This house was in existence in 1810, according to the diary of Rev. George Heim, which says "that in 1810 he organized the Lutheran congregation at Liverpool in the old schoolhouse." It will be noted that he calls it *old* even then, which implies that it must have been one of the first school buildings in the county. Teachers in this building were men named Mitchell, Rouse, Brink, John B. Porter and others. When this building became too crowded another was built and the town divided into two wards for school purposes, the pupils north of Race Street going to the new frame building, and those south going to the old log building. It so continued until about 1847, when a frame building with two rooms below and one above was erected, the upper floor later being divided into two rooms. This building was in use until 1878, when a new two-story, four-roomed building was erected. The first class to be graduated in the Liverpool High School was in 1884, under the principalship of Prof. E. Walt Snyder, who later became one of the county's leading physicians. The class was composed of Mattie Thompson, William Hamilton, Mary Charles, Lena Snyder, Sarah Williamson and Henry Williamson.

William Wallis, an early settler, was a cooper, and the ancestor of the present Wallis families. Christian Weirick, ancestor of the Weiricks, came about 1810. He was a cabinetmaker and had a large family, all of whom located in the West, except his son Henry. Michael Shank, a ship carpenter who built the first canal boat north of Harrisburg, located here in 1820. An early family was the Shulers, Samuel, John and Joseph, the latter becoming a prominent officeholder in the county. The late S. M. Shuler was a son of Samuel. Another early settler was John George Lutz, a German tailor. Peter Musselman came from Lancaster and erected a public house. Among early hotelkeepers were Richard and Abner Knight. The Walters' store was later owned by Jackson & English, and still later by Freeds. A family named Ellmaker, cabinetmakers and millwrights, resided at Liverpool at the time of the county's organization. Rev. David Grubb, an early United Brethren minister and cabinetmaker, was one of four brothers who moved to Perry County from Chester, and settled on a farm near Liverpool.

An act of the Pennsylvania Legislature of March 21, 1865, granted to William Inch, Sr., the right to ferry from the Borough of Liverpool to Liverpool Station.

When the canal was in course of construction, Rev. John A. Gear, from his pulpit in Liverpool, discoursed upon the evils of intemperance, with special emphasis upon drinking. In the audience was "a big Irishman," who stood up and retorted "Enough of that." George Tharp, a business man and himself from the Emerald Isle, arose and led him out. Tharp always stood for law and order, and at that period such men were priceless in a community. At that time liquor flowed pretty freely, there being nine taverns in the town. As the larger number of the workmen employed in building the canal were Irish Catholics, and as the hardships to which their employment subjected them took a heavy toll the Catholic Church purchased a plot of ground along the hillside and opened a cemetery. Tradition tells of their gay life and says there was always a frolic after a funeral.

The public square at Liverpool is sodded and occupied by rows of beautiful shade trees, planted there in 1876, the centenary of American Independence, commemorative of that event.

There was once a Knights of Pythias Lodge in Liverpool, its number being 386. On Odd Fellow Lodge, No. 259, was organized there in 1847. Neither are in existence.

John Staily entered the liquor business in Liverpool, and in 1865 erected a large brick building to extend accommodations to the traveling public, but in 1866, without even announcing his purpose to his family, he emptied all his liquors and closed the bar for good. It may seem strange to many that P. T. Barnum, the famous circus man, once exhibited at Liverpool, but such is the case. The circus troupe were entertained at Mr. Staily's hotel, and among them were a number of strong and rough men. A fight ensued between local roughs and these fellows, who threatened to turn loose the elephant. The town boys produced an old cannon which they loaded with scrap iron and told the management to "trot out its elephant." Mr. H. B. Staily, a son of John Staily's. establishes these facts.

When the large timber tracts in northern Pennsylvania were just starting to be cut, the logs were shipped down the river in rafts, and opposite Liverpool were three mills under one roof, according to Newton Williamson, an octogenarian.

The postmasters at Liverpool have been as follows:

1826-33—Henry Walters.	1866-69—William Staily.
1833-45—James J. Jackman.	1869-73—John D. Monroe.
1845-49—Henry W. Shuman.	1873-81—M. B. Holman.
1849-61—Joseph Shuler.	1881-85—Jacob E. Bonsall.
1862-63—Jacob Holman.	1885-96—Mrs. Laura J. Snyder.
1864-66—Abraham Grubb.	1896- —Geo. J. Tharp.

The first regular physician to locate at Liverpool was Dr. John W. Armstrong, who removed there from Petersburg (Duncannon) in 1824, having previously practiced at Duncannon. He was in Liverpool several years. He was a grandson of General John Armstrong, who commanded the expedition against the Indian town of Kittanning, which ended disastrously for the red skins, and who helped lay out the town of Carlisle, was a member of the Provincial Congress, and had command of the Pennsylvania troops at the Battle of the Brandywine in the Revolution. Dr. Armstrong's successor was Dr. James H. Case, who was born in the Wyoming Valley in 1801. He located in Liverpool in 1827 and practiced there until his death in 1882. He was a public-spirited citizen and a good doctor.

From 1828 to 1831 three different physicians located and stayed but short periods. They were Dr. Fitzpatrick, Dr. Sheedle and Dr. French.

About 1830 Dr. William Cummins, who was born in Belfast, Ireland, in 1804, and educated in Edinburgh, Scotland, located in Liverpool. He was educated for the ministry, but while teaching school read medicine with Dr. Mealy, of Millerstown, and later graduated at Jefferson Medical College. He practiced here until his death in 1846. He was twice married, his son, Hugh Hart Cummins, becoming president judge of Lycoming County. In 1846 Dr. Thomas G. Morris, a native of Sunbury, located at Liverpool. He was a surgeon of a Pennsylvania regiment in the War between the States, after which he practiced and conducted a drug store in New Bloomfield for two years, then resuming his Liverpool practice. He practiced there until his death in 1887. Dr. John Wright, a native of Juniata County, located in Liverpool in 1847, where he practiced until 1854, when he removed to Halifax. He was run down and killed by a train there in 1859. He was married to a daughter of George Blattenberger, one of the associate judges of Perry County.

Others who remained but short periods were Dr. John Rose, 1848; Dr. R. A. Simpson, 1857; Dr. A. A. Murray, 1876 to 1883; Dr. George Motter, 1866, and Dr. George Barlow, 1875. The latter sold his practice to Dr. James F. Thompson, of Centre County, who located in Liverpool in 1878. He graduated at the Jefferson Medical College in 1864. He served in the Sectional War as surgeon of a regiment of Ohio sharpshooters. He was one of the leading doctors of the county during the end of the last century. He practiced at Liverpool until his death, which occurred in 1913. His brother, Henry Adams Thompson, was once the nominee for the Vice-Presidency on the Prohibition ticket. Dr. H. F. Womer located at Liverpool in 1884. He was a graduate of the Jefferson Medical College, 1878. Dr. E. Walt Snyder, a Liverpool native, graduated from Jefferson Medical College in 1889, and located in Liverpool, where he practiced until 1899, when he located at Marysville. Dr. George Henry Bogar, Medico-Chi., 1910, and Dr. Wm. G. Morris are the present physicians, Dr. Morris locating here in 1899, and Dr. Bogar in 1915.

Hoover & Knisely started a shirt factory in the old U. B. church building, in 1905. H. F. Zaring and Park Holman purchased it in 1907, and operated it until 1913, when they sold to Chas. H. Snyder, who had built a new factory building in 1912. In 1914, Mr. Snyder sold it to Chas. E. Deckard, H. F. Zaring and James A. Wright, who operated it until 1917, when they sold the business and building to Jouvand & Lavigne, who had erected a silk mill here in that year. They discontinued the business and turned the building into a moving picture theater, known as the "Silk Mill Movies." The silk mill of this firm began operations in October, 1918. It employs over fifty persons.

The mercantile appraiser's report shows the following business places, the year being the date of connection with the business:

A. M. Shuler (1919), general store. This business was established in 1842 by Samuel and Joseph Shuler; in 1865 Samuel Shuler became proprietor and later it was Samuel Shuler & Son; in 1872 S. M. Shuler, and after his death S. M. Shuler estate.

J. Holman & Sons—Park and Willard Holman, proprietors, general store. Established over fifty years ago by Jacob Holman.

General stores, Wesley Coffman, H. M. Freed, J. A. Geist. A. E. Kerstetter (1907), J. W. Lutz, G. Y. Miller, F. E. Shuler, Long & Miller.

Miscellaneous: J. H. Kepner, groceries; R. F. Stailey, cigars; B. F Blattenberger, Chas. O. Mitchell, hotels; T. A. Stailey, John D. Miller, confectionery; J. J. Hamilton, shoes; John L. Ritter, baker; John D. Snyder, coal; Thomas Weirick & Co., meat market; J. L. Erlenmeyer, fertilizers;

O. C. Knisely, H. G. Long, Frank Potter, A. C. Tharp, auto supplies; George C. Hoffman (1895), succeeding Samuel R. Deckard (1875), furniture and undertaking; J. N. Ritter, paper and iron in bulk; E. C. Mengle, fertilizer; J. F. Deckard, oil.

When the county was organized in 1820, there was no church in Liverpool, the schoolhouse answering that purpose, as well as a little log house, privately owned and standing near the site of the present Lutheran Church. In 1827 the citizens of the village cut and hewed logs for a church. It was used by the German Reformed and Presbyterian people, but there was no settled ministry for a time. A minister from New Bloomfield and another from Millersburg, Rev. Isaac Gerhart, preached occasionally, according to tradition. Rev. William Cochran, a Millerstown boy who entered the ministry, was the first Presbyterian pastor. Rev. James Irvin and Rev. Britton Collins were his successors in turn, according to a historical article in the *Liverpool Sun* of October 6, 1881, probably compiled from local information from people then living. According to the Centennial Memorial of the Presbytery of Carlisle (1889) prepared by a committee, the Liverpool congregation was organized in 1818, by Rev. Nathaniel K. Snowden, who preached until 1820, after which it became vacant until 1828, when Rev. James F. Irvine was installed. Probably both statements are correct. Rev. Cochran was then studying for the ministry under the direction of Rev. Snowden, and it is probable that the young student frequently filled the pulpit at Liverpool. As most of his people had emigrated westward Rev. Irvine's appeal to the Presbytery to be relieved of the appointment was granted. Collins may then have gone over from his station at Millerstown and held occasional services, which practically makes the two statements dovetail, while at a glance they seem widely at variance. Rev. Gerhart was a Reformed minister, and the Reformed denomination held services at Barner's Church and various other points at that time, but time has effaced any records telling of the date of organization or other facts.

Liverpool Lutheran Church. There were early settlers who were Lutherans who had located between the two rivers, the itinerant ministers having appeared among them as early as 1764, the year after the last Indian invasion. The congregation at St. Michael's Church, in Pfoutz Valley, was organized in the early seventies, and the ministers on their way there held services at Liverpool, after the settlement there was begun. When John Huggins laid out the town he had reserved a plot for church and school purposes and a schoolhouse had been erected thereon. While on his way to Pfoutz Valley to preach at St. Michael's, Rev. Conrad Walter held services in the school building. That was between 1804 and 1809, according to Rev. Focht's "Churches Between the Mountains."

The second pastor was Rev. George Heim, whose charge included territory lying in the Tuscarora Valley west of Port Royal (then Perryville), in the vicinity of Mifflintown, Lewistown, and across the country to Lewisburg, and down to Liverpool. He had twelve places at which to preach, some of them forty to fifty miles apart. In 1810 the congregation at Liverpool was organized by Mr. Heim. He was succedeed by his brother, Rev. John William Heim, in June, 1814. The charge was so large that the Liverpool folks only heard him five times a year for several years.

The building of a church was not begun, however, until 1828, when the log frame was put up. It then stood in an unfinished condition until 1831, when it was put under roof. It had high galleries on three sides and a high bell-shaped pulpit, mounted on a post. It was painted white and had a cupola, bell and steeple. It was 35x40 feet in size, and the men most interested in its erection were George Lutz, George Barner, George Tharp, David Stewart, Christian Weirick and John Roush.

The Liverpool church was detached from the old charge in 1829, and with several other churches was supplied by visiting pastors. In 1833 it became a separate charge, with the following ministers since:

1833-42—Rev. Chas. G Erlenmeyer.	1870-72—Rev. Elias Studebaker.
1843 —Rev. Andrew Berg (6 mos.).	1874-81—Rev. D. S. Lentz.
Vacant until 1847.	1881-83—Rev. Herring.
1847-51—Rev. Wm. Weaver.	1883-87—Rev. Mumma.
Vacant until October, 1856.	1888-91—Rev. M. S. Romig.
1856-59—Rev. Josiah Zimmerman.	1891-93—Rev. W. H. Minnemyer.
1859-61—Rev. Jacob A. Hackenberger.	1896-00—Rev. J. M. Stover.
1862-65—Rev. John H. Davidson.	1901-04—Rev. W. H. Stahl.
1865-66—Rev. J. C. Hackenberger.	1904-15—Rev. M. S. Romig.
1866 —Rev. Kerr (supply).	1916-21—Rev. Clyde W. Sheaffer.
1867-70—Rev. W. H. Diven.	1922- —Rev. E. E. Gilbert.

The charge varied with the years, but latterly has included the White Church in Perry Valley, St. Michael's in Pfoutz Valley, and the church in Hunter's Valley. In 1882 a new brick church was erected on Front Street, costing $5,000. It is known as Trinity Church, and is 40x65 feet in size.

Liverpool M. E. Church. The first services in Liverpool by the Methodists were those held in the schoolhouse on the hill, between 1825 and 1830. For some years the organization was not effected, but the meetings were continued. On January 17, 1858, the first church was dedicated, being located at the corner of Market and Strawberry Streets. It was in use until 1877, when it was replaced with a more commodious structure, dedicated in 1878. M. B. Holman was largely instrumental for the building of the new structure. Until the year 1870 it was a part of the Newport charge, under which chapter are the ministers' names. Since that time the pastors have been:

1870-71—Rev. A. H. Mench.	1894-95—Rev. T. A. Elliott.
1872-74—Rev. J. W. Feight.	1896-99—Rev. E. L. Eslinger.
1875-76—Rev. T. S. Wilcox.	1900-01—Rev. F. C. Byers.
1877-78—Rev. B. H. Crever.	1902 —Rev. H. M. Ash.
1879-80—Rev. T. M. Griffeth.	1903-04—Rev. A. D. McCloskey.
1881 —Rev. J. W. Feight.	1905-07—Rev. J. E. Brenneman.
1882-83—Rev. J. R. Dunkerly.	1908-12—Rev. H. W. Hartsock.
1884 —Rev. Daniel Hartman.	1913-15—Rev. W. C. Robbins.
1885-86—Rev. Samuel Ham.	1916-17—Rev. Percy Boughey.
1887 —Rev. A. C. Forscht.	1918 —Rev. G. H. Knox.
1888-89—Rev. J. W. Forrest.	1919-20—Rev. A. E. Fleck.
1890-91—Rev. Edmund White.	1920-22—Rev. C. W. Rishell.
1892-93—Rev. J. P. Benford.	

Liverpool Evangelical Church. The Evangelical congregation at Liverpool erected its first church in 1867, being called St. Mary's Church. Rev. D. W. Miller was pastor when the church was built. Until 1873 it was a part of the Juniata Circuit, and the pastors' names until that time are not contained in the church records. It has since been remodeled on several occasions. With it, comprising the charge, is the Hunter's Valley church and two churches of Juniata County. The pastors since it became a separate appointment, have been:

1873-75—Rev. J. M. Price.	1891-93—Rev. D. P. Scheaffer.
1875-76—Rev. J. M. Ettinger.	1893-95—Rev. J. H. Welch.
1876-79—Rev. A. W. Kreamer.	1895-98—Rev. H. T. Searle.
1879-82—Rev. W. H. Lilly.	1898-00—Rev. E. W. Koontz.
1882-84—Rev. J. M. Dick.	1900-03—Rev. Walter J. Dice.
1884-86—Rev. H. A. Benfer.	1903-05—Rev. J. W. Bentz.
1886-88—Rev. E. D. Keen.	1905-09—Rev. F. H. Foss.
1888-89—Rev. P. F. Jarrett.	1909-11—Rev. A. S. Baumgardner.
1889-91—Rev. W. C. Bierly.	1911-13—Rev J. H. Kohler.

1913-15—Rev. **R. S. Daubert.**
1915   Rev. E. P. Markel (March
      to September).
1915-17—Rev. **C. A. Fray.**

1917-18—Rev. A. B. Coleman.
1918-19—Rev. G. C. Cramer.
1919-20—Rev. M. W. Dayton.
1920-22—Rev. J. E. Newcomer.

Liverpool U. B. Church. According to a historical article in the *Liverpool Sun,* many years ago, the entry of the United Brethren faith to Liverpool was soon after that of the Methodists, which is stated to have been between 1825 and 1830. The first church was erected at Pine Street and was 40x65 feet in size. This church was in use until 1904, having been remodeled several times. In 1904 it was replaced by a new church on Market Street. Among the ministers were Rev. Wm. Behel (1843), Rev. Geo. Wagner, Rev. Rankin, Rev. Samuel Snyder, Rev. ———— Snyder, Rev. J. L. Baker, Rev. Jacob Ritter, Rev. Sitman, Rev. Joshua Walker, Rev. Scott, Rev. Hartsock, Rev. Kirkpatrick, Rev. G. W. Miles Rigor, Rev. Wm. T. Ritchey, Rev. Shimp, Rev. Jackson, Rev. Woodward, Rev. A. E. Fulton, Rev. John Landis, J. F. Tallhelm, Rev. A. H. Spangler, Rev. Isaiah Potter, Rev. John A. Clemm, Rev. C. W. Raber, Rev. E. A. Zeek, Rev. C. B. Gruber, Rev. Keedy, Rev. A. W. Maxwell, Rev. B. C. Shaw, Rev. W. H. Mingle, Rev. W. H. Blackburn, Rev. C. C. Bingham, Rev R. Jamieson, Rev. J. F. Kelly, Rev. G. A. Sparks, Rev. Wm. Beach, Rev. J. E. Ott, Rev. T. H. McLeod, Rev. G. W. Rothermel, Rev. J. S. Emenheiser, Rev. J. C. Erb, Rev. H. B. Ritter and Rev. B. H. Arndt. Rev. David Grubb was not the regular pastor at any time, but was a local U. B. minister.

The official records with the dates were unobtainable and this list of ministers was compiled from information furnished by four members of long standing from the two Buck's Valley churches of the same charge, and, of course the names are not in consecutive order.

LIVERPOOL TOWNSHIP.

At the extreme northeastern section of the county is Liverpool Township, the eighth in order of formation and the first to be created after the establishment of the new county. It is bounded on the north by Juniata County, on the east by the Susquehanna River, on the south by Buffalo Township, and on the west by Greenwood Township, from which it was taken when formed in 1823. The eastern end of Perry Valley comprises a large part of the township. A small part of Pfoutz Valley lies within its borders, as also does Liverpool Borough, from which it took its name.

On the first Monday of December, 1822, to the Perry County courts convened in Landisburg, then the county seat, there was presented a petition signed by residents of Greenwood Township, stating that the township's boundaries were so extensive that it was inconvenient for the inhabitants thereof to attend to township affairs and praying for the court to appoint viewers to report on the advisability of erecting a new township. The viewers named were Meredith Darlington, George Monroe and George Elliott. The court records show that they were continued at the session of February 3, 1823. Further records are vague, but on the records of September 5, 1823, David Dechert (Deckard) was appointed constable of Liverpool Township, gave bond and was sworn in. The town of Liverpool had been laid out fifteen years prior, and from it the township took its name. Its boundaries have never changed, as have so many of the older townships.

On the Susquehanna River, below Liverpool, John Pfoutz took up 142 acres, March 3, 1755. It was a long, narrow strip joined on the south by Alexander McKee, who had warranted two tracts of 290 acres each on September 5 and 20, 1762. Prior to November, 1795, John and Jacob Huggins had located lands north of the present Borough of Liverpool.

The land on which part of the town of Liverpool is located was owned by John Staily, who sold it to John Huggins, October 25, 1808. The tract adjoining Staily on the north, bordering the river, was owned by Anthony Rhoades in 1820, and is now within the borough limits.

About 1790 Henry Grubb, the ancestor of the large and influential Grubb clan, located in Perry Valley. His descendants reside in many states. Among the first settlers was Henry Ulsh, who came from Germany and located during primitive times, when wild animals and Indians still infested the territory. John Hoffman, who was born in Germany, and came to America in early boyhood, was a United Brethren minister in Liverpool and Greenwood Townships, traveling the circuit on horseback. The Cauffmans were early residents. Henry Cauffman, born in Liverpool Township, August 14, 1796, is quoted as an example of early piety. He was a farmer, but found time to read the German Bible through five times and the English Bible, seven, during his long life. He was a great student and was married to Elizabeth Long. George Barner had located in the territory before the formation of the county in 1820. The Shumans came in about 1825. Many of these early residents builded well. The substantial stone farmhouse on the J. L. Kline farm was built in 1778.

An act of the Pennsylvania Legislature of March 7, 1841, provided "that the small island in the Susquehanna River, in Upper Paxton Township, Dauphin County, about four miles above Liverpool, in the county of Perry, be and the same is hereby attached to and declared to be a part of the common school district of Liverpool Township." This is known as Shuman's Island, and is now owned by Rev. B. H. Hart. The provision quoted was repealed on February 12, 1862. It will be noted that it was only for school purposes.

The McKenzie mill, known to many people of the present day, was erected upon lands warranted to Charles and James Dilworth in 1785, and conveyed by them in 1824 to Thomas Gallagher, who subsequently erected a gristmill, as in 1833 he conveyed the property "with gristmill and distillery thereon erected," to Elijah Leonard. In 1837 it passed to Abner C. Harding, of New Bloomfield, who in the same year sold it to David McKenzie, who died in 1856. His son, Daniel McKenzie, then became the owner, and it was in his possession until his death, after which, in 1902, his administrator conveyed it to Harry B. Ulsh. In 1912 Joseph M. Walborn bought it, and in 1918 sold it to Arthur E. Aucker, the present owner, who dismantled it. It was in the hands of the McKenzies, father and son, for sixty-five years, and as the McKenzie mill it was known to all. Its removal takes away another old landmark of eastern Perry.

At Dry Sawmill George W. Barner kept a feed and provision store, doing a large business with the passing boatmen in the old canal days. A small village in the township is locally known as Centreville. There was once a post office located there known as Berlee. The first store was kept there by Samuel and Fred Reen. Just below this village in earlier times there was a sawmill known as Wagner's, which had a large custom trade. During the middle of the past century there was a fulling mill located on the same stream. The post office known as Pfoutz Valley was established in 1884, in a storeroom located at the crossroads at that point. When the lime burning business was a leading industry in this community the highway from that point towards the Susquehanna River was dotted with homes, giving it the appearance of a village, the residents being employed in the kilns. At another crossroads, about two miles from this location, there is an old graveyard connected with the schoolhouse, which would imply that religious services were once held there.

Above Dry Sawmill, along the "Susquehanna Trail," the houses are close together and resemble a village street. The Kline Brothers conducted a steam sawmill there for a long time, doing a large business.

The oldest schoolhouse in the territory of Liverpool Township and borough was located where the Lutheran Church was located later, in the borough. Its usefulness had passed by 1828, when the church was built. According to the journal of Rev. J. W. Heim, he preached in a schoolhouse, which he called Stollenberger's, December 17, 1814. This building is supposed to have stood north of the schoolhouse later known as Barner's, at the foot of the hill. Among early teachers were John Buchanan, Abner Knight, George Grubb and John C. Lindsay. The late Abraham Cauffman, born in 1822, told of attending subscription schools in this district. His first teacher he named as "Ann Watts, who afterwards became a preacher." In the early forties of last century an old log schoolhouse still stood on the farm of Jacob Ulsh.

E. W. Lyter keeps a general store, which is the only place of business in the township.

Barner's Church. Barner's Church was once known as Dupes' Church, according to a historical sketch by Rev. M. H. Groh, once Reformed pastor at Landisburg, who also credits its building as early as 1786, and the organization of the congregation even before that. He names as its earliest ministers: Rev. George Geistweit, 1794-1804; Rev. John Dietrich Adams, 1808-12, and Rev. Isaac Gerhart, 1813-19. The more generally accepted history is that the church was organized by Rev. Gerhart, which would place its beginning between 1813-19. Had it been at the earlier period it would have been mentioned by many historians, among them Rev. Focht and Prof. Wright, as among the first churches.

Christ's Lutheran Church. Some of the residents of eastern Perry Valley who were of the Lutheran faith belonged to St. Michael's, a few were members of Newport and other churches. They were occasionally visited by the Rev. Mr. Heim and other ministers who held services in Grubb's schoolhouse. During the summer of 1844 they erected a church, which was dedicated June 8, 1845. It was a fine frame building and was painted white, which often caused it to be designated as "The White Church," while others called it Grubb's Church. The congregation remained unorganized and had no regular pastor until 1847, when the Liverpool pastor assumed charge, and it has been under that charge since, the pastors' names appearing in the Liverpool chapter.

As Liverpool Township surrounds Liverpool many of its citizens worship in the borough churches.

MADISON TOWNSHIP—INCLUDING SANDY HILL DISTRICT.

Madison Township, which was later divided into two districts, known as Northeast and Southwest Madison, is treated here as one district, as its history is practically identical, up until the division, which even then is only partial.

Madison, the twelfth township to be formed in the new county, was made so by an order of the courts in 1836, in response to a petition signed by George Rice, Solomon Haskel, John Hackett, George Rouse, Daniel Shaffer, William Miller, John Wormly, George Hench, William Owings, Samuel Ickes, Jr., Samuel Loy, Atchison Laughlin, Daniel Hall, Casper Wolf, Jacob Arnold, John Arnold, Daniel Ernest, Henry Ernest, James Hackett, Samuel Nesbitt, Henry C. Hackett, David Grove, John Urie, John S. McClintock, R. Hackett, Thomas Martin, Michael J. Loy, Abram Bower, John Zimmerman, William B. Anderson, John Garber and John Reed.

Madison Township was formed from territory principally taken from Toboyne Township, although Saville contributed a tract about a mile wide, extending from the Waggoner mill property to the Tuscarora Mountain, and Tyrone a small strip. The court appointed William West, Samuel Darlington and Alexander Magee as viewers. It was the intention to name the new township Marion, as that name appears on the draft of the survey of the viewers, but is crossed off. This report is dated August 25, 1835, but was not confirmed, owing to a remonstrance of interested landowners. Then, on November 5, 1835, the court appointed Jacob Smith, F. McCown and George Monroe to re-view the matter, and on July 8, 1836, they reported, the boundaries being designated as follows:

"Beginning at the line between Toboyne and Tyrone Townships, near William Miller's mill; thence adapting the line made by the first view and taking in a small part of Tyrone and a part of Saville Township, north 30¾ degrees, due west seven miles and fourteen perches to a pine on the Juniata County line on the top of Tuscarora Mountain; thence along said line and along the top of said mountain to Bailie's Narrows: thence by Toboyne township 31 degrees east eight miles and one hundred and eighty perches to a stone heap on the top of the Blue Mountain on the Cumberland County line (throwing off a space of one mile and eighty perches in breadth to the township of Toboyne, more than had been done by the former view); thence along said line to the intersection of the line between the townships of Tyrone and Toboyne; thence along said division line to place of beginning. which is hereby designated as a new township."

This second view changed but one thing, the locating of the western boundary of the new township one mile and eighty-four perches farther east. On their draft also appeared the name Marion, but the court in the decree, dated August 1, 1836, sagaciously changed it to Madison, in honor of former President of the United States James Madison, the fourth man to fill that exalted office, and the last to fill it before Perry became a county, and whose death had just occurred about five weeks previous to the court's session, on June 28th.

. The shape of Madison Township is almost that of a parallelogram, its greatest length being from north to south. The main part of the township is comprised in Sherman's Valley, but to the north, lying between the Conococheague Mountain and the Tuscarora Mountain, is Liberty Valley, and on the south, between Bower's Mountain and the Blue or Kittatinny Mountain, is Sheaffer's Valley. Including the Sandy Hill section, later fully described, the township contains nearly sixty square miles, with dimensions of seven by ten miles.

Across this township ran the earliest highway leading from Harris' Ferry (now Harrisburg) to the West, and in it stood the old frontier fort, known as Fort Robinson, and the first gristmill, that advance agent of civilization, first known as Roddy's mill, but for nearly a century as the Waggoner mill, in which family title still rests. However these are of such historical significance that they are fully covered in other chapters devoted to trails, landmarks, Indian history, etc.

The Robinsons, after whom Fort Robinson was named, as it was located on their farm, settled in this territory early. Three of the brothers were William, Robert and Thomas. To Robert posterity is indebted for the history pertaining to those early days when the red skins roamed the forests and made life for the pioneers a veritable land of affliction, grief and agony. The family resided in that vicinity at least nine years before warranting any lands, the first record being that of George Robinson, in May, 1763, who took up 209 acres, including his improvements, adjoining lands of Hugh Alexander, John Byers, James Wilson, and Alexander Roddy. This farm was for years in the name of Captain Andrew Loy, and is now owned by E. R. Loy. These Robinson brothers were interested in practically all the Indian troubles in what is now western Perry County and in many across the Tuscarora Mountain, in what is now Juniata County. George Robinson, who took up the land, was their father. In an engagement with the Indians along Buffalo Creek, in 1763, William and Thomas were killed, and Robert severely wounded. They were with a band of a dozen brave settlers and were ambushed at that point. In 1820 Nicholas Loy was assessed with 300 acres in Toboyne, of which this was a part. Andrew Loy, who owned it later, was his son, as also was George M., a prominent citizen of the vicinity of Andersonburg.

Alexander Roddy had settled in this vicinity before the Albany purchase, and was among those evicted by the provincial authorities. In 1755 he evidently was in possession of this mill property, as an adjoining warrant on the east is described as being bounded by lands of his on the west. He did not, however, warrant it until May, 1763, it being described as for "one hundred and forty-three acres, including his improvements, and adjoining John Byards (Byers), George Robinson, Roger Clarke, James Thorn and William Officier, in the Sherman's Valley." John Armstrong, the first surveyor of Cumberland County, surveyed it in 1765.

The farm just west of the Robinson farm was warranted by James Wilson, in August, 1766, originally containing two hundred acres. His wife, while making her way to the fort for protection, it being within sound of the human voice, was killed by the Indians. This property was owned from 1820 to 1824 by Alexander McClure, and was the birthplace of his son, A. K. McClure, the noted editor and close friend of Lincoln, to whom a chapter of this book is devoted. It was once owned by George Hench, and now by John Freeman. His mother was Isabella, a daughter of William Anderson, Esq., a noted citizen of the county's early days. She was a daughter of Isabella (Blaine) Anderson, who was a niece of James Blaine, grandfather of James G. Blaine.

The John Byers tract of 310 acres was warranted in July, 1762. About 1777, Rev. John Linn, one of the county's pioneer divines, purchased it. He preached at Centre Presbyterian Church from 1777 until 1820. His wife was Mary Gettys, daughter of the founder of Gettysburg. At Linn's death he owned large tracts of land.

What was later to become the Bixler mill tract was warranted by Hugh Alexander in 1755. It then comprised 344 acres. Whether he made his residence in the country before 1757 is now known, yet there is a tradition that his oldest child, Margaret, was born in Sherman's Valley in 1754, and that in her childhood her parents fled several times from Indian raids into the Sherman's Valley to their old home on the eastern shore of Maryland, returning to find their habitations burned. In 1752 he had married Martha Edmiston, who evidently was a daughter of David Edmiston, who took up a tract of three hundred acres adjoining Hugh Alexander, and on which the latter took up his residence, as Edmiston never located in the county. Hugh Alexander was a man of note, representing Cumberland County, which then also comprised Perry, in the Provincial Conference at Philadelphia in 1776, of the first Constitutional Convention necessitated thereby and of the first legislative assembly thus created. Margaret, this first-born of Hugh Alexander and his wife, later married John Hamilton, whose descendants to this day are among the prominent citizens of Harrisburg, where they had located and where he died in 1793. (See Bixler Mill, in "Old Landmarks, Mills and Industries").

George McCord is mentioned by Robert Robinson as living in the neighborhood of Alexander Logan's in 1863. He relates that "John Logan, Charles Coyle, William Hamilton and Bartholomew Davis followed the

63

Indians to George McCord's, where they were in the barn; Logan and all those with him were killed, except Davis, who made his escape." Davis warranted 187 acres in 1766 in the same township.

Three tracts lying south of Cisna's Run were taken up in 1762, 1767 and 1792, by Hugh Gibson, who was taken prisoner by the Indians in 1756. At the time of the attack on Fort Robinson, when his mother, the widow Gibson, the wife of James Wilson, and several others were killed and scalped. Adopted by the tribe, kept a prisoner for some time, he eventually effected an escape. John Byers, in 1767, took up 200 acres; in 1794 another one of 500 acres, and also a tract at Sandy Hill. Evidently he is the same man who was presiding justice of the Cumberland County court in 1763, when Toboyne Township was formed. Much of the land lying along the ridge north of Cisna's Run were taken up by Stephen Cessna, who resided here for a long time and whose name has been given to the locality. The Joseph B. Garber farm was warranted by Cessna and Henry Zimmerman. Dr. Reed Cisna and Captain G. C. Palm were descendants. The farm south of Centre post office was warranted in May, 1787, by James Maxwell. It contained 200 acres, and there was a "fulling mill and power mill" erected there. In 1835 it had passed to Joseph Eaton, who was assessed with a fulling mill, a carding machine and a still.

The Henry Bear mill is located on a tract warranted by John Scouller, in February, 1787, containing 200 acres. Englehart Wormley owned this property in 1814, being assessed with a mill and sawmill. The old mill was replaced by a brick mill in 1841, being built by John Wormley, who came into possession around 1835. In 1915 this mill was purchased by the Tressler Orphans' Home for its water rights for electric power. It had, however, ceased operations some years previous.

The Weaver mill was built by Rev. John William Heim, on lands taken up by John Dunbar, Jr., April 22, 1763, along Laurel Run, where his father had previously taken up a tract and later another. Its erection was about 1830. It is a stone structure, and at the death of Mr. Heim passed in turn to Joseph Bixler (in 1856), Anthony Firman and George Weaver. On January 1, 1919, it passed to the Tressler Orphans' Home, for $5,000, the power to be used in connection with that of the Bear mill plant to run the electric plant connected with that institution. The home also operates the mill both for custom work and as a manufacturing flour plant.

Robert Clark, a young fellow living in Carlisle, was among those who came over during the Indian depredations to help protect the pioneers and became familiar with the fine lands and excellent water in this part of the county. When the land office was opened he was not old enough to warrant land, but his father, Thomas Clark, performed that service and warranted for him in 1766. Robert married Mary Alexander, a daughter of Hugh Alexander, spoken of above, and became the progenitor of one branch of the numerous Clark family of what is now Perry County. W. S. Clark, now living near Everett, Bedford County, but a native Perry Countian, is the only one of the fourth generation still living. Mrs. E. R. Loy and Robert Morris Clark are also direct descendants. Of the three members of the first Provincial Assembly from Cumberland County, Hugh Alexander, Wm. Clark and John Brown, the first two were their ancestors.

In June, 1773, Abraham Lachta located 192 acres, and in May 1775, another claim. In February, 1755, Alexander Logan patented 549 acres, and in February, 1763, his son, John Logan, patented 150 acres. These lands are in the vicinity of the village of Kistler. After John Logan's death the three surviving sons of *Alexander Logan, George, Anthony and William,

---

*Alexander Logan, mentioned in this chapter, was murdered by the Indians, the same being fully described in "The French and Indian War."

created therefrom three farms of 150 acres each, which they owned until 1785, when the middle farm was sold to George McMillen, who had arrived from Dauphin County, but was a native of Ireland. The substantial McMillen families of the present and last generations are his descendants. The McMillens now own most of the Logan lands quoted above. These lands are already in the possession of the fifth generation of McMillens.

Adjoining the Alexander Logan tract on the west was located the lands of William Townsley, warranted September, 1755. During August, 1767, John McElheny warranted 73 acres, which later was owned by John Milligan, who settled there in 1770, from whom the Perry County Milligans are descended, among them being merchants and scholars of note. David Coyle, the progenitor of the well-known Coyles of Philadelphia, Carlisle and Newville, was a near neighbor of the Milligans. John Hamilton, in June, 1762, warranted a place, and Roger Clark, in August, 1766, warranted 251 acres. Where the old Indian trail crossed the Conococheague Mountain's end George Welch, in November, 1768, patented 124 acres. Other early warrants taken out were by Robert Potts, John Potts, James Toy, Henry Lewis, Jacob Grove, James and Alexander Watts, Lancelot Harrison, James Vardell, William McCord, Samuel McCord, John Brubaker, Henry Lewis, Samuel Lyons, Alexander Blaine, Alexander Murray, John McNeere (McAneer), Alexander McNeere, John Douglass, Robert Morrow, William Hamilton's widow, James Morrow, John Irvin, John Murray, John Nelson, John Blair, Bartholomew Davis, John Crawford, Robert Nelson, William Erwin, Christopher Bower, John Garner (Gardner), Hugh Gibson, James Brown, William McFarland, Stephen Cessna (Cisna), Henry Zimmerman, Jane McCreary, Joseph Neeper, William Neeper, William Dalzell, James Maxwell, John Baxter, James Baxter, William Baxter, Henry Lewis, James Dixon, John Scouller, William McClelland and William Hunter.

One of the earliest settlers in the township was William Anderson, the lands being patented in September, 1766, and May, 1757, the two tracts comprising 150 acres. He also purchased other lands, and one property is yet occupied by an Anderson descendant, Arthur Anderson, at Andersonburg, the village having taken the name of the Andersons. Each generation of Andersons has been represented in the civil affairs of the county. The 100-acre property is described as "including his improvements, adjoining the Limestone Ridge on the south, and Conococheague Mountain on the north, and a place called Crosses' Cabins on the west." William Anderson died in 1802. One of his children, Margaret, married James Johnston, of Toboyne Township, and became the mother of John Johnston, who attained considerable prominence as a member of the General Assembly of Pennsylvania, Another, his son, William Anderson, married Isabella Blaine, of the famous Blaine family, and was a member of the General Assembly before the creation of Perry County. Their daughter Isabella became the mother of Col. A. K. McClure, the noted editor, as previously stated. When Perry became a county, William Anderson was made an associate judge, which office he held until his death, in 1832. He was the Anderson after whom the village was named. In the year in which the county was created he was assessed with more property than any one in the township, and the only one assessed with a "negro slave." He had five children, two of whom became prominent. William B. was a member of the General Assembly and of the State Senate, and A. B. Anderson was an associate judge of the county. The stone house on the Anderson farm was erected in 1821, and the barn a year earlier. There is no deed to the Anderson farm, as it has remained in the Anderson family since warranted.

There are several villages within the confines of Madison Township, among them Andersonburg, Centre, Cisna's Run and Kistler.

Andersonburg was long known as Zimmerman, after the proprietor of a well-known old road house or tavern at that point, as early as 1822, and which was in operation until about 1875. When the township of Toboyne was still intact it was the lower voting place. When William Anderson, II, became a man of prominence the name was changed to Andersonburg. The first store was in an old log building known as "the barracks," on the Anderson farm. It was kept by William B. Anderson, who was succeeded by Bryner & Ernest, who in 1863 built the present store building. In 1869 Joseph B. Garber purchased this store. It is now kept by Wm. C. Garber, who succeeded his father in 1904. Andersonburg is one of the oldest post offices in Perry County, having been a post office already when the mail was carried on horseback from Landisburg to New Germantown. A marble works was once located there. Andersonburg was long an important centre, and Dr. B. F. Grosh practiced his profession there from 1844 until his death, in 1857. He was the father of the late Alexander Blaine Grosh. In 1861 Dr. G. W. Mitchell located there and practiced until 1902, since which time it has not been the headquarters of any physician. When the Newport & Sherman's Valley Railroad was built, Andersonburg was made a station. J. C. Martin conducts a large undertaking business there since 1889.

In 1801 James Gray settled in what is now called the Sandy Hill District. He did a weaving business and operated a still. He was the paternal ancestor of James A. Gray, who was sheriff in 1878, and of William B. Gray, who was a member of the board of county commissioners, 1891-93.

The old Hench tannery, located at Centre, was one of the most important in the county. It was located upon a part of the tract of 168 acres warranted by Jane McCreary and sons, on June 2, 1762. This tannery was erected before 1820, when Perry became a county, as Nicholas Loy was assessed with a tanyard in Toboyne Township (to which Madison then belonged) in that year. On December 17, 1825, John Loy purchased it from his father. It then consisted of a "log building, two stories high, containing two limes, one bate, beam house and currying shop." The bark was ground in an adjoining shed. "One pool, one leach and sixteen vats comprised the whole establishment." April 19, 1832, Atchison Laughlin purchased it, and on August 10, 1832, admitted George Hench into partnership, which lasted until 1837, when Mr. Hench became the entire owner upon the payment of $1,500 to Mr. Laughlin. Energetic, and a born tanner and business man, he began improving the plant. In 1842 he erected a large main building, and in 1851 put in steam, using the used tan as a fuel. In 1860 a sawmill was added. April 1, 1865, Atchison L. Hench, a son, was admitted into partnership, with a one-third interest. This lasted until April 1, 1872, when by mutual consent the son withdrew. At that time the assets of the firm had grown to $90,000. A few years later Mr. Hench removed to Carlisle, but continued in control of the tannery, which was operated until 1885. It passed to Henry Metz, and in 1894 the grounds and buildings were purchased by Robert Hench, who removed the vats. The original log mansion of Mr. Hench still stands, but has been remodeled by Mr. Robert Hench into what is one of the modern country homes of Perry County.

The 266-acre tract of Jacob Grove was warranted by him June 10, 1762, later having been owned by David Kistler, George I. Rice and Henry Kepner. The old Grove homestead was near the George I. Rice residence of recent years. As early as 1778, Jacob Grove had erected a gristmill and two stills on this property.

The James M. Moose mill, south of Cisna's Run, on Sherman's Creek, passed from Wm. Owings, in 1846, to James Marshall, who in turn sold to I. Graham McFarlane, in 1850. Daniel Hall owned it from 1854 to 1859, when it was owned for a year by Amos Stouffer. In 1860, it passed to Andrew Trostle, who was in possession until 1884. David Metz then purchased it, and in 1900 sold to James M. Moose. This mill is on lands taken up in 1767, by John Byers. The mill was erected by William Owings, in 1842.

The Bistline mill is located along Sherman's Creek, on the south bank, about a mile south of Cisna's Run. This tract was warranted by James Maxwell, May 7, 1787, and was originally 200 acres. Col. John Maxwell, who was county commissioner in 1824, and was a son of John Maxwell, was assessed with "a fulling mill and a power mill" in 1820, when the county was formed. In 1835, the assessment reads, "including a fulling mill, a carding machine and a still." From his heirs, in 1873, it was conveyed to Abraham Bistline, and it is now owned by Newton Flickinger. Just when the mill became a gristmill is problematical. This property later passed to Thomas Adams, by whose name the mill was long known.

Centre is a village and post office on the Newport & Sherman's Valley Railroad, and was the location of the once famous old Hench tannery, just described. William Welch had a store and was postmaster here as early as 1835. Robert Dunbar succeeded him, but sold in 1840 to James McNeal, who ran it until 1860, when he died. George Hench then bought the building, and his son, Atchison L., William Grier and William Hollenbaugh carried on business under the firm name of William Grier & Co., in 1863. Hollenbaugh and Grier sold their interest to J. L. Evinger, and the firm of Hench & Evinger continued for some years. John T. Robinson, John Wolf, George J. Hench and John J. Rice followed in turn. Edward Hull was postmaster for a long time. He was a blacksmith and became a county commissioner. George Barclay carried on wagonmaking. John E. Waggoner has been the merchant and postmaster there for the past fifteen years.

Cisna's Run, which once aspired to be the county seat, is another small village and a station on the Newport & Sherman's Valley Railroad. On the old land warrants made in 1755, it is known as Cedar Spring, being the location of a large spring, probably five feet deep, on the property of Wm. H. Loy. The lands lying around Cisna's Run were among the first to be warranted in the township. John Garner (Gardner) patented "two hundred acres, including his improvement on Cedar Spring, a branch of Sherman's Creek," in February, 1755, and 100 acres in 1767. As early as 1830 there was a store in the George Bryner house, kept by John Reed. Later merchants have been Daniel Garber, John H. Bryner and George Ernest, David Ernest, Elias Snyder and Samuel K. Morrow. R. A. Clarke started a store about 1860. George Bryner and sons for many years conducted a wagonmaker and blacksmithing business there.

Kistler is a village lying several miles from the Newport & Sherman's Valley Railroad, on the road to Juniata County, where it intersects with the road from Ickesburg to Blain. The village was named Kistler in honor of David Kistler, who was instrumental in getting a post office there in 1884. The post office was abandoned after rural free delivery was instituted. There were two stores there at one time. Henry Koppenheffer was the first merchant, starting about 1875.

In 1884 a post office was established at Bixler's mill and named Bixler, which also was discontinued with the advent of the rural free delivery system. Sandy Hill was also a post office and was discontinued for the same reason. Samuel Milligan built and kept the first store at Sandy Hill.

The first schoolhouses of which there was any knowledge were at Sandy Hill, Centre Church and Clark's. The Clark schoolhouse was a very old one, but its early history is veiled in obscurity. The Centre school was also a very old one and was located on the tract of the Centre Presbyterian Church. There is reason to believe that even before it was established that it had a predecessor on the lower Linn farm near the Waggoner mill. The Sandy Hill school was established before 1800, and tradition places the location as south of the store, near the spring at the edge of the old "camp meeting" grounds. In his report to the State Superintendent of Public Instruction, in 1877, Prof. Silas Wright, then county superintendent of schools, said of this school: "It is related that pupils attending this school from the west end of Liberty Valley, traveled across Conococheague Hill, in a path which is even to this day occasionally crossed by a bear. These pupils, in the short days of winter had to take their breakfast before daylight and the supper table awaited their return until long after dark." Before the free school act there was a "charity school" in the Anderson orchard at Andersonburg.

Madison Township was early the location of many mills, stills and tanneries. In 1762 Jacob Grove warranted 266 acres of land, near the village of Kistler. As early as 1778 he had erected a gristmill and two stills upon this property. This was one of the earliest mills to be built in the county and was found in all the assessments until 1820, when it was likely abandoned. In 1778 William McCord was assessed with a tanyard, and in the assessment of 1814 it is in the name of Samuel McCord.

In that part of Madison Township known as Liberty Valley, Wm. L. Beale and Samuel Milligan erected a large steam tannery in 1847. It burned in May, 1849, but was rebuilt at once. In 1858 it passed to Beale & Swearingen, who operated it until 1865, when they sold to Hollenbaugh & Lurtz, who later admitted Samuel Brickley as a partner. Ten months later, at sheriff's sale, it was purchased by Beale & Swearingen, who sold to George Cook. He formed a partnership with George Mohler and James Emory. In 1875 George Mohler & Son became the owners and operated it until "the eighties," when it was discontinued.

An early physician who resided midway between Sandy Hill and Centre Church was Dr. S. M. Tudor. He kept a colored slave who had escaped from the South, and caused no little trouble to those who condoned slavery. His practice covered forty years, including the third quarter of the last century. He was succeeded by Dr. Lewis Rodgers, a graduate of Cleveland Medical College, '70. Dr. J. Wesley Rowe, Jefferson Medical College, '71, was located at Centre for a short time.

There was once an old road house or tavern at the head of Waggoner's dam. It was owned and conducted by Daniel Shaffer. Dr. Theodore Meminger, a practicing physician of Philadelphia, desiring to retire, located in Liberty Valley in 1815. He was a member of the Society of Friends.

The business places of Madison Township, according to the mercantile appraiser, are as follows, the date being the time of entering business. Owing to the township being divided into two districts, known as Southwest Madison and Northeast Madison (or Sandy Hill District), the names are listed in their respective districts. They follow:

Southwest Madison—A. W. Clouse, R. A. Smith, W. C. Garber, D. Roy Moose, J. E. Waggoner, general stores; J. C. Martin, furniture; W. II. Waggoner, grain and feed; Moose & Junkin, flour and feed.

Northeast Madison—E. S. Adair, H. L. Bender, J. W. Heckendorn (1910), general stores; G. E. Beck & Sons, tobacco and feed.

St. Paul's Lutheran Church. There were many families of Lutheran people residing between Loysville and Blain, and in 1855 they decided to organize a new congregation in the vicinity of Andersonburg. Its officers were: Jacob Arnold, Jacob Kunkle, elders; J. B. Zimmerman, Samuel Arnold, deacons; George Hohenshilt, Henry Wolf, trustees. During the same year a church was built. Rev. Reuben Weiser resigned as pastor during its period of construction. On December 22, 1855, it was dedicated. It is built of brick, the size being 40x50 feet. From May, 1856 to 1858, Rev. Philip Willard as pastor. In 1858 it and Blain withdrew from the Loysville charge to unite and form the Blain charge. Its pastors, accordingly, have been the same as those of the Blain church. (See Blain chapter.)

Madison Township is usually listed for statistical purposes as Northeast and Southwest Madison Township, and is locally spoken of as Madison Township and Sandy Hill District. Twenty-one years after the erection of Madison Township the Court of Common Pleas, upon petition, divided it into two election districts—Madison District and Sandy Hill District. Then for some years matters moved along satisfactorily, both districts having but one set of township officers, but in 1866 an effort was made to divide the township. The petition praying for the division was presented to the court at the April session of 1866. The court appointed viewers and they reported on August 6th favoring two townships, whereupon the court ordered an election to be held on November 24, 1866. On December 3, 1866, the returns were presented to the court and showed a majority of thirty-three against the separation, opposition having developed.

Not content with the result, those who desired the division had a bill presented to the State Legislature which passed and was signed by Governor John W. Geary, on February 26, 1867. Considering the matter at issue the bill is more or less of a compromise, as no provision was made in the act for the election of justices of the peace. This fact, whether an oversight or not, withholds one essential of an independent township. That the act still holds it as one township is designated by the following language: "Provided, that the said township shall be and remain divided into two election districts, whilst it continues as one township." Those practically insignificant matters are the slight ties that bind Sandy Hill District to Madison Township, for while they otherwise elect two sets of officials, yet both districts vote for the same candidates for justice of the peace. It is a matter of conjecture whether or not there is in the whole State of Pennsylvania a similar example. The voting place of the Sandy Hill District, or Northeast Madison, is at the Sandy Hill store, and that of Madison Township, or the Southwest District, at Andersonburg.

Sandy Hill Reformed Church. This church was organized by Rev. F. S. Lindaman, September 14, 1873, by electing George L. Ickes and Samuel Bender, elders, and Jacob Kuhn and Samuel Showers, deacons. As early as the pastorate of Rev. C. H. Leinbach at Blain (1842-59), he had preached in the schoolhouse there. The newly organized congregation also worshiped in the schoolhouse until January 3, 1875, when the new frame church building was dedicated. It belongs to the Blain charge, whose pastors minister to its people. The list of pastors appears in the chapter devoted to Blain.

Stony Point United Evangelical Church. This church is located three miles west of Kistler, on the Blain road. About 1836 ministers of this faith first preached in a small schoolhouse, no longer there. They later preached at the house of Conrad Ernest, later, in a vacant "still house," and again in the schoolhouse. In 1866 they built the church. In 1903 it was remodeled. It is a part of the Perry Circuit, being served by the pastor who resides at Elliottsburg. See Spring Township for pastors.

Emory M. E. Chapel. The first Methodist organization in Madison Township (then a part of Toboyne), was at Bruner's mill (Trostle's), about 1815. The Bruner brothers, devout Methodists, are credited with being largely responsible for the establishment of Methodism in western Perry County. In the earlier years preaching services were held in schoolhouses. The church was built in 1838, among those interested being Jacob Bixler and John Flickinger, the latter giving the land upon which it was built. It is a part of the Blain charge, but up until 1875 was a part of the New Bloomfield charge, under which chapters the pastors' names appear.

St. Mark's Church. The Lutheran people residing at and around Kistler built a church in 1894, which was known as St. Mark's Church. Its territory was too narrow, with Loysville immediately below and St. Paul's almost against it above, with the attending result that it was soon found to be a heavy charge upon its supporters. The building was sold in 1919 and the church dismantled.

MARYSVILLE BOROUGH.

Marysville covers more territory than any borough in the county, extending from the Cumberland County line, at the crest of the Kittatinny or Blue Mountain, to the top of Cove Mountain, where it is bounded by Penn Township. It is located on the Susquehanna River, which is its eastern boundary, and extends westward a mile or more to Rye Township, from which its lands were taken for incorporation in 1865. It differs from every other town in the county from the fact that it is a "railroad town," its male citizens, with few exceptions, being employed by the Pennsylvania Railroad Company. It is not surrounded by any great amount of agricultural lands, the mountains shutting them off on two sides and the river on a third. This would not seriously affect its markets were it not that only eight miles to the south is Harrisburg—the State Capital—with a population of practically 100,000, to which trade naturally gravitates. Marysville is the only town in the county with a street car line and the advantage of the facilities afforded thereby. Its street car facilities extend up the Cumberland Valley to Newville, farther east than Lebanon, in the Lebanon Valley, and to Philadelphia, along the main line, via Hershey, Elizabethtown and Lancaster. The line to Marysville was opened on June 2, 1902.

The valley in which Marysville is located is known as Fishing Creek Valley, being drained by a creek of the same name which flows into the Susquehanna at Marysville. The lands at the mouth of this creek, on which Marysville is located, were first warranted by Samuel Hunter, on September 8, 1755, the tract extending two miles along the river and three miles up the valley. In 1766 and in 1767 he warranted adjoining tracts. Near the present site of Seidel's forge, on the creek, he erected a sawmill, which was Marysville's first industry. In 1767 he sold the property with the sawmill and other improvements, described as at the mouth of "West's Fishing Creek," to Elizabeth Stewart, for twenty pounds.

A portion of this land, after passing through several hands, came to R. T. Jacobs, who, on January 24, 1821, patented a tract containing 500 acres and allowance, extending a mile along the west bank of the Susquehanna and west about a mile and a half. Title later passed to Robert Clark, then to Frederick Watts; and later, to Jacob M. Haldeman was transferred "one undivided moiety," and to Jacob and Christopher C. K. Pratt, the other "moiety." Jacob Pratt sold his share to Hiram P. and Thomas W. Morley. Jacob M. Haldeman then bought out all these parties, and on December 1, 1860, sold to Margaretta D. Fenn.

The Seidels took it down and built a forge instead in 1862. Later the firm was Seidel & Sons, and still later Seidel Bros., being composed of A. J. Seidel and J. Harper Seidel, once a Member of Assembly from Perry County. About 1895 it was operated as a chain works for a few years.

The first schoolhouse was built within what is now the borough limits, in 1853, being located where the Holmes drug store stands. Harriet Singer was the first teacher. There was a single-room schoolhouse built on the river bank in 1868, costing $400, which was in use until 1885, J. L. Hain being the last to teach there. The two-room frame building below the railroad was built in 1871, at a cost of $2,300, and was in use until 1913. The old two-room building above the railroad was built in 1868, at a cost of $2,500, and was in use until 1885. The four-room building, on the site of the present large building, was erected in 1885, J. L. Hain having been the first principal. The new building, one of the best in the county, was erected in 1913 at a cost of over $25,000. R. R. Anderson, of York County, was the first principal at this building. There was also a two-story brick building on Lincoln Street, built in 1895, and in use until 1913, when it was sold to the Knights of Pythias. Marysville has a greater number of pupils in school than any other district in the county.

The first graduating class of the Marysville High School was that of April 6, 1888, under the principalship of J. L. Hain. The class was composed of Misses Nora Eppley, Mame Eppley, Minnie Shull, M. Ella Nevin and Mary Wox. An alumni association was organized in 1891, with ten members, and now numbers 187.

Marysville, with its extensive railroad yards, in 1862 had but a watering station for engines, called the "Y." In 1863 the wooden railroad bridge connecting the town of Dauphin and northern Marysville, was built, thus connecting the divisions of the Northern Central Railroad from Baltimore to the North. The northbound and southbound traffic then all passed through Marysville. The station at the west end of this bridge was known as Marysville, and the lower station, at the then village proper, as Haley's. The development of the freight traffic made necessary the building of the historic old roundhouse for the storage of engines, in 1868, from which time the railroad yards began to develop. Jeremiah Buzzard and Irvin Crane were the first yardmasters. This old Northern Central bridge burned in 1871, but was rebuilt and in use until 1886, when it was abandoned and torn away. Parts of three piers and the abutment still stand, notwithstanding the ravages of time. The present stone arch bridge of the Pennsylvania Railroad, the longest stone arch bridge in the world, was erected in 1900, taking the place of a steel structure which had been built in 1878.

As the business of the Northern Central and the Pennsylvania Railroads grew so did Marysville, and so did the number of tracks which had to be crossed by traffic at Valley Street, as the former corporation had its roundhouse there for the care and storage of its engines. This was a veritable death trap, and was eliminated by the erection of the subway when the roundhouse was removed in 1901, the Marysville yards remodeled and the Enola yards established.

In 1908 the yards were taken over by the Philadelphia Division of the road, and J. C. F. Geib and Simon Lick were made yardmasters, having filled the same positions when the yards were under the former management. In 1912 the Pennsylvania made the Marysville yards a preference freight yard, switching there the business that had formerly been done at Harrisburg. Before the patent couplers came into use in the railroad business many men were injured while coupling cars, by the loss of a hand or fingers. Robert C. Shaffer, now living in Lancaster, was the only one of sixteen brakemen once employed at the Marysville yards who was not so unfortunate. From the borough's southern limits the great stone arch bridge of the Pennsylvania Railroad crosses the Susquehanna River, 440,-000,000 tons of stones having been used in its construction. It is the longest stone arch bridge in the world.

When the Morley Brothers were in possession of the mill which stood where the Seidel forge stands, they were engaged in the manufacture of a left-handed plow, and did a large business. About 1884 a shoe factory was started at Marysville and operated for a few years, its passing occurring in 1889. In 1897 William H. Leonard operated a shirt and overall factory. It was in business a few years.

Marysville is supplied with water by the Marysville Water Company, which was incorporated April 5, 1895, with H. M. Horner as president, and John A. Herman as secretary and treasurer. The Marysville Light, Heat & Power Company was incorporated in 1897, with H. M. Horner, president; B. F. Umberger, secretary, and J. W. Beers, treasurer. It erected its own plant, but after a short time contracted with the Valley Railways Company for current, and in 1917 sold their franchise to the Juniata Public Service Company. Marysville owns its own brick municipal building.

Marysville's first lodge was Perry Lodge, No. 458, F. & A. M., organized December 27, 1869, with J. S. Funk, worthy master; A. J. Stahler, secretary, and H. H. Seidel, treasurer. Beuhler Lodge, K. of P., is almost as old, having been instituted November 3, 1870, with Wm. P. Price, chancellor, and Joseph McKenna, secretary.

During the earlier years the population of the vicinity of Marysville depended upon the physicians of Harrisburg, Dauphin, West Fairview, Duncannon and other places. In 1862 Dr. Heinsling located there and practiced for some years. Dr. Culp located there in 1868, and Dr. A. J. Traver in 1870, the latter practicing there until his death in 1885. In 1875 Dr. George W. Eppley located there, having previously practiced for a time at Elliottsburg. He was a graduate of the University of Pennsylvania, and practiced there until his death, which occurred July 27, 1887. He was a very successful practitioner. Dr. J. M. Boyd, a native of the county, located in Marysville in 1880, after graduating at Ohio Medical College, remaining a short time.

Dr. A. D. VanDyke, a native of Juniata County, located here in 1883, and remained until 1899, when he became connected with the medical department of the Pennsylvania Railroad, with which company he still remains, his headquarters being in the Pennsylvania Depot, New York City, since 1919. Prior to that time he had been connected with the company's offices at Harrisburg, Philadelphia, Elmira and Renovo. Dr. W. S. Ruch was located there a number of years, leaving about 1890, when he was succeeded by Dr. H. O. Lightner, who practiced until his death in 1915. Dr. E. Walt Snyder changed his location from Liverpool to Marysville, in 1899, where he practiced until 1919, and where he still resides. He was succeeded by his son, Dr. Chas. R. Snyder, May 1, 1919. Dr. George W. Gault, Baltimore Medical College, 1910, located at Marysville, upon his graduation. Dr. Snyder and Dr. Gault are now the practicing physicians. Dr. Frank Patterson and Dr. E. H. Mitchell were located here for a short time.

No other organization has done so much for Marysville as the Civic Club, organized January 28, 1913. Its first officers were Mrs. Mary E. Morley, president; Mrs. J. P. Lilley and Mrs. Pearl B. Hipple, vice-presidents; Mrs. F. W. Geib, recording secretary; Mrs. Nora Eppley, corresponding secretary, and Mrs. L. C. Wox, treasurer. Mrs. Wox has been president since January, 1914. Organizations of this character are wont to turn into social affairs and forget the object for which organized, but the record of this organization proves that it has not done so. In April, 1913, within ninety days of their organization, receptacles were placed at designated points for the collection of waste paper, etc. Although most of them were destroyed it stands to the credit of the new organization that they were provided. In 1914, at their instance and expense a better road was opened to the cemetery. The triangle known as the Marysville Square, had long been kept in an uninviting condition, and that was the next object upon which the Civic Club centered its efforts, in May, 1916, and ever since it is a beautifully sodded place surrounded by plants and shrubbery, seen by travelers from passing trains and visitors to town. Then, in 1920, after those who had defended their country, returned home, the club had erected upon the public school building a town clock, the only one in the county, save that upon the courthouse at the county seat, at an expense of over $2,000. Prior to this they had planted on the school lawn memorial trees in memory of Blaine Barshinger, Howard Spidel and James Brightbill, three local boys who lost their lives in the World War.

Upon the clock tower is this inscription:

> Built, A. D. 1920
> In Honor of the
> Boys and Girls
> Who Assisted in Winning
> The World War.

The present officers are: Mrs. L. C. Wox, president; Mrs. E. J. Sellers and Mrs. Chas. Clouser, vice-presidents; Mrs. Pearl B. Hipple, recording secretary; Mrs. Garfield Eppley, corresponding secretary, and Mrs. Wm. Dice, treasurer. Even now the organization is planning to pipe water to the Chestnut Grove cemetery. At the entrance to the cemetery, by the way, is a beautiful memorial gate, "presented by Jane Lanotte Wimer, 1908."

According to the report of the mercantile appraiser the following persons are identified with business in Marysville, the date following name being the date of their entry into business:

General stores, G. C. Bitting, A. J. Ellenberger (1901), J. L. Halbach, R. N. Hench, F. W. Roberts (1910; founded by W. L. Roberts, 1902), J. E. White (1903, in stand long kept by T. W. Morley; purchased Wise stand in 1907).

Groceries, Alice Ensminger, J. A. Fenicle, Jos. Stante.

H. E. Gault (1910) and C. J. Kistler, meat markets.

W. L. Roberts & Son, coal (1902).

Albert Bungden, stoves and tinware (1905).

L. F. Platt, cigars and tobacco (1910). Mr. Platt was killed in an aeroplane accident, November 5, 1920.

C. M. Dick, W. M. Straw, cigars and tobacco.

Margaret L. Bratton, H. A. Keim, confectionery.

H. J. Deckard, furniture.

C. H. Fortenbaugh, electrical supplies.

P. M. Skivington, flour, feed and coal.

R. H. Holmes, drugs.

There was once a United Brethren congregation located at Marysville, having dedicated its church May 15, 1875. The first services had been held in 1866. Rev. G. W. Lightner, who long made his home in Duncannon, was the pastor, covering a three-year period when the church was built. Early pastors were Rev. J. P. Bishop, Rev. J. X. Quigley, Rev. N.

Altman, Rev. G. A. Colestock, Rev. J. Neidig. Rev. W. Owen, Rev. J. S. Bradford, Rev. H. Brown. Rev. G. W. Lightner (3 years), Rev. J. R. Hutchinson, Rev. R. H. Whitlock, Rev. D. D. Lowrey, Rev. J. C. Crider. Rev. J. P. Anthony. The congregation having dwindled by removals and otherwise, the building was sold to the Lutheran congregation, April 16, 1887, for $1,200, it being used as their place of worship until 1901, when the enlargement of the railroad yards necessitated the purchase of more ground, which included that on which the church stood. It was then purchased by the railroad for $2,000, sold and removed to another location, where it was remodeled into a dwelling.

Bethany United Evangelical Church. Originally Perry County was divided into two sections by the Evangelical Church, and circuit riders carried the word to the entire faith. The members of the faith here were included in that part which finally narrowed down to Marysville, Newport and Rye Township's two churches—Salem and Bethel. The two latter were finally detached and made a part of the new Keystone charge. Then, until 1898 Marysville and Newport were united. In that year Marysville became a separate station, with C. W. Finkbinder as the first pastor.

A lot was presented to the Evangelical Association by Theodore and Margaretta D. Fenn, in 1866, and a movement started for the erection of an Evangelical church at Marysville. It was built and dedicated December 23d of that year, the building committee being Rev. John Cramer, Levi Dice and Leonard Swartz. The charge also once included the churches known as Salem and Bethel, in Rye Township. The ministers have been:

Rev. A. L. Reeser.	Rev. George Joseph.
Rev. L. K. Harris.	1881-82—Rev. P. S. Orwig.
Rev. J. C. Farnsworth.	1883-84—Rev. R. W. Runyan.
Rev. A. H. Irvine.	1885-87—Rev. I. C. Yeakel.
Rev. J. Young.	1888 —Rev. J. W. Bentz.
Rev. J. W. McGaw.	1889 —Rev. G. E. Zehner.
Rev. S. D. Bennington.	1890-92—Rev. S. P. Remer.
Rev. I. Y. Reid.	1893-94—Rev. Benj. Hengst.
Rev. S. T. Bucknell.	1895 —Rev. J. F. Douty.
Rev. W. E. Detwiler.	1896 —Rev. J. F. Dunlap.
Rev. S. Aurand.	1897-98—Rev. C. W. Finkbinder.
Rev. T. M. Morris.	1899-02—Rev. W. H. Lilley.
Rev. M. Sloat.	1903-04—Rev. D. L. Kepner.
Rev. S. E. Davis.	1905-07—Rev. L. E. Crumbling.
Rev. D. W. Miller.	1908-11—Rev. I. N. Bair.
Rev. W. H. Stover.	1912-14—Rev. W. E. Detwiler.
Rev. S. I. Shortess.	1915-17—Rev. L. A. Fuhrman.
Rev. Geo. E. Zehner.	1918- —Rev. C. D. Pewterbaugh.

In 1896 the congregation erected a new church on Valley Street. The building committee was composed of Rev. J. F. Dunlap, George Kocher, Jacob Kline, C. S. Wise and J. H. Souder. The parsonage was built in 1904, when Rev. D. L. Kepner was pastor.

Marysville Church of God. Rev. Thomas Still organized the first church of that faith in Marysville, in 1866, following a series of religious meetings held in the woods. It began with eight members. As early as 1850 several meetings were held, but with no result, as there were then but four dwelling houses there. In 1865 another effort was made, but again lapsed. For two years after 1866 the little flock worshiped in private dwellings and in the schoolhouse. When the Evangelical Association erected a church the members of the Church of God were allowed to hold meetings in it for some time, but this privilege was later denied on account of the doctrines of the Church of God. Again the meetings were held in homes, in the schoolhouse and on the picnic grounds. During April, 1869, a plot of ground located on the northwest corner of Myrtle Avenue and Chestnut

Street was purchased for the erection of a church. A frame building, 40x50 feet, was dedicated January 16, 1870. The building committee was composed of J. D. Miller, A. Hartman, D. Cowen, A. J. Brady, John Heaney and C. L. Amy. Since then the congregation has grown much larger and although worship is still conducted in that building, a plot has been purchased at the southwest corner of Maple Avenue and Chestnut Street, where a more commodius house of worship and a parsonage is being erected. Until 1904 Marysville was a part of the Duncannon charge, under which chapter a list of the pastors will be found. The pastors at Marysville since have been Rev. J. W. Miller, Rev. T. B. Tyler, Rev. E. M. Mell, Rev. S. C. Stonesifer, Rev. Charles Parsons, Rev. J. F. Wiggins, and Rev. Wesley N. Wright, the present pastor.

Trinity Reformed Church. The congregation of Trinity Reformed Church at Marysville is to some extent the outgrowth of the Fishing Creek church, just as the Duncannon Reformed Church is to some extent the successor of the church at Fio Forge. On February 4, 1868, Zion Classis, which included this territory in early days, met at New Bloomfield to establish a fourth charge in Perry County, to be called the Duncannon charge. The conclusion of Classis was that there should be four preaching points, Mt. Zion in Fishing Creek Valley, Marysville, Duncannon and St. David's at Dellville, the latter being the only organized congregation of the four, but Duncannon and Marysville being growing towns and a good field. Rev. William Dewitt Clinton Rodrick was assigned to the pastorate of the charge in April, 1868, but the Marysville church was not regularly organized until January, 1869. When the charge was organized there was but one member of the faith residing in Marysville, Mrs. Amelia A. Sloop, and at the organization of the church there were but four others. Later Dr. O. T. Everhart, who but recently passed away at Shrewsbury, Pennsylvania, joined, and it was decided to build a church. The building committee was composed of Rev. Rodrick, Dr. Everhart, George W. Kissinger and Lewis S. Lesh. Two town lots, which have ever since been the seat of worship of this people, were decided upon as a location, Mrs. Margaret D. Fenn, who owned the property, presenting the one, and the church purchased the other for $300. Excavation was made for the foundation of the first church by the membership during September, 1869, by the light of the moon, and on October 6, 1870, it was dedicated, having been built by a membership which then numbered only thirteen, at a cost of $4,500. This church was about 40x60 feet and in use until 1901, when it became necessary to replace it. The present modern brick building was then erected and dedicated on April 20, 1902. The building committee was composed of Rev. J. David Miller, E. B. Leiby, W. L. Roberts, W. T. White, C. B. Smith, P. M. Michener, L. C. Wox and Lucian Haas. In 1909 a fine brick parsonage was erected on Dahlien Street, and in 1914 a pipe organ was installed in the church. The pastors have been as follows:

1868-71—Rev. W. D. C. Rodrick.
1872-75—Rev. Harry Wissler.
1876-81—Rev. U. Henry Heilman.
1882-86—Rev. James R. Lewis.

1886-88—Rev. Samuel S. Meyer.
1889-16—Rev. J. David Miller.
1916-21—Rev. Ralph E. Hartman.

Zion Lutheran Church. The first Lutheran congregation at Marysville was served by Rev. M. L. Heisler, a supply of the Duncannon church, during 1870. The church seems not to have been regularly organized then, as Rev. G. W. Crist is accredited with its organization, during his pastorate, 1879-1882.

In 1901 a new brick church was erected on Front Street. The pastors have always been the same as those of the Duncannon church, save from 1900 to 1903, when the two churches did not form one charge. (See Duncannon chapter.) During that time the pastors of Zion at Marysville were Rev. P. T. E. Stockslager, June 1, 1900, to January 25, 1903, and Rev. J. G. Langham, March 1, 1903, to October 1, 1905, when the charges were reunited as the Marysville charge, the pastor being resident there and continuing under the restored charge. For list of pastors prior to 1901 and after 1902, see Duncannon chapter.

Methodist Episcopal Church. The Marysville Methodist Episcopal congregation was organized in .1872, by Rev. Cambridge Graham, who remained as pastor until 1873. Rev. E. A. Deavor succeeded him in 1873, during which year the church was built, the building being 35x50 feet in size. During the pastorate of Rev. Dickson (1897-1900) the church was remodeled. During 1919-20 a fine brick parsonage was built on a plot opposite the new school building. The members of the faith first worshiped in the schoolhouse on the river bank. The pastors from the beginning have been:

1872 —Rev. Cambridge Graham.	1894-95—Rev. E. A. Pyles.
1873-75—Rev. E. A. Deavor.	1896 —Rev. Samuel Fox.
1876-78—Rev. J. Y. Shannon.	1897-00—Rev. C. W. Dickson.
1879-80—Rev. E. T. Swartz.	1901-04—Rev. S. S. Carnill.
1881-82—Rev. J. P. Benford.	1905 —Rev. L. L. Snyder.
1883-84—Rev. H. N. Minnigh.	1906-07—Rev. H. W. Hartsock.
1885-87—Rev. G. A. Singer.	1908-09—Rev. A. O. Stone.
1888-90—Rev. E. M. Aller.	1910-13—Rev. A. C. Shue.
1891 —Rev. Owen Hicks.	1914-18—Rev. S. B. Bidlack.
1892-93—Rev. M. E. Swartz.	1919- —Rev. J. F. Glass.

MILLER TOWNSHIP.

Miller was the eighteenth township to be created in Perry County, but two—Tuscarora and Howe—being formed later. Part of it occupies a great bend in the Juniata River, and much of it is wooded. It is bounded on the north by Oliver Township and the Juniata River, on the east by the Juniata River, on the south by Wheatfield, and on the west by Centre and a bit of Oliver. A description by Prof. Claypole, the geologist, follows:

"Four distinct parallel ridges traverse Miller Township from east-northeast to west-southwest and determine the main features in its physical geography—Buffalo Hills, Limestone Ridge, Mahanoy Ridge and Dick's Hill. No stream of any importance is found within its limits. The largest is Losh's Run, which drains its southern portion and of which one arm forms its dividing line from Wheatfield Township. The basin of this stream is bounded by Mahanoy Ridge and Dick's Hill. Another stream of smaller size, Bailey's Run, drains the narrow basin between Mahanoy Ridge and Limestone Ridge and ends at Baileysburg.

"Miller Township is divided into two parts by the triple ridge that traverses it as mentioned. Its three parts diverge, from the central knob or focus at Pine Grove and Baileysburg."

It was erected by act of the State Legislature dated March 11, 1852. Joseph Bailey, who later became a congressman, is credited with naming the township, it being named in honor of David Miller. Bailey was in the Pennsylvania State Senate at the time of the township's erection as the representative of Perry and Cumberland Counties, and sponsored the bill, which follows:

"That all that portion of Oliver and Wheatfield Townships in the County of Perry, beginning at the Juniata River; thence along the line of Joseph Trimmer and Alexander's heirs, and between said Trimmer and David Smith and Bosserman's heirs to the middle of the back road; thence in a straight line to a hickory tree, a corner between the lands of Joseph Bailey and Cathcart and Deweese, on the top of Buffalo Ridge; thence westwardly along the top of said ridge to a point one-half mile west of the State road; thence in a straight line to the top of Limestone Ridge where the line dividing Oliver and Centre

Townships crosses said ridge; thence southwardly along said township line to a corner of Wheatfield Township; thence eastwardly along the top of Dick's Hill to the eastern termination of the same; thence in a straight line to the nearest point on Polecat Creek; thence down said creek to the Juniata near Losh's sawmill; thence up the middle of said river to the place of beginning."

In this bill Losh's Run is termed Polecat Creek, which may have been a very early name for it. At the time of the township's erection Senator Bailey had large holdings within this township's borders.

Among the early settlers Samuel Galbraith warranted 268 acres in 1790. George Losh later came into possession of this property. Back from the river John Elliot had 134 acres. On the river Samuel Martin warranted 68 acres in 1768. It had a river frontage of 207 rods, and Caroline furnace was built upon it. This was the Baileysburg tract. Back of it Francis Beelen had 328 acres warranted in 1814. Back of the Beelen tract was 129 acres warranted in 1766 to John Gilmore but surveyed to Marcus Hulings, in 1786. Matthew Hart warranted over 200 acres in 1784. Among other warrants were: William VanCamp, 70 acres in 1792; Hugh Miller, 150 acres in 1775; Frederick Nipple, 101 acres in 1767; John Anderson, 327 acres in 1767; John Ewalt, 162 acres in 1804; David English, 97 acres, including the big rock known as "Trimmer's," in 1766. In the big bend of the river Hugh Miller, Andrew Stephens and Robert Sturgeon warranted lands, Sturgeon's and Stephens' claims being for 100 acres each.

At the foot of Dick's Hill, on the north slope, Robert and John Woodburn, in 1786, took up large tracts later owned by the Harper and Barrick families. On this tract was the old road house known as "Woodburn's Tavern," to travelers on the old state road from Clark's Ferry to Pittsburgh. General Frederick Watts took up a tract in 1768 which in the last generation was owned by Thompson and Abraham Huss.

There was once a ferry at the farm lately owned by Oliver Rice, in the river bend. The old tavern on this place, the walls of which still stand, was known as Power's, as was the ferry and a fishery. On the other side of the river the ferry was known as Fetterman's. The Beelen farm, at Bailey's, of over 300 acres, was the militia parade grounds. The ferry at this point was known as Beelen's.

The John Anderson tract in the last generation was owned by Charles K. Smith, Henry Smith, William Evans and the VanCamp heirs.

There was an effort made at one time to put a bridge over the Juniata at Caroline furnace, now Bailey's Station. The Caroline Bridge Company was organized in 1838 by John D. Creigh and thirty-two others. There were to be 1,200 shares at $20 per share.

Joseph Bailey, State Senator, State Treasurer, and United States Congressman, was a mighty factor for many years in this township, where his holdings were large. He was the moving spirit in the management of Caroline furnace, and some of its walls still stand as a relic of a pioneer industry. The Bailey mansion is also standing. A station, called Bailey's, on the main line of the Pennsylvania Railroad, was established there when the road was laid out, and is in existence to this day. A sketch of Mr. Bailey appears elsewhere.

Ever since the railroad's establishment Bailey's has been the location of a watering station where the engines are replenished, and some years ago the old method of stopping for water was discontinued, and to-day trains running at fifty miles per hour take water on the fly by scooping it from long open schutes. A pumping station pumps the supply from the Juniata River.

The valley running westward from Losh's Run Station, on the Pennsylvania Railroad, was long known as Watts' Valley. In the palmy days of the Pennsylvania Canal there was located at Losh's Run a coal transfer known as the Ohio coal wharf, where all coal from the Susquehanna Valley was transferred from boats to railroad cars. It was discontinued about 1883. There was a large basin in the canal at that point for handling and turning boats. Many men found employment there.

The station at this point, on the Pennsylvania Railroad, is known as Losh's Run. The post office at Losh's Run is known as Logania. Long ago there was an office known as Beelen's Ferry, Francia Beelen being the postmaster, at the present site of Bailey's.

The earliest building in which school was conducted was, according to Prof. Silas Wright, the old Dick's Gap church, which was located near Pine Grove.

When traffic over the canal was the vogue the packet boats made a stop at Bailey's. The first settlements made there are credited to the Van-Camps, who came originally from Holland and settled at Kingston, New York, from whence they fled on horseback with all their effects in fear of an Indian uprising. The third railway station in the township, of the Pennsylvania Railroad, is named Iroquois, formerly known as Poor Man's Spring. There are no business places in the township. Farming and lumbering are the industries. An account of old Caroline furnace will be found in the chapter relating to Old Landmarks, Mills, etc. Sketches relating to Poor Man's Spring, the old canal, the physical features, etc., appear in appropriate chapters.

According to T. W. Campbell, there is a cave, supposed to have been used by the Indians, first as a place of concealment, and later as a burial place, located at the base of Mahanoy Ridge, about a half mile from the Pine Grove cemetery. It is closed by horizontal stones of considerable length, and so far as known has never been opened.

There are no business places within this township. Dr. George I. Crouse located at Losh's Run (Logania post office) in 1886, and practiced his profession, having been previously located at Richfield, Juniata County. He was a graduate of Jefferson Medical College, '84.

Pine Grove Church of God. The church records of the Pine Grove Church of God do not tell the time of its building, according to Mr. T. W. Campbell, who made a search of them, but from older residents the date is placed as in "the early sixties." It is a frame building, located upon lands once owned by William Holmes, and practically at the site of the early and rude enclosure, known as the Dick's Gap church, an account of which appears in the chapter devoted to "The Earliest Churches." It has been a part of the Lower Perry Circuit of the denomination. Rev. Samuel P. Campbell, long a near-by resident, was for many years a local preacher of this denomination, and to him belongs much of the credit for the continuation of this church in the neighborhood. During the pastorate of W. S. Smith, in 1891, the church was remodeled and rededicated. The following have been the ministers of this church and the Red Hill church in Howe Township:

1861-64—Rev. W. L. Jones.	1883-87—Rev. J. W. Miller.
1864-69—Rev. F. Still.	1887-89—Rev. O. E. Houston.
1869-71—Rev. Messinger.	1889-90—Rev. J. T. Fleegal.
1871-74—Rev. G. W. Seilhammer.	1890-92—Rev. W. S. Smith.
1874-76—Rev. J. W. Miller.	1892-96—Rev. Samuel Spurrier.
1876-78—Rev. W. J. Grissinger.	1896-97—Rev. J. A. Snyder.
1878-81—Rev. C. J. Behney.	1897-05—Rev. S. E. Kline.
1881-83—Rev. T. Still.	1905-08—Rev. G. H. Bowersox.

Beginning with 1906 the East Newport church was dedicated, and the persons named as pastors there also served Pine Grove and Red Hill, in Howe Township. See Oliver Township chapter.

64

Logania Church of God. The members of the Church of God residing in the vicinity of Logania first held meetings in their homes and in the schoolhouse. During 1889-90 a church building was erected. H. B. Cumbler, Andrew Watts and J. M. Peterman were the building committee. The first pastor of the new church was Rev. J. T. Flegal. It is connected with the Duncannon charge, where the names of the ministers will be found.

Mahanoy Union Church. Members of different denominations residing in the Mahanoy Valley erected a church in 1900. the building committee being John M. Smith, A. J. Burd, H. H. Yocum, J. R. Stewart and M. R. Clouser, who were also the board of trustees. The first officers of the board of trustees were H. H. Yocum, president; J. R. Stewart, secretary, and J. M. Smith, treasurer. The United Evangelicals of the Newport charge have been holding services in this church.

MILLERSTOWN BOROUGH.

*Millerstown Borough, the oldest town in Perry County, is located on the eastern bank of the Juniata River, thirty-three miles west of the capital of the state, the Pennsylvania Railroad station being located on the western side of the river. Millerstown was the first town in the territory now comprising Perry County to be plotted for the sale of lots, which was done in 1790. It is located on a tract of ground originally warranted to James Gallagher on September 23, 1766, although he had located there before that and had made improvements thereon. The old English custom of naming estates being still in vogue, it is named in the patent as "Smithfield." It is described as being a tract of two hundred acres on the north (east) side of the Juniata River, adjoining lands of John McBride. William Maclay, deputy surveyor, surveyed the tract.

While Greenwood Township was formed in 1767, and is generally supposed to have comprised all that part of Perry County lying east of the Juniata, yet such is not the case, as will be seen by referring to the chapter devoted to Greenwood Township, where the matter is fully described. That part of Greenwood Township lying north of Cocolamus Creek, which of course included the present location of Millerstown, was in Fermanagh Township, Cumberland County, and it so remained until the organization of Mifflin County on September 19, 1789. According to public records James Gallagher, of Fermanagh Township, sold to David Miller, an innkeeper, of Rye Township, on September 1, 1780, for twelve hundred pounds, "all that tract of land lying on the north (east) side of the river Juniata, in the Township of Fermanagh, containing 222 acres and 125 perches, and having a river front of one and one-half miles. Subsequently David Miller laid out the town. The original plot covered forty-two acres, but the entire acreage within the borough limits is four hundred and eighty-two.

The laying out of the town was after 1790, as the patent was not granted until March 25, 1790, and until then he could not have given legal title to the lots sold. Through older residents the time of settlement was fixed as

---

*The author is indebted to the historical articles of Rev. W. H. Logan, a former pastor of the Millerstown Presbyterian church, and H. G. Martin, James Rounsley and William T. Rounsley for data in reference to this chapter.

William Thompson Rounsley was born in 1876 and was a son of James and Ella (Thompson) Rounsley. He graduated from the Millerstown High School in 1893 and from the Millersville State Normal School in 1895. He taught the Grammar school in Millerstown the following term and the High school the succeeding year. He had been reëlected, but on August 26, 1897, he visited an uncle on the west side of the Juniata and on returning over the old grade-crossing he was run down by a train. During his short life he had amassed many historical facts relating to Millerstown and vicinity, which were kindly loaned to the writer, among which was a part of the original manuscript of Wright's History of Perry County. Mr. Rounsley was aged 21 years and 28 days.

McClung, joiner; Michael McGarra, butcher; Machlin & Ross, Joshua North, tanner; John Neeman, innkeeper; David Pfoutz, innkeeper of the stone house; Captain Ephraim Williams.

In the Greenwood Township assessment of 1814, among others were:

Abraham Addams, 320 acres of land and ferry at or near Millerstown; Thomas Cochran, 500 acres of land, store and distillery; Benjamin Lees, store; Edward Purcell, store; Henry Walters, store.

The stone hotel building, on the west side of the Square, was built by John Wood in 1800. In 1805 David Pfoutz was the innkeeper. In later years it was long the property of Henry Martin. Dr. S. T. Lineaweaver began the erection of a building for a home in 1869, but before its final completion in 1876, he changed the plans and made of it a hotel building. It was named the Juniata Valley Hotel, but financial misfortune soon closed its doors. It was a large brick building, three stories, with mansard roof, and was burned to the ground in February, 1877. Shuman Miller bought the lot and erected the present building on the same foundation, in 1881. In more recent years this hotel was kept by Huff Ward, and was known as the "Ward House."

About 1820 David Pfoutz built the Union tavern. It passed through many hands, the last being Shuman Miller, who kept it from 1875 to 1881, when it was closed as a public house. It is now owned by William Walker and Harry Beacham. When the old pike was in use David Rickabaugh kept a road house and the stage line office. Rev. Logan, a Presbyterian pastor at Millerstown, did a lot of historical research work in 1881 and 1882, and makes the statement that "when the canal was dug nearly all the houses in town were hotels." While this statement was overdrawn, yet there were actually seventeen hotels during that time. Among them was the residence of Mrs. S. C. Alexander. Millerstown had sixty houses in 1825, and eighty in 1832.

The first storekeepers were Thomas Cochran and Edward Purcell, the latter from 1800 to 1834. Cochran came to the territory from Ireland, in 1798, and became the first postmaster. He built the Alexander Goodman house in 1803, and the Stites house in 1813. This is now the John Ward house. Purcell also came from Ireland, and built the house which stood where the D. M. Rickabaugh house now stands. One of the earliest residents was Anthony Brandt, a blacksmith and an innkeeper, the ancestor of the numerous Brandt families in this part of Perry County.

In 1830 Samuel and Jacob Beaver built a warehouse and engaged in the purchasing and shipping of produce. A. H. Ulsh's sons are conducting the business now. Kirk Haines, T. P. Cochran and William Everhart were owners at different times during the interim. A. H. Ulsh assumed charge in 1883. E. P. Titzell was one of the town's former business men from 1870 to 1906.

The turnpike was built in 1822, the canal in 1827-28, and the first track of the Pennsylvania Railroad in 1848-49, each a great improvement in turn. Millerstown has more old substantial stone houses, many of them a century old, than any other town in the county. Such houses are numerous in the farming country of the extreme western end of the county. They are a monument to our ancestry, and their substantial construction shows the thoroughness which was common in those days—a quality, which I fear many of our present generation are losing.

In 1848 John H. Earnest built a foundry and carried on business until 1852. B. W. Page opened a shirt factory on High Street, in Millerstown, in 1904, with forty hands on the pay roll. It was located in a building which has since been turned into a double dwelling. In 1910 he took in his son as a partner, and in 1912 the firm erected a fine three-story brick shirt factory on Main Street, its size being 40x120 feet. In 1916 B. W. Page retired from the firm, and C. C. Page became the owner, later, in July, 1919, selling to the Phillips-Jones Corporation of New York City, and remaining as manager of their plants here and at Thompsontown and Mifflin.

In the early days there was a market house on the north side of the square, but when the canal was under construction it was removed. It was 25x60 feet in size, and had a comb roof, supported at a height of twenty feet by posts which rested upon stone pillars. It was purchased by Abram Addams and removed to his farm, where it was used for a wagon shed.

On April 4, 1838, the Millerstown Bridge Company was organized with six hundred shares of stock, the par value of which was twenty dollars per share. The commission to build it was composed of Thomas Cochran, John Fertig, Frederick Rinehart, David Kepner, John Rice and Jonas Ickes. It was built from the end of Sunbury Street, in 1839, by John Fertig and Henry Doughty. It has been swept away at various times, including its destruction by fire in 1902, an account of which appears in the chapters devoted to "Rivers and Streams." On March 28, 1814, an act passed the Pennsylvania Legislature authorizing the building of a bridge there by the Millerstown Bridge Company, but it was not then built.

John Fertig, who helped build the Millerstown bridge, was also one of the contractors who helped build the Pennsylvania Railroad. He settled here in 1829, and died in 1849, of Asiatic cholera. He was an early advocate of temperance. Another railroad contractor was William Goodman, who also built railroads in West Virginia and Tennessee, until the outbreak of the war between the North and the South.

Millerstown has been unfortunate a number of times through serious fires. The one in February, 1877, wiped out the Juniata Valley Hotel. Another on April 17, 1878, burned the Cluck corner and an adjoining building in which the post office was located. Four families were rendered homeless. The loss was $25,000, mostly covered by insurance. Mr. Cluck rebuilt, and Cathcarts succeeded him in business in 1883. Then on April 19, 1894, at 4 a. m., fire was discovered in the store of D. M. Rickabaugh, and before subdued had burned not only his store building but the shoe shop of J. B. Lahr, the drug store of C. W. Lahr, and the dwelling of U. H. Ward. The instruments of the Millerstown Band and the surgical instruments of Dr. W. H. Jones, who had their headquarters and offices in the burned buildings, were also destroyed. A drilled hole in the Rickabaugh safe, found in the ruins, showed that the fire was the result of burglary. A third, in June, 1902, burned the river bridge over the Juniata. The state erected a new bridge which was opened for traffic on January 1, 1906.

There was an early settlement of negroes located near Millerstown, which was known as "Washington City." About 1850 smallpox broke out in the settlement, and every one, save a man who had it before, got the disease. The place became practically quarantined, its people largely helpless and destitute. Dr. A. C. Stees, a local physician, aided by a number of men and women whose identity has never been disclosed, formed a relief party and ministered to the stricken people, carrying baskets of provisions to a point where the lone unstricken man in the settlement came to receive them. Dr. Stees changed his clothing in his barn before and after each visit to the settlement, which he brought through the scourge. Owing to the loathsomeness of the disease it was necessary to keep secret the names of these brave men and women, as they were meeting the public during the same time in a business and social way, and were thereby saved from being shunned.

Millerstown Borough was incorporated February 12, 1849, and the first meeting of the town council was held April 14, 1849. Abram Addams was the first chief burgess, and John M. Caufman, Christian Beck, James R. Gilmer and Jacob Emerick, members of the first borough council. Thomas P. Cochran was the first clerk to council, his salary being $2.50 a year. Abram Addams and John Fertig were named in the act as supervisors of the first election.

The first schoolhouse was also the first "meeting house," where religious services were held. It was built of logs in 1808, at the edge of the cemetery, on the Grave Street side. School was held there until 1856, when the new school building was erected on High Street, on grounds purchased of Joseph B. Carr. There was great opposition to the change of location at the time, but the more progressive element won. When the free school law went into effect Millerstown adopted the local option plan and held an election every third year to see whether schools would be held or not. The friends of education always won. The directors in office when the first public school building was built in 1856 were: William Kipp, president; Hiram Fertig, secretary; Henry Hopple, treasurer; Dr. D. M. Crawford, Samuel Gabel and George Keely. It was enlarged in 1869 by building an addition to the eastern end containing two rooms, the cost of which was $1,662. The first school building stood, but unused, until 1875.

Some of the earlier teachers whose names have been handed down are Messrs. McLaughlin, Belford, McDowell, John B. Porter, Cummins, Kinslow, Kintch, Joseph Jones, William J. Jones and Noble Meredith, all of whom taught in the old building in the cemetery. Prof. Silas Wright conducted a summer normal school here from 1868 to 1878, known as the Juniata Valley Normal School, an account of which appears in the chapter devoted to Academies, Institutions, etc.

One of the earliest teachers in what is now Perry County was Thomas Cochran, at Millerstown. He and three brothers came from Ireland to Chester County, where they laid out a town, calling it Cochransville, which name it has retained. The three brothers remained, but Thomas located in Millerstown in 1801. After teaching for some time he engaged in the mercantile business and also kept one of the first hotels. He was postmaster there during the War of 1812-14. A year later he sold out his hotel and was in other business until 1835, when he was succeeded by his son, Thomas P. Cochran. He and his wife were among the principal supporters of the Presbyterian Church there.

The first teachers in the present school building were D. A. Beckley, Jacob Gantt, W. W. Fuller and W. E. Baker. In 1869 there were three schools with Prof. Silas Wright as principal. Twenty-five years later (1894-95, 1895-96) he was again principal for two terms. J. S. Arnold served as principal six successive terms, from 1885-86 to 1890-91. In 1879 the principal's salary was was $35 per month, in 1880 it was $50. Three principals, Silas Wright, S. B. Fahnestock and E. U. Aumiller, became county superintendents of schools. The first graduating class was that of 1887. J. S. Arnold, principal. Its members were W. S. Snyder, S. Banks Taylor, Carrie McDuffie, Alton P. Diffenderfer and Clara Rippman. Of the male members of the class the first became an attorney, the second a physician, and the third an educator, all noted men in their line. This was the second town to graduate pupils from its high school. The largest graduating class was that of 1896, with fourteen members.

Millerstown postmasters, since the establishment of the office, have been Thomas Cochran, Edward Purcell, Beaver Brothers, Miss Margaret Clark,

munity had "gone over the top" in all the "drives" during the World War. The gun came from Fort Dupont, Delaware.

The tablet was dedicated at the time of the welcome home celebration, November 22, 1919, and the marker was erected late in 1920. It is the first marker in the county, save that to those who went forth in the long and harrowing Sectional War. The names upon the tablet are not only those of Millerstown's contingent, but of all those adjacent and along the rural routes which radiate therefrom. The first four named lost their lives in the service. Following is the inscription upon the marker:

"This Tablet is Dedicated in Honor of those of Millerstown
and Vicinity who Answered the Call
1917—of Our Country and Enrolled for Service—1919."

*Wilbur G. Anderson.	Sherman L. Fosselman.	George D. Newman.
*Robert H. Garman.	Emery R. Fry.	Warren V. Newman.
*Edward S. Knight.	Montgomery Gearhart.	Clarence E. Paden.
*Walter A. Smith.	Roscoe W. Hall.	Harry C. Pontius.
Ralph E. Acker.	Norman M. Grubb.	Clarence R. Powell.
Lee T. Allen.	J. L. Hogentogler	D. S. Powell.
Raymond S. Anderson.	A. L. Holman.	Charles W. Reisinger.
V. L. Aughe.	Edward L. Holman.	Simon L. Rhoads.
George A. Barner.	James R. Jones.	S. Nelson Rounsley.
John A. Barnes.	Henry M Keisling.	John W. Roush.
Ralph B. Beaver.	Lawrence L. Knight.	Raymond A. Rowe.
Frank R. Bixler.	James L. Kramer.	Warren R. Sarver.
Andrew S. Black.	Jacob A. Kretzing.	Roscoe L. Satzler.
Jonathan R. Black.	J. Banks Lahr.	Robert F. Shenk.
Frank A. Bostwick.	Carl Lauver.	Paul R. Smith.
Israel Brown.	Thomas P. Leonard.	Ernest B. Snook.
Emery A. Bucher.	C. W. Liddick.	Percy E. Stewart.
Harry R. Burkepile.	H. J. Liddick.	Casper W. Swartz.
George J. Cameron.	Wm. T. McConnell.	John H. Swartz.
Joseph C. Campbell.	M. Luther McDonald.	W. Rodney Taylor.
Emery J. Cauffman.	Robert C. McDonald.	Horace J. Troutman.
Wesley M. Cauffman.	Ralph N. McNaughton.	C. Kenneth Ulsh.
George Coffman.	Ross Mangle.	Edgar A. Ulsh.
Guy Diffenderfer.	Norman S. Markley.	James E. Ulsh.
Earl Dillman.	Leroy Marks.	Harry Wagner.
William R. Dimm.	Earl H. Miller.	D. Earl Ward.
John J. Doughten.	Ezra H. Minium.	Harry J. Yeigh.
Wm. H. Fahnestock.	Lewis M. Mitchell.	George G. Yohn.
J. Herbert Ferguson.		Annabelle D. Frey.

"With no selfish ends these served that the principles of right
might be established throughout the world."

Millerstown Borough owns its own water plant, bringing the water by gravity for a distance of over four miles from the Tuscarora Mountain. The plant was erected in 1897, at a cost of $7,000; later the cost totaled $9,000. The reservoir back of town has a capacity of two hundred thousand gallons, and the water pressure is one hundred and ten pounds. The borough was bonded for the purpose of building the plant and the proceeds are ample to pay off a bond of $1,000 each year.

Coincident with the introduction of water the Millerstown Fire Company was organized. It is a beneficial organization and is incorporated. J. H. G. Rippman has been the chief of the fire company since its organization. Its first officers were: J. H. G. Rippman, president; D. A. Lahr, vice-president; E. M. Kelly, secretary, and N. H. Ward, treasurer. The present officers are: C. C. Page, president; R. B. Thompson, vice-president; T. B. Diffenderfer, secretary; D. A. Lahr, treasurer. It was incorporated in 1907.

In 1894 Millerstown decided to put in its own light plant, and had already put up the power house when the project was abandoned. The town is lighted by electricity supplied by the Juniata Light & Power Company. The Pennsylvania Canal, now abandoned and considerably filled in and covered with sod and vegetation, has been leased to the borough for the payment of $1.00 annually. It is 1,275 feet in length, and will be turned into a park and community playground.

Millerstown's oldest lodge is Tuscarora Castle, No. 289, K. G. E., instituted October 24, 1888, with George D. Robinson, noble chief; J. Edgar Titzel, vice chief; Wm. Fenstemacher, master of records; O. D. Wingert, keeper of exchequer.

The first physician to locate in Millerstown was Dr. Henry Bucke, who was there as early as 1805. His successor was Dr. Samuel Mealy, evidently, as there is no record available of another. He was a son of a cooper from the western end of Perry County, and about 1793 worked with his father at his trade. Tradition has him as a very studious boy who carried his books along while following his avocation. He was with Captain Moreland's famous company on the Canadian frontier. He is reputed with saving the limb and probably the life of an officer in the command by refusing to agree to amputate, upon which the other surgeons insisted. After his return from the army in 1814 he located at Millerstown, where he practiced until 1832, when he removed to Iowa. He was married to Miss Margaret Blaine, one of the famous family of that name which had settled in western Perry County. Dr. Waterhouse located in Millerstown and practiced but a short time until he died, in 1821. Dr. John M. Laird practiced here between 1824 and 1840, when he removed to New Bloomfield, among whose physicians he is further spoken of. In 1827 Dr. McNeal located, but stayed only two years. Dr. Shellenberger read medicine with Dr. Mealy and practiced for about six years after 1830. Dr. Isaac Snowden, the son of Rev. Nathaniel Randolph Snowden, who was the first preacher ordained in Harrisburg, and later a member of the faculty of Dickinson College, located at Millerstown about 1824, being associated with Dr. Mealy. The partnership not being agreeable he went to Thompsontown about 1828, but again located in Millerstown in 1830. In 1834 he moved to Hogestown, Cumberland County. He was the father of A. Louden Snowden, long prominent in Pennsylvania politics. He was with General Jackson as a surgeon when he operated against the Seminole Indians in Florida.

Dr. John Irwin, born in Union County in 1809, and graduated from the University of Pennsylvania in 1832, succeeded Dr. Mealy in Millerstown in 1832, where he practiced until 1840, when he removed to his farm in Juniata County, retiring from practice. The late J. H. Irwin, of Newport, was a son. Dr. Kremer, who had read medicine with Dr. Mealy and married his daughter, and Dr. Ingleman were contemporaries of Dr. Irwin and were located here for nearly ten years. About 1841 Dr. Stilwell located in Millerstown and was associated with Dr. A. C. Stees, a native of Perry County, who graduated from Jefferson Medical College in 1836 and settled in Millerstown in 1841. At the end of a half dozen years the partnership was dissolved, Dr. Stilwell removing to Ohio. Dr. Stees remained in practice in Millerstown until his death, in 1854. Both these physicians were among the founders of the Perry County Medical Society. Dr. Stees was rated as a first-class physician and had a large practice. Dr. David Crawford practiced from 1851 to 1864, when he removed to Mifflin, Juniata County.

Dr. Samuel Stites was born in Northampton County in 1816. In 1856 he graduated from the University of Pennsylvania, and after studying in

Europe he located in Millerstown, where he practiced until his death in 1882. He was a surgeon of a Pennsylvania regiment during the War between the States. In the class of 1882 his son, Dr. George Stites, graduated from the College of Physicians and Surgeons, Baltimore, and succeeded his father in the practice of medicine. He located in Williamstown, Pa., about 1885.

Dr. S. T. Leinaweaver located in Millerstown in 1864 and practiced until 1877, when he located in Hagerstown, Maryland. He was a graduate of Jefferson Medical College. In the fall of 1877 he accepted an appointment from the Shah of Persia, as surgeon in the Turkish Army. He later resided at Lebanon. From 1868 to 1876 Dr. A. A. Murray practiced, when he removed to Liverpool.

Dr. Ellis Q. Kirk located in 1874 and practiced two years. Dr. John B. Oellig practiced from 1877 to 1881. Dr. P. Rundio practiced from 1877 to 1880. Dr. G. W. Campbell located in Millerstown in 1879, but removed to Newport the same year. Dr. G. C. Dean, a native of Perry County and a graduate of the University of Pennsylvania, practiced from 1879 to 1881, when he removed to Lewistown, where he died in 1892. Dr. J. L. Brubaker, a Maryland man and a graduate of Washington University at Baltimore, in 1874, practiced from 1879 to 1883. He had previously been at Markelville for several years. He was given a high rating in medical circles. Dr. J. C. Hall, a graduate of the College of Physicians and Surgeons, of Baltimore, '89, located at Millerstown in 1891, where he practiced until his death, February 11, 1903. Dr. S. R. Ickes located in Millerstown in 1882. He remained about a year, when he removed to Harrisburg and became interested in the traction business, later becoming president of the People's Traction Company. The present physician is Dr. M. Gearhart, who located here in 1912.

Among other physicians were Dr. W. E. Bonawitz, who had associated with Dr. Hall in practice, from 1898, and died in 1911; Dr. T. P. Cochran, Dr. L. S. Howard, Dr. J. H. Meyer, Dr. M. I. Stein and others.

According to the report of the mercantile appraiser the business places in Millerstown are as follows, the date being the time of starting business:

General stores, T. P. Cathcart, D. G. Rickabaugh & Co. The latter store was kept by D. G. Rickabaugh from 1865 until 1916.
Groceries, D. L. Farner. Rinehart & Heisey, William Rounsley (1908).
Confectionery, R. W. Hopple, Jennie Sheaffer, J. W. Cupp.
Drugs, D. A. Lahr (1913). Established by C. W. Lahr (1890), sold to J. B. Lahr (1895).
Ralph B. Thompson (1906). Established by E. P. Titzel.
A. H. Ulsh & Sons (1920), (L. G., P. B., and J. E. Ulsh). Purchased by A. H. Ulsh (1885), coal and feed.
W. C. Moore (1917), machinery. Established by William Kipp (1885), successors, Kipp & Moore (1917).
L. B. Meloy, saddlery.
G. W. Fry & Sons, furniture.
E. C. Reisinger (1913), stoves and tinware.
O. D. Wingert, clothing and shoes.
Cupp Bros., auto supplies and oils
A. L. Long, automobiles.

Millerstown Presbyterian Church. Presbyterianism in Millerstown is almost as old as the settlement itself. The first sermon was preached by Rev. John Hutchinson, of Mifflintown, in 1806, in the bar room of the Cochran tavern, on South Main Street, now owned by Mrs. S. C. Alexander. Later they were held throughout the town, and often in the same bar room. While the services were held as stated the members of the faith belonged to the churches at Middle Ridge and at Lost Creek (now Mc-

Alisterville), in Juniata County. The Lutheran residents attended church in Pfoutz Valley, and the Methodists had their services and camp meetings in the same valley, near the Cocolamus Creek.

The congregation was regularly organized in 1818, by Rev. N. R. Snowden, father of the late A. Loudon Snowden, who served two years. The organization took place in a building also used as a school building located in the northeast corner of the Millerstown cemetery plot. Nothing remains to tell just when this building was built, but there is record that it was conveyed to Thomas Cochran, William North and Amos Jordan, trustees, to hold for a Presbyterian church and burying ground, on May 4, 1808, and the building was likely erected immediately thereafter. There were no free schools and the building served for both church and school purposes. Rev. Snowden also taught a Latin school, among his pupils having been the late T. P. and William Cochran. He also served the members of his faith at Liverpool and New Buffalo. These churches were located upon the lands forming the delta between the Juniata and Susquehanna Rivers, which territory was attached to the Huntingdon Presbytery, where they remained until 1845.

After Rev. Snowden's pastorate, which terminated in 1820, for nine years there was no pastor. Revs. Hill, Gray and Lochman served as supplies. In 1829 Rev. Britton E. Collins, a licentiate of the Presbytery of Philadelphia and a graduate of Princeton Theological Seminary, accepted a call and remained almost ten years. During his pastorate the present stone church was built on grounds donated by Thomas Cochran, the building committee being John Boal, Abram Addams, Jacob Hoffman, John McGowan and Thomas Cochran. It was dedicated in May, 1832. The building was 50x55 feet in size. William Hunter was the contractor. The life of the church actually began with Rev. Collins. He owned and resided upon the present J. R. Wright farm in Greenwood Township, where he erected a house. Leaving Millerstown he removed to Shirleysburg, Pennsylvania, where he baptized in infancy one who was destined in after years to occupy his former pulpit at Millerstown, the late beloved Rev. S. C. Alexander. During his Millerstown pastorate he held several protracted services in the new church, and during his seven-year pastorate the net result was one hundred and fourteen members.

After his departure, in 1839, supplies were again sent by Presbytery. Among these were Rev. McKnight Williamson, 1840-42, and Rev. S. H. McDonald, 1842-44. Rev. Williamson also supplied the lower Tuscarora church. The success of the Millerstown church had not a little to do with the passing of the Middle Ridge church, as on May 14, 1842, thirty-three members were admitted, and all but two came from Middle Ridge church. After that services were held only occasionally at Middle Ridge. The forming of the New Bloomfield congregation, in 1834, under Rev. Dickey, had so weakened the Middle Ridge church that it was later abandoned. Of its membership the Millerstown church got fifty names.

Rev. George D. Porter became the regular pastor November, 1844, and remained until 1851. Emigration to the West—then at its height—about 1850, took from the roster the Bulls, Linns, McNaughtons, Merediths, Leonards and others of like prominence. This weakened it and a committee of Presbytery attached it to Upper (Blain) and Centre churches, but this action seems not to have been consummated. From 1851 to 1856 Rev. Hezekiah Hanson, of Petersburg (Duncannon), supplied it in addition to his own pulpit.

Rev. John B. Strain, a licentiate, who had preached for a seceding faction of the faith, supplied the pulpit from August, 1856, to December, when he was ordained by Carlisle Presbytery. He was then installed in charge of Millerstown and Buffalo, each church paying $250 annually. Prior to this time no records were kept of salaries. During the period from 1856-60 he also conducted a seminary or academy near St. Samuel's Church, where he resided. From 1860 to 1862 Rev. James Mahon and Elijah Wilson (the blind parson) were the stated supplies.

From May, 1862, to 1869, Rev. William P. Cochran, a boy born in Millerstown, served the church. The following is from a statement by him, and with a succeeding paragraph is reproduced as showing the tendency of the period: "In '61 I spent from January to May in that region and preached several times in Millerstown. Was with Dr. Thompson six weeks in a very powerful revival in Lower Tuscarora and Perrysville (a part of Liverpool)—some 300 inquirers, 150 uniting with the church."

"In May, '61, the war having commenced with its direful effects, I returned to Missouri, where I remained until May, '62. The church in Millerstown gave me a call in '61 and waited until I could honorably leave Missouri. I remained at Millerstown until May, '69. I found the church cold and dead, with fueds and heartburnings among the members. There was a kind of Sabbath school; no prayer meeting. In the winter of 1863-64 God poured out his spirit on the congregation. The occasion of my leaving was opposition that sprang up out of old fueds at the election of elders. I came back to Missouri in '69, where most of my ministerial life had been spent."

There is no mention of the state of religion in the church until the report of Presbytery in 1864, which says: "The congregations are good on the Sabbath and solemn, yet we have to lament the low state of piety in the church, the want of zeal and Godly living, while without, all around us, wickedness is on the increase, especially intemperance." During 1865 a ten days' meeting awakened new life, and the report is the reverse of the preceding year. During 1870 Rev. J. H. Downing was the stated supply, and Rev. J. J. Hamilton, until July, 1871, when he was installed. Millerstown paid him $600 for one-half of his time, the other half to be divided between Buffalo and Upper (Blain) churches. He resided near Ickesburg, and remained until 1875.

During 1875 the entire church was remodeled, a new Sunday school room added, the entrance changed to the east side of the building, etc., at a cost of $2,300. Dr. Murray had donated a lot of ground for the erection of a new church, but it was returned and the church remodeled. Rev. W. H. Logan served from 1876 to 1886. During 1877 the church was incorporated and the parsonage purchased. In 1887 Rev. S. C. Alexander was elected pastor and remained until his death, September 21, 1901. During his pastorate the church was again remodeled at a cost of $1,750, the entrance being placed upon the corner, with an additional entrance upon High Street; the interior arranged so that the lecture room could be used in connection with the auditorium, and memorial windows installed. The window on the east being known as "the governor's window," being a gift from General James A. Beaver, later governor of Pennsylvania, in memory of his mother. It bears the inscription, "In loving memory of Ann Eliza McDonald, daughter of Abram Addams, placed here by her children." Since then the ministers have been:

1902-08—Rev. H. G. Clair.   1909-17—Rev. Will H. Dyer.
1908-09—Rev. Henry Cunningham.   1917   —Rev. C. A. Waltman.

Millerstown Methodist Church. The members of the Methodist Episcopal faith began holding services here as early as 1832, and from then until 1840 worshiped in the schoolhouse which stood in the cemetery. The ministers who served them during this period were Rev. Wesley Howe, Rev. David Thomas and Rev. Hodges.

In 1840 the church was built and the organization became a part of the Newport charge and so remained until 1900.

The successive pastors were the same as those of the Duncannon church until 1857, and from then until 1900 the same as Newport. (See Duncannon and Newport chapters.) Since 1900 the pastors have been:

1900-01—Rev. John C. Bieri.	1912-14—Rev. Ray H Pierson.
1901-02—Rev. John J. Hunt.	1914-18—Rev. Chas. F. Himes.
1902-04—Rev. E. L. Williams.	1918-19—Rev. Victor T. Nearhoof.
1904-07—Rev. C. V. Hartzell.	1919-22—Rev. Chas. F. Berkheimer.
1907-12—Rev. John E. Beard.	

The charge comprises Millerstown, Donnally's Mills and Marsh Run. Until 1920 Ickesburg was also included, but the congregation having become very small, the work there was discontinued and the building sold to the school board in 1921.

NEW BUFFALO BOROUGH.

Before Perry County was formed a man named Jacob Baughman conceived the idea of laying out the site of a town where New Buffalo Borough is located, as the following advertisement will show:

"*A New Town*—The subscriber has laid out a town called New Buffalo, consisting of eighty-one lots, at Baughman's Ferry, in Buffalo Township, Cumberland County, at the junction of the roads leading from Sunbury and Lewistown. The site is elegant, being situate in a healthy part of the county, and in a neighborhood that, for the rapidity of its improvement for some years past, is not excelled by many in Pennsylvania. And as the boat and raft channel lies near the west side of the river, this place affords the only safe and convenient landing for many miles above Fahter's Falls.* It lies about fourteen miles above Harrisburg, and affords many inducements for the industrious mechanic and enterprising dealer. On the south margin of the town is a grist and sawmill. A lot, No. 61, the largest in the town, is reserved by the proprietor for the purpose of a place of worship and a schoolhouse for the use of the town."

In fact, the town was plotted and first called Baughmanstown, but it was changed to New Buffalo, being located in Buffalo Township at that time, before the public advertising was done. Adam Liddick, of Watts Township, helped to plot and stake off the lots, for which service he was paid with one lot. Mrs. McAlister, a daughter of Baughman's, assisted in carrying the chain in surveying the lots. Three of the first lots sold were to Jacob Baughman, Jr., Jacob B. Maus and Susan Steele. The first plan was to sell them by lottery at sixty dollars each, twenty dollars to be paid cash and the balance in five years.

Fronting the lots, between the river and Front Street, a space of ground was set apart to be used in common by the inhabitants for the purpose of piling lumber, plaster, merchandise, etc., upon. Jacob Baughman died, and in the *Perry Forester*, published at the new county seat at Landisburg, appeared the following advertisement:

"Agreeably to the last will and testament of Jacob Baughman (deceased), late of Buffaloe Township, Perry County, will be sold by way of public vendue, at the house of Jacob Baughman, innkeeper in the town of New Buffaloe, on Monday, the 2d of June next (1823), upwards of sixty lots of ground in said town. This town is laid out on the bank of the Susquehanna River, about five miles above Clark's Ferry, and eight miles below Liverpool on a beautiful and pleasant situation. There are already a number of buildings erected in the town: from the recent period of its commencement and its rapid growth, it is likely to become a town of considerable note in the county in a very short time."

*References fail to agree on the location of Fahter's Falls, as others name it as near the Patterson place in Howe township, later Juniata Falls.

The proprietor had reserved for himself and his heirs all the rights to the ferry and fisheries opposite to the town. At his death, by agreement of the heirs, his son Henry received seventy-one acres of land, four lots in the village, and all the ferry and fishery rights; his son Jacob got fifteen acres of land, the grist and sawmill and distillery, and his son John, ninety-four acres of land and a tract of land in Dauphin County. He had a fourth son, Christian, but it is not known what his patrimony was. It will be seen by the above that the father of New Buffalo was well-to-do in material things.

New Buffalo was incorporated as a borough, April 8, 1848. Urban's tannery was built in 1835 and was run for a number of years. New Buffalo had two boatyards where canal boats were built and repaired and was a town of considerable importance in the days of canal transportation, the Susquehanna Division of the Pennsylvania Canal passing through the town. G. W. and Robert Lesher opened the lower yard in 1854 and operated it for a period of six years. It was later owned by the Garnet heirs. It employed from ten to fifteen hands.

It will be noted that the will of Jacob Baughman disposed of a distillery, a gristmill and a sawmill. The dates of their erection is not known, but was prior to 1822. In 1861-62 the gristmill was rebuilt by Hilbish & Bowman. It had both water and steam power thereafter, and continued in business for several decades. Baughman's distillery was on the same street, opposite the gristmill.

The first schoolhouse was built about 1834, and located on Locust Street, on an open lot adjoining the church lot. It was in use until 1874, when the two-story brick building was erected on the same lot. The borough had two schools until after the closing of the Pennsylvania Canal. Prior to the erection of the first schoolhouse the pupils attended the school at Hill Church, in Watts Township.

The Baughman ferry landing was at Peach Alley, near the foot of the canal bridge. The landing in Dauphin County was at the old stone tavern. The fording was located near the ferry, and the fishery was opposite the boatyard. The first tavern was built by Jacob Baughman at the corner of Front Street and Blackberry Alley. He later built a hotel on an adjoining lot and kept a public house until his death. John Shaffer kept another hotel in the place at the same time that Baughman was in the business. In the old rafting days New Buffalo was a favorite place to "tie up" by the raftmen, and the hotels did a prosperous business.

The first store was kept by a Mr. Kepner. Before it was started the people generally did their buying in Halifax and Harrisburg, going in canoes. Other tradesmen in New Buffalo were Mrs. John Shaffer, Mrs. J. L. Arnold, William Hemperly and Jackson Bros., the members of the latter firm being William and J. B. Jackson, the latter a county commissioner in more recent years. This store was first established by William Jackson, who was born in 1815, and married in 1837. There is record that he started this store "soon after being married," which would date it to probably 1840. It was conducted by him and his sons until his death, in 1872, when it became the property of William and J. B Jackson, trading as Jackson Bros. They conducted it until the death of William H. Jackson, in 1910, when the surviving partner became the owner and conducted it until his death, in 1919. Since then it is in the possession of Mr. Jackson's daughter, Mrs. Edith Jackson Ober. W. E. Meck runs a general store, and W. J. Kines sells gas, these three business places being the only ones in the borough noted by the mercantile appraiser in his report.

New Buffalo is one of three places in Perry County of which there is record of the celebration of the fiftieth anniversary of American Independence, in 1826, the others being Landisburg and Bloomfield. The public meeting at New Buffalo was called to order by John H. Thompson, who was also made chairman. David T. Steel was the secretary. "The Buffaloe Volunteers," under command of Captain Christian Hays, paraded and firearms were discharged. Addresses and singing were a part of the program. The ever present toast of the period was brought into use. Among the volunteer toasts was one by Samuel Steele: "Our country girls who disdain to be imprisoned in corsets; may every 'Buffaloe Volunteer' have one in his nest."

At an early period New Buffalo was already the location for physicians. Dr. Patrick McMorris located there about 1840, and his brother, William McMorris, a little later. Both were natives of Ireland. The latter died before his brother, both practicing until their deaths. Dr. T. G. McMorris, who later located at Liverpool, practiced here in 1845. Physicians of a later date were Dr. Marshall, Dr. H. O. Orris and Dr. James B. Eby, who later located at Newport; Dr. Maxwell, Dr. B. F. Klugh and Dr. F. C. Steele, the latter locating in 1879, and was in practice until his death, in 1896.

New Buffalo Methodist Church. The New Buffalo Methodist Church is the only one in the town, a condition towards which modern efforts trend. Most towns have more churches than they can support in a proper manner, and one good, strong church far excels two weak, struggling ones. Miss Frances A. Urban gave the ground for its location and it was erected in 1841-42. Prior to that time services had been held in a private house rented for the purpose, until the building of the schoolhouse in 1834, when they were transferred there. This first church stood near the school building. It was purchased by the Brethren and moved to a plot near Newport and erected again.

The first pastor was Rev. Allan Brittain, and his successor was Rev. Daniel Hartman. At the time of its erection there were few members, but forty were added at one time shortly thereafter as the result of a revival meeting. The church was rebuilt in 1875-76. The first Sunday school superintendent was Owen Bruner, and the first teachers were Sarah F. Thompson, Mary S. Urban and Benjamin McKelvy.

In 1900, during the pastorate of Rev. Edwin L. Eslinger, it was replaced by the present fine edifice, known as the Elizabeth Livingston Rhoads Memorial Church, she having contributed about one-sixth of the cost of the church and its furnishings. Its cost was $3,435.66. Prior to its dedication Rev. Eslinger had been succeeded by Rev. F. C. Byers. The building committee was composed of E. B. Miller, president; J. B. Jackson, secretary and treasurer; G. W. Rider, I. B. Free, Thos. J. Free, Wm. H. Jackson, S. M. Weltmer and John W. Noblet. The church occupies a corner on the northern side of the public square. It belongs to the Liverpool charge, and its pastors have always been the same as those of the Methodist Church there. See Liverpool chapter.

NEWPORT BOROUGH.

Newport is the leading business town in Perry County, owing to its central location and shipping facilities. It has a greater number of business establishments than any other town and is surrounded by a larger agricultural district. Its streets meet at right angles and its dimensions are uniform. Few towns in the state are more prettily laid out than Newport.

It is located on the west bank of the Juniata River, within the limits of Oliver Township. It was incorporated as a borough in 1840. On Febru-

ary 8, 1775. *David English patented a tract of land where Newport is now situated. He had warranted it and another tract in December 30 and 31, 1762, one called "Antiqua," and the other. "Grenada." He sold 199 acres to his son. David English, on June 12, 1783, who on April 2, 1789, sold the same tract to Paul Reider. Through his will, dated August 6, 1804, the property descended to his sons, Paul, John, Daniel. Abraham and Ephraim. Of these sons, Paul, John and Daniel. after coming into possession, plotted the property into fifty-four lots, with the necessary streets and alleys. The first plan of the town extended only from Mulberry Street to Oliver, at the tannery, and from the river to Second Street. They kept the upper part and laid out the town along the Juniata River and Little Buffalo Creek. The town was first known as Reider's Ferry. and then as Reidersville, as houses began building. Paul Reider was the grandfather of the late O. H. P. Reider.

The Reiders established a ferry, which was in use until 1850, when its further use was ended by the diversion of traffic to the bridge. The Reider's Ferry Bridge Company was incorporated April 4, 1838, with six hundred shares of stock at $20 per share. The company was composed of the following: Thomas O. Bryan, James Black, Abraham B. Demaree. John Leas, Jonas Ickes, Jacob Leas, Jacob Loy, Samuel Sipe, Robert Mitchell, John K. Smith, John W. Bosserman, William Wallace, James Jackman, Charles Wright, Sr., George Kepner and Abraham Reider. The bridge was not built, however, until 1845, when the act of April 7th incorporated the Newport Bridge Company, with the following directors: Samuel Leiby, John Fickes, Robert Mitchell, John W. Bosserman, Benj. McIntire. Wm. Cumbler, Abram B. Demaree, Kirk Haines, John Wiley, John Patterson, James Jackman, Wm. Wallace, John Kibler, and Benjamin Musser. The shares were $20. These men were advance agents of modern progress and their names should go down to posterity, for that bridge and its successors have been of incalculable value to several generations of citizens whose homes were and are "between the rivers." As a boy, born and bred in that section, and later a resident of Newport, whose people of four generations have used it, the writer knows from a practical standpoint its value to that territory and to Newport in a business way. It was not, however, built until 1851. Garret Kirkpatrick was the contractor It was 700 feet long. All the river bridges in those days were toll bridges, and this one remained so until 1884, when it was purchased by the county and made free, at a cost of $13,583, a county jury deciding the amount, as viewers and owners failed to agree on a price. Perry County was one of the first counties in the state to free its bridges.

This ferry at Reider's was crossed by dispatch bearers on horseback from Washington, D. C., to Niagara, in the War of 1812-15. The exact date of plotting the town is unknown, but it is supposed to have been about 1804. Within what is now the borough's limits the first house to be erected was on Little Buffalo Creek, the second at Market and Water Streets, where Jesse Butz, Sr., was long in business, and the third where Hombach's marble works are located. The latter house was built by a Mr. Meredith, of Milford, and was later owned by James Smith. The fourth and a blacksmith shop were built by Fred Orwin.

---

*David English first patented a tract of land, on May 13, 1774, from Thomas Penn and John Penn, "True and absolute Proprietaries and Governors in chief of the Province of Pennsylvania, and the counties of Newcastle. Kent and Sussex, upon the Delaware." The document is made out to "David English, of Rye township," is signed by John Penn, "February 8, 1775, in the 15th year of the reign of King George, III," and calls for 102½ acres, which he named "Antiqua." This is not the Newport tract, but the one immediately north of it. The Newport tract was named "Grenada." The plot of these lands is yet in the possession of Mrs. Ephriam Rider and daughter, of Newport.

The old hotel, at the corner of Market and Water Streets, later owned by J. and B. H. Fickes, was built by Ephraim Bosserman in 1825. It was still standing in 1898. In 1825 there was also a house above the Jones warehouse, on Front Street. A man named Collar built the first hotel on the site of the Central Hotel (Mingle House), in 1827. In 1829 the land west of Second Street was all in wheat. The first house built above the line of the Pennsylvania Railroad through the center of the town, was where the Joshua S. Leiby house, more recently owned by H. H. Hain, and now by Hiram M. Keen, is located. The next was built where the old photograph gallery was later located. Samuel and H. Gantt built and owned them. The first house on Second Street was built by Dr. Dolan, where Mrs. John Fleisher resides. In 1829 Daniel Reider erected the first house built of sawed logs. It was located where William H. Hopple was so long in the undertaking business, now L. M. Kell's. There was only one store in Newport then, and that was kept by E. Bosserman and Samuel Beaver. Samuel Leiby went into business in Newport in 1826, then but twenty-two years of age.

With the opening of the canal, in 1829, the name of the cluster of houses was changed to Newport—for it was a new port and a busy one, as it was the gateway to Sherman's and Buffalo Creek Valleys.

In 1835 the first hotel was opened, by John Sipe, in a rented building on the old Jesse Butz corner. This was the first hotel along the Juniata from Duncan's Island to Lewistown where whiskey was sold. Prior to that it was necessary to go to Milford for "bitters." The second house on Second Street was the warehouse later operated by Kough's as a grain and commission house. In it was stored the first lot of flour ever placed on sale in Newport. It was shipped from the mouth of Little Buffalo Creek in an "ark," as the river boats were then known, to Port Deposit. Besides the flour the cargo consisted of pig iron from Juniata furnace, then operated by Mr. Everhart.

Samuel Sipe bought the plot where the Central Hotel stands and erected another building for a hotel. The opening of this house closed the other hotel (John Sipe's) and its proprietor went to Milford and took charge of that tavern. On March 6, 1856, this hotel in Newport was partly burned down. This building was later replaced by Jesse L. Gantt, father of the late W. H. Gantt, but on June 25, 1874, it was destroyed by fire. This fire was the most disastrous one that has ever taken place in Newport. It started in a small building standing next to the Jones warehouse, and consumed everything south to Market and along Market and up Second Street the entire length of the eastern side of the Square. Mr. Gantt then erected the present building. It was once known as the Gantt House, then the Central Hotel, and now the Mingle House. Mr. Gantt was the proprietor for thirty years. Among the earlier hotels were the "Farmers & Drovers" and the "Ninth Ward House."

The first tannery to be built in Newport was located upon the southeast corner of Water and Walnut Streets. It was built by Robt. B. Jordan in 1837. He later sold it to John Wiley, from whose estate Charles A. Rippman purchased it in 1865. Mr. Rippman conducted it until 1883, when it lay idle until it was destroyed by the great flood of 1889. Mr. Rippman is still in possession of part of the ground upon which it stood.

The first brick house was built by Philip Reamer, but was later torn down by Henry Myers to erect his new brick house, now the property of Samuel D. Myers, on South Second Street. The lands above Fourth Street were not settled until long afterwards.

The building of the Pennsylvania Railroad, in 1849, gave the town another impetus and was the occasion of much contention. The officials wanted to lay the tracks on Second Street, but were prevailed upon to locate the line on Third Street. The right of way was granted in 1847. On September 1, 1849, the first regular train passed through, the line having been opened to Lewistown on that date. With the building of the canal and railroad Newport became a great grain shipping centre, and as many as four large grain warehouses did a lucrative business at the same time, until the building of the narrow gauge railroad, which diverted much of that trade. It was no unusual thing to see on the streets of Newport from ten to thirty four and six-horse teams bringing grain or bark to market. They came from as far as the head of Sherman's Valley above New Germantown, a distance of thirty miles. These warehouses were operated by different men at different times, but will largely be remembered by the older folks as Jones Brothers (Alvin and D. Meredith), Fickes Brothers (Benjamin and Gibson), William Kough & Sons, and W. F. H. Garber. In the chapter entitled "River and Canal Transportation," there is an account of a shipment of flour and pig iron from Newport in the old-time ark, the forerunner of the canal boat. That Jones' warehouse was built before the canal days must be a fact, if the statement is correct that the Reformed Church congregation was organized in the building in 1820. The business of the Jones firm, however, dates only to 1866, when John Jones—a grandson of the founder of Milford—started in business. later taking in his sons, D. Meredith and Alvin. This business was in the names of the Jones family until the present century's first decade had passed.

The Bloomfield *Advocate and Press* of April 13, 1859, has a report of the work of the Perry County Medical Society, signed by Drs. Isaac Lefevre, James Galbraith and J. E. Singer. Among other things it tells of the unhealthy condition of Newport prior to the building of the Pennsylvania Railroad, in 1849, especially mentioning "remittent fevers epidemically during the autumnal months." The draining of a marsh of six or eight acres at the west end of town (west of Walnut Street) by the railroad authorities is given credit for the healthier condition.

Newport was incorporated in 1840, the act having been signed by Governor David Rittenhouse Porter, on March 10th. The first borough election was held on March 20, 1840. Samuel Leiby, Sr., was the first burgess. The school directors elected were Henry Switzer, George Zinn, John W. Bosserman, Samuel Leiby, Samuel Sipe and A. W. Monroe. The first school tax of the new borough totaled only $144.68. William Kinsloe taught the school four months at $25 per month. It had an early experience at expansion, but not of a permanent nature. An act of the Pennsylvania Legislature, dated April 9, 1856, extended the limits "to include mills and residence of John Kibler, the farms of Catharine Loy, Samuel Leiby, Benjamin Himes, Isaiah Corl, and so much of the lands of John Fickes as lies south of the Ickesburg road." In 1859 another act repealed this one and threw these lands back into Oliver Township. The town was extended northward in 1897.

Newport had a brass band as early as 1850, John S. Demaree being the leader. It was known as the Newport Sax Horn Band.

There was an early school building in Newport known as "the Old Mansion," where the children of Reidersville parents were taught to "read, write and cypher," by George Monroe. Then for a few years they attended the various places in Oliver Township, of which it was a part. until 1826, when the school was removed from the Henry S. Smith place to a small, one-story house belonging to John Reider, east of the street leading to Little Buffalo and near the creek. This is the successor to the school spoken of in the history of Oliver Township, which had originated in the old Josiah Fickes residence. John Ruth and John Ferguson taught here from 1825 to 1828. This house was swept away by the waters of the creek. Then there was a school at Clouser's, near the present home of Capt. James Hahn. This building was later destroyed by fire. A. W. Monroe, John Ferguson and Jacob Gantt taught there.

In 1832-33 Dr. Dolan kept a school in a building known as "the Barracks," located between the Central Hotel and the Pennsylvania Canal, with two rooms, one for the boys and one for the girls. The old brick schoolhouse on Second Street was built by contributions in 1834, and in it the next season was held the last pay or select school, as the free school law was passed the following year. John Ferguson taught that year. The lower schoolhouse was built in 1841, by Joseph Tate, contractor, for $190. In it Arnold Lobaugh was a teacher. Other early teachers were Stewart Low, C. P. Barnett, Isaac Mutch, Margaret A. Monroe, R. Wolf, Jesse L. Butz, John Adair, H. G. Milan, I. H. Zinn, J. D. C. Johns, A. M. Gantt, J. E. Bonsall, Isaac T. Woods and Miss H. Cooper.

In the fall of 1842, the borough's second year, the school term was made three months, and two schools opened, the teachers being C. P. Bonsall and Joseph Meetch. The salaries were $18 and $16, respectively. Later there was only one school again.

The old school building which was superseded by the present one, not including the wings on either side, was built in 1865, George and John Fleisher being the contractors. Its cost was $6,000. George W. Bretz was the first teacher in this building. In 1867 the number of schools had increased to three, and were graded for the first time. During the summer of 1867 Silas Wright, later county superintendent of schools, opened his Normal School in this building. The one wing or addition to this old building was built in 1874, and the other, in 1888. This entire building was demolished in May, 1911, and during the summer, the present building—the finest one in Perry County—was erected.

The first graduating class of the Newport High School was graduated May 10, 1887, under Prof. Silas Wright. Its members were: Jene F. Boyer, Jessie E. Charles, Wm. C. Hombach, Willis G. Mitchell, Turie S. Ickes, Curtis H. Gantt and Edwin H. Constantine.

The business men of the last half century would include Jesse Butz, who first opened a store on May 22, 1861; James B. Leiby, who first opened in the spring of the same year, and with the exception of one year was continuously in business until his death; Philip Bosserman, one of the pioneer merchants of the period; J. W. Frank, T. H. Milligan, Marx Dukes, David H. Spotts, William Henry Bosserman, Joshua Leiby, B. M. Eby, Rudolph Wingert, O. H. P. Rider, John Fleisher, W. H. Hopple, A. V. Hombach, A. B. Demaree, A. Fred Keim, R. H. Wingert, William Wertz, W. H. Gantt, B. F. Demaree (after 1882), J. C. Barrett and others. John C. Hetrick was a contractor for a thirty-year period following 1866. He erected the Episcopal and Reformed churches in Newport, the Methodist church in Duncannon, and the Juniata County courthouse. Miss M. L. Bell kept a millinery store there as early as the fall of 1854. Dr. S. H. Whitmer long practiced dentistry, prior to his death, in 1902.

Up until about 1832 the territory around Newport depended upon Milford and Millerstown for medical attention. About that time Dr. John H. Doling located here and remained several years. He then removed to Milford, where he practiced the balance of his life, except for a short period gold hunting in California. Dr. Bell succeeded him and practiced there two years. In 1837 Dr. S. R. Fahnestock was located here. Joshua E. Singer was born in Sunbury, in 1809, and graduated from Jefferson Medical College, locating in Newport in 1838, where he practiced until within a few years of his death, which occurred in 1881. Dr. Singer was a remarkable man, a good physician, interested in business and in church work. He was the moving spirit in the organization of the People's Bank, the forerunner of the present First National Bank, and was the organizer of the first Bible class in the county—it being formed in the Newport Reformed Church. Dr. Robert S. Brown settled in Newport before 1850, and was in practice here until 1860, when he died, part of the time being associated with Dr. Singer. Dr. William R. Howe, a native of the county, commenced practice here in 1857 as an associate of Dr. Brown, a brother-in-law. After a few years he removed to Blain, where he died in 1860. Both were graduates of Jefferson Medical College. Dr. R. B. Hoover located here in 1856, and Dr. W. O. Baldwin in 1859, neither remaining long. In 1860 Dr. Joseph Eby located here, coming from Milford, where he had practiced three years. He was born near New Germantown, in 1830, and graduated at the Eclectic Medical College in Philadelphia. He was married to a daughter of Dr. Jonas Ickes, of New Bloomfield. He died in 1872. Mrs. Gibson Fickes, still residing in Newport, is a daughter. Dr. William Mateer located there in 1860, and practiced for a few years. Dr. George W. Mitchell, after graduation in 1860, practiced here a year or two, and then removed to Andersonburg. From about 1862 to 1868 Dr. J. M. Miller practiced here, then going West. Several years prior to 1866 Dr. Williams practiced at Newport.

Dr. James B. Eby was born in New Bloomfield, in 1840. He graduated in 1866 from the University of Pennsylvania, and located at Newport, being associated with Dr. Joseph Eby. After a year he removed to New Buffalo, where he remained until 1870. He then returned to Newport, where he practiced until his death, which occurred in 1911. He was a skillful practitioner and had large business interests. He was the father of Lieut. Colonel Charles McHenry Eby, U. S. A. Dr. Fishburn located at Newport about 1866, where he practiced for several years, then removing to the West. Dr. H. O. Orris, still in active practice in Newport, located there in 1867, the year of his graduation. He has had a large practice in the county and is a successful physician. In 1867 Dr. Harry Stites, a son of Dr. Samuel Stites, of Millerstown, located there, where he practiced for several years, leaving to become a surgeon in the United States Army. After practicing for a short time in Millerstown Dr. George W. Campbell, a graduate of Jefferson Medical College, located here in 1879, where he continued in practice until his death in 1912. During the last few years of his practice he had associated with him Dr. Lenus Carl, mentioned below. Dr. Campbell had a large practice and was successful. Dr. C. E. DeLancy's location in Newport dates to 1883. Dr. W. H. Hoopes came later and practiced until about 1917, when he was found dead in his sleigh while making a professional call. In 1908, as stated above, Dr. Carl located here. The present physicians are Dr. Orris, Dr. DeLancey and Dr. Carl.

One of the industries of a past generation which is yet remembered by many is the W. R. S. Cook planing mill, which was located in west Newport, Oliver Township. In June, 1875, this industry was started on lands purchased from Dr. J. E. Singer, with a twenty-five horse-power, portable sawmill, with a capacity of ten thousand feet of lumber a day. It was located along the Pennsylvania Canal, and soon thereafter a sawmill and a shingle mill were added. In 1881 the two-story mill was built, and in 1885 the planing mill was added. These mills jointly had a capacity of over sixty thousand feet of finished product per day. The capacity of the mill was being continually increased.

The wagon manufacturing plant of the late J. C. Frank had its beginning when his father, Philip Frank, mastered wagonmaking and opened a shop at Girty's Notch, in Buffalo Township, in 1843. In that shop J. C. Frank learned the business, later opening a shop near Newport, and in 1876 erecting a manufacturing plant in Newport, which, for the next quarter of a century, was one of the town's busy industrial plants. Snyder & Kahler later erected a factory at Fourth and Mulberry Streets, and also did a large business for a like period.

The Newport Planing Mill. In 1863, eighteen or twenty citizens of Newport organized the Newport Manufacturing & Building Company, which built a planing mill and operated it until 1865. At that time the remaining stockholders sold out to George Fleisher, John W. Smith, Henry C. Smith, Wm. Henry Bosserman and B. F. Miller. Gradually George Fleisher purchased the other interests until 1885, when sole ownership rested with him. He operated it successfully until 1900, when he in turn sold it to his son, J. Emory Fleisher, who operated it until 1920, when it was sold to a newly organized corporation known as the Newport Planing Mill Company, of which C. Z. Moore is president, and E. B. Callow, secretary. The product of this mill during the long ownership of the Fleishers—father and son— and since, has been high-grade mill work for building purposes. From twenty-five to forty men have found employment there for many years. An everlasting credit to this plant is the fact that Daniel W. Gantt served in the capacity of foreman from 1865 to the present (1920). As an experienced mill man Mr. Gantt's equals are seldom found. George Fleisher attained his boyish ambition, which was to own a planing mill. He erected many homes in Newport during his lifetime and helped make the town what it is.

The Oak Extract Company. Through the efforts of Mr. H. H. Bechtel, a practical tanner and a resident of Newport for many years, who afterwards located at Cincinnati, Ohio, and became vice-president of the American Oak Leather Company of that city, the Oak Extract Company was incorporated in Pennsylvania for the manufacture of tannic acid, and the plant located at Newport, of which Mr. Bechtel was also first vice-president. This company was chartered March 17, 1899, the business being really an auxiliary one of the American Oak Leather Co. of Cincinnati, having plants at New Decatur, Alabama; Harriman, Tennessee; Louisville, Ky., and at Cincinnati. Also having leather stores at Boston, Chicago and St. Louis.

Fifteen acres of the Gibson Fickes farm, lying immediately north of Newport Borough, were leased and subsequently purchased by the Oak Extract Company, upon which the plant was to be erected and the construction of the plant started March, 1899, and manufacture began March 10, 1900, and the plant has been in continuous operation up to the present time with the exception of occasional shutdowns for repairs, etc., such as all manufacturing plants are subjected to. Its present acreage also comprises the old Clemsen property adjoining, containing four and one-half acres. Ten larger and smaller buildings comprise the plant. Fifty to eighty men have been continually employed. Until January 1, 1921, its general disbursements have been over $3,500,000, of which amount $2,-157,000 was paid for wood alone.

The several plants and leather stores enumerated are largely the result of the industry and financial capacity of Mr. James E. Mooney, of Cincinnati, who was president of the American Oak Leather Co. of that place until his death, which occurred in his eighty-fourth year, up to which time he had been active in business. It might be considered in this connection that Mr. Mooney was the father of the extract business in this country, having established the first one in Alabama, and the second one at Newport. In 1900, when the Oak Extract Company began operations, it was paying $2.25 per cord of 128 cubic feet for chestnut wood, while in 1920 the price had risen to $7.50 per cord. The history of the Newport tannery appears in Chapter XV.

The Newport Hosiery Mill is located on South Fifth Street, and is a result of the Board of Trade, organized in Newport in 1902. Through this organization the building was erected and turned over to H. A. Romberger, of Philadelphia, for a three-year period, rent free. Prior to the expiration of the three-year lease Mr. Romberger agreed to purchase the interests of all the stockholders at eighty per cent of the value of their holdings, and thus secured entire control of the plant. It first started operation July 21, 1902, with but fifteen employees. Soon after its beginning Aaron D. Hoke became the manager and part owner of the business, and from then on its strides were rapid. In fact, the writer has always considered this business a monument to the business ability of Mr. Hoke, whose death occurred November 19, 1915, while in the prime of his usefulness in the community. Mr. Hoke had charge of the Middletown mill of Mr. Romberger before coming to Newport. After the death of Mr. Hoke, E. M. Buffington was made manager, and still holds the position. Upon the death of Mr. Hoke, his interest in the mill was sold to Mr. Romberger. The mill is a substantial brick structure, 100x140 feet in size. It has been enlarged twice since 1902 and has its own electric plant, the power being furnished by a ninety-horse-power steam engine. The greatest period of expansion was in 1914 and 1915, when the pay roll mounted to 115 persons, mostly female help. The production was then nine hundred dozen per day. During the past three years the production has been about three hundred dozen per day, and the pay roll numbers about fifty. This mill passed into the ownership of Wilbur D. Gring, November 1, 1920.

The Moorehead Knitting Company, Incorporated, of Harrisburg, opened a branch mill in Newport on February 27, 1920, citizens of the town investing in stock of the company to induce its location. The resident manager is Wilmer B. Hoke, a son of the late A. D. Hoke, who was superintendent and part owner of the Romberger mill on Fifth Street. It is located in the Smith garage building, on Penn Avenue, near the Pennsylvania Railroad Station. It started with seven employees, and at the present time (1921) employs thirty, mostly females. The Moorehead people conduct an immense plant at Harrisburg and several other branches, and no doubt their Newport plant will, in time, become one of Newport's valued industries.

The Newport Shirt Factory was started by H. W. Shumaker, in 1904. In 1906 a one-story factory was built, to which another was added in 1914. It was later owned by J. K. Saucerman, and now, by the Phillips-Jones Corporation of New York.

Newport has a live Chamber of Commerce. It was organized on March 15, 1920, as a result of a meeting held on March 1st, which was attended by over two hundred business men and citizens. On the date of its organization 135 members had enrolled. The membership fee is $10 annually. It is affiliated with both the State Chamber of Commerce and that of the United States. Its first officers were Dr. L. A. Carl, president; A. L. Gelnett, vice-president; George R. Fry, secretary; G. P. Bistline, treasurer.

Of the Newport organizations the Civic Club is most noted for accomplishments of a public nature. It was organized April 20, 1906, with these officers: Mrs. J. E. Fleisher, president; Mrs. Alvin Jones, vice-president; Mrs. Delphine Pennell, secretary, and Mrs. T. H. Butturf, treasurer. It began with fourteen members, and at the end of a year had thirty-six.

During 1906-07 it initiated its program by having the old graveyard cleaned and fenced. It also had waste paper receptacles placed throughout the town, donated $10 to Mt. Alto Sanatorium, and contributed $200 to the fund for the improvement of the river road opposite town, for which Newport business men had obligated themselves heavily. During 1908 organs were purchased for the primary and intermediate schoolrooms. In 1909 the club obligated themselves to pay annually for four years to the McNight scholarship at State College. During 1909-11 various projects were helped, principally adding to a town foundation fund, started in 1909. In 1911 a contribution was made to the Titanic Memorial Fund. In 1912 a fountain was placed in the public square, at a cost of $525.63. In 1914. through permission of the school board, a room was obtained in the public school building and fitted with shelves and other library equipment. and a public library opened. On November 23, 1915, it was first opened to public use. The members took turns as librarian at first, its hours being from two to four, and to be open one day each week. About 1,600 books are already upon its shelves. The secretary, Mrs. Pennell, is there much of the time, both her time and labor being given gratuitously. Mrs. W. J. Flickinger, for the past two years, has been assisting along the same line The club is now aiming for a building large enough for community service. Many other local projects have been aided financially. Mrs. Fleisher was president from the organization until 1919, save for two years when she was abroad, and Mrs. Pennell has been secretary during the entire time. It now has seventy-three members, and six honorary male members. Its officers now are : Mrs. J. E. Fleisher, honorary president; Mrs. J. S Eby, president; Mrs. Wm. J. Flickinger and Mrs. D. B. Howanstine. vice-presidents; Mrs. Delphine Pennell, secretary; Mrs. George Fry, corresponding secretary, and Mrs. Edna Boyer, treasurer. This library project should be encouraged by citizens and former residents by the contribution of at least a book a year, which would eventually give the town a large library. Let it be a "Book a Year Club."

Newport has two clubs which maintain club rooms and incidentally engage in community projects. The Calumet Club was organized in 1908, and the Phi Epsilon Kappa Fraternity, on June 18, 1909. The latter is a high school fraternity, but in Newport was not confined strictly to such students. It has been responsible for the community Christmas tree for the past several years, among its other activities.

Newport has by far the largest number of business places of any Perry County town. According to the report of the mercantile appraiser the following business places are located there, the dates following the names being the year of entering the business :

General stores, J. M. Flickinger (1889), succeeding E. B. Weise.

Groceries, C T Albright, C. L. Bair (1899 to 1920), succeeding William Emenheiser (1877); M. C. Bower, C F. D'Olier, Philip Fickes, S. J. Horting (1901). A. W. Kough (1881), succeeding E. B. Weise, elected county treasurer; W. W. Manning, E. S. L Soule (1908), succeeding I. H. Souders (1904), and C. T Rice (1895); W. G. Wilson (1890), established by Jackson Rhoads (1883), Chas. L. Fleck.

Druggists John S. Eby (1910), established by H. M. Singer (before 1855), whose successor was B. M. Eby (1864); Chas. E. Bosserman (1920), established by E. C. Beach (1878), successors W. H. Hoopes, J. N. C. Hetherington.

Dry goods, W. R. Bosserman, established by Philip Bosserman and in his charge until his death (1899), C. V. Bosserman & Co., until her death (1916) ; J. B. Leiby & Sons (1901), established by J. B. Leiby (1861), at Market and Water Streets as a small general store.

Hardware. C. T. Rice & Son (1905), established by C. T. Rice ; J. M. Smith & Sons (1807), established by B. F. Miller & Son, succeeded by J. W.

Frank (1871), who located in present building in 1878; F. E. Taylor (1910), established by T. H. Milligan (1886), later owned by H. B. Wilson.

Stoves and tinware, T. W. Bassett, S. W. Burd (1894), J. W. Davis & Son

Furniture and undertaking, S. D. Myers (1907), succeeding John Fleisher (1875); L. M. Kell (1915), succeeding W H. Hopple (1888) and Jacob Hopple.

Clothing, J. S. Butz (1880); Fleck & Hyman, succeeding David Spotts, who succeeded Marx Dukes; Newport One Price, succeeding Peter Schlomer, Ira Meminger, H. Lipsett.

Restaurants, L. E. Gannt (1913); Noll Bros.

Hotel, C. F. Kloss.

Confectionery, J. C. Berger, E C. Sheibley, C. F. Smith Estate.

Jewelers, F. C. Gannt (1914), succeeding W. H. Gannt (1872); Chas. P. Keim (1901), formerly C. P. McClure's.

Meat markets, Chas. A. Oren (1914), established by Silas W. Clark (1911); J. A. Jackson, Mrs. Thad. Stephens.

Wholesalers, Rice Produce Co. (1915), William Fickes, C. F. Smith Estate, J. Frank Fickes. S. A. Sharon, Newport Planing Mill, Henry Shull, George Boova.

Automobiles and supplies, Gelnett Bros. (W. L. and A. L., 1915), established by their brothers, Daniel L. and Benj. L., 1910; Roy Keller (1917), C. H. Rebert, J. S. Smith, H. R. Kell.

Cigars, C. R. Horting. Geo. J. Wagenseller, F. P. Witmer.

Musical instruments, H. M. Kough, W. A. Smith (1887).

Miscellaneous, R. T. Smith, coal; W. H. Kepner (1891), grain and feed; F. M. Snyder & Co., coal and feed; Jacobs & Wright, machinery; R. T. Beatty, furniture; B. F. Horting, fertilizers; Harry McKee, plumbing supplies (1906); Sarah A. Adams, Anna Hibbs and Mrs. Geo. J. Wagenseller, millinery; D. A. Hockenberry, fish; W. J. Morrow, photographer (1910), established by W. A. Keagy (1890); J. J. Newberry & Co. (1919), succeeding Banks Bros. (1908), 5 and 10 cent store; Juniata Public Service Co., electrical supplies; Fickes & Wolfe, coal and feed; Paul Hombach, marble works, established by A. V. Hombach (1867); J. W., Leonard, marble works.

The Photoplay Theatre was opened in 1910 by Zinn & Frank, whose successor was H. E. Williams. In 1918 purchased by John S. Kough and W. J. Morrow, the former succeeding to ownership in 1921.

The Newport Union Church. The Lutheran, Reformed and Presbyterian folks residing about Newport held a conference early in 1846 and agreed to erect a joint church. On May 1, 1846, John Wiley and Barbara, his wife, deeded to Andrew B. Maxwell, John Loy and John Titzel, a plot of ground for church purposes at the corner of Second and Walnut Streets. The corner stone was laid on May 12, 1846, and it was dedicated May 23, 1847. In 1868, the Reformed congregation desiring to build a church, sold their one-third interest to the Lutherans and the Presbyterians for $900. In 1877 the Presbyterians purchased the other half-interest from the Lutherans for $2,380, and became sole owners. From then on the history of this church building will be found under that of the Newport Presbyterian Church. This was Newport's first church.

Newport Lutheran Church. As early as 1830 Rev. John William Heim was preaching in the homes and in the schoolhouses in the vicinity. In 1842 he was requested to also preach in the English language, his previous exhortations having been in German. On January 14, 1844, the congregation was regularly organized, under the care of Rev. Levi T. Williams, who became pastor in November, 1843, preaching in the old brick schoolhouse. The first officers were Daniel Rider, elder; Godfrey Lenig and Henry D. Smith, deacons. In connection with the Reformed and Presbyterian congregations the old Union church was built by them and dedicated in May, 1847. In 1877 the Lutherans sold their interest in the church to the Presbyterians for $2,380.

A contract was made with Joshua Sweger for the erection of a new church on Market Street, for the sum of $10,000. Including the ground

and furnishings its cost was over $15,000. This church still stands, having
been one of the best in the county. Its Sunday school room is on the first
floor, and the second floor is occupied by the ample auditorium, which seats
five hundred people.

This church was connected with the New Bloomfield charge until 1868,
when a separate pastorate was formed, of which it was the head, the other
churches being St. Samuel's, in Oliver Township, and the Lutheran Church
in Buck's Valley. This church belongs to the Synod of Central Pennsylvania and was the first church in that synod to have a pipe organ, which
it had installed as early as 1885. This was also the first pipe organ in
Perry County. The ministers have been:

1830-42—Re.. John William Heim.	1876-81—Rev. M. Colver.
1843-45—Rev. Levi T. Williams.	1881-85—Rev. W. B. Glanding.
1845-49—Rev. Lloyd Knight.	1885-88—Rev. J. T. Gladhill.
1849-52—Rev. Jacob Martin.	1889-94—Rev. S. E. Smith.
1852-53—Rev. Wm. Gerhardt.	1895-00—Rev. Geo. M. Diffenderfer.
1853-54—Rev. Adam Height.	1900-01—Rev. J. Henry Harms.
1855-63—Rev. David H. Focht.	1902-05—Rev. J. H. Musselman.
1863-66—Rev. P. P. Lane.	1906-09—Rev. Joseph B. Baker.
1866-71—Rev. Geo. F. Sheaffer.	1910-20—Rev. William C. Ney.
1871-76—Rev. A. H. Aughe.	1920- — Rev. L. Stoy Spangler.

Reformed Church. The Reformed people in Newport began holding
services in the homes and schoolhouses before the organization of the
county and while the place was still known as Reider's Ferry. In the
same year as the county's formation, 1820, the congregation was regularly
organized, its first meeting place being in the old Jones warehouse, and its
first pastor being Rev. Jacob Scholl, who remained as such until his death
in 1847. Until the pastorate of Rev. William F. Cauliflower, the congregation worshiped in the old Union church, which was owned jointly by the
Reformed, the Lutheran and the Presbyterian organizations, and was dedicated May 23, 1847. In June, 1869, the Reformed interest in this church
was sold to the Presbyterian and Lutheran people for $900, and the same
year a new church building was erected at a cost of nearly $7,000. It was
named Christ's Reformed Church. The building committee of this first
Reformed church was composed of William Bosserman, Sr., John W.
Smith, Dr. Joshua Singer, Josiah Fickes, Charles K. Smith, Charles Bressler and Isaiah Carl. It was dedicated January 16, 1870.

The organization was incorporated in 1868, and in 1874, during the pastorate of Rev. James Crawford, a parsonage was built at a cost of $2,518,
which is to-day one of Newport's attractive homes and which would cost
several times that amount to build. The building committee included
James B. Leiby, John W. Smith, Elias B. Leiby and Jacob Saucerman.
The first Sunday school was organized in 1869, George Ickes being the
first superintendent.

Unfortunately the foundations of the first church were faulty, and although it had been in use but twenty years it was abandoned, torn away
and replaced with the present fine structure of brick, which was dedicated
September 7, 1890. It was then named the Reformed Church of the Incar-
nation. Its cost was about $10,000. The building committee was composed
of J. B. Leiby, C. K. Smith, Daniel Smith, Josiah Fickes and Jeremiah V.
Fickes.

In 1897, Carlisle Classis, the governing body, detached the New Bloomfield church from the pastorate, and during the pastorate of Rev. Meixell
the Markelville church was detached and placed with New Bloomfield. Dr.
Deatrich continued as pastor at New Bloomfield, after the charge was
divided, and remained until his death in 1900.

The ministers in charge of the congregation have been:

1820-47—Rev. Jacob Scholl.
1848-50—Rev. Daniel Gans.
1851-63—Rev Samuel Kuhn.
1863-67—Rev. David W. Kelley.
1867-70—Rev. Wm. F. Colliflower.
1871-75—Rev. James Crawford.
1876-81—Rev. John Kretzing.

1881-97—Rev. W. R. H. Deatrich.
1897-00—Rev. James M. Mullan.
1900-02—Rev. Edwin D Meixell.
1903-08—Rev. Frank L. Kerr.
1908-15—Rev. James M. Runkle
1915-   —Rev. U. O. H. Kerschner.

Newport Presbyterian Church. When the first Presbyterian meetings were held in Newport is not recorded, but the Presbyterian people were, in connection with the Lutherans and the Reformed people, the builders of Newport's first church, the old Union church. The Reformed people sold their interest, in 1868, to the Lutherans and Presbyterians, and the Presbyterians eventually purchased the interests of the Lutherans, and thus the building became theirs.

It was dedicated May 23, 1847, as a Union church, and since then the Presbyterians have worshiped at this location, where their new edifice is also located. The Sunday school dates to 1873.

While the church was owned jointly by the Presbyterians, Lutheran and Reformed people, yet it seems not to have been a regularly organized congregation at first, as the folowing will show.

The Session record of the Presbyterian Church at Newport, commencing from its origin, has this entry:

April 18th, 1863. The following petition was presented to the Carlisle Presbytery at their meeting in Middletown, Pa., April 12th, 1863: "We the undersigned members of the Presbyterian Church residing in the town of Newport and its vicinity do most respectfully petition your Reverent Body to organize us into a Presbyterian Church. We would suggest Saturday the 18th day of April as a suitable time and that the Lord's Supper be administered to us on the following Sabbath. Signed

GEORGE JACOBS,
MARGARET JACOBS,
WILLIAM MATEER,
MARGARET LOWTHER,
SARAH MARLIN,
MARGARET MITCHELL,
ANN MITCHELL, Wife of Robert,
MARTHA MITCHELL.

JOHN PATTERSON,
JANE PATTERSON,
HENRIETTA PATTERSON,
CAROLYN ENGLISH.
JANE DUNBAR,
SARAH REYNOLDS,
MARGARET MITCHELL. Wife of William.

Some of those named had been members of the Middle Ridge church long before, among them being the Mitchells. The movement to organize the church was the work of a Perry Countian, a minister gone abroad and returned on account of sectional feeling, Rev. William P. Cochran, of Missouri. The war was on, and Unionist that he was, Rev. Cochran had returned to his boyhood home at Millerstown and became the stated supply for the pulpits there and at Buffalo (Ickesburg). When not busy elsewhere he held meetings in Newport in the Union church, in which the Presbyterians had an interest, and the above petition resulted. He and Elder W. L. Jones were appointed to organize the church. On April 18, 1863, the church was organized with the fifteen members, named in the petition.

In 1869, upon the payment of $450, and in 1877, for a consideration of $2,380, according to the deed, the interests of others in the Union church were bought and the church became the Presbyterian Church. In 1885 an addition was built and the entire church remodeled, being dedicated December 13th. Its location is a fine one, on the corner of Second and Walnut Streets. The pastors since the organization have been:

1863-69—Rev. William P. Cochran.
1869-71—Rev. J. G. Downing.
1872-75—Rev. Albert C. Titus.
1876-86—Rev. William H. Logan.
1887-01—Rev. S. C. Alexander.
1902-09—Rev. A. F. Lott.

1909-11—Rev. R L. Williams.
1911-18—Rev. R. M. Ramsey.
1919-20—Rev. J. C. Clarke (stated supply).
1921- —Rev. Harry M. Vogelsonger.

Newport M. E. Church. About 1830 the Methodist people began holding meetings in their homes, but the church was not built until 1836, when, October 19th, James Black gave a deed for a lot on which to build the church, the site being the location of the former Evangelical Church. This first church was a plain one-room frame building, being then the only church building in the town. The first class leader was John Ernest. At a conference in 1845, the New Bloomfield Circuit, to which it had belonged, was divided and it was made a part of a circuit consisting of Newport, Liverpool, Millerstown, New Buffalo and Petersburg (Duncannon). In 1856 this circuit was divided into the Newport and Duncannon Circuits. The first Methodist church was sold in 1869 to the Evangelical denomination for $1,450. On January 8, 1871, the new church at Fourth and Market Streets was dedicated. It was a two-story building, costing $15,000. There were two pastors until 1871, when Liverpool and New Buffalo were separated from the circuit and made a separate charge. In 1900 Millerstown was separated from Newport and with Donally's Mills became a station. The walls of the church having become unsafe, a new church was built and dedicated on June 10, 1904. The building committee was composed of Rev. L. Dow Ott, B. M. Eby, G. H. Frank, A. Fred Keim, Henry Smith and H. L. Tressler. The names of the pastors from 1833 to 1856 will be found under the Duncannon chapter. Since that time they have been as follows:

1857	—Rev. Geo. Stevenson. Rev. Chas. H. Zigler.	1869	—Rev. Alexander R. Miller. Rev. J. M. Meredith.
1858	—Rev. Frederick E. Crever. Jas. T. Wilson.	1870	—Rev. Alexander R. Miller.
1859	—Amos C. Smith. Rev. Isaac C. Stevens.	1871-73	—Rev. H. C. Cheston.
		1874-75	—Rev. H. M. Ash.
1860	—Rev. Amos C. Smith. Rev. J. Clark Hagey.	1876-78	—Rev. J. W. Buckley.
		1879-81	—Rev. N W. Colburn.
1861	—Rev. G. W. Bouse. Rev. Milton K. Foster.	1882	—Rev. B. P. King.
		1883-84	—Rev. John Vrooman.
1862	—Rev. G. W. Bouse.	1885-87	—Rev. E E. A. Deaver.
1863	—Rev. H. S. Mendenhall. Rev Robt. R. Pott.	1888-91	—Rev. Jared Y. Shannon.
		1892	—Rev. Amos S. Baldwin.
1864	—Rev. H. S. Mendenhall. Rev. Samuel R. Deach.	1893-94	—Rev. Peter P. Strawinski.
		1895-96	—Rev. John L. Leilich.
1865	—Rev. John W. Cleaver. Rev. John Donahue.	1897-99	—Rev. Furman Adams
		1900-02	—Rev. Elmer G Baker.
1866	—Rev. John W. Cleaver. Rev. A. Duncan Yocum.	1903-05	—Rev. Lorenza Dow Ott.
		1908-10	—Rev. J. Vernon Adams.
1867	—Rev. John W. Cleaver. Rev. J Milton Akers.	1911-16	—Rev. John C Collins.
		1917	—Rev. John W. Glover.
1868	—Rev. Alexander R. Miller Rev. W. N. Houghtelin.	1918-21	—Rev. Frank T. Bell.
		1921-	—Rev R. Frank Ruch.

Calvary Evangelical Church. The Evangelical people of Perry County were originally served by two circuit riders, the one section finally narrowing down to Marysville, Newport and Rye Township's two churches—Salem and Bethel. The latter two were finally detached and made the nucleus of Keystone charge. Marysville and Newport then continued as one charge until 1898, when they were separated. The work at Newport dates back to "the sixties."

This people evidently were organized somewhat before the time of the purchase of the old Methodist church, but records are lacking. From 1870 to 1874 the pastor of Perry Circuit, residing at Elliottsburg, served the Newport church, but in that year it became a part of the Marysville Circuit. In 1898 Newport was made a separate charge. The first services were held at various places, but in 1869 the congregation purchased the old Methodist church which stood on a lot fronting Walnut Street, and extending along an alley, between Second and Third Streets, for $1,450. They repaired and used it until 1878, when they erected a new brick church, 32x60, upon the same site. Its cost was $2,500. In 1919-20 the congregation erected a handsome church building upon a plot of ground located at the corner of Fourth and Oliver Streets, at a cost of about $35,000. Adjoining the church, in 1919, a fine brick parsonage was erected.

The earlier pastors, under the Perry Circuit, whose pastors resided at Elliottsburg, were: Rev. S. W. Seibert, Rev. D. W. Miller, Rev. M. Sloat, Rev. H. A. Deitterick, Rev. U. F. Swengel. These pastors then followed: Rev. R. W. Runyan, Rev. A. Stapleton, Rev. G. W. Currin, Rev. C. E. Zehner, Rev. P. S. Orwig, Rev. E. Swengel and Rev. J. C. Reeser, who resided at Newport.

The pastors from then on who resided at Marysville and served both churches were: Rev. S. P. Remer, Rev. B. Hengst, Rev. H. H. Douty, Rev. J. F. Dunlap and Rev. C. W. Finkbinder.

Those since who have resided in Newport, it having been made a separate pastorate: Rev. W. J. Dice, Rev. George Joseph, Rev. J. T. Pettit, Rev. C. S. Raffensperger, Rev. A. F. Weaver, Rev. W. H. Brown, Rev. E. Fulcomer, Rev. M. W. Stahl, and Rev. W. K. Shultz.

Newport Episcopal Church. The first Episcopal services in Newport were held in the parlor of Mrs. H. H. Bechtel, through her efforts and those of Mrs. Peter Heistand, on March 28, 1875. Later a Sunday school was organized there, but soon transferred into what is now the office of the supervisor of the Pennsylvania Railroad, which was fitted up for church services and where this people worshiped. Rev. T. O. Tongue was the first rector. The Sunday school the following year had over a hundred pupils, and Mrs. Bechtel was long its superintendent. The lot for a church was bought in 1887. It is located on South Second Street. The church was dedicated November 14, 1889. Rev. C. E. D. Griffiths, under whose charge the building had been started, died in March, 1889, and was succeeded by Rev. J. E. C. Schmedes, D.D., who served this church in connection with Mechanicsburg. In August, 1891, Rev. Wm. Dorwart took charge, in connection with Steelton, but in October of the same year relinquished the Steelton appointment and moved to Newport, where he is still rector. The rectory was erected in 1893. Others who served in the earlier years were Alfred J. Billow, John Gregson, S. K. Boyer and James Stoddard.

OLIVER TOWNSHIP.

Oliver Township was the thirteenth to be formed in the territory now comprising Perry County. Its original domain was much larger than the present township, as it included all of Howe Township—which had been a part of Buffalo—and part of Miller. At the January sessions of the Perry County court, in 1836, a petition signed by eighty-nine residents of the territory was presented, praying for the erection of a new township. The petition:

"The petition of the subscribers, inhabitants of the townships of Buffalo, Juniata and Centre, in said county, respectfully represents that they labor under great inconvenience in many respects for want of a new township to be erected out of the townships of Buffalo, Juniata and Centre, and therefore pray the court to appoint persons to view and lay out the same according to law, and the boundaries of the General Election District of Newport, which are as follows, to wit.

"Beginning at the Juniata River at the line between Centre and Wheatfield Townships; thence across the Juniata River at the line to Buffalo Township; thence up the said river to the house of James Shield, including the same; thence a northerly course to Thomas Boyd's, including his house; along the line of said Boyd and Swift north, till they intersect the line between Buffalo and Greenwood Townships; thence along said line to the Juniata River; thence up the same to the Rope Ferry; thence across the Juniata River to the house of Abraham Reider, including the same; thence a through course to the house of Samuel Murray, including the same; thence a straight line to the house of Peter Werts (probably Wertz), including the same; thence a straight southerly line to the house of John Bressler, and including the same; thence a south course to the top of Limestone Ridge in Centre Township; thence an easterly course to a sawmill, known as 'Stengle's old sawmill'; thence the same course till it intersects the line between Wheatfield and Penn Townships; thence along said line to the place of beginning. And we, as in duty bound, will pray."

Accordingly, on January 6, 1836, the court appointed William West, Andrew Linn and Robert Irvine as viewers. Almost two years elapsed before the report of the viewers was presented at the November sessions in 1837. The report was signed by William West and Robert Irvine and favored the establishing of the new township, with practically the same boundaries as outlined in the petition. On November 11, 1837, the report was confirmed by the court, and the township was named Oliver, in further honor of Oliver Hazard Perry, the county already bearing his last name.

Oliver Township is bounded on the north by Tuscarora, on the east by the Juniata River, which it borders for about six miles between the Tuscarora line and the great bend in the river between Newport and Bailey's Station; on the south by Miller Township, and on the west by Centre and Juniata. It is one of the smaller townships in the county, its area being less than twenty square miles. Newport Borough lies within its borders. At its southern end Limestone Ridge touches it. The Buffalo Hills run parallel a short distance north. Still further north is Middle Ridge, much of which is under tillage. Between it and Limestone Ridge flows Little Buffalo Creek, which empties into the Juniata at Newport's southern boundary. In the northern part of the township high cliffs border the river, the lands on the opposite side being comparatively low, while farther down—just above the Newport bridge—the opposite condition prevails.

As early as 1788 David English took up fifty-two acres on the Juniata as a fishery. William Darlington warranted 292 acres on the Juniata River and Buffalo Creek, adjoining William West, which was transferred to David English, who also took up the following tracts: on the same creek 200 acres, in 1766 two tracts of 220 and 235 acres, 110 acres in 1774, 219 acres in 1766, 400 acres in 1785, and 236 acres in 1768. These claims total almost 2,000 acres.

Adjoining his lands John English had 803 acres, one warrant being for 252 acres in 1767. The tract upon which Newport stands was taken up by David English under three warrants granted May 14, 1775, and December 30 and 31, 1762, for 144 acres, 238 acres, and 115 acres, a total of 497 acres. These tracts have a frontage of 248 rods on the Juniata, and extend from Buffalo Creek to Little Buffalo Creek.

The tract of 185 acres, on which Eshelman's mill stands, was warranted in 1772, by William West, Jr., who sold to David English, in 1790.

Oliver Township is the home of a number of towns and villages. Besides Newport, the incorporated borough within its boundaries, are East Newport, West Newport and Everhartville. East Newport was formerly known as Habeckertown, by reason of it being plotted by J. B. Habecker in 1866. Besides the homes of many thrifty people it has been the location of Eshelman's mill, the Marshall furnace, Butturf's bottling works and ice plant, and Morrow's glue factory. William Wertz and Elias Fisher had the first stores there. West Newport once comprised all that section west of Oliver Street and extending to the fair grounds road, where Front and Fourth Streets merge. It was never laid out in lots, but "just grew" along the two highways, the upper end being known as Singertown, by reason of the houses being erected by Dr. Singer, who owned the lands. In its earlier days most of the homes were occupied by mechanics employed in the local industries. The tannery was once in Oliver Township, but borough extension located it in Newport Borough. The W. R. S. Cook saw and planing mill was another industry of importance. The Flurie brick yards flourished many years and gave employment to many men.

When Oliver was yet a part of Rye Township it contained the voting place of the "Sixth District, comprising Rye and Greenwood Townships." With poor roads, no railroads and distances extending from Newport to Sterrett's Gap to be traveled to vote, those old pioneers should set to shame forever those able-bodied voters who want to be hauled to the elections. It was located on Buffalo Creek, about a mile and a half west of Newport, at the old "English Mill." The act of 1787 located it there. The English mill is obscure. It must have been built before 1787, as the act says "late the property of Daniel English." It was torn down when Reaves & Company built a forge below the road. J. B. Habecker was the superintendent of this forge. It was abandoned in a few years.

The Mitchell property, now owned by J. Emory Fleisher, was the early residence of Robert Mitchell, the son of a Revolutionary War officer, Colonel John Mitchell, of whom more elsewhere.

The first school within the limits of the township was usually held in some part of a building that could be rented. The earliest record is that of a school in 1812, in the old Josiah Fickes residence. John English was the teacher. Later teachers were David McConaughey, Richard Henry Swayne, Thomas Butler, Valentine Varnes and Jonas Schofield. Varnes had a disabled arm caused by trying to gain entrance into a schoolroom at Millerstown during a "barring out the teacher" process. This school was later removed to the residence of Henry S. Smith (at the Henry Wilson farm of later years), where Jonas Schofield was a teacher. From there it was removed to the Reider schoolhouse in Newport, which comes under the history of Newport Borough.

Prior to 1830 there was a schoolhouse at the residence of Harvey L. Troup, which was attended by pupils from the other side of the Juniata, in Greenwood Township. Heil North was the first teacher. It was later removed to the residence of David Mitchell and was taught by James English, in 1830. In 1831 it was taught at B. Baltozer's, later known as the Gish farm, by John Jones. In 1832, at John Deardorff's, by A. W. Monroe. Surveying, in addition to the common branches, was taught in this school. In 1834 the school was taught at the Jacob Fleisher place of our day, by Henry Beatty. After that until Newport became a borough the pupils of this school were permitted to attend the old brick schoolhouse on Second Street.

The first public schoolhouse in the township of which there is record is in 1839. Mt. Fairview was built on a plot of four square rods, purchased of Abraham Deardorff. C. P. Barnett was the first teacher. Part of the district having no facility in that line available Evergreen, near the present fair grounds, was built in 1842 to meet the need, and Dr. R. S. Brown was

the first teacher. Others who taught early at Mt. Fairview were John
McCullough, in 1842; Joel Lobaugh, in 1844-45; George W. Bosserman,
in 1846; Ezra Patton, in 1847, and A. M. Gantt, in 1850. The term was
three months, and the salary $16 and $18 per month.

In 1881 James Morrow erected a glue factory near the Marshall furnace, which was operated for many years, even as late as 1900 An account of the Eshelman or Butturf mill appears in the chapter relating to
Old Industries, likewise that of Marshall furnace. The Newport cemetery
is located on the crest of Middle Ridge, in Oliver Township, and was
opened in 1875. Its beginning is traced back to March 31, 1863, when
Henry L. Smith and Mary Ann, his wife, deeded to Samuel Bressler,
George Fleisher and Philip Bosserman, trustees of the Newport Cemetery
Association, over three acres of ground for that purpose. Prior to this
purchase, on January 26th, an organization had been effected by selecting
George Campbell, president; J. Don I. Gantt, secretary, and Capt. A. C.
Clemson, Henry L. Smith, Watson I. Gantt, Dr. J. B Eby, Jacob Miller,
Wm. T. Fickes and Benjamin Fickes, trustees. In 1875 another addition
was added, and in more recent years another one.

There was once a humming industry in West Newport, the Cook planing
mill. During June, 1875, W. R. S. Cook purchased a plot of ground from
Dr. J. E. Singer and built thereon a portable steam sawmill, with a capacity of 10,000 feet of lumber per day. He soon added a shingle mill, and in
1881 he purchased additional land and replaced the first mill with a two-
story mill. In 1885 he erected a planing mill adjoining and increased the
capacity of all the mills. The lumber was brought down the Susquehanna
and towed up the Pennsylvania Canal to Newport. The capacity in a single year was over four million feet. It employed twenty-five hands. Later
it was owned by Sweger & Shreffler.

In 1881 James Everhart erected the Everhart steam grist and sawmill
upon his farm, west of Newport, on the Bloomfield road, where a small
village soon grew, he building the houses for his employees. It was changed
from a burr to a roller mill at the end of a year, being the first mill in
the county to install rolls. Its capacity was twenty-five barrels per day.
It operated for several decades, when it burned.

The following business places are noted in the mercantile appraisers'
report:

Theo. H. Butturf, grain and feed.

M. D. Clouser, groceries.

M. W. Miles, coal and cement.

Snyder Carriage Co.

J. F. Wilt, merchandise.

W. S. Shade, general store. This store was founded by Mrs. Flora Middleton, 1902, and later owned by C. F. D'Ober and Walter Kell, in turn, the
latter selling to Mr Shade in 1916, who added to the grocery stock a line of
general merchandise.

East Newport Church of God. The early meetings of the members of
the Church of God of East Newport were held in the public school building there. The new brick church building was erected during 1905 and
was dedicated on January 12, 1907. There was no building committee, the
bethel being erected under the supervision of the pastor, Rev. G. H.
Bowersox, to whom is due much of the credit for the raising of funds
and the ultimate erection of the church. The pastors have been:

1906-08—Rev. G. H. Bowersox.	1914-16—Rev. J. C Witmer.
1908-09—Rev. W. H. Dressler.	1916-17—Rev. E. L. Ditzler.
1909-11—Rev. H. J. Carmichael.	1917-18—Rev J. H. Gilbert.
1911-14—Rev. C. D. Collins.	1918-22—Rev. J. A. Staub.*

*Died early in 1922.

Mt. Olivet Church of the Brethren. A number of members of the Church of the Brethren formerly known as German Baptists, residing in northern Oliver Township, first held meeting in their homes, and later on in the schoolhouse. When the Methodists at New Buffalo built their new church, the members of the Church of the Brethren in Oliver Township purchased the old building, razed it and removed it to a site west of Newport, opposite Mt. Fairview schoolhouse. It was dedicated January 3, 1915.

As Oliver Township surrounds Newport most of its citizens worship in those churches.

PENN TOWNSHIP.

Penn Township lies west of the junction of the Juniata and Susquehanna Rivers, almost in the form of a triangle. It is bounded on the north by Wheatfield Township, on the east by the rivers, as stated, on the opposite side of which is Dauphin County; on the south by Rye Township, and on the west by Rye and Wheatfield.

Penn Township contains a unique physical formation within its borders, "The Cove." Peters Mountain, from the break at the Susquehanna River below Duncannon, runs southwest for probably ten miles, where it makes a beautiful "horseshoe curve" and tends eastward to the banks of the Susquehanna, above Marysville. This was originally known as Barnett's Cove, after Thomas Barnett, who warranted 400 acres of land there in 1785, as well as the property on which the county seat is located. He had lived there prior to that, however, as he was assessed with fifty acres of land in Rye (now Penn) Township, in 1767. Later it was known by the name of Allen's Cove, and now is ordinarily spoken of as "The Cove." Prof. Claypole, the geologist, thus describes it:

"The district enclosed by the mountain is drained by a small stream rising at the Horse Shoe Bend and receiving the waters of both slopes. The district is peculiarly isolated from the rest of the country by its physical formation. Surrounded on two sides by the mountain, and on the third by the river, access to it is very difficult. Two roads zigzag across the range to the south, from Rye Township, and one enters from the north, through the gap of the Susquehanna, and passes out by the same outlet. The Pennsylvania Railway has taken advantage of the same natural pathway to enter and leave the valley. These excepted, there is no practicable road from the outside world into this secluded district, which is, as it were, a little world by itself."

The township is well drained, the waters of both Sherman's Creek and Little Juniata Creek passing through and emptying into the Susquehanna. From 1766 until 1826 the territory comprising Penn Township was a part of Rye. It then became a part of Wheatfield, and so remained until 1840, when, upon petition to the courts it was made a township with the lines as they now exist, being the fourteenth township.

Further references to early settlers will be found in the chapters devoted to the Indians in the early pages of this volume. John Harris had formed a temporary settlement in this vicinity, but it was not in Penn Township. Marcus Hulings had holdings in what is now Penn Township, but the reader will find the history of his early settlements under the chapters devoted to Duncan's and Haldeman's Islands and Watts Township, his place of abode.

James Baskins, who is mentioned by Hulings in his communications with the secretary of the province, was a resident here before 1762, but did not warrant land until 1766, when he took up 300 acres, upon which the northern part of Duncannon is located and which was long known as Baskinsville. He also owned lands on the island and was the owner of a ferry. His daughter married Alexander Stephens, who was a soldier under Braddock, and from this marriage was born at Duncannon, Andrew

66

Stephens, who became the father of Alexander Stephens, Vice-President of the Confederacy. That topic is covered by a chapter in this book. Also refer to description of Juniata Township and Old Ferries. James Baskins' descendants conducted ferries in the vicinity until they were replaced with bridges. The old Presbyterian graveyard on the bluff above Duncannon was originally known as Baskins' graveyard, and there sleep these Baskins pioneers. An act of the Pennsylvania Legislature, dated April 4, 1838, provided for the building of the first bridge "at the Juniata's mouth," and named George Stroop, Robert Clark, Amos A. Jones, Thomas Duncan, Jacob Keiser, Wm. Clark, Alex. Branyan, Henry Hackett, James Black, Robert Mitchell, John Wagner, Jacob Shively, Benj. McIntire, Daniel Grove, George Barnett and Fred'k Rinehart, as stockholders.

Above the James Baskins tract was a place known as "Barren Hills," which contained 300 acres, and was taken up by William Baskins in 1766. On Little Juniata Creek was 263 acres taken up by Isaac Jones in 1766. This is the Haas' mill tract. East of it Andrew Berryhill took up 331 acres in 1766. It is named in the warrant "Sherman's Valley." He sold the right and it passed to John Shearman, who is the first man by that name to patent land in the county (November 24, 1781), although the western part of the county was known as "Shearman's Valley" and the creek as "Shearman's Creek" as early as 1750.

In The Cove lands were warranted by Joseph Watkins (1774), Thomas White, James White, Elizabeth Branyan, Alexander Gailey and Israel Jacobs. David and William Ogle warranted 500 acres in 1792. David Stout settled along the river, his warrant being dated March 14, 1755. George Allen resided here before 1762, and from him is derived the names of Allen's Cove and Allen's Island. Allen never warranted the lands, and it is likely that the tract taken up by Thomas Barnett was negotiated for through Allen and was one and the same tract. On June 4, 1762, Thomas Barnett took out a warrant for 317 acres, and resided there until 1787, when he purchased the right of David Mitchell for 418 acres, upon a part of which the county seat is now located. Mr. Barnett had two sons, Frederick and George. His Cove lands he conveyed to his son Frederick, who lived and died there, leaving the property to his descendants, one of whom, Joseph Barnett, long postmaster at Cove, still resides there. Thomas Barnett then lived upon the Bloomfield tract until his death, in 1814, when that property passed to his other son, George Barnett. The island, known as the Wister Island, was a part of his Cove holdings, its acreage being stated as sixty-four. Another early warrantee was Alexander Branyan.

Among other lands warranted were: Samuel Goudy, 215 acres in 1766; Richard Coulter, 217 acres in 1762, later owned by Rev. James Brady; Alexander Rutherford, 300 acres in 1787; Robert Nicholson, 682 acres in 1769; Joseph Kirkpatrick, 100 acres in 1790; Isaac Kirkpatrick, 300 acres in 1814, and Benjamin Abraham, 207 acres on both sides of Sherman's Creek at "the loop," in 1766.

On the Little Juniata Creek, above Duncannon, which is located on the John Brown warrant, was a tract of 263 acres surveyed to Isaac Jones in 1766. His son, Robert Jones, erected a sawmill and a gristmill, whose son, Cadwallader Jones, owned it when the county came into existence. From him it passed to Frederick Albright, who sold it to Jacob Bruner. Mr. Bruner erected a woolen mill with fulling and carding machinery, and did a large manufacturing business in the making of cloth. It later passed to John and Benjamin Shade, Samuel Shull and Samuel Haas, the latter being the last owner to conduct the milling business. Sylvester S. Sheller purchased the property in 1898, and erected a large ice dam in 1900. He sold the property in 1919 to Thomas Mutzabaugh, who is the present owner.

On an order of survey, dated April 27. 1787, Alexander Rutherford located 300 acres of land above the Isaac Jones tract, on Little Juniata Creek. Here Frederick Speck built an oil and fulling mill about 1840, which he operated for a few years. In 1846 it passed to Robert King, who changed it to a gristmill. It passed to William C. King, and is known to this day as King's mill. After passing from the Kings it was sold to Philip Cook. whose executors, in 1884, conveyed it to James Everhart. It is now owned by Maria Rumbaugh.

H. and E. Mager were operating a woolen goods factory in the Cove in 1841.

The Goudy location, at the mouth of Clark's Run, became the western landing of Clark's ferry, described elsewhere in this volume. The warrant of 100 acres to Joseph Kirkpatrick passed from him to his brother Moses, who accumulated 600 acres of land, which, at his death in 1820, passed to his eight children. Isaac, the oldest son (known in later years as Elder Isaac). on May 23, 1814, warranted 300 acres of lands adjoining some of those of his father. In 1876 he was assessed with 476 acres, mostly in present Carroll Township. He died September 8, 1865, in his ninetieth year, having been an elder in the Presbyterian Church for sixty-one years. An act of the Pennsylvania Legislature, dated March 13, 1795, authorized William Beatty to erect a dam across from Sheep Island to the west bank of the Juniata River. This island lies in the Juniata River a short distance above the iron bridge at the north end of Duncannon. An act of March 21, 1868, annexed Wister's Island to Penn Township. detaching it from Dauphin County. It lies in the Susquehanna River, almost opposite Covallen Station. The first bridge over Sherman's Creek, near the Duncannon Iron Company plant, was built in 1832.

In reference to education the first record of a schoolhouse in Penn Township was contained in a law regulating election districts, which passed the legislature in 1797, and was signed by Thomas Mifflin. the first governor of the State of Pennsylvania. which declared that the Union schoolhouse at Petersburg (now Duncannon) should be the voting place for the district then formed. Its erection naturally is farther back than that time. It was built of logs, the spaces between the logs being closed with mortar. It was about twenty-five feet square. There was a broad fireplace at one side and the seats were of slabs and without backs. It stood where the Duncannon National Bank now stands. It was in use until about 1845, at which time a four-room building was erected upon the site of the present building, but later was removed to the corner of Ann Street and Church Avenue and turned into tenements, being still used in that capacity.

Before the public school law of 1834 became operative there was a school where the Michener schoolhouse now stands. There was an early school at Young's mill, which was attended by pupils within a radius of four miles. Joseph McIntire was a teacher in that building. The old Methodist church at Young's graveyard, near Duncannon, was bought in 1840 and used as a school building for many years.

An early resident of "The Loop" was David Carnes, who came from York County. He had two sons, David and John, and three daughters. Catharine (Mrs. Castlebury Harris), Hannah (Mrs. Jonathan Michener) and Maria (Mrs. Doane Michener), whose descendants are widely located.

Among the merchants of the end of the century was W. R. Swartz. located at the extreme northern end of what was then Baskinsville, long in business there and once a member of the General Assembly from Perry County. For years that was the only store in the section known as Baskinsville. The Duncannon Iron Company store did the business of the lower end, which did not get by to the Duncannon shopping district. It likewise was the mart where traded the many employees of that great concern. According to the late report of the mercantile appraiser, Daniel Miller has a general store, established 1910; George M. Krick and H. E. Reidlinger have grocery stores, and S. L. Clouser operates a meat market.

In Penn Township are located two summer colonies, at Cove Station and Perdix, where many cottages and bungalows have been erected by city people. There was once a fertilizer works located at Perdix, but it has not been operated for forty years, the Pennsylvania Railroad now owning the grounds. In 1891 J. S. Sible purchased a farm in the Cove and erected a large ice dam, covering half the place, which passed to the United Ice & Coal Company in 1902. It was in use until 1916. That part containing the dam was sold to the Pennsylvania Railroad in 1917. The construction of the railroad tracks along the river made necessary the building of a wagon road around the mountain above Marysville. When first constructed it was a very poor and dangerous highway, but in 1921 it was macadamized and a retaining wall erected. It was also widened.

The members of the Presbyterians, first noted as "seceders," and later as the United Presbyterian Church, had erected a small church near Hickory Grove schoolhouse many years ago. They later removed to Church Avenue, Duncannon, and still later their church was purchased by the German Reformed congregation. Early in "the nineties" a Church of God was erected on the Leedy place, near the new Lower Cove schoolhouse, at which services were held for ten or more years. It has been torn down and removed. The township has no other churches, as it surrounds Duncannon, where its people worship.

Perdix Chapel. With the growth of Perdix as a summer colony there seemed need of services of some character, and song services were held in various cottages, the result of which was the erection of an interdenominational chapel during 1920. It is a community church, and is now presided over by Rev. Sloan, a Dickinson College student. The first trustees of the organization were B. F. Allen, E. C. Keller, George Shope, H. B. Baker and W. U. Aldinger.

RYE TOWNSHIP.

Long before Perry was a county Rye was created as a separate township of Cumberland County, there being but two older townships of the territory now comprising Perry County, the townships of Tyrone and Toboyne. Rye was created out of a part of Tyrone in 1766. Tyrone originally contained all the lands in the county lying west of the Juniata. At the January sessions of the courts of Cumberland County, in 1766, a petition was presented asking for the erection of a new township out of the lower end of Tyrone. Upon due consideration the following order was issued by the court at the March term:

"Upon petition of Severall of the Inhabitants of Tyrone Township to this Court, Setting forth that Said Township is too large, it is adjudged and ordered by the said Court, that from the North Mountain to the Tuskarora Mountain by Mr. West's, and from that to Darlington's and to Strack the Tuskarora about William Noble's be the line, and the name of the Lower be called Rye Township."

It will be of interest to note that Rye Township, as then created, contained besides its present territory, the townships of Penn, Wheatfield, Miller, Oliver, Juniata, Tuscarora, and parts of Centre and Carroll. It remained to such extent until 1793, when Juniata Township was created, with its southern boundary at the top of Mahanoy Ridge, which automatically became the northern boundary of Rye. Rye Township is bounded on the north by Wheatfield and Penn Townships, on the east by Marysville Borough, on the south by Cumberland County, and on the west by Carroll Township.

Colonel Samuel Hunter, of Dauphin County, warranted lands in the lower end of the township, including the location of the Borough of Marysville, in 1755, 1756 and 1757 His holdings covered a tract extending two miles along the river and three miles westward in Fishing Creek Valley. Adjoining Hunter on the south William Swanzey warranted 322 acres with a river frontage of only thirty rods, and below him on the river as far south as the county line Hartley Wormley warranted 312 acres in 1792. His warrant, dated September 8, 1755, was the first in the township as now constituted. Other warrants were those of John W. Kittera, 372 acres in 1792; Alexander Berryhill, a tract; Duncan Stewart, 142 acres; Barefoot Bronson, 91 acres in 1784; Henry Robison, 240 acres; James Starr, 359 acres; William Swanson, 322 acres; William Davis, 327 acres; George McLaughlin, 442 acres; John Bowman, a tract on which he had a gristmill, a sawmill and a carding machine; John Wiley and John Bolton, 307 acres, in 1792; Alex. Johnson, 400 acres; Humphrey Williams, 311 acres; James McFarlane, 329 acres in 1792; Thomas Buchanan, 329 acres in 1793; William McFarlane, 322 acres in 1793; David Ralston, 323 acres in 1792, on which for years was the post office called Keystone; John Clous (or Cless), 281 acres in 1789; Robert Wallace, 337 acres; Robert Whitehill, 105 acres in 1795, on which was located for years the Grier's Point post office.

Ralph, John and James Sterrett during 1788 warranted 400 acres extending for a distance of three miles east of Croghan's Gap, which later took their name, and by which it is known to this day. The main valley road was laid out by the pioneers and was used as a post road, Peter, Samuel and John Harold being postriders. Thomas Burney warranted 300 acres in 1765; Robert Allen, 50 acres in 1795; Martin Dubbs, 400 acres in 1793, and William Glover, 150 acres in 1774.

Nancy Bovard took up two tracts, one of 150 acres, and one of 250 acres, in 1815, and her father, Charles Bovard, in the same year warranted 250 acres. Bovard had come from Carlisle, in 1815, and settled in the valley. Here he built a tavern which he conducted until 1834. It was located on the old road from Carlisle to Sunbury. Keystone is located partly on this tract. One of Bovard's daughters married Zachariah Rice, who was an early mail route contractor in Perry County. This hotel was the only one in the valley from Sterrett's Gap to Marysville. The store and post office there were long kept by Charles Barshinger.

The Gambers and Ensmingers were early settlers of the Fishing Creek Valley, practically all of which lies within Rye Township. However, the entire section just north of the Kittatinny Mountain, east of the Susquehanna River, to Schuylkill County, bears this same name.

In the year of its erection—1766—the assessment list of Rye Township was as follows:

John Adams, 100 acres; John Anderson, 100; Cornelius Atkinson, 100: Thomas Armstrong, 100; James Baskins, 150; Thomas Barnett, 50; John Black, 200; Roger Brown, 100; Johnathon Cummins, 100; Neale Dougherty, 50; John Dougherty. 50; Thomas Dougan, 100; Edward Elliot, 100; David English, 400; Francis Ellis, 100; Samuel Galbreath, 150; Samuel Goudy, 100; Robert Hearst, 100; Tobias Hendricks, 100; Samuel Hunter, 200 and sawmill; Joseph Junkin, 100; James Irwin, 150; Thomas Johnston, 100; Joseph Jacobs, 100; James Loudon, 100; John Montgomery, Esq., 100; Henry Moile, 100; Michael Marshall, 200; Joseph Marshall, 100; John McCune, 100; Finlaw McCune, 100; Neale McKay, 50; John Mitchell, 100; Robert Meek, 50; William McPherson, 150; Robert McGrory, 50; Francis McGuire,

100; William McCroskey, 200; William McNitt, 100; David Miller, 100; John Orr, 50; William Power, 150; William Parkinson, 100 Samuel Power, 75; James Patton, 150; John Parkinson, 100, Mary Quillon, 50; William Richardson, 200 and sawmill, Samuel Robinson, 100; William Stewart, 200; Robert Stewart, 50; John Stewart, 100; Andrew Steen, 100; William Smiley, 100; Archibald tewart, 100; Frederick Watts, 200; Robert Watson, 100, Francis West, 100.

Grier's Point, once a post office, is located in Rye Township, over a mile east of the Carroll Township line, nine miles from Marysville. It was named after Samuel Grier, who settled there shortly after the creation of the new county. Mr. Grier kept a hotel known as the "Hunters' Home." Captain William Messinger kept the first store here, Samuel Grier succeeding him. David P. Lightner succeeded Grier upon his death. It is now owned by Harry A. Miller.

On the old Valley road, near the George Kocher property, now owned by the James Bell estate, a log schoolhouse was built before 1800. It was lighted by inserting panes of glass between the logs, and was covered with a clapboard roof. Fourteen miles west of Marysville, on the old Valley road at Daniel Cowen's, were located at different times two schoolhouses, one built long before 1800, and the other in 1805. The latter was in use in 1830. Among the teachers were Isaac Gray and Samuel Coble.

On February 2, 1819, Jacob Sidle sold forty perches of land to Christian Ensminger, William Messinger, Peter Foulk, Conrad Sloop, Peter Gamber, George Albright, Conrad Yohe, Philip Hench, George Shade, Daniel Yohe, David Shade, Solomon Finicle, David Myers, James White, Peter Billow and Jacob Sidle for the purpose of erecting a schoolhouse thereon. The deed recites that they were to pay "unto Jacob Sidle the sum of one dollar fur their shears of said school, and the said subscribers is to pay an Eaquel Portion fur building said house and to keep the said house in good Repear."

On the Bovard lands a schoolhouse was built before 1828, and was named "Congruity." On June 28, 1828, Bovard deeded the ground on which it stood to the school trustees.

In 1797 Christian Ensminger was possessed of about 600 acres of land lying between Fishing Creek and Pine Hill, on which he built a sawmill, which was in use long after 1820. Jacob Sidle, an early settler of Fishing Creek, in 1820 was the owner of 480 acres, a sawmill and a gristmill. He then lived in the upper end of the valley, in Rye Township. Shortly after 1820 he took down his gristmill and moved it across Pine Hill to the present site of Dugan's mill.

Jacob Bishop built a sawmill about 1835, about four miles west of Marysville, which stood until 1878. Charles Bovard built the sawmill later known as Keller's, located west of Keystone. It burned many years ago. Captain William Messinger built the chop and sawmill, east of Keystone, about 1835. Peter Billow built a sawmill about 1835

The mill in Rye Township known to the older generation as Hartman's mill, was one of the mills erected in the county's territory before 1800. It was built in 1798 by Nicholas Wolf and his son-in-law, John Bowman. At the same time and place they built a carding mill and a sawmill, which have long since disappeared. The gristmill was destroyed in 1880, being then owned by Neihart & Son, who rebuilt it and sold it to Alexander Hartman, who in turn remodeled it and installed rolls. From Hartman it passed to John Cowns, then to Henry Fisher, from whose estate it was transferred to P. H. Heishley, the present owner, in 1910. The community surrounding the mill is now known as Glenvale, and the mill as the Glenvale Roller Mills.

According to the mercantile appraiser's report the following business houses exist in Rye Township, the date following being the time of entering the business:

General stores, Mrs. E. L. Bell (1906), established by C. Barshinger (1866); J. W. Hummel, Mervin Swinn (1919), H. A. Miller, L. I. Leonard Estate. James Bell Estate, fertilizer and groceries; P. H. Heishley, flour and feed.

As early as 1825 Dr. Frederick Klineyoung located at Keystone, where he practiced until his death in 1846. Dr. F. A. Koughling succeeded him in 1846, and practiced there until his death in 1855. Dr. Kaechline, a German, began practice at Grier's Point in 1853, but was found frozen to death while in the performance of professional duties, three years later. Dr. Joseph Swartz succeeded him in 1857, practicing there for three years, when he removed to Duncannon. Dr. Edward Ebert practiced at Grier's Point for several years, beginning about 1857. Dr. Theodore Lightner was here for a short time in 1880. Dr. Chas. W. Dean, a graduate of the Eclectic Medical School, 1871, located near the top of the Blue Mountain at Dean's Gap, and practiced in both Perry and Cumberland Counties.

About 1838 or 1840 the Evangelical people had built a church about a mile west of Marysville, at the Sitterly graveyard, but it was removed about 1867, its membership being the nucleus of the Marysville church.

Bethel Evangelical Church. Bethel Evangelical Church came to be erected through the results of meetings held in schoolhouses during the few years previous to its erection. For a period it was served by the pastors of the Marysville Evangelical Church. It was known as the Fishing Creek charge until 1907, since which it has been known as Keystone charge. The first church was erected in 1846, at a cost of $800. Among the first members were Martin Souder, Mary Souder, George Fenicle, Sarah Fenicle, B. F. Leonard, Elizabeth Leonard and George Kocher, Sr. This church was replaced by a new one in 1889. The pastors have been:

1862-69—Rev. W. C. Bierly.	1892-96—Rev. L. K. Harris.
1869-71—Rev. W. E. Detwiler.	1896-97—Rev. S. E. Davis.
1871-73—Rev. J. M. Young.	1897-00—Rev. W. N. Fulcomer
1873-74—Rev. W. H. Stover.	1900-03—Rev. E. W. Koontz.
1874-75—Rev. T. M. Morris.	1903-07—Rev. G. S. Albright.
1875-77—Rev. S. I. Shortess.	1907-10—Rev. M. W. Stahl.
1877-79—Rev. G. E. Zehner.	1910-14—Rev. J. E. Newcomer.
1879-82—Rev. George Joseph.	1914-16—Rev. F. D. Sherman.
1882-85—Rev. L. K. Harris.	1916-17—Rev. B. G. Hoffman.
1885-86—Rev. I. C. Yeakle.	1917-19—Rev. W. E. Yingling.
1886-87—Rev. Wm. Minsker.	1919-20—Rev. L. E. Teter.
1887-89—Rev. J. W. Bentz.	1920-21—Rev. H. H. Jacobs.
1889-91—Rev. J. H. Welch.	1921- —Rev. F. F. Mayer.
1891-92—Rev. W. C. Bierly.	

From this charge there entered the ministry of the denomination, Reverends B. F. Keller, J. M. Dick, H. A. Benfer, J. M. Dice and others.

Salem Evangelical Church. The first meetings of the Evangelicals of the Salem territory were held in conjunction with those of the Bethel Evangelical Church in the valley. In 1856 a church was built and was in use until 1905, when it was replaced by a new one. Among the first members were Israel Dick, Elizabeth Dick, Henry Foulk, Jacob Bitner, Sr., Frances Bitner, Emanuel Keller, Chas. Barshinger, John Kreamer, Sarah Kreamer, David Benfer and Matilda Benfer. It was a part of the Fishing Creek charge until 1907, since which it has been known as Keystone charge. The pastors are the same as those of Bethel Evangelical Church, mentioned previously.

Glenvale Church of God. Services of this denomination were first held in the Oak Grove schoolhouse at Hartman's mill, or Glenvale, as it is now known, long prior to 1882, when the new church was built there, costing $1,800. This was largely made possible through the will of a Mr. Welty, who willed $1,000 towards building a church there. A Mr. Bowman donated the plot of ground where the church and cemetery are located. Prior to the erection of the church James Wagner held a successful revival in a wagonmaker shop. Rev. McDonald was the pastor at the time of the erection of the church. Among the original membership were Jacob Fortenbaugh, Sr., and Alexander Hartman and their wives. David Maxwell, Henry Clay, Wm. McFadden and A. Swartz were early ministers. The Marysville ministers of the same faith have served this people.

SAVILLE TOWNSHIP.

Saville Township was the seventh township to be formed in the territory which comprises Perry County and the last to be formed while it still was a part of Cumberland. Saville's territory was a part of Tyrone Township from the time of its formation in 1754, until 1817, when it was made a township. It has retained its original formation, with the exception of contributing a part of Centre and a strip on the west, which became a part of Madison Township when that township was formed. It is bounded on the north by the Juniata County line, on the east by Tuscarora, Juniata and Centre Townships, on the south by Centre, Spring and Tyrone Townships, and on the west by Madison.

At the April term of the Cumberland County courts, in 1817, a petition signed by citizens asking that Tyrone Township be divided, was presented. The court appointed John Darlington and David Grove as viewers, and at the November term they presented their report, of which this is the last paragraph:

"That by confirming the division of said township agreebly to the draft presented, would conduce greatly to the convenience of the inhabitants of the respective sections thereof, and that the limestone ridge, along which the division line runs the whole distance from east to west, is the natural and proper division of said township."

It was dated June 24, 1817, and was confirmed at the November term, being named Saville. It is one of the largest townships in the county, containing about forty square miles of land. Its principal stream is Buffalo Creek, noted in many provincial affairs as the location of depredations by the Indians.

On the day of the opening of the land office, February 3, 1755, for the location of lands in Perry County, Thomas Elliot, whose father had settled seven miles north of Carlisle, warranted 200 acres. At the same time William Waddell warranted the adjoining tract. These locations were for the low lands along Buffalo Creek, later owned by the Bodens and others. On the same day Mr. Elliot took up an adjoining tract of fifty acres, and in 1767 another fifty acres. When he first located lands he was but twenty-five years of age, and probably his knowledge of "the lay of the land" came from being one of the many parties of citizens from south of the Blue Mountain who came to the aid of their more unfortunate fellows who were suffering at the hands of the Indians. The Indian uprisings that followed Braddock's defeat drove all the settlers out of the county, and Elliot was of course included. It was 1762 before it was again safe to return, and then he brought with him Edward, Charles and John Elliot. Edward located lands later owned by Jonathan Swartz. As will be noted in a chapter on the Indians, it was at this place that the men were harvesting when apprised that hostile Indians were in the neighborhood. A party of men organized to send aid to the less fortunate were ambushed at the Nicholson place—later the Orris farm—and five of them were killed.

In the party were Charles Elliot and Edward McConnell, who escaped but were shot while ascending the bank of Buffalo Creek a little later. Rev. Dr. Elliot, an account of whose life appears elsewhere in this book, is a descendant.

In 1793 Robert Elliot, a descendant of this first Elliot family, warranted forty-one acres and bought the adjoining 187 which had been warranted by John Sanderson in 1767. William and James Elliot warranted lands in 1793. The Hall place was owned by John Black before 1774, as other warrants name his lands as "adjoining." Robert and James Irvine came from Ireland in 1752, and in 1774 Robert warranted 300 acres of land on the west side of Buffalo Creek, adjoining lands of Edward Elliot and John Black on the east and Conococheague Hill on the north. He accumulated other lands, and at his death 330 acres passed to his son James, who patented it in 1812; 250 passed to another son, William, who patented it the same year, this being the tract on which the old stone house stands, and another 200 to his son John.

Part of the land taken up by William Elliot, Jr., was later in possession of former county superintendent of schools, Lewis B. Kerr. In 1755 John Smith warranted fifty acres, in 1774 Alexander Sanderson warranted 300 acres, and James Sanderson fifty acres, and in 1786 Charles Weise and James Bartley, 300 acres, the latter tract being near the Saville and Juniata Township line.

Located along Buffalo Hills David McClure warranted 125 acres in 1762, fifty acres in 1770, and forty-eight acres later. In 1774 these lands were surveyed to William Power. John McClure warranted 220 acres in the same vicinity. Thomas Patton took up 250 acres on both sides of Buffalo Creek.

James Adair had made an improvement on a tract, which was sold to Col. Thomas Hartley, of York, Pennsylvania, an officer in the Revolution and a member of the United States Congress for twelve years, who warranted the tract, containing 300 acres in 1786. This tract was on Buffalo Creek, above Roseburg. Michael Loy warranted 200 acres in 1793, adjoining the Hartley tract. The same year Andrew Crouse warranted 200 acres adjoining Loy's, and Thomas McKee warranted 200 acres adjoining Crouse on the side of the mountain, including Winn's Gap. Thomas Robinson warranted a tract in 1796, and had another before 1794. Mary Buchanan, of Tyrone Township, owned an adjoining tract.

The Nicholson lands which passed in later years to the Orris family, lay north of Ickesburg. The roads which now meet near "the gap" at an earlier day met there. This was the scene of the Indian skirmish of 1763. The first Orris was Adam, who was the father of three sons, his son Adam attaining possession of the homestead. He also had three sons, Captain D. C. Orris succeeding to the title of the home. Of his other sons, H. O. became a physician at Newport, and Solomon Stanhope Orris became a college professor and one of the greatest Greek scholars then known. In 1785 William Linn, a brother of Rev. John Linn, warranted 178 acres on Buffalo Creek, and in 1793 he warranted 400 acres adjoining Archibald and Andrew Kinkead. Here a mill was built which has always borne the name of the Buffalo mill. The Lutheran and Reformed church is located here. The Kinkeads, named above, warranted 300 acres of lands in 1786, and others later.

In 1772 David Sample warranted 220 acres. It is described as including a survey made by Samuel Finley in 1761, and situated "on the north side of Limestone Ridge, opposite to Samuel Fisher's house." This tract is in the southwest corner of the township, north of Elliottsburg. The Fisher tract adjoining was also an adjoining tract of John Sanderson's, which is described in Spring Township and which was the subject of much early litigation in so far as the title was concerned.

Among other early warrants were those of William McMeen, for 150 acres in 1766; David Hamilton, for fifty acres in 1775; Lawrence Mealy, for 300 acres in 1786; William Marshall, for 258 acres in 1786; Robert Kearney, for 200 acres in 1789; John D. Creigh, for 300 acres in 1792; Patrick Duffield, for 200 acres in 1792; William Robinson, for 150 acres in 1794, and Adam Hays, for eighty acres in 1796.

The Milligan, Elliot, Hench, Dromgold, Rice, Ickes, Hartman, Shull, Boden, Flickinger, Blair and Liggett families are of Saville's earliest and most substantial settlers. Jacob Hartman, who emigrated from Chester County, took up a tract of land and erected upon it a house of hewed logs. In the center of it was a large chimney surrounded by three fireplaces, one in the parlor, one in the bedroom, and one in the kitchen. This house stood as late as 1900. The log barn, erected at the same time, is yet in use.

On September 18, 1810. Andrew Shuman warranted 328 acres on Buffalo Creek, where Eshcol is located. He had located here in 1804, and shortly thereafter built a mill. In 1824 he erected a mill further up the creek. In 1830 he donated ground for a Union church, which was built the next year. He died in 1852, and the upper mill passed to his son John, and the lower mill to his son Andrew. In 1867 Andrew Shuman sold the lower mill to Isaac Weaver. The upper mill was sold in 1871 to John Kendig and John Hostetter. These mills are no longer in business. The adjoining tract above was of the John Hays warrant, and in 1852 William Rosensteel purchased forty-three acres from the lands of both Hays and Shuman and erected thereon a tannery with a capacity of fifteen hundred hides annually. Prior to 1870 the tannery had passed to Jacob Spanogle. It was sold to Samuel Hench and Henry Duffield, under whose ownership it ceased to operate.

When the county was formed Robert Hackett had a distillery in Saville. At that time Andrew Linn was conducting a store, a distillery, a gristmill and a sawmill. In 1882 Edward Miller built a fulling mill on Buffalo Creek, two miles south of Ickesburg, and in 1831 was conducting a store and a sawmill at the same place.

George Sanderson was assessed with a tanyard in both 1821 and 1831. In 1820 Henry Trostle was operating a distillery, and two years later a sawmill, but in 1831 the distillery was no longer in use. In the assessment of 1820 there were 194 taxpayers in Saville, which included four stores, five sawmills, five gristmills, five distilleries, one fulling mill, seven blacksmith shops, four wagonmakers, one tanyard, and three cooper shops.

About 1897 the Hench and Dromgold families, which were nurtured on Perry County soil, but now spread over many states, began holding annual reunions or picnics in Perry County. Other families were added, until it included the families of Hench, Dromgold, Rice, Ickes, Hartman and others. John Hench, the progenitor of the Perry County families, attended St. Vincent German Reformed Church in Chester County, where he resided, and among those on that church record who emigrated to Perry County, are Hench, Shull, Happle, Yeager, Acker, Foose, Hartman, Wagner, Miller, Kepner, Reiss, Haas, etc. John Hench was one of 114 farmers who lost his land by the foreclosure of an old English mortgage which had not been satisfied when they purchased their lands. Another who lost his farm in the same manner was Zachariah Rice, the father of twenty-one children, John Hartman and others, when then located in Perry and Juniata Counties. John Rice, a son of Zachariah, was married to a daughter of Mr. Hench, and located in Perry County about 1790 and worked as a blacksmith, carrying his tools and anvil from place to place. He died in 1800, and lies in the Loysville churchyard. Nicholas Ickes left Montgomery County in 1795 and settled in Perry County on 230 acres of land bought of Robert Robinson. He also purchased 260 acres of mountain land from Dr. Mailey, and 130 from Charles Elliot. He purchased 170 acres from George Sanderson in 1816, on which he lived and where he died in 1848, aged eighty-four years. Ickesburg is located on part of this tract, hence the name—Ickesburg. It was laid out in 1816. Thomas Dromgold, progenitor of the Perry County Dromgolds, was from near Dublin, Ireland, and located at Donnally's Mills, making his way on foot from New Castle, Delaware, to the Chesapeake Bay, and thence up the rivers. He purchased a farm near Ickesburg in a short time, and at his death had 600 acres which descended to his son, John Dromgold. Thomas Dromgold was naturalized in the Perry County courts, January 5, 1830. In Ireland he had been a millwright, merchant and farmer, and the old stone house and mill owned by him still stood in 1900, when W. A. Dromgold made a trip to the ancestral home and was entertained by relatives yet in possession. While at Donnally's Mills he wooed and won the fair Elizabeth Donnally, and, as he was a miller, was no doubt in the employ of the Donnally family in milling. The fifth generation of Donnallys, as represented by L. A. Donnally, a former member of the legislature, reside at Donnally's Mills, where he still operates the mill.

The date of the earliest school in this township is shrouded in mystery, so long ago was it already in use. It was located on a small plot of ground opposite the lane leading from the old Ickes mill to the public road, where the Boden farm joined, and one of the corner stones was there yet at the end of the century, a mute relic of the "schoolhouse by the road," as immortalized by Henry W. Longfellow, the poet. From districts as far away as "Mountain Home," Roseburg and Eshcol, came boys and girls seeking knowledge. The mother of the late Nicholas Hench attended school here as early as 1785, and the schoolhouse had been in use before that. Among the teachers before 1800 were John Bolton. Thomas Stevenson, J. Watts, Thomas Meldrum and George Williams.

In 1800 Linn's school was started, near the residence of Thomas Shull. It was still in use in 1825, as there is record of a Sunday school there in that year. The building was later sold and moved away. In 1803 a Mr. Jamison taught a school at Duffie's Hill.

There was quite a fight in this township on the question of the adoption or rejection of the free school system in 1836, although it had been in operation the previous year. Robert Elliot, associate judge of the county at the time, favored it, and Andrew Shuman, with considerable following, opposed it. The western part of the township voted almost unanimously against it, and the northern part strongly for it, but a majority was against it. In 1835 there were three male and two female teachers, whose salary for one and one-fourth month's services was $16.50. There were sixty-eight male and seventy-one female pupils.

Summit schoolhouse, near Ickesburg, was thrice burned, the first being a frame building, and two years later a brick building. It burned again in 1911. It was first used about 1800.

On the Harry C. Boden farm, near Ickesburg, is a cave 250 feet long, 12 feet wide, and 18 feet in height. There are several apartments. It was first discovered in January, 1857.

According to the report of the mercantile appraiser the following are in business in Saville Township, the dates being the time of starting:

General stores, Kochenderfer & Bro., S. A. Rice. R. B. Rodgers (1897), postmaster at Saville, 1900-1920; Samuel H. Swab, Lloyd Smith.

Dr. William R. Cisna followed. He was a graduate of Dickinson College as well as a graduate in medicine. After getting his medical diploma in 1865 he located in Ickesburg, where he practiced until about 1882, when he located in Chicago. Dr. Charles Delancey succeeded Dr. Cisna, but soon moved to Loysville. Then Dr. Dean was there a short time, but moved to Millerstown. Dr. Newton Bryner, son of George Bryner, of Cisna's Run, a graduate of the University of New York, located in Ickesburg in 1881, where he practiced until his death, which occurred April 29, 1877, aged twenty-nine years. Dr. J. H. Bryner graduated at Columbus Medical College in 1885, and located at Ickesburg, where he practiced until 1912, when he removed from the county. Dr. E. Kenneth Wolff located here in 1910, and practiced until 1917, since which time Dr. George Kinzer has been located here. Dr. Kinzer is a graduate of the College of Physicians and Surgeons of Baltimore, '92.

Eshcol. Eshcol is a hamlet surrounding the Shuman church and mill, named after the scriptural Eshcol, owing to the features suggesting it, according to the late William E. Baker. It was long known as "The Narrows," then as "Shuman's Church," and "Gaylortown." It has had several stores, a tannery, a blacksmith shop and a few houses. The post office was originally at the upper Shuman mill. It was transferred to the settlement and named Eshcol. John D. Baker was the first postmaster. He was succeeded by Jacob Kleckner. The first stores were kept by John D. Baker and John Harmon. The tannery was built by Michael Gaylor, and was later operated by Rev. L. A. Wickey. In 1889 George McC. Long and I. Lane Long erected a store building and went into business, the latter buying out the former six years later and continuing in business there until 1910, when he sold out to Mrs. Lucy Campbell, and located at Dauphin, Pennsylvania, where he opened a large general store and where he is vice-president of the Dauphin National Bank. The Longs descended from Henry Long, who came from York or Adams County in 1795, and settled in what is now Saville Township.

Dr. John D. Baker, a graduate of American University of Philadelphia, began practice at Eshcol in 1880, and continued until his death, in 1915.

United Brethren Churches. Many years ago there had been a United Brethren Church at Ickesburg, which on June 2, 1883, was sold to a cornet band then in existence. After that period, following the Sectional War, there was a charge known as the Eshcol charge, which comprised the churches at Eshcol, Mannsville, Otterbein chapel, near Donnally's Mills, and Gingrich's church, between Ickesburg and Donnally's Mills. The Eshcol church was erected in 1870. One of the pastors, Rev. L. A. Wickey, left his impress on the community. He was located there six years, and was stricken with paralysis in his pulpit, January, 1898, dying four days later. He was an able man. Rev. J. N. Crowell was the last pastor. In 1916 the church was sold to Harry C. Boden, who removed it.

The Reformed Church at Buffalo. Before this church was built the members of the Reformed faith worshiped at Loysville and at St. Peter's Church, in Spring Township. During the pastorate of Rev. Scholl, on the Sherman's Valley charge (1819-40), he began holding services in the territory of Buffalo church, the meetings being held in the homes of members of the faith. He also held services in the old log schoolhouse located "on the rise, just south of Buffalo Mills." The congregation was organized in 1839, but was then known as "the New Church." It is not mentioned as Emanuel Church in synodical reports until 1843. The first officers were Jonathan Swartz and Philip Kell, elders, and Adam Orris and Henry Kell, deacons. With the building of the church entire families belonging to the Loysville Lutheran Church withdrew and connected with the Buffalo

Church, the Lutherans assuming the unpaid portion of the building. The church was built of stone and was erected in 1840. Conrad Rice and Jonathan Swartz composed the building committee. Henry Hartman and Henry Kell were long faithful pillars of this church. Jointly these two peoples—Reformed and Lutherans—worshiped here until 1886-87, when each erected its own edifice. This Reformed congregation has had the reputation of having been one of the leading churches of that faith in the county to do things, according to Rev. Groh's historical sketch.

The new church was dedicated on March 7, 1886, the stained glass memorial windows having been designed by Prof. J. C. Miller, the penman, himself a member of the congregation. It was a part of the Blain charge from the beginning, which was known as the Sherman's Valley charge until 1841. The list of pastors appears under the Blain chapter.

Buffalo Church, Lutheran Congregation. This people occupied, with the Reformed congregation, the stone church at Buffalo, built in 1840, as stated above. Rev. Heim preached for them in private dwellings, but discouraged their building a church and never preached in it when built. For about a year a Rev. Boyer preached there occasionally. They were unorganized at that time. Then for several years, or until 1847, the Lutherans attended the Reformed services in the church. On June 12, 1847, the Lutherans organized by electing Benjamin Rice and John Buttorff, elders, and George Rice and John Peck, deacons. Conrad Rice was made trustee. The pastors from then on have been:

1847-49—Rev. Lloyd Knight.   1854   —Rev. Adam Height.
1849-52—Rev. Jacob Martin.   1855-59—Rev. D. H. Focht.
1852-53—Rev. Wm. Gerhardt.

As the Buffalo church lay nearer the Loysville field, on June 1, 1860, it was attached to that charge. The pastor was Rev. G. M. Settlemoyer, 1860-61. The congregation then withdrew from the Loysville charge and became a part of the Blain charge, with the same ministers as Blain until 1886, when it became a part of the newly formed Ickesburg charge. The names of the later ministers appear in the history of Blain and Ickesburg churches, elsewhere in this book. A new brick-cased church was built in 1886-87, but later burned and was then replaced with a frame structure.

Buffalo Presbyterian Church. This church was organized in April, 1823. In that year a log church was built upon lands secured from Philip Kell, located one and one-fourth miles west of Ickesburg. Rev. John Linn, the pastor of Centre Church, had previously been holding services in the vicinity. Several histories credit its organization to Rev. James M. Olmstead, but the History of Presbytery, by Rev. William West, names Rev. Nathan Harned as the first pastor, 1823, with Rev. Olmstead following in 1825-32, and Rev. John Pomeroy, 1832-33. In 1834, when Rev. John Dickey came to New Bloomfield, Buffalo church was added to that pastorate and so remained until 1855, under Mr. Dickey. It was then united with Millerstown and was served by Rev. John B. Strain, 1856-60, and Rev. Thomas P. Cochran, D.D., 1862-67. In 1868 Buffalo and Blain united and called Rev. J. J. Hamilton, who made his residence in Saville Township. The History of Presbytery then places the name of Robert McPherson as stated supply during 1877-81. Rev. John H. Cooper, 1884-85, resided at Blain, but filled both pulpits. The four churches, Buffalo, Blain, Centre and Landisburg, were then served by Rev. William M. Burchfield from 1887 until 1895, when he was retained by Centre, and the churches at Buffalo, Blain and Landisburg formed a charge.

St. Andrew's Lutheran Church. This Lutheran Church is really the cradle in which was nurtured the religious faith of that denomination in so far as Saville Township is concerned. When the last century was born there were settling around the vicinity of present-day Ickesburg the Ickes, Lyons, Shuman, Long, and many other families of that faith. Their nearest churches were from eight to twelve miles, and at stated periods a minister would come into the district and preach, usually in some home or a school building. About 1806 Rev. Frederick Oberhauser began holding regular services near Ickesburg, as well as at many other points in western Perry. In 1815 he conducted a catechetical class at Andrew Shuman's home, at Shuman's mill, conducted a communion service and confirmed twelve members. Owing to the infirmities of age he soon ceased preaching here. He died in 1821. From then until 1828 Rev. John William Heim preached occasionally. In that year Mr. Heim settled at Loysville and still preached occasionally at Shuman's thereafter.

The log church was not built until 1831. It was erected on an acre of land donated by Andrew Shuman for a Union church (Lutheran and Reformed) and a graveyard. Andrew Shuman and Jacob Bealor were the building committee. The first council was as follows: Frederick Anders, elder; John Beistlein, deacon; Peter Long, John Swartz, trustees. The pastors since then have been Rev. Heim, who served until 1849; Jacob Martin. until 1852; Rev. Wm. Gerhardt, Rev. Adam Height, Rev. David Focht and the successive pastors of the New Bloomfield congregation, until 1866, for which see the chapter devoted to that town. Under Rev. Martin and the beginning of Rev. Focht's pastorate the services were held alternately in English and German. In 1886 it became a part of the newly formed Ickesburg charge, the pastors being the same. See Ickesburg Lutheran Church.

St. Andrew's Reformed Church. This congregation's place of worship was the same as that of the Lutheran Church, described immediately preceding. Rev. Jacob Scholl was the pastor from the time of its building in 1831 to the time of his death, September 4, 1847. Rev. Daniel Gans followed until 1851, and Rev. Samuel Kuhn. until 1862. It was then united with the Blain charge and so continued for a few years, when it was abandoned as a regular pulpit by the members of that faith on account of its close proximity to Ickesburg and Buffalo.

Ickesburg Lutheran Church. Although the Buffalo church. three miles away, was the home of a Lutheran congregation, and St. Andrew's Lutheran Church existed at Eshcol, still closer, the Lutheran families of Ickesburg organized a congregation and built a church. which was dedicated December 6, 1885. Its cost was $4,500. Most of the elder Lutheran families then residing at Ickesburg were members of one of these two churches, and other families moving in would not unite with churches three miles away, neither would the young people. which resulted in the building of the Ickesburg church. A congregation was organized and also a Sunday school, the United Brethren Church being rented and the pastor from Blain, Rev. Clair, filled the pulpit. The Presbyterians then offered their church, and in it the meetings were held until the church was dedicated. Following Rev. Clair, came Rev. Frazier, Rev. Heisler, and Dr. Neff. Blain and New Bloomfield showed a tendency to release Buffalo and St. Andrew's Churches. with the result that Ickesburg charge was formed of the three churches. For a short time a fourth church, St. Mark's. at Kistler, was attached. but it soon dropped out, and to-day even the building is gone. The new Ickesburg charge has been served by Rev. Trostle, Rev. Deitterich, Rev. Nichols, Dr. Diven, Rev. Romig. Rev. Dauhenspeck, and the present pastor, Dr. A. C. Forscht.

The Reformed Church of Ickesburg. Settlements did not always follow the location of churches, and this was true of Ickesburg. To the west was Buffalo Reformed Church, and to the south was Shuman's Reformed

Church. The former was three miles away and the latter was at the period of its disintegration. The members of the faith residing in Ickesburg organized April 10, 1869, with George Orris, Peter Swartz and John Simonton as elders, and Alexander Barnes, G. W. Kochenderfer and Thomas M. Kochenderfer, as deacons. It was named St. Luke's, and in 1871 erected a brick church. In the beginning the Ickesburg congregation was subordinate to the Buffalo Church. The Blain pastor serves this church, and in the Blain chapter will be found a list of the pastors.

Ickesburg Methodist Church. The Ickesburg Methodist Church was built in 1843. It was long served by the pastors of the New Bloomfield charge, but of later years was connected with the Millerstown church. Services were held in it until 1920. During 1921 it was sold to the school board.

Spring Township.

While there appears to be no authentic account in the court records relating to Spring Township there is evidence that the preliminary petition to the court asking for the formation of the new township was presented at the January sessions in 1848. The viewers appointed were Richard Adams, James Black and Wm. B. Anderson. The report signed by Mr. Adams and Mr. Black, recommended the creation of the new township and named it Lawrence, but at the August sessions of court when the report was confirmed, although almost 200 citizens protested, it was made a township and named Spring. It was formed from lands taken from Tyrone Township.

Spring Township is bounded on the north by Saville and Centre, on the east by Centre and Carroll, on the south by Cumberland County, and on the west by Tyrone Township. Its outline on the north and east is irregular. At the census of 1850, succeeding its formation, it had a population of 1,281, 105 farms, 215 houses, and 14 productive establishments.

On February 4, 1755, one day after the lands which now comprise Perry County were opened to settlers, John Sanderson warranted 150 acres, the eastern end of Elliottsburg now being located on this property, and the road from the present hotel to the north being the line between him and Samuel Fisher, who patented his tract on May 1, 1755. A note signed by John Lukens, surveyor general, attached to Fisher's warrant, says: "I understand the land called Samuel Fisher's in this warrant to be the land first settled by Richard Kirkpatrick, and that there was a line marked between said Kirkpatrick and Sanderson by consent." Accordingly both Kirkpatrick and Sanderson must have been upon the grounds before the lands were open to settlement. As far as Kirkpatrick is concerned there is evidence to that effect, as quoted in one of the chapters in this book relating to the Indians, he having been one of those removed from the lands by the provincial authorities. John Sanderson warranted other tracts in 1785 and 1789. He resided on this original claim but owned 1,100 acres in one plot. In 1782 he was assessed with two stills and a gristmill, which was run as late as 1873 by John Snyder. When he died, in 1790, he bequeathed to his nephew, George Elliot, 400 acres. In 1829 George Elliot sold this property to George S. Hackett, who kept a hotel in what is stated to be the first brick house in Perry County, it having been built by Sanderson before his death in 1790. It stood until 1884.

Near the limestone ridge, east of Elliottsburg, Thomas Fisher, a son of Samuel Fisher, referred to above, took up 337 acres. William Power warranted eighty-six acres south of Elliottsburg and adjoining it, in 1788. Abraham Smith and Casper Comp took up 150 acres. The farm long known as the John Reapsome place, and the John Rice place, south of Elliottsburg, was taken up by Matthias Pierson, June 28, 1788, and comprised 216 acres. It was described as being three miles in length and the shape of a horseshoe, the width at one end being ten rods, and at the other sixty-one. James Baxter warranted 207 acres. The "Little Germany" tracts were taken up by John Fuas (Foose) in 1794. In 1820 he was assessed with 300 acres, a sawmill and a distillery. Edward Irvine, in 1766, took up a large tract, and in 1765 Casper Comp took up sixty acres, including an improvement of Hermanus Alricks, who, with his brothers, James and West, had taken warrants for adjoining lands in 1784. In February, 1803, George Stroop warranted 250 acres adjoining lands, which he had purchased, east of Landisburg. While living in this vicinity Stroop was sheriff of Cumberland County. When the county was formed his heirs were assessed with over 1,300 acres of land.

Stroop's main tract, passed to Martin Swartz in 1822, and in the same year to John Junkin, of Cumberland County, who located there and was associate judge of Perry County for nineteen years, after the death of the first incumbent, William Anderson. Mr. Junkin, in 1854, with his entire family, except B. F. Junkin, who later became president judge, removed to Iowa. When sold in 1822 it had erected thereon "a large brick house, gristmill, sawmill, five tenant houses, etc." On his removal Mr. Junkin sold to John Brown, who in 1866 conveyed it to Wm. P. Heckendorn. After his death it was conveyed to Jos. M. Bolze, in 1906. A year later it passed to C. E. Kuller, after whose death, in 1911, it passed to Edward Cless, the present owner. This farm passed to John Brown, in 1854, and a few years later to Samuel Spotts. Mr. Spotts sold twenty acres of it, on which had been built a gristmill and a sawmill, to William Heckendorn, a few years later. This property eventually passed to M. L. Rice & Brother, who abandoned the mill about 1900.

In 1755 James Diven warranted 195 acres on which he later built a tannery. David Beard, in 1763, took up 150 acres, and in 1791 another sixty-five acres. Hugh Kilgore, in 1755, warranted 217 acres, and in 1766 an additional claim of 123 acres. In 1784 David Robb took up 100 acres, and in 1785 an additional seventy acres adjoining it. There was a pine mill and a still on one of these properties, probably where the Wetzell mill later stood. Near Bridgeport four Ross brothers—Jonathan, John, Samuel and Thomas—warranted almost a thousand acres from 1762 to 1784. These lands extended almost to Landisburg. John Waggoner, the head of the family prominent in the milling industry of the county from then until now, purchased 500 acres of these Ross lands lying on both sides of the creek, and in 1805 erected the mill, now known as the B. P. Hooke mill. See "Old Landmarks, Mills and Industries."

Near the line where Spring is joined by Carroll Township, along Sherman's Creek, George Gibson took up fifty acres in February, 1785, and another fifty acres in 1787. Ann West Gibson took up 100 acres in April, 1793. This was the Falling Springs property. She was the wife of George Gibson, who was killed in 1791 in battle, and took up the claim after his death. Her father, Francis West, and Ross Mitchell owned adjoining claims. George Gibson and his wife, Ann West Gibson, were the parents of five children, two of whom became prominent, John Bannister Gibson being a Chief Justice of the Supreme Court of Pennsylvania, and George Gibson, Commissary General of the United States. See chapter devoted to their lives. The old Gibson mill was built by Ann West Gibson prior to 1782, its history being embraced in the chapter on Old Landmarks, Mills, etc. When the county was formed in 1820, the Gibson heirs were assessed with 450 acres of land, a sawmill and a gristmill. The Wests, of which family Mrs. Gibson was a member, were descendants of Francis West, who came over with William Penn on his second voyage to America, from

67

the family seat at "Westover," England. They took up large tracts along Sherman's Creek. William West warranted 323 acres in May, 1755; Francis West, several tracts in 1755 and 1757; Ann West Gibson, a tract in 1787; Edward West, 100 acres in 1792, and a tract called "Trouble Ended," in 1790. The 100-acre tract he called "Quaker Hill."

Francis West, one of the family, was a "squatter" prior to taking out a warrant for his land. His old hut was still standing a dozen years after the formation of the county. At the outbreaking of the Revolution he resided at Carlisle and was judge of the courts. During the war he moved to his lands here, where he died in 1784.

In March, 1794, James McCord warranted 200 acres. In August, 1784, Hugh Ferguson warranted a tract which he named "Bachelor's Retreat." Henry Gass, one of those driven from the county by the provincial authorities at the behest of the Indians in 1750, returned and warranted lands, parts of which have been in the hands of the Dunkleberger families of recent generations. On the north side of Quaker Hill, Robert Kelley warranted fifty acres. In August, 1793, Christian Heckendorn and Thomas McKee warranted 400 acres, but a year later McKee sold his portion to Heckendorn. When the county was formed Heckendorn was one of the largest landowners, being assessed with over 700 acres.

John McBride, in 1767, warranted 224 acres, and William Nelson, during the period from 1787 to 1793 warranted 550 acres, both tracts being near Oak Grove furnace, which was located on part of the Christian Heckendorn place. Later these lands were known as the "Thudium tract," and still later passed to the ownership of the McCormick estate. In February, 1794, William Long took up 400 acres, adjoining the Long's Gap road. In September, 1766, Hance Ferguson patented 304 acres, and John Johnson warranted lands in 1766 and 1771 totaling 237 acres. Adam Junkin warranted a plot, and he and Benjamin Junkin, as early as 1773, purchased the Johnston lands, later part being sold to John Carl.

Elliottsburg, a village located on the line of the Newport & Sherman's valley Railroad, which is located on parts of the original grants of William Power and Samuel Fisher, was named after George Elliott, who inherited 400 acres of the Sanderson grants. Evidently it already bore that name before 1828, when the post office was established, Henry C. Hacket being the first postmaster. Peter Bernheisel was the first merchant, being succeeded by Cadwallader Jones. Mrs. Gilbert Moon moved from Landisburg and kept the first tavern. When the county seat agitation was on one of the sites proposed was located here. The first subscription school here was taught in the kitchen of the mill tenant house, by Alex. Peale, Alex. Topley and Alex. Roddy, in succession. The Hershey Creamery Company, of Harrisburg, built a milk condensory here in 1918.

Elliottsburg has at times been the location of physicians, among them having been Dr. Conrad, of Northumberland County, a graduate of Jefferson Medical College, who later located in Florida; Dr. G. W. Eppley, who was here a short time before locating at Marysville; Dr. Boyer and Dr. G. W. Byers, the last named removing to McVeytown in 1888; and Dr. L. M. Shumaker, who later located in Harrisburg, practicing there until his death in 1919.

Two other Spring Township physicians were Henry Von Haken, a graduate of the University of Berlin, who located there in 1865, and Dr. Louis Ellerman, of Prussia.

Bridgeport is located on the north bank of Sherman's Creek on lands originally warranted by the Ross brothers. About 1832 James Ball erected a blacksmith shop, and in 1838 Wilson Welsh started a store. It became a local centre from then on.

In 1795 Casper Comp took up sixty acres, including an improvement of Hermanus Alricks, who with his brothers James and West Alricks, had warranted adjoining lands in 1784. Conrad Holman bought this tract in 1800 and built a sawmill and a fulling mill. The adjoining settlement became known as "Slabtown" (also "Milltown") by reason of the fact that most of the houses were built of slabs from the Holman mill. It later passed to the McAfees, who operated the fulling mill in its final stages. It is now owned by the Bolze family.

At an early date Abraham Shively erected a brick house and kept a tavern known as the Blue Ball Hotel, the sign being large blue balls. Wilson McClure erected the mill later known as the Fry mill.

James Diven warranted 195 acres in 1755, and later built a tannery thereon. He died in 1818. This property later passed to Daniel Spotts, and then to Frank Spotts. In 1784 David Robb warranted a tract of 100 acres, including a "pine hill." This was probably at or near the site of Wentzell's mill, which was one of the pioneer mills. It was long owned by Robert Crozier. An old distillery was located on the place and operated until the period of the War between the States.

It was in present Spring Township that Secretary Peters, of the Province of Pennsylvania, reported in 1750 that he had found "on Sherman's Creek, about six miles over the Blue Mountain, James Parker, Thomas Parker, Owen McKeib, John McClare, Richard Kirkpatrick, James Murray, John Scott, Henry Gass, John Cowan, Simon Girtee (Girty), and John Kilough, who had settled and erected cabins or log houses there."

There was once a tannery on the Carlisle-Landisburg road, over a mile above Falling Springs, built by George Kepner, who sold to Samuel K. Dunkelberger and T. M. Dromgold. They sold it to Abram Wertz, who rebuilt it and operated it until his death. The property was then purchased by Alfred Dunkelberger, who built a home there.

Located in that part of Spring Township known as "Little Germany" as early as 1780 was a schoolhouse, which had been erected by Henry Ludolph Spark, a German teacher, who taught there until his death, when he bequeathed the property for school purposes. It contained seventeen acres. Israel Carl taught for a period of about twenty years thereafter, the school thereby acquiring that name. It was a log building, including the dwelling house of the teacher, under the same roof. When J. B. Cooper taught there, prior to 1850, a partly finished gravestone occupied a position on a table in the center of the room, at which the teacher worked when not teaching. Another building was built almost at the same spot in 1851. William Grier, who died in 1919, and who resided in New Bloomfield, where he was proprietor of the academy for so many years, was the teacher of the first two sessions in it.

Woomer's Cave, an extensive subterranean cavern, is located in Spring Township. It contains a number of rooms, and has been explored by the more daring of several generations. It is on the farm known as the Wentzel place, later owned by John W. Kell, and was first discovered by W. H. Kell.

In 1798 a schoolhouse was erected in Pisgah Valley, and in 1859 a brick building took its place. This school is known to this day as the Pisgah schoolhouse. About 1800 another was built at St. Peters' Church. It too was a log house and the congregations of the Lutheran and Reformed Churches used it as a place of worship until 1817, when their church was completed. It was in use until about 1849, when it was replaced by a new one. There was a schoolhouse known as West's (later known as Union), which stood as late as 1830, the time of its erection being obscure. It was at this school that Chief Justice John Bannister Gibson was a pupil. There was a schoolhouse where Springdale is now located, which was in use as late as 1835, and at that time was a very old building. Its early history is unknown. It was located on the original grant of George Stroop and on the farm later owned by the father of Judge B. F. Junkin, who attended school there as a boy. Among the teachers at that period were James B. Cooper, William Power, John Ferguson and Henry Thatcher.

When Colonel George Gibson fell at the defeat of General St. Clair, the United States Government, then in its very beginning, probably gave little attention to pensions, and his widow, Ann West Gibson, and her little sons had only the small earnings of a primitive gristmill between them and poverty. Nothing daunted, the young widow built a schoolhouse near her home and herself became the teacher of the little neighborhood, from whence went forth her son, John Bannister, later the celebrated chief justice of Pennsylvania.

As stated elsewhere, several efforts have been made to discover oil on Perry County soil, but without success. At this time over 18,000 acres have been leased in Spring and Tyrone Townships, and a well is being sunk on the F. P. Spotts farm. The company is known as the Perry Oil and Gas Company, whose directors are: W. R. Graupner, president; E. O. Meadows, vice-president; Job J. Conklin, secretary-treasurer; Alvin Fraim, Elmer Ehler and E. C. Dile, the latter from Perry County and the others residents of Harrisburg.

The old Thudium or Fry mill, south of Alinda, dates back prior to 1820, when Perry County was still a part of Cumberland County. Hermanas and James Alricks conveyed these lands to Wilson McClure in 1801. Wilson McClure sold to Martin Swartz, who upon his death in 1824 devised to his son, John Swartz, the gristmill and sawmill. John Swartz, in 1834 conveyed to John Diven, and his administrator passed title to Christian Thudium in 1841. Mr. Thudium sold to Col. Wm. J. Graham in 1875. About 1878 they passed to Frederick Fry, and to Albert Fry in 1887. His wife, Elizabeth Fry, became owner in 1892, and passed the title to her son, John Fry, the present owner.

According to the mercantile appraiser the following firms are doing business in Spring Township, the dates being time of entering the business:

General stores, J. M. Bolze, one each at Milltown and Lebo; J. A Bower & Son, W. H. Gray, J. E. Garber, J. B. Gibson

Groceries, D. A Dunkelberger, R. T. Thompson.

Flour and feed, S. V. Dunkelberger, B. P. Hooke.

Charles A. Dum, fertilizer; J. F. Frye, feed; James H. Rice, fertilizer; J. W. Rice, meat market; Ed. Reapsome, Jr. (1920), cigars; C. G. Reiber (1918), established by M. H. Sheibley (1907), fencing; J. R. Rhoads, produce; H. R. Wentzel, grain; R. F. Thompson, poultry.

Ludolph Church, in Little Germany. Carl's schoolhouse, located in Little Germany, Spring Township, was a preaching station as early as 1837, Rev. John William Heim, of the Lutherans, and Rev. Jacob Scholl, of the Reformed faith, holding services there. A joint church was built there in 1842 on the tract of Ludolph Sparks, and in his honor was named Ludolph Church. Both faiths worshiped there until 1869, when the Lutheran Church at Elliottsburg—a near-by point—was completed. The Reformed people continued to worship there until 1872, when the Reformed Church was built in Elliottsburg, when they too abandoned it. It still stands and is sometimes used for funeral services.

Church of God—Oak Grove and Little Germany. The Church of God was organized at Oak Grove, in Spring Township, in 1833, by Archibald Young. The one at Little Germany was organized somewhat later. Until 1858 both congregations worshiped in schoolhouses, but then a stone church was built a half-mile north of Lebo. Since then the members of that

faith have worshiped there. The building committee was composed of
Abraham S. Baker, George Reiber, Sr., and Jacob Dentler. Stephen Losh
was the contractor. The elders and ministers have been the same as those
of the Landisburg Church of God. See Landisburg chapter.

Elliottsburg Lutheran Church. This church was first regularly organized in 1840, by Rev. John William Heim, at Ludolph's Church, in the section known as Little Germany, although he had held services there for
several years previous in Carl's schoolhouse, as described above. The
location is about a mile and a half east of Elliottsburg. As the years
passed settlement in this district remained stationary or perhaps became
less, while the village of Elliottsburg, located on the main valley road,
grew in size. Accordingly the congregation was incorporated on January
7, 1867, and arrangements begun for the building of a new church at
Elliottsburg for the congregation. One-half an acre of land was purchased from W. S. Snyder for $125, and one-fourth an acre from Jacob
Dum for $62.50, as a site during 1868. In May of that year the corner
stone was laid, the services being held in the barn of Thomas Gray,
near by. Rev. Peter Sahm, the pastor, officiating. It was dedicated in
1869. Henry Fleisher and Michael Noll, Jr., composed the building committee. Abram W. Kistler was the contractor, the price being $2,350. It
was remodeled in 1885.

Elliottsburg Reformed Church. St. John's Reformed Church at Elliottsburg, like the Lutheran Church, is the result of the earlier congregation
which worshiped in the joint church in Little Germany. The membership
coming largely from the vicinity of Elliottsburg, which had attained the
proportions of a village, it was decided to build a new church there. A
lot was purchased from Jacob Sheibley, and almost an acre of ground for
burial purposes, from Jacob Dum, and a church built, which was dedicated
October 13, 1872, Rev. E. V. Gerhardt then being the pastor. The pastors
have been the same as those of the Landisburg Reformed Church, for
which see Landisburg chapter. The contract price of the church was
$2,950. The building committee consisted of George Hoobaugh, Julius
Gurskey, George Rheem and Wm. Sheibley.

Mt. Zion United Evangelical Church. This church is located at Elliottsburg. Prior to the building of the first church, services were held in homes
for a number of years. The first church was built in 1856, the building
committee being John Dum and William Nelson. It is a part of Perry
Circuit, and the pastor resides here. The church was rebuilt in 1907, when
C. W. Hipple was pastor, the building committee ·being Margaret Dum,
W. R. Dum and T. L. Hench. Pastors have been as follows, since 1881 :

1881-82—Rev. J. M. Brader.	Rev. W. J. Dice.
1882-83—Rev. J. F. Shultz.	1899-03—Rev. J. H. Hertz.
1883-85—Rev. J. W. Bentz.	1903-05—Rev. A. L. Burkett.
1885-87—Rev. George Josephs.	1905-06—Rev. W. M. Sanner.
1887-89—Rev. W. W. Rhoads.	1906-10 - Rev. C. W. Hipple.
Rev. Wm. Minsker.	1910-13—Rev. M. T. Crouch.
1889-92—Rev. J. R. Sechrist.	1913-15—Rev. Earl P. Markel.
1892-95—Rev. H. T. Searle.	1915-20—Rev. W. E. Smith.
1895-97—Rev. E. L. Kessler.	1920-22—Rev. L. E. Teter.
1897-99—Rev. A. S. Baumgardner.	1922- —Rev. D. P. Smeltzer.

TOBOYNE TOWNSHIP.

Until 1763 Toboyne Township was a part of Tyrone Township, when in
accordance with a petition of residents to the court of Cumberland County,
it was created a separate township. The action of the court was not very
specific in designating boundary lines, as this order would indicate: "Upon
application of some of the inhabitants of Tyrone Township to this court,

setting forth that said township is too large, it is adjudged by the said court that Alexander Roddy's mill run be the line, and the name of the upper, Toboyne, Alexander Logan being in Toboyne Township." Accordingly, Toboyne became the second township in what is now Perry County. Its area was reduced by the formation of Madison, in 1836, and of Jackson, in 1844, yet it remains one of the largest in the county, its area being about seventy-five square miles. Located at the extreme west end of the county, it reaches from Juniata County, on the north, to Cumberland County, on the south. On the west it is bounded by Franklin County, and on the east by Jackson Township. It is the only township in the county which borders on three counties, other than the one in which it is located.

The Waggoner gristmill, two miles west of Loysville, occupies the site of the Alexander Roddy mill, and Alexander Logan lived on the farm of Preston J. McMillen, at Sandy Hill. A line running through these points was practically north and south, which evidently was the intention of the court. Constituted as it was then Toboyne Township comprised about one-fourth of the territory of the county as later formed.

Among early warrants for land in Toboyne were: John Wilson, 200 acres in 1755; John Rhea, 100 acres in 1767; John Thomas, 113 acres in Horse Valley, in 1765; William Wallace, 292 acres in 1765; John Watt, 209 acres in 1766, and 150 in 1767. On this latter tract the first gristmill in what is now Toboyne Township was built in 1800, by Samuel Leaman. Other early warrants were granted to John Glass, William Adams, John Jordan, Archibald Watts, John Farrier, Patrick and John Culbertson and Robert McKee. Although the warrant of John Wilson, dated in 1755, is the earliest on record, yet there must have been others, as Wilson's lands are described as being "bounded by those of John Watt, Joseph McClintock, Brown's Run, Robert Morrow and Anthony Morrison."

Stephen, Francis and John Johnston settled as early as 1780, and John Clendennin in 1792. When the county was formed in 1820, the population of Toboyne was 1,955, and the valuation $342,179. Tavern licenses were held in 1821 by Peter Shively and James Baird; in 1822, by John Snell, Henry Zimmerman and David Koutz, and in 1823, by John Strawbridge. In those days it was a common custom for merchants to take out a liquor license in connection with their stores, so that it is not always possible to make a clear distinguishing mark between the two lines of traffic. Anthony Black was licensed in 1825, as was Henry Zimmerman, who kept a place at Andersonburg, where he was also postmaster.

When the township was first created Tyrone and Toboyne voted at the same place, but in 1803 they were formed into two election districts, the house of Henry Zimmerman being named as the polling place for Toboyne. In 1830, Jackson and Madison having not yet been separated from Toboyne, there were two polling places, according to a proclamation in the *Perry Forester*, at the schoolhouse in New Germantown, and at Zimmerman's tavern. Early merchants were Anthony Black, B. Fosselman & Co., James Ewing and James Morrison. Ewing had a store in New Germantown, and also for a time at Mt. Pleasant. Black's store was at his home, near Mt. Pleasant, and later at Blain.

Toboyne Township was early an important location for tanneries. The Adams tannery, located about two miles south of New Germantown, was the first one, being built before 1814, in which year Thomas Adams was assessed with it. In 1824 it was burned to the ground. It was assessed in 1835 in the name of James Adams, and was operated until about 1840. The New Germantown tannery was built by John Stewart about 1820. In 1835 it was assessed as the property of Noah Elder, who ran it many years. It was later owned by James Humes, and was then bought by the

Morrison Brothers, who ran it until about 1865. Fairview tannery, near the head of the valley, with a large capacity, was erected between 1835 and 1840, by John Hoover and Arnold Faughs. In 1848 William Elder and son Filson, became the owners. The latter later became the owner. After running it eight years he sold it to Ephraim McLaughlin, who operated it until 1870, when it was abandoned, owing to the lack of railroad communication. In 1847 Israel and Samuel Lupfer built the Monterey tannery at the upper end of the narrow valley lying at the base of Bower's Mountain. The brothers gained a competence through it. Israel Lupfer purchased his brother's share in 1858, and ran it until 1880. In connection with John Wiley, Charles H. Rippman purchased it. They sold it to Hans Reese' Sons, in 1881, who abandoned it in 1889. Prior to the construction of the Newport & Sherman's Valley Railroad through western Perry Mr. Rippman hauled leather in wagons down the valley on the way to market, and on the return trip he hauled hides for tanning.

The first gristmill to be built within the present limits of Toboyne Township was erected about 1800, by Samuel Lehman, at a point on Sherman's Creek, about two miles west of New Germantown. In the year of the county's erection he was assessed with a gristmill, a sawmill and 277 acres of land. Rev. Peter Long, of Huntingdon County, purchased it in 1843, and while in his possession, in 1885, the mill burned. He rebuilt it, and in 1890, his executor, E. D. Book, sold it to Ernest Blemel, who operated it until 1895, when it again burned. It was not again rebuilt.

The New Germantown gristmill had much to do with the location of New Germantown, which was laid out in 1816, as to it came the trade from the surrounding territory. The mill was then already established, and its owner, Jacob Kreamer, had his home within the present limits of New Germantown. It is now known as the Snyder mill. It is located on Sherman's Creek, a short distance southeast of the town. While Mr. Kreamer had occupied the lands before and erected the mill, his patent only dates to 1827. In 1857 he sold to Lydia and James E. Gray, who in 1874 sold to Abraham Snyder. In 1903 the property was purchased by John W. Fry. In the assessment list of 1767, when Toboyne yet retained its original area —including what is now Jackson and Madison—the following names appear:

James, Thomas, William and Robert Adams, each 100 acres; John Baxter. 50; John Brown, 200; James Brown, 50; John Blair, 100; Barnett Cunningham, 200; · Thomas Clark, 100: Bartholomew Davis, 100; John Crawford, 100; "A Dutchman," 100; William Ewings, 100; John Glass, 100; William Gardner, 100; Jacob Grove, 200 and a grist and sawmill; Thomas Huett, 150; Andrew Helander, 200; James Morrison, 150; Anthony Morrison, 150; Joseph McClintock, 150; James Murray, 100; John Mitchell, 200; John McNeere, 100; William McClelland, 100; Robert Adams, 100; William Anderson, 200; James Boal, 100; Adam Boal and John Whiting, 150; James Blain, 300; Robert Brown, 100; John Byers, 200; Robert Caldwell, 100; James McCord, 100; Alexander Roddy, 100; George Sanderson, 200: Andrew Taylor, 200; John Watt, 150; Thomas White, 100; William Harkness, 100.

In 1814 the assessment list, still including Madison and Jackson, shows the following industries:

Abraham Groves, gristmill; Jacob Gunkle, sawmill; George Hollenbaugh, grist and oilmill, where the Abram Bistline mill was later located, in present Madison Township; Bailey Long, gristmill; David Moreland, merchant, gristmill; James Maxwell, fulling mill; John Moreland, grist and sawmill; Englehart Wormley, grist and sawmill; Thomas Adams, tanyard; Solomon Bower. distillery; Jacob Bryner, still; John Brown, sawmill; Frederick Bryner, grist and sawmill, known as the Waggoner mill; Abram Bower. still, located on the George Loy farm; Owen Bruner, gristmill, later Trostle's; Jacob Creamer.

gristmill, later the Abram Snyder mill; William Cook, sawmill; George Ebright, tanyard; John Musselman, still; Samuel Lemon, gristmill.

The number of industries was 4 stills, 6 sawmills, 10 gristmills, 2 tanneries and a fulling mill.

John Clendenin, a settler in what is now Toboyne Township, was killed and scalped by the Indians, about one-fourth mile southwest of the Monterey tannery site. He evidently had located lands which the Indians considered an encroachment. In July, 1772, his son, also John Clendenin, warranted 109 acres, and in January, 1792, 178 acres. This first tract may have been one claimed by the father.

Toboyne Township furnished the officers for two companies, the fourth and eighth, of the famous Frederick Watts battalion of Cumberland County Militia during the Revolution, and practically all the men   See chapter on the subject. During the War of 1812 Captain David Moreland's company contained a large proportion of Toboyne men. Captain Moreland was from what is now Blain.

For variety of physical features Toboyne Township leads the county, but as many of them are described in the chapter on "The Tuscarora Forest," the reader will do well to refer there. Within its borders is the head of Sherman's Valley, parts of Horse and Henry's Valleys, Little Illinois Valley. Sherman's Creek, Houston's Run (locally known as Sheaffer's Run), Brown's Run (locally known as Fowler Run), Patterson's Run, parts of the Tuscarora and Kittatinny or Blue Mountains, Conococheague Mountain, Rising Mountain, Bowers Mountain, Big Round Top, Little Round Top, Buck's Hills, Chestnut Ridge (locally known as Shultz Ridge), and others of lesser note. A mile north of New Germantown is a small settlement known as Seagertown.

Many years ago William Stump, father of Jesse Stump, came across the Kittatinny Mountain to locate. He carried a willow cane, which he stuck into the soil near the creek at the farm now known as the Philip Sheaffer place, about two miles west of New Germantown. From that little cane, used to mark a line, there grew a large willow tree. which the writer measured in July, 1919, while collecting material for this volume. At a height of five feet from the ground the circumference was twenty-four feet, nine inches. The ravages of time have started its disintegration.

Toboyne Township was also the home of the Blaines, one of America's noted families, which gave to the country both then and since distinguished services, but as the lands taken up by these pioneers of that name were in that part of Toboyne which later became Jackson Township. The history pertaining to them is included in that of Jackson Township and the chapter devoted to the Blaine Family.

As early as 1800 records show two schoolhouses in that part of Toboyne Township which constitutes it at present. One was located at the western end of New Germantown, and Anthony Black and two men named Johnston and Steele were teachers before the county was created. The other was near the farm now owned by Samuel B. Trostle. It had a clapboard roof, slab benches and desks, a wooden chimney, and two windows, the lights of which were of greased paper. The ceiling was of poles, and the floor of hewed logs. About 1805 another schoolhouse was erected at the farm now owned by D. Dervin Hollenbaugh. As early as 1814, a bill dated March 28th, passed the Pennsylvania Legislature relating to Toboyne, as follows:

"Section 1. The land officers to make a title clear of purchase money and fees to trustees for schools to be established in the township of Toboyne for a piece of land.
"Section 2. A majority of subscribers to supply vacancies of trustees"

There is record of a schoolhouse "built of mud," located near New Germantown, and taught by a man named Thatcher, among the pupils being children of James Johnston, then a prominent citizen of that community, one of whose sons, George Johnston, was later Perry County's representative in the State Legislature.

The business places of Toboyne Township, according to the report of the mercantile appraiser, are as follows:

General stores, Vernon Smith, C. W. Bistline, J. A. Rhea.

Stambaugh & Smith, coal; M. E. Morrison, millinery, Kirby Moose, meat market.

New Germantown. Joseph McClintock warranted much land and bought more until he owned a large tract. The Kern farms and the Wilhide lands were a part of his holdings, as were also the lands on which New Germantown to-day stands. He took up most of them before 1767. Solomon Sheibley came into possession of the property on which the town stands and which he laid out in lots March 1, 1816. The original plan was four blocks of six lots each, eighty feet wide by one hundred and fifty feet in depth. A public sale of lots was held on March 18, 1816.

Among the earliest residents of which there is record were J. Kuntz, shoemaker; John Leiby, carpenter; J. Smith, hatter, and William and Mathias Stump, blacksmiths. The lots for taxation purposes were valued at ten dollars. Jacob Kreamer, who once owned the mill southeast of town, was another resident.

At the east end of the town, on the George Kern farm, now owned by George M. Smith, is a remarkably large spring—one of the noted springs of the county—and which gave to the immediate vicinity the name of Limestone Spring, before the town was laid out. It is so named on Mitchell's old map of Pennsylvania. One of the early settlers of the town was William A. Morrison, who located there in 1830, father of the present Morrisons residing there, who was a county auditor, postmaster for eleven years, and for a period of thirty years a justice of the peace. In 1830 there were two taverns there, the "Old Stone Castle" or "Blue Ball Hotel" of David Koutz, and another kept by Thomas B. Jacobs, who died in 1833. It was then purchased by Mrs. Emily Gray, grandmother of the Morrisons, who kept a licensed house, known as "Travelers' Rest," until 1860, when she decided to run the place as a temperance house, which shows that over a half century ago the temperance question was already a matter of issue in Perry County. The Koutz place was unlicensed from 1831 to 1875, when William A. Shields was licensed. Samuel Kern and John Sanderson were once proprietors. From then on until the county "went dry" in 1918, there was a license at times and at times not. It was once known as the "Blue Ball" tavern, the sign being two large globes.

John Kooken was appointed a justice of the peace in 1822, and served many years. The tannery in the early years of the county's history, was operated by Noah A. Elder.

On June 18, 1842, the town was incorporated as a borough by an act of the legislature, but failure to fulfill all the provisions of the act caused the charter to be forfeited. Its existence as a separate unit must have been longer than usually stated, as an act of the Pennsylvania Legislature, March 12, 1849, creates it a special election district, and an act of May, 1850, authorizes New Germantown Borough and Toboyne Township jointly to sign liquor applications. During the existence of the town there have been two serious conflagrations. On March 3, 1876, the stores of Dr. F. A. Gutshall and J. Morrison & Son and the dwellings of Barbara Kreamer and Jane Morrison's heirs were destroyed by fire, and in 1885 J. E. Rumple's store burned.

New Germantown is located twenty-eight miles west of Newport, almost at the extreme west end of Sherman's Valley, and is the western terminus of the narrow gauge railroad. It is on the state highway leading from New Bloomfield, Perry County, to Chambersburg, Franklin County.

Rev. Dr. Frederick Oberholtzer was the first physician at New Germantown, being also pastor of the Lutheran Church. This was prior to 1821, in which year he died. Dr. J. R. Scott began practice there in 1824, but there is no record of the length of his practice in point of time. In 1843 Dr. William C. Hays located in New Germantown, where he practiced for six years. Dr. F. A. Gutshall, who graduated from the University of Pennsylvania in 1866, located in New Germantown, but some years later removed to Blain, where he is still in active practice. Dr. A. R. Johnston, reared in the vicinity, located here in 1883, but removed to New Bloomfield a year later. Dr. Milton Shull located here in 1885, but later removed to Hummelstown, where he was successful. Dr. W. J. Allen, Baltimore University, '76, was located here for a while, when he transferred to Landisburg. Dr. Russell Campbell, Medico-Chi., '09, was also here for a year or two, until his death. Dr. B. F. Grosh, an able and learned physician, came from Lancaster County and located at Andersonburg in 1844. He married into the well-known Anderson family and practiced here until his death in 1857. He was the father of Alexander Blaine Grosh, later a prothonotary of the county, and successor of the late John A. Baker as editor of the *Perry County Freeman*. After Dr. Grosh's death Dr. E. B. Hotchkin was located there for about two years. Previous to locating in Ickesburg Dr. Jonathan Jackson practiced in Andersonburg in 1859. Dr. George W. Mitchell, a native of the county, located at Andersonburg at the close of the War between the States, having graduated in 1860, and served in the war as a surgeon of one of the Pennsylvania regiments. He practiced until about 1900.

New Germantown Lutheran Church. A number of Lutheran families having been residents of New Germantown and vicinity, a meeting was held March 12, 1893, at which an organization was effected. The church was built in 1894, its first officers having been: Solomon Gutshall and J. K. Shoemaker, elders; S. A. Gutshall, William Hollenbaugh and P. G. Beighler, deacons. It belongs to the Blain charge, and has the same ministers.

New Germantown M. E. Church. The first Methodist organization was effected in 1841, and at that time the congregation was connected with the Concord (Franklin County) Circuit. The church was built in 1843 on land donated by Solomon Sheibley, who also gave the land for the cemetery. Until then the congregation had worshiped in the school building, but was refused its further use. They also worshiped in a discarded schoolhouse owned by James Adams. The church later belonged to the New Bloomfield Circuit until about 1875, when the Blain charge was formed, and it became a part. (See Bloomfield and Blain chapters for list of pastors.)

Horse Valley M. E. Church. A Methodist Episcopal church was built in Horse Valley in 1857, being located on lands of Benjamin Scyoc, who donated them. It was dedicated December 27, 1857. It was then designated as "Scyoc Chapel." Among those interested in its erection were Elias Cook, Benjamin Scyoc, William Widney and Jacob Seibert. It is still in use, the pastor from East Waterford holding services.

TUSCARORA TOWNSHIP.

Tuscarora Township, with the single exception of Howe, was the last division in so far as the townships of Perry County are concerned. It was at the October term of the courts in 1858 that the matter of the formation of a new township from parts of Greenwood and Juniata Townships was presented. The court ordered an election to be held, which was the only instance in the entire list of townships where such a course was taken, and it was accordingly held on November 30, 1858.

The result of the election being favorable the court at the session of January 3, 1859, issued the following decree:

"Whereupon, January 3, 1859, the Clerk of the Court of Quarter Sessions having laid the within return before the court, it is ordered and decreed that a new township be erected agreeably to the lines marked out by the commissioners, whose report is filed, and that the said township be named "Tuscarora," and further, the court do order and decree that the place of holding the elections shall be at the house of Michael Donnally, at Donnally's Mills, and do appoint Jacob Yohn, Judge, and James H. Deavor and David Leonard, Inspectors, to hold the spring elections for the present year, and also appoint John S. Kerr, constable."

Tuscarora Township is bounded on the north by the Juniata County line, on the east by the Juniata River, on the south by Oliver and Juniata Townships, and on the west by Saville Township. Its territory is considerably of wooded land, being traversed its entire length by four ridges of more or less importance. At the north is the Tuscarora Mountain, its crest being the township line as well as the county line. Ore Ridge, comparatively low, and running parallel, comes next. Then south of the fertile Raccoon Valley lies Raccoon Ridge, and south of that is Hominy Ridge, which separates it from Juniata Township.

Raccoon Valley is drained by Raccoon Creek, which empties into the Juniata River below Millerstown. The streams from the Tuscarora Mountain all flow into Raccoon Creek, and the streams from Raccoon Ridge and Hominy Ridge flow into Sugar Run in Buckwheat Valley. The soil in the latter valley is not so fertile as that of Raccoon Valley.

Among the early warrants for lands was that of Robert Larimer for 219 acres, opposite Millerstown and above Raccoon Creek, in 1766. The next property northward was warranted by Lewis Gronow in 1775, and contained fifty-three acres, and still further north Thomas Craig warranted 214 acres in 1794. Up the valley to the north, James Black warranted 251 acres in 1763; John Black, Jr., 366 acres in 1790; Robert Cochran, 212 acres in 1767, and Samuel Atlee, 200 acres in the same year. The John Black tracts were occupied in recent generations by Jonathan Black and James G. Kreamer. The tannery built by John Black and operated by him, and later by his son Jonathan, was located here.

The mill property known as Donnally's Mills, and still in possession of a member of that family, L. E. Donnally, who once represented his county in the General Assembly of Pennsylvania, was warranted by Henry Bull in 1763. He built the gristmill and sold to Michael Donnally about 1840. The William Fosselman and B. H. Inhoff farms were warranted to William Bull in 1767. Other warrants were granted A. Thomas White, Janet Brown in 1763, Robert McCrary in 1767, and George Robinson in 1763. The Loudons took up almost a thousand acres, as follows: James Loudon, 266 acres in 1767; Matthew Loudon, 372 acres in 1768, and Archibald Loudon, 296 acres in 1784. Another warrant was that of John Murray, for 130 acres in 1766.

In Buckwheat Valley Cornelius Ryan warranted lands in 1792, George Leonard in 1782, and Edward O. Donnally, the ancestor of the Perry County Donnallys, in 1782. John Miller warranted lands in 1794, and Robert Campbell's heirs in 1767. This is, no doubt, the Robert Campbell referred to in one of our chapters on the Indians, in which a house was attacked while six men were at dinner, and all of them, including Campbell, were murdered, except one George Dodds, who escaped. The cabin was burned by the redskins.

A thousand acres of ridge lands were warranted by Peter Jones, Philip Jones and William White. The John and Matthew Louden lands were later known as the Devor tract. Colonel John McKenzie built the gristmill there about 1840. In 1845 it passed to Devors. On Sugar Run, William Brown warranted 416 acres. The Archibald Loudon named here as warranting lands was doubtless the author of the famous Loudon's Narratives, reference to which is made a number of times in this book. The William Bull named as warranting lands, had three sons. On one occasion he and his son William were in a field planting corn when they were surprised by the Indians and taken captive, being held for a year. One of William Bull's children, Rebecca, later became Mrs. William Neilson, who was the grandmother of the late Judge William Neilson Seibert. Bull's Hill graveyard, which was a burying ground for a hundred years, was named after this family. This place of burial was started by the burial of a man who was crossing the old Indian path over the Tuscarora Mountain and was frozen to death. The graves in earlier days were covered with stones to prevent the wolves from digging up the remains. The oldest stone in this graveyard is dated 1783, to the memory of James Loudon, who was the father of Archibald Loudon, author of Loudon's Narratives. Colonel Bull was killed after the surrender of Fort Erie on July 4, 1814, being ambushed by the Indians. See chapter on the War of 1812.

Ward's mill was located in Tuscarora Township, near the mouth of Raccoon Creek, and not far from the line of the Pennsylvania Railroad, on lands once owned by Jacob F. Markley, which passed to George Rothrock in 1844, and to others in 1858. In 1868 Fietta Ward, wife of John Ward, became the owner. Just when it was built cannot be stated but, in the deed of 1868, from Wm. and Jacob Rothrock and William J. Jones, it is described as having thereon erected "a frame gristmill and sawmill." About 1886 it was burned down, ownership at that time resting in the Wards. It was never rebuilt.

The oldest schoolhouse in Tuscarora Township was situated in "the narrows," along the road from Donally's Mills to Buckwheat Valley. It was built in 1780. Owing to defective wooden chimneys three houses were burned on this site. There was an old-time house in Buckwheat Valley and another known as Bull's, at Donally's Mills, in an old carpenter shop.

Donnally's Mills M. E. Church. The Donnally's Mills M. E. Church was erected in 1868, under the pastorate of Rev. A. R. Miller. It then belonged to the Newport Circuit, but in 1904 it was assigned to the Millerstown Circuit, whose pastors serve it.

The Gingerich Church. This church was formerly an old stone school building which was remodeled for church purposes about 1861, for the U. B. denomination. In 1892 it was replaced by a new church while Rev. Barshinger was pastor. Henry Harman, Samuel Buchanan, Andrew Paden and Chas. Gutshall were then the officials. The split in the U. B. denomination caused it to be sold, in 1910, to the Methodists who are served by the pastor of the Millerstown church.

According to Wright's History, that part of Tuscarora Township known as Raccoon Valley was settled by the Blacks, the Nobles and the Robinsons, in the order named from the Juniata River westward. We quote: "In this selection certain distinctions gave precedence of location. Their pastor, Rev. Wm. B. Linn, having the preference, chose his portion near Robinson's Fort; the father of the Irvin families in Saville Township, chose their old mansion property; he was joined by Elliot's on the west, and he in turn by a younger man, until we reach the Robinson, Noble and Black farms in Raccoon Valley, extending to the Juniata River. The chain of settlements extended more than twenty miles, and included some of the best and most highly respected citizens of the county. It is historic for its arrangement of families in chronological order, as well as the noble record made during every war in which its own or the general welfare was endangered."

The business firms, according to the report of the mercantile appraiser, are as follows, the date being the time of entering the business:

L. E. Donnally, flour and feed; J. Logan Jones, general store; R. H. Kerr (1913), groceries, old location of Marsh Run postoffice; I. B. Secrist (1910), coal, feed, flour, etc.

There was once a United Brethren Church near Donally's Mills, known as Otterbein Chapel, which was then a part of Eshcol Circuit, long since out of existence. The church was sold on April 3, 1900, to Harriet Hogentogler, for $500.

Donnally's Mills United Evangelical Church. Services by the members of this faith were first held in the homes. About 1870 the first church was built, the building committee being Mr. Inhoff, John Bressler and Joseph Lesh. It has always been a part of Perry Circuit, whose minister resides at Elliottsburg. The names of the pastors will be found under the chapter relating to Spring Township.

TYRONE TOWNSHIP.

After the Albany treaty of 1754, which included the lands which now comprise Perry County, we find the following upon the records of Cumberland County, in reference to new townships: "And we do further erect the settlements called Sherman's Valley and Bofolo's Creek into a separate township and nominate the same the township of Tyrone, and we appoint John Scott Linton to act as constable therein for the remaining part of the current year."

No definite boundaries were fixed, but it included all of that part of Perry County as now constituted lying west of the Juniata River. The same territory is now divided into fifteen townships and six boroughs. It was often referred to in its pioneer days as "the eternal state of Tyrone." When Perry County was erected it had already been divided by the creation of Toboyne, Rye, Juniata and Saville. As now constituted Tyrone Township is bounded on the north by Saville, on the east by Spring, on the south by Cumberland County, and on the west by Southwest Madison Township.

As Tyrone Township comprised such an extensive domain at the time of its creation and long afterwards, of the places named and the descendants some are likely to be found in other townships, since created from parts of Tyrone.

There is an assessment list in existence which shows the names of property holders in the year 1767, as follows:

Hugh Alexander, Hermanus Alricks, John Black, Robert Brotherton, David Beard, Henry Cunningham, David Carson, John Darlington, John Dunbar, Sr., James Diven, James Dunbar, Thomas Elliot, Edward Elliot, Samuel Fisher, Hance Ferguson, Thomas Fisher, Henry Gass. James Glass, Obadiah Garwood, John Hamilton. John Johnson, Thomas Hamilton, John Kilkead, Hugh Kilgore, the Widow Kennedy, Patrick Kinsloe, the Widow Kinkead, Robert Kelly, John Kennedy, Samuel Lamb. Thomas Maney, William McClure, Owen McKeab, David McClure, William Miller, John McConnell, William Noble, Richard Nicholson, William Officer, James Orr, William Patterson, John Perkins, James Purdy, Thomas Ross, Jonathon Ross, George Robinson. Alexander Roddy, Robert Robinson. Robert Vin, William Sanderson, John Sanderson, Alexander Sanderson, John Sharps, Andrew Simonton, John Scott, Peter Stone, John Simonton, Peter Titters, Francis West, William Waugh, Daniel Williams. John Williams, Robert Welsh, John Wilson, Thomas Wilson.

As early as 1779 Obadiah Garwood was assessed with a sawmill, Widow Robinson with a gristmill, and Francis West with a grist and sawmill.

West resided on the line between Tyrone and Rye. By 1782 the assessment on mills and distilleries was as follows:

Hugh Brown, John Black, Robert Irwin, Sr. (2), Robert Irwin, Jr. (2), George Hamilton, William Neilson, and Robert Scott, stills; James Fisher, malt kiln; Alexander Roddy. sawmill; Robert Garwood and Francis West, gristmills; John Sanderson, two stills and a gristmill.

After a period of thirty-two years had elapsed the assessment roll of industries included the following in the year 1814, six years before Perry became a county:

James Diven, Samuel Nickey, Robert Thompson, tanyards; Francis Gibson, two distilleries. John Linn, Francis Portzline, Josiah Roddy, Samuel Smiley, Henry Shoemaker, Jacob Stambaugh, Frederick Shull, Englebart Wormley, Adam Webley, stills; John Foos, sawmill and still; Christian Heckendorn, sawmill and still; Nicholas Ickes, sawmill and two stills; Zalmon and Azariah Tousey, saw and gristmill and still; John Waggoner, saw and grstmill and still; George Elliot, Widow Gibson's heirs, Zachariah Rice, gristmills; Conrad Halleman, Nicholas Loy, Samuel McCord, Francis Patterson, John Shafer, Jacob Shatto, Frederick Smiley, George Waggoner, sawmills; Samuel and Andrew Linn, grist and sawmill; Peter Mores, tilt hammer; William Power, store; Thomas Purdy, stores; Adam Seller, Martin Swartz and Shuman & Utter, saw and gristmills; George Stroop, sawmill.

Alexander Roddy, named above, who later built the mill known to this day as Waggoner's mill, lived at several places before taking up the mill tract, which is covered rather extensively in the chapter devoted to "Old Landmarks, Mills and Industries."

The land office opened in 1755 for the settlement of lands in the new purchase, and when James Wilson, Andrew Simeson and others came in at that time their warrants name Alexander Roddy as "adjoining," which is evidence that although he had been ordered out before the lands were available, that he had come back. These locations were west of Montour's Run. He lived there several years before taking up the Waggoner mill tract, May 13, 1763, on Roddy's Run. He purchased other lands adjoining his on both sides of "the run," and in 1767 was assessed with 100 acres and a gristmill in Toboyne Township, and 300 acres and a sawmill in Tyrone Township, part of this 300 acres being the original tract warranted by him on Montour's Run. His sons, Josiah and Alexander Roddy, warranted 175 acres in 1786, and in 1789 the Roddys took out a warrant for 312 acres adjoining the county home tract. Robert and James Wilson, whose descendants yet live about Landisburg, took up four hundred acres in 1755, which they describe as located "where Thomas Wilson and Alexander Roddy have presumed to settle on Montour's Run, adjoining the dwelling plantation of Andrew Montour." The Andrew Simeson place was later known as the John Albert and the John Creigh farms.

In the early chapters of this book, among the matters and disputes between the Indians and the provincial authorities, there will be found an account of the encroachment of the pioneers on lands which the Indians still claimed and which those in authority decided should be vacated by all settlers. Under the authority of the province this was done, and Andrew Montour was then authorized to settle somewhere in that territory to see that the law would be observed. He located in what is Tyrone Township, near a large stream which flows into Sherman's Creek and which to this day bears his name—Montour's Run. He took out a warrant for 143 acres of land lying between where the town of Landisburg now stands and Sherman's Creek and Montour's Run, which was surveyed to William Mitchell, June 13, 1788, and passed to Abraham Landis soon thereafter. This is what has been known for a century as the Rice mill property, the old mill still being in operation. The history of this old landmark also appears in the chapter entitled "Old Landmarks, Mills and Industries." As settlers came in and Indians vanished Montour found his occupation as a trader gone, and he then left.

In 1787 Abraham Landis warranted a tract of 116 acres, which he combined with the Montour tract, and in 1795 both tracts were patented to him. Landis laid out Landisburg, but probably never lived in Tyrone Township or Landisburg, as all the deeds mentioned his home as in Lancaster County. On March 10, 1813, Landis sold his property to George Stroop, who laid out an addition to the town, but died before 1828. His heirs failed to comply with the terms of sale made by Landis and the property again reverted to Landis. Matters were compromised with lot purchasers and the remaining farm lands were sold to Dr. Samuel Moore, General Henry Fetter and Zachariah Rice. Peter Fahnestock, a son-in-law of Landis, who transacted the latter's business by power of attorney after Stroop's death, later (before 1830) built a scythe and edge tool factory and also had a tilt hammer at the old Francis Patterson mill.

William Patterson, the progenitor of the Patterson families in that section of the county, settled in 1753 on Laurel Run, and Francis Patterson had a sawmill there in 1814, and later an oil mill, and in 1825 Thomas Patterson was in possession of both and also a chopping mill. It was at this location where Fahnestock, as stated above, erected his scythe and edge tool factory, about 1838. About 1840 Solomon Hengst conducted a foundry at that point for several years. John Waggoner, of Kennedy's Valley, was once the owner and he was the man who changed the oil and chopping mill to a gristmill. It was later owned by William A. and James F. Lightner.

The two John Dunbars—father and son—took up tracts as early as 1763 and 1768. On one of these Dunbar tracts Rev. J. W. Heim built a stone gristmill about 1830, which his administrator in 1852 sold to Joseph Bixler. It later passed to Anthony Firman and George Weaver in turn, and is known as Weaver's mill to this day, being now owned by the Tressler Orphans' Home since January 1, 1919.

William McClure warranted 264 acres in 1763, which he sold to Martin Bernheisel prior to 1794. He had six children by his first marriage, the first-born being Alexander, who settled near where the Centre Presbyterian Church is located. He became the father of the celebrated editor, A. K. McClure. To William McClure, by his second marriage, there were born ten children. After the death of Martin Bernheisel the old McClure tract passed to his son Adam, who in 1810 sold the place to the poor directors of Cumberland County, and went West. This is to-day the site of the Perry County Home, the history of which appears in the chapter devoted to "Academies and Public Institutions."

Bell's Hill derives its name from James Bell, who in 1768 took up 223 acres on and near it. James Galbreath in 1750 took up 400 acres. Simon Girty (father of Simon Girty, the renegade), who trespassed and was evicted by the provincial authorities, later became a tenant upon this Galbreath tract, the owner living in Carlisle. This property passed to Charles Stewart, whose heirs in 1800 sold it to George Waggoner, where he lived until his death in 1824. In 1810 he built a sawmill upon Montour's Run, which was in use until 1884. A bark and sumac factory was built in 1850 and operated until 1864.

Obadiah Garwood, who in 1767 was assessed with 125 acres, and in 1779 with a sawmill, lived in Kennedy's Valley. Robert Garwood in 1782 was assessed with a gristmill. About 1785 John Wagner purchased the property, including the small stone mill. In 1814 he had there a gristmill, sawmill and distillery. He resided there until 1834, when he died. He was the father of ten children, his son Benjamin buying the Roddy mill about 1839, from whence it derives its name. Benjamin Roddy died, and his brother Moses purchased it. John Waggoner, another son, bought the Patterson mill and ran it. John Waggoner, the father, had also built a mill in 1805, at Bridgeport, later known as Snyder's mill, and now owned by B. P. Hooke. To give an entire list of these early settlers would fill a book in itself, but among others were the following pioneers: James Blaine, in 1785, 300 acres; John Carrothers, in 1766, 300 acres, later known as the Caldwell still house tracts; John Simonton, in 1755, 400 acres; William Anderson, in 1786, 200 acres; James Smith, in 1768, 300 acres; Michael Kinsloe, in 1795, 200 acres, and in 1800, 200 acres adjoining. David Carson, in 1762, took up a tract which he later sold to Peter Sheibley, from whom the many Sheibley families in Perry County have descended. Mr. Sheibley was the father of twenty children.

On Sherman's Creek, on the line of Spring and Tyrone Townships, Thomas Ross, an elder of Centre Presbyterian Church, located 200 acres in 1762, and Jonathan Ross, 150. Mount Dempsey was once known as Scott's Knob. Prior to 1775 it was owned by John and Christian Tussey, and changed hands several times until 1792, when it came into possession of Charles Dempsey, from whom it takes its name. In 1813, Philip Fosselman built a stone tannery on a branch of Montour's Run, and carried on the tanning business until 1832, when he sold to Jacob Shearer, who operated it until 1856, when the business was discontinued. In 1849 Mr. Shearer went to California, from where he shipped great quantities of hides to be tanned at this small plant.

In Kennedy's Valley, several miles from McCabe's Run, Colonel William Graham, in 1842, erected a tannery on land formerly belonging to Abraham Wagner, and operated it until 1849, when he sold it to James L. and John L. Diven. They operated it until 1867, when it again came into possession of Colonel Graham, who was in business there until 1872, when it was no longer run. James Baxter took up two hundred and seven acres and erected a tannery before 1820, which he ran for several years, selling it to John Titzel in 1828. He conducted it until about 1855, when it was abandoned.

About 1790 Peter Sheibley removed from Berks to Perry County territory, settling in Tyrone Township. He received payment for his farm in Berks County in Continental money, which soon became worthless. He had been a private in the Continental Army, and lived until December, 1824. He was aged eighty-four years.

Occasions where three brothers marry three sisters are rare indeed, yet one such instance is recorded in Perry County. Jacob Briner, of Berks County (grandfather of George S. Briner, now of Carlisle), married Magdalena Hammer about 1806, and with his brother George came to what is now Perry County and located about two miles south of Loysville, where they began farming. Some time later George Briner returned to Berks County and brought with him the second Miss Hammer. After a lapse of another two years Peter Briner, who had joined his brothers, returned to Berks County and brought along back as his wife the third of the Hammer sisters.

In a very early day there were four brothers, John, Henry, Jonathan and George Rhinesmith, who located in Tyrone Township, and from them have sprung the numerous Rhinesmith families of Perry County and elsewhere.

In 1826 John Bernheisel erected a clover mill, in which clover-seed and sumac were ground, upon his farm, located in Tyrone Township, between Elliottsburg and Green Park. Some time between 1830 and 1840 he added a sawmill. In 1874 his son, Sololmon Bernheisel, changed the mill to a gristmill, refitting it with steam in 1878, and as such it was in use until the latter part of the century. Martin J. Bernheisel, of the next generation, operated the mill after the death of his father.

The first schoolhouse of which there is record in Tyrone Township was at the Lebanon Church, at Loysville, which was built about 1794. Rev. D. H. Focht, in his historical work, says of it:

"A short time after the church was built a large schoolhouse was erected on the same lot of ground and near the church. A partition divided the schoolhouse inside and a large chimney occupied the centre. One end of the house was occupied by the teacher and his family and the other by the school. For many years a sort of congregational school was kept there."

That old schoolhouse was in use until 1837, when the first public school built there took its place. In 1853 the Loysville Academy was begun in the basement of this church, and later merged into the Tressler Orphans' Home. Of the Landisburg schoolhouse we have spoken in the chapter devoted to that town. There was a schoolhouse as early as 1815 in the vicinity of Rheem's foundry, at Green Park. In 1842 a brick house was built. There was a log house west of Sherman's Creek, near the Morrow farms, and one near Patterson's mill. Near the Church of God there was a frame house long in use. and in 1851 one was built on the Waggoner farm, north of Landisburg. There was one in Kennedy's Valley, on the Crull farm, and one on the old William Allen farm. The one at Bridgeport was built of brick before Spring Township was organized.

Loysville. Besides Landisburg Borough, which lies within its borders, Tyrone Township has two other towns which are not incorporated, Loysville and Green Park, the largest being Loysville. It was early known as Red Rock.

Loysville is laid out on parts of two original tracts, the east part being on the McClure tract, warranted in 1763, and the west part on the John Sharp tract, warranted the same year. Martin Bernheisel and Michael Loy later came into possession of them, and donated several acres for church and school purposes. At this point the Lutheran and Reformed Church, a parsonage, and a parochial school stood. On July 20, 1840, the directors of the poor of Perry County surveyed a block of eight lots, 60x150 in size, on the County Home tract, on the east side of the road leading to Heim's mill, and named it Andesville. Martin Kepner, Robert Dunbar and Andrew Welch were early business men. A hotel was opened by James Gracey. In 1822 Michael Loy gave a half acre of ground for the Loysville cemetery.

A post office named Andesville was established about 1842, but a few years later the name was changed to Loysville, in honor of Michael Loy. Early postmasters were Jacob Rickard, David Kochenderfer, George F. Orrel, David K. Minich, Samuel Shumaker, Isaac P. Miller, Davis S. Asper, Joseph Newcomer, John W. Heim.

Michael Loy, Jr., who died in 1846, provided in his will that his executors, George and William Loy, should lay out a row of lots from where the Lutheran parsonage stood, to the New Bloomfield road. These lots were laid out about 1848. John Ritter purchased a number of lots, and on two of them he built the present brick hotel, in 1852, now in possession of Wm. H. Power. His son, Benjamin Ritter, occupied this hotel from 1852 to 1884, when it passed to the hands of the third generation, George E. Ritter, later sheriff, becoming the proprietor.

The history of the Lutheran and Reformed Churches appears in the chapter entitled the Earliest Churches. The pastorate of Rev. John Wil-

68

liam Heim, of Lebanon Lutheran Church, covered the period from May, 1815, until his death, December 27, 1849. The church erected a monument at his grave and celebrated its centennial at the same time, in 1894, largely through the efforts of Rev. W. D. E. Scott, Samuel Ebert and Jacob Wolf.

Loysville Castle, No. 111, Knights of the Golden Eagle, was instituted here February 13, 1907.

The Women's Welfare Club was organized at Loysville in January, 1921, with the following officers: Mrs. Wm. T. Morrow, president; Mrs. George Kell, vice-president; Miss Ida Kleckner, secretary, and Mrs. Robert Eaton, treasurer, who are the officers at this time (1921). Shortly after organizing, the Welfare Club went in for improved streets through the town, and arranged with the State Highway Departmens to jointly make a crushed limestone highway through it. The work is about completed. Future plans are for the improvement of the town—which is not a borough—and aid in case of an epidemic. This organization has started well and has a fertile field, as a town of that nature does not have the organization of a borough to cover many matters needing attention.

The history of the Loysville Academy, the Soldiers' Orphans' School and the Tressler Orphans' Home, which developed from one to the other, appears under "Academies and Institutions." The group of buildings are visited by thousands annually.

In 1896, Dickinson, Gilbert & Keen opened a creamery here, which was a pioneer in its line. It has operated continuously since. The share of Hiram Keen was purchased from his heirs by B. Stiles Duncan, who, in conjunction with I. H. Dickinson and Amos Gilbert, now owns the plant, under the firm name of the Loysville Creamery Company. H. P. Dyson is the secretary and treasurer.

There was no resident doctor in Loysville until 1842, when Dr. Isaac Lefevre located there. In 1855 he removed to New Bloomfield. He later was located at Mechanicsburg and Harrisburg. Dr. A. E. Linn was his successor, and practiced here until he removed to Shermansdale, in 1857. Dr. B. P. Hooke graduated from the University of Pennsylvania in 1855, and located at Loysville a year later. He practiced there successfully until his death, which occurred March 10, 1903. Dr. C. E. Delancey, who graduated from the University of the City of New York in 1878, after practicing a short time at Ickesburg, located here in 1883. He removed from here to Newport, where he has a large practice. Dr. George L. Zimmerman, born at Andersonburg, followed Dr. Delancey. He later located at Bloserville, Cumberland County, and still later at Carlisle. He graduated at Jefferson Medical College in 1889. Dr. Alburtis T. Ritter, of Franklin County, who graduated from Baltimore Medical College in 1893, located at Loysville and practiced until his death, which occurred February 11, 1911. Soon after the death of Dr. Ritter, Dr. William T. Morrow, a native of the vicinity, located there. Dr. Morrow graduated from the Baltimore Medical College in 1908. He is the only practicing physician at Loysville.

Green Park. The west part of Green Park is on a fifty-three-acre tract warranted originally to Ludwig Laird, in 1755, and surveyed to Henry Shoemaker in 1814. The east part is on a tract of fifty acres warranted to James Moore, in 1766. The first house was built by William Reed, about 1834. About 1857 Martin Motzer and John Bernheisel built a store building and opened a store. They were succeeded in the business by Frank Mortimer, George Ernest, William B. Keck, W. W. McClure, Samuel Stambaugh, George Bernheisel and William Hoobaugh. Jacob Bernheisel built a grain cradle factory and a shingle mill where the Rheem foundry is located, in 1857, turning it into a foundry later. In 1874 Rheem Bros. purchased it and conducted business there for many years.

The business places within the bounds of Tyrone Township are designated as follows by the mercantile appraiser, the date being the time of entering the business:

General stores, A. N. Billman (1913), successor to W. W. Minich; B. F. Kell (1891). erected present building in 1905; J. G. Minich.

Groceries, Ira Evans, D. E. Emlet & Sons.

H. A. Dunkelberger, confectionery; J. B. Lightner, grain and coal; Casper C. Nickel, furniture; D. W. Raffensperger, fertilizers; J. A. Sausaman (1915), feed, established 1786 as the Rice mill; Wells Stewart, eggs; Tressler Orphans' Home, feed; J. W. Wolfe, stoves and spouting.

Loysville Methodist Church. A short distance west of Loysville a Methodist Episcopal church was erected in 1865 through the efforts of Rev. J. Riddle, but the field was never a very fruitful one. The ministers of the New Bloomfield Circuit supplied it until 1883, when it was torn down and removed to Mansville, a village in Centre Township, and reerected.

Sheaffer's Valley Church of God. The Church of God in Sheaffer's Valley, was built about 1830, on lands of Michael Murray. It was remodeled in 1885. It is served by the pastor of the Landisburg charge, where a list of pastors appear.

Kennedy's Valley Church of God. The Kennedy's Valley Church of God was built in 1886, the corner stone having been laid on July 7th. Rev. W. J. Grissinger was then pastor. Pastors appear under the Landisburg chapter.

Tyrone Township surrounds Landisburg, where many of its citizens also worship.

WATTS TOWNSHIP.

For picturesque location Watts Township cannot be beaten. It lies between the Juniata and Susquehanna Rivers where they join on their way to the sea. Much of its lands are considerably elevated and all of them lie south of the Half-Fall Mountain. The lands gradually taper to the rivers, where they are elevated but little above the high-water level. Its boundaries are on the north by Buffalo Township, and on the east, south and west by the two rivers.

The channel, however, where the rivers joined, thus forming Duncan's Island, has long since been filled up, and over it went the Pennsylvania Canal in the days when it was the main line of traffic between the anthracite coal fields and the seaboard. There was a third island known as Hulings', but the construction of the canal caused the intervening channel to fill up, thus uniting it permanently physically with Perry County, at low tide. It is still assessed in Dauphin County, its extent being twenty-five acres. Over this channel there was once a toll bridge, operated by Marcus Hulings, who also owned a ferry over the Juniata. Later Rebecca H. Duncan and David Hulings were joint owners.

Among the first settlers were John Eshelman, who warranted 160 acres in March, 1792; Robert Ferguson, sixty-four acres in June, 1774; William Thompson, 216 acres in March, 1775; Frederick Watts, 110 acres in December, 1794; and before this a tract of 102 acres in October, 1766; Benjamin Walker, 201 acres in January, 1767, which was later owned by Robert Thompson and Levi Seiders. Southeast of this tract Marcus Hulings warranted 199 acres in November, 1766. Hulings also had another tract of 200 acres located at the junction of the Juniata and Susquehanna Rivers, warranted in August, 1766. This is the farm long owned by Dr. George N. Reutter, who represented Perry County in the legislature. It is known as Amity farm, and is now in the possession of McClellan Cox. In the stone house on this farm, almost opposite Aqueduct Station, on the Pennsylvania Railroad, Marcus Hulings, Jr., and Thomas Hulings kept a tavern, the old sign still being on the attic of the house only a few years ago. North of this, along the river for almost two miles, and reaching almost to New Buffalo, Samuel Neaves had two tracts containing 512 acres, warranted in March and June, 1755. Immediately above Neaves, on the river, Francis Ellis warranted a tract in 1767, which passed to Jacob Steele when surveyed.

The next tract up the river is now the site of New Buffalo Borough. It contained 183 acres, and was warranted in November, 1767, by Christopher Mann. Above this tract Andrew Long warranted 110 acres, in July, 1762, and next above was the tract of Stophel Munce, containing 124 acres, warranted in May, 1763. He was the first collector of Greenwood Township, in 1767, Watts then being a part of Greenwood, which took its name from Joseph Greenwood, who is mentioned by Marcus Hulings as one of his closest neighbors. Immediately above Munce's claim was that of George Etzmiller, containing 162 acres, and warranted in November, 1767. John Miller had 131 acres back of the claims of Etzmiller, Munce, Long and Mann, warranted in December, 1773. Everhard Liddick warranted lands in 1868, adjoining the church, and Joseph Nagle, 150 acres, adjoining Liddick, in April, 1775. John Finton warranted sixty-six acres in 1839.

The reader, by referring to the chapter entitled "Duncan's and Haldeman's Islands," will find further interesting historical matter relating to the movements of Marcus Hulings, the pioneer. Owing to the proximity of these islands to Watts Township, their early history is largely contemporaneous.

Prior to the Revolutionary War, General Frederick Watts, of Revolutionary fame, was a landowner in the territory now comprising Watts Township, his daughter Elizabeth being the first wife of Thomas Hulings. General Watts owned part of the lands warranted to William Stewart and George Lennff, in November, 1772. From him ownership passed to Thomas Hulings, by purchase from the heirs. From Hulings, the Watts son-in-law, it passed by will to David Watts, an eminent lawyer located at Carlisle, but who had been born in that part of Cumberland which became Perry, and in that part of Greenwood Township which became Watts. It was for David Watts that the township was named. When the petition for the new township came before the court, in 1849, Judge Black was presiding in the absence of Judge Frederick Watts, and upon his suggestion it was named Watts, in honor of David Watts, the eminent lawyer who was the son of General Frederick Watts and the father of Judge Frederick Watts, then serving in that capacity. The Watts family's history is to be found elsewhere in this book. In 1839 this property passed to Alexander McAlister, by purchase.

Further evidence that the property spoken of above was in the possession of David Watts is contained in an act of the Pennsylvania Legislature, passed March 8, 1799, in reference to a ferry, the western landing of which was located thereon:

"Whereas, Mathias Flamm owns land on the west side of the Susquehanna, opposite the mouth of Juniata, and David Watts on the west side, where the State road crosses the Susquehanna, and that they have established and maintained a ferry at the place for a number of years, they are empowered by law, at this date to establish and keep same in repair, and build landings, etc."

An early schoolhouse in what is now Watts Township was on the church grounds. It was a log house without a floor, and was rebuilt on the same foundation when it had become so low that the teacher could not stand erect in it. These early log schoolhouses were usually built hastily by the communities in which they were located, and the workmanship was very crude. At the old schoolhouse near Colonel Thompson's was the first free school in Pennsylvania to be opened under the free school act, as will be noted in the chapter on "The County Schools, Past and Present," also under the life of Chief Justice Gantt, who then was the teacher. In later years the township had three schools, known as McAllister's, Centre and Livingston's. In the old schoolhouse which was located in Alexander McAllister's meadow, the teacher of the term of 1852-53 was Prof. S. B. Heiges, who later became principal of the Cumberland Valley State Normal School.

Dr. George N. Reutter, a native of Perry and a graduate of the University of Maryland, in 1858, was located at the junction of the Juniata and Susquehanna Rivers, and practiced in the surrounding community, including New Buffalo. He was once the representative of Perry County in the General Assembly and was the father of Dr. H. D. Reutter, who practiced for so many years in Duncannon. He was preceded at the Junction by his father, Dr. Daniel N. Reutter, who died October 15, 1846.

There are two small stores within the limits of the township, kept by Mrs. Belle Lowe and James C. Wright, the latter started in 1898. E. H. Derr conducts a summer resort near Girty's Notch, and retails cigars and confectionery. There was a post office in Watts Township many years ago, being known as "Thompson's Crossroads." When the William Penn Highway is completed it will join the Susquehanna trail at the township's south, where the ways diverge. This will be the only township in the county to be traversed by these two great highways.

The Hill Cemetery Association was incorporated January 18, 1915, in order to maintain the cemetery connected with this church, so that it might be kept in order and its use supervised in accordance with the warrant granted Samuel Albright, September 28, 1840. Both Presbyterian and Lutheran congregations had ceased to exist, and the Hill U. B. Church had no ownership in the cemetery, although their church adjoins it and it is used by their people. The incorporators were John H. Huggins, A. R. Thompson, D. A. Miller, H. L. Thompson and J. W. Ulsh, Jr. (recorded Deed Book 85, page 634). The seventh section of the Articles of Incorporation provides that tri-annually after the last Saturday of July, 1917, an election shall be held for trustees, and that all citizens of the age of twenty-one and upwards residing in Watts Township and New Buffalo, and all persons having relatives buried in said cemetery, shall have the right of ballot. The cemetery is kept in order by voluntary contributions.

The Union Church. In the survey of Everhard Liddick, made in 1800, for tract No. 5004, it is described as adjoining "vacant land for church and school purposes," a tract comprising over three acres. This is the location of the churches and the burial ground in Watts Township. A schoolhouse was once located here, which tradition says eventually sunk in the ground so far that the teacher could not stand straight—evidently only tradition. Like other places in the county, this schoolhouse may have been used for both church and school purposes. There was no legal right granted, in so far as known, until 1840, when Samuel Albright was granted a warrant, in trust for the Presbyterian and Lutheran congregations, its dates being September 28th. Mr. Albright accordingly deeded it to these congregations. But previous to this there was a Union church erected, in the period between 1804 and 1809. It was built of logs, and was 36x40 feet in size. It was in use until 1860, when it was removed. In it worshiped Lutherans and Presbyterians, the former probably having also held services in the old Gap Church. See "the Earliest Churches."

Lutheran Church. The Watts Township congregation of Lutherans probably dates back to the old Half-Falls Gap Church, described in "the Earliest Churches." From there the members of the faith went to the Union Church, which stood on the site of the Lutheran Church. In 1860 they erected a new church, which was in use until 1865, when the membership had so dwindled that the field was abandoned by the Lutherans. In the list of ministers we find Mathias Guntzel, 1789-96; John Herbst, 1796-1801; Conrad Walter, 1804-09; John William Heim, 1814-30. In 1833 the Liverpool pastorate was formed, and it was connected with that pastorate, having as ministers:

1833-42—Rev. Charles G. Erlenmeyer. 1843-47—Vacant.
1842-43—Rev. Andrew Berg (6 mos.).

In 1847 this church seems to have been dropped from the Liverpool Circuit, as the newly called pastor did not preach here, nor did any of his successors of that charge. In the meantime, while the Liverpool pastorate was vacant, according to Rev. Focht's "Churches Between the Mountains," Rev. Lloyd Knight, who took charge of the Duncannon pastorate on October 1, 1845, also served New Buffalo, as this church was known by reason of its location not far from that town. Rev. Knight served until 1849. Rev. Jacob Martin succeeded him in July, 1849, and the following year the Duncannon charge was regularly formed at a convention held at New Bloomfield, and New Buffalo made an integral part. Rev. Martin remained one year, and in November, 1850, Rev. John P. Heister became the pastor, but according to the "Churches Between the Mountains," at New Buffalo "he preached seldom, if any at all." He remained until November, 1853. From June, 1854, to May, 1858, Rev. George A. Nixdorff was pastor of the Duncannon charge, and again preached at New Buffalo, but at first only occasionally. August 27, 1858, Rev. Wm. H. Diven became pastor, and in May, 1859, at Synod held at Mifflinburg, Union County, reported four congregations, and New Buffalo as a "preaching station." When Rev. Focht's book was issued, June 1, 1862, Rev. Diven was still in charge of the Duncannon pastorate, but concluded his services that year. Records are unavailable, but local tradition tells of the discontinuance of services there by both the Lutherans and Presbyterians about 1870, when the United Brethren organized and used the church until their own was built in 1876. The last board of trustees of this old church were N. C. Heyd, Joseph Hammaker and J. W. Ulsh, Sr. The church had long been idle, until about 1895, when Rev. J. M. Axe held services there for a period covering six months, preaching every fourth week, in the afternoon. As the congregations had disintegrated by death, removals and lack of a shepherd, the old church gradually became a victim of the ravages of time. Occasionally funerals were held within its walls, however. During the winter of 1916-17 heavy snows crushed in the roof, and it was torn down and removed by the Cemetery Association. In this church Rev. Harry N. Bassler, a noted minister of the Reformed Church, preached his first sermon, when but twenty years of age.

The Hill U. B. Church. The United Brethren people began holding services in Watts Township about 1870, as the other denominations seemed to be letting the field take care of itself. Their meetings were held in the Lutheran Church until 1876. On January 9, 1875, Isaac Huggins deeded the grounds for a church, to Isaac Motter, James Wright, Wm. Fenicle and Leonard Jones, trustees of the U. B. congregation, and during 1875-76 the church was erected. It was a part of the Duncannon Circuit from 1870 to 1874. It was then attached to the Liverpool Circuit, where the names of the later ministers may be found. The pastors while under the Duncannon Circuit were Rev. G. W. Lightner and Rev. J. W. Hutchison.

In 1874 the latter held a revival and had over a hundred converts, adding ninety members to the church. J. L. Huggins and Alfred Jury were long among those who helped sustain this congregation as a working body.

New Buffalo Presbyterian Church. During the pastorate of Rev. Nathaniel Snowden, at Millerstown Presbyterian Church, he also organized churches at Liverpool and (at the Hill) near New Buffalo, the period being between 1818 and 1820. After his leaving, in 1820, the Liverpool and Buffalo churches were without a pastor until 1828, when Rev. James F. Irvine was installed as their pastor. During the next year that part of Perry County lying between the Juniata and Susquehanna Rivers was taken from the Huntingdon Presbytery and placed in the Carlisle Presbytery. In 1830, Rev. Irvine sought his release through Presbytery, as there were so many removals that he deemed the remainder unable to pay his salary. A committee visited both the New Buffalo and Liverpool fields and found but eight responsible people left to pay the salary. It was during the period when the Scotch-Irish were emigrating, and the newcomers were mostly Germans. And thus passed two early congregations. The New Buffalo Church, as it was known in Presbyterian circles, used the old Union church, the same building that the Lutherans occupied, its location being in Watts Township, a mile west of New Buffalo, at Hill cemetery.

WHEATFIELD TOWNSHIP.

Between 1793, when Juniata Township was erected from territory taken from Rye Township, and 1826, when Wheatfield Township was formed from territory also taken from it, there were various efforts made in the courts of both Cumberland and Perry Counties to divide the township by the creation of another, for the territory was yet a part of Cumberland for the first twenty-seven of these thirty-three years. After Juniata Township's erection, Rye embraced the territory bounded by Mahanoy Ridge on the north, the Juniata and Susquehanna Rivers on the east, Cumberland County on the south, and Tyrone Township on the west.

In 1824, at the May sessions of the Perry County courts, a petition was presented asking the erection of a new township. The court appointed Meredith Darlington, Jacob Stroop and William Wilson as viewers. What happened in the interim to delay the matter is not clear, but the order of the court granting the petition is dated January 5, 1826—over two years later. The township was named "Wheatfield," which tradition attributes to the fact that during one of the trips of the viewers over it the entire township's lands were fields of waving grain. At that time it embraced all of Penn Township and parts of Miller, Centre and Carroll. A small strip was later added to Wheatfield, being taken from Rye, it being located between Sherman's Creek and the crest of Pine Hill. Wheatfield is a long, narrow township, except at its western end, where it has a breadth of eight miles.

Wheatfield is bounded on the north by Centre and Miller, on the east by the Juniata River and Penn Township, on the south by Penn and Rye, and on the west by Carroll and Centre. At the north Losh's Run is the boundary. It is also drained by Little Juniata and Sherman's Creeks. It had 298 taxables at the time of its erection.

The original frontage on the Juniata of the township as it now exists was comprised in two warrants, one of 331 acres being granted to Frederick Watts, a native of Wales, whose history is covered in our chapter relating to the Revolutionary War and by a sketch. The warrant is dated June 4, 1762. He died in 1795, and his remains and that of his wife were interred in a burial ground on the farm. They had seven children, a daughter, Elizabeth, being married to a son of Marcus Hulings. The farm recently owned by the heirs of Noah Hertzler was comprised in the Watts holdings. The other tract also extended into Miller Township, and was for 199 acres, and was warranted by John Smith in 1788. It was later owned by Dr. J. P. Singer.

In 1766, William Baskins warranted 238 acres on Little Juniata Creek, above King's mill. The old Montebello furnace was built on it, and adjoining tracts were purchased by the owners. Eve Baker warranted 133 acres of land in 1767, which shortly passed to Levi Owen, the progenitor of the many families of that name within the county, and many located elsewhere. Owen, in 1791, warranted the adjoining 150 acres. He later purchased other lands and was a large landowner. The Owen family has been prominent in the civil affairs of the county since its erection.

Arnold VanFossen warranted 123 acres in 1766. A pioneer United Brethren pastor, Rev. John Snyder, warranted 189 acres below the Owen and VanFossen claims, in 1828, but an improvement had been made there as early as 1800. He died in 1845. What later became the Daniel Bornman farm, was comprised in a warrant for 189 acres, granted in 1767, to Robert Ramsey, but later surveyed to Alexander Shortess. Below, in what is known as "dark hollow," 228 acres were warranted in 1793, by John McBride. East of this tract, William Bothwell, in 1811, warranted 450 acres, which was later increased to 500. In 1815, John Light warranted 231 acres, which afterwards was known as the Samuel McKenzie tract. On Sherman's Creek, embracing "The Loop," and in both Penn and Wheatfield Townships, Benjamin Abram warranted 207 acres in 1766. Fio Forge was later located on a part of this tract, purchased by Israel Downing and James B. Davis, in 1827. Where Dellville is located, was included in the warrant of George Moser. George Mills warranted a tract above Dellville, and Samuel Graham one along Sherman's Creek. Andrew Boyd warranted lands in 1767, but they were patented to Matthew Henderson, in 1787. The greater portion of this tract lies in Carroll Township. John Stewart, an early settler and a Revolutionary soldier, came in from Carlisle prior to 1800, and Samuel Potter and Andrew Pennell settled in the eastern end of the township soon after 1820. Descendants of these three families have been prominent in that section of the county ever since.

As early as 1773, Alexander Power, a schoolmaster who came from Philadelphia, was in possession of a large tract of land. His lands lay in the vicinity of the road leading from Weaver's Station, on the Susquehanna River & Western Railway, to Centre schoolhouse. John, George and Jacob Clay later resided in this vicinity.

Before 1800 Christian Ensminger was in possession of over 500 acres of land in Rye, but some of which extended into Wheatfield His son David settled in Wheatfield and was one of its substantial citizens. Alexander Shortess, in 1815, took up 186 acres, and made many purchases of lands in addition.

Montebello furnace was located on Little Juniata Creek, on a tract of land warranted in 1766, to William Baskins, its history appearing under the chapter devoted to "Old Landmarks, Mills and Industries." Fio forge's history appears at the same place. Jacob Seidel, of Fishing Creek, purchased property on Sherman's Creek, and dismantled his mill in Rye Township, and shortly after 1820 erected a mill from the same lumber at the location known to this day as Dugan's. About 1850 he sold it to a man named Shapley, who five years later sold it to Dugan & Zorger. The latter firm tore down the old mill, in 1856, and erected the present mill. Then Adam H. Zorger and Emanuel Dugan operated it until the death of Mr. Zorger, when, in 1895, Mr. Dugan purchased the other interest. After

Mr. Dugan's death, in 1896, James A. Shearer purchased it and still is in possession.

Farther up the stream, where Dellville is located, on the George Moser tract of 102 acres, Christian Smith and Isaac Kirkpatrick purchased a small tract, and in 1841 erected a gristmill, which they operated until 1853, when Smith sold his interest to Daniel Ristine. The other interest passed to John Souder. In 1856, Mr. Ristine sold his interest to Eli Young, and it came to be known as Young's mill to that generation. The other interest also came into the possession of Mr. Young in 1878, and after his death, it was conveyed to Amos N. Hunsecker, in 1894. In 1911 he sold to Roy Rice, the present owner.

Griffeth Owen, a native of Wales, who came to America about the same time as William Penn, was the grandfather of Levi Owen, who settled on a large tract of land between New Bloomfield and Duncannon, about 1770. The story that he helped convey the Indians over the Allegheny Mountains when they moved farther west, of course, is fiction, as the Indians were not in the habit of being "conveyed."

The post office at Dellville was established in 1860, with Eli Young as postmaster. The first store at Dellville was opened in 1855, by Adam Billow, who has had many successors.

The greater part of the land between Pine Hill and Sherman's Creek was patented to Samuel Funk, in 1805. He soon sold 106 acres to John Minich, who sold it to Adam Fultz, in 1809. In 1812, it passed to Peter Billow, who died in 1829, George Billow then coming into possession. Prior to 1820 there was a tavern and distillery on the place. The tavern was a well-known stopping place, and after the erection of the county, in 1820, for many years the name of George Billow appears as the proprietor. The place was locally known as "Billow's Fording" until 1836, when a bridge, the length of which was 160 feet, was erected at a cost of $2,000. It was proposed to locate a town there as late as 1843, when Joseph Marshall advertised lots for a town "on the north bank of Sherman's Creek, at Billow's Inn, Wheatfield Township." On February 22, 1854, it was advertised for sale by R. E. Shepley, then the owner. It no longer exists.

One of the longest continuous records of holding a public office in Perry County was that of Joseph Lepperd, father of John R. Lepperd, merchant at Roseglen, who was a justice of the peace for ten terms, covering forty-eight years.

In Wheatfield Township resided Gen. Frederick Watts, one of the Executive Committee of the Colony of Pennsylvania, which was the governing body during those year between the Declaration of Independence and the formation of the American Union. In 1813, Gen. Henry Miller, a Revolutionary hero, also located in this township. He became prothonotary of Perry County at the first election in 1821, and died in Carlisle, April 5, 1824, in his ninety-fifth year.

There are not many business places within the township. The mercantile appraiser names Roy E. Rice, flour and feed; J. R. Lepperd, and Philip People, general stores, and J. N. Crouse, grocery store. Mrs. Maria Price had once kept a small store at Roseglen, where Mr. Lepperd started in 1907, succeeding H. D. Banks, who built the building and opened the business in 1901. Mr. Crouse's location is near Losh's Run Station, at the Wheatfield-Miller line and the Juniata River. He has long been located there, and is postmaster at Logania.

On the lands of Levi Owen a schoolhouse was built about 1810, where sessions were held until about 1820, when a log schoolhouse was built near Snyder's Church. It was in use until 1848, when the schoolhouse on the Wallace farm was moved nearer and its usefulness was a thing of the past. Wheatfield accepted the common school act in 1835, and received $148.20 appropriation from the state. In November, 1835, the school directors met at the Clay schoolhouse to examine the teachers. This house stood near the present location of the Roseglen store, on the New Bloomfield-Duncannon road, and was abandoned long ago. The Potter (now Pennell's) schoolhouse was in use before the free school law came into existence.

Near Aqueduct Station is a notable summer colony composed principally of Harrisburg business men, whose cottages line the banks of the Juniata for almost a half-mile.

A Methodist church once stood on the top of the hill, west of Fio forge, not far from Sherman's Creek, on the Carlisle road, west of the present residence of Henry Grubb (then August McKenzie's place). A. S. Hays, a Duncannon merchant, now eighty-two years of age, attended meetings there when a boy, and distinctly recollects it. The graveyard is located close by the buildings of the Sausaman farm. It was built in 1840, and in use until 1875. It was served by Reverends Jordan, Holmes, Wright, Swengler, Hamilton, Thompson and White. The U. B. congregation used it a few years after 1875.

Snyder's U. B. Church. Snyder's Church, that historic old structure located along the Duncannon-Bloomfield road, is one of the churches of distinction within the county limits. It was built as a Union church, in 1814, in conjunction with the Methodists, who soon dropped out and left it to the United Brethren alone. It was the first church of that faith to be located north and west of the Kittatinny Mountain and west of the Susquehanna River. In other words, it is the oldest United Brethren church in the Juniata Valley, and in all that part of the country lying to its west. Prior to 1846 this church was included as a part of the Carlisle Circuit, of Cumberland County. At that time the Shermansdale charge was formed by the churches at Young's, near Shermansdale, and Snyder's. Rev. John (Schneider) Snyder, the first pastor, from whom it took its name, warranted a tract of 129 acres of land below the Owen and VanFossen warrants, on April 12, 1828, and it is described as "on which an improvement had been made before 1800." Rev. Snyder's successor was William Sholty. Rev. Snyder died in 1845, and sleeps in the burial ground adjoining the church. The church was remodeled and rebuilt in 1904. The list of pastors appears under the Carroll Township chapter, in connection with Young's United Brethren Church.

St. David's Lutheran Church. Located near the site of old Fio forge, about five miles southwest of Duncannon, was St. David's Church, which was dedicated in November, 1845. The Lutheran people residing in this neighborhood originally belonged to Mt. Zion and Mt. Pisgah churches, in Carroll Township, and to Christ's, at Duncannon. The long distances from their homes to these churches impelled them to make an effort to have a church nearer home. Rev. L. T. Williams preached in the Fio forge schoolhouses in 1845, and a church was erected at once by members of the Lutheran and Reformed faiths. While the church was built in 1845, the Lutherans did not organize the St. David congregation until June 20, 1846, when it was organized with a membership of twenty-seven. Rev. Lloyd Knight, the New Bloomfield pastor, began holding regular services every four weeks, he being the first pastor. He served until June, 1849, when he was succeeded by Rev. Jacob Martin, who preached every three weeks. In February, 1850, this congregation and others united to form the Petersburg (Duncanon) charge, whose pastors have since served it. See chapter on Duncannon Borough.

St. David's Reformed Church. The Reformed congregation at St. David's was organized between 1843 and 1845, but preaching had been conducted there before that time, in the schoolhouses and at irregular intervals. It was organized by Rev. Jacob Scholl. From its beginning the pastors of the New Bloomfield charge had charge of the services until April, 1867, the close of Rev. Kelley's ministry. (See Bloomfield chapter.) From then until the early part of 1868 they were without a pastor, and from that time were made a part of the newly formed Marysville-Duncannon Reformed charge, the pastors having since been the same, the list of ministers appearing in the chapter relating to Marysville.

This church was first known as Billow's Church. It was a well built frame structure, 30x40 feet in size.

Pennell's Church. During 1845 Andrew Pennell donated a plot at the corner of his farm, in Wheatfield Township, for the purpose of erecting a Methodist church. The present stone church was erected on this site, the building committee being Robert Jones, George Bruner and Andrew Pennell. Since then this pulpit has been supplied by the Duncannon Methodist pastors at intervals. The church is the property of the Duncannon congregation.

INDEX

CPSIA information can be obtained
at www.ICGtesting.com
Printed in the USA
BVHW040326190621
609908BV00008B/1410

9 780343 148492